Lecture Notes in Computer Science 3758

Commenced Publication in 1973
Founding and Former Series Editors:
Gerhard Goos, Juris Hartmanis, and Jan van Leeuwen

Editorial Board

David Hutchison
  Lancaster University, UK
Takeo Kanade
  Carnegie Mellon University, Pittsburgh, PA, USA
Josef Kittler
  University of Surrey, Guildford, UK
Jon M. Kleinberg
  Cornell University, Ithaca, NY, USA
Friedemann Mattern
  ETH Zurich, Switzerland
John C. Mitchell
  Stanford University, CA, USA
Moni Naor
  Weizmann Institute of Science, Rehovot, Israel
Oscar Nierstrasz
  University of Bern, Switzerland
C. Pandu Rangan
  Indian Institute of Technology, Madras, India
Bernhard Steffen
  University of Dortmund, Germany
Madhu Sudan
  Massachusetts Institute of Technology, MA, USA
Demetri Terzopoulos
  New York University, NY, USA
Doug Tygar
  University of California, Berkeley, CA, USA
Moshe Y. Vardi
  Rice University, Houston, TX, USA
Gerhard Weikum
  Max-Planck Institute of Computer Science, Saarbruecken, Germany

Yi Pan   Daoxu Chen   Minyi Guo
Jiannong Cao   Jack Dongarra (Eds.)

Parallel and Distributed Processing and Applications

Third International Symposium, ISPA 2005
Nanjing, China, November 2-5, 2005
Proceedings

 Springer

Volume Editors

Yi Pan
Georgia State University, Department of Computer Science
Atlanta, GA 30302-4110, USA.
E-mail: pan@cs.gsu.edu

Daoxu Chen
Nanjing University, Department of Computer Science
Nanjing 210093, China
E-mail: cdx@nju.edu.cn

Minyi Guo
The University of Aizu, School of Computer Science and Engineering
Tsuruga, Ikki-machi, Aizu-Wakamatsu City, Fukushima 965-8580, Japan
E-mail: minyi@u-aizu.ac.jp

Jiannong Cao
Hong Kong Polytechnic University, Department of Computing
Hung Hom, Kowloon, Hong Kong
E-mail: csjcao@comp.polyu.edu.hk

Jack Dongarra
University of Tennessee, Computer Science Department
1122 Volunteer Blvd., Knoxville, TN 37996-3450, USA
E-mail: dongarra@cs.utk.edu

Library of Congress Control Number: 2005934458

CR Subject Classification (1998): F.1, F.2, D.1, D.2, D.4, C.2, H.4, K.6

ISSN   0302-9743
ISBN-10   3-540-29769-3 Springer Berlin Heidelberg New York
ISBN-13   978-3-540-29769-7 Springer Berlin Heidelberg New York

This work is subject to copyright. All rights are reserved, whether the whole or part of the material is concerned, specifically the rights of translation, reprinting, re-use of illustrations, recitation, broadcasting, reproduction on microfilms or in any other way, and storage in data banks. Duplication of this publication or parts thereof is permitted only under the provisions of the German Copyright Law of September 9, 1965, in its current version, and permission for use must always be obtained from Springer. Violations are liable to prosecution under the German Copyright Law.

Springer is a part of Springer Science+Business Media

springeronline.com

© Springer-Verlag Berlin Heidelberg 2005
Printed in Germany

Typesetting: Camera-ready by author, data conversion by Scientific Publishing Services, Chennai, India
Printed on acid-free paper   SPIN: 11576235   06/3142   5 4 3 2 1 0

Preface

Welcome to the proceedings of ISPA 2005 which was held in the city of Nanjing. Parallel computing has become a mainstream research area in computer science and the ISPA conference has become one of the premier forums for the presentation of new and exciting research on all aspects of parallel computing. We are pleased to present the proceedings for the 3rd International Symposium on Parallel and Distributed Processing and Applications (ISPA 2005), which comprises a collection of excellent technical papers, and keynote speeches. The papers accepted cover a wide range of exciting topics, including architectures, software, networking, and applications.

The conference continues to grow and this year a record total of 968 manuscripts (including workshop submissions) were submitted for consideration by the Program Committee or workshops. From the 645 papers submitted to the main conference, the Program Committee selected only 90 long papers and 19 short papers in the program. Eight workshops complemented the outstanding paper sessions.

The submission and review process worked as follows. Each submission was assigned to two Program Committee members for review. Each Program Committee member prepared a single review for each assigned paper or assigned a paper to an outside reviewer for review. In addition, the program chairs, vice program chairs, and general chairs read all papers when a conflicting review result occured. Given the large number of submissions, each Program Committee member was assigned roughly 15–20 papers. Based on the review scores, the program chairs along with the vice program chairs made the final decision.

The excellent program required a lot of effort from many people. First, we would like to thank all the authors for their hard work in preparing submissions to the conference. We deeply appreciate the effort and contributions of the Program Committee members who worked very hard to select the very best submissions and to put together an exciting program. The effort of the external reviewers is also deeply appreciated. We are also very grateful to Prof. Sartaj Sahni, Prof. Pen-Chung Yew, and Prof. Susumu Horiguchi for accepting our invitation to present keynote speeches. Thanks go to the workshop chairs for organizing eight excellent workshops on several important topics related to parallel and distributed computing and applications.

We deeply appreciate the tremendous efforts of the vice program chairs, Prof. Ivan Stojmenovic, Prof. Mohamed Ould-Khaoua, Prof. Mark Baker, Prof. Jingling Xue, and Prof. Zhi-Hua Zhou. We would like to thank the general co-chairs, Prof. Jack Dongarra, Prof. Jiannong Cao, and Prof. Jian Lu, for their advice and continued support. Finally, we would like to thank the Steering Committee chairs, Prof. Sartaj Sahni, Prof. Yaoxue Zhang, and Prof. Minyi Guo for the opportunity to serve as the program chairs as well as their guidance through the process. We hope that the attendees enjoyed this conference, found the technical program to be exciting, and had a wonderful time in Nanjing.

Yi Pan and Daoxu Chen
ISPA 2005 Program Co-chairs

Conference Organization

ISPA 2005 was organized mainly by the State Key Laboratory for Novel Software Technology, Nanjing University, China.

General Co-chairs

Jack Dongarra, University of Tennessee, USA
Jiannong Cao, Hong Kong Polytechnic University, China
Jian Lu, Nanjing University, China

Program Co-chairs

Yi Pan, Georgia State University, USA
Daoxu Chen, Nanjing University, China

Program Vice-Chairs

Ivan Stojmenovic, University of Ottawa, Canada
Mohamed Ould-Khaoua, University of Glasgow, UK
Mark Baker, University of Portsmouth, UK
Jingling Xue, University of New South Wales, Australia
Zhi-Hua Zhou, Nanjing University, China

Steering Committee Co-chairs

Sartaj Sahni, University of Florida, USA
Yaoxue Zhang, Ministry of Education, China
Minyi Guo, University of Aizu, Japan

Steering Committee

Jiannong Cao, Hong Kong Polytechnic University, China
Francis Lau, University of Hong Kong, China
Yi Pan, Georgia State University, USA

Li Xie, Nanjing University, China
Jie Wu, Florida Altantic University, USA
Laurence T. Yang, St. Francis Xavier University, Canada
Hans P. Zima, California Institute of Technology, USA
Weiming Zheng, Tsinghua University, China

Local Arrangements Chairs

Xianglin Fei, Nanjing University, China
Baowen Xu, Southeast University, China
Ling Chen, Yangzhou University, China

Workshops Chair

Guihai Chen, Nanjing University, China

Tutorials Chair

Yuzhong Sun, Institute of Computing Technology, CAS, China

Publicity Chair

Cho-Li Wang, University of Hong Kong, China

Publication Chair

Hui Wang, University of Aizu, Japan

Conference Secretary

Xuan Xu, Nanjing University, China

Program Committee

Selim G. Akl	Queen's University, Canada
Amy W. Apon	University of Arkansas, USA
Hamid R. Arabnia	University of Georgia, USA
Eduard Ayguade	UPC, Spain
David A. Bader	Georgia Institute of Technology, USA

Mark Baker	University of Portsmouth, UK
Anu Bourgeois	Georgia State University, USA
Wentong Cai	Nanyang Technological University, Singapore
Xing Cai	Univ. of Oslo/Simula Research Lab, Norway
Emmanuel Cecchet	INRIA, France
Weng-Long Chang	Southern Taiwan Univ. of Tech., Taiwan
Guihai Chen	Nanjing University, China
Su-Hui Chiang	Portland State University, USA
Yuanshun Dai	Purdue University, USA
Andrzej M. Goscinski	Deakin University, Australia
Dhrubajyoti Goswami	Concordia University, Canada
Ning Gu	Fudan University, China
Jieyue He	Southeast University, China
Yanxiang He	Wuhan University, China
Hung-Chang Hsiao	National Tsing-Hua University, Taiwan
Jenwei Hsieh	Dell Inc.
Ching-Hsien Hsu	Chung Hua University, Taiwan
Chun-Hsi Huang	University of Connecticut, USA
Tsung-Chuan Huang	National Sun Yat-sen University, Taiwan
Constantinos Ierotheou	University of Greenwich, UK
Stephen Jarvis	University of Warwick, UK
Chris Jeshsope	Universiteit van Amsterdam (UvA), Netherlands
Beihong Jin	Institute of Software, Chinese Academy of Sciences, China
Hai Jin	Huazhong University of Science and Technology, China
Weijia Jia	City University of Hong Kong, China
Ajay Katangur	Texas A&M University at Corpus Christi, USA
Hatsuhiko Kato	Shonan Institute of Technology, Japan
Daniel S. Katz	JPL, California Institute of Technology, USA
Jacques Chassin de Kergommeaux	INPG, LSR-IMAG, Grenoble, France
Raj Kettimuthu	Argonne National Laboratory, USA
Chung-Ta King	National Tsing-Hua University, Taiwan
Dieter Kranzlmueller	Linz University, Austria
Sy-Yen Kuo	National Taiwan University, Taiwan

Chokchai Leangsuksun	Louisiana Tech University, USA
Jie Li	University of Tsukuba, Japan
Minglu Li	Shanghai Jiao Tong University, China
Yamin Li	University of Hosei, Japan
Xiaola Lin	Sun Yat-sen University, China
Zhen Liu	Nagasaki Institute of Applied Science, Japan
Peter Kok Keong Loh	Nanyang Technological University, Singapore
Jianhua Ma	Hosei University, Japan
Praveen Madiraju	Georgia State University, USA
Geyong Min	University of Bradford, UK
Michael Ng	University of Hong Kong, China
Jun Ni	University of Iowa, USA
Manish Parashar	Rutgers University, USA
Andrea Passarella	University of Pisa, Italy
Rolf Rabenseifner	Rechenzentrum, Universität Stuttgart, Germany
Alex Shafarenko	University of Hertfordshire, UK
Yuzhong Sun	Institute of Computing Technology, CAS, China
Peiyi Tang	University of Arkansas at Little Rock, USA
David Taniar	Monash University, Australia
Ruppa K. Thulasiram	University of Manitoba, Canada
Xinmin Tian	Intel, USA
Lorenzo Verdoscia	ICAR, Italian National Research Council (CNR), Italy
Frederic Vivien	INRIA, France
Guojung Wang	Hong Kong Polytechnic University, China
Xingwei Wang	Northeastern University, China
Allan Wong	Hong Kong Polytechnic University, China
Chengyong Wu	Chinese Academy of Sciences, China
Bin Xiao	Hong Kong Polytechnic University, China
Nong Xiao	National University of Defense Technology, China
Cheng-Zhong Xu	Wayne State University, USA
Dongyan Xu	Purdue University, USA
Jianliang Xu	Hong Kong Baptist University, China
Xinfeng Ye	Auckland University, New Zealand

Kun-Ming Yu	Chung Hua University, Taiwan
Jun Zhang	University of Kentucky, USA
Yao Zheng	Zhejiang University, China
Bingbing Zhou	University of Sydney, Australia
Wanlei Zhou	Deakin University, Austraia
Xiaobo Zhou	University of Colorado at Colorado Springs, USA
Jianping Zhu	University of Akron, USA
A.Y. Zomaya	University of Sydney, Australia

Table of Contents

Keynote Speech

Data Structures and Algorithms for Packet Forwarding and
Classification
 Sartaj Sahni 1

Using Speculative Multithreading for General-Purpose Applications
 Pen-Chung Yew 2

Towards Peta-Bit Photonic Networks
 Susumu Horiguchi 3

Tutorial

Technologies and Considerations for Developing Internet and
Multiplayer Computer Games: A Tutorial (Extended Abstract)
 Wanlei Zhou 17

Routing in 2-D Meshes: A Tutorial (Extended Abstract)
 Zhen Jiang 19

Session 1A: Cluster Systems and Applications

RDIM: A Self-adaptive and Balanced Distribution for Replicated Data
in Scalable Storage Clusters
 Zhong Liu, Nong Xiao, Xing-Ming Zhou 21

Modeling and Analysis of a Parallel Nested Loop Join on Cluster
Architectures
 Erich Schikuta 33

Scheduling Efficiently for Irregular Load Distributions in a Large-scale
Cluster
 *Bao-Yin Zhang, Ze-Yao Mo, Guang-Wen Yang,
 Wei-Min Zheng* 39

A Content-Based Load Balancing Algorithm for Metadata Servers in
Cluster File Systems
 Junho Jang, Saeyoung Han, Sungyong Park, Jihoon Yang 49

Reducing the Overhead of Intra-Node Communication in Clusters of SMPs
   Sascha Hunold, Thomas Rauber 58

Session 1B: Performance Evaluation and Measurements

On Service-Oriented Network Measurement Architecture with Mobile Agent
   Zhi Wang, Bo Yu, Chuanshan Gao 66

Pathtrait: A Tool for Tight Link Location and End-to-End Available Bandwidth Measurement
   Dalu Zhang, Ye Wu, Jian Xu 78

Performance Evaluation of a Self-organized Hierarchical Topology for Update of Replicas in a Large Distributed System
   Jesús Acosta-Elias, B. Pineda Reyes, E. Chavez Leos,
   Alejandro Ochoa-Cardiel, Mario Recio, Omar Gutierrez-Navarro 90

A Proposal of Reconfigurable MPI Collective Communication Functions
   Luiz E.S. Ramos, Carlos A.P.S. Martins 102

Session 1C: Distributed Algorithms and Systems

Design and Evaluation of Network-Bandwidth-Based Parallel Replication Algorithm
   Yijie Wang, Yongjin Qin 108

A Quorum Based Group k-Mutual Exclusion Algorithm for Open Distributed Environments
   Armin Lawi, Kentaro Oda, Takaichi Yoshida 119

An Efficient Implementation of the Backtesting of Trading Strategies
   Jiarui Ni, Chengqi Zhang 126

Reconfigurable Object Consistency Model for Distributed Shared Memory
   Christiane V. Pousa, Luís F.W. Góes, Carlos A.P.S. Martins 132

Session 1D: Fault Tolerance and Reliability

ER-TCP: An Efficient Fault-Tolerance Scheme for TCP Connections
   Zhiyuan Shao, Hai Jin, Bin Cheng, Wenbin Jiang 139

Online Adaptive Fault-Tolerant Routing in 2D Torus
  Yamin Li, Shietung Peng, Wanming Chu 150

Replicating Multithreaded Web Services
  Xinfeng Ye, Yilin Shen 162

Design Schemes and Performance Analysis of Dynamic Rerouting
Interconnection Networks for Tolerating Faults and Preventing
Collisions
  Ching-Wen Chen, Chang-Jung Ku, Chih-Hung Chang 168

RRBS: A Fault Tolerance Model for Cluster/Grid Parallel File System
  Yan-mei Huo, Jiu-bin Ju, Liang Hu 180

Session 2A: High-Performance Computing and Architecture I

Fast Parallel FFT on CTaiJi: A Coarse-Grained Reconfigurable
Computation Platform
  LiGuo Song, YuXian Jiang 188

Integrating Local Job Scheduler – LSF^{TM} with $Gfarm^{TM}$
  *Xiaohui Wei, Wilfred W. Li, Osamu Tatebe, Gaochao Xu, Liang Hu,
  Jiubin Ju* 196

Cache Management for Discrete Processor Architectures
  Jih-Fu Tu 205

Enhancing DCache Warn Fetch Policy for SMT Processors
  Minxuan Zhang, Caixia Sun 216

Aggressive Loop Fusion for Improving Locality and Parallelism
  Jingling Xue 224

Session 2B: Parallel Algorithms and Systems I

An Upper Bound on Blocking Probability of Vertical Stacked Optical
Benes Networks
  Jiling Zhong, Yi Pan 239

It's Elementary, My Dear Watson: Time-Optimal Sorting Algorithms
on a Completely Overlapping Network
  *Sanpawat Kantabutra, Wattana Jindaluang,
  Prapaporn Techa-angkoon* 252

Lock-Free Parallel Garbage Collection
  H. Gao, J.F. Groote, W.H. Hesselink 263

Adaptive Parallel Ant Colony Optimization
  Ling Chen, Chunfang Zhang 275

Collective Communications for Scalable Programming
  Sang Boem Lim, Bryan Carpenter, Geoffrey Fox, Han-Ku Lee 286

Session 2C: Network Routing and Communication Algorithms I

A Fast and Scalable Conflict Detection Algorithm for Packet Classifiers
  Xin Li, Zhenzhou Ji, Mingzeng Hu 298

Loss Rate Aware Preferential Treamtment Scheme at the Congested Router
  Dongping Zhao, Deyun Zhang, Jiuxing Cao, Weibin Zheng, Zhiping An 308

A Heuristic Routing Algorithm for Degree-Constrained Minimum Overall Latency Application Layer Multicast
  Baoliu Ye, Minyi Guo, Daoxu Chen, Sanglu Lu 320

DIRA: Distributed Insertion and Relocation Routing Algorithm for Overlay Multicast in Diffserv Domain
  Xiao Chen, Huagang Shao, Weinong Wang 333

Load Balancing Based on Similarity Multi-paths Routing
  Wuping Xu, Puliu Yan, Delin Xia, Ming Wu 345

Session 2D: Security Algorithms and Systems I

Secure Real-Time Transaction Processing with Timeliness Guarantees in Mobile Distributed Real-Time Database Systems
  Yingyuan Xiao, Yunsheng Liu, Guoqiong Liao, Xiaofeng Liu 358

A New Data Fusion Model of Intrusion Detection-IDSFP
  Junfeng Tian, Weidong Zhao, Ruizhong Du, Zhe Zhang 371

The Application of Collaborative Filtering for Trust Management in P2P Communities
  Min Zuo, Kai Wang, Jianhua Li 383

Intelligent DDoS Packet Filtering in High-Speed Networks
   Yang Xiang, Wanlei Zhou 395

Session 3A: High-Performance Computing and Architecture II

2L-MuRR: A Compact Register Renaming Scheme for SMT Processors
   Hua Yang, Gang Cui, Xiao-zong Yang 407

Scheduling Convex Bipartite Communications Toward Efficient GEN_BLOCK Transformations
   Ching-Hsien Hsu, Shih-Chang Chen, Chao-Yang Lan,
   Chao-Tung Yang, Kuan-Ching Li 419

A Chronological History-Based Execution Time Estimation Model for Embarrassingly Parallel Applications on Grids
   Chao-Tung Yang, Po-Chi Shih, Cheng-Fang Lin, Ching-Hsien Hsu,
   Kuan-Ching Li 425

Developing High-Performance Parallel Applications Using EPAS
   Mohammad Mursalin Akon, Ajit Singh, Xuemin (Sherman) Shen,
   Dhrubajyoti Goswami, Hon Fung Li 431

On Utilization of the Grid Computing Technology for Video Conversion and 3D Rendering
   Chao-Tung Yang, Chuan-Lin Lai, Kuan-Ching Li, Ching-Hsien Hsu,
   William C. Chu 442

Session 3B: Parallel Algorithms and Systems II

Communication-Free Data Alignment for Arrays with Exponential References Using Elementary Linear Algebra
   Weng-Long Chang, Minyi Guo, Michael (Shan-Hui) Ho,
   Sien-Tang Tsai 454

Parallel Unstructured Quadrilateral Mesh Generation
   Jianjun Chen, Yao Zheng 467

Container Problem in Burnt Pancake Graphs
   N. Sawada, Y. Suzuki, K. Kaneko 479

A Cost Optimal Parallel Quicksorting and Its Implementation on a Shared Memory Parallel Computer
   Jie Liu, Clinton Knowles, Adam Brian Davis 491

Session 3C: Network Routing and Communication Algorithms II

Near Optimal Routing in a Small-World Network with Augmented Local Awareness
Jianyang Zeng, Wen-Jing Hsu, Jiangdian Wang 503

Systolic Routing in an Optical Fat Tree
Risto T. Honkanen 514

Fast Total-Exchange Algorithm
Anssi Kautonen 524

MFLWQ: A Fair and Adaptive Queue Management Algorithm for Scavenger Service
Xiaofeng Chen, Lingdi Ping, Zheng Wan, Jian Chen 530

Session 3D: Security Algorithms and Systems II

CBTM: A Trust Model with Uncertainty Quantification and Reasoning for Pervasive Computing
Rui He, Jianwei Niu, Guangwei Zhang 541

An Authentication Protocol for Pervasive Computing
Shiqun Li, Jianying Zhou, Xiangxue Li, Kefei Chen 553

A Hybrid Neural Network Approach to the Classification of Novel Attacks for Intrusion Detection
Wei Pan, Weihua Li 564

Efficient and Beneficial Defense Against DDoS Direct Attack and Reflector Attack
Yanxiang He, Wei Chen, Wenling Peng, Min Yang 576

Session 4A: Grid Applications and Systems

Study on Equipment Interoperation Chain Model in Grid Environment
Yuexuan Wang, Cheng Wu 588

Grid Accounting Information Service with End-to-End User Identity
Beob Kyun Kim, Haeng Jin Jang, Tingting Li, Dong Un An, Seung Jong Chung 596

Performance Analysis and Prediction on VEGA Grid
  *Haijun Yang, Zhiwei Xu, Yuzhong Sun, Zheng Shen,
  Changshu Liu* 608

An Accounting Services Model for ShanghaiGrid
  Jiadi Yu, Qi Qian, Minglu Li 620

An Agent-Based Grid Computing Infrastructure
  Jia Tang, Minjie Zhang 630

Session 4B: Database Applications and Data Mining

Dynamically Mining Frequent Patterns over Online Data Streams
  *Xuejun Liu, Hongbing Xu, Yisheng Dong, Yongli Wang,
  Jiangbo Qian* 645

Clustering Mixed Type Attributes in Large Dataset
  Jian Yin, Zhifang Tan 655

Mining Association Rules from Multi-stream Time Series Data on
Multiprocessor Systems
  *Biplab Kumer Sarker, Toshiya Hirata, Kuniaki Uehara,
  Virendra C. Bhavsar* 662

Mining Frequent Closed Itemsets Without Candidate Generation
  Kai Chen 668

Distribution Design in Distributed Databases Using Clustering to Solve
Large Instances
  *Joaquin Perez Ortega, Rodolfo A. Pazos Rangel,
  Jose A. Martinez Florez, J. Javier Gonzalez Barbosa,
  E. Alejandro Macias Diaz, J. David Teran Villanueva* 678

Session 4C: Distributed Processing and Architecture

Modeling Real-Time Wormhole Networks by Queuing Theory
  Lichen Zhang, Yuliang Zhang 690

A Discrete Event System Model for Simulating Mobile Agent
  Xuhui Li, Jiannong Cao, Yanxiang He, Jingyang Zhou 701

A Holistic Approach to Survivable Distributed Information System for
Critical Applications
  H.Q. Wang, D.X. Liu, D. Xu, Y.Y. Lan, X.Y. Li, Q. Zhao ... 713

A Personalized and Scalable Service Broker for the Global Computing
Environment
  *Kyung-Lang Park, Chang-Soon Kim, Oh-Young Kwon,
  Hyoung-Woo Park, Shin-Dug Kim* 725

Distributed Network Computing on Transient Stability Analysis and
Control
  Chenrong Huang, Mingxue Chen 737

Session 4D: Sensor Networks and Protocols

A Distributed Power-Efficient Data Gathering and Aggregation
Protocol for Wireless Sensor Networks
  Ming Liu, Jiannong Cao, Hai-gang Gong, Li-jun Chen, Xie Li 743

A Key Management Scheme for Cross-Layering Designs in Wireless
Sensor Networks
  Bo Yu, Haiguang Chen, Min Yang, Dilin Mao, Chuanshan Gao 757

A Clustering Mechanism with Various Cluster Sizes for the Sensor
Network
  Yujin Lim, Sanghyun Ahn 769

Percentage Coverage Configuration in Wireless Sensor Networks
  Hongxing Bai, Xi Chen, Yu-Chi Ho, Xiaohong Guan 780

Session 5A: Peer-to-Peer Algorithms and Systems I

A Fault-Tolerant Content Addressable Network
  Daisuke Takemoto, Shigeaki Tagashira, Satoshi Fujita 792

Effective Resource Allocation in a JXTA-Based Grid Computing
Platform JXTPIA
  *Kenichi Sumitomo, Takato Izaiku, Yoshihiro Saitoh, Hui Wang,
  Minyi Guo, Jie Huang* 804

A Generic Approach to Make Structured Peer-to-Peer Systems
Topology-Aware
  Tongqing Qiu, Fan Wu, Guihai Chen 816

A Workflow Management Mechanism for Peer-to-Peer Computing
Platforms
  Hong Wang, Hiroyuki Takizawa, Hiroaki Kobayashi 827

Session 5B: Internet Computing and Web Technologies I

DDSQP: A WSRF-Based Distributed Data Stream Query System
  Jia-jin Le, Jian-wei Liu 833

Quantitative Analysis of Zipf's Law on Web Cache
  Lei Shi, Zhimin Gu, Lin Wei, Yun Shi 845

An Adaptive Web Caching Method Based on the Heterogeneity of Web Object
  Yun Ji Na, Il Seok Ko, Gun Heui Han 853

Supporting Wireless Web Page Access in Mobile Environments Using Mobile Agents
  HaiYang Hu, JiDong Ge, Ping Lu, XianPing Tao, Jian Lu 859

Session 5C: Network Protocols and Switching I

TCP and ICMP in Network Measurement: An Experimental Evaluation
  Wenwei Li, Dafang Zhang, Gaogang Xie, Jinmin Yang 870

Fuzzy Congestion Avoidance in Communication Networks
  F. Habibipour, M. Khajepour, M. Galily 882

A New Method of Network Data Link Troubleshooting
  Qian-Mu Li, Yong Qi, Man-Wu Xu, Feng-Yu Liu 890

Ethernet as a Lossless Deadlock Free System Area Network
  Sven-Arne Reinemo, Tor Skeie 901

Session 5D: Ad Hoc and Wireless Networks I

An Anycast-Based Geocasting Protocol for Mobile Ad Hoc Networks
  Jipeng Zhou 915

A Mesh Based Anycast Routing Protocol for Ad Hoc Networks
  Shui Yu, Wanlei Zhou 927

Research of Power-aware Dynamic Adaptive Replica Allocation Algorithm in Mobile Ad Hoc Networks
  Yijie Wang, Kan Yang 933

GCPM: A Model for Efficient Call Admission Control in Wireless
Cellular Networks
  Lanlan Cong, Beihong Jin, Donglei Cao, Jiannong Cao 945

Session 6A: Peer-to-Peer Algorithms and Systems II

Cross-Layer Flow Control Based on Path Capacity Prediction for
Multi-hop Ad Hoc Network
  Yongqiang Liu, Wei Yan, Yafei Dai 955

Constructing the Robust and Efficient Small World Overlay Network
for P2P Systems
  Guofu Feng, Ying-chi Mao, Dao-xu Chen 966

Transparent Java Threads Migration Protocol over Peer2Peer
  *Edgardo Ambrosi, Marco Bianchi, Carlo Gaibisso, Giorgio Gambosi,
  Flavio Lombardi* 972

Analytic Performance Modeling of a Fully Adaptive Routing Algorithm
in the Torus
  Mostafa Rezazad, Hamid Sarbazi-azad 984

Redundancy Schemes for High Availability in DHTs
  Fan Wu, Tongqing Qiu, Yuequan Chen, Guihai Chen 990

VIP: A P2P Communication Platform for NAT Traversal
  Xugang Wang, Qianni Deng 1001

Session 6B: Internet Computing and Web Technologies II

Hyper-Erlang Based Model for Network Traffic Approximation
  Junfeng Wang, Hongxia Zhou, Fanjiang Xu, Lei Li 1012

Prediction-Based Multicast Mobility Management in Mobile Internet
  *Guojun Wang, Zhongshan Gao, Lifan Zhang,
  Jiannong Cao* 1024

A Rule-Based Workflow Approach for Service Composition
  Lin Chen, Minglu Li, Jian Cao 1036

Manage Distributed Ontologies on the Semantic Web
  *Peng Wang, Baowen Xu, Jianjiang Lu, Dazhou Kang,
  Yanhui Li* 1047

Session 6C: Network Protocols and Switching II

Next Generation Networks Architecture and Layered End-to-End QoS
Control
  Weijia Jia, Bo Han, Ji Shen, Haohuan Fu 1055

FairOM: Enforcing Proportional Contributions among Peers in
Internet-Scale Distributed Systems
  Yijun Lu, Hong Jiang, Dan Feng 1065

An Efficient QoS Framework with Distributed Adaptive Resource
Management in IPv6 Networks
  Huagang Shao, Weinong Wang, Rui Xie, Xiao Chen 1077

Scheduling Latency Insensitive Computer Vision Tasks
  Richard Y.D. Xu, Jesse S. Jin 1089

Session 6D: Ad Hoc and Wireless Networks II

Throughput Analysis for Fully-Connected Ad Hoc Network with
Multiuser Detection
  Xiaocong Qian, Baoyu Zheng, Genjian Yu 1101

Dynamic Traffic Grooming for Survivable Mobile Networks - Fairness
Control
  Hyuncheol Kim, Sunghae Kim, Seongjin Ahn 1113

An Efficient Cache Access Protocol in a Mobile Computing Environment
  Jae-Ho Choi, SangKeun Lee 1123

Implementation and Performance Study of Route Caching Mechanisms
in DSR and HER Routing Algorithms for MANET
  K. Murugan, Sivasankar, Balaji, S. Shanmugavel 1135

An Effective Cluster-Based Slot Allocation Mechanism in Ad Hoc
Networks
  Tsung-Chuan Huang, Chin-Yi Yao 1146

Author Index 1159

Data Structures and Algorithms for Packet Forwarding and Classification

Sartaj Sahni

Department of Computer and Information Science and Technology,
University of Florida, USA
Sahni@cise.ful.edu

Abstract. We review the data structures that have been proposed for the forwarding and classification of Internet packets. Data structures for both one-dimensional and multidimensional classification as well as for static and dynamic rule tables are reviewed. Sample structures include multi-bit one- and two-dimensional tries, quad trees, binary trees on binary trees, and list of hash tables.

Using Speculative Multithreading for General-Purpose Applications

Pen-Chung Yew

Department of Computer Science and Engineering,
University of Minnesota, USA
yew@cs.umn.edu

Abstract. As multi-core technology is currently deployed in computer industry primarily for limiting power consumption and improving system throughput, continued performance improvement of a single application on such systems remains an important and challenging task. Using thread-level parallelism (TLP) to improve instruction-level parallelism (ILP), i.e. to improve the number of instructions executed per clock cycle, has shown to be effective for many general-purpose applications. However, because of the program characteristics of these applications, effective speculative schemes at both thread and instruction levels are crucial. In the past few years, we have seen significant progress being made in the architectures and the compiler techniques to support such thread-level speculative execution model. In this talk, we will discuss these architectural and compiler issues, in particular, the compiler techniques that could support speculative multithreading for general-purpose applications.

Towards Peta-Bit Photonic Networks

Susumu Horiguchi[*]

Graduate School of Information Sciences, Tohoku University,
Aoba 6-3-09, Sendai, 980-8579, Japan
susumu@ecei.tohoku.ac.jp

Abstract. With a tremendous growth in the Internet traffic, next generation network have been requiring a large increase in transmission capacity, switching-system high-throughput and high-performance optical networking. Wavelength Division Multiplexing (WDM) technology has been increased to the number of wavelengths per fiber hundreds or more with each wavelength operating at the rates of 10Gbps or higher. Thus, the use of all-optical (photonic) networks based on the WDM technology is considered promising to provide peta-bit bandwidth for next generation Internet. To enable the future peta-bit photonic networks, deliberate studies are deserved for some key techniques, such as the ultra-high speed all-optical switching, high performance routing and wavelength assignment (RWA), efficient restoration and protection, etc. This paper provides you with the knowledge about dense WDM networks, high-speed optical switching architectures, high performance routing and wavelength assignment, efficient restoration, as well as prospective vision of future photonic Internet.

1 Introduction

The Internet is experiencing an exponential growth in bandwidth demand from large numbers of users in multimedia applications and scientific computing, as well as in academic communities and military. Also, recent broadband service delivery such as; high capacity contents delivery services, video stream transport, large volume file transfer, and numerous broadband/wideband data services have been pushing carriers and internet service providers to provide an end-to-end optical network from a huge numbers of users home to enterprises. With the development of Wavelength Division Multiplexing (WDM) technology, the number of wavelengths per fiber has been increased to hundreds or more with each wavelength operating at the rates of 10Gbps or higher. Thus, the use of photonic networks based on the WDM technology is considered promising to provide peta-bit bandwidth for next generation Internet [1].

To enable the future peta-bit photonic networks, deliberate studies are deserved for some key techniques, such as the ultra-high speed photonic switching, high per-

---

[*] This research is supported partially by JSPS Grand-in-Aid Scientific Research 17300010 and The Telecommunications Advancement Foundation.

formance routing and wavelength assignment (RWA), efficient restoration and protection, etc. This paper provides you with the knowledge about dense WDM networks, high-speed optical switching architectures, high performance routing and wavelength assignment, efficient restoration, as well as prospective vision of future photonic Internet.

2 Photonic Networks

An optical network is a communications network in which information is transmitted entirely in the form of optical or infrared transmission signals. In a true photonic (all-optical) network, every switch and every repeater works with infrared transmission or visible-light energy. Photonic networks have several advantages over electrical and optical transmission. A single optical fiber can carry hundreds or more of different wavelengths, each beam having its own set of modulating signals. This is known as Wave-Division Multiplexing (WDM).

2.1 Wavelength Division Multiplexing (WDM)

The very high carrier frequency of light also allows the use of multiple different frequency carriers on the same light beam or in the same optical fiber. During the late 1970s to the middle 1990s, fiber transmission roughly capacity doubled each year. In the late of 1990s, WDM technology achieved the significant enhancement in aggregate transmission bit-rate to terabits-per-second. It also provides multiply network capacity, increases the capacity of the interconnection system, and reduces the amount of cabling required in the system. More recent WDM researches have been achieving practical high-speed WDM systems deployable over long distance and dense wavelength division multiplexing (DWDM) [2]. In modern DWDM systems, each wavelength is used as s separate client channel to establish path connectivity in an optical network [3].

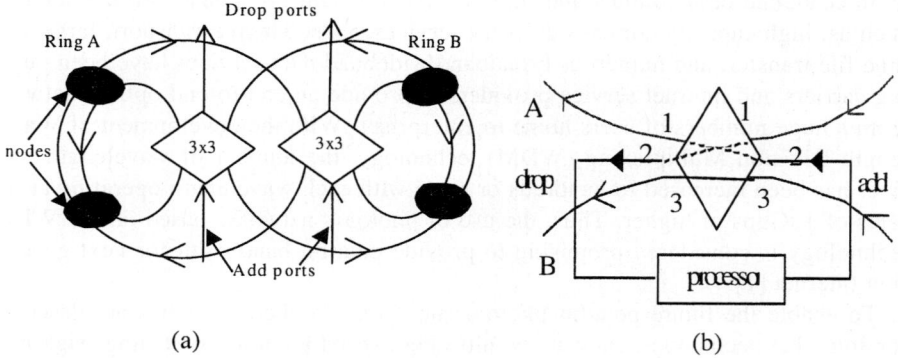

Fig. 1. (a) Two 3x3 switches used to connect two self-healing rings. (b) Working of *add/drop* ports.

With rapid advances in WDM technology such as DWDM add/drop multiplexers(ADMs), wideband optical amplifiers, stable single frequency laser, novel optical cross-connects (OXCs), optical networking has been more focused. Khandker and Horiguchi [4] proposed WDM self-healing ring networks using 3x3 widesense nonblocking optical switches. Figure 1 shows two 3x3 nonblocking optical switches of WDM add/drop. Thus, WDM networks with mesh topology have recently caught much more interest than ever due to the mesh-in-nature Internet backbones that are considered more capacity-efficient and survivable. In WDM mesh networks, all-optical photonic switch is a key network element equipped with a WDM switching node.

2.2 Photonic Packet Switching

One of the most widely adopted photonic switching technologies is based on circuit-switching, in which a lightpath is set up between two nodes for relatively a long period of time. In such a network also called a wavelength-routed (WR) network, the lightpaths provisioned along fibers are switched according to their wavelengths. In the past, the WR approach could be effective and acceptable in the Internet backbone. The network control architecture is overlaid by multiple existing protocols, such as IP over ATM over WDM or IP over ATM over SONET over WDM. The existence of the immediate layer(s) together has solved the discrepancy between the upper IP and the underlying WR based WDM layer. With the emergence of GMPLS protocols, people started to think about IP over WDM architecture in which IP packets are launched directly upon the WDM infrastructure such that it eliminates the overhead and redundancy caused by overlaying multiple protocols.

In such a circumstance, Photonic Packet Switching (PPS) is the most straightforward way to the photonic Internet. It statistically multiplexes the incoming IP packets to a common wavelength channel in the optical domain. It also bears most of the advantages inherent from the conventional IP networks. Figure 2 illustrates photonic

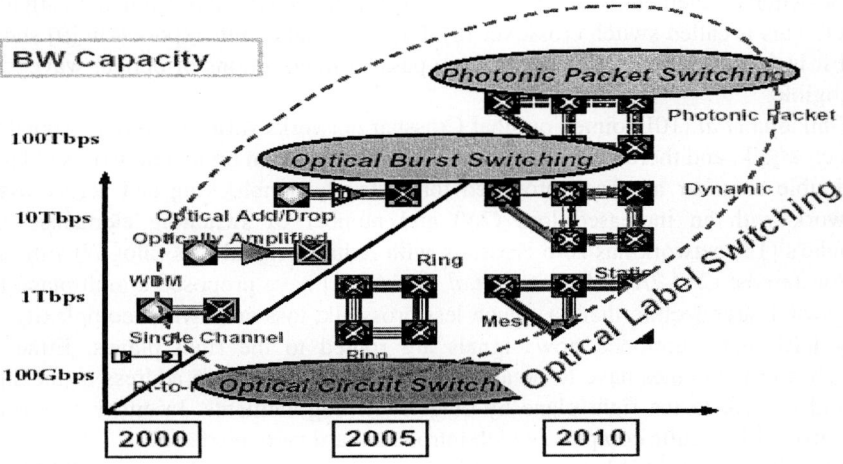

Fig. 2. Photonic network evolution from point-to-point WDM to photonic packet

network progress and evolution from per-to-per WDM to photonic packets. However, due to the fact that the current technology barrier in practically implementing PPS is still huge [5], Optical Burst Switching (OBS) [6][7] is a very promising alternative for the future optical network data plane to deal with the burst and dynamic Internet traffic with high efficiency.

Optical switching technologies are viable for the next generation Internet where high-performance packet transport is facilitated by switching in the optical layer.

3 Optical Switches

Optical switches are useful in designing optical cross-connect to reduce the cell loss probability. For applications that require a high data transmission rate, low error rate and low delay, rearrangement of the states of switching elements in the optical network is not desirable, making nonblocking switching increasingly important for optical networks. Besides, if traffic arrives at input ports asynchronously then a switching network is required to be nonblocking to handle the traffic efficiently. In such cases signals at each input port can be instantly delivered to their destination ports if the destination ports are free and rearrangement of states of internal switching elements will thus be minimized. Thus, nonblocking switching provides a promising technology for the development of photonic networks.

3.1 Nonblocking Optical Switches Using Directional-Coupler (DC)

The basic 2×2 switch element in optical switching systems is usually a directional-coupler (DC) that is created by manufacturing two waveguides close to each other. There are two ways in which optical paths can interact in planar switching networks. First, two optical channels on different waveguides cross each other in order to obtain a particular topology. We call this a channel crossover. Alternatively, two paths sharing a switching element will experience some undesired coupling from one path to the other. This is called switch crossover [8]. Experimental results reported in [9] showed that it is possible to make crosstalk from passive intersections of optical waveguides negligible.

Chikama *et al.*[10] pointed out that Crossbar networks suffer from huge signal loss and crosstalk, and therefore cannot be directly employed in optical networks [11][12]. A double crossbar has been proposed for a strictly nonblocking and zero crosstalk network with an increased loss ($2N$) and number of switching elements ($2N^2$). Spanke's [13] network has zero crosstalk with reduced signal loss ($2\log_2 N$) with huge hardware cost ($2N^2-2N$). M. Vaeze *et.al* in [14][15] have proposed a multiplane banyan switch architecture that has much less crosstalk, loss and switch complexity. But they have not mentioned how signals are routed to the right planes. Either the switches in the planes have to be able to decode the destination address or the signal should be sent to the right plane by other switching elements. In either case access circuitry will be quite complex, which introduce hardware overhead.

Khandker *et. al.* [16] have proposed a recursive network architecture, RN(N,m) in which an $N \times N$ strictly nonblocking switch network can be constructed with given

$m \times m$ size of strictly nonblocking switch. They have expanded $RN(N,m)$ into $GRN(N,M,n,m)$ with $N \times M$ switch size [17]. Figure 3 shows $RN(N,2)$ network. They also proved that even with a 2×2 optical switch as the building block the $RN(N,2)$ has $O(\log_2 N)$ signal loss and constant crosstalk for switch crossover.

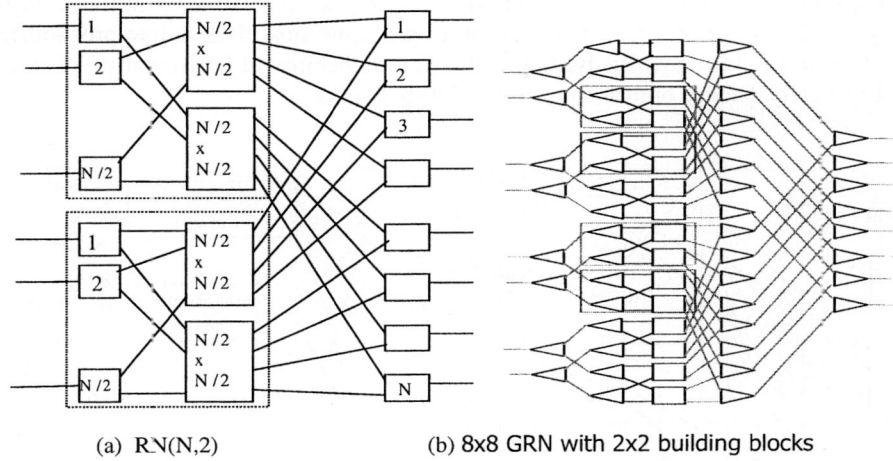

Fig. 3. Nonblocking Recursive Optical Switching Networks

3.2 Vertically Stacked Optical Banyan (VSOB) Networks

A large-scale optical switch is usually composed of numerous basic switching elements (SEs) grouped in multiple stages along with the optical links arranged in a specified interconnection pattern. Figure 4 shows a novel optical switch structure is the vertical stacking of multiple copies (planes) of a banyan network [18]. The resulting networks, namely vertically stacked optical banyan (VSOB) networks, preserve all the good properties of the banyan networks, such as simple switch setting ability (self-routing) and small depth [19][20]. These properties are attractive for DC-based optical switching systems because loss and attenuation of an optical signal are proportional to the number of couplers that the optical signal passes through. In this paper, we focus on the VSOB networks that are free of first-order crosstalk in SEs (we refer to this as crosstalk-free hereafter).

Lot of results are available for VSOB networks, such as [21][22][23], and their main focus has been on determining the minimum number of planes required for nonblocking VSOB networks. Analytical models have also been developed to understand the blocking behaviors of VSOB networks that do not meet the hardware requirement for nonblocking. None of these models, however, have considered the probability of network components failing in their determination of blocking probability. With the gain in importance of fault-tolerant capability of optical switching networks, performance modeling of VSOB networks in presence of network failure becoming critical for the adoption of VSPB networks in practical applications.

Jiang et al. [24][25][26][27] have proposed an analytical model for the blocking probability of VSOB networks that incorporates link failure probability. The new model can guide network designers to determine the effects of link failure and reduction in the number of planes on the blocking behaviors of VSOB networks. They also conducted simulation to validate the model. The analytical and simulation results indicate that our model is accurate and the blocking behavior of a VSOB network is very similar to that of a fault-free one for a reasonable small link failure probability. Chen et al. [28][29] have analyzed the blocking probability of horizontally expanded and vertically stacked optical banyan (HVOB) networks.

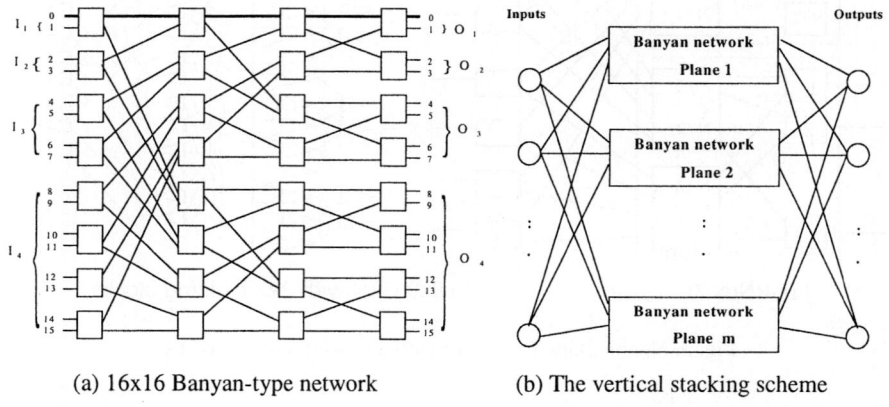

(a) 16x16 Banyan-type network   (b) The vertical stacking scheme

Fig. 4. Vertical stacked optical Banyan nonblocking network (VSOB)

3.3 MEMs and SOA Optical Switches

A number of current researches in photonic switching present challenges to product a large scale matrix switches in low-cost as well as high-speed optical switches in highly reliable system. NTT [30] developed 8x8 optical matrix switch employs Mach-Zehnder interferometer with thermo-optic phase shifter as switching unit. Thermo-Optic switch is featured by smaller package and lower power consumption than mechanical switches. The switching time is around 2 msec, which is acceptable for use in optical cross-connect (OXC) and optical add/drop multiplexing (OADM) nodes.

Matxer et al. [31] proposed thermo-optical digital switch array integrated in silica on silicon. The switch is composed of two interacting waveguide arm though which light propagates. Heating one of the arms changes its refractive index, and the light is transmitted down one path rather than the other. However, the scalability of this technology is limited by the relative high power consumption due to heating waveguides.

Micro-electro-mechanical systems (MEMs) are use for telecommunication applications recently. Since MEMs creates so many mirrors on a single chip, the cost per switching element is relatively low, but MEMS is fairly slow to switching due to moving parts. Lucent Technologies developed two-axis motion MEMs optical cross-connect mirror and also developed large-scale 2D-MEMs switches with 256 x 256 OXC switching array. The optical loss varies with the selected input and output ports in 2D-MES because of the difference in optical path length.

Fujitsu [32] developed 3D-MEMs optical switch by a government-supported OBS R&D initiative in 2001-2005. A large-scale matrix switch of 128x128 with a *msec*-order switching time was fabricated in one chip using the 3D-MEMs free-space transmission type switch. For the high-speed switching, they developed comb-driven MEMS mirror whose speed is over 10 times faster than that of conventional parallel plate mirror. 3D-MEMs optical switch is more suitable for use in fabricating a large-scale 1000x1000 switching system than a digital optical switch and the optical loss in the 3D-MEMs is lower than in the 2D-MEMs.

A semiconductor (laser) optical amplifier (SOA) is now emerging from laboratories into commercial availability. SOA production for use in optical add/drop optical switching is rising rapidly. SOA optical switching is achieved by changing between two stages of SOA. The SOA response time is very fast with switching speed of *nsec*-order. For implementation of SOA optical switch, many technical problems and fabrication problems are still remained. SOA assemblies for wavelength conversion will be a key factor in future all-optical networks.

4 High-Performance Routing and Wavelength Assignment

Photonic networks using wavelength-division- multiplexing (WDM) technology are now considered very promising to meet the huge bandwidth demand of next generation Internet. In WDM wavelength-routed networks, data is switched and routed in all-optical domain via lightpaths. The Routing Wavelength and Assignment (RWA) problem concerns in determining a path and a wavelength to establish lightpaths for connection requests. RWA problem play an important role in improving the performance of WDM networks [33][34]. Without wavelength converters, the same wavelength must be assigned on every link of a lightpath, this referred to as the wavelength-continuity constraint. RWA problem can be classified into the static RWA and dynamic RWA problems. In the static RWA problem, the connection requests are given in advance. In contrast, the dynamic RWA considers the case where the connection requests arrive randomly. The dynamic RWA is more challenging; therefore, heuristic algorithms are usually employed in resolving this problem.

4.1 Dynamic RWA

In this paper, we focus on the dynamic RWA problem under the wavelength-continuity constraint. To solve this problem, there are static routing approaches such as shortest-path routing (SP) or alternate shortest-path routing (ASP) [35]. These approaches compute statically a set of shortest paths without acquiring the current network state. One advantage of alternate shortest-path routing is its simplicity, e.g. small setup time and low control overhead, while providing a significantly lower blocking probability than shortest path routing [36]. Adaptive routing approaches such as adaptive-unconstraint routing using exhaustive search (AUR-E) [37] or least-loaded routing (LLR) [38] are more efficient than static routing methods in terms of blocking probability. However, the main problems of these adaptive routing methods are longer setup delay and higher control overhead, including the requirement of global network's state on each node. To solve this problem, Li et al. [39] proposed an alternate dynamic routing algorithm, called fixed-paths least congestion (FPLC). This algorithm routes a connection request on the least congested path out of a set of pre-determined paths. It is shown that FPLC outperforms the fixed-alternate routing method. The authors also proposed furthermore the FPLC-N(k) method using neighborhood information from only k links on each searched path. This method is employed as a trade-off between network performance versus setup delay and control overhead [40].

4.2 Hybrid Ant-Based Routing and RWA

We proposed a hybrid ant-based routing algorithm (HABR) using mobile agent approach [41] [42] in combining with alternate method to solve the dynamic RWA problem. Inspired from the behaviors of natural ant system, a new class of ant-based algorithms for network routing is currently being developed. We developed an alternate dynamic routing and wavelength assignment algorithm using ant-based mobile agent approach and to compare its performance with other alternate methods. Our motivation is that alternate routing methods such as ASP or FPLC are based on a set of fixed pre-computed paths, which can limit the network performance in terms of blocking probability. Thus, we proposed to use a new routing table structure P-route

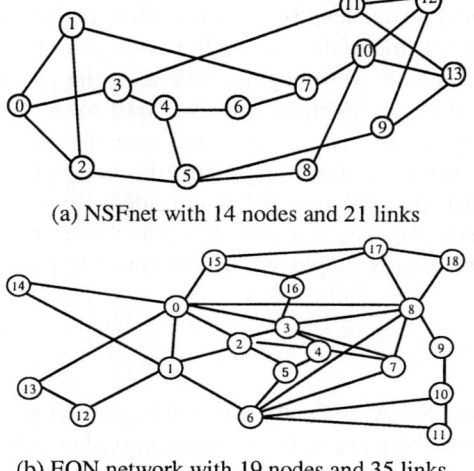

(a) NSFnet with 14 nodes and 21 links

(b) EON network with 19 nodes and 35 links.

Fig. 5. Network examples

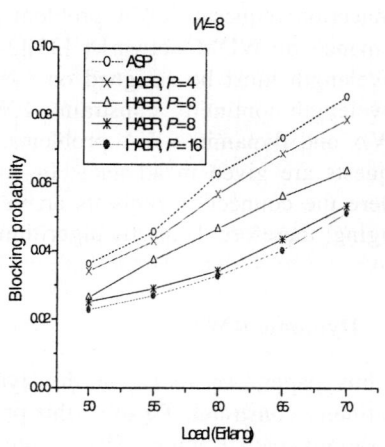

Fig. 6. Performance of HABR on difference value of P when k=2

on each network node that contains a set of P feasible paths between a source-destination pair. Based on the current information of network congestion, ant-based mobile agents will continuously update these routing tables so that the alternate routes are more likely the candidates for a connection request. Thus, this can reduce the blocking probability while still maintaining a small setup time like other alternate methods.

Figure 5 shows the example networks. Figure 6 shows simulation results on the Network Simulator (NS-2). It is seen that with a suitable number of ants and small value of P, our algorithm can outperform alternate shortest-path (ASP) and the fixed-paths least congestion (FPLC) routing algorithm in terms of blocking probability.

5 Survivability in WDM

WDM networks have the capability of provisioning huge bandwidth, and it is expected that the WDM will be a dominant technology for the next generation photonic Internet. As WDM networks carry more and more data, failure of any part in such networks and the resulting inability to move data around quickly may have tremendous economic impacts. For this reason, survivability issues in high bandwidth WDM networks have become an important area of research in recent years.

5.1 Active Restoration

In the active restoration scheme [43], a Dijkstra algorithm- based two-step-approach [44] is used to compute for each connection request a primary lightpath and multiple backup paths that start from the nodes along the primary path and end at the source node of the path, respectively. Here, a backup path starting from a node of the primary path is just the shortest path from that node to the source node that is link-disjoint with the primary path. If enough wavelength channels are available along the primary path, the connection request is accepted and the routing information of all backup paths is then stored in the nodes of the primary path for possible restoration.

On the other hand, if the primary path can not be established due to the lack of resource, the connection is blocked. In this scheme, we define a node along the primary path a supported node if there do exists a backup path from the node to the source node; an unsupported node, otherwise. The active scheme works as follows. Upon a link failure happens along the primary path, the immediate downstream node next to the failure checks successively the availability of the pre-defined downstream backup paths until it finds the first available backup path (in this case, the corresponding supported node is referred as the restoration node) or it fails to find a free backup path among all these downstream backup paths. In the former case, the immediate downstream node next to the failure will send a Failure Notification Message (FNM) to the restoration node which then send a setup message to the source node through the backup path. In the later case, the restoration of this lightpath fails.

We use the example in Figure 7 to illustrate the main idea of active restoration. Let node v_0 be the source node and node v_4 is the destination node, and the primary path is $(v_0\text{-}v_1\text{-}v_2\text{-}v_3\text{-}v_4)$. Suppose the link between v_0 and v_1 fails, the node v_1 will detect a *LOL (Loss of Light)* failure. Since node v_1 is an unsupported node, it will check successively which backup path can be employed for traffic restoration. If the first backup path (e.g. $v_2\text{-} v_5\text{-} v_0$) is available for restoration, node v_1 will send a *FNM* to the restoration node v_2. As soon as node v_2 receives the *FNM*, it will immediately send a set up message to the source node through the backup path $(v_2\text{-} v_5\text{-} v_0)$. Once the source node v_0 accepts the set up message, it reroutes all data to the backup path $v_0\text{-}v_5\text{-}v_2$, then data will go through the rest of primary path to the destination node. If the backup path of the first supported node is not available for restoration, the backup paths of the following supported nodes will be investigated (e.g. $v_3\text{-}v_7\text{-}v_2\text{-}v_5\text{-}v_0$ then, $v_4\text{-}v_7\text{-}v_2\text{-}v_5\text{-}v_0$). If none of these backup paths is available due to the lack of network resources, the restoration of this lightpath fails.

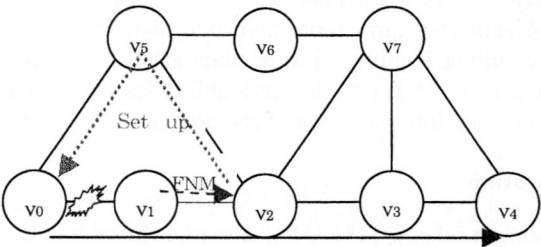

Fig. 7. Active restoration

5.2 Proactive and Reactive Restoration

The approaches to ensuring survivability can be generally classified as *proactive protection* and *reactive restoration*. With the former, a backup lightpath is computed and wavelength channels are reserved for it at the time the primary lightpath is established. If both primary and backup lightpaths are available for a demand, the demand is accepted. Extensive research has been done on proactive protection of WDM networks [45] [46]. While proactive protection yields a 100% restoration guarantee since a backup lightpath is always available to carry the disrupted traffic when a primary lightpath fails, it usually suffers a high blocking probability and resource redundancy. In the reactive restoration, a backup lightpath is searched after the primary lightpath is interrupted. Several lightpath restoration schemes for WDM networks have been reported recently [47] [48]. Although reactive restoration is more efficient in terms of capacity usage and blocking probability, it may lead to an unacceptable long restoration time due to its global search for a backup lightpath. As the proactive protection experiences a very high blocking probability and huge network resource redundancy while the reactive restoration results in a very long restoration time, a novel active restoration scheme, in which a primary lightpath is guarded by multiple backup paths that are predefined but not reserved along the primary path, was proposed recently [49] to compromise the proactive protection and reactive restoration schemes such that good performance can be achieved. Probabilistic modeling is an efficient approach to analyzing network performance, and many analytical models have been proposed for calculating the blocking probability in WDM networks [50] [51].

6 Conclusions

The key for success of photonic networks is a high level of integration with low-cost, highly reliable and standardized optical components. MEMs and array technologies have been manufacturing large-scale optical switches such as 3D-MEMs switches. Advanced technologies realize SOA switches, hybrid integration of active and passive optical components in Photonic Integrated Circuits (PICs) as well as and Planar Lightwave Circuits (PLCs). These advanced, highly functional, integrated, and low-cost photonic components are making the evolution of photonic networking technologies from mesh optical transport network to photonic packet network in next-generation photonic Internet.

References

1. S. Horiguchi, K. Ochiimizu and T. Katayama edited: The Proceeding of the International Symposium on Towards Peta-Bit Ultra-Networks, ISBN4-9900330-3-5, A&I Ltd. (2003) pp.1–188
2. S. V. Karalopulos ,"DWDM: Networks, Devices, and Technology," Wiley Iterscience and IEEE Press, Hoboken, NJ, 2003.
3. S. V. Karalopulos, "Elastic Bandwidth", IEEE Circuits ans Devices, vol.18, No.1, Jan. 2002, pp.8-13.
4. M. R. Khandker and S. Horiguchi, "3x3 Wide Sense Non-blocking Optical Switch for WDM Self-healing Ring Networks," Proc. Int'l Conf. On Electrical and Computer Engineering, Icece 2001, pp. 222-225.
5. C. Qiao, M. Yoo, "Optical burst switching (OBS): A new paradigm for an optical internet", Journal of high speed networks (JHSN) on WDM Networks, vol. 8, no. 1, 1999.
6. Y Chen, C. Qiao, X. Yu, "An optical burst switching: a new area in optical networking research," IEEE Network, vol. 18, 2004, pp. 16-23.
7. Y. Xiong, M. Vandenhoute, and H. Cankaya, "Control architecture in optical burst-switched WDM networks,' IEEE Journal on Selected Areas in Communications (JSAC), Vol. 18, 2000, pp. 1838-1851.
8. A. Jajszczyk, "A Class of Directional-Coupler-Based Photonic Switching Networks", IEEE Transactions on Communications, Vol. 41, No. 4, 1993, pp. 599-603.
9. K. Padmanbhan and A. N. Netravali, "Dialated Networks for Photonic Switching", IEEE Transaction on Communications, Vol. COM-35, No.12, 1987, pp. 1357-1365.
10. T. Chikama, H. Onaka and S. Kuroyanagi, "Photonic Networking Using Optical Add Drop Multiplexers and Optical Cross-Connects", Fujitsu Science and Technology Journal, Vol. 35, No. 1, 1999, pp. 46-55.
11. H. S. Hinton, "A Nonblocking Optical Interconnection Network using Directional Couplers," 1984 IEEE Globecom, Nov. 1984, Vol.2, pp. 885-889.

12. H. S. Hinton, "An introduction to Photonic Switching Fabrics", Plenum publishing co., 1993, pp. 83- 158.
13. R. A. Spanke, "Architectures for Guided-wave Optical Switching Systems", IEEE Communications Magazine, Vol. 25, No. 5, 1987, pp. 42-28.
14. M. Mehdi Vaez and Chin-Tau Lea, "Wide-Sense Nonblocking Banyan-Type Switching Systems Based on Directional Couplers", IEEE Transactions on Communications, Vol. 16, No. 7, 1998, pp. 1327-1332.
15. M. Mehdi Vaez and Chin-Tau Lea, "Strictly Nonblocking Directional-Coupler-Based Switching Networks Under Crosstalk Constraint", IEEE Transactions on Communications, Vol. 48, No. 2, 2000, pp. 316-323.
16. M. R. Khandker, X. Jiang, H. Shen, S. Horiguchi, " A New Architecture for Nonblocking Optical Switch Networks", Photonic Network Communications, Vol .3, No.4, 2001, pp. 393-400.
17. M. R. Khandker, X. Jiang, H. Shen and S. Horiguchi, "A New Self-routing Nonblocking Optical MIN", HPC ASIA 2001, 26th, Stream B, September, 2001, Queensland, Australia.
18. C.-T. Lea, "Muti-log_2N networks and their applications in high speed electronic and photonic switching systems," IEEE Trans. Commun., vol.38, pp.1740-1749, Oct. 1990.
19. F. T. Leighton, Introduction to Parallel Algorithms and Architectures: Arrays, Trees, Hypercubes, Morgan Kaufmann, 1992.
20. J. H. Patel, "Performance of processor-memory interconnections for multiprocessors," IEEE Trans. Comput., vol.C-30, Oct.1981, pp.771-780.
21. G.Maier and A.Pattavina, "Design of photonic rearrangeable networks with zero first-order switching-element-crosstalk, " IEEE Trans. Commun., vol.49, no.7, July.2001. pp.1268-1279.
22. M.M.Vaez and C.-T. Lea, "Strictly nonblocking directional-coupler-based switching networks under crosstalk constraint," IEEE Trans. Commun., vol.48, no.2, Feb. 2000, pp.316-323.
23. M.M.Vaez and C.-T. Lea, "Wide-sense nonblocking Banyan-type switching systems based on directional couplers, " IEEE J. Select. Areas Commun., vol.16, Sept.1998, pp.1327-1332.
24. X. Jiang, M. R.Khandker, H. Shen and S. Horiguchi," Modeling the Blocking Probabilities of Crosstalk-free Optical MINs with Vertical Stacking ", Proc. of IEEE Region 10 (IEEE TENCON'02) Oct.2002, Beijing, China.
25. X. Jiang, M. R. Khandker and S.Horiguchi, "Upper-bound for blocking probabilities of a Class of Optical MINs Under Crosstalk-free Constraint," Proceedings of the 2001 IEEE Workshop on High Performance Switching and Routing, pp.203-207, May.2001, Dallas, USA.
26. X. Jiang, H. Shen, M. R. Khandker and Susumu Horiguchi, " Blocking Behaviors of Crosstalk-free Optical Banyan Networks on Vertical Stacking," IEEE/ACM TRANSACTIONS on NETWORKING, 11 (2003), 982-993.
27. X. Jiang, H. Shen, and S. Horiguchi," Blocking Probability of Vertically Stacked Optical Banyan Networks Under Random Routing," Proc. of GLOBECOM 2003, Dec.1-5, San Francisco, USA.
28. Y. Chen, X. Jiang, Pin–Han Ho, S. Horiguchi and H. T. Mouftah, "Blocking Probability Modeling of Distensible Optical Banyan Networks," Accepted by the International Conference on Communications, May 15-21, 2005, Seoul, Korea (the best paper award in ICC 2005).

29. Y. Chen, X. Jiang and S. Horiguchi, "Analysis of Blocking Probability for Vertically Stacked Optical Banyan Networks with Extra Stage", Proceedings of the 4th IASTED International Multi-Conference, WIRELESS AND OPTICAL COMMUNICATIONS, pp.845-850, July 8-10, 2004, Banff, Canada
30. T. Maruno, "Recent Progress in Optical Switching Device technologies in NTT," NTT Technical review, Vol. 1, No. 7, pp.12-19, Oct. 2003.
31. Matxer et al. "Thermooptical digital switch array in silica on silicon with defined zero voltage state," IEEE Hournal of Lightwave Technology, Vol. 16, No.3, 1998, pp. 395-400.
32. O. Tsuboi et al.,"A Rotational Comb-driven Micro Mirror with Large Deflection ad Lowe Drive Voltage", Optical MEMs, pp.532-535.
33. R. Ramaswami and K. Sivarajan, Optical networks: A practical perspective, Morgan Kaufman Publishers Inc., San Francisco, CA, 2002
34. H. Zang, et al., "A review of routing and wavelength assignment approaches for Wavelength-Routed Optical WDM Networks," in Optical Networks Magazine, Vol. 1 pp. 47-63, Jan. 2000.
35. A. Birman, "Computing approximate blocking probabilities for a class of all-optical networks," IEEE J. Sel. Areas Communication, vol. 14, no. 5, pp. 852-857, June 1996.
36. S. Ramamurthy and B. Mukherjee, "Fixed-alternate routing and wavelength conversion in wavelength-routed optical networks," in Proc. IEEE GLOBECOM, pp. 2295-2302, Nov. 1998
37. H.T. Mokhtar and M. Azizoglu, "Adaptive wavelength routing in all-optical networks," IEEE/ACM Trans. Networking, vol. 6, pp. 197-206, April 1998.
38. B. Zhou, and H.T. Mouftah, "Adaptive least loaded routing for multi-fiber WDM networks using approximate congestion information," in Proc. IEEE ICC, vol. 5, pp. 2745-2749, 2002.
39. L. Li and A.K. Somani, "Dynamic wavelength routing using congestion and neighborhood information," IEEE/ACM Trans. Networking, vol. 7, No. 5, pp. 779-786, October 1999
40. M. Dorigo and V. Maniezzo, "Ant system: Optimization by a colony of cooperating agents," IEEE Trans. Systems, Man, and Cybernetics-Part B, vol. 26, No. 1, pp. 29-41, 1996
41. S. H. Ngo, X. Jiang, S. Horiguchi, "Adaptive routing and wavelength assignment using ant-based algorithm," in Proc. 12th IEEE ICON, vol. 2, pp 482-486, Singapore, Nov. 2004.
42. V.T. Le, X. Jiang, S.H. Ngo, S. Horiguchi, "Dynamic RWA based on the combination of mobile agents technique and genetic algorithm in WDM networks with sparse wavelength conversion", 19th IEEE IPDPS, Colorado, USA, April 2005
43. M. A. Azim, X.Jiang, M. R. Khandker, S. Horiguchi and P.H. Ho, "Active Light-path Restoration in WDM Networks", OSA Journal of Optical Networking, Vol.3/4, pp. 247-260, (2004).
44. R. Bhandari, Survivable Networks: Algorithms for Diverse Routing, Kluwer Academic Publishers, Boston, 1999.
45. Pin-Han Ho and H. T. Mouftah, "A Framework of Service Guaranteed Shared Protection for Optical Networks, "IEEE Communications Magazine, Feb. 2002, pp. 97-103.
46. G. Maier, S. D. Patre, A. Patavina, M. Martinelli, "Optical Network Survivability: Protection Techniques in the WDM Layer", Photonic Network Communications, Volume4, Issue3/4, pp. 251-269, July-December 2002.

47. S. Ramamurthy, B. Mukherjee, "Survivable WDM Mesh Networks, Part II - Restoration", in: Proc. ICC99, Vol. 3, pp. 2023-2030.
48. G. Mohan and C. Siva Ram Murthy, "Lightpath Restoration in WDM Optical Networks", IEEE Network, vol. 14, no. 6, pp. 24-32, Nov/Dec 2000.
49. M. A. Azim, X. Jiang, P.-H. Ho, and S. Horiguchi, "Performance Analysis of WDM Networks Employing Active Restoration," the IASTED international conference on Optical Communication Systems and Networks (OCSN'04), July 2004.
50. A. Birman, Computing Approximate Blocking Probabilities for a Class of All-Optical Networks, IEEE Journal on Selected areas in Communications, Vol. 14, No. 5, June 1996, pp. 853-857.

Technologies and Considerations for Developing Internet and Multiplayer Computer Games: A Tutorial (Extended Abstract)

Wanlei Zhou

School of Information Technology,
Deakin University, Melbourne, Australia
wanlei@deakin.edu.au

Games are universal and probably as old as humankind. Today the development of computer technology, especially the development of fast networks and the Internet, brings games a faster growth than ever before. Game design and development is now a fast-growing entertainment field, with a lot to offer professionally and creatively. In fact, from IT professional's point of view, creating computer games provides us with all the usual technical challenges associated with software development, such as requirement analysis, architectural design, rapid prototyping, HCI, parallel and distributed processing, code reuse, programming, performance evaluation, testing and maintenance. It also provides challenges on other exciting aspects, such as storyboarding, screenplays, illustration, animation, sound effects, music, and social impact. By developing a computer game from start to finish, one would be able to acquire multi-disciplinary knowledge to become an IT professional for the modern era.

The main aim of this tutorial is to survey the major theory and techniques behind the design and implementation of multiplayer and Internet games, and to understand the application of the knowledge to the development of working multiplayer and Internet games. Upon completion of this tutorial, people should have a basic understanding of the technologies used in multiplayer and Internet game development, along with the ability to expand on this knowledge to carry out further research and development of Internet and multiplayer computer games

This tutorial has four parts. The first part discusses theoretical issues in developing Internet and multiplayer computer games. Topics in this part include: chronology of game programming, essentials for game design and development; design strategies for multiplayer computer games (MCGs); basic architectures of MCGs and MCG components; tools for MCG development, and challenges for developing MCGs. The second part focuses on the technological issues in developing Internet and multiplayer computer games. Topics in this part include: game servers, networking technologies, Internet database technologies, and security issues. The third part deals with a number of considerations in developing Internet games. Topics in this part include: design considerations for Internet games, development considerations for Internet games, and launching and managing an online game. The last part of the tutorial briefly discusses the rationales and the structure of a university course in games design and development.

The audience of this tutorial includes researchers, practitioners, and technical officers from academic, business and government. No specific knowledge is required.

Anyone with a basic knowledge of computing and an interest in the Internet and multiplayer computer games will be able to understand the materials presented in the tutorial. The length of the tutorial will be three hours.

Outline

Part 1: Theoretical Issues in Developing Internet and Multiplayer Computer Games
1. Chronology of game programming
2. Essentials for game design and development
3. Design strategies for multiplayer computer games (MCGs)
4. Basic architectures of MCG and MCG components
5. Tools for MCG development
6. Challenges for developing MCG

Part 2: Technological Issues in Developing Internet and Multiplayer Computer Games
7. Game servers
8. Networking technologies
9. Internet database technologies
10. Security issues

Part 3: Considerations in Developing Internet Games
11. Design considerations for Internet games
12. Development considerations for Internet games
13. Launching and managing an online game

Part 4: A Course in Games Design and Development
14. Rationales for university courses in games design and development
15. An example course design: Bachelor of Information Technology (Games Design and Development)

Routing in 2-D Meshes: A Tutorial
(Extended Abstract)

Zhen Jiang

Computer Science Department,
Information Assurance Center,
West Chester University of PA,
West Chester, PA 19335, U.S.A.
zjiang@wcupa.edu

As we know, the performance of networks systems is dependent on the end-to-end cost of communication mechanisms. Routing is a process of finding a path from the source node to the destination node in a given network system. The ability to route message efficiently becomes increasingly important. Routing in mesh-connected networks, such as 2-D meshes, has been commonly discussed due to the structural regularity for easy construction and the high potential legibility for variety of algorithms.

This tutorial will provide a survey of the existing routings which can be applied in 2-D meshes, including a variety of wireless network routings and sensor network routings. We will focus on the use of network topology information in the routing process. Our current research on information model for routing in 2-D meshes is also introduced. The main aim is to offer the audience another chance to understand the importance of information technology, as well as the opportunities in further research.

The tutorial has three parts. In the first part, the 2-dimentional mesh networks, simply 2-D meshes, will be introduced. A 2-D mesh interconnection network is one of direct networks, which are also called router-based networks. Then, the wormhole routing and agent routing in such 2-D meshes will be discussed. After that, we present a cost-effective way using information models to ensure the existence of a minimal path and form a minimal path by routing decision at each intermediate node along the path. A minimal routing always routes the packet in an efficient way to the destination through the shortest path. Wireless networks is an emerging new technology. In the second part, we will focus on how to collect and distribute network topology information to facilitate the routing process and its development stages of reducing cost expense. Most existing literature discusses the wireless network routing in the 2-D plane. By using the graphical data structure, the wireless networks can be described in 2-D meshes. Based on this topology description, we will introduce the existing proactive routings, reactive routings, hierarchical routings, and geographical routings. Recent advances in micro-electromechanical systems, digital electronics, and wireless communications have enabled the development of low-cost, low-power, and multifunction sensor devices. These devices can operate autonomously to gather, process, and communicate information about their environments. They constitute a wireless sensor network or simply sensor network. In the last part, we will introduce the problem of saving energy consumption, fault tolerance, scalability, network dynamics, and connectivity, and complete coverage in sensor networks. These make the inherence of wireless network routing in sensor networks inefficient. We will introduce our connected dominating set solution and discuss the future work on information model for routing in sensor networks.

Outline

Part 1: The Introduction to 2-D Meshes and its information based routing
1. 2-D mesh interconnection network
2. Wormhole routing and agent routing
3. Adaptive routing and fault tolerant routing
4. Minimal routing, detour and backtracking
5. Orthogonal fault block model, extended safety level model, and boundary model
6. Minimal connected component model

Part 2: Wireless network routing
7. Introduction to wireless networks: (infrastructured and infrastructureless networks)
8. Proactive routings (DBF, TBRPF, GSR, WRP, DSDV, CGSR, LANMAR, FSR, and OLSR)
9. Reactive routings (AODV, DSR, FORP, LMR, TORA, ABR, and SSA)
10. Hierarchical routings (ZRP, CEDAR, DDR, BRP, SHARP, CBRP, and HSR)
11. Geographical routings (LAR, GLS, RDMAR, DREAM, and ZHLS)

Part 3: Sensor network routing
12. Introduction to sensor networks
13. Energy saving, fault tolerance, scalability, network dynamics, and connectivity in sensor networks
14. Future work on sensor network routing

RDIM: A Self-adaptive and Balanced Distribution for Replicated Data in Scalable Storage Clusters[*]

Zhong Liu, Nong Xiao, and Xing-Ming Zhou

Institute of Computer, National University of Defense Technology,
Changsha, China, 410073
Liuzhong@zhmail.com

Abstract. As storage systems scale from a few storage nodes to hundreds or thousands, data distribution and load balancing become increasingly important. We present a novel decentralized algorithm, RDIM (Replication Under Dynamic Interval Mapping), which maps replicated objects to a scalable collection of storage nodes. RDIM distributes objects to nodes evenly, redistributing as few objects as possible when new nodes are added or existing nodes are removed to preserve this balanced distribution. It supports weighted allocation and guarantees that replicas of a particular object are not placed on the same node. Its time complexity and storage requirements compare favorably with known methods.

1 Introduction

As the use of large distributed systems and large-scale clusters of commodity computers has increased, significant research has been devoted toward designing scalable distributed storage systems. Its applications now span numerous disciplines, such as: higher large-scale mail system, online numeric periodical, digital libraries, large online electric commerce system, energy research and simulation, high energy physics research, seismic data analysis, large scale signal and image processing applications, data grid application and peer-to-peer storage application, etc. Usually, it will no longer be possible to do overall upgrades of high performance storage systems. Instead, systems must grow gracefully over time, adding new capacity and replacing failed units seamlessly—an individual storage device may only last five years, but the system and the data on it must survive for decades. Since the capacities of storage nodes usually are non-uniform and storage nodes are dynamically changed in large-scale distributed storage systems, systems must distribute data objects among the storage nodes according to their capabilities and afford to immediately rebalance data objects distribution according to weight of storage nodes when storage nodes are changed. So we study the problem of designing flexible, adaptive strategies for the distribution of objects among a heterogeneous set of servers. Ideally, such a strategy should be able to adapt with a minimum amount of replacements of objects to changes in the capabilities of the servers so that objects are always distributed among

---

[*] Supported by the National Basic Research Program 973 of China (No.2003CB317008).

the servers according to their capabilities. Finally, Xin, et al.[1] reports that the mean time to failure (of a single disk) in a petabyte-scale (10^{15} bytes) storage system will be approximately one day. In order to prevent data loss, we must allow for data replication. Furthermore, the data replication scheme should guarantee that replicas of the same object get placed on different servers, or the effect of replication will be nullified.

Previous techniques are able to handle these requirements only in part. For example, a typical method to map data object to storage nodes in an optimally balanced way is a simple Round-Robin (RR) assignment. The storage node number assigned to a given data object can be easily calculated using modular arithmetic: h(id)=id mod n, where id is object ID and n is the number of storage nodes in system. If storage nodes have the uniform capabilities, it can be used to distribute data objects evenly among n servers. However, they usually do not adapt well to a change in the capabilities. Moreover, If a new server is added, approximately the fraction n/(n+1) of the data objects must be moved from one storage node to another before the data can be accessed using the new mapping. For a large storage system, this leads to a long period of unavailability of data, which is not acceptable to many applications. In contrast, the minimum fraction that must be relocated to obtain a balanced mapping is approximately 1/(n+1). A different approach is to maintain object-to-node mapping in a stored directory (SD). In this case, a directory of B entries is maintained in which the ith entry contains the node number assigned to object i, where B is the total number of objects and is usually a fairly large integer. Thus, each object can be individually assigned or reassigned to any storage node. When new storage nodes are added, individual objects are selected for relocation to the new nodes so that only the minimum amount of object is moved. However, this approach suffers from severe performance bottleneck problems and consumes a significant amount of memory. Litwin, et al. [2] has developed many variations on Linear Hashing (LH*), the LH* variants are limited in two ways: they must split buckets, and they have no provision for buckets with different weights. LH* splits buckets in half, so that on average, half of the objects on a split bucket will be moved to a new empty bucket, resulting in suboptimal bucket utilization and a "hot spot" of bucket and network activity between the splitting node and the recipient and the distribution is unbalanced after replacement. Moreover, the LH* variants do not support weighted allocation and data replication. Other data structures such as DDH [3] suffer from similar splitting issues. Choy, et al. [4] describes algorithms for perfect distribution of data to disks that move an optimally low number of objects when disks are added. However, these algorithms do not support weighting of disks, removal of disks and data replication. Brinkmann, et al. [5, 6] proposes a method for pseudo-random distribution of data to multiple disks using partitioning of the unit range. This method accommodates growth of the collection of disks by repartitioning the range and relocating data to rebalance the load. However, this method does not move an optimally number of objects of replacement, and does not allow for the placement of replicas. Honicky, et al. [7,8] presents algorithms for balanced distribution of data to disks that move an optimally low number of objects when disks are added, which supports weighting of disks and replication, but do not support removal of disks [7], however, the methods relies upon iterating for producing the same sequence of numbers regardless of the number actually required, and the large-scale iterations increase the lookup time. We present an algorithm for balanced distribution of data to nodes that move probabilistically an optimally number of objects when nodes are added or removed, which supports weighting of nodes, but do not support replication [9].

In the algorithm, data objects are always distributed among the storage nodes according to their weights. When new nodes are added or existing nodes are removed, it distributes objects to nodes evenly, and redistributing as few objects as possible and preserves this balanced distribution. Moreover, our algorithm almost always moves a statistically optimal number of objects from every storage node in the system to each new storage node, rather than from one storage node to one storage node. It supports data replication and guarantees that replicas of a particular object are not placed on the same node. The algorithm is very fast, and scales with the number of storage nodes groups added to the system. Its time complexity and storage requirements compare favorably with known methods. The rest of the paper is organized as follows. Section 2 contains definitions, including descriptions of the measures of "goodness" of a mapping method that are of interest to us. Section 3 presents a self-adaptive data objects placement algorithm supporting weighted allocation and replication. Section 4 gives performance analysis and simulation results. Section 5 summarizes the paper.

2 The Model and Definitions

Given a positive integer B, the number of data objects, and a positive integer N, the number of storage nodes, and a positive integer R, the maximum degree of replication for an object, the problem is to construct a mapping f from the set of object id's (0, 1,2, ..., B-1) and the replica number r ($0 \leq r < R$) of the object in question to the set of node id's (0, 1,2, ..., N-1). Typically, B is much larger than N. When an expansion occurs, the number of storage nodes increases from N to some N', we have to construct a new mapping f' to reassign the node number in N' for data access. We can view a mapping method as a function M (x, r, p) that takes a data object id x, the replica number r and a representation p of a particular mapping, and returns a storage node id. That is, f (x, r) = M (x, r, p) where p is the representation of f. For example (no replication), for the RR method mentioned in the Introduction, the representation p is simply n, and M (x, p) = x mod n; for the SD method, p is a list ($y_0, y_1, \ldots y_{B-1}$) of integers, and M (x, p) = y_x.

Let the size of storage node i under the mapping f is l_i, which is the number of data objects that f maps to i. Let the weight of storage node i is w_i. Measures of the goodness of a solution include the following:

(1) Balance. A mapping f from B objects onto N nodes is said to be balanced if for every pair of nodes in the system i and j, the expected ratio between the size of i and j is equal to the ratio of the weights assigned to i and j (i.e. $\dfrac{l_i}{l_j} = \dfrac{w_i}{w_j}$).

(2) Mapping Complexity. This is the number of operations needed to compute f (x), given an object id x.

(3) Mapping Storage. This is the amount of storage needed to store a representation of the mapping. In placing upper bounds on the mapping storage of a particular

mapping method M (x, p), we bound only the storage needed for the representation p (which can, in general, depend on N, B, and the number of expansions), and we ignore the (constant) storage needed to hold an algorithm for computing M.

(4) Object Relocation. When a mapping f is replaced with another mapping f' as the result of an expansion, the object relocation of the expansion is the number of objects that are assigned to different nodes by f and f', i.e., the number of object id's x such that $f(x) \neq f'(x)$ and $0 \leq x < B$.

3 Replication Under Dynamic Interval Mapping

3.1 Representation of the Mapping

We assume that system storage nodes are partitioned into sub-clusters; sub-clusters consist of identical storage nodes that are added, removed, and reweighed as a group. The entire storage system consists of multiple server sub-clusters, accreted over time. In most systems, sub-clusters of storage nodes have different properties—newer storage nodes are faster and have more capacity. We must therefore add weighting to the algorithm to allow some storage nodes to contain a higher proportion of objects than others. We assign weight factor w_j to a single storage node in sub-cluster j. This factor will likely be a number that describes the power (such as capacity, throughput, or some combination of the two) of the storage node. Suppose that we are in a situation where m expansions have occurred. Part of the representation of the mapping is the sequence $N_0, N_1, N_2, \ldots, N_m$, where $N_0 > 0$ is the number of storage nodes initially, and N_j is the total number of storage nodes after the jth expansion. It is convenient to define $N_{-1}=0$. Let $d_j = N_j - N_{j-1}$ for $0 \leq j \leq m$. Thus, at the jth expansion, d_j storage nodes are added to the existing N_{j-1} storage nodes to create a new total of N_j storage nodes. Note that $d_j > 0$ for $0 \leq j \leq m$, since $N_{j-1} < N_j$. In what follows, we assume that the numbers d_j is also stored, although an alternative is to recompute a particular d_j whenever it is needed. Define the jth sub-cluster, for $0 \leq j \leq m$, to be storage nodes with id's in the interval $[N_{j-1}, N_j)$. (For integers z_1 and z_2 with $z_1 < z_2$, the interval $[z_1, z_2)$ contains all integers z with $z_1 \leq z < z_2$.) Thus, d_j is the number of storage node in the jth sub-cluster.

Suppose that we have a random function H: $\{0, 1, \ldots, M\} \rightarrow [0,1)$, the function H maps the data object's id uniformly at random to real numbers in the interval [0,1). The basic idea of the mapping is to map the space [0, B) of data object id's into intervals in [0,1) and divide the interval [0, 1) into different length intervals according to weight of sub-clusters; All objects mapped to the same interval are mapped to storage nodes that belong to the same sub-cluster. A storage node can contain objects from several different intervals. When sub-clusters are changed, current intervals are divided into more small intervals rather than the interval [0,1) is redefined and different intervals are reassigned into new sub-clusters, resulting in data objects replacement.

In addition to m, the N_j's, and the d_j's, the rest of the representation of the mapping consists of the following:

(1) An integer $k \geq 1$, the number of intervals.
(2) Real numbers a_i for $0 \leq i \leq k$ where
$0 = a_0 < a_1 < a_2 < \ldots < a_k = 1$

The ith interval is $[a_{i-1}, a_i)$, for $1 \leq i \leq k$. We imagine that the intervals are ordered from left to right, and we say that the ith interval is to the left of the jth interval (and that the jth is to the right of the ith) if $i < j$.

(3) Nonnegative integers b_i, for $1 \leq i \leq k$. For the ith interval $[a_{i-1}, a_i)$, the number b_i is the sub-cluster number associated with this interval. Thus, $0 \leq b_i < m$. All data objects $H(x)$ in $[a_{i-1}, a_i)$ are mapped to storage nodes in sub-cluster b_i, Define sub-cluster(x) = b_i, for all $H(x)$ in $[a_{i-1}, a_i)$.

In general, several intervals can be mapped to the same sub-cluster; that is, we can have $b_i = b_j$, for different i and j.

(4) Nonnegative real numbers c_i, for $1 \leq i \leq k$. For each i, the number c_i, is the total length of intervals of objects x's $H(x)$ in intervals to the left of the ith interval (i.e., $H(x) < a_{i-1}$) such that x is mapped to a sub-cluster b_i, (i.e., sub-cluster(x) = b_i). The c_i's are helpful in computing the mapping. Note that c_i is the total length of intervals of objects x in intervals to the left of the ith such that x is mapped to sub-cluster b_i. We call c_i the offset adjustment of the ith interval.

3.2 Computation of the Mapping

The algorithm becomes slightly more complicated when we add replication because we must guarantee that no two replicas of an object are placed on the same server, while still allowing the optimal placement and migration of objects to new sub-clusters. Given a data object id x and its replica number r, the way to compute the mapping is first to determine the number of replicas which belong in each sub-cluster according to its weight, and find the interval $[a_{i-1}, a_i)$ to which x belongs, and then to compute the mapping using b_i, N_{j-1}, and d_j (j=b_i). Once it has determined that a particular sub-cluster should contain u replicas of an object, it selects u storage nodes randomly from that sub-cluster. Pseudo-code for the mapping computation is given by Algorithm 1 in Figure 1, where $0 = u_0 < u_1 < u_2 < \ldots < u_m = 1$, the interval length of $[u_{j-1}, u_j)$ is the weight rate of the jth sub-cluster.

Algorithm 1: Mapping Computation
Input: A object id x and its replica number r
Find i such that H(x) is in $[a_{i-1}, a_i)$
j = b_i
if (r = 0)
    Return N_{j-1} + x mod d_j
else
    Find j such that H(r) is in $[u_{j-1}, u_j)$
    choose a random prime number p > d_j
    Return N_{j-1} + (x + r*p) mod d_j
end if

Fig. 1. Algorithm for mapping computation

3.3 The Initial Representation

Initially, when there are no expansions have occurred, the representation is given by $m=0$, $k=1$, $a_0=0$, $a_1=1$, $b_1=c_1=0$, and $d_0=N_0$, Thus, the mapping is exactly given by $y=x+r*p \bmod N_0$. where p is a random prime number ($p > N_0$)

When the number of storage nodes is changed, the representation of the mapping must be modified Assume that we are in a situation where m expansions have occurred previously (for some $m \geq 0$) and that we have a representation of the mapping, from B data objects to N_m storage nodes, as described above; call this mapping the old mapping. There are two cases.

3.4 Adding Sub-cluster

Suppose that the (m+1)th sub-cluster is added, which consists of storage nodes in $[N_m, N_{m+1})$. The basic idea is, for each sub-cluster j with $0 \leq j \leq m$, to move the proper number of objects from sub-cluster j to the (m+1)th sub-cluster so as to produce a new balanced mapping from B objects to N_{m+1} nodes. Among the objects in sub-cluster j, the ones with a larger random number H(x) are moved. This has the effect that if an object stays in the same sub-cluster, then it remains mapped to the same node. So for each sub-cluster j with $0 \leq j \leq m$, there will be a splitting point s_j such that, for each object x mapped to sub-cluster j in the old mapping, if $H(x) < s_j$, then object x remains in sub-cluster j in the new mapping, and if $H(x) \geq s_j$, then object x is moved to the new

---

Algorithm 2: Computation of Adding Cluster Actions
Input: A new number N_{m+1} of Nodes

$$\text{total} = \sum_{j=0}^{m+1} d_j * w_j$$

for j = 0 to m
    $t_j = d_j * w_j / \text{total}$
end for
w = 0
for i = 1 to k
    $j = b_i$
    if $t_j \geq (a_i - a_{i-1} + c_i)$ then
        A_i = Null
    else if $t_j \leq c_i$ then
        A_i = Move(w)
        $w = w + a_i - a_{i-1}$
    else
        $s = a_{i-1} + t_j - c_i$,
        A_i = Split(s,w)
        $w = w + a_i - s$
end for

Fig. 2. Algorithm for computing adding cluster actions

(m+1)th sub-cluster in the new mapping. If $a_{i-1} < s_j < a_i$, for some interval $[a_{i-1}, a_i)$ with $b_i = j$ in the representation of the old mapping, then this interval will be split into two intervals, $[a_{i-1}, s_j)$ that remains mapped to sub-cluster j, and $[s_j, a_i)$ that is mapped to the (m+1)th sub-cluster. To make the following description of mapping expansion independent of implementation, the result is given as a set of actions to be performed. There is an action A associated with each interval $[a_{i-1}, a_i)$ in the representation of the old mapping. There are three types of actions:

1. If A_i = Null, then objects in the interval $[a_{i-1}, a_i)$ do not move. The sub-cluster number and the offset adjustment of the interval do not change.
2. If A_i = Move(c), then all objects in the interval $[a_{i-1}, a_i)$ are moved to the (m+1)th sub-cluster. The sub-cluster number of the interval is changed to m, and c becomes the new offset adjustment of the interval.
3. If A_i = Split(s, c), then the interval $[a_{i-1}, a_i)$ is split into two intervals, $[a_{i-1}, s)$ and $[s, a_i)$. Objects with H(x) in $[s, a_i)$ are moved to the (m+1)th sub-cluster, and c is the offset adjustment of the interval $[s, a_i)$. Objects in $[a_{i-1}, s)$ do not move; the sub-cluster number and offset adjustment of $[a_{i-1}, s)$ are identical to those of $[a_{i-1}, a_i)$ in the old mapping.

Pseudocode for computing the appropriate actions is given by Algorithm 2 in Figure 2.

Algorithm 3: Computation of Removing Cluster Actions
Input: A removed rth cluster

$$\text{total} = \sum_{j=0, j \neq r}^{m} d_j * w_j$$

for j =0, j≠r to m
    $t_j = d_j * w_j / \text{total}$
end for
j = 0
for each interval $[a_{i-1}, a_i)$ with $b_i = r$
    if j≠r then
        t = total interval length of the cluster j
        if $(t_j - t) \geq (a_i - a_{i-1})$ then
            A_i = Move (t)
            $t = t + a_i - a_{i-1}$
        else
            $s = t_j - t + a_{i-1}$
            A_i = Split(s, t)
            j = j + 1
    end if
end for

Fig. 3. Algorithm for computing removing cluster actions

3.5 Removing Sub-cluster

Suppose that the rth sub-cluster is removed, which consists of storage nodes in $[N_{r-1}, N_r)$. The basic idea is to move the proper number of objects from sub-cluster r to other sub-cluster j with $0 \le j \le m$ and $j \ne r$, so as to produce a new balanced mapping from B objects to $N_m - d_r$ nodes. So for each interval $[a_{i-1}, a_i)$ of the rth sub-cluster, either the all the interval $[a_{i-1}, a_i)$ is moved to some sub-cluster j with $0 \le j \le m$ and $j \ne r$, or there will be a splitting point s such that, $[a_{i-1}, s)$ is moved to some sub-cluster j, $[s, a_i)$ is remained to next movement To make the following description of mapping expansion independent of implementation, the result is given as a set of actions to be performed. There is an action A associated with each interval $[a_{i-1}, a_i)$ of the rth sub-cluster. There are two types of actions:

1. If $A_i = \text{Move}(c)$, then all objects in the interval $[a_{i-1}, a_i)$ are moved to sub-cluster j. The sub-cluster number of the interval is changed to j, and c becomes the new offset adjustment of the interval.
2. If $A_i = \text{Split}(s, c)$, then the interval $[a_{i-1}, a_i)$ is split into two intervals, $[a_{i-1}, s)$ and $[s, a_i)$. Objects with $H(x)$ in $[a_{i-1}, s)$ are moved to sub-cluster j, and c is the offset adjustment of the interval $[a_{i-1}, s)$. Replace the interval $[a_{i-1}, a_i)$ of the rth sub-cluster with $[s, a_i]$ and continue.

Pseudocode for computing the appropriate actions is given by Algorithm 3 in Figure 3.

The RDIM method has the following property:

- The number of objects placed in a sub-cluster is proportional to the total length of intervals mapped to the corresponding sub-cluster.
- The number of objects placed in any sub-cluster is proportional to its weights.
- When storage nodes are changed, the number of objects migrated is the minimum.

Since objects are distributed evenly to storage node in any sub-cluster by the algorithm for mapping computation. So we draw the conclusion that the dynamic interval mapping is balanced algorithm and the number of objects relocated is the minimum.

4 Performance and Simulation Results Analysis

4.1 Performance

Since both mapping complexity and mapping storage depend on the number k of intervals, it is useful to have an upper bound on k as a function of m. The following gives such a bound.

THEOREM 1. If k intervals are produced as the result of m expansions to the number of storage nodes, then

$$k \le \frac{1}{2} m*(m+1) + 1$$

Proof. The proof is by induction on m. Initially (when m=0) there is one interval. Assuming that the bound holds for m expansions, we prove it for m+1 expansion. Just before the (m+1)st expansion, there are m+1 sub-clusters, 0 through m. For each of these sub-clusters, there will be at most one interval that is mapped to the sub-cluster and that is split during the (m+1)st expansion. So the (m+1)st expansion causes at most m+1 intervals to be split, thus creating at most m+1 new intervals. Therefore, using the induction hypothesis, the total number of intervals after m+1 expansions is at most $\frac{1}{2}$ m*(m+1)+1+(m+1)=$\frac{1}{2}$ (m+1)*(m+2)+1.

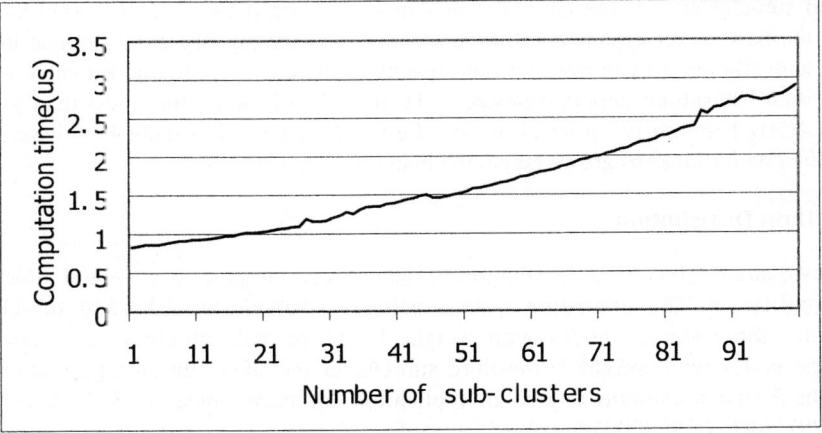

(a) Time per lookup per replica as the number of sub-clusters increases

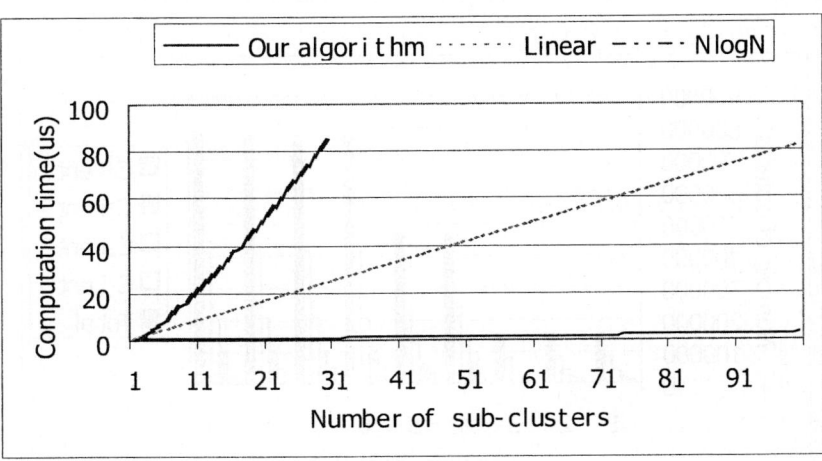

(b) Time per lookup compared to linear and nlogn functions

Fig. 4. Time for looking up an object versus the number of sub-clusters in the system

In the implementation, the numbers a_i, b_i, c_i, d_j, and N_j, are stored in random-access tables or tree, The Find operation in Algorithm 1 is done by binary search in the table or the tree. Obviously, mapping complexity is $O(\log k)$ and mapping storage is $O(k)$. By Theorem 1, mapping complexity is $O(\log m)$ and mapping storage is $O(m2)$.

In our algorithm, we need a random function H, which maps the objects uniformly at random to real numbers in the interval [0,1). We select the Mersenne Twister[10] as the random function H in the implementation of our algorithm.

In order to quantify the real world performance of our algorithm, we tested the average time per lookup under many different configurations for a system with 1000000 objects and 4 replicas per object. First, we ran a test starting with 10 storage nodes in a single sub-cluster and computed the average time for these 4000000 lookups, and then added sub-clusters, 10 storage nodes at a time, and timed the same 4000000 lookups over the new server organization. Figure 4(a) shows the per-object per-replica lookup time with slightly growth rates for the capacity of the most recently added sub-clusters, even with 100 sub-clusters in the system, the amortized lookup time is less than 3 μs on the 1.4GHz Pentium IV on which we ran these experiments; In Figure 4(b), we can see that the line for lookups grows far slower than linear and NlogN.

4.2 Data Distribution

We evaluate the balanced distribution of data objects supporting weighted allocation and replication. The simulation system includes 3 sub-clusters; the first sub-cluster includes three storage nodes with weight 1, the second sub-cluster includes two storage nodes with weight 3, the third sub-cluster includes four storage nodes with weight 5, the maximum degree of replication for each object is 3. The 100000, 200000, 400000, 800000 data objects from four clients are sent respectively to storage nodes. Figure 5 show that data objects sent from four clients and the total sums are always distributed among the storage nodes according to their weights.

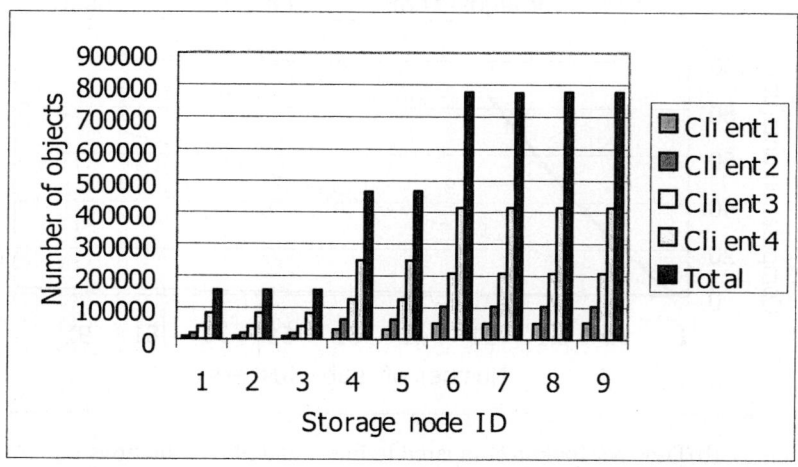

Fig. 5. The distribution of data objects according to nodes weight

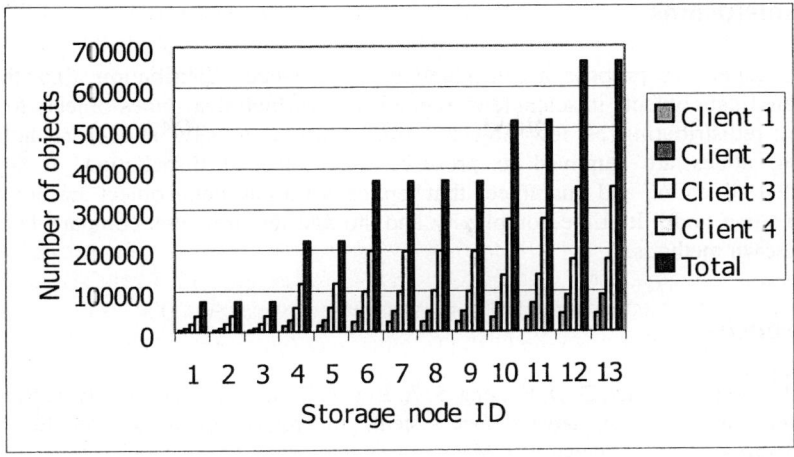

Fig. 6. The redistribution of data objects after adding two clusters

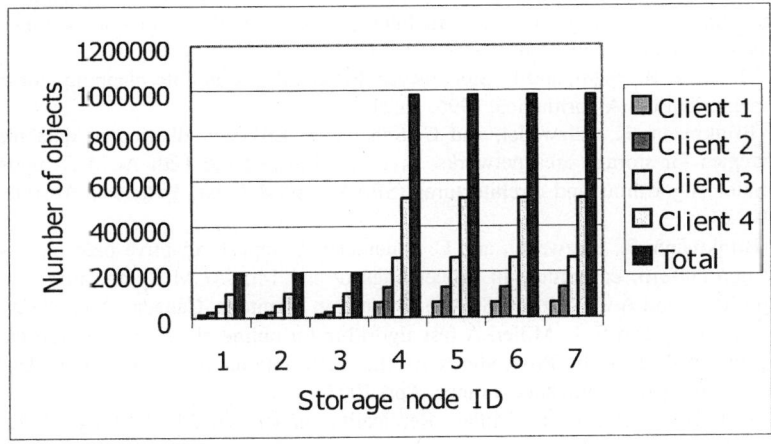

Fig. 7. The redistribution of data objects after removing one cluster

Then, we evaluate the balanced redistribution of data objects supporting weighted allocation by adding two sub-clusters and removing one sub-cluster respectively. (1) Add two sub-clusters, the first sub-cluster includes two storage nodes with weight 7; the second sub-cluster includes two storage nodes with weight 9. (2) Remove the second sub-cluster, which includes two storage nodes with weight 3. Figure 6 and Figure 7 show that data objects sent from four clients and the total sums are always redistributed among the storage nodes according to their weights after adding or removing sub-cluster.

5 Conclusions

In this paper, we propose a self-adaptive and balanced distribution algorithm for replicated data objects in scalable storage clusters, which distributes objects to nodes evenly, redistributing as few objects as possible when new nodes are added or existing nodes are removed to preserve this balanced distribution. It supports weighted allocation and guarantees that replicas of a particular object are not placed on the same node. Its time complexity and storage requirements compare favorably with known methods.

References

[1] Q. Xin, E. L. Miller, D. D. E. Long, S. A. Brandt, T. Schwarz, and W. Litwin. Reliability mechanisms for very large storage systems. In Proceedings of the 20th IEEE / 11th NASA Goddard Conference on Mass Storage Systems and Technologies, pages 146–156, Apr. 2003.
[2] W. Litwin, M.-A. Neimat, and D. A. Schneider. LH*—a scalable, distributed data structure. ACM Transactions on Database Systems, 1996, 21(4): 480-525.
[3] R. Devine. Design and implementation of DDH: A distributed dynamic hashing algorithm. In Proceedings of the 4th International Conference on Foundations of Data Organization and Algorithms, pages 101–114, 1993.
[4] D. M. Choy, R. Fagin, and L. Stockmeyer. Efficiently extendible mappings for balanced data distribution. Algorithmica, 1996, 16:215-232.
[5] A. Brinkmann, K. Salzwedel, and C. Scheideler. Efficient, distributed data placement strategies for storage area networks. In Proceedings of the 12th ACM Symposium on Parallel Algorithms and Architectures (SPAA), ACM Press. Extended Abstract. 2000, 119-128.
[6] A. Brinkmann, K. Salzwedel, and C. Scheideler. Compact, adaptive placement schemes for non-uniform capacities. In Proceedings of the 14th ACM Symposium on Parallel Algorithms and Architectures (SPAA), Winnipeg, Manitoba, Canada , Aug. 2002. 53-62.
[7] R. J. Honicky and E. L. Miller. A fast algorithm for online placement and reorganization of replicated data. In Proceedings of the 17th International Parallel & Distributed Processing Symposium, Nice, France, Apr. 2003.
[8] R. J. Honicky and E. L. Miller. Replication under scalable hashing: A family of algorithms for scalable decentralized data distribution. In Proceedings of the 18th International Parallel & Distributed Processing Symposium (IPDPS 2004), Santa Fe, NM, Apr. 2004. IEEE.
[9] Zhong Liu, Xing-Ming Zhou. An Adaptive Data Objects Placement Algorithm For Non-Uniform Capacities, In Proceedings of the 3rd International Conference on Grid and Cooperative Computing, WuHan, Oct. 2004.
[10] M. Matsumoto and T. Nishimura, "Mersenne Twister: A 623-dimensionally equidistributed uniform pseudorandom number generator", ACM Trans. on Modeling and Computer Simulation Vol. 8, No. 1, January pp.3-30 1998.

Modeling and Analysis of a Parallel Nested Loop Join on Cluster Architectures

Erich Schikuta

Research Lab on Computational Technologies and Applications,
Institute of Knowledge and Business Engineering, University of Vienna,
Rathausstraße 19/9, A-1010 Vienna, Austria
erich.schikuta@univie.ac.at

Abstract. We develop a concise but comprehensive analytical model for the well-known Nested Loop Join algorithm on cost effective cluster architectures. We concentrate on a limited number of characteristic parameters to keep the analytical model clear and focused. We believe that a meaningful model can be built upon only three characteristic parameter sets describing main memory size, the I/O bandwidth and the disk bandwidth. We justify our approach by a practical implementation and a comparison of the theoretical and real performance values.

1 Introduction

The most important operation in a relational database system is the join due to its inherent expressive power. It allows to combine information of different relations according to a user specified condition, which makes it the most demanding operation of the relational algebra. Thus the join is the central point of research for performance engineering in database systems.

In this paper we present an analysis and evaluation of the Nested Loop Join. This work is part of a running project for a comprehensive analysis of parallel join operations [1]. We did a similar research for all important parallel join operations (e.g. Hybrid Hash Join [2]). A focus on analyzing hardware characteristics of the underlying system is beyond the scope of this paper. So we are interested in the specifics of the algorithms and not of the machines.

2 Nested Loop-Join

Basically the join operation 'merges' two relations R and S via two attributes (or attribute sets) A or B (respective relations R and S) corresponding to a certain join condition. The join attributes have to have the same domain. In the following we focus on the equi-join (i.e. the join condition is equality).

Generally three different approaches for the realization of join algorithms are distinguished: nested loop, sort merge, and hash based join.

The nested loop algorithm is the simplest approach to join two relations. Basically each tuple of one relation is probed to each tuple of the other relation. However its simple layout and thus low constant cost factors (overhead) makes it quite attractive in database systems for specific situations (e.g. one relation is very small).

Our parallel version of the nested loop approach is realized by a conventional client-server scheme. The server stores both relations to join and distributes the tuples among the available clients. The clients perform the specific join algorithm on their sub relations and send the sub results back to the server. The server collects the result tuples and stores the result relation.

Specifically a parallel nested loop join partitions first the, so called, inner relation R among the clients. At the clients the tuples are stored in a temporary file. Secondly the outer relation S is distributed among the disks using the same hash function as in the first step. In the third phase both relations are joined. Step by step the main memory is filled with tuples of relation R. With every step the complete relation S is read and every tuple of S probes the content (tuples of R) in the main-memory. In case of a match result tuples are built.

3 Analytical Model

A realistic assumption of our model is that the relations of the database system are too large to fit into the main memory of the processing units. Consequently all operations have to be done externally and the I/O costs are expected to be the dominant factor for the system performance.

In the following (see Table 1) we specify several parameters and a few derived terms, which describe the characteristics of the model environment and build the basis for the cost functions to develop.

Table 1. Parameters of the cost model

m	number of tuples of relation R (inner relation)
n	number of tuples of relation S (outer relation)
p	number of processors
n_t_m	number of tuples per message
b	bucket size (tuples per bucket)
s	selectivity factor (percentage of the product of m and n giving the result size
l_f	loop_factor (number of loops necessary to build hash buckets due to number of open file limitations)
read	read one tuple from disk
write	write one tuple to disk
receive	receive one message
send	send one message
find_target	find the right target client
hash	store a tuple into a main memory hash table
probe	probe a main memory hash table with a tuple
fill	fill a tuple into main memory
compare	compare the keys of two tuples in main memory and build a result tuple if keys match.

3.1 Server Cost Model

The server distributes the data among the clients. Thus it reads the two input relations (1),

$$server\_read = (m+n) * read \qquad (1)$$

calculates the respective target client using a distribution function (2)

$$server\_compute = (m+n) * find\_target \qquad (2)$$

and sends the tuples (packed in messages) to the target client (3).

$$server\_send = (\frac{m}{n\_t\_m} + \frac{n}{n\_t\_m}) * send \qquad (3)$$

After sending the messages the server is in an idle-state. It waits for the results of the clients (4).

$$server\_receive = \frac{m * n * s}{n\_t\_m} * receive \qquad (4)$$

The received tuples are written to disk (5).

$$server\_write = m * n * s * write \qquad (5)$$

Thus the total costs of the server are described by (7) and are the sum of (1) to (5).

$$server\_cost = server\_read + server\_compute+ \qquad (6)$$
$$+ server\_send + server\_receive + server\_write$$

The costs of the server, I/O-costs (read,write), message-costs (send, receive) and computational costs, are obviously independent of the number of processors used. Figure 1 shows this situation graphically by splitting the total server execution costs into the shares on I/O costs (read and write operations), communications costs (send and receive operations) and pure computational costs.

3.2 Client Cost Model

The costs for the clients start with receiving the tuples of the inner and outer relation from the server. Every client gets only $\frac{m}{p}$ tuples of the inner relation R and $\frac{n}{p}$ tuples of the outer relation S. The costs for receiving are described by (7).

$$client\_receive = \frac{\frac{m}{p}}{n\_t\_m} * receive + \frac{\frac{n}{p}}{n\_t\_m} * receive \qquad (7)$$

Afterwards the received tuples are written to the local disk, which is (8).

$$build\_temp\_files = \frac{m}{p} * write + \frac{n}{p} * write \qquad (8)$$

The filling of the memory and the probing of the tuples is depicted by (9) and (10) respectively.

$$build\_mem = \frac{m}{p} * (read + fill) \qquad (9)$$

$$probe\_mem = (\frac{\frac{m}{p}}{b}) * (\frac{n}{p} * read + \frac{n}{p} * b * compare) \qquad (10)$$

Finally the client has to write the result tuples back to the server (11).

$$send\_result = (\frac{m}{p} * \frac{n}{p}) * \frac{s}{n\_t\_m} * send \qquad (11)$$

The cost of the client is the sum of (7),(8),(9),(10) and (11), which is (12).

$$client\_nested\_cost = client\_receive + build\_temp+ \qquad (12)$$
$$+ build\_mem + probe\_mem + send\_result$$

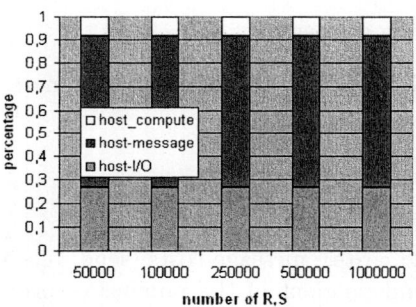

Fig. 1. Percentage of server-side cost types

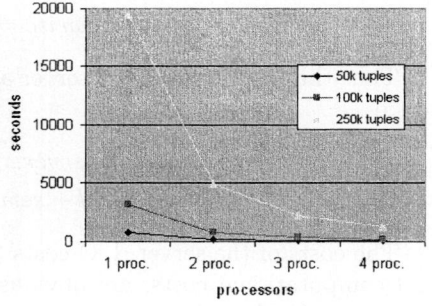

Fig. 2. Theoretical speed-up

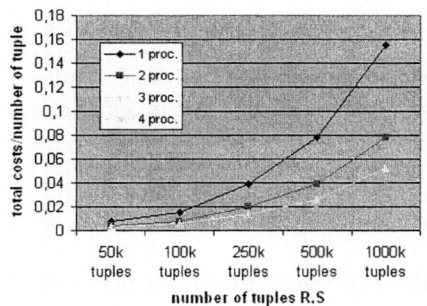

Fig. 3. Theoretical cost per tuple

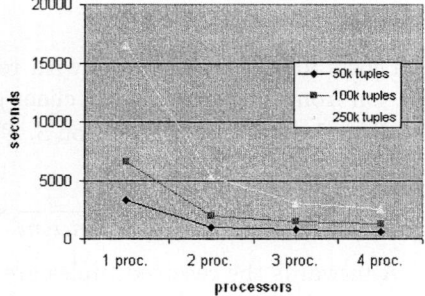

Fig. 4. Real speedup

Finally the total cost of the nested loop join is the sum of the cost of the server and the clients and is defined by (13).

$$nested\_cost = server\_cost + client\_nested\_cost \qquad (13)$$

Figure 2 shows the performance of the nested loop join using different numbers of processors and different numbers of input tuples.

Next we want to know if the costs per tuple change when the number of input tuples increase. We expect that the costs per tuple rise because the main parts of nested loop join develop with $O(m+n*m)$ where $|n| < |m|$. The results can be seen in Figure 3 for 1 to 4 clients.

Further we checked the percentage of I/O-costs, message costs and computational costs in relation to the total client costs. It shows a nearly even distribution of the different parts of costs while changing the number of input tuples. At least we want to know if there is a change in the percentage of I/O-costs, message costs and computational costs in relation to the total client costs when changing the number of used processors. Again it shows an even distribution of the different parts of costs. Most of the execution time is used for computing.

4 Model Justification

To justify the presented model we evaluate and compare it to a practical performance analysis were we realized the algorithm according to the preceding section.

We realized the client-server architecture so that one of the nodes implemented the server, starting the operations, distributing the workload and collecting the result, and 4 client nodes, processing the distributed workload. At the beginning of each test run the relations R (inner relation) and S (outer relation) reside on a server. In the tests we used an integer variable as join attribute.

Test-bed for our analysis was an off-the-shelf "el-cheapo" PC cluster consisting of 5 single processor nodes (computational units) running the Linux operating system. The algorithms were realized with the C language and PVM as communication library. We used a test module to determine the values of the basic parameters and the derived functions of our cost model. Figure 4 shows the real execution times for the Nested Loop Join. All given values are the averages of at least 20 runs.

The real values correspond to the theoretical values amazingly well. The asymptotic runtime behavior for increasing workloads and processing nodes (speed-up) of the model and the reality is about same. Not only the trend of the data is the same, but also the real execution values match the ones calculated by the model. The difference between the two values was about 10 percent, which is due to the simplified model ignoring operating system specifics. Summing up this result shows that the simplified approach described in the previous section models the reality very well and justifies it as basis for the analysis on cluster architectures.

5 Conclusions

By the presented analysis of the proposed concise, but obviously comprehensive model and the justification by the comparison to real implementation results, we could prove the stated assumptions at the beginning of the paper: For building up an analytical model for relational operations on cluster systems it is sufficient to concentrate on the characteristics of *main memory, IO bandwidth and disk bandwidth*.

As a side effect of our analysis we gave a case for the usage of cluster systems as architecture for parallel database systems. With the development of faster and cheaper network interfaces clusters can deliver an un-beatable price/performance ratio for the administration and manipulation of very large data sets.

Acknowledgements

I would like to express my thanks to Peter Kirkovits, who helped in designing the algorithms and the programming of the test suite. The work described in this paper was partly supported by the Special Research Program SFB F011 AURORA of the Austrian Science Fund.

References

1. Kirkovits, P., Schikuta, E.: Parallel Join Algorithms on Clusters. In: Parallel I/O for Cluster Computing. Hermes Science Publishing Limited (2004) 133–155
2. Schikuta, E., Kirkovits, P.: Cluster based hybrid hash join: Analysis and evaluation. In: Proc. IEEE International Conference on Cluster Computing, Chicago, IEEE Computer Society Press (2002)

Scheduling Efficiently for Irregular Load Distributions in a Large-scale Cluster*

Bao-Yin Zhang[1], Ze-Yao Mo[1], Guang-Wen Yang[2], and Wei-Min Zheng[2]

[1] Institute of Applied Physics and Computational Mathematics,
Beijing, 100088, P.R. China
[2] Department of Computer Science and Technology, Tsinghua University,
Beijing, 100084, P.R. China
zby@tsinghua.edu.cn

Abstract. Random stealing is a well-known dynamic scheduling algorithm. However, in a large-scale cluster, an idle node must randomly steal many times to obtain a task from another node, especially, this problem severely affects performance in systems where only a few nodes generate most of the system workload. In this paper, we present an efficient dynamic scheduling algorithm, Transitive Random Stealing (TRS) based on random stealing, which makes any idle node rapidly obtain a task from another node for irregular load distributions in a large-scale cluster. Then by the random baseline technique, we experimentally compare TRS with Shis, one of load balance policies in the EARTH system, and random stealing for different load distributions in the Tsinghua EastSun cluster and show that TRS is a highly efficient scheduling algorithm for irregular load distributions in a large-scale cluster. Finally, TRS is implemented in the Jcluster environment, a high performance Java parallel environment, and an experiment result is given in the HKU Gideon 300 cluster.

Keywords: Scheduling, irregular load distribution, large-scale cluster, transitive random stealing.

1 Introduction

The availability of high speed networks and increasingly powerful commodity microprocessors is making the usage of clusters of computers an appealing vehicle for cost-effective parallel computing. The scale of the clusters is becoming more and more large, which is up to hundreds of and thousands of nodes. In order to achieve scalable performance, it is important to evenly schedule the workload among the processing nodes. Two basic approaches [6] to dynamically scheduling task loads can be found in current literature - *random stealing* and *work sharing*.

Random stealing attempts to steal a task from a randomly selected node when a node finds its own task queue empty, repeating steal attempts until it succeeds. Random stealing is provably efficient in terms of time, space, and communication

---

* This work is supported by Chinese NSF for DYS granted by No. 60425205 and National Postdoctor Science Foundation of China.

for the class of fully strict computations [4, 13]; and the natural work stealing algorithm is stable [2]. Communication is only initiated when nodes are idle. When the system load is high, no communication is needed, causing the system to behave well under high loads. Some systems that implement random stealing include Cilk [3], Jaws [8], and Satin [9]. Cilk [3] provides an efficient C-based runtime system for multithreaded parallel programming with a random stealing scheduler. JAWS [8] efficiently schedule load over a dynamically varying computing infrastructure with random stealing algorithm, Satin [9] presents a system for running divide-and-conquer programs on distributed memory systems with random stealing. The EARTH runtime system [7] supported several dynamic load balancer policies, which goal is to design simple balancers that deliver good load distribution with minimum overheads. But a virtual ring network topology is adopted in all the balancers with nodes numbered clock-wise. The authors of the paper [5] evaluate these load-balancing schedulers for a fine-grain multithreading environment.

In this paper, we study the dynamic scheduling algorithms for a large-scale cluster. For random stealing in a large-scale cluster, an idle node must randomly steal many times to obtain a task from another node. Especially, this problem severely affects performance in systems where only a few nodes generate most of the system workload [12]. For overcoming this problem, *Shis*, one of load balance policies in the EARTH system [5], which slightly modifies random stealing was to remember the originating node (history information) from which a task was last received, and to send requests directly to that node. The authors of the paper [11], present two relatively complicated adaptive location policies which record more history information for global scheduling algorithms.

Here we present a scheduling algorithm, Transitive Random Stealing (TRS), which further improves Shis not only remember the originating node from which a task is stolen but also *forward* the information of the node to other remote nodes which want to steal a task from it. With the transitive policy, TRS can make any node obtain a task faster with less times to steal in a large-scale cluster, reduce the idle time for all nodes and improve the overall performance of the system. Then by the random baseline technique, we experimentally compare the performance of TRS with Shis and random stealing for different load distributions in the Tsinghua EastSun cluster, and show that TRS outperforms Shis and random stealing in all test cases. Finally, TRS is implemented in the Jcluster environment [1], a high performance Java parallel environment, and an experiment result is given on HKU Gideon 300 cluster.

In the rest of this paper, we first give the transitive random stealing algorithm in next section. Section 3 evaluates the performance of TRS, Shis and random stealing by the random baseline technique. We show an experiment result on HKU Gideon 300 cluster in Jcluster environment in Section 4. Finally, Section 5 concludes our works.

2 Design the Transitive Random Stealing Algorithm

Our design philosophy for scheduling algorithms is to reduce the idle time for all nodes, rather than balancing work loads equally on all nodes. A node is said to be in the idle state when it has no tasks to execute. Distributing the workload during application execution is achieved by sending the *tokens* to the schedulers on remote nodes. A token contains all the necessary information to create a new *task*. A Task is a piece of code that is to executed, possibly in parallel with other tasks. Tokens are stored in the task queue on each node.

In the following, we give the transitive random stealing algorithm in detail. First, we show you a figure to illustrate an architecture of a task scheduler based on TRS.

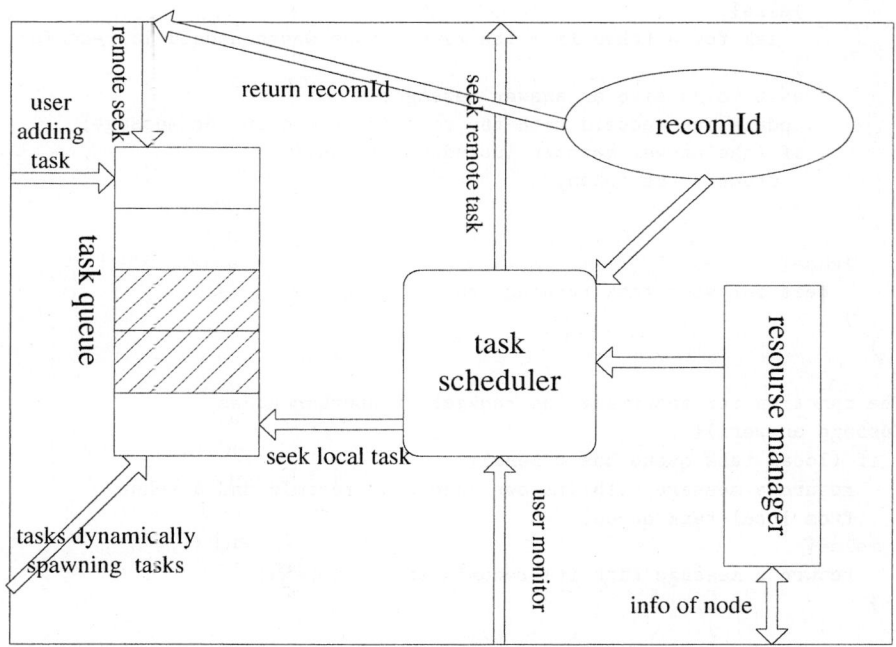

Fig. 1. An architecture of a task scheduler based on TRS

Here resource manager is responsible for adding or deleting nodes and maintains an active list of nodes in the cluster. Task queue is a double-ended queue to store tokens that have been spawned dynamically by tasks or have been added by user, but not yet executed. New tokens spawned dynamically by tasks are pushed into the queue from one end and tokens are also popped from the same end for execution on the local node. On the other hand, new tokens added by user are pushed into the queue from the other end, and a token is also popped from the other end of the task queue when remote nodes asks for tasks. The recomId is a variable which remembers the nodeId of other remote node.

The transitive policy is simple and TRS can be easily implemented. But with this simple transitive policy, TRS can make any idle node obtain a task from

```
The main-loop function for stealing tasks from another nodes:
void run(){
  While(true){
    if (idle of node){
      if (local task queue has tokens){
        get a token to execute;
      }else{
        if (recomId is blank){
          randomly select a remote node from the list of nodes,
          and ask for a token from it;
        }else{
          ask for a token from the remote node whose nodeId is recomId;
        }
        wait to receive an answer message;
        update its recomId with the recomId in the answer message;
        if (the answer message includes a token){
          execute the token;
        }
      }
    }else{
      wait for some task running over;;
    }
  }
}
The function for answering the request of another nodes:
Message answer(){
  if (local task queue has tokens){
    return a message with its own nodeId as recomId and a token
    from local task queue;
  }else{
    return a message with its recomId and no tokens;
  }
}
```

Pseudo code of the transitive random stealing algorithm

another node with less times to steal in a large-scale cluster. As a result, this will greatly reduce the idle time for all nodes and improve the scalability of the system. At the same time, TRS inherits the advantages of simple random stealing policy: communication is only initiated when nodes are idle. When the system load is high, no communication is needed, causing the system behave well under high loads.

As we can see, a few more bytes (recomId) is sent in the replying message for TRS than Shis and RS. But the time and bandwidth of the communication are very similar for those messages with little different sizes. In a sense, the key factor which influences the network communication overhead is the times of sending messages.

Note. In some very special conditions, there may be a loop transition of the recomId. In order to avoid this case, the implementation of the algorithm can limit the times of transition of the recomId. In fact, in the later experiments, we empirically limit the times of transition of recomId by $\max\{\lceil \log_2 n - 3\rceil, 1\}$, where n is the number of the nodes in the cluster.

3 Performance Evaluation Based on Random Baseline Technique

In this section, by the random baseline technique, we experimentally compare TRS with Shis, one of load balance policies in the EARTH system, and random stealing for different load distributions on the Tsinghua EastSun cluster which has 32 nodes (4×Xeon III 700s, Fast Ethernet, Redhat 8.1). Here we implement each of the three algorithm as an MPI application in which a process simulates a node. The processes implement two threads except the process with rank 0, one thread for dealing the main loop, the other for handling the request. The process with rank 0, by the random baseline technique, implements a task generator which distributes the same load distributions to the other processes for the three algorithms respectively.

In order to stress to test the performance of algorithms on the different load distributions, we make use of the task generator generating different load distributions instead of scheduling some real parallel programs. The task generator generates three types of load distributions uniformly distributed on all

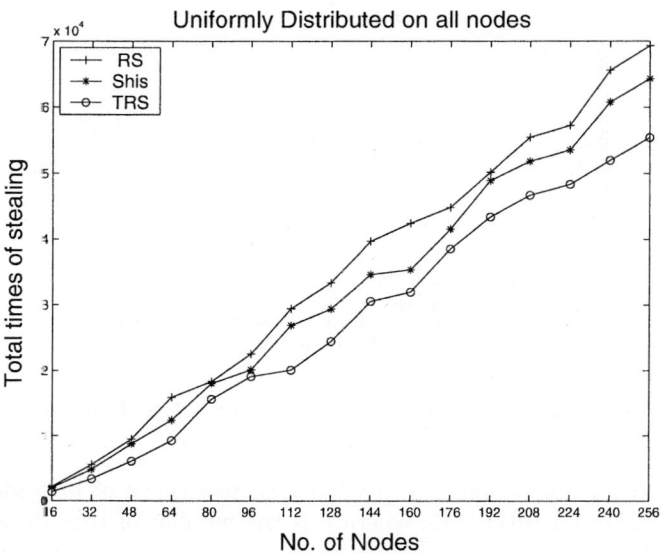

Fig. 2. Task load uniformly distributed on all nodes

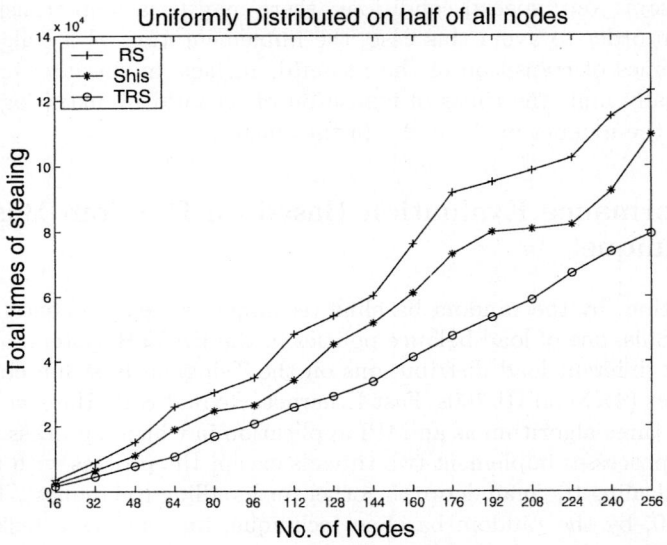

Fig. 3. Task load uniformly distributed on half of all nodes

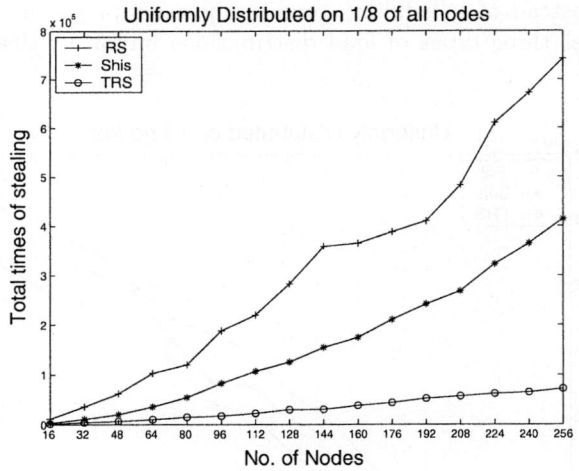

Fig. 4. Task load uniformly distributed on 1/8 of all nodes

nodes, half of all nodes and 1/8 of all nodes, two types of binomial distributions, $Bi(n, 1/3)$ and $Bi(n, 1/8)$, where n is the number of the nodes. From the knowledge of Statistics, the binomial distribution $Bi(n, p)$ approaches the Poisson distribution, when the number n is large, and the probability p is small. The five types of load distributions all distribute $5n$ tasks to the nodes for 10 times,

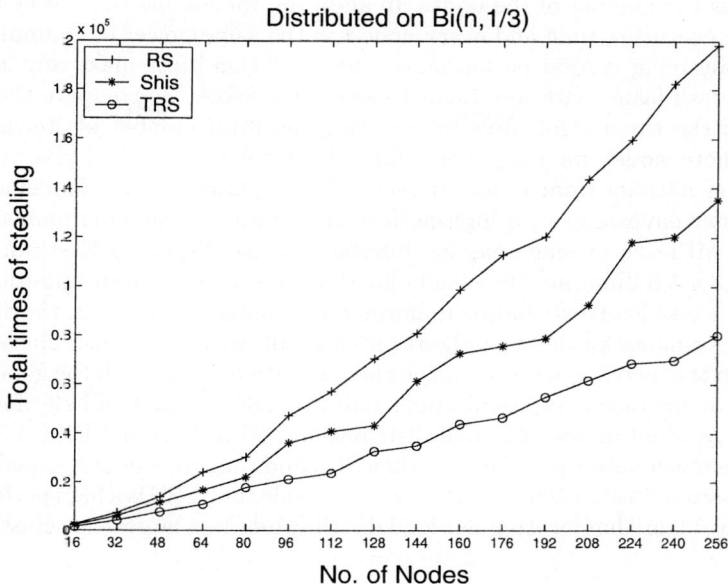

Fig. 5. Task load distributed on $\text{Bi}(n, 1/3)$

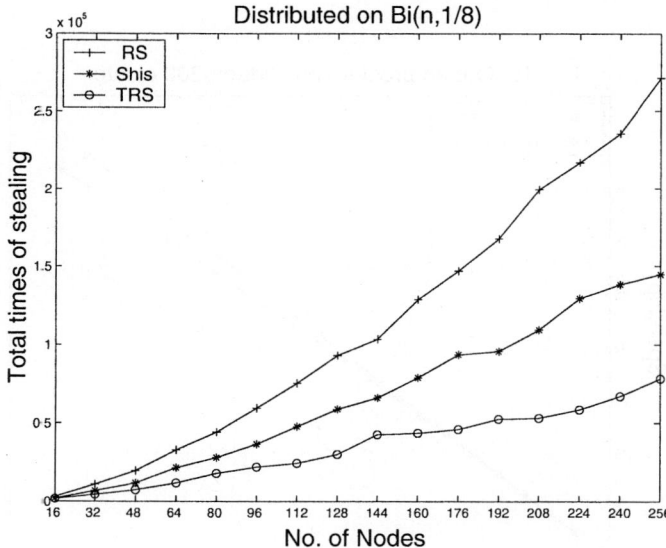

Fig. 6. Task load distributed on $\text{Bi}(n, 1/8)$

where n is the number of the nodes. In addition, we assume that every task has the same executing time and every node has the same power of computing.

For obtaining a good performance, the algorithm must make any idle node obtain a task faster with less times to steal. Therefore, we compare the performance of the three algorithms by counting the total number of stealing tasks from remote nodes for each algorithm (the total number includes the times of stealing nothing from remote nodes). The experiments are implemented in the Jcluster environment, a high performance Java parallel environment which provides MPI-like message passing interface on the Tsinghua EastSun cluster. Figure 2,3,4,5,6 illustrate the results for the five type of load distribution.

For the task load distribution uniformly distributed on all nodes, the difference of the performance for the three algorithms is small on the small-scale clusters, however, with the increase of the size of the nodes, TRS behaves with the good performance. For the task load distributions uniformly distributed on half of all nodes and on 1/8 of all nodes, binomial distributions, $Bi(n, 1/3)$ and $Bi(n, 1/8)$, TRS exhibits a much better performance than Shis and random stealing, especially, for the large-scale clusters. Therefore, we can conclude that TRS is a high performance scheduling algorithm for irregular load distributions in a large-scale cluster.

4 An Experiment Result in the Jcluster Environment

Jcluster environment [1] that provides a high performance PVM-like and MPI-like message passing interface implements the TRS algorithm to schedule the

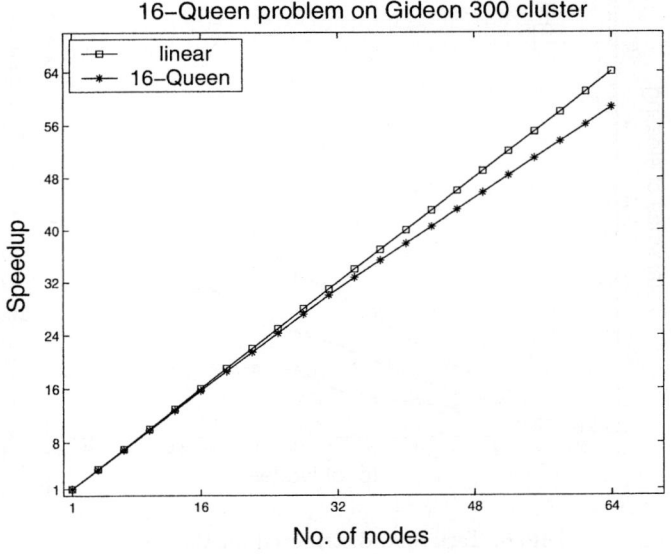

Fig. 7. 16-Queen problem on HKU Gideon 300 cluster

tasks dynamically in a large-scale cluster. Here a divide-and-conquer program, 16-Queen problem, is used to stress to test the task scheduler based on TRS. There are more than 2,200 subtasks which will be dynamically spawned on some nodes to be scheduled. With the help of Prof. Francis C.M. Lau, Prof. C.L. Wang and Weijian Fang, the test for 16-Queen problem has been held on HKU Gideon 300 cluster (Pentium IV 2.0 GHz, Fast Ethernet, redhat 8.0, Jdk 1.4.0) at the University of Hong Kong. Figure 7 illustrates the results.

The efficiency of the speedup reaches up to 91.73% on 64 nodes, which exhibits an efficient scheduling of TRS on the real platform.

5 Conclusion and Further Works

In this paper, we present the Transitive Random Stealing algorithm (TRS) which provides an efficient scheduling policy making any idle node rapidly obtain a task from other remote node for irregular load distributions in a large-scale cluster. Then by the random baseline technique, we experimentally compare TRS with Shis, one of load balance policies in the EARTH system, and random stealing for different load distributions on the Tsinghua EastSun cluster and conclude that TRS is a highly efficient scheduling algorithm for irregular load distributions in a large-scale cluster. Finally, Jcluster environment implements a task scheduler based on TRS to obtain a good experiment result for 16-Queen problem on HKU Gideon 300 cluster. In the future, more real parallel applications will be developed to evaluate the algorithm on some real platforms.

Acknowledgements

We are very grateful to Prof. Francis C.M. Lau, Prof. C.L. Wang and Weijian Fang in the University of Hong Kong for their warmhearted help.

References

1. http://vip.6to23.com/jcluster/
2. Berenbrink, P., Friedetzky, T., Goldberg, L.A., "The Natural Work-Stealing Algorithm is Stable", SIAM Journal on Computing, Vol. 32(5), pp. 1260-1279, 2003.
3. Blumofe, R.D., Joerg, C.F., Kuszmaul, B.C., Leiserson, C.E., Randall, K.H., and Zhou, Y., "Cilk: An efficient multithreaded runtime system", Proceedings of the 5th ACM SIGPLAN Symposium on Principles and Practice of Parallel Programming, PPoPP'95, Santa Barbara, California, pp. 207-216, July 1995.
4. Blumofe, R.D., and Leiserson, C.E., "Scheduling Multithreaded Computations by Work Stealing", Proceedings of the 35th Annual IEEE conference on Foundations of Computer Science (FOCS'94), Santa Fe, New Mexico, November 20-22, 1994.
5. Cai, H., Olivier Maquelin, Prasad Kakulavarapu, and Gao, G.R., "Design and Evaluation of Dynamic Load Balancing Schemes under a Fine-grain Multithreaded Execution Model", Proc. of the Multithreaded Execution Architecture and Compilation Workshop, Orlando, Florida, January 1999. Delaware, May 1999.

6. Eager, D.L., Lazowska, E.D., and Zahorjan, J., "A Comparison of Receiver-Initiated and Sender-Initiated Adaptive Load Sharing", Performance Evaluation, Vol. 6, pp. 53-68, 1986.
7. Herbert H.J. Hum, Olivier Maquelin, Kevin B. Theobald, Xinmin Tian, Xinan Tang, Guang R. Gao, Phil Cupryk, Nasser Elmasri, Lau-rie J. Hendren, Alberto Jimenez, Shoba Krishnan, Andres Marquez, Shamir Merali, Shashank S. Nemawarkar, Prakash Panangaden, Xun Xue, and Yingchun Zhu. "A design study of the EARTH multiprocessor", Proceedings of the IFIP WG 10.3 Working Conference on Parallel Architectures and Compilation Techniques, PACT '95 (Lubomir Bic, Wim Bohm, Paraskevas Evripidou, and Jean-Luc Gaudiot, eds.), Limassol, Cyprus, ACM Press, pp. 59-68, June 27-29, 1995.
8. Mao, Z.M., So, H.S.W., Woo, A., "JAWS: A Java Work Stealing Scheduler Over a Network of Workstations", Technical report, The University of California at Berkeley, June 1998.
9. Rob V. van Nieuwpoort, Kielmann, T., and Bal, H., "Satin: Efficient Parallel Divide and Conquer in Java", Proc. Euro-Par 2000, Munich, Germany, pp. 690-699, Aug. 29-Sep. 1, 2000.
10. Sanders, P., "Randomized receiver initiated load balancing algorithms for tree shaped computations", The Computer Journal, Vol. 45(5), pp. 561-573, 2002.
11. Shivaratri, N.G., and Krueger, P., "Two Adaptive Location Policies for Global Scheduling Algorithms", IEEE International Conference on Distributed Computing Systems, 1990.
12. Shivaratri, N.G., Krueger, P., and Ginghal, M., "Load Distributing for Locally Distributed Systems", IEEE Computer, Vol 25(12), pp. 33-44, Dec. 1992.
13. Wu, I.C., and Kung, H., "Communication Complexity for Parallel Divide and Conquer", 32nd Annual Symposium on Foundations of Computer Science (FOCS'91), San Juan, Puerto Rico, pp. 151-162, Oct. 1991.

A Content-Based Load Balancing Algorithm for Metadata Servers in Cluster File Systems*

Junho Jang, Saeyoung Han, Sungyong Park, and Jihoon Yang

Department of Computer Science and
Interdisciplinary Program of Integrated Biotechnology,
Sogang University, Seoul, Korea
{jj, syhan, parksy, yangjh}@sogang.ac.kr

Abstract. A metadata service is one of the important factors to affect the performance of cluster file systems. We propose a content-based load balancing algorithm that dynamically distributes client requests to appropriate metadata servers based on the types of metadata operations. By replicating metadata and logging update messages in each server rather than moving metadata across servers, we significantly reduce the response time and evenly distribute client requests among metadata servers.

1 Introduction

It is reported from SPEC that up to 60% of user requests in cluster files systems are metadata operations [1]. Due to the large amount of metadata operations, some cluster file systems use a separate metadata server or a cluster of metadata servers for scalability and availability [2][3][4][5].

A key question in the design of such systems is how to partition the metadata among metadata servers to maintain both high performance and scalability. The first approach, known as directory sub-tree partitioning, partitions the metadata along the directory sub-tree, which suffers from severe bottleneck due to the hot spots. As an alternative, a pure hashing approach [2] is introduced. This approach hashes the filename to distribute the namespace among the metadata servers evenly. This requires metadata servers to maintain the directory hierarchy, and further requires them to repartition the namespace among the servers whenever a metadata server is added or removed from the cluster. Another approach such as Lazy Hybrid (LH) [3] combines both approaches to address the problems above. However, all the approaches above are based on the static mechanism such that a metadata server is designated when a new metadata structure is created. This prevents client requests from being distributed fairly among the metadata servers based on current load conditions.

This paper proposes a content-based load balancing algorithm for metadata servers that dynamically distributes client requests to appropriate metadata servers based on the types of metadata operations. In order to distribute client requests dynamically, a dispatcher is used. In addition to distributing client requests dynamically, the

---

* This work was supported by grant No. R01-2003-000-10627-0 from the Basic Research Program of the Korea Science & Engineering Foundation.

dispatcher also shares Indirect Metadata Table (ITL) with all the metadata servers and adjusts assigned entries among metadata servers, reflecting current load conditions. Although the capacity of the dispatcher is critical to the overall cluster system performance, emerging hardware technologies for switching reduces the relaying overhead significantly, which ensures us to assume sufficient capacity of dispatcher.

The rest of this paper is organized as follows. In chapter 2 we present an overview of metadata management schemes used in cluster file systems. Chapter 3 presents the detail mechanism of content-based load balancing algorithm. Its analysis and experimental result are presented in chapter 4. Chapter 5 summarizes our work and concludes this paper.

2 Related Work

The first approach to allocating metadata among metadata servers in cluster file systems is the hierarchical directory sub-tree partitioning. This approach partitions the file system namespace according to the structure of directory sub-tree and the metadata of each directory sub-tree is managed by individual metadata server. This technique suffers from severe bottleneck when a single file, directory, or directory hierarchy must be traversed to determine the permissions of each file that is accessed.

The second approach, pure hashing, distributes the namespace among metadata servers by hashing the file identifier, file name, or other related values. This results in more balanced workloads than directory sub-tree partitioning. Vesta parallel file system [2] is a representative method of pure hashing. The hash function of Vesta file system uses the full pathname as an input key, and outputs the identifier of the metadata server and the location of the metadata inside the server. This pure hashing guarantees direct accesses to metadata without traversing all the metadata servers along the directory hierarchy, but it does not support the directory path-based file permission using access control list. Moreover, for some expensive operations such as changing directory name, removing directory, and adding or removing of metadata servers, a large number of metadata should be moved across metadata servers, which leads to long response time and clients should wait for a long period of time for their requests.

Lazy Hybrid (LH) [3] addresses the above problems by combining the advantages of both approaches and adding capabilities such as global logging and delayed updates. The metadata location is determined by hashing the full pathname, which allows direct accesses to the metadata without traversing all of the metadata servers that stores directories along the path. However, hierarchical directories are maintained in order to provide standard directory semantics and operations such as *ls*. Lazy update policies allow for efficient metadata updates when the file/directory names or their permissions are changed or when metadata servers are added to or removed from the system. Moreover, a dual-entry access control list structure is maintained for any file permissions to be determined directly without traversing the entire path. When a large amount of metadata has to be moved at a time, the real location is globally logged in all the metadata servers, instead of moving metadata. Later, upon the first access after global logging, the metadata is actually moved. By using the delayed updates, the initial operation is very fast and only a little overhead is incurred at the time when each of the modified metadata is accessed first. On the other hand, when the requests generated by the clients are bursty, this scheme leads to the concentration of the requests on a particular metadata server holding the real metadata, and suffers from the performance degradation due to the overhead incurred by forwarding client requests.

To address these shortcomings due to the static determination of metadata servers on each client, we propose a dynamic load balancing algorithm based on a dispatcher. The dispatcher periodically collects load information from the metadata servers and forwards client requests to appropriate server based on the content of each request.

3 Content-Based Load Balancing Algorithm

In this section, we present the detailed schemes used in the content-based dynamic load balancing algorithm.

3.1 Architecture

Fig. 1 shows the structure of the metadata server cluster. This cluster consists of several metadata servers and a dispatcher that relays the request from clients to appropriate metadata servers. Given the information of the file included in a request, the dispatcher hashes the full pathname of the file to produce a hash value indicating the index into the Indirect Lookup Table (ILT). The index found in the entry of the ILT specifies which metadata server currently stores the metadata for that file. After determining appropriate metadata server, the dispatcher forwards the requests to the selected metadata server or broadcasts it to all the metadata servers depending on the content of the request. The detailed operations will be described in the next section.

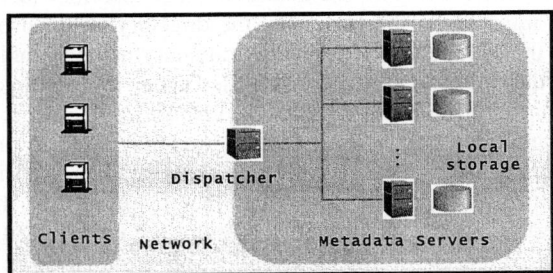

Fig. 1. Architecture for load balancing

In this architecture, all the metadata servers and the dispatcher should share the same ITL as well as the same hash function. Using these, each metadata server determines independently whether it is responsible for the requested file or not, and then stores, retrieves, or modifies the metadata of the file. Moreover, each metadata server caches the inode information of all the files and directories, and stores the directory hierarchies in order to improve the performance of metadata operations.

In order to efficiently distribute the load among metadata servers, all metadata servers report their load conditions to the dispatcher periodically. Based on this information, the dispatcher adjusts the ILT and then redistributes it to all the metadata servers.

3.2 Metadata Operations

To ensure the consistency of metadata among metadata servers, our algorithm writes and logs metadata write operations on every metadata servers. Since our algorithm uses a full pathname as an input into the hash functions, some operations, such as changing directory name, adding or removing of metadata server, and ITL adjustment, result in a large amount of metadata movement across the metadata servers. To reduce the overhead incurred by moving metadata, we replicate metadata among all the metadata servers, and log all the metadata modification messages. While the requests such as simply looking up metadata for files or directories are handled by one designated metadata server, the requests for writing metadata or logging some operations are broadcast to all the metadata servers concurrently. As a result, all the metadata servers have the same metadata information. For some retrieval operations for directories or file attributes that require metadata modification (i.e., update "last access time" field), we divide the operations into two steps: looking up metadata and updating the "last access time" field.

When a file or a directory needs to be retrieved, the dispatcher uses a hash function (using the full pathname) to locate the appropriate metadata server in constant time and ask the designated server to reply with the metadata information related to the file or the directory. The modification message for the "last access time" field is then broadcast and all the servers update and log the information. On the other hand, except for the operations related to the attribute manipulation, all the metadata operations related to changing directory structure require the modification of directory hierarchy in addition to updating inode information. For example, the directory removal operation requires the deletion of all the subdirectories. Changing directory name should rearrange all the metadata for the files, subdirectories, and the files under the subdirectories across the metadata servers since the hash values need to be changed.

It should be noted that changing the directory hierarchy requires the movement of a large amount of metadata. In our approach, each metadata server is supposed to execute the operation at the same time and thereby eliminate the movement of metadata. Considering that the file system operations are mostly read operations (with the ratio of 9:1 in office environments), replication is much more reasonable than metadata movement in general cluster file system environment [8].

Unlike the directory write operations, the writing operations for files do not require any modification of the directory hierarchy. However, they are also carried out concurrently at each metadata server to ensure the metadata coherency.

3.3 Adjustment of Indirect Lookup Table (ILT)

Since each file system operation requires different amount of computational power and each file has different access frequencies, some metadata servers may be overloaded more than the others. This may cause longer response time and decrease overall system performance. Moreover, since the entire metadata server may not have the same computing power, we should adjust the imbalance through reconstructing the ITL.

The goal of our algorithm is that all the metadata servers have similar load conditions approaching to the average load and minimize the change of designated metadata server. In order to do this, our algorithm should first determine the metadata servers whose load exceeds the overall average, and calculate the amount of extra load for each metadata server, $Extra(mds_i)$, by subtracting the average load from its own load. The metadata server with negative $Extra(mds_i)$ value can handle more metadata by assigning more ILT entries taken from the metadata server with positive $Extra(mds_i)$. In order to distribute the overloaded entries to other metadata servers, based on the load per entry $Load_e(mds_i)$, we determine the maximum number of ILT entries EE_i for any overloaded metadata server i, satisfying that

$$Extra\ (mds_i) - Load_e\ (mds_i) \times EE_i \geq 0,$$

where $0 \leq EE_i \leq$ the number of ILT entries handled currently by mds_i.

Any metadata server j with negative $Extra(mds_i)$ may take the entries from i as many as maximum EE_j. That is, the following should be satisfied

$$Extra\ (mds_j) + Load_e\ (mds_j) \times EE_j \leq 0,$$

where $EE_j \geq 0$. In order to take the load more aggressively, we allow each metadata server with more available capacity than $Load_e\ (mds_j) / 2$ to take one more entry. Therefore, the above formula can be changed like this.

$$Extra\ (mds_j) - Load_e\ (mds_j) / 2 + Load_e\ (mds_j) \times EE_j \leq 0,$$

where $EE_j \geq 0$. Fig.2 shows an example of the adjustment of ITL so that all the metadata servers have quite evenly distributed load around the average load.

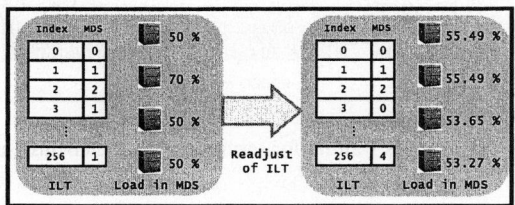

Fig. 2. Example of ILT Adjustment

4 Performance Evaluations

4.1 Experimental Environment

We evaluate our algorithm using CSIM 9.0, a process-oriented discrete-event simulator [8]. The simulations are performed on Intel Pentium-III (800 MHz dual CPU) running Linux Kernel 2.6. The detailed parameters are presented in Table 1.

In this evaluation, we measure the load of each metadata server to see how well the client requests are distributed. The average response time from the clients is also measured. The ratio of read accesses and write accesses is 9:1. We evaluate our algorithm and compare it with those of Vesta and LH3.

Table 1. Parameters for the simulation

The number of MDS	8
Metadata size	256 Bytes
Average memory cache search time	0.155 msec for 10MB
Memory cache hit ratio	90%
Disk access time	1.561 msec for 1 metadata
Network transfer time	0.209 msec for 1 metadata

4.2 Results

Figures 3 through 5 show the load condition of each metadata server for Vesta, LH3, and our approach, respectively. In order to obtain current load at each metadata server, we measure the number of requests waiting to be processed at each server for a period of 20,000 milliseconds.

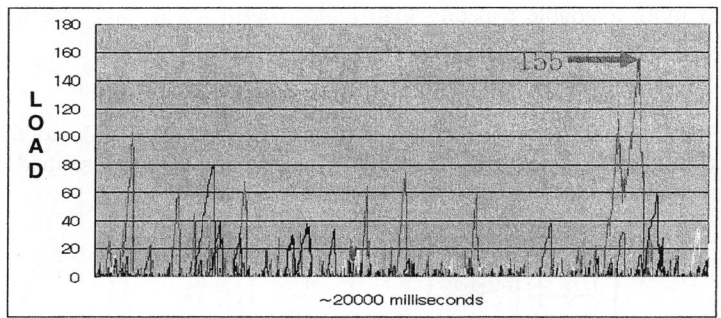

Fig. 3. Number of requests waiting for services in each metadata server (Vesta)

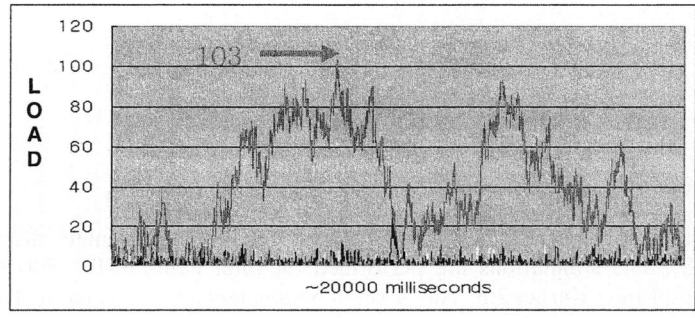

Fig. 4. Number of requests waiting for services in each metadata server (LH3)

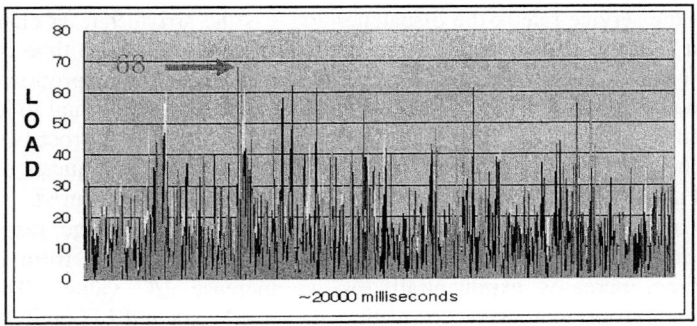

Fig. 5. Number of requests waiting for services in each metadata serer (proposed approach)

As you can see from Fig. 3 and Fig. 4 (Vesta and LH3 cases), for some of metadata servers, the number of waiting requests is much larger than those of the others. This implies that the client requests are forwarded heavily onto some metadata servers and the load is not fairly distributed among all the metadata servers. On the other hand, Fig. 5 (our approach) shows that the requests are well distributed all over the metadata servers. Moreover, while the average load of our approach is a little bit higher than that of Vesta, the variance is remarkably smaller (see Table 2). This also indicates that replicating metadata is more efficient for distributing client requests than moving metadata throughout the network.

Table 2 shows the average response time of all three approaches. As the table shows, our approach has minimum average response time although it doesn't include the processing time at the dispatcher. Under the assumption that we can implement the dispatcher with quite good performance, the processing time at the dispatcher can be ignored. Table 3 also shows that our approach significantly outperforms other approaches.

Table 2. Average numbers of requests waiting for services and the variances

	Vesta	LH3	Our approach
Average # of requests waiting	2.11	4.35	3.13
Variance	10.56	95.10	0.14

Table 3. Average response time for each approach

	Vesta	LH3	Our approach
Average response time (msec)	11.93	32.04	6.39

In order to explain the relationship between the performance of dispatcher and the response time of client requests, we introduce a formula using queuing theory. For example, the response time at the dispatcher R can be written as

$$R = \frac{1}{C - \lambda},$$

where C is the service rate at the dispatcher and λ is the arrival rate of client requests [10]. When λ is unchanged, the only factor that affects the response time is C. If C is much larger than λ, a dispatcher can forward the client requests to appropriate metadata server immediately on receiving a request. If C is approximately equal to λ but is not smaller than λ, the response time increases rapidly because of the processing delay at the dispatcher. If C is smaller than λ, the arrival rate of client requests exceeds the capacity of a dispatcher, and thereby the response time can't be measured.

Based on the fact described above, we measure the average response time including the processing time at the dispatcher. As you can see from Fig. 6, the response time increases exponentially as we increase 1/C values. The average response time of our approach is lower than those of Vesta and LH until 1/C is up to 0.8. However, our approach suffers from long response time when 1/C goes close to λ, which implies that the performance of dispatcher becomes the bottleneck of overall cluster system. On the other hand, we can expect performance improvement when the arrival rate of client requests is below 93% of service rate of the dispatcher in this experiment.

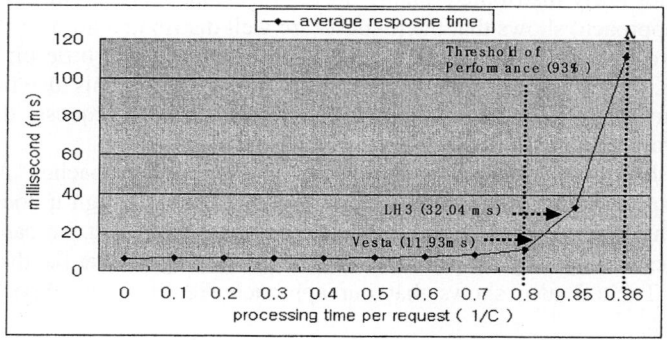

Fig. 6. Effect of the performance of dispatcher

5 Conclusion

In this paper, we have proposed a content-based load-balancing algorithm for metadata servers in cluster file system, where the client requests are handled differently according to their contents, and the loads of the metadata servers are redistributed by dynamically adjusting the indirect metadata table periodically. By replicating the metadata and logging update messages, all the metadata servers concurrently execute the update operations on metadata, which minimizes the metadata movements.

Through our performance evaluation, we have showed that our dynamic load balancing algorithm outperformed existing metadata management schemes used in traditional cluster file systems. We are currently investigating further about the effect of the performance of dispatcher on the overall system performance in the metadata cluster.

References

1. SPEC, SFS 3.0 Documentation Version 1.0, Standard Performance Evaluation Corporation, 2001.
2. Peter F. Corbett et al., The vesta parallel file system, ACM Transactions on Computer Systems(TOCS), 14(3), pp.225-264, Aug. 1996.
3. Scott A. Brandt et al., Efficient Metadata Management in Large Distributed Storage Systems, Proceedings of the 11th IEEE NASA Goddard Conference on Mass Storage Systems and Technologies, Apr. 2003.
4. Peter J. Braam et al., The Lustre Storage Architecture, Cluster File Architecture, Cluster File System. Inc, Mar. 2003.
5. Jin Xiong et al., Design and Performance of the Dawning Cluster File System, IEEE International Conference on Cluster Computing(Cluster'03), Dec. 2003.
6. Bourke T., Server Load Balancing, O'Reilly and Associates, Sebastopol, 2001.
7. Daniel P. Bovet et al., Understanding the Linux Kernel, O'Reilly and Associates, Sebastopol, 2003.
8. http://www.mesquite.com

Reducing the Overhead of Intra-Node Communication in Clusters of SMPs

Sascha Hunold and Thomas Rauber

Department of Mathematics, Physics and Computer Science,
University of Bayreuth, Germany
{hunold, rauber}@uni-bayreuth.de

Abstract. This article presents the C++ library vShark which reduces the intra-node communication overhead of parallel programs on clusters of SMPs. The library is built on top of message-passing libraries like MPI to provide thread-safe communication but most importantly, to improve the communication between threads within one SMP node. vShark uses a modular but transparent design which makes it independent of specific communication libraries. Thus, different subsystems such as MPI, CORBA, or PVM could also be used for low-level communication. We present an implementation of vShark based on MPI and the POSIX thread library, and show that the efficient intra-node communication of vShark improves the performance of parallel algorithms.

Keywords: clusters of SMPs, parallel programming models, message passing between threads.

1 Introduction

Clusters of SMPs (Symmetric Multiprocessors) have become very popular in high performance computing (HPC). Due to the huge number of different cluster systems, the message passing libraries such as MPICH or LAM are usually not machine optimized. One disadvantage of MPI (Message Passing Interface) libraries is their low performance for intra-node communication. The communication on a single SMP node is either done via shared memory (system calls like shmget) or socket-based. Intra-node communication via sockets or shared memory at operating system level is more expensive than copying data directly between lightweight threads. vShark provides an effective realization of the communication requirements of an application that can be adapted to the memory and network system of the parallel or distributed platform without help from the programmer. In particular, vShark reduces the overhead of intra-node communication in clusters of SMPs by introducing a thread-based architecture. Instead of starting a number of processes on SMP nodes, the vShark system starts the same number of threads. Since those threads live in the same address space of the same process, communication between them is much faster than going through the communication stack of the message-passing library. The communication between physically distributed threads in vShark is performed by a separate communication thread. Each physical SMP node has exactly one communicator thread which handles communication requests from local worker-threads and polls for requests from remote communicator threads.

The next section gives a short overview of the vShark framework. The rest of the paper describes the C++ implementation of the vShark interface using the MPI standard and the POSIX thread library. The article introduces a simple but effective communication protocol to ensure thread-safe communication between worker-threads. We also evaluate the performance of vShark and present experimental results.

2 Programming Model of vShark

The vShark library is an improved message-passing framework for distributed memory machines. Thus, the programming model is the same as for common message-passing environments like MPI, i.e. explicit messages-passing between participating processes is required.

The vShark library consists of different layers to provide maximum flexibility. Parallel programs based on vShark have a common interface to the top layer runtime interface. The layer below is the transportation layer of the vShark runtime. The transportation layer binds the vShark runtime to a particular communication device like MPI or PVM. The programmer does not have access to the communication layer directly. Instead, he must use abstract functions of the vShark runtime library to send or receive data.

In this article we can only give a coarse introduction of the system. vShark provides a message-passing API which is similar to MPI. It contains methods for sending and receiving messages like `int send(Envelope *env)`, and it also contains entities such as `VSharkGroup` which is the logical equivalent to an MPI communicator. The code below is an example of how a processor would send its own rank to processor 1 in vShark.

```
Runtime& re = get_runtime();                        // get vShark runtime handle
VSharkGroup *group = re.get_group();                // handle to world communicator
Message *msg = new IntMessage(&rank, 1, 0);         // int of length 1 and with tag 0
group->send(group->create_envelope(msg, rank, 1));  // blocking send
```

Fig. 1. Sending an integer message in vShark

3 vShark Implementation with MPI and POSIX Threads

vShark can be implemented on top of different communication libraries. In this section, we describe a vShark implementation based on MPI and the POSIX thread library.

General Communication Scheme. The MPI standard does not guarantee thread-safety. Therefore, the vShark driver for MPI has to ensure thread-safe communication between worker threads. Thread-safe communication in this context is achieved when only one thread per node is transferring data at a time. Several solutions were proposed in literature, e.g. protecting all MPI calls with locks to ensure mutual exclusion, see [4] for a detailed analysis. Another solution for thread-safe communication is an auxiliary communicator thread that manages communication requests. This thread is the only one with access to the MPI layer. vShark uses such a communicator thread. A distinct communicator not only ensures thread-safe communication, but more importantly, it also allows us to change the communication path (channel) at runtime (shared-memory or socket-based). When a virtual processors (worker thread) wants to send or receive data, it appends a request to the communicator's request queue. We explicitely indicate that vShark does not copy messages into a separate buffer. Instead, the virtual processor passes a memory reference to the communicator. After the data transfer is completed, the communicator signals the virtual processors that the requests have been fulfilled.

Message Transfer Protocol. There are two performance-critical decisions to make. The first is, how and when communication between two communicators takes place, i.e. how often does the communicator need to poll for inter-node requests. Secondly, does the system support buffering of messages?

vShark does not buffer incoming messages to reduce the memory requirements and to avoid deadlocks through insufficient free memory. Such a scenario may occur if a communicator thread constantly polls for incoming messages and receives a large amount of incoming data within a short time interval. However, the time at which the data is actually requested is unknown, and so, the message has to be kept in the buffer. Especially in numerical applications with messages of hundreds of megabytes the fast growing buffer would quickly exceed the memory limit.

vShark uses a communication protocol to avoid deadlocks and extra memory requirements. The transfer of messages is always initiated by the the sending communicator. The communicator sends a request message to the node where the receiver resides. This message contains the id of the virtual processor of the sender and the receiver. The communicator of the receiver checks its local queue if the corresponding virtual processor has already requested this data. If so, the communicator sends an acknowledgment-message (ACK) to the initiator and immediately starts receiving data (MPI_Irecv) into the message buffer of the virtual processor. If there is no such request, the communicator enqueues the request in a waiting list. When a virtual processor later dispatches the matching receive request, the ACK will immediately be sent to the initiator. In order to find the corresponding request to each ACK and vice versa, the ACK message also contains the identifiers of the sending and receiving virtual processors. This protocol has two basic advantages: (1) No additional message buffering is required. (2) The initiating communicator can select which message is sent first. That makes it possible to reschedule and optimize the message transfer respecting the message-passing constraints such as order and fairness (subsequent messages may not overtake each other).

Realization of the Communicator Thread. As discussed before, the communicator constantly polls for incoming requests. The central performance question is, when and for how long the communicator thread will be suspended. This sleep time must be short enough to guarantee quick message delivery, but also long enough that worker threads can get the CPU and perform their tasks. In case of shared-memory, we could use a consumer/producer model. The consumer would be suspended until produced items are available for consumption and so, it would not consume CPU time. Unfortunately, we cannot apply this model in a distributed memory environment. Thus, active waiting for incoming messages is necessary which may consume CPU time. Since we want to minimize this wait overhead, we introduce a sleep time for the communicator. The communicator sleeps for the given amount of time when all local queues are empty and no remote request has yet been received. We will see that this timeout parameter is very performance-critical. The timeout settings (minimum, maximum, default) of the MPI driver can be changed in a configuration file called vshark_mpi.conf.

Running vShark Programs over MPI. An MPI-based vShark program can be started by calling mpirun on each participating node. The runtime system of vShark reads the node configuration file vshark.conf. For compatibility reasons, this file has the same syntax as the machine configuration files of MPICH (node:#processors). According to the number of processors specified in the file, the vShark runtime starts the virtual processors. After the runtime is loaded on each node, the actual vShark program is passed to the virtual processors which then start to execute the program.

4 Experimental Results of the MPI Version of vShark

For a performance comparison of vShark with traditional MPI programs, we ran several benchmarks from the ParkBench collection [9]. The original ParkBench code is written in Fortran 77. We ported the benchmarks to C++ and replaced MPI calls with the corresponding vShark function.

In the diagrams that follow, "parkbench" denotes the results of the original benchmark and vShark stands for the rewritten benchmark. The range $(x-y)$ after the vShark label denotes the chosen minimum and the maximum timeout of the communicator, e.g. for $1-10$ the communicator waits at least $1\ ms$ and at most $10\ ms$ when all queues are empty.

COMMS1 Benchmark. The COMMS1 benchmark is a so called ping-pong benchmark and measures the time a message is transferred between two nodes back and forth, i.e. the master processor sends a message of variable length to a slave processor that immediately returns the message after receiving it.

Fig. 2 (left) presents the throughput results for the intra-node communication of vShark and ParkBench. It can be observed that the communication between two MPI processes (original ParkBench) is fast for smaller messages. When the message size increases, vShark's thread-based copying significantly boosts the performance. For a message size of about 20.000 bytes, the throughput of vShark becomes clearly superior to MPI.

COMMS3 Benchmark. The website www.top500.org characterizes the benchmark as follows: each processor of a p-processor system sends a message of length n to the other $(p-1)$ processors. Each processor then waits to receive the $(p-1)$ messages directed at it. The timing of this generalized ping-pong ends when all messages have been successfully received by all processors; although the process will be repeated many times to obtain an accurate measurement, and the overall time will be divided by the number of repeats. Figure 2 (right) compares the bandwidth which was measured for the MPI version of COMMS3 and the vShark version. When utilizing four processors,

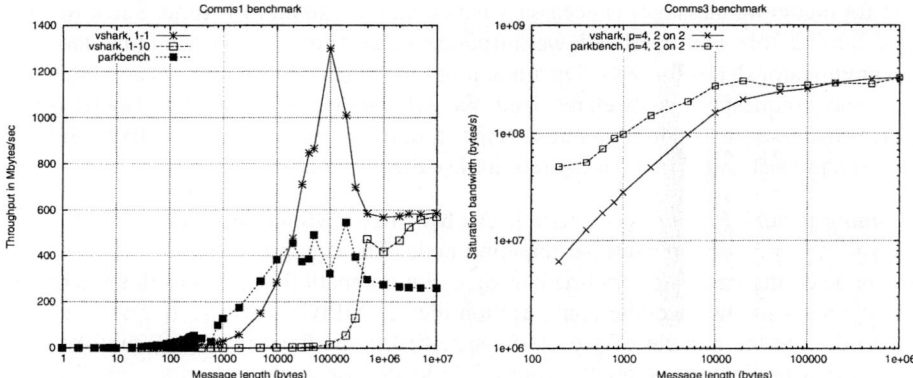

Fig. 2. Left: Throughput measured with the COMMS1 benchmark (intra-node, SMP). Right: Two virtual vShark processors on two SMP nodes compared to two MPI processes on two SMP nodes. System: Dual Xeon cluster, SCI network, ScaMPI.

the bandwidth achieved by vShark is slightly lower than the MPI version. Yet, when the message length is larger than 50.000 bytes vShark is as fast as the original ParkBench. Due to the additional communication protocol, the bandwidth of vShark decreases for a larger number of processors.

Testing with a Real Application. We examine the real-world application performance on the basis of tpMM (task parallel matrix multiplication). The tpMM algorithm uses a hierarchy of multiprocessor groups where it is assumed that matrix A is decomposed into p blocks of rows and B into p blocks of columns, where p denotes the number of processors. tpMM recursively updates matrix panels to compute the result matrix $C = A \times B$, see [6] for a more detailed description of tpMM and [7] for an overview of how tpMM can be used as a building block in multi-level matrix multiplication algorithms.

The runtime results for tpMM on vShark and on MPICH are shown in Figure 3 (left). We can see that tpMM running on vShark outperforms the C/MPI version (note the logarithmic scale). This algorithm benefits from the vShark runtime since most of the communication required happens on an SMP node.

In order to evaluate the performance of vShark on larger SMP nodes, tpMM was further tested on a four-way Xeon (2.0 GHz) running Linux and MPICH 1.2.5. Figure 3 (right) compares the MFLOPS per processor of the vShark-based and the MPICH-based versions of tpMM. The MPICH results include statistics for the P4 device (shared memory enabled) as well as for the VMI device. On a multi-way SMP machine, vShark clearly outperforms the MPICH versions, either using the VMI or the P4 driver.

5 Related Work

The combination of message passing in a multi-threaded environment and its advantages has already been examined and published. For example, Sun Microsystems offers

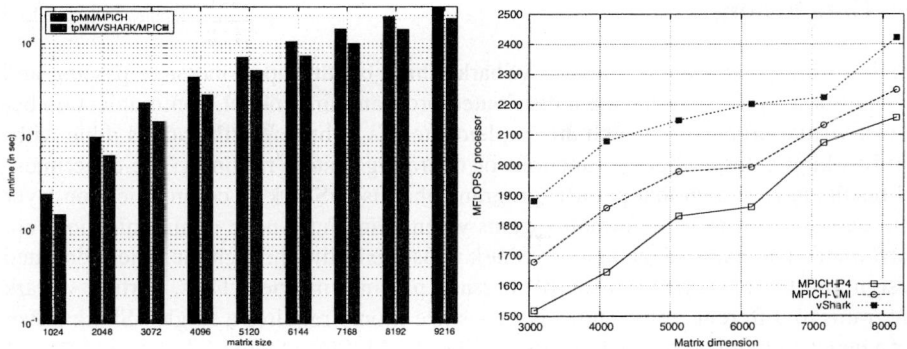

Fig. 3. Left: Comparison of the performance of tpMM running on vShark and directly on MPI (8 virtual processors, 2 thread per node), system: dual Xeon cluster, MPICH 1.2.5.2 (-with-comm= shared). Right: tpMM performance with MPICH-P4, MPICH-VMI, and vShark, system: 4-way Xeon.

thread-safe MPI libraries for Solaris [13] where threads can concurrently call MPI functions but may only refer to processes as senders or recipients. Multi-threaded approaches to MPICH have been discussed in [11]. The article [4] describes how to use threads in an MPI environment efficiently to improve the performance of irregular algorithms on distributed systems. In general, there are two approaches for exploiting threads in distributed systems. One way is to create a virtual shared model of the parallel system. Since the programmer sees only one big memory, the complexity of writing parallel program decreases because explicit message passing is omitted. MuPC is an example of such programming language [12]. Another approach is to extend the POSIX thread model and to add message passing capabilities to each thread [3]. In [1] the authors proposed a thread-only implementation of MPI and it aims at the development stage of program where tests are performed on a single machine. The work in [10, 14] goes one step further and rewrites parts of MPICH to shift the original process-only model to a thread-only model. The disadvantage of these approaches is the dependency on the operating system and the MPICH version. Another multi-threaded MPI implementation is called AMPI and has been discussed in [5]. AMPI uses the same notation of virtual processors as vShark. Each virtual processor is a lightweight user-thread and has its own private memory. AMPI optimizes the mapping of virtual processors to real processors. The objective of AMPI is to reduce the complexity of writing parallel programs for systems where the number of processors differs from the number of processors that the algorithms require. [2] introduces TPVM as a multi-threaded version of PVM. Similar to vShark, TPVM uses threads as units of parallelism and the communication between threads is done via explicit message passing with a unique thread id. Since TPVM is a modified version of PVM, it is restricted to the PVM library and the operating systems to which it has been ported. The Virtual Machine Interface (VMI) is also equipped with the support for multiple communication interconnects including shared memory, TCP/IP, Myrinet [8]. In contrast to vShark, VMI is a middleware layer between MPI and the network device drivers.

6 Conclusions

We have presented the C++ library vShark which is built upon message passing and thread libraries. Despite having a distributed programming model, communication between virtual processors which are implemented as lightweight threads is done without invoking external library functions or operating system routines. The experimental results have shown that parallel programs that use vShark as communication layer can lead to significant performance gains when many intra-node communications are performed. The main advantage of vShark is its flexibility through the object-oriented design and the placement on top of message passing libraries. Thus, porting vShark programs to different architectures is easy since it only requires a single vShark driver for a new communication interface like MPI or PVM. Since there is already an MPI 1.1 binding available, vShark will work with any MPI compliant library.

References

1. Erik D. Demaine. A Threads-Only MPI Implementation for the Development of Parallel Programs. In *Proc. of the 11th International Symposium on High Performance Computing Systems (HPCS'97)*, pages 153–163, Winnipeg, Manitoba, Canada, July 1997.
2. Adam Ferrari and V. S. Sunderam. Multiparadigm Distributed Computing with TPVM. *Concurrency: Practice and Experience*, 10(3):199–228, 1998.
3. Matthew Haines, David Cronk, and Piyush Mehrotra. On the Design of Chant: A Talking Threads Package. In *Proc. of the 1994 conference on Supercomputing*, pages 350–359. IEEE Computer Society Press, 1994.
4. Judith Hippold and Gudula Rünger. A Communication API for Implementing Irregular Algorithms on SMP Clusters. In *Proc. of the 10th EuroPVM/MPI 2003*, LNCS 2840, pages 455–463, Berlin Heidelberg, 2003. Springer.
5. Chao Huang, Orion Lawlor, and L. V. Kalé. Adaptive MPI. In *Proc. of the 16th International Workshop on Languages and Compilers for Parallel Computing (LCPC 03)*, LNCS 2958, pages 306–322, College Station, Texas, October 2003. Springer.
6. Sascha Hunold, Thomas Rauber, and Gudula Rünger. Hierarchical Matrix-Matrix Multiplication based on Multiprocessor Tasks. In *Proc. of the International Conference on Computational Science ICCS 2004, Part II*, LNCS 3037, pages 1–8. Springer, 2004.
7. Sascha Hunold, Thomas Rauber, and Gudula Rünger. Multilevel Hierarchical Matrix Multiplication on Clusters. In *Proc. of the 18th Annual ACM International Conference on Supercomputing, ICS'04*, pages 136–145, June 2004.
8. Scott Pakin and Avneesh Pant. VMI 2.0: A Dynamically Reconfigurable Messaging Layer for Availability, Usability, and Management. In *The 8th International Symposium on High Performance Computer Architecture (HPCA-8), Workshop on Novel Uses of System Area Networks (SAN-1)*, Cambridge, Massachusetts, February 2, 2002.
9. PARKBENCH Committee/Assembled by R. Hockney (Chairman) and M. Berry (Secretary). PARKBENCH report: Public international benchmarks for parallel computers. *Scientific Programming*, 3(2):101–146, Summer 1994.
10. Jari Porras, Pentti Huttunen, and Jouni Ikonen. The Effect of the 2nd Generation Clusters: Changes in the Parallel Programming Paradigms. In *Proc. of the International Conference on Computational Science ICCS 2004, Part III*, LNCS 3037, pages 10–17. Springer, 2004.

11. Boris V. Protopopov and Anthony Skjellum. A Multithreaded Message Passing Interface (MPI) Architecture: Performance and Program Issues. *Journal of Parallel and Distributed Computing*, 61(4):449–466, 2001.
12. J. Savant and S. Seidel. MuPC: A Run Time System for Unified Parallel C. Technical report, Department of Computer Science, Michigan Technological University, September 2002.
13. Sun Microsystems Computer Company. Sun MPI 4.1 Programming and Reference Guide, March 2000.
14. Hong Tang and Tao Yang. Optimizing Threaded MPI Execution on SMP Clusters. In *Proc. of the 15th International Conference on Supercomputing*, pages 381–392. ACM Press, 2001.

On Service-Oriented Network Measurement Architecture with Mobile Agent

Zhi Wang, Bo Yu, and Chuanshan Gao

Department of Computer Science and Engineering,
Fudan University, Shanghai, China, 200433
zhi_wang@163.com, yubosmail@163.com, cgao@fudan.edu.cn

Abstract. Interoperability and adaptability are two major problems that embarrass network measurement practices today on how to finely integrate heterogeneous measurement systems and functionalities. This paper proposes a service-oriented approach based on Web Service for building integrated network measurement architecture that's scalable and adaptable for change. Measurement functionalities are wrapped in Web Service that can be described in WSDL, discovered by UDDI and accessed through SOAP openly. Mobile Agent, as an autonomous entity, is employed to implement the global control of network measurement, which migrates from site to site calling these Web Services to perform the measurements and returns with the data collected from them. This approach de-couples network measurement control and supporting network measurement functionalities thus introduces flexibilities into the implementation of both sides. The architecture promised by this approach allows not only fast deployment of network measurement functionalities but also simple introduction of measurement control policies.

Keywords: Network Measurement, Service-Oriented Architecture, Web Service, UDDI, SOAP and Mobile Agent.

1 Introduction

Network performance is always of network service provider's concern when planning networks to provide differentiated services and deliver quality of services (QoS). In 1998, IP Performance Metrics (IPPM) Working Group of IETF proposed a framework of Internet Protocol (IP) performance metrics in [1]. Under the framework, metrics such as one-way packet delay [2] and loss pattern [3], are put forward to satisfy the needs for observing Internet performance from different perspectives. As most of these metrics are generally associated with distinct measurement methodologies, adaptable network measurement architecture becomes of primary concern that's required not only be able to integrate all these metrics seamlessly, but also allow introducing new ones flexibly on demand.

NIMI [4] and Surveyor [5] are two examples that deploy similar network measurement architecture. They both have a group of probing sites (PS) geographically distributed across the networks. Each pair of PSs establishes a connection at a well known UDP port. End-to-end packet transfer delays, loss, and bulk throughputs are measured by One-Way Delay and Packet Loss (OWDP) [6] or Round-Trip Delay and

Packet Lost (RTDP) [7] test protocols, which probes network performance by sending/receiving small packets over these connections. Besides, a central server is designated to distribute measurement functionalities (MF) to PSs and coordinates their measurement exercises.

Although it simplifies the management of PSs and measurement functionalities, the centralized control model weakens the architecture's adaptability. Firstly a PS must meet specific software or hardware requirements in order to support designated MFs, which limits the possibility of recruiting a lot of PSs to widen the coverage of network clouds. Secondly, constraints on PS's platform narrow the scope of metrics and MFs that can be introduced into the architecture. Actually Surveyor and NIMI are designed to support active measurements only. If to deploy passive measurement such as traffic monitoring on backbones, PSs must reinstall the network interceptor devices and measurement control software as well.

In this paper, a service-oriented network measurement architecture, SONA is proposed to address these problems. It builds an extensible network measurement platform based on Web Service [8]. Now PS plays a positive role other than simply being reactive to central server's control. MF can be deployed by PS independently but is provided as a Web Service for central server's use. Web Service isn't tied to any operating systems or programming languages thus offers an open facility to realize remote procedure call (RPC). They can be called through SOAP [9], which is a standard XML messaging protocol that simplifies the access to Web Service. To support such a platform, a UDDI (Universal Description Discovery and Integration) database server (UDS) is employed for PSs to publish their Web Services in WSDL. WSDL is a formal language to describe a web service from the perspectives of WHAT the service is, HOW to use the service and WHERE to locate the service. Based on all these, SONA is not only extensible as MF can now be deployed and called in a standard way; but also it's adaptable since it separates the measurement control with MF deployment, which means the central server can only be responsible for organizing a measurement, while PS caring for providing the proper MF.

The paper is organized as following. In Section 2, we will have an overview of SONA's architecture. Then a brief survey of current network measurement approaches is presented in Section 3, also it introduces Mobile Agent as an effective way for their measurement control. In Section 4, Web Service implementation of network measurement functionality is illustrated by an example of round-trip packet delay test service. Section 5 describes Mobile Agent in detail and illustrates how it works in SONA. In Section 6, possible security issues in SONA are evaluated. Future work is presented briefly in the Conclusion section.

2 Architecture Overview

SONA is architected upon a few PSs that are geographically distributed on the networks. Each PS installs a HTTP server with SOAP support. In Figure 1, a typical topology of SONA is illustrated. Two PSs are deployed in the domain. Each one provides a Web Service for its supported measurement functionality and publishes the service to the UDS (WS1 and WS2). Generally PS is purposely placed near the network element that's in observation, such as ATM switches, core/edge routers and DSL access multiplexers for collectively measuring their performance. The Network

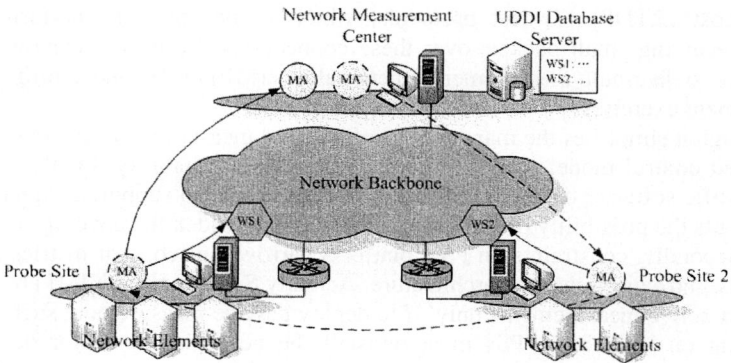

Fig. 1. SONA Architecture. SONA is architected on a few probe sites distributed across the networks. Each probe site provides their network measurement functionalities through a few standard web services and publishes them to a public UDDI database. Mobile Agent dispatched by NMC migrates in SONA to organize the network measurement practice over a wide scope.

Measurement Center (NMC) is responsible for organizing the measurements that may involve a few PSs based on the service profiles they publish to the UDS.

NMC can notify a PS to perform a measurement by directly calling its Web Service through a SOAP request. But it isn't an effective way for most of the cases because SOAP is still a RPC like protocol, that is, NMC will be blocked by the call until it returns. For measurement that lasts for a short time, this approach is fine. For example, to get the IP datagram forwarding speed on a router, a Web Service can be called on the PS around to watch on the "ipForwDatagrams" variable in the router's management information base (MIB) for 5 minutes and apply following formula $(ipForwDatagrams_y - ipForwDatagrams_x) / (5 * 60s)$ to get the result, where x is the measurement end time and y is the start time. But for most measurements that need to run for a long time, such as to derive the average packet delay or lost rate along a network route within 2 hours, this approach can't be applied when there are many such measurements to be performed at the same time.

To deal with this problem, Mobile Agent (MA) comes up as a rescue. As an autonomous entity, Mobile Agent can migrate with its code (or execution logic) and data and continue its execution at other hosts. In SONA, Mobile Agent is dispatched by NMC to the PS and calls PS's web service locally on behalf of NMC. With Mobile Agent, NMC can gain a flexible control of the measurement. For each measurement, it can generate a PS list for MA to visit, and for each PS, it prepares a Web Service list for MA to call. These two lists together make up a mission list for MA. MA with the list then travels from PS to PS to accomplish the job one by one. In Fig.1, NMC designates a MA to visit PS2 and then PS1. MA will call WS2 at PS2 and WS1 at PS1, and then go home. After NMC sends out the MA, it doesn't need to wait for result back continuously, while Mobile Agent can do the things for it. Besides this, Mobile Agent can do a lot of other important jobs such as network topology discovery, fault diagnose and resource trading. Such functions are open for MA developers to realize as value-added components to SONA.

3 Measurement Control Based on Mobile Agent

Generally network measurement approaches can be divided into two groups. One is active measurement. Another is passive measurement. For active measurement, a PS normally establishes a test connection with another PS at a well-known TCP or UDP port and actively sends/receives test packets. All PSs must synchronize their time clocks through Network Time Protocol [10] or Global Positioning System. Each test packet is time stamped and indexed so that packet delay, lost percentage and throughput can be easily extracted and recorded. Ping, OWDP and IPMP [11] are examples for this approach. As it injects extra network traffics, this approach may disturb the network's normal operations. So in order to achieve unbiased results, sampling and analysis methods must be carefully studied [12][13].

Active measurement can also be realized in two ways. One is unicast-based, another is multicast-based. For unicast-based measurement [14][15], there is a test connection for each pair of PSs. Its complexity is $O(N^2)$, and when a new PS joins, N test connections must be created accordingly. OWDP is such a kind of unicast-based test protocol. But for multicast-based measurement [16], a multicast tree is established upon a group of PSs. Test packet ejected by a PS is multicasted down the tree to all related PSs in the group. This approach generate less traffic into the network than the Unicast because the test packet appears only once per link in the multicast tree. Thus its complexity is $O(N)$.

For passive measurement, through special network sniffer devices or SNMP [17] and RMON, PS simply keeps watch on the traffics flowing over the wire and/or on specific performance variables in network element's MIB. For example, OCXmon and FDDI monitors are utilized in NLANR [18] passive measurement project. OCXmon have two measurement cards installed so that they can capture traffic in both directions of a full duplex connection. Based on the traffics traces captured, bidirectional transaction analysis and flow analysis can be done. In the case of SNMP, network performance information such as interface speed and IP packet error rate can be derived directly from network element's MIB.

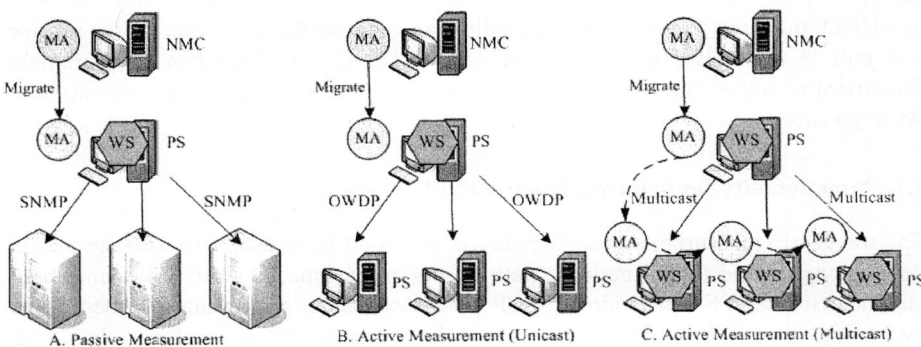

Fig. 2. Measurement Organization by Mobile Agent. Mobile Agent can flexibly organize passive or active measurement by migration from host to host.

By Web Service technology and Mobile Agent, all these kinds of measurements can be easily realized and controlled. Figure 2 illustrates how to deploy the Web Service and Mobile Agent to organize the measurement practices.

For passive measurement, a PS can provide a measurement web service that accesses network element's MIB through SNMP, or accesses special hardware devices to retrieve the performance data. Mobile Agent can migrate to there, call its service, derive some statistics and return with the result.

For unicast active measurement, taking OWDP for example, a measurement service can be deployed on the PS that sets up a test connection with other PSs and send test packets to them in given time. Other parameters can also be accepted such as time-out constraints and TCP/UDP port. Mobile Agent can return to NMC with the measurement of packet delay or packet loss.

For multicast active measurement, three kinds of Web Services are to be deployed. One is multicast establishing (ME) service for all involved PS. Another is multicast testing (MT) service for the sender PS. The last one is measurement collection (MC) service for all receiver PSs. In (C) of, four PS are involved in the multicast measurement. NMC can delegate an MA that firstly visits all PSs in the multicast tree to call each one's ME service thus establish the multicast membership, then returns to the sender PS's location to call its MT service to start the measurement, and after the measurement is over, visits each receiver PS to call its MC service to get the result, and finally returns to NMC.

4 Measurement Functionality as Web Service

Implementing network measurement functionality as Web Service follows quite a different way other than before. Firstly, we must implement the functionality in a specific programming language such as Java and C++. Then we need to write a configuration file for the implementation and deploy it to a web server with SOAP support such as Tomcat with Axis, a SOAP request dispatch engine. If deployed successfully, a web service is created for the functionality and can be called through the server. We need also to create a WSDL file for the service and publish it to a UDDI database server, so that the caller can generate the stub code for the service and call it remotely. In this section, we will study a round-trip measurement functionality and go through the development cycle in Java for its implementation in Web Service.

4.1 Functionality Implementation and Deployment

The round-trip measurement functionality is supposed to measure the average packet delay along an end-to-end network path over a given time. It needs following input parameters: peer PS's IP address, TCP port, test packet size, waiting timeout and measuring time. We can implement such functionality in a Java class, i.e. *RoundTripTestService*. For simplicity, we only give its pseudo codes.

```
public class RoundTripTestService {
    public double roundTripDelayTest(String peerPSIpAddr, int udpTestPort, int packetSize,
            int waitingTimeout, int measureTime) {
        create a stream socket S;
        bind S to <peerPSIpAddr, tcpTestPort>;
        while(measureTime isn't up) {
            Packet P = new Packet(packetSize);
            Set P's Timestamp with current time;
            Set P's Sequence No. with current Sequence No.;
            Send the P through S;
            while(no packet is received on S && waitingTimeout isn't up) { }
            if(no packet is received) continue
            else {
                extract the packet's timestamp;
                compare the timestamp with current time and record the delay;
                sleep for a random time;
            }
            increase current Sequence No.;
        }
        return ∑(delay of each packets received) / number of packet received;
    }
}
```

RoundTripTestService provided a measurement functionality named *roundTripDelayTest*, which is a public method in the class. Such a service class can be deployed to any web server that supports SOAP. Following is a sample deployment description file used by Apache Tomcat server to install the service.

```
<?xml version="1.0"?>
<isd:service xmlns:isd="http://xml.apache.org/xml-soap/deployment"
    id="urn:RoundTripTestWebService">
    <isd:provider type="java" scope="Application" methods="roundTripDelayTest">
        <isd:java class="RoundTripTestService" static="false"/> </isd:provider>
    <isd:faultListener>org.apache.soap.server.DOMFaultListener</isd:faultListener>
</isd:service>
```

It tells the server that a *RoundTripTestService* class that provides the measurement functionality *roundTripDelayTest* is to be deployed as a Web Service. Its name is *RoundTripTestWebService* and given a universal resource identifier (URI) *"urn:RoundTripTestWebService"*. As Java Virtual Machine (JVM) limits Java program from directly accessing local systems, so for specific measurement functionality that heavily depends on specialized devices, we can still write a few C/C++ libraries to handle their hardware interactions, and depend on Java Native Invocation (JNI) to wrap these in a seamless way.

4.2 Network Measurement Service in WSDL

WSDL is an important XML document that contains a set of definitions that describes a Web Service. Basically there are three parts in a WSDL file: the **WHAT** part, consisting of the *types*, *message*, and *portType* elements, defines the messages and data types exchanged between client and server; the **HOW** part, consisting of the *binding* elements, describes the technical implementation details of the Web Service; finally the **WHERE** part, consisting of the *service* element, pulls together the port type, the binding, and the actual location of the Web Service. Following is a sample WSDL for the *RoundTripTestService*.

```
<definitions name="RoundTripTestService" xmlns="http://schemas.xmlsoap.org/wsdl/"
     xmlns:soap="http://schemas.xmlsoap.org/wsdl/soap/">
 <types><xsd:schema xmlns:xsd="http://www.w3.org/2001/XMLSchema">
   <xsd:element name="peerPSIpAddr"      type="xsd:string"/>
   <xsd:element name="tcpTestPort"       type="xsd:int"/>
   <xsd:element name="packetSize"        type="xsd:int"/>
   <xsd:element name="waitingTimeout"    type="xsd:int"/>
   <xsd:element name="measureTime"       type="xsd:int"/>
   <xsd:element name="double_Response"   type="xsd:double"/>
  </xsd:schema></types>
 <message name='RoundTripTestService_roundTripDelayTest_Response'>
   <part name='response'    element='ns0:double_Response'/></message>
 <message name='RoundTripTestService_roundTripDelayTest_Request'>
   <part name='peerPSIpAddr' element='peerPSIpAddr'/>
   <part name='tcpTestPort'  element='tcpTestPort'/>
   <part name='packetSize'   element='packetSize'/>
   <part name='waitingTimeout' element='waitingTimeout'/>
   <part name='measureTime'  element='measureTime'/>
 </message>
 <portType name='RoundTripTestService'>
   <operation name='roundTripDelayTest' parameterOrder='peerPSIpAddr
          tcpTestPort packetSize waitingTimeout measureTime'>
     <input message='tns:RoundTripTestService_roundTripDelayTest_Request'/>
     <output message='tns:RoundTripTestService_roundTripDelayTest_Response'/>
   </operation></portType>
 <binding name='RoundTripTestService' type='tns:RoundTripTestService'>
   <soap:binding transport='http://schemas.xmlsoap.org/soap/http' style='rpc'/>
   <operation name='roundTripDelayTest'>
     <soap:operation soapAction=" style='rpc'/>
     <input>
       <soap:body parts='peerProbeIp tcpTestPort packetSize waitingTimeout
            measureTime' use="encoded" encodingStyle='...' /></input>
     <output>
       <soap:body parts='response' use='encoded' encodingStyle='...' /></output>
   </operation></soap:binding>
 </binding>
 <service name='RoundTripTestService'>
   <port name='RoundTripTestService' binding='tns:RoundTripTestService'>
   <soap:address location='http://myprobe.org/soap/servlet/rpcrouter'/></port>
 </service>
</definitions>
```

A *message* is the basic communication element of SOAP. It consists of one or more *parts*, each part representing a typed parameter. All messages are grouped into *operations* in an entity called a *portType*. A *portType* represents the interface, a concrete set of operations supported by the Web Service. A Web Service can have multiple interfaces represented by different *portType*. Here there is only one *portType* with an operation *roundTripDelayTest*. The client sends a *RoundTripTestService_roundTripDelayTest_Response* message to call the method, which contains many parts that are the input parameters for *roundTripDelayTest*. *RoundTripTestService_roundTripDelayTest_Response* message as a reply contains one *part* (the return value) called *response*. In the *SOAP binding* element, *RPC* communication style is specified for the operations in *portType*. It supports automatic marshalling and demarshalling of messages, permitting developers to specify a request as a method call with a set of parameters that returns a response containing a return value. Based on this WSDL file, we have all the information needed to create a client application to access the Web Service

4.3 Publish Network Measurement Service to UDDI Registry

Only with its WSDL file, NMC can know how to call a measurement web service. UDDI database server provides a mechanism for PS to advertise their Web Services in WSDL and for NMC to search the WSDL file for a Web Service. It contains categorized information about the businesses and services that a PS offers, and associates these with corresponding WSDL. Because most of measurement services are mission-critical, UDDI database server must impose extra security controls on unauthorized access to all the entries for published Web Services in the database.

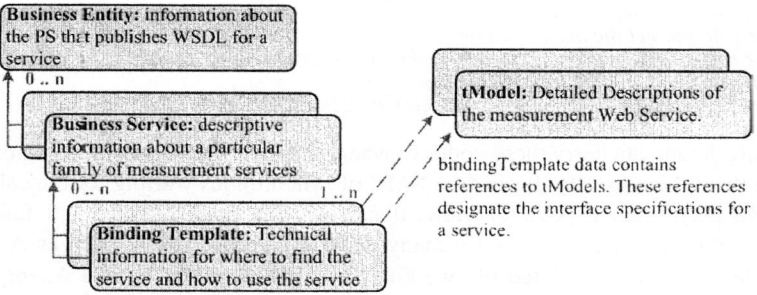

Fig. 3. A PS's Entry in UDDI Database. Each PS has an entry in the UDDI database, which includes Business Entity, Business Service and Binding Template information for a combinative description of its services.

Each PS has an entry in the UDDI database. Figure 3 illustrates the structure of a PS's entry. The **Business Entity** normally contains description information for the PS, such as its identification, affiliated organization, and administrator's contact address. The **Business Service** describes a family of services in the same category such as Passive Measurement, Unicast-based Active Measurement and Multicast-based Active Measurement. Associated with each business service entry is a list of **Binding Templates** that provide information on where to find the service and how to use the service. For example, a binding template may specify the access point for *RoundTripTestService* and provides a reference to a construct of **tModel** that describes the measurement Web Service in detail, such as its name and service category. A web service's WSDL is generally attached to the **tModel**. That is, with the tModel, the WSDL file for the *RoundTripTestService* can be retrieved.

4.4 Call a Network Measurement Service

To make a call, we need to specify URI for given measurement web service, signature of desired measurement functionality and input parameters. Apache SOAP is a powerful toolkit that provides abundant client-side APIs for users to create SOAP request, transfer SOAP message and interpret SOAP response. Following code illustrates a call to the *roundTripDelayTest* measurement functionality in the *RoundTripTestService* web service. The measurement is desired to be done within 30 minutes by this PS with another PS (202.114.71.25) at TCP port 7000. Each test packet is 100 bytes long and deemed as lost when not received within 60s.

```
/*packaging a SOAP request*/
Call call = new Call();
call.setTargetObjectURI("urn:RoundTripTestWebService");
call.setMethodName("roundTripDelayTest");
Vector params = new Vector();
params.addElement(new Parameter("peerPSIpAddr", String.class, "202.114.71.25", null));
params.addElement(new Parameter("tcpTestPort", Integer.class, new Interger(7000), null));
params.addElement(new Parameter("packetSize", Integer.class, new Interger(100), null));
params.addElement(new Parameter("waitingTimeout", Integer.class, new Interger(60), null));
params.addElement(new Parameter("measureTime", Integer.class, new Interger(1800), null));
call.setParams(params);
/*make a call and get the SOAP response*/
Response resp = call.invoke ("http://myprobe.org/soap/servlet/rpcrouter", "" );
Parameter result = resp.getReturnValue ();
double measureResult = ((Double) result.getValue()).doubleValue());
```

Mobile Agent can carry these codes to where the measurement service is hosted and execute them there locally. It can free NMC of synchronous waiting for the call return, and from performance point of view, it narrows the possibility of call failure and reduces network traffics. Currently many Mobile Agent systems, such as Aglet [19] and Mole [20], are formulated by two kinds of Agents, one is Mobile Agent that can move around, and another is Service Agent (SA) that is stationary to provide services to MA. MA speaks with SA through Java RMI. In SONA, things are simplified as MA directly speaks to a Web Service through SOAP other than interacts with SA. This new mechanism keeps the communication between MA with desired services in a standard way so that MA can easily interact with a lot of heterogeneous services without explicit needs for code changes and recompilation.

5 Mobile Agent

Having received all those parameters such as service URI, method name and parameter list from NMC, Mobile Agent can make a call upon the MF exposed by PS's web service. In SONA, for each PS to be visited by Mobile Agent, NMC uses a so-called "Mission" to formulate all these information. The mission is made up of a few jobs for Mobile Agent to do, each of which addresses a measurement functionality on the destined PS. Fig.4 illustrates Mobile Agent, Mission and Job.

Mobile Agent is uniquely identified by its *agentID* and an *nmcAddr*. All the missions assigned by NMC are kept in Mobile Agent's *missionList* field. The *Mission* gives the address for the PS in its *probeSiteAddr*, which can guide Mobile Agent's migration from host to host. A few jobs are maintained in the *jobList* of Mission, each of which corresponds to a call for a given MF exposed by the Web Service hosted on PS. The *Job* contains all the parameters to generate the call, such as SOAP Address, Service URN, Method Name and Input Parameter List.

Upon arriving, Mobile Agent extracts the *Mission* from its mission list that's corresponding to the PS it's now running on. Then it executes the assigned jobs by calling designated MFs one by one and stores the measurements in each *Job*'s *Result* field. Fig.5 illustrates how a Mobile Agent migrates from host to host to accomplish its missions. There are 3 hosts for Mobile Agent to visit according to its Mission List. For each host, there is a job list for the agent to do. On PS1, the agent will call MF1 and MF2 provided by the web service *urn:WS1*. Then the agent will migrate to PS2 to call MF1 of *urn:WS1* and MF2 of *urn:WS2*. At the last stop of its itinerary, agent will call WF1, WF2 and WF3 provided by *urn:WS1* of PS3. Finally the agent returns to NMC with all these results.

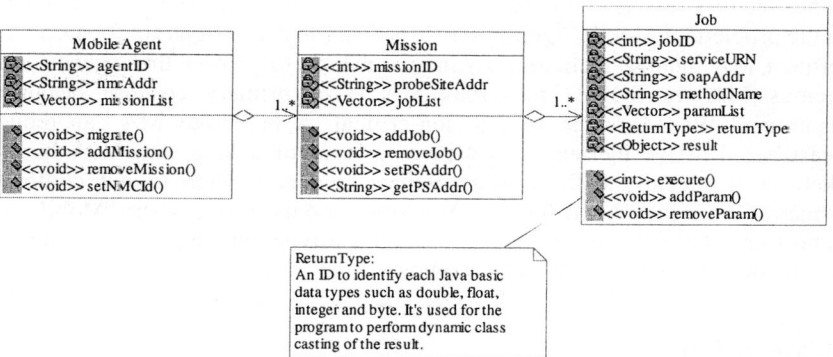

Fig. 4. Mobile Agent, Mission and Job Class. Mobile Agent is assigned a list of missions by NMC, which are to be accomplished during its traveling. Every mission is endowed with a list of jobs, each of which contains all the information for calling a MF within PS's web service.

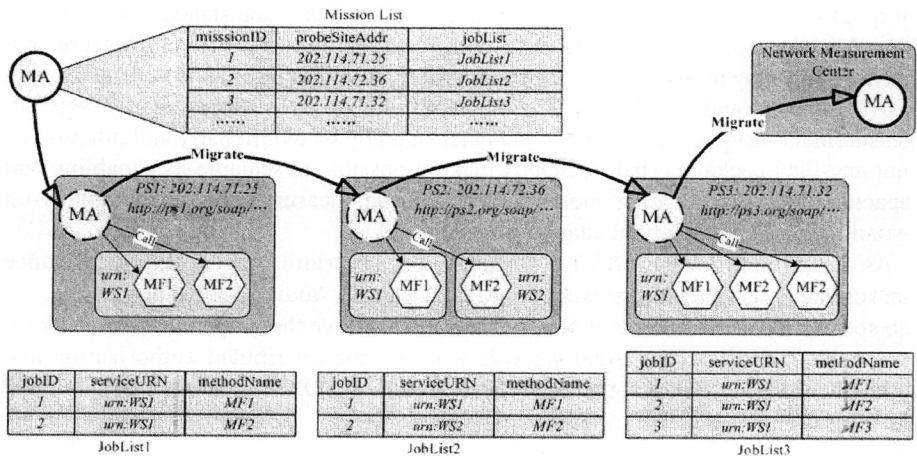

Fig. 5. Mobile Agent migrates to accomplish its missions. Based on its mission list, Mobile Agent migrates from host to host to accomplish missions one by one. It calls the measurement functionality based on the information provided by the job list in each mission, and finally returns to NMC with the result.

6 Security Considerations

There are two security issues to be considered within SONA. Firstly, as SONA aims to achieve a wide participation of network measurement in a scalable way, new PS to SONA must be authorized and authenticated, or else, unauthorized PS that hosts malicious Web Service can initiate Denial of Service attacks or spy on the confidential information from NMC to PS. So before a new PS can join in, it's reasonable that PS be required to present a X.509 certificate signed by the NMC. Another security leak is on the Mobile Agent. A lot of works have been done to deal with the problem of Mobile Agent's security [21]. Most questions are focused on how to protect MA against malicious Agency and how to protect the Agency against malicious MA. In SONA, malicious MA is of primary concern because all measurement Web Services are mission-critical. A malicious MA can request a Unicast-based active measurement service to run for a long time with large test packet, or it illegally calls a passive measurement service to get confidential information from prohibited sources. Thus we not only need a secure Mobile Agent transport protocol here, but also have to find a way appending each Mobile Agent with a credential signed by its birth Agency.

7 Conclusion

We studied SONA, a Web Service based network performance measurement architecture in this paper to deal with the interoperability and adaptability issues of current network measurement projects. Wrapping traditional network measurement functions as a Web Service makes SONA a standardized service oriented architecture for quick deployment of network measurement functionality and standard invocations. Also Mobile Agent enriches SONA with flexible controls of the measurement activities. To play in SONA, a probe site is only required to install a HTTP server with SOAP support and a Mobile Agent agency for receiving the agent. Network measurement services can be developed independently by a third party and offered as a plug-and-play package. That is, SONA make it possible to scalable its capability and capacity of accommodating more probe sites and measurement functionalities on demand without architectural changes.

As the future work, XML schemas for describing network performance measurement service and measurement result will be studied. With the schema, we can specify the service in a much standard way and have them open to other network management applications. Also we will work on the distributed authorization and authentication mechanism that can be applied in SONA to make it a reliable platform.

References

1. V. Paxson, G. Almes, J. Mahdavi, and M. Mathis, Framework for IP performance metrics, RFC 2330, May 1998
2. G. Almes, S. Kalidindi, A one-way delay metric for IPPM, RFC 2679, Sept. 1999.

3. R. Koodli, R. Ravikanth, One-way Loss Pattern Sample Metrics, Internet Draft, draft-ietf-ippm-loss-pattern-05.txt, Jan 2001.
4. V. Paxson, J. Mahdavi, A. Adams, and M. Mathis, An architecture for large-scale internet measurement, IEEE Communications Magazine, vol. 36, no. 8, pp. 48–54, Aug. 1998.
5. S. Kalidindi and M. Zekauskas, Surveyor: An infrastructure for Internet Performance Measurements, in Proceedings of the INET'99, CA, USA, 1999.
6. S.Kalidindi, OWDP: A Protocol to Measure One-Way Delay and Packet Loss, Surveyor Technical Report, Sept. 1998
7. L. Ciavattone, A. Morton, and G. Ramachandran, Standardized Active Measurements On A Tier 1 IP Backbone," IEEE Comm. Mag., June 2003.
8. W3C, Web services, http://www.w3.org/2002/ws/
9. SOAP Specification 1.2, http://www.w3.org/TR/2003/REC-soap12-part1-20030624/, W3C Recommendation, June 2003
10. D. L. Mills, Network time protocol (version 3): Specification, implementation and analysis, RFC 1305, Mar. 1992.
11. Luckie, M.J. and A. J. McGregor. IPMP: IP Measurement Protocol. Proceedings PAM2002 Passive & Active Measurement Workshop, Fort Collins, Colorado, pp. 168-176, Mar. 2002.
12. V. Paxson, On calibrating measurements of packet transit times, in Proceedings of ACM SIGMETRICS'98, Madison, WI, Jun. 1998, pp. 11–21.
13. S. Moon, P. Skelly and D. Towsley, Estimation and Removal of Clock Skew from Network Delay Measurements, Proc. of Infocom '99, New York, NY, Mar. 1999.
14. M. J. Coates and R. Nowak. Network Delay Distribution Inference From End-to-end Unicast Measurement. in Proc. of the IEEE International Conference on Acoustics, Speech,and Signal Processing, May 2001.
15. M. J. Coates and R. Nowak. Network Loss Inference Using Unicast End-to-end Measurement. in Proc. ITC Conf. IP Traffic, Modeling and Management, Monterey, CA, Sept. 2000.
16. A. Adams, T. Bu, R. Caceres, N.G. Duffield, T. Friedman and J. Horowitz, F. Lo Presti, S.B. Moon, V. Paxson, D. Towsley, The Use of End-to-End Multicast Measurements for Characterizing Internal Network Behavior, IEEE Communications Magazine, May 2000.
17. J. Case, M. Fedor, M. Schoffstall, and J. Davin, A Simple Network Management Protocol (SNMP), RFC 1157, May 1990
18. A. McGregor, H-W.Braun, and J. Brown. The NLANR Network Analysis Infrastructure. IEEE Communications Magazine, Vol. 38 (5): pp. 122-128, May 2000.
19. P.E.Clements, T. Papaioannou and J. Edwards, Aglets: Enabling the Virtual Enterprise, In the Proceedings of ME-SELA'97, July 1997, pp.425-432.
20. J. Baumann, F. Hohl, K. Rothermel and M. Strasser: Concepts of a Mobile Agent System, WWW Journal, Special issue on Applications and Techniques of Web Agents, 1998
21. Karnik, Neeran, Security in Mobile Agent Systems, Ph.D. dissertation. Department of Computer Science and Engineering, University of Minnesota, 1998

Pathtrait: A Tool for Tight Link Location and End-to-End Available Bandwidth Measurement

Dalu Zhang[1], Ye Wu[2], and Jian Xu[3]

[1] Department of Computer Science and Engineering, Tongji University
daluz@acm.org
[2] Department of Computer Science and Engineering, Tongji University
beatles_v@hotmail.com
[3] Department of Computer Science and Engineering, Tongji University
discoveryxj@online.sh.cn

Abstract. Estimating the end-to-end available bandwidth along a network path is of great significance in congestion control, streaming applications, QoS verification, server selection. Knowing the exact locations of tight links, network operators can apply traffic engineering, routing policy optimization and fault diagnosis. In this paper we present *Pathtrait*, a tool that allows end users to accurately locate the tight link along a network path and efficiently estimate the end-to-end available bandwidth through the information of tight link location. *Pathtrait* is based on a novel probing technique that generates three different sorts of probing trains. We utilize a original probing structure to capture the input rate and output rate of a single probing train at certain link among the estimated network path, which can infer the tight link and estimate the available bandwidth of the tight link.

Keywords: Network measurements, available bandwidth, tight link, pathtrait.

1 Introduction

Knowledge of available bandwidth on end-to-end paths and the location of tight links can effectively enhance the performance of network applications. The tight link along a network path is the link that has the minimal end-to-end available bandwidth. Unfortunately, it is quite hard to identify the exact location of the tight link unless we are able to keep link load information for every involved link. However such information is hardly attainable due to the decentralized property of the Internet which discourages link information sharing, it is impossible for end users to obtain the link information through traditional passive measurement techniques. Therefore, so as to meet the needs of end-based network applications, it is necessary to observe the internal dynamics of general Internet paths from the end-to-end measurements.

Tight link location and accurate available bandwidth estimation techniques extend existing measurement methodologies of available bandwidth and benefit the design of resource-aware network applications and the strategies of network management and diagnosis.

1.1 Main Contributions

In this paper, we present an original end-to-end available bandwidth estimation and tight link location measurement methodology, called *pathtrait*. It utilizes a novel probing structure to capture the input rate and output rate of a single probing train at certain hop, which leads to the discovery of tight link and accurate estimation of available bandwidth along a network path. We have also evaluated *pathtrait* in a controlled and reproducible environment using NS simulations. The results of the simulations show that *pathtrait* accurately locates the first tight link when the path includes several tight links and attains the available bandwidth with high accuracy.

1.2 Overview

This paper is organized as follows. Section 2 summarizes previous works on available bandwidth estimation and tight link location. Section 3 explains the *pathtrait* probing methodology. Section 4 presents the *pathtrait* implementation and algorithms. Section 5 describes the NS simulations and analyzes the results of the simulations. Section 6 summarizes and discusses future work.

2 Related Work

2.1 Available Bandwidth Measurement

Carter *et al.* presented a tool called cprobe [2] to estimate the available bandwidth based on the dispersion of long packet trains at the receiver. Later, Dovrolis [3] pointed that cprobe actually measured a metric called the asymptotic dispersion rate (ADR) other than the available bandwidth.

Melander *et al.* proposed a measurement methodology called TOPP (Trains of Packet Pairs) [4]. It estimates both the available bandwidth and the capacity of the tight link by analyzing the relation between the input and output rates of different packet pairs.

Another recent estimation technique is Self-Loading Periodic Streams (SLoPS) [1] proposed by Jain *et al.* The basic idea of is that one-way delays of packets show an increasing trend when the input rate of the probing stream is higher than the available bandwidth of the path. Pathchirp [5] is proposed to improve the measurement speed of pathload.

Hu *et al.* proposed a tool called IGI [6] that measures the cross-traffic intensity other than directly calculating the available bandwidth.

2.2 Tight Link Location Techniques

A recent proposal [7] used a tool, BFind, to locate the tight link of a path. It essentially induces network congestion through continuous transmission of UDP traffic and determines the location of the tight link from traceroute round-trip times. However, the traffic intrusiveness of BFind tool can not be neglected.

Ribeiro et al. proposed a tool called STAB [8], which measures the sub-path available bandwidth and the last thin link that has the least available bandwidth on the entire path is the tight link.

D. Zhang et al. proposed a probing technique for tight link location called dual rate periodic stream (DRPS) [10] probing. DRPS probing provides a periodic stream with two rates. It can adjust the rate shift time to control the link congestion.

Another interesting probing technique is recursive packet train (RPT) [11]. It relies on the fact that load packets interleave with cross traffic on the links along the path and changing the length of the packet train.

3 Pathtrait Probing Methodology

In this section, we present the underlying idea of *pathtrait* probing. We first discuss the preliminary knowledge of *pathtrait* probing and basic definition. Next, we describe the *pathtrait* probing theory.

3.1 Basic Definition

Basic Assumption. As enumerated below, there are four basic assumptions, which are common to most recent related studies [1, 11]:

1. FIFO queuing at all routers along the path;
2. Cross traffic follows a fluid model;
3. Average rates of cross traffic change slowly and are constant for the duration of a single measurement.
4. All routers along the path can generation ICMP packets, the ICMP packet generation time is pretty small [13, 14].

Available Bandwidth. We first define the available bandwidth of a network link and then of an end-to-end path. Generally, we consider a store-and-forward network link i with capacity C_i. Let $\lambda_i(t)$ be the instantaneous utilization of the link at t. When the link i is idle, $\lambda_i(t)$ is equal to zero. When the link i is utilized, $\lambda_i(t)$ is equal to one.

Theoretically, the available bandwidth at link i during time interval $(t, t + \tau)$ is defined as its unutilized capacity in that duration,

$$A_i(t, t + \tau) = \frac{1}{\tau} C_i \int_t^{t+\tau} [1 - \lambda_i(t)] dt \qquad (1)$$

Thus, consider now a network path with n links, the end-to-end available bandwidth of the network path during the same time interval is defined as the minimum available bandwidth of all traversed links,

$$A(t, t + \tau) = \min_{i=1...n} \{A_i(t, t + \tau)\} \qquad (2)$$

The tight link of a network path is the link with the end-to-end available bandwidth along the path.

Proportional Shared Bandwidth. In practical, it is hard to directly obtain the link utilization information along a network path through end-to-end measure techniques due to the property of a general network path which discourages sharing of link information. Therefore, we use a more practical available bandwidth definition.

Proportional shared bandwidth of a network path is the rate that the link provides to a new probing train in a proportional shared fashion, *i.e.*

$$R_O = \begin{cases} R_I & R_I < A \\ C_t \frac{R_I}{R_I + \lambda} & b \geq R_I \geq A \end{cases} \quad (3)$$

where b is the second minimum surplus link bandwidth along the path, R_I and R_O are the input rate and output rate of the probing train respectively, A is the end-to-end available bandwidth of the path and C_t is the capacity of the tight link.

3.2 Pathtrait Probing

Some Definitions. We now describe underlying idea of our probing methodology and probing construct. A probe [12] is a sequence of one or more packets transmitted from a common origin. Let us consider 3 types of probing packets closely related to the *pathtrait* probe. A packet that can successfully reach the specific destination from a common origin TYPE I probe. We consider that a packet is hop-limited if its TTL is manually set to a smaller value so as not to reach the destination and be dropped at the specific hop along the probed path. We refer to the hop-limited packets as TYPE II probe. A hop-limited packet that can be used to trigger an ICMP response from a specific intermediate router is referred to as TYPE III probe.

The size and the destination of each packet p with a probe are parameterized as $s(p)$ and $D(p)$ respectively. If a packet p is hop-limited, the manually set value is $h(p)$. To denote a probe, we refer to each probe packet with a distinct lowercase letter, and represent the sequential order in which they are transmitted from the probing host by writing them from left to right. With $[pq]$, we denote that two packets p and q are transmitted back-to-back. $\{pq\}_\delta$ shows that two packets p and q are transmitted with inter-packet gap δ. A probe of form $\{[pq][pq]\}_\delta$ denotes that a pair of two-packet probes transmit with inter-probe gap δ, then the rate of the probe is $R = \frac{s(p)+s(q)}{\delta}$. Next, we discuss the main properties of *pathtrait* probe.

Packet Tailgating Property. For each link, the technique sends a large TYPE II packet followed by a very small TYPE I packet that will queue continuously behind the large packet until the previous packet expires. It provides us a basic idea of tracking the variation of output rates with different input rates with two types of *pathtrait* probes.

Lemma 1 (Tailgating Property). *Let us consider a path of n links $L_1, L_2, \ldots, L_n$ with available bandwidth $A_1, A_2, \ldots, A_n$, and a probing train with two TYPE I probes*

p and q. If a probe of the form $[pq]$ is injected at L_1, with $D(p) = D(q) = L_n$ and if $\forall k \leq n, \frac{s(p)}{s(q)} \geq \frac{A_{k+1}}{A_K}$, then $[pq]$ will remain back-to-back along the entire path.

Proof. The proof of Lemma 1 can be found in [12]. □

Self-Loading Periodic Streams Property. Self-Loading Periodic Streams (SLoPS) [1] provides an effective methodology for estimating the end-to-end available bandwidth.

Lemma 2 (SLoPS Property). *Consider a path of n links $L_1, L_2, \ldots, L_n$ with available bandwidth $A_1, A_2, \ldots, A_n$ and a probing train with a TYPE I probe p. If a probe of the form $\{pp\}_{\delta_1}$ (The form at hop i is $\{pp\}_{\delta_i}$.) is injected at L_1, with $D(p) = L_n$ and if $\delta_n > \delta_1$, then the input rate of the probe $R = \frac{s(p)}{\delta} > \min_{k=1\ldots n} A_k$.*

Proof. From the definition of proportional shared bandwidth and formula (3), we have

$$\frac{R_1}{R_n} = \frac{s(p)/\delta_1}{s(p)/\delta_n} = \frac{\delta_n}{\delta_1} = \begin{cases} 1 & R_1 < A \\ > 1 & R_1 \geq A \end{cases}$$

If $\frac{\delta_n}{\delta_1} > 1$, then $R_1 (= s(p)/\delta_1) > \min_k A_k$ □

Lemma 2 shows that we can analyze the available bandwidth of the path by sending periodic probing train.

Dual Rate Property. Dual Rate Periodic Streams (DRPS) [10] is designed for locating tight links in a network path. A DRPS probe has both dual rate property and SLoPS property. Dual rate property. It can mark the position of tight links with different input rates injected. Initially, the dual rate probe goes through the path with a higher rate. As arriving at the objective hop of the path, it shifts its rate to a lower rate and keeps the rate until arriving at the receiver.

Given a path of n links $L_1, L_2, \ldots, L_n$ with available bandwidth $A_1, A_2, \ldots, A_n$, and a probing train with a TYPE I probe q and a TYPE II probe p. We inject the probing train with the form $\{pqpq\}_{\delta_1}$ at L_1 and assume that the probing train enters L_i with the form of $\{pqpq\}_{\delta_i}$. Given that $h(p) = m < n, D(q) = L_n, s(p) = s(q)$.

For each link $L_k, 1 \leq k \leq m$, the rate at L_k satisfies $R_k = R_k^p = R_k^q = s(p)/\delta_k$, and for each link $L_k, m < k \leq n$, the form of the probing train becomes $\{qq\}_{2\delta_k}$ with the rate satisfying $R_k = R_k^p = s(q)/2\delta_k$.

Theorem 1 (Dual Rate Periodic Streams Property I). *Consider a path of n links $L_1, L_2, \ldots, L_n$ with available bandwidth $A_1, A_2, \ldots, A_n$ and a probing train with a TYPE I probe q and a TYPE II probe p. We inject the probing train with the form $\{pqpq\}_{\delta_1}$ at L_1 and assume the probing train enters L_i with the form of $\{pqpq\}_{\delta_i}$. Given that $h(p) = m < n, D(q) = L_n, s(p) = s(q)$. In addition, let the location of the tight link be hop j, and the input rate R_I satisfies $R_I > \min_{k=1\ldots n}\{A_k\}, R_I < \min_{k=1\ldots n}(\{A_k\}-\{A_j\})$, then*

a If $m > j$, then $2\delta_1 < 2\delta_n$.

b *If $m < j$, then $2\delta_1 = 2\delta_n$.*

Proof. The proof of Theorem 1 can be deduced from [10]. We denote $2\delta_1 < 2\delta_n$ instead of $\delta_1 < \delta_n$ to indicate the inter-packet gap changes from δ to 2δ. □

Corollary 1 (Dual Rate Periodic Streams Property II). *Consider the same path and available bandwidth of all the links along the path as Theorem 1. We inject the probing train that consists of TYPE I probe q and TYPE II probe q with the form $\{[pq][pq]\}_{\delta_1}$. Given that $h(p) < m = n, D(q) = L_n, s(q) \ll s(p)$. Let the location of tight link be hop j, and the input rate R_I satisfies $R_I > \min_{k=1...n}\{A_k\}$, $R_I < \min_{k=1...n}(\{A_k\} - \{A_j\})$, then*

a *If $m > j$, then $\delta_1 < \delta_n, R_I = \frac{s(p)}{\delta_1} > \frac{s(p)}{\delta_n}$.*
b *If $m < j$, then $\delta_1 = \delta_n, R_I = \frac{s(p)}{\delta_1} = \frac{s(p)}{\delta_n}$.*

Proof. From Lemma 1 and $s(q) \ll s(p)$, the size of packet q can be neglected and the initial inter-packet gap between two consecutive packet p is δ_1. Then, from Theorem 1, we get Corollary 1. □

We now change the form of the injected probe form to $\{[pe][pe]\}_{\delta_1}$, where e denotes a TYPE III packet. The inter-packet gap between two TYPE III probes can reflect the variation of the length of probing train and obtain the information without requiring access to the destination. According to Corollary 1, we get our dual rate property III.

Corollary 2 (Dual Rate Periodic Streams Property III). *Consider the same path and available bandwidth of all the links along the path as Theorem 1. We inject the probing train that consists of TYPE I probe p and TYPE III probe e with the form $\{[pe][pe]\}_{\delta_1}$. Given that $h(e) = m < n, D(q) = L_n, s(e) \ll s(p)$. Let the gap between two ICMP echo reply be σ, and the location of the tight link be hop j, and the input rate R_I satisfies $R_I > \min_{k=1...n}\{A_k\}$, $R_I < \min_{k=1...n}(\{A_k\} - \{A_j\})$, then*

a *If $m < j$, then $\delta_1 < \sigma, R_I = \frac{s(p)}{\delta_1} > \frac{s(p)}{\sigma}$.*
b *If $m > j$, then $\delta_1 = \sigma, R_I = \frac{s(p)}{\delta_1} = \frac{s(p)}{\sigma}$.*

Proof. The gap between two ICMP echo reply σ denotes the output inter-packet gap of link m-1, that is, the input inter-packet gap of link m. Therefore, we have $\sigma = \delta_m$. Then from Corollary 1, we get Corollary 2. □

Input Rate Selection. In practice, the key problem of applying Theorem 1, Corollary 1,2 is how to select the appropriate input rate.

Theorem 2 (Rate Selection Property I). *Consider the same path and available bandwidth of all the links along the path as Theorem 1. We inject the probing train that consists of TYPE I or TYPE II probe p and two TYPE III probes e_{m-1}, e_m with the form $\{[pe_{m-1}e_m][pe_{m-1}e_m]\}_{\delta_1}$. Given that $h(e_{m-1}) = m - 1, h(e_m) = m, 2 \leq m \leq n + 1$, $D(q) = L_n, s(e_{m-1}) = s(e_m) \ll s(p)$. Let the gap between two ICMP echo reply triggered by e_{m-1} be σ_{m-1}, and the gap between two ICMP echo reply triggered by e_m be σ_m, then If $\sigma_m > \sigma_{m-1}$, then $R_m = s(p)/\delta_m > A_m$. If $\sigma_m = \sigma_{m-1}$, then $R_m = s(p)/\delta_m \leq A_m$*

Proof. If $\sigma_m > \sigma_{m-1}$, then $\delta_{m+1} > \delta_m$, $R_{m+1} < R_m$. From formula 3, we have $R_m = s(p)/\delta_m > A_m$. If $\sigma_m = \sigma_{m-1}$, then $\delta_{m+1} = \delta_m$, $R_{m+1} = R_m$. From formula 3, we have $R_m = s(p)/\delta_m \leq A_m$ □

Theorem 2 provides a way to identify the relationship of the available bandwidth between two continuous links along the path. At the sender, we first probe the path with a higher input rate. After the ICMP echo replies returns, we adjust the input rate with a lower input rate and probe the path again. Repeatedly, we can find the tight link.

Theorem 3 (Rate Selection Property II). *Consider the same path and available bandwidth of all the links along the path as Theorem 1. We inject the probing train that consists of TYPE I or TYPE II probe p and three TYPE III probes e_{m-2}, e_{m-1}, e_m with the form $\{[pe_{m-2}e_{m-1}e_m][pe_{m-2}e_{m-1}e_m]\}_{\delta_1}$. Given that $h(e_1) = 1, h(e_2) = 2, h(e_{m-2}) = m-2, h(e_{m-1}) = m-1, h(e_m) = m, 3 \leq m \leq n$ $D(q) = L_n, s(e_{m-1}) = s(e_m) \ll s(p)$. Let the gap between two ICMP echo reply triggered by e_{m-2} be σ_{m-2}, the gap triggered by e_{m-1} be σ_{m-1}, and the gap triggered by e_m be σ_m, then If $\sigma_{m-2} = \sigma_{m-1}$ and $\sigma_{m-1} = \sigma_m$, then $A_m < A_{m-1}$.*

Proof. From Theorem 2, if $\sigma_{m-2} = \sigma_{m-1}$, then $R_{m-1} = R_m \leq A_m$, and if $\sigma_{m-1} < \sigma_m$, then $R_m > A_m$, so we get $A_m < A_{m-1}$. □

Theorem 3 provides a method to compare the available bandwidth between consecutive two links.

4 Pathtrait Implementation and Algorithm

In this section, we describe the *pathtrait* implementation. The algorithm is explained throughly.

4.1 Pathtrait Train Structure

Pathtrait train consists of load packets, each of which is followed back to back by one backward packet or one forward packet alternatively, as depicted in figure 1. Let q denote measurement packets, and p denote load packets, $s(q) \ll s(p)$. Let $s(q) = 40$ Byte and $s(p) = 1000$ Byte. We refer packet size as IP-layer payload. That is, load packets have large size 1000 Byte and measurement packets have small size 40 Byte. Measurement packets are sent back to back after load packets. *Pathtrait* sends 100 load packets with constant inter-packet time δ, the rate of the load packets is $s(p)/\delta$.

Pathtrait consists of 3 phases. In the first phase, *pathtrait* finds the hop count of the current path, and determine the maximum probing rate. *Pathtrait* sends a pathtrait train with a TTL 128, at the receiver the TTL in packets is examined, and determines the hop count from the decrement of TTL. Let the bandwidth of the outgoing interface as the maximum rate of load packets. In the second and third phase, *pathtrait* locate the tight link and measure the available bandwidth respectively. In the next two subsections, we describe the second phase and the third phase thoroughly.

Pathtrait Train Construction

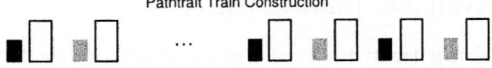

Fig. 1. Pathtrait train structure: white rectangles represent load packets, gray rectangles represent forward packets, black rectangles represent backward packets.

4.2 Locating the Tight Link

Let *choke link* be the link where congestion occurred during *pathtrait* probing, *choke count* as the count of choke link during one *pathtrait* probing train and *last choke link* as the choke link that is closest to the receiver in one *pathtrait* probing train. *Pathtrait* employs the algorithm depicted in figure 2 to locate the tight link. It works as follows, it probes each hop along the path, get the choke count, if for hop *i* the input rate is greater than output rate by 5% (We let delta 5%). If choke count is one, the choke link is reported as the tight link. Otherwise, *pathtrait* proceeds to another locating with adjusted probing rate.

```
do
    backward_rate[0] = rate
    for (i = 0; i < hop_count; i++)
        send_stream(i+1, rate,
                    forward_rate, backward_rate)
    for (i = 0; i < hop_count; i++)
        if (backward_rate[i] - forward_rate[i]
            > backward_rate[i] * delta)
            choke++
            tight_link = i
            min_rate = forward_rate[i]
            max_rate = backward_rate[i]
    if (choke == 0)
        rate = (min_rate + max_rate) / 2
    else
        rate = min_rate
while (choke != 1)
```

Fig. 2. The pathtrait locating tight link algorithm

Pathtrait starts locating the tight link with maximum rate obtained in the first phase. Then it gets the choke count of this train. If choke count equals one, the tight link is at the unique choke link. Otherwise it needs another train. It adjusts the rate of load packets by setting it to the input rate at the last choke link. As a result, it gets a new choke count. If this new one equals 1, it terminates its locating phase with the tight link at choke point or it sends another train of *pathtrait* train with adjusted rate. This process is repeated until it finds the tight link or exceeds a maximum times. Currently we set the maximum times to 15. The last probing rate is used in the following phase.

4.3 Measuring Available Bandwidth

Pathtrait sends probing train toward the tight link periodically 15 times with different rate. Their rate is calculated as:

$$R_i = (1 + (8-i)\epsilon)R \tag{4}$$

where R is the last probing rate in locating the tight link, R_i is the rate of the ith probing train.

Thus we get 15 samples of input rate and output rate of the tight link. By equation 3, we get:

$$\frac{1}{R_O} = \begin{cases} \frac{1}{R_I} & R_I < A \\ \frac{1}{C_t} + \frac{\lambda}{C_t}\frac{1}{R_I} & b \geq R_I \geq A \end{cases} \tag{5}$$

where R_I is the input rate and R_O is the output rate at the tight link, C_t is the bandwidth of tight link and λ is the rate of cross traffic at tight link. There is a linear relationship between $1/R_O$ and $1/R_I$, if $b \geq R_I \geq A$. Using a linear regression on the 15 pairs of $1/R_0$ and $1/R_I$, we get C_t and λ, from which we deduce the available bandwidth A as $C_t - \lambda$. Currently ϵ is set to 2%.

5 Simulation and Validation

Pathtrait is verified in ns2 simulation environment. First, we develop an ns version of *pathtrait* as two agent along with an echo agent. Next, we do substantial simulation with various topology and cross traffic conditions.

In the following, we simulate the topology of the 10-hop path, illustrated in figure 3. The *pathtrait* packets enter the path at hop 1 and exit at hop 10. The tight link is located at link 3 or link 7, link 3 is near, link 7 is far respectively. For each link, let the capacity be 10Mbps and link delay be 10ms. The topology we used in simulation is summarized in table 1. The experiment is grouped into CBR, Pareto and Exponential group. Exp#1 – Exp#7 are CBR scenario, the cross traffic are all CBR, the tight link is 3. Exp#8 – Exp#14 are CBR scenario, the tight link is 3 and 7. Exp#15 – Exp#21 are Pareto scenario, the cross traffic are of type Pareto, the tight link is 3. Exp#22 – Exp#28 are all Exponential scenario, the cross traffic are of type Exponential, the tight link is 3. We used default parameters for the traffic generators.

5.1 Constant Cross Traffic Environment

In table 1, exp#1 – exp#7 are grouped as suit#1. In this suit, all cross traffic are constant bit rate (CBR) traffic sources. The tight link is the third link, that is the near one. The results are summarized in table 2, with the tight link location at link 3, which is correct according to topology.

We analyze the last experiment of suit#1. Figure 5.1(a) depicted the process of locating tight link. Figure 5.1(b) depicted the process of regression to available bandwidth. The rates of the two probing trains are 10, and 3.073 Mbps respectively.

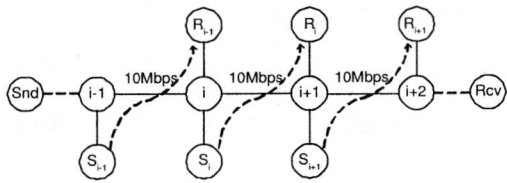

Fig. 3. The topology used in simulation. All the links have 10Mbps bandwidth and 10ms link delay. The traffic types are CBR, Exponential or Pareto.

Table 1. The simulation topology. Exp#1 – Exp#7 is of suit#1, and has one tight link 3. Exp#8 – Exp#14 is of suit#2, and has two tight links 3 and 7. Exp#15 – Exp#21 is of suit#3, and has one tight link 3. Exp#22 – Exp#28 is of suit#4, and has one tight link 4.

Exp#	Non Tight Link Rate (Mbps)	Tight Link Rate (Mbps)
1 | 8 | 15 | 22	3	5
2 | 9 | 16 | 23	3	7
3 | 10 | 17 | 24	1	3
4 | 11 | 18 | 25	1	2
5 | 12 | 19 | 26	3	9
6 | 13 | 20 | 27	5	9
7 | 14 | 21 | 28	7	9

Table 2. Suit#1-#4's simulation results

Exp#	Tight Link Reported	Av-bw (Mbps)	%Error
1| 8|15|22	3|3|3|3	5.073|5.107| 5.39|5.415	1.5| 2.0 | 7.8| 8.3
2| 9|16|23	3|3|3|3	2.97|3.073|3.242|2.733	-1.0| 2.5 | 8.1|-8.9
3|10|17|24	3|3|3|3	7.063|6.883|6.447|7.658	0.9|-1.7 |-7.9| 9.4
4|11|18|25	3|3|3|3	7.895|7.848|7.728|7.184	-1.3|-1.9 | -3.4|-10.2
5|12|19|26	3|3|3|3	1.017|1.019|1.109|1.077	1.7| 1.9 |10.9| 7.7
6|13|20|27	3|3|3|3	1.018|1.021|1.081|1.092	1.8| 2.1 | 8.1| 9.2
7|14|21|28	3|3|3|3	1.016|1.025|1.093|1.101	1.6| 2.5 | 9.3|10.1

The locating tight link phase of exp#7 consists of 2 trains. The first train is sent at full rate, that is 10 Mbps. After this we find congestion occurred at 5 hops. Next we adjust the load packets rate to 3.073 Mbps, and measure again. We find choke count 1, which means we should terminate *pathtrait* locating phase. In fact, the reported tight link location is correct.

Next we begin the analysis of suit#2. In suit#2, there are two tight link, link#3 and link#7, according to our theory, we should locate the first one as the tight link. The measurement results is shown in table 2.

We analyze the last experiment exp#14. Figure 5.1 depicts the process of locating tight link. The rates of the five probing trains are 10, 2.486, 1.918,

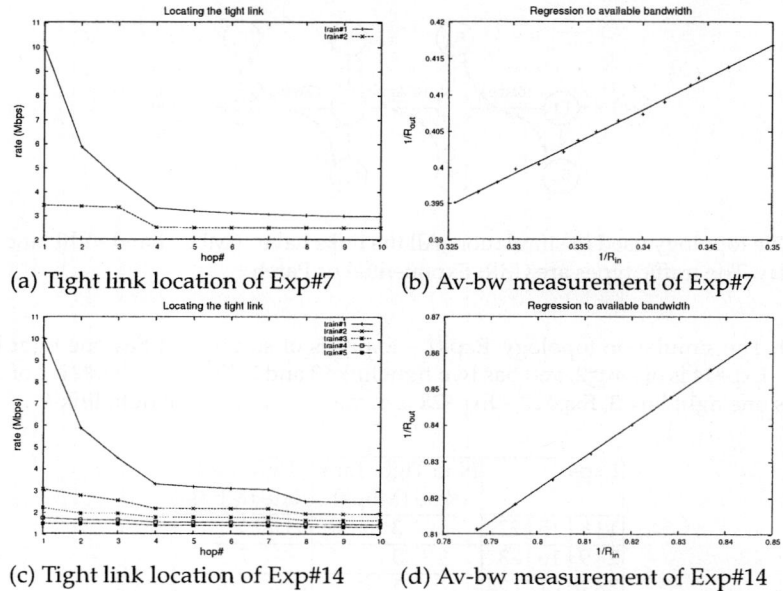

(a) Tight link location of Exp#7 (b) Av-bw measurement of Exp#7

(c) Tight link location of Exp#14 (d) Av-bw measurement of Exp#14

1.617, and 1.436 Mbps respectively. From table 2, the relative error of available bandwidth measurement is within 3%, and the tight link location is all correct, which validate the accuracy of *pathtrait* in suit#2.

The locating tight link process in multi tight link environment can be quite long, but the result is accurate. It takes 5 probing trains for *pathtrait* to locate the tight link. The regression to available bandwidth is quiet accurate.

5.2 Bursty Environment

In this subsection, we validate *pathtrait* in the bursty environment.

In table 2, we present the simulation results. The results in bursty environment is not as accurate as that in constant cross traffic environment. The relative error of measuring available bandwidth in suit#3 and suit#4 is less than 11%, which is still acceptable. The tight link location is all accurate.

6 Conclusion and Future Work

In this paper, we present a novel probing tool – *pathtrait* – that measures the location of tight link and available bandwidth along end-to-end paths. We show that *pathtrait* is able to locate the tight link with high accuracy and measures the available bandwidth effectively. We have illustrated the power of combining the two efforts together.

However the exploration is not complete in some aspects. The large scale measurement of tight link and available bandwidth on Internet is required to be one of our future work. Furthermore, the configuration parameters such as the load packet size, the number of load packets should be studied henceforth. We are working to improve the accuracy of *pathtrait* by modifying the *pathtrait* probing structure.

References

1. M. Jain and C. Dovrolis. End-to-end available bandwidth: Measurement methodology, dynamics, and relation with tcp throughput. In *Proceedings of ACM SIGCOMM*, August 2002.
2. R. Carter and M. Crovella. Measuring Bottleneck Link Speed. In *Packet-Switched Networks, International Journal on Performance Evaluation*, 2728,1996.
3. C. Dovrolis, P, Ramanathan, and D. Moore. What Do Packet Dispersion Techniques Measure? In *Proceedings of IEEE INFOCOM*, April 2001.
4. B. Melander, M. Bjorkman, and P. Gunningberg. Regression-based Available Bandwidth Measurements In *Proceedings of SPECTS*, July 2002.
5. V. Ribeiro, R. Riedi, R. Baraniuk, J. Navratil, and L. Cottrell. pathChirp: E cient Available Bandwidth Estimation for Network Paths. In *Proceedings of Passive and Active Measurement Workshop*, 2003.
6. N. Hu and P. Steenkiste. Evaluation and Characterization of Available Bandwidth Probing Techniques. IEEE JSAC Special Issue in Internet and WWW Measurement, Mapping , and Modeling, 3rd Quarter 2003.
7. A. Akella, S. Seshan, and A. Shaikh. An empirical evaluation of wide-area Internet bottlenecks. Internet Measurement Conference, 2003.
8. V. Ribeiro, R. Riedi, R. Baraniuk. Spatio-Temporal Available Bandwidth Estimation with STAB. In *ACM SIGMETRICS Performance Evaluation Review*, June 2004.
9. K. Lai and M. Baker. Measuring Link Bandwidth Using a Deterministic Model of Packet Delay. In *Proceedings of ACM SIGCOMM*, 2000.
10. D. Zhang, W. Huang, C. Lin. Locating the tightest link of a network path. In *ACM SIGMETRICS Performance Evaluation Review*, June 2004.
11. N. Hu, L. Li, Z. Mao, P. Steenkiste, J. Wang. Locating Internet Bottlenecks: Algorithms, Measurements, and Implications. In *ACM SIGCOMM Computer Communication Review*, October 2004.
12. K. Harfoush, A. Bestavros and J. Byers. Measuring bottleneck bandwidth of targeted path segments. In *Proceedings of IEEE INFOCOM*, March 2003.
13. K. Anagnostakis, M. Greenwald and R. Ryger. Cing: Measuring Network–internal Delays Using Only Existing Infrastructure. In *Proceedings of IEEE INFOCOM*, April 2003.
14. R. Govindan and V. Paxson. Estimating Router ICMP Generation Delays. In *Proceedings of PAM*, March 2002.

Performance Evaluation of a Self-organized Hierarchical Topology for Update of Replicas in a Large Distributed System

Jesús Acosta-Elias, B. Pineda Reyes, E. Chavez Leos,
Alejandro Ochoa-Cardiel, Mario Recio, and Omar Gutierrez-Navarro

Universidad Autónoma de San Luis Potosí,
Alvaro Obregon 64, San Luis Potosí, SLP 78000, México
mrecio@galia.fc.uaslp.mx, {jacosta, bpineda, echavez, aochoa}@uaslp.mx

Abstract. In this paper we evaluate our own weak consistency algorithm, which is called the "Fast Consistency Algorithm", and whose main aim is optimizing the propagation of changes introducing a preference for nodes and zones of the network which have greatest demand. Weak consistency algorithms allow us to propagate changes in a large, arbitrary changing storage network in a self-organizing way. These algorithms generate very little traffic overhead; they have low latency and are scalable, in addition to being fault tolerant. The algorithm has been simulated over ns-2, and measured its performance for complex spatial distributions of demand, including Internet like self-similar fractal distributions of demand. The impulse response of the algorithm has been characterized. We conclude that considering application parameters such as demand in the event or change propagation mechanism to: 1) prioritize probabilistic interactions with neighbors with higher demand, and 2) including little changes on the logical topology (leader interconnection in hierarchical topology), gives a surprising improvement in the speed of change propagation perceived by most users. In other words, it satisfies the greatest demand in the shortest amount of time.

1 Introduction

In this paper[1] we evaluate "Fast Consistency" (FC), a weak consistency algorithm for the dissemination of changes considering application-level demand. In this scenario, each network node provides service to a group of subscribers, and nodes are only required to know a few neighbor nodes (autonomy and self-organization). FC gives priority to sessions with neighbors with higher demand, and introduces little changes in the logical topology.

We have found considerable improvement with the exchange of very little additional signalling information: with a low number of anti-entropy sessions it is possible to deliver consistent content to a greater number of clients (satisfying most demand in less time).

---
[1] Partially supported by the Mexican Ministry of Education under contract P/PROMEP/103.5/03/2557 and the FAI-UASLP, México.

A replica is a host which provides exactly the same services as the principal host. In this paper we will use the terms server and replica in the same sense. When changes in data are introduced, the distribution of changes or events to all nodes is required to keep all the replicas consistent, with the same content. Several issues have to be considered:

Consistency: There are strong consistency algorithms, and weak consistency algorithms. Strong consistency algorithms (see [1], [6], [11] and [18]) are suitable for synchronous systems with a small number of replicas, where it must be guaranteed that all the replicas are in a consistent state (i.e. all the nodes possess exactly the same content) before any transaction can be carried out. Therefore they are costly, non-scalable on unreliable networks, generating considerable latency and a big amount of traffic. By contrast, weak consistency algorithms (see [1], [15] and [12]) generate very little traffic, have low latency, and are more scalable. They do not sacrifice either availability or response time in order to guarantee strong consistency, but only need to ensure that the nodes eventually converge to a consistent state in a finite, but not bounded, period of time. They are very useful in systems where it is not necessary for all the nodes to be totally consistent in order to carry out transactions (systems that withstand a certain degree of asynchrony).

Distribution of Demand: We cannot assume that demand is the same in all locations. Demand is dynamic: there may be hot spots of demand at some locations, meanwhile somewhere else demand could be several orders of magnitude smaller. If changes arrive first to hot spots, more demand will be satisfied with fresh data.

In replication with weak consistency each node from time to time chooses a neighbor to start an update session. In an update session two nodes mutually update their contents. At the end of the session both nodes will have the same content. These are called anti-entropy session because in each session between nodes, the total entropy in the network is reduced. In this paper it will be referred to simply as a "session". The usual metric principle to evaluate weak consistency algorithms is the amount of sessions necessary for a change brought about in a node to be propagated to all the others.

In simple regions with only one hot spot, giving priority to sessions with neighbors with higher demand gives very good results [8], whereas in multiple regions of high demand its performance advantage is reduced due to the formation of islands of locally consistent replicas. To tackle this problem successfully, we proposed a mechanism to alter the logical topology [10] for converting multiple zones of high demand into a single zone: interconnecting the leaders of every zone of high demand(a self-organized hierarchical topology). The combined effect gives the best possible performance for our fast consistency algorithm.

Given that the worst case demand has a combination of high and low demand zones, the value of demand could be viewed as a landscape consisting of mountains and valleys of demand(Fig. 1). For this purpose, we have developed a random demand generator with self-similar characteristics, in the form of mountains and valleys, using the diamond-square algorithm [2] from computer graphics.

To evaluate the performance of the algorithm presented in this paper, a fast and weak consistency algorithm simulator has been constructed, over Network Simulator 2 [17].

To take into account the demand of clients at every node we use additional metrics: the speed of demand satisfaction (the rate of demand satisfied with consistent information), an utility function (based on economic theory). We conclude that FC improves the distribution of changes by prioritizing nodes with greatest demand, rather independently of demand distribution and topology. In other words, our algorithm satisfies the greatest demand in the shortest amount of time, while sending the same amount of messages (better value at the same cost).

The rest of the paper is organized as follows: Section 2 describes our system model. In section 3 we describe the Fast Consistency algorithm(FC), In section 4 we explain the methodology of simulation of our algorithms in terms of network topology, demand workload and performance metrics. In section 5 we discuss the simulation results for several cases. The paper concludes in section 6.

2 System Model

The model of our distributed system consists of a number of N nodes (principals) that communicate via message passing. By simplicity we assume a fully replicated system, i.e., all nodes must have exactly the same content.

Every node is a server that gives services to a number of local clients. Clients make requests to a server, and every request is a "read" operation, a "write" operation, or both. When a client invokes a "write" operation in a server, this operation (change) must be propagated to all servers (replicas) in order to guarantee the consistency of the replicas. An update is a message that carries a "write" operation to the replica in other neighboring nodes.

In this model, the demand of a server is measured as the number of service requests by their clients per time unit or simply the number of clients "subscribed to".

3 The Fast Consistency Algorithm

The following section describes an extended Time-Stamped Anti-Entropy (TSAE) [15] weak consistency algorithm with a "fast update" step for faster propagation of changes to nodes of higher demand.

3.1 The Basic FC Algorithm

In a network with an arbitrary large number of nodes N, every node n knows his local demand and the demand on t neighbors: $n.demand$ or d_n, and $n.neighbors[ni] =$

$d0, d1, dn, dt,$. Demand at node n : dn, in our model and simulations it has been defined simply as the number of clients that node n provides service. The value of t is typically in the range of $1..log(N)$. Every message m can be identified by a $MessageId$ and a Timestamp: $m = m.id, m.tstmp, m.data$ Every node n has a summary vector of the history of messages it has received: $n.SV[]$.

Figure 1 describes the protocol with an example among three neighbor nodes, where n has a new message m and $n''.demand > n'.demand > n.demand$, with all values of demand observed at the nodes at the same time. n randomly initiates a session of exchange of summary vectors with n', and n' immediately sends a fast update with n'' because it has greater demand.

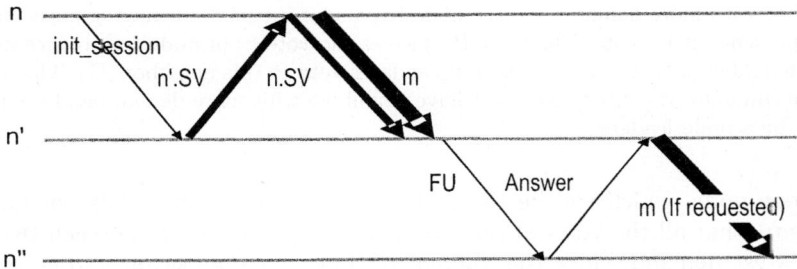

Fig. 1. An anti-entropy session followed by a fast-update notification to a node with higher demand

3.2 High Demand Zones Interconnection

In order to improve performance when there are several regions of high demand surrounded by regions of lower demand that act as barriers slowing down the propagation of messages (See Fig. 2), the basic Fast Consistency algorithm builds a logical topology to interconnect the high demand zones. In order to reach this objective, the nodes in high demand zones choose a leader node by means of a decentralized voting algorithm[10].

In this algorithm each node executes the same local algorithm, which consists in first sending messages (announcing its demand) to its neighbors via the corresponding (adjacent) links, awaiting the arrival of the messages (neighboring demand) and processing them. The messages are transmitted in all directions and arrive after an unpredictable but finite delay.

Each node at a random time will cast its vote for the neighboring node having the greatest demand, and will send it a message notifying it that the vote has been cast(See Fig. 2). Each vote is unique and unrepeated; it has the ID of the node casting it, a time stamp, and a time to live necessary for avoiding loops or for preventing the vote from circulating infinitely around the network.

Each node that receives a vote passes the vote on to whichever of its neighbors has the largest demand, and so on successively, until after an unbounded but finite period of time the majority of votes cast on a high demand zone have

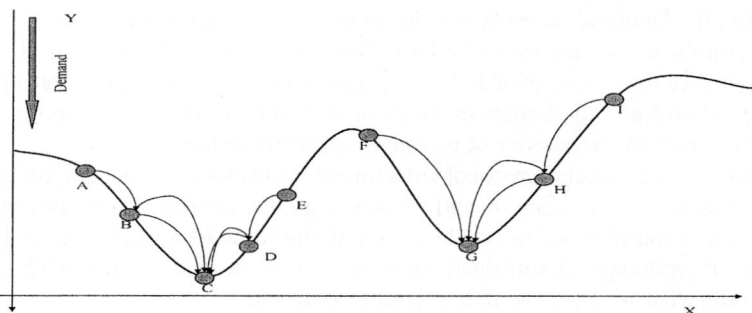

Fig. 2. A demand based election of leader nodes. Every node cast its vote for the neighbor with more demand, i.e. the node I votes for its neighbor having most demand (H) and sends it its vote. The node H receives the vote from node I and since node H has a neighbor with greater demand, it sends I's vote to this neighbor (G). The node G only accumulate votes because don't have neighbors whit more demand and eventually it will be a node leader.

only one node, which will be the node selected (the leader). It is not possible to ensure that all the votes of the nodes on a high demand zone reach the node of greatest demand, since the number of nodes that make up a zone of high demand is not known. Neither do we know how many votes are still travelling without having arrived at the node of greatest demand. However, it is possible to ensure that the votes in a high demand zone will not travel to other zones, since only replicas of higher demand are propagated, and never toward the zones of lower demand. In order for a node to take on the role of a leader node, it is sufficient that, in a $time = t$, the number of accumulated votes be different from zero.

However, not all the nodes possessing votes can be considered leaders, since there will be nodes with more votes and others with very few votes. Thus, from this subset of nodes, all those having fewer votes under a certain threshold will be discarded.

In this way we obtain a new set of nodes which represent the greatest zones of high demand, but as sometimes occurs in a democratic political election, the nodes with the largest number of votes are not necessarily those with greatest demand, although they may represent a high demand zone because they are the nodes in this zone with greatest demand.

The node that knows it is the leader now has the task of finding other leader nodes, if they exist. It must also announce itself so that other nodes become aware of its existence.

The mechanism by which a leader node announces itself is by sending a message as part of the weak consistency protocol. This protocol ensures that the message arrives to all the nodes in a finite, but unbounded, period of time, and therefore to the leader nodes as well, assuming these exist.

When a leader node receives a message from another leader node, it keeps the Id of the node sending the message in a table. Each leader node has a table containing the data of the other leader nodes that know of its existence. This table is replicated in each leader node and is reconstructed dynamically. The Id of a leader node is included in the table on arrival of a message of announcement. It is not necessary to remove a node from the table of leaders because the table is dynamically reconstructed periodically, the period of time being at least equal to the time (expressed in sessions) necessary for the message to cross the entire network of replicas. These leader nodes establish connection among themselves(logic topology) in order to speed up the exchange of messages among all the zones of high demand. Therefore, the logical communication topology is slightly transformed into the equivalent of one zone of high demand, that is the most favorable situation for our algorithm.

4 Simulation Methodology

To evaluate the performance of the fast consistency algorithm compared to Golding's algorithm[15], we simulate the behavior of the algorithms on a system network with synthetic demand. In this section, we discuss the network topology and demand workloads that we use in our simulations. We then describe the performance metrics that we use as a basis for comparing the algorithms in terms of how demand is satisfied per time unit.

4.1 Network Topology

In order for the data obtained from simulation approximates to reality, it is essential that the number of nodes, and other topological properties of the network used in the simulations, resemble those of the phenomenon under investigation. However, we are limited by the computational power available. For this reason, and because the array dimension for the fractal algorithm should be a power of two plus one, the scenario consists of a square-sectioned mesh of $(2^4+1)*(2^4+1)$ or 17*17 nodes, in which each node receives the total number of messages in different anti-entropy sessions. For example, the nodes in the center of the mesh become consistent in far fewer sessions than those found towards the edges of the mesh. We have observed a certain degree of independence of the network organization: other experiments using different topologies and different number of nodes (linear, ring, random networks generated with Brite [13]) have shown similar results. In addition, our results are related to the network diameter. Therefore, results for our network with diameter=17 could be applicable to a network topology similar the Internet. Danesh et al. [4] claim that informed random address probing with TTL up to 15 discovers most of the network hosts, and the number of new hosts using probes with values of TTL between 15 and 30 does not grow significantly.

4.2 Demand Workload

In the works of Yook et al. [16], and in [3] Anukool et al. demonstrated a similar fractal dimension (≈ 1.5) of routers, ASes, and population density. The coinci-

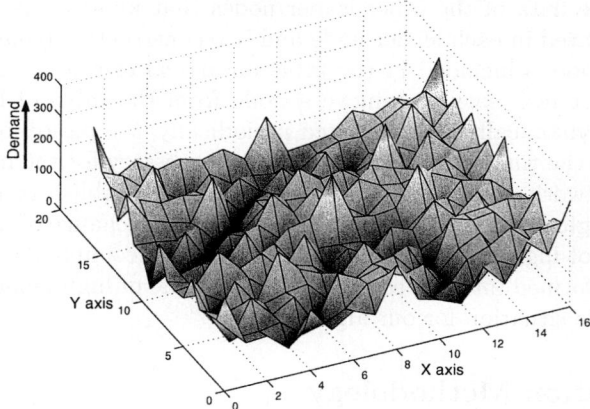

Fig. 3. An example of 100 generated Landscapes. Z-axis corresponds to the demand and the hills are high demand zones.

dence between the fractal dimension of the population and the Internet nodes (router and AS) is not unexpected: high population density implies higher demand for Internet services, resulting in higher router and domain density. The demand is generated by the Internet users. If the geographic location of Internet users have fractal properties, we can infer that the demand have the same fractal properties. Other important characteristic is the existence of high demand regions and large regions of low demand [7]. We use as scenarios for applying our algorithm, 100 random demand surfaces(see fig. 1) on which the different levels, representing the demands, are synthetically generated by the diamond-square algorithm [2], which is a classic algorithm for generating fractal surfaces that resemble landscapes with scaling properties or self-similar. In this way, we achieve a scenario sufficiently general to ensure that the results obtained in the simulations do not depend on the particular or local conditions of a specific scenario. To reduce the effects of randomness, and to prevent the results from depending on the characteristics of a particular fractal surface, each experiment has been run 1000 times for every (100) random demand surface.

4.3 Performance Metric

The purpose of the "fast consistency" algorithm is to improve the performance of the weak consistency algorithms, with particular emphasis on increasing the speed with which these algorithms convey the changes to the zones of greatest demand, so that a greater number of clients may have access to fresh content in a shorter period of time. It is for that reason that our experiments are centered on measuring these speeds.

The performance (speed) is measured in terms of the anti-entropy sessions needed for all the zones to receive the messages with the changes generated in the rest of the nodes that make up the network. If the number of users in each node of the network is used as a measure of demand, then a node with a high number of users which reaches a consistent state will benefit the community more than another node with a low number of users which reaches the same state. The availability of up-to-date information on a data intensive distributed system will be higher if high demand nodes have higher priority than low demand ones.

Every simulation calculates the pair (d_i, c_i) for all nodes, where d_i is the demand at node i, and c_i is the time when node i has received all changes. This pair can be expressed by the $c(n_i, t)$ function (an impulse function of value d_i):

$$c(n_i, t) = \begin{cases} d_i : t = c_i \\ 0 \end{cases} \qquad C(t) = \sum_{i=0}^{N} c(n_i, t) \qquad (1)$$

$C(t)$ is the sum of demand for all nodes that have reached a consistent state at a certain time t. In economic terms, we can define a utility function for each node $u(n_i, t)$. It represents the value of demand satisfied with up-to-date information at time t (a step function of value d_i).

$$u(n_i, t) = \begin{cases} d_i : t \geq c_i \\ 0 \end{cases} \qquad U(t) = \sum_{i=0}^{N} u(n_i, t) \qquad (2)$$

$U(t)$ is the sum of utility for all nodes that are consistent in time t. $U(t)$ expresses the satisfaction or benefit perceived by the community of users of our system. $U(t)$ roughly corresponds in economic terms with the Social Welfare function (SWF) defined in terms of global values as Benefit - Cost, given that the cost (total number of messages exchanged) does not change significantly. In time $t = 0$, all the nodes are in a non-consistent state, and as time passes more and more nodes will reach a consistent state and thus they will contribute to the SWF with their local demand d_i.

5 Simulation Results

In this section, we evaluate the performance of the various parts of the algorithm on a mesh topology using various demand workloads.

5.1 System with Fractal Demand

A fractal demand with fractal dimension similar to which has Internet is assigned to each node. In other words, each node no longer possesses the same demand as the rest of the nodes on the grid, with several random regions of high and low demand. In this scenario, the basic "fast consistency" (FC) shows a better performance than the weak consistency algorithms (WC), but without being optimal[9], owing mainly to the presence of multiple high and low demand zones which cause the messages carrying the changes to move quickly towards the high demand zones, and at the speed of the WC algorithm towards the low demand zones.

5.2 Leader Interconnection

In order to improve performance when there are several regions of higher demand surrounded by regions of lower demand, the nodes in high demand zones choose a leader node by means of a decentralized voting algorithm[10]: each node casts a vote for its neighbor with greatest demand. At the end of the voting process there exists a set of nodes that have accumulated votes. However, not all the nodes possessing votes can be considered leaders, since there will be nodes with more votes and others with very few votes. Thus, from this subset of nodes, all those having fewer votes under a certain threshold will be discarded.

In this way we obtain a new set of nodes which represent the greatest zones of high demand. These leader nodes establish connection among themselves in order to speed up the exchange of messages among all the zones of high demand. Therefore, the logical communication topology is slightly transformed into the equivalent of one zone of high demand, that is the most favorable situation for our algorithm.

Since we now have the leader nodes, experiments to determine the improvement caused by the leader interconnection algorithm and the effects of the topologies of leader nodes can now be carried out.

5.3 Leader-node Interconnection in Ring Topology

Leader nodes having a number of votes greater than or equal to the average are selected and interconnected in a ring topology(top level of hierarchical structure), which joins together the zones of high demand. In this topology, each leader node sees the same network diameter. However, there exists the disadvantage that the diameter is very large for the same number of nodes than other topologies. Simulation results can be seen in Figure 4. We can see in terms of $C(t)$ or $U(t)$ that FC has a better performance than WC. With the FC algorithm $C(t)$ begins to grow in less sessions than the weak consistency. $U(t)$ have similar results.

5.4 Leader-node Interconnection in Star Topology

The same experiments have been carried out when the leader nodes are interconnected in star topology (Fig. 5). In this topology the diameter of the leader-node network is very low, with a maximum of two. We initially though that the behavior would be better than that obtained by the leader nodes connected in a ring topology. However, this is not the case. In the following experiments, the leader node star topology is not included since it shows a performance inferior to that of the leader nodes connected in a ring topology.

Performance Evaluation of a Self-organized Hierarchical Topology   99

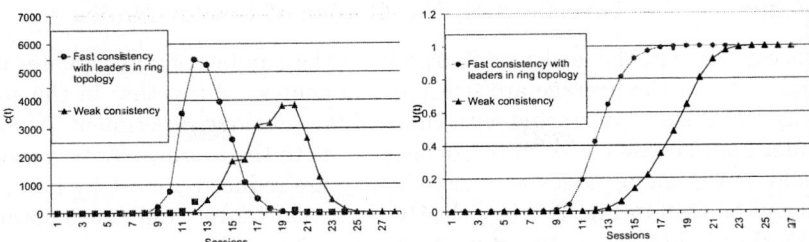

Fig. 4. $C(t)$ and $U(t)$ to separate contributions of fast consistency versus weak consistency

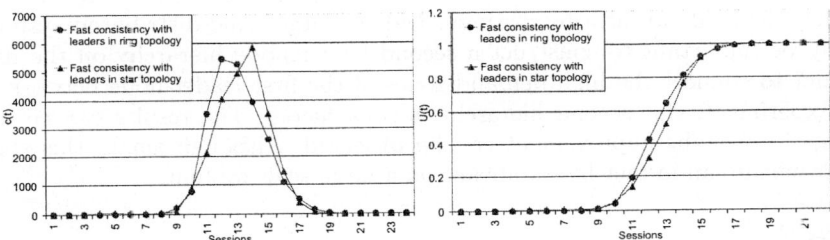

Fig. 5. $C(t)$ and $U(t)$ for leader interconnection in ring and star topology (ring is better)

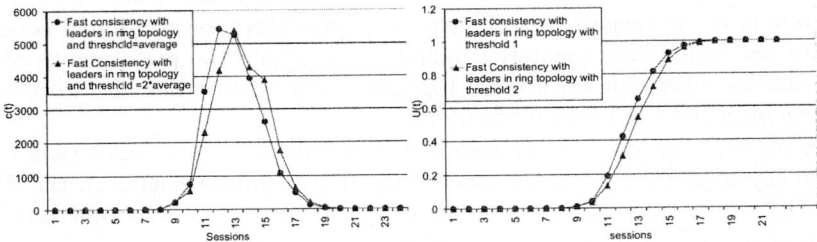

Fig. 6. $C(t)$ and $U(t)$ for threshold of leader selection (average='more leaders' is better)

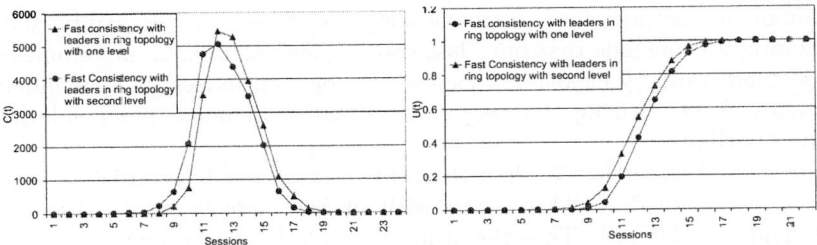

Fig. 7. $C(t)$ and $U(t)$ for one or two levels of leader interconnection (two slightly better)

5.5 Effect of the Threshold on the Choice of Leader Nodes

For this experiment, the leader nodes receiving the number of votes greater than or equal to twice the average are selected and connected together in the shape of a ring. Results are contrasted with those of the previous experiment, in which the leader nodes chosen were those corresponding to the average. With a greater threshold, fewer leader nodes are elected; they are reduced almost by half. The results can be seen in Fig. 6. They clearly show that better results are obtained with the threshold fixed at the average of votes obtained.

5.6 Second Leader Hierarchy

In the leader-node network in our fractal demand distributions, zones of high and low demand can also be distinguished. In large scale distributed systems, it may be important to construct a second leader node hierarchy on the first, in order to connect the high demand zones of the first leader-node network. In this experiment, this second hierarchy is constructed. The results can be seen in Fig. 7. A slight improvement can be observed. Although small, this slight improvement can in fact be significant on a large scale system.

6 Conclusions

In this paper, we study the problem of propagating changes of replicated data on a Decentralized System in a system of any scale, with only little knowledge of a few neighbor nodes, using our "Fast consistency algorithm" and whose main aim is the propagation of changes with preference for nodes and zones of the network which have greatest demand. We evaluate the performance of the algorithm by simulation on a mesh topology using various demand workloads. We have obtained the following results:

We see that fast consistency algorithm has a better performance than weak consistency algorithm. We may observe significant improvements in the SWF when fast consistency algorithm is used with the leader nodes connected in a ring topology(a logical and hierarchical topology), although several alternative leader interconnection topologies provide similar values of improvement as a result of the effect of communicating several high demand zones into a virtually one single high demand zone.

Employing, among other economic concepts, those such as utility and social welfare, we conclude that our "fast consistency" algorithm, interconnecting high demand zones by means of a logical topology, optimizes the dissemination of changes by prioritizing the nodes with greatest demand, independently of demand distribution.

In other words, in the FC algorithm, the network reach a consistent state in a shorter period of time. This occurs without any increase in use of resources for carrying out this task. Thus the utility function $U(t)$ grows much faster with Fast Consistency algorithm over a self-organized hierarchical topology which interconnect the high demand zones in a large distributed system.

References

1. Atul Adya: Weak Consistency: A Generalized Theory and Optimistic Implementations for Distributed Transactions, PhD thesis M. I. T., Department of Electrical Engineering and Computer Science, March 1999.
2. Alain Fournier, Don Fussell, and Loren Carpenter: Computer Rendering of Stochastic Models, Comm. of the ACM, Vol. 6, No. 6, June 1982, pages 371-384.
3. Anukool Lakhina, John Byers, Mark Crovella, Ibrahim Matta: On the Geographic Location of Internet Resources. Internet Measurement Workshop 2002 Marseille, France, Nov. 6-8, 2002
4. Arman Danesh, Ljiljana Trajkovic, Stuart H. Robin Michael H. Smith: Mapping the Internet, 2001.
5. C.Neuman, "Scale in Distributed Systems. In Readings in Dist. Comp. Syst.", IEEE Computer Society Press, 1994
6. J. Dietterich: DEC data distributor: for data replication and data warehousing. In Int. Conf. On Management of data, pp 468, ACM, May 1994.
7. Jean Laherrere, D Sornette (1998): Stretched exponential distributions in Nature and Economy: 'Fat tails' with characteristic scales, European Physical Jour., B2:525-539.
8. Jesús Acosta Elias, Leandro Navarro Moldes. A Demand Based Algorithm for Rapid Updating of Replicas, IEEE Workshop on Resource Sharing in Massively Distributed Systems (RESH'02), July 2002.
9. Jesús Acosta Elias, Leandro Navarro Moldes: Behaviour of the fast consistency algorithm in the set of replicas with multiple zones with high demand, Simp. in Informatics and Telecommunications, SIT 2002.
10. Jesús Acosta Elias, Leandro Navarro Moldes: Generalization of the fast consistency algorithm to multiple high demand zones, in proc. of the Int.Conference on Computational Science 2003 (ICCS2003). St.Petersburg, Russia, June. 2-4, 2003.
11. K. P. Birman: The process group approach to reliable distributed computing, Communications of ACM, December 1993/Vol. 36, No. 12.
12. K. Petersen, M. J. Spreitzer, D. B. Terry, M. M. Theimer, and Demers: Flexible Update Propagation for Weakly Consistent Replication, Proc. of the 16th ACM Symposium on Operating Systems Principles (SOSP-16), Saint Malo, France, October 5-8, 1997, pages 288-301.
13. Medina, A. Lakhina, I. Matta, and J. Byers, "BRITE: Universal Topology Generation from a User's Pers.".
14. Michel D. Schroeder, Andrew D. Birrel, and Roger M. Needham, Experience with Grapevine: The Growth of a Distributed System, ACM Transactions of Computer Systems, Vol. 2, No. 1, February 1984, Pages 3-23.
15. R. A. Golding, "Weak-Consistency Group Communication and Membership", PhD thesis, University of California, Santa Cruz, Comp. and Inf. Sciences Tech. Report UCSC-CRL-92-52, Dec.1992.
16. Soon.-Hyung. Yook, H. Jeong, and A.-L. Barabsi. Modeling the internet's large-scale topology. Tech. Report cond-mat/0107417, Cond. Matter Archive, xxx.lanl.gov, July 2001.
17. The Network Simulator: http://www.isi.edu/nsnam/ns/
18. V. Duvvuri, P. Shenoy and R. Tewari, "Adaptative Leases: A Strong Consistency Mechanism for the World Wide Web", IEEE INFOCOM 2000, pages 834-843.

A Proposal of Reconfigurable MPI Collective Communication Functions

Luiz E.S. Ramos[1] and Carlos A.P.S. Martins[2]

[1] Rutgers University
luizesramos@ieee.org
[2] Pontifical Catholic University of Minas Gerais
capsm@pucminas.br

Abstract. Message Passing Interface (MPI) Collective Communication Functions (MCCF) are usually implemented in programming libraries utilizing invariable algorithms. Not always do such algorithms yield the best performance with all kinds of applications and over all execution environments. In this paper, we present, simulate, analytically model, verify and analyze reconfigurable MCCF that present variable structures and behaviors, in order to provide optimized configurations, flexibility and performance. In this paper we propose and present a set of optimized reconfigurable MCCF, which add flexibility and high performance to collective communications. We simulate, analytically model, verify and analyze the proposed functions, and compare them with invariable implementations. Our results show that reconfiguration at the algorithm level really yields flexibility and performance gains in MCCF.

1 Introduction

The performance of Message Passing Interface (MPI) collective communication functions (MCCF) is a critical factor for most of the MPI based applications [1] [4]. There are several related works addressing this issue [2] [3] [4] [5] [6] [7] [8] [9], many of them, by adding flexibility to the implementations of MCCF. However not always do such algorithms yield the best performance with all kinds of applications running on all execution environments.

In this paper, we propose and present a set of optimized reconfigurable MCCF (RMCCF), which add greater flexibility (algorithmic level) and improve the performance of collective communications. We simulate, analytically model, verify and analyze the proposed functions, and compare them with invariable implementations.

2 Reconfigurable MPI Colective Communication Functions

The performance optimization of MPI collective communication functions (MCCF) has been intensely studied in the latest years. In literature, there are several works related to ours in different aspects [2] [3] [4] [5] [7] [8], which remarks the importance of optimizing MCCF. According to those works, the main **strategies** for addressing this issue are: **(1)** proposing algorithms for specific architectures, networks and topologies [3] [7]; **(2)** selecting and changing communication algorithms within a limited set of options, based on input parameters [2] [3] [4] [5]; **(3)** message segmentation [7]; **(4)** message combination, suitable for high latency networks [5] [7]; **(5)** network links redundancy [7] [8]; **(6)** heuristics for algorithm selection [5] [7]; **(7)** component specification of MCCF [6] [8]; and **(8)** small granularity components [5] [8]. However none of them combined all these strategies. In the literature we find countless works that use the terms "reconfigurable system/software/algorithm", but none of them focus on the algorithmic level.

In this work improve our initial proposal of Reconfigurable MPI Collective Communication Functions (RMCCF) [9], by exploring further the flexibility and high performance in the algorithmic level of MCCF. An RMCCF is divided three in hierarchical layers, namely: Basic, Reconfigurable and Configuration Control.

The **Basic Layer** (BL) is composed of data storage structures and frames. A frame is a generic algorithmic structure (implemented as function, classes, etc) with an interface having two possible finalities: (1) supporting the execution of algorithm parts which can be changed or replaced (action frame); or (2) controlling the functioning, by acting upon or managing data structures. Our proposal of RMCCF has three frames. **Algorithm Assembly** (action) is responsible for creating a logical topology between processes by selecting, combining and configuring communication patterns, addressing strategies 1 and 2 for adding flexibility. Message **Combination & Segmentation** (control) is responsible for combining messages, in order to reduce the communication latency, or segmenting them, in order to favor packet switching, flow control, error control and message buffering (strategies 3 and 4). **Maximum Degree of Primitives** (action) configures the degree of the communication primitives in order to take advantage of the fact that the network may have a communication degree greater than one (strategy 5).

The Reconfigurable Layer (RL) is a configuration or an instance of the BL, in which every frame is filled in with one or more compatible building blocks at a certain moment. A block is a possible implementation of a frame (i.e. a set communication pattern among which we can select an option). A block may have one or more options (it is configurable) and may also be static or dynamically replaced. The building blocks for the first frame are collective communication patterns, compatible with the behavior of each communication operation.

The Configuration Control Layer (CCL) is responsible for selecting and swap-ping the building blocks that fill in the frames at a given moment. It is also responsible for configuring those blocks. Thus, the functioning of the RA and the configurations are decided within this layer. Its decisions are made upon input parameters, dynamic workload information, commands from the operating system or user etc. Our initial CCL proposal is implemented as a table that keeps up the best configuration according to some static (e.g.: network topology) or dynamic system information and workload parameters (message size, number of processes).

This proposal of RMCCF as a whole assesses the strategies (5), (6) and (7). Thus, our proposal is flexible enough to combine all highlighted strategies, which add flexibility to MCCF aiming to improve their performance.

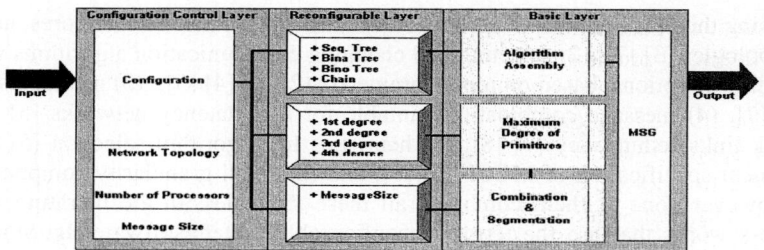

Fig. 1. Architecture of a reconfigurable MPI collective communication function

3 Results

In order to reduce the number of experiments and analyses, we simplified our simulations and analytical models. The simulation response times were obtained with ClusterSim [9], which simulates parallel and distributed systems. Our simulation environment is a homogeneous 16 PIII (1GH) nodes workstation cluster with a Fast Ethernet network (bus and switch topologies). On the other hand, the analytical modeling considered the same cluster using other network topologies: full-connected, star, 2D-mesh and ring [10]. The metric was the number of hops.

In the simulations the workload is composed of parallel jobs, containing different communication patterns (Algorithm Assembly frame). They were based on first-degree point-to-point communication primitives and transmitted messages from 1 byte to 256KB. No message segmentation or combination was used. These patterns implement MPI_Bcast (one-to-all), MPI_Reduce (all-to-one) and MPI_Allgather (all-to-all), which represent all MPI cardinality classes. In the analytical modeling we also varied the degree of the communication primitives (Maximum Degree of Primitives frame). We used first- and optimal-degree primitives. We remark that analyzing the Combination & Segmentation frame is a future work.

In the simulation of the clusters using bus and switch, RMReduce (Reconfigurable MPI_Reduce) was compared with four invariable implementations utilizing other

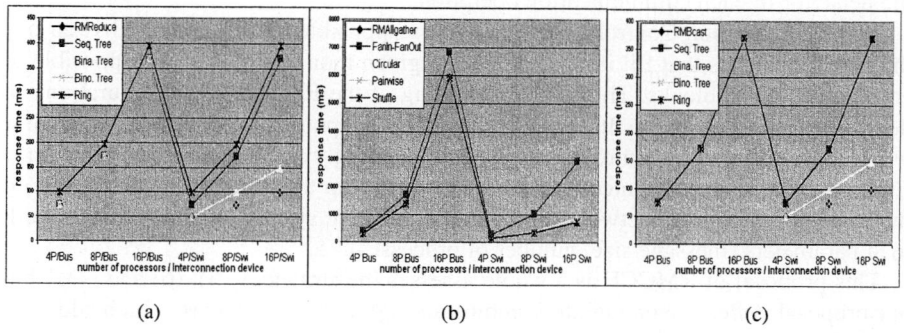

Fig. 2. Simulated response times for MPI (a) Reduce, (b) Allgather, (c) Bcast

communication patterns: Sequential, Binary, Binomial and Ring [3]. According to Fig.2a, RMBcast provided the best response time. That function assumed the Sequential and Binomial configurations, respectively running on the bus and the switch-based clusters, because those functions yielded the best results. Binomial yielded the lowest response times on the switch because it explores the parallelism within the interconnection device. However on the bus, Binomial presented dependency between transmissions, and Sequential performed better. Ring yielded the worst results due to its sequential nature and to the dependency between its transmissions.

Suppose an application with 50% of the calls to MPI_Reduce executed on the bus, and 50% on the switch. RMReduce would produce a speedup of 2.37 and of 1.0013 regarding Sequential and Binomial respectively. We remark that even an optimized algorithm such as Rabenseifner's [5] may perform worse than another one, depending on the features of the system where it is executed.

In the simulation of the clusters using bus and switch, RMAllgather was compared with four invariable implementations utilizing the following communication patterns: FanIn-FanOut, Circular, Pairwise and Shuffle [3]. According to Fig.2b, the best results were provided by RMAllgather assuming a Pairwise configuration. Considering the simulated network, the transmitted message sizes and the communication patterns utilized, we noticed that the reconfigurable function performs at least as good as the best average algorithm for that situation. Among the invariable patterns, Pairwise yielded the best results because it transmits the smallest number of messages (hub) and because it explores the parallelism within the interconnection device (switch). In both cases, RMAllgather there would present no extra performance gains over the MPI_Allgather implemented with the invariable Pairwise pattern.

In the simulation of the clusters using bus and switch, RMReduce (Reconfigurable MPI_Reduce) was compared with four invariable implementations utilizing the following communication patterns: Sequential, Binary, Binomial and Chain [5]. According to Fig.2c, the RMBcast provided the best results assuming a Binomial configuration both in bus and switch. The reason is the fact that these patterns are very similar to those used in MPI_Reduce, but they work reversely.

In the analytical modeling we considered the best and the worst cases of mapping between processes and the cluster's nodes. Respectively, the messages would take the smaller and the longest path to get to their destinations. Analyzing Table 1, we notice that Binomial presented the best results in all cases. Thus we could wrongly suppose that choosing a single invariable algorithm to implement MPI_Bcast would always provide the best performance. That statement is false when we analyze the best case:

Table 1. Worst and best mappings between processes and network topology (number of hops)

Topology	Mapping -Worst Case					Mapping -Best Case				
	Seq	Bina	Bino	Chain	RMbcast	Seq	Bina	Bino	Chain	RMbcast
Full-Connected	15	6	4	15	4	15	6	4	15	4
Star	29	12	8	29	8	15	11	7	29	7
2D-Mesh	48	26	20	55	20	32	10	7	15	7
2D-Mesh + WA	32	21	13	49	13	32	8	4	15	4
Ring	120	70	53	255	53	120	26	19	15	15

on a Ring topology, Chain performs better than Binomial. In this case, Chain would present a 1.04 speedup regarding Binomial, although the latter has a speedup of 4.11 regarding the first in the worst case of mapping.

Suppose a workload composed of a great amount of broadcast function calls. It is executed on several 16-node clusters, found at a data processing center. Considering that 80% of the clusters use a Ring topology and the other 20% use equally the other four network topologies that we modeled. If we simultaneously execute the workload in all clusters of the center considering the best case of mapping between processes and network nodes, RMBcast would present a speedup of 1.24 regarding Binomial and 1.20 regarding Chain. This fact means that RMBcast presented a better performance than both other algorithms, remarking that both were the best option in each case. Thus it is clearer that the use of RMCCF yield greater performance gains than those possibly achieved with a single invariable algorithm. As suggested in [10], if the network's topology varied, there might be further performance gains. Suppose a parallel application composed of 8 processes and utilizing 100 calls to the function MPI_Bcast. This workload is executed in a network with a topology that can vary along time between: Star, Ring, and 4x4 2D Mesh without wraparound. In this case, the speedup of RMBcast would vary from 1.38 to 2.9. The flexibility increases using the Primitive Degree frame of the RMCCF, so that the greatest speedups are obtained utilizing the optimal degree for each type of network topology. We notice that Binomial presented the best performance in the computational simulations involving the broadcast operation. However in the analytical modeling, sometimes that communication pattern presents a worse performance than the worst average algorithms used in the computational simulations (i.e. Chain).

4 Conclusions

In this work we proposed, presented, simulated, analytically modeled, verified and analyzed a set of RMCCF. Their flexibility at the algorithmic level can be used to improve performance, since they can alter their behavior by changing their structure. RMCCF yielded better performance than invariable functions based on traditional algorithms, at all tested situations. In some cases, there was a considerable performance gain (3.7 average speedup and 7.8 peak speedup).

Our results also show that an algorithm, which is commonly considered the best, may perform worse at some situations than other algorithms, which commonly yield the worst performance. Although the traditional algorithms we modeled are very simple, we conclude that even more complex algorithms behave similarly [5]. An important aspect of reconfigurable functions is the fact that any behavior can be changed or replaced, thus providing optimized results for each execution environment. RMCCF's performs as good as the best algorithm, and can be much better. The concept of reconfigurability makes it possible to add previously inexistent configurations to the algorithm, and is applicable to other architectural levels.

The main disadvantage of RMCCF lies in the CCL, which may present a great computational and storage costs, thus demanding simplifications. Nevertheless, there are several heuristics assessing this drawback [5] [7].

The main **contributions** of this work are: (1) the proposal, presentation, simulation, analytical model, verification and analysis of RMCCF; (2) the comparative analysis of different MCCF based on reconfigurable and invariable algorithms; and (3) the successful use of the concept of reconfigurability on MCCF, which provided optimized performance, and some considerable performance gains.

Our **future works** include: (1) adding reconfigurability into real implementations of the MPI standard; (2) exploiting dynamic reconfiguration; (3) comparing RMCCF with functions based on the state-of-the-art algorithms; (4) utilizing multi-criteria decision in the CCL; (5) evaluating and analyzing the reconfiguration overhead; (6) applying the discussed concepts in other contexts.

References

1. Gorlatch, S.: Send-Receive Considered Harmful: Myths and Realities of Message Passing, ACM TOPLAS'04, ISSN:0164-0925, vol. 26(1), (2004) 47-56
2. Huse, L.P.: Collective Communication on Dedicated Clusters of Workstations, Euro PVM/MPI (1999) 469-476
3. Tan, W.B., Strazdins, P.: The Analysis and Optimization of Collective Communications on a Beowulf Cluster, ICPADS (2002) 659-666
4. Thakur, R., Gropp, W.: Improving the Performance of Collective Operations in MPICH, Euro PVM/MPI (2003) 257-267
5. Vadhiyar, S.S., Fagg, G.E., Dongarra, J.: Automatically Tuned Collective Communications, SuperComputing 2000: HPNC, CD-ROM, ISBN 0-7803-9802-5, 2000
6. Squyres, J.M., Lumsdaine, A.: A Component Architecture for LAM/MPI, Euro PVM/MPI (2003) 379-387
7. Kielmann, T., et al.: Network performance-aware collective communication for clustered wide-area systems, Parallel Computing, vol. 27(11), (2001) 1431-1456
8. Barnett, M., et al.: Building a High-Performance Collective Communication Library. SuperComputing (1994) 107-116
9. Ramos, L.E.S., Martins C.A.P.S.: Reconfigurable MPI Collective Communication Functions. WSCAD'04, 2004 (in Portuguese)
10. Freitas, H.C.: Proposal and Development of a Network Processor with Reconfigurable Crossbar Switch, M.Sc. thesis, PPGEE, PUC-MG, 2003 (in Portuguese)

Design and Evaluation of Network-Bandwidth-Based Parallel Replication Algorithm*

Yijie Wang and Yongjin Qin

National Laboratory for Parallel and Distributed Processing, Institute of Computer,
National University of Defense Technology, Changsha, China, 410073
wwyyjj1971@vip.sina.com

Abstract. Data replication can be used to reduce bandwidth consumption and access latency in the distributed system where users require remote access to large data objects. In this paper, according to the intrinsic characteristic of distributed storage system, the parallel replication algorithm NBPRA (Network-Bandwidth-based Parallel Replication Algorithm) is proposed. In the NBPRA, according to the network state, several replicas of a data object are selected, which are of the least access cost; then the different parts of the data object are transferred from these replicas, and they are used to make a new replica. The results of performance evaluation show that the NBPRA can utilize the network bandwidth efficiently, provide high data replication efficiency and substantially better access efficiency, and the improvement of system performance is related to the number of different data objects accessed by jobs.

1 Introduction

There is a growing demand for the automatic, online archiving of data resources. For decades, industry and other users have relied on tape to back up their critical data, but this scheme requires a human administrator to maintain the tape drivers, file drivers, and the tapes themselves. As the amount of data resources in the world explodes, this maintenance will become too costly to be feasible. At present, how to aggregate the geographically distributed heterogeneous storage resources to form the virtual storage space and provide secure efficient data storage service is becoming a challenging research topic in the worldwide.

The replication scheme of distributed storage system determines how many replicas of each data object are created, and to which nodes these replicas are allocated. This scheme critically affects the performance of distributed storage system, since reading a data object locally is less costly than reading it from a remote node, especially for large data objects. There are two major motivations for replication—increasing availability and increasing system performance. Replication creates redundant information in the network, which allows the system to remain operational in spite of node and link failures and thus increase reliability. Also, if data is replicated near the node where it is

---

* This work is supported by the National Grand Fundamental Research 973 Program of China (No.2002CB312105), A Foundation for the Author of National Excellent Doctoral Dissertation of PR China (No.200141), and the National Natural Science Foundation of China (No.69903011, No.69933030).

accessed, communication cost is greatly reduced. Due to the dynamic of network, sometimes the network bandwidth is relatively very low. That leads to a focus on reducing network transmission cost, on utilizing the redundant network bandwidth sufficiently, and hence on the performance issue.

Peer-to-peer distributed storage systems are positioned to take advantage of gains in network bandwidth, storage capacity, and computational resources to provide longterm durable storage infrastructures. Systems such as Farsite([1]), Intermemory([2]), Freenet([3]), CFS([4]), PAST([5]), and OceanStore([6]) seek to capitalize on the rapid growth of resources to provide inexpensive, highly-available storage without centralized servers. The designers of these systems propose to achieve high availability and long-term durability, in the face of individual component failures, through replication techniques.

Optimising the use of Grid resources is critical for users to effectively exploit a Data Grid. Data replication is considered a major technique for reducing data access cost to Grid jobs([7],[8],[9]). Replication involves the creation of identical copies of data files and their distribution over various Grid sites. This can reduce data access latency and increase the robustness of Grid applications.

In the most research projects on peer-to-peer distributed storage system and Data Grid, the traditional replication technology is utilized to achieve the high availability and durability. In the traditional replication technology, if a new replica R' of data object DO is to be made on node A, the best replica R of data object DO should be found, then make a copy of R and transfer it to node A, that is replica R'. If the network bandwidth is relatively low and the data object need to be replicated is very large, the efficiency of replication will be low, thus the availability and system performance will be reduced.

In this paper, according to the intrinsic characteristic of distributed storage system, the parallel replication algorithm NBPRA is proposed. Section 2 describes the parallel replication algorithm NBPRA. Section 3 presents the results of performance evaluation. Section 4 provides a summary of our research work.

2 Parallel Replication Algorithm NBPRA

In the parallel replication algorithm NBPRA (Network-Bandwidth-based Parallel Replication Algorithm), firstly, according to the network state, NUM replicas of data object DO are selected, which are of the least access cost; secondly, different parts of data object DO are transferred from different replicas, then these parts are combined to make the new replica of data object DO. Compared with the traditional replication technology, NBPRA utilizes several network links to transfer a copy of data object, thus the availability of network bandwidth is improved, and the efficiency of data replication is improved, so the efficiency of data access is improved efficiently.

NBPRA includes two strategies: the replica selection strategy and the data quantity assignment strategy.

2.1 The Replica Selection Strategy

The replica selection strategy decides which replicas are used to make the new replica. Firstly, the access cost of each replica should be evaluated; secondly, the number of replicas to be selected should be decided; lastly, the replicas with the least access cost are selected.

The access cost of replica lies on the network bandwidth and the distance between the two nodes. In figure 1, a new replica of data object DO will be made on node A, and there is a replica R of data object DO on node B, and the number of hops between node A and node B is k+1, the available bandwidth of each link between any two nodes is bw_1, bw_2, bw_3, ...,bw_k, bw_{k+1}, thus the access cost of replica is $\sum_{i=1}^{k+1}\left(size(R)/bw_i\right)$.

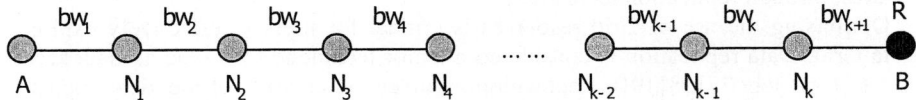

Fig. 1. The access cost of replica

In fact, it is not true that more replicas selected will get more profit. If more than one replica will be transferred through the same link, then the available bandwidth of each replica will be relatively low. On the other hand, if one replication occupies too many links, the other replications will be affected badly. In view of the system performance, the number of replicas selected will be decided according to the degree of node A.

The basic idea of the replica selection strategy is as follows:

1. Calculate the access cost of each replica R, which is $\sum_{i=1}^{k+1}\left(size(R)/bw_i\right)$.
2. Select the replicas used to make the new replica of data object DO. The selection conditions include:
   a) The replicas selected are of the least access cost;
   b) The replicas selected do not share the same links;
   c) The number of replicas selected is not more than the degree of node A.

2.2 The Data Quantity Assignment Strategy

The efficiency of replication is decided by not only the replicas selected, but also the data quantity transferred from each replica. There are two fundamental principles of data quantity assignment: 1) the access cost of replica is less, the data quantity transferred from it is larger; 2) the data transfer of all replicas finish simultaneously.

The basic idea of the data quantity assignment strategy is as follows:

1. Calculate the transfer rate of each replica selected by the replica selection strategy. In figure 1, the access cost of replica R is $Cost_R = \sum_{i=1}^{k+1}\left(size(R)/bw_i\right)$, the transfer rate of replica R is $TR_R = 1/Cost_R$.

2. Calculate the sum of transfer rate of selected replicas. Assume the number of selected replicas is NUM, the selected replicas are $R_1, R_2, \ldots, R_{NUM}$, and the transfer rate of them are $TR_1, TR_2, \ldots, TR_{NUM}$, so the sum of transfer rate of selected replicas is $SUM\_TR = \sum_{j=1}^{NUM} TR_j$.

3. According to the transfer rate of each selected replica, assign the data quantity of each replica. The data quantity of replica R_k is assigned to $size(DO) \dfrac{TR_k}{SUM\_TR}$, $size(DO)$ is the size of data object DO.

In the traditional replication strategy, a replica of the least access cost is selected, so the time of replication is $size(DO) / \max(TR_1, TR_2, \ldots, TR_{NUM})$.

In NBPRA, the NUM replicas are selected, which are of the least access cost. The different parts of data object DO are transferred from the different replicas, so the time of replication is $size(DO)/SUM\_TR$.

It is clear that NBPRA utilizes the network bandwidth more efficiently than the traditional replication strategy, and can improve the efficiency of replication evidently.

2.3 Algorithm Description

The description of NBPRA is as follows.

BEGIN
Step_1: Get the degree of node A on which a new replica of data object DO will be made, let DG denote the degree of node A.
Step_2: Get the replica set of data object DO from metadata catalog, let Set_R denote the replica set of DO, let Num_Set_R denote the number of replicas in Set_R.
Step_3: Evaluate the access cost of each replica in Set_R. Let $Cost_R$ denote the access cost of replica R, $Cost_R = \sum_{i=1}^{k+1} \left(size(R) / bw_i \right)$.
Step_4: Initialization: i = 0, Set_Selection = ∅.
Step_5: Num_Selection = min(Num_Set_R, DG).
Step_6: DO
{
    Select the replica R_Selection from Set_R, the access cost of which is the least in Set_R, $Cost_{R\_Selection} = \min(Cost_R, R \in Set\_R)$;
    $Set\_Selection = Set\_Selection + R\_Selection$;
    i = i + 1;
    $Set\_R = Set\_R - R\_Selection$;
    FOR each R'∈ Set_R

{
       IF R_Selection and R' share the same links
       THEN $Set\_R = Set\_R - R'$;
}
}WHILE (i< Num_Selection AND Set_R $\neq \varnothing$)

Step_7: Calculate the transfer rate of each selected replicas.

$$TR_R = \frac{1}{Cost_R}, \quad R \in Set\_Selection,$$

TR_R denotes the transfer rate of replica R.

Step_8: Calculate the sum of transfer rate of selected replicas.

$$SUM\_TR = \sum_{R \in Set\_Selection} TR_R.$$

Step_9: Assign the data quantity of each replica R in Set_Selection to $size(DO)\dfrac{TR_R}{SUM\_TR}$.

END

2.4 The Case Study

In figure 2, there are 6 replicas of data object DO in the network, and they are distributed on node D, F, H, I, J, K, denoted as R_D, R_F, R_H, R_I, R_J, R_K. According to the access requirements, a new replica of DO will be made on node A. The relative available bandwidth of each link is marked in the figure, for example, the relative available bandwidth of link between node A and B is 3. There is a tuple ($Cost_R$, TR_R) for each replica R, which denotes the access cost and transfer rate of each replica, for example, (1.33, 0.75) of replica on node F means that the access cost of the replica is 1.33, and that the transfer rate of the replica is 0.75.

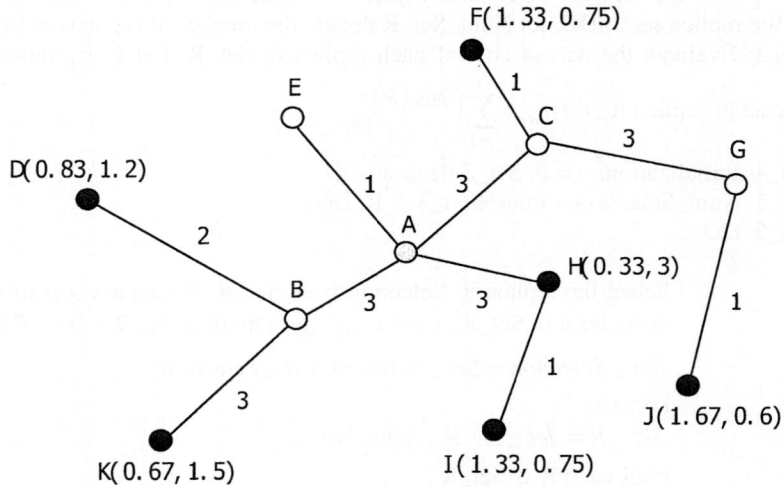

Fig. 2. The access cost and transfer rate of replicas

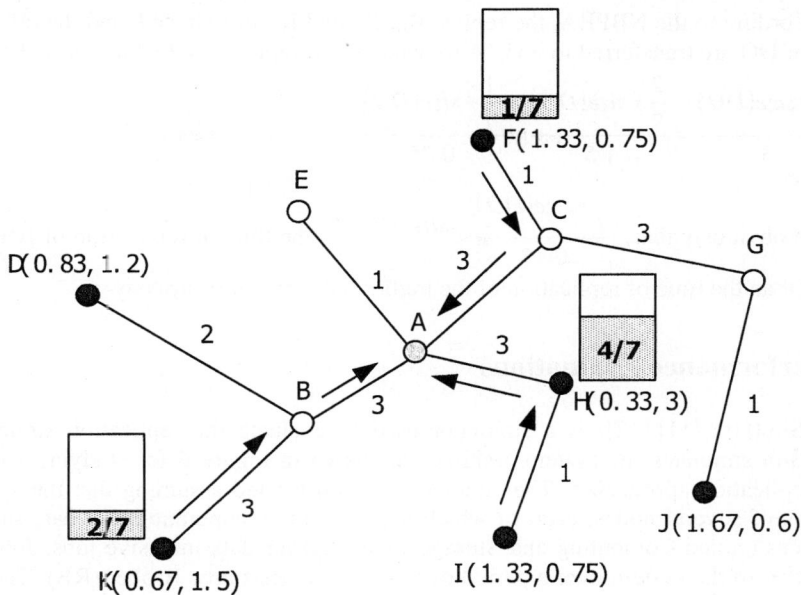

Fig. 3. The data quantity of the selected replicas

According to the NBPRA, initially, Set_R={R_D, R_F, R_H, R_I, R_J, R_K}, Set_Selection=∅. The degree of node A is 4, the number of replicas in Set_R is 6, so the number of selected replicas should be not more than 4.

Firstly, the replica R_H is selected, the access cost of which is 0.33, and it is of the least access cost among Set_R, so Set_Selection={R_H}. Because the replica R_H and R_I share the same link, the Set_R changes to { R_D, R_F, R_J, R_K }.

Secondly, the replica R_K is selected, the access cost of which is 0.67, and it is of the least access cost among Set_R, so Set_Selection={R_H, R_K}. Because the replica R_K and R_D share the same link, the Set_R changes to {R_F, R_J}.

Thirdly, the replica R_F is selected, the access cost of which is 1.33, and it is of the least access cost among Set_R, so Set_Selection={R_H, R_K, R_F}. Because the replica R_F and R_J share the same link, the Set_R changes to ∅. Therefore, the selected replicas are R_H, R_K, R_F.

Lastly, the data quantity of each selected replica is assigned. Figure 3 shows the assignment, the data quantity of replica R_H is $\frac{4}{7}*size(DO)$, the data quantity of replica R_K is $\frac{2}{7}*size(DO)$, the data quantity of replica R_F is $\frac{1}{7}*size(DO)$.

According to the traditional replication strategy, the replica R_H is selected, and it is transferred to node A to make a new replica of data object DO, so the time of replication is $size(DO)/3$.

According to the NBPRA, the replica R_H, R_K and R_F are selected, and the different parts of DO are transferred to node A to make a new replica, so the time of replication is $\dfrac{\frac{4}{7}*size(DO)}{3} = \dfrac{\frac{2}{7}*size(DO)}{1.5} = \dfrac{\frac{1}{7}*size(DO)}{0.75}$.

It is obviously that, $\dfrac{\frac{1}{7}*size(DO)}{0.75} < {size(DO)}/{3}$, the time of replication of NBPRA is less than the time of replication of the traditional replication strategy.

3 Performance Evaluations

OptorSim([10],[11],[12]) is a simulator used to evaluate the replication strategies. OptorSim simulates the system architecture shown in Figure 4 for studying various data replication approaches. The simulation is constructed assuming that the system consists of several nodes, each of which may provide computation and data-storage resources (called Computing and Storage Elements) for data intensive jobs. Jobs are submitted to the system over a period of time via the Resource Broker (RB). The RB schedules each job to the Computing Elements (CE) with the goal to improve the overall throughput of the system. A Replica Manager (RM) at each node manages the data flow between nodes and interfaces between the computing and storage resources. The Replica Manager (RM) is responsible for the selection and dynamic creation and deletion of replicas.

In our simulation, the system topology (see Figure 5) comprises 11 nodes. Each SE of node has a capacity of 150 GB. Each data object has size of 1 GB and the total size of the data object set is 120 GB.

We assume that initially each data object has only one physical instance referred to as master copy, and the number of replicas of each data object is a random number between 0 and 2. The initial data object distribution is that all master copies and replicas are randomly distributed among all nodes. If the access frequency of a data object from one node reaches the threshold, then a new replica of data object should be made on the node.

Access pattern determines the order in which a job requests data objects. The following two access patterns are considered in our simulation:

1. sequential access pattern: all data objects are requested in a predetermined order;
2. Gaussian random walk access pattern: successive data objects are selected from a Gaussian distribution centred on the previous data objects.

The economy-based replication strategy ([9],[13]) is proposed for Data Grid, it optimises both the selection of replicas for running jobs and the dynamic creation of replicas in the nodes. In this strategy, optimization agents are located on nodes and use an auction protocol for selecting the optimal replica of a data object and a prediction function to make informed decisions about local data replication. Data

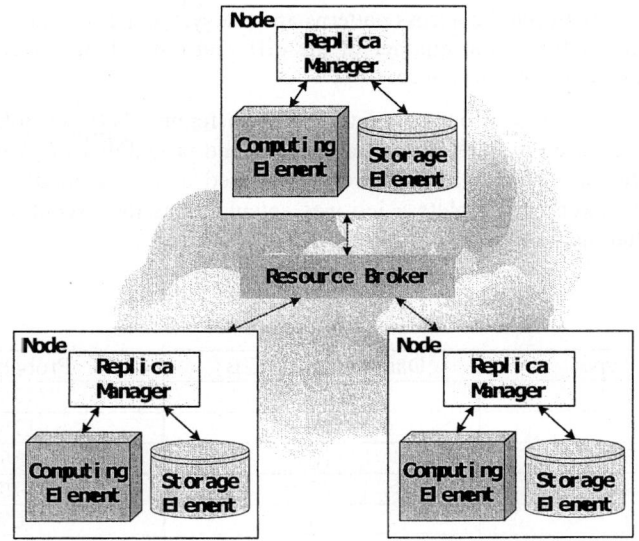

Fig. 4. Simulated system architecture

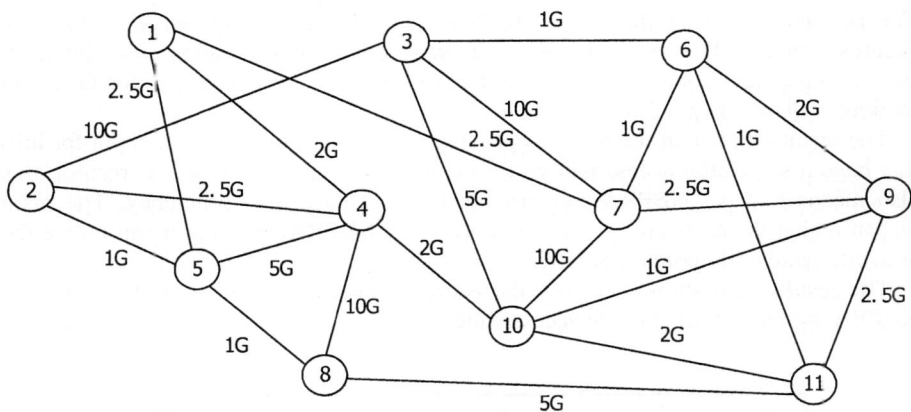

Fig. 5. System topology for simulation

objects are "purchased" by CEs for running jobs and by SEs to make an investment that will improve their expected future revenue. These data objects are sold by SEs to either CEs or other SEs. CEs try to minimize the data object purchase cost, while SEs attempt to maximise their profits. CEs and SEs interact with intelligent optimization agents which perform the reasoning required in the strategy.

The performance comparison between the economy-based replication strategy and the NBPRA includes two aspects:

1. Relation between the access patterns and the system performance;
2. Relation between the number of the different data objects accessed by jobs and the system performance.

There are 6 job types in our simulation. The difference between job types is the data quantity accessed by jobs. The data quantity and probability distribution of each job type is shown in Table 1. Jobs were submitted at five seconds intervals. The estimated time taken to complete a job was calculated as the execution time on the node, not including the time waiting in the queue at the node.

Table 1. Job types

Job Type	Data Quantity (GB)	Probability
1	1	17%
2	5	17%
3	10	16%
4	25	17%
5	30	16%
6	50	17%

3.1 Access Patterns

The results comparing the two algorithms for each access pattern are shown in Figures 6 and 7. The total job time is averaged over 10 simulation runs. Figure 6 shows results for sequential access pattern and Figure 7 shows results for Gaussian random walk access pattern.

The results show that the NBPRA provides substantially better throughput for jobs that have a sequential access pattern or a Gaussian random walk access pattern, this also means that the NBPRA can provide higher data access efficiency. The main reason is that the replication is parallelized in the NBPRA, and that it can utilize the network bandwidth more efficiently.

The results also show that both the economy-based replication strategy and the NBPRA are not sensitive to the access patterns.

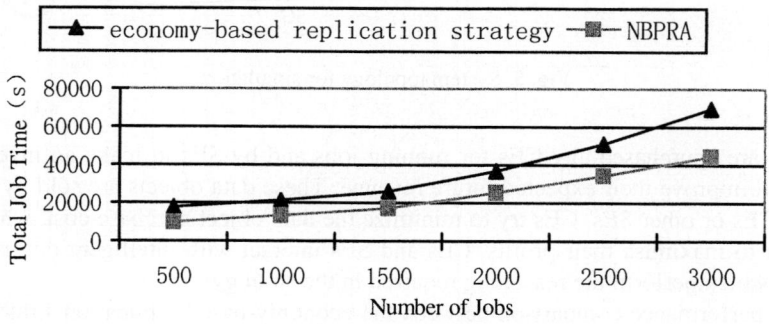

Fig. 6. Total job times for sequential access pattern

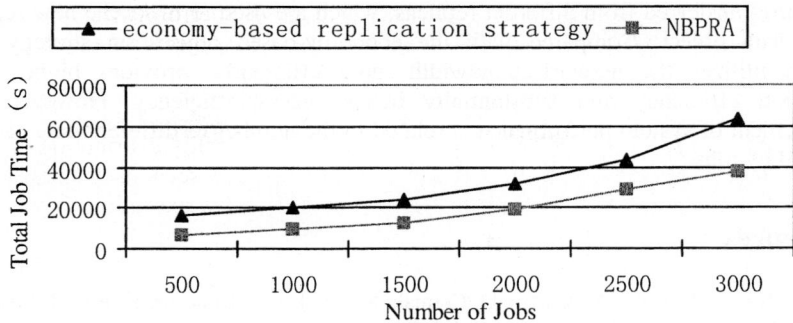

Fig. 7. Total job times for Gaussian random walk access pattern

3.2 Number of Data Objects

The results comparing the two algorithms for the number of the different data objects accessed by jobs are shown in Figure 8. 1000 jobs are executed. The access pattern of jobs is sequential access pattern. The number of the different data objects accessed by jobs is changed from 50 to 120. The total job time is averaged over 10 simulation runs.

The results show that the difference between the NBPRA and the economy-based replication strategy is decreased as the number of the different data objects accessed by jobs increases. In the NBPRA, if there are more different data objects to be replicated, the interference between different replications will be more serious. So the improvement of replication efficiency is limited, and it will affect the improvement of system performance indirectly.

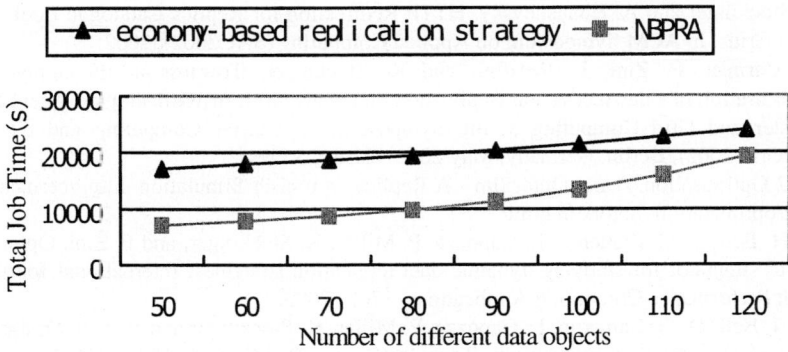

Fig. 8. Relation between the number of different data objects and total job times

4 Conclusions

In the parallel replication algorithm NBPRA, in order to utilize the network bandwidth efficiently, the replication is parallelized, the different parts of a data object are transferred from different replicas, which are used to make the new replica of the data object. Compared with the economy-based replication strategy, the NBPRA utilizes the network bandwidth more efficiently, provides higher data replication efficiency and substantially better access efficiency. However, the improvement of system performance is related to the number of different data objects accessed by jobs.

References

1. A. Adya, W. Bolosky, M. Castro, G. Cermak, R. Chaiken, J. Douceur, J. Howell, J. Lorch, M. Theimer, and R. Wattenhofer. FARSITE: Federated available and reliable storage for incompletely trusted environments. In 5th Symp on Operating Systems Design and Impl., December 2002.
2. Chen, Y., Edler, J., Goldberg, A., Gottlieb, A., Sobti, S., and Yianilos, P. A prototype implementation of archival intermemory. In Proceedings of the 4th ACM Conference on Digital libraries (Berkeley, CA, Aug. 1999), pp. 28--37.
3. CLARK, I., SANDBERG, O., WILEY, B., AND HONG, T. Freenet: A distributed anonymous information storage and retrieval system. In *Proc. of the Workshop on Design Issues in Anonymity and Unobservability* (Berkeley, CA, July 2000), pp. 311–320.
4. DABEK, F., KAASHOEK, M. F., KARGER, D., MORRIS, R., AND STOICA, I. Wide-area cooperative storage with CFS. In *Proc. of ACM SOSP* (October 2001).
5. DRUSCHEL, P., and ROWSTRON, A. Storage management and caching in PAST, a largescale, persistent peer-to-peer storage utility. In *Proc. of ACM SOSP* (2001).
6. KUBIATOWICZ, J., ET AL. Oceanstore: An architecture for global-scale persistent storage. In *Proc. of ASPLOS* (Nov. 2000), ACM.
7. H. Lamehamedi, B. Szymanski, Z. shentu, and E. Deelman, "Data Replication Strategies in Grid Environments," Proc. Of the Fifth International Conference on Algorithms and Architectures for Parallel Processing (ICA3PP'02), 2002.
8. H. Stockinger and A. Hanushevsky. HTTP Redirection for Replica Catalogue Lookups in Data Grids. In ACM Symposium on Applied Computing (SAC2002), 2002.
9. M. Carman, F. Zini, L. Serafini, and K. Stockinger. Towards an Economy-Based Optimisation of File Access and Replication on a Data Grid. In Workshop on Agent based Cluster and Grid Computing at Int. Symposium on Cluster Computing and the Grid (CCGrid 2002), Berlin, Germany, May 2002. IEEE-CS Press.
10. WP2 Optimisation Team. OptorSim - A Replica Optimiser Simulation. http://cern.ch/edg-wp2/optimization/optorsim.html/.
11. W. H. Bell, D. G. Cameron, L. Capozza, P. Millar, K. Stockinger, and F. Zini. Optorsim - a grid simulator for studying dynamic data replication strategies. International Journal of High Performance Computing Applications, 17(4), 2003.
12. W. H. Bell, D. G. Cameron, L. Capozza, P. Millar, K. Stockinger,and F. Zini. Design of a Replica Optimisation Framework. TechnicalReport DataGrid-02-TED- 021215, CERN, Geneva, Switzerland, December 2002.
13. W. H. Bell, D. G. Cameron, R. Carvajal-Schiaffino, A. P. Millar, K. Stockinger, and F. Zini. Evaluation of an Economy-Based File Replication Strategy for a Data Grid. In Proceedings of 3nd IEEE Int. Symposium on Cluster Computing and the Grid (CCGrid'2003).

A Quorum Based Group k-Mutual Exclusion Algorithm for Open Distributed Environments

Armin Lawi, Kentaro Oda, and Takaichi Yoshida

Porgram of Creation Informatics, Kyushu Institute of Technology,
680-4 Kawazu, Iizuka, Fukuoka 820, Japan

Abstract. This paper presents a quorum-based group k-mutual exclusion algorithm for open distributed computing systems that can evolve their behavior based on membership changes in the environment. The algorithm consists of two main layers; the quorum-consensus and quorum-reconfiguration. The quorum consensus layer is used to handle requests from and to the application layer, and it directly adopts a proposed k-coterie based algorithm of the group k-mutual exclusion in the static environments without any change to its protocol. Thus, the message complexity and quorum availability are the same as in the static environments. The quorum reconfiguration reconstructs information structure of the k-coterie by simply implementing the properties of two quorum input operations called coterie-join and coterie-cross. The reconfiguration layer is simple to use and has a great ability to complete any operation during reconfiguration powerfully thus system does not enter the halt state.

1 Introduction

The *distributed mutual exclusion* is one of the most fundamental issues in the study of distributed control and management problems that arises when multiple computing nodes compete for a shared resource in an uncoordinated way. The problem is to design a safety synchronization such that at most one node is allowed to use the resource at a time. The problem of k-*mutual exclusion* (k-mutex) and *group mutual exclusion* (GME) are the two well studied natural generalizations of the mutual exclusion. The k-mutex guarantees at most k (≥ 1) nodes can be allowed to use a single resource simultaneously, and the GME synchronizes conflicting nodes in sharing m resources such that at most one resource can be used by some concurrent nodes. Recently, Vidyasankar [1] introduced group k-mutex as the generalization of the k-mutex and GME problems in a shared-memory environment. The problem is to design a conflict resolution such that at most k (out of m) resources can be used by some concurrent nodes.

As mentioned, let us consider a distributed system consisting of n nodes, which share undetermined number of resources[1]. The system is said to be *group k-mutual exclusive* if the following requirements hold:

---

[1] The paper have further relaxed the assumption of the original problem that the nodes have no knowledge about the entire set of the shared resources.

- **k-mutual exclusion:** at most k resources are allowed to be used by some concurrent nodes at a time.
- **concurrent entering:** nodes which request the allowable resources can use them simultaneously at a time.
- **liveness:** a node requesting a resource will eventually succeed.

Quorum consensus approaches are the well-known solution to any conflict resolution which is generalized from the mutual exclusion. The class of these solutions gives a significant interest in fault-tolerant of node and communication failures that may lead to network partitioning [2, 3]. Coterie based algorithm is a typical quorum consensus for mutual exclusion: A node can use the resource only if it obtains permissions from all nodes in any quorum of a coterie, and since each quorum intersects with each other and each node only issues one permission, the mutual exclusion can be guaranteed. In the GME, Joung [4] have proposed an m-group quorum system for GME quorum consensus, however, construction of such a good quorum system (i.e., a non-dominated m-group quorum system) arises a more difficult problem. Moreover, the coterie based of the mutual exclusion can directly be adopted to this problem; i.e., the conflicting nodes simply use a coterie to manage their mutual exclusive accessions to the requested resources. The k-coterie based algorithms are a particular quorum consensus on the k-mutex problem. There at most k pairwise disjoint quorums in a k-coterie, thus at most k nodes can use it so as to achieve the k-mutex safety requirement. Furthermore, the k-coterie based algorithm can also be used for the group k-mutex in the static environments. In this paper, we firstly present a k-coterie based group k-mutex algorithm in the static environments and adopt it forward to the open distributed environments.

Open distributed computing systems are built on the highly volatile networks in the sense that the rate of membership changes (i.e., nodes joining and leaving the system) is very high. The system consists of a set $\mathcal{P}$ of an undetermined number of nodes which communicate in a message passing manner using a reliable FIFO bidirectional link and share a nonempty set $\mathcal{R}$ of an undetermined number of resources. A node can be created and removed either by user or by another node or even joining and leaving the system by itself. We assume that each node has its own memory and it may fail according to fail-stop failure model in [5]. If a node is created (or join), removed (or leave) or get fails then it can be detected by some other nodes in the system. When a new node is created or joining to the system, it should firstly verify the current configuration of the system.

The existing distributed quorum consensus can run correctly on top of network layer of the open distributed environments, since they are designed as a resilient solution against node and communication failures. However, the membership changes by the leaving and joining nodes will adversely decrease availability of the quorum system. The contention is the reliability that can be gained by developing a core set of distributed algorithms that are aware of the underlying volatility in the network. Lawi et al.[6] have proposed a wait-avoidance mechanism in reconfiguring quorum system for mutual exclusion so as to prevent this drawback. Their algorithm mainly consists of two layers that separately works; the quorum-consensus and -reconfiguration. The quorum consensus layer is used to handle requests from and to the application layer, and it directly adopts the coterie based algorithm for group mutual exclusion in the static environments. The quorum reconfiguration layer reconstructs information structure of the coterie by implementing the two quorum input operations called coterie-join and -cross operations. The coterie join operation is used when a set of nodes have leaved from the system while some others are joining, and the coterie cross is implemented to the algorithm when there is only a set of joining nodes enter the system. In this paper, we extend the results in [6] by showing that the k-coterie based algorithm of the group k-mutex can also be used in their quorum consensus layer, and the quorum reconfiguration layer can also be adopted in reconfiguring k-coteries.

2 The Quorum Consensus Layer

2.1 k-Coteries

Definition 1. [7] A nonempty set of sets, $\mathcal{C}$, is a k-*coterie* under a set of nodes $\mathcal{P}$ iff $\mathcal{C}$ satisfies the following properties:

1. **Non-intersection:** For any h-set $\mathcal{H} = \{Q_1, \ldots, Q_h \in \mathcal{C} \mid Q_i \cap Q_j = \emptyset, i \neq j\}$, $h < k$, there exists $Q \in \mathcal{C}$ such that $Q \cap Q_i = \emptyset$, $1 \leq i \leq h$.
2. **Intersection:** For any $(k+1)$-set $\mathcal{K} = \{Q_1, \ldots, Q_{k+1}\} \subseteq \mathcal{C}$, there exists a pair $Q_i, Q_j \in \mathcal{K}$ such that $Q_i \cap Q_j \neq \emptyset$, $1 \leq i, j \leq k+1$, $i \neq j$.
3. **Minimality:** $Q_i \not\subseteq Q_j$, $\forall Q_i, Q_j \in \mathcal{C}, i \neq j$. □

The quorum consensus layer has two sections that alternate accessed repeatedly: a possibly nonterminating *noncritical section* (NCS) and a terminating *critical section* (CS). The layer stays in the NCS when there is no request to use a resource from the application layer and enters the CS whenever it has an *access right* to a requested resource. The CS is a specified part of the code in which node uses the resource. A node executes a *trying* protocol to entreat an access right so as to enter the CS, and executes an *exit* protocol after leaved the CS and thus returns back to the NCS again. Therefore, the problem in this layer is to design a safety synchronization in the form of *trying* and *exit* protocols to be executed, respectively, immediately before and after the CS which satisfies the safety requirements of group k-mutex (as mentioned in Section 1).

Let $\mathcal{C}$ be a k-coterie. Each node in $\mathcal{P}$ has local variables AGREE, DISAGREE, PERM and QUEUE, respectively, keeps the set of nodes which have agreed (by message ack), the set of nodes which have not yet agreed (by message wait), the set of requests in which p_i has give its permission but has not yet received a message rec_aim, and the ordered set of requests in which p_i has replied wait messages. For conciseness, we roughly give a curt description how the k-group mutex algorithm works for this layer in Figure 1.

Trying Section { // When node p_i wishes to access a resource r_i
1: Selects a quorum Q from C;
2: send $\text{req}(t_i, p_i, r_i)$ to $\forall p \in Q$; // t_i is the p_i's current logical time
3: Inserts $p_j (\in Q)$ answering ack into AGREE;
4: if $(\exists Q \in C, Q \subseteq \text{AGREE})$ then $state := $ **Critical Section**;
5: else-if { // If there exists $p_j (\in Q)$ answers wait
6: Inserts p_j answering wait into DISAGREE;
7: Selects another quorum $Q' \in C$ such that
  $(Q' \cap \text{DISAGREE} = \emptyset)$ and $(Q' = \max\{|Q \cap \text{AGREE}|\})$;
8: if (there is no quorum satisfy) then $state := $ **Wait**;
9: $Q := (Q' - Q)$ and goto line 2; } }

Exit Section { // When node p_i leaves resource r_i
1: send exit to $\forall p_j \in (\text{AGREE} \cap \text{DISAGREE})$ }

When p_i receives $\text{req}(t_j, p_j, r_j)$ message {
1: // Let $\langle t_y, p_y \rangle$ is the highest priority in QUEUE;
2: if (PERM $= \emptyset$ or $r_j = r_y$) then
3:   send ack to p_j and inserts $\text{req}(t_j, p_j, r_j)$ to PERM;
4: else-if { // If there exists $\text{req}(t_x, p_x, r_x)$ in PERM and $r_j \neq r_y$
5:   Inserts $\text{req}(t_j, p_j, r_j)$ into QUEUE;
6:   if $\langle t_j, p_j \rangle > \min\{\langle t_x, p_x \rangle, \langle t_y, p_y \rangle\}$ then send wait to p_j;
7:   else-if // If $\langle t_j, p_j \rangle$ is the highest priority in QUEUE
8:     send reclaim to p_y; } }

When p_i receives exit message from p_j {
1: Removes $\text{req}(t_j, p_j, r_j)$ from PERM;
2: if (PERM $= \emptyset$ and QUEUE $\neq \emptyset$) then {
3:   // Let $\langle t_y, p_y \rangle$ is the highest priority in QUEUE;
4:   for each $(\text{req}(t_j, p_j, r_j) \in \text{QUEUE}$ and $r_j = r_y)$ {
5:     Moves $\text{req}(t_j, p_j, r_j)$ from QUEUE to PERM;
6:     send ack to p_j; } } }

When p_i receives reclaim message from p_j {
1: if (p_i not in CS and $p_j \in$ AGREE) then {
2:   Moves p_j from AGREE to DISAGREE;
3:   send relinquish to p_j; } }

When p_i receives relinquish message from p_j: {
1: // Let $\langle t_y, p_y \rangle$ is the highest priority in QUEUE;
2: send ack to p_y;
3: Inserts $\text{req}(t_y, p_y, r_y)$ into PERM }

Fig. 1. A distributed group k-mutex algorithm for static environments

2.2 Non-dominated k-Coteries

Definition 2. [3] C is a *dominated* k-coterie under $\mathcal{P}$ iff there exists a k-coterie $\mathcal{D}$ (under $\mathcal{P}$) such that

1. $C \neq \mathcal{D}$,
2. $\forall Q \in C, \exists S \in \mathcal{D}, S \subseteq Q$.

If there is no such $\mathcal{D}$, then C is *non-dominated* (or, an ND k-coterie). □

It is easy to observe that if a system using a dominated k-coterie is operational in the occurrence of failures then a system using an ND k-coterie is also operational, but the opposite is not always true. Hence, reliability of an ND k-coterie is better then the dominated one. Another advantage of ND k-coteries is the lower cost of message complexity (since every quorums in an ND k-coterie are subset of the quorums in the dominated k-coterie).

Neilsen [8] have proposed a helpful theorem to check whether a coterie is dominated or not. The theorem can be relaxed to further the k-coteries as well.

Theorem 1. $\mathcal{C}$ is a dominated k-coterie under a set of node $\mathcal{P}$ iff there exists a set $X \subseteq \mathcal{P}$ such that the following conditions hold.

1. **Non-intersection:** There exists h-set $\mathcal{H} = \{Q_1, \ldots, Q_h \in \mathcal{C} \mid Q_i \cap Q_j = \emptyset, i \neq j\}$, $h < k-1$, such that $X \cap Q_i = \emptyset$.
2. **Intersection:** For any k-set $\mathcal{K} = \{Q_1, \ldots, Q_k\} \subseteq \mathcal{C}$, there exist $Q_i \in \mathcal{K}$ such that $Q_i \cap X \neq \emptyset$.
3. **Minimality:** $\forall Q \in \mathcal{C}, Q \nsubseteq X$. ∎

3 Quorum Reconfiguration

The quorum reconfiguration layer mainly based on the reconfiguration algorithm posed by Law et al.[6] which uses two quorum input operations in reconfiguring the quorum system of the mutual exclusion; i.e., coterie-join and -cross. We have extended their results for k-coteries and directly adopt them in this layer.

For the following subsections, let $\mathcal{C}_1$ and $\mathcal{C}_2$ be k-coteries under $\mathcal{P}_1$ and $\mathcal{P}_2$, respectively, and $\mathcal{P}_1 \cap \mathcal{P}_2 = \emptyset$.

3.1 Coterie Join Operation

Definition 3. [8] Let x be a node in $\mathcal{P}_1$. A *coterie join* operation for inputs $\mathcal{C}_1$ and $\mathcal{C}_2$ produces a quorum set $(\mathcal{C}_1 \odot_x \mathcal{C}_2)$ defined by

$$(\mathcal{C}_1 \odot_x \mathcal{C}_2) = \{(Q_1 - \{x\}) \cup Q_2 \mid Q_1 \in \mathcal{C}_1, Q_2 \in \mathcal{C}_2 \text{ and } x \in Q_1\}$$
$$\cup \{Q_1 \mid Q_1 \in \mathcal{C}_1 \text{ and } x \notin Q_1\}. \qquad \square$$

Jiang and Huang [9] have proved the following results.

Theorem 2. Let $\mathcal{C}_3 = (\mathcal{C}_1 \odot_x \mathcal{C}_2)$, then

1. $\mathcal{C}_3$ is a k-coterie under $\mathcal{P}_3 \subseteq \mathcal{P}_1 \cup \mathcal{P}_2$.
2. $\mathcal{C}_3$ is an ND k-coterie only if $\mathcal{C}_1$ and $\mathcal{C}_2$ are both ND k-coteries.
3. $\mathcal{C}_3$ is dominated, if either $\mathcal{C}_1$ or $\mathcal{C}_2$ is dominated. ∎

The following can easily be proved using mathematical induction.

Corollary 3. Let $\mathcal{C}_1, \mathcal{C}_2, \ldots, \mathcal{C}_m$ be k-coteries under $\mathcal{P}_1, \mathcal{P}_2, \ldots, \mathcal{P}_m$, respectively. For any $X = \{x_1, x_2, \ldots, x_{m-1} \mid x_i \in \mathcal{P}_i\}$, then $\mathcal{C} = (\mathcal{C}_1 \odot_{x_1} \cdots \odot_{x_{m-1}} \mathcal{C}_m)$ is a k-coterie under $\mathcal{P} \subseteq \cup_{i=1}^{m} \mathcal{P}_i$. ∎

3.2 Coterie Cross Operation

Definition 4. [6] A *coterie cross* operation for inputs $\mathcal{C}_1$ and $\mathcal{C}_2$ produces a quorum set defined by, $(\mathcal{C}_1 \otimes \mathcal{C}_2) = \{Q_1 \cup Q_2 \mid Q_1 \in \mathcal{C}_1 \text{ and } Q_2 \in \mathcal{C}_2\}$. $\square$

Theorem 4. [6] Let $\mathcal{C}'$ and $\mathcal{C}''$ be *coteries* under $\mathcal{P}'$ and $\mathcal{P}''$, respectively, and $\mathcal{P}' \cap \mathcal{P}'' = \emptyset$. If $\mathcal{C} = (\mathcal{C}' \otimes \mathcal{C}'')$, then

1. $\mathcal{C}$ is a coterie under $\mathcal{P} \subseteq \mathcal{P}' \cup \mathcal{P}''$.
2. $\mathcal{C}$ is an ND-coterie only if $\mathcal{C}'$ and $\mathcal{C}''$ are both ND-coteries.
3. $\mathcal{C}$ is dominated, if either $\mathcal{C}'$ or $\mathcal{C}''$ is dominated. ∎

We have extended results in Theorem 4 for k-coteries as follows.

Theorem 5. Let $\mathcal{C}_4 = (\mathcal{C}_1 \otimes \mathcal{C}_2)$. Then,

1. $\mathcal{C}_4$ is a k-coterie under $\mathcal{P}_4 \subseteq \mathcal{P}_1 \cup \mathcal{P}_2$.
2. $\mathcal{C}_4$ is an ND k-coterie only if both $\mathcal{C}_1$ and $\mathcal{C}_2$ are ND k-coteries.
3. $\mathcal{C}_4$ is dominated only if either $\mathcal{C}_1$ or $\mathcal{C}_2$ is dominated k-coterie.. ∎

3.3 The Reconfiguration Algorithm

The quorum reconfiguration layer simply implements the two operations introduced in the previous two subsections, but for the conciseness, we roughly outline how it works as follows. Let $\mathcal{C}$ be the the current k-coterie of the system.

1. *When there are sets joining nodes X and leaving nodes Y*: The algorithm firstly partitions the set X into m ($\leq |Y|$) disjoint sets and constructs m independent k-coteries $\mathcal{C}_1, \ldots, \mathcal{C}_m$ under $X_1, \ldots, X_m$, respectively, and creates a new coterie $\mathcal{C}_{\text{temp}} = \mathcal{C}$. Each node $y_i \in Y$ is replaced by $\mathcal{C}_i$ iteratively using coterie cross operation, $\mathcal{C}_{\text{temp}} = \mathcal{C}_{\text{temp}} \odot_{y_i} \mathcal{C}_i$, $i = 1 \ldots, m$. The iterated result of $\mathcal{C}_{\text{temp}}$ is stored to $\mathcal{C}$ as the new quorum configuration.
2. *When there is only a set X of joining nodes*: The algorithm simply creates a k-coterie $\mathcal{C}'$ under X and restores $\mathcal{C}$ with $(\mathcal{C} \otimes \mathcal{C}')$ as the new configuration.

Note that the coterie cross operation can also be implemented in case 1, however, the result k-coterie will be dominated. Let $\mathcal{C}'$ be k-coterie under the set X of joining nodes and $\mathcal{P} \cap X = \emptyset$. Let $x \in \mathcal{P}$ is the leaving node, then

$$(\mathcal{C} \otimes \mathcal{C}') = (\mathcal{C} \odot_x \mathcal{C}') \setminus \{Q \mid Q \in \mathcal{C} \text{ and } x \notin Q\}$$

Thus, there exists a set $Z \in \{Q \mid Q \in \mathcal{C} \text{ and } x \notin Q\}$ satisfies the Theorem 1.

4 Performance Analysis

The number of messages required per entry to the CS is the same as for the mutual exclusion [10] and hence for the k-mutex algorithm [7] in the static environments. The message complexity of the algorithm in the best case is 3ϵ and can be bounded from above by 6ϵ in the worst case, where $\epsilon = \max\{|Q| \mid Q \in \mathcal{C}\}$.

Let $\mathcal{C}_1$ and $\mathcal{C}_2$ be k-coteries under $\mathcal{P}_1$ and $\mathcal{P}_2$, respectively, and $\mathcal{C} = \mathcal{C}_1 \odot_x \mathcal{C}_2$, $x \in \mathcal{P}_1$, or $\mathcal{C} = \mathcal{C}_1 \otimes \mathcal{C}_2$.

Theorem 6. $|Q| \leq 2 \max\{|Q'| \mid Q' \in \mathcal{C}_1 \text{ or } Q' \in \mathcal{C}_2\}$, $\forall Q \in \mathcal{C}$. ∎

Now, let $\|\mathcal{C}\|$ (resp., $\|\mathcal{C}_1\|$ and $\|\mathcal{C}_2\|$) defines rank of coterie $\mathcal{C}$ (resp., $\mathcal{C}_1$ and $\mathcal{C}_2$); i.e., the number of quorums in coterie $\mathcal{C}$ (resp., $\mathcal{C}$ and $\mathcal{C}$).

Theorem 7. If $\mathcal{C}_1$ and $\mathcal{C}_2$ are majority ND k-coteries, then

1. $\|\mathcal{C}\| = \|\mathcal{C}_1\| \times \|\mathcal{C}_2\|$, when $\mathcal{C} = \mathcal{C}_1 \otimes \mathcal{C}_2$, and
2. $\|\mathcal{C}\| \geq \|\mathcal{C}_2\| \times \binom{|\mathcal{P}_1|-1}{q-1}, q = \lceil \frac{|\mathcal{P}_1|+1}{k+1} \rceil$, when $\mathcal{C} = \mathcal{C}_1 \odot_x \mathcal{C}_2$. ∎

5 Conclusions

We have proposed a quorum based group k-mutex algorithm for open distributed environments in this paper. The algorithm consists of two main parts, i.e., the quorum-consensus and quorum-reconfiguration, each of which placed in different layers and work separately. The quorum consensus layer directly adopts a k-coterie based algorithm for group k-mutex in the static environments which is also proposed in this paper. Thus, its message complexity and quorum availability performances are the same as in the static environments.

References

1. Vidyasankar, K.: A simple group mutual ℓ-exclusion algorithm. Information Processing Letters **85** (2003) 79–85
2. Agrawal, D., Abbadi, A.E.: An efficient and fault-tolerant algorithm for distributed mutual exclusion. ACM Trans. Computer Systems **9** (1991) 1–20
3. Garcia-Molina, H., Barbara, D.: How to assign votes in a distributed system. Journal of the ACM **32** (1985) 841–860
4. Joung, Y.J.: Quorum-based algorithms for group mutual exclusion. IEEE Transaction on Parallel and Distributed Systems **14** (2003) 463–476
5. Schlichting, R., Schneider, F.: Fail-stop processors: an approach to designing fault-tolerant computing systems. ACM Trans. Computer Systems **1** (1983) 222–238
6. Lawi, A., Oda, K., Yoshida, T.: A simple quorum reconfiguration for open distributed environments. In: Proc. International Conference on Parallel and Distributed Systems (ICPADS). Volume II. (2005) 664–668
7. Fujita, S., Yamashita, M., Ae, T.: Distributed k-mutual exclusion problem and k-coteries. In: Proc. 2nd International Symposium on Algorithms, Lecture Notes in Computer Science 557. (1991) 22–31
8. Neilsen, M.L., Mizuno, M.: Coterie join algorithm. IEEE Trans. Parallel and Dist. Systems **3** (1992) 582–590
9. Jiang, J.R., Huang, S.T.: Obtaining nondominated k-coteries for fault-tolerant distributed k-mutual exlusion. In: Proc. International Conference on Parallel and Distributed Systems (ICPADS). (1994) 582–587
10. Maekawa, M.: A $\sqrt{N}$ algorithm for mutual exclusion in decentralized systems. ACM Trans. Computer Systems **3** (1985) 145–159

An Efficient Implementation of the Backtesting of Trading Strategies

Jiarui Ni and Chengqi Zhang

Faculty of Information Technology,
University of Technology, Sydney,
GPO Box 123, Broadway, NSW 2007, Australia
{jiarui, chengqi}@it.uts.edu.au

Abstract. Some trading strategies are becoming more and more complicated and utilize a large amount of data, which makes the backtesting of these strategies very time consuming. This paper presents an efficient implementation of the backtesting of such a trading strategy using a parallel genetic algorithm (PGA) which is fine tuned based on thorough analysis of the trading strategy. The reuse of intermediate results is very important for such backtesting problems. Our implementation can perform the backtesting within a reasonable time range so that the tested trading strategy can be properly deployed in time.

1 Introduction

Backtesting also known as Systems Testing is the concept of taking a strategy and going back in time to see what would have happened if the strategy had been faithfully followed. The assumption is that if the strategy has worked previously, it has a good but not certain chance of working again in the future and conversely if the concept has not worked well in the past, it probably will not work well in the future.

The backtesting of trading strategies is important for brokers and investors to judge if the strategies are profitable under certain circumstances. It helps the users learn how a trading strategy is likely to perform in the marketplace. It also provides the users with the opportunity to improve a trading strategy. A detailed discussion of the benefits of backtesting is given by [6].

Due to the many benefits of backtesting, it is widely used by brokers and investors. And there are a lot of backtesting systems available in the market, for example, MetaStock from Equis International (www.equis.com) and TradeStation from TradeStation Securities (www.tradestation.com), etc. These systems help the users develop and back test their own trading systems.

Early trading strategies such as Moving Average Crosses were relatively simple and easy to implement and test. As more and more people join in the game of searching for better trading systems, more complicated trading strategies are investigated. Intraday data instead of interday data are utilized, which increases the data to be processed by a factor of hundreds or even thousands. More complicated indicators that are hard to calculate are exploited. Furthermore, people sometimes have to try a strategy against multiple stocks and even multiple markets. All these factors make the backtesting of these trading strategies much more time-consuming, and the ready-for-use commercial products become incapable of dealing with them. People need more efficient implementations in order to perform the backtesting of such trading strategies within an acceptable time range.

In the following sections, we will analyze a simplified trading strategy in detail and present an efficient implementation of it using parallel genetic algorithm (PGA) based on the analysis.

2   A Simplified Trading Strategy

Today's trading strategies tend to exploit several indicators and filters in combination to make the final decision. To make the discussion easier, we will introduce a simplified trading strategy in this section.

Our simplified trading strategy exploits a modified Bollinger band only. Bollinger band is among the most popular technical analysis techniques. It includes 3 lines: the upper band, the lower band, and the center line. The center line is simply the moving average, and the upper and lower bands are, respectively, the center line plus/minus twice the standard deviation [5]. In our strategy, the standard deviation is no longer timed by a fixed coefficient of 2. Instead, the coefficient becomes a variable to be optimized, and its value can be different for upper and lower bands. Given the price series $P_n (n = 1, 2, 3, \cdots)$, the center line C_n, upper band U_n and lower band L_n of a p-period Bollinger band can be calculated as follows:

$$C_n = \frac{1}{p} \sum_{i=n-p+1}^{n} P_n , \qquad (1)$$

$$U_n = C_n + V_u \times \sqrt{\frac{\sum_{i=n-p+1}^{n}(P_n - C_n)^2}{p-1}} , \qquad (2)$$

$$L_n = C_n - V_l \times \sqrt{\frac{\sum_{i=n-p+1}^{n}(P_n - C_n)^2}{p-1}} , \qquad (3)$$

where V_n and V_l are variables to be optimized, and we assume they vary between 1.0 and 2.0 with a step of 0.1. Besides, we assume that p can take any integer value between 11 and 50.

The financial explanation for Bollinger band is as follows: the closer the prices move to the upper band, the more overbought the market, and the closer the prices move to the lower band, the more oversold the market. Based on this understanding, we derive our simple trading rules as follows:

During the normal trading hours, at the end of each bar (a short time period, e.g., 10 or 30 minutes), we evaluate the current price. If the price crosses over the lower band, i.e., $P_{n-1} <= L_{n-1}$ AND $P_n > L_n$, buy 100 shares at the beginning of the next bar. If the price crosses under the upper band, i.e., $P_{n-1} >= U_{n-1}$

AND $P_n < U_n$, sell all shares in hand at the beginning of the next bar. To make the discussion simple, we assume that our trading volume is small enough that our buy/sell orders can be executed at the current price without delay. We also ignore the brokerage fee here. Of course, the real trading strategies have to deal with all these issues.

The purpose of the backtesting of this trading strategy is to answer the following questions: 1) Can this strategy make profit when applied to certain stocks for a time period such as one year (the training period)? 2) If it can make profit for a certain stock, what values for the parameters p, V_u, V_l can give the most profit? 3) Can these values also give a reasonable profit during the following time period such as the next six months (the testing period)?

Question 3 is a simple yes-or-no question which can be easily answered by running the trading strategy once with the values given by question 2. However, because the trading strategy is very sensitive to the change of any parameter, there is no simple relation between the profit and the parameters. Therefore, question 1 and 2 can not be easily answered before trying all the possible triples of (p, V_u, V_l).

3 A Direct Implementation of the Backtesting Problem

The simplest approach to the above optimization problem can simply loop through all the possible triples of (p, V_u, V_l) and run the trading strategy with each triple. The following pseudo-code illustrates this approach.

```
Algorithm 1
for(p = 11; p <= 50; p ++) {
    Calculate Cn and standard deviation Dn;
    for(Vu = 1.0; Vu <= 2.0; Vu += 0.1) {
        Un = Cn + Vu * Dn;
        for(Vl = 1.0; Vl <= 2.0; Vl += 0.1) {
            Ln = Cn - Vl * Dn;
            Run trading strategy with Cn, Un, and Ln;
        }
    }
}
```

Note that C_n and D_n only have to be calculated once for each value of p, and that U_n only has to be calculated once for each pair of (p, V_u). The idea is to reuse the intermediate results as much as possible. Even in this simple case, experiments show that the execution time is reduced by a factor of 10 with the reuse of intermediate values of C_n, D_n and U_n.

Alg. 1 is easy to implement and understand. However, the running time is too long for really complicated trading strategies. While backtesting one trading strategy provided by our industrial partner, our initial try with such an approach took 8 hours to work thru only 1/40 of the whole search space on one single stock. Obviously, The users can not wait that long for the backtesting result. We have to reduce the computing time.

4 Using PGA

A straightforward way to speed up Alg. 1 is to parallelize its execution. Once a triple of (p, V_u, V_l) is given, a processing element (PE) can execute the whole trading strategy by itself. If we have N PEs, we can easily partition the search space into N equal subspaces and then start one process to deal with each subspace. Because there are no communication or synchronization requirements, the parallelization causes almost no overhead in this problem. However, this approach is limited by the number of available PEs. Normal brokers or investors can not expect to have more than 1 or 2 CPUs ready for use at any time. We need better software solutions.

Genetic algorithms (GAs) have demonstrated to be particularly successful in the optimization, classification and control of very-large-scale and varied data. PGAs further provide the basis for tackling problems in a wider range of fields [4]. GAs and PGAs have been widely used in many disciplines from astronomy [2] to molecular design [1]. [3] discusses many ways in which GAs can be parallelized, including the master-slave model. Based on this model, a basic PGA for our backtesting problem is developed as follows:

```
Algorithm 2 -- Master process
Generate random population of n triples;
While(true) {
    Partition the population into N equal groups;
    Send the triples in each group to one slave process;
    Receive the fitness value for each triple from the slaves;
    Exit if no better fitness value is found;
    Select triples with better fitness from the population;
    Generate new population by crossover and mutation;
}

Algorithm 2 -- Slave process
While(true) {
    Receive a triple of (p, Vu, Vl) from the master process;
    Calculate Cn and standard deviation Dn;
    Un = Cn + Vu * Dn;
    Ln = Cn - Vl * Dn;
    Run trading strategy with Cn, Un, and Ln;
    Send the profit (fitness) to the master process;
}
```

The crossover and mutation operations used here are very simple. Suppose we have two triples (p_1, V_{u1}, V_{l1}) and (p_2, V_{u2}, V_{l2}), the crossover operation randomly select p, V_u and V_l independent of each other from the first or second triple and form a new triple. And the mutation operation just randomly change the value of one variable in a given triple to create a new triple.

Note that because the triples are randomly generated in Alg. 2, we can no longer reuse the intermediate values of C_n, D_n and U_n in the way we did in

Alg. 1. This decreases the efficiency of the algorithm. To alleviate this unwanted effect, we have to refine the algorithms to take advantage of the intermediate results as much as possible. The only change to the master process is that the population should be sorted by p and V_u before it is partitioned into N equal groups. The refined algorithm for the slave process is showed below:

```
Algorithm 3 -- Slave process, refined
p_old = Vu_old = Vl_old = newpFlag = 0;
While(true) {
    Receive a triple of (p, Vu, Vl) from the master process;
    if(p != p_old) {
        Calculate Cn and standard deviation Dn;
        p_old = p; newpFlag = 1;
    }
    if(newpFlag > 0 || Vu != Vu_old) {
        Un = Cn + Vu * Dn;
        Vu_old = Vu;
    }
    if(newpFlag > 0 || Vl != Vl_old) {
        Ln = Cn - Vl * Dn;
        Vl_old = Vl;
    }
    Run trading strategy with Cn, Un, and Ln;
    Send the profit (fitness) to the master process;
}
```

5 Performance Evaluation

For the simplified trading strategy described in this paper, we have carried out a set of experiments for all the algorithms described above to illustrate the effect of each algorithm. We performed the backtesting of each algorithm over 1 year's period against one stock ANZ from the Australian stock market. 30-minutes bar data (open price, close price, best bid, best ask) were used in the experiment. The data were stored in a text file and read by the algorithms at startup. To count the execution time more accurately, each algorithm was repeated 20 times. The average execution time is shown in the upper half of Table 1.

The parallelization introduces some overhead. And for this simple trading strategy, the overhead is quite noticeable. When running in parallel on 4 CPUs, it took Alg. 1 much longer than a quarter of the time it needed when running sequentially. And 8 CPUs make hardly any difference than 4 CPUs.

The crossover and mutation operations in the PGAs also result in some overhead that is noticeable in the backtesting of this simple strategy. Alg. 2 is much slower than Alg. 1 when both running in parallel on 8 CPUs. However, Alg. 3 shows less running time that Alg. 1. It means that the PGA can reduce the execution time. The difference between Alg. 2 and Alg. 3 emphasizes the importance of reusing the intermediate results wherever possible.

Table 1. Execution time for different algorithms

Trading strategy	Algorithm	Execution time
Simplified	Alg. 1 (sequential)	87 s
	Alg. 1 (parallel on 4 CPUs)	24 s
	Alg. 1 (parallel on 8 CPUs)	22 s
	Alg. 2 (parallel on 8 CPUs)	32 s
	Alg. 3 (parallel on 8 CPUs)	18 s
Real	Alg. 1 (sequential)	ca. 300 h
	Alg. 1 (parallel on 8 CPUs)	40 h
	Alg. 3 (parallel on 8 CPUs)	$1 \sim 2$ h

For the real trading strategy we tested for our industry partner, we have got the following results as shown in the lower half of Table 1. In this case, the speedup factor of multiple PEs is very apparent. When executed in parallel on 8 CPUs, the execution time of Alg. 1 is reduced to near 1/8. The PGA achieves an speedup factor of at least 20 comparing with the parallel version of Alg. 1. Finally we are able to back test the trading strategy against one stock within $1 \sim 2$ hours. This makes the backtesting of the complicated trading strategy against multiple stocks and multiple markets feasible.

6 Conclusion

In this paper, we have demonstrated step by step the implementation of the backtesting of a complicated trading strategy. We have shown that PGAs can speedup the backtesting process greatly. Furthermore, the reuse of intermediate results is very important for accelerating the backtesting of complicated trading strategies. We believe that the same principles used in this paper can and should be applied in the implementation of the backtesting of other complicated trading strategies as well to make the backtesting feasible.

References

1. Clark, D. E. (Ed): Evolutionary Algorithms in Molecular Design, Wiley-VCH, Weinheim, 2000.
2. Metcalfe T. S., Charbonneau, P.: Stellar structure modeling using a parallel genetic algorithm for objective global optimization, Journal of Computational Physics, Volume 185, Issue 1, p. 176-193., 2003
3. Nowostawski M., Poli R.: Parallel genetic algorithm taxonomy, Proc. of 3rd Int. Conference on Knowledge-based Intelligent Information Engineering Systems (KES'99), Adelaide, Australia, 1999
4. Stender J.: Parallel Genetic Algorithms: Theory & Applications, IOS Press, Amsterdam, 1993
5. stockcharts.com/education/IndicatorAnalysis/indic_Bbands.html
6. www.traids.com

Reconfigurable Object Consistency Model for Distributed Shared Memory

Christiane V. Pousa, Luís F. W. Góes, and Carlos A. P. S. Martins

Graduation Program in Electrical Engineering, Computational and Digital Systems Group,
Pontifical Catholic University of Minas Gerais, Minas Gerais, Brazil
pousa@ieee.org, lfwgoes@yahoo.com.br, capsm@pucminas.br

Abstract. The consistency models are responsible for managing the state of shared data for the applications of a distributed shared memory (DSM) systems. The already proposed consistency models are inflexible and cannot adapt to the workload and environments characteristics. So, they cannot achieve the best performance for the workloads and environments in all the cases. In this work, we propose, present and analyze a reconfigurable consistency model (ROCoM –Reconfigurable Object Consistency Model) for object based DSMs. ROCoM behavior was represented using a reconfigurable algorithm (RA) and its analysis was made using a simulation tool. Our results show that ROCoM, on average, had 34% (upper bound) better performance than other ones.

1 Introduction

Distributed shared memory (DSM) is an abstraction that provides an illusion of a shared memory in a distributed system [1][2][3]. Some DSMs are implemented to manage objects. In these DSMs, the read and write operation semantics (consistency model) guarantee that objects will be consistent for the application [4].

A consistency model can be defined as a contract that has rules about how and when a process of an application can access the shared object [5][6][7]. Consistency models should have a low response time, in order to maximize the system's performance for all workloads. The main problem is that workload and environment change continuously. In order to solve this problem, some flexible and adaptable consistency models were proposed [8][9][10]. A poorly explored solution is the use of reconfigurable algorithms to represent a consistency model [11][12][13] [14].

Our proposal in this paper is to use a reconfigurable algorithm to represent the behavior of a reconfigurable object consistency model (ROCoM). ROCoM is a reconfigurable consistency model for asynchronous distributed systems that manage concurrent access in shared objects [7]. Ideally, this model may assume infinite configurations and it reconfigures itself according to entry parameters such as: performance metrics and workload characteristics.

The **main objectives** of this paper are: to present the ROCoM, represent its behavior using a RA, analyze its performance using simulation and show the use of a RA is better than the use of a traditional algorithm. The **main goals** are: the implementation and performance analysis of ROCoM.

2 Reconfigurable Object Consistency Model

ROCoM is a reconfigurable object consistency model for asynchronous architectures that execute an object-based software DSM [7]. This consistency model manages the state of a set of shared objects. ROCoM can have its behavior reconfigured considering the workload and environment characteristics. So, it can adapt to them improving flexibility and increasing performance.

Any consistency model can be decomposed into parts or frames (coherence protocols, consistency constraints, events ordering policy, access policy, replication protocol) [7]. Each frame is responsible for one part of the consistency model. A constructive block implements a frame solution of our consistency model. ROCoM has five frames (event ordering policy, constraint policy, coherence protocol, replication protocol and access policy) and some constructive blocks that are combined to reconfigurable it.

The reconfiguration in ROCoM is done during the workload execution, but it is important to say that this reconfiguration is done after an application execution ends. In our system, a workload is composed of n applications, and between these applications, ROCoM can be reconfigured to assume the best form or configuration to the next application. The actual version of ROCoM can be reconfigurable to assume some sequential consistency model variations. So, a consistency model is said to be reconfigurable if: i) it can assume different consistency models variations during the workload execution and ii) it cannot assume more than one consistency at a time.

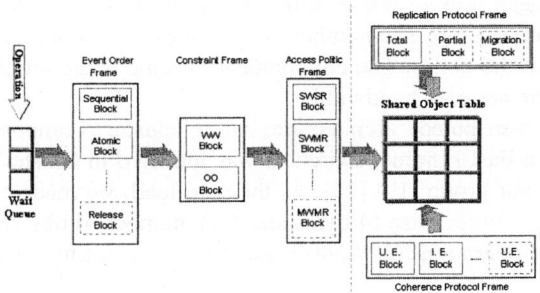

Fig. 1. The Basic Layer of the ROCoM and some possible constructive blocks

A reconfigurable algorithm was used to represent ROCoM's behavior. RA has the characteristics (frames, constructive blocks etc) that were necessary to represent the presented consistency model. In Figure 1, we can observe the RA that represents our consistency model. The configuration control layer (CCL) of our RA controls the constructive blocks that are active in a moment; it is implemented with a selection structure. The basic layer (BL) has the implementation of every consistency model's parts, constructive blocks and structures (shared objects and wait queues). Finally, the reconfigurable layer (RL) is an instance of the BL. In this paper the Access Policy Frame can be filled out with single writer/multiple reader (SWMR) policies. The

Event Ordering Frame is filled out with the sequential ordering. The Constraint Frame can use the WW or OO approach. The Replication Protocol Frame can be filled out with total replication protocol. Finally, the Coherence Protocol Frame can be filled out with the update eager or invalidate eager (UE and IE).

3 Related Works

In this research, we found many works about consistency models [6][8][9][10][15][16][17][18], few works about reconfigurable software and algorithms [8][15], and none about reconfigurable consistency models. In this work, we will discuss some papers that are more relevant and close to our work [8][6].

In [8], a flexible consistency algorithm is proposed and implemented. As well as our proposal, it uses a different algorithm depending on the user choice. The consistency algorithm implements three-consistency models (Sequential, Causal, Cache), but it uses just the traditional implementation of each one. And, in [6], a sequential consistency algorithm with dynamic protocols switching is proposed and verified by means of formal proofs.

4 Experimental Results

In order to analyze a consistency model, we can use different metrics. The most common are: response time, communication time and number of messages [7] [14] [15] [16]. The mean job response time is the mean time interval between the submission and end of a job. The number of messages is the total number of messages exchanged between the nodes. The communication time is the number of transmitted bytes divided by the network bandwidth.

The selected distributed architecture is a cluster composed of 8 nodes interconnected by a Fast Ethernet switch. It was modeled in ClusterSim, a simulation tool developed by our group [19] [20]. As the workload, we made combinations with some characteristics: object size (4 bytes and 4K), number of objects (1, 4 and 8) and percentage of write operations (20%, 40% and 60%), generating 9 workloads.

Table 1. ROCoM configurations

Configurations	Constraint
Conf 1	WW, UE, SWMR, Total
Conf 2	WW, IE, SWMR, Total
Conf 3	OO, UE, SWMR, Total
Conf 4	OO, IE, SWMR, Total

In order to test and analyze the performance of the ROCoM, we created some configurations (Table 1). It is important to note that each ROCoM configuration is a traditional sequential consistency model. In these models, its parts are fixed and cannot be changed over time. For example, in Table 1, Conf01 has the WW constraint, Write Update protocol, and it cannot changes over time. Through the rest of this paper, traditional algorithm and configuration will be treated as synonyms.

Due to the limited number of pages, we present only the results for the response time (in seconds). In Figure 2, we present the response time for every workload with objects of 4 bytes. We can see that the Conf2 had the best results on average for almost all workloads. In some workloads (1 object-20% writes, 1object – 40%writes and 4 objects – 40%writes) the Conf4 had better or equal results of the configuration two. The Conf2 uses WW constraint of consistency and invalidation coherence protocol. The WW (Write->Write) constraint is a sub set of the OO (Write->Write, Read->Write and Write->Read) constraint.

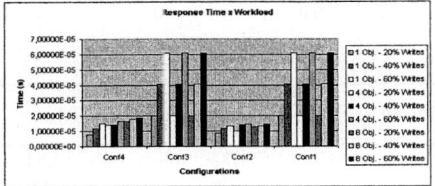 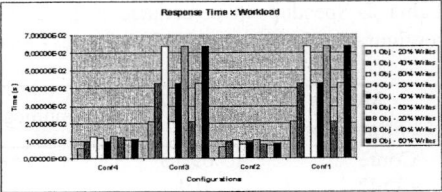

Fig. 2. Response Time x 4 Bytes   **Fig. 3.** Response Time x 4K bytes

So, the WW constraint serializes fewer operations than the OO constraint. With this constraint the Conf2 has a low probability of remote operations happen and the response time became smaller than in the other configurations. Furthermore, with the invalidation coherence protocol, the messages sent through the network are smaller than the messages sent by the update coherence protocol (Conf1 and Conf3) and with the WW constraint is not necessary to sent many objects in the configuration two.

In the configurations that use invalidate coherence protocol and have a large number of remote operations, the read operations spent more time with the network than with the write ones. Because, in invalidation protocol, all replicas are invalidate in a write operation. So, in each remote read, the object has to be sent to the process that is executing the read operation. We can conclude that, in relation of response time for workloads with object size smaller than the network packet, number of writes and objects increases the response time. Because large number of writes means smaller number of consecutive reads.

In Figure 3, we present the response time of workloads with object size of 4K bytes. We can observe that in the Conf1 and Conf3, the number of objects has no influence in the response time. This happen, because the number of write operations are equal for all workloads (20%, 40% and 60%). In this case, in each write operation, the object replicas are updated with the new object value. As the replicas of objects are never invalidated with this protocol, just local operations have to be executed. Just update messages are sent through the network. We can also observe that the Conf2 and Conf4 got the best results for response time, as in the workload with objects of 4 bytes. However, the Conf4 presented the smallest response time for the workload of one object and 20% of writes, because with this configuration and workload, the OO constraint did not have to restrict many conflicting operations.

It is important to observe that in the Conf2 and Conf4, the response time for the workloads with 8 objects and 40%/60% of writes did not present regularity as in the other workloads. These configurations present smaller response time for 40%/60% of writes than for 20% of writes. In this case, the number of objects and write operations are bigger and this decreases the number of conflicting and read operations. So, the number of messages of invalidation sent is bigger than the messages of objects.

In order to analyze the performance of ROCoM, we need to compare it to each configuration and/or sequential consistency model individually. As we said in the proposal of ROCoM, the CCL evaluates the entry parameters, reconfiguring ROCoM to the best configuration.

Table 2. Speedup, in percentage (%), of the ROCoM performance when compared to each configuration for the workload of 4 bytes objects

Metrics Configurations	Response Time	Communication Time	Number of Messages	Mean
Conf1	69,13	68,2	24,11	53,81
Conf2	0,96	0,93	11,56	4,48
Conf3	69,13	68,2	24,11	53,81
Conf4	15,34	12,8	20,15	16,09
Mean	38,64	37,53	19,98	32,05

In Table 2, we observe that on average, considering all metrics and workloads with an object size of 4 bytes, ROCoM is 32,05% better than other 4 traditional consistency algorithms. Note that if we had chosen Conf2 (the best configuration on average), ROCoM would still be 4,48% better. Now, we analyze another example, in which the workload is composed of 4KB objects. According to Table 3, on average, the speedup of ROCoM increases to 36,31%. If we consider only the number of messages metric, the speedup of ROCoM over Conf2 increases from 3,63% to 9,94%.

Table 3. Speedup, in percentage (%), of the ROCoM performance when compared to each configuration for the workload of 4Kbytes objects

Metrics Configurations	Response Time	Communication Time	Number of Messages	Mean
Conf1	80,63	80,63	24,5	61,92
Conf2	0,48	0,48	9,94	3,63
Conf3	79,55	76,6	24,5	60,21
Conf4	18,89	18,89	20,65	19,47
Mean	44,88	44,15	19,89	36,31

5 Conclusions

In this paper, we proposed, presented, implemented (in a simulation tool) and analyzed the performance of ROCoM by simulation. As general conclusions about the

ROCoM frames, we can highlight: a) Considering the Constraint Frame, the OO blocks had better performance in the aplications with a bigger number of writes. b) In the Coherence Protocol Frame, the invalidate eager block presented the better results.

On average, the performance of ROCoM was around 34% (upper bound) better than the other consistency models for all tested workloads. Using a reconfigurable algorithm, developers don't need to create a monolithic algorithm and it is possible to propose new consistency models.

The **main contributions** of this paper are: the presentation, implementation and performance analysis of ROCoM, comparing it with other consistency models for different workloads. As future works we can highlight: the inclusion of new frames and blocks in ROCoM; an adaptive CCL; compare ROCoM with other consistency models, simulation with different workloads and real tests.

References

1. Adve V. S. and Garachorloo K., "Shared Memory Consistency Models: A Tutorial", Technical Report 95/7, DEC Western Research Laboratory, University Avenue, 1995.
2. Mosherger D., "Memory Consistency Models", Technical Report TR 92/11, University of Arizona, 1992, pp. 18-26.
3. Melo A. C. M. A., "Defining Uniform and Hybrid Memory Consistency Models on a Unified Framework", Proc. of the 32th HICSS, Vol VIII-Software Technology, 1999, p. 270-279
4. Ahuja S., Carriero N., and Gerlernter D.,: "Linda and Friends", IEEE Computer 19:8, 1986.
5. Shi W., Hu W. and Tang Z., "An Interaction of Coherence Protocols and Memory Consistency Models in DSM Systems". ACM Operating Systems, 1997, pp. 41 – 54.
6. Raynal M., "Sequential Consistency as Lazy Linearizability", Fourth Annual ACM Symposium on Parallel Algorithms and Architectures, 2002, pp. 151-152.
7. Pousa C. V., Góes L. F. W., Martins C. A. P. S.: "Reconfigurable Object Consistency Model", 7th Advances in Parallel and Distributed Computational Models, 2005. (in Press)
8. Jiménez E., Fernández A., and Cholvi V., "A Parametrized Algorithm that Implements Sequential, Causal, and Cache Memory Consistency", Workshop on Parallel, Distributed and Network-based Processing, 2002, pp.437-444.
9. Raynal M., and Vidyasankar K., "A Distributed Implementation of Sequential Consistency with Multi-Object", 24th International Conference on Distributed Computing Systems, 2004, pp. 544-551.
10. Singh G., "Invariant Consistency: A Mechanism for Inter-Process Ordering in Distributed Shared Memory Systems", 22th International Conference on Distributed Computing Systems, 2002, pp. 447-450.
11. Góes L. F.W. and Martins C.A.P.S., "Reconfigurable Gang Scheduling Algorithm", 10th Workshop on Job Scheduling Strategies for Parallel Processing, LNCS, 2004.
12. Ramos L. E. S., Martins C. A. P. S., "Reconfigurable Collective Communication MPI Functions", High Performance Computational Systems, 2004. (in Portuguese)
13. Góes L. F., "Proposal and Development of a Reconfigurable Parallel Job Scheduling", M.Sc. Thesis Graduation Program in Electrical Engineering, Pontifical Catholic University of Minas Gerais, 2004. (in Portuguese)
14. Pousa C. V., Góes L. F. W., Penha D. O., Martins C. A. P. S.: "Reconfigurable Sequential Consistency Algorithm", in 12th Reconfigurable Architecture Workshop, 2005. (in Press)

15. Monnerat L. R. and Bianchini R., "Efficiently Adapting to Sharing Patterns in Software DSMs", Proceedings of the 4th IEEE International Symposium on High-Performance Computer Architecture, 1998.
16. Shah S.K. and Fleisch B.D., "A Comparison of DSM Coherence Protocols using Program Driven Simulations", Proc. Int'l Conf. Parallel and Distributed Processing Techniques and Applications, (PDPTA), Vol. 3, CSREA Press, 1998, pp. 1546-1553.
17. Wang D., Chen I. and Chu C., "Analyzing reconfigurable algorithms for managing replicated data with strict consistency requirements: a case study", 24th Annual International Computer Software and Applications Conference, 2000, pp.608 – 613.
18. Lamport L., "How to make a multiprocessor computer that correctly executes multiprocess programs", IEEE Trans. Comput.1979, pp. 28:690-691.
19. Pousa C. V., Ramos L. E. S., Goes L. F. W., Martins C. A. P. S.: "Extending ClusterSim with MP and DSM Modules", In International Symposium on High Performance Computational Science and Engineering, 2004.
20. Góes L. F. W., Ramos L. E. S., Martins C. A. P. S.: "ClusterSim: A Java Parallel Discrete Event Simulation Tool for Cluster Computing", IEEE International Conference on Cluster Computing, 2004.

ER-TCP: An Efficient Fault-Tolerance Scheme for TCP Connections[*]

Zhiyuan Shao, Hai Jin, Bin Cheng, and Wenbin Jiang

Cluster and Grid Computing Lab.,
School of Computer Science and Technology,
Huazhong University of Science and Technology, Wuhan, 430074, China
hjin@hust.edu.cn

Abstract. This paper proposes a novel scheme, called ER-TCP, which transparently masks the failures on the server nodes in a cluster from clients at TCP connection level. Connections at the server side are actively and fully replicated to remain consistency. A log mechanism is designed to cooperate with the replication to achieve small sacrifice on the performance of communication and makes the scheme scale beyond a few nodes, even when they have different processing capacities. The scheme is justified by experiments conducted on prototype implementation.

1 Introduction

As a reliable point-to-point transport level protocol, TCP has been gaining more and more users in the Internet nowadays. Years of enhancement and fine-tuning have made it very efficient and robust. However, it is difficult to tolerate the faults of the TCP connections and totally mask them from the users, since there are no widely adopted standards or specifications for that purpose.

Fault-tolerance of the TCP connections is turning increasingly important for many real applications. For example, many organizations and enterprises enhance their throughput by clusters, whose availability is usually guaranteed by using a front-end approach. The front-end approach employs software packages (e.g. LVS [7]) or industry solutions (e.g. Cisco LocalDirector [5]) as dispatchers to direct incoming TCP connections to the back-end real servers, and guarantees the service availability by avoiding new connections to the crashed nodes. However, it does not guarantee the connection availability, since the connections processed by the failed server will be simply lost. Therefore the front-end approach may expose clients to connection failures.

In order to solve this problem, many research works [1][3][8][10][11][13][15] have been conducted in past a few years. FT-TCP [1] uses a logger to record the on-going connections and reincarnates the connections of the crashed server by replaying the log on a new server. In this way, the connection sustains and failure could be masked from the clients. However this solution introduces another single point of failure (the logger). Furthermore, this fault-tolerance approach is time-costly.

To overcome the shortcomings of FT-TCP, ST-TCP [8], HARTS [10] and so forth adopt the primary-backup approach to fully replicate and synchronize the TCP con-

---

[*] This paper is supported by National 863 Hi-Tech R&D Project under grant No.2002AA1Z2102.

nections in the communication among the replicas. The primary-backup approach masks the failures of server nodes by failing the connections over healthy servers. However, the ST-TCP approach only tolerates single failure and requires identical processing speed of the replicas. HARTS and other schemes of this class usually result in high penalty on the performance of communication.

In this paper, we propose a novel scheme, named as ER-TCP, which combines primary-backup replication with logging mechanism to achieve fault-tolerance on the server side TCP connections. The scheme minimizes the performance penalty resulted by replication and makes itself scale beyond a few replicas so as to tolerate multiple failures. Moreover, ER-TCP works even when the replicas have different processing capacities.

The paper goes as follows. Section 2 presents the architecture of our scheme. Section 3 briefly surveys the related works. In Section 4, we explain how our scheme works during the failure free phase. Section 5 addresses the case of failures. Section 6 presents the results of experiments conducted on the prototype implementation. Section 7 concludes this paper.

2 Cluster Architecture for ER-TCP

For the convenience of discussion, we take the share-nothing cluster architecture shown in Fig. 1 as the hardware configuration. In this configuration, we consider only the TCP connections initiated from the clients to the cluster. As shown in Fig. 1, each server node connects to all the other server nodes of the cluster and the outside world by a switch or router. The *local area network* (LAN) used by the cluster supports IP multicasting as well as point-to-point communication.

Among the server nodes, there is a unique primary server, a unique logger server and multiple backup servers. Primary server possesses the portal IP address of the cluster. All the server nodes in the cluster have their own IP addresses (*IP1, IP2, ..., IPn*), which belong to a private subnet. Incoming request is relayed to all the backup server nodes by the primary, and connections running on the server nodes are fully replicated. To guarantee the reliability, the primary and logger server work together to log the incoming packets. In case of two server nodes in the cluster, no backup server exists.

In this paper, we assume the network is always available and consider only crash failures (fail-stop). If the primary server crashes on a fly, the logger server is promoted

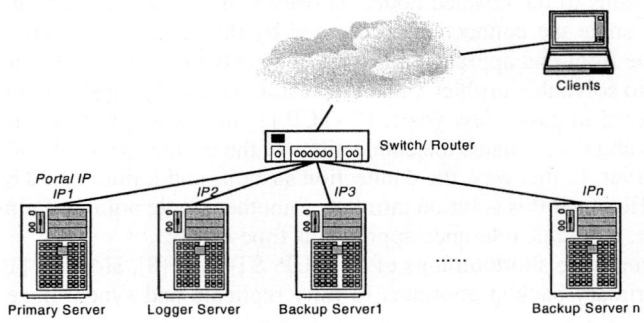

Fig. 1. Cluster Architecture for ER-TCP

as the new primary and one of the backup servers is chosen to be the new logger. The strategy of failure detection and failover will be discussed in Section 5.

To simplify and facilitate the discussion in this paper, some assumptions are made. First, we assume the primary and the logger server will not crash simultaneously. This is reasonable as the possibility for this is very small. We assume that the execution of the application is deterministic and all copies of the application have identical responses when processing the same request. We assume the application protocol is interactive. The client interacts with the server with sending requests and obtaining responses, and it must wait until obtaining the response of preceding request from the server before sending a new one. Most legacy applications and protocols, which follow the client/server model, adopt the interactive communication paradigm, e.g., the database applications, HTTP, POP and SMTP. We further assume the time consumed by the server to process a request is evenly distributed. As our scheme can adopt any external failure detectors, we assume the failure detector used in the scheme is perfect, i.e., satisfies strong accuracy and strong completeness properties [4].

3 Related Works

The objective of HydraNet-FT [11] is to provide fault tolerant services in a completely client-transparent fashion. To achieve this objective, HydraNet-FT proposed an infrastructure of dynamically duplicating services over inter-network by replicating TCP communications. In HydraNet-FT, traditional one-to-one paradigm of TCP is changed to be one-to-many from the client to the servers and many-to-one from the servers to the client. At this point, the solution of HydraNet-FT is very similar to ours. But there are two drawbacks in HydraNet-FT compared with our proposals. First, this scheme requires modifications of the applications at server side. That means it is necessary for HydraNet-FT to obtain the source code of the server applications. But this is infeasible in some cases. Second, HydraNet-FT uses a proxy-like redirector between the client and the servers to replicate the TCP connections. By this means, the redirector itself becomes a single point of failure.

ST-TCP [8] proposes an extension of TCP to tolerate TCP server failures. It uses an active backup server to keep track of the state of TCP connection and takes over the TCP connection whenever the primary fails. The migration of the TCP connection to the backup server is completely transparent to the client. The scheme proposed by ST-TCP is very close to ours. But it has to assume the backup server has the identical response to every incoming request as the primary, and the buffer of the primary needs further reliability guarantee. The scheme tolerates only single failure as it has only one backup.

Over the last decade, many reliable multicast protocols have been designed and studied, including MTP [2], RMF [14], SRM [6], RTP [9], and so froth. Most of these protocols target very large scale multicast applications, and brings out lots of challenging research topics. Some of these protocols are designed for certain applications. For example, SRM has been designed for large-scale white-board applications, and RTP for real-time data, such as audio and video, transportation in the Internet. Despite such tremendous efforts, there is still not a consensus on the standard deployable protocol for the common multicast applications, especially the medium scale ones.

4 Failure-Free Phase

In ER-TCP, there are multiple units keeping track of the status changing of the TCP connection at the server side during the failure-free phase. This requires our scheme to guarantee the reliability of message delivery among them. Fig.2 illustrates the communication paradigm adopted in ER-TCP.

Connection Management (CM) module of the primary server intercepts all incoming TCP packets from the client, and after legality check on connections, it relays them to all the backup servers. We use an IP multicast tunnel to improve the efficiency of relaying. The tunnel masks all the details about fragmentation and reassembling so that the backup servers feel like receiving packets from the clients directly.

In order to synchronize the communication among all the server nodes, conservative method that requires the primary gather all responses from the backup servers, such as in HARTS [10], can be used. However, this method decides the speed of communication by the slowest node within the cluster and thus knocks down the performance of communication by increasing the latency.

In ER-TCP, the primary server needs only to wait the corresponding responses from the logger server before it sends its responses back to the clients. The logger server needs to wait the responses from rest of the backup servers when the establishing and destroying a connection. For long connections, the logger server needs also to wait the responses from the backups at each predefined times of iteration (K times, and $K = 100$ in our implementation). That is, the primary and logger server are strictly synchronized at the communication, and all server nodes are re-synchronized only at the startup and termination or at each K times iterations of every connections. If no backup server exists in the system (i.e., there are only two server nodes), the logger server need no longer wait for the responses from the backups.

Compared with the conservative method, our scheme improves the speed of communications by two means. First, the primary server does not need to gather all responses from the rest server nodes, which alleviates the overhead at the primary. If the primary and logger server are carefully chosen, the slowest node of the cluster will no longer decide the speed of communication. Second, the backup servers do not need to send out their responses at all the iterations of the connection, which saves lots of time. This advantage even permits the group to harbor slower backups.

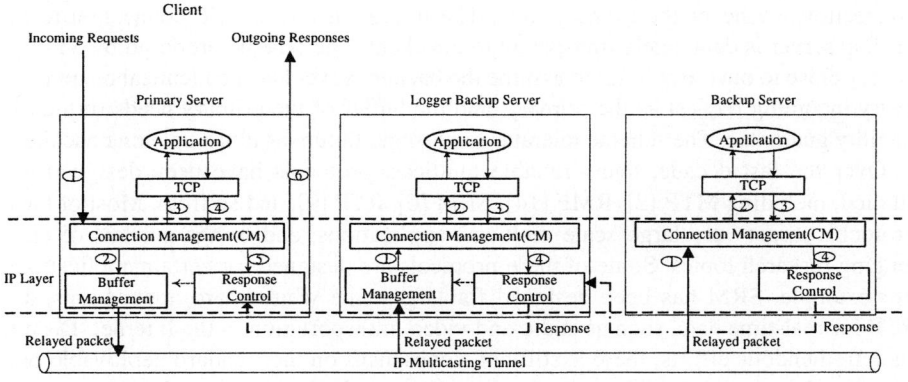

Fig. 2. Communication Paradigm of ER-TCP

However, the scheme raises a new problem to be solved. If a backup server is slower than the primary and logger server, after some times of iteration, it may lag behind and lose some requests. In this case, retransmission of the lost request messages is required. The logger server in our scheme is designed to handle these retransmissions. Buffer Management module of the logger server (see Fig.2) is designed to log the requests unconfirmed by the backups. These logged requests are duplicated in the primary to tolerate faults. Since we have all backup servers synchronized with the primary and logger server at K times of iterations at each connection, this means the length of buffer to log incoming requests is K for all connections. However, for the applications serving large audience, thousands of connections may be established at the same time, and great quantity of memory will be consumed for logging at the primary and logger server.

Actually, when the primary and logger server process the requests, the backup servers process the requests also. Therefore, logging all request messages is not necessary. The most ideal solution is to log only the request messages that will be required for retransmission by the backups. But without accurate knowledge about the request processing progress on the backups during the fly, the size of the logging buffer has to be predicted. The predicted size should be smaller than K to alleviate the load for logging and larger than the number of requests required for retransmission so as to make the scheme safe. In this paper, based on the evenly distributed request processing time assumption, we design a method to predict the logging size.

In order to explain the method, a quantity analysis on the communication is needed. Let T_{client} be the average time required for the client to process a response from the primary server. $T_{priamry}$ be the average time required for the primary to process a request, T_{logger} be that of the logger server, and T_{backup} be that of the slowest backup. Let T_{packet_send} be the average time required for the kernel to send a TCP/UDP packet, $T_{packet\_receive}$ be that for receiving, T_{tunnel_send} be that for the kernel to send an IP multicasting tunnel packet, $T_{tunnel\_receive}$ be that for receiving. For convenience, we ignore the time spent by a packet on the wire, as it is comparably small.

As we have assumed that the pattern of communication is interactive, the interval for which two requests arrive at the cluster ($Interval_{Arrive}$) should equal to the message *Round Trip Time* (RTT) between the client and the cluster. If we assume both the request and the response could be contained in single packet, the interval of request arriving can be expressed in the Equation 1:

$$Interval_{Arrive} \approx RRT_{client\text{-}cluster} \approx T_{client} + 2 \times (T_{packet\_send} + T_{packet\_receive}) + T_{tunnel\_send} \\ + MAX(T_{primary}, T_{tunnel\_receive} + T_{logger} + T_{packet\_send}) \quad (1)$$

For the backup servers, they receive requests via the IP multicast tunnel from the primary server. This means the rate of request arriving should be $1/Interval_{Arrive}$ at all backup servers. The server utilization rate of the slowest backup server can be expressed in Equation 2:

$$\rho_{utilization} = T_{backup}/Interval_{Arrive} \quad (2)$$

Increasing the utilization rate of the slowest backup server means it becomes busy and this may results in losing request messages. In this case, some request messages should be logged at the logger server for retransmission, and this requires the logger server to retain the queue of unprocessed requests that should originally be kept by the slowest backup itself. According to the queuing theory, the length of logging buffer (defined as L_{queue}) should be:

$$L_{queue} = \rho_{utilization}^2/(1-\rho_{utilization}) \qquad (3)$$

In order to guarantee the reliability, our scheme expands the logging buffer with a "margin of safety" M ($M = 10$ in our implementation). The length of logging buffer at the primary and logger server of our scheme, defined as L_{buffer}, can be expressed in Equation 4:

$$L_{buffer} = L_{queue} + M \qquad (4)$$

The upper bound of the buffer length for logging is K, so if L_{buffer} turns greater than K, it will be set to be K. According to the queuing theory, inequality 5 should be satisfied, if the system is called "stable". However, in ER-TCP, the server nodes get to be re-synchronized after a certain number of iterations, so the inequality results in only increment at the length of buffer needed at the logger server and the latency on communication.

$$T_{backup} < Interval_{Arrive} \qquad (5)$$

It is possible that the backup server undergoes a load surge during the fly, and loses more requests than that can be retransmitted from the primary or logger server. In this case, we have the backup server dropped from the group. The primary and the logger server get to know the process capabilities of all the nodes in the cluster via the heartbeat messages, which will be discussed in the next section.

5 Handling Failures

Our scheme adopts heartbeat as the failure detector. A thread built within the OS kernel of each server node periodically (interval = 1 second) multicasts a heartbeat message to the group. The heartbeat message also contains local information, i.e., node ID number and the processing speed, to differentiate each other and facilitate further decision-making (such as group management, predicting buffer size for logging and failover). If one of the server nodes cannot receive heartbeat message from another for a specific interval (failure detection interval), the latter is suspected to be dead by the former. The failure detection interval is set to be 4 seconds in our implementation.

Although the heartbeat failure detection cannot be proven as a perfect failure detector as we have assumed, it is practically feasible. Since we use kernel threads to multicast the heartbeat messages, this method can guarantee the emission of these heartbeat messages even the server node is busy. Furthermore, in LAN environment, the possibility of a message to be continuously dropped for 4 times is very small. As the processing capacities of server nodes are piggybacked in the heartbeat messages, at the startup of the system, the fastest two nodes of the group will be chosen as the primary and the logger server. The system administrator can also define the roles in advance.

The failures we consider in this paper include those of the primary, the logger, and the backup servers.

1. The Failure of Primary Server

If the primary crashes, a round of adjustment will be started among the remaining healthy nodes. The logger server will be promoted to be the new primary, and at the same time, the fastest backup server will win the election to be the new logger server. Portal IP address will be bound at the NIC of the new primary server, and serials of gratuitous ARP packets will be broadcasted to facilitate the IP takeover. After that, the entire logging buffer content will be copied from the new primary server to the new logger server. As we assume the primary and logger server will not crash simultaneously, the logged requests will not be lost. With the help of the retransmission mechanism of TCP, current requests of the clients arrive again at the new primary.

2. The Failure of Logger Server

If the logger server crashes, the primary server will appoint the remaining fastest backup server to be the new logger server. The entire buffer content will be copied from the primary server to the new logger server.

3. The Failure of Backup Server

It is also possible that some of the backup servers crash during the fly. After getting to know that, all the remaining healthy servers will proceed to get rid of all the related information of that crashed backup server within all the connections.

6 Performance Evaluation

We implement ER-TCP in a four-node cluster for evaluation. Section 6.1 will present and analyze the penalty on communication. In section 6.2, we will analyze the overhead put on the CPU of both the primary and the logger backup during the communications. In section 6.3, we will discuss the length of the logging buffer in different cases.

The server nodes of the cluster are PCs running Redhat Linux of kernel version 2.4.7-10, with hardware configuration of Intel Pentium III 1GHz CPU, 516MB Memory and 100Mbps 3COM 3c59x NICs. Client is a PC running Windows 2000 professional (service pack 4), with hardware configuration of Intel Celeron CPU running at 1.7 GHz, 516MB Memory and RTL8139A NIC. A 3COM 100Mbps switch is used to connect all these PCs.

6.1 Communication Penalty

In Fig. 3, we compare the performance of TCP connections by ER-TCP with that of standard TCP. The performance is evaluated by Netpipe-2.4 [12] with different number of replicas. The *round trip time* (RTT) between the client and the cluster is used to demonstrate the latency of communication.

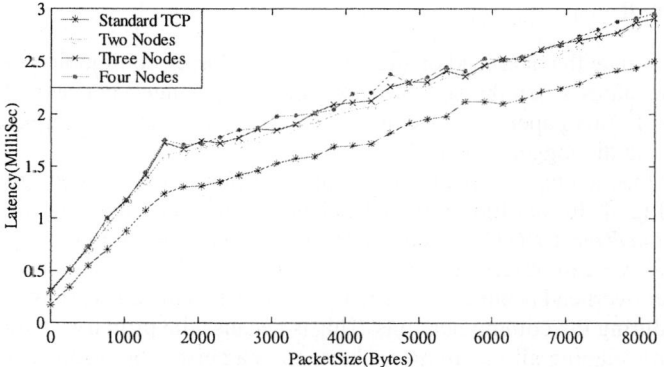

Fig. 3. Communication Performance

From Fig.3, we can see that when there are two server nodes in the cluster, the latency increases about 15% compared with that of standard TCP. The increment of latency is incurred by the time paid at sending message via IP Multicast tunnel and waiting for the responses from the logger server as discussed in Section 4.

When the number of server nodes increases, the latency turns higher than that when there are two servers. The increment is resulted for more time will be spent on re-synchronization all of the backup servers. But if we compare it with the latency when there are two servers, we can find that the increment is very small. This is because IP multicast tunnel is used to relay the incoming request message, and this greatly improves the efficiency of relaying. Moreover, the primary server of ER-TCP does not need to gather all responses from the backups to send the final version to the clients. This means that ER-TCP can scale beyond a few nodes without imposing very high penalty on communication.

Table 1 compares the announced performance penalties between ER-TCP and other schemes.

Table 1. A Comparision of the Announced Peroramnce Penalties between ER-TCP and Other TCP Fault-tolerance Schemes

Scheme	Design Choice	Announced Penalty
FT-TCP	Logging	28%-76%
HotSwap	Active Replication	54.3%
HydraNet-FT	Active Replication	50%-90%
HARTS	Active Replication	30%
ST-TCP	Active Replication	below 5%
ER-TCP	Active Replication + Logging	15%

From Table 1, we can see that ER-TCP achieves a small penalty on communication performance. Although ST-TCP even has smaller penalty, it can tolerate only single failure and requires the primary and the backup server have same processing capacities, which is difficult to be satisfied in the real world.

6.2 CPU Load

In order to evaluate the overhead on the server nodes during communication, we record the CPU load status when the size of packet being exchanged between client and the server varies. In this paper, we concentrate our discussion on the overhead of the primary server and the logger server.

The CPU load status of primary server under different cluster configurations is illustrated in Fig. 4. In this figure, the CPU load is calculated by using the formula of $1-IdleCPUTime/TotalCPUTime$, and this method is also used in Fig.5.

From Fig.4, we can observe that compared with that of single server node (standard TCP), heavier overhead is put on the primary server when the cluster has more than one server node during the communications. This is because the primary server of ER-TCP is in charge of relaying all incoming packets, and gathering the response packets from the logger server (synchronization), while the speed of communication is close to that of standard TCP (see Fig. 3). However, when the number of server nodes in the cluster

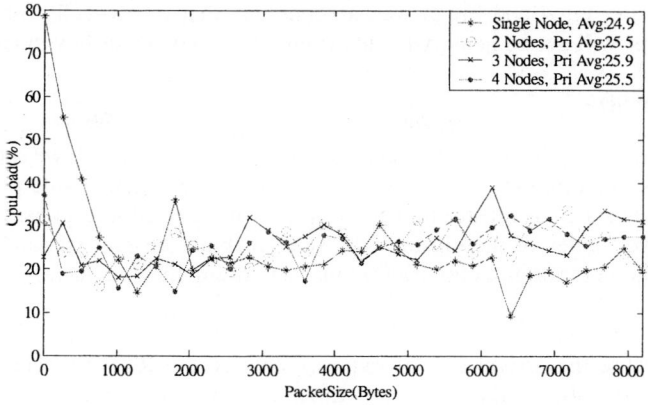

Fig. 4. CPU Load of Primary Server under Different Cluster Configurations

continues to increase, the overhead put on the primary server does not increase very much. This is because in ER-TCP, the primary server does not need to handle the responses from the backup servers.

The CPU load status of logger server under different cluster configuration is shown in Fig.5. From Fig.5, we can observe that in a 2-nodes cluster (primary plus logger server configuration), the logger server has even lighter overhead than the standard TCP during the communications. This is because in such a cluster, the speed of communication is slower than the standard TCP (see Fig.3), and thus consumes less CPU resources. However, when the number of backup server nodes in the cluster increases, the overhead on the logger server grows. This is because the logger server is in charge of gathering the response packets of these backup servers (synchronization) and handling the requests of retransmission. Nevertheless, the size of growth is small, which can be told from Fig.5.

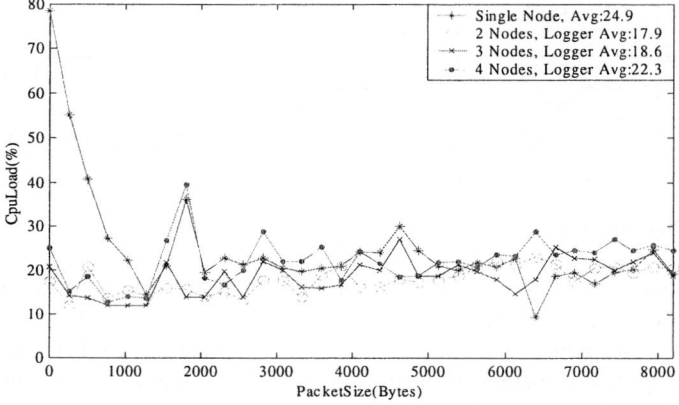

Fig. 5. CPU Load of Logger Server under Different Cluster Configurations

Considering Fig.4 and Fig.5, we can conclude that in ER-TCP, both primary and logger server will not be heavily loaded even the cluster scales beyond a few nodes.

6.3 Buffer Size

In order to evaluate the logging mechanism discussed in section 4, we set up a program, which works in a ping-pong model, for experiments. The client side program sends a request to the six-node cluster immediately after it received a response, and vice versa for the server nodes of the cluster. The sizes of both the requests and responses are 1KB, and the iteration lasts for 10000 times. By doing this, we have:

$$T_{client} \approx T_{primary} \approx T_{logger} \approx T_{backup} \approx 0 \qquad (6)$$

We measure the arrival rate of requests, that is, the RTT between client and the cluster as in Equality 1. By repeating 5 times we have the average:

$$Interval_{Arrive} \approx RTT_{client\_cluster} \approx 1.1438 \ (ms) \qquad (7)$$

After that, we increase the processing time required (T_{backup}) of the server side program at one of the backups by placing an artificial delay in each loop. In this way, the slowest backup server is imitated, and its server utilization rate could be calculated by using $T_{backup}/Interval_{Arrive}$. At different values of utilization rate, we compare the number of retransmitted requests in the experiments and the predicted value of Equation 4 in Table 2.

From Table 2, we find that the number of retransmitted requests in the experiments is always smaller than that of predicted by Equation 4. This means the strategy we use to save the buffer at the primary and logger server is safe, although it wastes some memory.

Table 2. Buffer Length under Different Backup Utilization Rate

T_{backup}	Utilization Rate	Retransmitted requests	Predicted Buffer Length
0.915	80%	2	3+10
1.023	90%	7	8 + 10
1.087	95%	12	18+10
1.121	98%	31	48+10
1.144	100%	39	100

7 Conclusions

In this paper, we propose a scheme, called ER-TCP, to tolerate failures happened at the TCP connections at the server nodes of cluster by having them fully replicated among the server nodes. The scheme can be implemented in the kernels of the server nodes so as to be transparent to legacy applications. To justify our design, we conduct experiments on the prototype implementation based on the ideas of the proposed scheme, and find that the scheme imposes small penalty on the performance of communication. Logging mechanism is designed in ER-TCP to synchronize slower server nodes and guarantee the reliability. The strategy plotted to save the buffer size for logging is proven to be safe by experiments.

References

1. L. Alvisi, T. C. Bressoud, A. El-Khashab, K. Marzullo, and D. Zagorodnov, "Wrapping Server-Side TCP to Mask Connection Failures", *Proceedings of IEEE INFOCOM*, Anchorage, Alaska, USA, 2001, pp.329-337.
2. S. Armstrong, A. Freier, and K. Marzullo, *Multicast Transport Protocol*, Internet RFC 1301, IETF, February 1992.
3. N. Burton-Krahn, "HotSwap - Transparent Server Failover for Linux", *Proceedings of USENIX Sixteenth Systems Administration Conference (LISA'02)*, Berkeley, California, November 2002, pp.205-212.
4. T. D. Chandra and S. Toueg, "Unreliable failure detectors for asynchronous systems", *Proceedings of the 10th ACM Symposium on Principles of Distributed Computing*, Montreal, Quebec, Canada, 1991, pp.325-340.
5. Cisco White Papers, http://www.cisco.com.
6. S. Floyd, V. Jacobson, C. Liu, S. McCanne, and L. Zhang, "A Reliable Multicast Framework for Lightweighted Sessions and Application Level Framing", *IEEE/ACM Transactions on Networking*, 1997, 5(6): 784-803.
7. Linux Virtual Server, http://linuxvirtualserver.org.
8. M. Marwah, S. Mishra, and C. Fetzer, "TCP Server Fault Tolerance Using Connection Migration to a Backup Server", *Proceedings of the 2003 IEEE International Conference on Dependable Systems and Networks (DSN'03)*, San Francisco, CA, 2003, pp.373-382.
9. H. Schulzrinne, S. Casner, R. Frederick, and V. Jacobson, *RTP: A Transport Protocol for Real-Time Applications*, Internet RFC 1889, 1996.
10. Z. Shao, H. Jin, B. Chen, J. Xu, and J. Yue, "HARTS: High Availability Cluster Architecture with Redundant TCP Stacks", *Proceedings of the International Performance Computing and Communication Conference (IPCCC'03)*, Phoenix, Arizona, USA, 2003, pp.255-262.
11. G. Shenoy, S. K. Satapati, and R. Bettati, "HydraNet-FT: Network Support for Dependable Services", *Proceedings of the 20th IEEE International Conference on Distributed Computing Systems (ICDCS 2000)*, Taipei, 2000, pp.699-706.
12. Q. O. Snell, A. Mikler, and J. L. Gustafson, "Netpipe: A Network Protocol Independent Performance Evaluator", *Proceedings of IASTED International Conference on Intelligent Information Management and Systems*, Washington, DC, USA, 1996, pp.196-204.
13. F. Sultan, K. Srinivasan, D. Iyer, and L. Iftode, "Migratory TCP: Connection migration for service continuity in the Internet", *Proceedings of the International Conference on Distributed Computing Systems (ICDCS'02)*, Vienna, Austria, 2002, pp.469-470.
14. Z. Whang, J. Crowcroft, C. Diot, and A. Ghosh, "Framework for Reliable Multicast Application Design", *Proceedings of High Performance Protocol Architecture (HIPPARCH)*, Uppsala, Sweden, 1997, pp.123-131.
15. R. Zhang, T. F. Abdelzaher, and J. A. Stankovic, "Efficient TCP connection failover in web server clusters", *Proceedings of the IEEE INFOCOM*, Hong Kong, China, 2004, pp.1220-1229.

Online Adaptive Fault-Tolerant Routing in 2D Torus

Yamin Li[1], Shietung Peng[1], and Wanming Chu[2]

[1] Hosei University, Tokyo 184-8584 Japan
yamin@k.hosei.ac.jp, speng@k.hosei.ac.jp
[2] University of Aizu, Aizu-Wakamatsu 965-8580 Japan
w-chu@u-aizu.ac.jp

Abstract. In this paper, we propose efficient routing algorithms for 2D torus with possible large number of faulty nodes. There is no presumption on the number and the distribution of faulty nodes. The proposed algorithms find a fault-free path between any two nonfaulty nodes with high probability in linear time by using only the local routing information of the network. The results of our empirical analysis through simulations show that the algorithms can find a fault-free path between any two nonfaulty nodes with high probability. For example, in a torus of size up to 128×128, where, the number of faulty nodes up to 15%, the heuristuc-square routing algorithm finds a fault-free path with a probability of 90% or higher. The experimental results are impressive for 2D torus with only four links per node.

1 Introduction

The two dimensional mesh/torus has constant node degree, recursive structure, simple communication algorithms, and good scalability. Due to these attractive properties, the mesh/torus has been the common interconnection network for several commercially available parallel computers, such as MPP (Goodyear Aerospace), Paragon (Intel), Victor (IBM), AP3000 (Fujitsu), and Toroidal Net (IRECE), Alpha 21364 [9].

A 2D mesh can be laid out on a VLSI chip in an area that increases linearly with the number of processors. Since the implementation of 2D mesh uses short, local links only, it is possible to perform communication at very high speed. A 2D torus has wraparound links. However, the method of folding can be used to lay out a 2D torus in such a way that it uses only short, local links too.

In this paper, we focus our designs on 2D torus. However, the ideas used in the proposed algorithms should be applicable to higher dimensional torus. The 2D torus has been and will continuously be a popular interconnection network for high-performance parallel computers due to its high bandwidth nearest neighbor connectivity for efficient computation and fast communication in many scientific applications.

Fault-tolerant routing is a dominant issue facing the design of interconnection networks for large-scale parallel computers [10]. There are many fault models used for designing fault-tolerant routing algorithms [1][2][3][6][7][8][11][12][13].

Some of these algorithms set conditions on the number of faulty nodes or the shape of faulty components. Others use global fault information (off-line) or partially global information. Chen et. al [4][5] introduced the concept of local-subcube connectivity for hypercubes. In this paper, we develop fault-tolerant routing algorithms on 2D torus using local information only (on-line), and allow arbitrary number of faulty nodes with no restriction on the shape of the faulty nodes (blocks). Our algorithms find a fault-free path between any two non-faulty nodes with high probability in linear time.

The rest of this paper is organized as follows: In the next section, we give necessary definitions used throughout the paper. We also show a theorem that is a theoretical ground of the proposed routing algorithms. In Sections 3, 4, and 5, respectively, three fault-tolerant routing algorithms are proposed on 2D torus with possible large number of faulty nodes. In Section 6, simulations are performed and the results are analyzed and discussed. Finally, in the last section, we conclude this paper with some remarks.

2 Locally-Safe Torus

A kD n-torus T_n^k has k dimensions, n nodes per dimension, and $N = n^k$ nodes. Each node is uniquely indexed by a radix-n k-tuple. Each node is connected via communication links to two other nodes in each dimension. The neighbors of node $s = (s_0, \ldots, s_{k-1})$ in dimension i are $(s_0, \ldots, s_{i-1}, s_i \pm 1, s_{i+1}, \ldots, s_{k-1})$, where addition and subtraction are performed modulo n. For simplicity, throughout this paper, all arithmetics on the indices of nodes in a given torus should be modulo n implicitly. The distance between two nodes s and t in T_n^k is $d(s,t) = \sum_{i=0}^{k-1} \min(|s_i - t_i|, n - |s_i - t_i|)$. In this paper, we work on 2D torus only. For simplicity, we use term T, instead of T_n^2, to denote a 2D n-torus if no confusion arises.

For a given node $s = (s_0, s_1)$ in T, we denote its two neighbors in dimension i by s^{i+} and s^{i-}, respectively. For example, $s^{0+} = (s_0 + 1, s_1)$ and $s^{0-} = (s_0 - 1, s_1)$. An m-square M_m^2, or simply M, in a 2D torus T is a subgraph of T, and M is a 2D mesh of width m (m nodes in each dimension). T is locally-m-safe if the following conditions are satisfied:

1. for every m-square M in T, the subgraph formed by all nonfaulty nodes in M is connected, and
2. every boundary line segment of an m-square in T contains at least one nonfaulty node.

If there exists an integer m, $2 \leq m \leq n$, such that T is locally-m-safe then we say that T is locally-safe. The following theorem shows that local-safety implies connectedness of T.

Theorem 1. *If a 2D torus T is locally-safe then T is a connected graph.*

Proof. Let $s = (s_0, s_1)$ and $t = (t_0, t_1)$ are two nonfaulty nodes in T. Without loss of generality, we assume that $s_i < t_i$ for $i = 0, 1$. We also assume that s^{i+}

and s^{i-} be the neighbors of s on dimension i such that s^{i+} is the neighbor of s closer to t, that is, $d(s^{i+}, t) = d(s,t) - 1$. Since T is locally-safe there exists an integer m, $2 \leq m \leq n$, such that T is locally-m-safe. Let $P = (s \to t)$ be the shortest path from s to t constructed by the dimension-order routing (routing along dimension 0, and then dimension 1). We construct an L-shape chain of width m that contains the path P as shown as in Figure 1.

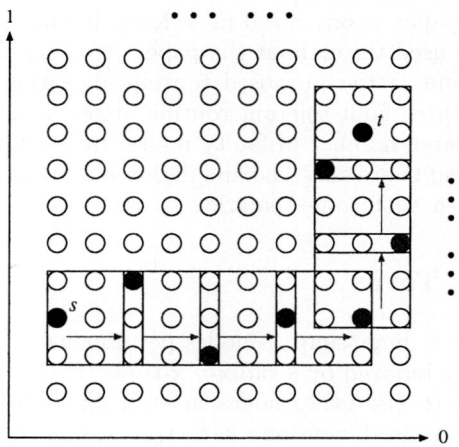

Fig. 1. Routing in chains

Let $P = P_0 \cup P_1$, where P_0 and P_1 are the line segments $s \to u$ and $u \to t$ along 0 and 1 dimensions, respectively, where $u = (u_0, u_1) = (t_0, s_1)$. The chain contains ch_0, and ch_1 defined as follows:

1. $ch_0 = \{v \in T \mid s_0 \leq v_0 \leq t_0,$ and $s_1 - \lfloor m/2 \rfloor \leq v_1 \leq s_1 + \lceil m/2 \rceil - 1$; and
2. $ch_1 = \{v \in T \mid u_1 - \lfloor m/2 \rfloor \leq v_1 \leq t_1$ and $u_0 - \lfloor m/2 \rfloor \leq v_0 \leq u_0 + \lceil m/2 \rceil - 1$.

Consider ch_0 as a sequence of m-squares $M_i, 0 \leq i \leq p$, where $p = \lceil (t_0 - s_0)/(m-1) \rceil$, such that

1. $L_i = M_{i-1} \cap M_i$, $1 \leq i \leq p$, are line segments of length $m - 1$ and $ch_0 \subset \cup_{i=0}^{p} M_i$;
2. $s \in M_0$ and $u \in M_p$.

Let $L_u = \{v \in ch_0 \mid v_0 = u_0\}$. Obviously, we have $L_u \subset M_p$. Since T is locally-m-safe, there exist nonfaulty nodes $v^i \in L_i$, $1 \leq i \leq p$, $u' \in L_u$, and fault-free paths: $(s \to v^1) \subset M_0, (v^1 \to v^2) \subset M_1, \ldots, (v^{p-1} \to v^p) \subset M_{p-1}, (v^p \to u') \subset M_p$. Then, the path $(s \to v^1 \to v^2 \ldots \to v^p \to u')$ is the fault-free path from s to u'. From the definition of ch_1, we have $u' \in ch_1$. By the similar argument, we can find a fault-free path in ch_1 from u' to t. Therefore, s and t can be connected through the fault-free path $s \to u' \to t$. We conclude that T is connected. ◇

The proof of the theorem is a constructive one. It provides the necessary background for our first fault-tolerant routing algorithm to be presented at next section.

3 Chain Routing Algorithm

For practice, we do not presume that T is locally-safe. The number of faulty nodes or its distribution is arbitrary. Our routing algorithms are local-information-based: no global information about the situation of the network is needed. If T is locally-m-safe then from theorem 1, the algorithm will generate a fault-free path Otherwise, it will either generate a fault-free path or report a failure.

The algorithm follows the constructive proof of theorem 1. A chain of meshes with width m that contains the shortest path P is used for the fault-tolerant

---

Algorithm 1 (Channel_Routing(T_n, m, s, t))
Input: 2D n-torus T_n, width of local mesh m, source node
  $s = (s_0, s_1)$, and destination node $t = (t_0, t_1)$
Output: a fault-free path $P = (s \to t)$ or report failure
begin
  $P = \phi$;
  $r = s$;
  $dir_0 = dir_1 = 1$;   /* determine routing direction */
  if $(0 \leq r_0 - t_0 \leq n/2)$ OR $(0 \leq t_0 - r_0 > n/2)$ $dir_0 = -1$;
  if $(0 \leq r_1 - t_1 \leq n/2)$ OR $(0 \leq t_1 - r_1 > n/2)$ $dir_1 = -1$;
  for $i = 0, 1$ **do**   /* for each dimension i */
    /* determine $mesh$ boundaries of i and j dimensions */
    $j = (i + 1) \bmod 2$;   /* dimension j */
    $b_j = (r_j - dir_j + n) \bmod n$;   /* $[b_j, B_j]$ in dimension j */
    $B_j = (r_j + (m-2) \times dir_j + n) \bmod n$;
    while $r_i \neq t_i$ **do**
      /* determine $mesh$ boundaries of i dimension */
      $b_i = r_i$;   /* $[b_i, B_i]$ in dimension i */
      $B_i = (r_i + (m-1) \times dir_i + n) \bmod n$;
      if t is in $mesh$
        if there is a fault-free path $P' = (r \to t)$ in $mesh$
          $P = P \cup P'$;
          return P;   /* path constructed */
        else return failure;   /* failed */
      else
        if there is a fault-free path $P' = (r \to r')$ in $mesh$
          such that $(r'_i = B_i)$ OR $(r'_i = t_i)$
          $P = P \cup P'$;
          $r = r'$;   /* continue */
        else return failure;   /* failed */
    endwhile
  endfor
end

routing. While routing from source s to destination t, the path is allowed to move inside the chain through a sequence of squares as specified in the proof of theorem 1. However, for routing with higher successful routing rate, we construct the ch_0 such that, for any $v \in ch_0$, $d(v_1, t_1) \leq d(s_1, t_1) + 1$. The ch_1 is constructed similarly. The details are specified in Algorithm 1. We call this algorithm Chain_Routing (see Algorithm 1). The rate of successful routing of the algorithm will be analyzed empirically and the simulation results will be used to compare with that of the other routing algorithms proposed in this paper.

In Algorithm 1, we route source node $s = (s_0, s_1)$ to destination node $t = (t_0, t_1)$ through an L-shape chain. The chain is divided into a sequence of m-squares. A square is uniquely determined with two nodes: b and B, as shown as in Figure 2.

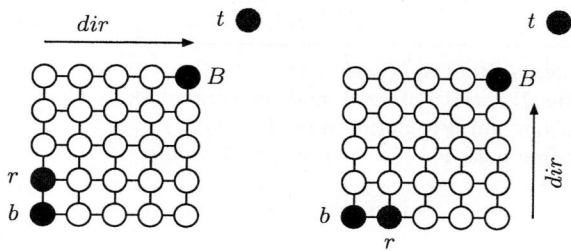

Fig. 2. Boundary of square ($m = 5$)

If routing in the first part of the chain succeeds, a node $r = (t_0, r_1)$ will be reached where r_1 is in the line segment bounded by b_0 and B_0. The path $(s \to r)$ may goes through many squares. To route in an m-square, we can use any search algorithm, depth-first search (DFS) or breadth-first search (BFS) algorithm for instance. If two parts of the chain are routed successfully, a fault-free path $(s \to t)$ is found. Whenever the routing in a square fails, the algorithm reports a failure and terminates. Assuming that the local routing inside a 2D m-mesh takes constant time, the algorithm runs in $O(n)$ time. We summarize these results into the following theorem.

Theorem 2. *The Chain_Routing algorithm will terminate in $O(n)$ time. When the algorithm terminates, it either generates a fault-free path from s to t or reports that the path cannot be found.*

4   Adaptive-Square Routing Algorithm

In this section, we describe another local-information-based, fault-tolerant routing algorithm, called Adaptive_Square Routing. The idea is as follows. Instead of arranging the sequence of m-squares as an L-shape chain, a sequence of squares is found recursively such that the routing direction of each square should be along the dimension i such that the distance $d(r_i, t_i)$ is a maximum, where r is the new source node after a local routing. Intuitively, the sequence of squares is arranged to contain a ladder-shaped shortest path that might have many turns, Each square will adapt itself such that the new source node r and the path segment along dimension i are inside the square (not at the boundary of the square).

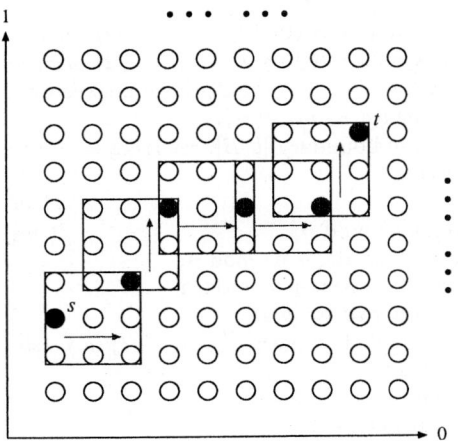

Fig. 3. Routing with Squares

To describe the algorithm, we need a notation to show the position of an m-mesh inside T. Referring to Figure 3, we associate each node r in T with a unique m-square M_r to be used by the algorithm. The M_r is determined by two nodes b and B, representing the lower-leftmost node b and an upper-rightmost node B of the two boundary lines along the routing direction.

More precisely, let i be the current routing direction, and dir_j be the unit direction ($+1$ or -1) of the shortest path along dimensions j. Then, we have $b_i = r_i$ and $b_j = r_j - dir_j$, $B_i = r_i - (m-1) \times dir_i$ and $B_j = r_j - (m-2) \times dir_j$ (all arithmetics are modulo n).

The proposed recursive algorithm is similar to that of the chain approach. The difference is that the square is adaptable in all dimensions instead of just in the dimension of the chain. Let $r = s$. The algorithm first determines the routing dimension i and the local m-square M_r, and then performs local routing in M_r that routes node r to a nonfaulty node r', a node located at the opposite boundary line of M_r from r along the ith dimension. If the local routing $r \rightarrow r'$ successes then we consider r' as a new source r and route from r recursively. If the local routing fails, the algorithm terminates unsuccessfully and reports a failure. The algorithm is formally specified as in Algorithm 2.

Algorithm 2 (Adaptive_Square_Routing(T_n, m, s, t))
Input: 2D n-torus T_n, width of local mesh $m \geq 3$, source node
$s = (s_0, s_1)$, and destination node $t = (t_0, t_1)$
Output: a fault-free path $P = (s \rightarrow t)$ or report failure
begin
    $P = \phi$;
    $r = s$;
    while $r \neq t$ **do**
        $dir_0 = dir_1 = 1$;   /* determine routing direction */
        if $(0 \leq r_0 - t_0 \leq n/2)$ OR $(0 \leq t_0 - r_0 > n/2)$ $dir_0 = -1$;
        if $(0 \leq r_1 - t_1 \leq n/2)$ OR $(0 \leq t_1 - r_1 > n/2)$ $dir_1 = -1$;
        Find the dimension i so that the distance between r_i and t_i
            $d(r_i, t_i) = \max(d(r_0, t_0), d(r_1, t_1))$;
        /* determine *mesh* boundary $[b, B]$, referring to Figure 3 */
        $j = (i + 1) \bmod 2$;   /* dimension j */
        $b_i = r_i$;   /* $[b_i, B_i]$ in dimension i */
        $b_j = (r_j - dir_j + n) \bmod n$;   /* $[b_j, B_j]$ in dimension j */
        $B_i = (r_i + (m - 1) \times dir_i + n) \bmod n$;
        $B_j = (r_j + (m - 2) \times dir_j + n) \bmod n$;
        if t is in *mesh* bounded by $[b, B]$
            if there is a fault-free path $P' = (r \rightarrow t)$ in *mesh*
                $P = P \cup P'$;
                return P;   /* path constructed */
            else return failure;   /* failed */
        else
            if there is a fault-free path $P' = (r \rightarrow r')$
                in *mesh* such that $(r'_i = B_i)$ OR $(r'_i = t_i)$
                $P = P \cup P'$;
                $r = r'$;   /* continue */
            else return failure;   /* failed */
    endwhile
end

Next, we show that the algorithm will terminate in $O(n)$ time, and either finds a fault-free path from s to t or reports a failure.

Theorem 3. *Adaptive_Square_Routing algorithm terminates in $O(n)$ time, and either outputs a fault-free path from source s to destination t or reports a failure.*

Proof. We first show that, for $m \geq 3$, the local routing always makes progress toward destination t. Since the box M_r for node r is constructed in the way that the farthest upper node B is toward to t. That is, $B = (r_i + (m-1) \times dir_i, r_j + (m-2) \times dir_j)$. The worst case is that r is routed to $r' = (r_i + (m-1) \times dir_i, r_j - dir_j)$. Since $d(r, t) - d(r', t) = (m - 1) - 1 = m - 2 > 0$ for $m \geq 3$, the local routing always makes progress toward t. Therefore, the algorithm will terminate after at most $O(n)$ local routings. For a fixed m, the running time of the local routing is a constant. Therefore, the total running time of the algorithm is $O(n)$. ◇

5 Heuristic-Square Routing Algorithm

In this section, we make an effort to improve the performance of Adaptive_Square_Routing algorithm by allowing the routing to continue when the local routing along the dimension of the longest distance, say i, fails. In the new algorithm, the routing continues by trying the local routings in the squares set along the other dimension when the distance between r and t along that dimension is nonzero. If the distance between r and t along the other dimension, say j, $d(r_j, t_j) < m - 1$ then the local routing will route r to r', where $d(r_j, r'_j) = d(r_j, t_j)$. Once the local routing along the dimension j successes, the square constructed for the new source should be arranged along dimension i again. The algorithm that adds this heuristic strategy to the Adaptive_Square Routing is called Heuristic_Square routing. In the next theorem, we show that Heuristic_Box routing works.

Theorem 4. *Heuristic_Square_Routing algorithm terminates in $O(n)$ time, and either outputs a fault-free path from s to t or reports a failure.*

Proof. In the new algorithm, we continue to route along dimension j when the local routing along dimension i fails. The local routing along dimension j might not make progress when $d(r_j, t_j) = 1$ and $d(r', t) = d(r, t)$. However, the next local routing will be along dimension i and make progress as shown in Theorem 3. Therefore, the number of local routing in the new algorithm is at most twice of that of the adaptive-square routing algorithm. For fixed m, the running time for the local routing is a constant. Therefore, the running time of the algorithm is $O(n)$. ◇

6 Simulation Results

We have performed a set of simulations on the performance of the proposed algorithms. For the experiments concerning the sizes of the 2D torus and the local squares used, we divide the values of the parameters n and m into two groups. In the first group, we set $n = 16$, 32 and $m = 3, 4, 5$, while in the second group, $n = 64$, 128 and $m = 6, 7, 8$. That is, the size of the m-square used for local routing is larger in the second group than that in the first group. In any case, the values of m is still small compared with the values of n. For the performance of each routing algorithm, two figures (one per group) are used to show the successful routing rate and/or improvement of the algorithm. For the fault model, we use uniform distribution of node failures. The number of faulty nodes generated range between 5% and 25% with a 5% increment. For each case, we simulate 10,000 times. The simulation results of the successful routing rate, improvement, and the length of the routing path for the set of parameters specified above are shown in the figures below.

Figure 4 and Figure 5 plot the successful routing rate of the simplest algorithm, Chain_Routing, where the two numbers in brackets in the figures are n and m, respectively. We can see that for a given n, increasing m improves the

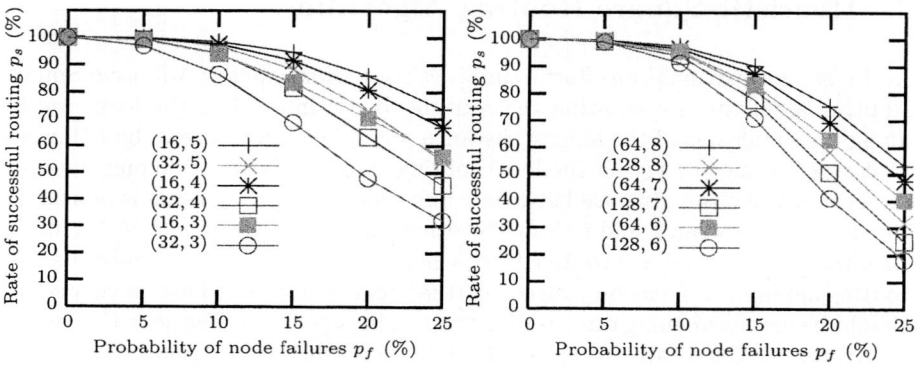

Fig. 4. Chain_Routing: Group #1   **Fig. 5.** Chain_Routing: Group #2

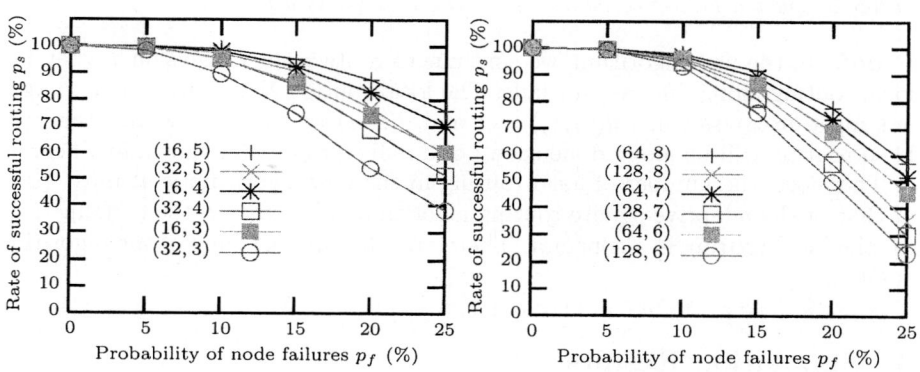

Fig. 6. Square_Routing: Group #1   **Fig. 7.** Square_Routing: Group #2

successful routing. On the other hand, for a given m, routing in a small torus has higher successful routing rate than that in a large torus.

Figure 6 and Figure 7 show the successful routing rate of the Adaptive_Square_Routing algorithm. Figure 8 and Figure 9 show the performance improvement of the adaptive-square algorithm compared to that of the chain algorithm. From the figures, we conclude that the adaptive-square approach is better than the chain approach in most of the cases.

The *improvement* in Figure 8 and Figure 9 is defined as

$$\frac{\text{Successful routing rate of adaptive-square algorithm}}{\text{Successful routing rate of chain algorithm}}$$

When n is small and m is large, $n = 16$ and $m = 4$ for instance, the adaptive-square algorithm is not much better than the chain algorithm. However, when m is smaller, especially as n increases, the improvement of the adaptive-square

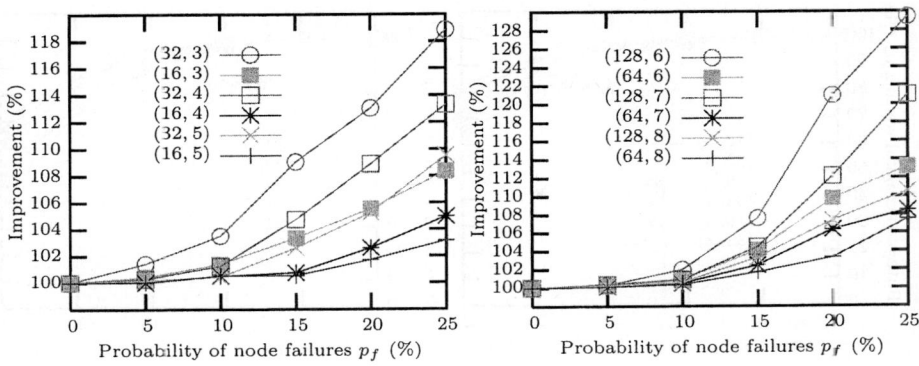

Fig. 8. Square vs Chain: Group #1

Fig. 9. Square vs Chain: Group #2

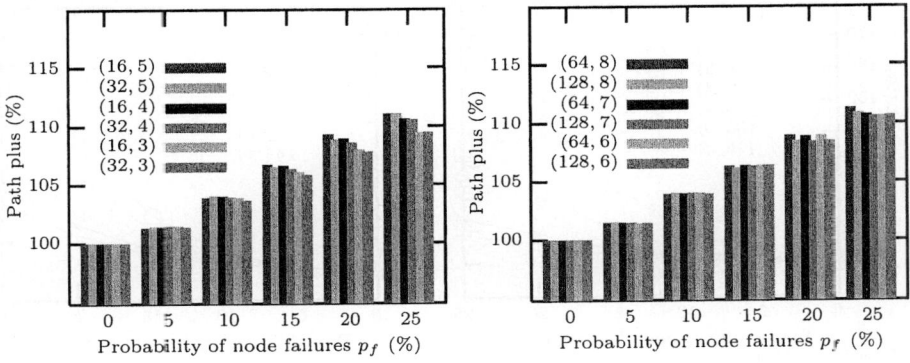

Fig. 10. Square_Routing: Group #1

Fig. 11. Square_Routing: Group #2

algorithm grows faster. As an example, when the number of faulty nodes is 25%, the improvement are about 1.2 and 1.3 for $n = 32$, $m = 3$ and $n = 128$, $m = 6$, respectively, in two groups. For fixed n, using a larger square will have a better performance with a cost of increasing time complexity at a rate proportional to m^2.

Figure 10 and Figure 11 display the path plus of the adaptive-square algorithm, which is calculated by

$$\text{Path plus} = \frac{\text{Path length of } P = (s \to t)}{\text{Distance between } s \text{ and } t}$$

Figure 12 and Figure 13 plot the successful routing rate of the heuristic-square routing algorithms. Figure 14 and Figure 15 depict the improvement of successful routing rate gained by using the heuristic-square routing algorithms to that of the adaptive-square algorithm. From the figures, we conclude that the

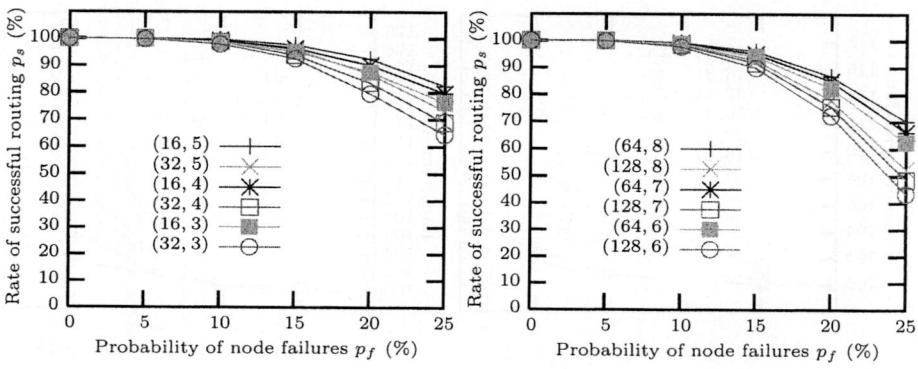

Fig. 12. Heuristic_Routing: Group #1   **Fig. 13.** Heuristic_Routing: Group #2

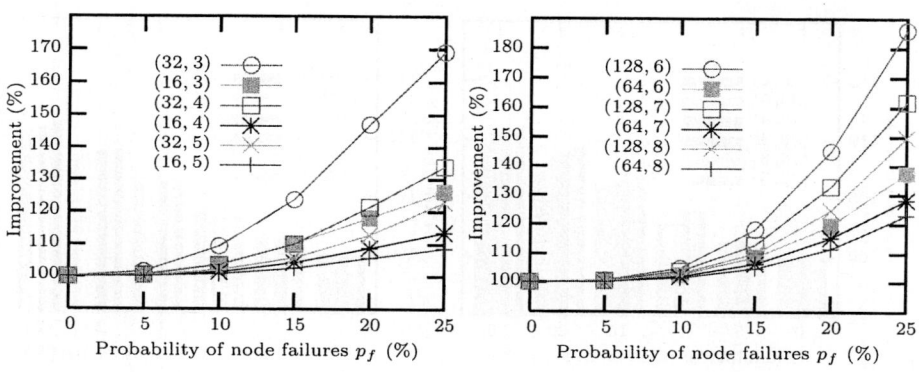

Fig. 14. Heuristic vs Square: Group #1   **Fig. 15.** Heuristic vs Square: Group #2

improvement of the heuristic-square routing over the adaptive-square is significant. For example, when the number of faulty nodes is 25%, the improvement are about 1.7 and 1.85 for $n = 32$, $m = 3$ and $n = 128$, $m = 6$, respectively, in two groups. It is worth to adopt the heuristic-square routing algorithm when the probability of faulty nodes is high.

7 Conclusions

In this paper, we first presented a concept of local-safety for a kD n-torus. Then, we proposed two different approaches for fault-tolerant routing in a 2D n-torus with possible large and arbitrarily faulty nodes. The algorithms are online (only local information is used) and efficient ($O(n)$ time assuming that the local routing is $O(1)$). The simulation results show that the rates of successful routing of the algorithms are quite high considering that there are only four links per node in a 2D torus. The possible directions of the further research include 1) Provide theoretical analysis on the performance of the proposed algorithms; and 2) Investigate the practical issues (e.g., deadlock-free) while implement the proposed routing algorithms on certain switching models.

References

1. L. D. Aronson. Homogeneous routing for homogeneous traffic patterns on meshes. *IEEE Transactions on Parallel and Distributed Systems*, 11(8):781–793, August 2000.
2. R. V. Boppana and S. Chalasani. Fault-tolerant wormhole routing algorithms for mesh networks. *IEEE Transactions on Computers*, 44(7):848–864, July 1995.
3. S. Chalasani and R. V. Boppana. Fault-tolerant wormhole routing in tori. *IEE Proc.: Computers and Digital Techniques*, 142(11):386–394, Nov 1995.
4. Jianer Chen, Guojun Wang, and Songqiao Chen. Routing in hypercube networks with a constant fraction of faulty nodes. *Journal of Interconnection Networks*, 2(3):283–294, September 2001.
5. Jianer Chen, Guojun Wang, and Songqiao Chen. Locally subcube-connected hypercube networks: Theoretical analysis and experimental results. *IEEE Transactions on Computers*, 51(5):530–540, May 2002.
6. Q-P Gu and S. Peng. Fault tolerant routing in toroidal networks. *IEICE Transactions on Information and Systems*, E-79D:1153–1159, August 1996.
7. Q-P Gu and S. Peng. Unicast in hypercubes with large number of faulty nodes. *IEEE Transactions on Parallel and Distributed Systems*, 10:964–975, October 1999.
8. Z. Jiang and J. Wu. Fault-tolerant broadcasting in 2D wormhole-routed meshes. *The Journal of Supercomputing*, 25(3):255–275, July 2003.
9. Shubhendu S. Mukherjee, Peter Bannon, Steven Lang, Aaron Spink, David Webb The Alpha 21364 Network Architecture *IEEE Micro* 22(1):26-35, January/February 2002.
10. V. Puente, J. A. Gregorio, F. Vallejo, and R. Beivide Immunet: a cheap and robust fault-tolerant packet routing mechanism *Proceedings of The 31st Annual International Symposium on Computer Architecture*, pages 198-209, June 2004.
11. M.-J. Tsai and S.-D. Wang. Adaptive and deadlock-free routing for irregular faulty patterns in mesh multicomputers. *IEEE Transactions on Parallel and Distributed Systems*, 11(1):50–63, January 2000.
12. J. Wu. Fault-tolerant adaptive and minimal routing in mesh-connected multicomputers using extended safety level. *IEEE Transactions on Parallel and Distributed Systems*, 11(2):149–159, February 2000.
13. D. Xiang. Fault-tolerant routing in hypercube multicomputers using local safety information. *IEEE Transactions on Parallel and Distributed Systems*, 12(9):942–951, September 2001.

Replicating Multithreaded Web Services

Xinfeng Ye and Yilin Shen

Department of Computer Science, Auckland University, New Zealand
{xinfeng, yshe026}@cs.auckland.ac.nz

Abstract. Replication is a widely used technique for providing high-availability and fault-tolerance of critical services. Multithreaded implementation of services presents a challenge to the replication technique, since managing the execution order of the threads on different replication sites for consistency purpose is not a trivial task. This paper presents a middleware that transparently support reliable web services built on active replication. The middleware is responsible for maintaining the consistency of the replicas' states. It also handles issues relating to multithreaded implementation of web services.

1 Introduction

Web services are self-contained, modular applications that can be located and invoked over the Internet [2]. As more and more applications are built on web services, providing reliable web services is becoming an important issue [4]. Replication is a widely used technique for providing high-availability and fault-tolerance of critical services. Multithreaded implementation of services presents a challenge to the replication technique. This is because the executions of threads are normally scheduled by the operating system or Java virtual machines. Thus, managing the execution order of the threads on different replication sites for consistency purpose without modifying the operating system or Java virtual machine is not a trivial task. This paper presents a middleware that transparently supports reliable web services built on active replication. The middleware is implemented in Java and does not require any change to operating system kernel.

The rest of the paper is organized as below. §2 presents the middleware. §3 shows the performance of the middleware. A conclusion is given in §4.

2 The System

Passive and active replication are commonly used replication techniques [1]. In active replication, services are replicated on several sites. A client sends its request to all replica sites, which all handle the request and send back the response to the client. Compared with passive replication, the advantage of active replication is its speedy recovery from failure. This is because, as long as the client receives one reply, the client can carry on with its task. The other advantage of active replication is that it provides the potential to balance the workload across the system. This is because some operations, e.g. retrieving a file, do not need to be carried out on all the replica sites. Thus, for this kind of operations, the client only needs to send its requests to a subset of all the sites in the system as long as there is a high probability that the client will get at least one response from the sites in the subset. Due to these advantages of the active replication, it is used in our system.

Sending a client's request to all replicas is equivalent to multicast the request to all replicas. Multiple clients might send requests to replicas simultaneously. To ensure that the replicas' states are consistent, a *total order* is needed when multicasting clients' requests to the replicas. Total order means all requests are delivered to the replicas in the same order even if the senders of the requests are different. The system in this paper uses the TOPBCAST multicast protocol [3]. The protocol ensures the total order of multicast messages. It also guarantees message delivery in the presence of message loss and site failure.

2.1 An Overview of the System Model

To provide reliable web services, the system uses the active replication technique. Services specified in a WSDL file are replicated at several sites. Each replica consists of two entities: a proxy web service site (PWSS) and a web service site (WSS). The WSS is a conventional web service provider. It hosts the code and data that provide the functionality of the web services. The PWSS is a middleware between clients and the WSS. It is responsible for ensuring the consistency and coping with failures of its corresponding WSS. Clients interact with the PWSSs. A client only needs to send its service requests to one PWSS. The PWSSs are responsible for multicasting clients' requests to other replicas and returning results to the clients. To maintain the consistency of the WSSs' states, the PWSSs must ensure that all clients' requests are executed on the WSSs in the same order. The replicas form a group, called *service group*. Fig. 1 shows a conceptual diagram of the system.

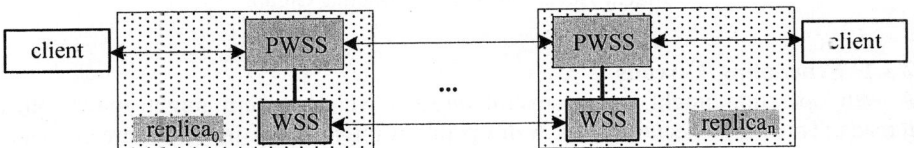

Fig. 1. A Middleware for Replicated Web Services

The system provides a Java package, *RWS*, which includes classes for handling the interactions between a client and a PWSS. Programmers can use the package when writing client applications. With these classes, the client views a service group as a single web service site. When a client sends a service request, say m, m is sent to a PWSS. The PWSS multicasts m to all the other PWSSs using the TOPBCAST protocol. As a result, m can be executed on all replicas. Since the TOPBCAST protocol ensures total order of all clients' requests, the PWSSs forward m to their corresponding WSSs in the order determined by the protocol. The WSSs return the responses to m to their corresponding PWSSs. If a PWSS receives m from a client directly, the PWSS sends the response to the client. If m does not come from a client directly (i.e. m is received from another PWSS in a multicast), the PWSS stores the response in its buffer in case the response needs to be sent to the client in the presence of a system failure.

2.2 Controlling Multithreaded Web Services

A multithreaded web service implementation means, when a web operation is called, multiple threads are created to carry out the task implemented by the web operation. When multithreading is used to implement web services, in order to ensure the consistency of the replicas' states, the replicas need to agree on the execution order of some of the threads. For example, assume that a web service is replicated on two sites S_1 and S_2. During the execution of a web operation, two threads, say T_1 and T_2, are created on both S_1 and S_2. If T_1 and T_2 modify shared data items, S_1 and S_2 should ensure that T_1 and T_2 are executed in the same order on both sites. Otherwise, the states of S_1 and S_2 might become inconsistent.

Instead of modifying the OS kernel or Java virtual machine, a scheduler is developed to control the execution of the threads. The scheduler resides on each WSS. Before a thread starts its execution, it registers with the scheduler asking the scheduler schedule its execution. The schedulers on the WSSs use a timestamp-based algorithm to reach an agreement on the order in which the threads should be executed. Once an agreement is reached, the schedulers instruct the threads execute in the agreed order.

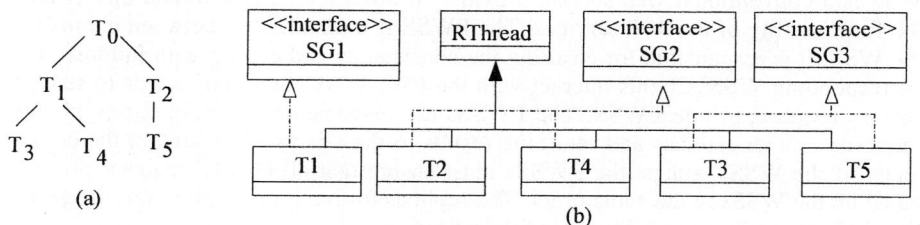

Fig. 2. Thread Trees and Scheduling Groups

2.2.1 Scheduling Threads

A web operation might create several threads, which in turn might spawn other threads. Thus, the execution of a web operation might result in many threads being created. Fig. 2(a) shows a thread tree. Each node represents a thread. The child node in the tree represents a thread created by its parent node. The executions of a set of threads only need to be ordered if the threads share data. Thus, threads are divided into several scheduling groups. Threads in one scheduling group all share the same set of data items. One thread can only belong to one scheduling group. Threads in the same scheduling group must be executed in the same order on all sites. Threads from different scheduling groups can be executed in any order.

When a thread registers with a scheduler, the scheduler needs to find out which scheduling group the thread belongs. To enable the scheduler to discover a thread's scheduling group, programmers are required to (a) define Java interfaces representing scheduling groups (these interfaces are called *scheduling interfaces*), and, (b) make the thread in a scheduling group implement the corresponding scheduling interface. For example, in Fig. 2(a), assume that there are three scheduling groups SG_1, SG_2 and SG_3. The three groups are represented by interfaces *SG1*, *SG2* and *SG3* respectively. T_1 belongs to SG_1. T_2 and T_4 are in SG_2. SG_3 consists of T_3 and T_5. The hierarchy of the classes representing the five threads is shown in Fig. 2(b). When a thread registers with a scheduler, the scheduler uses Java reflection API to discover which scheduling group the thread belongs to and schedules the thread accordingly. To facilitate the scheduler to identify the scheduling interfaces, the names of the scheduling interfaces must have prefix *SG*.

When a thread, say *T*, registers with a scheduler on a WSS, the scheduler assigns a *local timestamp*, which is greater than the timestamps of all the threads already known by the scheduler, to the thread. On the other WSSs, the threads that correspond to *T* are also given local timestamps by the schedulers on those WSSs. The schedulers exchange the local timestamps of *T* and *T*'s counterparts. The largest local timestamps are chosen as the *global timestamp* for the threads. Thus, the global timestamps of *T* and *T*'s counterparts are the same on all WSSs. Global timestamps are used to determine the execution order of the threads. That is, a thread with a smaller timestamp is executed before a thread with a larger timestamp. It can be seen that, if the WSSs execute the threads in their global timestamps order, the threads are executed in the same order on all WSSs.

We provide a package *MWS* which includes classes for programmers to use when they write multithreaded web services. In order to distinguish the threads in the system, each thread must be given a unique name. Class *RTName* in package *MWS* allows the programmers specify the root's name of a thread tree. Class *RThread* in package *MWS* includes code that assigns a name to a thread when the thread is created. When programmers write thread applications, the classes defining threads should extend *RThread*. With *RThread* class, assigning names to threads are carried out mostly transparently to the programmers. Thus, the programmers do not need to track the forming of the thread trees. The following code snippet shows the main steps in writing a thread class, say T1 in Fig. 2(b), which interacts with the scheduler.

```
1.   interface SG1 {}
2.   class T1 extends RThread implements SG1 {
3.       public void run() {
4.           Scheduler.start(currentThread());
5.           // code implementing the thread's logic
6.           Scheduler.terminate(currentThread());
         }
7.       // other code for T1
     }
```

Interface *SG1* (line 1) is used to mark a scheduling group. Since it does not do any work itself, its body is empty. *T1* is in scheduling group *SG1*. Thus, *T1* needs to implement *SG1* (line 2). All threads should extend *RThread* for naming purpose (line 2). *Scheduler* is a static class in package *MWS* (line 4). When a thread is started, the programmer should register the thread with the scheduler by calling the *start* method of the *Scheduler* class (line 4). One scheduler runs on each MSS. The *start* method of *Scheduler* creates an instance of the scheduler on the WSS if no such instance exists. Otherwise, the method simply registers the thread with the scheduler. After calling the *start* method, the thread waits for the scheduler's response. When the scheduler decides that it is the thread's turn to run, the scheduler returns the thread's call to the *start* method. As a result, the thread can carry on executing the thread's logic (line 5).

At the end of the execution, the thread notifies the scheduler by the *terminate* method of class *Scheduler* (line 6). As a result, the scheduler removes the thread from its queue. Calling the *start* and *terminate* methods are the only two statements that a programmer needs to add to the thread's logic. Hence, very little extra efforts are required from the programmers when writing thread classes used in web operations.

3 Performance

Performance tests are carried out to measure the overheads of the PWSS and the thread scheduler when the service group is deployed over a LAN. The TOPBCAST implementation assumes that message lost rate is 5%, site failure rate is 1%, and, a site sends its gossiping messages to three other sites in each gossiping round. With these assumptions, using a Markov chain, it is calculated that, for a group consisting of up to 45 sites, once a message is sent, there is a high probability (over 99%) that the message is received by all its destinations after two rounds of gossiping about the message. Thus, in the experiment, a message's delivery order is decided after two rounds of gossiping about the message when running the TOPBCAST protocol.

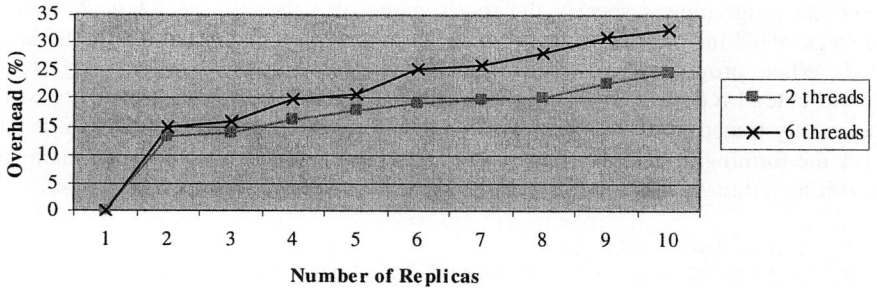

Fig. 3. Overheads of the Middleware

Java SDK 1.4.2 is used in our implementation. The PWSS also uses JAXM 1.2 while Java WSDP 1.3 is needed to implement the WSS. Tomcat 5.0 is used to host PWSSs and WSSs. In the experiment, it is configured that (a) each PWSS and its corresponding WSS reside on different machines, (b) all machines are connected by a 100Mbps Ethernet, and, (c) each machine is a Compaq Evo W4000 with one 1.8GHz P4 CPU. Overhead is defined as $(t_n - t_1)/t_1$ where t_n is the service response time when the service group has n replicas and t_1 is the service response time when no replication is used.

The experiment assumes that the web operation runs for 4000ms when (a) there is a single site in the service group and (b) a single thread carries out the operation. Two sets of tests are carried out. In the first set of tests, two threads are used to implement the web operation where each thread lasts 2000ms. In the second set of tests, six threads are used to implement the web operation where each thread runs for about 666ms. In each set of tests, we vary the number of replicas in the service group from 1 to 10. Since there is only one CPU on each WSS, increasing the number of threads for executing a web operation will only increase the execution time of the operation due to thread scheduling cost. From Fig. 3, for both tests, the overhead appears to be "moderate" when there are up to five replicas in a service group. The overhead of the system can reach about 33% in the worst case when there are ten replica sites and the operation consists of six threads. The experiment appears to show that the middleware can be used efficiently in systems in which the number of replicas in a service group and the number of threads used to implement the web operations are kept at a reasonable level.

4 Conclusion

The middleware discussed in this paper supports reliable web services based on active replication. The middleware ensures the consistency of the replicas. Unlike many existing work, the middleware also addresses issues relating to multithreaded web services. For multithreaded web services implementation, programmers are required to follow some programming conventions when coding web services. This allows the middleware determine which threads' executions need to be ordered and ensure that these threads are executed in the same order on all replicas. Empirical data show that, for services that require relatively long running time, the overhead of the middleware is reasonably low.

References

1. Felber P., Schiper A., Optimistic active replication, Proc. Of 21st International Conference on Distributed Computing Systems, pp333 – 341, 2001
2. Gardner T., An Introduction to Web Services, Ariadne Issue 29, 2001
3. Hayden M.G., Birman K. P., Probabilistic Broadcast, Tech. Rep. TR96-1606. Dept of Computer Science, Cornell University, 1996
4. Tartanoglu F., Issarny V., Romanovsky A., and Levy N., Dependability in the Web Services Architecture, Proc. of Workshop on Architecting Dependable Systems, 2002

Design Schemes and Performance Analysis of Dynamic Rerouting Interconnection Networks for Tolerating Faults and Preventing Collisions*

Ching-Wen Chen[1],**, Chang-Jung Ku[2], and Chih-Hung Chang[2]

[1] Department of Information Engineering and Computer Science,
Feng Chia University, Taichung City, Taiwan 40724, ROC
Tel: +886-4-24517250 Ext. 3729 Fax: +886-4-24516101
chingwen@fcu.edu.tw

[2] Department of Computer Science and Information Engineering,
Chaoyang University of Technology,
Wufong, Taichung County, Taiwan 413, ROC
{s9327608, s9227610}@csie.cyut.edu.tw

Abstract. In fault-tolerant multistage interconnection design, the method of providing disjoint paths can tolerate faults, but it is complicated and hard to choose a collision-free path in disjoint paths networks. A disjoint paths network can concurrently send more identical packets from the source node to increase the arrival ratio, but the method might increase the collision ratio. In contrast, a dynamic rerouting method finds an alternative path that tolerates faults or prevents collisions. In this paper, we present methods of designing dynamic rerouting networks. This paper presents 1) three kinds of dynamic rerouting networks designed to tolerate faults and prevent collisions; 2) design schemes that enable a dynamic rerouting network to use destination tag routing to save hardware cost in switches for computing rerouting tags; and 3) simulation results of related dynamic rerouting networks to realize the factors which influence the arrival ratio including the fault tolerant capability and the number of rerouting hops. According to our proposed design schemes and according to our analysis and simulation results, a designer can choose an applicable dynamic rerouting network by using cost-efficient considerations.

Keywords: Parallel computing, multistage interconnection network (MIN), dynamic rerouting, fault tolerance, collision, performance, destination tag routing.

1 Introduction

Interconnection networks are critical to parallel systems because their performance has great impact on system latency and throughput. Multistage inter-

---

* This work was supported partially by the National Science Council, Taiwan (NSC-92-2213-E-324-006-).
** Corresponding Author.

connection networks (MINs) are considered cost-effective ways of providing high-bandwidth communication in multiprocessor systems [1].

To enhance the reliability of MINs, many researchers have investigated fault tolerance issues [2-8]. Previous works provided disjoint paths [3-5] and used dynamic rerouting [6-8] enable MINs to have fault tolerance capability. The method of providing multiple disjoint paths which used to tolerate faults are used in two ways: 1) to know in advance the location of a faulty element before a packet is sent; therefore, one fault-free path can be taken to deliver message packets; and 2) to send multiple identical packets simultaneously from the source to the destination to tolerate faulty elements. However, the first method, which chooses one fault-free path, cannot know in advance whether a collision will occur during routing and the second method, which sends multiple packets simultaneously, causes a high collision ratio.

The dynamic rerouting method provides alternative paths to a destination when a packet encounters a faulty or busy element. Thus, this method does not need to know the locations of faulty elements before a packet is sent. In previous works, many 3x3 or more complicated switches are provided to construct dynamic rerouting networks [6-8]. For example, the Gamma network [6] uses 3x3 crossbar switches at the middle stages to provide multiple paths, but they can not reroute packets when the packets encounter a faulty or busy element in a straight link; that is, they cannot not guarantee one fault tolerance and cannot prevent collisions in the straight link. The B-network [7] uses a backward link to the switch at the previous stage for rerouting, but the B-network cannot guarantee one fault-tolerance, and it takes two rerouting hops at least. Although the Enhanced IADM [8] can guarantee one fault tolerance, it uses 5x5 crossbar switches at the middle stages to achieve zero rerouting hops. In addition, in the Enhanced IADM, the method of computing the rerouting tag and rerouting control in the switches at the middle stages require more hardware cost. There are some networks that add some extra stages to provide fault tolerance capability or prevent collisions, but the packets traverse more links to the destination regardless of whether the packets encounter a faulty or busy element. Thus, the collision ratio increases in such a design.

In this paper, we address these important issues and propose methods of designing dynamic rerouting networks. In particular, we propose three kinds of dynamic rerouting networks designed to tolerate faults and prevent collisions. In addition, we aslo propose the design schemes of destination tag routing networks to save hardware cost in the switches for computing the rerouting tag. Simulation results are presented of related dynamic rerouting networks to realize the factors that influence the arrival ratio including the fault tolerant capability and the number of rerouting hops.

The rest of this paper is organized as follows. In Section 2, we introduce routing methods which use pre-computing tags in the ICube network that is equivalent to the most important multistage networks and in other cube-like networks. In Section 3, we present the schemes used to design dynamic rerouting networks based on the researchable set concept and propose three kinds of dynamic rerouting networks. In addition, we also introduce how to design a destination tag routing function for easy rerouting. In Section 4, we simulate our three proposed dynamic rerouting networks and other previous dynamic rerouting networks and compare their arrival ratio under one-fault and fault-free situations. Section 5 concludes this work.

2 Preliminaries

In this section, we present the method of pre-computing routing tags in the indirect binary n-cube network (ICube network) [9] and in other cube-like networks. We also introduce the rerouting conditions that exist at a switch when a packet encounters a faulty element or when a packet is involved in a collision. In Section 2.1, we present the topology and the routing method of the ICube network. In Section 2.2, we show the distance tag routing method in other cube-like network.

2.1 Indirect Binary n-Cube Network (ICube Network)

An ICube network of size $N=2^n$ consists of $n+1$ stages labeled from 0 to n. Each stage involves N switches [9]. Switches of sizes 1x2 and 2x1 are coupled with the first and last stages, respectively. Moreover, each switch located at the intermediate stages is a 2x2 crossbar. Switch $j = j_{n-1}j_{n-2}\cdots j_2j_1j_0$, at stage i has two output links connected with two switches at stage $(i+1)$ based on the plus or minus 2^i function; that is, the non-straight link of switch j at stage i connects the switch $[(j - 2^i) \mod N]$ at stage $i+1$ if j_i is 1. Otherwise, the output non-straight link of switch j at stage i connects the switch $[(j + 2^i) \mod N]$ at stage $i+1$.

With regard to the routing behavior, if switch j $(= j_{n-1}j_{n-2}\cdots j_2j_1j_0)$ at stage i delivers a packet to the non-straight link and the $(n-i)$-th bit of switch j, j_i, is 1/0, the $(n-i)$-th bit of the switch that the packet is delivered to at the next stage is 0/1. Accordingly, we can pre-compute the routing tag, $D=d_{n-1}d_{n-2}\ldots d_2d_1d_0$, by an XOR operation of the source and the destination tags. Thus, the routing tag can be used to deliver packets from the source to the destination in such a way that the straight/non-straight link at stage i is taken if d_i is 0/1. Example 1 show the routing situation when the source is 1 (=001), the destination is 6 (=110) and the routing tag is 111 (001 XOR 110).

Example 1. In an ICube network of size $N=8$, the source is 1, and the destination is 6. The routing tag is 111 generated by an XOR operation of the source and the destination tags. The routing condition is shown in Figure 1(a) and is described as follows: *0(stage 1)→1(stage 0)→2(stage 2)→6(stage3)*

2.2 Distance Tag Routing in Cube-Like Networks

A cube-like network with distance tag routing of size $N=2^n$ consists of $n+1$ stages labeled from 0 to n. Each stage involves N switches. Switches of sizes 1x2 and 2x1 are coupled with the first stage and the last stage, respectively.

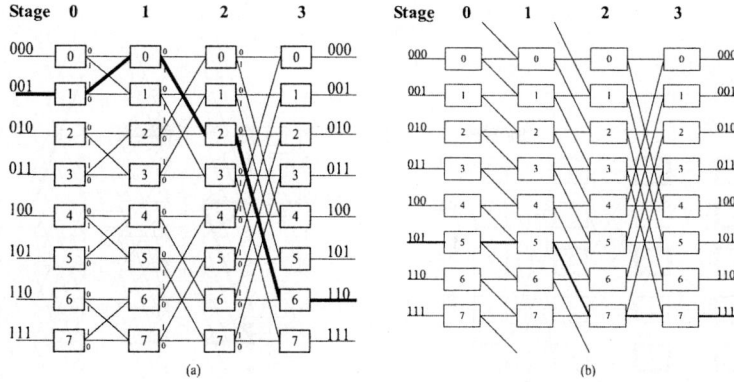

Fig. 1. (a) An ICube network of size $N=8$ and the routing condition when the source is 1 and the destination is 6. (b) A cube-like network of size $N=8$ and the routing condition when the source is 5 and the destination is 7.

Moreover, each switch located at intermediate stages is a 2x2 crossbar. Switch number j at stage i has two output links connected with switches at stage $(i+1)$ based on the plus-2^i function; that is, switch j at stage i has two output links to switches j and $[(j+2^i) \bmod N]$ at the consecutive stage.

With regard to the distance tag routing in such a network, an n-digit tag determines the path connecting the source S with the destination T where each tag digit can be 1 or 0. An n-digit tag $D = d_{n-1}d_{n-2}\ldots d_2 d_1 d_0$ represents the difference between T and S, i.e., $D = T - S$ (if D is less than 0, then D is equal to D plus N). Digit d_i of the routing tag D is used at stage i in such a way that the non-straight connection is taken if d_i is equal to 1, and the straight connection is selected when d_i is 0. For example, when N is 8, the source node S is 5, the destination node T is 7, and the routing tag D is 010, as shown in Figure 1(b).

3 Dynamic Rerouting Networks and Destination Tag Routing Designs

In this section, we present the dynamic rerouting network design scheme based on the concept of the researchable set presented in Section 3.1. Section 3.2 describes a method of designing a destination tag routing network.

3.1 Dynamic Rerouting Network Design Scheme

In Section 2, we introduced the routing methods that pre-compute a routing tag in a cube-like network. In cube-like multistage interconnection networks, the routing behavior at a switch at stage i eliminates the 2^i vertical distance to approach the destination if the routing bit d_i is 1; that is, once a packet is

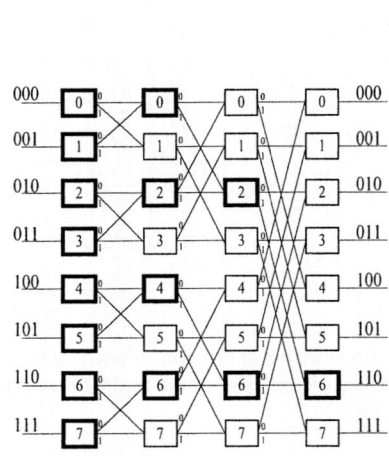 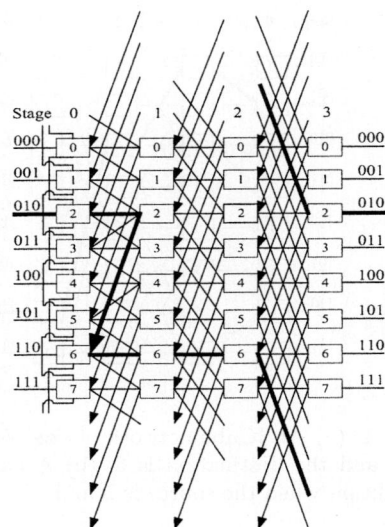

Fig. 2. The switches in the reachable set S_6

Fig. 3. Topology of our first kind of proposed dynamic rerouting network, with size $N=8$

delivered from stage i to stage $i+1$, the last $(i+1)$-th bit of the switch index at stage $i+1$ is the same as the last $(i+1)$-th bit of the destination. As a result, after n ($=\log_2 N$) routing hops, a packet can arrive at a destination from any source. In other words, in a cube-like network, if a packet is at switch j at stage i from some source node, the last i bits of the switch index j are the same as the last i bits of the destination tag.

According to the routing behavior, we can easily find the reachable switches for some specific destination. In Definition 1, we define the reachable set to include the switches that can deliver packets to a specific destination.

Definition 1. The switches at stage i whose last i bits of the index are the same as the last i bits of the destination T $(=t_{n-1}t_{n-2}\ldots t_2 t_1 t_0)$ are called reachable switches at stage i for a destination T. A reachable set for a destination T $(=t_{n-1}t_{n-2}\ldots t_2 t_1 t_0)$, denoted S_T, means all reachable switches at all stages.

In Figure 2, the reachable set S_6 for destination node 6 is shown. In Theorem 1, we prove that any switch in the reachable set S_T can deliver a packet to the destination T.

Theorem 1. The switch at stage i belonging to S_T can deliver a packet to the destination T.

Proof. We assume that a packet is delivered from some source and reaches switch j at stage i. Switch j that belongs to the reachable set S_T. By Definition 1, the last i bits of the switch index j are the same as the last i bits of the destination T, because the switch at stage i can deliver a packet to the switch at stage $i+1$, whose last $(i+1)$-th bit is the same as the last $(i+1)$-th bit of the destination T. Thus, after routing $(n - i)$ hops from stage i, the packet can arrive at the destination T.

From Theorem 1, all the switches in the reachable set S_T can deliver packets to the destination T if the packet does not encounter a faulty or busy element. As a result, if a faulty element exists or a collision occurs, the switch can easily reroute a packet to the switches belonging to the same searchable set for rerouting; that is, we can add extra links in a switch to connect the switches belonging to the same reachable set as alternative links for rerouting.

In the following, we use this concept to construct and propose dynamic rerouting networks for tolerating faults and preventing collisions. We create three kinds of dynamic rerouting networks by adding an extra link to the switch at the previous stage, adding an extra link to the switch at the current stage, and adding two extra links to two switches at the latter stage.

Adding an Extra Link to the Switch at the Previous Stage

The scheme of designing dynamic rerouting networks by adding extra links to the switches at the previous stage is proposed in this section. First, we analyze the result of Theorem 1 to propose the design scheme. In addition, we propose related important issues for preventing collisions.

When switch j at stage i wants to reroute a packet to a switch at stage i-1, $N/2^{i-1}$ switches at stage i-1 can be considered because at stage i-1, there are $N/2^{i-1}$ switches whose last $(i-1)$ bits are the same as the last $(i-1)$ bits of switch j; that is, the $N/2^{i-1}$ switches at stage i-1 and the switch j at stage i belong to the same reachable set no matter which destination is desired. Hence, we can add an extra link to switch j at stage i. The extra link connects to one of the $N/2^{i-1}$ switches at stage i-1 and is an alternative link for rerouting. We show in Figure 3 this kind of dynamic rerouting networks that is created by adding one backward link from stage i to stage i-1 at each switch, where i is from 1 to n ($=\log_2 N$).

This kind of dynamic rerouting network sends a packet to the added link when the packet encounters a faulty or busy element. However, some important problems should be carefully solved when designing such a dynamic rerouting network. 1) The switches at stage 0 cannot send a packet to the previous stage for rerouting. To solve this problem, a switch at stage 0 can add extra links by adding a link to a switch at the current stage or by adding two links to the switches at the latter stage. 2) If a rerouting behavior occurs because a packet encounters a faulty element in the middle stages, the situation of a packet re-encountering a faulty element again after rerouting should be prevented to reduce the number of rerouting hops to reduce the number of collisions. We discuss the situations and propose solutions in Section 3.2.

Adding an Extra Link to the Switch at the Current Stage

In the following, we present the second kind of dynamic rerouting network, in which an extra link is added in each switch to connect the switches at the same stage.

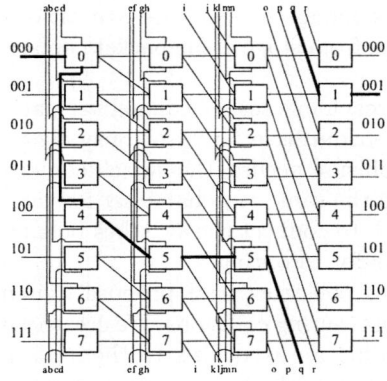
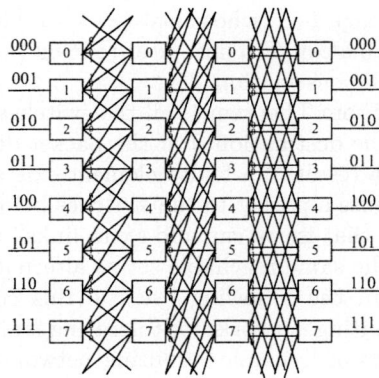

Fig. 4. The topology of the second kind of dynamic rerouting network, with size 8 and the routing situation when the source is 0, the destination is 1, and switch 1 at stage 1 is fully faulty

Fig. 5. The topology of the network with switches connecting the latter stage's switches with size $N=8$

When a switch at stage i wants to reroute a packet to the switches at the same stage, $N/2^i$ switches whose last i bits are the same as the last i bits of the current switch can be considered as the rerouting targets. Moreover, these $N/2^i$ switches, whose last i bits are the same as the current switch, belong to the same reachable set regardless of the destination of a packet. Similarly, the situation of a packet re-encountering a faulty element after rerouting should be prevented to reduce the number of rerouting hops. We show in Figure 4 this kind of dynamic rerouting network that is made by adding one link to each switch, a link which connects two switches at the same stage by a 2^{n-1} vertical distance from stage 0 to stage n-1. The network takes at least one rerouting hop for the rerouting behavior. In Figure 4, the routing and rerouting example is shown where the source is 0, the destination is 1, and switch 1 at stage 1 is fully faulty.

Adding two Extra Links to the Switches at the Latter Stage

In the following, we present the third kind of dynamic rerouting network, in which two extra links are added in each switch to connect two switches at the next stage.

This kind of dynamic rerouting network is different from the previous two kinds in which only one extra link is added for rerouting. If switch j $(=j_{n-1}j_{n-2}\cdots j_2j_1j_0)$ at stage i wants to reroute a packet to the next stage, two extra links corresponding to routing bits 0 and 1 are needed. The connection rules for switch j at stage i for the two extra links are described as follows: 1) choose $N/2^i$ switches at stage i+1 whose last i-bits are the same as the last i-bits of the current switch j, $j_{i-1}\cdots j_2j_1j_0$; 2) split these switches into two sets according to the value (0 or 1) of the last $(i$+1)-th bit of the switch index; 3) individually choose a switch from these two sets; 4) connect these two switches from switch

j at stage i and use them as the alternative links; and, finally, 5) mark the alternative links 0 or 1 as follows: if the last $(i+1)$-th bit of the chosen switch at stage $i+1$ is the same as the last $(i+1)$-th bit of the switch index j at stage i, j_i, mark the alternative link 0; otherwise, mark the alternative link 1. In Figure 5, we show a network that two extra links added at each stage to connect two switches at the next stage. In Figure 6, we present the connection conditions in detail from stage i to stage $i+1$ for Figure 5.

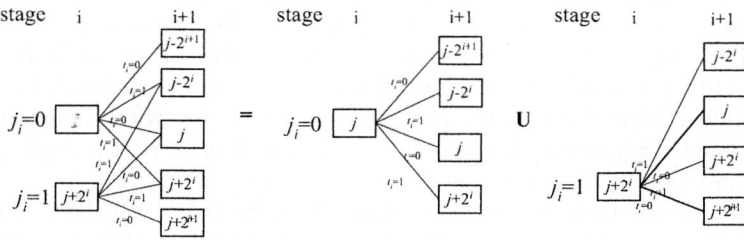

Fig. 6. All output links in a switch at stage i for the case of two extra links to connect the next stage's switches

In general, when a switch at stage i wants to connect the switches at the next stage, $N/2^{i+1}$ likely switches can be considered for routing bits 0 and 1. This kind of dynamic rerouting network does not take any extra rerouting hops, but the switch architecture between stage 0 and stage n-1 uses 4x4 crossbar hardware. When switch j at stage i wants to choose a switch as the alternative switch from a set for routing bit 0 or 1, $N/2^{i+1}$ switches can be considered, but we avoid choosing the switch which has already been connected by switch j. However, at stage n-1, there is only one switch in a set. Thus two duplicated links are established to connect two switches between stage n-1 and stage n.

Rather than requiring two extra links in each switch for this kind of dynamic rerouting network, in the first two kinds of dynamic rerouting networks, in which an extra link is added to connect to the switch at the current stage and the previous stage, there is a cost of one extra link for rerouting. However, the penalty, the extra rerouting hops, for these two kinds of rerouting networks affects the system performance. In Section 4, we simulate and analyze the arrival ratio of these three kinds of dynamic rerouting networks with the factors which include one fault tolerance, and rerouting hops.

In the next section, we present how to design the destination tag routing method to save hardware cost associated with computing the rerouting tag in the switch for rerouting behavior.

3.2 Destination Tag Routing Designing Schemes

In this section, we present a method on how to make pre-computing tag networks use the destination tag routing method to save hardware cost at switches for the rerouting process. According to the pre-computing tag method in the ICube network or the other cube-like networks, the routing behavior in the switch at stage i delivers a packet to the switch at stage $i+1$ whose last $(i+1)$-th bit is the same as the last $(i+1)$-th bit of the destination; that is, if a packet is delivered from stage 0 to switch j $(=j_{n-1}j_{n-2}...j_0)$ at stage i, the last i bits, $j_{i-1}\,j_{i-2}Kj_0$, are the same as the last i bits of the destination index. As a result, we can know that a packet at switch j at stage i is sent to a non-straight link if the last $(i+1)$-th bit of the switch index, j_i, is different from the last $(i+1)$-th bit of the destination index; that is, if j_i is the same as the last $(i+1)$-th bit of the destination index, a packet is sent to the straight output link. Accordingly, a switch at stage i can deliver a packet to the next stage according to the last $(i+1)$-th bit of the destination tag and the last $(i+1)$-th bit of the current switch index. Thus, because the last $(i+1)$-th bit of the switch index at stage i is permanent, we can easily mark the two output links 0 or 1 according to the last $(i+1)$-th bit of the current switch, j_i.

The marking rule is described as follows: 1) If the last $(i+1)$-th bit of a switch index at stage i is 1, mark the non-straight link 0 and the straight link 1. 2) If the last $(i+1)$-th bit of a switch index at stage i is 0, mark the non-straight link 1 and the straight link 0.

In the following, we apply this marking rule to the ICube network [9] and the cube-like network to enable these two networks to use a destination tag routing scheme. According to the marking rules, we mark the non-straight link output link in a switch at stage i 0/1 and the straight link output link in a switch at stage i 1/0 if the last $(i+1)$-th bit of the switch index at stage i is 1/0. Figure 7(a) and Figure 7(b) show the marked results and the destination tag routing behavior from the source index 1 to the destination index 6.

Since the ICube network [9] is equivalent to many important multistage interconnection networks [11]; for example, the Omega network, the Shuffle Exchange, and so on [11], the principle that is followed to enable the ICube network to use

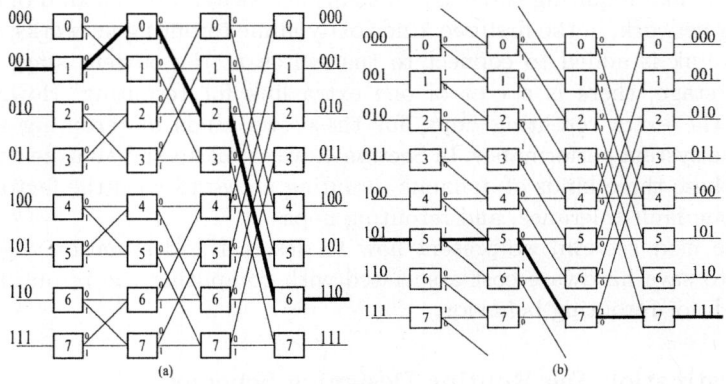

Fig. 7. (a) An ICube network of size N=8 (b) A cube-like network of size N=8, and the destination routing behavior with source 1 and destination 6

the destination tag routing method can also be applied and explained in these equivalent networks.

We can easily apply the schemes mentioned above to enable our three proposed dynamic rerouting networks mentioned in Section 3.1 to use the destination tag routing method to save the hardware cost during rerouting behavior. Although the three kinds of dynamic rerouting networks have the capability to tolerate faults and prevent collisions, the hardware cost in terms of the switches and the number of rerouting hops are different. In the next section, we compare and discuss the differences between the three kinds of networks and other previous works and present the comparisons of the arrival ratio according to our simulations.

4 Simulation Results

In this section, we present our simulation, results and discussions. We compared our three proposed dynamic rerouting networks, the Gamma network (GIN), the B-network, and CGIN (providing two disjoint paths networks to tolerate a fault) in a 6.25% to 100% traffic load condition, with a network size of $N=16$. Our three proposed dynamic rerouting networks, GIN, and the B-network use the dynamic rerouting method to tolerate a fault and prevent collisions, while CGIN sends two copy packets at a time via two disjoint paths to enhance fault tolerance capability and to prevent collisions.

For our simulation, the term "traffic load" means the number of packets that are to be sent simultaneously by the different sources. For example, if two packets in two different sources are to be sent to two different destinations, the traffic load is 12.5%, where the network size is 16. As a result, the maximum traffic load means that each of the 16 source nodes has a packet to be sent to 16 different destination nodes. However, in the CGIN, each source sends two identical packets to the destination via two disjoint paths.

In our simulation, we continuously and randomly generated the different source-destination requests in each cycle and continuously ran 10,000 cycles to compute the arrival rate, the collision rate, and the successful rerouting rate under a fixed traffic load. When a faulty element exists in the network, we assumed the faulty switch was fully faulty, and we performed simulations with each switch at the middle stage being a fully faulty switch; that is, we ran 3*16 simulations and averaged these results to get the simulation results under a fixed traffic load because there are three middle stages and 16 switches at every stage with a network size of 16. In addition, we preformed simulations with various traffic loads to get our final results.

We also showed the improvements in the arrival ratio in the case of a network with a link added to the current stage when a fully faulty switch element exists in the network. With regard to the disjoint paths network, if none of the two packets arrives at the destination, the route failed. Figure 8 show the arrival rates and the collision rates of these networks without and with a fault, respectively. From the simulation results, the arrival rate of the two disjoint paths network,

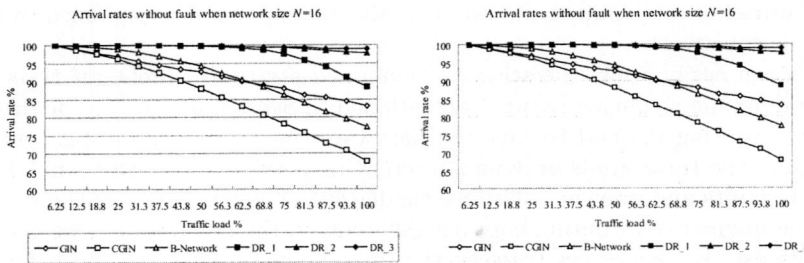

Fig. 8. Arrival ratio comparisons of our proposed networks and other previous networks widh and without a faulty element when the network size is $N=16$

CGIN, is fine under low traffic loads because the case of two packets being sent concurrently via two disjoint paths does not increase the collision rate. However, because twice the number of packets is sent, the collision rate grows. In Figure 8, the disjoint paths network (CGIN) exhibits a more rapid decrease in the arrival ratio than other networks. Because of the reasons listed above, the dynamic rerouting networks perform better than a disjoint paths network. However, the title DR_1 refers to the first of our three proposed networks, DR_2 refers to the second, and DR_3 refers to the third kind of our three proposed networks.

Figure 8 show the arrival ratio of dynamic rerouting networks, including the Gamma network, the B-network, DR_1, DR_2, and DR_3 with and without a faulty element. Although the B-network performs a good arrival ratio in fault-free networks in light traffic, the lack of guaranteed fault tolerance and the penalty in more rerouting hops degrade the arrival ratio quickly in the B-network. With regard to DR_2, and DR_3, DR_2 performs with a little lower arrival ratio than DR_3 when there is no faulty element in the network. When there is one faulty switch in the network, DR_2 has an arrival ratio that is a little 5% less than that of DR_3 because of 1 rerouting hops.

5 Conclusions

In this paper, we presented 1) three kinds of dynamic rerouting networks design that have the capability of tolerating faults and preventing collisions; 2) design schemes that enable a dynamic rerouting network to use destination tag routing to save hardware functions of computing the rerouting tag in the switches; 3) simulation results of related dynamic rerouting networks to realize the factors which influence the arrival ratio including the fault tolerant capability and the number of rerouting hops.

In the simulation results, we simulated these dynamic rerouting networks and one disjoint paths network under various traffic loads with and without faulty element considerations. From our experimental results, the third of our three proposed networks perform best in terms of the arrival ratio, with or without a faulty element, but it requires 4x4 crossbar switches in the middle stage. Although our second proposed second dynamic rerouting network show a little lower arrival ratio than the third proposed network, it uses 3x3 crossbar switches at the middle stages. In addition, if the traffic load is not very heavy, it performs with almost the same arrival ratio as the third proposed network.

In addition, we also compared the dynamic rerouting networks with two disjoint paths network that sends two identical packets from a source to a destination to tolerate one fault and prevent collisions. From our results, the two disjoint paths network has a good arrival ratio if the traffic load is light; however, the arrival ratio decreases very quickly when the traffic load increases.

With regard to the dynamic rerouting networks, the B-network, and the Gamma network, because of the lack of fault tolerance guarantee in the Gamma network and the B-network, these two networks have a worse arrival ratio than our proposed networks. Based on our proposed design schemes and according to our analysis and simulation results, a designer can choose an applicable dynamic rerouting network by using cost-efficient considerations.

References

1. T. Y. Feng, "A survey of interconnection networks", IEEE Computer 14, Dec. 1981, pp. 12-27.
2. G. B. III Adams, D. P. Agrawal, and H. J. Siegel, "A Survey and Comparison of fault-tolerant Multistage Interconnection Networks," IEEE Transactions cn Computer Vol. 20, No. 6, June 1987, pp. 14-27.
3. K. Yoon and W. Hegazy, "The Extra Stage Gamma Network," IEEE Transactions on Computers, Vol. 37, No. 11, November 1988, pp.1445-1450.
4. P. J. Chuang "CGIN: A Fault Tolerant Modified Gamma Interconnection Network," IEEE Transactions on Parallel and Distributed Systems. Vol. 7, No. 12, December 1996, pp. 1301-1306.
5. S. W. Seo and T. Y. Feng, "The Composite Banyan Network," IEEE Transactions on Parallel and Distributed Systems, Vol. 6, No. 10, October 1995, pp.1043-1054
6. D. S. Parker and C. S. Raghavendra, "The Gamma Network," IEEE Transactions on Computers, Vol. C-33, April 1984, pp.367-373.
7. K. Y. Lee and H. Yoon, "The B-network: A Multistage Interconnection Network with Backward Links," IEEE Transactions on Computers vol. 39, no. 7, July 1990, pp. 966-969
8. R. J. McMillen and H. J. Siegel, "Performance and Fault Tolerance Improvements in the Inverse Augmented Data Manipulator Network," 9th Symp. Computer Architecture, Apr. 1982, pp. 63-72.
9. M. C. Pease III, "The indirect binary n-cube microprocessor array." IEEE Trans. Computer, vol. C-26, May 1977, pp.458-473.
10. D. H. Lawrie, "Access and alignment of data in an array processor", IEEE Trans. Computers 24, Dec. 1975, pp. 1145-1155.
11. C. L. Wu and T. Y. Feng, "On a class of multistage interconnection networks", IEEE Trans. Computer 29, Aug. 1980, pp. 694-702.

RRBS: A Fault Tolerance Model for Cluster/Grid Parallel File System*

Yan-mei Huo, Jiu-bin Ju, and Liang Hu

Department of Computer Science & Technology, Jilin University,
Changchun, China, 130012
{huoym, jjb, hul}@jlu.edu.cn

Abstract. Parallel file systems stripe the data from a single file across multiple cluster/grid nodes so that the systems can access file in parallel. In such a system, if an I/O node or the storage device of that node doesn't work, all the subfiles on the node can't be accessed. In this paper, we introduce a special fault tolerance model for parallel file systems called Round-robin Redundant Backup of Subfile (RRBS). This model ensures the accessibility of the parallel files even when an I/O node is failure. In order to test the usability of RRBS, we also developed a prototype of parallel file system called WPFS on a PC/Windows cluster.

1 Introduction

I/O bottlenecks have always been a major issue in computer science. As early as 1967, [1] addressed the issue of storage and computation efficiency. Almost forty years later, this lack of performances is confirmed in [2] and this trend is likely to continue as I/O hardware performances increase slower than CPU and memory. Furthermore, this gap is amplified by the increasing use of clusters of work-stations or PCs [13]. Therefore, it is necessary to improve I/O performance so that to balance it with CPU performance.

One way of improving I/O performance is to carry out I/O operations in parallel, which is supported by parallel file systems. Parallel file systems logically aggregate multiple independent storage devices of a cluster/grid into a single high performance storage subsystem[3][14]. Striping the data from a single file across multiple devices allows the system to access files in parallel.

Till recently, many parallel file systems have been developed. Most parallel file systems were built on clusters [6][7][12][8][9][10] or computing grids [14] [6] [15] . The cluster/grid architecture, as a distributed system environment, generates some constraints such as fault tolerance. For example, damage to the magnetic disk on which the parallel files are stored will produce unthinkable loss. Fault tolerance of a parallel file system ensures the accessibility of files even when an I/O node is failure.

---

* This research work is supported by National Natural Science Foundation of China under Grant No.60473099 and by Outstanding Youth Science Foundation of Jilin Province under Grant No.20040119.

In this work, we present a fault tolerance model called Round-robin Redundant Backup of Subfile (RRBS). In this model, every subfile in a parallel file system will have a backup copy on another I/O node. Thus all the subfiles can be rebuilt and accessible even when an I/O node is failure or the magnetic disk is damaged.

In order to test the usability of RRBS, we also developed a prototype of a parallel file system called WPFS on a PC/Windows cluster. The experimental results show that RRBS works well. Moreover, RRBS is suitable to every parallel file system built on cluster/grid.

The rest of the paper is organized as follows: section 2 shows the design and implementation of the parallel file system prototype WPFS. Then section 3 describe the details of our fault tolerance model RRBS. Next, section 4 gives some experimental results and in section 5 some related works are discussed. Eventually, section 6 concludes and describes future works.

2 Design and Implementation of WPFS

Before we describe the details of RRBS, we'll show the prototype WPFS roughly so that some keywords will be clear.

2.1 WPFS Structure

Like most of the cluster parallel file systems, WPFS is implemented as client-server model. WPFS consists of three components: the service manager(SM), the I/O server (IOS), and the application library (wpfs_lib).

Figure 1 shows the structure of WPFS.

SM handles permission checking for file creation, open, close, and remove operations. The IOS handles all file I/O without intervention of the service manager. Through the wpfs_lib, the applications communicate with the WPFS system.

The three components of WPFS communicate and cooperate with each other. All the communications rely on TCP to provide reliable end-to-end data stream service. WinSock2 has been used in all the communication programs of the system.

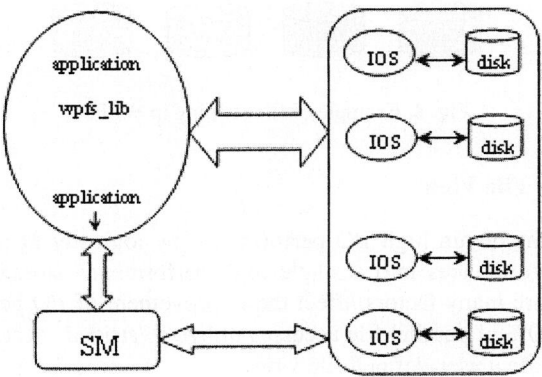

Fig. 1. TPFS file system

WPFS runs on PC clusters. Every node in the cluster is an independent computer system, which has processors and local storage devices of its own. The nodes are connected with each other by high speed network. On each node can run the SM, the IOS or user applications. According to the software running on it, the node is called management node (MN), I/O node (ION) or compute node (CN). Of course, one node can play multiple roles at the same time. But this will impact on the performance.

2.2 File Stripe and Data Storage

In WPFS, the parallel files are implemented. One parallel file is a logically single file and physically consisting of multiple discontiguous subfiles striped across different IONs. The user applications can visit these subfiles in parallel.

The number of subfiles is equal to the number of IONs that store the file. Each subfile is a physically contiguous byte stream. But logically it consists of a lot of discontiguous units which are called striping-units. In other words, a parallel file is divided averagely into multiple striping-units, a subfile is the collection of striping-units belonging to a given file that reside on a single ION. The size of the striping-unit is specified (as a parameter by the user application or by default) at the time the file is built and will never change. Striping-units are allocated to IONs with a round robin scheme.

Figure 2 shows an example of file striping in WPFS.

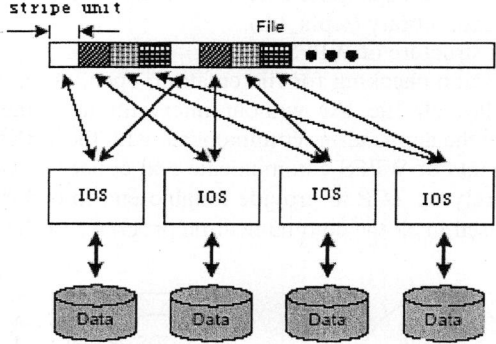

Fig. 2. Example of file striping in WPFS

2.3 User Defined File View

Parallel file systems obtain high I/O performance by logically aggregating multiple independent storage devices into a single high performance storage subsystem [3]. But in fact, there are many factors affect the improvement of I/O performance. Studies showing that 80% of parallel file accesses utilize a "strided" access pattern [4]. So in WPFS, we provide a user-defined file view.

This allows for noncontiguous file regions to be accessed with a single function call. The concept is similar to logical file partitioning in Vesta[9] and PVFS [7] and file views in MPI-IO[5]. An application can partition a WPFS file, effectively limiting the view of the file to a subset of the complete byte sequence.

Figure 3 shows a user-defined file view of a WPFS file: file.dat. According to the three parameters: ro,rs and sd provided by the user application. Then a user file view consisting of three records is got.

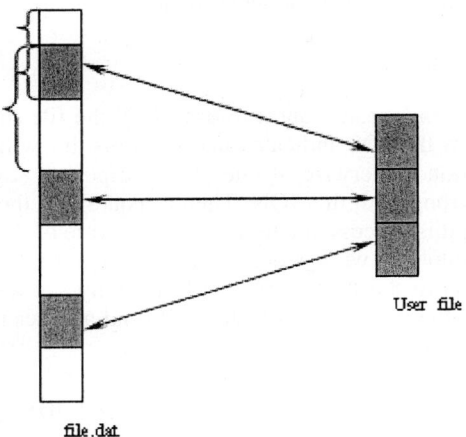

Fig. 3. A User-defined file view

3 A Fault Tolerance Model: RRBS

In a cluster/grid parallel file system, a single parallel file will spread across N (N>=1) IONs. If a storage device or a node or an IOS program or the network equipment connecting the ION is disabled, all the subfiles on that node will be unaccessible. If it is the damage of magnet media, the whole parallel file is broken only because one of its subfiles is spread across this node, despite that the other N-1 subfiles are right and accessible.

The failure of one node causes so bad effect, but there is little probability of two nodes failure at the same time. In WPFS, to ensure the validity of the system, we implement a mechanism of fault tolerance called Round-robin Redundant Backup of Subfiles(RRBS).

In this section, we'll show RRBS model in detail.

3.1 Design and Implementation of RRBS

Each subfile of a parallel file has a copy. A subfile is called the source and it's copy is called the copy The source and the copy are stored separately on the No. m and the No. n ION. Suppose the numbering of the I/O nodes of WPFS is as: 1,2, ...,N. The relationship between m and n is as follows:

When $m < N : n = m + 1$; and
When $m = N : n = 1$

When a parallel file is opened, every source and its copy will be opened together. Usually, WPFS will access the source, and the copy is accessed only when the source is unaccessible. Through cooperations between wpfs_lib and IOS, the access to the subfile and the update to the copy is completed.

When the API wpfs_read/wpfs_write is called by the application, wpfs_lib is responsible for mapping the I/O request to the I/O requests to multiple subfiles. Following are the processes of wpfs_read and wpfs_write.

3.2 Process of Wpfs_Read

At first, the wpfs_lib sends read request to each ION the file striped on. If all the responses returned from the IOS indicate success, wpfs_lib will return a success respond to the application. Otherwise, if one of the responses suggests a failure, there must be something wrong with that ION. Then a request for the copy will be send to the next ION. During this process, the user won't be aware of the failure.

Figure 4 is an example of wpfs_read. In this example, the node n is power down. After sending requests to the three IOSs, wpfs_lib only get responses from IOSn-1 and IOSn+1. So after the overtime, wpfs_lib will send another request to IOSn+1 for data from the copy of subf n.

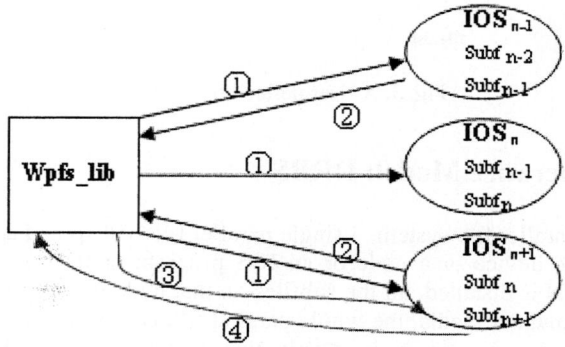

Fig. 4. Fault Tolerance model of wpfs_read

3.3 Process of Wpfs_Write

Comparing to wpfs_read, the process of wpfs_write is more complex. When a subfile is written, the copy will be update synchronously. And if there is a node failure, the source and the copy will be inconsistent.

Synchronous Updating of Copy: Wpfs_lib sends write requests and the data that will be written to the subfiles. The IOSs are responsible for writing the data to the right location of the subfiles and send response messages. Then the IOS send update requests and the data to the next ION to update the copy. Thus, updating of copy is completed by the ION where the subfile is located and the application gets the response message in time.

Figure 5 shows the process:

Fig. 5. Synchronous updating of copy

Inconsistency of Source and Copy: If every IOS sends an affirmative response to the wpfs_lib, the wpfs_lib will return an affirmative response to the application indicating the write request has been performed successfully. Otherwise, if one of the responses suggests a failure, there must be something wrong with that ION. Then the wpfs_lib will send another request for the copy. Thus the source and the copy will be inconsistent.

Delay Update of Subfile: Our method to ensure the consistence of the source and the copy is called delay update of subfile. Namely update when open next time.

If either the source or the copy of a subfile is updated but the other one is not, a log file about the details of that update will be built. The following write operation to the same source or copy will also be logged to the log file.

The parameters logged include the IP address of the I/O node needs to be updated, the service port of the IOS and the offset and length of every write operation. The offset is the offset from the beginning of the whole parallel file.

Next is the content of a logfile: parafile3log.txt.

202.198.67.150:7000 1020 100

From the request of the wpfs_lib, the IOS gets the IP address and the service port number. Once an IOS opens a subfile, the corresponding log file is also opened. The inexistence of log file indicating there is no inconsistency between the source and the copy. If the log file exists, the IOS will read the IP address and the port number logged in the file, connect to the IOS on that host by SOCKET, and read the records in the log file one by one to update the source or the copy. When all the updates completed, the IOS will delete the log file. In this way, we do delay update of the subfile when it is opened, the consistent of the source and the copy is ensured.

In addition, once the disk of an ION is damaged, the lost subfile can be rebuilt from its copy. Thus the damage of one subfile won't do harm to the whole parallel file.

4 Experimental Results

In this section we present the results of two experiments designed to show the usability of WPFS and RRBS.

The system used for testing was a PC cluster, consisting of a number of PCs, each with 128MB of RAM and 20G of local disk. The network is fast Ethernet which provides full duplex links between PCs. The operating system running on the PCs is Windows NT.

Experiment 1: In the first experiment, the throughput of WPFS with one, two and three IONs was tested. In any case, we tested different read request sizes.

Figure 6 shows a comparison of overall throughput for WPFS reads with various numbers of I/O nodes. A 128K stripe size was used in all tests. When the request size is small, the cost of network communication is considerable, increasing the number of the I/O nodes results in a drop of throughput. But when the request size is large enough, the cost of the network communication can almost be ignored, more I/O nodes provides better throughput. The result shows the ability of WPFS to improve I/O performance.

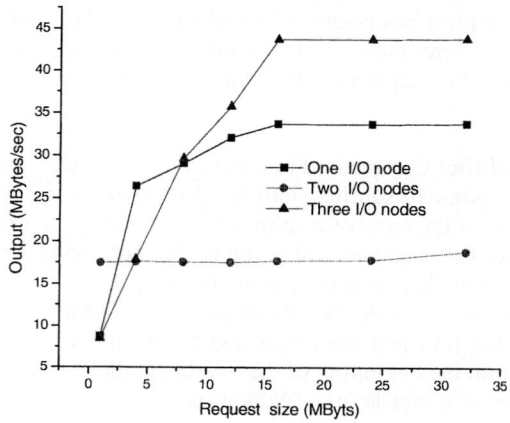

Fig. 6. Read Performance under Different Number of I/O Nodes

Experiment 2: In this experiment, we tested RRBS over a cluster of three IONs. A parallel file was striped over the three IONs. A 128K stripe size was used in the test.

We tried wpfs_read when one of the IONs didn't work. The result showed that all the requests to the failed ION can complete by reading from the copy on the next ION.

Then we tried wpfs_write when one of the IONs didn't work. The copy was written and a corresponding logfile was built.

The results showed that RRBS works well.

5 Related Works

Fault tolerance of a parallel file system ensures the accessibility of files even when an I/O node is failure. Only a few parallel file systems have considered fault tolerance. PIOUS provides a dynamically-selectable fault tolerance level [8] [3], Vesta provides a file checkpoint facility that is efficient and simple to use[9], and GPFS[6] is designed to be configured so that single points-of-failure can be avoided. A recent and advanced project of cluster file system is Lustre[10][11]: it aims at handling both distributed system constraints such as availability and fault tolerance and parallel I/O considerations.

But all of the above methods are incapable to cope with the I/O node failure, and the damage of the magnetic disk will produce unthinkable loss.

6 Conclusions and Future Work

In this paper, we introduce a special fault tolerance model RRBS of parallel file systems.

The cluster/grid architecture is a distributed system environment. So the parallel file systems built on the cluster/grid have to face some constraints such as fault tolerance. The Round-robin Redundant Backup of subfile improves the validity of the parallel file systems.

In a parallel file system, a single read or write operation can generate data accesses on multiple independent storage devices, so next we plan to design an effective concurrency control mechanism in WPFS.

References

1. G. Amdahl. Validity of the single-processor approach to achieving large scale computing capabilities. pages 483–485, 1967
2. J. L. Hennessy and D. A. Patterson. Computer architecture: A quantitative approach, 1996
3. Steven A. Moyer and V. S. Sunderam. Characterizing concurrency control performance for the PIOUS parallel file system, Technical Report CSTR-950601,Emory University , June 1995
4. N. Nieuwejaar and D. Kotz,Low-level Interfaces for High-level Parallel I/O, Workshop for I/O in Parallel and Distributed Systems, IPPS 1995, pp 47-62, 1995
5. R. B. Ross, Providing Parallel I/O on Linux Clusters, Second Annual Linux Storage Management Workshop, Miami, FL, October 2000
6. Frank Schmuck, Roger Haskin, GPFS: A Shared-Disk File System for Large Computing Clusters, Proceedings of the Conference on File and Storage Technologies (FAST'02), Monterey, CA, pp. 231–244, January 2002
7. Ligon, III, W.B., and Ross, R. B.,PVFS: Parallel Virtual File System, Beowulf Cluster Computing with Linux, Thomas Sterling, editor, pages 391-430, MIT Press, November, 2001
8. N. Nieuwejaar, D. Kotz.,PIOUS: A Scalable Parallel I/O System for Distributed Computing Environments, Proceedings of the Scalable High-Performance Computing Conference, pages 71--78, 1994
9. Peter F. Corbett, Sandra Johnson Baylor, Dror G. Feitelson, Overview of the Vesta Parallel File System. ACM SIGARCH Computer Architecture News, Pages: 7 - 14,1993
10. P. Schwan. Lustre : Building a file system for 1,000-node clusters. In Proceedings of the Linux Symposium, Ottawa, July 2003
11. F. Wang, Q. Xin, B. Hong, S. A. Brandt, E. L. Miller, D. D. E. Long, and T. T. McLarty. File system workload analysis for large scale scientific computing applications. In Proceedings of the 21st IEEE / 12th NASA Goddard Conference on Mass Storage Systems and Technologies, College Park, MD, Apr. 2004
12. Avery Ching, Alok Choudhary, Wei-keng Liao, Robert Ross, and William Gropp, "Noncontiguous I/O through PVFS," Proceedings of 2002 IEEE International Conference on Cluster Computing, September, 2002
13. MARK BAKER AND RAJKUMAR BUYYA, Cluster Computing: The Commodity Supercomputer, Software Practice and Experience, 29(6):551-557,1999
14. Ron Oldfield, David Kotz, Armada: a parallel I/O framework for computational grids, Future Generation Computer Systems 18 (2002) 501–523,2002
15. I.Foster, C. Kesselman (Eds.), The Grid: Blueprint for a New Computing Infrastructure, Morgan Kaufmann, Los Altos, CA,1998

Fast Parallel FFT on CTaiJi: A Coarse-Grained Reconfigurable Computation Platform

liGuo Song[1] and YuXian Jiang[2]

Department of Automatic Control,
Beijing University of aeronautics and astronautics,
Beijing, 100083
[1] songlg123456@sohu.com, [2] jiangyx@263.com

Abstract. Traditional microprocessors are today getting more and more inefficient for a growing range of applications that are mainly about processing data-stream. These applications have two character characteristics: one is that lots of intensive computation tasks need to be processed, another is that the running time of these tasks occupy more than 90% of total time. Coarse grained reconfigurable computation is very fitful for these tasks and can achieve very high performance. This paper presents implementation of the task of fast parallel complex FFT on CTaiJi, the 16bits Reconfigurable computation platform, which is targeting on streamed applications such as multi-media and DSP (digital signal processing). The proposed mapping comprises fast store-address transformation and configuring the function of PEA (processing element array) to fit for FFT. More-over, the performance is scalable according to FFT sizes. Since there is no functionality specifically tailored to FFT, the results demonstrate the capability of CTaiJi architecture to extract parallelism from streamed applications. Further ration- ales are given based on the concepts of scalar operand networks.

1 Introduction

Toward a coming billion-transistor era, today's computation platforms design has already foreseen the end of the road for conventional micro-architectures [1], and numerous new approaches have arisen above the horizon, such as EPIC[2], RAW [3], Imagine [4], VIRAM [5] and XPP-64 [6], etc. ALL of them target on streamed applications, in which more than 90% of total processing-time is spent on loop and regular data processing. The biggest challenge of architecture design is the scalability, only with which can one follow up the step of Moore's Law. The difficulty of scalability is imposed by slower decrease of wire transmission delay than that of transistor switching delay. This discrepancy requires a new philosophy on design of scalar operand network [7] and memory hierarchy.

Reconfigurable Computing (RC) is emerging as an important new organization structure for implementing intensive computations. This area is consolidating itself as a real alternative to application specific integrated circuits (ASICs) and general purpose processors. The main advantage of RC devices comes from its unique combination of broad applicability, provided by the reconfiguration capacity, and achievable performance, through the potential parallelism exploitation. The coarse-grain RC is not usually suitable for applications with many bit-level manipulations. One the contrary, it is usually a good choice for arithmetic operations at the byte level and can change the device configuration *on the fly* during system operation through dynamic reconfiguration. Therefore, some tasks which have regular structure and data can be implemented efficiently by coarse-grained RC. As we know, FFT is the most import ant algorithm in DSP (digital signal processing). In this paper we present a fast, efficient and scalable implementation of FFT algorithm on a coarse-grained RC platform called CTaiJi. It has a scalar operand network bandwidth even higher than RAW and the memory is organized as a loose-couple distribute address space (DAS). The plat form is described briefly in section 2 and the comparison between it and other fixed architectures is given. In order to demonstrate the capability of CTaiJi, a complex point Fast Fourier Transformation (FFT) algorithm with different sizes is mapped onto CTaiJi architecture in section 3. Section 4 addresses related works and performance comparisons with other platforms. Conclusion is drawn in the last section.

2 Coarse-Grained RC Platform----CTaiJi

2.1 CTaiJi Architecture

CTaiJi is a highly scalar and flexible 16bits coarse grained RC architecture, with the applications that are commonly addressed in multimedia applications (like image or video processing). CTaiJi architecture consists of two main subsystems: configuration system and data-processing system. Configuration system are composed of one central-reconfigurable controller (CRC) and four sub-reconfigurable controllers

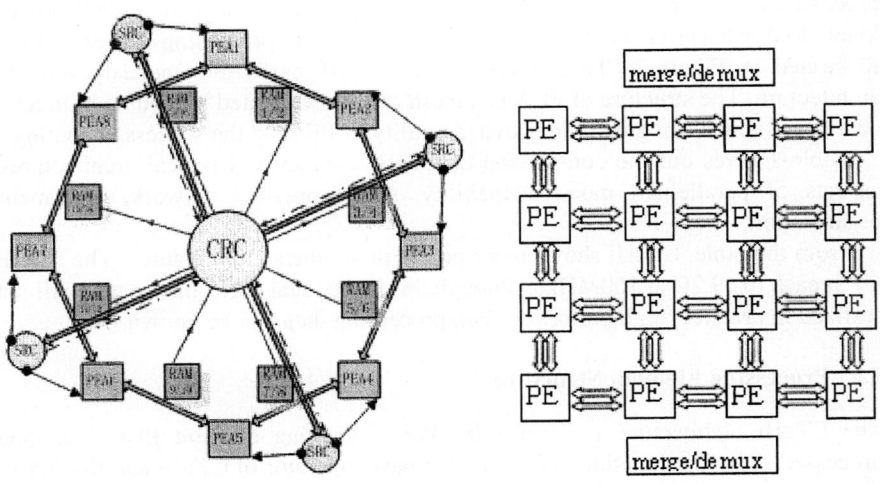

Fig. 1. CTaiJi architecture   **Fig. 2.** PEA organization

Table 1. Comparison of CTaiJi with other architectures

	VIRAM	Imagine	RAW	MorphoSys	XPP64	CTaiJi
Parallelism model	Vector	SIMD	MIMD	SIMD	SIMD	SIMD
Peak OPS	6.4G	23.7G	3.6G	28.8G	12.48G	59.2G
Clock Speed MHz	200	296	225	450	65	100
Network nodes	8 (banks)	8	16	64	64	16/8[*2]
Total band-width(Gbps)	51.2	75.8	922	922	399.4	1638.4
1stlevel size	64KB	96KB	16.4KB	16.4KB	12KB × 16	128KB ×8
2stlevel size	104MB	1MB	16MB	2MB		/

*1 : plan to use 0.18μm ;
*2 : 16/8 indicate that there are eight PEAs in CTaiJi, and each PEA is composed of 16 PEs.

(SRCs), with the responsibility of reading configurable data, distributing them into PEA and send the configuration-demand for reconfiguring the function of PEA. Data-processing system is composed of eight PEAs. They can connected end-to-end to form a ring, as illustrated in Figure 1.When the number of needed PEs exceed the capacity of one PEA, some adjacent PEAs will link together. The data that are being processed can be moved between PEAs. PEA is the least macro-module that can run lonely to finish a task, and its structure is made up of 4x4 processing elements (PEs), as illustrated in Figure 2. Thus, there are eight task can simultaneously run in the architecture. The structure of PEA is a mesh of PEs connected by double bidirectional data buses which can greatly improve the utility of PEs and the success of routing.

Table-1 gives out the comparison of CTaiJi with several typical architectures, in aspects of parallelism model, capability, scalar operand network, and memory organization.

From the table, CTaiJi shows more power than others architectures. The ma ximal OPS reach to 59.2G at 100MHz. Although this is the ideal performance that will not be realized in practice, high performance in processing data can be known.

2.2 Processing Element Structure

The CTaiJi architecture is formed by 128 processing element PEs. The data is processed in it. The functions of PE are the basic operator of CTaiJi and the functions that can be map onto the PE are listed in table 2.

Table 2. PE functions

Add	Subtract	Multiply	division
Multi-bit Add	And(logic)	Or(logic)	Not(logic)
Bool operation	Loop control	If-else control	Shifter bit

3 Mapping FFT on CTaiJi

FFT algorithm is the most important algorithm in DSP and is often used in practice. In order to utilize the maximum parallelism of CTaiJi for FFT, an efficient mapping approach is very important. In this section FFT algorithms is described briefly and the parallelism in the algorithm that fits for CTaiJi architecture is pointed out. Consequently an efficient mapping scheme is presented.

3.1 FFT Algorithm

Fast Fourier Transform (FFT) is a fast algorithm for computing DFT to reduce number of multiplications from N^2 to $NlgN$. FFT is defined as:

$$X_K = \sum_{m=0}^{N-1} x_m W_N^{mk} \tag{1}$$

$$W_N^{mk} = e^{-j\frac{2\pi mk}{N}} \quad k = 0,1,\cdots N-1 \tag{2}$$

If radix-2 FFT length N equal to 2^m, m stages of permutation and storage is needed, and each level have (2m-1) butterfly operations. For general-purpose processor, it will need three nest loops to accomplish FFT: the outside loop deal with level from the first to the m^{st}; In the p stage, there are 2^{p-1} twiddles and the processor take turns to calculate the 2^{m-p} operations for each twiddle. As the size of FFT increases, the number of operations will improve greatly. Therefore, the FFT algorithm is often implemented by hardware in reconfigurable computing architecture.

3.2 Effective Memory Addressing Scheme for FFT

By far, There are two ways to realize FFT in configurable architecture: one is directly map FFT algorithm onto the architecture, utilizing the configurable PEs and data-path to realize the algorithm. The other is utilizing two special data store units called Frame Buffer (FB) and the function of the two FBs alternates when processing FFT. When FB1 stores last operation data and FB2 is empty, data of FB1 is transmitted to the PEs for processing and FB2 receive the output of PEs till FB1 sends over [7]. The function of FB1 and FB2 exchanges when FB1 sends data over, and FB2 begin to send data and FB1 receive the output. The first way is only suitable for small size of FFT. For example, if the length of FFT equal to 64 in XPP64A1, the processing is very fast and efficient. However, if the length of FFT is larger than 64, the performance will became bad. The second way can handle with different length FFT. But because it has two FBs and need to read out twiddles and data from them, the special design and route wire will be very complex, and can not achieve the general-purpose.

Figure 4 is the distortion of data flow graph (DFG) of FFT. From this figure, we can see that the structure in the dashed-line box is same. Therefore, The PEAs can be configured to the same function as figure 4. The complex numbers of FFT-point send to PEA in order. Only the store-address of data that the function structure outputted need to be adjusted before processing in the next stage. Therefore, the computing result of last PEA should be stored in an adjacent RAM, and the data in the RAM can not be read out and send to the next PEA till all the results of FFT points have been stored. Because each PEA can be configured to accomplish the function as shown in figure 5, PEA can deal with 2 stages of FFT. Therefore, if using all the eight PEAs, the maximal level is up to 16 and the size of FFT reach to 2^{16}. Owing to the capacity of RAM, the maximal length of FFT is limited to 2^{13}.

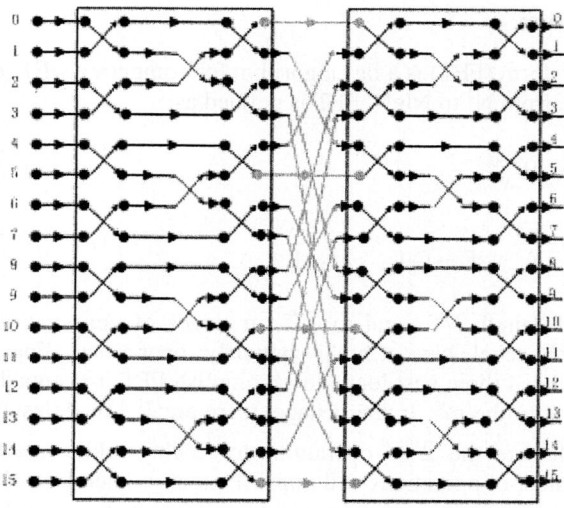

Fig. 4. FFT data flow graph

Two operation formulae are defined before the relation between output-order and store-address is founded.

Definition 1. $LSH(X,i)$ indicate that binary data X shift i bits towards left.

Let $X = (x_n \cdots x_1 x_0)_2$, then $LSH(X,i) = (x_{n-i} \cdots x_0 x_n \cdots x_{n-i+1})_2$.

Definition 2. $REVB(X)$ indicate that binary data X bit reversed.

Let $X = (x_n \cdots x_1 x_0)_2$, $Y = (y_n \cdots y_1 y_0)_2$,

if $Y = REVB(X)$, then $Y = (y_n \cdots y_1 y_0)_2 = (x_0 x_1 \cdots x_n)_2$.

The relation between store-address and output-order after $2q$ ($2q < m$) stages FFT butterfly operations is formulated as below:

$$Addr = \begin{cases} u_m \cdots u_{(2q+2)} 0 \cdots 0 + \\ LSH(u_{(2q+1)} u_{2q} \cdots u_0, 2) \end{cases} \text{OR} \quad \begin{array}{l} m \text{ is even } \quad 2q < m; \\ m \text{ is odd } \quad 2q < m-1; \end{array} \\ REVB(u_m \cdots u_1 u_0) \quad \begin{array}{l} m \text{ is odd} \\ 2q = m-1; \end{array} \\ REVB(LSH(u_m \cdots u_1 u_0, m-1)) \quad \begin{array}{l} m \text{ is odd} \\ p = m; p \text{ is stage number} \end{array} \end{cases} \quad (3)$$

3.3 Mapping Statistics

After the adjustment of store-address, every 2 stages structure of FFT is the same. Therefore, utilizing the characteristic of CTaiJi architecture, the function of PEA can be configured as figure 5. A very good feature of the proposed FFT engine is its scalability. FFT with the size not exceeding 8K can be mapped to CTaiJi with the same mapping methodology by connecting together diverse PEAs. It not only can satisfy the 64 points of IEEE 802.11a but also 4096 points of DVB-T.

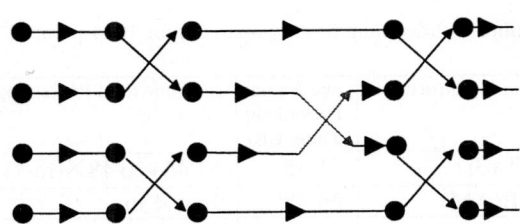

Fig. 5. The configurable function of PEA

Table 3. Cycle numbers and processing time for FFT

FFTsize	cycle count	processing time (us)	PEA number needed
64	207	2.07	3
128	532	5.32	4
256	1044	10.44	4
512	2585	25.85	5
1024	5145	51.45	5
2048	12318	123.18	6
4096	24606	246.06	6
8192	57379	573.79	7

Table 3 shows different cycle numbers and processing time for different sizes of FFT on CTaiJi platform. When processing FFT of different size, the number of PEA that participated in is different. If the size of FFT is 64, only 3 PEAs is needed. While 7 PEAs is needed when the size of FFT is 8192. Since there are 8 PEAs in CTaiJI architecture, besides the PEAs that are in for the FFT, the others can accomplish other task.

When processing FFT of different size, the number of PEA that participated in is different. If the size of FFT is 64, only 3 PEAs is needed. While 7 PEAs is needed when the size of FFT is 8192. Since there are 8 PEAs in CTaiJi architecture, besides the PEAs that are in for the FFT, the others can accomplish other task.

4 Benchmark Comparisons

Streamed multimedia applications are inherently computation intensive and favor from data level parallelism. Multimedia processors incorporate large number of processing units and huge memory bandwidth to achieve high performance. Very Long Instruction Word (VLIW), Vector Processing, SIMD Extensions, and Super-Scalar are main design themes for DSP processors; for instance Texas Instruments' TMS320C62x™ is based on VelociTI™; an advanced 8-slot VLIW architecture[8]. m frame 1024-point FFT on different platforms are compared in table 4 for comparison. Owing to only concerning about the tiptop performance of the platforms, the clock for every platform is the highest working-frequency.

Table 4. Processing time comparison for 1024-point FFT

platform	one frame Processing Time (us)	m frame total Processing Time (us)
CTaiJi	51.45	$51.45+20.48\times(m-1)$
VIRAM	26.4*[1]	$26.4\times m$
Imagine(Float)	7.4*[1]	$7.4\times m$
TMS320C6201	104	$104\times m$

*1 : data quote from [7]

From the table 4, owing to the clock frequency for CTaiJi architecture is only 100MHz and the processing time of 1024 points FFT reaches up to 51.45us, and only better than TMS320c6201. But the total processing time will be evidently decreased as the number of FFT frames increase. When processing 10 frames, the total time needed is almost equal to the time needed for VIRAM. This is because the CTaiJi architecture is designed for data-stream and it begins to process data of next frame before last frame processing over. The number of clock that PEA need to wait for before processing next frame data equal to the FFT size(the RAM which store last frame computing-result sends data to next PEA in the time). The output sequence of FFT input and output data of m frame is shown in figure 6. Additionally, the total power of architecture will be lowest for its lowest clock frequency and spatial design.

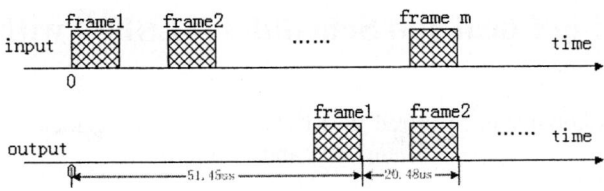

Fig. 6. Output sequence of m frame FFT

5 Conclusion

Coarse-grained reconfigurable computing architecture achieves both the performance of ASICs and the flexibility of general purpose processors and has broad application in DSP. FFT is the classic algorithm in DSP, In practice, the size of FFT varied from 64 point to 4096 point. The CTaiJi architecture is good at scalability and is fitful for the diversification of FFT size. As the number of FFT frame increase, the advantage of the RC architecture is displayed evidently. Since every PEA can lonely take charge of a task, when some PEAs answer for an special algorithm, others could be configured to finish another task.

References

1. Agarwal, Hrishikesh, Keckler, Burger, "Clock rate versus IPC: the end of the road for conventional microarchitectures," Computer Architecture, Proceedings of the 27th International Symposium on, 2000, pp. 248 -259.
2. Schlansker, Rau, "EPIC: Explicitly Parallel Instruction Computing," *IEEE Computer*, Vol. 33, No. 2, Feb 2000 pp. 37 -45.
3. Taylor, et al "The Raw microprocessor: a computational fabric for software circuits and general-purpose programs," *IEEE Micro*, Vol. 22, No. 2, Mar/Apr 2002, pp. 25 -35.
4. Rixner, et al. "A bandwidth-efficient architecture for media processing," *Microarchitecture, Proceedings of 31st Annual ACM/IEEE International Symposium on*, Nov/Dec 1998, pp. 3-13.
5. Kozyrakis, Patterson, "Vector vs. superscalar and VLIW architectures for embedded multimedia benchmarks," *Microarchitecture, Proceedings of 35th Annual IEEE/ACM International Symposium on*, 2002, pp. 283-293.
6. http://www.pactcorp.com December, 29,2004
7. Amir H. Kamalizad, Chengzhi Pan, Nader Bagherzadeh, "Fast Parallel FFT on a Reconfigurable Computation Platform," Proceedings of the 15th Symposium on Computer Architecture and High Performance Computing(SBAC-PAD'03), 2003,
8. http://www.ti.com December, 29,2004

Integrating Local Job Scheduler – LSF™ with Gfarm™

Xiaohui Wei[1], Wilfred W. Li[2], Osamu Tatebe[3], Gaochao Xu[1],
Liang Hu[1], and Jiubin Ju[1]

[1] College of Computer Science and Technology, Jilin University, Changchun 130023, PRC
{weixh, xugc, hul, jjb}@jlu.edu.cn
[2] University of California, San Diego, 9500 Gilman Dr. La Jolla CA 92093, USA
Wilfred@sdsc.edu
[3] Grid Technology Research Center, AIST, Tsukuba, Ibaraki 3058568, Japan
o.tatebe@aist.go.jp

Abstract Applications that both access and generate large data sets increasingly draw our attention in high energy physics, astronomy, genomics and other disciplines. The Data Grids, like Gfarm, seek to harness geographically distributed resources for such large-scale data-intensive problems. However, scheduling is a challenging task in this context. In this paper, we discuss the integration of LSF with Gfarm. We will discuss how to enable LSF to support Gfarm applications requiring GSI authentication, the design and implementation of data aware scheduling and data management. The system is able to find data-affinity hosts for Gfarm jobs and to adjust the distribution of the data replicas dynamically according to the job load. Before job running, the system will setup the proper credential for it. Using the LSF scheduler plugin mechanism, we do not need to write a new scheduler from scratch or make a lot of changes to an existing scheduler.

Keywords: data grid, data aware scheduling, GSI, LSF, Gfarm.

1 Introduction

Grid is considered as the infrastructure for the next generation of Internet. Computing grid and data grid play key roles in grid technologies. Computing grid is designated to facilitate CPU-intensive jobs, whose core functionalities are job scheduling, resource management and job execution. The well known batch systems, such as Condor[1], LSF[2], SGE[3], and PBS[4], etc, focus on local job scheduling and resource management, while Condor-G[5] and CSF[6] work at the grid level.

With the fast developing computer commodity technology, CPU is no longer expensive. Emerging classes of data-intensive applications that both access and generate large data sets are drawing much more attention. High-performance data-intensive computing and networking technology has become a vital part of large-scale scientific research projects in areas such as high energy physics, astronomy, space exploration, and human genome projects. One example is the Large Hadron Collider (LHC) [7] project at CERN. The so-called Data Grids provide essential infrastructure for such applications. Grid Datafarm (Gfarm)[8], for example, is one of them.

Gfarm architecture is designed for global petascale data-intensive computing. It provides a global parallel file system with online petascale storage, scalable I/O bandwidth, and scalable parallel processing, and it can exploit local I/O in a grid of clusters with tens of thousands of nodes. Gfarm parallel I/O APIs and commands provide a single file system image and manipulate file system metadata consistently.

If a huge amount of data I/O is involved, a network system's performance will be degraded by network congestions without proper data management and job scheduling. In Gfarm, *gfrun* and *gfmpirun* commands are able to allocate the file-affinity hosts for optimum execution of applications based on available metadata. However, the manual method is not scalable in a production environment with a large number of users running jobs concurrently. It is imperative to have an automated job scheduling and data management mechanism.

Gfarm provides two security models, share key model and GSI model. GSI model is encouraged to be used in real production environment. In this model, proxy certificates are required for applications to access Gfarm file system. Since we do not want to duplicate a user's proxy certificate on every computing node, a credential automatic setup/clean mechanism is compulsory.

In this paper, we describe the design and implementation of such credential automatic setup/clean mechanism as well as data aware scheduling in Gfarm by using a LSF scheduler plugin mechanism. The system is able to reserve the best hosts for job execution, setup and clean up the credential, and performs data stage-in and stage-out. Moreover, it can adjust the distributions of the data replicas based on the actual requirements of jobs, and balance the load for each data replica dynamically. With the plugin approach, the new scheduling policy is provided as a module to be dynamically loaded, and it can cooperate with other scheduling policies in the system as well.

In the rest of the paper, we discuss the credential automatic setup/clean mechanism first, after that the LSF's scheduler plugin mechanism is briefly introduced, then we discuss the architecture of the data aware schedule module. In section 5, the design principles of the scheduling algorithm and its implementation are explained. Section 6 is the experiment result. In section 7, some related works are discussed. Finally we present our plan in the near future.

2 The Job Credential Automatic Setup/Clean Mechanism

Whenever an application trying to access a Gfarm file, it need communicate with Gfarm daemon, gfsd. If Gfarm configured in GSI security model, gfsd requires the application to provide its credential, the user's proxy certificate, for GSI authentication. Otherwise, gfsd will deny any request from the application. A real production cluster may consist of thousands of hosts, and a job can be dispatched to any host by scheduler. We need a solution to guarantee the jobs can access Gfarm on execution hosts.

During the design stage, we considered four alternative solutions. (1) Configuring Gfarm in share key model. In this model, gfsd does not require a GSI authentication. It is quite simple in that we do not need worry about authentication at all. However, this model is not secure. (2) Implementing a mechanism to automatically duplicate a user's certificate on every computing node in the cluster. Then the user's job can run on any host. The disadvantage of the solution is that it introduces a lot of overhead to duplicate every user's certificate and keep these certificates valid on each host. It is not secure either in that there are many copies of certificate in the cluster. (3) Generating a new user proxy certificate on execution host for a job before its running. It's the safest way. However, it is hard to implement as it requires the job to be able to get its owner's password somehow. (4) Passing a user's proxy certificate from the job submission host to job execution host. After the job being finished, delete the certificate from the execution host.

The last solution is a compromise of solution 2 and 3. It is acceptable to require a user to set up its proxy certificate before submitting jobs. It is safer than solution 2 as a user's certificate will reside in the execution host during the job running period only. It's easier to implement than solution 3 in that it doesn't require the job to know the user's password for certificate. Therefore, we chose solution 4 in our prototype. In terms of implementation, LSF's esub is used to get a user's proxy certificate at job submission time, and LSF's eexec is used to set up the credential for the job on the execution host. We take advantage of LSF's post-exec mechanism to clean up the job's credential after it is finished. With the above job credential automatically setup/clean mechanism, a Gfarm job can run everywhere in the cluster. The more implementation details of this part will be discussed in another paper.

3.1 LSF Scheduler Plugin Mechanism

In the real world, each user has different requirements. No matter how many scheduling polices are provided, no resource management system can meet all users' needs. Hence, in version 5.0, LSF designed the scheduler plugin feature to allow users to write their own scheduling policies.

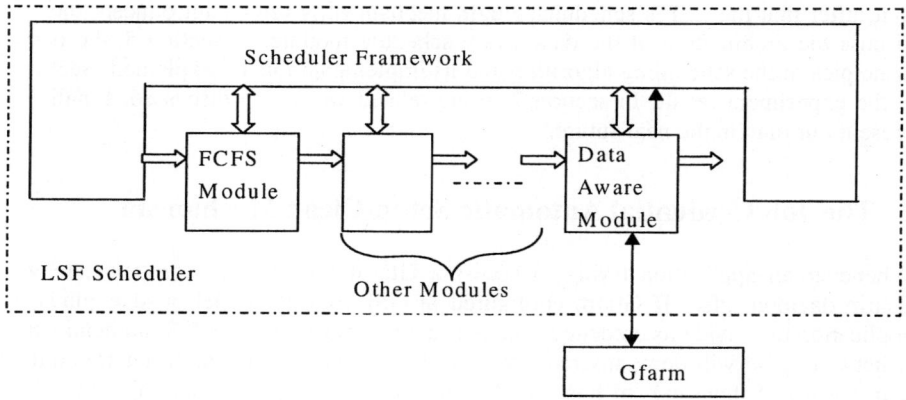

Fig. 1. LSF scheduler plugin mechanism

The LSF plugin mechanism consists of the scheduler framework and a number of scheduler plugin modules. See figure 1. The scheduler framework works as a motherboard with slots to hold scheduler plugin modules. The framework maintains the elementary information, like pending jobs, available hosts etc, for all plugin modules. Plugin modules are able to access those data inside scheduler framework via a LSF scheduler API. The particular scheduling policies are implemented inside plugin modules. FCFS module, for example, provides the first come first serve policy, which is the default policy of LSF.

The plugin modules are loaded dynamically by the framework at run time. The user can indicate which modules to be loaded via configuration. Using this mechanism, the users do not need to write a customized scheduler from scratch, but to provide just a plugin module with the desired policy. In this paper, we describe a plugin module to perform data aware scheduling and data management in Gfarm.

4 Architecture of Data aware Scheduling Module

The data aware scheduling module is implemented as a LSF plugin. It communicates with LSF via the LSF scheduler framework API. The module takes the pending jobs and the available hosts in the system as input from LSF and gets the data replica information from Gfarm. To Gfarm, the module is simply a normal Gfarm application. Any Gfarm API and command can be used. The output of the module is a series of schedule decisions, such as host reservation, replica creation, job execution and so on. These decisions are executed by LSF and Gfarm respectively.

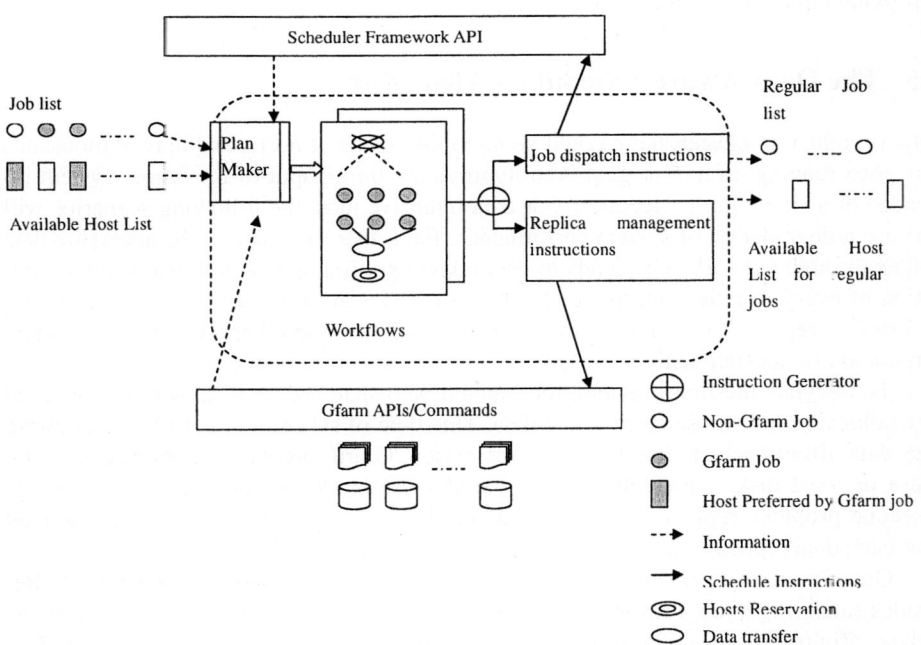

Fig. 2. The data aware plugin module

The data aware module consists of three components, the Plan Maker, the Workflow Container and the Instruction Generator. See figure 2. The Plan Maker is responsible for making job scheduling and data management decisions. The decisions are described as workflows and maintained by the Workflow Container. At the end of a scheduling session, the Instruction Generator issues the corresponding LSF or Gfarm commands to execute the workflows.

The data aware module handles Gfarm applications only, and the other jobs are scheduled by other modules. Hence, the Plan Maker has to be able to recognize Gfarm jobs. In our work, a special tag is attached to each Gfarm job at submission time. A tag is a string with the format of "Gfarm Files=$f1,..fn$", which indicates the files to be accessed by the job. This is done via LSF *bsub –ext* command.

The Plan Maker is the brain. It decides when and where to start a Gfarm job, and whether to create a new replica for a data set. The Plan Maker follows the data aware scheduling policy and writes its decisions into the workflows maintained by the Workflow Container. A workflow is a job execution plan for a data replica. Besides the jobs to be launched, a typical workflow consists of host reservation, file transfer (stage-in), and file elimination (stage-out) operations as well. New jobs can be dynamically added into an existing workflow.

The Instruction Generator is the decision executor, generating concrete jobs or data operations based on the workflows. Those instructions are issued to LSF/ Gfarm via appropriate APIs/commands at the end of each scheduling session. More details are provided in the following section.

5 The Data-Aware Scheduling Algorithm

In a production cluster, there could be up to thousands of hosts, and tens of thousands of jobs running on it. Our goal is to improve the throughput of the whole system instead of a single job's execution. For data-intensive jobs, the following scenarios will cause a degradation of system performance. First, there are many jobs accessing data files through network. This leads to network congestion and slow down of the execution of every job. Second, the loads of data replicas are imbalanced. Some data files with few replicas are being accessed heavily, while some other data files with more replicas are not frequently accessed.

To alleviate the first problem, jobs should be dispatched to hosts with the required data locally or to those close to the data. This type of scheduling is called data aware or data affinity scheduling. For the same reason, Gfarm insists on users making good use of local disks, although network parallel I/O is also supported. To resolve the second problem, replica management should be able to dynamically balance the load of each data replica based on a job's actual requirement.

Our algorithm resolves these two problems above in the following ways: 1. Besides satisfying a job's resource requirements, like host/OS type, it always selects the data affinity hosts for job execution, 2. It supports data stage-in and stage-out, 3. It adjusts dynamically the number of data replicas and their locations according to the real load of the jobs in the system, 4. It avoids creating multiple data replicas concurrently to reduce the possibilities of the network access conflicts.

Both job scheduling and data replica management strategies are embodied in the algorithm. The algorithm is executed by the Plan Maker periodically. Each execution is called a scheduling session. In each session, more jobs will be inserted into existing workflows, and some new workflows could be created. All the jobs belong to the same workflow have to be started in sequence, and normally they do not start within one schedule session. The jobs from different workflows can run concurrently. See Figure 3.

5.1 Algorithm

1. Select a Gfarm job from the pending job list. Other jobs are ignored by the algorithm. The pending job list includes all the jobs waiting to run, and it is maintained by LSF scheduler framework.
2. If the job state is *scheduled*, it must belong to an existing workflow. Check the workflow, if a reserved host is available, and there is no job in the workflow to be executed before it, change the job's state to *launching*. The job will be started in this schedule session.
3. If the job state is not *scheduled*, then try to insert it to an existing workflow. If successful, change the job state to *scheduled*. Otherwise, log the data files (also called data set) used by the job and do statistic using the following formula,

$$\text{Sum}(ds) = \sum_{i=1..n} P_i * T_i$$

(Pi is the job's priority, ds is the data sets used by the job, (1)
Ti is the job's running time)

Note: There is a limit for the number of jobs that a workflow can have. If a workflow is full, no more jobs can be inserted into it unless some jobs are launched. Such a limit can avoid load imbalance among data replicas.

4. If there are more pending jobs, go to 1.
5. After going through all the pending jobs, the algorithm will decide whether to create new replicas in this session according to the statistic results in 3. If there is a data set whose Sum(ds) is larger than a pre-defined value, then the data set needs a new replica. However, in order to decrease the chance of network congestion, only one new replica will be created in a schedule session. The following actions will be taken to perform the replica creation for the data set with the largest Sum(ds) value,
   a) Select the best location (hosts) for the new replica according to job's resource requirement. If there is no host with spare disk space, the obsolete data replicas will be overwritten based on the LRU algorithm.
   b) Create a null workflow
   c) Insert host reservation operation to the workflow to reserve the selected hosts
   d) Insert the data transfer operation to the workflow to create the replica on the selected hosts

At the end of a scheduler session, the Instruction Generator goes through all the workflows: notify LSF to start all the jobs with *launching* state; notify LSF to execute the host reservations for the new replicas; notify Gfarm to start copying data to reserved hosts. Subsequently, the new workflow is used by the Plan Maker to schedule jobs during the next session.

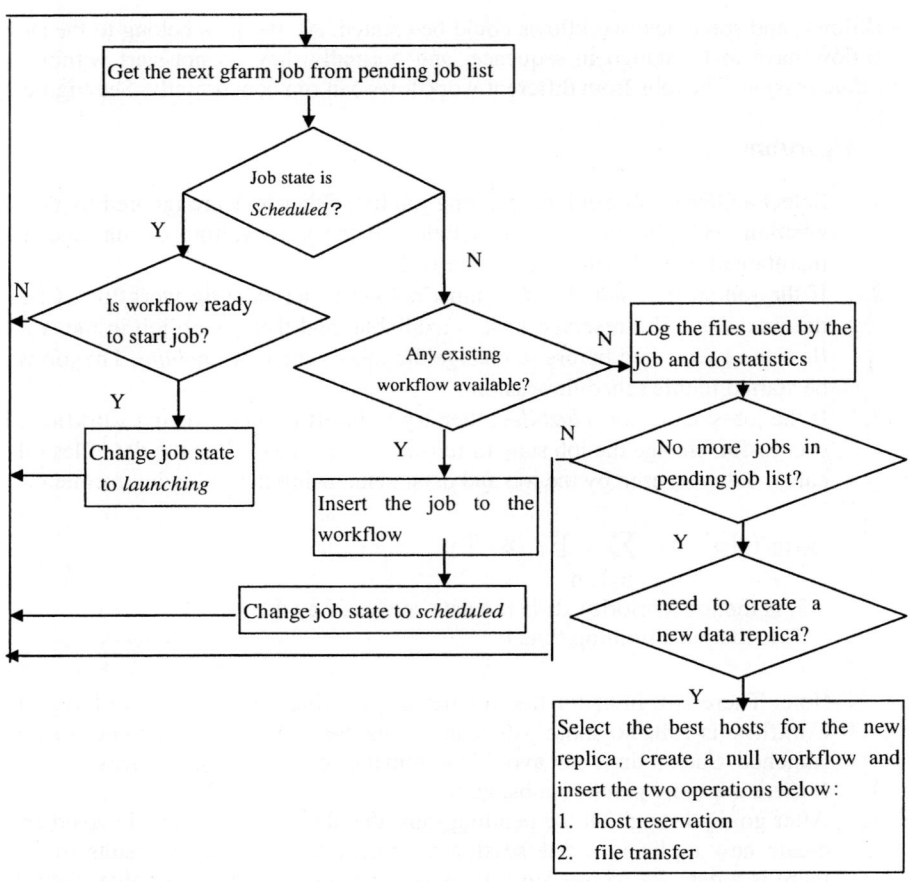

Fig. 3. Data aware algorithm

6 Experiment Result

The system prototype is realized using C language in Linux Red Hat 9. The experiment cluster consists of 6 Linux boxes running LSF6.0 and Gfarm1.0.3 connected by 100M Ethernet. To simplify the test, we assume that all the jobs have the same priority value 1. The data aware plugin algorithm will generate a new data replica once its Sum(ds)>= 1500 which is configurable.

The experiment results depend on the characteristics of the applications to be tested. In our test case, there are three kinds of jobs submitted to the system. Accordingly, three input data files are located in different hosts' disks. All the jobs are using the same algorithm to process its input data, and all the data files have the same size-900MB. Running on the host with the input file locally, a job is completed in 32 seconds in average. In contrast, the job normally spends 132 seconds if to access input file remotely. In each test, we submit 300 jobs(100 for each type) to the system. After 10x of such test, we got the following results,

With the data aware plugin, the system takes 1650s in average to finish 300 jobs. Compared with 2640s without data aware plugin, the system performance is improved by 37.5%. The result looks positive. However, many factors, like job patterns and network topology etc, have impact on the performance of the algorithm. We are planning to run our prototype on PRAGMA test bed to collect more data.

7 Related Works

In [9], job scheduling and data management modules are separate components. In [10], a data aware scheduling mechanism is implemented in a peer-to-peer computing model: job scheduling and data management are implemented as two loose-coupled components. In our work, job scheduling and data management are integrated together. In our case, the scheduler knows both jobs and data well, therefore, is able to make a better plan to improve the system's performance overall.

Plan based scheduling is introduced in some recent works. The focus of [11] is on the scheduling for a single complex task with multiple components in the computing grid. AI plan is used to generate workflows to execute components of a task. Our work is an extension of [11]. Instead of focusing on a single job, workflows are used to plan the execution of a number of data-intensive jobs. Many works, like [12], introduced methods to balance the load for a parallel job to overcome the performance heterogeneity betweens the nodes in a cluster. In this paper, we achieve dynamic load balancing for data replicas based on the needs of jobs in the system. Moreover, our use of a LSF scheduler plugin mechanism has the following advantages: no need to write a scheduler from scratch, because the data aware scheduling policy is implemented as a plugin module; the new policy can co-operate with other policies, like FCFS, fair share, and preemption etc.

8 Conclusion and Future Work

This paper describes the integration of LSF6.0 and Gfarm1.0.3 on Linux RedHat9.0. A job credential automatically setup/clean mechanism is introduced to support Gfarm GSI authentication. The data aware scheduling and data replica management functionalities are implemented using a LSF scheduler plugin mechanism. The following features are provided by the data aware plugin: 1. A queuing mechanism for Gfarm jobs is provided and to the ability to allocate data-affinity hosts for job execution. 2. The stage-in and stage-out functionality. 3. Dynamic adjustment of the distribution of data replicas according to actual job requirement. 4. Cooperation with other scheduling policies and ease of extension with new scheduling features.

Our team has finished the project to port CSF[6] from GT3-OGSI to GT4-WSRF. CSF is a grid level scheduling framework. In the near future, we are going to introduce data aware scheduling policy into CSF. Our research will identify the different focuses between the grid level data aware scheduling and cluster level data aware scheduling, and how to make the two kind of policies work together efficiently. We will also add other job schedulers like SGE and Open PBS to our test bed.

Acknowledgment

Xiaohui Wei would like to acknowledge the support from JiLin University grant 419070200053 and 420010302338.

W. W. Li would like to acknowledge the support from NSF grant INT-0314015 for PRAGMA and NIH/NCRR program grant P41 RR08605 for NBCR.

References

1. Jim Basney and Miron Livny, "Managing Network Resources in Condor". *Proceedings of the Ninth IEEE Symposium on High Performance Distributed Computing (HPDC9)*, Pittsburgh, Pennsylvania, August 2000, pp 298-299.
2. Songnian Zhou, Xiaohu Zheng, Jingwen Wang et al. Utopia: a Load Sharing Facility for Large, Heterogeneous Distributed Computer Systems. SOFTWARE—PRACTICE AND EXPERIENCE, Dec 1993: 23(12), 1305-1336.
3. James, P. J, Portable Batch System: Exterernal Reference Specification Altair PBS Pro 5.3. http://www.mta.ca/torch/pdf/pbspro54/pbsproers.pdf, March 2003.
4. Sun Microsystems, Inc. Sun Grid Engine 5.3 Administration and User's Guide. http://gridengine.sunsource.net/project/gridengine-download/SGE53AdminUserDoc.pdf, April, 2002.
5. James Frey, Todd Tannenbaum, and Ian Foster *et al*, "Condor-G: A Computation Management Agent for Multi-Institutional Grids", Journal of Cluster Computing volume 5, pages 237-246, 2002.
6. Platform Computing Co. Open source metascheduling for Virtual Organizations with the Community Scheduler Framework (CSF). http://www.cs.virginia.edu/~grimshaw/CS851-2004/Platform/CSF_architecture.pdf , 2004.
7. MONARC Collaboration. Models of Networked Analysis at Regional Centres for LHC experiments: Phase 2 report. Technical Report CERN/LCB-001, CERN. http://www.cern.ch/MONARC/, 2000.
8. Osamu Tatebe, Youhei Morita, Satoshi Matsuoka et al. Grid Datafarm Architecture for Petascale Data Intensive Computing. Proceedings of the 2nd IEEE/ACM International Symposium on Cluster Computing and the Grid, pp.102-110, 2002.
9. Kavitha Ranganathan, Ian Foster. Decoupling Computation and Data Scheduling in Distributed Data-Intensive Applications. Proceedings of 11th IEEE International Symposium on High Performance Distributed Computing (HPDC-11), Edinburgh, Scotland, http://www.globus.org/research/papers/decouple.pdf, July 2002.
10. Florian Schintke, Thorsten Schutt, Alexander. A Framework for Self-Optimizing Grids Using P2P Components. Proceedings of the 14th International Workshop on Database and Expert Systems Applications (DEXA'03), http://www.zib.de/reinefeld/Publications/dexa03.pdf , 2003.
11. Jim Blythe, Ewa Deelman, Yolanda Gil et al. The Role of Planning in Grid Computing. 13th International Conference on Automated Planning and Scheduling (ICAPS), Trento, Italy, http://www.isi.edu/~gil/papers/icaps03-submission.pdf , June 2003.
12. Yoshiaki Sakae, et al. Preliminary Evaluation of Dynamic Load Balancing Using Loop Repartitioning on Omni/SCASH. The 3rd International Symposium on Cluster Computing and the Grid, Tokyo, Japan, May 2003: 463-471.

Cache Management for Discrete Processor Architectures

Jih-Fu Tu

Department of Electronic Engineering,
St. John's University,
499, Sec. 4, Tam-King Road, Tamsui, Taipei, Taiwan

Abstract. Many schemes had been used to reduce the performance (or speed) gap between processors and main memories; such as the cache memory is one of the most methods. In this paper, we issue the structure of shared cache, which is based on the multiprocessor architectures to reduce the memory latency time that is the one of major performance bottlenecks of modern processors. In this paper, we mix two schemes, sharing cache and multithreading, to implement this proposed multithreaded architecture with shared cache, to reduce the memory latency and, furthermore improve the processor performance. In this proposed multithreaded architecture, the shared cache is achieved in level-1 (L1) data cache. The L1 shared data cache is combination of cache clock in the single space address and a cache controller to solve the required data transmitting, data copies simultaneously, and reduce memory latency time.

Keywords: Discrete processor architectures, cache coherency, multithreading, memory latency, shared cache, write-invalidate (WI), and cache block.

1 Introduction

The speed gap is growing up between the CPU and memory, which is the bottleneck of performance of processor. Thus, There are several methods issued for tolerating or hiding the memory latency between the processor and main memory to reduce the needed data access latency, Such as adding a small fast I- and D-cache (i e. cache memory), or exploiting multithreading scheme continually execute the thread while context switch occurrence. Cache memory was a proved effective technique to reduce memory latency and had been implemented in all the known high-performance multiprocessor architectures [1, 2, 8, 9]. A shared cache is a fast RAM-type memory positioned between the relatively fast CPU and slower main memory (usually implement DRAM memory). The shared cache [4, 21] is a hardware solution that makes the cache invisible to the operating system and the application software.

The structure of shared cache is combination of several processors, memory management units (MMU), bus arbiters, and a shared cache. In the shared cache, accesses of all bus arbiters are routed to main memory through the same shared-cache. The shared cache is exploited in a number of processors systems to solve the cache coherency and to reduce the memory latency.

In shared cache system, the processors share the cache memory as well as the main memory. The shared cache is partitioned several shared blocks in the same address area. It should have speed compatible to that of the processors. To make the shared cache competitive that should offers simultaneous read/write property to allow the processors and main memory (DRAM) to access the same cache block at the same time [5,20]. The shared cache is located between processor and main memory to reduce and hide the main memory latency while the needed data of processors is transmitted inter-processor of multiprocessor systems.

To maintain the copied data are coherence in cache block of the shared cache. An effective cache coherency is enforced on the multiprocessor systems. A cache coherency protocol is a set of rules that ensure the cached data to be distributed among individual processor coherently. For the system performance of multiprocessor systems, which depend on the effectively the data-caching coherence scheme.

The proposed architecture is innovated to the multiprocessor systems, then on multithreaded architectures with shared cache. We construct the execution unit to each processor, called threading processor unit (TPU), of multiprocessor systems, in which each TPU is combination of the program counter, general purpose registers, and stacks (shown in Figure 1). In this paper, we also issue a cache controller for this multithreaded processor with shared cache. The shared cache is construct of 4-way set-associative, write-invalidate (WI) protocol for cache coherency of cache blocks, and write through strategy read/write for cache and memory simultaneously [7,11,15,16,19].

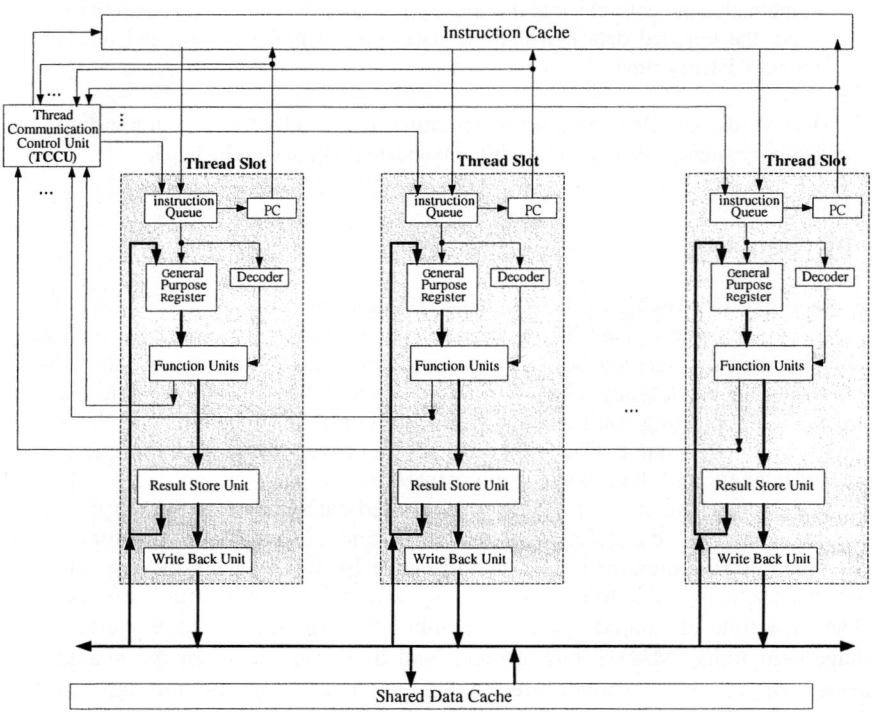

Fig. 1. The shared cache based on multithreaded processors

The proposed multithreaded processors (MTP) with shared cache is constructed and simulated with trace-driven simulation tools, SES/*workbench* [18]. We compare the performance of this proposed MTP with shared cache to that of the MTP without shared cache. Both have the same specification and simulate with the same environment, parameters, and workbench. We find this proposed MTP with shared cache has higher performance than the MTP without shared cache.

The main contribution of this paper, we use a bus arbiter to handle the request/grant signals, furthermore to access the needed data from cache blocks or other thread processing unit. The remained of this paper is organized as follows. We investigate the issued designs and papers of shared cache in Section 2. The structures of the shared cache of MTP, cache controller, and the cache coherency protocol are illustrated in Section 3. The simulation model and the results are analyzed in Section 4. Finally, we remark the conclusions in Section 5.

2 The Previous of Shared Cache Design

A cache memory contributes in both hiding memory latency and reducing the traffic on the processor interconnection network of shared cache and shard memory on the multiple processors but it cause causes the coherence problems [6].

The shared cache is the one approach of hardware-based techniques to solve the cache coherency. In shared cache, we split the single address space shared cache into several cache blocks, which are uniformly shared accessed by the thread processing unit (TPU) that is all processors have equal access time to the cache lines.

The shared cache approach was exploited in multiprocessors, such as, in 1993s, Chaudhry and Han [3] exploited the concept of shared cache and private cache techniques and used the P-Bus and S-Bus via network to control the data access from /to private block cache and shared block cache, respectively.

In 1994s, Sawchuk and Cheng [17] used the optoelectronic devices in parallel computers to increase the effective processing rate. In those shared cache systems, the processors shared the cache as well as the main memory through two levels of interconnection networks. In 1995s, Kang and Rim [10] had implemented the shared cache, shared system interface, dispatcher, and multiprocessor to built on-chip multiprocessor to improve the performance.

In 1996s, Nuyfeh et al. [14] proposed a clustering shared cache. Though the access latency is reduced intro-cluster shared cache, a longer latency time is needed in the inter-cluster shared cache. The needed data is accessed both in the intro- and inter-cluster shared cache are thoroughly the networking techniques.

As for the application of shared cache, fewer papers are issued. Referred to the previous works of shared cache, we find that both used a network to manage the shared cache blocks. Thus, the hit latency and needed data access latency are existed on inter-processor communication for the interconnection networking. In this paper, we discard the networking and replace by an arbitration controller with buffer techniques. In 1996s, Chen et al. [4] used a trace-driven simulation to study shared cache performance on multithreaded architectures. In that article, two conclusions are issued, more cache size and more set-associative in order to maintain comparable cache performance.

In 1999s, Tasi et al. [21] constructed superthreaded processor architecture, in which includes several thread processing unit, and the shared I-and D-shared cache.

Each thread-processing unit is a logic pipeline processor to be added to a communication unit. In this paper, the thread is sequenced fork via and transfers the needed data between the private communication units of thread-processing unit. The data update not immediately between communication block and shared cache, thus the invalided data could be stored in the shared cache block and read by the other thread-processing unit. In 2004, Tu [22] issued the concept of the shared cache for multiprocessor systems.

In our proposed shared cache based on multithreaded architectures, we exploit the write-invalided strategy for shared cache and a common thread communication unit to cohere the cache blocks and to reduce the communication delay inter-processors, respectively.

3 The Structure of Shared Cache Controller

The MIMD (multiple instructions and multiple data) is classed into processor-level architectures and thread-level architectures. The most of thread-level architectures have been built or proposed with shared memory, such as Denelor HEP [12] and MIT Hybrid Machine, and distributed shared memory systems, such as Tera, *T [13], P-RISC, and EM-4 [23]. There are fewer multithreaded machine with shared cache, example of superthreaded processor architecture.

In this paper, we construct a shared cache based on multithreaded architectures, which is the revolutionary the structure of superthreaded processor architecture [21], in which is improved having a thread communication unit to handle the context switch and needed data communication inter-thread processing units. The structure of this proposed multithreaded architecture is shown in Figure 2. The detail schematic of the proposed multithreaded architecture, the proposed multithreaded architectures is combination of several thread-processing units, thread communication unit, and the shared cache. The thread-processing unit is a logic pipeline processor having instruction queue (IQ) and encoder, general-purpose register (GPR), program counter, ALU, result store buffer (RSB), and write back unit. Any thread is executed in thread-processing unit as a process in pipeline processor until the data dependency occurs. Thus, context switching happens among thread-processing unit to be controlled by the thread communication unit.

The thread communication unit includes two elements, there are bus arbiter and data communication unit. The bus arbiter handles and records the context switching and the status of thread of thread-processing unit, respectively. The data communication unit is constructed as buffer to temperately store the address of needed data in where of the cache block during the requesting stilly stupendous. Until the requesting thread of the requesting thread-processing unit is to be awaken.

The shared cache is split into I-cache and D-cache. All the threads are shared a L1 cache. The results of any thread-processing unit are written into data result buffer (DSB) and the shared cache block, simultaneously. When the data is updated, an invalided signal is sent to the copied cache block to avoid this un-update data to read by the other thread-processing unit. The detail of control and data flow between thread processing unit (TPU) and thread communication unit (TCU) is shown in Figure 2. For the needed data is accesses from three paths, there are written back from the data store buffer (DSB), directly fetch from the shared cache block, and remote access from the DSB of other TPU.

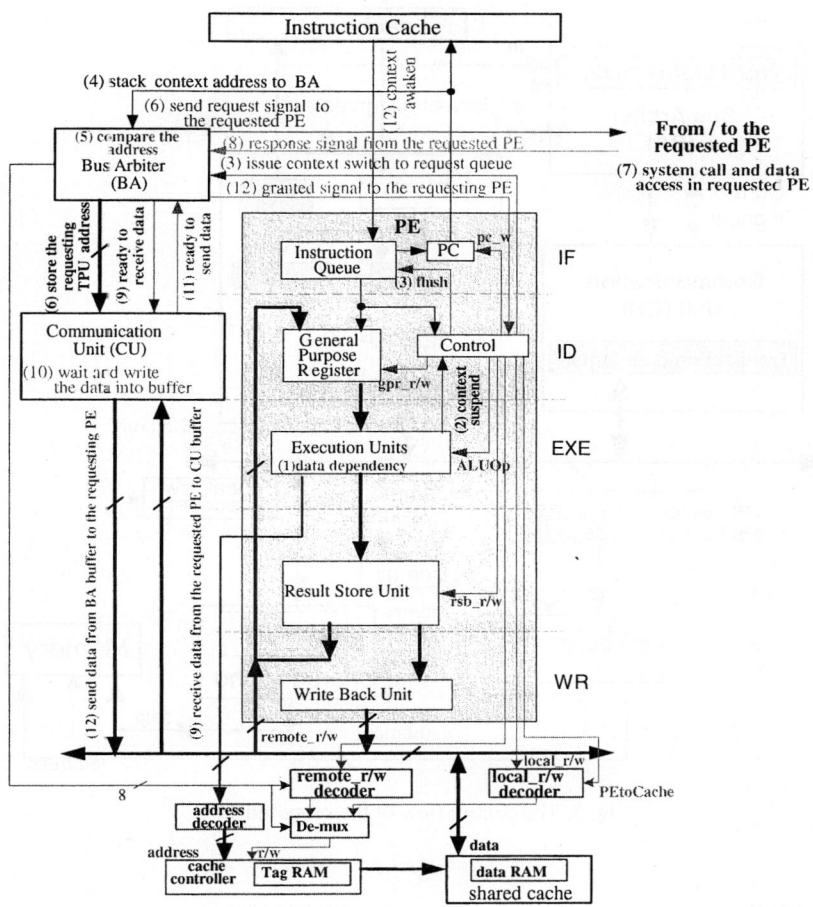

Fig. 2. The control and data flows between TPU and TCU

The shared data cache is split to several blocks associative to the number of TPUs. When the data dependency is occurred, an exception request is issued from ALU to the control unit, then to the bus arbiter. Furthermore this requesting thread is suspended and a context switching in its concurrent TPU. When the needed data have remotely accessed from other TPU, but the requesting thread do not awaken.

The address of the needed data is store in the buffer of the communication unit. When the requesting thread awakens, the communication unit issues this address of needed data to its concurrent TPU to access the needed data from the valid cache block. The produce of thread control flow and its protocol are shown in Figure 5, in which the needed data request is issued when data dependency occurs in thread processing unit (TPU), the bus arbiter manages the handshaking among TPUs, and the communication unit transfers the address of needed data in shared cache.

Figure 6 show the structure of communication unit, in which is combination of several tri-state control registers and data buffer. The address of needed data of cache

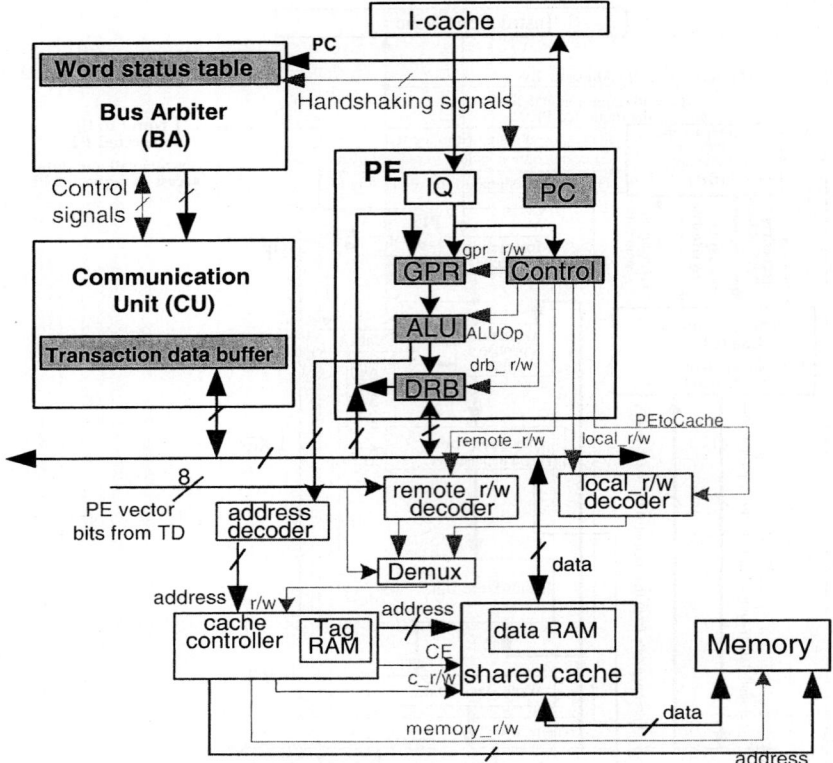

Fig. 5. The control flow of the proposed TPU

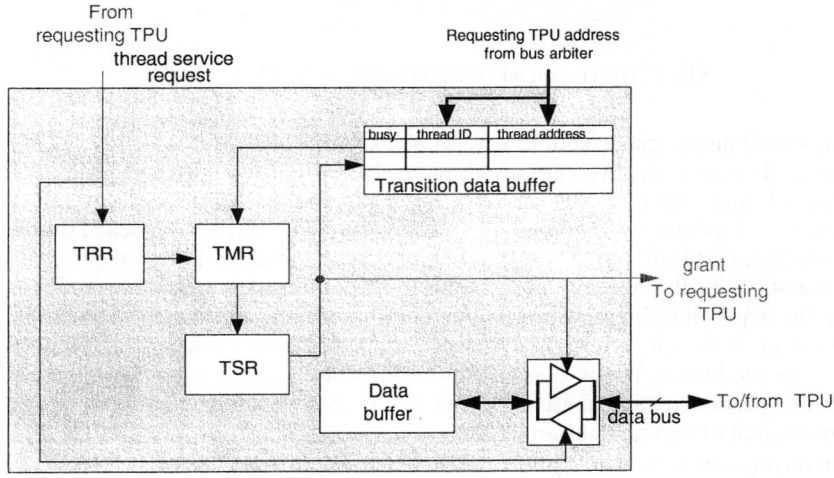

Fig. 6. The structure of communication unit

block is temporality store in the transition data buffer of communication unit. The L1 data cache is split into several blocks. In order to maintain the coherence data in shared cache, we exploit the write invalidation strategy to void the old data to be read by TPU. For the cache controller, it is designed and shown in Figure 7.

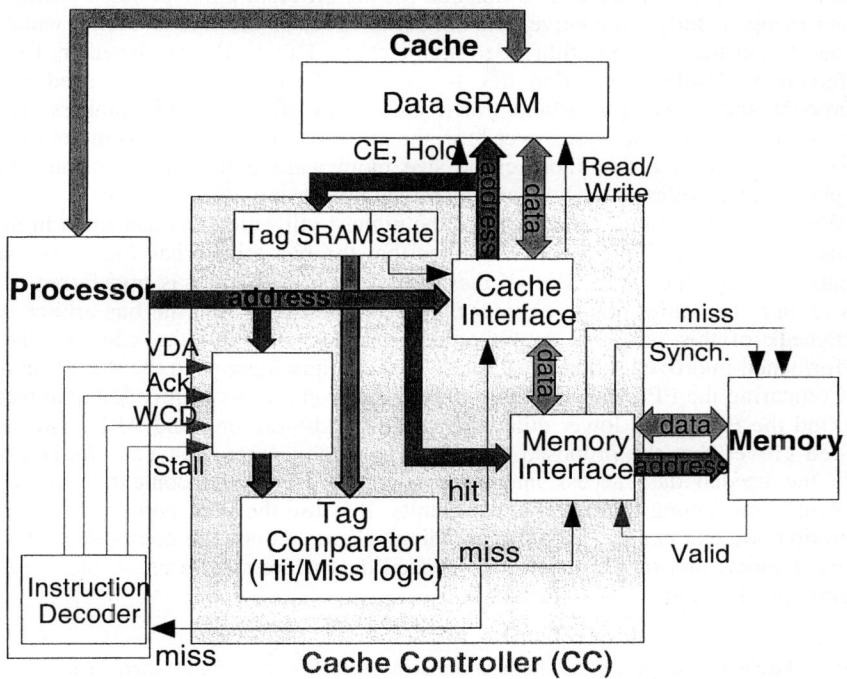

Fig. 7. The structure of cache controller

4 The Simulation Results

The experiments have conducted on a detailed, cycle accurate, performance simulator that is derived from the SES/*workbench* tools set. The simulator takes binaries compiled with gcc for the hierarchical model. A statistical simulation uses populations, utilization, and throughput rate to characterize the simulated model parameters: *Populations* are the number of transactions, called *samples*, present at the node, which in a SES/*workbench* model represents the manipulation of a physical or logical resource or some other processing step, in a model or sub-model. *Utilization* is the number of servers or resources in use on a model of a sub-model. *Throughput rate*, abbreviation *rate* in the result of this paper, *the total amount of transactions done in a give simulated time*, is defined as the average number of transactions executed by the nodes, such as function unit of SES/*workbench*, per unit time step.

The throughput rate multiplies to a number of the workload machine operating frequency, which I calculated by MHz, we could obtain the throughput in MIPS [11].

We compare the utilization and throughput to each unit in the different kinds of configures of L1 shared cache and different instruction size in the assume parameters.

4.1 Comparing the Utilization for Different Configure of Shared Cache

In this section, we illustrate the utilization for the different kinds of cache configures, direct-mapped, fully associative, and set-associative, of the shared cache, which are embedded in the same multithreaded architecture. The results are listed in Table 1. Referring to Table 1, we find the 4-way set-associative has lower used rate of submodel and instruction access traffic time than others thread numbers. As we increase the scalar of set value over four, the utilization of submodel is increased, too. This reason tells me that more cache size more waiting time when occurs thread suspended and context switching among thread processing units.

We also find that the bus arbiter has the highest utilization to other units in the all kinds of configure. The reason illustrates that the bus arbiter has higher operation frequency than other units. For all message of each thread slot is transferred to this bus arbiter. This information express two facts, the one is that the bus arbiter is the bottleneck of this proposed multithreaded architectures, and the other is that the performance-improved scheme exploits TLP technique superior to the ILP technique.

Comparing the FPU unit to other units of the proposed multithreaded architecture, we find the FPU's has lower utilizations than Load/Store unit and ALU. This result envied proves that the proposed multithreaded architecture with bus arbiter effects hide the needed data access latency time while occurs the context switching or asynchronous among thread processing units. Because the float point has complexly operation, we can exploit the multithreading scheme reduce the computing time, the access latency, and rapidly obtain the needed data address from cache block via the communication unit.

Table 1. The transactions number are using in different configure shared cache

	Direct-mapped	Fully-associative	Set-associative			
			2-way	4-way	6-way	8-way
Instr_queue	33	33	29	33	33	32
Bus arbiter	215	215	214	236	233	234
Reuse_store	15	15	21	17	17	16
ALU	21	21	16	24	24	24
L/S unit	20	20	21	18	18	18
FPU	7	7	6	8	8	8
Total	313	311	307	336	333	332

4.2 Comparing MIPS with Different Configures of Shared Cache

Secondly, we describe the speedup for different Configures of Shared Cache of the proposed multithreaded architecture; the results are shown in Table 2. For instance, the system throughput rate, defined the transactions per simulation time unit rates, multiply the number of the operating frequency in MHz. Thus, we can obtain the system throughput in MIPS. We find the best case is 4-way set-associative.

Table 2. The throughput rate in different configure shared cache

	Direct-mapped	Fully-associative	Set-associative			
			2-way	4-way	6-way	8-way
Instr_queue	0.00132	0.00132	0.0012	0.0013	0.00132	0.0013
Bus arbiter	0.0043	0.0043	0.0043	0.0047	0.00475	0.0047
Reuse_store	1.461	1.461	1.57	1.56	1.56	1.56
ALU	0.3	0.3	0.3	0.3	0.3	0.3
L/S Unit	0.2	0.2	0.2	0.2	0.2	0.2
FPU	0.5	0.5	0.5	0.5	0.5	0.5
Total Rate	2.46662	2.46662	2.5758	2.566	2.566	2.566

4.3 Comparing the Utilization to Networking Scheme Multithreaded Architectures

Finally, we compare the utilization of the multithread architecture with 4 thread slots and 8 instruction sizes to the networking multithreaded architectures (single thread processor). Besides, the thread slot and the instruction sizes are consisted in multithreaded architecture; both the multithreaded architecture and the networking multithreaded architecture have the same features. Figure 8 illustrates the utilization between the proposed multithreaded architecture and the networking multithreaded architecture.

Observing the results, we obtain that the multithreaded architecture has higher utilization than the networking multithreaded architectures, especially the FPU and Load/Store node of multithreaded architecture. Referring to Figure 8, expect the I-queue and D-cache nodes, in the advantage; the utilization t of the multithreaded architecture is higher than the networking multithreaded architectures. This result expresses that the shared data cache improving the data latency and access traffic.

This result also tells us that the multiple threads can achieve speedup to the computers; the times are decided to the thread slot numbers. In addition, the FPU unit specifically highlight, the reason is clearly described in Section 4.1.

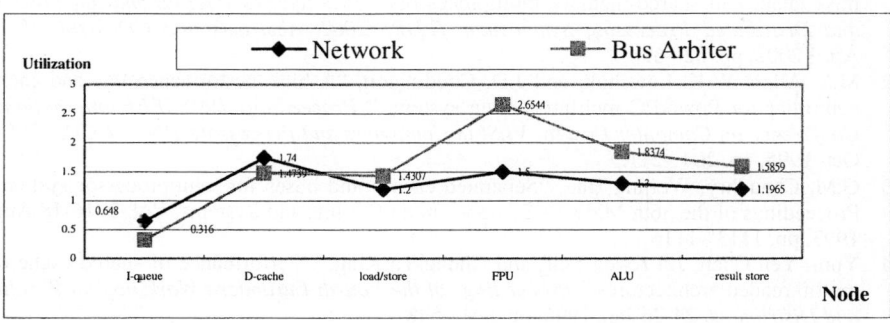

Fig. 8. The utilizations between the proposed cache controller and the network of shared cache multithreaded architecture

Refer to Figure 9, we find the proposed multithreaded architecture has 4-TPU, in which has the fastest run-time, on average. Even if we increase the size of TPU number up to 16-TPU, the performance of the proposed multithreaded architecture does not evidently improvement. This result due to the handshaking between the shared data cache to be handed the bus arbiter, more the TPU number more loading to the bus traffic. Whereas, the address of the needed data of request TPU's are directly pre-store in the buffer of communication unit. Furthermore, the information is delivered to the requesting TPU while the suspended thread is awakening.

5 Conclusions

The major purposes of shared data cache are used to reduce the cache-hit latency and remain the cache coherency among cache block to reduce the needed access latency. For the must previous multithreaded processor systems exploit distributed shared memory. Those multithreaded architectures have the same characters to the multiprocessor systems; using multithreading and networking techniques to implement the context switching and the dependent data access among each processor units, respectively. In this paper, we proposed an on-chip multithreaded architecture, in which each thread processing unit has private L1 instruction cache and the L1 data cache is based on the shared cache scheme.

We simulate this proposed multithreaded architecture using a trace-driven simulation tools. We analyze the simulation result to find this proposed multithreaded architecture more effective than the private cache based on multithreaded architectures. The best configuration of the shared L1 data cache is constructed of 64 KB, 4-way set-associative 64 bits line.

There is much room for the shared cache based on multithreaded architectures, such as the control method of shared cache, the bus configuration of shared cache, and single bus or multiple buses?

References

1. M.E. Acacio, J. Gonzalez, J. M. Garcia, and J. Duato, "A. novel approach to reduce L2 miss latency in shared-memory multiprocessors," *Proceedings International on Parallel and Distributed Processing Symposium, IPDPS 2002, Abstracts and CD-ROM*, 15-19 April 2002, pp. 62 –69.
2. M.S. Allen, W.K. Lewchuk, and J.D. Coddington, "A high performance bus and cache controller for PowerPC multiprocessing systems," *Proceedings 1995 IEEE International Conference on Computer Design: VLSI in Computers and Processors 1995, ICCD '95*, 2-4 Oct. 1995, pp. 204 –211.
3. G.M. Chaudhry, Weijing Han, "Separated caches and buses for multiprocessor system," Proceedings of the 36th Midwest Symposium on Circuits and Systems, Vol. 2, 16-18 Aug. 1993, pp. 1113 –1116.
4. Yunn-Yen Chen, Jih-Kwon Peir, and Chung-Ta King, " Performance of shared cache on multithreaded architectures," *Proceedings of the Fourth Euromicro Workshop on Parallel and Distributed*, 24-26 Jan. 1996, pp. 541 –548.
5. Q. Chunming and R. Melhem, "Reducing communication latency with path multiplexing in optically interconnected multiprocessor systems," *IEEE Transactions on Parallel and Distributed Systems, Volume: 8 Issue: 2*, Feb. 1997, pp. 97 –108.

6. P. Foglia, R. Giorgi, C. A. Prete, "Analysis of sharing overhead in shared memory multiprocessors," Proceedings of the Thirty-First Hawaii International Conference on, Volume: 7, 6-9 Jan. 1998, pp. 776 –777.
7. D. Hsieh and Lai Feipei, "Design and test of memory management unit and cache controller chip," Proceedings. IEEE Region 10 Conference on Computer, Communication, Control and Power Engineering. TENCON '93. Issue: 0, 19-21 Oct. 1993, pp. 10 –13.
8. L. Ivanov and R. Nunna, "Modeling and verification of cache coherence Protocols," The 2001 IEEE International Symposium on Circuits and Systems, 2001. ISCAS 2001, Volume: 5, 6-9 May 2001, pp. 129 –132.
9. Tao Jie, M. Schulz, and W. Karl, "A simulation tool for evaluating shared memory systems," 36th Annual Simulation Symposium, 30 March-2 April 2003,pp. 335 –342.
10. Jun-Woo Kang; Kee-Wook Rim,"VLSI implementation of multiprocessor system," IEEE Region 10 International Conference on Microelectronics and VLSI, TENCON '95, 6-10 Nov. 1995,pp. 480 -483
11. D. Keen, M. Oskin, and J. Hensley, F. T. Chong, " Cache coherence in intelligent memory systems," IEEE Transactions on Computers, Volume: 52 Issue: 7, July 2003, pp. 960 –966.
12. R. S. Nikhil and Arvind, "Can Dataflow Subsume von Neumann Computing," Proc. 16th Annu. Int. Symposium. Computer Architecture, 1989, pp. 262-272.
13. R. S. Nikhil and G. M. Papadopulos, "*T: A Multithreaded Massively Parallel Architecture," Proc. 19th Annual Int. Symposium. Computer Architecture, May 1992, pp. 361-372.
14. B.A. Nayfeh, K. Olukotun, and J.P. Singh," The impact of shared-cache clustering in small-scale shared-memory multiprocessors," Proceedings. Second International Symposium on High-Performance Computer Architecture, 3-7 Feb. 1996, pp. 74 –84.
15. J. A. Reisner and T. S. Wailes, "A cache coherency protocol for optically connected parallel computer systems," Proceedings of Second International Symposium on High-Performance Computer Architecture, 3-7 Feb. 1996, pp. 222 –231.
16. J. Sahuquillo and A. Pont, "Impact of reducing miss write latencies in multiprocessors with two level cache," Proceedings. 24th Euromicro Conference, Volume: 1, 25-27 Aug. 1998, pp. 333 –336.
17. A.A. Sawchuk, L. Cheng, " Considerations for optoelectronic shared cache parallel computers," Proceedings of the First International Workshop on Massively Parallel Processing Using Optical Interconnections, 26-27 April 1994, pp. 241 –251.
18. Scientific and Engineering Software, inc., SES/workbench User's Manual, Release 2.1 Scientific and Engineering Software Austin, TX, USA, 2, 1992.
19. S. Selvakumar and P. Prabhakar, "Implementation and comparison of distributed caching schemes," Proceedings of the IEEE International Conference on Networks, 2000. (ICON 2000), 5-8 Sept. 2000, pp. 491.
20. M. Shalan and V. J. Mooney, "Hardware support for real-time embedded multiprocessor system-on-a-chip memory management," Proceedings of the Tenth International Symposium on Hardware/Software Codesign, CODES 2002, 6-8 May 2002, pp. 79 –84.
21. Jenn-Yuan Tsai, Jian Huang, C. Amlo, D.J. Lilja, Pen-Chung Yew, "The superthreaded processor architecture," IEEE Transactions on Computers, Volume: 48 Issue: 9, Sept. 1999, pp. 881 –902.
22. Jih-Fu Tu, "SMTA: A Next Generational High Performance Multithreaded Architecture," IEE Proceedings- Computer and Digital Techniques, Vol. 149, No. 5, September 2002, pp.213-218.
23. Y. Yamaguchi, S. Sakai, and Y. Kodama," Synchronization Mechanism of a Highly Parallel Dataflow Machine EM-4," IEICE Transactions, Vol.74, No. 1 1991, pp. 204-213.

Enhancing DCache Warn Fetch Policy for SMT Processors

Minxuan Zhang[1] and Caixia Sun[2]

[1] College of Computer, National University of Defense Technology,
Changsha 410073, Hunan, P.R. China
mxzhang@nudt.edu.cn
[2] College of Computer, National University of Defense Technology,
Changsha 410073, Hunan, P.R. China
cxsun1979@163.com

Abstract. Simultaneous Multithreading (SMT) processors improve performance by allowing running instructions from several threads simultaneously at a single cycle. These threads executing simultaneously share the processor's resources, but at the same time compete for them. A thread missing in L2 cache may allocate a large number of resources which other threads could be using to make forward progress. And as a result, the overall performance of SMT processors is degraded. To prevent this situation, many instruction fetch policies are proposed. DWarn is among the most efficient fetch policies to handle L2 cache misses. In this paper, we present an enhanced version of the DWarn policy called DWarn+. Results show that our policy significantly improves the original one in throughput and fairness when not more than four threads run. When the number of threads running is higher than 4, our policy enhances the original one mainly for memory bounded workloads, and the average improvement for all types of workloads is very limited.

Keywords: SMT, L2 cache miss, I-fetch Policy, Fetch Priority, Resource Allocation.

1 Introduction

Simultaneous Multithreading (SMT) processors [1,2,3] improve performance by allowing running instructions from several threads simultaneously at a single cycle. Co-scheduled threads share some resources, such as issue queues, physical registers, and functional units. The way of allocating shared resources among the threads will affect the overall performance of SMT processors. Currently, shared resources allocation is dynamically decided by the instruction fetch policy.

In SMT processors, the number of shared resources is limited, so if a thread holds critical resources for a long time, other threads may run slower than they could or even stall because of lack of resources. A load missing in L2 cache usually causes this happen. An efficient fetch policy should be able to prevent this situation. DWarn [4] is among the most efficient fetch policy to handle L2 cache misses. DWarn uses L1 data misses as indicators of L2 misses, giving higher priority to threads with no outstanding L1 data cache misses. It can avoid harming a thread when L1 misses do not lead to L2 misses. So DWarn policy is able to prevent the negative effects caused by loads missing in L2 cache as well as can reduce the resource under-use. However, using DWarn, a thread with L2 cache missing can still have some opportunity to fetch instructions into the processor, especially when the number of threads running is small. Although DWarn gates the threads with L2 cache missies when there are less than three threads running, it may be so late that shared resources have been clogged. Furthermore, there may exist idle cycles of the processor when all threads are experiencing L2 cache misses.

In this paper, we propose an enhanced version of DWarn fetch policy called DWarn+. In our policy, when a load misses in L1 data cache, its thread is given lower fetch priority than threads with no outstanding data cache misses. If the load finally misses in L2 cache, its thread's fetch priority is reduced further. Hence, as long as the number of co-scheduled threads is big enough, the threads with L2 cache misses almost have no chance to fetch instructions into the processor. When less than three threads run, our modification is restricting the resources allocated to threads with cache misses, and gating these threads only when they attempt to exceed their assigned resources. In this way, on one hand, the threads with L2 cache misses can be prevented from clogging the shared resources; on the other hand, idle cycles of the processor would not be produced even if all threads are experiencing L2 cache misses.

This paper is organized as follows. Section 2 introduces the DWarn policy and explains its main drawback. In Section 3, we detail our DWarn+ policy. Sections 4 and 5 present the methodology and the results. Finally, concluding remarks are given in Section 6.

2 The DWarn Policy

DWarn policy is based on the combination of two ideas, namely, classification of threads, and prioritization of threads. At first, at each cycle, available threads are classified into two groups: Dmiss group, containing the threads that have at least one in-flight L1 data cache miss (Of course, the thread with L2 cache misses belongs to this group.), and Normal group, to which the remaining threads belong. Once the classification is done, the fetch priority of the less-promising (Dmiss) threads is reduced. This is done by prioritizing the Normal threads, and fetching instructions from the Dmiss threads only when there are not enough available instructions from the Normal threads. Threads in the same group are sorted using ICOUNT [2].

Threads are never stalled, and as a result, even if a thread is in the Dmiss group, it has some opportunity to fetch instructions into the processor. In SMT processors using ICOUNT2.8 as the basic fetch policy, when 2-thread workloads run, DWarn may fail to prevent the Dmiss thread clogging the shared resources. To address this problem, DWarn uses a hybrid mechanism. If there are less than three threads running, the priority of the thread experiencing an L1 data cache miss is reduced. After that, if the L1 miss finally turns to an L2 miss, its thread is gated. If the number of execution threads is higher than 2, DWarn will only reduce the fetch priority of the Dmiss threads.

There are two problems with DWarn fetch policy:

First, DWarn does not distinguish the threads experiencing L2 cache misses from those only experiencing L1 data cache misses. These two kinds of threads are all belong to Dmiss group, so these threads can only be sorted by ICOUNT. Maybe threads with L2 cache misses are chosen to fetch instructions prior to those only with L1 data cache misses. In fact, we hope to prioritize the latter because the latter is less likely to clog the shared resources than the former.

Second, when less than three threads run, the threads having in-flight L2 cache misses are gated. So there may exist idle cycles of the processor when all threads are experiencing L2 cache misses. Furthermore, threads are not stalled until L2 miss is declared, which may be so late that these threads have clogged the shared resources before being gated.

3 Enhancing the DWarn Policy

3.1 Basic Idea

To address the first problem of DWarn, we distinguish the threads experiencing L2 cache misses from those only experiencing L1 data cache misses. That is to say, we classify Dmiss group in DWarn into two new groups: L2miss group, containing the threads having at least one in-flight L2 cache miss, and L1Dmiss group, containing the threads having at least one in-flight L1 data cache miss but having no L2 cache misses belong. Normal group keeps unchanged. The fetch priority of threads in Normal group is highest and the threads in L2miss group have the lowest fetch priority. The L2miss threads are chosen to fetch instructions only if there are not enough available instructions from both the Normal threads and the L1miss threads, so the threads with L2 cache misses almost have no chance to fetch instructions into the processor when the number of co-scheduled threads is big.

Obviously, our method still fails to handle L2 cache misses when less than three threads run. So, we also use a hybrid mechanism like the one used by DWarn. The difference is that when less than three threads run, we restrict the resources allocated to threads with cache misses and gate these threads when they attempt to exceed their assigned resources. Because the resources allocated to threads with cache misses are limited, it is impossible that shared resources are monopolized by these threads. Furthermore, as long as the thread with cache misses does not exceed its assigned resources, it would still be able to fetch instructions, and as a result, idle cycles of the processor are reduced.

Now we summarize our policy, DWarn+, as follows: if there are less than three threads running, the priority of the thread experiencing an L1 data cache miss is reduced, and at the same time the number of resources allocated to this thread is restricted to a certain value. After that, if the L1 miss finally turns to an L2 miss, its thread's fetch priority is reduced further, but the number of resources allocated to this thread keeps unchanged. The threads in Normal group are allowed to allocate as many resources as that are available. If the number of co-scheduled threads is higher than 2, DWarn+ will only reduce the priority of the threads in L2miss group and L1Dmiss group.

3.2 Implementation

To implement DWarn+, each thread requires an L1 data miss counter, which is also needed in DWarn. Beyond that, DWarn+ requires an L2 miss counter and 5 resources usage counters per thread. Each instruction occupies an active list entry and maybe a physical register before committing. It uses an entry in the issue queues if its operands are not ready, and also require a functional unit. But each thread can have its own active list and functional units are pipelined. Therefore we only need to restrict the usage of issues queues and physical registers by threads with cache misses. There are three kinds of issue queues: integer, fp and load/store, so each thread requires three issue queues usage counters. Two more resources usage counters are required to track physical registers (integer and fp) per thread. The additional complexity required to introduce these counters depends on the particular implementation, but we do not expect it to be more complex than other hardware counters already present in most processors [6]. L1 data miss counters are incremented every time a thread experiences an L1 data cache miss and decremented when the data cache fill occurs. L2 miss counters are incremented every time an L1 miss turns to an L2 miss and decremented when L2 cache fill occurs. If the L2 miss counter of a thread is nonzero, this thread belongs to L2miss group, otherwise if the L1data miss counter is nonzero, it belongs to L1Dmiss group. Only when the L1 data miss counter and the L2 miss counter are all zeros, does the thread belong to Normal group. Issue queues usage counters are incremented in the decode stage and are decremented when an instructions is issued for execution. Physical registers usage counters are incremented in the decode stage and are decremented in the commit stage.

Now there is a question. How many resources can be allocated to the threads with cache misses when less than three threads run? In our policy, we use a static resources allocation policy. Supposed that the total number of some shared resource is T, and the number of co-scheduled threads is N (N=1, 2). The number of this resource allocated to a thread with cache misses is equal to T divided by N. If a thread with cache misses is exceeding its assigned resources, stall fetching from this thread. It is better to allocate dynamically resources between threads based on cache behaviors of threads. But that will be more complex, and we leave it as the future work.

4 Methodology

Execution is simulated on an out-of-order superscalar processor model derived from SMTSIM [7]. The simulator models all typical sources of latency, including caches, branch mispredictions, TLB misses, etc. It also carefully models execution down the wrong path between branch misprediction and branch misprediction recovery. The baseline configuration of our simulator is shown in Table 1.

Table 2 summarizes the benchmarks used in our simulations. All benchmarks are taken from the SPEC2000 suite [8] and use the reference data sets as inputs. It is time-consuming to simulate the complete SPEC benchmark suit. So we follow the idea proposed in [9] to run the most representative 300 million instruction segment of each benchmark. Benchmarks are divided into two groups based on their cache behaviors:

Table 1. Baseline configuration of the simulator

Parameter	Value
Fetch Width	8 instructions per cycle
Basic Fetch Policy	ICOUNT2.8
Instruction Queues	32 int, 32 fp, 32 load/store
Functional Units	6 int, 3 fp, 4 load/store
Physical Registers	384 int, 384 fp
Active List Entries	256 per thread
Branch Predictor	2K gshare
Branch Target Buffer	256 entries, 4-way associative
RAS	256 entries
Min Branch Misprediction Penalty	6 cycles
L1I cache, L1D cache	64KB, 2-way, 64-bytes lines, 1 cycle access
L2 cache	512KB, 2-way, 64-bytes lines, 10 cycles latency
Main Memory Latency	100 cycles

Table 2. Benchmarks used

Type	Benchmark
MEM	mcf, twolf, vpr, parser, ammp, applu, art, swim
ILP	aspi, fma, eon, gcc, gzip, vortex, crafty, bzip2

Table 3. Multithreaded Workloads used

Num of threads	Type	Applications
2	ILP	{gzip, bzip2}, {gcc, aspi}, {vortex, fma}, {eon, crafty}
	MIX	{gzip, vpr}, {gcc, ammp}, {art, vortex}, {fma, parser}, {aspi, twolf}, {crafty, art}, {bzip2, swim}, {eon, applu}
	MEM	{mcf, vpr}, {ammp, parser}, {twolf, art}, {mcf, swim}
4	ILP	{aspi, fma, eon, gcc}, {gzip, vortex, crafty, bzip2}, {fma, eon, gcc, crafty}
	MIX	{fma, eon, parser, ammp}, {aspi, gzip, mcf, art}, {crafty, bzip2, vpr, parser}, {eon, gcc, twolf, art}, {vortex, aspi, mcf, ammp}, {gcc, fma, parser, applu}
	MEM	{vpr, parser, ammp, applu}, {mcf, art, vpr, twolf}, {twolf, vpr, art, swim}
6	ILP	{aspi, fma, eon, gcc, gzip, vortex},{fma, eon, gcc, gzip, vortex, crafty}
	MIX	{fma, eon, gcc, vpr, parser, ammp}, {aspi, fma, eon, twolf, vpr, parser}, {eon, gcc, gzip, mcf, art, vpr}, {aspi, gcc, eon, vpr, swim, parser}
	MEM	{mcf, twolf, vpr, parser, ammp, applu}, {twolf, vpr, parser, ammp, applu, art}
8	ILP	{aspi, fma, eon, gcc, gzip, vortex, crafty, bzip2}
	MIX	{eon, gcc, gzip, aspi, mcf, twolf, ammp, applu}, {vortex, crafty, bzip2, fma, vpr, parser, art, swim}
	MEM	{mcf, twolf, vpr, parser, ammp, applu, art, swim }

those experiencing between 0.02 and 0.12 L2 cache misses per instruction, on average, over the simulated portion of the code are considered memory-intensive applications, and the rest have lower miss rates and higher inherent ILP. Table 3 lists the multi-threaded workloads used in our simulations. All of the simulations in this paper either contain threads all from the first group (the MEM workloads in Table 3), or all from the second group (ILP), or an equal mix from each group (MIX). To avoid our results are biased towards a specific set of threads, each type of workloads may include multiple sets. The final result of each type workload is shown as the average of these sets.

We use two metrics to make a fair comparison: IPC and the Harmonic Mean (Hmean) [10]. Just as stated in [5], IPC may be a questionable metric if a fetch policy favors high IPC threads. The Hmean is the harmonic mean of the relative IPC of the threads in a workload and it attempts to avoid artificial improvements achieved by giving more resources to threads with high ILP.

5 Results

5.1 Throughput Results

Figure 1(a) shows the throughput increment of DWarn+ over DWarn. The results indicate that DWarn+ outperforms DWarn for all types of workloads.

As an enhanced version of DWarn, DWarn+ also attempts to handle L2 cache misses. For the ILP workloads, the threads all have low L2 cache misses rate. So, our policy has little effect on ILP workloads, and the average improvement is only by 0.7%. For MEM workloads, the throughput increment of DWarn+ is greatest, by 5.5% on average. The main reason is that for MEM workloads, the pressure on shared resources is very high; hence it is preferable to prevent threads with L2 cache misses competing for shared resources by reducing further the fetch priority of these threads. The special case is for 2-thread workloads, the improvement of MEM workloads is lower than that of MIX workloads. This is because restricting the resources used by threads with cache misses will favor the other threads with no outstanding misses, while the two threads in MEM workloads all have higher cache misses rate than the ILP thread in MIX workloads.

Another conclusion is the improvement of DWarn+ decreases as the number of co-scheduled threads increase. This is because the higher the number of threads running is, the less likely the threads with cache misses are chosen to fetch instructions. And

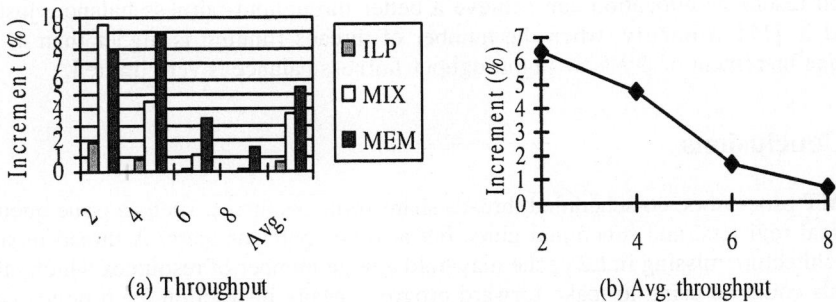

(a) Throughput (b) Avg. throughput

Fig. 1. The improvement of DWarn+ over DWarn

our policy outperforms DWarn only when there are some opportunities to fetch from the threads with cache misses. However, there is a little specialness for MEM workloads. The increment of 4-thread MEM workloads is higher than that of 2-thread MEM workloads. The main cause is the mechanisms used to improve throughput are different. For 2-thread MEM workloads, the improvement owns to resource allocation between threads and the increase of resource utilization, and for 4-thread ones, preventing threads with L2 cache misses competing for resources lightens the pressure on shared resources. Figure 1(b) shows the average increment of DWarn+ over DWarn as the number of co-scheduled threads changes. We can see that the average improvement of our policy in throughput is very limited when more than four threads run.

5.2 Hmean Results

Figure 2(a) depicts the Hmean increment of DWarn+ over the DWarn policy. The results imply that our policy would not sacrifice some thread severely when improving the performance of another thread. The Hmean increment of MEM workloads is still greatest, by 3.9% on average.

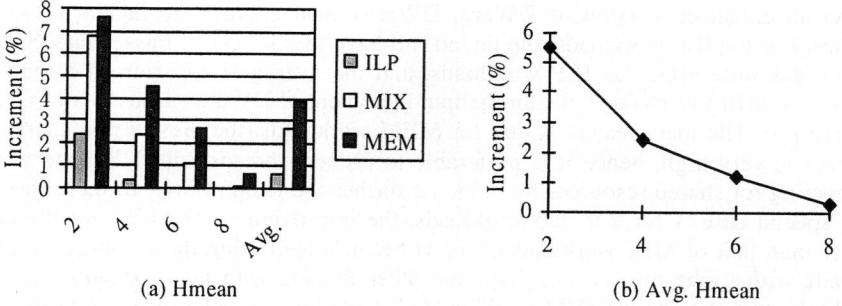

(a) Hmean   (b) Avg. Hmean

Fig. 2. The improvement of DWarn+ over DWarn

Figure 2(b) shows the average Hmean increment of DWarn+ over DWarn as the number of co-scheduled threads changes. For 2-thread workloads, the Hmean increment is very significant, by 5.6% on average. This is because explicitly controlling shared resources allocation can achieve a better throughput-fairness balance, just as stated in [11]. Similarly, when the number of threads running is higher than 4, the average increment of DWarn+ in throughput-fairness balance is very limited.

6 Conclusions

In SMT processors, co-scheduled threads share some resources, such as issue queues, physical registers, and functional units, but also compete for them. A thread in such an architecture missing in L2 cache may hold a large number of resources which other threads could be using to make forward progress. Many instruction fetch policies are proposed to prevent this situation. DWarn is a very efficient fetch policy to handle L2 cache misses. However, there are some problems with DWarn. The first problem is the threads with L2 cache missed still have some opportunity to fetch instructions into the processor. The second one is there may exist idle cycles of the processor when less than three threads run.

Our contribution is that we propose an enhanced version of DWarn, called DWarn+. By reducing further the fetch priority of the threads experiencing L2 cache misses, these threads almost have no opportunity to fetch instructions. If there are few threads running, we restrict the resources allocated to the threads with cache misses to avoid both the monopolization of shared resources and idle cycles of the processor.

The results show that DWarn+ achieves a significant improvement over DWarn in both throughput and fairness, especially for MEM workloads, by 5.5% and 3.9% on average, respectively. Another conclusion is the increment of our policy decrease as the number of co-scheduled threads increases. Not more than four threads run, the improvement is remarkable. When the number of threads running is higher than 4, our policy enhances the original one mainly for MEM workloads, and the average improvement for all types of workloads is very limited.

Acknowledgements

This work was supported by "863" project No. 2002AA110020, Chinese NSF No. 60376018, No. 60273069 and No. 90207011. The authors would like to thank Hongwei Tang for his comments on the draft. And we also would like to thank Peixiang Yan and Yi He for their work on the simulator.

References

1. D. Tullsen, S. Eggers and H. Levy: Simultaneous multithreading: Maximizing on-chip parallelism. In Proc. ISCA-22(1995)
2. D. Tullsen, S. Eggers, J. Emer, H. Levy, J. Lo and R. Stamm: Exploiting choice: Instruction fetch and issue on an implementable simultaneous multithreading processor. In Proc. ISCA-23(1996)
3. S. J. Eggers, J. S. Emer, et al.: Simultaneous Multithreading: a Platform for next-generation processors. IEEE Micro, 17(5):12-19(1997)
4. F. J. Cazorla, A. Ramirez, et al.: DCache Warn: an I-Fetch policy to increase SMT efficiency. In Proc. IPDPS-18(2004)
5. D. Tullsen and J. Brown: Handling long-latency loads in a simultaneous multithreaded processor. In Proc. MICRO-34(2001)
6. F. J. Cazorla, A. Ramirez, et al.: Dynamically controlled resource allocation in SMT processors. In Proc. MICRO-37(2004)
7. D. Tullsen: Simulation and modeling of a simultaneous multithreading processor. In Proceedings of 22nd Annual Computer Measurement Group Conference (1996)
8. The standard performance evaluation corporation. WWW site. http://www.specbench.org
9. T. Sherwood, E. Perelman and B. Calder: Basic block distribution analysis to find periodic behavior and simulation points in applications. In Proceedings of the International Conference on Parallel Architectures and Compilation Techniques (2001)
10. K. Luo, J. Gummaraju, and M. Franklin: Balancing throughput and fairness in SMT processors. In Proceedings of the International Symposium on Performance Analysis of Systems and Software (2001)
11. F. J. Cazorla, P. M. W. Knijnenburg, et al.: Implicit vs. explicit resource allocation in SMT processors. In Proceedings of the Euromicro Symposium on Digital System Design (2004)

Aggressive Loop Fusion for Improving Locality and Parallelism

Jingling Xue

Programming Languages and Compilers Group,
School of Computer Science and Engineering,
University of New South Wales,
Sydney, NSW 2052, Australia

Abstract. Existing loop fusion algorithms fuse loop nests only when the dependences in the loop nests are not violated. This paper presents a new algorithm that is capable of fusing loop nests in the presence of fusion-preventing anti-dependences. We eliminate all these violated dependences by automatic array copying. In this work, such an aggressive loop fusion strategy is applied to a Jacobi program. The performance of such iterative methods is typically limited by the speed of the memory system. Fusing the two loop nests in the Jacobi program into one reduces data cache misses, and consequently, improves the performance results of both sequential and parallel versions of the Jacobi program, as validated by our experimental results on an HP AlphaServer SC45 supercomputer.

1 Introduction

Due to the increasing performance mismatch between processors and main memories, modern computer systems are equipped with increasingly more levels of caches (e.g., three levels in the Intel IA-64 processors) to prevent performance degradation. However, caches help speed up only those programs that exhibit good data locality. For programs that do not reuse data, their execution times are limited by the poor latency and bandwidth values of the main memory. Therefore, cache-conscious programs are important for CPU-intensive applications, where the most computations are carried out inside loop nests.

There has been a great deal of work on the exploitation of cache locality for performance enhancement. For example, the design of LAPACK is influenced by efficiency considerations in the presence of caches. The main motivation of LAPACK was to recast the algorithms in EISPACK and LINPACK into blocked versions in terms of calls to BLAS [1]. In parallel with the development of LAPACK, compiler researchers have successfully automated many of the loop transformations, such as loop tiling or blocking [9, 11, 12] (for generating blocked algorithms), loop fusion and loop distribution [10], used in LAPACK in a compiler.

However, one fundamental limitation of existing loop transformations is that they are dependence-preserving and thus inapplicable when the data dependences in the program are violated. In [13], we introduced a new loop fusion compiler algorithm that allows arbitrary loop nests with affine loop bounds and array subscript expressions to be fused. In the fused program, all fusion-preventing flow (i.e., true) and output dependences are eliminated by loop tiling and all fusion-preventing anti-dependences by automatic array copying. Such an aggressive loop fusion strategy has two important benefits. First, by fusing the two loop nests that cannot be fused conventionally, we are able to exploit the data reuse across the two loop nests. Second, by creating perfect loop nests that cannot be obtained conventionally, we are able to exploit the data reuse within perfect loop nests by further applying loop tiling to these perfect nests. In [13], we demonstrated that our aggressive loop fusion can improve program performance significantly on uniprocessors with cache memories. In this paper, we show that our aggressive loop fusion can also improve the performance of parallel applications running on multi-processor computer systems. Our example is an MPI program that uses the Jacobi method to solve the Helmholtz equation. Iterative solvers for partial differential equations (PDEs) such as Jacobi are typically implemented using global sweeps over the whole data set. As a result, their performance is limited by the speed of the memory system. Improving the cache performance of iterative solvers is absolutely essential to achieving good performance for these solvers on modern computer systems. We report and analyse the performance results of our Jacobi application before and after loop fusion is applied. The fused program yields improved performance due to improved data locality and also slightly reduced message communication cost.

Like Gauss-Seidel and SOR (Successive Over-Relaxation) methods, Jacobi is a classic iterative solver for PDEs. These solvers ares still important today because they are useful either as models for more complex methods or as building blocks from which more advanced methods, such as multigrid, can be constructed. This paper is not concerned with designing fast iterative solvers. Instead, the thesis of this work is that an aggressive loop fusion strategy can improve the performance of parallel applications for which the existing loop fusion is inapplicable. One future work is to apply our technique to multigrid methods.

The rest of this paper is organised as follows. Section 2 introduces an algorithm that fuses loop nests in the presence of violated anti-dependences. In Section 3, we apply this algorithm to transform a Jacobi program consisting of two loop nests into one perfect loop nest. Section 4 presents and analyses our experimental results on uniprocessor and multi-processor systems. Section 5 compares with the related work. Section 6 concludes the paper.

2 An Aggressive Loop Fusion Algorithm

We consider array-dominated programs consisting of multiple loop nests whose loop bounds and array subscript expressions are affine expressions of the surrounding loop variables. The fusion of two perfect loop nests is legal iff all dependences from the first (i.e., the lexically earlier) nest to the second nest are not reversed in the fused program [10–p. 315]. The dependences that are reversed are known as the *fusion-preventing dependences*. There are three kinds of fusion-preventing dependences: flow (i.e., write before read) dependences, output (i.e., write before write dependences) and anti- (i.e., read before write) dependences.

Suppose we are given two perfect loop nests that are to be fused by embedding the iteration space of one nest inside that of another in a certain way. The two nests may not have the same loop bounds in a common dimension or even the same number of loops. We propose to eliminate all the fusion-preventing dependences between the two nests in two steps. We eliminate all the fusion-preventing flow and output dependences by applying loop tiling or loop shifting to the first loop nest. In [13], loop tiling is used. This first step is omitted here. We eliminate all the fusion-preventing anti-dependences by inserting array copy operations inside the second loop nest. This second step is discussed below.

In the case of multiple loop nests, our fusion strategy is applied iteratively bottom-up, starting from the last two nests. Let there be K perfect loop nests, identified by $\mathcal{L}_1, \ldots, \mathcal{L}_K$, from the beginning to the end of the program:

$$\begin{aligned}
\mathcal{L}_1: &\ \text{do } I_1 = L_{1,1},\ U_{1,1} \\
&\qquad \vdots \\
&\quad \text{do } I_{n_1} = L_{1,n_1},\ U_{1,n_1} \\
&\qquad BODY_1(I_1, \ldots, I_{n_1}) \\
&\qquad \vdots \\
\mathcal{L}_K: &\ \text{do } I_K = L_{K,1},\ U_{K,1} \\
&\qquad \vdots \\
&\quad \text{do } I_{n_K} = L_{K,n_K},\ U_{K,n_K} \\
&\qquad BODY_K(I_1, \ldots, I_{n_K})
\end{aligned} \quad (1)$$

where the loop bounds of each loop nest are assumed to be affine. Two different loop nests may not have the same loop bounds in a common dimension or even the same number of loops. Let IS_k be the n_k-dimensional iteration space of the k-th loop nest $\mathcal{L}_k$. Let $n = \max\{n_k \mid 1 \leqslant k \leqslant K\}$. If the dependences in the program (1) are ignored for the moment, it is always possible to fuse the K nests into one perfect loop nest whose n-dimensional iteration space is:

$$IS = \{(I_1, \ldots, I_n) \mid \forall\, 1 \leqslant i \leqslant n : L_i \leqslant I_i \leqslant U_i\} \quad (2)$$

This consists of finding an injective mapping from IS_k to IS for every nest $\mathcal{L}_k$:

$$F_k : IS_k \mapsto IS \quad (3)$$

The fused program becomes one single perfect loop nest as follows:

$$\begin{aligned}
&\text{do } I_1 = L_1,\ U_1 \\
&\qquad \vdots \\
&\quad \text{do } I_n = L_n,\ U_n \\
&\qquad \text{if } (I_1, \ldots, I_n) \in F_1(IS_k) \\
&\qquad\quad BODY_1(F_1^{-1}(I_1, \ldots, I_n)) \\
&\qquad \vdots \\
&\qquad \text{if } (I_1, \ldots, I_n) \in F_K(IS_K) \\
&\qquad\quad BODY_K(F_K^{-1}(I_1, \ldots, I_n))
\end{aligned} \quad (4)$$

Aggressive Loop Fusion for Improving Locality and Parallelism

```
1   ALGORITHM: ElimRW(P)
2   INPUT: A program P of the form given in (1)
3   OUTPUT: A fused program P' with same input/output behavior as P
4   Let P' be the fused program (4) obtained from P
5   for every array A in the program P
6       for k = K − 1, 1
7           for k' = k + 1, K
8               Compute $RW_A(k, k')$
9               $\overline{RW}_A(k) := \bigcup_{k'=k+1}^{K} \{(I', k', s') \mid (I, I', s') \in RW_A(k, k')\}$
10              Compute $\min_{\prec} \overline{RW}_A(k)$
11              Introduce a new array for A, $H_{A,k}$, of size $|\min_{\prec} \overline{RW}_A(k)|$ in P'
12              Insert the copy operations at the beginning of $\mathcal{L}_{k+1}$'s loop body in P'
```
$$\text{if } (I, k', s') \in \min_{\prec} \overline{RW}_A(k)$$
$$H_{A,k}(f_{k',s'}(I)) = A(f_{k',s'}(I))$$
```
13              for read reference $s \in Reads_A(k)$, i.e., $A(f_A^{k,s}(I))$ in $\mathcal{L}_k$
14                  $C_A^{k,s} := \{I \mid I \in S_A^{k,s} \wedge k' > k \wedge s' \in Writes_A(k') \wedge I' \in S_A^{k',s'}$
                              $\wedge I' \prec I \wedge f_A^{k,s}(I) = f_A^{k',s'}(I')\}$
15                  Replace $A(f_A^{k,s}(I))$ by:
```
$$\text{if } I \in C_A^{k,s}$$
$$H_{A,k}(f_A^{k,s}(I))$$
$$\text{else}$$
$$A(f_A^{k,s}(I))$$

Fig. 1. An algorithm for fixing all the fusion-preventing data dependences

where all original K loop nests "share" the same iteration vector $I = (I_1, \ldots, I_n)$.

The loop fusion used for transforming the program (1) to the fused program (4) are illegal when some dependences in the original program (1) are violated. Figure 1 gives an algorithm for eliminating all the fusion-preventing anti-dependences so that both programs have the same input/output behaviour. As we discussed earlier, we assume that the violated flow and output dependences have already been eliminated by some other means such as loop tiling [13] and/or loop shifting.

Our algorithm makes use of the following notations. A denotes an arbitrary but fixed array in the original program (1), which may be accessed in all its K loop nests, $\mathcal{L}_1, \ldots, \mathcal{L}_K$. All p_k read references of A in $\mathcal{L}_k$ are identified by integers consecutively, starting from 1. Thus, a read reference identified by s signifies that it is the s-th read reference accessed among all p_k read references. Let $Reads_A(k) = \{1, \ldots, p_k\}$. Similarly, $Writes_A(k) = \{1, \ldots, q_k\}$ denotes the set of all q_k write references in $\mathcal{L}_k$. $S_A^{k,s}$ denotes the set of iterations at which the s-th read or write reference is accessed and $f_A^{k,s}(I)$ its array subscript expression, where $I = (I_1, \ldots, I_n)$ is the iteration vector of the fused program (4).

Consider two loop nests $\mathcal{L}_k$ and $\mathcal{L}_{k'}$, where $k < k'$. $RW_A(k, k')$ is the set of anti-dependences of A that prevent $\mathcal{L}_k$ and $\mathcal{L}_{k'}$ from being fused:

$$\begin{aligned}RW_A(k,k') = \{(I,I',s') \mid \; &s \in \mathit{Reads}_A(k) \wedge I \in S_A^{k,s} \\
\wedge \; &s' \in \mathit{Writes}_A(k') \wedge I' \in S_A^{k',s'} \\
\wedge \; &I' \prec I \wedge f_A^{k,s}(I) = f_A^{k',s'}(I')\}\end{aligned} \qquad (5)$$

where $\prec$ denotes the lexicographc "less than" order between iteration vectors.

To eliminate the violated anti-dependences from $\mathcal{L}_k$ to $\mathcal{L}_{k'}$, where $k < k'$, we insert array copy operations to copy the values of A just before they are incorrectly overwritten by a write reference in Writes_A so that all read references in Reads_A can be modified to access the original values of A correctly.

Let us explain the basic idea behind our algorithm *ElimRW* given in Figure 1. Here RW stands for Read before Write dependences. Given the fused program (4), we eliminate all the violated anti-dependences iteratively bottom-up across the K loop nests starting from the last two loop nests $\mathcal{L}_{K-1}$ and $\mathcal{L}_K$. First, we eliminate all the violated anti-dependences from $\mathcal{L}_{K-1}$ to $\mathcal{L}_K$. Next, we eliminate all the violated anti-dependences from $\mathcal{L}_{K-2}$ to $\mathcal{L}_{K-1}$ and $\mathcal{L}_K$. This process is repeated until $\mathcal{L}_1$ is processed, in which case, we eliminate all the violated anti-dependences from $\mathcal{L}_1$ to the last $n-1$ nests from $\mathcal{L}_2$ through $\mathcal{L}_K$.

ElimRW takes as input a program P of the form (1) and produces as output a fused program P' that has the same input/output behavior as P. In line 4, we obtain the fused program P' of the form (4) from P as discussed earlier. In line 5, we process all arrays in the program, one by one, in any order. In the **for** loop starting at line 6, we eliminate iteratively all violated anti-dependences bottom-up across all K loop nests. During the k-th iteration of this **for** loop, we aim at eliminating all the fusion-preventing anti-dependences from $\mathcal{L}_k$ to $\mathcal{L}_{k+1}, \ldots, \mathcal{L}_K$. In lines 7 – 9, $\overline{RW}_A(k)$ is calculated to be the set of all such violated anti-dependences. To insert the required copy operations correctly, we must know the earliest iteration at which a particular anti-dependence is violated. The set of all these earliest points is given by $\min_\prec \overline{RW}_A(k)$ in line 10, where the iteration vector I is treated as a parameter and the iteration vector I' as a variable. If all constraints involved in defining $\overline{RW}_A(k)$ are affine expressions of I' and I, $\min_\prec \overline{RW}_A(k)$ can be computed parametrically (in terms of I) using the PIP [4] or Omega Calculator [7] (both tools) are based on integer programming).

By definition, $\min_\prec \overline{RW}_A(k)$ contains the earliest writes at which some anti-dependences are violated in the program P. In lines 11 – 12, we insert the copy statements to copy the old values of A at these iterations just before they are overwritten. In lines 13 – 15, we make sure that the copied values are used correctly only at the iterations defined by the predicate $C_A^{k,s}$ in line 14.

Note that the correctness of *ElimRW* relies on the fact that all the fusion-preventing flow and output dependences have been eliminated first.

Theorem 1. *The input program P to and the output program P' from ElimRW have the same input/output behaviour.*

Proof. As a loop invariant at the beginning of the k-th iteration of the **for** loop in line 6, all the violated anti-dependences in $\overline{RW}_A(k+1), \ldots, \overline{RW}_A(K)$ have been eliminated. During the k-th iteration, the violated anti-dependences in $\overline{RW}_A(k)$

are all eliminated by array copying. In addition, the copy array, $H_{A,k}$, introduced in line 10 will not affect the values in the copy arrays, $H_{A,k+1}, \ldots, H_{A,K}$, that may have been introduced in the earlier iterations of the **for** loop in line 6. □

The number of copying arrays introduced for an existing array depends only on the number of fused loop nests. If array expansion [5] is used to eliminate output and anti-dependences, the amount of extra space introduced often depends on the problem size. For example, a 2-D array of size $N \times N$ is often expanded into a 3-D array of size $N \times N \times N$. In our case, the worst-case scenario is $N \times N \times L$, where L is the number of loop nests in the program.

3 A Jacobi Program

Figure 2 gives a Fortran90 program for solving the Helmholtz equation on a regular mesh, using an iterative Jacobi method with over-relaxation. The program is taken from [2] except that the roles of u and unew are swapped. There are two loop nests in the while, i.e., the time loop. The two-dimensional array u is used to store the results of the previous iteration and the two-dimensional array unew is used to store the results of the current iteration. In the first loop nest, the sweep operation is executed, including the sum of the squared residuals used for the error estimation and the termination condition of the surrounding while loop. In the second loop nest, unew is copied to u.

The two loop nests in the while loop cannot be fused by the conventional loop fusion transformation because the cross-nest anti-dependences from the two read references u(i-1,j) and u(i,j-i) in the first loop nest to the write reference u(i,j) will be violated. Therefore, the inter-nest data reuse for the two arrays cannot be exploited for a reasonably large mesh.

We can apply *ElimRW* to fuse the two loop nests legally as follows. The input program P consists of the two loop nests in the Jacobi program. In line 4, we obtain the fused loop nest, P', as depicted in Figure 3. There is only one variable, u, whose anti-dependences may be violated. So the **for** loop in line 5 has only one iteration. There are only two nests. So $K = 2$. The **for** loop in line 6 also executes for only one iteration. Let the four read references of u in the first nest be numbered as u(i-1,j)[1], u(i+1,j)[2], u(i,j-1)[3] and u(i,j+1)[4]. So $Reads_u = \{1, 2, 3, 4\}$. There is only one write reference, u(i,j), in the second loop nest. So $Writes_u = \{1\}$. We note that all anti-dependences from u(i+1,j)[2] and u(i,j+1)[4] to u(i,j) are respected. But all the anti-dependences from u(i-1,j)[1] and u(i,j-1)[3] to u(i,j) are violated. In line 8, we obtain:

$$\begin{aligned}
RW_u(1,2) &= \{((j',i'),(j,i),1) \mid 2 \leqslant j, j' \leqslant m-1 \wedge 2 \leqslant i, i' \leqslant n-1 \\
&\quad \wedge (j',i') \prec (j,i) \wedge ((j',i') = (j-1,i) \vee (j',i') = (j,i-1))\} \\
&= \{((j',i'),(j,i),1) \mid 2 \leqslant j, j' \leqslant m-1 \wedge 2 \leqslant i, i' \leqslant n-1 \\
&\quad \wedge ((j',i') = (j-1,i) \vee (j',i') = (j,i-1))\}
\end{aligned} \quad (6)$$

In line 9, we have $\overline{RW}_u(1) = RW_u(1,2)$. In the fused program given in Figure 3, all elements of u except those in row n-1 and column m-1 are written too earlier before their values have been actually consumed by u(i-1,j)[1] and u(i,j-1)[3].

```
      subroutine jacobi (n,m,dx,dy,alpha,omega,u,f,tol,maxit)

      double precision dx,dy,f(n,m),u(n,m),alpha, tol,omega
      double precision error,resid,ax,ay,b
      double precision unew(n,m)

      ax = 1.0/(dx*dx) ! X-direction coef
      ay = 1.0/(dy*dy) ! Y-direction coef
      b = -2.0/(dx*dx)-2.0/(dy*dy) - alpha ! Central coeff

      error = 10.0 * tol
      k = 1

      do while (k.le.maxit .and. error.gt. tol)
         error = 0.0
         do j = 2,m-1
           do i = 2,n-1
             resid = (ax*(u(i-1,j) + u(i+1,j)) &
    &            + ay*(u(i,j-1) + u(i,j+1)) &
    &            + b * u(i,j) - f(i,j))/b
             unew(i,j) = u(i,j) - omega * resid
             error = error + resid*resid
           end do
         enddo

         do j=2,m-1
           do i=2,n-1
             u(i,j) = unew(i,j)
           enddo
         enddo

         k = k + 1
         error = sqrt(error)/dble(n*m)
      enddo ! End time loop

      print *, 'Total Number of Iterations ', k
      print *, 'Residual ', error

      maxit = k - 1

      return
      end
```

Fig. 2. A Jacobi program for solving the Helmholtz equation

To fix these violated anti-dependences, we compute $\min_{\prec} \overline{RW}_u(1)$ in line 10. In this case, we actually have $\min_{\prec} \overline{RW}_u(1) = \overline{RW}_u(1)$. The subscript expression for u(i.j) is $f_u^{2,1}(i,j) = (i,j)$. According to lines 11 – 12, we introduce a new array, H, and insert the following copy statement just before u(i,j)=unew(i,j):

$$\boxed{\begin{array}{l}\text{if (j .ne. m-1 .and. i .ne. n-1) then}\\\quad\text{H(i,j)=u(i,j)}\\\text{end if}\end{array}} \quad (7)$$

```
            . . .
            do while (k.le.maxit .and. error.gt. tol)
              error = 0.0
              do j = 2,m-1
                do i = 2,n-1
                  resid = (ax*(u(i-1,j) + u(i+1,j))  &
           &            + ay*(u(i,j-1) + u(i,j+1))  &
           &            + b * u(i,j) - f(i,j))/b
                  unew(i,j) = u(i,j) - omega * resid
                  error = error + resid*resid
                  u(i,j) = unew(i,j)
                enddo
              enddo

              k = k + 1
              error = sqrt(error)/dble(n*m)
            enddo ! End time loop
            . . .
```

Fig. 3. The code obtained by fusing the two loop nests given in Figure 2

where the if conditional is obtained from the specifying constraints of $\min_{\prec} \overline{RW}_u(1)$ simplified under the context $2 \leqslant j \leqslant m-1 \wedge 2 \leqslant i \leqslant n-1$, which defines the iteration space of the fused loop nest in Figure 3.

In lines 13 – 15, we need to examine all the four references u(i-1,j)[1], u(i+1,j)[2], u(i,j-1)[3] and u(i,j+1)[4] to see how they should be modified to read the copied values in H. We find that $C_u^{1,2} = C_u^{1,4} = \emptyset$, meaning that the antidependences originating from the second and fouth read references are not violated. However, $C_u^{1,1} = C_u^{1,3} \neq \emptyset$. Under the context $2 \leqslant j \leqslant m-1 \wedge 2 \leqslant i \leqslant n-1$, the specifying constraint for $C_u^{1,1}$ is simplified to $i \geqslant 3$ and that for $C_u^{1,3}$ to $j \geqslant 3$. Therefore, in line 15, the read reference u(i-1,j)[1] should be replaced by:

$$
\boxed{\begin{array}{l}\text{if (i .ge. 3) then} \\ \quad \text{H(i-1,j)} \\ \text{else} \\ \quad \text{u(i-1,j)} \\ \text{end if}\end{array}} \tag{8}
$$

Similarly, the read reference u(i,j-1)[1] should be replaced by:

$$
\boxed{\begin{array}{l}\text{if (j .ge. 3) then} \\ \quad \text{H(i,j-1)} \\ \text{else} \\ \quad \text{u(i,j-1)} \\ \text{end if}\end{array}} \tag{9}
$$

In practice, if we choose to copy redundantly some boundaries elements of an array, then the if conditionals like those in (7 – (9) can often be simplified

```
        ...
        double precision H(n,m)
        ...
        do j=2,m-1
          H(1,j) = u(1,j)
        enddo
        do i=2,n-1
          H(i,1) = u(i,1)
        enddo
        do while (k.le.maxit .and. error.gt. tol)
           error = 0.0
           do j = 2,m-1
             do i = 2,n-1
               resid = (ax*(H(i-1,j) + u(i+1,j)) &
     &                + ay*(H(i,j-1) + u(i,j+1)) &
     &                + b * u(i,j) - f(i,j))/b
               H(i,j) = u(i,j)
               tmp = u(i,j) - omega * resid
               error = error + resid*resid
               u(i,j) = tmp
             enddo
           enddo
           k = k + 1
           error = sqrt(error)/dble(n*m)
        enddo ! End time loop
        ...
```

Fig. 4. Final code from *ElimRW* with all violated anti-dependences of u fixed

or even completely eliminated. Under such optimisations, which can be incorporated into *ElimRW*, we obtain the final fused version of our Jacobi program shown in Figure 4. By choosing to copy row n-1 and column m-1 redundantly, the if conditional in (7) is removed. Similarly, by copying row 1 and column 1 redundantly just before the while loop, the if conditionals in (8) and (9) have been removed. Note that the array unew is no longer needed. So the access unew(i,j) has been replaced by a scalar, tmp. The copy array H has the same size as unew. In this example, loop fusion has not caused any extra memory space increase.

In the final program, the two arrays u and H are accessed within a single loop nest. Therefore, their data elements exhibit better data reuse in cache memories.

4 Experiments

We evaluate this work using the Jacobi example on a 126-node HP AlphaServer SC45 supercomputer. Each node has four 1GHz ev68 (Alpha 21264C) CPUs running OSF1 sc0 V5.1. Each CPU has a 64KB (on-chip) write back and write allocate data cache with FIFO replacement policy. The L1 data cache is 2-way set-associative with a cache line size of 64B. Each CPU also has an (off-chip) L2 unified cache, which is direct-mapped and has a capacity of 8MB. Each node has between 4GB and 16GB of RAM and between 2 and 6 36GB SCSI disks. Due to the use of the fat-tree interconnect of the Quadrics "Elan3" network, the SC45 computer system achieves an MPI latency of less than 5 usecs and an MPI bandwidth of 250 Mbytes/sec (bi-directional).

In all our experiments, maxit=1000 is fixed and the while loop has always completed in exactly 1000 iterations. The regular mesh on which the Jacobi method operates is defined by two problem size parameters, m and n. In all our experiments, a square mesh is used: n=m. All arrays are of double precision. So an array of size 90 × 90 fills up roughly the 64KB L1 data cache and an array of size 1024 × 1024 fills up exactly the 8MB L2 cache for the Alpha 21264 CPU.

In Section 4.1, we discuss our experimental results on a single CPU. In Section 4.2, we discuss our experimental results on multi-processor platforms.

4.1 Uniprocessors

There are two sequential programs, Org and Fused, where Org is the original program given in Figure 2 and Fused denotes the fused program shown in Figure 4. We demonstrate the performance benefits of our aggressive loop fusion algorithm using the Jacobi example on a single 21264 CPU. Both programs are compiled by the HP Fortran90 compiler (V5.5A) at the optimisation level "-fast".

Figure 5 compares the execution times of Org and Fused. The speedups of fused program Fused over Org range from 19.62% to 29.27% with an average of 24.38%. Figure 6 compares the L1 data cache misses of both programs. The cache misses are estimated using the DineroIV cache simulator for the array accesses only. In Org, the inter-nest data reuse for the two arrays u and unew cannot be exploited. By fusing the two loop nests, the single loop nest in Fused also contains two arrays of the same size. But better data reuse for the two arrays can now be exploited. As a result, we observe some significant reductions

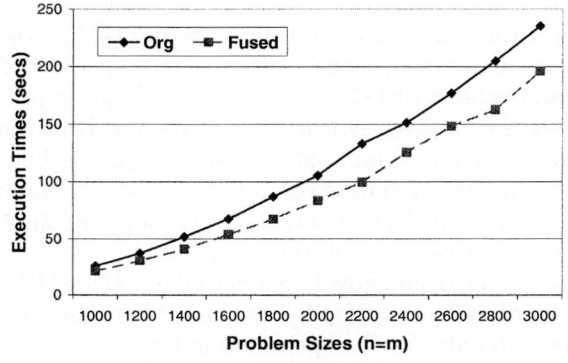

Fig. 5. The execution times of Org and Fused

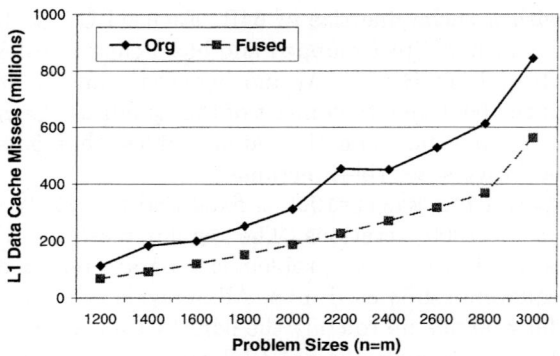

Fig. 6. The simulated L1 data cache misses of Org and Fused

in the L1 cache misses across all the problem sizes used. In comparison with the original program Org, Fused enjoys an average of 40% L1 cache miss reduction for the problem sizes simulated. The decreases in cache misses have translated into the performance improvements as shown in Figure 5.

4.2 Multiple Processors

The MPI versions of sequential programs Org and Fused are obtained using a 1D domain decomposition. This choice is made primarily to facilitate a simple boundary condition implementation. Suppose that $\mathcal{P}$ processors are available. The regular mesh n x m is divided into $\mathcal{P}$ vertical strips, with one being allocated to one processor. In other words, the columns of each array are blocked distributed among the $\mathcal{P}$ processors. As a result, the part of the global array u(n,m) allocated to the p-th processor, where $0 \leqslant p < \mathcal{P}$, is u(n,mlo:mhi), where $\texttt{mlo} = p \times (\texttt{m} - 2)/\mathcal{P} + 1$ and $\texttt{mhi} = \min(p+1) \times (\texttt{m} - 2)/\mathcal{P} + 2, \texttt{m})$. The array unew(n,m) in the program Org and the array H(n,m) in the program Fused are both distributed in the same manner.

The processor p is responsible for computing the values for the sub-mesh n x (mlo+1:mhi-1). During each iteration of the while, i.e., the time loop, the processor p first sends asynchronously column mlo+1 to its left neighbouring processor $p-1$ and column mhi-1 to its right neighbouring processor $p+1$. In addition, the processor receives synchronously column mlo from its left neighbouring processor $p-1$ and column mhi from its right neighbouring processor $p+1$. Only after having received both columns, can the processor p start working on its allocated columns. At the end of each while loop, MPI_ALLREDUCE is called to calculate the error for the current iteration.

The MPI versions of Org and Fused are referred to as Org-MPI and Fused-MPI, respectively. Both programs are compiled by the HP Fortran90 compiler (V5.5A) on the SC45 supercomputer at the optimisation level "-fast". The SC45 uses a version of MPI that is based on MPICH 1.2.4. In this particular supercomputer, we are allowed to use a maximum of 60 CPUs. In all our experiments on MPI

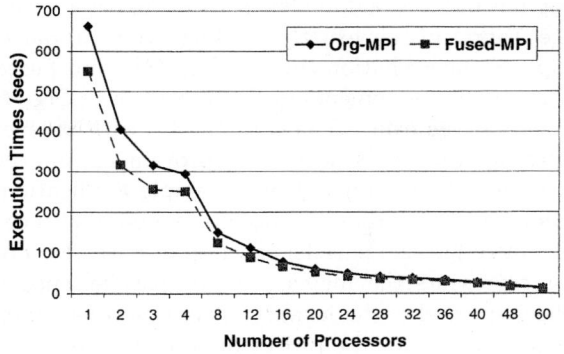

Fig. 7. The execution times of Org-MPI and Fused-MPI

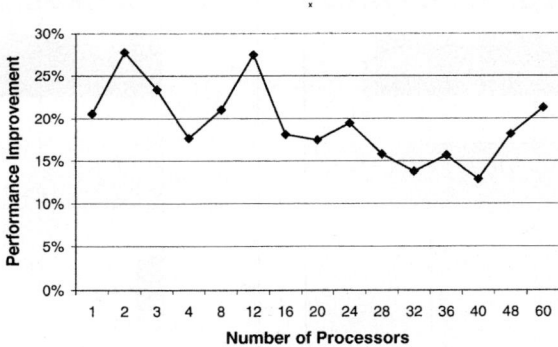

Fig. 8. The performance improvements of Fused-MPI over Org-MPI

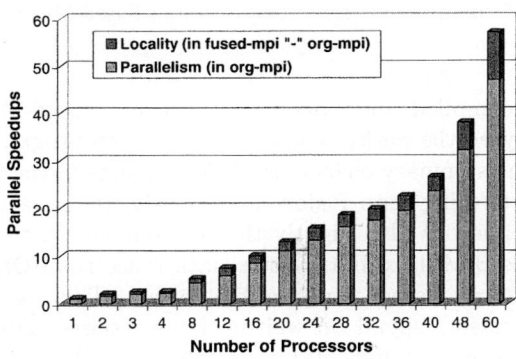

Fig. 9. Effects of improving cache locality in Fused-MPI on parallel speedups

applications, a regular mesh of 5000 × 5000 is used. As before, we set `maxit=1000` so that the `while loop` runs for exactly 1000 iterations in our experiments.

Figure 7 compares the execution times of Org-MPI and Fused-MPI. Figure 8 shows the performance improvements of Fused-MPI over Org-MPI. The performance improvements range from 12.85% to 27.74% with an average of 19.35%. Figure 9 illustrates quantitatively how the improvements in cache locality have contributed to the overall speedups of our example application. For each processor configuration, the bottom bar represents the parallel speedup of Org-MPI over Org and the entire bar the parallel speedup of Fused-MPI over Org. Therefore, the top bar represents the increase in the parallel speedup (in absolute terms) due to the improved cache locality. These increases range from 0.21 to 7.66 with an average of 2.38 for the processor configurations used.

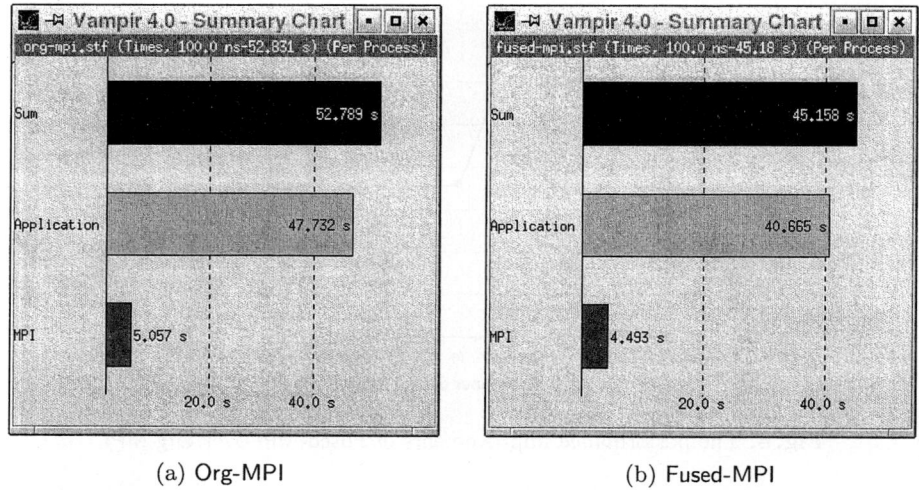

(a) Org-MPI   (b) Fused-MPI

Fig. 10. Performance analysis of Org-MPI and Fused-MPI when $\mathcal{P} = 24$

We have also compiled and linked Org-MPI and Fused-MPI with Vampirtrace 4.0 and analysed the performance results of both programs using Vampir. Figure 10 shows the summary charts for both programs in the 24-processor configuration. By performing loop fusion aggressively, we have reduced not only the computation time but also slightly the communication time for the Jacobi program. Since Fused-MPI exhibits better data reuse than Org-MPI, each processor completes its allocated computations earlier. This may reduce the idle time that the processors spend on waiting for messages. Therefore, the overall communication time in Fused-MPI is slightly reduced compared to Org-MPI. Note that Vampirtrace does incur some instrumentation overhead. So the execution times shown in Figure 10 are not exactly the same as those shown in Figure 7.

5 Related Work

Loop fusion is a standard compiler optimisation employed in a number of research and commercial compilers. Some earlier work on the topic can be found in [3, 6, 10] and the references therein. However, loop fusion is applicable only when the dependences in the program are not violated. In [13], we presented the first algorithm that allows arbitrary affine loop nests to be fused in the presence of the fusion-preventing flow, output and anti-dependences. The motivation of our earlier work was to improve the cache performance of sequential programs on uniprocessors. In this paper, we investigate the performance benefits of this aggressive loop fusion algorithm for parallel applications.

Many scientific and engineering applications require the solution of partial differential equations (PDEs). A common approach discretises the input domain, thereby transforming a PDE problem into one of solving a linear system. For large systems with several millions of unknowns, the methods of choice are all iterative. Classic iterative solvers are Jacobi, Gauss-Seidel and SOR (Successive Over-Relaxation) methods. These solvers remain important because they are useful either as models for more complex methods or as building blocks from which more advanced methods, such as multigrid, can be constructed.

However, iterative methods do not exhibit good data reuse since they are typically implemented using global sweeps over the whole data set. Song and Li [8] describe special-purpose techniques for tiling Jacobi-like codes to achieve good performance improvements on uniprocessors. In this paper, we show that fusing the loop nests in Jacobi-like codes can achieve good performance results on both uniprocessor and multi-processor systems.

6 Conclusion

This paper presents a loop fusion algorithm that is capable of fusing loop nests even when the conventional loop fusion optimisation fails. In the presence of fusion-preventing anti-dependences, we eliminate all these violated dependences by means of automatic array copying. We assume that all violated flow and output dependences have been eliminated before our algorithm is applied. In [13], we demonstrated that such an aggressive loop fusion strategy achieves good performance improvements on uniprocessors with cache memories. Taking a Jacobi program as an example, we show in this paper that such a strategy is also effective for improving the performance of MPI applications on multi-processor systems. In general, the performance of stencil codes is limited by the speed of the memory system. Our experimental results indicate that better performance results for stencil codes can be obtained if the data reuse in these codes is improved. One future work is to investigate the performance benefits of our technique for more advanced methods such as multigrid. How to effectively combine loop fusion and loop tiling for multigrid methods is another interesting topic.

Acknowledgments

This work is supported by an ARC Grant DP0452623.

References

1. E. Anderson, Z. Bai, C. Bischof, S. Blackford, J. Demmel, J. Dongarra, J. Du Croz, A. Greenbaum, S. Hammarling, A. McKenney, and D. Sorensen. *LAPACK User's Guide*. SIAM, Philadelphia, 3rd edition, 1999.
2. The OpenMP Architecture Review Boards (ARB). http://www.openmp.org.
3. A. Darte. On the complexity of loop fusion. *Parallel Computing*, 29(6):1175 – 1193, 2000.
4. P. Feautrier. Parametric integer programming. *Operations Research*, 22:243–268, 1988.
5. P. Feautrier. Dataflow analysis for array and scalar references. *Int. J. of Parallel Programming*, 20(1):23–53, Feb. 1991.
6. N. Manjikian and T. S. Abdelrahman. Fusion of loops for parallelism and locality. *IEEE Trans. on Parallel and Distributed Systems*, 8(2):193–209, Feb. 1997.
7. W. Pugh. The Omega test: A fast and practical integer programming algorithm for dependence analysis. *Comm. ACM*, 35(8):102–114, Aug. 1992.
8. Y. Song and Z. Li. New tiling techniques to improve cache temporal locality. In *ACM SIGPLAN'99 Conference on Programming Language Design and Implementation (PLDI'99)*, pages 215–228, May 1999.
9. M. J. Wolfe. More iteration space tiling. In *Supercomputing '88*, pages 655–664, Nov. 1989.
10. M. J. Wolfe. *High Performance Compilers for Parallel Computing*. Addison-Wesley, 1996.
11. J. Xue. On tiling as a loop transformation. *Parallel Processing Letters*, 7(4):409–424, 1997.
12. J. Xue. *Loop Tiling for Parallelism*. Kluwer Academic Publishers, Boston, 2000.
13. J. Xue, Q. Huang, and M. Guo. Enabling loop fusion and tiling for cache performance by fixing fusion-preventing data dependences. In *International Conference on Parallel Processing*, 2005.

An Upper Bound on Blocking Probability of Vertical Stacked Optical Benes Networks

Jiling Zhong[1] and Yi Pan[2]

[1] Department of Math, Physics, CS and Geomatics, Troy University,
Troy, AL 36082, USA
billzhong@hotmail.com
[2] Computer Science Department, Georgia State University,
Atlanta, GA 30303-3080, USA
pan@cs.gsu.edu

Abstract. Directional coupler (DC)-based optical switching networks can switch signals at the rate of several terabits per second. Benes networks are widely employed for their small depth and self-routing capability. Crosstalk between two optical signals passing through the same DC is an intrinsic drawback in DC-based optical networks. Vertical stacking of multiple copies of an optical Benes network has been intensively studied by researchers to build non-blocking optical networks. The resulting network is called vertically stacked optical Benes network (VSOBN). However, no rigorous analysis has been done to predict the behavior of VSOBN. In this paper, we study the deterministic conditions for strictly non-blocking VSOBN with and without worst case scenarios. We further analyze the blocking probabilities of VSOEN networks under a fixed load and develop their upper bound with respect to the number of planes in the networks. These performance measures can be used to predict the performance of VSOBN.

Index Terms: Benes networks, blocking probability, multistage interconnection networks (MINs), directional coupler (DC), switching networks, vertical stacking.

1 Introduction

Multistage Interconnection Network (MIN) is very popular in switching and communication applications. This network consists of N inputs, N outputs, and n stages ($n = \log_2 N$). Each stage has N/2 Switching Elements (SEs), each SE has two inputs and two outputs connected in a certain pattern. The most widely used MINs are the electronic MINs. There are three types of nonblocking networks: strictly nonblocking, wide-sense nonblocking and rearrangeable nonblocking. [4]

As optical technology advances, there is a considerable interest in using optical technology to implement interconnection networks and switches [1, 2, 3]. In electronic MINs electricity is used, where as in optical MINs light is used to transmit the messages. Optical switching network is an essential part in an optical network, which has the capability of switching huge data at an ultra-high speed. The 2x2 switching element (SE) in optical switching networks is usually a directional coupler

(DC) that is created by manufacturing two waveguides close to each other [4]. The *cross* (*bar*) state of a DC can be implemented by applying a suitable voltage (no voltage) to it. Crosstalk in DC is a major shortcoming in DC-based optical networks, which occurs between two signals carried by the two waveguides of a DC [5], [9].

Banyan-type networks have a single path between an input–output pair. A common design technique for creating alternate paths is to append x extra stages to the back of a regular Banyan-type network in which case the number of paths between an input–output pair becomes 2^x (see Fig. 1). The maximum number of stages that can be added to such network is ($\log N - 1$), which corresponds to the *Benes* network.

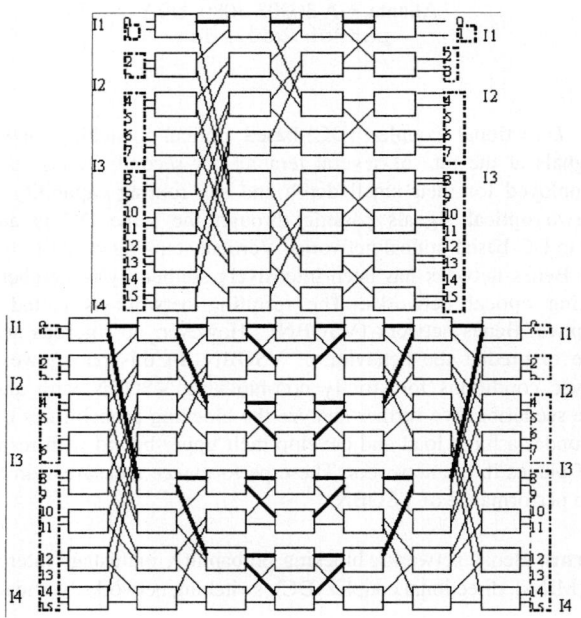

Fig. 1. A stacked Banyan networks and a Benes networks. By appending extra stages, alternative routes are available.

A Benes network has a simple switch setting ability (self routing) and also a small number of SEs along a path between an input–output pair. These characteristics have made Benes networks attractive for constructing DC-based optical switching networks. In this paper, we will focus on the optical Benes networks that are free of first-order crosstalk in SEs (we refer to this as crosstalk-free hereafter). In Benes networks, there are many paths between an input-output pair. For a fixed routing strategy, when two connections intend to use the same link, one of them will be blocked. This is called link-blocking. There is, however, another type of blocking in optical Benes networks, namely crosstalk-blocking. Since the crosstalk-free constraint requires that only one signal is allowed to passes through a SE at a time, thus it has a larger contribution to the overall blocking probability than that of link-blocking.

An Upper Bound on Blocking Probability of Vertical Stacked Optical Benes Networks 241

Vertical stacking of multiple copies of an optical Benes network is a novel scheme for constructing nonblocking (crosstalk-free) optical switching networks with neither increasing the number of stages nor sacrificing the self-routing property of the Benes network [6]. We use VSOBN to denote vertically stacked optical Benes networks and VSOBN(N,m) to denote an VSOBN network that has m stacked copies (planes) of an NxN Benes network. Previous results [6],[7] focus on determining the minimum number of planes required for nonblocking VSOBN(N,m) networks. These results indicate that the vertical stacking scheme, although is attractive, requires a prohibitively high hardware cost for building a nonblocking VSOBN network.

Analysis of blocking probability of a network that does not meet the hardware requirement for nonblocking is an effective approach to studying network performance. In [8], blocking probability of stacked banyan networks is analyzed.

In this paper, we will analyze the blocking probability of stacked Benes networks.

In section 2, we will describe the deterministic condition for strictly nonblocking VSOBN networks. In particular, we derive the blocking probabilities of VSOBN in the worst case, second worst case, and third worst case. In section 3, we will derive the upper bound of the blocking probability. Section 4 will summarize the paper.

We follow the same assumptions held by [8]. We neglect the correlation among signals arriving at input (output) ports and consider that the statuses (busy or idle) of individual input (output) ports in the network are independent. This assumption is justified by the fact that the correlation among signals at inputs (outputs), though it exists for fixed communication patterns, becomes negligible for arbitrary communication patterns in large-size networks.

2 Strictly Nonblocking Without Worst Case Scenarios

In this section, we briefly describe the deterministic condition for the strictly nonblocking VSOBN network that is obtained based on worst-case and second worst case analysis. We also evaluate the probability that the worst-case scenario occurs to motivate the work of this paper.

Due to their topological symmetry, all paths in a Benes network have the same property in terms of blocking. To study the blocking probability, we can arbitrarily select an input and an output in the network and set up a connection between them. Through out this paper, we will select the path between the first input and the first output and try to set up a connection between them. We call the path between this input-output pair the *tagged path*. All the SEs on the tagged path are called *tagged SEs*. In Benes networks, all paths between the targeted pair are called the tagged paths.

The flow of information through the network is assumed to be from left to right—all the inputs being on the left-hand side and all the outputs on the right-hand side of the network. The stages of SE's are numbered from left (stage 1) to right (stage 2logN -1). The stages of links are also numbered from left to right, but starting from 0 (input links) to 2logN -1 (destination links). For a tagged path, an *input intersecting set* (IIS) I_i associated with stage i ($1<=i<=2logN-1$) is defined as the set of all inputs that intersect a tagged SE at stage i. Likewise, an *output intersecting set* O_i (OIS) associated with stage i is the set of all outputs that intersect a tagged SE at stage

2LogN-i. Fig. 1 shows some examples. In the figure, a tagged path and a tagged SE are displayed in solid lines or dark. Input intersecting sets and output intersecting sets are also labeled.

We are interested in an optical network that is nonblocking and crosstalk-free. This can be achieved at the cost of extra hardware. For a VSOBN network, the following theorem gives the deterministic condition for strictly nonblocking [6], we are going to discuss the noblocking requirement without the worst case scenarios.

Theorem 1[6]: VSOBN is strictly nonblocking if the following condition is true:

$$m >= 2x + (2N/2^x)^{1/2} - 1 \text{ in which } x = \log N - 1$$

The above result was obtained based on worst-case analysis. That is, to find the maximum possible number of connections that will conflict the tagged path and let each of these connections block a distinct plane.

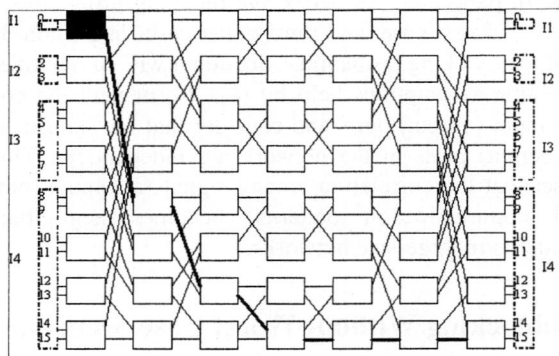

Fig. 2. Different input (output) links have different blocking capabilities

From figure 2, we know that different input (output) links have different blocking capabilities. Inputs (outputs) in I_1 have the capabilities to block the whole plane; inputs (outputs) in I_2 have the capabilities to block only ½ plane…; inputs (outputs) in I_k have the capabilities to block only $1/2^{k-1}$ plane. When a connection is set up between an input from I_i and an output from O_j, the connection will block $1/2^{\min\{i,j\}-1}$ plane. In the following, symbols "{" and "}" are used to define a set and symbols "(" and ")" are used to define a relation. Therefore, the problem of finding the worst-case traffic pattern can be formulated as follows:

Given a set Γ: {1, ½, ½, ¼, ¼, ¼, ¼, …, 1/ N/2 ,…, 1/ N/2}, find a relation $\Gamma \times \Gamma$, such that $\Sigma \max(\Gamma \times \Gamma)$ is maximized.

It is clear that in order to maximize the sum, the relation must be as unbalanced as possible. For example, for set {1, ½}, relations (1, ½) and (½, 1) would be a better choice than relations (1, 1) and (½, ½) since the former will block 2 plane, but the latter will only block 1½ planes.

Therefore, in order to maximize the sum, we must pick up the relation pairs from the two ends of the set. And the relations are (1,1/N/2), (1/2, 1/N/2),(1/2, 1/N/2),(1/2,

1/N/2),(1/2, 1/N/2),(1/4, 1/N/2),..., (1/N/4, 1/N/2) ,..., (1/N/4, 1/N/2), their respective inversions and (1/N/2, 1/N/2). Add 1, 1, ½, ½, ½, ½, ½, ½, ½, ½, ¼, ..., 1/N/4 ,...,1/N/4 , and 1/N/2 together, we will get the result of theorem 1.

From Theorem 1, it is clear that the hardware cost for a strictly nonblocking VSOBN network is high. Let us find out the probability that the worst-case scenario could occur. Let the probability that an input (output) port is busy be r (r is basically the traffic rate at the input line) and denote by P_{worst} the probability that the worst-case scenario occurs. P_{worst} is then given in the following lemma under the assumption that statuses of individual input (output) ports are independent.

Lemma 1: In an NxN optical Benes network, we have

$$P_{worst} = \left(r^{n/2-1} \frac{N/2}{\binom{N-1}{N/2-1}} r \right)^2$$

When r=0.9 and N =64 and r=0.9 and N=128, P64 = 2.63 e − 34, and P128 = 3.97 e − 77. This indicates that the probability of worst case from happening is very small or even can be ignored in most cases.

Table 1 and Figure 3 show the relationship between the number of inputs and the number of planes required. The blocking requirement is the value calculated from Theorem 1. This shows that a lot of planes are needed to make VSOBN absolutely non-blocking. We would like to investigate the blocking behavior without considering some rare cases.

Table 1. Blocking requirement and actual number of planes needed

No. of inputs	16	32	64	128	256
Blocking requirement	6 1/8	8 1/16	10 1/32	12 1/64	14 1/128
No. of planes required	7	9	11	13	15

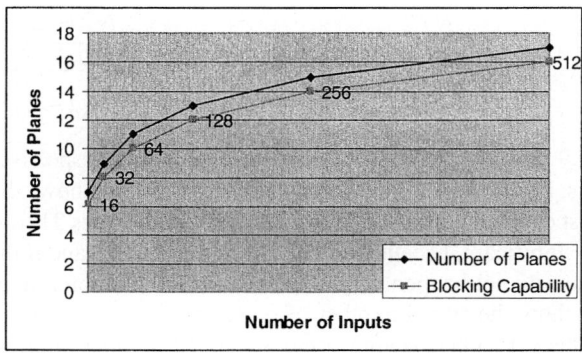

Fig. 3. Blocking requirement and actual number of planes needed

In this paper, we define the term second worst case scenario as follows: Second worst case is the case(cases) in which the second largest blocking capability occurs.

It is also important to find out the probability that the second worst-case scenario could occur. The reason is explained as follows:

Take when N = 16 as an example,

I1: {1}   O1: {1}
I2: {½, ½}   O2: {½, ½}
I3: {¼, ¼, ¼, ¼}   O3: {¼, ¼, ¼, ¼}
I4: {1/8,1/8,1/8,1/8,1/8,1/8,1/8,1/8}   O4: {1/8,1/8,1/8,1/8,1/8,1/8,1/8,1/8}

The worst-case is when inputs (outputs) in I1, I2, and I3 are connected to outputs (inputs) in I4. There will be one pair in I4 and O4 left and this pair accounts for the 1/8. In order to be strictly nonblocking, we need 7 planes.

Now let's consider the second worst-case. In the second worst-case, the blocked planes will be 6. The second worst case happens either when I1, I2, I3 going to O4 and O1, O2, O3 going to I4 while the remaining one pair in I4 and O4 is not connected or one pair in I3 and O3 is connected while rest of the inputs(outputs) are connected to O4(I4). Therefore, in the former case, the blocking capability is reduced by 1/8 because the remaining pair in I4 and O4 is not connected; in the latter case, because one pair in I3 and O3 is connected, while in the worst case these two are both connected with one in I4 or O4, the capability of blocking is reduced by ¼. At the same time, the pair in the I4 and O4 must be connected together, which increased the blocking capability by 1/8. So, blocking difference between the worst-case and the second worst-case will be ¼-1/8 = 1/8.

This proves Theorem 2.

Theorem 2: A VSOBN network is strictly nonblocking with m = 2*(logN −1) when worst and second worst case do not occur.

Now it is the time to find out the probability that second worst-case could happen.

Lemma 2: In an NxN optical Benes network, we have

$$P_{\text{second-worst}} = \left(r^{n/2-1} \frac{N/2}{\binom{N-1}{N/2-1}} (1-r) \right)^2 + \left(r^{n/2-2} \frac{\binom{N/2}{N2/-2}}{\binom{N-1}{N/2-2}} r^2 \right)^2$$

When r = 0.9 and N = 64 and r = 0.9 and N = 128 respectively, we have the following results, P_{64} = 3.91 e -34, and P_{128} = 8.38 e -74. This shows that the probability that second worst case happens is still very small, which justifies Theorem 2.

The result is significant, because we can save one whole plane if the worst case and second worst-case do not happen very often and could be ignored in our design. Table 2 and Figure 4 show the actual number of planes needed without considering the 2nd worst case and the percentage saving compared to the number of planes required in an absolutely non-blocking environment.

Table 2. Savings (percentage) without 2nd worst case

No. of inputs	16	32	64	128	256	512	1024
No. of planes	6	8	10	12	14	16	18
Blocking requirement	6 1/8	8 1/16	10 1/32	12 1/64	14 1/128	16 1/256	18 1/512
Saving(percentage) w/o 2nd worst case	14.3%	11.1%	9.1%	7.7%	6.7%	5.9%	5.3%

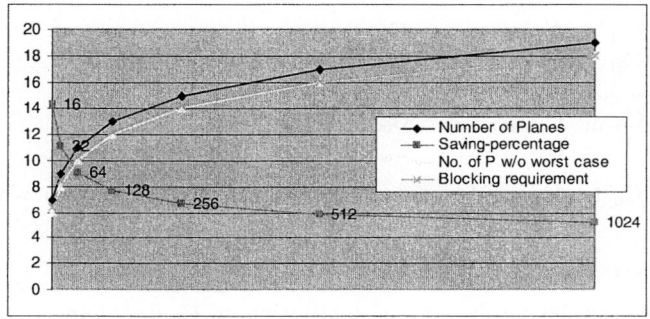

Fig. 4. Savings (percentage) without 2nd worst case

The table shows that even when N = 1024, which is a quite large network, we can still save 5.3% if we neglect first and second order worst-cases. This motivates us to further investigate the possibility of saving of planes when we ignore other rare cases of blocking.

Lemma 3: In an NxN optical Benes network, further neglecting third order worst-case does not save a plane.

For example when N = 16, in the third worst-case, the blocked planes will be 4.875. The reason is that 1/8 is the smallest residue in this system and in order to get the blocked planes in the third worst case, all needs to be done is to let two pair in I3 and O3 to be connected; while in the second worst case only one pair is connected, the other pair is connected with one in I4 or O4. Therefore, the capability of blocking is reduced by ¼. And at the same time, the pair in the I4 and O4 must be connected together, which increases the blocking capability by 1/8. So, blocking difference between the second worst-case and the third worst-case will be ¼-1/8 = 1/8. Therefore, further neglecting third order worst-case is meaningless.

From the above analysis, it is seen that spending a large amount of extra hardware in order to guarantee the strictly nonblocking property is not cost-effective in most cases. This motivates us to find out the blocking probability of a VSOBN network with respect to the number of planes (hardware cost), and to seek an approach to making tradeoff between hardware cost and blocking probability.

3 Upper Bound on Blocking Probability

Since exact blocking probability is hard to obtain, in this section we will derive various formulas to get an upper bound on the blocking probability of a VSOBN in terms of the number of planes. This bound can be considered as the estimate for the worst case blocking probability. In the following discussion, we give a few definitions and notation which will be used in the analysis.

For an N x N network, a matrix of logN x logN is proposed. An element in the matrix C_{ij} stands for the connection from Ii to Oj.

$$\begin{matrix} C_{11} & C_{12} & \ldots & C_{1n} \\ C_{21} & C_{22} & \ldots & C_{2n} \\ \ldots & & & \\ C_{(n-1)1} & C_{(n-1)2} & \ldots & C_{(n-1)n} \\ C_{n1} & C_{n2} & \ldots & C_{nn} \end{matrix}$$

We use C_{Ii} to denote the sum of coefficients of C_{ij} in row i where j>=i. For example:

$$C_{I2} = C_{22} + C_{23} + \ldots + C_{2n}.$$

We use C_{Oj} to denote the sum of coefficients of C_{ij} in column j where i>=j. For example:

$$C_{O2} = C_{22} + C_{32} + \ldots + C_{n2}.$$

By this definition, C_{Ii} stands for the connections coming from input group i going to ouput groups j (j>=i). C_{Oj} stands for the connections going to ouput group j coming from input groups i (i>=j). The total blocking capability BC is therefore

$$C_{I1} + C_{O1} - C_{11} + \tfrac{1}{2}*(C_{I2} + C_{O2} - C_{22}) + \tfrac{1}{4}*(C_{I3} + C_{O3} - C_{33}) + \ldots + 1/2^{\log n - 1}*(C_{In} + C_{On} - C_{nn}).$$

In the above formula, C_{I1} stands for the connections coming from input group to every output group, and C_{O1} stands for the connections coming from every input group to output group 1. And any connection in C_{I1} and C_{O1} will block a whole plane. But there are some overlaps in these two groups and the overlap is C_{11} (which are the connections coming from input group 1 to output group 1), since it has been counted twice in C_{I1} and C_{O1}.

C_{I2} stands for the connections coming from input group 2 to every output group other than group 1. Similarly, C_{O2} stands for the connections coming from every input group other than input group 1 to output group 2. And any connection in C_{I2} and C_{O2} will block 1/2 of a whole plane. But there are some overlaps in these two groups and the overlap is C_{22} (which are the connections coming from input group 2 to output group 2), since it has been counted twice in C_{I2} and C_{O2}. Similar consideration will apply to $C_{I3}, C_{O3}, \ldots, C_{In}, C_{On}$.

Clearly there will be no blocking if $C_{I1} + C_{O1} - C_{11} + \tfrac{1}{2}*(C_{I2} + C_{O2} - C_{22}) + \tfrac{1}{4}*(C_{I3} + C_{O3} \, C_{33}) + \ldots + 1/2^{\log n-1}*(C_{In} + C_{On} - C_{nn}) < m.$ (1)

An Upper Bound on Blocking Probability of Vertical Stacked Optical Benes Networks 247

Therefore we have

$$P(\text{nonblocking}) = \sum_{C_{I1}=0}^{\min(2^0, m-1)} \sum_{C_{I2}=0}^{\min(2^1,(m-1)*2)} \cdots$$

$$\sum_{C_{In}=0}^{\min(n/2,(m-1)*2^{\log n-1})} \sum_{C_{O1}=0}^{\min(2^0,m-1)} \sum_{C_{O2}=0}^{\min(2^1,(m-1)*2)} \cdots \sum_{C_{On}=0}^{\min(n/2,(m-1)*2^{\log n-1})} P(C_{I1}, C_{O1}, C_{I2},$$

$C_{O2}, \ldots, C_{In}, C_{On}) * P(C_{I1} + C_{O1} - C_{11} + \tfrac{1}{2}*(C_{I2} + C_{O2} - C_{22}) + \tfrac{1}{4}*(C_{I3} + C_{O3} - C_{33}) +$
$\ldots + 1/2^{\log n-1}*(C_{In} + C_{On} - C_{nn}) \le m-1 | C_{I1}, C_{O1}, C_{I2}, C_{O2}, \ldots, C_{In}, C_{On})$ (2)

The lower bound of C_{I1} is 0 since it can not be negative. On the other hand, C_{I1} must not be greater than 2^0, since there is only 2^0 input in I_1; and C_{I1} must not be greater than m-1, since there are only m planes in the networks and if C_{I1} is greater than m-1, then the network will be blocked. Therefore, C_{I1} must not be greater than the minimum of 2^0 and m-1.

The lower bound of C_{I2} is 0 since it can not be negative. On the other hand, C_{I2} must not be greater than 2^1, since there is only 2^1 inputs in I_2; and C_{I2} must not be greater than $2*(m-1)$, since there are only m planes in the networks and if C_{I2} is greater than $2*(m-1)$, then the network will be blocked. Therefore, C_{I1} must not be greater than the minimum of 2^1 and $2*(m-1)$.

And the ranges of other connections can be derived accordingly.

From (1)

$C_{11} + C_{O1} - C_{11} + \tfrac{1}{2}*(C_{12} + C_{O2} - C_{22}) + \tfrac{1}{4}*(C_{13} + C_{O3} - C_{33}) + \ldots + 1/2^{\log n-1}*(C_{In} + C_{On} - C_{nn}) \le m-1$,

by simple algebraic manipulation,

We have $C_{11} + \tfrac{1}{2} C_{22} + , \ldots, + 1/2^{\log n-1} C_{nn} \ge C_{I1} + C_{O1} + \tfrac{1}{2}*(C_{I2} + C_{O2}) + \ldots + 1/2^{\log n-1}(C_{In} + C_{On}) - m + 1$ (3)

Therefore,

$$P(\text{nonblocking}) = \sum_{C_{I1}=0}^{\min(2^0,m-1)} \sum_{C_{I2}=0}^{\min(2^1,(m-1)*2)} \cdots$$

$$\sum_{C_{In}=0}^{\min(n/2,(m-1)*2^{\log n-1})} \sum_{C_{O1}=0}^{\min(2^0,m-1)} \sum_{C_{O2}=0}^{\min(2^1,(m-1)*2)} \cdots \sum_{C_{On}=0}^{\min(n/2,(m-1)*2^{\log n-1})} P(C_{I1}, C_{O1}, C_{I2}, C_{O2},$$

$\ldots, C_{In}, C_{On}) * \sum_{C_{11}+1/2C_{22}+1/4C_{33}+\ldots+1/2^{\log n-1}C_{nn}=Lower}^{Upper} P(C_{11}, C_{22}, \ldots, C_{nn} | C_{I1}, C_{O1}, C_{I2},$

$C_{O2}, \ldots, C_{In}, C_{On})$

Where

Lower = max[0, $C_{I1} + C_{O1} + \tfrac{1}{2}*(C_{I2} + C_{O2}) + \ldots + 1/2^{\log n-1}(C_{In} + C_{On}) - m + 1$]
and
Upper = $\min(C_{I1}, C_{O1}) + \tfrac{1}{2}*\min(C_{I2}, C_{O2}) + \ldots + 1/2^{\log n-1}*\min(C_{In}, C_{On})$.

From (3) $C_{11} + \frac{1}{2} C_{22} + ,..., + 1/2^{\log n-1} C_{nn} \geq C_{I1} + C_{O1} + \frac{1}{2}*(C_{I2} + C_{O2})+...+1/2^{\log n-1}(C_{In} + C_{On}) - m + 1$, we can see that the lower bound of $(C_{11}+ \frac{1}{2} C_{22}+ \frac{1}{4} C_{33} + ...+1/2^{\log n-1}C_{nn})$ is $C_{I1} + C_{O1} + \frac{1}{2}*(C_{I2} + C_{O2})+...+ 1/2^{\log n-1}(C_{In} + C_{On}) - m + 1$.

On the other hand, C_{11} must not be greater than C_{I1} or C_{O1}; $1/2\, C_{22}$ must not be greater than $1/2 C_{I2}$ or $1/2 C_{O2}$ ... and so forth. Here so derives the upper bound of $(C_{11}+ \frac{1}{2} C_{22}+ \frac{1}{4} C_{33} + ... +1/2^{\log n-1}C_{nn})$.

And,

$P(\text{nonblocking}) = P(C_{I1}, C_{O1}, C_{I2}, C_{O2}, ..., C_{In}, C_{On}) P(C_{11}, C_{22},..., C_{nn} | C_{I1}, C_{O1}, C_{I2}, C_{O2}, ..., C_{In}, C_{On})$
$= P(C_{11}, C_{22},..., C_{nn}, C_{I1}, C_{O1}, C_{I2}, C_{O2}, ..., C_{In}, C_{On})$
$= P(C_{I1}\, C_{11})P(C_{22},..., C_{nn}, C_{O1}, C_{I2}, C_{O2}, ..., C_{In}, C_{On} | C_{I1}\, C_{11})$
$= P(C_{I1}\, C_{11})P(C_{22},..., C_{nn}, C_{O1}, C_{I2}, C_{O2}, ..., C_{In}, C_{On} | C_{I1})$

We drop C_{11} in the above formula under the assumption that the connections in C_{I1} are independent with all others, which can be justified if the amount of traffic under consideration is huge. Thus, we have

$P(\text{nonblocking}) = P(C_{I1}\, C_{11})P(C_{I1}, C_{22},..., C_{nn}, C_{O1}, C_{I2}, C_{O2}, ..., C_{In}, C_{On})/P(C_{I1})$
$= P(C_{I1}\, C_{11}) P(C_{O1}\, C_{11})P(C_{22},..., C_{nn}, C_{I2}, C_{O2}, ..., C_{In}, C_{On} | C_{O1}\, C_{11})/P(C_{I1})$
$= P(C_{I1}\, C_{11}) P(C_{O1}\, C_{11})P(C_{22},..., C_{nn}, C_{I2}, C_{O2}, ..., C_{In}, C_{On} | C_{11})/P(C_{I1})$

Similarly, we drop C_{O1} under the assumption that the connections in C_{O1} are independent with all others, which can be justified if the amount of traffic under consideration is huge. Now, we have

$P(\text{nonblocking}) = P(C_{I1}\, C_{11}) P(C_{O1}\, C_{11})P(C_{11}, C_{22},..., C_{nn}, C_{I2}, C_{O2}, ..., C_{In}, C_{On})/P^2(C_{I1})$
$= ...$
$= P(C_{I1}\, C_{11}) P(C_{O1}\, C_{11}) P(C_{I2}\, C_{22}) P(C_{O2}\, C_{22})... P(C_{In}\, C_{nn}) P(C_{On}\, C_{nn})P(C_{11}, C_{22}, ..., C_{nn})/ P^2(C_{I1}) P^2(C_{22})... P^2(C_{nn})$

Since $C_{11}, C_{22}, ,..., C_{nn}$ are independent of each other, $P(C_{11}, C_{22}, ,..., C_{nn}) = P(C_{11})P(C_{22}),..., P(C_{nn})$.

Therefore, $P(\text{nonblocking}) = P(C_{I1}\, C_{11}) P(C_{O1}\, C_{11}) P(C_{I2}\, C_{22}) P(C_{O2}\, C_{22})... P(C_{In}\, C_{nn}) P(C_{On}\, C_{nn})P(C_{11}, C_{22}, ,..., C_{nn})/ P^2(C_{I1}) P^2(C_{22})... P^2(C_{nn})$
$= P(C_{I1}\, C_{11}) P(C_{O1}\, C_{11}) P(C_{I2}\, C_{22}) P(C_{O2}\, C_{22})... P(C_{In}\, C_{nn}) P(C_{On}\, C_{nn}) P(C_{11})P(C_{22}),..., P(C_{nn})/ P^2(C_{I1}) P^2(C_{22})... P^2(C_{nn})$
$= P(C_{I1}\, C_{11}) P(C_{O1}\, C_{11}) P(C_{I2}\, C_{22}) P(C_{O2}\, C_{22})... P(C_{In}\, C_{nn}) P(C_{On}\, C_{nn}) / P(C_{11}) P(C_{22})... P(C_{nn})$.

In general, $P(C_{kk})$ stands for the probability of C_{kk} connection coming from input group k going to output group k. Therefore, $P(C_{kk})$ is $P(C_{kk}) = \binom{2^{k-1}}{C_{kk}} \alpha_k^{C_{kk}} (1-\alpha_k)^{2^{k-1}-C_{kk}}$, where α_k is the probability that a connection from input group k going to the out put groups k. So α_k is $r * (2^{k-1})/(N-1)$ in this case.

An Upper Bound on Blocking Probability of Vertical Stacked Optical Benes Networks 249

In general, P(C_{Ik} C_{kk}) is the probability of C_{Ik} connections from input group K to output groups K and above while there are C_{kk} connections from input group K to output group K. It can be calculated as:

$$P(C_{Ik}\ C_{kk}) = \binom{2^{k-1}}{C_{kk}} \alpha_k^{C_{kk}} * \binom{2^{k-1}-C_{kk}}{C_{Ik}-C_{kk}} * \gamma_k^{C_{Ik}-C_{kk}} * (1-\alpha_k-\gamma_k)^{2^{k-1}-C_{Ik}}$$

where α_k is the probability that a connection from input group k going to the output group k. So α_k is r * 2^{k-1}/N-1 in this case. γ_k is the probability that a connection from input group k going to the output groups above k and γ_k is r * (N-2^k / N-1).

In general cases, P(C_{Ok} C_{kk}) is the probability of C_{Ok} connections from input group K to output groups K and above while there are C_{kk} connections from input group K to output group K. We have the general formula to calculate it:

$$P(C_{Ok}\ C_{kk}) = \binom{2^{k-1}}{C_{kk}} \alpha_k^{C_{kk}} * \binom{2^{k-1}-C_{kk}}{C_{Ok}-C_{kk}} * \gamma_k^{C_{Ok}-C_{kk}} * (1-\alpha_k-\gamma_k)^{2^{k-1}-C_{Ok}}$$

where α_k is the probability that a connection from input group k going to the output group k. So α_k is r * 2^{k-1}/N-1 in this case. γ_k is the probability that a connection going into output group k coming from the input groups above k and γ_k is r * (N-2^k / N-1).

Based on the above formulas, we can calculate the blocking probability with various numbers of planes, as in Figure 5.

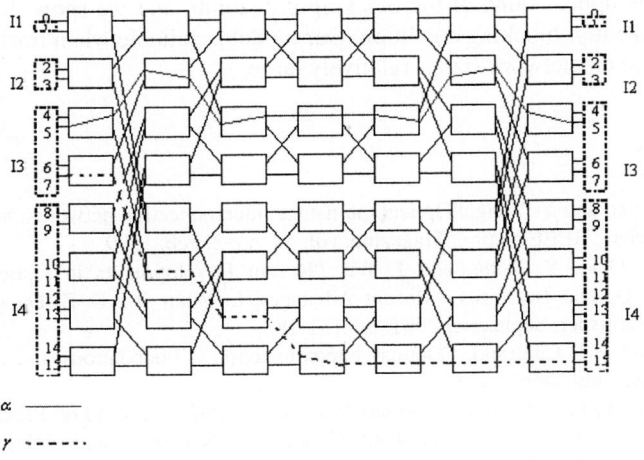

Fig. 5. Illustration of paths for calculating α and γ

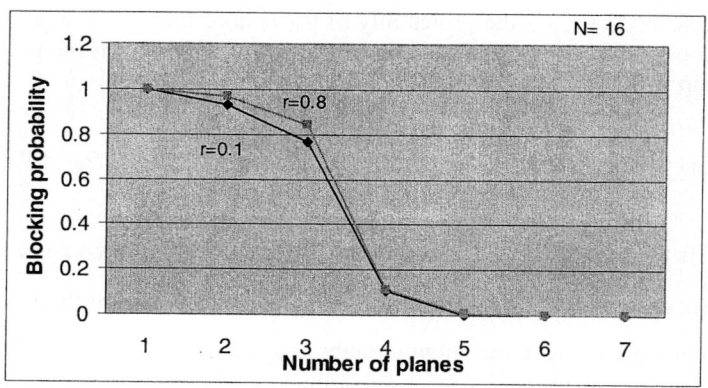

Fig. 6. Blocking Probability

Now we show some analytical results based on the formulas obtained in this section. Figure 6 shows the blocking probability with different number of planes. From the figure, it can be seen that when n =16, the blocking probability is very close to 0 even the number of planes is 5. Hence, in most practical cases, we do not need a full number of planes to guarantee non-blocking, and our analysis will show what the probability of blocking if a smaller number of planes is used. This figure can be used as guidance when a designer makes a trade-off between performance and cost.

4 Conclusion

In this paper we discuss the blocking probability of stacked Benes network. We show that by neglecting worst case traffic pattern, we can save one whole plane. We further investigate the upper bound of the blocking probability and we show that our theory conforms to the non-blocking condition. Our model is suitable when traffic load is not very heavy and the network size is relatively large.

References

1. Y.Pan, C. Qiao and Y. Yang, "Optical multistage interconnection networks: new challenges and approaches," IEEE comm.. Magazine, vol. 37, no. 2, Feb. 1999.
2. Y. Pan, C. Qiao, Y. Yang, and J. Wu, "Recent Developments in Optical Multistage Networks," Optical Networks - Recent Advances, L. Ruan and D.-Z. Du (Eds), Kluwer Academic Publisher, September 2001, pp. 151-185.
3. C. Tocci and H.J. Caulfield, "Optical Interconnection – Foundations and Applications," Artech House Publishers, 1994.
4. H. S. Hinton, *An Introduction to Photonic Switching Fabrics*. New York: Plenum, 1993.
5. V.E. Benes, Mathematical Theory of Connecting Networks and Telephone Traffic, Academic Press, New York, 1965.

6. M. M. Vaez and C.-T. Lea, "Strictly nonblocking directional-coupler-based switching networks under crosstalk constraint," *IEEE Trans. Commun.*, vol. 48, pp. 316–323, Feb. 2000.
7. M. M. Vaez and C.-T. Lea, "Wide sense nonblocking banyan-type switching systems based on directional couplers," *IEEE J. Select. Areas Commun.*, vol. 16, pp. 1327–1332, Sept. 1998.
8. X Jiang, H Shen, M Khandker, S Horiguchi, "Blocking Behaviors of Crosstalk-Free Optical Banyan Networks on Vertical Stacking" *IEEE/ACM Trans. Networking.*, vol. 11, No. 6, Dec. 2003.
9. V. R. Chinni *et al.*, "Crosstalk in a lossy directional coupler switch," *J. Lightwave Technol.*, vol. 13, pp. 1530–1535, July 1995.

It's Elementary, My Dear Watson: Time-Optimal Sorting Algorithms on a Completely Overlapping Network

Sanpawat Kantabutra, Wattana Jindaluang, and Prapaporn Techa-angkoon

The Theory of Computation Group,
Computer Science Department, Chiang Mai University,
Chiang Mai, 50200, Thailand
sanpawat@alumni.TUFTS.edu
http://www2.cs.science.cmu.ac.th/person/sanpawat/theory.html

Abstract. Several parallel architectures exist in computer science literature. Motivated by the experimental overlapping connectivity network, we propose a new theoretical network called a completely overlapping network (CON). This network is an extension of the overlapping connectivity network with multiple buses. In this paper we investigate some properties of this network and demonstrate the use of CON and its usefulness by solving two toy problems: decimal number and one-digit binary number sortings.

1 Introduction

The concept of parallel computation has been around for decades and parallel computation itself has increasingly become even more important in the era of information-dependent world. Thousands of parallel applications and architectures are available for use. However, parallel architectures such as hypercube and mesh are generally expensive [1] and hence their use is limited to only those who can afford them. Some attempts have been made to find an alternative to these expensive parallel machines.

One alternative is called a cluster of workstations and personal computers. Research in parallel computation on a cluster of workstations abounds. Examples can be found in [2–4]. A typical cluster of workstations is essentially a group of numerous workstations and personal computers connected through a single communication line. Each computer can send a message, bit by bit, when the communication line is free. If the communication line is currently occupied, the computer must wait before it is allowed to send its message.

One chief problem with this model of communication via a single communication line is the line can only serve one computer at any time. To lessen this problem, during the recent decade or so, a group of computer scientists in the United States, led by Wilkinson, has developed an experimental network called *an overlapping network* [5–7]. They have worked on the concept of using multiple bus lines in some certain configurations. Figure 1 shows one such example.

It's Elementary, My Dear Watson: Time-Optimal Sorting Algorithms

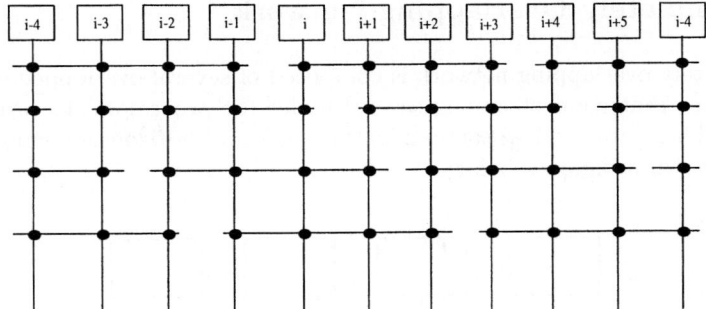

Fig. 1. Multiple bus network with overlapping connectivity

These configurations are in the general classification of overlapping connectivity networks. Overlapping connectivity networks have the characteristic that regions of connectivity are provided and the regions overlap so as to provide parallelism. The overlapping connectivity scheme is suitable for processors having local memory and can be applied to both *fine-grained* and *coarse-grained* processors.

In this paper we extend the network model of Wilkinson one step further to provide *complete* overlapping of communication and use a set of *fine-grained* processors connected through CON. Our theoretical network model is more general than but similar to the experimental overlapping network in figure 1. Henceforth, we will refer to this model as *a completely overlapping network*. From now on, we will also use an abbreviation "CON" interchangeably with its full name "completely overlapping network". Because Wilkinson's multiple bus network model yields a good result [5], it is worth studying properties of CON and investigating its potential. We do this by using two toy problems; namely, *decimal number and one-digit binary number sortings*. This will in fact be the central theme of our paper.

We now discuss a little bit about parallel sorting. Sorting is a fundamental problem with many important practical applications. Several parallel sorting algorithms exist in computer science literature depending on the kinds of network architectures they use. Most existing parallel algorithms are described in the context of networks such as mesh [8–11], line [12, 13], hypercube [14–17], torus [18], etc. The rest are mostly in the environment of cluster of workstations with one communication bus, i.e., LANs [19–22]. As of today, we are not aware of any sorting algorithm on an architecture similar to CON.

In the following sections the definition and rules of operations of our completely overlapping network are firstly given. Secondly, a decimal number parallel sorting algorithm on our completely overlapping network is shown. We prove that this algorithm is time-optimal on CON. Thirdly, we show another parallel sorting algorithm on CON but this time it will sort only binary numbers. We again prove that this binary number sorting algorithm is time-optimal on CON. Fourthly, we compare the two parallel sorting algorithms. Finally, we conclude our paper with a summary and some comment on practicality of our theoretical network.

2 Completely Overlapping Network

A completely overlapping network is composed of several overlapped communication lines that connect among several nodes (or processors) to provide parallelism. There are vertical communication lines and horizontal communication lines as shown in figure 2 below.

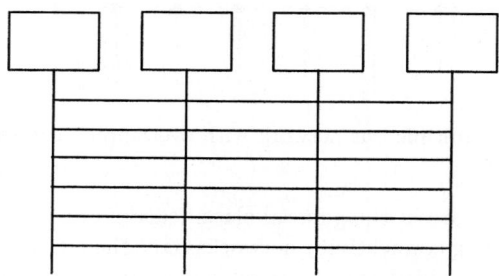

Fig. 2. Four-node completely overlapping network

The number of vertical lines is equal to the number of nodes N and the number of horizontal lines is equal to $\frac{N(N-1)}{2}$. One straight line *segment* equates one step horizontally and vertically. (Note that a line in CON comprises several line segments.) For instance, figure 3 shows a communication of 9 steps between the leftmost node and the rightmost node.

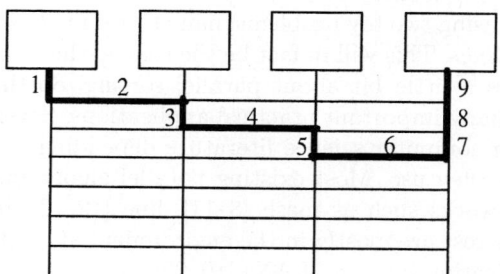

Fig. 3. Nine-step communication between nodes

Like any other networks, there are rules of operations. These rules are reasonable and can certainly be implemented. The rules are as follows.

– Horizontal and vertical line segments cannot be shared. That is, any line segment can be used only one at a time.
– Each line segment is bidirectional.
– Each node has a constant memory size.

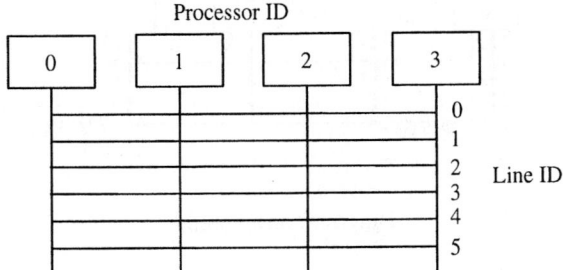

Fig. 4. Numbering scheme for a four-node CON

- A same message can be concurrently sent from one node to several destination nodes as long as there is no collision of messages.
- If there exists contention for a communication line segment, some kind of priority can be applied.

In order to enable readers to understand our communication method, a numbering of both nodes and communication lines is necessary. Our numbering scheme is illustrated in figure 4. This figure shows a four-node CON with node and line identification numbers. It is easy to generalize this numbering scheme for a N-node CON. Hereafter, we will regularly refer to this numbering scheme when explaining our algorithms.

3 Decimal Number Parallel Sorting Algorithm on CON

Our Decimal Number Parallel Sorting Algorithm is specifically designed to suit the completely overlapping network and thus is unique and interesting in its own right. The definition of our Decimal Number Parallel Sorting Algorithm on CON is given as follows. We borrow some of pseudocode conventions from [23].

Decimal Number Sorting Algorithm for Process P_i
1. **for** $i = 0$ to $N - 1$ and $i \neq myID$
2.   **send**($myNum$, P_i, $myID$)
3. $myCounter = 0$
4. **for** $i = 0$ to $N - 2$
5.   **recv**(num, P_{ANY})
6.   **if** $myNum > num$
7. $myCounter = myCounter + 1$
8. **if** $myCounter \neq myID$
9. $twoItems = $ **pack**($myNum, myCounter$)
10.   **for** $i = 0$ to $N - 1$ and $i \neq myID$
11.   **send**($twoItems, P_i, myID$)
12. **while recv**($packedItems, P_{ANY}$) $\neq NULL$
13.   **unpack**($packedItems, num, counter$)
14.   **if** $counter = myID$
15. $myNum = num$

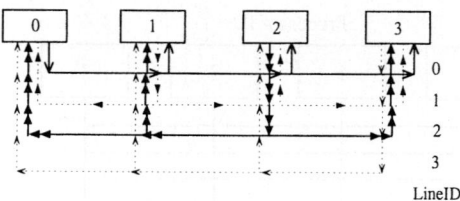

Fig. 5. Overall steps

It is assumed that each processor (or node) has a number stored in it initially and there is a total of $N > 2$ processors in the CON where N is the number of *distinct* items to be sorted. We also assume one process per one processor and $myID$ is its own process identification number. There are two communication subroutines in the algorithm: **send**(*data, destination process, communication line number*) and **recv**(*data, source process*). These subroutines require identification numbers for both lines and nodes. These identification numbers were described in the previous section. Also note that **pack**(*item1, item2, ..., itemN*) is a subroutine that packs all stated items together as one larger item and the subroutine **unpack**(*packedItems, item1, item2, ..., itemN*) does just the opposite.

One of the arguments in subroutine **send**() indicates the communication lines to use. (There is no such argument in **recv**().) Figure 5 shows how the lines are used in this sorting algorithm. Four different sources of communication are denoted by four different arrow patterns. There is a total of 11 communication steps. This communication scheme can be easily generalized for a N-node CON.

Like any communication scheme, it is vital that there be no collision of messages on any of these communication lines (or any line segment) at any point in the algorithm. Lemma 1 shows that our communication scheme produces no collision.

Lemma 1 (Collision-Free All-to-All). *The communication scheme used in the Decimal Number Parallel Sorting Algorithm produces no collision.*

Proof. We use the proof by contradiction. Suppose there is a collision of messages in the CON network. Since one time step equates one line segment, there must exist *at least* two paths of equal length that the messages use to traverse from different sources to the point of collision (i.e., the line segment that messages collide). But the algorithm ensures that the path lenghts in the algorithm from different sources differ *at least* one step before *any* common line segment is used (lines 2 and 11). This is true because node i always uses line i to communicate. Thus, this is a contradiction. We conclude that lemma 1 is true.

After designing an algorithm, a computer scientist needs to know whether his algorithm is provably correct. That is, whether the remaining decimal numbers in each node are in increasing order at the end of the algorithm. Theorem 1 shows that our algorithm works correctly.

Theorem 1 (Algorithm's Correctness). *The Decimal Number Parallel Sorting Algorithm is correct.*

Proof. Let P_i be an arbitrary process i, $0 \le i \le N-1$, in the completely overlapping network. In the algorithm each process P_i initially sends out its own number $myNum$ to the other processes P_j, $j \ne i$ (lines 1-2). Upon receiving these numbers, each process P_i counts the numbers less than its own number $myNum$ and keeps this count in $myCounter$ (lines 4-7). If $myCounter$ is equal to the positional number $myID$ of the process P_i, it implies that there are exactly $myCounter$ numbers that are less than $myNum$ and thus $myNum$ is in correct position. If $myCounter$ is not equal to the positional number $myID$, both $myNum$ and $myCounter$ are sent to the other processes P_j, $j \ne i$ (lines 8-11). Upon receiving these numbers, each process P_i checks if the just-received variable *counter* is equal to $myID$. If it is, the process P_i replaces $myNum$ with the just-received variable *num*. If it is not, the process P_i waits for the next number to arrive and checks. One of these numbers must have its variable *counter* equal to $myID$ (lines 12-15). With lemma 1, each process P_i eventually keeps the number whose rank is i.

In addition to being correct, the algorithm should be efficient in order to be applicable to real-life applications. The following theorem shows that this sorting algorithm has a running time of $O(N)$.

Theorem 2 (Running Time). *The Decimal Number Sorting Algorithm on CON has a running time of $O(N)$ where N is the size of the items to be sorted.*

Proof. In parallel algorithm running time is divided into communication time τ and computation time δ. For simplicity, assume that one step in communication is equal to one step in computation. There is a total of four phases in this algorithm.

Phase 1 (Communication): Each process sends its own number to the other processes (lines 1-2). Since this sending is done in parallel, the time of the longest communication path dominates the whole communication.

$$\tau_1 = 3N - 1 \tag{1}$$

Phase 2 (Computation): Each process counts the number of smaller numbers than its own number $myNum$ (lines 3-7).

$$\delta_1 = N - 1 \tag{2}$$

Phase 3 (Communication): Each process sends its own number and its own counter $myNum$ and $myCounter$ respectively to the other processes (lines 8-11). For simplicity, assuming that time of sending one item and two items are the same[1], we therefore have

$$\tau_2 = 3N - 1 \tag{3}$$

---

[1] This assumption does *not* affect the time complexity since the time of sending two items is constant.

Phase 4 (Computation): Each process checks for a counter that is equal to its $\overline{\text{ID}}$ (lines 12-15). There are in the worst case a total of $N-1$ counters to check. Therefore, we have

$$\delta_2 = N - 1 \tag{4}$$

Hence, the total time complexity ξ is $\xi = \tau_1 + \delta_1 + \tau_2 + \delta_2 = O(N)$.

Naturally the question that comes to the mind of computer scientists is whether this parallel sorting algorithm is the best possible or time-optimal on CON. Theorem 3 nicely answers this question.

Theorem 3 (Optimality). *The Decimal Number Parallel Sorting Algorithm is time-optimal on CON.*

Proof. In order to solve *any* sorting problem on CON, the parallel sorting algorithm must *at least* communicate between the two farthest nodes 0 and $N-1$. Let us call the shortest distance between the two farthest nodes a *diameter*. In CON the diameter is $N+1$ steps. This establishes the lower bound $\Omega(N)$ for the sorting problem on CON. Theorem 2 states that the Decimal Number Parallel Sorting Algorithm has a time complexity of $O(N)$. Hence, theorem 3 holds.

4 Binary Number Parallel Sorting Algorithm on CON

Given a set of 1's and 0's, can we, without any modification, use the Decimal Number Parallel Sorting Algorithm in the previous section to sort it? The answer is no. This is because there are repeated numbers of 1's and 0's and this violates the assumption of having *distinct* numbers as the input to the algorithm. Hence, we need to invent a new algorithm specifically for sorting binary numbers. At the first glance one might suspect that sorting one-digit binary numbers may be computationally easier than sorting decimal numbers because we have some prior knowledge about our input. That is, only two kinds of numbers (i.e., 0's and 1's) are possible. But our suspicion may not necessarily be true. We will later illustrate this point in this section.

Several binary number sorting algorithms on different parallel architectures exist in computer science literature [24]. However, most algorithms work with d-digit binary numbers where $d > 1$. Few algorithms are designed to work specifically with only one-digit binary numbers. In [24] an algorithm for sorting N k-bit binary numbers on a complete binary tree was described and it was shown that, by counting, the hypothesized lower bound of $\Omega(Nk)$ bit steps can be beaten if k is equal to 1. This case is similar to ours because our binary number sorting algorithm deals also with one-digit binary numbers. The theoretically interesting question is *"Can we beat the lower bound $\Omega(N)$, too?"*.

The definition of the Binary Number Sorting Algorithm on CON is given as follows. Once again it is assumed that each processor has a single-digit binary number stored in it initially and there is a total of $N > 2$ processors in the CON where N is the cardinality of the set of one-digit binary numbers to be sorted.

Binary Number Sorting Algorithm for Process P_i

1. myCounter = myNum
2. **for** $i = 0$ to $N - 1$ and $i \neq myID$
3.   send($myNum, P_i, myID$)
4. **for** $i = 0$ to $N - 2$
5.   recv(num, P_{ANY})
6.   **if** $num = 1$
7.   myCounter = myCounter + 1
8. **if** $myID < N - myCounter$
9.   myNum = 0
10. **if** $myID \geq N - myCounter$
11.   myNum = 1

As a computer scientist, we would like to know whether this algorithm is provably correct. First, we note that lemma 1 also applies to this algorithm because it uses the same **send**(...) and **recv**(...) subroutines. Theorem 4 will show the rest.

Theorem 4 (Algorithm's Correctness). *The Binary Number Parallel Sorting Algorithm is correct.*

Proof. Let P_i be an arbitrary process i, $0 \leq i \leq N-1$, in the completely overlapping network. In the Binary Number Parallel Sorting Algorithm, each process P_i counts the number of 1's from its initial variable $myNum$ and keeps this count in $myCounter$ (line 1). Each process P_i then sends out its own number $myNum$ to the other processes P_j, $j \neq i$ (lines 2-3). Upon receiving these binary numbers, each P_i continues to count the number of 1's and keeps this count in $myCounter$ (lines 4-7). At this point the total number of 1's (i.e., $myCounter$) in the network is known to each process P_i. Given its positional number $myID$ and $myCounter$, each process P_i can identify the number, either 1 or 0, to be kept in $myNum$. If $myID < N - myCounter$, process $P_{i=myID}$ falls into the range of 0's and if $myID \geq N - myCounter$, process $P_{i=myID}$ falls into the range of 1's (lines 8-11). Hence, with lemma 1, the Binary Number Parallel Sorting Algorithm is correct.

This algorithm indeed looks simpler than the decimal number sorting counterpart. After all, this algorithm has only 11 lines, executes a pair of **send**(...) and **recv**(...) subroutines only once, and does not use **pack**(...) and **unpack**(...) subroutines. In addition, each process in our Binary Number Parallel Sorting Algorithm only needs to count the number of 1's and does not need to send this count to the other processes because it can immediately determine what number, either 0 or 1, should be in its position. But the important question to computer scientists is *"What about the time complexity? Are they asymptotically equivalent?"*. Theorem 5 shows the running time of our Binary Number Parallel Sorting Algorithm.

Theorem 5 (Running Time). *The Binary Number Parallel Sorting Algorithm on CON has a running time of $O(N)$ where N is the size of one-digit numbers to be sorted.*

Proof. In the Binary Number Parallel Sorting Algorithm running time is divided into communication time τ and computation time δ. We assume once again for simplicity that one communication step is equal to one computation step. There is a total of two main phases in this algorithm.

<u>Phase 1 (Communication)</u>: Each process sends its own number to the other processes (lines 2-3). Since this sending is done in parallel, the time of the longest communication path dominates the whole communication.

$$\tau = 3N - 1 \tag{5}$$

<u>Phase 2 (Computation)</u>: Each process counts the number of 1's from the just-received binary number (lines 4-7).

$$\delta = N - 1 \tag{6}$$

Therefore, the total time complexity ξ is $\xi = \tau + \delta + \iota = O(N)$ where ι is a constant.

At this point we want to be able to claim that our algorithm is time-optimal on CON. We would particularly like to know whether this claim is true because it will confirm the best possible performance of our algorithm on theoretical network CON and, as a consequence, we will be able to answer the question of complexity between this algorithm and its decimal number counterpart. Theorem 6 proves this claim nicely.

Theorem 6 (Optimality). *The Binary Number Parallel Sorting Algorithm is time-optimal on CON.*

Proof. In order to sort *any* instance of the binary number sorting problem on CON, all nodes in CON must necessarily assemble together some collective information about states in the CON network (i.e., the locations of 1's (or 0's) in the network or the total number of 1's (or 0's) in the network). To achieve this in CON, there must *at least* be communication among all N nodes in the network in some fashion. In other words, each node must at least send some piece of information either *directly* or *indirectly via some intermediate nodes* to all the other $N-1$ nodes.

The number of steps required for a node to send a message to all the other $N-1$ nodes in CON is at least $\lfloor \frac{N}{2} \rfloor + 2$ (i.e., a node in the middle of CON sends a message to all the other $N-1$ nodes where N is odd.). This implies *at least* $\lfloor \frac{N}{2} \rfloor + 2$ steps of communication must occur. We know of *one* way to achieve the assembling of this information, which is the way we described in figure 5. This method takes $3N - 1$ steps.

Let S_{min} be the *minimum* number of steps required to achieve the assembling of this information. Therefore, $\lfloor \frac{N}{2} \rfloor + 2 < S_{min} \leq 3N - 1$. This establishes the lower bound $S_{min} = \Omega(N)$ for any binary number sorting problem on CON. Theorem 5 states that the Binary Number Parallel Sorting Algorithm has a time complexity of $O(N)$. Thus, theorem 6 holds.

5 Comparison of the Two Parallel Algorithms

In section 4 we alluded a little bit to the question of time complexity of the two parallel algorithms. It at first seems that the Binary Number Parallel Sorting Algorithm is easier computationally than the decimal number counterpart. But, as theorems 2, 3, 5, and 6 have shown, they are actually equivalent asymptotically (i.e., when $N \to \infty$). In addition, methods of optimality proofs also differ. It is easy for one to fall into the trap of using the same proof of optimality for both cases. After a few more thoughts, one will notice that we *cannot* use the same argument of the case of decimal numbers for the binary number case, even though the lower bound is asymptotically the same. In the case of decimal numbers, there must necessarily be an exchange of two numbers residing in nodes 0 and $N-1$ in order to sort *any* instance of the decimal number sorting problem. On the other hand, knowing that the input is only a set of 1's and 0's, the binary numbers residing in nodes 0 and $N-1$ do not necessarily need to exchange the numbers *physically* via the network in order to sort any instance of the binary sorting problem. Therefore, we cannot use the diameter to establish the lower bound in this case.

6 Conclusion

We were originally motivated by Wilkinson's multiple bus networks with overlapping connectivity to increase parallelism. A theoretical network CON is an extension of Wilkinson's model. We illustrated the use of CON and its usefulness by solving two toy problems: decimal number and binary number sortings. In the decimal number parallel sorting we showed that our time-optimal algorithm has a speedup of $\frac{O(NlgN)}{O(N)} = O(lgN)$ over the fastest sequential sorting algorithm. This speedup is considered fairly good. For example, suppose $N = 1,000,000$ and logarithm base 10 is used, we have $\log N = 6$. This is already 6 times as fast as the fastest sequential algorithm. For the case of binary number parallel sorting algorithm, there is no speedup over the fastest sequential sorting algorithm, but, theory-wise, we can take satisfaction in knowing that there is no faster algorithm for solving the one-digit binary number sorting problem on CON. Because both sorting problems have a lower bound of $\Omega(N)$, it behooves us to ask whether or not there is a problem that can be solved on CON with a lower time complexity than $\Omega(N)$. This will be our future research question. On a final note, this paper is done from a purely theoretical perspective. It would be nice if some engineers actually implement this CON network. We would be very pleased to learn of any result!

Acknowledgement

We would like to thank the reviewers of this paper for their valuable comments.

References

1. Anderson, T.E., Culler, D.E., Patterson, D.: A case for NOW (Networks of Workstations). IEEE Micro. **15** (1995) No. 1 (Feb.) 54–64
2. Kantabutra, S., Couch, A.: Parallel K-means clustering algorithm on NOWs. NECTEC Technical Journal. **1** (2000) No. 6 (Jan.)

3. Drozdowski, M., Wolniewicz, P.: Experiments with scheduling divisible tasks in clusters of workstations. Lecture Notes in Computer Science. **1900** 311–319
4. Hamdi, M., Lee, C.K.: Dynamic load-balancing of image processing applications on clusters of workstations. Parallel Computing. **22** Issue 11 (1997) 1477–1492
5. Wilkinson, B.: On crossbar switch and multiple bus interconnection networks with overlapping connectivity. IEEE Transactions Computers. **41** (1992) 738–746
6. Wilkinson, B., Farmer, J.M.: Reflective interconnection networks. Computer and Electrical Engineering. **20** (1994) 289–308
7. Hoganson, K., Wilkinson, B., Carlisle, W.H.: Applications of rhombic multiprocessors. In Proc. of the International Conference on Parallel and Distributed Processing Techniques and Applications. (1997)
8. Schnorr, C., Shamir, A.: An optimal sorting algorithm for mesh connected computers. In Proc. of the 18th ACM Symposium Theory Computing. (1986)
9. Nassimi, D., Sahni, S.: Bitonicsort on a mesh connected parallel computer. IEEE Transactions on Computers. **c-28** (1987) 408–419
10. Lang, H.W., Schimmler, M., Schmeck, H., Schroder, H.: Systolic sorting on a mesh-connected network. IEEE Transactions on Computers. **34** No. 7 (1985) 652–658
11. Marberg, J.M., Gafni, E.: Sorting in constant number of row and column phases on a mesh. Algorithmica **3** (1988) 561–572
12. Sasaki, A.: A time-optimal distributed sorting algorithm on a line network. Information Processing Letters. **83** (2002)
13. Knuth, D.E.: The art of computer programming (sorting and searching). **3** Addison-Wesley. (1973)
14. Abali, B., Ozguner, F., Bataineh, A.: Balanced parallel sort on hypercube multiprocessors. IEEE Transactions **4** (1993) 572–581
15. Varman, P.J., Doshi, K.: Sorting with linear speedup on a pipelined hypercube. IEEE Transactions **41** (1992) 97–103
16. Tang, T.: Parallel sorting on the hypercube concurrent processor. In Proc. of Distributed Memory Computing Conference. (1990) 237–240
17. Lan, Y., Mohamed, M.A.: Parallel quicksort in hypercubes. In Proc. of the 1992 ACM/SIGAPP Symposium on Applied Computing. (1992)
18. Gu, Q.P., Gu, J.: Algorithms and average time bounds of sorting on a mesh-connected computer. IEEE Transactions on Parallel and Distributed Systems. **5** (1994) 308–315
19. Andrea, C., Arpaci-Dusseau, R., Arpaci-Dusseau, H., Culler, D.E., Hellerstein, J.M., Patterson, D.: High performance sorting on networks of workstations. In Proc. of the 1997 ACM SIGMOD International Conference on Management of Data. **26** (1997)
20. Brest, J., Vreze, A., Zumer, B.: A sorting algorithm on a PC cluster. In Proc. of the 2000 ACM Symposium on Applied Computing. (2000) (Mar.)
21. Salehmonamed, M., Luk, W.S., Peters, J.G.: Performance evaluation of LAN sorting algorithms. ACM SIGMETRICS Conference on Meaurement and Modeling of Computer Systems. **15** (1987) (May)
22. Luk, W.S., Ling, F.: An analytical/empirical study of distributed sorting on a local area network. IEEE Transactions on Software Engineering. **15** (1989)
23. Cormen, T.H., Leiserson, C.E., Rivest, R.L.: Introduction to algorithms. MIT Press. (1990)
24. Leighton, F.T.: Introduction to parallel algorithms and architecture: arrays • tree • hypercube. Morgan Kaufmann. (1993)

Lock-Free Parallel Garbage Collection

H. Gao[1], J.F. Groote[2], and W.H. Hesselink[1]

[1] University of Groningen, P.O. Box 800, 9700 AV Groningen, The Netherlands
[2] Eindhoven University of Technology,
P.O. Box 513, 5600 MB Eindhoven, The Netherlands

Abstract. This paper presents a lock-free parallel algorithm for *garbage collection* in a realistic model using synchronization primitives offered by machine architectures. *Mutators* and *collectors* can simultaneously operate on the data structure. In particular no strict alternation between usage and cleaning up is necessary, contrary to what is common in most other garbage collection algorithms.

We first design and prove an algorithm with a coarse grain of atomicity and subsequently apply the reduction theorem developed in [11] to implement the higher-level atomic steps by means of the low-level primitives.

1 Introduction

A *lock-free* (also called *non-blocking*) implementation of a shared object guarantees that within a finite number of steps always some process trying to perform an operation on the object will complete its task, independently of the activity and speed of other processes [12]. Since lock-free synchronizations are built without locks, they do not suffer from performance bottlenecks, which are often caused by locks and which can easily have a performance degrading effect of several orders of magnitude. In addition, lock-free synchronizations can offer progress guarantees. A number of researchers [1, 3, 12, 18] have proposed techniques for designing lock-free implementations. Essential for such implementations are advanced machine instructions such as *compare-and-swap* (*CAS*), or *load-linked* (*LL*)/*store-conditional* (*SC*).

In this paper we propose a lock-free implementation of mark&sweep *garbage collection* (GC). Garbage *collectors* are employed to identify at run-time which objects are no longer referenced by the *mutators* (i.e. user programs). The heap space occupied by these objects is said to be *garbage* and must be re-cycled for subsequent new objects. The garbage collectors reclaim all garbage by adding them to a so called *free-list*, which keeps track of free memory.

There are several basic strategies for GC: reference counting, mark&sweep and copying. Reference counting algorithms can do their job incrementally (resulting in shorter collection pauses), but impose overhead on the mutators and fail to reclaim circular garbage. Mark&sweep algorithms can reclaim circular structures, and don't place any burden on the mutators like reference counting algorithms do, but tend to leave the heap fragmented. Copying algorithms can reduce fragmentation, but add the cost of copying data from one space to another and require twice as much memory as a mark&sweep collector. Moreover, copying also requires that the programming language restrict address manipulation operations, which isn't true for C or C++.

One often encounters GC algorithms (e.g. [7,8]) that employ stop-the-world mechanisms, which suspend all normal running threads and then perform GC. Such an algorithm introduces a global synchronization point between all threads and tends to become a scaling bottleneck that limits program performance and processor utilization. It is unacceptable when the system must guarantee response time of interactive applications. Therefore, to achieve parallel speed-ups on shared-memory multiprocessors, lock-free algorithms are of interest [17, 21].

There are several lock-free GC algorithms in the literature. The first one is due to Herlihy and Moss [13]. They present a lock-free copying GC algorithm, which uses excessive copying for moving objects to avoid blocking synchronization. In their algorithm, the failure of a participating thread can indefinitely prevent the freeing of unbounded memory. In [15], Hesselink and Groote give a wait-free (wait-freedom is stronger than lock-freedom) GC algorithm using reference counting. However, this collector applies only to a restricted programming model, in which objects are not allowed to be modified between creation and deletion, and is therefore generally limited. Detlefs et. al. [5] provide a lock-free GC algorithm using reference counting. The approach relies on a strong hardware primitive, namely *double-compare-and-swap (DCAS)* for atomic update of two distinct words in memory. Michael [20] presents an efficient lock-free memory management algorithm that does not require special operating system or hardware support. However, his algorithm only guarantees an upper bound on the number of removed nodes not yet freed at any time. This is undesirable because a single garbage node might use a large amount of resources and might never be reclaimed.

Mark&sweep algorithms do not move objects. They can thus coexist well with C/C++ code, where one never dares to move an object because of possible address computations, and are gaining popularity. Our lock-free mark&sweep algorithm is non-intrusive and features high-performance and reliability. Moreover, unlike most previously published Mark&sweep algorithms [2, 6, 7], we make no assumption on the maximum numbers of mutators and collectors that can operate concurrently. As far as we could find, no similar algorithm exist.

The correctness properties of any concurrent implementation are seldom easy to verify. This is in general even harder for lock-free algorithms. Our previous work [9] shows that providing correctness proofs for such algorithms require huge amounts of effort, time, and skill. In [11], we have developed a reduction theorem that enables us to reason about a lock-free program to be designed on a higher level than the synchronization primitives. Using the reduction theorem, fewer invariants are required and some invariants are easier to discover and formulate without considering the internal structure of the final implementation.

2 Specification

We assume a fixed set Node of nodes (cf. Fig. 1), each of which is identified with a unique label between 1 and N for some $N \in \mathbb{N}$. The nodes in the set free are the

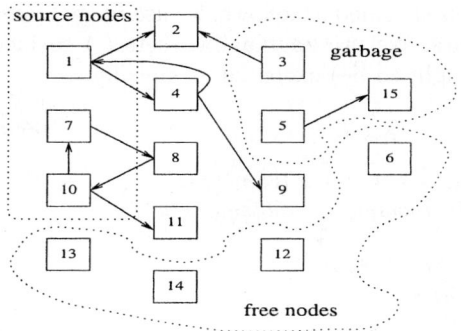

Fig. 1. A graph representation of the memory

free nodes. We model the heap as a finite directed graph of varying structure with a set of non-free nodes. Each node in the graph points to zero or more children (nodes), and the descendent relation may be circular. In the following context, we regard the attributes of nodes as arrays indexed by $1 \ldots N$. The number of children of a node x is indicated by its arity, which is denoted by arity$[x]$. We let C be the upper bound of the arities of the nodes. The expression child$[x, j]$ stands for the pointer to the jth child of node x, where $1 \leq j \leq$ arity$[x]$.

A node is called a *root* when some process has direct read access to it. Each application process p maintains a private set $roots_p$ that holds its root nodes. The set *Roots* is the union of all $roots_p$ for all processes p.

Access to nodes can be transferred between processes. We assume that there is a two-dimensional array Mbox indexed with a pair of processes that serves as mailboxes. If process p allows process q to access some node x, it writes x at Mbox$[p, q]$ using *Send*. Then, process q can claim the access by calling *Receive*.

We call a node a *source node* if the node is either in *Roots* or in some mailbox. A node is called *accessible* iff it is reachable by following a chain of pointers from a source node. Free nodes must not be accessible. Only nodes in the free set are allowed to be allocated by the mutators. A node is said to be a *garbage node* if it is neither accessible nor in the free set. Garbage collectors compute the set of nodes reachable from a set of source nodes and reclaim all garbage nodes by placing them into the free set. More formally, we define

$$R(p, x) \equiv (\exists z \in roots_p : z \xrightarrow{*} x),$$
$$R(x) \equiv (\exists z \in Roots : z \xrightarrow{*} x) \vee$$
$$(\exists p, q \in \text{Process} : \text{Mbox}[p, q] \xrightarrow{*} x),$$

where the reachability relation $\xrightarrow{*}$ is the reflexive transitive closure of relation $\to$ on nodes defined by: $z \to x \equiv (\exists k : 1 \ldots \text{arity}[z] : \text{child}[z, k] = x)$. The fact that a node x is a garbage node is formalized by: $\neg R(x) \wedge x \notin \text{free}$.

The interface of the mutators consists of a shared data structure of nodes, and a number of procedures that can be called in the application processes. We assume there are in total P concurrently executing sequential processes. In the text of the procedures specified as follows, we use *me* to stand for the process that invokes the procedure. We use angular brackets ⟨ ⟩ to indicate that embraced statements are (thought to be) executed atomically.

proc *Create*(): Node
    local x : Node;
    ⟨ **when available extract** x **from free**;
      $\text{arity}[x] := 0$; $roots_{me} := roots_{me} \cup \{x\}$; ⟩
    return x;

proc *AddChild*(x, y: Node): Bool
{ $R(me, x) \wedge R(me, y)$ }
    local *suc* : Bool;
    ⟨ *suc* := ($\text{arity}[x] < C$);
      if *suc* **then** $\text{arity}[x]$++; $\text{child}[x, \text{arity}[x]] := y$; **fi** ⟩
    return *suc*;

proc *GetChild*(x: Node, *rth*: ℕ): Node ∪ {0}
{ $R(me, x)$ }
    local y : Node ∪ {0};
    ⟨ **if** $1 \leq rth \leq \text{arity}[x]$ **then** $y := \text{child}[x, rth]$; **else** $y := 0$; **fi** ⟩
    return y;

proc *Make*(c: **array** [ ] **of** Node, n: $1 \ldots C$): Node
{ $\forall j: 1 \leq j \leq n: R(me, c[j])$ }
    local x : Node; j : ℕ;
    ⟨ **when available extract** x **from free**;
      for $j := 1$ **to** n **do** $\text{child}[x, j] := c[j]$ **od**;
      $\text{arity}[x] := n$; $roots_{me} := roots_{me} \cup \{x\}$; ⟩
    return x;

proc *Protect*(x: Node)
{ $R(me, x) \wedge x \notin roots_{me}$ }
    ⟨ $roots_{me} := roots_{me} \cup \{x\}$; ⟩
    return;

proc *UnProtect*(z: Node)
{ $z \in roots_{me}$ }
    ⟨ $roots_{me} := roots_{me} \setminus \{z\}$; ⟩
    return;

proc *Send*(x: Node, r: Process)
{ $R(me, x) \wedge \text{Mbox}[me, r] = 0$ }
    ⟨ $\text{Mbox}[me, r] := x$; ⟩
    return;

proc *Receive*(r: Process): Node
{ $\text{Mbox}[r, me] \neq 0$ }
    local x : Node;
    ⟨ $x := \text{Mbox}[r, me]$;
      $\text{Mbox}[r, me] := 0$; $roots_{me} := roots_{me} \cup \{x\}$; ⟩
    return x;

The application programmers are responsible for ensuring that an offered procedure is called only when its precondition (enclosed by braces { } if there is any) holds. The condition "available" in *Create* and *Make* is implementation dependent. When an allocation request cannot be met from the free memory, the mutator either waits, or invokes a new round of GC to free more garbage. The threshold value that determines whether or not to invoke a new round of GC can be customized by the user.

Behind this abstract "user system" there is a collection of garbage collecting processes. A garbage collector does not modify the memory graph but only manipulate the `free` set. To specify that GC does happen and is eventually exhaustive, we give the liveness property, i.e. every garbage node will be eventually put into the `free` set by a garbage collector.

3 A Higher-Level Implementation

The idea behind most GC algorithms in use is to first recursively trace all reachable nodes starting from root nodes, then nodes not reached are considered garbage and can be collected. We present a lock-free implementation that comes close to the classical mark&sweep algorithms.

We first extend the specification to a high-level implementation, where all actions on shared variables are separated into distinct atomic accesses except for some special commands enclosed by angular brackets $\langle \ldots \rangle$. In order to be able to finally transform the higher-level algorithm into the low-level algorithm using our reduction theorem developed in [11], we require that every labeled atomic group of statements in the higher-level algorithm refer to at most one shared node.

3.1 Data Structure

The data structure we use in the higher-level implementation is shown in Fig. 2. Besides fields `arity` and `child`, each node has one of three colors: *white*, *black* and *grey*. All *black* nodes reachable from a source node are interpreted as accessible nodes and all other *black* nodes are garbage. *Grey* is a transient color that only occurs during GC. The `free` set is implemented as a virtual set that contains all *white* nodes.

Since any accessible node must not be freed as garbage, the system needs to keep track of source nodes that are created by a process and may still be referred to by other processes. We introduce a field `srcnt` for each node to count all references (processes and mailboxes) to the node as a source node.

To avoid possible interference between mutators and collectors, the updates of the field `srcnt` of the node, upon deletion from the *roots* set, is postponed. We use the field `freecnt` to count the postponed decrementings of `srcnt`. The fields `ari` and `father` record the number of children a node has at the beginning of GC and the parent node of a node in a tree traversed from a source node by collectors, respectively.

We use a shared variable `shRnd` to hold the round number of the current GC, together with an additional field `round` in the record of a node. The private variable *rnd* is a private copy of the shared variable `shRnd`. The global private variable *toBeC* is used to transfer information about checked nodes between

Constant
    $P = $ number of processes; $N = $ number of nodes;
    $C = $ upper bound of number of children;
Type
    colorType: {*white, black, grey*};
    nodeType: **record** =
        arity, srcnt, freecnt, ari, round: $\mathbb{N}$;
        child: **array** $[1\ldots C]$ **of** $1\ldots N$;
        color: colorType; father: $\mathbb{N} \cup \{-1\}$;
    end
Shared variables
    Mbox: **array** $[1\ldots P,\ 1\ldots P]$ **of** $0\ldots N$;
    Node: **array** $[1\ldots N]$ **of** nodeType; shRnd: $\mathbb{N}$;
Private variables
    roots, toBeC: **a subset of** $1\ldots N$; *rnd*: $\mathbb{N}$;
Initialization:
    shRnd $= 1 \wedge \forall x\colon 1\ldots N$: round$[x] = 1$;

Fig. 2. Data Structure

internal calls. There is also a local private variable *toBeD* for representing the set of source nodes to be tracked from.

3.2 Algorithm

In this section, we give a higher-level implementation for the collectors and the mutators. Since the same sequential program can be executed by all processes, we adopt the convention that every private variable name can be subscripted by the process identifier. In particular, pc_p is the program counter of process p. We do not write Node$[x].f$ but $f[x]$. We denote color$[x] = $ *white* by *white*(x), and similarly for the other two colors. Brackets ⟦ ⟧ and the actions between parenthesis ⦇ ⦈ can be ignored in the implementation. They only serve in the proof of correctness. We will explain this in section 4.

Collectors. Our garbage collectors are encoded in the procedure *GCollect* as shown in Fig. 3. It consists of three phases: (1) initialization: paint all *black* nodes *grey*, (2) marking: paint all *grey* nodes reachable from the source nodes back to *black* after traversing the memory graph, and (3) sweeping: reclaim all garbage by painting all remaining *grey* nodes *white*.

In the first phase, the processes only need to paint the *black* nodes *grey* since the *white* nodes can not be garbage. Moreover, we let the field father of each node with positive srcnt be 0, and that of other nodes be -1. As the algorithm allows parallel use of mutators, being a source node is not stable. For simplicity, we call a node x with father$[x] = 0$ an *old source node*.

In line 108, a delayed initialization on node x will be skipped since round$[x]$ is never decreased. As usual with version numbers, here we assume that sufficient

```
proc GCollect() =
    local x: 1...N; toBeD: a subset of 1...N;
100:    rnd := shRnd; toBeC := {1,...,N};
101:    while shRnd = rnd ∧ toBeC ≠ ∅ do
            choose x ∈ toBeC;
108:        ⟨ if round[x] = rnd then
                    round[x] := rnd + 1; ari[x] := arity[x];
                    if black(x) then color[x] := grey; fi;
                    if srcnt[x] > 0 then father[x] := 0; else father[x] := −1; fi; fi; ⟩
            toBeC := toBeC \ {x}; od;
121:    toBeC := {1,...,N}; toBeD := {1,...,N};
122:    while shRnd = rnd ∧ toBeD ≠ ∅ do
            choose x ∈ toBeD;
126:        toBeD := toBeD \ {x};
            ⟨ if father[x] = 0 then Mark_stack(x); fi; ⟩ od;
129:    while shRnd = rnd ∧ toBeC ≠ ∅ do
            choose x ∈ toBeC;
134:        ⟨ if round[x] = rnd + 1 ∧ grey(x) then
                    color[x] := white;
                    ⦃ assert ¬R(x) ∧ x ∉ free; free := free ∪ x; ⦄ fi; ⟩
            toBeC := toBeC \ {x}; od;
135:    ⟨ if rnd = shRnd then shRnd := rnd + 1; fi; ⟩
137:    return
end GCollect.
```

Fig. 3. Procedure *GCollect*

bits are allocated for the version numbers to ensure that they cannot "wrap around" during the interval of a process's GC cycle.

In the second phase, lines 121-126, the processes build a forest in the set of all reachable nodes starting from the old source nodes. Trees in the forest are mutually disjoint. Each of them is rooted by a chosen old source node, and is established via calling *Mark_stack* (see Fig. 4) in a *while* loop. During *Mark_stack*, all the *grey* nodes on the tree are painted *black* in the order from the leaf to the root.

The procedure *Mark_stack* is mainly a form of graph search, and it was initially designed as a recursive procedure. Since we want to prove the correctness of our algorithm with PVS, we eliminated the recursion in favor of an explicit stack. The private variable *toBeC* serves to ensure that the search of a collector traverses every node at most once. This is important since the memory graph may have cycles and nodes may be reachable from different old source nodes.

In *Mark_stack*, lines 151-163, the tree is established by setting the father pointers. Since the memory graph may have cycles, the processes must reach consensus about the tree. The processes starting from the same old source node cooperate with each other, and are in competition with others to expand the tree to all nodes reached.

```
proc Mark_stack(x: 1...N) =
     local w, y: 1...N; suc: Bool; j, k: ℕ;
     stack: Stack; head: ℕ; set: a subset of 1...N;
     ch: [1...C] of 1...N;
150: toBeC := toBeC \ {x}; set := {x}; head := 0;
151: while shRnd = rnd ∧ set ≠ ∅ do
157:    choose w ∈ set; set := set \ {w};
        ⟨ if grey(w) ∧ round[w] = rnd + 1 then
            k := ari[w];
            for j := 1 to k do ch[j] := child[w, j] od; ⟩
          head++; stack[head] := w; j := 1;
158:      while shRnd = rnd ∧ j ≤ k do
            y := ch[j];
            if y ∉ toBeC then j++;
            else
163:          ⟨ if father[y] ∈ {−1, w} ∧ grey(y)
                    ∧round[y] = rnd + 1 then
                  father[y] := w; ⟩ set := set ∪ {y};
                toBeC := toBeC \ {y}; fi;
              j++; fi; od; fi; od;
168: while shRnd = rnd ∧ head ≠ 0 do
175:    y := stack[head]; head--;
        ⟨ if grey(y) ∧ round[y] = rnd + 1 then
            srcnt[x] := srcnt[x] − freecnt[x];
            color[y] := black; freecnt[x] := 0; fi; ⟩ od;
180: return
end Mark_stack.
```

Fig. 4. Procedure Mark_stack

The order for choosing an element from the local variable *set* is irrelevant for correctness, but relevant for efficiency. The search is a depth first search if the order is first in last out. The search is a breadth first search if the order is first in first out. Starting from the chosen old source node, all nodes on the tree are pushed onto the local stack after their children have been stored. The order of the elements pushed onto the stack is essential for correctness.

After the tree has been established, the process paints all *grey* nodes *black* in the order in which they are popped from the *stack* (lines 168-175). When a node in the tree is painted *black*, its descendants (with respect to the *father* relation) in the tree must have been painted *black* already. So the other processes need not trace or paint the subtree starting from that node. At the end of *Mark_stack*, the process returns to the procedure *GCollect* to traverse another tree from another old source node.

In the third phase, lines 129-134, processes try to re-cycle all remaining *grey* nodes by coloring them *white* (i.e. adding them to the free set). The main proof obligation for the algorithm is that all nodes being freed are not accessible. When the fastest process executes line 135, the shared variable shRnd is incremented to notify all other collectors that this round of GC is completed.

Mutators. The higher-level implementations of the procedures for the mutators are relatively easy. For reasons of space, in Fig. 5 we only provide the code for procedure Make (see [10] for the remainning). In the code, "time to do GC" indicates that some variable, like time or the amount of free memory, reaches a threshold value.

proc *Make*(c: **array** [ ] **of** $1\ldots N$, n: $1\ldots C$): $1\ldots N =$
$\{\ \forall\ j:\ 1\ldots n$: $R(me,\ c[j])\ \}$
      local x: $1\ldots N$; j: $\mathbb{N}$;
      while *true* **do**
300:      **choose** $x \in [1\ldots N]$;
306:      $\langle$ **if** *white*(x) **then**
              color$[x] :=$ *black*; srcnt$[x] := 1$;
              $(\!|$ **assert** $x \in$ free; free $:=$ free $\setminus x$; $|\!)$
              $[\![$ **for** $j := 1$ **to** n **do** child$[x,\ j] := c[j]$; **od**
              arity$[x] := n$; roots $:=$ roots $\cup \{x\}$; $]\!]\ \rangle$
              break;
308:      **elseif** *time to do GC* **then** *GCollect*(); **fi**; **od**;
310:      $[\![$ **return** $x\ ]\!]$
end *Make*.

Fig. 5. Procedure *Make*

4 Correctness

The main issue of the algorithm is how to ensure the correct execution of collectors and mutators when they concurrently compete with each other for the same data structure. The algorithm is correct if it behaves properly for all interleavings. Here we only give a sketch of the correctness of the algorithm. For the complete mechanical proof, we refer to [14].

We need to distinguish safety properties and liveness properties. The main aspect of safety is functional correctness and atomicity, say in the sense of [19]. We prove partial correctness of the implementation by showing that each procedure of the implementation executes its specification command exactly once and that the resulting value of the implementation equals the resulting value in the specification. As shown in Fig. 3 to Fig. 5, we extend the implementations with auxiliary variables and commands used in the specification. For simplicity, we use brackets $[\![\ ]\!]$ to enclose the specification commands that perform the same actions as the implementation, and parenthesis $(\!|\ |\!)$ to enclose the specification commands that can be deleted in the implementation.

GC is an internal affair not relevant for the users of the routines. *GCollect* cannot be invoked explicitly, but will only be invoked implicitly in, e.g. *Make*. This means we only need to prove the match of the specifications and implementations for all user programs, but not for *GCollect*. Instead, the main safety property we have proved for *GCollect* is that the system only collects garbage, i.e. that an accessible node is never freed. This is expressed in the invariant $I1$: $white(x) \Rightarrow \neg R(x)$.

Furthermore, we also need to prove that all preconditions of the interface procedures are stable under the actions of the other processes. Process p can ensure its rights to have access to node x by checking the predicate $R(p, x)$, independently.

A liveness property asserts that program execution eventually reaches some desirable state. In our case, we want to ensure it is always the case that every garbage node is eventually collected. That is, $\neg R(x) \leadsto white(x)$, where $\leadsto$ is the "leads-to" relation defined by: $(P \leadsto Q) \equiv \Box(P \Rightarrow \Diamond Q)$.

We actually prove something stronger, viz., that, every inaccessible node is painted *white* within two rounds of GC.

Theorem 1. *For any integer m,*
$shRnd = m \wedge \neg R(x) \leadsto shRnd \leq m + 2 \wedge white(x)$.

5 The Low-Level Implementation

Synchronization primitives LL and SC, proposed by Jensen et. al. [16], have found widespread acceptance in modern processor architectures (e.g. MIPS II, PowerPC and Alpha architectures). These instructions are closely related to the CAS, and together implement an atomic Read/Write cycle.

At the cost of copying an object's data before an operation, Herlihy [12] introduced a general methodology to transfer a sequential implementation of any data structure into a lock-free synchronization by means of synchronization primitives LL and SC.

In [11], we formalize Herlihy's methodology [12] and develop a reduction theorem that enables us to reason about a general lock-free algorithm to be designed on a higher level than the synchronization primitives. A reduction theorem is a general rule for deriving an "equivalent" higher-level specification from a lower-level one in some suitable sense [4]. The big advantage is that substantial pieces of the concrete program can be dealt with as atomic statements on the higher level and thus the correctness can be more easily verified.

In the higher-level implementation (from Fig. 3 to Fig. 5), instruction 135 is simply a CAS instruction offered by machine architectures. Each of all other special commands enclosed by angular brackets ⟨...⟩ only refer one shared node and some private variables, and therefore can be transformed into low-level lock-free implementations using our reduction theorem. The transformation is straightforward, and we refer the reader to [14].

6 Conclusions

We present a lock-free parallel algorithm for mark&sweep GC in a realistic model by means of synchronization primitives *compare-and-swap* (CAS) and *load-linked* (LL)/*store-conditional* (SC) offered by machine architectures. Our algorithm allows to collect a circular data structure and makes no assumption on the maximum number of mutators and collectors that can operate concurrently during GC. The efficiency of GC can be enhanced when more processors are involved in it.

Formal verification is desirable because there could be subtle bugs as the complexity of algorithms increases. To ensure our correctness proof presented in the paper is not flawed, we use the higher-order interactive theorem prover PVS for mechanical support. For the complete mechanical proof, we refer the reader to [14].

In the interface we did not provide a procedure for deleting a child of a node. However, this extension is rather straightforward after we have done the following two steps. First, introduce an additional field of a boolean array in the record of a node to record whether a child of a node is deleted. The boolean array should restrict only the mutators not the collectors from accessing a "deleted" child via the pointers of children. Secondly, similarly to what we did with unprotecting a source node, we need to modify line 175 to let the deletions of some "deleted" children be really operated. Since we don't think deleting a child is a main operation of GC, we didn't incorporate it. However, the correctness of this extension should not be difficult to verify.

The entrenched problem inherited from classical mark&sweep algorithms is that our algorithm may also result in severe memory fragmentation, with lots of small blocks. It is possible that there will be no block of memory on the free list large enough to hold a large object, such as an array. Thus, it is important to move free blocks that happen to be adjacent in memory. We plan in the future to incorporate some appropriate copying technique in our algorithm.

References

1. G. Barnes. A method for implementing lock-free data structures. In *Proceedings of the 5th ACM Symposium on Parallel Algorithms and Architectures*, pages 261–270, June 1993.
2. M. Ben-Ari. Algorithms for on-the-fly garbage collection. *ACM Transactions on programming Languages and Systems*, 6(3):333–344, 1984.
3. B.N. Bershad. Practical considerations for non-blocking concurrent objects. In *Proceedings of the Thirteenth International Conference on Distributed Computing Systems*, pages 264–274, 1993.
4. E. Cohen and L. Lamport. Reduction in TLA. In *Proceedings of the 9th International Conference on Concurrency Theory*, pages 317–331, 1998.
5. D.L. Detlefs, P.A. Martin, M. Moir, and G.L. Steele Jr. Lock-free reference counting. *Distributed Computing*, 15(4):255–71, December 2002.
6. E.W. Dijkstra, L. Lamport, A.J. Martin, C.S. Scholten, and E.F.M. Steffens. On-the-fly garbage collection: An exercise in cooperation. *Communications of the ACM*, 21(11):966–975, November 1978.
7. T. Endo, K. Taura, and A. Yonezawa. A scalable mark-sweep garbage collector on large-scale shared-memory machines. In *Proceedings of the 1997 ACM/IEEE conference on Supercomputing (CDROM)*, pages 1–14. ACM Press, 1997.

8. C. Flood, D. Detlefs, N. Shavit, and C. Zhang. Parallel garbage collection for shared memory multiprocessors. In *Usenix Java Virtual Machine Research and Technology Symposium (JVM '01)*, Monterey, CA, April 2001.
9. H. Gao, J.F. Groote, and W.H. Hesselink. Almost wait-free resizable hashtables (extended abstract). In *Proceedings of 18th International Parallel & Distributed Processing Symposium (IPDPS)*, April 2004.
10. H. Gao, J.F. Groote, and W.H. Hesselink. Lock-free parallel garbage collection by mark&sweep. Technical Report CS-Report CSR-04-31, Eindhoven University of Technology, The Netherlands, 2004.
11. H. Gao and W.H. Hesselink. A formal reduction for lock-free parallel algorithms. In *Proceedings of the 16th conference on Computer Aided Verification (CAV)*, July 2004.
12. M. Herlihy. A methodology for implementing highly concurrent data objects. *ACM Transactions on Programming Languages and Systems*, 15(5):745–770, November 1993.
13. M.P. Herlihy and J.E.B. Moss. Lock-free garbage collection for multiprocessors. *IEEE Transactions on Parallel and Distributed Systems*, 3(3):304–311, 1992.
14. W.H. Hesselink. http://www.cs.rug.nl/~wim/mechver /garbage_collection
15. W.H. Hesselink and J.F. Groote. Wait-free concurrent memory management by Create, and Read until Deletion. *Distributed Computing*, 14(1):31–39, January 2001.
16. E.H. Jensen, G.W. Hagensen, and J.M. Broughton. A new approach to exclusive data access in shared memory multiprocessors. Technical Report UCRL-97663, Lawrence Livemore National Laboratory, January 1987.
17. P.C. Kanellakis and A. A. Shvartsman. *Fault-Tolerant Parallel Computation*. Kluwer Academic Publishers, 1997.
18. V. Luchangco, M. Moir, and N. Shavit. Nonblocking k-compare-single-swap. In *Proceedings of the fifteenth annual ACM symposium on Parallel algorithms and architectures*, pages 314–323. ACM Press, 2003.
19. N. A. Lynch. *Distributed Algorithms*. Morgan Kaufmann Publishers, 1996.
20. M. M. Michael. Safe memory reclamation for dynamic lock-free objects using atomic reads and writes. In *Proceedings of the twenty-first annual symposium on Principles of distributed computing*, pages 21–30. ACM Press, 2002.
21. H. Sundell and P. Tsigas. Scalable and lock-free concurrent dictionaries. In *Proceedings of the 2004 ACM Symposium on Applied computing*, pages 1438–1445, 2004.

Adaptive Parallel Ant Colony Optimization[*]

Ling Chen[1,2] and Chunfang Zhang[1]

[1] Department of Computer Science, Yangzhou University,
225009, Yangzhou, China
[2] National Key Lab of Novel Software Tech, Nanjing University,
210093, Nanjing, China
lchen@yzcn.net

Abstract. In this paper an adaptive parallel ant colony optimization is developed. We propose two different strategies for information exchange between the processors: selection based on sorting and on distance, which make each processor choose a partner to communicate and update the pheromone according to the partner's pheromone. In order to increase the ability of search and avoid early convergence, we also propose a method of adjusting the time interval of information exchange adaptively according to the convergence factor of each processor. Experimental results based on traveling salesman problem on the massive parallel processors (MPP) Dawn 2000 demonstrate the proposed APACO are superior to the classical ant colony optimization.

1 Introduction

Social insects(e.g. birds, fish, ants etc.) have high swarm intelligence [1]. Among the social insects' many behaviors, the most widely recognized is the ants' ability to find good solution to the shortest path problems between the nest and a food source. By simulating ant's swarm intelligence, Dorigo, M. et al. were the first to apply the ant colony optimization algorithm (ACO)[2] to solve TSP problem [3,4]. In ACO, artificial ants are created to emulate the real ants in the process of seeking food and information exchanging. The successful simulation has been applied in many applications such as job-shop scheduling [5], quadratic assignment problem [6], data mining [7], network routing [8], network load balancing [9] and robotics [10].

Ant colony optimization is a good candidate for parallelization. The rapid development of the technology in the computer hardware and parallel processing has established the material foundation for parallel ant colony optimization. In order to parallelize the ACO into a parallel ant colony optimization ((PACO), it is more important to modify the structure of ACO to get better optimization effect rather than to transfer the sequential ACO into a parallelization schema. The modification of ant colony structure to fit the parallel computational model involves three aspects: (1)

---

[*] This paper is supported in part by the Chinese National Natural Science Foundation under grant No. 60473012, Chinese National Foundation for Science and Technology Development under contract 2003BA614A-14, and Natural Science Foundation of Jiangsu Province under contract BK2005047.

Dividing the single ant colony of sequential ACO into several mutually independent sub colonies; (2) Controlling and managing the information exchange between the sub colonies; (3) Determine the time interval of information exchange between the sub ant colonies. Different methods of dividing colony and exchanging information generate different parallel ant colony algorithms. Our goal of parallelization is to obtain the high speedup and efficiency while the convergence and the ability of optimization are maintained or even improved.

Some authors have studied parallel versions of ACO algorithm. Two parallelization strategies of synchronous and asynchronous were proposed in the paper [11]. In the synchronous strategy, every processor exchanges information after every iteration, while in the asynchronous strategy every processor exchanges information after a certain time interval regularly. A fine grained parallelization with synchronous strategy was presented to solve quadratic assignment problem [12]. Randall, M. [13] introduced a synchronous parallel strategy, which assigned only one ant on each processor. D.A.L.Piriyakumar [14] introduced an asynchronous parallel Max-Min ant colony algorithm and tested it on the TSP benchmarks using the parallel computer Cray-T3E. Merkle, D. [15] first proposed a parallel ant colony algorithm on reconfigurable processor arrays. The running time of the algorithm is quasi-linear with the problem size n and the number of ants on a reconfigurable mesh with n^2 processor. Dorigo, M. [16] advanced a parallel ant colony algorithm on the hyper-cube architecture, this new approach enhances the ability of the ant colony algorithm to deal with complicated objective functions theoretically and practically.

To parallelize the ant colony algorithm, the most important factors to be considered are the pattern and the time interval of information exchange between the processors. These factors affect not only the speed of convergence of algorithm, but also the optimization ability of the algorithm. In the algorithms of [11-14], the global best solution is computed and broadcasted to all the processors in information exchange. Then every processor updates the pheromone matrix according to the global best solution. This method of information exchange could probably create some similar solutions in different processors, which cause large amount of pheromone on some trails. These trails could be considered to be the "optimum solution", and this will reduce the searching ability of the processors. Shu-Chuan Chu [17] and Middendorf, M.[18] proposed several different strategies of exchange information in order to enhance the performance of the algorithm. In addition, the processors exchange information is a constant time interval in the papers [11-14]. Although paper [11] acknowledged that this constant time interval of information exchange could affect the optimization speed, diversity and convergence of the algorithm, the detailed analysis of the effect and the method to reduce it have not been provided. Since this constant time interval information exchange do not take the distribution of the solutions into account, it may influence the diversity of the solutions and the convergence speed.

In this paper, we present an efficient adaptive parallel ant colony algorithm (APACO). Two strategies for information exchange and one method for adjusting the time interval of information exchange are proposed for APACO. Experimental results based on the traveling salesman problem on the massive parallel processors (MPP) Dawn 2000 confirm the efficiency and effectiveness of the proposed APACO.

2 Massively Parallel Processors

Our parallel ant colony algorithm is based on the computational model of massively parallel processors (MPP), which adopts the message passing method. MPP system has several features as follows [19]: (1) Adopt the commercialized microprocessor in processing nodes, and there are one or more microprocessors in each node; (2) Use the physically distributed memory, namely, each node has its own local memory system which could not be shared with other nodes; (3) The nodes are connected by a communication network with high bandwidth and short delay; (4) The system is extensible and can be expended to hundreds and thousands processors; (5) It is an asynchronous MIMD where a procedure consists of several processes each of which has its own memory space. Communication between the processes is implemented by message passing. The data distribution is usually not transparent to the users.

Due to these features of MPP system, it is very suitable for implementing the parallel ant colony algorithms. The local memory on each node is used for storing the information of each sub colony, such as pheromone matrix and the best solution. MPP supports standard programming mode, such as PVM, MPI, which are suitable to carry out information exchange between the ant sub colonies by the message passing interface. We use MPI with C bounding programming mode to implement our algorithm APACO on the MPP machine Dawn 2000.

3 The Adaptive Parallel Ant Colony Optimization

In our adaptive parallel ant colony optimization (APACO), the ant colony is divided into P colonies, and every processor holds a colony of ants. First, the ants in each sub colony search for the best solution in its own processor independently. After several generations, the processors exchange information with its partner. Instead of randomly choosing a processor to exchange information, each processor dynamically determines its partner by an adaptive method to make full use of the best gene from other processors. This enables each processor to select the partner according to the quality of its solution and to direct its further searching. In addition, the time interval of information exchange between processors is determined dynamically according to the convergence factor of each processor instead of a constant time interval. The strategy of information exchange and the time interval of information exchange are the critical factors influencing the convergence speed of algorithm, the quality of solution, the efficiency of computing and the speedup.

3.1 The Framework of the Algorithm of APACO

Including two stages, the framework of the proposed algorithm APACO is as follows:

Algorithm: Adaptive Parallel Ant Colony Optimization (APACO)
```
Begin
  Stage1:
    Initialize the pheromone matrix, the initial value of
    the time interval of information exchange g₀, and other
    parameters;
```

```
      Set the cycle counter i=0, the counter of exchange in-
      formation t=0;
    Stage2:
      While  (not termination) do
        For every processor do in parallel
          For (each ant)
            Construct the solution;
            Evaluate the solution;
          End for
          Local pheromone update;
          If (i==g_t)
            { t=t+1;
              Find a processor to exchange information;
              Update the pheromone according to its part-
ner;
              Adjust the time interval of information ex-
              change g_t;
              i=0;
            }
          i=i+1;
        End for
      End do
End
```

3.2 Adaptive Strategies of Information Exchange Between Processors

After several generations of local optimization, the solutions of a group could become stagnate and probably no the better solutions could be generated, so it is necessary to exchange information between the processors. The purpose of information exchange is to propagate the information to other processors. When the algorithm of one processor falls into a convergence state, it can get rid of local optimum by the information absorbed from other processors, then evolve towards the best solution. Information exchange plays an important role in APACO, it may enhance the probability of getting the optimum solution. Instead of choosing a neighboring [18] or a random processor to exchange information, two adaptive strategies for information exchange is proposed in this section, which offer a direction for each processor in further searching towards the optimal solution.

(1) Exchange Information Based on Fitness Sorting

This strategy enables each processor choose its partner according to the average fitness of the solutions obtained by the processors. The average fitness of solutions on processor i on current iteration is defined as $f_{ave}(i) = \frac{1}{N_i} \sum_{k=1}^{N_i} f(i,k)$, where N_i is the number of ants on processor i, $f(i,k)$ is the fitness of ant k. When information exchange is taken, the average fitness $f_{ave}(i)$ of every processor is sorted in descent order. We denote the indices of the processors after sorting as $rank_1, rank_2, \ldots, rank_P$. The partner of information exchange for the processor $rank_i$ ($i \in [1, \ldots, P]$) is the processor $rank_{P+1-i}$. For instance, the processor $rank_1$ which has the maximum average fitness would exchange information with processor $rank_P$ which has the minimum average fitness.

Once the processor $rank_i$ ($i \in [1, \ldots, P]$) finds the partner of information exchange, the elements $\tau(j,k)$ of its pheromone matrix is updated according to the pheromone $\tau^*(j,k)$ of processor $rank_{P+1-i}$:

$$\tau(j,k) = \frac{1}{2}[\tau(j,k)^{\delta_1} + \tau^*(j,k)^{\delta_2}]. \tag{1}$$

Here, $\tau^*(j,k)$ denotes the pheromone on edge (j,k) of processor $rank_{P+1-i}$, $\delta_1 = 1 - \frac{rank_i}{P}$ and $\delta_2 = \frac{rank_i}{P}$. δ_1 and δ_2 are the pheromone weights to determine the relative influence of the trail strength $\tau(j,k)$ and $\tau^*(j,k)$. The weight of pheromone on processor $rank_i$ is $1 - \frac{rank_i}{P}$, while that of pheromone on processor $rank_{P+1-i}$ is $\frac{rank_i}{P}$. If average fitness of processor $rank_i$ is relatively low, then its pheromone weight δ_1 will be relative small, while its partner's pheromone has a large influence δ_2. By information exchange, processor $rank_i$ of low average fitness can improve the searching speed effectively and enhance the optimization ability by combining with the information comes from the processor $rank_{P+1-i}$ of high average fitness. Meanwhile, The processor with higher average fitness can extend the searching space to avoid falling into the local optimum on the process of search.

(2) Exchange Information Based on Distance

This strategy enables each processor choose its exchange partner which has the most different best solution. To measure the difference of the best solutions, we use $dis(i,j)$ to denote the distance between processor i and processor j. Let $best(i)$ be the best solution of processor i and a_{ik} be the kth city of $best(i)$. Then $dis(i,j)$ is defined as:

$$disf(i,j) = \sum_{k=1}^{n} x(i,j,k), \text{ where } x(i,j,k) = \begin{cases} 0 & \text{if } a_{ik} = a_{jk} \\ 1 & \text{otherwise} \end{cases}. \tag{2}$$

From the equations above, we can see that the larger the distance between processors, the less similarity of these two processors. Processor i chooses the partner of information exchange according to (3).

$$j = \arg\max_{\substack{1 \le k \le P \\ k \notin tabu}} \left\{ \frac{dis(i,k)}{L(k)} \right\}. \tag{3}$$

Here $tabu$ is the set of processors that have not been chosen, $L(k)$ is the length of the best tour that processor k gets. From Eq.(3), we can see that processor i inclines to choose the processor j with higher quality solution and larger distance between other processors.

After the processor i determines the partner to exchange information, updating pheromone matrix is taken on processor i:

$$\tau(u,v) = \frac{1}{2}[\tau(u,v)^{\delta_3} + \tau^*(u,v)^{\delta_4}]. \tag{4}$$

where

$$\delta_3 = \frac{\sum_{k=1}^{P} dis(i,k)}{n \cdot P}, \quad \delta_4 = \frac{\sum_{k=1}^{P} dis(j,k)}{n \cdot P}. \tag{5}$$

Here, $\tau^*(u,v)$ denotes the pheromone on edge (u, v) of the partner of processor i, δ_3 and δ_4 are also the pheromone weights to measure the relative influence of the trail strength $\tau(u,v)$ and $\tau^*(u,v)$. $\sum_{k=1}^{P} dis(i,k)$ and $\sum_{k=1}^{P} dis(j,k)$ are the sums of distance between processor i, j and other processors respectively. The more the difference is, the larger the pheromone weight is. This strategy of information exchange will strengthen the influence of the better solutions while the diversities of solutions in the processors are maintained.

3.3 The Strategy of Adjusting the Time Interval of Information Exchange

The time interval of the adjacent information exchanges is the other critical factor that influences the performance of parallel ant algorithm. With short time interval of information exchange, since the processors communicate with other processors frequently, the information on one processor can be often sent to other processors, which can offer a guide for the processor to evolve and enhance the quality of the solutions. But on the other hand, due to the heavy overhead caused by the communications, the speed up of the algorithm could be reduced. In addition, the dominant influence of the best solutions will have a negative impact on the diversity of solutions. On the contrary, the long time interval of information exchange will reduce the overhead caused by the communications and increase the convergence speed in each processor. Since the processors get less global information of the information from the other processors, they will have a high probability getting trapped in a local optimum solution.

To get a proper time interval of information exchange, an adaptive method of adjusting the interval of information exchange is presented in this section. In our method, the time interval is no longer a fixed constant, but is adjusted adaptively by a certain rule which is helpful to get balance between the diversity of solutions and the convergence of algorithm.

To adjust the time interval of information exchange adaptively, we define a convergence factor $con(k)$ to denote the degree of convergence on processor k. The convergence factor is a function of the pheromone values, which is computed as follows:

$$con(k) = 2\left(\left(\frac{\sum_{i=1}^{N}\sum_{j=1}^{N}\max\{\tau_{max}^k - \tau_{ij}^k, \tau_{ij}^k - \tau_{min}^k\}}{N \times N \times (\tau_{max}^k - \tau_{min}^k)}\right) - 0.5\right). \quad (6)$$

where

$$\tau_{max}^k = \max\{\tau_{ij}^k \mid 1 \leq i \leq N, 1 \leq j \leq N\}. \quad (7)$$

$$\tau_{min}^k = \min\{\tau_{ij}^k \mid 1 \leq i \leq N, 1 \leq j \leq N\}. \quad (8)$$

τ_{max}^k and τ_{min}^k are the maximum and minimum pheromone on processor k respectively. At the initial stage of the algorithm, the pheromone value on each edge of every processor is set to 0.5, then the convergence factor $con(k) = 0$. When the algorithm on processor k has converged, then $con(k) = 1$. The convergence factor reflects the distributing of pheromone on the edges. The more the $con(k)$ is, the more concentrated the pheromone on processor k is, the more probability of processor k falling into the local optimum is. We adjust the time interval of information exchange according to this convergence factor:

$$g_{t+1} = \begin{cases} \max\{g_t + (0.5 - con_{ave}) \cdot k_1, 1\} & \text{if } con_{ave} \geq 0.8 \text{ or } con_{ave} \leq 0.2 \\ g_t & \text{otherwise} \end{cases} \quad (9)$$

Here k_1 is positive constant, g_{t+1} is the new time interval for the next information exchange, $con_{ave} = \frac{1}{P}\sum_{k=1}^{P} con(k)$. con_{ave} indicates the average degree of convergence of all the processors. When con_{ave} becomes larger, the tour that the ants choose are concentrated on some edges, and the pheromone of the majority processors is very concentrated. Since the solutions of the whole system lack of diversity, the time interval of information exchange should be reduced in order to frequently interchange the information between the processors to get rid of local optimum solution by absorbing the information from other processors. If con_{ave} value increases, the pheromone of the majority processors is evenly scattered, and solutions of the processors become well diversified, the time interval should be increased so that the overhead of communication can be decreased and each processor can continue searching in its own environment of evolution.

4 Experimental Results and Analysis

In this section, we show the test results on TSP benchmarks [20] to compare our method with that of ant colony algorithm. Our parallel algorithm is implemented on the passive parallel processors Dawn 2000 using MPI (C bounding). The basic parameters are set as: $\rho = \gamma = \xi = \lambda = 0.1$, $\alpha = 1$, $\beta = 2$, $k=16$, $k_1=0.5$, the number of ants is equal to the number of cities. If not stated otherwise, the number of processors is 6, and all given results are averaged over 50 trials each over 2000 iterations. In following tables and figures, S-APACO stands for APACO which adjust the time interval and exchange information based on fitness sorting, while D-APACO based on distance.

It can easily be seen from Table 1 that the best value (the length of the shortest path) of the best solutions of S-APACO and D-APACO are much smaller than that of classical ACO. In most trials, our algorithms need less computation time to get the high quality solutions. It is indicated that our parallel algorithms have higher optimization ability because of the reasonable the parallel strategies. The parallel strategies and the adaptive strategies for information exchange that we presented can enhance the quality of solutions and accelerate the convergence speed.

Table 1. The comparison result of ACO, S-APACO and D-APACO

Problem	Algorithm	Best value	Average value	The number of trials reaching the best solution	Time (s)
eil76	ACO	556.28	561.74	44	84.78
	S-APACO	538.37	539.93	48	15.98
	D-APACO	538.37	539.12	49	16.54
kroA100	ACO	21679.75	21762.41	36	96.29
	S-APACO	21282.44	21285.27	46	16.95
	D-APACO	21282.44	21284.56	48	17.87
d198	ACO	16819.59	16904.64	41	120.53
	S-APACO	15780.03	15783.58	47	21.62
	D-APACO	15780.03	15781.73	47	22.37
lin318	ACO	43001.57	43098.54	37	203.81
	S-APACO	42029.14	42033.73	46	34.67
	D-APACO	42029.14	42031.82	48	35.68
pcb442	ACO	51324.67	51417.52	34	432.82
	S-APACO	50778.13	50782.15	45	73.51
	D-APACO	50778.13	50780.36	46	74.93

Table 2 shows the results of four TSP problems that obtained with different number of processors by using D-APACO. From Table 2 we can see that when the number of processors is increased, the computing time can be reduced due to the less ants assigned on each processor. But due to the overhead of communication which increases the total time of algorithm, the speedup of our algorithm can not increase linearly with the increasing of processor exactly. This is in conformity with the Amdahl's Law. In order to show how the number of processors influences the time of the algorithm, we use Fig.1 to describe the relationship between them. Fig.1 graphically show that problems with small size can not get high speedup because the communication overhead is relatively larger than the computations. However, with the scale of the problem increased, the speedup is increased. For instance, the speedup of problem pcb442 is much greater than that of problem eil76.

Table 2. The comparison result of different processors on each problem using D-APACO

Problem	Number of processors	Best value	Average value	The number of trials reaching the best solution	Time(s)
eil76	3	538.37	547.49	42	29.51
	6	538.37	539.12	49	16.54
	10	538.37	549.54	41	9.43
d198	3	15780.03	15820.76	36	40.61
	6	15780.03	15781.73	47	22.37
	10	15780.03	15804.39	42	13.75
lin318	3	42029.14	42086.41	35	65.17
	6	42029.14	42031.82	48	35.68
	10	42029.14	42051.69	42	21.72
pcb442	3	50778.13	50842.61	35	147.68
	6	50778.13	50780.36	46	74.93
	10	50778.13	50807.84	42	49.53

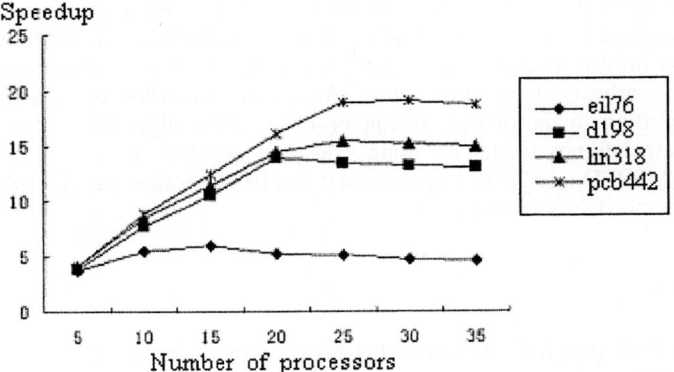

Fig. 1. Speedup on different problem using D-APACO

The influence of different time interval of information exchange is shown in Table 3. The Table shows that without adjusting the time interval, there is less communication overhead and hence the time cost can be reduced, but it can't keep balance between the diversity of solutions and the convergence of algorithm since the information between the processors can't be exchanged immediately, which would influence the search ability of the algorithm. Since S-APACO can make full use of the information come from other processors in a rational time interval according to the degree of convergence of the algorithm, its quality is better than others.

Table 3. The comparison result of different interval of information exchange

Problem	Evaluation standard	The time Interval of information exchange			
		4	6	8	S-APACO
eil51	Best Value	427.15	429.86	434.37	426.21
	Time(s)	9.91	9.87	9.73	10.02
kroA100	Best Value	21287.56	21294.18	21301.34	21282.44
	Time(s)	15.84	15.76	15.61	16.95
lin318	Best Value	42035.14	42043.14	42051.14	42029.14
	Time(s)	34.34	33.29	33.01	34.67
pcb442	Best Value	50796.81	50815.46	50829.35	50778.13
	Time(s)	73.41	72.01	71.53	73.51

5 Conclusion

To parallelize the ant colony algorithm, the most important factors to be considered are the pattern and the time interval of information exchange between the processors. These factors affect not only the speed of convergence of algorithm, but also the optimization ability of the algorithm. In this paper, we propose two different strategies for information exchange between processors: selection based on sorting and on distance, which make each processor dynamically determines its partner by an adaptive method to make full use of the best gene from other processors. This enables each processor to select the partner according to the quality of its solution and to direct its further searching each processor. In addition, a good time interval not only makes the best solution on one processor to send to other processors in proper time, but also reduces the overhead of communication. An adaptive method to adjusting the time interval according to the degree of convergence of the algorithm is presented. We apply these techniques to the traveling salesman problem, on the massive parallel processors (MPP) Dawn 2000. Experimental results show that our algorithm has high convergence speed, high speedup and efficiency.

References

1. Kennedy J. Eberhart R.C.: Swarm Intelligence.San Francisco, CA:Morgan Kaufmann Publishers (2001)
2. Dorigo M., Maniezzo V., Colomi A.:Ant system :Optimization by a colony of coorperating agents, IEEE Transactions on Systems, Man, and Cybernetics-Part B Vol. 26(1), (1996) 29-41
3. Dorigo, M., Gambardella, L.M.: Ant colony system: a cooperative learning approach to the traveling salesman problem. IEEE Transaction. On Evolutionary Computation, Vol. 1(1), (1997) 53-66
4. Dorigo, M., Gambardella, L.M.: Ant colonies for the traveling salesman problem. BioSystems , Vol. 43(2), (1997) 73-81
5. Colorni, A. Dorigo, M, Maniezzo, V.: Ant colony system for job-shop scheduling. Belgian J. of Operations Research Statistics and Computer Science, Vol. 34(1), (1994) 39-53

6. Maniezzo, V.: Exact and approximate nondeterministic tree search procedures for the quadratic assignment problem. Informs Journal of Computer, Vol. 11(4), (1999) 358-369
7. Parpinelli, R.S., Lopes, H.S., Freitas, A.A.: Data mining with an ant colony optimization algorithm, IEEE Transactions on Evolutionary Computation, Vol. 6(4), (2002) 321-332
8. Di Caro G.,Dorigo M., AntNet: A mobile agents approach for adaptive routing, Technical Report,IRIDIA (1997) 97-12
9. Schoonderwoerd R.,Holland O.,Bruten J.: Ant-like agents for load balancing in telecommunications networks. Proc.of Agents'97. Marina del Rey,CA:ACM Press (1997) 209-216.
10. Holland O.E , Melhuish C.: Stigmergy, self-organization, and sorting in collective robotics, Artificial Life, Vol. 5 (1999) 173-202
11. Bullnheimer, B., Kotsis, G., Steauss, C.: Parallelization strategies for the ant system. High Performance and Algorithms and Software in Nonlinear Optimization, Applied Optimization , Vol. 24, (1998) 87-100
12. Talbi, E-G., Roux, O., Fonlupt, C., Robilard, D.: Parallel ant colonies for the quadratic assignment problem. Future Generation Computer Systems, Vol. 17, (2001) 441-449
13. Randall, M., Lewis, A.: A parallel implementation of ant colony optimization. Parallel and Distributed Computing, Vol. 62, (2002) 1421-1432
14. Piriyakumar. D.A.L., Levi, P.: A new approach to exploiting parallelism in ant colony optimization. Proceedings of 2002 International Symposium on Micromechatronics and Human Science, (2002) 237-243
15. Merkle, D., Middendorf, M.: Fast ant colony optimization on runtime reconfigurable processor arrays. Genetic Programming and Evolvable Machine, Vol. 3, (2002) 345-361
16. Blum, C., Dorigo, M.: The Hyper - Cube framework for ant colony optimization. IEEE Transactions on SMC, Vol. 34(2), (2004) 1161-1172
17. Shu-Chuan Chu, John F.Roddick, Jeng-Shyang Pan: Ant colony system with communication strategies, Information Science, Vol. 167, (2004) 63-76
18. Middendorf M., Reischle, F., Schmeck, H.: Multi colony ant algorithms. Heuristics, Vol. 8, (2002) 305-320
19. Harry F. Jordan, Alaghband, Gita: Foundations of Parallel Processing, Prentice Hall (2003)
20. TSPLIB WebPage, http://www.iwr.uni-heidelberg.de/groups/comopt/software/ TSPLIB95 / tsp/

Collective Communications for Scalable Programming

Sang Boem Lim[1], Bryan Carpenter[2], Geoffrey Fox[3], and Han-Ku Lee[4],*

[1] Korea Institute of Science and Technology Information (KISTI), Daejeon, Korea
slim@kisti.re.kr
[2] OMII, University of Southampton, Southampton SO17 1BJ, UK
dbc@ecs.soton.ac.uk
[3] Pervasive Technology Labs at Indiana University, Bloomington, IN 47404-3730
gcf@indiana.edu
[4] School of Internet and Multimedia Engineering, Konkuk University, Seoul, Korea
hlee@konkuk.ac.kr

Abstract. HPJava is an environment for scientific and parallel programming using Java. It is based on an extended version of the Java language. One feature that HPJava adds to Java is a multi-dimensional array, or multiarray, with properties similar to the arrays of Fortran. We are using Adlib as our high-level collective communication library. Adlib was originally developed using C++ by the Parallel Compiler Runtime Consortium (PCRC). Many functionalities of this high-level communication library is following its predecessor. However, many design issues are reconsidered and re-implemented according to Java environment. Detailed functionalities and implementation issues of this collective library will be described.

1 Introduction

The basic features of HPJava [10] [11] [12] have been described in several earlier publications. In this paper we will jump straight into a discussion of the implementation of some collective communications in HPJava.

The main characteristic change from Java to HPJava is to add a concept of multi-dimensional arrays, called "*multiarrays*". And to support parallel programming, HPJava creates "multiarrays" by extending multiarrays. These "multiarrays" are very closely modeled on the arrays of High Performance Fortran (HPF). The new distributed data structures are cleanly integrated into the syntax of the language. In other word, new distributed data structure doesn't interfere with the existing syntax and semantics of Java-for example ordinary Java arrays are left unaffected.

New syntaxes in the source HPJava program is translated to an intermediate standard Java file and this Java file is compiled using ordinary Java compiler. The preprocessor that performs this task is reasonably sophisticated. During the

* Corresponding author.

preprocessor phase, it performs a complete static semantic check of the source program, following rules that include all the static rules of the Java Language Specification [9]. So it should not normally happen that a program accepted by the HPJava preprocessor would be rejected by the backend Java compiler. The translation scheme depends on type information, so we were essentially forced to do a complete type analysis for HPJava (which is a superset of standard Java). Moreover we wanted to produce a practical tool, and we felt users would not accept a simpler preprocessor that did not do full checking.

The current version of the preprocessor also works hard to preserve line-numbering in the conversion from HPJava to Java. This means that the line numbers in run-time exception messages accurately refer back to the HPJava source. Clearly this is very important for easy debugging.

A translated and compiled HPJava program is a standard Java class file, ready for execution on a distributed collection of JIT-enabled Java Virtual Machines. All externally visible attributes of an HPJava class can be transparently reconstructed from Java signatures stored in the class file. This makes it possible to build libraries operating on distributed arrays, while maintaining the usual portability and compatibility features of Java. The libraries themselves can be implemented in HPJava, or in standard Java, or as JNI interfaces to other languages. The HPJava language specification documents the mapping between distributed arrays and the standard-Java components they translate to.

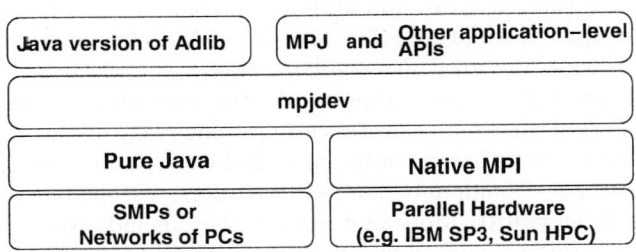

Fig. 1. An HPJava communication stack

Currently HPJava is supplied with one library for parallel computing-a Java version of the *Adlib* library of collective operations on distributed arrays [14]. A version of the *mpiJava* [1] binding of MPI can also be called directly from HPJava programs. Figure 1 summarizes an HPJava communication libraries stack. This figure shows how high-level collective libraries and low-level device library are working together.

2 Related Works

UC Berkeley is developing Titanium [3] to add a comprehensive set of parallel extensions to the Java language. Support for a shared address space and compile-time analysis of patterns of synchronization is supported.

The Timber [2] project is developed from Delft University of Technology. It extends Java with the Spar primitives for scientific programming, which include multidimensional arrays and tuples. It also adds task parallel constructs like a foreach construct.

Jade [8] from University of Illinois at Urbana-Champaign focuses on message-driven parallelism extracted from interactions between a special kind of distributed object called a Chare. It introduces a kind of parallel array called a ChareArray. Jade also supports code migration.

HPJava differs from these projects in emphasizing a lower-level (MPI-like) approach to parallelism and communication, and by importing HPF-like distribution formats for arrays. Another significant difference between HPJava and the other systems mentioned above is that HPJava translates to Java byte codes, relying on clusters of conventional JVMs for execution. The systems mentioned above typically translate to C or C++. While HPJava may pay some price in performance for this approach, it tends to be more fully compliant with the standard Java platform.

3 High-Level Collective Communications

A C++ library Adlib [6] was completed in the Parallel Compiler Runtime Consortium (PCRC) [7] project. It was a high-level runtime library designed to support translation of data-parallel languages. It incorporated a built-in representation of a distributed array, and a library of communication and arithmetic operations acting on these arrays. The array model supported general HPF-like distribution formats, and arbitrary regular sections.

The Adlib series of libraries support *collective operations* on distributed arrays. All members of some active process group, which may or may not be the entire set of processes executing the program, must invoke a call to a collective operation simultaneously. Communication patterns supported include HPF/Fortran 90 intrinsic such as **cshift**. More importantly they include the regular-section copy operation, **remap**, which copies elements between shape-conforming array sections regardless of source and destination mapping. Another function, **write-Halo**, updates ghost areas of a distributed array. Various collective **gather** and **scatter** operations allow irregular patterns of access. The library also provides essentially all Fortran 90 arithmetic transformational functions on distributed arrays and various additional HPF library functions.

Figure 2 shows how collective communication is used in HPJava. It creates a general purpose matrix multiplication routine that works for arrays with any distributed format. This program takes arrays which may be distributed in both their dimensions, and copies into the temporary array with a special distribution format for better performance. A collective communication schedule **remap()** is used to copy the elements of one distributed array to another. From the viewpoint of this paper, the most important part of this code is communication method. One of the most characteristic and important communication library methods, **remap()**, takes two arrays as arguments and copies the elements of the source array to the destination array, regardless of the distribution format of the two arrays.

```
public class Comm {
  public void matmul(float [[-,-]] c, float [[-,-]] a, float [[-,-]] b) {

    Group2 p = c.grp();
    Range  x = c.rng(0);
    Range  y = c.rng(1);

    int N = a.rng(1).size();

    float [[-,*]] ta = new float [[x, N]] on p;
    float [[*,-]] tb = new float [[N, y]] on p;

    Adlib.remap(ta, a);
    Adlib.remap(tb, b);

    on(p)
      overall(i = x for : )
        overall(j = y for : ) {

          float sum = 0;
          for(int k = 0; k < N ; k++)
            sum += ta [i, k] * tb [k, j];

          c[i, j] = sum;
        }
  }
}
```

Fig. 2. A general Matrix multiplication in HPJava

3.1 Implementation of Collectives

By using a characteristic example of collective communication, we will discuss implementation of the Java Adlib collectives. For illustration we concentrate on the important **remap** operation. Although it is a powerful and general operation, it is actually one of the more simple collectives to implement in the HPJava framework.

General algorithms for this primitive have been described by other authors. For example it is essentially equivalent to the operation called **Regular_Section_Copy_Sched** in [4]. In this section we want to illustrate how this kind of operation can be implemented in terms of the particular **Range** and **Group** hierarchies of HPJava (complemented by a suitable set of messaging primitives).

Constructor and public method of the remap schedule for distributed arrays of float element can be described as follows:

```
class RemapFloat extends Remap {
  public RemapFloat (float # dst, float # src) {...}

  public void execute() {...}
  . . .
}
```

```
public abstract class BlockMessSchedule {

  BlockMessSchedule(int rank, int elementLen,boolean isObject) { ... }

  void sendReq(int offset, int[] strs, int[] exts, int dstId) { ... }
  void recvReq(int offset, int[] strs, int[] exts, int srcId) { ... }

  void build()    { ... }
  void gather()   { ... }
  void scatter()  { ... }
  ...
}
```

Fig. 3. API of the class `BlockMessSchedule`

The remap schedule combines two functionalities: it reorganizes data in the way indicated by the distribution formats of source and destination array. Also, if the destination array has a replicated distribution format, it broadcasts data to all copies of the destination. Here we will concentrate on the former aspect, which is handled by an object of class **RemapSkeleton** contained in every **Remap** object.

During construction of a **RemapSkeleton** schedule, all send messages, receive messages, and internal copy operations implied by execution of the schedule are enumerated and stored in light-weight data structures. These messages have to be sorted before sending, for possible message agglomeration, and to ensure a deadlock-free communication schedule. These algorithms, and maintenance of the associated data structures, are dealt with in a base class of **RemapSkeleton** called **BlockMessSchedule**. The API for the super class is outlined in Figure 3. To set-up such a low-level schedule, one makes a series of calls to **sendReq** and **recvReq** to define the required messages. Messages are characterized by an offset in some local array segment, and a set of strides and extents parameterizing a multi-dimensional patch of the flat Java array. Finally the **build()** operation does any necessary processing of the message lists. The schedule is executed in a "forward" or "backward" direction by invoking **gather()** or **scatter()**.

The implementation details of **BlockMessSchedule** will not be discussed in greater detail here because they are not particularly specific to our HPJava system, and the principles are fairly well known (see for example [4]).

However we do wish to describe in a little more detail the implementation of the higher-level **RemapSkeleton** schedule on top of **BlockMessSchedule**. This provides some insight into the structure HPJava distributed arrays, and the underlying role of the special **Range** and **Group** classes.

To produce an implementation of the **RemapSkeleton** class that works independently of the detailed distribution format of the arrays we rely on virtual functions of the **Range** class to enumerate the blocks of index values held by each process. These virtual functions, implemented differently for different distribution formats, encode all-important information about those formats. To a large extent the communication code itself is distribution format independent.

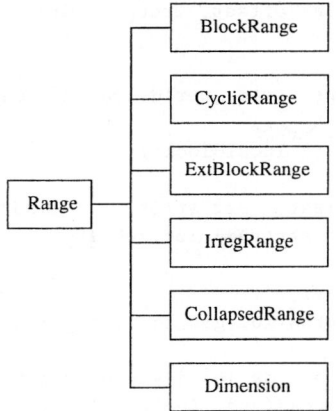

Fig. 4. The HPJava Range hierarchy

```
public abstract class Range {
    public int size() {...}
    public int format() {...}
    ...
    public Block localBlock() {...}
    public Block localBlock(int lo, int hi) {...}
    public Block localBlock(int lo, int hi, int stp) {...}

    public Triplet crds() {...}
    public Block block(int crd) {...}

    public Triplet crds(int lo, int hi) {...}
    public Block block(int crd, int lo, int hi) {...}

    public Triplet crds(int lo, int hi, int stp) {...}
    public Block block(int crd, int lo, int hi, int stp) {...}
    ...
}
```

Fig. 5. Partial API of the class `Range`

The range hierarchy of HPJava is illustrated in Figure 4 and some of the relevant virtual functions are displayed in the API of Figure 5. The most relevant methods optionally take arguments that allow one to specify a contiguous or striped subrange of interest. The **Triplet** and **Block** classes represent simple struck–like objects holding a few **int** fields describing respectively a "triplet" interval, and the strided interval of "global" and "local" subscripts that the distribution format maps to a particular process. In the examples here **Triplet** is used only to describe a range of *process coordinates* that a range or subrange is distributed over.

```
private void sendLoop(int offset, Group remGrp, int r){

  if(r == rank) {
    sendReq(offset, steps, exts, world.leadId(remGrp));
  } else {
    Block loc = src.rng(r).localBlock();

    int offsetElem = offset + src.str(r) * loc.sub_bas;
    int step       = src.str(r) * loc.sub_stp;

    Range rng = dst.rng(r);
    Triplet crds = rng.crds(loc.glb_lo, loc.glb_hi, loc.glb_stp);

    for (int i = 0, crd = crds.lo; i < crds.count; i++, crd += crds.stp){
      Block rem = rng.block3(crd, loc.glb_lo, loc.glb_hi, loc.glb_stp);

      exts[r]  = rem.count;
      steps[r] = step * rem.glb_stp;

      sendLoop(offsetElem + step * rem.glb_lo,
               remGrp.restrict(rng.dim(), crd), r + 1) ;
    }
  }
}
```

Fig. 6. sendLoop method for Remap

Now the **RemapSkeleton** communication schedule is built by two subroutines called **sendLoop** and **recvLoop** that enumerate messages to be sent and received respectively. Figure 6 sketches the implementation of **sendLoop**. This is a recursive function-it implements a multidimensional loop over the **rank** dimensions of the arrays. It is initially called with r = 0. There is little point going into full detail of the algorithm here, but an important thing to note is how this function uses the virtual methods on the range objects of the source and destination arrays to enumerate blocks-local and remote-of relevant subranges, and enumerates the messages that must be sent. Figure 7 illustrates the significance of some of the variables in the code. When the offset and all extents and strides of a particular message have been accumulated, the **sendReq()** method of the base class is invoked. The variables **src** and **dst** represent the distributed array arguments. The inquiries **rng()** and **grp()** extract the range and group objects of these arrays.

Of the collective communication schedules currently implemented in Adlib, all except **WriteHalo** share with **Remap** this property that their implementation code does not explicitly depend on the distribution format of the arrays. All rely heavily on the methods and inquiries of the **Range** and **Group** classes, which abstract the distribution format of arrays.

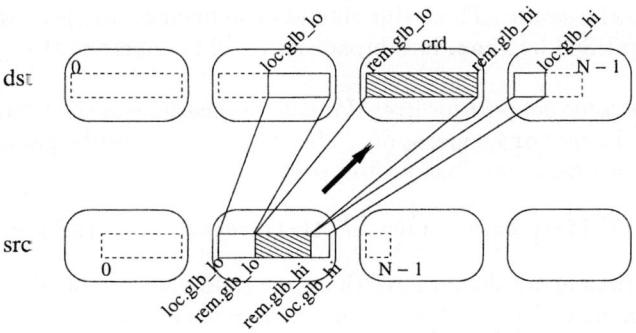

Fig. 7. Illustration of sendLoop operation for remap

3.2 Other Schedules in Adlib

We described main characteristic example of the regular communications, **remap()**. This section we will overview functionalities of all collective operations in Adlib. The Adlib has three main families of collective operation: regular communications, reduction operations, and irregular communications. We discuss usage and high-level API overview of Adlib methods.

The method **shift()** is a communication schedule for shifting the elements of a distributed array along one of its dimensions, placing the result in another array. In general we have the signature:

> void shift(T # destination, T # source,
> int shiftAmount, int dimension)

where the variable T runs over all primitive types and Object, and the notation T # means a multiarray of arbitrary rank, with elements of type T. The shiftAmount argument, which may be negative, specifies the amount and direction of the shift. In the second form the dimension argument is in the range $0, \ldots, R-1$ where R is the rank of the arrays: it selects the array dimension in which the shift occurs. The source and destination arrays must have the same shape, and they must also be *identically aligned*.

The function **broadcast()**, which is actually a simplified form of **remap()**. There are two signatures:

> T broadcast(T [[]] source)

and

> T broadcast(T source, Group root)

The first form takes rank-0 distributed array as argument and broadcasts the element value to all processes of the active process group. Typically it is used with a scalar section to broadcast an element of a general array to all members of the active process group. The second form of **broadcast()** just takes an ordinary

Java value as the source. This value should be defined on the process or group of processes identified by `root`. It is broadcast to all members of the active process group.

Adlib has some support for irregular communications in the form of collective `gather()` and `scatter()` operations. The simplest form of the `gather` operation for one-dimensional arrays has prototypes

```
void gather(T [[-]] destination, T [[-]] source, int [[-]] subscripts) ;
```

The `subscripts` array should have the same shape as, and be aligned with, the `destination` array. In pseudocode, the `gather` operation is equivalent to

```
for all i in {0,...,N - 1} in parallel do
    destination [i] = source [subscripts[i]] ;
```

where N is the size of the `destination` (and `subscripts`) array.

The basic `scatter` function has very similar prototypes, but the names `source` and `destination` are switched. Currently the HPJava version of Adlib does not support combining scatters, although these could be added in later releases.

You can find complete list of Adlib schedules in [12]. Information, API, and usage on the each schedule are described in this paper.

4 A Multigrid Application and Benchmark Results

The multigrid method [5] is a fast algorithm for solution of linear and nonlinear problems. It uses a hierarchy or stack of grids of different granularity (typically with a geometric progression of grid-spacings, increasing by a factor of two up from finest to coarsest grid). Applied to a basic relaxation method, for example, multigrid hugely accelerates elimination of the residual by restricting a smoothed version of the error term to a coarser grid, computing a correction term on the coarse grid, then interpolating this term back to the original fine grid. Because computation of the correction term on the fine grid can itself be handled as a relaxation problem, the strategy can be applied recursively all the way up the stack of grids.

The experiments were performed on the SP3 installation at Florida State University. The system environment for SP3 runs were as follows:

- System: IBM SP3 supercomputing system with AIX 4.3.3 operating system and 42 nodes.
- CPU: A node has Four processors (Power3 375 MHz) and 2 gigabytes of shared memory.
- Network MPI Settings: Shared "css0" adapter with User Space(US) communication mode.
- Java VM: IBM's JIT
- Java Compiler: IBM J2RE 1.3.1

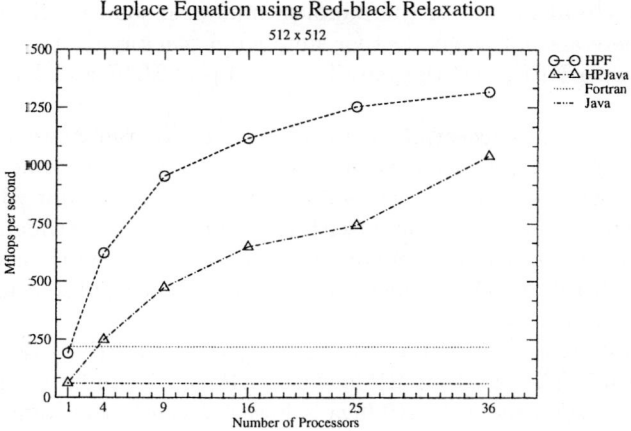

Fig. 8. Laplace Equation with Size of 512^2

For best performance, all sequential and parallel Fortran and Java codes were compiled using -O5 or -O3 with -qhot or -O (i.e. maximum optimization) flag.

First we present some results for the computational kernel of the multigrid code, namely unaccelerated red-black relaxation algorithm. Figure 8 gives our results for this kernel on a 512 by 512 matrix. The results are encouraging. The HPJava version scales well, and eventually comes quite close to the HPF code (absolute megaflop performances are modest, but this feature was observed for all our codes, and seems to be a property of the hardware).

The flat lines at the bottom of the graph give the sequential Java and Fortran performances, for orientation. We did not use any auto parallelization feature

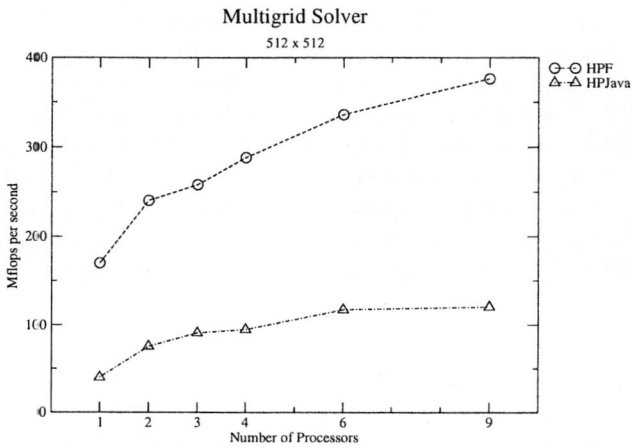

Fig. 9. Multigrid solver with size of 512^2

here. Corresponding results for the complete multigrid code are given in Figure 9. The results here are not as good as for simple red-black relaxation-both HPJava speed relative to HPF, and the parallel speedup of HPF and HPJava are less satisfactory.

The poor performance of HPJava relative to Fortran in this case can be attributed largely to the naive nature of the translation scheme used by the current HPJava system. The overheads are especially significant when there are many very tight overall constructs (with short bodies). Experiments done elsewhere [11] leads us to believe these overheads can be reduced by straightforward optimization strategies which, however, are not yet incorporated in our source-to-source translator.

The modest parallel speedup of both HPJava and HPF is due to communication overheads. The fact that HPJava and HPF have similar scaling behavior, while absolute performance of HPJava is lower, suggests the communication library of HPJava is slower than the communications of the native SP3 HPF (otherwise the performance gap would close for larger numbers of processors). This is not too surprising because Adlib is built on top of a portability layer called *mpjdev*, which is in turn layered on MPI. We assume the SP3 HPF is more carefully optimized for the hardware. Of course the lower layers of Adlib could be ported to exploit low-level features of the hardware (we already did some experiments in this direction, interfacing Java to LAPI [13]).

5 Conclusions and Future Work

We have explored enabling parallel, high-performance computation-in particular development of scientific software in the network-aware programming language, Java. Traditionally, this kind of computing was done in Fortran. Arguably, Fortran is becoming a marginalized language, with limited economic incentive for vendors to produce modern development environments, optimizing compilers for new hardware, or other kinds of associated software expected by today's programmers. Java looks like a promising alternative for the future.

We have discussed in detail the design and development of high-level library for HPJava-this is essentially communication library. The Adlib API is presented as high-level communication library. This API is intended as an example of an application level communication library suitable for data parallel programming in Java. This library fully supports Java object types, as part of the basic data types. We discussed implementation issues of collective communications in depth. The API and usage of other types of collective communications were also presented.

References

1. mpiJava Home Page. http://www.hpjava.org/mpiJava.html.
2. Timber Compiler Home Page. http://pds.twi.tudelft.nl/timber.
3. Titanium Project Home Page. http://www.cs.berkeley.edu/projects/titanium.

4. A. Agrawal, A. Sussman, and J. Saltz. An integrated runtime and compiletime approach for parallelizing structured and block structured applications. *IEEE Transactions on Parallel and Distributed Systems*, 6, 1995.
5. William L. Briggs, Van Emden Henson, and Steve F. McCormick. *A Multigrid Tutorial*. The Society for Industrial and Applied Mathematics (SIAM), 2000.
6. Bryan Carpenter, Guansong Zhang, and Yuhong Wen. NPAC PCRC runtime kernel definition. Technical Report CRPC-TR97726, Center for Research on Parallel Computation, 1997. Up-to-date version maintained at http://www.npac.syr.edu/projects/pcrc/doc.
7. Parallel Compiler Runtime Consortium. Common runtime support for high-performance parallel languages. In *Supercomputing '93*. IEEE Computer Society Press, 1993.
8. Jayant DeSouza and L. V. Kale. Jade: A parallel message-driven java. In *Proceedings of the 2003 Workshop on Java in Computational Science*, Melbourne, Australia, 2003. Available from http://charm.cs.uiuc.edu/papers/ParJavaWJCS03.shtml.
9. James Gosling, Bill Joy, Guy Steele, and Gilad Bracha. *The Java Language Specification*, Second Edition. Addison-Wesley, 2000.
10. HPJava project home page. www.hpjava.org.
11. Han-Ku Lee. *Towards Efficient Compilation of the HPJava Language for High Performance Computing*. PhD thesis, Florida State University, June 2003.
12. Sang Boem Lim. *Platforms for HPJava: Runtime Support for Scalable Programming in Java*. PhD thesis, Florida State University, June 2003.
13. Sang Boem Lim, Bryan Carpenter, Geoffrey Fox, and Han-Ku Lee. A device level communication library for the hpjava programming language. In *the IASTED International Conference on Parallel and Distributed Computing and Systems (PDCS 2003)*, November 2003.
14. Guansong Zhang, Bryan Carpenter, Geoffrey Fox, Xiaoming Li, Xinying Li, and Yuhong Wen. PCRC-based HPF compilation. In Zhiyuan Li et al, editor, *10th International Workshop on Languages and Compilers for Parallel Computing*, volume 1366 of *Lecture Notes in Computer Science*. Springer, 1997. http://www.hpjava.org/pcrc/npacWork.html.

A Fast and Scalable Conflict Detection Algorithm for Packet Classifiers

Xin Li, Zhenzhou Ji, and Mingzeng Hu

School of Computer Science and Technology,
Harbin Institute of Technology, Harbin, China
{lixin, jzz, mzhu}@pact518.hit.edu.cn

Abstract. Packet filters are rules for classifying packets based on their header fields. A filter conflict occurs when two or more filters overlap, creating an ambiguity in packet classification. There has been prior works on conflict detection for multi-dimensional classifiers, but their efficiency and scalability are not good. A new algorithm is proposed, which uses hashing-based PATRICIA trie. The new algorithm can fast detect conflicts in classifiers and have high scalability. The technology of processing transport-level ports can bring more security than existed algorithms.

1 Introduction

CIDR, IntServ and DiffServ QoS, Firewalls and VPNs are all examples of technologies which have extended the internet forwarding table lookups, from fixed length lookups to sophisticated 5 tuple lookups with wildcarding [1]. Both packet classification problem and filter conflicts detection problem are under active study these days. The filter conflict is possible because a packet might match multiple filters, each with a different associated action. It is important to consider filter conflict resolution in any scheme involving filters, since filters, if not handled correctly, can cause packets to be subject to the wrong actions. For example, incorrectly matching packets to filters in firewalls can cause security problems. Adding resolve filters for each pair of conflicting filters is the most common solution.

Conflict detection has become an important problem as router vendors offer larger classifier tables and the filters are used for potentially conflicting purposes such as QoS, security [1][2][3][4]. In many of these applications, some service may dynamically insert a new filter that can conflict with existing security or QoS policy. While the majority of added filters will not conflict [5][6], a mechanism to warn managers of potential conflicts seems necessary to avoid breaches of the security or QoS policies. Clearly, the time to add filters and detect conflicts is important [1].

It could be argued that since resolving conflicts by adding new resolve filters would require policy input and possibly human input, there is no need for a fast conflict detection and resolution algorithm. However, for the next generation signaling protocols, the conflict detection is done at one site and the conflict resolution is done elsewhere. It is important for routers to be able to process signaling messages as fast as possible in order to leave enough processing power for other tasks like packet forwarding, scheduling, routing updates and other signaling requests [1].

2 Filter Conflict Detection—Problem Statement

Definition. Filter F_x is in conflict with Filter F_y if every field in F_x is a subset or a superset or equal to the corresponding field in F_y, and actions of F_x and F_y are different. Formally, F_x is conflict with F_y iff

$$\forall i: F_x[i] \Vdash F_y[i], \text{ and actions of } F_x \text{ and } F_y \text{ are different}$$

Where $\Vdash \in \{\subset, \supset, =\}$, $i \in \{\text{protocol, src\_ip, src\_port, dst\_ip, dst\_port}\}$.

[4][7][8] defined all 5 relations that relate two or more packet filters, completely disjoint, exactly matched, inclusively matched, partially matched and correlated. Both relation of completely disjoint and relation of partially matched can never result in conflicts, and both relation of exactly matched and relation of inclusively matched cannot result in security problems. So, the main work of *Detecting and Resolving Packet Filter Conflicts* is to find filters which are in correlated relation.

3 Previous Works

BV [9], ABV [10], SBV [5] and IBV [5] are four algorithms for detecting conflicts. All of them are on the base of Bit Vector(BV) scheme. SBV use two separately tries for each dimension, which can improve BV's performance which only uses a trie. ABV and IBV use aggregation scheme to eliminate redundant reads to words that have no bits set, which can both improve performance and reduces the size of the memory. But all above Bit Vector based algorithms use precomputation to speed up filter search, this makes filter updates slow.

[1] develop a *2-dimensional recursive trie* data structure to solve the filter conflict problem, which we call it GoT algorithm in this paper. A general solution is presented for the 5-tuple filter, and an optimized version is described for the more common 2-tuple filters consisting of source and destination addresses [1]. It use two Grid of Tries(GoT) to organize src_ip and dst_ip, which has more scalability and better performance than BV based algorithms when the size of filters is very big. We will use the example database B shown in Table 1 and Fig.1 to illustrate GoT scheme. GoT algorithm needs two complementary data structures, one for each of the following two cases.

1. $G[1]$ is a prefix of $F[1]$ and $F[2]$ is a prefix of $G[2]$, or
2. $F[1]$ is a prefix of $G[1]$ and $G[2]$ is a prefix of $F[1]$

In particular, one data structure can efficiently isolate the filters whose source field is a prefix of F's source field, and then organize these filters to quickly determine if any of them has the destination field with $F[2]$ as a prefix. The second data structure reverses the roles of source and destination fields. Fig.1 shows the complete construction for case 1 of the set in Table 1. Nodes of destination tries are labeled with the filters associated with that destination address. GoT algorithm needs not much precomputation, it has good scalability than BV based algorithm.

Table 1. An example 2-tuple filter database

Filter	F[1]	F[2]
F_1	100*	001100*
F_2	1001*	0010*
F_3	100001*	0011*
F_4	1001110*	0010000*
F_5	1000111*	0011*
F_6	1000111*	001101*
F_7	1000111*	001100*

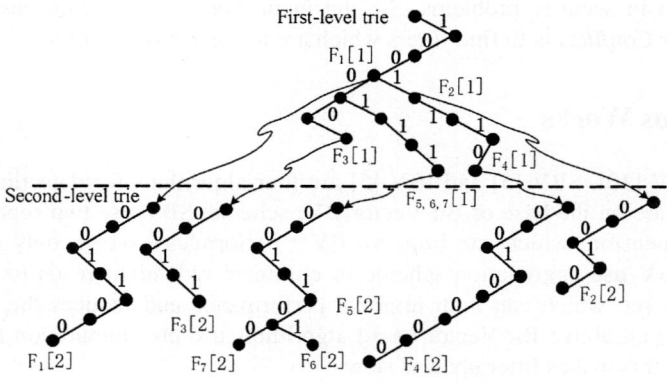

Fig. 1. Recursive Trie 1 for the example database of Table 1

4 A New Algorithm for Conflicts Detection

4.1 PATRICIA Trie

We develop a *2-dimensional recursive PATRICIA trie* data structure to solve the filter conflict problem. PATRICIA trie is the shallowest trie [11], which is very often used for the information retrieval systems [12][13].

Recursive PATRICIA Trie 1 can efficiently isolate the filters whose source field is a prefix of *F*'s source field, and then organize these filters to quickly determine if any of them has the destination field with *F*[2] as a prefix. *Recursive PATRICIA Trie 2* reverses the roles of source and destination fields.

The average depths of source trie and destination trie in Fig.1 are separately 5.9 and 5.3. The average depths of source PATRICIA and destination PATRICIA trie in Fig.2 are separately 3.6 and 1.7. Above example use short strings, for 32 bits IP addresses, it can more efficiently reduce the trie's depth.

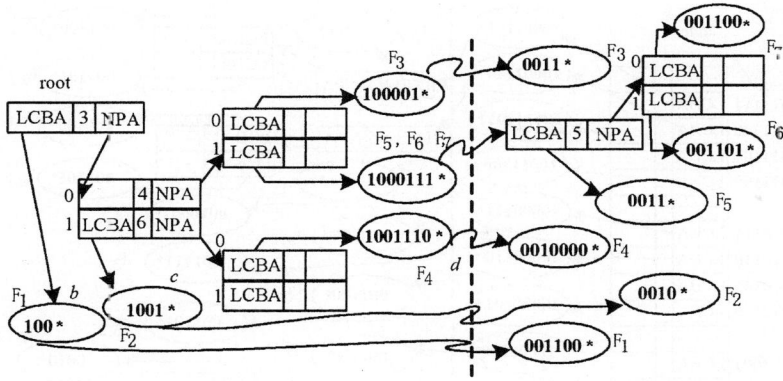

Fig. 2. Recursive PATRICIA Trie 1 for the set in Table 1

4.2 Hashing Technology and Data Structure

To use hashing technology to improve the performance, we restrict the prefix lengths of IP addresses only be 32, 28, 24, 20, 16, 12, 8 and 4, other lengths' prefix can be transformed to be these lengths. Table 2 shows an example of transforming prefix to restricted lengths. By restricting IP prefix's length, we can use hashing to improve performance further. We only restrict src_ip's prefix in the *Recursive PATRICIA Trie 1*, and dst_ip's prefix in the *Recursive PATRICIA Trie 2*.

For the filter set in Table 1, we get Table 2 by restricting the length of src_ip prefix. By hashing, we can construct multiple PATRICIA tries, and each PATRICIA trie is very shallow. If using 3 bits length code and the lowest 4 bits of IP prefix as hashing index, we can get 128 PATRICIA tries. For example, the hashing index of $F_{3,l}$ is 0010100, the high 3 bits "001" refers the length of prefix is 8 bits, and the low 4 bits "0100" refers the low 4 bits of $F_{3,l}$=10000100*. Because all prefix lengths are equal in a PATRICIA trie, the first-level PATRICIA trie is fixed-length PATRICIA trie, which have better performance than prefix PATRICIA trie. Fig.3 shows the new data structure, which the average depth of $S(B)$ and $D(B)$ are 1 and 1.9 respectively.

Table 2. An example 2-tuple filter database

Filter	Source	Destination
$F_{1,1}, F_{1,2}$	1000*, 1001*	001100*
F_2	1001*	0010*
$F_{3,1}, F_{3,2}, F_{3,3}, F_{3,4}$	10000100*, 10000101*, 10000110*, 10000111*	0011*
$F_{4,1}, F_{4,2}$	10011100*, 10011101*	0010000*
$F_{5,1}, F_{5,2}$	10001110*, 10001111*	0011*
$F_{6,1}, F_{6,2}$	10001110*, 10001111*	001101*
$F_{7,1}, F_{7,2}$	10001110*, 10001111*	001100*

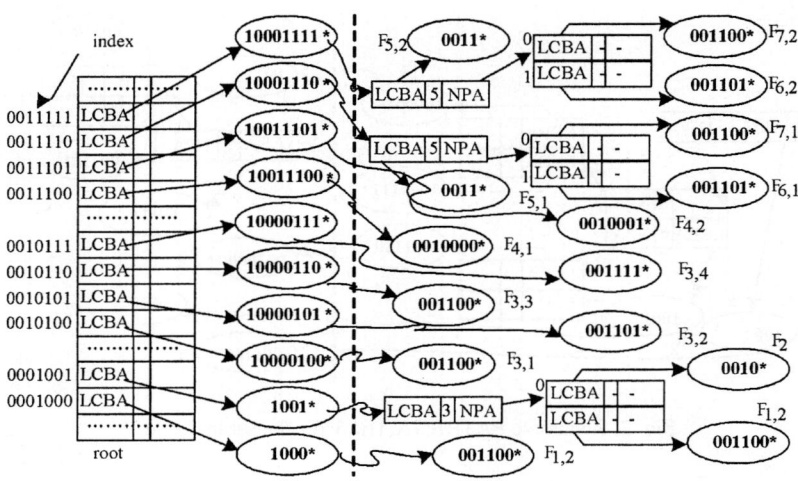

Fig. 3. hashing based Recursive PATRICIA Trie 1 for the example database of Table 2

4.3 Pseudocode of Conflict Detection Algorithm for 2-Tuple Filters

```
program FastDetect(F, B)
1.    Initialize C(F) = {F};
      /* Search Recursive PATRICIA Trie 1 */
2.    Transform F[1] for Recursive PATRICIA trie 1, get N₁
      filters from F;
3.    for i=1 to N₁ do
4.        Hashing to get the index root of PATRICIA tries on the
          term of Fᵢ[1] and its length;
5.        Matching Fᵢ[1] in the PATRICIA trie of the root index;
6.        if(no matched) goto (9);
              else get the matched node u;
7.        Determine all nodes in D(u) which F[2] is a prefix of
          destination field of these nodes;
8.        Add these nodes to C(F);
9.        if(there are other PATRICIA trie whose length is
          shorter than length(Fᵢ[1]))
                  transform Fᵢ[1] to the shorter length;
                  goto 4;
      /*Search Recursive PATRICIA Trie 2 is omitted */
      . . . . . .
10.   If C(F) only contains F , then add F to B, and
      return "No Conflict";
11.   for each filter F'∈C(F) do
12.       Add ResolveFilter(F,F') to B;
13.   end.
```

As an example, suppose we want to add a filter $F=(10011100*, 0010*)$ to the set in Table 1. When looking up in the Fig.3, there are following steps:

(1) Hashing on the term of $F[1]$ and its length and get root index = "0011100".
(2) Using the root index 0011100 to lookup corresponding 2-level PATRICIA trie, find that $F_{4,1}[1]= F[1]$. Continue to access $F_{4,1}[2]$, because $F[2]$ is a prefix of $F_{4,2}[2]$, F conflicts with $F_{4,1}$.
(3) Because existing shorter index 4, transform F to $F=(1001*, 0001*)$, and get the new index is 0001001.
(4) Use the root index 0001001 to lookup corresponding 2-level PATRICIA trie, get that F conflicts with F_2.

The search in the second structure, Recursive PATRICIA Trie 2, is similar, except the roles of source and destination fields are reversed.

4.4 Theoretical Analyses

Now, we will analyze the performance of the new algorithm. For an original filter set B which has N filters, by compressing IP's prefix length with parameter ω, we will get a new filter set C which has ρN filters. Without hashing, both the average depth of PATRICIA trie and the number of memory accesses when detecting conflicts in B will be $log_2 N$. If we hash the set C to M bits index, which we get 2^M PATRICIA tries. For full 2-ary PATRICIA trie, the average depth of each PATRICIA trie will be

$$D_{average} = \log_2 \frac{\rho N}{2^M}$$

As described in algorithm FastDetect, for a new added filter F, it will be transformed to several new filters which have fixed length. Let refers to the number of transformed filters of F. Furthermore, Step 9 of FastDetect may look up multiple PATRICIA trie when conflicts detecting. When detecting conflict amongst C, the number of memory accesses of FastDetect will be

$$M_{access} = \rho \theta \log_2 \frac{\rho N}{2^M}$$

In order that FastDetect have better performance of conflicts detection, following relation should be existed.

$$log_2 N > \rho \theta \log_2 \frac{\rho N}{2^M}$$

So, to decrease ρ and θ and ω, and to increase M can improve the performance of HBPP algorithm. But small ω causes small θ but big ρ, and big M causes big memory space. In experiment of section 7 we use $M=9$ and $\omega=4$.

We know that there are $\rho=\omega$ at averagely for full random filters. As firewalls locate in edge networks, and its filters are not random but very characteristic. The value of ρ is only related with the length of IP prefixes and ω, and the value of θ is only related with the number of different lengths of IP prefixes.

Generally, all IP addresses in Intranet zone of filters have same length IP address prefix, and all IP addresses in DMZ of filters may have fixed 32 bits IP address.

Furthermore, for a filter which corresponding to a specified flow from an ingress to an egress of the firewall, IP prefix length in Internet have little variable. For example, a filter corresponding to a flow from Intranet to Internet, the IP prefix of Internet zone often are fixed server, which have 32 bits length. So if introducing the ingress and egress of flow corresponding to filters, the ρ and θ can be very small.

In order to decrease ρ we utilize both the ingress and egress of flow of filters. When configuring filters, besides the common 5-tuple information, both ingress and egress of flow which will match this new filter are considered. For example, there are 3 interfaces in firewall of Fig.4. Each filter has a fixed ingress and a fixed egress.

Then, the first-level PATRICIA trie is fixed-length PATRICIA trie. We proposed a new PATRICIA trie which has optimal insertion, search and deletion performance for 2-ary trie based algorithms [14].

5 Extending FastDect to 5 Tuples

The protocol field is processed as [1]. We restrict the source and destination ports to be either >1023 or <1024, or fully specified. For multiple filters with same source and destination IP prefix and protocol and differing only in source and destination ports, we divide them into multi-sets and organize them in a single linked list, and use a pointer pointing to the head of list from the node in the PATRICIA trie corresponding to the source and destination prefixes of the filter in the sets.

For example, consider a new filter F=(src_ip, dst_ip, TCP, >1023, 80), in which the source port is >1023 and the destination ports is well specified as 80. We begin by traversing the tries containing TCP filters. Assume we are traversing the PATRICIA trie with the source address on the first level. At a given step on the second level, assume *SrcPrefixLen* is set to *longer* and the *DstPrefixLen* is set to *shorter*. What that means is that the source address prefix of the filter is longer and the destination address prefix shorter than any filter stored at that node. In the 2-tuple case, this would automatically cause a conflict. However, in the 5 tuple case, this can cause a conflict only if the source and destination ports and the protocol fields overlap too. The protocol field is already the same, because of the way the filters are partitioned. Thus we need to check if the source and destination ports overlap with the existing filter. As can be easily seen, they overlap when the stored filter has the source port ">1023", or a specified port which >1023, and the destination port 80 or "<1024".

[1] restrict the source and destination ports to be either fully wildcarded or fully specified. Because most filters' source port are ">1023", and many filters' destination port are "<1024". Restricting port either fully wildcarded or fully specified will cause security problem. We improve filters' security by restricting the source and destination ports to be either >1023 or <1024, or fully specified.

We process ingress and egress of filters as same as protocol field. The key idea here is to partition the set of 5-tuple filters with ingress and egress information into disjoint sets of 5-tuple filters without ingress and egress information.

Consider 5-tuple filters consisting of IP source and destination address prefixes, the protocol type and source and destination port, ingress and egress of filters need be given when configuring filters. For example, in Fig.4 we restrict the ingress and egress either internal interface or DMZ interface or Internet interface. Thus, we can partition the set of filters into 9 disjoint sets upon flow's directions. Clearly, there is no overlap or conflict between any two sets. Given a new 5-tuple filter with ingress and egress, we can see which set of filters to check for conflicts on the base of the ingress and egress information.

6 Experimental Results

We use common firewall case in Fig.4 as an example. Considering the generality of filters configured, we reference the characteristic of IP prefix in [15], and obey following rules.

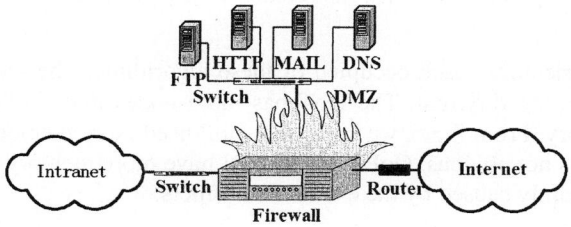

Fig. 4. Common firewall topology

(1) Prefixes length of IP addresses in DMZ are fixed 32 bits, ports are also fixed.
(2) All IP addresses in Intranet has same high 24 bits, their low 8 bits are randomly generated. Their prefix length are randomly generated too, and ports are ">1023".
(3) All IP addresses in Internet have fixed high 20 bits, their low 12 bits and their prefix lengths are randomly generated. For filters from Internet to DMZ, the Ports values of Internet are ">1023", for filters from Intranet to Internet the ports values are fixed 80 port. Ingress, egress, protocol and action of filters are randomly generated.

We compared the performances of GoT and the new algorithm. For the new algorithm, we test the performances of the case of only using PATRICIA trie(GoP), the case of using PATRICIA trie and hashing but without ingress and egress(GoPB), and the case of use PATRICIA trie and hashing with ingress and egress(GoPBI). Because memory accesses are most time-consuming, we measured their performances with the number of memory accesses. Fig.5 shows their performances. The number of memory accesses is an average value, for example, the first column of Fig.5 is the average value of memory accesses for the first 500 inserted rules.

From Fig.5, we can know that the numbers of memory accesses of GoP and GoPBI are obviously smaller than GoT algorithm. Because firewall locates on the edge of network as Fig.4, prefixes of local network IP addresses are same. PATRICIA trie can efficiently reduce the depth of trie, so GoP have better performance than GoT. GoPB has worse performance than GoP and GoPBI, because without ingress and egress the value of θ is very big. GoPBI use two technologies to improve performance, one is hashing, and the other is the optimal 2-ary PATRICIA trie [14]. We use 9 bits hashing index to generate 512 PATRICIA tries, which causes the depth of each PATRICIA is reduced obviously. Furthermore, an optimal 2-ary PATRICIA trie for fixed-length match is proposed and used to organize the first-level PATRICIA, which can improve performance further [14].

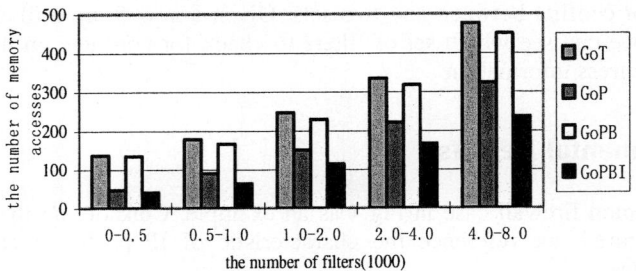

Fig. 5. Conflict enumeration using Fast Detect

Fig.6 shows memory space occupied of these algorithms. The memory spaces of above algorithms are different. The GoT has more nodes than GoP, but each node needs less memory. From Fig.6, we know that GoP need more memory than GoT, but their difference is not obvious. GoPB and GoPBI have more memory consuming than GoP, which is mainly caused by the extension of filters.

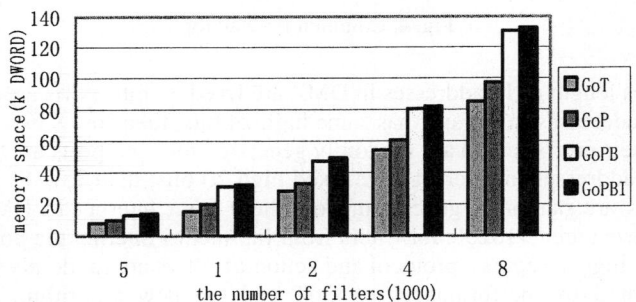

Fig. 6. Conflict detection memory space

Both the GoP and GoPBI algorithms can improve the time performance of conflicts detecting. GoP causes memory space improvement just a little, but has obvious performance improvement. GoPBI needs much memory space than GoT, but can improve performance further.

7 Conclusions

Confliction-free filters are the precondition of packet classification. The performance of detecting conflicts determines the performance of filters constructing and incremental updating. So, good algorithm should be able to fast detect conflicts in filters. PATRICIA trie based algorithm can efficiently reduce the depth of trie, so it can improve trie's performance. Hashing based algorithm can further improve performance, but the cost is that it needs more memory space.

Both the new algorithms and GoT algorithm need little of precalculation than BV based algorithms. So, they have better scalability and can suit for huge filters. Furthermore, we implement a new method to process transport level ports, which have more security than existed algorithms.

References

1. Hari A., Suri S., Parulkar G.: Detecting and resolving packet filter conflicts. 19th Annual Joint Conf of the IEEE Computer and Communications Societies (2000)
2. Srinivasan V.: A packet classification and filter management system, IEEE INFOCOM 2001.
3. Wool A.: A quantitative study of firewall configuration errors, IEEE Computer (2004)
4. Al-Shaer E., Hamed H.: Firewall policy advisor for anomaly discovery and rule editing. In IFIP/IEEE Eighth International Symposium on Integrated Network Management (2003) 17–30,
5. Baboescu F., Varghese G.: Fast and Scalable Conflict Detection for Packet Classifiers, 10th IEEE International Conference on Network Protocols (2002)
6. Gupta P., McKeown N.: Packet classification on multiple fields, in: Proceedings of ACM Sigcomm (1999)
7. Al-Shaer E., Hamed H.: Design and Implementation of Firewall Policy Advisor Tools, DePaul CTI Technical Report, CTI-TR-02-006 (2002)
8. Al-Shaer E., Hamed H.: Modeling and Management of Firewall Policies, in IEEE Transactions on Network and Service Management, Volume 1-1 (2004)
9. Lakshman T. V., Stidialis D.: High speed policy-based packet forwarding using efficient multi-dimensional range matching, in Proceedings of ACM Sigcomm (1998)
10. Baboescu F., Varghese G.: Scalable packet classification, in Proceedings of ACM Sigcomm (2001)
11. Shishibori M., Okuno M., Ando K., Jun-Ichi Aoe: An efficient compression method for Patricia tries. In: Proc of IEEE International Conference on Computational Cybernetics and Simulation (1997) 12-15
12. Wooguil P., Saewoong B.: Flexible and fast IP lookup algorithm. IEEE International Conference on Communication. Volume: 7, 11-14 (2001) 2053-2057
13. Cho K., Kaizaki R., Kato A.: An aggregation technique for traffic monitoring. Applications and the Internet(SAINT)Workshops (2002) 74 – 81
14. Xin Li, Zhen-Zhou Ji, and Ming-Zeng Hu: Stateful Inspection Firewall Session Table Processing, ITCC (2005) Las Vegas, NV, USA
15. Marcel Waldvogel, George Varghese, Jon Turner: Scalable high speed IP routing lookups[C]. ACM Sigcomm (1997) 27(4):25-36

Loss Rate Aware Preferential Treamtment Scheme at the Congested Router

Dongping Zhao[1,2], Deyun Zhang[1], Jiuxing Cao[3], Weibin Zheng[1], and Zhiping An[1]

[1] Department of Computer Science and Technology, Xi'an Jiaotong University, Xi'an,China
[2] Xi'an Research Institute of High Technology, Xi'an, China
{zdp, dzhang, zwb, anzp}@xanet.edu.cn
[3] Department of Computer Science and Technology, Southeast University, Nanjing, China
jx.cao@seu.edu.cn

Abstract. One weakness of the RED algorithm typical of routers is that at any given time, it imposes the same loss probability on all flows, regardless of their QoS. In this paper, we propose an improved packet discard algorithm based on RED for real-time multimedia service, which does its endeavor to avoid dropping packets from the same flow continuously in terms of instantaneous loss rate and short-time average loss rate. It traces the concerned flow's state whenever every packet's arrival and then dynamically adjusts the packet drops to achieve a given loss rate. When network is congested, it drops all packets of certain invalid flows mandatorily to avoid a majority of applications being invalidated simultaneously because of packet loss. Our evaluation results indicate that the proposed algorithm provides better QoS for real-time multimedia service, whether network is congested or not.

1 Introduction

With the fast development of Internet and the wide deployment of Internet applications, network congestion is becoming more and more serious. One solution to it is to equip network routers with some active queue management mechanism. Active queue management refers to the practice of manipulating the queue at an outbound interface in a router to bias the performance of flows that transit the router. By dropping packets before buffers overflow, active queue management allows routers to control when and how many packets to drop, thus providing all connections with an efficient and effective service.

As a recommended active queue management mechanism, random early detection (RED) [1, 2] makes it possible that data packets will be dropped out with certain probability when it detects that router packet queue will begin to congest, while the traditional tail-drop (TD) FIFO scheme simply drops out all the arriving data packets when router output queue is overflowed. Compared with TD, RED can avoid congestion, global synchronization and total drop of sudden traffic flow.

For most real-time multimedia applications, acknowledging and re-transmitting lost data are impractical while a certain dropping packets rate is generally tolerated. One of the important network management issues it to find how data can be dropped without unduly affecting the QoS. These applications will not be seriously affected if the dropping packet rate is within a certain range, while when it is beyond the range, the normal applications will not be available. For example, when the dropping packets rate of IP telephony is below 10%, the speech quality is good; when ranging from 10% to 20%, it still works; when beyond 20%, it fails to accept. Therefore dropping packets continuously will result in QoS of the application being degraded and application's terminating.

However, RED algorithm cannot avoid continuous packet-drops of the same flow. When the Internet congests, by dropping all packets of the flow with the same probability, RED mechanism may lead to the decrease of QoS for most real-time services in a short time, and even their interruption, thus making enormous bandwidth waste. So the uniform dropping policy is inefficient for multimedia services.

To solve the above problem, this paper presents an enhanced RED algorithm, preferential packet discard (PPD), which is applicable to real-time multimedia services. We define three states and three stages for each flow or aggregated flow by monitoring its corresponding instantaneous loss rate and short-time average loss rate. From the two rate values we can obtain each flow's quality of service during a period of time due to past packet loss, and then to decide how to drop packets by using calculated probability according to each flow's state and router's queue occupancy. Under congestion, our proposed algorithm tries to drop all packets of poor QoS service's flow to alleviate congestion and share more bandwidth for other better performance services. One contribute of this paper is that each flow's QoS due to packet loss can be obtained cleverly and easily to circumvent packet dropping's ignorance of QoS. The QoS objective is to guarantee a majority of flows' packet loss percentage as low as possible at the sacrifice of a small number of invalid flows.

The rest of the paper is organized as follows. In Section 2 we generally review related works. Section 3 details our proposed PPD algorithm for real-time multimedia service, including theoretic analysis and algorithm design. Next, in Section 4 we present evaluation results done to verify our analysis and design recommendations. Finally, Section 5 summarizes our work and discusses possible future work.

2 Related Works

The traditional queue management algorithms, such as TD, have some important problems, for instance, bias against the burst traffic, global synchronization and full queue for long periods of time [3]. The RED algorithm was introduced to overcome these problems. It detects congestion by monitoring the average output queue size of the router and avoids congestion by dropping some data packets with certain probability. Transient congestion is accommodated by a temporary increase in the queue. Longer-lived congestion is reflected by an increase in the computed average queue size, and results in randomized feedback to some of the connections to decrease their windows.

The RED algorithm consists of two main parts: estimation of the average queue size and the decision of dropping probability function. The average queue size avg is estimated using an exponential weighted moving average which is equivalent to the low pass filter:

$$avg \leftarrow (1-w_q) \times avg + w_q \times q \tag{1}$$

where w_q is a fixed (small) parameter and q is the instantaneous queue size. The dropping probability of data packets in the RED algorithm is a function of the average queue size. Comparing avg with the two thresholds (minimum threshold min_{th} and maximum threshold max_{th}), one can work out the dropping probability of data packets, namely:

$$P(avg) = \begin{cases} 0 & \text{if } avg < min_{th} \\ max_p \times \dfrac{avg - min_{th}}{max_{th} - min_{th}} & \text{if } min_{th} \leq avg < max_{th} \\ 1 & \text{if } avg \geq max_{th} \end{cases} \tag{2}$$

Here max_p is the packet dropping probability with the average queue size being the maximum threshold. min_{th} specifies the average queue size below which no packets will be dropped, while max_{th} specifies the average queue size above which all packets will be dropped. The dropping probability increases as the estimated average queue size grows. As the average queue size varies from min_{th} to max_{th}, packets will be dropped with a probability that varies linearly from 0 to max_p.

When a packet arrives at the queue, if avg is less than min_{th}, no drop action will be taken and the packet will simply be enqueued. If the average is greater than min_{th} but less than max_{th}, the packet will be dropped at the dropping probability. If the average is greater than max_{th}, a forced drop operation will occur. The forced drop is also employed when the queue is full but avg is still less than max_{th}.

The design of RED is such that during the drop phases of the algorithm, high bandwidth flows will have a higher number of packets dropped since their packets arrive at a higher rate than lower bandwidth flows (and thus are more likely to be dropped in an early drop action). However, all flows experience the same loss rate under RED. By using probabilistic drops, RED maintains a shorter average queue length, avoiding lockout and repeated penalization of the same flows when a burst of packets arrives.

Many researches have analysis its performance by using different way. After vast simulation experiments, some argue that RED should be not deployed and need a thorough analytic research [4-6] due to inexact parameter tuning or no clear advantage under some situations. A number of research efforts have focused on possible short-comings of the algorithms in RED and have proposed modifications and alternatives. Numerous RED variants [7-13] have been proposed, perhaps motivated by the difficulty in understanding the dynamics of RED completely. For example, Adaptive RED [8] makes RED much more robust to the setting of the parameters. SRED mechanism [10] identified misbehaving flows for statistically estimating the number of active flows at a link. Weighted RED (WRED) [13] preferentially drops lower-priority packets by setting different drop-probability functions for each priority level. It is so meaningful for multimedia service differentiation that we have integrated this idea into our scheme here.

Some variants of RED also use per-active-connection accounting to make different dropping decisions, such as FRED [7], Balanced-RED [12] and RED-PD [14], mainly to achieve different bandwidth allocation. However, RED-PD mechanism uses the packet drop history at the router to detect high-bandwidth flows in times of congestion, and preferentially penalize these flows. REDBA [15] surveys packet-drop history to find non-TCP-friendly flows and drops arriving packets from these flows. We also exploit packet drop history to reject invalid flows to mitigate other flows' packet loss.

There are also several queue management algorithms been proposed to obtain a reasonable bandwidth fair share [16, 17]. We should note that our proposed PPD scheme is different from them, though they are all based on RED algorithms. PPD does improve QoS for individual connections in the presence of network congestion by monitoring their relative packet loss and rejecting those invalid flows, while others guarantee the fair share of bandwidth. Random rate-control RED [16] aims to limit those flows consuming more bandwidth to guarantee a fair share among all the present flows by using per-active-flow accounting to enforce on each flow a loss rate than depend on the flow's own rate. The objective of weighted fair discard scheme [17] is similar with ours. It can also estimate possible data losses in advance and control them in real time, but compared to our proposed scheme it is highly complicated as the authors have stated.

3 Preferential Packet Discard Scheme

We now present our PPD scheme in this section. First of all, we define the instantaneous loss rate and short-time loss rate for one flow to trace one of its QoS parameters, that is, recent packet loss during some periods of time.

3.1 Instantaneous Loss Rate

The dropping packets rate measures the average number of packets dropped during a period of time, which cannot reflect packet loss of one flow effectively during the latest small period of time when it fluctuates severely due to congestion. So we define instantaneous loss rate as the latest dropping packets rate:

Definition 1. Whenever a packet arrives, the instantaneous loss rate of the concerned flow this packet belongs to is calculated according to the following formula:

$$L_{t+1} = \begin{cases} L_t \cdot (1-\omega) & \text{if this packet is not dropped} \\ L_t \cdot (1-\omega) + \omega & \text{otherwise} \end{cases} \quad (3)$$

Here L_{t+1} is the latest instantaneous loss rate; L_t is the instantaneous loss rate when the previous packet arrived and $L_0=0$; ω is computational weight constant with its value ranging from 0 to 1. Let ω be 0.5, Formula 3 is simplified to be:

$$L_{t+1} = \begin{cases} L_t \cdot \frac{1}{2} & \text{if this packet is not dropped} \\ L_t \cdot \frac{1}{2} + \frac{1}{2} & \text{otherwise} \end{cases} \quad (4)$$

That is to say, whenever a new data packet arrives, the previous instantaneous loss rate decreases by 1/2. Therefore the instantaneous loss rate can be expressed with a binary decimal fraction $0.X_n X_{n-1} X_{n-2} \cdots$. Based on the properties of the binary decimal, we draw the following conclusions:

Theorem 1. If the latest n packets of one flow are all dropped, the instantaneous loss rate L_t of this flow should satisfy the following inequation: $L_t \geq 1 - \frac{1}{2^n}$.

Proof: we use mathematical induction to proof it. (1) If the last packet is dropped, $n=1$, $L_t = L_{t-1} \cdot \frac{1}{2} + \frac{1}{2} \geq \frac{1}{2} = 1 - \frac{1}{2^1}$; (2) Suppose $L_t \geq 1 - \frac{1}{2^k}$ when $n = k$; (3) When $n = k+1$, $L_{t+1} = L_t \cdot \frac{1}{2} + \frac{1}{2} \geq (1 - \frac{1}{2^k}) \cdot \frac{1}{2} + \frac{1}{2} = 1 - \frac{1}{2^{k+1}}$. So the inequation $L_t \geq 1 - \frac{1}{2^n}$ is verified.

Theorem 2. If the latest n packets of one flow are not all dropped, the instantaneous loss rate L_t of this flow should satisfy the following inequation: $L_t < 1 - \frac{1}{2^n}$.

Proof: as we have pointed out above, the instantaneous loss rate can be expressed with a binary decimal fraction $0.X_m X_{m-1} X_{m-2} \cdots X_{m-n+1} \cdots$. If the latest n packets are not all dropped, there is least one zero among the series of bits $X_m, X_{m-1}, X_{m-2}, \cdots, X_{m-n+1}, \cdots$. Suppose $X_k = 0$, $m-n+1 \leq k \leq m$, then $L_t = 0.X_m X_{m-1} X_{m-2} \cdots 0 \cdots X_{m-n+1} \cdots < 0.X_m X_{m-1} X_{m-2} \cdots 1 \cdots X_{m-n+1} \cdots \leq 1 - \frac{1}{2^n}$.

So we can get the number of latest drop continuously from instantaneous loss rate according to Theorem 1 and Theorem 2. We also can draw the following conclusions:

Theorem 3. If none of the latest n packets of one flow is dropped, the instantaneous loss rate L_t of this flow should satisfy the following inequation: $L_t < \frac{1}{2^n}$.

Theorem 4. If one of the latest n packets of one flow is dropped, the instantaneous loss rate L_t of this flow should satisfy the following inequation: $L_t \geq \frac{1}{2^n}$.

We can estimate whether there are some packets dropped of the latest n packets according to Theorem 3 and Theorem 4. From the two theorems above, we can easily draw the following theorem:

Theorem 5. If the instantaneous loss rate of one flow is L_t, then the number of consecutively non-dropped packets x since the last dropped packet is:

$$x = \lfloor \log_{1/2}(L_t) \rfloor - 1 \tag{5}$$

Thus we see, when the value of ω is 0.5, the packet drop measurement in the last period of time can be obtained easily according to instantaneous loss rate. The old rate value is shifted right one bit and the newly highest bit is set or unset according to this new packet's drop. We show that our proposed algorithm can also be implemented efficiently, with only a small number of add and shift instructions for each packet arrival. Hence the value of constant ω is 0.5 in this paper otherwise stated.

3.2 Short-Time Average Loss Rate

For real-time application, our algorithm remains two loss rate thresholds: L_{min} and L_{max}. When the loss rate is below L_{min}, the real-time application works well; when the loss rate is beyond L_{max}, the application becomes impossible; when it is between L_{min} and L_{max}, the system could work, and it is acceptable to the users. In this paper, the short-time average loss rate $\tilde{L}$ is considered as the average loss rate of one flow. The definition of the short-time average loss rate $\tilde{L}$ is as follows:

Definition 2. The short-time average loss rate $\tilde{L}$ of the flow k is defined as this flow's average loss rate since its last packet dropped.

As the number of the latest continuous non-dropped packet can be obtained by using Theorem 5, we can calculate short-time average loss rate according to instantaneous loss rate.

Theorem 6. If the instantaneous loss rate of flow k is $L_t(k)$, its short-time average loss rate is:

$$\tilde{L}(k) = \frac{1}{x+1} = \frac{1}{\left\lfloor \log_{1/2} L_t(k) \right\rfloor} \tag{6}$$

After we have obtained its short-time loss rate for each real-time flow, we can differentiate it into one QoS-aware state due to packet loss. For flow k, if $\tilde{L}(k) < L_{min}$, we define that the state of this flow is *good*; if $L_{min} \leq \tilde{L}(k) < L_{max}$, it is *critical*; if $\tilde{L}(k) \geq L_{max}$, it is *invalid*. As we will show later, our scheme should avoid dropping packets continuously of one flow to keep this flow from invalid state.

3.3 PPD Algorithm

Based on the aforementioned discussion, we now present our improved algorithm. For simplicity, we first classify all real-time service flows into three priorities: high, medium and low priority. Each priority flow's dropping packet probability is shown as Fig.1. As the general RED algorithm does, we also define three stages according to the calculated average queue length *avg*.

(1) Loose dropping stage: $avg < \min_{th}$

The queue length is comparatively short, which indicates no congestion will occur in the near future, so drop is conducted with a comparatively low probability:

$$P = \min_p \times \frac{avg}{\min_{th}} \tag{7}$$

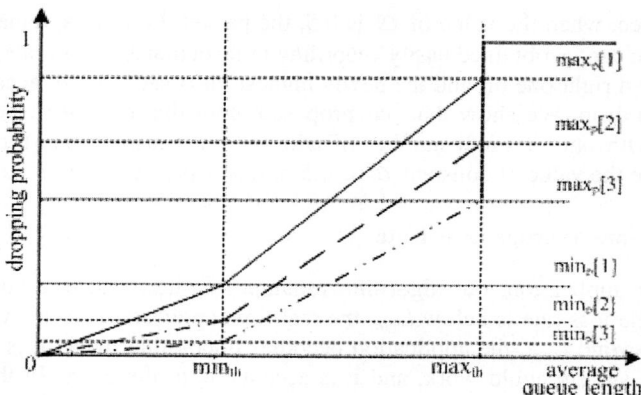

Fig. 1. Packet dropping probability function of PPD algorithm. The parameters $max_p[1]$ and $min_p[1]$ are corresponding to low priority, $max_p[2]$ and $min_p[2]$ to medium priority, $max_p[3]$ and $min_p[3]$ to high priority, respectively.

(2) Strict dropping stage: $min_{th} \leq avg < max_{th}$

The queue length is increasing, which indicates that congestion may occur, so some packets need to be dropped to mitigate the latent tendency. As the queue length increases, the packet dropping probability increases linearly. The packet dropping probability is calculated by:

$$P = \min_p + (\max_p - \min_p) \times \frac{avg - \min_{th}}{\max_{th} - \min_{th}} \quad (8)$$

(3) Congestion stage: $avg \geq max_{th}$

Once congestion occurs, packet dropping should be conducted at a large scale. We first conduct packet dropping from flows with high loss rate. If the congestion still occurs, we continue to drop the packets of those flows with medium loss rate until congestion is alleviated. In this way we can avoid simultaneous failure of a majority of applications.

Here, min_p denotes the packet dropping probability when the average queue length is less than min_{th}, and max_p represents the packet dropping probability when the average queue length is equal to max_{th}. For different priority flows, these two values are different. The value of max_p is still set as recommended in the standard RED algorithm [2], and min_p is set to half of max_p.

To avoid one application failure resulting from consecutive packet drops of its concerned flow during a short period of time, we should check this flow's state before certain packets are dropped. If this flow is in the critical or invalid state, our algorithm should try to avoid dropping its subsequent packets.

During the loose dropping stage, if the corresponding flow is in the critical or invalid state, the packet which should be dropped in terms of estimation of dropping probability is enqueued. We just add one to the number of the packets which need to be dropped for this flow.

During the strict dropping stage, if the flow is in the invalid state, just do the same as above. When the number of the packets that need to be dropped for concerned flow is over zero, if the coming packet is not to be dropped according to the computed probability, we choose to drop it and subtract one from the number of the packets which need to be dropped. The dropping process is same as the standard RED algorithm.

While during the congestion stage, if one flow is in the critical state, its arrival packet which needs to be dropped is dropped and then we mark this flow invalid. Once a flow is marked invalid, all packets belonging to that flow since then will be dropped during the congestion stage. That is to say, we choose to drop data packets of invalid flows as possible as we can. To avoid simultaneous failure of most applications, we mark those flows invalid with a certain probability, which increases linearly as the queue length increases. The probability to mark a flow invalid is computed by:

$$P_m = \begin{cases} \frac{avg}{3s} \cdot f(k) & \text{if flow } k \text{ is with high priority}, \\ \frac{2avg}{3s} \cdot f(k) & \text{if flow } k \text{ is with medium priority}, \\ \frac{avg}{s} \cdot f(k) & \text{if flow } k \text{ is with low priority} \end{cases} \qquad (9)$$

Here s is the maximum size of the output queue. The value of the function $f(k)$ depends on the state of flow k: if it is critical, $f(k)=1/2$, else if it is invalid, $f(k)=1$.

4 Simulation and Analysis

In this section we carried out the simulation using the ns network simulator [18] and then analyzed its results.

4.1 Simulation Environment

The simulation network is showed as Fig.2. Sources 1~4 simulate a multimedia service terminal respectively and send data to sink 6. Source 5 is used to generate background traffic. The bandwidth of the gateway is restricted to 2 Mbps; its buffer of the output queue is 500 packets; the maximum and minimum thresholds are 200 and 100 respectively. In the experiment, a multimedia service achieves good effect when its dropping packets rate is below 10%, just acceptable to the users when below 20%, and unacceptable when over 20%.

In our experiment, the employed multimedia traffic flow capacity is 40 frames per second. The size of each data frame obeys to the exponential distribution with the average value 10^3 bytes. The average capacity of one flow is about $10^3 \times 8 \times 40 = 320$ kbps. The background traffic flow obeys to the exponential distribution with the average value 640 kbps. Source 1, 2, 3, 4 and 5 will start to transmit data packets from 11s, 31s, 51s, 71s and 91s respectively and stop at 110s. Sources 1, 2 and 4 all take medium priority while source 3 takes low priority. The background traffic flow of source 5 takes medium or low priority randomly.

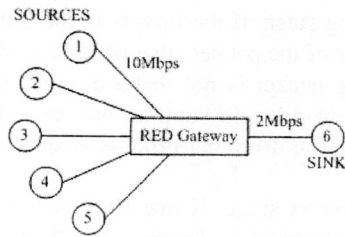

Fig. 2. Simulation network

We calculate the average queue length according to Formula 1, and take the queue weight 0.002 as recommended by Floyd [2]. Throughout our experiments, the max_p and min_p are set to 0.1 and 0.05 for low priority traffic, 0.08 and 0.04 for medium priority traffic, respectively.

4.2 Results and Analysis

From the results we obtain Table 1 and Table 2. We see from Table 1 that the dropping packets rate rises as the flow increases when RED algorithm is employed. During 71~90s, while four sources send data simultaneously without background traffic, the dropping packets rate is about 8% and all applications works well. During 91~110s, four sources send data simultaneously and source 5 also sends background traffic flow, the dropping packets rate of sources 1~4 rises up to 25% and 10 packets dropped, which is so intolerable that all services come to invalid state. The reason for the rate rising is that the total traffic of all flows is larger than the total bandwidth of the router, thus causing enormous packets dropped.

Table 2 shows the standard variance of the number of the dropped packets for both algorithms. The standard variance where the PPD algorithm is employed is obviously smaller than that where RED is employed. This indicates that the dropping packets rate is relatively steady when using PPD. The reason is that the PPD algorithm tries to avoid discarding packets of the same data flow continuously.

Fig.3 depicts the number of dropped packets per second during 0~110s for sources 1~4 when RED and our enhanced algorithm PPD are exploited respectively. We see that when the RED algorithm is employed, the packets dropping rate may be over

Table 1. Average number of packet-drops per second

time (s)	Source 1 RED	Source 1 PPD	Source 2 RED	Source 2 PPD	Source 3 RED	Source 3 PPD	Source 4 RED	Source 4 PPD
11-30	1.05	0.95	—	—	—	—	—	—
31-50	1.35	1.35	1.90	1.95	—	—	—	—
51-70	2.65	2.15	3.15	2.25	2.60	2.60	—	—
71-90	3.35	3.20	3.15	2.85	4.50	3.75	4.35	3.00
91-110	9.80	3.25	10.15	3.65	11.3	37.15	10.4	3.80

Table 2. Average variance of packet-drops per second

time	Source 1		Source 2		Source 3		Source 4	
(s)	RED	PPD	RED	PPD	RED	PPD	RED	PPD
11-30	0.94	0.83	—	—	—	—	—	—
31-50	1.42	0.93	1.52	0.89	—	—	—	—
51-70	2.96	1.79	2.28	1.41	2.76	1.54	—	—
71-90	3.27	1.40	3.20	1.63	2.52	1.89	2.92	1.84
91-110	—	1.89	—	2.18	—	—	—	2.04

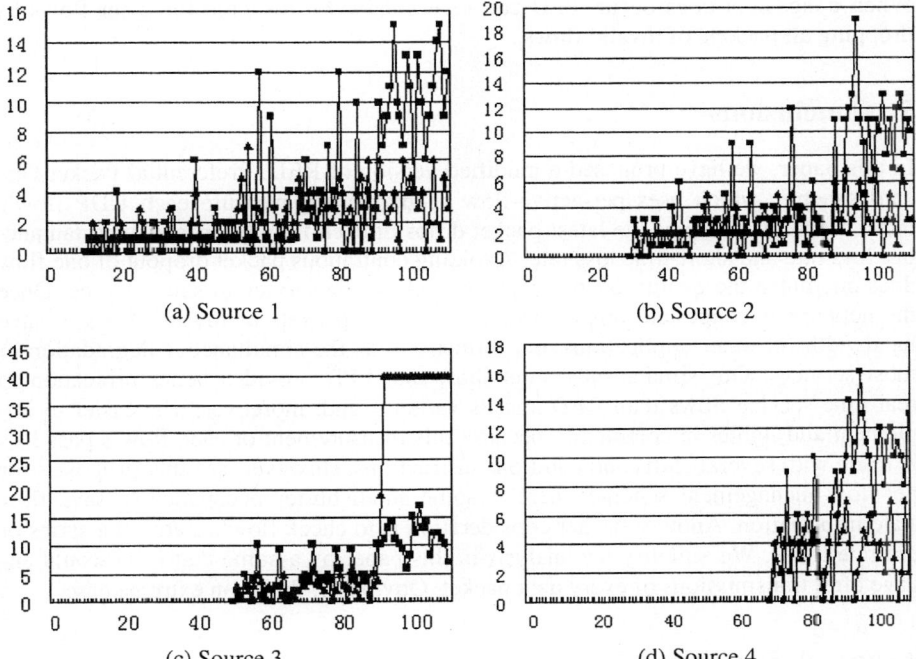

Fig. 3. Number of packet-drops of each source. The x-axis represents simulation time(s), and the y-axis represents the number of packets dropped of corresponding source. The square legend represents RED scheme, and the triangle legend represents PPD scheme.

10% or even 20% at some periods, thus causing the temporary break off of the real-time multimedia service; while when PPD is employed, except that the packets dropping rate of the flow 3 during 91~100s is beyond 20%, the packets dropping rate of all flows is never beyond 20% during other periods of time. Without background traffic, there is no obvious difference in the dropping packets rate between PPD and RED algorithm. During 91~110s, when source 5 transmits background traffic, the packets from source 3 are all dropped, while without background traffic the dropping packets rate of source 1, 2 and 4 approximates to that during 71~90s.

Hence, when network load is heavy, RED rejects the packets of all flows in an average way, which may cause the dropping packets rate of most flows to become too high to accept and make enormous application fail. On the contrary, our proposed PPD scheme can save bandwidth for well-worked flows by dropping selectively all packets of some invalid flows. Therefore, we conclude that the PPD algorithm presented in this paper could effectively avoid continuous data packet drops in a short period of time, thus improving quality of service.

The experiment results also show that our PPD scheme is better in performance than RED, whether the network is congested or not. Before congestion occurs, PPD can avoid continuous drop of data packets of the same flow during a short period of time, thus improving the service quality of the real-time multimedia application. When congestion does occur, PPD can save bandwidth resource for other flows by dropping all packets of invalid flows.

5 Conclusions

In this paper, we have proposed a modified version of RED, Preferential Packet Discard scheme, which uses per-active-flow accounting to measure each UDP flow's latest drops. It measures the latest packet drops of each flow by means of instantaneous loss rate and short-time loss rate. Avoiding continuous packet dropout of one flow does guarantee the quality of the real-time multimedia service to some degree. Once the network is congested, this algorithm rejects all packets of invalid flows to save bandwidth for other applications and further avoids the simultaneous degradation of most services. Our simulation results show that PPD provides better protection to real-time service flows than RED and its variants, and, moreover, it is easier to implement and lighter in complexity because this measurement of each flow's pass loss is made with several shifts and additions instructions. However, as other proposals for per-flow management scheme, there is some small buffer occupancy to save flow state information. Another further consideration is to check flow's status at a series of discrete times. We simplify the analysis in this paper by assume that PPD would engage after transmissions of every data packet. Obviously, this is an extreme case.

Acknowledgments

The authors would like to thank Gao Lei and Jing Bin for their useful advice and inspiring discussions. The work reported in this paper was supported in part by the National Science Foundation under Grant 60403028.

References

1. B.Braden, D.Clark, J.Crowcroft, et al.: Recommendations on Queue Management and Congestion Avoidance in the Internet. RFC 2309, Apr. 1998
2. S.Floyd, V.Jacobson.: Random Early Detection Gateways for Congestion Avoidance. IEEE/ACM Transactions on Networking, vol. 1, no. 4, Aug. 1993, pp. 397-413

3. A.Mankin, K.Ramakrishnan.: Gateway Congestion Control Survey, RFC 1254, Aug. 1991
4. M.May, J.Bolot, C.Diot, B.Lyles.: Reasons not to Deploy RED. IWQoS'99, London, U.K., June 1999, pp. 260-262
5. M. Christiansen, Kevin Jeffay, David Ott, F. Donelson Smith.: Tuning RED for Web Traffic. ACM/SIGCOMM 2000, Stockholm, Sweden, 2000, pp. 139-150
6. G.Iannaccone, C.Brandauet, T.Ziegler et al.: Comparison of Tail Drop and Active Queue Management Performance for Bulk-data and Web-like Internet Traffic. IEEE ISCC, July 2001, pp. 122-129
7. Dong Lin, Robert Morris.: Dynamics of Random Early Detection. ACM/SIGCOMM, Cannes, France, Sept. 1997, pp. 127-137
8. W.Feng, D.D.Kandlur, D.Saha, K.G.Shin.: A Self-configuring RED Gateway. IEEE INFOCOM 1999, vol. 3, New York, USA, Mar. 1999, pp. 1320-1328
9. Jinsheng Sun, King-Tim Ko, Guanrong Chen, Sammy Chan, Moshe Zukerman.: PD-RED: to Improve the Performance of RED. IEEE Communications Letters, vol. 7, no. 8, Aug. 2003, pp. 406-408
10. Teunis J. Ott, T.V.Lakshman, Larry H. Wong.: SRED: Stabilized RED. IEEE INFOCOM'99, vol. 3, New York, USA, Mar. 1999, pp. 1346-1355
11. R.Pan, B.Prabhakar, K.Psounis.: CHOKe: A Stateless Active Queue Management Scheme for Approximating Fair Bandwidth Allocation. IEEE INFOCOM 2000, Tel Aviv, Israel, Mar. 2000, pp. 942-951
12. F.M.Anjum, L.Tassiulas.: Fair Bandwidth Sharing Among Adaptive and Non-Adaptive Flows in the Internet. IEEE INFOCOM, vol. 3, New York, USA, Mar. 1999, pp. 1412-1420
13. Cisco Systems Inc.: Weighted Random Early Detection on the Cisco 12000 Series Router. Mar. 2002
14. R.Mahajan. S.Floyd, D.Wetherall.: Controlling High-bandwidth Flows at the Congested Router. IEEE/ACM 9th ICNP, Riverside, CA, Nov. 2001, pp. 192-201
15. Shushan Wen, Lemin Li, Hairong Sun.: An Algorithm to Protect TCP Bandwidth Based on Packet-drop History in RED. IEEE CCS/WSE 2002, vol. 1, June 2002, pp. 700-704
16. Diego Teijeiro-Ruiz et al.: On Fair Bandwidth Sharing with RED. ISCIS 2003, Lecture Notes in Computer Science, Springer. vol. 2869, Oct. 2003, pp. 892-899
17. Luo Tao, K.R. Subramanian, He Feng, XiaoFan Deng.: Weighted Fair Discard Scheme for Buffer Management in the Presence of Network Congestion. Computer Communications, vol. 25, no 10, June 2002, pp. 944-953
18. S. McCanne and S. Floyd.: Ns2 Network Simulator. http://www.isi.edu/nsnam/ns

A Heuristic Routing Algorithm for Degree-Constrained Minimum Overall Latency Application Layer Multicast

Baoliu Ye[1,2], Minyi Guo[1,2], Daoxu Chen[2], and Sanglu Lu[2]

[1] Department of Computer Software, the University of Aizu,
Aizu-Wakamatsu City, Fukushima 965-8580, Japan
{yebl, minyi}@u-aizu.ac.jp
[2] State Key Laboratory for Novel Software Technology, Nanjing Uiversity,
Nanjing 210093, P. R. China
{cdx, sanglu}@nju.edu.cn

Abstract. Application Layer Multicast (ALM) shifts multicast functionality from routers to end hosts and has the potential to address most problems associated with IP multicast. It has attracted wide attention in research community in recent years. However, as an end host based solution, the applicability of ALM to realtime applications such as streaming services is constrained by node bandwidth and transmission latency. How to guarantee QoS is still a challengeable problem. In this paper, we think overall latency is a more effective metric for evaluating the QoS perceived by most users and explore the optimization problem of Degree-Constrained Minimum Overall Latency Spanning Tree (DCMOLST). We divide the optimization process into initialization phase and dynamic adjustment phase. In the former stage, we propose a heuristic algorithm through giving a more consideration to both transmission delay and node bandwidth, so as to avoid QoS degradation caused by single metrics. In the later, we present a set of distributed iterative optimizing operations for further optimization. Experimental results show that our proposal can improve overall performance efficiently and is able to cope with network dynamics.

1 Introduction

Multicast plays an important role in group communication applications, such as audio/video conferencing, multi-party game, and content distribution. In the last decade, researchers have made great efforts on IP multicast techniques. However, due to some fundamental issues related to its scalability, reliability and deployment, IP multicast is not widely employed after its initial proposal. Recently, with the flurry of Peer-to-Peer (P2P) computing research, the research community began to revisit the issue of whether IP layer is indeed the right layer to implement multicast functionality and advocated using overlay network architecture as an alternate solution to support multicast. This kind of techniques is always referred as *Application Layer Multicast* (ALM) which integrates all the multicast related functions into end hosts through software approach. Since all data flows are transmitted as unicast packets, ALM deployment may be accelerated. However, although ALM has the potential to address most of the problems associated with IP multicast, it is not as efficient as IP multicast. It cannot completely prevent multiple logical edges from traversing the same physical link in overlay network. Thus some redundant traffic on physical links is unavoidable. Furthermore, the target environment of overlay network is dynamic, heterogeneous and unpredictable, overlay topology management is another challenge. Meanwhile, typical streaming media applications such as video/audio services always have stringent requirements on bandwidth, delay and other performance parameters. There is an urgent need to explore multicast routing algorithms capable of satisfying these QoS requirements.

In this paper, we deem that the overall latency is a more effective metric for evaluating the QoS of ALM and focus on the problem of *Degree-Constrained Minimum Overall Latency Spanning Tree (DCMOLST)*. In fact, end hosts are always heterogeneous in their available bandwidth and the edge delay among nodes is non-uniform. It is essential to capture the relative importance of different nodes according to edge delay as well as node degree when constructing ALM tree. To achieve the optimizing objective, we provide a heuristic algorithm for multicast tree initialization by extending the Prim algorithm and present several distributed optimization operations for further improvement during the multicast session.

The rest of this paper is organized as follows: in the next session, we discuss the related work. Section 3 gives the network model and problem definition. Section 4 describes the details of the heuristic algorithm. Section 5 presents our simulation results. Finally we summarize the work of this paper in section 6.

2 Related Work

Most of existing ALM protocols (such as Narada [1], NICE [2], Yoid [3] and Scribe [4]) assume that all the end hosts participating in a multicast session are homogeneous in their capability. The objective of protocol design is to address network dynamics so as to reduce topology maintenance cost and improve resource utilization. However, as a streaming application oriented technique, it is essential to satisfy QoS constraints. In the past, a lot of work on QoS-aware IP multicast routing has been done. Bellman-Ford algorithm and Dijkstra algorithm [5] are two well-known algorithms used to solve the Shortest Path Tree (SPT) problem. Prim algorithm [5] is a classical algorithm for the Minimum Spanning Tree (MST) optimization problem. KMB heuristic [6] is a good candidate for generating a Steiner tree. Zhu *et al.* [7] proposed a bounded shortest multicast algorithm to solve the delay constrained tree optimization problem. Kompella *et al.* [8, 9] and Jia [10] also presented several algorithms to construct a delay constrained Steiner tree.

Since data duplicate and forward are performed by end hosts, end hosts' network interface bandwidth is the main constraint in ALM routing design. This makes previous QoS-aware IP multicast algorithms unsuitable. And how to construct a bandwidth constrained multicast tree along with other special requirements becomes one of the key issues of ALM research. This is usually termed as the *degree-constrained multicast tree problem*. EMS [11] is a QoS-driven ALM protocol which uses a variant of the shortest widest path algorithm presented in [12] to simultaneously consider both bandwidth and latency, but it prioritizes bandwidth over latency. The authors of [13] proposed centralized greedy heuristics to two degree-constrained multicast tree related problems: Minimum Diameter Degree-Bounded Spanning Tree (MDDBST) and Bounded Diameter, Residual-Balanced Spanning Tree (BDRBST). The MDDBST problem is in essence the same as the min max-latency problem. OMNI [14] proposed an iterative distributed solution to the min average-latency problem. However, this schema is for infrastructure based ALM, rather than for P2P computing based systems.

3 Problem Description

An overlay network is a logical network built on top of the existing IP network infrastructure. For any pair of nodes, there must exist a unicast and the latency between them corresponds to the unicast transfer delay over the underlying physical network. An overlay network can be depicted as an undirected weighted graph $G=(V, E)$, where V is a node set and E is a set made up of overlay links. $|V|$ and $|E|$ denote the number of nodes and overlay links in the network, respectively. Let $delay(e)$ represent the end-to-end delay of e ($e \in E$) and $b(v)$ denote the available bandwidth of v ($v \in V$). For simplicity, we first give some concepts related to our work.

Definition 1: Node Degree is the maximum number of children that a node can support in a multicast session (or tree). Let $d_n(T)$ denote the node degree of node n in a multicast session T. $d_n(T)$ implies that node n can concurrently forward incoming packet at most to $d_n(T)$-1 other nodes.

Node degree is a non-negative integer determined by the bandwidth capability of a node. If r is the transmission rate of a multicast session T, then $d_n(T)$ can be calculated by formula (1):

$$d_n(T) = \max\{\lfloor (b(n))/r \rfloor, 0\} \qquad (1)$$

Definition 2: Overlay Latency is the transfer delay between two nodes along an ALM tree. Let $l_T(i, j)$ represent the overlay latency between node i and j over T. $l_T(i, j)$ is always larger than their IP unicast delay.

Definition 3: An ALM Tree is a subgraph of $G=(V, E)$ that spans all the nodes in V and can be represented by $T(s, M, E')$, where $s \in V$ is a source node, $M=V-\{s\}$ is a set of the receiver nodes and $E' \subset E$ is a set of edges forming the multicast tree. We define several property functions related to tree T as follows:

- $P_n(T)$: the parent of node n in tree T.
- $G_n(T)$: the grandfather of node n in tree T.
- $C_n(T)$: the number of children of node n in tree T, i. e., $C_n(T)=|n':P_{n'}(T)=n|$. For degree-constrained ALM tree, $C_n(T)$ must satisfy with $C_n(T) <= d_n(T)$-1.
- $L_n(T)$: the overlay latency from source node s to node n in tree T. Here we have $L_s(T)=0$, $L_n(T) = L_{P_n(T)}(T) + delay(P_n(T), n)$.
- $N_n(T)$: the total number of nodes in the subtree rooted at node n. here $N_n(T) = \sum_{\forall P_i(T)=n} N_i(T)$. For conciseness, we denote the subtree of tree T which rooted at node n as $S_n(T)$.

Definition 4: Overall Transfer Latency is the sum of overlay latency from the source node to all other nodes in the ALM tree. Let $D_s(T)$ be the overall transfer latency of ALM tree T that rooted at source node s, $D_s(T) = \sum_{n \in M} L_n(T)$.

According to Definition 3, $D_s(T)$ can also be computed as follows:

$$D_s(T) = \sum_{\forall P_i(T) = s} ((N_n(T)+1) \times l(s,i) + D_i(S_i(T))) \quad (2)$$

Overlay latency provides a metrics for evaluating the overvall QoS performance perceived by most users and is one of the important optimizing objectives in ALM QoS routing. Definition 5 states the DCMOLST problem in a more formal manner.

Definition 5: The optimization problem of **Degree-Constrained Minimum Overall Latency Spanning Tree (DCMOLST)** is to find an ALM tree $T_{min}(s, M, E')$ which satisfies the following conditions:

1) $E' \subset E$, $V = M \cup \{s\}$;
2) $C_n(T_{min}) < d_n(T_{min})$ for any node $v \in M$;
3) $D_s(T_{min}) \leq D_s(T')$ for any other trees T' that satisfies with both 1) and 2).

Obviously, this is a NP-complete problem which cannot be optimized by previous solutions, such as min max-latency algorithm. For example, figure 1(a) depicts an ALM tree constructed by the centralized greedy heuristic proposed in [15] for the MDDBST problem. The overall transfer latency of figure 1(a) is 4×5+3×6+2+2+3=45. If we make a tradeoff between edge delays and node degrees when determining the relative position of end hosts, then it's possible to get an ALM tree as figure 1(b). Obviously, this is a superior one whose overall transfer latency is 4×6+6+2+2+3=37.

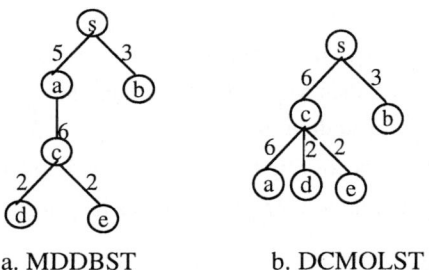

a. MDDBST   b. DCMOLST

Fig. 1. An Example of DCMOLST Tree

4 The Heuristic Routing Algorithm of DCMOLST

4.1 Heuristics for ALM Tree Initialization

Typically, a multicast data distribution is scheduled to start at a specific time. Suppose m nodes sent the data request to the source node s prior to this instant. Firstly we must organize these nodes into an initial ALM tree with respect to the optimizing objective. We think the joining order of each node should be determined by the edge delay as well as the node degree. Concretely, the priority ought to be proportional to the node degree and in inverse proportion to the edge delay. We develop a heuristic initialization DCMOLST algorithm by extending the Prim algorithm.

The heuristic DCMOLST algorithm maintains the following three node sets. M_{avail} consists of all the nodes already attached to the tree and still have free node degree, M_{off} includes all the nodes to be attached, M_{full} is a node set where all nodes have been connected to the tree but cannot accept any additional children due to its degree constraints. Initially, $M_{avail}=\{s\}$, $M_{off}=M$, $M_{full}=\phi$. During the initialization phase, M_{avail}, M_{off}, M_{full} are mutual exclusive sets satisfying with $M_{avail} \cup M_{off} \cup M_{full} = \{s\} \cup M$. Before describing the heuristic DCMOLST algorithm in detail, we first give the concept of the minimum ALM distance from an off-tree node to the source node s.

Definition 6: The minimum ALM distance from an off-tree node n_1 ($n_1 \in M_{off}$) to the source node s is the shortest overlay path from n_1 to s through any nodes already in T with free degree. Let $\delta(n_1,T)$ denote this distance, it can be expressed as follows:

$$\delta(n_1,T) = min(L_{n'}(T) + l(n',n_1)), \forall n' \in M_{avail} \quad (3)$$

Here node n' is termed as the **access node** of node n_1.

Similar to the Prim algorithm, the initializing process starts from the source node s. During the initialization phase, our heuristic algorithm performs the following procedure repeatedly till $M_{off} = \phi$.

1) Select a node n ($n \in M_{off}$) with the highest priority and add it to the existing component T through its access node n'. Let $d_n(T) = d_n(T)-1$, $d_{n'}(T) = d_{n'}(T)-1$.

2) Node n computes and saves the overlay latency from the source node s to itself in the current component T, i.e. $L_n(T)$.

3) Let $M_{off} = M_{off} - \{n\}$. If $d_n(T) \geq 1$, then $M_{avail} = M_{avail} \cup \{n\}$; Otherwise $M_{full} = M_{full} \cup \{n\}$. If $d_{n'}(T)=0$, then $M_{full} = M_{full} \cup \{n'\}$ and $M_{avail} = M_{avail} - \{n'\}$.

4) If node n joins M_{avail} or node n' moves from M_{avail} to M_{full}, then each node n_o in M_{off} recomputes its $\delta(n_o,T)$ according to formula (3) and updates its access node.

5) If $M_{off} \neq \phi$, then each node $n_o \in M_{off}$ recalculates its priority as follows:

$$p_T(n_o) = \alpha \times \frac{\delta_{min}}{\delta(n_o,T)} + (1-\alpha) \times \frac{d_{n_o}(T)}{d_{max}}, \forall n_o \in M_{off} \quad (4)$$

where α ($0 \leq \alpha \leq 1$) is a tunable parameter used to negotiate the weight ratio between edge delay and node degree, δ_{min} and d_{max} are the minimum value of $\delta(n_o',T)$ and the maximum value of $d_{n_o'}(T)$ for all node n_o' ($n_o' \in M_{off}$), respectively.

Algorithm 1 gives the pseudo-code of the heuristic DCMOLST algorithm.

Algorithm 1. The heuristic DCMOLST algorithm

```
for each n∈V
    if (dₙ<1) exit();
    else D_T=D_T+dₙ;
if (D_T <2(v-1)) exit();
M_avail={s};M_off=M;M_full= φ;
while(M_off≠ φ){
    for each n∈M_off
        for each n₁∈M_avail
```
$$\text{if } (L_{n_1}(T)+l(n,n_1)<\delta(n,T)) \quad \delta(n,T)=L_{n_1}(T)+l(n,n_1);$$
$$\delta_{min}=min(\delta(n,T)); \quad d_{max}=max(d_n(T));$$
```
    for each n∈M_off
```
$$p_T(n)=\alpha\times\frac{\delta_{min}}{\delta(n,T)}+(1-\alpha)\times\frac{d_n(T)}{d_{max}};$$
```
    let n∈M_off be the node with maximum p_T(n)·
    n joins T via its access node n₁;
    M_off=M_off -{n};
    dₙ= dₙ-1;
    dₙ₁= dₙ₁-1;
    if (dₙ=0) M_full=M_full ∪ {n};
    else M_avail= M_avail ∪ {n};
    if (dₙ₁=0) M_full=M_full ∪ { n₁};
}
```

4.2 Iterative Optimizing Operations

Since our heuristic initialization algorithm is not a greedy one, there may still have available degree on some branch nodes near the root. Thus it's possible to further optimize the overall latency by adjusting the position of local subtrees/nodes with these available degrees. Furthermore, nodes join and leave the multicast session dynamically, so it's necessary to maintain the topology adaptively, so as to improve the reliability and performance of the system. We present four local iterative optimizing operations for this situation. Each node in the ALM tree attempts to perform these operations periodically.

Parent-Child Position Swap. This operation needs available degree at the child node. Assume node g and node p are the grandparent and parent of node c, respectively. Parent-Child swap operation is performed if and only if formula (5) is true:

$$N_p(T)\times L_p(T)>(L_g(T)+l(g,c))\times N_p(T)+(N_p(T)-N_c(T))\times l(c,p) \quad (5)$$

Figure 2 demonstrates a parent-child position swap operation. In figure 2(a), since node c has free degrees, it initiates a parent-child position swap test according to formula 5, then sends a swap request to its parent node p. figure 2(b) shows the resulted tree after swapping.

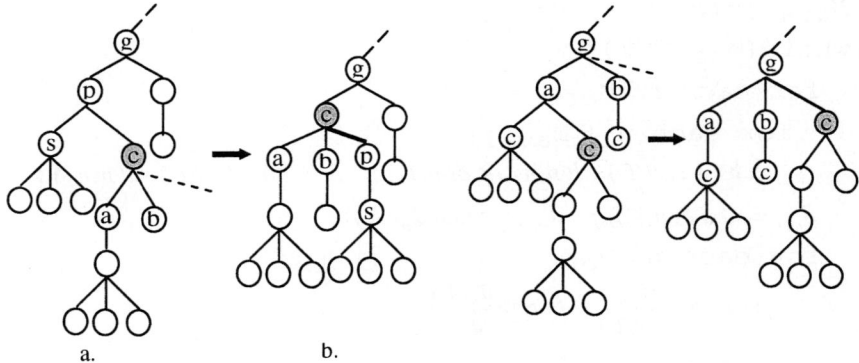

Fig. 2. Parent-child position swap   **Fig. 3.** Grandchild node promotion

Grandchild Node Promotion. This operation is a grandfather-driven operation. If node g has residual degrees, then one of its grandchildren is promoted as a direct child of g. Suppose C is a node set consisting of all the grandchildren of g, i.e., $C=\{c|G_c(T)=g\}$. In order to maximally reduce the overall latency, node g chooses a node from C with algorithm 2.

Algorithm 2: Grandchild selection algorithm
| ```
CanNode=null;
totalCost=0;
for each c∈C
  if (L_C(T)-L_g(T)>0)
    if(((L_C(T)-L_g(T))×N_C(T)> totalCost) {
      totalCost=(L_C(T)-L_g(T))×N_C(T);
      CanNode=c;
    }
``` |

Figure 3 shows an example of grandchild node promotion operation. Note that node c_2 is moved from node a to node g.

Nephew Node Movement. We call node n is a nephew of node u and u is the uncle of n if $G_n(T)=P_u(T)$ and $P_n(T) \neq u$. Nephew node movement is an uncle-driven operation and moves one of its nephew nodes to be a direct child of itself if having available degree. Algorithm 3 gives the pseudo-code of this operation. Note that S is a set about all the nephew nodes of node u.
```

Algorithm 3: Nephew selection algorithm

```
CanNode=null;
totalCost=0;
for each n∈S
  p=Pn(T);
  if (Lp(T)+1(p,n)- Lu(T)-1(u,n)>0)
    if((Lp(T)+1(p,n)- Lu(T)-1(u,n))×Nn(T)> totalCost) {
      totalCost=(Lp(T)+1(p,n)- Lu(T)-1(u,n))×Nn(T);
      CanNode=n;
    }
```

Figure 4 gives an instance of this operation.

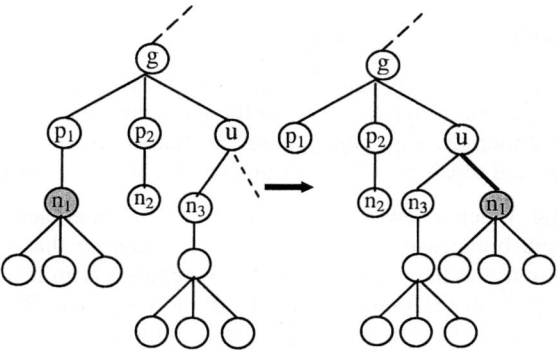

Fig. 4. Nephew node movement

All the above three operations must be initiated by the node with available degrees. In order to avoid collision and reduce optimizing cost, we define the priori of these operations as follows: parent-child position swap, grandchild node promotion and nephew node movement. Each eligible node performs these operations orderly.

Cousin Nodes Swap. We call node c_1, c_2 as cousin nodes if they share the same grandfather but with different parents. Cousin nodes swap operation exchanges the position of cousin nodes. This operation is performed if and only if the following inequation is true:

$$N_{c_1}(T) \times L_{c_1}(T) + N_{c_2}(T) \times L_{c_2}(T) > \\ (L_a(T) + l(a,c_2)) \times N_{c_2}(T) + (L_c(T) + l(c,c_1)) \times N_{c_1}(T) \tag{6}$$

Note that this operation may sacrifice some nodes' overlay latency so as to improve the overall benefits of the multicast tree. Figure 5 illustrates an example of this operation. Before swapping, $P_{c1}(T)=a$, $P_{c2}(T)=c$; After executing this operation, $P_{c1}(T)=c$ and $P_{c2}(T)=a$.

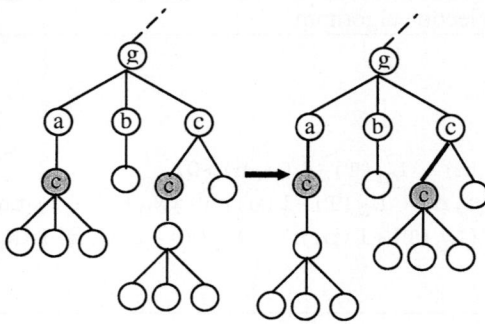

Fig. 5. Cousin nodes swap

4.3 Group Membership Management

One of the key differences between ALM tree and IP multicast tree is that the overlay multicast network is more dynamic due to the autonomy attribute of end hosts. This section presents a membership management mechanism to support new node to join the multicast tree and repair possible partitions caused by member leaving or failure.

Member Joining. When a new host want to join the multicast session, it first contacts source node s and broadcasts a joining request message to the whole multicast tree through s. In response to the joining request, all members with residual degrees return their overlay latency in the multicast tree to the joining host. Then the joining host computes its minimum ALM distance to s (as definition 6) and attaches to the multicast tree through its access node.

Member Exiting. There are two different cases of member exit: friendly leaving and abrupt failure. In the former case, a member notifies its neighbors before leaving. Abrupt failure is an exception event caused by some unpredictable reasons and should be detected locally and propagated to the rest of the group. Many distributed failure detection algorithms have been proposed in recent years [1-3, 15]. We only concern with the case of friendly leaving and give our approach for partition repair here.

A leaf node should only inform its parent node when leaving a multicast session. However, it's not as simple for branch nodes. The leaving of a branch node splits the multicast into several parts. To remerge these partitions, we employ a local repair scheme where only the children of the leaving node participate in the reconstruction and all the subtrees rooted at these children still keep their current topologies and states. Suppose node g is the leaving node, node p is the parent of g and C is a set about g's children. To repair the multicast tree, our algorithm first selects a node $c_1 \in C$ with the minimum distance from p to replace the position of g, then updates the overlay latency of all the nodes in the subtree $S_{c_1}(T)$. Following that we try to connect all the other subtrees $S_{c_i}(T)$ ($c_i \in C$) to the existing component tree T through available degrees in subtree $S_{c_1}(T)$ as possible. In the case of no sufficient degrees, the unconnected subtrees will contact source node s so as to determine their access nodes.

5 Performance Evaluation

In this section, we evaluate the performance of our heuristic routing algorithm. We generate a transit-stub network with the GT-ITM topology generator [16] for our experiments. End hosts randomly select a router from stub domains and connect to it. Our simulation scenarios consist of 200 nodes. The IP unicast delay between two nodes varies from 10ms to 200ms. Node degree ranges from 1 to 20 and the averaged value is 5.

Figure 6 shows the performance comparison over different α. The mean latency corresponding to each α is the averaged result over several trails. Each trail is conducted with a different average node degree. We see that $\alpha = 0.4$ is preferable to either $\alpha = 1$ or $\alpha = 0$. This result proves that we could produce a better tree by giving a more consideration to both transmission delay and node degree. When $\alpha = 1$, the heuristic DCMOLST algorithm is similar to the MDDBST algorithm [15] and gives priority to nodes with minimal latency from the source node. When $\alpha = 0$, the heuristic gives priority to nodes with larger available degree and chooses the one with minimal latency preferentially when they have the same available degrees.

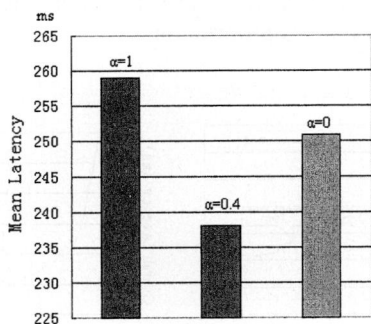

Fig. 6. Performance comparison over different weight ratio

Figure 7 depicts the effect of iterative optimizing operations for the overall performance. Note that we suppose no node joins/exits the multicast tree during this experiment and members perform these optimizing operations periodically. From this figure, we can see that the overall latency is decreased and converged to a stable level over time. Since our heuristics is not a greedy algorithm, the available degrees near the root provide more opportunities for performing iterative optimizing operations after the ALM tree initialization. Thus, initially the overall latency drops rapidly over optimizing operations. At the same time, these operations exhaust the eligible free degrees gradually, so later the curve reaches to a converged state. This result indicates that the iterative optimizing operations can improve the overall performance effectively.

Figure 8 compares the overall latency of different averaged node degree. We observe that the higher averaged node degree could result in a lower overall latency ALM tree. The reason is twofold. First, large averaged node degree provides more

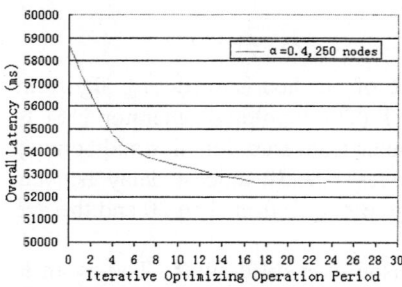
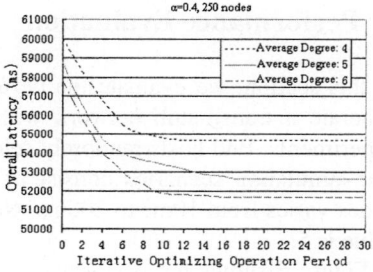

Fig. 7. Effect of iterative optimizing operations

Fig. 8. Effect of different averaged node degree

feasibility to create a broad ALM tree through available degrees near the root. Therefore the overlay latency from the source node to each node in the initial ALM tree is less than the case of small averaged node degree. Second, increasing node degree provides more possibility to further shrink the depth of multicast tree through residual degrees. And the execution of optimizing operations is more likely to be limited in an ALM tree with low averaged degree. Thus, the higher averaged degree tree still retains lower overall latency after optimization.

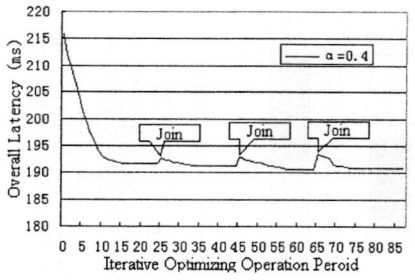
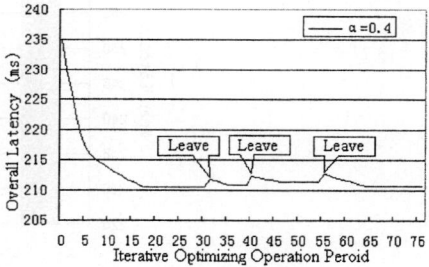

Fig. 9. Impact of node join

Fig. 10. Impact of node leave

We also examine our solution under dynamic environment. To simulate the node join scenario, we first generate a multicast tree consisting of 120 nodes with DCMOLST algorithm. Then we periodically inject new nodes into the tree, each time inserts 30 nodes. Figure 9 illustrates the impact of node join. We can see that the average latency curve fluctuates with the join operations and then gradually drops to a balanced state. Since most of the top nodes near the root are saturated under steady state and new nodes can only attach to the lower nodes. Thus the average latency increases at first. Later, the optimizing operations work and improve the performance. Figure 10 shows the impact of node exit. The initial multicast tree includes 200 nodes. A few nodes are randomly selected to friendly leave the session. Figure 10 indicates that node leaving has negative impact on the overall performance, but this situation could be improved partially by the optimizing operations.

6 Conclusions

Different from previous work on QoS routing, we take a new angle of view for evaluating the performance of degree-constrained application layer multicast routing, with the purpose to provide better QoS for most users. Especially, we study the optimizing problem of the degree-constrained minimum overall latency spanning tree. To achieve the optimizing objective, our solution divides the optimizing procedure into different stages and presents corresponding algorithms for them. Concretely, we provide a heuristic DCMOLST algorithm for multicast tree initialization and define a set of distributed iterative optimizing operations for further improvement. The philosophy of our heuristic DCMOLST algorithm is to avoid QoS degradation caused by single metrics by weighing both transmission delay and node bandwidth. And the idea of our iterative optimizing operations is that tries to improve the overall performance at the cost of sacrificing partial nodes' benefits. This paper describes the details of our scheme. The simulation results demonstrate that our approach is reasonable and is a promising means for providing low delay, high performance application layer multicast services.

Acknowledgement. This work is partially supported by the National Basic Research Program of China (973) under Grant No. 2002CB312002; the National Natural Science Foundation of China under Grant No. 60402027; the National High-Tech Research and Development Program of China (863) under Grant No. 2004AA112090.

References

1. Y. Chu, S. G. Rao, S. Seshan, H. Zhang, "A Case for End System Multicast," in the Proceedings of ACM SIGMETRICS, June 2000.
2. Y. Chawathe, "Scattercast: An Architecture for Internet Broadcast Distribution as an Infrastructure Service," Ph.D. Thesis, University of California, Berkeley, December 2000.
3. P. Fracis, "Yoid: Extending the Internet Multicast Architecture, P. Francis," April 2000, White Paper, http://www.aciri.org/yoid.
4. M. Castro, P. Druschel, A-M. Kermarrec, and A. Rowstron, "SCRIBE: A large-scale and decentralized application-level multicast infrastructure," IEEE Journal on Selected Areas in communications (JSAC), 2002.
5. T. H. Cormen, C. E. Leiserson, R. L. Rivest, "Introduction to algorithms," MIT Press, 1997.
6. L. Kou, G Markowsky, L. Berman, "A fast algorithm for Steiner trees," ACTA Informatica, pp. 141-145, 1981.
7. Q. Zhu, M. Parsa, J. Garcia-Luna-Aceves, "A souorce-based algorithm for delay-constrained minimal-cost multicasting," in Proceedings of IEEE INFOCOM'95, pp.377-384, 1995.
8. V. Kompella, J. Pasquale, G. Polyzo, "Multicast routing for multimedia communication," IEEE/ACM Transactions on Networking, pp. 286-292, 1993.
9. V. Kompella, J. Pasquale, G. Polyzo, "Two distributed algorithms for multicasting multimedia information," in Proceedings of ICCCN'93, pp.343-349, 1993.
10. X. Jia, "A distributed algorithm of delay-bounded multicast routing for multimedia applications in wide area networks," IEEE/ACM Transaction on Networking, 1998,6(6): 828~837.

11. Y. H. Chu, S. G. Rao, S. Seshan, H. Zhang, "Enabling conferencing applications on the Internet using an overlay multicast architecture," In proceedings of ACM SIGCOMM 2001, San Diago, CA, August 2001.
12. Z. Wang, J. Crowcroft, "Bandwidth-delay based routing algorithms," In *IEEE GlobeCom*, November 1995.
13. S. Y. Shi, J. S. Turner, "Routing in Overlay Multicast Networks," In proceedings of IEEE INFOCOM 2002, June 2002.
14. B. Suman, C. Kommareddy, K. Kar *et. al.*, "Construction of an efficient overlay multicast infrastructure for real-time applications," IEEE 2003, pp. 1521-1531.
15. B. Zhang, S. Jamin, and L. Zhang, "Host multicast: A framework for delivering multicast to end users," In Proc. of IEEE INFOCOM, New York, NY, June 2002.
16. E. W. Zegura, K. Calvert, and S. Bhattacharjee, "How to model an internetwork," in Proceedings of IEEE INFOCOM. San Francisco, CA, 1996.

DIRA: Distributed Insertion and Relocation Routing Algorithm for Overlay Multicast in Diffserv Domain

Xiao Chen, Huagang Shao, and Weinong Wang

Regional Network Center of East China,
Department of Computer Science and Technology,
Shanghai Jiao Tong University, China
{shawn, hgshao, wnwang}@sjtu.edu.cn

Abstract. Traditional multicast routing algorithms require routers to be specially designed such that they can forward the same copy of packet onto different output links simultaneously. This idea conflicts severely with the core-stateless principle in most QoS network architectures, such as Diffserv. Meanwhile, overlay multicast emerges as an effective alternative to the traditional approaches. In this paper, we combine the overlay multicast technique with the Diffserv architecture seamlessly and design an overlay multicast routing algorithm, which generates a multicast tree at a pretty low cost incrementally. Owing to its distributed nature, the computation of the tree can be executed efficiently. Through a large amount of simulations, we have shown that our algorithm is quite competitive in terms of network resource utilization and other metrics.

1 Introduction

In today's Internet, a large amount of novel applications, such as multimedia broadcast and teleconference, depend heavily on a multicast style network service. However, the traditional multicast protocols assume that each router in the network is able to send the same packet to multiple destinations at the same time. This assumption requires the routers to have special routing entries to forward the packet onto different links[6]. In terms of routing information, these approaches infer that routers should keep some state information, such as group membership, for each multicast session. This requirement also contradicts sharply with the core-stateless principle adopted in most QoS architectures, such as Diffserv[2]. In contrast with so many drawbacks of the traditional multicast schemes, the advantages of the overlay multicast make it a promising alternative to the old methods.

In brief, overlay multicast is to perform multicast upon overlay network. An overlay network is composed of a selective collection of the underlying physical nodes. All these nodes are connected by overlay links, each of which equals to a unicast path in the underlying network. Because the overlay network only focuses on a specific part of the whole network, it is easier for us to carry out multicast routing on it without changing the underlying infrastructure. Some famous applications of this kind include peer-to-peer file sharing and end-host-based multicast in the Internet[3],[5]. Unfortunately, the overlay network doesn't address all problems perfectly. According to QRON[7], a majority of the overlay networks are based on end hosts[3],[5]. They are confronted with great difficulties in enabling multicast in the current Internet environment for following reasons:

1. The scope of the overlay network is not defined clearly. It means the nodes in an overlay network may belong to several different autonomous systems (ASes). This situation often leads to a centralized routing algorithm, which inevitably suffers from the scalability problem.
2. The topology of the overlay network changes frequently. Since the end host is free to join or leave a session, the routing algorithm has to take great trouble to keep a reasonable balance between the routing efficiency and the membership flexibility.
3. The underlying QoS cannot be guaranteed. For most of the end host users, they only have limited bandwidth resource available to the overlay network applications. As the upper layer applications become more demanding, this disadvantage could be a fatal one for developing valuable overlay multicast applications.
4. The overlay network layer is built at a high level. In order to take advantage of the flexibility offered by the overlay network, most of the proposed schemes[1] have the overlay network layer built above the normal network layer. However, the extra computational workload near the application layer is inevitable when organizing an overlay network topology.

In this paper, we try to address these problems by constructing the overlay network over the edge routers within a Diffserv domain as they join the multicast session. On one hand, the Diffserv architecture has advantages with regard to the scalability and QoS capability. On the other hand, the overlay network is also a suitable complement to enable multicast within the Diffserv domain because it complies with the core-stateless principle and asks for no change in the core routers. Thus the objective of our effort is to design a routing algorithm, which will generate an overlay multicast tree efficiently at a possibly low cost.

The rest of the paper is organized as follows: Section 2 reviews the related works on this topic. Section 3 formulates the network model and specifies the related difficulties to achieve our objective. In section 4, we describe our algorithm through the basic idea as well as the pseudocode routine function. The performance of our algorithm is evaluated through a large amount of simulations in section 5. Finally we draw the conclusions in section 6.

2 Related Works

With regard to the overlay multicast, a lot of solutions have been proposed. One group among them(e.g. Narada[3]) focuses on the application level end-hosts based implementations. While these solutions could be flexible in heterogeneous network environment, they will incur the difficulties we have mentioned in section 1. On the other hand, several schemes have been designed, such as [8], [1] and [4], to place some Multicast Service Nodes(MSNs) into the underlying physical network and organize an overlay network through them to support the upper layer multicast applications. These solutions are similar to ours in that they employ some fixed nodes in the physical network to provide the overlay network service. However, they are different in many other aspects.

In [1] and [4], the authors use centralized heuristics to minimize the maximal diameter of the tree. However, they don't deal with the issue of the dynamic membership. In [8], this problem is resolved by an iterative distributed solution. By means of five different local transformation operations and random swaps, [8] adapts the routing tree for a minimal average latency among the clients in a distributed style. However, because different MSNs could apply for a transformation simultaneously, it is difficult to coordinate such an operation without a mediator. Furthermore, it's even harder to collect the information of the partial topology as the position of MSNs changes constantly. In contrast to this approach, we limit the overlay network within the scope of a Diffserv domain and adapt the tree each time a new join or departure request arrives. This method contributes to a stable topology and reduces the control message overhead drastically. In [7], the overlay service network(OSN) is proposed as a general framework for supporting a variety of overlay applications. In this framework, each overlay broker (OB) assumes several responsibilities during the QoS-aware routing process, such as bandwidth measurement and resource allocation. In fact, all the QoS-related functionalities have already been defined in the Diffserv architecture. Since we can safely rely on the edge routers and the bandwidth broker (BB) to fulfill these tasks, our algorithm imposes fewer requirements on the overlay nodes. Another work most similar to ours is described in IIA[9]. It generates the tree by appending the new node to an in-tree node or inserting it into an overlay link, whichever leads to a least cost gain. It is a centralized algorithm, which requires a new node to compare all cost gains throughout the whole tree. In addition, it doesn't take care of the edge links in the Diffserv domain, which may reduce the tree cost hugely. In contrast, our algorithm carries out the computation in a distributed style and imposes no intensive burden for any single node.

3 Network Model and Problem Specification

3.1 Physical Network Model

Without loss of generality, we model the underlying network in question by an undirected connected graph G (V, E) with the vertexes representing routers and the edges standing for links. As it is defined in the Diffserv[2] architecture, each node is either an edge node or a core node. Edge nodes are located on the border of a domain. In Diffserv architecture, it is assumed that edge nodes only deal with the traffic related to their adjacent domains. Thus they work in a comparatively low speed network environment and we grant them the responsibility to keep the state information for each flow into their concerned domains. In contrast with edge nodes, core nodes, which stand within a domain, are convergence points for network traffic from all surrounding domains so that they are kept stateless. We also define that a link that is built between two edge nodes is called an edge link, while the other links are referred to as core links. All these concepts can be illustrated in Fig. 1.

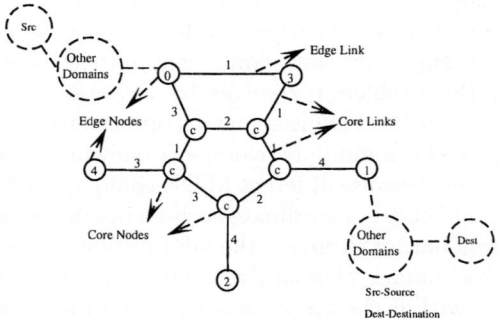

Fig. 1. This figure shows the topology of a Diffserv domain

The cost of each link between node a and b is denoted by $C(l_{ab})$. The core path between edge node a and b, denoted by $CPath(a,b)$, is a unicast path between them, which is composed of a collection of core links and has a least accumulated cost. Because the edge links are built mainly to enhance the communication capacity between edge nodes, we have the following assumption:

Assumption 1. *The cost of any edge link is lower than that of any core path. Formally we have the following inequality(a and b are edge nodes):*

$$\max\{C(l_{ab})|l_{ab} \in E\} \leq \min\{\Sigma_{l_{ab} \in CPath(a,b)} C(l_{ab})\} \quad (1)$$

From Fig. 1 we can see that a Diffserv domain usually plays as an intermediate domain and contains no end receivers or end senders. The multicast sessions we deal with here all belong to source specific multicast(SSM). Thus the objective of our effort is to multicast the data efficiently among all those edge nodes, which serve as the designated receivers, from the designated source. Hereinafter all nodes we will mention are within the same domain.

3.2 Overlay Network Model

Overlay multicasting is to send one copy of the data from the source node to several receiver nodes and then retransmit it from those nodes to other receiver nodes. Therefore, overlay multicast routing is to construct an overlay multicast tree, which is rooted at the source node and covers all the receiver nodes. Note that this tree only consists of the edge nodes, which are members of the multicast session. So we call such an overlay multicast tree a virtual tree, in contrast with any other multicast tree, which may contain intermediate nodes.

Before we can go further, some definitions are necessary. First we denote the overlay network by a virtual graph of $VG(\,V', E'\,)$, which consists of all edge nodes within a Diffserv domain. The cost of a virtual link between node a and b in the virtual graph, denoted by $VC(l'_{ab})$, can be expressed as:

$$VC(l'_{ab}) = \begin{cases} \sum_{l \in CPath(a,b)} C(l) & l_{ab} \notin E \\ C(l_{ab}) & l_{ab} \in E \end{cases} \quad (2)$$

3.3 Objectives of Our Routing Algorithm

The main focus of this paper is to construct a virtual tree at a low cost that covers and only covers those participant edge nodes. In other words, we don't bother other edge nodes to serve as intermediate nodes for carrying packets unrelated to them. In addition, such an algorithm should satisfies following requirements:

1. It is able to accept dynamic membership. This is a big obstacle for most overlay routing algorithms because the arrival or departure of a new member may cause the topology of the whole virtual tree change drastically.
2. It must be efficient in the computation of the virtual tree. Since the algorithm computes the tree incrementally, it has to be executed in a short time. Otherwise, the continuous join or leave requests may cause the algorithm impractical.

4 Our Algorithm

4.1 Definitions in Our Algorithm

In this paper, relocation means the operation of breaking the connection between a node and its current parent node and appending it to another one in the virtual tree. This is a basic operation adopted in our algorithm to generate the virtual tree for a low cost. We will give several definitions related to this notion as follows:

Definition 1. *Relocation cost gain for node s to c, denoted by $RG(s,c)$, can be formulated as:* $RG(s,c) = VC(l_{cs}) - VC(l_{ps})$. *Here, p is the parent of node s.*

Definition 2. *Relocation scheme of node s, denoted by $RS(s)$, is a binary tuple of (CostGain, AppendToNew). These two fields can be calculated as follows:*

$$RS(s).CostGain = min(RG(s,i), RG(s,c))$$

$$RS(s).AppendToNew = \begin{cases} true & RG(s,i) \leq RG(s,c) \\ false & RG(s,i) > RG(s,c) \end{cases}$$

Here, i stands for a new member requesting to join the session while c is the candidate parent for node s. All these notions will be explained in detail in the next section.

Definition 3. *Graft scheme of node s, denoted by $GS(s)$, is a quarternary tuple of (CostGain, GraftPoint, RelocatedNode, AppendToNew).*

CostGain represents the least cost gain we can obtain by grafting the node i to the *GraftPoint* under the subtree rooted at node s and relocating the *RelocatedNode*. If *RelocatedNode* is null, then *CostGain* means the cost gain for appending the new node i directly to the *GraftPoint* without relocating any other node. *AppendToNew*, which is similar to that of Relocation scheme, stands for whether we should append the *RelocatedNode* to the new coming node of i. We will show the computation of the graft scheme in our algorithm in detail.

4.2 Basic Idea

The basic idea behind our algorithm is as follows. In case that the parent node fails for some reason or relocation occurs, each node except the source node chooses one adjacent node in the virtual tree as its candidate parent. Note that the candidate parent of a node cannot be its descendant node in the tree.

Whenever we want to append a new node i to a non-leaf node s in the virtual tree, we have three choices. One is to append node i directly to node s without relocating any other node. The second way is to insert the new node between node s and one of its child nodes. The last choice is to append the new node to s and relocate one of the child nodes to the child's candidate parent. Suppose node s has n child nodes appended to it in the virtual tree. Then we will have 2n+1 cost gains in 2n+1 different situations, which are described above. If we refer to the minimal value among the 2n+1 cost gains as the least cost gain for node s, we can easily calculate the least cost gain for the tree by comparing the least cost gains for all nodes and selecting the minimal one. In order to build the virtual tree at a cost as low as possible, we calculate the least cost gain for the tree each time a new node wants to join and insert it into the tree accordingly. We now illustrate this idea by an example in Fig. 2.

Suppose the topology of the underlying network we employ for illustration is shown in Fig. 1. The designated source is node 0 and other edge nodes are

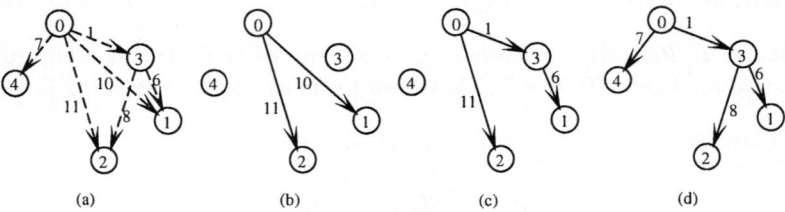

Fig. 2. Tree building process

numbered in the order they join the session. According to this topology, we demonstrate the process of the virtual tree construction through (a) to (d). In these figures the solid lines indicate the current virtual tree topology while the dotted lines represent the virtual links in the virtual graph. The cost of all lines are as marked in the figures. We can see in (b) that at first the virtual tree only consists of three nodes. When node 3 comes in, we will obtain the least cost gain of -3 by inserting it between node 0 and node 1. After node 3 is inserted, the candidate parent of node 2 should be changed to node 3. Thus (c) outlines the virtual tree after node 3 joins the session. We assume at this moment node 4 requests to join. Because the candidate parent of node 2 is closer to it than its current parent, node 2 will turn to node 3 for connection as node 4 is connected to node 0. The final virtual tree is shown in (d).

4.3 Complete Algorithm

Scenario 1. If an edge node, who wants to join a multicast session, is the first subscriber, then its request might be sent to another edge node, which will later become the designated source of the session in this domain. After source node has established its connection to the multicast session, it will inform its only subscriber for the intra-domain connection. At this time, the virtual tree is just a unicast connection between two edge nodes.

Scenario 2. After the first connection is established, each time a new join request arrives the source node will propagate the information about the new subscriber throughout the current virtual tree in a top-down manner. When the leaf nodes are informed of the new node, the algorithm in Fig. 3 will be executed in each leaf node. Then the output will be submitted to their parents, which in turn execute the same algorithm. After each node has carried out such a computation, the relocation scheme for the whole tree with regard to the new node can be obtained in a bottom-up way. At this step, source node will instruct the nodes involved in the relocation scheme to behave accordingly. Once the new node settles down, the source node, informed of this change, will spread the topology of the new tree among the in-tree nodes. This action is needed for two reasons. One is that some nodes may expect the new node to be their candidate parent. The other is that each node should check if their candidate parent has become a descendant of itself due to the relocation. If the latter occurs, the node should select another node from the tree as its candidate parent.

Scenario 3. When a node is going to quit the tree, it must order all its child nodes, if it has any, to be relocated. Intuitively, this process doesn't demand any further computation for each of the child nodes because they will turn to their respective candidate parents for connection. Once all these child nodes have settled down with their new parents respectively, the node, which is about to quit, will inform the source node of its departure from the tree and completely break its connection to its parent node. It is also necessary that all those relocated nodes inform the source node of their new parents respectively. After the source node has collected all information about the change of the tree, it will

```
Program DIRA (Node i)
   //i-the new coming node
   Var
      Node p,c,this;
      //p-parent node;
      //c-candidate parent;
      //this-this node;
   Begin
      Initialization of node p and c;
      GS(this).CostGain = VCost(this,i);
      GS(this).GraftPoint = this;
      GS(this).RelocatedNode = Null;
      If this is not a leaf node Then
         Inform all child nodes of node i;
         For each child node m do
            //GS(m) and RS(m) returned from every child node m
            If GS(this).CostGain > VCost(this,i) + RS(m).CostGain Then
               GS(this).CostGain = VCost(this,i) + RS(m).CostGain;
               GS(this).RelocatedNode = m;
               GS(this).AppendToNew = RS(m).AppendToNew;
            End If
         End For
         For each child node m do
            If GS(this).CostGain > GS(m).CostGain Then
               GS(this).CostGain = GS(m).CostGain;
               GS(this).GraftPoint = GS(m).GraftPoint;
               GS(this).RelocatedNode = GS(m).RelocatedNode;
               GS(this).AppendToNew = GS(m).AppendToNew;
            End If
         End For
      End If
      If p != Null Then
         //this is not the root node
         RS(this).CostGain = min(RG(this,i), RG(this,c));
         If RG(this,i) <= RG(this,c) Then
            RS(this).AppendToNew = True;
         Else
            RS(this).AppendToNew = False;
         End If
      Else
         RS(this) = Null;
      Return RS(this) and GS(this);
      //to parent node if there is one
   End.
```

Fig. 3. DIRA algorithm for each node

once more propagate the new topology among the in-tree nodes. The reason for it is similar to that we stated in scenario 2. Of course if the node to quit is the last subscriber in the session, all actions above are not necessary. After the last member breaks its intra-domain connection, the source node will also finish its inter-domain connection to the multicast session.

4.4 Discussion

The first thing we want to talk about is the cost analysis of our algorithm. The cost involved in our algorithm comprises message overhead and time overhead. Owing to the message propagation throughout the virtual tree, the number of messages necessary in one round of the algorithm execution is proportional to the number of the nodes in the tree. If the current tree has m nodes, the magnitude should be about $O(m)$. On the other hand, because the computation can be carried out in parallel among the nodes, the time overhead only depends on the longest branch in the virtual tree. On average, the magnitude of the time cost of our algorithm should be approximately $O(\log m)$.

Although the algorithm we have mentioned so far doesn't take into account some of the critical issues in the overlay network routing, such as fan-out degree limitation and diverse QoS provisioning, it's almost a trivial work to enhance the simplest version to support these different functions. In order to limit the fan-out degree of each overlay node, we can just forbid those nodes, who have already run out of free fan-out degrees, to accept any node as their new child without relocating any of their current child nodes. As far as QoS diversity is concerned, we only need to block the message propagation at those nodes that are incapable to provide sufficient QoS service to the new node. Fortunately, all these different limitations imposed on our algorithm doesn't change its overhead significantly. According to the methods we have described above, it's easy to infer that the message cost and the time cost is kept at the same order of magnitude.

5 Evaluation

In this section, we evaluate the proposed DIRA algorithm using simlations. The goal of our simulations is to evaluate the performance of our algorithm in terms of the following metrics:

1. Cost of the whole tree
2. Average latency of each node

The algorithms we adopt for comparison include the IIA[9] and the PIM[10]. As we have mentioned in section 2, IIA has a common goal as ours. However it only tries to insert the new node into the tree without adjusting the existing topology. Therefore, we regard it as an upper bound benchmark for tree cost. On the other hand, PIM is a popular multicast protocol for the multicast-enabled network. Thus we consider it as a lower bound for our algorithm. One thing all these algorithms have in common is that they follow an incremental approach in the tree building process.

5.1 Simulation Setup

In order to generate a network model for the Diffserv domain, we first create a network that only consists of the core nodes according to the Waxman approach[11]. Next we add the edge nodes into the graph in a similar way. Each edge node is connected to the core network by no more than 2 fanout links. After all edge nodes are connected to the core network, the edge links are built between them. The number of the edge links is given as a parameter and their positions are chosen randomly. While generating the topology in a random style, this approach avoids the situation, where some edge node stands in the way between another pair of edge nodes.

The topology we use in this section has 100 nodes that include all edge nodes and core nodes. In each simulation scenario, we obtain the final result through the average value of 1000 sample tests. To evaluate the performance of our algorithm in different network environments, we repeat our simulations in the following two different network scenarios:

1. 30% of the nodes are edge nodes
2. 50% of the nodes are edge nodes

In each sample session, one edge node serves as the source while all other edge nodes play as members. That means in scenario 1 the overlay tree consists of 30 nodes while in scenario 2 the tree comprises 50 nodes.

5.2 Simulation Results and Discussions

In each of the above scenarios, we measure the three algorithms (DIRA, IIA, PIM) along with their modified version (DIRA*, IIA*, PIM*) for comparison. Here DIRA* and IIA* have taken into account the degree limitation such that each physical link between an edge node and a core node can never carry more than 3 overlay traffic flows in the same direction in one session. PIM* is a modified version of PIM, where an edge link is not used for tree construction unless it connects a new node to the tree directly. All these diverse versions of algorithms allow us to have a better understanding of the performance of the algorithms under different limitations.

According to assumption 1, one feature of our algorithm is to take advantage of the edge links to generate the overlay tree at a cost as low as possible. Therefore, our first simulation aims to find the relationship between the tree cost and

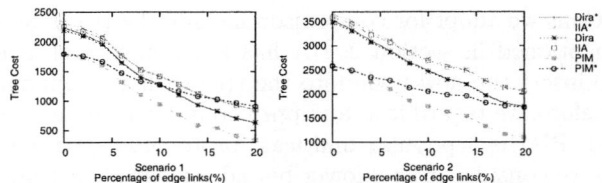

Fig. 4. Percentage of edge links VS Tree cost

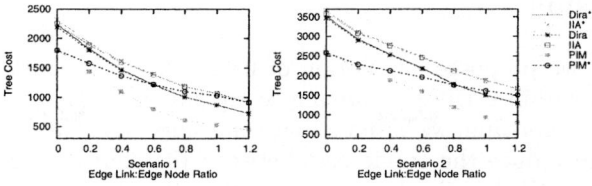

Fig. 5. Ratio of edge links to edge nodes VS Tree cost

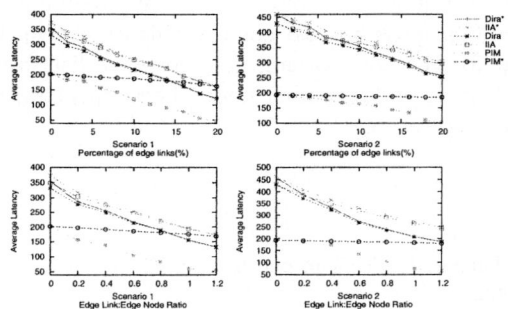

Fig. 6. Average latency in all experiments

the percentage of the edge links among all physical links. We show the simulation results for all six algorithms in Fig. 4 for the two scenarios respectively.

From Fig. 4, we can infer that the performance of DIRA is better than that of IIA in terms of tree cost and approaches that of PIM as the percentage of the edge links increases. We also observe that as an increasing number of edge links are built within the network, the degree limitation for edge nodes makes little difference in tree cost. In addition, we notice that the curve of PIM* changes slowly in comparison with other curves. It means that PIM* makes little use of the edge links for cost reduction. Thus we should believe that PIM won't work well in a Diffserv domain, where the edge links are not open to public usage.

Comparing these two figures, we find that the result in scenario 2 is not so satisfying as that in scenario 1. This observation leads to another simulation, which measures the tree cost based on the change of the ratio of the edge links to the edge nodes. We show the results in Fig. 5.

Without regard to the extra overhead introduced by different topology settings, the curves here in scenario 1 and scenario 2 have a similar trend in the change of the tree cost. This similarity indicates that the ratio of the edge links to the edge nodes is a dominant factor for the tree cost.

The average latency for the edge nodes in each of the simulations above is presented in Fig. 6. It is interesting that all these figures also lead us to the same conclusions we have obtained above.

6 Conclusion

In this paper, we proposed the notion of using DIRA to construct an overlay multicast tree within a Diffserv domain to support QoS-aware multicast applications. In our algorithm, we assume that some edge links are built between the edge routers to reduce the traffic cost between the connected nodes. Through these edge links, DIRA builds the tree efficiently while keeping the physical links less burdened.

The focus of this paper is DIRA. DIRA is designed as an overlay multicast routing algorithm, whose goal is to find an overlay tree spanning all member nodes at a cost as low as possible. To achieve this objective, DIRA computes the best access point for the new coming member in a distributed manner and keeps a candidate parent in each member node. These mechanisms makes DIRA not only efficient but also resilient.

References

1. S.Y.Shi and J.S. Turner: Routing in overlay multicast networks. *Proc. IEEE INFOCOM*, June 2002.
2. S.Blake, et. al.: An Architecture for Differentiated Services. RFC2475, December 1998.
3. Y.-H. Chu, S. G. Rao, and H. Zhang: A Case for End System Multicast. *Proc. ACM Sigmetrics*, June 2000.
4. S. Shi, J. Turner, and M. Waldvogel: Dimensioning server access bandwidth and multicast routing in overlay networks.*Proceedings of NOSSDAV*, June 2001.
5. Gnutella [Online]. Available: http://www.Gnutella.com
6. Deering, S.: Multicast Routing in Internetworks and Extended LANs. *SIGCOMM Summer 1988 Proceedings*, August 1988.
7. Li , P. Mohapatra: QRON: QoS-aware routing in overlay networks. *IEEE JSAC*, 2003
8. S. Banerjee, C. Kommareddy, K. Kar, B. Bhattacharjee, and S. Khuller: Construction of an efficient overlay multicast infrastructure for real-time applications. *IEEE INFOCOM*, San Francisco, CA, April 2003
9. Baijian Yang and Abdol H. Esfahanian and Lionel Ni: A Tree Building Technique for Overlay Multicasting in DiffServ Domains. *International Conference on Internet Computing* 2003
10. Estrin, et. al.: Protocol Independent Multicast-Sparse Mode (PIM-SM): Protocol Specification", RFC 2362, June 1998
11. B.M. Waxman: Routing of multipoint connections.*IEEE J. Select. Areas Commun.*, vol.6, no. 9, Dec. 1988.

Load Balancing Based on Similarity Multi-paths Routing*

Wuping Xu [1,2], Puliu Yan [1], Delin Xia [1], and Ming Wu [1]

[1] School of Electronics Information, Wuhan University, Wuhan Hubei P.R. China
[2] School of Computer, Wuhan University, Wuhan Hubei P.R. China
whwp@tom.com

Abstract. To load balance in Internet, we need more valid routing paths to share load in the case of no long-term routing loops to be introduced. It is acknowledged to adopt near or relaxed best routing to extend the number of available paths in multi-path routing. However, it is difficult to determine the degree of approximation or relaxed. A new distributed algorithm (which is called similarity multi-paths routing, SMR) for the dynamic computation of multiple paths from source to destination in a computer network is presented in this paper. SMR uses similarity principle to computes similarity coefficient between the shortest path and other paths, and then makes use of similarity coefficient to estimate the degree of approximation. Simulations show us it is robust for SMR to select near or relaxed best paths. Based on SMR, we also propose a traffic balancing algorithm. Its average performance is analyzed by simulation and compared against Equal Cost Multi-path (ECMP).

Keywords: Similarity, Multi-Paths Routing, Traffic split, Load Balancing.

1 Introduction

Most of the routing solutions to date are unsuitable for load balancing. The current Internet routing architecture is rather straightforward: within individual Internet domains, all links are assigned link costs, which are used as a basis for the calculation of network paths. Paths between any two nodes in the domain are determined by minimizing the sum of link costs over all path candidates. But, in most operational networks, the link cost values are usually kept static for several hours or days, however traffic always takes the same path from source to destination, even if other uncongested paths exist. This may lead to unbalanced utilize networks.

In order to solve this problem, many approaches have been developed. One is the global optimization of link costs for a given traffic matrix [2]. This method enables performance gains in operational networks, but unfortunately the optimization problem is NP-hard and thus heuristic methods must be employed.

In contrast to shortest/best routing, many papers show that multi-path or adopting backup route can balance the network's loading and improve performance [1,2,3,4,5]. For example, the Equal Cost Multipath (ECMP) [3] offers a router multiple choices for

---

* Foundation item: Supported by the National Natural Science of China (90204008).

packet forwarding when those choices offer the minimum distance. However, when there is fine granularity in link costs metric, as in the case of optimal routing, there is less likelihood that multiple paths with equal distance exist between each source-destination pair, which means the full connectivity of the network is still not used for load-balancing. So Optimized Multi-path (OMP) [4, 5] and many papers [3,7] trend to adopt near or relaxed minimum distance to extend the number of available paths. But the problem is how to determine the degree of approximation or relaxed to the best path. If it is too small, it is just the shortest paths. Otherwise, long-term routing loops can occur, causing routing instability with the risk of oscillation.

In this paper, we described a load-balancing routing framework to obtain "near-optimal" performance. A key component of the frame is SMR (Similarity Multi-Paths Routing). SMR extends the number of available paths using similarity principle to determine the degree of approximation or relaxed to the best path. It selects multiple successor choices for packet forwarding, and the routing graphs implied by the routing tables are DAGs (directed acyclic graphs) in SMR. By load-balancing traffic over these multiple next-hop choices, congestion is alleviated, and delay is significantly reduced.

The remainder of the paper is structured as follows: Section 2 introduces the elements of the SMR algorithm. Section 3 presents a number of simulation results. Section 4 concludes the paper with summarizing remarks.

2 Load Balancing Based on SMR

2.1 Problem Formulation

A network is modeled as a graph $G = (N, L)$, where N is set of nodes (routers) and L is the set of edges (links). Let N^i be the set of neighbors of node i. The problem consists of finding the successor set at each router i for each destination j. The successor set includes two sub-sets: primary successor set, denoted by $S_j^i \subseteq N^i$, which provides the shortest/best path for destination j. And the secondary successor set, denoted by $S'^i_j \subseteq N^i$, which provides the near shortest/best paths for destination j. When router i receives traffic load for destination j, it can split traffic proportionally among the neighbor routers in the successor set $S_j^i \cup S'^i_j$. By repeating this operation at every router, the traffic is expected to reach the destination. If the routing graph SG_j^i implied by S_j^i and SG'^i_j implied by S'^i_j, respectively, a directed acyclic sub-graph of G is defined by the directed link set $\{(m,n) \mid m_{init} = i, n \in S_j^m, m \in N\}$, where m_{init} is the first node of DAG, a traffic load destined for j follows multiple paths in $S_j^i \cup S'^i_j$.

2.2 Algorithm of SMR

1) SMR Overview: SMR use the method called *diffusing computations* suggested by Dijkstra's [9] to spread routing messages. In a word, given a DAG, each node updates its routing table based on messages reported by the "downstream" nodes and reports its routing information to "upstream" nodes. Nodes exchange routing messages with its neighbors periodically.

When a node receives all routing messages about a destination from its neighbors, it computes the shortest path using these routing messages firstly. Then, according to loop-free invariant (LFI) conditions [11], it eliminates paths which loop with the shortest path. Lastly, it selects several paths among the paths left as secondary routing based on similarity principle.

In order to judge whether a path is similar to the shortest path, SMR uses similarity coefficient to describe the similar degree. Simulations results show that it is relatively easy to determine the degree of approximation or relaxed to best path.

2) Computing of the Shortest Path: Given that there are many potential paths for a given destination in a graph, a question arises as to which path must be used? The natural choice is the one defined by the shortest paths. SMR defines D_j^i as the shortest length of a DAG denoted by routing graph SG_j^i, and is measured (metrics) as the weighted average of the hops and the average costs of the links on the shortest path in SG_j^i, and denoted by as following.

$$D_j^i = \beta \cdot h_j^i + (1-\beta) \cdot \frac{C_j^i}{h_j^i} \quad (1)$$

h_j^i is the hops of the shortest path for j in SG_j^i, and C_j^i is the sum of costs of the links on the shortest path in SG_j^i. Here, SMR uses hops to avoid routing vibration. The value of β is decided by experience at present, usually between 0.4 and 0.5.

The cost of link is denoted by a link performance parameter—*normalized queue length* [8]. Let $Q_{j,k}^i$ is the mean length of sub-queue from i to j passing by k in a fixed statistic interval, and $BW_{j,k}^i$ is the bandwidth from i to j passing k. *normalized queue length* $q_{j,k}^i$ is defined as following:

$$q_{j,k}^i = \frac{Q_{j,k}^i}{BW_{j,k}^i} \quad (2)$$

The sum costs of the shortest path from i to j passing k (denoted as $C_{j,k}^i$) is that of neighbor k to j as reported by k to i add $q_{j,k}^i$, defined as follows:

$$C_{j,k}^i = C_j^k + q_{j,k}^i \quad (3)$$

And then SMR can get the length of a DAG from i to j passing k (denoted as $D_{j,k}^i$) is formulated by:

$$D_{j,k}^i = \beta \cdot h_{j,k}^i + (1-\beta) \cdot \frac{C_{j,k}^i}{h_{j,k}^i} \quad (4)$$

$h_{j,k}^i$ is the hops the shortest path from i to j passing k. So we can define $D_j^i = \min(D_{j,k}^i), k \in N^i$, and get the successor set $S_j^i = \{k \mid D_{j,k}^i \leq D_j^i, k \in N^i\}$.

According to *diffusing computations*, to compute D_j^i in a DAG, each node computes its length using length reported by the "downstream" nodes and reports its length to "upstream" nodes.

3) Loop-free Multi-paths: The shortest length routing graph SG_j^i implied by S_j^i is the *primary multi-path*. In order to balance traffic load, SMR need more valid multi-paths. SMR also defines the routing graph SG''_j implied by S''_j is called the *secondary multi-paths*. The paths included in SG''_j are approximate or relaxed to the shortest path in SG_j^i. Furthermore, $SG_j^i \cup SG''_j$ must be a DAG.

To ensure $SG_j^i \cup SG''_j$ is a DAG, We generalize the work to date on loop-free routing over single paths or multiple paths by means of the following loop-free invariant (LFI) conditions, which are applicable to any type of routing algorithm. We modify the terminology and nomenclature first introduced for DUAL[11], and describe the LFI conditions as follows.

Loop-free Invariant (LFI) Conditions: *Any routing algorithm designed such that the following two equations are always satisfied, automatically provides loop-free paths at every instant, regardless of the type of routing algorithm being used:*

$$FD_j^i \leq D_{ji}^k, k \in N^i \qquad (5)$$

$$S_j^i \cup S''_j = \{k \mid D_j^k < FD_j^i \wedge k \in N^i\} \qquad (6)$$

Where D_j^k is the length reported to i by its neighbor k; and FD_j^i is called the feasible distance of router i for destination j and is an estimate of D_j^i, in the sense that FD_j^i equals D_j^i in steady state but is allowed to differ from it temporarily during periods of network transitions.

4) Computing of Similarity: assume there are many loop-free paths for a given destination reported by neighbors, which of them will be used as secondary routing? It is universally acknowledged that the paths with approximate cost to the shortest path should be adopted. But the problem is how to determine the degree of approximation. SMR tries to overcome this question by using similarity coefficient.

To compute similarity coefficient, SMR needs several parameters to describe a path. Let $P_{j,k}^i$ denotes a path from i to j passing k. SMR uses a binary group $(h_{j,k}^i, C_{j,k}^i)$ to describe the path $P_{j,k}^i$, where $h_{j,k}^i$ is the hop of this path and $C_{j,k}^i$ is the cost of the path from i to j passing k as stated above. Then SMR makes $(h_{j,k}^i, C_{j,k}^i)$ normalized, that means to make $h_{j,k}^i, C_{j,k}^i \in [0,1]$. And let $h''_{j,k}$ denotes the normalized value of $h_{j,k}^i$, $C''_{j,k}$ denotes the normalized value of $C_{j,k}^i$.

$$h''_{j,k} = h_{j,k}^i / h_{j,\max}^i, k \in S_j^i \cup S''_j \wedge h_{j,\max}^i \geq h_{j,k}^i \qquad (7)$$

$$C''_{j,k} = C_{j,k}^i / C_{j,\max}^i, k \in S_j^i \cup S''_j \wedge C_{j,\max}^i \geq C_{j,k}^i \qquad (8)$$

```
00.procedure ProcessEntry( i, m, j, h, C)
01.{i: thisnode, m: neighbor who send the message, j: destination,
    h: hops, C: cost}
02.begin
03.    $D_j^m = \beta \cdot h + (1-\beta) \cdot \frac{C}{h}$;
04.    $h_{j,m}^i = h+1, C_{j,k}^i = C+1, D_{j,m}^i = \beta \cdot h_{j,k}^i + (1-\beta) \cdot \frac{C_{j,k}^i}{h_{j,k}^i}$;
05.       if $D_{j,m}^i < D_j^i$ then $D_j^i = D_{j,m}^i$, $S_j^i = \{m\}$; endif
06.       if $h_{j,m}^i > h_{j,\max}^i$ then $h_{j,\max}^i = h_{j,m}^i$; endif
07.       if $C_{j,m}^i > C_{j,\max}^i$ then $C_{j,\max}^i = C_{j,m}^i$; endif
08.       if (last message is received for j) then
09.         $S''_j = \emptyset, \rho_j^i = \frac{V_j^i}{\sum BW_{j,k}^i}, k \in S_j^i$;
10.         if $\rho_j^i > Lth$ then
11.            foreach $k \in N^i \wedge k \notin S_j^i \cup S''_j$ do
12.               if $D_j^k \leq D_j^i$ then $S''_j = S''_j \cup \{k\}$; endif
13.            done
14.            $h'_j^i = \frac{h_{j,k}^i}{h_{j,\max}^i}, C'_j^i = \frac{C_{j,k}^i}{C_{j,\max}^i}, k \in S_j^i$;
15.            foreach $k \in S''_j$ do
16.               $h'_{j,k}^i = \frac{h_{j,k}^i}{h_{j,\max}^i}, C'_{j,k}^i = \frac{C_{j,k}^i}{C_{j,\max}^i}$;
17.               $r_{j,k}^i = 1 - 0.5 \cdot [(|h''_j - h''_{j,k}| + |C''_j - C''_{j,k}|)]^{1/2}$
18.               if $r_{j,k}^i < rth$ then $S''_j = S''_j - \{k\}$; endif
19.            done
20.         endif
21.       endif
22.end
```

Fig. 1. Algorithm of SMR

Now SMR can define $r_{j,k}^i$ as the similarity coefficient between $P_{j,k}^i$ and P_j^i as follows, here P_j^i denotes the shortest path from i to j, $P_j^i = P_{j,k}^i, k \in S_j^i$.

$$r_{j,k}^i = 1 - c(d(P_j^i, P_{j,k}^i))^\alpha, k \in S''_j \qquad (9)$$

Where c and α are parameters, the values of them make $r_{j,k}^i \in [0,1]$. $d(P_j^i, P_{j,k}^i)$ is various distance. In general, SMR adopts Minkowski distance, denoted as follows:

$$d(P_j^i, P_{j,k}^i) = (|h''_j - h''_{j,k}|^p + |C''_j - C''_{j,k}|^p)^{1/p}, k \in S''_j \qquad (10)$$

h''_j, C''_j is the hop and cost of path P_j^i respectively. When $p=1$, $d(P_j^i, P_{j,k}^i)$ is Hamming Distance, and when $p=2$, it is Euclidean Distance. Both of them is usually configure in our simulations. SMR sets a similarity threshold (rth). If $r_{j,k}^i < rth$, which means the path $P_{j,k}^i$ is not similar to the shortest path P_j^i, SMR would not select $P_{j,k}^i$ as secondary routing and let $S''_j = S''_j - \{k\}$. If $r_{j,k}^i \geq rth$, $P_{j,k}^i$ is similar to P_j^i. When there are no many paths to select, such as in low connectivity network, set $rth = 0.5$, other wise, in high connectivity network, set $rth = 0.75$.

5) Algorithm of SMR: In SMR, every router usually uses primary multi-path routing. Only when the traffic load increases greatly, such as greater than a threshold Lth, node begins discovery secondary multi-paths to share load. In order to describe the degree of load, SMR introduces a parameter ρ_j^i called *load coefficient*. It defined as:

$$\rho_j^i = \frac{V_j^i}{\sum BW_{j,k}^i}, k \in S_j^i \bigcup S''_j \tag{11}$$

Here, V_j^i specializes the mean import traffic load for destination j through i in a fixed statistic interval, and $BW_{j,k}^i$ be the available bandwidth from i to j passing k. When $\rho_j^i > Lth$, here, Lth is a load threshold (usually between *0.9* and *1.1*), SMR begins discovery secondary multi-paths to share load. Nodes executing SMR exchange information using messages periodically. Every message can have one or more entries. An entry is of the form $\{j,h,C\}$, where j is destination, h is the hops and C is the sum costs of the shortest path form the node sending the message to destination. Nodes invoke the procedure *ProcessEntry* shown in Fig.1 to process entries. In this algorithm, the parameters of similarity coefficient formula (9) are specified as $c = 0.5, \alpha = 0.5$, and $d(P_j^i, P_{j,k}^i)$ is specified as Hamming Distance.

2.3 The Algorithm of Load Balancing

We improved the adaptive traffic distribution model in Ref. [10] as follows.

1) Link Cost: In traffic split, we will use the cost of the link defined by formula (2).

2) Path Cost: The cost of the path from i to j pass k (denote as $C_{j,k}^i$) is that of neighbor k to j as reported by k to i add $q_{j,k}^i$, defined as formula (3).

3) Traffic Split for Load Balancing: The ideal of distributing traffic proportionally among multi-paths is adopted. The goal of traffic split is to make performance of multi-paths improved as much as possible. The problem can be come down to find a group optimal proportion α_j^k to minimize the sum of distances of all multi-paths, which is described as follows:

$$\begin{aligned} &\min \sum C_{j,k}^i, k \in S_j^i \bigcup S''_j \\ &S.T: \sum \alpha_j^k = 1, k \in S_j^i \bigcup S''_j \end{aligned} \tag{12}$$

Obviously, this problem belong to non-linear optimize. The procedure of computing the optimal proportion is generally quite complex to implement in practice. To circumvent this problem, we consider one alternative strategy: *Equalizing Path Cost*. The objective of this strategy is to find a group of proportions, and make the cost of all multi-paths equal.

SMR first computes the mean cost $\overline{C_j^i}$ over all multi-paths.

$$\overline{C_j^i} = \frac{\sum Q_{j,k}^i + V_j^i}{\sum BW_{j,k}^i}, k \in S_j^i \cup S_j^{\prime\prime\prime} \quad (13)$$

V_j^i is the traffic load of node i for j in a fixed statistic interval. And then, SMR can obtain the proportion α_j^k in a interval:

$$\alpha_j^k = \frac{BW_{j,k}^i \cdot \overline{C_j^i} - Q_{j,k}^i}{V_j^i}, k \in S_j^i \cup S_j^{\prime\prime\prime} \quad (14)$$

3 Simulations and Analysis

3.1 Simulation Environment

Simulation includes two environments. One is shown in Fig.2(a), which has three sources (S_1, S_2, S_3) and one destination (node 5).

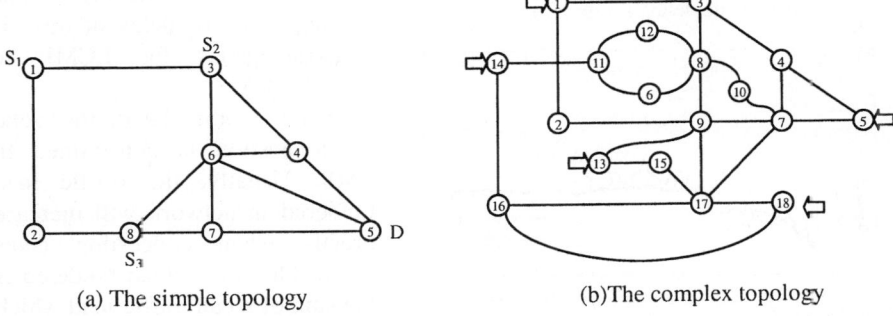

(a) The simple topology   (b)The complex topology

Fig. 2. The topology of simulation

The other environment is shown in Fig.2(b). The topology is more close to practical network. For simplicity, all the links are assumed to be bidirectional and of the same capacity. There are five source nodes (1, 5, 13, 14, 18), the destination node is chosen randomly from the other four source nodes. Using these two topologies, we will compare the performance of SMR and ECMP in load balancing. And evaluate the robust of SMR.

The simulation is mainly to demonstrate algorithms, and drops a lot of details of the realization of the protocol.

3.2 Comparing SMR with ECMP

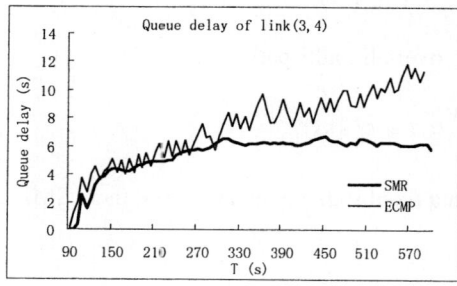

(a) Queue delay of link (3,4)

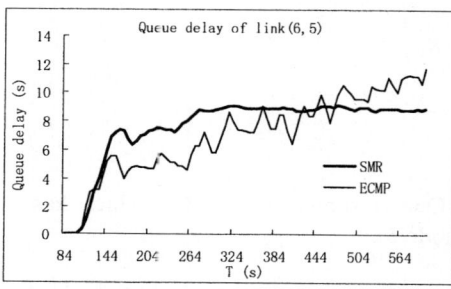

(b) Queue delay of link (5,6)

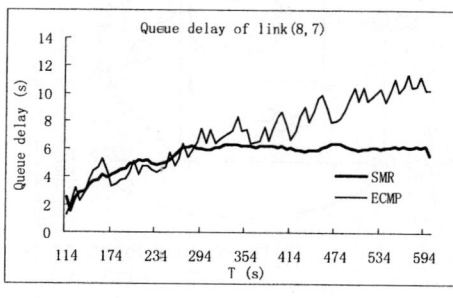

(c) Queue delay of link (8,7)

Fig. 3. Queue delay of links in simulation (1)

First, we compare the ability of SMR and ECMP on load balancing.

Simulation (1): using the topology in Fig.2(a), The link(3,4), link(6,5) and link(8,7) are focuses. The queue delay curves of them increase continually in ECMP, but become smooth comparatively in SMR. That is due to SMR can adopts secondary multi-paths sharing the load in time. For example, in SMR, node 3 adopts paths {(3,4),(4,5)} and {(3,6),(6,5)} simultaneity. But in ECMP, because there is less likelihood that multiple paths with equal distance exist between each source-destination pair, node 3 can only adopt path {(3,4),(4,5)} and {(3,6),(6,5)} alter- nately, which can be seen from the waving of curves as shown in Fig.3. The waving of queue delay of links is disadvantageous for ECMP to provide QoS.

On the other hand, the trend of congestion is constrained in SMR. Usually, the traffic load hindered in network will increase greatly when congestion takes place. The traffic load hindered is the sum of mean traffic load which have not been forwarded and stay at export queue of nodes in a fixed statistic interval all over the network. The quantity of traffic load hindered in network of SMR and ECMP are shown in Fig.4. It can be seen that the quantity of traffic load hindered of SMR goes up slowly and begins to go down. But the traffic load hindered of ECMP rises continually with waving of curve, which tells us the trend of congestion in ECMP grows gradually.

Through simulation (1), we can conclude rough that the SMR is more valid than ECMP on load balancing and resolving congestion.

3.3 Analysis on the Robust of SMR

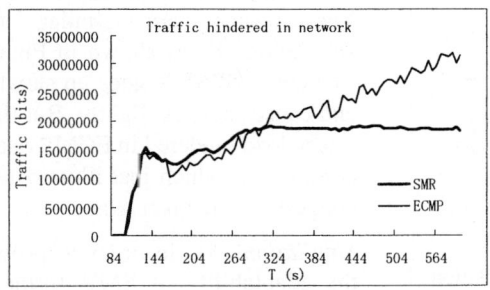

Fig. 4. Comparing traffic hindered in simulation (1)

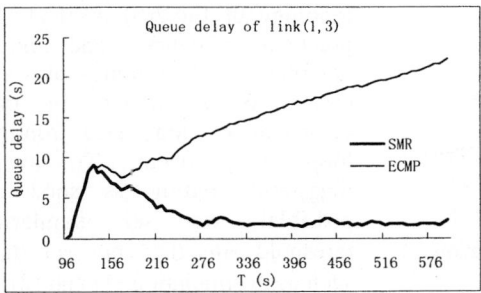

(a) Queue delay of Link (1,3)

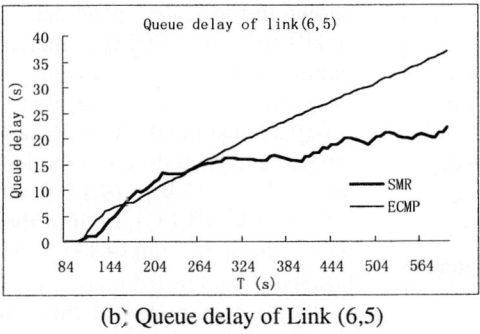

(b) Queue delay of Link (6,5)

Fig. 5. Queue delay of links in simulation (2)

The analysis of the robust includes two sides: one is the adaptability of SMR to deal with the changing of environment; the other is the range of the value of similarity threshold.

Adaptability Analysis: to evaluate the adaptability of SMR, the cost of the shortest path is set as traffic aware or unaware, and both simple and complex topologies are used.

Simulation (2): still using the topology of Fig.2(a), set $\beta = 1.0$ in formula (1), which is similar to the case of the link cost values usually keeping static (traffic unaware) in some networks. In simulation (2), the computing of the shortest path is decided by hops both in SMR and ECMP. But the simulation results are very different, as shown in Fig.5.

In ECMP, according to hops, node 3 adopts paths $\{(3,4),(4,5)\}$ and $\{(3,6),(6,5)\}$ for destination node 5. node 8 adopts paths $\{(8,7),(7,5),\}$ and $\{(8,6),(6,5),\}$ for node 5. ECMP splits traffic averagely between two paths at node 3 and 5 respectively, which results in a half of the traffic load of node 3 and 5 going through link(6,5). So the queue delay of link(6,5) rises quickly as shown in Fig.5(b).

In addition, node 1 can only forward packets through node 3 because the path passing node 2 has more hops, which results in link(1,3) congesting gradually, see Fig.5(a). But in SMR, node 1 selects node 2 and 3 as successors simultaneity based on similarity coefficient, the curve of queue delay of link(1,3) decreases quickly after a peak (Fig.5(a)). And SMR splits traffic proportionally according to performance of paths at node 3 and 5. The curve of link(6,5) in Fig.5(b) becomes smooth compared to that of ECMP.

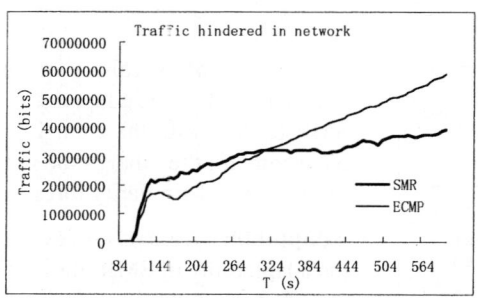

Fig. 6. Comparing traffic hindered in simulation (2)

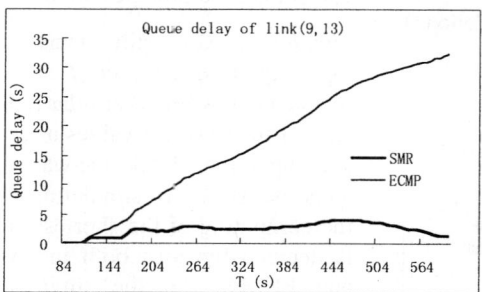

Fig. 7. Queue delay of link(9,13) in simulation (3)

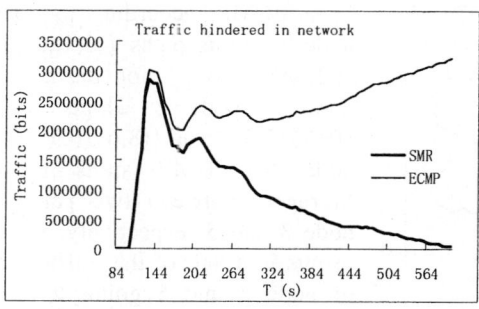

Fig. 8. Comparing traffic hindered in simulation (3)

Finally, we compare the traffic load hindered in SMR and ECMP. The results are similar to simulation (1), as shown in Fig.6. The curve of SMR goes up slowly and causes congest lightly. But the traffic load hindered in ECMP rises continually, which just illuminates congest having taken place.

Simulation (3): in order to prove the adaptability of SMR further, the topology of Fig.2(b) is used. Still set $\beta = 1.0$ in formula (1), Compared to Fig.2(a), the topology of Fig.2(b) is closer to practical network, and more complex, in which multi-paths are easier to be found. In this environment, long-term routing loops may occur. To avoid long-term routing as soon as possible, we set similarity threshold $rth = 0.75$ not $rth = 0.5$ such as in simulation (1) and (2).

Simulation (3) shows us that the problem lies in link(9,13). As shown in Fig.7, the queue delay of link(9,13) in ECMP increase continually. The reason of congestion is similar to that of link(6,5) in simulation(2). Because the paths from node 1, 5 to node 13 are {(1,2), (2,9), (9,13)} and {(5,7), (7,9), (9,13)}, both of them pass through link(9,13). And because the paths from node 14, 18 to 13 all pass node 17, there are two paths to node 13 at node 17, they are {(17,15), (15,13)} and {(17,9), (9,13)}. ECMP divide traffic somewhat evenly at node 17, which results in a majority of traffic for node 13 goes through link(9,13).

But in SMR, node 17 splits traffic reasonably according to paths performance. Thus, the congestion of link(9,13) is eliminated successfully, and its queue delay becomes smooth comparatively, as shown in Fig.7.

Fig.8 shows us the comparing of traffic load hindered of SMR and ECMP in simulation (3). The advantage of SMR is obvious. The trend of congestion is resolved quickly.

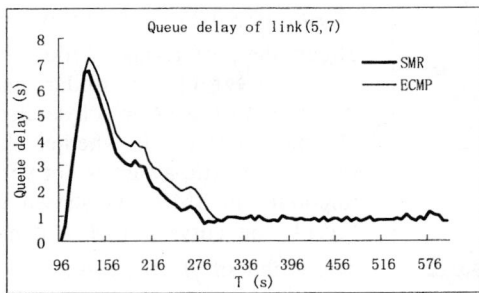

Fig. 9. Queue delay of link(5,7) in simulation (4)

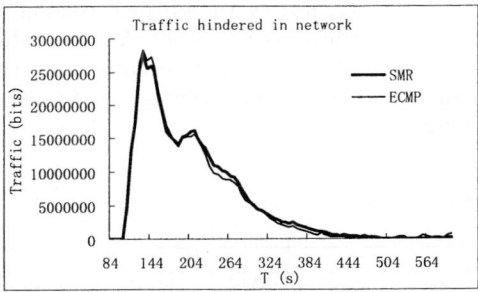

Fig. 10. Traffic hindered in simulation (4)

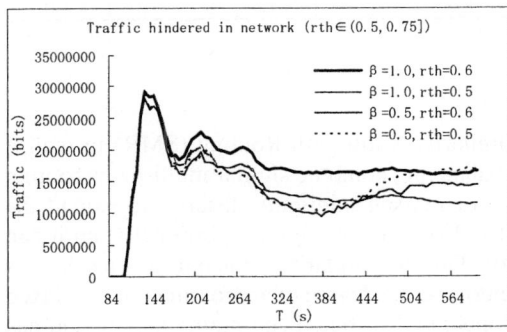

Fig. 11. Traffic hindered with Similarity threshold between 0.5 and 0.75

Simulation (4): the only different between simulation (4) and (3) is $\beta = 0.5$ in simulation (4), that means the selection of the shortest length path is traffic aware. ECMP works well considerably in simulation (4), there is no congest, and no problem link. SMR operates well also, the performance of some links are even better than that of ECMP, such as link(5,7), as shown in Fig.9. The queue delay of link(5,7) is the highest all over the network either in SMR or in ECMP. The performance of whole network is still compared by traffic hindered shown in Fig.10.

Based on the results of four simulations above, it can be concluded: whether the shortest length of path is traffic aware or not, whether the topology is simple or complex, the adaptability of SMR is more powerful than that of ECMP.

Analysis of Similarity Threshold: The range of the value of similarity threshold is decided mainly by the complexity of environment. However, it is difficult to distinguish the complexity of environment. Usually we consider the network with less than 10 nodes is simple environment, and with more than 10 nodes is complex.

In sample environment, the similarity threshold can be set between 0.5 and 0.75. We often set $rth = 0.5$ because there is little different when similarity threshold takes other values between 0.5 and 0.75. And in complex environment, the similarity threshold can be set between 0.75 and 0.9. We often set $rth = 0.75$ due to the same reason.

Fig.11 and Fig.12 show the comparing of traffic hindered in environment of Fig.3. It can be seen that the performance of whole network is related to the range of value of similarity threshold. When Similarity threshold is between 0.75 and 0.9 as shown in Fig. 12, the performance of network is better than that of Fig.11. But if $rth \in (0.75, 0.9]$

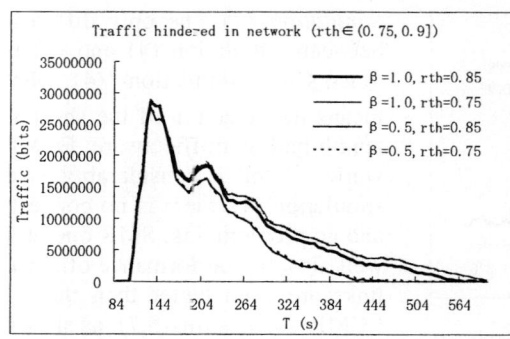

Fig. 12. Traffic hindered with similarity threshold between 0.75 and 0.9

or $rth \in (0.5, 0.75]$, the value of rth effects the performance little. The curves in Fig.11 are similar, and the cures in Fig.12 are close also. On the other hand, whether the routing is traffic aware is not very important in SMR. As shown in Fig.11, the curves of $\beta = 1.0$ are near to that of $\beta = 0.5$ also.

As what have been shown above, SMR has capacity to deal with the changing of environment, regardless of whether routing is traffic aware or not. And the value of similarity threshold does not require us to choice elaborately. So we think that SMR is robust compared to ECMP.

Table 1 lists the main parameters of simulations.

Table 1. The parameters of simulations (1)~(4)

Simulation parameters	(1)		(2)		(3)		(4)	
	ECMP	SMR	ECMP	SMR	ECMP	SMR	ECMP	SMR
topology	Fig.2(a)	Fig.2(a)	Fig.2(a)	Fig.2(a)	Fig.2(b)	Fig. 2(b)	Fig. 2(b)	Fig. 2(b)
rth	-	0.5	-	0.5	-	0.75	-	0.75
β	0.5	0.5	1.0	1.0	1.0	1.0	0.5	0.5
Lth	-	1.0	-	1.0	-	1.0	-	1.0

4 Conclusions

This paper concentrates on adopting Similarity Multi-path Routing (SMR) to realize load balancing. We apply SMR to load balancing, combine similar multi-paths routing to traffic split. This scheme adopts near or relaxed minimum distance to extend the number of available paths and split traffic load among them proportionally, so it can provide better performance than ECMP. Due to similarity principle are used, it is relatively easy and robust for SMR to determine the degree of approximation or relaxed to best path. In addition, the scheme adopts the distributed computing model, and has many properties such as: low costing, easily realization, highly efficiency and so on. In a word, it is a valid routing algorithm for load balancing.

References

[1] Nelakuditi S, Zhi-Li Zhang, Tsang R P. Adaptive Proportional routing: a localized QoS routing approach[A]. INFOCOM 2000[C]. Tel-Avio, Israel: INFOCOM, 2000. 1566-1575.
[2] Guoliang Xue. Optimal Multi-path end-to-end data transmission in networks[A]. ISCC'00 [C]. Antibes, France: ISCC, 2000

[3] J. Moy, "OSPF Version 2", Request For Comments 2328, Internet Engineering Task Force, April 1998.
[4] C. Villamizar, "MPLS Optimized Multipath MPLS-OMP)", Internet Draft, February 1999.
[5] C. Villamizar, "OSPF Optimized Multipath (OSPF-OMP)", Internet Draft, February 1999.
[6] Gojmerac, I.; Ziegler, T.; Ricciato, F.; Reichl, P. Adaptive multipath routing for dynamic traffic engineering IEEE GLOBECOM 2003, Page(s): 3058- 3062
[7] J.J. Garcia-Luna-Aceves and J. Behrens, "Distributed, Scalable Routing based on Vectors of Link States," IEEE Journal on Selected Areas in Communications, Vol 13, No. 8, October 1995.
[8] Basu Anindya, Lin Alvin, Ramanathan Sharad, Routing using potentials: A Dynamic Traffic-Aware Routing Algorithm, ACM SIGCOMM'03, Karlsruhe, Germany: ACM SIGCOMM, 2003.37-48.
[9] E.W.Dijkstra and C.S.Scholten. Termination Detection for Diffusing Computations. Information Processing Letters, 11:1–4, August 1980.
[10] Wuping Xu, Puliu Yan, Ming Wu, Multi-Path Routing and Resource Allocation in Active Network. Wuhan University Journal of Natural Sciences, Vol.10, No.2, March 2005, 398-404.
[11] J.J. Garcia-Luna-Aceves. Loop-Free Routing Using Diffusing Computations. IEEE/ACM Trans. Networking, 1:130–141, February 1993.

Secure Real-Time Transaction Processing with Timeliness Guarantees in Mobile Distributed Real-Time Database Systems

Yingyuan Xiao, Yunsheng Liu, Guoqiong Liao, and Xiaofeng Liu

School of Computer Science and Technology, Huazhong University of Science and Technology, Wuhan, Hubei, P.R. China
xyyacad@tom.com

Abstract. Mobile distributed real-time databases are needed in security-critical applications, e.g., e-commerce, stock trading system, and military applications. In these applications, mobile distributed real-time database systems have to simultaneously satisfy two requirements in guaranteeing data security and minimizing the deadline miss ratio for admitted transactions. Multilevel secure database system based on mandatory access control can prevent direct unlawful information flows between transactions belonging to different clearance levels. However, it cannot prevent the covert communications between transactions belonging to different clearance levels. This paper presents a secure hybrid optimistic real-time concurrency control protocol (SHORTCC). The protocol not only considers carefully the inherent characteristics of mobile environment and the timing constraints of time-critical applications, but also achieves data security without sacrificing real-time performance significantly.

1 Introduction

A mobile distributed real-time database system (MDRTDBS) is, in general, defined as a distributed real-time database system (DRTDBS) supported by a mobile environment [1], where an DRTDBS is defined as a distributed database system within which transactions and data have timing characteristics or explicit timing constraints and the system correctness depends not only on the logic results, but also on the time at which the logic results are produced. The timing constraints of transactions in an MDRTDBS are typically specified in the form of deadlines that require a transaction to be completed by a specified time. For soft real-time transactions, failure to meet a deadline can cause the results to lose their value, and for firm or hard real-time transactions, a result produced too late may be useless or harmful. In an MDRTDBS, transactions are given priorities which are used when scheduling transactions and resolving data conflicts. The priority assigned to a transaction is directly related to the deadline of the transaction. For instance, transactions are assigned priorities that are directly proportional to their deadlines in Earliest Deadline First (EDF) assigning policy. The transaction with the nearest deadline gets the highest priority. Owing to the inherent characteristics of mobile environment, such as mobility, frequent disconnection and high delay of wireless network etc., it will became more difficult for mobile real-time transactions to meet their timing constraints.

MDRTDBS is usually applied to the safety-critical applications, e.g., e-commerce, stock trading systems and military systems. In these applications, transactions and data items can be classified according to their clearance and sensitivity levels, and it is essential to prevent unlawful information flows between different security levels. Conventional mobile real-time database systems mainly focus on minimizing the ratio of mobile real-time transactions missing their deadlines, and don't consider the secure requirements of the safety-critical applications. Most secure database systems have access control mechanisms based on the Bell-LaPadula model, which is specified in terms of subjects and objects [2]. An object is a data item, whereas a subject is an active process, i.e., a transaction in databases, which requests access to an object. Each object in the system has a classification level (e.g., Top Secret, Secret, Classified, Public, etc.) based security requirements. Similarly, each subject has a corresponding clearance level based on the degree to which it is trusted by the system. According to Bell-LaPadula model, a transaction can read an object only if the transaction's clearance level is equal to or higher than the object's classification level, and a transaction can write an object only if the transaction's clearance level is equal to or lower than the object's classification level.

The Bell-LaPadula access restrictions can prevent direct unlawful information flows between transactions belonging to different clearance levels. However, it is not sufficient to prevent indirect unlawful information flows, called covert channels [3], in which transactions can conspire for an illegal inter-level information transfer. For example, if a low clearance level transaction T_1 requests access to an exclusive resource (e.g., lock), which has already been held by a high clearance level transaction T_2, T_1 will be delay. The presence or absence of the delay can be used to encode information by T_2 that is conspiring to pass on information to T_1.

Covert channels based on data and resource can be prevented by improving the non-secure concurrency control strategy. When inter-level data conflict which occurs between transactions belonging to different clearance levels happens, the system guarantees favoring low clearance level transaction in the conflict resolution. In this strategy, low clearance level transactions can't know the presence of high clearance level transactions, i.e., no covert channel. However, this may violate the timing constraints, thereby resulting in increasing the deadline miss ratio. In the above example, suppose that T_1 has a low priority, and T_2 has high priority. When data conflict happens between T_1 and T_2, the high priority transaction T_2 will be aborted for security purposes. Whereas, for real-time purposes, the low priority transaction T_1 should have been blocked in order to favor the high priority transactions. A secure mobile distributed real-time database system (SMDRTDBS) has to simultaneously satisfy the two goals of ensuring the timing constraints are satisfied and the security constraints are satisfied. However, these two goals can conflict with each other and to achieve one goal is to sacrifice the other, so the concurrency control strategy must make a tradeoff between these two goals according to the application requirements.

In recent years, many real-time concurrency control protocols have been put forward to meet timing constraints of transaction, such as DHP2PL [4], Priority Ceiling [5], and real-time concurrency control method based on similarity [6] etc. These protocols all consider carefully timing constraints of transactions, but don't take into account the security constraints and the characteristics of mobile environment. The research on secure real-time concurrency control protocols aimed at mobile environment is very infrequent. The current researches on secure real-time concurrency control protocols are mainly based upon centralized database systems or distributed environment [7][8][9][10], and don't combine the characteristics of mobile environment. This paper presents a secure hybrid optimistic real-time concurrency protocol (SHORTCC) on the basis of the proposed mobile real-time transaction-processing model. The SHORTCC combines optimistic concurrency control with high priority two-phase locking in mobile real-time transaction processing, and introduces the notion of similarity in order to minimize the number of missed transaction deadlines. In the validation-commitment phase, the security check is executed. If exists the possibility of violating the security constraints, the decision of blocking or aborting the validating transaction is made by comparing the total severity degrees of violating the security constraints, which are caused by blocking the validating transaction, with the total severity degrees of violating the timing constraints, which are caused by aborting the validating transaction.

The rest of the paper is organized as follows. Section 2 describes secure control factors and real-time control factors. In section 3 we describe our mobile distribute real-time database system model. Section 4 presents our mobile real-time transaction-processing model. Section 5 presents our secure hybrid optimistic real-time concurrency control protocol. Simulation results are given in Section 6. Section 7 concludes the paper.

2   Secure Control Factor and Real-Time control Factor

In the following depiction, we use CL(T) to denote the clearance level of the transaction T, P(T) to denote the priority of T, ST to denote the set of transaction in the system.

Definition 1. $\forall$ T_i, $T_j \in$ ST, if exist a pair of conflict operations which belong to T_i and T_j respectively, we define T_i and T_j as a pair of conflict transactions, notated by T_i CF T_j.

Definition 2. Suppose $T_i \in$ ST, $ST_1 \subseteq$ ST. If the following condition is met:
$$\forall T_j \in ST_1 (T_i \ CF \ T_j)$$
ST_1 is said to be the Conflict Set of T_i, notated by $CS(T_i)$.

Definition 3. Suppose $T_i \in$ ST, $ST_2 \subseteq$ ST. If the following condition is met:
$$(\forall \ T_j \in ST_2 (T_i \ CF \ T_j)) \wedge (\forall \ T_j \in (ST - ST_2) (\neg (T_i \ CF \ T_j)))$$
ST_2 is defined as the Maximal Conflict Set of T_i, notated by $MCS(T_i)$.

Definition 4. We define $| f(CL(T_i)) - f(CL(T_j)) |$ as Clearance Difference Degree of between T_i and T_j, notated by $CDD(T_i, T_j)$. Where f is a mapping from the set of different clearance levels to the set of natural number.

Definition 5. We define $|P(T_i) - P(T_j)|$ as Priority Difference Degree of between T_i and T_j, notated by $PDD(T_i, T_j)$.

Definition 6. Suppose $T_i \in$ ST, $MCS1(T_i) \subseteq MCS(T_i)$. If the following condition is met:

$(\forall\ T_j \in\ MCS1(T_i)\ (CL(T_j) > CL(T_i))) \land (\forall\ T_j \in (\ MCS(T_i) - MCS1(T_i))\ (CL(T_j) \leq CL(T_i)))$

$MCS1(T_i)$ is defined as the High Clearance Maximal Conflict Set of T_i, notated by $HCMCS(T_i)$.

Definition 7. Suppose $T_i \in ST$, $MCS2(T_i) \subseteq MCS(T_i)$. If the following condition is met:

$(\forall\ T_j \in\ MCS2(T_i)\ (P(T_j) < P(T_i))) \land (\forall\ T_j \in (\ MCS(T_i) - MCS2(T_i))\ (P(T_j) \geq P(T_i)))$

$MCS2(T_i)$ is defined as the Low Priority Maximal Conflict Set of T_i, notated by $LPMCS(T_i)$.

Definition 8. We define $\sum_{T_j \in HCMCS(T_i)} (\ |\ f\ (CL(T_i)) - f\ (CL(T_j))\ |\ )$ as Clearance Difference Degree of between T_i and $HCMCS(T_i)$, notated by $CDD(T_i, HCMCS(T_i))$.

The value of $CDD(T_i, HCMCS(T_i))$ reflects the total severity degrees of violating the security constraints caused by blocking T_i in the conflict resolution. $CDD(T_i, HCMCS(T_i))$ is said to be secure control factor of T_i.

Definition 9. We define $\sum_{T_j \in LPMCS(T_i)} (\ |\ P(T_i) - P(T_j)\ |\ )$ as Priority Difference Degree of between T_i and $LPMCS(T_i)$, notated by $PDD(T_i, LPMCS(T_i))$.

The value of $PDD(T_i, LPMCS(T_i))$ reflects the total severity degrees of violating the timing constraints caused by aborting and restarting T_i in the conflict resolution. $PDD(T_i, LPMCS(T_i))$ is said to be real-time control factor of T_i.

3 Mobile Distributed Real-Time Database System Model

A typical MDRTDBS consists of the mobile hosts (MHs), the fixed hosts (FHs), the location server (LS), the mobile support base stations (MSSs), high speed fixed network and mobile network. The FHs, LS and MSSs are connected by high speed fixed network. Each FH and MSS has a database server that manages the relevant database. The LS is responsible for managing and tracking the status and current location of each MH. The mobile network is assumed to be a radio cellular network. Each MSS has a wireless communication interface and serves a cell site, which covers a definite geographical area in which MHs can communicate with the MSS. All database servers form a distributed database system together to support the mobile distributed real-time transaction processing. MHs have local database functionality and support local transactions processing. MHs can transparently accesses the distributed database located at the fixed network via the MSSs. In this paper, we call FH and MSS uniformly as FDS (fixed database server).

As a component of a distributed database system, each MSS also act as a coordinator of the mobile transactions. It receives operations of mobile transactions from MHs, transmits the operations to the relevant FDS, and supervises the executions and commitments of the mobile transactions. At the same time, it feeds back the results of executions to the MHs. Each MH can move freely within a cell site or between cell sites. Owing to the limit of the energy and the cost of communication, MHs often disconnects voluntarily. After the MHs renew to connect, they may retake the result transmitted by the MSS and continue to transmit the latter operations. The LS records the current location of each MH. The coordinator of the mobile transactions can obtain the current location of the MH through querying the LS. Thereby, the result of a transaction execution can be transmitted to the correct MH.

In order to meet the deadlines of mobile real-time transactions, our MDRTDBS adopts a Main Memory Database (MMDB) as its ground support. In an MMDB, the "working copy" of the database is placed in the main memory and the "secondary copy" of the database on disks serves as backup. An MMDB can eliminate disk I/O during a transaction execution by certain data exchange policy.

4 Mobile Real-Time Transaction Processing Model

A mobile real-time transaction (MRTT) is a real-time transaction that is initiated by an MH, and a real-time transaction T is defined as a 3-tuple: $T ::= (O, C, <)$, where $O ::=$ the operation set of T ; $C ::=$ the timing constraints of T; $< ::=$ the temporal ordering of O.

An MRTT initiated by an MH is firstly preprocessed by the MH to extract the deadline and information of data that will be accessed by the MRTT, to establish the operations requests of the MRTT based on the order of execution, and then orderly to transmit these operations requests to the corresponding MSSs.

Due to the mobility of an MH, the processing of an MRTT may involve several MSS. An MRTT begins with the operation of *BEGIN MTID* where MTID represents the identification of the MRTT. We designate the MSS received an operation of *BEGIN MTID* as the coordinator of the relevant MRTT, and the other MSSs at which some operations of the MRTT will be executed as participators of the corresponding MRTT. Usually, an MSS is a coordinator of some MRTTs and also a participator of some other MRTTs. When a coordinator receives an operation of *BEGIN MTID*, it stores MTID in its transaction queue and broadcasts the message of (MTID, MADDR). Here, MADDR stands for the network address of the coordinator. Other MSSs received this message store the message in their Route Table (ROT).

An MSS maintains two kinds of transaction operation queues: CTOQ (Coordinator Transaction Operation Queue) and ETOQ (Executor Transaction Operation Queue). When the coordinator of an MRTT receives a data operation, it inserts the operation into its CTOQ if possible for it to perform this operation, or dispatches the operation to some participator based on a scheduling strategy. When an MSS as a participator receives an MRTT's operation, it stores the operation in its ETOQ and sends the message of (MTID, N, MADDR) to the coordinator by querying the ROT, where N is the order number of the operation. The coordinator inserts the message of (MTID, N, MADDR) into its CTOQ orderly. Therefore, a CTOQ covers two types of information of the MRTT operations: actual operations themselves, and the message (MTID, N, MADDR), which represents an operation with order number N to be performed at the participator with network address MADDR.

For an MRTT, each related FDS (coordinator or participator) creates an agent subtransaction for the MRTT. All the agents on an FDS form the local transactions set processed and controlled by the relevant database server.

5 Secure Hybrid Optimistic Real-Time Concurrency Control Protocol

5.1 Introduction of Similarity

The traditional conflict serializability criterion is no longer suitable in a real-time database system. We relax the criterion in our secure hybrid optimistic real-time concurrency control protocol (SHORTCCP) by introducing the data similarity and operation similarity.

Definition 10. For data object D, suppose $V_1(D)$ and $V_2(D)$ are two values of D. If the distance between $V_1(D)$ and $V_2(D)$, notated by DIS $(V_1(D), V_2(D))$, meets the condition:

$$\text{DIS}(V_1(D), V_2(D)) \leq \sigma$$

$V_1(D)$ and $V_2(D)$ are said to be similar, notated by $V_1(D) \approx V_2(D)$. Where σ is the threshold that depends on the application semantics, and

$$\text{DIS}(V_1(D), V_2(D)) = |g(V_1(D)) - g(V_2(D))|$$

Where g is a mapping from the domain of D to the real number space.

Definition 11. Suppose that OP_i and OP_j are two operations of concurrent transactions T_i and T_j on the same data object D, respectively. If $V_{OPi}(D) \approx V_{OPj}(D)$, then operations OP_i and OP_j are said to be similar, notated by $OP_i \approx OP_j$. Where $V_{OPi}(D)$ and $V_{OPj}(D)$ are the values of D produced by the OP_i and OP_j, respectively.

Definition 12. Assume that the operations $OP_1, OP_2, \ldots, OP_n$ of concurrency transactions $T_1, T_2, \ldots, T_n$ act on the same data object D, and $V_{OP1}(D), V_{OP2}(D), \ldots, V_{OPn}(D)$ are respectively the values of D that are produced by the operations $OP_1, OP_2, \ldots, OP_n$. If the following conditions is met:

$$\forall\ V_{OPi}(D), V_{OPj}(D) \in \{V_{OP1}(D), V_{OP2}(D), \ldots, V_{OPn}(D)\},\ \text{DIS}(V_{OPi}(D), V_{OPj}(D)) < \sigma$$

we define that the operation set $\{OP_1, OP_2, \ldots, OP_n\}$ is similar.

Definition 13. Let SDi and SDj be two different states of the database DB, if the following condition is held:

$$\forall D \in \text{DB}\ (\exists V_i(D) \in \text{SD}i,\ V_j(D) \in \text{SD}j\ (V_i(D) \approx V_j(D)))$$

then SDi and SDj are referred to as similar, notated by SD$i \approx$ SDj. Where $V_i(D)$ and $V_j(D)$ are the values of D in SDi and SDj, respectively.

Definition 14. Let SCH_a be any schedule for a transaction set $ST = \{T_1, T_2, ..., T_n\}$ and SD_a be the states of the database produced by SCH_a. Iff

$$\exists\ SCH_b\ (SD_a \approx SD_b)$$

hold, SCH_a is called a similar serializable schedule, where SCH_b is any serial schedule for ST and SD_b is the database state produced by SCH_b.

5.2 Concurrency Control Protocol

An MRTT execution is divided into two phases: optimistic execution and validation-commitment. During the optimistic execution phase, all the subtransactions of an MRTT are distributed and optimistically executed on its participator FDSs. Once entering the validation-commitment phase, each of these FDSs triggers a base transaction for validating consistency, security constraints and committing the data locally, replacing the subtransaction. With the support of an MMDB, these base transactions have no I/O in their executions. Thus the execution time of a base transaction is decreased greatly, and so is the time for a base transaction to hold locks.

An optimistic subtransaction *OPST* is a 5- tuple: *OPST::=(PID, TID, P, O, C)*, where *PID* stands for the ID of MRTT; *TID* denotes the ID of this subtransaction; *P* denotes the sequence of the operations of *OPST*; *O* denotes the data set to be accessed; *C* denotes the timing constraints of the MRTT.

For a write operation, an *OPST* just write a new value into its Write Set (WS), instead of update the database. For a read operation, an *OPST* reads the data required first from its WS and then from the database if the data required has not been in the WS, and records the value of data object into Read Set (RS).

During the execution of an *OPST*, the MH may disconnect to any MSS and thus the coordinator will fall into waiting without result. And further, the other *OPSTs* of this MRTT will also fall into waiting state. In order to avoid this situation to occur, when the coordinator is in waiting state, it sends a message of detecting network link state to the MH every other regular time interval. If the coordinator makes sure that the MH has been in disconnection or the MRTT has expired its deadline, it broadcasts a message to abort the MRTT and delete the MRTT's information from corresponding data structures. After the corresponding participators receive the abort message, they abort the corresponding *OPSTs* immediately.

Definition 15. Let $OPST_i$ be an optimistic subtransaction, the corresponding base transaction be BT_i and ROS be the Read Operation Set of $OPST_i$ and BT_i. Suppose RS_o and RS_b represent the RS of $OPST_i$ and BT_i, respectively. We say that there exists a Conflict of Read Set (CRS) if one of the following conditions is true:

(1) $\exists\ r \in ROS\ (RS_o \neq RS_b)$

(2) $(\exists\ r \in ROS) \wedge (\exists\ D \in (RS_o \cap RS_b)\ \neg(V_o(r(D)) \approx V_b(r(D))))$

Where $V_o(r(D))$ and $V_b(r(D))$ represent the values of the read operation r on D in $OPST_i$ and BT_i, respectively.

Once all of $OPST_i$ ($1 \leq i \leq m$) of an MRTT have finished, the MRTT enters validation-commitment stage and two-phase commit protocol is adopted. The coordinator firstly sends a message of PREPARE to all the participators, and after receiving the message, every participator triggers the relevant base transaction BT_i. The BT_i inherits the priority of the corresponding MRRT. For the all BT_i on the same FDS, the high priority two-phase lock protocol based on similarity combined with security check (HP2PL-SS) is adopted to control their concurrent executions, and detects CRS. Therefore, we design four kinds of locks: R lock (read lock), X lock (write lock), I lock (information lock) and S lock (similarity lock). The lock compatibility matrix is shown in Table 1. From table 1, we can know that I lock don't influence other transactions to apply for any kind of locks. During MRTT's optimistic execution stage, each $OPST_i$ firstly applies for I lock to data object that will be accessed. The main function of I lock is that when a base transaction updates the data object D on which a $OPST_i$ has had a I lock and $V_o(D) \approx V_b(D)$ isn't true, the base transaction sends a conflict message to the coordinator of the $OPST_i$; After receiving this message, the coordinator will terminate the MRTT at once. S lock includes SR (similarity read lock) and SW (similarity write lock). R locks, X locks and S locks are designated for base transactions in validation-commitment stage. When a base transaction executes read operation or write operation on certain data object D, it has to first apply for an R lock or X lock on D. If CCM (concurrency control manager) detects no operation conflict, it grants the transaction the corresponding lock; or else if the conflict operations are similar, CCM grants the transaction the corresponding SR lock or SX lock.

Table 1. Compatibility Matrix of Lack

Hold / Request	I	R	X	S
I	Y	Y	N	N
R	Y	Y	N	N
X	Y	N	N	N
S	Y	Y	Y	Y

Let BTS denote the set of base transactions at a FDS, $T_i \in$ BTS and $MCS(T_i) = \{T_{i,1}, T_{i,2}, \ldots, T_{i,m}\}$. Suppose that T_i is requesting a lock on data object D, and each $T_{i,k}$ ($k=1,2,\ldots, m$) has held the lock on data object D. $OP(T_i)$ denotes the T_i's operation of requesting the lock on D and $OP(T_{i,k})$ denotes the $T_{i,k}$'s operation locking D. We use $PCS(T_i)$ to denote the operation set conflicting with $OP(T_i)$, i.e. $PCS(T_i) = \{OP(T_{i,1}), \ldots, OP(T_{i,m})\}$. The HP2PL-SS may be described as follows:

```
IF (P(T_i) > max (P(T_i, k)))    // k=1, 2 ,..., m
{ IF (∀OP(T_i, k) ∈ PCS(T_i)( OP(T_i, k) ≈ OP(T_i)))
    T_i obtains the S lock that T_i is requesting;
  ELSE
    T_i obtains the corresponding lock (R lock or X
    lock), and T_i, k is terminated. If T_i, k is a base
    transaction of MRTT_k, the abort message is sent
    to the coordinator of MRTT_k and the coordinator
    decides to terminate the MRTT_k permanently or to
```

```
            restart the MRTT_k according to its deadline;
    }
    ELSE
    { IF (∀OP(T_{i,k}) ∈ PCS(T_j) ( OP(T_{i,k}) ≈ OP(T_j)))
         T_i obtains the S lock that T_j is requesting;
      ELSE
      { IF (ω×CDD(T_i,HCMCS(T_i))>(1-ω)× PDD(T_i,LPMCS(T_i)))
           Abort T_i and send the abort message to the
           coordinator of MRTT_i ;
        ELSE
           Block T_i ;}}
```

In the above description, ω and $(1-\omega)$ denotes the weight of security constraints and timing constraints, respectively. The value of ω can be adjusted dynamically according to the requirements of applications.

During a base transaction execution, for every read operation, the MRTM (mobile real-time transaction manager) validates if any CRS has been happened. If a CRS is detected, the MRTM aborts the base transaction and sends a message "Non-OK" to the coordinator. After receiving the message, the coordinator decides to abort the corresponding MRTT and broadcasts the decision to all the related participators of the MRTT, and then aborts itself and releases all the system resources. After aborting an MRTT, the MRTM may decide to restart it if possible, instead of permanently terminating it. If a base transaction passes the validation, the corresponding participator sends a message "OK" to the coordinator. After receiving an "OK" from all the participators, it sends a message of Global Commit to all the participators. When a participator receives the message of Global Commit, it ends the corresponding base transaction and sends a message of ACK to the coordinator.

Let SCH be a schedule of the set of transaction in the system. There exists the following theorem:

Theorem 1. SCH is a similar serializable schedule, if SCH obeys SHORTCC protocol.

Proof: (1) Suppose $G = (V, E)$ is the precedence graph of SCH where $V = \{T_1, T_2, ..., T_n\}$, $E = \{(T_i \rightarrow T_j) \mid T_i, T_j \in V$, OP_i and OP_j which belong to T_i and T_j respectively are a pair of conflict operations and OP_i is executed before $OP_j\}$. Let $G^1 = (V, E^1)$ is the directed graph that is gotten by throwing away the directed edges of G that are caused by conflict operations of similarity. Obviously, G^1 is acyclic according to 2PL.

(2) Take out a directed edge e from $(E - E^1)$ and join e into G^1. Obviously, e is caused by a pair of conflict operations of similarity. Suppose this pair of conflict operations are OP_k from T_k and OP_m from T_m, namely $e = (T_k \rightarrow T_m)$. If G^1 becomes cyclic, owing to $OP_k \approx OP_m$, the database state caused by exchanging the executing order of OP_k and OP_m is similar with the original database state. So the ring in G^1 can be eliminated and thus the similarity of the database state is assured.

(3) Repeat step (2), until $(E - E^1)$ becomes empty.

(4) Through the above steps, we can assure that the final G^1 is acyclic. Suppose the certain schedule corresponding to the final G^1 is SCH^1. Obviously, SCH^1 is conflict serializablity.

(5) Because the database state produced by SCH is similar to the database state produced by SCH^1, SCH is a similar serializable schedule.

6 Performance Simulation Experiments and Result

In our simulation system, each MH has a transaction generator, a transaction manager, a message server, a handoff handler and a disconnection handler. Each FDS has a mobile real-time transaction manager, a local transaction manager, a message server, a concurrency control manager, a data exchange manager implementing data exchange between MMDB and disk database, and a main memory database manager. MMDB at each FDS is modeled as a collection of data page in main memory.

In our experiments, we mainly compare SHORTCC protocol with non-secure DHP2PL protocol, which cannot be free from covert channels. Main parameters are presented in Table 2. The main performance metrics used for the evaluations are the ratio of transactions missing their deadlines, denoted as TMDR, and total average number of low clearance level transactions blocked by high clearance level transaction per 5 seconds, notated as NLCB. TMDR is defined as follows: TMDR = (Number of transactions missing their deadlines) / (Total number of transactions in the system). TMDR reflects the real-time performance, and NLCB reflects the severity degree of violating the security constraints. We use HCTMDR to denote the TMDR of high clearance level transactions, and LCTMDR to denote the TMDR of low clearance level transactions. LCTMDR and HCTMDR are respectively defined as

Table 2. Simulation Parameters

Parameter	Value	Description
NMH	10	Number of mobile hosts
NFH	5	Number of fixed hosts
NMSS	5	Number of mobile support bases
NWCell	10	Number of wireless cell
SDB	200 pages	Size of MMDB at each FDS
PD	0.05	Probability of disconnect
PH	0.02	Probability of handoff
Rate	[5, 40]	Arrival rate of the transactions
P_U	0.4	Probability of update operation
ThinkT	0	Time interval which MH waits for transmitting the next transaction after the former has committed
Slack	U (2.0, 6.0)	Slack factor
NCL	6	Number of different clearance levels (level 1~level 6)
RDCL	1/6	Ratio of different clearance level transactions
ω	0.5	The weight value of security constraints
P_S	0.4	Similarity probability between operations of different transactions

follows: LCTMDR = (number of low clearance level transactions missing their deadlines) / (Total number of transactions in the system); HCTMDR = (number of high clearance level transactions missing their deadlines) / (Total number of transactions in the system). High clearance level includes level 4, level 5 and level 6, and low clearance level includes level 1, level 2 and level 3.

In the Table 2, U(i, j) denotes a uniformly distributed random variable in the range [i, j]. In our simulation experiments, priority-assigning policy adopts EDF policy and the deadline of mobile real-time transaction T is set using the following formula: $D(T) = AT(T) + \text{Slack} \times ET(T)$, where $AT(T)$ is the arrival time of T; Slack is a uniformly distributed random variable; $ET(T)$ denotes an estimated execution time of T.

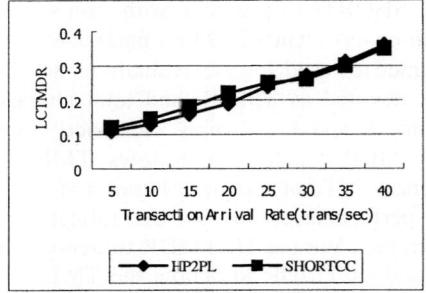

Fig. 1. LCTMDR Comparison   Fig. 2. HCTMDR Comparison

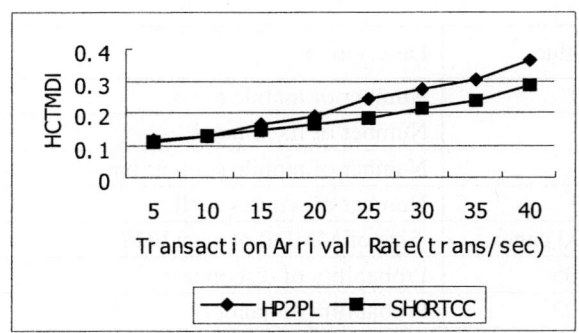

Fig. 3. NCLB Comparison for HP2PL and SHORTCC

The performance results are shown in Fig.1–Fig.3. Fig.1 illustrates the ratio of low clearance level transactions missing their deadlines (LCTMDR) for 2PLHP and SHORTCC. When transactions arrival rates is below 25, 2PLHP slightly gets an advantage over SHORTCC. The reason is that for SHORTCC, when a low clearance level transaction conflicts with a high clearance level transaction, the low clearance level transaction is usually aborted in order to be free from covert channels. However, after an arrival rate of 25, SHORTCC has an advantage over 2PLHP slightly. This can be illustrated by that when transaction arrival rate increases, many conflict operations between low clearance level transactions and high clearance level transactions may be similar, thereby avoiding abort. As shown in Fig. 2, when arrival ratio of transaction enhances, HCTMDR of both 2PLHP and SHORTCC increase, but performance of SHORTCC obviously gets an advantage over DHP2PL. Fig.3 illustrates the total average number of low clearance level transactions blocked by high clearance level transaction per 5 seconds (NLCB) for 2PLHP and SHORTCC. Obviously, SHORTCC excels 2PLHP in NLCB.

7 Conclusion

An SMDRTDBS has to simultaneously satisfy the two goals of guaranteeing data security and minimizing the deadline miss ratio for admitted transactions. However, these two goals can conflict with each other and to achieve one goal is to sacrifice the other. This paper presents a secure hybrid optimistic real-time concurrency protocol (SHORTCC) on the basis of the proposed mobile real-time transaction-processing model. According to the SHORTCC, the execution of an MRTT is divided into optimistic execution stage and validation-commitment stage based on high priority two-phase locking, and introduces the notion of similarity in order to improve the concurrency of transactions. In the validation-commitment phase, data consistency and security constraints are ensured by high priority two-phase locking protocol integrated with the security check. If exists the possibility of violating the security constraints, the decision of blocking or aborting the validating transaction is made by comparing the total severity degrees of violating the security constraints, which are caused by blocking the validating transaction, with the total severity degrees of violating the timing constraints, which are caused by aborting the validating transaction. According to the application requirement, the SHORTCC can make a tradeoff between security constraints and timing constraints by adjusting the weight of security constraints.

Simulation experiments show that the SHORTCC not only achieves data security, but also guarantees high real-time performance.

References

1. Kayan, E., Ulusoy, ö.: An Evaluation of Real-time Transaction Management Issues in Mobile Database Systems. The Computer Journal (1999) 501–510
2. LaPadula, L., Bell, D.: Secure computer systems: Unified exposition and multics interpretation. The Mitre Corp (1976)
3. Lampson, W.: A note on the confinement problem. Comm. of ACM (1973)
4. Lam, K.Y., Kuo, T.W.: Concurrency control in mobile distributed real-time database systems. Information Systems (2002) 261–286
5. Sha, L., Rajkumar, R., Son, S.H., et al: A Real-Time locking protocol. IEEE Transactions on Computers (1991) 793–800
6. Guohui Li, Yunsheng Liu: Concurrency control in real-time database. MINI-MICRO SYSTEM (2001) 1501–1502 (in Chinese)

7. Quazi, N.A., Suan, V.V.: Maintaining security and timeliness in real-time database system. The journal of Systems and Software (2002) 15–29
8. Kang, K.D., Son, S.H., Stankovic, J.A.: STAR: Secure real-time transaction processing with timeliness guarantees. Proceedings of the 23rd IEEE REAL-TIME SYSTEMS SYMPOSIUM (2002)
9. Binto, G., Jayant, H.: Secure transaction processing in firm real-time database systems. SIGMOD'97 AZ, USA (1997)
10. David, R., Son. S.H., Mukkamala, R.: Supporting security requirements in multilevel real-time databases. IEEE Transactions on Knowledge and Data Engineering (2000) 865–879

A New Data Fusion Model of Intrusion Detection-IDSFP

Junfeng Tian, Weidong Zhao, Ruizhong Du, and Zhe Zhang

Faculty of Mathematics and Computer Science, Hebei University, Baoding 071002, China
zwdeasenet@163.com

Abstract. Based on the multi-sensor data fusion technology, a new Intrusion Detection Data Fusion Model-IDSFP is presented. This model is characterized by correlating and merging alerts of different types of IDSs, generating the measures of the security situation, and thus constituting the evidence. Current security situation of network is estimated by applying the D-S Evidence Theory, and some IDSs in the network are dynamically adjusted to strengthen the detection of the data that relate to the attack attempt. Consequently, the false positive rate and the false negative rate are effectively reduced, and the detection efficiency of IDS is accordingly improved.

Keywords: Network Security, Intrusion Detection, Alert Correlation, Data Fusion, D-S Evidence Theory, Situation Estimation.

1 Introduction

Intrusion Detection System (IDS) is a new generation of security assurance technology after the traditional security measures such as firewall, data encrypt etc. By analyzing data, which relate to the system security, IDS can detect the intrusion behaviors. The current IDS products can be divided into two major categories: Network-based IDS and Host-based IDS. But there are some problems in practical application, for example the false positive rate and the false negative rate are high [1].

To improve the detection accuracy of IDS, some scholars try to apply data fusion technology to IDS in recent years. Tim Bass discusses the multi-sensor data fusion technology for next generation distributed intrusion detection systems [2][3]. The research project EMERALD [4] of SRI International merges alerts of different types of IDSs by using Bayesian Methods. But in practical application, it is very difficult to set meta alerts accurately. The MIRADOR Project [1] defines the similarity function which is used for calculating the similarity between two alerts by using Expert System Method, then merges them, but the performance of real time is low. Moreover, Burroughs, Wilson and Cybenko consider the intrusion behaviors from an attacker-centered viewpoint, and present a new approach which track and identify the attacker by using Bayesian Method [5]. But the identification rate of the attack is over 89%. At the same time, the false rate reaches about 20%.

The research of applying data fusion technology to IDS in our country is seldom concerned. How to apply data fusion technology to IDS are discussed from different aspects and some data fusion models are presented in the reference 6, 7 and 8, but the concrete fusion methods are rarely presented.

Based on the multi-sensor data fusion technology, a new fusion model-IDSFP (IDS Fusion and Precaution) is presented in this paper. This model can merge alerts of different types of IDSs, make intelligent inference and estimate the current security situation according to the fusion result. At the same time, it can strengthen the detection of the data which relate to the attack attempts. Consequently, the false positive rate and the false negative rate are effectively reduced, and the detection efficiency of IDS is improved.

2 Fusion Model-IDSFP

In order to judge the intrusion behaviors in the network accurately, we need to combine the information from Network-based IDS and Host-based IDS. Furthermore, the attacking methods have changed from single-host attack to distributed correlation attack. To protect the network security against the attack effectively, we also need to gather quantity of suspicious and intrusive information. Fig.1 shows a physical diagram that IDSFP is applied to intrusion detection.

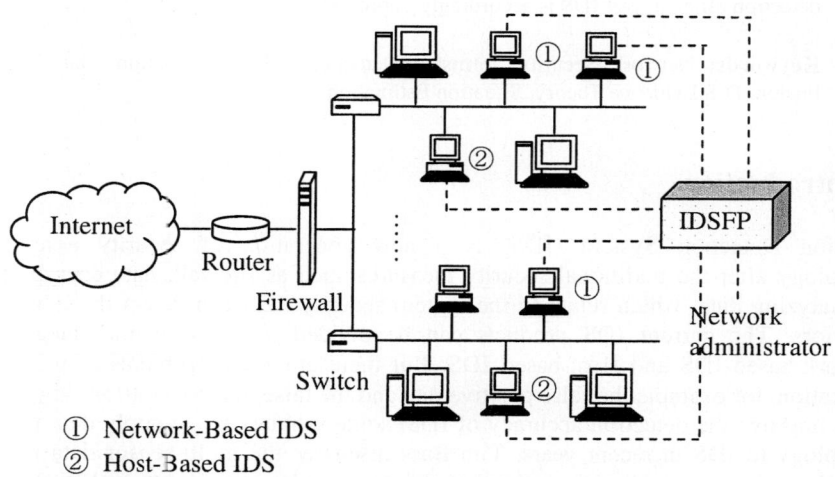

① Network-Based IDS
② Host-Based IDS
----describes the communication between IDSs and IDSFP

Fig. 1. The physical diagram that IDSFP is applied to the intrusion detection

To process them in uniform format, we suppose that alerts which are processed by IDSFP accord with the alert instances which were defined in IDMEF [9]. The fusion model-IDSFP is analyzed as follows: alert correlation module, security situation estimation module and management & control module (see Fig.2).

Define1: Alert track describes a set of alerts which relate to an attack event.

By correlating and merging the alerts of the different types of IDSs or other security products in this model, the alert track database possibly has many alert tracks. On the base of it we can estimate the current security situation by applying the D-S Evidence Theory, and then identify the attack classifications or attack attempts. This information is conveyed to the management & control module, and some IDSs in the network are adjusted automatically or semi-automatically (network administrators also can do this). As a result, the false positive rate and the false negative rate are effectively reduced, and the accurate rate of detection of IDSs is improved.

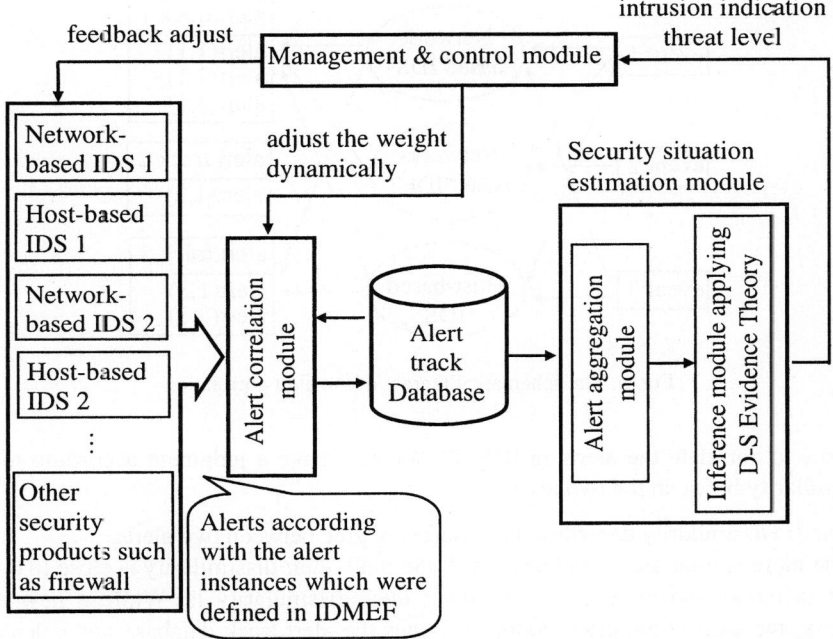

Fig. 2. The logical diagram of IDSFP

2.1 Alert Correlation Module

When an attack is occurring in the network, a great deal of alerts may be triggered by the different types of IDSs or other security products. This module processes each alert corresponding to these attack events and there are exactly two possibilities with regard to the alerts produced:

Rule1: The event also produced other alerts that already belong to an alert track. This means that the alert being processed is associated with that particular alert track.

Rule2: None of the existing alert tracks is the result of the event that produced the alert. In other words, the alert is the result of the observation of a new event and forms its own alert track.

These two possibilities are shown in Fig.3. In this figure, Host-based IDS and Network-based IDS1 detects attack event 1 and event 3. Network-based IDS2 detects event 1 and event 2.

Define2: Alert(x,y) describes that the alert is triggered by an attack event y, which number is x.

So, alert(1,1), alert(2,1) and alert(3,1) are the result of attack event 1, which number is 1, 2 and 3. Hence they are correlation alerts. Alert(1,2) is the only alert produced by attack event 2. Alert(1,3) and alert(2,3) are the result of attack event 3, which number is 1 and 2. Hence they are correlation alerts.

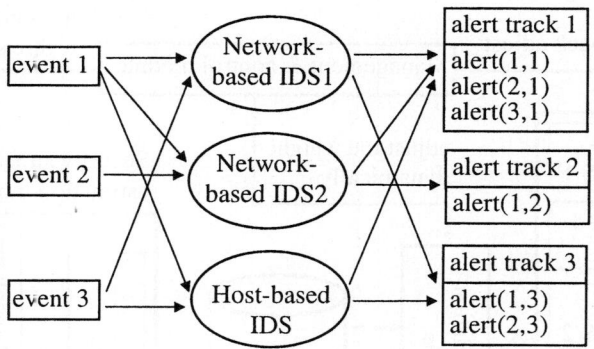

Fig. 3. The schematic diagram of the alert correlation

How to correlate the alerts in IDSFP? We can make a judgment according to the dissimilarity between the two alerts.

Define3: Dissimilarity describes the different degree between two alerts.

The more similar alert i and alert j are, the more their dissimilarity is close to 0. The more different two alerts are, the higher their dissimilarity is. While a new alert coming, the alert correlation module searches the alert track database and calculates the dissimilarity between the new alert and each alert of database. Then, we obtain all the dissimilarities resulting from every two possible correlating alerts. The most likely correlation is the pair of alerts with the lowest dissimilarity. When the dissimilarity is low enough, the alert correlation module decides to assign the new alert to the alert track which the existing alerts belong to. Or we obtain a new alert track, when every dissimilarity which is calculated by the new alert and each alert of database, is higher than the maximum dissimilarity (according to the experience, we suppose an expert value in advance). This new alert is considered to be triggered by a new attack event, and there is not an alert track that relate to this attack event before this.

We calculate the dissimilarity in IDSFP by using the Probability-based method. For the important attributes of two alerts (less important attributes do not attend the calculation), we define a dissimilarity function to calculate the dissimilarity, and the total dissimilarity is calculated by dissimilarity of those important attributes of two alerts.

While calculating the dissimilarity between two alerts, these attributes that will attend the calculation can be described as p attributes such as Source IP address, Destination IP address, Protocol type, Alert identification and Create time etc. The alert has some different types of attributes such as numerical variable, boolean variable and enumerated variable. The method of calculating the dissimilarity of different types of attributes is firstly introduced [10] and then the total calculating formula is given.

2.1.1 The Method of Calculating the Dissimilarity of Different Types of Attributes
(1) Numerical variable
Numerical variable is a continuous variable. We can adopt Euclidean Distance to describe the different degree of two numerical variables. Here, we suppose two alert sets: $(x_{i1}, x_{i2}, ..., x_{ip})$ and $(x_{j1}, x_{j2}, ..., x_{jp})$. These alerts are P-dimensional variable, and their calculating dissimilarity method is given as formula (1).

$$d(i,j) = \sqrt{w_1 |x_{i1} - x_{j1}|^2 + w_2 |x_{i2} - x_{j2}|^2 + ... + w_p |x_{ip} - x_{jp}|^2} \ . \tag{1}$$

Where w_i is the weight of attribute i of the alert, and a method how to determinate the weights of attributes is given in the next section.

(2) Boolean variable
Boolean variable has two values: "0" or "1". We adopt the famous brief match coefficient method to calculate the dissimilarity, and the calculating method is given as formula (2).

$$d(i,j) = \frac{r+s}{q+r+s+t} \ . \tag{2}$$

Where q is the number of the corresponding attribute values which the alert i and alert j are equal to "1". t is the number of the corresponding attribute values which the alert i and alert j are equal to "0". r is the number of the corresponding attribute values which the alert i is "1"and alert j is "0". s is the number of the corresponding attribute values which the alert i is "0"and alert j is "1".

(3) Enumerated variable
Enumerated variable is different from boolean variable, and it has many values. But we may also use the famous brief match coefficient method. The calculating method is given as formula (3).

$$d(i,j) = \frac{p-m}{p} \ . \tag{3}$$

Where m is the matching number of alert attributes, and this means that m is the number of corresponding attributes which alert i and alert j have the same value. p is the number of all enumerated variables of alert i and alert j.

2.1.2 The Method of the Total Calculating Dissimilarity
We suppose that alert i and alert j include p different types of attributes. Then, the $d(i,j)$ which describes the dissimilarity between alert i and alert j, is defined as formula (4).

$$d(i,j) = \frac{\sum_{f=1}^{p} w^{(f)} d_{ij}^{(f)}}{p}. \tag{4}$$

Where p is all the attribute number of alert i and alert j (the number which attend to calculate dissimilarity between two alerts). f is one of the p attributes. $w^{(f)}$ is the weight of attribute f. $d_{ij}^{(f)}$ is the dissimilarity while calculating the dissimilarity of attribute f between alert i and alert j.

2.1.3 The Method of Distributing the Weights for the Attributes of an Alert

In the course of calculating the dissimilarity between two alerts, how to determine the weights of alert attributes is an inverse problem of the synthetic decision model [11] in Fuzzy Mathematics. According to the experience of the expert in practice, the dissimilarity evaluation of each attribute of two alerts is given at first, and then the total dissimilarity evaluation of two alerts is also given. At this time, we can get the fuzzy equation according to the synthetic decision model and list the fuzzy relation equation. With the equation being worked out, we can get the weight of each attribute that is used for calculating the dissimilarity between two alerts.

A simple example is given here. Suppose that the evaluation set $U=\{$Source IP address, Destination IP address, Alert identification$\}$, the factor set $V=\{$strong dissimilar, dissimilar, weak dissimilar, not dissimilar$\}$, and the weight set $W=\{w_1, w_2, w_3\}$.

According to the experience of the experts and network administrators in practice, the dissimilarity evaluations of three attributes of two alerts are given as far as single factor:

Take the Source IP address for example, the result of evaluation is given as follows: 20% of persons think two alerts strong dissimilar, 70% think them dissimilar, and 10% think them weak dissimilar. So we can get the set.

Source IP address $\mapsto$ (0.2 0.7 0.1 0)

We receive the following sets in the same way.

Destination IP address $\mapsto$ (0.2 0.7 0.1 0)

Alert identification $\mapsto$ (0.2 0.3 0.4 0.1)

Combining all above evaluation of the single factor, we get a fuzzy matrix R

$$R = \begin{pmatrix} 0.2 & 0.7 & 0.1 & 0 \\ 0 & 0.4 & 0.5 & 0.1 \\ 0.2 & 0.3 & 0.4 & 0.1 \end{pmatrix}.$$

Then, for the overall alert, the total evaluation is given as follows: 17% of persons think two alerts strong dissimilar, 34% think them dissimilar, 40% think them weak dissimilar, and 9% think them not dissimilar.

the total evaluation set $b=(0.17\ 0.34\ 0.40\ 0.09)$

At this time, we can list the following fuzzy equation

$$(x_1, x_2, x_3) \times \begin{pmatrix} 0.2 & 0.7 & 0.1 & 0 \\ 0 & 0.4 & 0.5 & 0.1 \\ 0.2 & 0.3 & 0.4 & 0.1 \end{pmatrix} = (0.17, 0.34, 0.40, 0.09).$$

The final weight set W can be derived from this equation

$$W = \{0.2, 0.5, 0.3\}$$

We have got the weights of three attributes, which are used for calculating the dissimilarity between two alerts. The weight of source IP address is 0.2, the weight of Destination IP address is 0.5, and the weight of Alert identification is 0.3. The weights got in this way are more rational than those appointed at random. Moreover, they can accurately reflect the weights of attributes in calculating the dissimilarity between two alerts.

2.1.4 The Algorithm of the Alert Correlation Module

Step1: When a new alert coming, the initial dissimilarity $d = +\infty$

Step2: The dissimilarity d' between the new alert and the alert which get from the alert track database is calculated.

    IF $d' < d$ THEN
        BEGIN
            modify d, $d = d'$
        END

Step3: IF the whole alert track database have not been searched THEN
        BEGIN
            $j = j+1$ (get the next alert from the alert track database)
            GOTO Step2
        END

Step4: IF $d >$ the maximum dissimilarity THEN
        BEGIN
            a new alert track is added to the alert track database
        END
    ELSE BEGIN
            the alert track database is modified, and the new alert is added to alert track which has already existed
        END

Step5: Stop

2.2 Security Situation Estimation Module

2.2.1 Alert Aggregation Module

After the correlation module processing, an alert track possibly has many alerts which are triggered by the different types of IDSs. There are mainly two types of relations. In other words, two types of alert aggregations:

1. Alerts that together make up an attack
2. Alerts that together represent the behavior of a single attacker

These are different types of aggregations, because a single attacker can be involved in multiple attacks and multiple attackers can be involved in a single attack. Furthermore, not all attacker behavior is necessarily part of an attack. Why we did see this becomes clear when the relationships between attackers and attacks are analyzed. This shows which attackers are involved in which attack.

2.2.2 D-S Evidence Theory Introduce [12]

(1) Frame of Discernment

The frame of discernment (FOD) Θ consists of all hypotheses for which the information sources can provide the evidence. This set is finite and consists of mutually exclusive propositions that span the hypotheses space.

(2) Basic Probability Assignment

A basic probability assignment (*bpa*) over a FOD Θ is a function $m: 2^{\Theta} \to [0,1]$ such that

$$m(\phi) = 0$$

$$\sum_{A \subseteq \Theta} m(A) = 1.$$

The elements of 2^{Θ} associated to non-zero values of m are called focal elements and their union core.

(3) Belief Function and Plausibility Function

The belief function given by the basic probability assignment is defined as:

$$\text{Bel}(A) = \sum_{B \subseteq A} m(B).$$

The value $Bel(A)$ quantifies the strength of the belief that event A occurs.

Let $Bel: 2^{\Theta} \to [0,1]$ be the belief function, the plausibility function is defined as

$$Pl(A) = 1 - Bel(\overline{A}), \text{ for all } A \subseteq \Theta.$$

$Pl(A)$ is called the plausibility of A, which quantifies the strength how we don not doubt A or A is reliable.

(4) Dempster's Rule of Combination

Dempster's rule of combination represents the conjunctive operation of the evidence. Given several belief functions on the same frame of discernment based on different evidences, if they are not entirely conflict, we can calculate a belief function using Dempster's rule of combination. It is called the orthogonal sum of the several belief functions.

The orthogonal sum $Bel_1 \oplus Bel_2$ of two belief functions is a function whose focal elements are all the possible intersections between the combining focal elements and whose *bpa* is given by

$$m(A) = \begin{cases} 0 & \text{when} \quad A \neq \phi \\ \dfrac{\sum\limits_{A_i B_j = A} m_1(A_i) m_2(B_j)}{1 - \sum\limits_{A_i B_j = \phi} m_1(A_i) m_2(B_j)} & \text{when} \quad A = \phi \end{cases}$$

The orthogonal sum can be easily extended to the general case of combining several belief functions.

2.2.3 Inference Module Applying D-S Evidence Theory

(1) Intrusion diction data fusion based D-S Evidence Theory

In the IDS data fusion, the targets are propositions that are all the possible estimation of the current security situation (where and when the attacks happen). The alerts triggered by every IDS result in the measure of the security situation, which constitute the evidences. Fig.4 illustrates how to estimate the intrusion situation by applying D-S Evidence Theory. In the figure, $m_{s1}(A_j)$, $m_{s2}(A_j)$, ..., $m_{sk}(A_j)$, ($s=1,2,...,n$; $j=1,2,...,m$) is the *bpa* the *s*th IDS assigns to proposition A_j in the *i*th ($i=1, 2, ..., k$) detection cycle, $m_1(A_j), m_2(A_j),...,m_k(A_j)$ is the conjunctive *bpa* calculated from the aggregation of the *n* *bpa*s in each of the *k* detection cycles by using Dempster's rule and $m(A_j)$ is the conjunctive *bpa* calculated from the *k* *bpa*s.

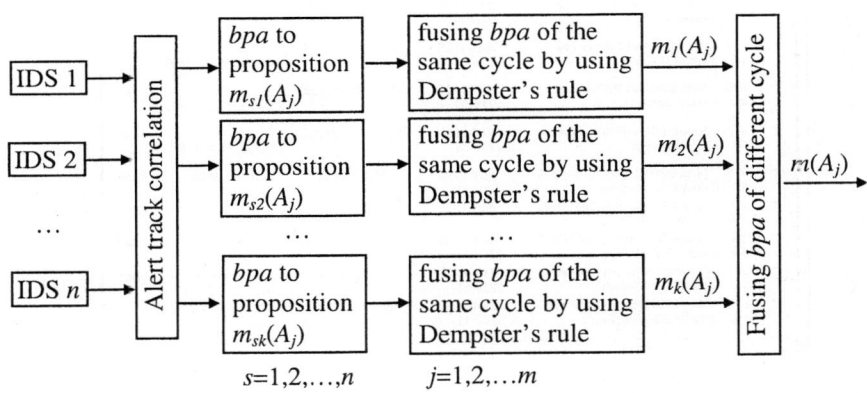

Fig. 4. Data Fusion Model Based on D-S Evidence Theory

(2) The course of fusion applying D-S Evidence Theory

In IDSFP, the fusion process by applying D-S Evidence Theory like this: at first, we ought to determinate the FOD, consider all possible kinds of result and list all possible propositions. Then, the total conjunctive *bpa* will be calculated using the Dempster's rule of combination, based on the *bpa* of each proposition obtained according to the evidence that the IDSs provide in the cycle. At last, we get the belief function and inference by a certain rule from these combined results, and estimate the current security situation.

2.3 Management and Control Module

After processing of the security situation estimation module, we can judge the attempts and the threat levels of the attacks, and whether the new attack events happen. A report to the network administrator will be formed. This module adjusts some IDSs of the network dynamically to strengthen the detection of the data that relate to the attack, and adds the new attack rules to the IDS feature database. Then, the detection quality would be improved. On the other hand, according to the current security situation, it can dynamically adjust the weights of some alert attributes so that we pay more attention to some specific alerts.

3 Experiments and Analysis

We configure the LAN with Snort and E-Trust, and attack one of computers in the LAN. Two IDSs produce the 111 alerts, which are obtained as follows: 85 for Snort

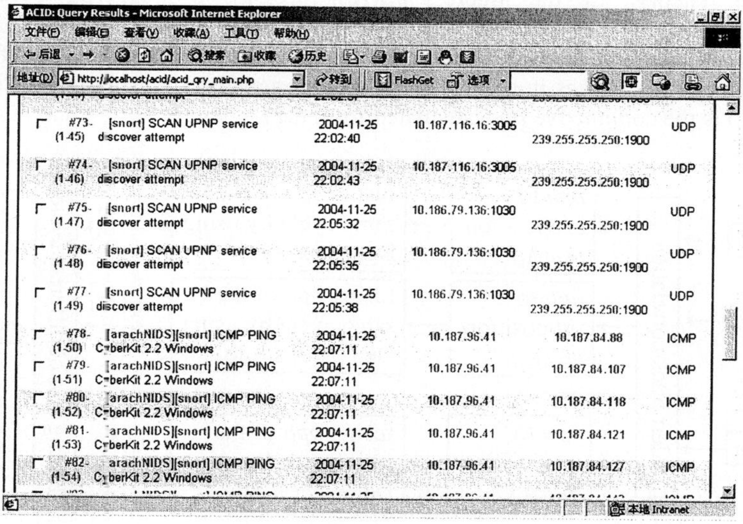

Fig. 5. Alerts that Snort produced in the LAN

Table 1. Alert track database after correlation

Alert track	E-Trust	Snort	Description in detail
1	11	31	Port-scan
2	3	18	ICMP Flood
3	4	8	Scan UPNP service discover attempt
4	3	8	WEB-PHP content-disposition
5	4	14	Udp-flood
6	0	4	Web-Iss attack attempt
7	1	2	RPC sadmind Udp ping

(see Fig.5) and 26 for E-Trust. Here, we uniform the format of these different types of alerts and calculate the dissimilarity between these alerts, and get the alert track according to the calculating result. See Table 1.

At this time, we get the intrusion situation which possibly has 7 attacks as follows: Port-scan, Udp-flood, Scan UPNP service discover attempt, WEB-PHP content-disposition, ICMP Flood, Web-Iss attack attempt, and RPC sadmind Udp ping. The value m of bpa that the two IDSs assign to the proposition is shown as follow:

Table 2. m of bpa is assigned by two IDSs

Alert track	1	2	3	4	5	6	7
m of bpa assigned by Snort	0.268	0.038	0.392	0.029	0.201	0.029	0.043
m of bpa assigned by E-Trust	0.341	0.061	0.182	0.036	0.340	0.024	0.016

The total conjunctive bpa is calculated by applying the D-S Evidence Theory.

Table 3. The fusion result

Propositions	m of total conjunctive bpa
Port-scan	0.354
ICMP Flood	0.014
Scan UPNP service discovers attempt	0.338
WEB-PHP content-disposition	0.007
Udp-flood	0.278
Web-Iss attack attempt	0.003
RPC sadmind Udp ping	0.006

From the result we can find out the belief of the Port-scan, Scan UPNP service discover attempt and Udp-flood are much greater than that of ICMP Flood, WEB-PHP content-disposition, Web-Iss attack attempt and RPC sadmind Udp ping. So we can confirm that attackers are attacking the network by Port-scan, Scan UPNP service discovers attempt and Udp-flood. If judging only the attacks by the number of alerts we may be wrong (as above). Therefore we must judge the intrusion behavior from many aspects. The above ICMP Flood is a false alert produced by the IDS, and a number of ICMP Echo data pockets are produced when the route can not be reached is the possible reason.

4 Conclusions

The current IDS products have existed some problems. For example, the false positive rate and the false negative rate are higher, and too many alerts are triggered in practical application. The multi-sensor data fusion technology is an effective solution to these problems. A new fusion model-IDSFP is presented in this paper. It merges these alerts of different IDSs and makes intelligent inference according to the fusion results. Consequently, the number of raw alerts decreases effectively. The false positive rate and the false negative rate are reduced. The security situation is timely estimated, and the security of network is improved. But how to determinate the weights of the attributes of alert more properly, and identify the very similar alerts which have no logical relation (the similar alerts describe the different attack events) and dissimilar alerts which have logical relation (the different alerts describe the same attack event) will be studied in our further work.

References

1. Frédéric Cuppens.: Managing Alerts in a Multi-Intrusion Detection Environment. In Proceedings of the 17th Annual Computer Security Applications Conference, December (2001) 22-32.
2. Tim Bass.: Intrusion Detection Systems and Multisensor Data Fusion. Communications of the ACM, Vol. 43, April (2000) 99-105.
3. Tim Bass, Silk Road.: Multisensor Data Fusion for Next Generation Distributed Intrusion Detection Systems. IRIS National Symposium Draft (1999) 24-27.
4. Alfonso Valdes, Keith Skinner.: Probabilistic Alert Correlation. In Proceedings of the 4th International Symposium on Recent Advances in Intrusion Detection (2001) 54-68.
5. Daniel J. Burroughs, Linda F. Wilson, and George V.: Cybenko. Analysis of Distributed Intrusion Detection Systems Using Bayesian Methods, in Proceedings of IEEE International Performance Computing and Communication Conference, April (2002).
6. Jiaqing Bao, Xianghe Li, Hua Xue.: Intelligent Intrusion Detection Technology. Computer Engineering and Application. (2003) Vol. 29 133-135.
7. Jianguo Jiang, Xiaolan Fan.: Cyber IDS-New Generation Intrusion Detection System. Computer Engineering and Application. (2003) Vol. 19 176-179.
8. Guangchun Luo, Xianliang Lu, Jun Zhang, Jiong Li.: A Novel IDS Mechanism Based by Data Fusion with Multiple Sensors. Journal of University of Science and Technology of China (2004) Vol. 33 71-74.
9. Intrusion Detection Working Group.: Intrusion detection message exchange format data model and extensible markup language (XML) document type definition. Internet-Draft, Jan (2003) 21-26.
10. Ming Zhu.: Data Mining. Hefei: University of Science and Technology of China Press. (2002) 132-136.
11. Peizhuang Wang.: Fuzzy Sets and Application. Shanghai: Shanghai Scientific & Technical Publishers. (1983) 105-123.
12. Jinhui Lan, Baohua Ma, Tian Lan etc.: D-S evidence reasoning and its data fusion application in target recognition. Journal of Tsinghua University (2001) Vol. 41 53-55.

The Application of Collaborative Filtering for Trust Management in P2P Communities

Min Zuo*, Kai Wang, and Jianhua Li

Department of Electronic Engineering, Shanghai Jiaotong University, Shanghai, China
{zuomin, smile_shining94, lijh888}@sjtu.edu.cn

Abstract. The open and anonymous nature of P2P services opens the door to malicious peers who cause the loss of trust by providing corrupted data or harmful services. The introduction of a trust management system is one of the possible ways to combat this problem. This paper presents some new ideas for the design of a P2P trust management system. Its main contributions include: a recommendation-aggregating model based on collaborative filtering (CF), a polling protocol for trust queries and responses, and the use of identity-based cryptosystem to secure recommendations. Simulations show that our CF-based trust model performs pretty well even when malicious peers make the majority.

Keywords: P2P, Trust management, Reputation system, Collaborative filtering.

1 Introduction

Since the appearance of Napster in 1999, P2P (Peer-to-Peer) applications, especially file-sharing applications such as Gnutella, KaZaa, eDonkey and BitTorrent, have become the largest traffic source on the Internet. According to a report by CacheLogic [1], in the first half of year 2004, P2P traffic volumes in Europe are at least double that of HTTP during peak evening periods and as much as tenfold at other times, and at the same time, P2P traffic is continuing to grow despite the disturbances from recording industry (RIAA and others) every now and then.

P2P is a great appeal mainly because it is more efficient than any other ways to distribute large volumes of data through Internet connections. Another reason for P2P's popularity is that, P2P is less dependent on central servers, thus makes it easy for everyone to share information or to work together with others. The increasing availability of broadband Internet connections and low-cost PCs, together with improved multimedia compression technologies, also stimulates the adoption of P2P file sharing and exchanging technologies.

However, P2P services nowadays are still far from being satisfying, and there are yet many people and companies who are hesitating to use them.

Problems with P2P mainly concern security, reliability, privacy or copyright. P2P communities are often established dynamically with peers who are unknown to each

---

* Supported by the National High-Tech Research and Development Plan of China (863) under Grant No.2003AA142070.

other. These peers communicate directly with each other to exchange information, distribute tasks, or do businesses. Usually there is no authoritative supervision over the trading process and the involving two parties. For a peer who wants to transact with others, there is no guarantee that other peers will act properly as they have claimed. Therefore, P2P systems are extremely vulnerable to malicious users trying to poison the system with corrupted data or harmful services for personal or commercial gains, or just for monkeyshines. And it is up to the peers to protect themselves.

When facing these problems, users of P2P applications must be wary of the quality and validity of the resources or services they wish to order. They need a mechanism to guide them in making decisions such as whether or where to download a file, and whether or with whom to do a business. In other words, they need a mechanism to evaluate the trustworthiness of an item (a peer, a file, a service, etc.) *before* they actually get to it. That is the main purpose of so called P2P trust management systems.

The above-mentioned problem is quite similar to that of collaborative filtering (CF) in recommender systems. CF-based recommender systems try to predict which items a given user might like without using any information about the actual content of the items. But rather, they use a database of users' preferences (implicit ratings or explicit ratings). Similarly, in a P2P community, a peer can gather from other peers the feedback ratings about trustworthiness of the items it is interested in *before* it actually gets to them, then it can operate over these feedback ratings using a CF-like technology, and pick out items that might be trustworthy from its point of view.

Starting from this point, in this paper, we will borrow the ideas from the research field of collaborative filtering and put forward our P2P trust model. The rest of this paper is organized as follows: firstly we discuss some related work in section 2; then we present our CF-based model in section 3, followed by the distributed communication protocol in section 4; we discuss the security issues (identities and keys) in section 5, where we propose the use of an identity-based public key system; finally, we give some experimental results in section 6 and conclude this paper in section 7.

2 Related Work

Along with the rapid development of P2P technologies, a large body of literature on P2P trust management has sprung up in the past three to four years. Similar to [2], we classify most of the existing P2P trust management systems into three categories: police-based systems, social network-based systems, and reputation-based systems.

Some typical examples of policy-based trust management system are PolicyMaker [3] and KeyNote [4]. To our best knowledge, the notion of trust management was first introduced by M. Blaze et.al. in 1996[3]. In that paper, trust management problem is defined to be a collective of security policies, security credentials and trust relationships. The authors also designed an architectural framework named PolicyMaker for distributed trust management. Later in [4], the same authors presented the successor of PolicyMaker which is called KeyNote. KeyNote has been accepted as a RFC standard. However, these frameworks focus more on access control than on resource/peer selection, so they are not suitable for the scenario we are discussing.

Social network-based systems make use of social relationships to evaluate trust. They try to reconstruct a social network which represents the relationships within the community, and then draw conclusions about peers' trustworthiness based on different aspects of this social network. Examples of such trust management systems include group-identifying systems [5] and expert-identifying systems [6], etc.

There are two mainstreams of reputation-based trust management systems. One is based on so called "web of trust". The other is based on reputation ratings.

"Web of trust" is a phenomenon reflecting the fact that trust is conditionally transitive. For example, if A trusts B and B trusts C, then A will probably trust C to some degree. A typical example of "web of trust" is the PGP community [7]. Some distributed trust management schemes, such as [8] and [9], are based on this model. The main point of these systems is to find out at least one path from the truster to the trustee, and evaluate the degree of trust using some aggregating methods along the paths.

The validity of "web of trust" is limited by the length of the paths because degree of trust declines rapidly when the number of intermediators increases. When this happens, it will be a better way to base a trust decision on reputation ratings. The main point is to gather a number of others' ratings on the target, and aggregate these ratings to draw conclusions about the target's trustworthiness. A brief overview of such systems is presented in [10]. The eBay's feedback forum is a successful de facto example of server-based centralized online reputation system. A considerable fraction of P2P trust management schemes belong to this category. Typical examples include P-Grid [11], P2Prep [12], EigenTrust [13], PeerTrust [14] and RobustRep [15], etc.

3 Model Description

3.1 Rating Matrix

Suppose there are n peers in a P2P community, and m items rated by them. Here the items could be peers or resources (for example, files), depending on the specific application and requirements.

Let **R** be the matrix of the peers' ratings, where R_{ij} is the rating given by peer i to item j ($i \in \{1,2,...,n\}, j \in \{1,2,...,m\}$). We set $R_{ij} = 0$ if peer i has not rated item j, and require the actual ratings to be non-zero. A row vector $\vec{R}_i$ consists of peer i's ratings for all the m items. Note that this vector represents peer i's personal judgment from direct experiences. Typically **R** is a *sparse* matrix with many missing ratings, especially for a large-scale P2P community perhaps with millions of peers.

When a peer a wants to evaluate the trustworthiness of an item x which it has not rated, it will have to ask for recommendations from others who have rated the item.

Those recommendations, however, are probably not all honest and reliable. On the one hand, malicious peers may give misleading recommendations for personal or commercial gains. For example: a "badmouthing" peer may give bad ratings to all the others; a bunch of malicious peers may collude to give good ratings to each other and bad ratings to outside peers; etc. On the other hand, personal experiences may differ. For example: peers may feel differently about a file and make subjective judgments on its "trustworthiness" which could be different or even contradicting; some peers may act honestly to reputable peers but dishonestly to newcomers; etc. Therefore, peer a needs some algorithm to have these recommendations properly aggregated so that it can work out a best evaluation of the target x's trustworthiness.

Typical aggregating algorithms include threshold decision, majority voting and weighted summation. Threshold decision is a kind of heuristic algorithm. Some preset threshold values are required, and this usually makes the most difficult part in application. We refer the readers to [11] for an example. Majority voting is an intuitive method to deal with large number of ratings or votes. It works pretty well if honest peers are the majority. But if the total number of malicious peers exceeds that of honest ones, then a reputation system based on majority voting can be easily subverted. An improvement of majority voting is weighted summation, where recommendations form honest peers are honored while those from dishonest peers are punished before summing up. For example, EightTrust [13] weights peers' opinions by the evaluator's trust on them, and RobustRep [15] keeps a separate recommender trust vector and weights the recommendations using the values in this vector.

Here we propose a weighted summation algorithm using the personal similarities between the evaluator and the recommenders – a CF-based aggregating algorithm.

3.2 Collaborative Filtering Algorithms

Collaborative filtering is widely adopted in recommendation applications for music, news, commodities etc. With collaborative filtering, users can get personalized predictions and suggestions to help them find what they want with a higher probability.

Most of today's collaborative filtering algorithms are based on ratings from most "similar" users. According to [16], these algorithms can be classified into two categories: memory-based algorithms and model-based algorithms.

Model-based algorithms are based on an operation called dimensionality reduction. This kind of algorithm first builds a model of user preferences (low dimension) from the rating database (high dimension), then makes predictions using this established model. Bayesian networks [16] and SVD (Singular Value Decomposition) [17] are typical examples. Because the model is usually a low dimensional one, these algorithms can be very instant in making online recommendations after the model is established. But these algorithms all need a learning phase, which may take several hours, even several days long. Therefore, these algorithms can't adapt easily to dynamic rating databases, so we won't use them in our P2P trust management system.

Memory-based algorithms, in contrast, build no prediction models but operate over the entire rating database to make each recommendation. In this case, the predicted rating of user a for item x is a weighted sum of other users' ratings, as in formula (1).

$$R_{ax}^{predicted} = \overline{R}_a + k\sum_{i=1}^{n} w(a,i)(R_{ix} - \overline{R}_i) \qquad (1)$$

Here $\overline{R}_a$ and $\overline{R}_i$ is the averaged rating of user a and user i respectively, $w(a,i)$ is the weight between user a and user i, and k is a normalizing factor.

The weights $w(a,i)$ usually reflect distance, correlation or similarity between users' personal experiences. Users with high weights to a given user can be seen as "neighbors" of that user. Therefore memory-based algorithms are also called neighbor methods. There are several different ways to define the weights $w(a,i)$, typical examples are Pearson correlation and Cosine similarity [16].

Memory-based algorithms may be slower in making online recommendations because the whole rating database must be checked to find neighbors of a given user.

However, they need no learning phases, so they can adapt more easily to the dynamic rating database of a P2P trust management system. Moreover, memory-based collaborative filtering algorithms are known to be more accurate than model-based algorithms [16]. Therefore, we will choose some algorithm of this kind as our recommendation-aggregating algorithm. As for the choice of the weighting function, it will depend on the features of the specific application, such as, the density of the rating matrix, the form of the ratings (binary, discrete or continuous), etc.

4 Polling Protocol

Today's collaborative filtering systems are mostly server-based systems. User ratings are collected by a central server and stored at the server as a centralized database. The collaborative filtering algorithm is executed at the server in response to users' queries. However, things are different on P2P networks. Usually there are no central database servers or computing servers in a P2P environment. So, users' ratings are distributed in the community and computing tasks should also be fulfilled by the peers themselves or in a distributed fashion. This urges an appropriate mechanism for peers to communicate with each other and gather the data they need for trust decisions.

Some researchers propose the use of DHT (Distributed Hash Table) to store the reputation ratings [11,13,14], but DHTs seem to be not suitable for unstructured P2P systems such as BitTorrent, KaZaa and eDonkey, which are the most popular P2P applications. First, maintaining a DHT is too costly when peers frequently join and leave the system. Second, some incentive mechanism is needed to ensure that peers would like to take their responsibility as part of the DHT, but this incentive problem appears to be even more troublesome than the problem of evaluating trust itself [18]. Third but not last, strong cryptological methods must be adopted to prevent peers in the DHT from modifying the data they stored, and this can be too complicated to implement.

In contrast to DHTs, we argue that a broadcast or multicast polling protocol will fit better into an unstructured P2P system. And we've tried to develop a protocol which works in a Gnutella-like unstructured purely distributed fashion. It's a derivation of Damiani et al's polling protocol in [12]. This protocol runs as follows:

Step1: A peer (noted as A) uses the searching mechanism provided by the P2P community to find the resources he wants. When this searching finishes, A gets a list of candidate resources and/or their owners' IDs.

Step2: Peer A picks out some limited number (for fear the query message might be too long) of target items in the list from step1, and broadcasts a request-for-recommendation querying message containing the following information:

      Request::=Issuer_ID | Target_SET | Desired_length
      Target_SET::= SET OF {Target_ID}

Issuer_ID is the ID of peer A. Target_ID is the ID of the target items (resources and/or their owners). Desired_length is the desired number of ratings in a recommendation vector. This vector contains the recommender's ratings for several other items as well as one or more of the target ones. It is used to compute the similarity.

Step3: When another peer (noted as B) receives this query message and is willing to give a recommendation, he first checks his "blacklist" to make sure that the issuer

A is not in that list. Then he looks for the target IDs in his own transaction history log. If there are at least one hit, then he constructs a response message like the follow:

    Response::=Responser_ID | Item_SET | Rating_vector
    Item_SET::= SET OF {Item_ID}
    Rating_vector::=VECTOR OF {Rating}

Responser_ID is the ID of peer B. Item_SET contains the IDs of the target item(s) hit in B's log, and some other randomly chosen items in order to reach the "Desired_length" in the query message. Rating_vector contains the ratings corresponding to the items in Item_SET.

Peer B encrypts the Item_SET field with A's public key and signs the whole message with B's private key, and then transmit the message to A. (The problem of identity and key management will be discussed in section 5.)

Step4: Peer A waits for responses until timeout or enough recommendations have been gathered. It checks the signature for each received response. If the signature is invalid, the message will be discarded as a fake recommendation. Otherwise, the encrypted part will be decrypted using A's private key. After that, it reconstructs a rating matrix from these recommendations and carries out a CF-based aggregating algorithm to draw conclusions of the target items' trustworthiness.

Step5: If A is satisfied about some of the targets, it will begin to requests for them directly from the owners. Otherwise, another round of querying will be carried out for some other limited number of items in the list from step1.

In this polling protocol, signatures on the response messages ensure the integrity and authenticity the recommendations. This not only prevents malicious peers from modifying other peers' response messages during transmission, but also can be a disincentive for them to give too many misleading recommendations, because that can put them into other peers' blacklists.

Encryption on Item_SET in the response message aims at protecting the recommender's privacy. Due to the encryption, only the peer issuing this query message can read the content and have some knowledge about the recommender's personal transaction history. Together with the randomicity in the choice of items in his log, the recommender can feel safe that no one else can get his full transaction history.

5 Identity and Key Management

An identity and key management mechanism is necessary for the polling protocol described in section 4. We do not recommend the use of PKI public key certificates, because certificate management is too costly and inefficient for a distributed P2P system. To avoid using public key certificates, we propose a key management system based on so-called "identity-based" cryptography.

Identity-based cryptography was first introduced by Shamir in 1984 [19]. His original motivation was to simplify certificate management in e-mail systems. In an identity-based cryptosystem, instead of generating a random pair of keys and publishing the public one, a user chooses his name or other personal identification information as his public key. Because the public key is the ID itself, there will be no need for a certificate to bind the public key to the user's ID. A user can authenticate himself to a KGC (Key Generation Center) and obtain his private key. The only purpose of a KGC is to fix the system parameters and give each user a personal "card" when he first joins the community. The KGC can be closed after all the users have got their "cards", and the system can continue to function in a totally independent way.

Here we suppose a certain number of register servers in a P2P community. They act as a distributed KGC of an identity-based cryptosystem. The master-key of the KGC is distributed among the servers using techniques of threshold cryptography so that no single location can get the whole master-key [20].

Every peer in this community should register on one of these servers in order to get a unique ID (it is also the public key) and a corresponding private key, if he wants to participate in the trust management system. There can also be unregistered peers, but these peers can't use the function of the trust management system.

Note that peers only need to contact a register server for once. They don't have to do the logins and logouts each time they get online and offline, as in a centralized system like eBay. As long as the peers finish the registering, they can authenticate each other using their IDs and private keys without the interference of a central authentication server. So the existence of a register server is not a contradiction with the philosophy of P2P. Moreover, the existence of a register server can increase the cost of pseudonyms and so to some extent solve the problem of so-called "sybil attack"[21], which is a great threat to the functioning of a reputation system.

6 Simulations and Experiments

We evaluate our CF-based recommendation-aggregating algorithm by simulation experiments. These simulations are done using MatLab 5.3 on a PC machine with a P4 1.4G CPU and 256M RAM. Our concentration is on the algorithm's effectiveness when facing various kinds of malicious users. We didn't simulate the distributed polling protocol because it only influences the time efficiency and traffic overload but has little impact on the accuracy.

6.1 Threat Models

We consider three kinds of malicious peers (similar to those in [22]):

1. *badmouthing*: these peers always act dishonestly and give bad ratings to everyone else (good or bad).

2. *colluding*: these peers cluster into one or more collusion groups. They act dishonestly to all the good or bad peers outside their group, deliberately give good ratings to the malicious peers in their group, and give bad ratings to all the others.

3. *front peers*: so called "front peers" usually belong to some collusion group. They act honestly during transactions to gain a good reputation, and then spread their malicious ratings to subvert the functioning of the reputation system.

We make the assumption that a malicious peer always acts maliciously according to some of the above patterns. That is to say, we didn't consider the dynamic personality of the users, or the misbehaviors caused by the users' incidental carelessness.

6.2 Simulation Setup and Description

Our simulated P2P community consists of 1,000 peers. (We also did the same experiments with a community of 100 and 10,000 peers, and the results were largely the same.) The peers rate each other about their trustworthiness in transactions. The rating matrix **R** is a 1000*1000 square matrix.

We randomly choose x% (x = 10 ~ 90) of the peers as malicious ones. We assume that good peers always act honestly in transactions and provide honest feedback afterwards, while malicious peers act according to the different threat models described in section 6.1.

We use a binary feedback system similar to that of eBay. If a peer thinks another peer is trustworthy, *1* will be given as the rating; otherwise, *-1* will be the rating value. If a peer has no experience with another peer, the corresponding value in the rating matrix will be *0* meaning ignorance.

To accumulate enough ratings before implementing the aggregating algorithms, we perform 10,000 transactions between randomly chosen pairs. Because the chosen pairs may be the same in different transactions, the density of the resulting rating matrixes should be less than 2% (each transaction results in 2 ratings in the matrix). They are quite sparse matrixes meaning most of the peers do not know each other.

For each of the resulting rating matrixes, a good peer is randomly selected as the observer (or evaluator). Four algorithms are executed by the observer to evaluate the trustworthiness of all the other peers in the community:

Algorithm 1: The observer only trusts his own direct experiences. No recommendation is accepted.

Algorithm 2: For peers he has rated, the observer trusts his own ratings. And for each peer he has not rated, all the non-zero ratings in the corresponding column are summed up followed by an application of function sign(x), where

$$\text{sign}(x) = 1(\text{if } x > 0) \text{ or } -1(\text{if } x < 0) \text{ or } 0(\text{if } x = 0) \tag{2}$$

This is equivalent to majority voting.

Algorithm 3: For peers he has rated, the observer trusts his own ratings. And for each peer he has not rated, a weighted summation of all the non-zero ratings in the corresponding column are computed followed by an application of function sign(x). The weight of the rating in the *i*th row, written as w(i), is the dot product of row vector $\vec{R}_{observer}$ and $\vec{R}_i$:

$$w(i) = \vec{R}_{observer} * \vec{R}_i \tag{3}$$

The dot product reflects the similarity between the two peers' opinions. Thus, algorithm 3 can be seen as an application of neighbor-based CF technology.

Algorithm 4: For peers he has rated, the observer trusts his own ratings. And for each peer he has not rated, the function sign(x) is applied to the dot product of the corresponding column vector and the row vector $\vec{R}_{observer}$. This operation stands for a weighted summation by the observer's direct trust placed on the recommenders.

After the evaluation, an aggregated trust vector is compared with the peers' real reputations (1 for good peers, and -1 for malicious peers) to compute an error rate (error ratings divided by total number of peers) and a coverage rate (non-zero ratings divided by total number of peers).

A brief overview of the simulation setup is presented in Table 1.

Table 1. Simulation setup

Decription	value
Number of peers in the community	1,000
Percentage of malicious peers	10% ~ 90%
Percentage of front peers in a collusion group (if any)	10%
Number of transactions	10,000
Number of aggregating algorithms compared	4

6.3 Results and Discussion

The results are presented in figure1 to figure 3 for the three different threat models described in section 6.1. All the results have been averaged over ten runs of the experiments.

First look at the left part of figure1 through figure 3. The least error rate is achieved by algorithm 1 under all the three threat models, and the error rate remains stable when the percentage of malicious peers increaces. The performance of algorithm 3 and 4 is also not bad in the terms of error rate. On the contrary, the error rate of algorithm 2 increases rapidly when the percentage of malicious peers increases, and it is even worse off if malicious peers collude (figure2 and figure3). This implies that one's own experiences are the most valuable and reliable foundation when making trust decisions, especially in an untrustworthy environment where majority rating will lead to error results.

Then look at the right part of these figures. Although algorithm 1 achieves the lowest error rate, its coverage rate is the lowest, too. In contrast, the error rate of algorithm 4 is similar to that of algorithm 1, but the coverage rate is considerably increased. The best coverage rate is achieved by algorithm 2 and 3. We know that algorithm 1 means depending only on one's own judgement, while the other algorithms mean asking for advices from other peers if one can't make a judgement by oneself. This tells us that personal experiences are always limited, so experience-sharing is necessary for a successful trust management system.

Coverage rate is a very important metric for a trust management system. Algorithm 1 is the most conservative one, and algorithm 4 makes only one step further. They both suffer from a low coverage rate (less than 40%). That means they fail to give an evaluation result in most of the cases. Algorithm 2 and algorithm 3 outperform them as far as this is concerned.

On the other hand, if we compare the performance of algorithm 2 and algorithm 3, we can see that: firstly, our CF-based algorithm (algorithm 3) achieves a comparable coverage rate with majority voting (algorithm 2) even when the rating matrix is very sparse (with a density less than 2%); secondly, it performs far better than majority voting in terms of error rate when malicious peers make the majority. The error rate of our CF-based algorithm increases very slowly (figure 1) or remains stable (figure

2,3) when the percentage of malicious peers increases. It achieves an error rate lower than 10% even when 90% of the peers are malicious. The advantage of our CF-based algorithm is even more remarkable when malicious peers collude (figure 2,3).

Here we can reach the conclusion that our CF-based algorithm can reach a good balance between error and coverage, thus is the best one among the above 4 kinds of algorithms.

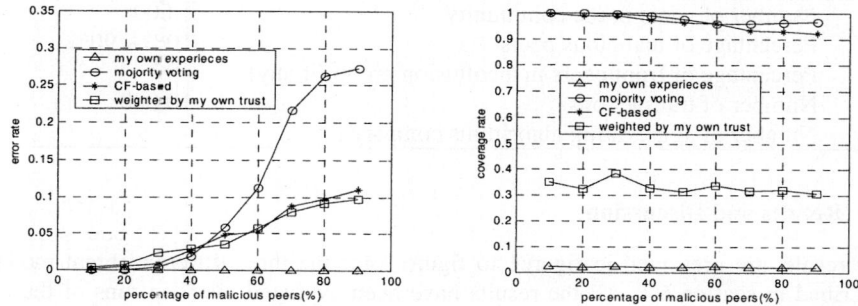

Fig. 1. Badmouthing malicious peers

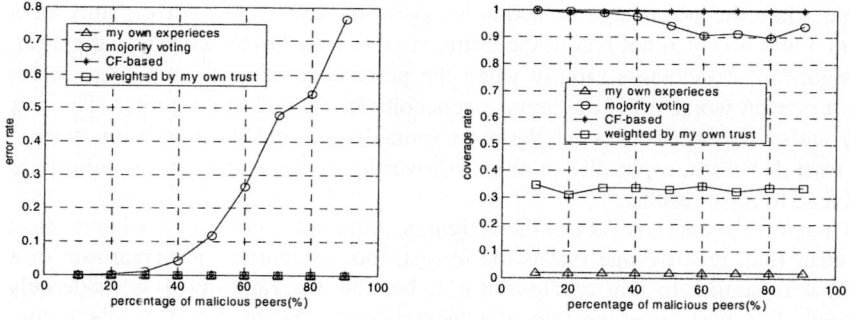

Fig. 2. Colluding malicious peers

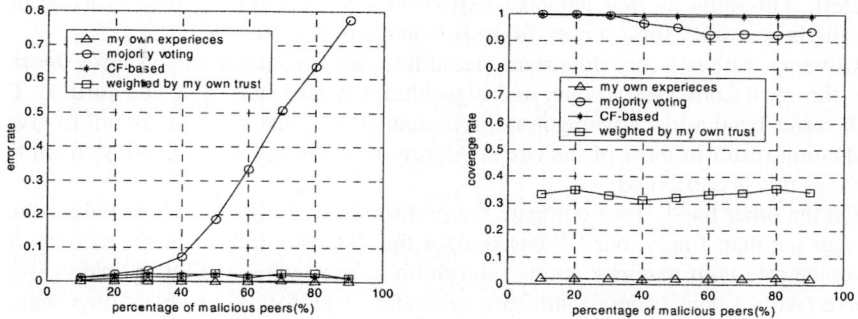

Fig. 3. Colluding malicious peers with 10% of the malicious peers as front peers

7 Conclusion

In this paper, we present a trust management scheme for distributed P2P communities. This scheme includes three main parts: a CF-based recommendation-aggregating algorithm, a polling protocol for gathering recommendations, and an identity-based key management system to ensure the confidentiality, integrity and authenticity of trust recommendations.

The application of identity-based cryptography can greatly simplify key management in a distributed environment. We believe that it is a promising technology not only in e-mail systems, but also in trust management systems on P2P networks.

Our polling protocol makes use of identity-based encryption and signatures. Together with a randomization mechanism, users' privacy can be protected while they make recommendations.

We evaluate our CF-based recommendation-aggregating algorithm by simulation experiments. And the results show that it performs pretty well even when malicious peers make the majority.

We haven't test out scheme in a real P2P application. Neither have we simulated all the possible threat models (for example, whitewashing, dynamic personalities, etc.). The traffic overload induced by the polling also need further study. We will examine these problems in a future paper.

References

1. CacheLogic. http://www.cachelogic.com/research/index.php
2. Suryanarayana G, Taylor R N. "A Survey of Trust Management and Resource Discovery Technologies in Peer-to-Peer Applications". Technical report, UC Irvine, (2004)
3. Blaze M, Feigenbaum J, Lacy J. "Decentralized Trust Management". In: Proc. of IEEE Conference on Security and Privacy, Oakland, CA (1996)
4. Blaze M. "The KeyNote Trust Management System (Version 2)". RFC2704. http://www.crypto.com/papers/rfc2704.txt, (1999)
5. Khambatti M, Ryu K, Dasgupta P. "Efficient Discovery of Implicitly formed Peer-to-Peer Communities". International Journal of Parallel and Distributed Systems and Networks, 5(4) (2002), pp155-164.
6. Pujol J, Sanguesa R, et al. "Extracting reputation in multi agent systems by means of social network topology". In: Proc. of First International Joint Conference on Autonomous Agents and Multi-Agent Systems, Bologana, Italy (2002).
7. Capkun S, Buttyan L, Hubaux JP. "Small worlds in security systems: an analysis of the PGP certificate graph". In: Proc. of ACM New Security paradigms Workshop'02, Virginia (2002), pp28-35
8. Capkun S, Buttyan L, Hubaux JP. "Self-organized public-key management for mobile ad hoc networks". IEEE Transactions on Mobile Computing, 2(1) (2003), pp52-64
9. Richardson M, Agrawal R, and Domingos P. "Trust management for the semantic web". In: Proc. of ISWC 2003, Sanibel Island, Florida (2003)
10. Resnick P, Zeckhauser R, Friedman E, et al. "Reputation Systems: Facilitating Trust in Internet Interactions". Communications of the ACM, 43(12) (2000), pp45-48
11. Aberer K, Despotovic Z. "Managing Trust in a Peer-2-Peer Information System". In: Proc. of CIKM 2001, Atlanta, Georgia (2001), pp310-317

12. Damiani E, Vimercati SDC, Paraboschi S, et al. "Managing and Sharing Servents' Reputations in P2P Systems". IEEE Transactions on Knowledge and Data Engineering, 15(4) (2003), pp840-854
13. Kamvar SD, Schlosser M T, Garcia-Molina H. "The EigenTrust Algorithm for Reputation Management in P2P Networks". In: Proc. of WWW2003, Budapest, Hungary (2003)
14. Xiong L, Liu L. "PeerTrust: Supporting reputation-based trust in peer-to-peer communities". IEEE Transactions on Knowledge and Data Engineering, 16(7) (2004), pp843-857
15. Buchegger S, Boudec J Y. "A Robust Reputation System for P2P and Mobile Ad-hoc Networks". In: Proc. of P2PEcon 2004, Harvard University, (2004)
16. Breese JS, Heckerman D, Kadie C. "Empirical analysis of predictive algorithms for collaborative filtering". Technical report, Microsoft Research, (1998)
17. Sarwar BM, Karypis G, Konstan JA, et.al. "Application of dimensionality reduction in recommender system – a case study". In: Proc. ,ACM WebKDD'2000 Web Mining for E-Commerce Workshop, Boston, MA (2000)
18. Lai K, Feldman M, Stoica I, et.al. "Incentives for Cooperation in Peer-to-Peer Networks". In: Proc. of 1st Workshop on Economics of Peer-to-Peer Systems, UC Berkeley (2003)
19. Shamir A. "Identity-based Cryptosystems and Signature Schemes". In: Advances in Cryptology – Crypto'84, LNCS 196, Springer-Verlag, pp47-53 (1984).
20. Boneh D, Franklin M. "Identity-based Encryption from the Weil Pairing". In: Pro. of Crypto 2001, LNCS 2139, Springer-Verlag, pp213-229 (2001).
21. Douceur JR. "The Sybil Attack". In: Proc. of IPTPS'02, (2002)
22. Marti S, Garcia-Molina H. "Limited Reputation Sharing in P2P Systems". In: Proc. of ACM EC'04, New York (2004), pp91-101

Intelligent DDoS Packet Filtering in High-Speed Networks

Yang Xiang and Wanlei Zhou

School of Information Technology, Deakin University,
Melbourne Campus, Burwood 3125, Australia
{yxi, wanlei}@deakin.edu.au

Abstract. Currently high-speed networks have been attacked by successive waves of Distributed Denial of Service (DDoS) attacks. There are two major challenges on DDoS defense in the high-speed networks. One is to sensitively and accurately detect attack traffic, and the other is to filter out the attack traffic quickly, which mainly depends on high-speed packet classification. Unfortunately most current defense approaches can not efficiently detect and quickly filter out attack traffic. Our approach is to find the network anomalies by using neural network, deploy the system at distributed routers, identify the attack packets, and then filter them quickly by a Bloom filter-based classifier. The evaluation results show that this approach can be used to defend against both intensive and subtle DDoS attacks, and can catch DDoS attacks' characteristic of starting from multiple sources to a single victim. The simple complexity, high classification speed and low storage requirements make it especially suitable for DDoS defense in high-speed networks.

1 Introduction

Computer networks and the Internet have now evolved into a ubiquitous information infrastructure. High-speed backbones and local area networks (wired or wireless) provide the end-user with bandwidths that increase rapidly, linking millions of end-users to many critical services. In the past a few years, companies, organizations and government agencies have been attacked by successive waves of Distributed Denial of Service (DDoS) attacks [7] [23]. A DDoS attack is characterized by an explicit attempt from an attacker to prevent legitimate users from using the desired resource [4].

The rapid development of high-speed networks has spurred new applications and has in turn been driven by the popularity of those applications. However, it also provides DDoS attackers advantages to start an attack. Although many defense approaches have been proposed to fight against DDoS attacks, such as filtering [5] [25], traceback [1], congestion control [6] [8] and replication [33] [27]. It is still difficult to separate unambiguously the attack traffics from legitimate traffics, and then remove the attack traffic, especially when the traffic volume is high. There are two major challenges on DDoS defense in the high-speed networks. One is to sensitively and accurately detect attack traffic, and the other is to quickly filter out the attack traffic, which mainly depends on high-speed packet classification [11]. Here packet classification means the process of categorizing packets into normal or attack flows in a router. Since packet classification has been one of the major bottlenecks in routers that provide security services, a fast packet classification algorithm is critical to a router-based DDoS defense system.

We use neural network to differentiate normal and abnormal traffic. By the aid of the marks of a traceback scheme, Flexible Deterministic Packet Marking (FDPM), in the IP header [30], the system separates the attack packets from the legitimate packets. Our contributions are that we explore neural network methods on DDoS defense in high-speed networks and propose a Bloom filter-based packet classification scheme for the implementation of the filtering system. The experimental evaluations show that the system can sensitively and accurately detect DDoS packets, quickly filter out the packets in a high-speed network (eg. 7.6 Gb/s), accordingly greatly improve the legitimate traffic throughput and reduce attack traffic throughput.

2 Related Work

Many methods have been proposed to detect network anomalies caused by DDoS attacks. Statistical method requires a strong assumption that the network traffic variables obey a Normal Distribution [17] to detect anomalies. Nonparametric Cumulative Sum (CUSUM) method [26] is stateless, lightweight, and sensitive to persistent sudden changes caused by DDoS attacks instead of Internet flash crowd. However, this method can only consider one network feature, and can only deal with the change point problem (eg. sudden increase of a variable). If the network anomaly is not an intensive flood, this method may not discover the attack timely. Rather than analyzing the change of features such as traffic volume, multivariate correlation analysis [14] [34] that is proposed to detect subtle DDoS attacks considers the correlations among the features. However, there is no theoretical proof to decide which features are valid for the correlation models and how important each feature is. Additionally, these methods can only represent the changes of correlation, but not the causality between those changes and attacks.

Many researches have been done on building the rules to filtering the DDoS packets, such as Ingress filtering [5], Distributed Packet Filtering (DPF) [25], Hop-Count Filtering (HCF) [13], RED [6] and RED-related schemes [24] [18], Path Identifier (PI) [32] and Deterministic Bit Marking (DBM) [15]. However, these approaches are mostly affected by the distance in number of router hops, resulting in low detection rate if the attacks come from hosts that are far away from the victim. Additionally, they limit the attack bandwidth by the rate of attack-bearing path signatures, which is based on the assumption that the more attack traffic the more legitimate traffic can pass through.

Fast packet classification is another important issue to deal with the DDoS attacks, which is inherently difficult. The task of packet classification is to forward packets according to the set of rules quickly. Linear time search or parallelisms are used to search through all rules sequentially, such as multi-dimensional range matching [16] and Ternary-CAMs [19]. However, these solutions will be expensive when the DDoS filtering rule sets are large. Heuristic methods such as Recursive Flow Classification (RFC) [9], Hierarchical Intelligent Cuttings (HiCuts) [10], and Tuple Space Search [28] have lower complexity in worst-case time requirements than linear search schemes. However, other limitations such as storage requirements and scalabilities make them unsatisfactory for fast packet filtering on DDoS problems.

3 System Design

3.1 Overview

We are not going to discuss the Flexible Deterministic Packet Marking (FDPM) [30] in detail in this paper. The FDPM encoding modules are deployed at the edge routers that are close to the attack source end. When packets enter the network, they are dynamically marked by the encoding modules. The real source IP addresses of the entry points are stored in the marking fields. When the packets reach the victim end, the source IP addresses of entry points can be reconstructed. As it is shown in figure 1, the system is deployed between the source end (one hop behind FDPM encoding module) and the victim end. Incoming packets are tapped into both Offline Training System (OTS) and Online Filtering System (OFS). OTS is a lightweight neural network [22] with back-propagation algorithm [12], which consists of three parts, data collecting part, training part and rules generating part. It is usually deployed close to the victim end, in order to obtain better training result. The trained neural networks are transferred back to OFS for testing. Once the packets are identified as the attack packets, they can be filtered out by the Bloom filter-based packet processing part.

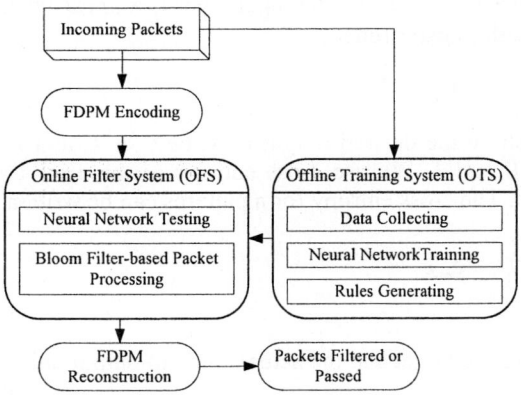

Fig. 1. System architecture

There are two key ideas to solve the challenges we introduced in Section 1. One is the application of neural network to detect network anomalies. As it is shown before, in the marks that FDPM uses, the address digest bits in different IP packets are always the same for one entry point. If the attacker sends attack packets, in a large traffic volume (eg. 3GBps), or in a certain rate (eg. 300KBps), through one entry point, there will be a special pattern of marked packets with the same destination IP address and address digest bits. Therefore, in a global view, there will be a pattern with several groups of packets with corresponding address digest bits, and the same destination IP address. The pattern reflexes clearly the character of DDoS traffics that come from multiple sources and aggregate at one destination.

The other is the fast packet classification by using Bloom filter [3]. In DDoS packet filtering problems, packet classification becomes a two-category classification process. While Bloom filter provides good space and speed efficiencies with low false positives, it gives a fast decision making function to filter the attack packets. The OFS can be deployed at any point in the protected network. If it is deployed close to the attack source end, it can protect even better the rest of network from it to victim, because the attack traffic has been removed before it travels to the victim, without causing overall network congestion.

3.2 Neural Network

A 3-layer neural network is used in this DDoS defense system. Here we introduce the design of this neural network. More details such as parameter tuning can be found in [31]. There are input layer, hidden layer and output layer in this neural network. The number of the units in the input layer is dictated by the dimensionality of the input vectors (features of traffic). There is one unit in the output layer, representing a value between 0 and 1 (legitimate and attack traffic, respectively). Theoretically, more hidden units can deal with more complex nonlinear problem. However, the training error and test error should be small enough while moderate number of hidden units is chosen. After tuning in the experiments, we found the optimal value of number of hidden units is between 19 and 21. The input layer is a linear layer and the other two are sigmoid layer with transfer function

$$y = 1/(1+e^{-x}), \quad y \in (0,1) \tag{1}$$

In the training phase the desired output must be 0 or 1, and in the test phase the output is between 0 and 1. We use cross entropy as the error criterion function to control the iteration. The cross entropy for n patterns can be written as

$$J(\mathbf{w}) = \sum_{m=1}^{n} t_m \ln(t_m / z_m) \tag{2}$$

where t_m and z_m are the target and the actual value of output unit for pattern m, when there is 1 output unit; w is the weight. The optimal learning rate η_{opt} that satisfies the requirement of convergence and minimum training error can be written as

$$\eta_{opt} = (\frac{\partial^2 J}{\partial w^2})^{-1} \tag{3}$$

In terms of minimum Bayes error [2] the features of input with good discriminatory power can be chosen. However, selecting features by Bayes error is much less effective in non-linear classifiers than linear classifiers because in practice it is difficult to know the class probability densities. In [21] a Support Vector Machine (SVM) approach is used to rank the features. In this paper we use some extracted network traffic features with high ranks in the previous reference and some features by experience, as the input of the neural network for training and test (as shown in table 1), and let the output as the likelihood of attack packets. We apply time window to collect the information of network traffic. Besides the common packet features, the mark (address digest bits) that the FDPM writes into the IP header, is also concerned. Let

$$x_{mark} = Number\_of\_Packets / Number\_of\_digests \tag{4}$$

This feature means the concentration of the packets that have same digest bits. In practice, we adjust the scale of this special feature, to make the neural network adjust weights from it more than other features during training, because if the neural network prefers this feature over the others, it will be more sensitive to DDoS attacks, according to our experiments. We just simply let

$$x'_{mark} = \beta x_{mark} \tag{5}$$

where x'_{mark} and x_{mark} are the adjusted mark feature and the original mark feature respectively, and β is the scaling ratio.

Table 1. Features used in neural network

Feature	Description	Protocol
SrcIP	Number of source IP address	Any
DestIP	Number of destination IP address	Any
SrcPort	Number of source port	Any
DestPort	Number of destination port	Any
Length	Total length of packets	Any
Chksum	Number of wrong checksum	Any
SYN	Number of SYN flag	TCP
FIN	Number of FIN flag	TCP
ACK	Number of ACK flag	TCP
Mark	Concentration of the packets with same digest bits	Any

3.3 Bloom Filter

A Bloom filter is a simple space-efficient randomized data structure for representing a set in order to support membership queries [3]. The space efficiency is achieved at the cost of a small probability of false positives. Here we briefly first introduce the Bloom filter theory and then the application of it in packet classification.

A Bloom filter has a set $S = \{x_1, x_2, \ldots, x_n\}$ of n elements by an array of m bits, initially all set to 0. It uses k independent hash function $h_1, \ldots h_k$ with range $\{1, \ldots, m\}$. Here we have an assumption that hash functions are perfectly random. For each element $x \in S$, the bits $h_i(x)$ are set to 1 for $1 \leq i \leq k$. A location can be set to 1 multiple times, but only the first change has an effect. For the membership query if $y \in S$, we check if $\forall i, h_i(y) = 1$. If $\exists h_i(i) \neq 1$, then $y \notin S$. If $\forall i, h_i(y) = 1$ is true, we can assume $y \in S$ with a false positive rate as

$$f = \left(1-\left(1-\frac{1}{m}\right)^{kn}\right)^k \approx \left(1-e^{-\frac{kn}{m}}\right)^k = \exp(k\ln(1-e^{-kn/m}))$$

(6)

Let $g = k\ln(1-e^{-kn/m})$ and we have

$$\frac{dg}{dk} = \ln(1-e^{-kn/m}) + \frac{kn}{m}\frac{e^{-kn/m}}{1-e^{-kn/m}}$$

(7)

Because minimizing the f is equivalent to minimizing g with respect to k, we have when the above equation equals 0, $k = \ln 2 \cdot (m/n)$. The optimized false positive is $(0.6185)^{m/n}$.

3.4 Online Filtering System (OFS)

The Online Filtering System (OFS) is key sub-system that enables the filtering function. We test the incoming packets by the trained neural network that transferred from the Offline Training System. If the output indicates anomalies, we further investigate the composition of marked packets. If the number of packets that have the same address digest bits exceeds a threshold N_{drop} (this value is decided by experience), this flow of packets will be filtered. This two-step design can not only protect legitimate traffic that shares a large portion of bandwidth but also punish entirely the attack traffic. First, because the anomaly detection is performed by a nonlinear neural network classifier with the assistance of concentration of the packets of same digest bits, the legitimate traffic will be less likely decided as an anomaly than by other coarse granite classifier such as statistical model. Second, once the attack traffic flow is identified, this flow can be totally filtered by differentiating the identity – address digest bits that FDPM marks.

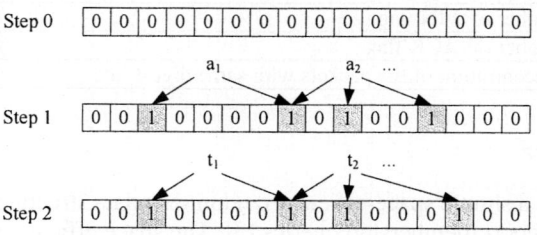

Fig. 2. Bloom filter-based packet classification

After the attack packets are identified, it turns into the packet classification phase. As it is shown figure 2, the filter begins as an array of all 0's in step 0. The attack packets $a_i, i \in [1, n]$ are hashed k times, with each hash the corresponding bit turns into 1 in step 1. Then in step 2, for each incoming packet $t_i, i \in [1, m]$, if any hashed bit is not equal to the corresponding bit in the preset array, then it means the packet does not belong to attack packets. On the other side, if all hashed bits are within the bits of value 1, then the packet is either an attack packet or a false positive.

4 Performance Evaluations

4.1 Detection Performance

To test the capability of the neural network to find anomalies, we conduct experiments by using public data sets. Two sources of data sets are used in the experiments. One is 1998 DARPA Intrusion Detection Evaluation Data Set at Lincoln laboratory, MIT [20]. The other is sanitized UCLA CSD traffic traces from D-WARD project [29]. We train the neural network by clean training data, and then apply the trained neural network to test the attack data.

The MIT data sets are in tcpdump format, we extract the features of interest with time window of 10 seconds. The training data include one week data and a four-hour subset of training data. The features include all the features in table 1 except Mark. We will investigate effects of the mark feature in the later section. The UCLA data sets are in plain text format, each row represents a packet. The features extracted are SrcIP, DestIP, SrcPort, DestPort, and Length. The attack traffic is generated by TFN DDoS tool. We test different types of attacks (maximum attack rate is 300KBps) as in table 2.

Table 2. Attack type in UCLA data sets

Attack type	Description
Constant rate attack	The maximum rate is achieved immediately and maintained until the attack is stopped
Pulsing attack	The attack rate oscillates between the maximum rate and zero. The duration of active and inactive period is the same - 100 seconds
Increasing rate attack	The maximum rate is achieved gradually over 300 seconds and is maintained until the attack is stopped

By using different training data set and testing data set, we obtain the fitted ROC curves as follows. A ROC curve is a plot with the false positive rate on the X axis and the true positive rate on the Y axis. It can reflect the sensitivity of the neural network by measuring the area below the curve. The point (0, 1) is the perfect classifier: it classifies all positive cases and negative cases correctly. It is (0, 1) because the false positive rate is 0 (none), and the true positive rate is 1 (all). From the following figures we can see under each situation the area below the curve is nearly equal to 1, which proofs the neural network approach can detect anomalies sensitively and accurately.

4.2 Filtering Performance

\The ultimate goals are to find out the attack traffic as accurately as possible, and to filter out the attack traffic as much as possible and at the mean time let as much legitimate traffic pass through as possible (but not to detect anomalies). Therefore, the performance metrics are average value of legitimate traffic passed rate (LTPR) and attack traffic passed rate (ATPR) of distributed filtering systems. Let

$$LTPR = Number\_of\_legitimate\_packets\_passed / Number\_of\_total\_legitimate\_packets \qquad (8)$$

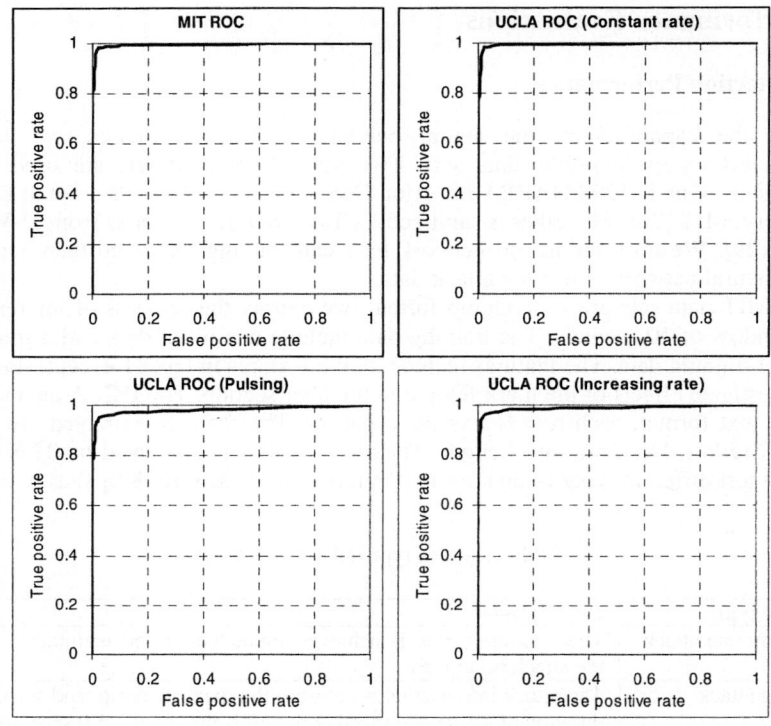

Fig. 3. MIT and UCLA ROC curves

$$ATPR = {Number\_of\_attack\_packets\_passed}/{Number\_of\_total\_attack\_packets} \tag{9}$$

We deploy the mark-aided distributed filtering system at different distances from the victim and conduct experiments based on both TFN2K and Trinoo DDoS simulator tools. Random algorithms in SSFNet are used to generate legitimate traffic. After the neural network is trained, the DDoS tools are initiated to start the attack with 300KBps attack rate. Then the traffics on the deployment points are monitored. The following figures show the average values of LTPR and ATPR at routers that locate at different hops from the victim. From the figures we can see our scheme can filter out most of the attack traffic and let most of the legitimate traffic pass through. These two figures also show that both LTPR and ATPR decrease slightly if the defense systems are deployed close to the attack source end. This proofs our system can be deployed at any place in the protect network. Actually, if the filtering system is deployed close to the attack source end, it can protect the rest of the network from congestion.

FDPM can change its marking rate dynamically at its encoding modules according to the load of participating routers. This ability can intelligently find the most possible attack packets to be marked. From figure 5 we can see that the performance of LTPR

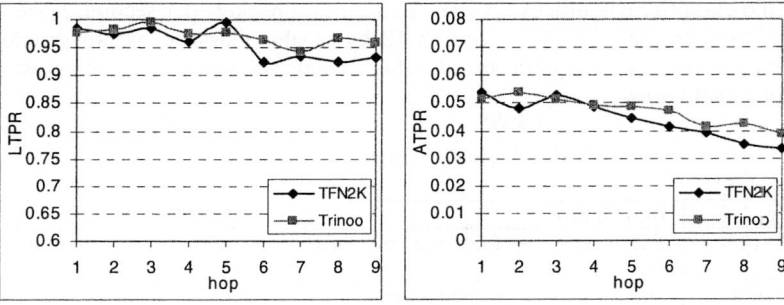

Fig. 4. Average LTPR and ATPR at different distances

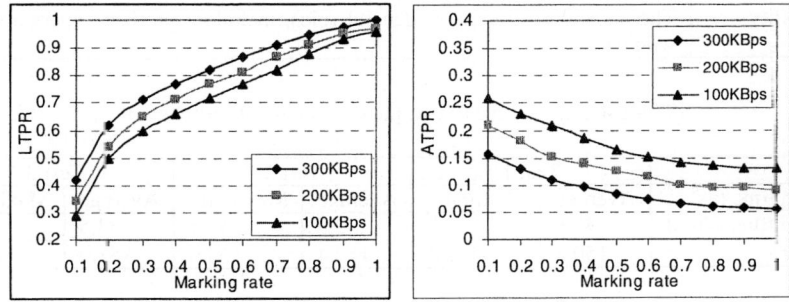

Fig. 5. Average LTPR and ATPR at marking rate at hop=1

and ATPR change according to the marking rate. Moreover, if attacking packet rate increases, our scheme can let even more legitimate packets pass through, and filter more attacking packets.

4.3 Packet Classification Performance

There are many metrics for packet classification algorithms [11] such as search speed, low storage requirements, fast updates, scalability and flexibility. We summarize these metrics in table 3. Different classification applications have different requirements. For our application, search speed and low storage requirements are two major goals. For fast updates, a relative low update rate is sufficient because the there is no need to change the rules all the time, which require very frequent updates. We only need classify packets into two categories, attack packets and normal packets. We also consider the scalability and flexibility are not obligatory requirements because the classification problem here is not a general purpose application.

For comparison, the Hierarchical Tries algorithm is implemented. This algorithm is an extension of the one dimensional radix trie data structure. Table 4 shows the search time of 3 different tests. On average, the Bloom-filter-based classifier is 354% faster than a traditional H-Trie classifier. The Bloom-filter-based classifier can achieve the average search time at about 33ns and the maximum search time at about 42ns. This means the classifier can process at least 23.8 million packets per second. If we assume the minimum length of an IP packet is 40 bytes, this classifier is power enough to process packets at the 7.6 Gb/s speed, which meets the requirement of most current high-speed networks.

Table 3. Metrics for packet classification

Metric	Description
search speed	The speed to find the matched rules. Faster links require faster classification.
low storage requirements	Small storage requirements enable the use of fast memory technologies like static random access memory (SRAM).
fast updates	The classifier changes from time to time, therefore fast and incrementally update of the data structure is essential to a good classification algorithm.
scalability	The number of IP header fields used for classification.
flexibility	The capability to support general rules, including prefixes, operators and wild cards.

Table 4. Search time of two packet classification schemes

Test	Test 1		Test 2		Test 3	
Search time (ns)	Average	Maximum	Average	Maximum	Average	Maximum
Bloom filter-based	33.8	43.6	32.9	41.5	33.5	42.7
H-Trie	150.4	167.4	152.4	164.6	151.9	168.1

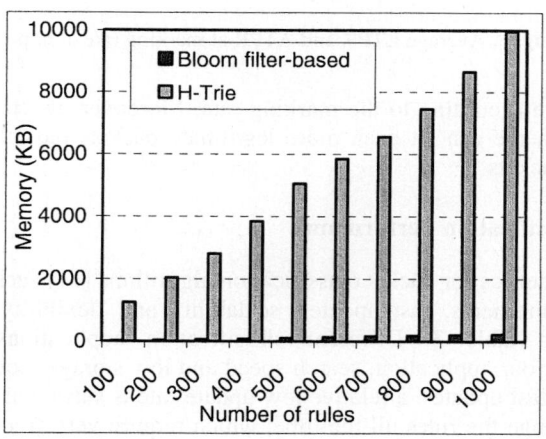

Fig. 6. Comparison of memory consumption

Although in our tests the memory consumption is not a remarkable issue, because there are usually less than 500 rules to be used in the classification for DDoS filtering in the experiments, the Bloom filter-based classifier still shows good storage efficiency compared with the H-Trie classifier. For example, for the 500-rule test in figure 6, our classifier consumes only 2.259% of what an H-Trie classifier needs. On the scalability, even if tested by up to 10000 artificial generated rules (not by DDoS tests) the Bloom filter-based classifier only needs less than 3M memory. This proves it has potential to be applied for other more memory-consuming applications.

5 Conclusions

In this paper we present an intelligent DDoS filtering system by using neural network technology and Bloom filter. It solves two major challenges on DDoS defense in high-speed networks: It can sensitively and accurately detect the network anomalies and filter quickly the attack packets at a gigabit speed.

References

[1] H. Aljifri, "IP Traceback: A New Denial-of-Service Deterrent?", IEEE Security & Privacy, Vol.1, No.3, 2003, pp.24-31.
[2] J. M. Bernardo, and A. F. M. Smith, Bayesian Theory, John Wiley and Sons, England, 1994.
[3] A. Broder, and M. Mitzenmacher, Network Applications of Bloom Filters: A Survey, Internet Mathematics, Vol. 1, No. 4, 2003, pp. 485-509.
[4] Computer Emergency Response Team, CERT, http://www.cert.org, 2004.
[5] P. Ferguson, D. Senie, "RFC 2267 - Network Ingress Filtering: Defeating Denial of Service Attacks which employ IP Source Address Spoofing", Network Working Group, 1998.
[6] S. Floyd, and V. Jacobson, "Random Early Detection Gateways for Congestion Avoidance", IEEE/ACM Transactions on Networking, Vol.1, No.4, 1993, pp.397-413.
[7] Lee Garber, "Denial-of-Service Attacks Rip the Internet", Computer, Vol.33, No.4, 2000, pp. 12-17.
[8] P. Gevros, J. Crowcroft, P. Kirstein, and S. Bhatti, "Congestion Control Mechanisms and the Best Effort Service Model", IEEE Network, Vol.15, No.3, 2001, pp. 16-26.
[9] P. Gupta, and N. McKeown, "Packet classification on Multiple Fields", ACM SIGCOMM, pp. 147-160, 1999.
[10] P. Gupta, and N. McKeown, "Classification Using Hierarchical Intelligent Cuttings", IEEE Micro, Vol. 20, No. 1, pp. 34-41, 2000.
[11] P. Gupta, and N. McKeown, "Algorithms for Packet Classification", IEEE Network, Vol. 15, No. 2, 2001, pp. 24-32.
[12] S. Haykin, Neural Networks: A Comprehensive Foundation, 2nd Edition, Prentice Hall, 1998.
[13] C. Jin, H. Wang, and K. G. Shin, "Hop-count Filtering: An Effective Defense Against Spoofed DDoS Traffic", Proc. of the 10th ACM Conference on Computer and Communication Security (CCS 2003), pp.30-41.
[14] S. Jin, D. S. Yeung, "A Covariance Analysis Model for DDoS Attack Detection", 2004 IEEE International Conference on Communications, Vol. 4, 2004, pp.1882-1886.
[15] Y. Kim, J.-Y. Jo, F. L. Merat, "Defeating Distributed Denial-of-Service Attack with Deterministic Bit Marking", IEEE GLOBECOM 2003, pp.1363-1367.
[16] T. V. Lakshman, and D. Stidialis, "High speed policy-based packet forwarding using efficient multi-dimensional range matching", ACM SIGCOMM, pp. 191-202, 1998.
[17] M. Li, C. Chi, W. Jia, W. Zhao, W. Zhou, J. Cao, D. Long and Q. Meng, "Decision Analysis of Statistically Detecting Distributed Denial-of-Service Flooding Attacks", International Journal of Information Technology and Decision Making, Vol.2, No.3, 2003, pp.397-405.

[18] R. Mahajan, S. M. Bellovin, S. Floyd, "Controlling High Bandwidth Aggregates in the Network", Computer Communications Review, Vol.32, No.3, 2002, pp.62-73.
[19] Memory-Memory, http://www.memorymemory.com
[20] MIT 1998 DARPA Intrusion Detection Evaluation Data Set, http://www.ll.mit.edu/IST/ideval/data/1998/1998_data_index.html
[21] S. Mukkamala, and A. H. Sung, "Detecting Denial of Service Attacks Using Support Vector Machines", The IEEE International Conference on Fuzzy Systems 2003, pp.1231-1236.
[22] B. Müller, J. Reinhardt, M.T. Strickland, Neural Networks : An Introduction, 2nd Edition, New York : Springer-Verlag, 1995.
[23] Peter G. Neumann, "Denial-of-Service Attacks", Communications of the ACM, Vol.43, No.4, 2000, pp.136.
[24] T. J. Ott, T.V. L., and L. Wong , "SRED: Stabilized RED", IEEE INFOCOM 1999, pp.1346-1355.
[25] K. Park, and H. Lee, "On the Effectiveness of Route-based Packet Filtering For Distributed DoS Attack Prevention in Power-law Internet", ACM SIGCOMM 2001, 2001, pp.15-26.
[26] M. Pollak, ' Optimal detection of a change in distribution", Ann. Statist., Vol. 13, 1986, pp. 206-227.
[27] C. Sangpachatanaruk, S. M. Khattab, T. Znati, R. Melhem, and D. Mosse, "A Simulation Study of the Proactive Server Roaming for Mitigating Denial of Service Attacks", Proc. of the 36th Annual Simulation Symposium 2003 (ANSS 2003).
[28] V. Srinivasan, S. Suri, and G. Varghese, "Packet Classification Using Tuple Space Search", ACM SIGCOMM, pp. 135-146, 1999.
[29] Sanitized UCLA CSD traffic traces, http://lever.cs.ucla.edu/ddos/traces/
[30] Y. Xiang, W. Zhou, and J. Rough, "Trace IP Packets by Flexible Deterministic Packet Marking (FDPM)", 2004 IEEE International Workshop on IP Operations & Management (IPOM 2004).
[31] Y. Xiang, and W. Zhou, "Mark-Aided Distributed Filtering by Using Neural Network for DDoS Defense", IEEE GLOBECOM 2005.
[32] A. Yaar, A. Perrig, and D. Song, "Pi: A Path Identification Mechanism to Defend against DDoS Attacks", 2003 IEEE Symposium on Security and Privacy, pp93-107.
[33] J. Yan, S. Early, R. Anderson, "The XenoService A Distributed Defeat for Distributed Denial of Service", Proc. of ISW 2000.
[34] Z. Zhang, C. N. Manikopoulos, "Detecting Denial-of-Service Attacks through Feature Cross-Correlation", 2004 IEEE/Sarnoff Symposium on Advances in Wired and Wireless Communication, pp.67-70.

2L-MuRR: A Compact Register Renaming Scheme for SMT Processors

Hua Yang, Gang Cui, and Xiao-zong Yang

PBox 320, School of Computer Science and Technology,
Harbin Institutue of Technology, 150001, China
{yangh, cg}@ftcl.hit.edu.cn, xzyang@hit.edu.cn

Abstract. In simultaneous multithreaded (SMT) processors, a larger multi-ported rename register file is indispensable for holding more intermediate results of in-flight instructions. However, larger rename register file incurs longer access delay and more power consumption, which are becoming a bottleneck in future SMT processors. To tackle these problems, we propose *2L-MuRR*, the abbreviation of *Multi-usable Rename Register with 2-Level renaming and allocating*, which focuses on more efficient utilization of a fewer number of rename registers. Based on the fact that the effective bit-width of most operands is narrower than the full-bit width of a register entry, 2L-MuRR partitions each rename register into several fields of different widths. Either single field or field combination can hold an operand, thus making each rename register *multi-usable*. The simulations show that 2L-MuRR improves the efficiency of the rename register file significantly, achieving higher performance with much fewer rename registers.

1 Introduction

Modern dynamically scheduled superscalar processors examine a large window of in-flight instructions to find and issue multiple ready instructions every cycle. And in simultaneous multithreading architecture (SMT), the instruction window size and issue width should be much larger, because SMT executes instructions from multiple threads simultaneously and converts thread-level-parallelism (TLP) into instruction-level-parallelism (ILP) dynamically [1]. However, supporting a larger instruction window requires larger structures within the processor, namely, larger reorder buffer (ROB), larger issue queue, more execution units, and larger multi-ported rename register file (RRF).

RRF is used for holding the renamed register values, i.e., the intermediate (uncommitted yet) results of in-flight instructions. The minimum size of RRF should be greater than the product of the pipeline depth (between the rename and commit stages) and issue width. For example, a processor with 7-stage pipeline (5-stage from rename to commit) which supports 8-wide issue would need at least O(5X8=40) rename registers. In practice, the size of RRF should be much bigger because of the long-latency instructions, such as cache misses, which hold rename registers for the entire duration of cache misses and delay the release of them to subsequent instructions. E.g., in the 4-wide 7-stage pipeline Alpha21264, beyond the 32 integer and 32 floating-point user-visible registers (non-speculative), an additional 41 integer and 41 floating-point registers are available to hold the renamed register values prior to instruction retirement [2]. Deeper pipelines due to higher frequency, wider issue for more ILP, and multiple threads for TLP exacerbate the design of RRF [3][4]. Future SMT processors with deeper pipeline and wider issue will probably need hundreds of rename registers. However, a larger multi-ported RRF incurs longer access delays and more power consumption, both of which are critical to the overall performance. Being significantly affected by the size and port number, the access time and power-consumption of register file are very likely to become one of the bottlenecks of future SMT processors.

Many techniques has been proposed to tackle these pressing problems, and we classify them coarsely into 3 categories. The first is to reduce the port number and accelerate the access time by decentralizing register file organization, for instance, register caching [5], hierarchical solutions [4], and multi-banked register files [6]. The second is to reduce the demand for bigger size and port number by delayed allocating or earlier releasing of rename registers. Exploiting program semantics to release registers early was studied in [7], while checkpoint schemes that enable early releasing of registers and other resources was described in [8]. A scheme called VPR (virtual-physical register) postpones the allocation of rename register to a later stage when the renamed value is known [9]. The third is to reduce the demand for bigger size through value-based optimizations. In a scheme called physical-register-inling [10], if a register value can be expressed with fewer bits than the bits the register map table would need to specify a physical register number, the value is stored directly in the table, thus avoiding the indirection and saving space in the RRF. In [11], the temporal locality of register values was exploited by correlating several logical registers that contain a same value with just one physical register.

This paper focuses on more efficient utilization of a fewer number of rename registers, and our work relies on two facts. First, most operands can be represented with much fewer bits than the full-bit width (usually 32-bit or 64-bit) of a register entry. Fig. 1 shows (for Alpha AXP ISA) the cumulative distribu-

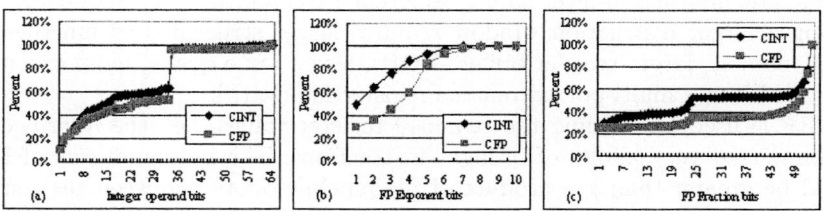

Fig. 1. Register Operand Distribution. The cumulative distribution of the number of bits needed to represent: (a) integer, (b) floating-point's exponent, (c) floating-point's fraction respectively, for the SPEC2000 *CINT* average and *CFP* average.

tion of the number of bits needed to represent integer operand, floating-point operand's exponent and fraction respectively, for the SPEC2000 CINT average and CFP average separately. Second, rather than traditionally being allocated during decode/rename stage, a rename register can be allocated at the end of execute-stage when the destination value is known. A scheme called VPR exploits this fact and reduces the average rename register occupancy time greatly [9]. In this paper, we propose a compact RRF organization called *2L-MuRR*, the abbreviation of *Multi-usable Rename Register with 2-Level renaming and allocating*. In 2L-MuRR, each rename register is partitioned into several fields of different widths, and either single field or field combination can hold an operand. Therefore, each rename register in 2L-MuRR can hold multiple operands simultaneously. Depending on its value, the destination operand selects which fields to use in the RRF at write-back stage, effectively eliminating its meaningless register file occupancy.

2 Review of Register Renaming

Register renaming was first proposed in the IBM 360/91, and nowadays is considered to be a standard feature of superscalar processors [12]. By dynamically renaming logical registers that specify control and data flow through a program to physical registers implemented in the machine, register renaming eliminates false name dependencies—Write-After-Read or Write-After-Write—that remarkably limit the amount of parallelism in a program.

2.1 Register Map Table

In traditional register renaming process, a rename (physical) register is allocated for each logical destination register in an instruction at the decode stage, and this mapping is recorded in a structure called *register map table*, so that logical input registers in subsequent instructions will correctly reference the rename register that holds the latest value.

As shown in Fig. 2, the two most common types of register map table are RAM (random addressed memory) and CAM (content addressed memory) tables. In RAM table, the total number of entries is equal to the number of *logical*

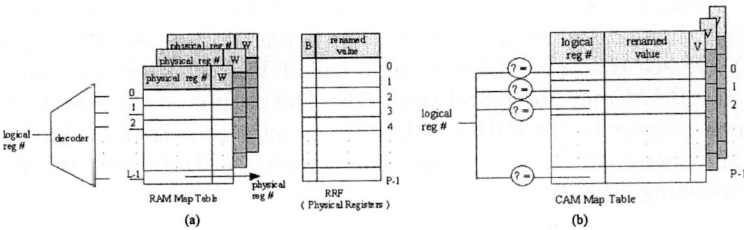

Fig. 2. Traditional Register Renaming: (*a*) *RAM Map Table*, (*b*) *CAM Map Table*. The shallow copy entries are needed for controlling speculation and precise exceptions.

registers. A logical register number is decoded to select a single entry that points to the physical register location holding the latest value for that logical register, and a W-bit in each entry indicates whether the value is ready (written-back). In CAM table, the total number of entries is the number of *physical* registers in the machine. An associative lookup is required, and a valid-bit V is needed in each entry to find latest allocation for the given logical register.

2.2 Layout of Rename Registers

As for the layout of RRF, there are commonly three types of implementations [12]. The first is the *merged* register file, in which ARF (architectural register file) and RRF dynamically share a same physical register file. One advantage of this type is that no data transfer is required for updating the ARF when instructions commit. Power1 and Alpha21264 are examples of this type. The second type has *stand-alone* RRF and ARF, which is explicit, but need data transfer for updating the ARF. This type was exploited by PowerPC603/620, Power3 and Pentium4. The third type can be viewed as *embedding* RRF into the ROB. Since each in-flight instruction has a ROB entry, it is natural to have ROB entries extended for holding the renamed values, but this will increase the ROB complexities and also need data transfer when instructions commit. K5, K6, Pentium II and Pentium III chose this type.

3 Architecture of 2L-MuRR

In this section, we will discuss 2L-MuRR in detail. We adopt RAM table because CAM does not scale well to larger number of rename registers. For simplicity, we choose the stand-alone RRF and ARF, that is, there also exists a stand-alone ARF for holding the committed register values.

3.1 Basic Structure of 2L-MuRR

Fig. 3 illustrates the basic structure of 2L-MuRR. Each entry in the RRF is partitioned into N fields of different widths: $field\_1, field\_2, \ldots, field\_N$. A single field, or a combination of several fields in a entry, can hold an operand. Thus, each rename register in 2L-MuRR is *multi-usable*, that is, it may hold multiple operands simultaneously. Besides, each rename register has a N-bit *busy_flag* to indicate which fields are occupied, one bit per field. Comparing with Fig. 2(a), we see that Fig. 3 has a table called V2P map (virtual-to-physical) between the RAM map table and the RRF. The output of the RAM map table is no longer pointer to the RRF entries, but pointer to entries in the V2P map. We call the entries in the V2P map *virtual registers*, and each virtual register has the following 4 fields:

- B *bit*: busy bit, indicates whether this entry has been allocated;
- *rename reg#*: identifier of the rename register that hold the corresponding renamed value; meaningless when the W bit is 0;

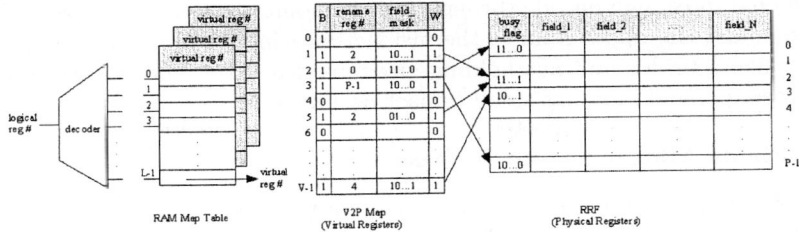

Fig. 3. Basic Structure of 2L-MuRR. A virtual register (entry in *V2P Map*) is allocated to be alias of the logical destination of an instruction at decode stage. At write-back stage, some fields in a rename register (entry in *RRF*) are allocated for holding the destination value.

- *field_mask*: indicates which fields in the rename register hold the renamed value; meaningless when the *W* bit is 0;
- *W bit*: write-back bit, indicates whether the renamed value has been written-back to a rename register.

For instance, 2# virtual register is related to 0# rename register, while both 1# and 5# virtual registers are related to 2# rename register, etc.

Like the VPR scheme [9], the V2P map acts as a bridge between the RAM map and the RRF, through which the allocation of rename registers can be postponed to a later stage in the pipeline. When an instruction is decoded, a virtual register is allocated to be alias of its logical destination. However, in 2L-MuRR, no rename register is related to this virtual register until the instruction enters the write-back stage when its destination value is already known. At write-back stage, the instruction tries to find a suitable rename register to hold its destination value. If succeed, the *rename reg#*, *field_mask*, *W* bit in the virtual register, and the *busy_flag* of the selected rename register, will be updated to keep track of the states of the V2P map and RRF. At commit stage, the completed instructions move their destination values from the RRF to the ARF, releasing the entries in V2P map and the corresponding fields in RRF. Since the RRF usually has fewer entries than the V2P map, there are possibilities (although rarely) that an instruction can not find a suitable rename register during write-back. In this case, the instruction is marked as "uncompleted" and re-enqueued, waiting to be re-executed later. Fig. 4 shows the pipeline stages for 2L-MuRR.

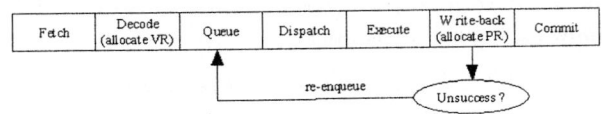

Fig. 4. Pipeline for 2L-MuRR. Upon unsuccess at write-back stage, the instruction will be *re-enqueued*, waiting to be re-executed later.

To guarantee high decode throughput, the number of virtual registers should be large, and the upper limit is the instruction window size. However, just behaving like a bridge and not holding any renamed value, the structure of V2P map is simple and only has small impact on hardware cost.

3.2 Fields Allocation and Release

In contemporary computers, integer is represented in 2's complement and floating-point in *IEEE-754* format. Since each field in 2L-MuRR is usually much narrower than an operand's normal representation, an operand must be compressed before being stored into some fields of a rename register. Based on the statistics shown in Fig. 1, we compress the operands just by truncating its leading or trailing repeating bits. The detailed operand truncation and fields allocation policies are shown below:

- For integer, its higher-order repeating bits (0s or 1s) can be viewed as its sign and truncated before being stored into some fields in a rename register;
- For floating-point, because its exponent and fraction differ in distributing, we deal with them separately. Taking the double-precision floating-point for example, normally its value is $(-1)^S(1 + fraction)2^{(exponent-1023)}$, where S denotes the sign bit and 1023 is a *bias* and should be subtracted from the exponent. Due to the fact that exponent is biased, we keep bit $<62>$ as the exponent's sign bit (ES bit) and only compress bit $<61:52>$ as an integer. Then the truncated representation of bit $<61:52>$ is fit into a field, with the highest bit set to ES. The fraction is compressed by cutting the trailing repeating 0s before being stored into some fields;
- All the fields related to an operand must be in an identical rename register;
- For simplicity of implementation, floating-point's exponent and fraction occupy different fields, that is, a floating-point occupies at least two fields. Due to the fact that in most cases 8-bit is enough to hold the exponent (worst case, 11-bit), we predefine that the exponent can occupy only one field, and it must be the leftmost one of all the fields occupied by the floating-point;
- An instruction tries to find the "smallest" field combination to hold its destination value, that is, to store the destination value with as few bits as possible. This is carried out by examining the *busy_flags* of all rename registers.

Fig. 5 shows a example of how a 64-bit integer and a double-precision floating-point are truncated and stored into a same rename register.

When an instruction commits (update the ARF) or is discarded due to misspeculation, its V2P entry and the corresponding fields in the RRF are released through the following logical operations:

RR.busy_flag := RR.busy_flag Xor VR.field_mask;
VR.Busy:= 0;

where RR and VR denote the corresponding RRF entry and V2P entry respectively.

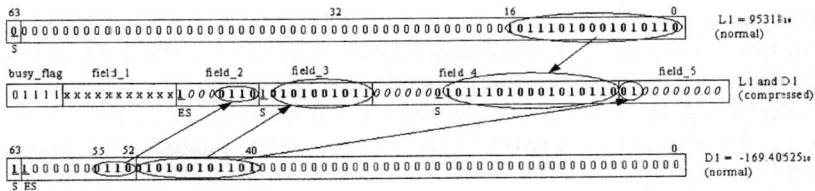

Fig. 5. Operand Compression Example. A 64-bit integer ($L1=95318_{10}$) and a double-precision floating-point ($D1=-169.40625_{10}$) are truncated and stored into a same rename register. $L1$ is stored into $field\_4$. For $D1$, its exponent is stored into $field\_2$, and its fraction is stored into $field\_3$ and $field\_5$. Here, the bold bits are *key* bits and can be used to preserve the value, while the italic bits are *padding* bits for filling up a field. S denotes the sign bit, and ES is viewed as the exponent's sign bit. The field-pattern is *11-8-11-24-10* and the $busy\_flag$ is 5-bit.

3.3 Field Partitioning

How rename register file is partitioned, i.e., how many fields in each rename register and how many bits in each field, will certainly affect the overall performance. To be comparable, we set the rename register in 2L-MuRR to have the same sum-width as a traditional register (64-bit in Alpha AXP). There are two opposite choices in partitioning the rename registers: more fields that are narrower, or less fields that are wider. The first choice will certainly improve the efficiency of all fields because of fewer *padding* bits on average. However, too many fields will increase the complexities of both implementation and field allocation due to: (1) more opportunities when big operands cannot find a wide enough field and has to find a field combination; (2) more different field combinations to select from; (3) wider $busy\_flag$ and $field\_mask$ (see Fig. 3); etc. Contrarily, the second choice has more bits wasted in each field, but increases the opportunities when operands occupy just one field and decreases complexities. A degenerate case of the second choice is to have only one field in each rename register, which is similar to the VPR scheme. Therefore, a compromise between field number and field width should be found.

We exploited the operand distribution features described in Section 1 to find out rational field-patterns. Fig. 1 shows that there are some representative points that can be used for field partitioning: 8-bit, 10-bit, 24-bit and 34-bit. Upon these observations, we chose the field-pattern *11-8-11-24-10* in our simulations, which is 64-bit in total: 11-bit for $field\_1$, 8-bit for $field\_2$, etc. Accordingly, the $field\_masks$ and $busy\_flags$ are 5-bit wide.

3.4 Deadlock Avoidance

As shown in Fig. 4, in 2L-MuRR, an instruction that can't write-back is marked as "uncompleted" and re-enqueued, waiting to be re-executed later. When this instruction finishes execution again, it may probably succeed in writing-back because other committed instructions have released some fields during this period of time. However, in dynamically scheduled processors, instructions execute out-of-order, but commit in-order. Therefore, if the re-enqueued instructions are the oldest ones, they will probably never get opportunities to write-back. The reason is that the already written-back instructions are younger and cannot commit and release their occupied rename registers. To avoid this deadlock, we use the *NRR* (*number of reserved register*) proposed for VPR [9], which preserves *NRR* rename registers particularly for the oldest instructions. Although simple, it works well in our simulations.

4 Simulation Environment and Results

We modified the SimpleScalar/Alpha ver3.0d [13] to build three SMT simulators using 2L-MuRR, TRAD (traditional register renaming) and VPR respectively. Table 1 summarizes the key parameters of these three SMT machines, all which are 12-issue and support 4-thread running simultaneously with ICOUNT scheduling policy [14]. Alpha AXP was designed as a 64-bit RISC architecture—all registers are 64-bit in length and all operations are performed between 64-bit registers [2]. We compose 6 test-suites using 24 SPEC2000 benchmarks, and each test-suite consists of 2 integer and 2 floating-point benchmarks. All simulations use the SPEC2000's ref sets. After *fast-forward* the first 1 billion instructions for each thread, the simulations run until a thread commits 100M instructions. For comparison, we define a baseline machine, which is TRAD with infinite rename

Table 1. Hardware parameters for TRAD, VPR, 2L-MuRR

	TRAD	VPR(256-entry V2P map)	2L-MuRR(256-entry V2P map)
Deadlock Avoidance	—	1-entry NRR per thread	1-entry NRR per thread
L1 Inst. Cache	128K bytes, 32-byte block, 4-way associative, 2-cycle latency, LRU replace		
L1 Data Cache	128K bytes, 64-byte block, 2-way associative, 2-cycle latency, LRU replace		
Unified L2 Cache	1M bytes, 64-byte block, 4-way associative, 12-cycle latency, LRU replace		
Branch predictor	Gshare (2K-entry), 32-entry RAS, 4-way 512-set BTB		
Main memory	Infinite capacity, 36-cycle latency for first chunk, 2-cycle inter-chunk latency		
Fetch/Decode/Issue/ Commit width	12 inst/cycle, 4-thread contexts, ICOUNT scheduling		
Out-of-order Execution	6 Int. ALU, 3 Int. Multiply/Divide, 6 FP ALU, 3 FP Multiply/Divide, 4 Read-port, 2 Write-port, 256-entry ROB, 128-entry LSQ		

Table 2. Test-suites and their Baseline IPC

	1#	2#	3#	4#	5#	6#	
Test-suite	gzip vpr wupwise swim	gcc mcf mgrid applu	crafty parser mesa galgel	eon perlbmk art equake	bzip2 twolf lucas fma3d	sixtrack apsi gap vortex	Avg
Baseline IPC	6.11	7.66	6.27	5.76	5.78	7.08	6.44

registers and can be viewed as owning peak performance. Table 2 shows the test-suites and their baseline IPC (instruction per cycle).

4.1 Performance Comparison

Fig. 6(a) shows the IPC comparisons of TRAD, VPR and 2L-MuRR when RRF size is 50. It's evident that 2L-MuRR outperforms TRAD and VPR for all test-suites. The average IPC are 4.28 (TRAD), 5.54 (VPR), 6.12 (2L-MuRR) respectively. The superiority of 2L-MuRR over VPR is more noticeable for 1# and 6# test-suites, because they have more "narrow" values to enjoy the multi-usable rename registers in 2L-MuRR.

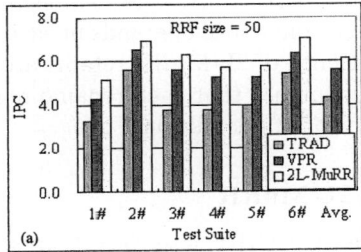
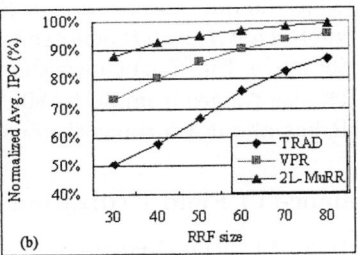

Fig. 6. (a) IPC comparison of TRAD, VPR and 2L-MuRR when $RRF\ size=50$; (b) Normalized Average IPC when $RRF\ size$ ranges from 30 to 80, the data are average IPCs normalized to the baseline average IPC (6.44)

Fig. 6(b) shows the average IPC of all test-suites when RRF size ranges from 30 to 80; all data here are normalized to the baseline average IPC (6.44, see Table 2). Compared with 2L-MuRR, the performances of TRAD and VPR are more sensitive to the RRF size. 2L-MuRR with RRF size being 50 achieves 95.0% of the baseline's performance, which is nearly equal to VPR with 80 and outperforms TRAD with 80 significantly. With RRF size being 60, 70 and 80, 2L-MuRR achieves 96.7%, 98.1% and 99.1% respectively of the baseline's performance. In summary, by using 2L-MuRR, SMT processors can achieve the same high performance with much fewer rename registers.

4.2 Efficiency of 2L-MuRR

Fig. 7(a) shows the occupancy rate of rename registers (RR_busy_rate) as a function of the RRF size, for TRAD, VPR and 2L-MuRR respectively. The RR_busy_Rate of 2L-MuRR is much lower than that of TRAD and VPR. E.g., when RRF size is 50, they are 99.2% (TRAD), 67.3% (VPR) and 53.1% (2L-MuRR) respectively. Furthermore, the actual occupancy of RRF in 2L-MuRR is even lower, because a rename register is viewed as "busy" when its $busy\_flag$ is not 0, but it may still has some free fields.

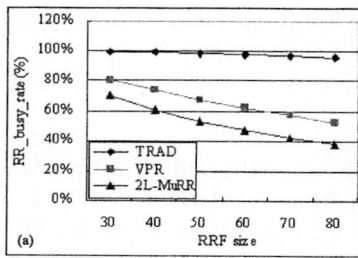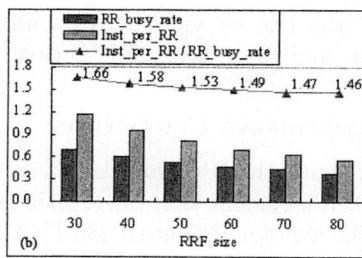

Fig. 7. (a) RR_busy_rate comparison of TRAD, VPR and 2L-MuRR; (b) Efficency of 2L-MuRR

We define the quotient $Inst\_Per\_RR/RR\_busy\_Rate$ as the *efficiency* of 2L-MuRR, where $Inst\_Per\_RR$ denotes average amount of operands in each rename register per cycle. Fig. 7(b) shows the efficiency of 2L-MuRR retains around 1.5 when RRF size ranges from 30 to 80. This implies that each rename register in 2L-MuRR has about 1.5 times the "capacity" of a traditional one.

4.3 Balance of Field Utilization in 2L-MuRR

The relative utilization frequency of each field (RRF size=50) is presented in Fig. 8. This figure reveals that *11-8-11-24-10* is a rational field-pattern, which have a balanced utilization of all fields. *Field_5* (10-bit) is occupied less frequently, because most operands will find a "suitable" location in the front 4 fields during field allocating.

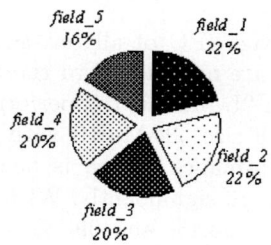

Fig. 8. Relative utilization frequency of each field

4.4 Saving on Writing to RRF

Because each accessing to a rename register may read or write multiple values in it, 2L-MuRR can reduce the accessing to the RRF, somewhat alleviating the read/write ports pressure. For simplicity, we only give the statistic of the savings on write-back to the RRF in our simulations. At write-back stage, if multiple instructions choose identical rename register to store their destination values, their destination values are combined together and write to the selected rename register just once. The simulations present an average saving of 8% (best case 14%, worst case 4%) on writing to the RRF.

5 Conclusions

SMT requires a large register file to support multiple thread contexts. This raises a difficult design tradeoff, because large register file will greatly impact such aspects as cycle time, die size and power consumption.

This paper proposes a novel rename register file organization called 2L-MuRR. Fundamental to 2L-MuRR is the sharing of each rename register among multiple truncated operands. As revealed in its name, 2L-MuRR possesses two features. The first is the delayed register allocation, through which each instruction undergoes *2 level* of register renaming and allocating before write-back its destination value. The second is the partitioned rename registers, in which any field combination can hold an operand, thus making each rename register *multi-usable*. Our results show these two features significantly improve the efficiency of RRF, making each rename register has about 1.5 times "capacity" of a traditional one. With the same RRF size, 2L-MuRR outperform TRAD scheme and VPR scheme significantly, implying SMT processors using 2L-MuRR can achieve the same high performance with much fewer rename registers. In addition, 2L-MuRR alleviates the pressure on the read/write ports.

References

1. Tullsen, D.M., Eggers, S.J., Levy, H.M.: Simultaneous Multithreading: Maximizing On-Chip Parallelism. In Proceedings of the 22nd Annual International Symposium on Computer Architecture (1995) 392–403
2. Kessler, R.E.: The Alpha 21264 Microprocessor. IEEE Micro 19(2)(1999) 24–36
3. Sprangle, E., Carmean, D.: Increasing Processor Performance by Implementing Deeper Pipelines. In Proceedings of the 29th Annual International Symposium on Computer Architecture (2002) 25–34
4. Balasubramonian, R., Dwarkadas, S., Albonesi, D.H.: Reducing the Complexity of the Register File in Dynamic Superscalar Processors. In Proceedings of the 34th Annual International Symposium on Microarchitecture (2001) 237–248
5. Postiff, M., Greene, D., Raasch, S., Mudge, T.N.: Integrating Superscalar Processor Components to Implement Register Caching. In Proceedings of the International Conference on Supercomputing (2001) 348–357

6. Cruz, J.L., González, A., Valero, M., Topham, N.P.: Multiple-Banked Register File Architectures. In Proceeding of the 27th Annual International Symposium on Computer Architecture (2000) 316–325
7. Lo, J.L., Parekh, S.S., Eggers, S.J., Levy, H.M., Tullsen, D.M.: Software-Directed Register Deallocation for Simultaneous Multithreaded Processors. IEEE Transactions on Parallel and Distributed Systems 10(9) (1999) 922–933
8. Martinez, J.F., Renau, J., Huang, M.C., Prvulovic, M., Torrellas, J.: Cherry: Checkpointed Early Resource Recycling in Out-of-order Microprocessors. In Proceedings of the 35th Annual IEEE/ACM International Symposium on Microarchitecture (2002) 3–14
9. González, A., González, J., Valero, M.: Virtual-Physical Registers. In Proceedings of the 4th International Symposium on High-Performance Computer Architecture (1998) 175–184
10. Lipasti, M.H., Mestan, B.R., Gunadi, E.: Physical Register Inlining. In Proceedings of the 31st Annual International Symposium on Computer Architecture (2004) 325–335
11. Jourdan, S., Ronen, R., Bekerman, M., Shomar, B., Yoaz, A.: A Novel Renaming Scheme to Exploit Value Temporal Locality through Physical Register Reuse and Unification. In Proceeeding of the 31st IEEE/ACM Symposium on Microarchitecture (1998) 216–225
12. Sima, D., The Design Space of Register Renaming Techniques. IEEE Micro 20(5) (2000) 70–83
13. Burger, D.A., Austin, T.M.: The SimpleScalar Tool Set, Version 2.0. Computer Architecture News 25(3) (1997) 13
14. Tullsen, D.M., Eggers, S.J., Emer, J.S., Levy, H.M., Lo, J.L., Stanm, R.L.: Exploiting Choice: Instruction Fetch and Issue on an Implementable Simultaneous Multithreading Processor. In Proceedings of the 23rd Annual International Symposium on Computer Architecture (1996) 191–202

Scheduling Convex Bipartite Communications Toward Efficient GEN_BLOCK Transformations*

Ching-Hsien Hsu[1], Shih-Chang Chen[1], Chao-Yang Lan[1],
Chao-Tung Yang[2], and Kuan-Ching Li[3]

[1] Department of Computer Science and Information Engineering,
Chung Hua University, Hsinchu, Taiwan 300, R.O.C.
chh@chu.edu.tw

[2] Department of Computer Science and Information Engineering,
Tunghai University, Taichung, Taiwan, R.O.C.
ctyang@mail.thu.edu.tw

[3] Department of Computer Science and Information Management,
Providence University, Taichung, Taiwan, R.O.C.
kuancli@pu.edu.tw

Abstract. Irregular data redistribution is used to enhance data locality and algorithm performance on heterogeneous processor systems. In this paper, we present an efficient scheduling algorithm based on convex bipartite communications for irregular GEN_BLOCK transformations. The proposed technique consists of two phases: *degree reduction phase*, schedules communications involved in processors with degree greater than two; and *coloring phase*, schedules remaining communications of all processors with degree-2 and degree-1. To evaluate the performance of our algorithm, we have implemented the proposed technique along with three scheduling methods. The simulation results show improvement of total communication costs by the proposed algorithm.

1 Introduction

In many parallel programs, dynamic data re-decomposition is needed when applications running from one sub-algorithm to another during run-time. Many data parallel programming languages support run-time primitives for changing a program's array decomposition. Since data re-decomposition is performed at run-time, there is a performance trade-off between the efficiency of the new data decomposition for a subsequent phase of an algorithm and the cost of redistributing data among processors. Thus efficient methods for performing data re-decompositions are of great importance for the development of distributed memory compilers for those languages. High Performance Fortran version 2 (HPF2) provides GEN_BLOCK distribution format which facilitates generalized block distributions and redistributions. GEN_BLOCK allows unequal sized data segments of an array to be mapped onto processors. This

---

* The work of this paper was supported by National Science Council of Taiwan under grant number NSC-93-2213-E-216-028.

makes it possible to let different processors dealing with appropriate data quantity according to their computation ability.

Recently, there are some studies focuses on the problem of irregular data redistribution. These researches can be divided into two categories: communication set generation [1] and communication schedule. Guo *et al.* [2] presented a symbolic analysis method for reducing communication cost of irregular array redistribution. Lee *et al.* [3] presented a logical processor reordering algorithm on irregular array redistribution. Algorithms were compared in various redistribution environments for illustrating the reducing communication cost. Wang *et al.* [4, 5] proposed a method based on divide-and-conquer algorithm. This method separated data array into groups by *Neighbor Message Set* (*NMS*), then these groups will be merged for resulting the schedule. Yook *et al.* [6] presented a scheduling algorithm including list scheduling phase and relocation phase. The list scheduling phase sorts messages by size and then allocates them in decreasing order. Relocation phase finds appropriate positions for current messages while contentions happen. The above research reflected that the communication scheduling is one of the most important issues on developing runtime array redistribution techniques. In this paper, we present an efficient algorithm for scheduling communications of irregular data redistribution based on convex bipartite graph concept. Upon the device that communication patterns of GEN_BLOCK transformation were configured as convex bipartite graph, the proposed scheduling technique can minimize total message size of communication steps and avoid nodes contentions.

2 Notations and Terminologies

Definition: Given a bipartite graph $G = (V, E)$ to represent the communication patterns of an irregular array redistribution on $A[1:N]$ over P processors, vertices of G are used to represent the source and destination processors. Edge e_{ij} in G denotes the message sent from SP_i to DP_j, where $e_{ij} \in E$, $0 \le i, j \le P-1$. $|E|$ is given as the total number of communication messages through the redistribution. The maximal degree of G denoted by $Degree_{max}$ is defined as $Degree_{max} = \max(degree(v))$, for all $v \in V$.

Definition: The length of a communication step i is the maximal size of messages that transmitted at step i.

An example of communication patterns of irregular data redistribution on an array A[1:100] is shown in Figure 1. Figure 1(a) gives two distribution schemes of source and destination processors. Figure 1(b) illustrates communications between processors upon the transformation of GEN_BLOCK given in (a). Figure 1(c) sketches a simple schedule result. To avoid node contention, while one source processor sends message to a destination processor, it can't send other messages at the same time. It is the same to a destination processor; one can't receive two messages at the same time. Those messages that can not be scheduled at the same time are called conflict tuple[5]. For example, $\{m_4, m_5, m_6\}$ and $\{m_6, m_7, m_8\}$ are conflict tuples since m_4, m_5 and m_6 have the same source processor, m_6, m_7 and m_8 have the same destination processor. In general, communication time consists of startup time and data transmission time. To minimize communication steps can be achieved by applying graph coloring mechanism. The coloring mechanism is an efficient method to determine minimal communication steps. However, it ignored the total length of communication steps. Optimizing both total length and minimal steps is usually the objective in developing efficient communication techniques for irregular data redistribution.

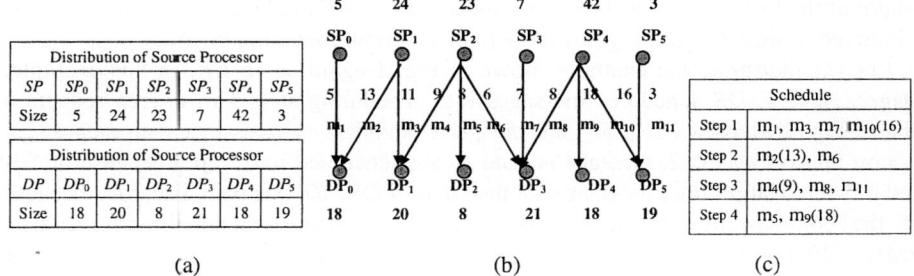

Fig. 1. Example of irregular data redistribution. (a) Data distributions mapped onto source and destination processors (b) A directed bipartite representation used to denote all communications. (c) Simple schedule. The length of step 1, 2, 3 and 4 are 16, 13, 9 and 18. Total length of scheduling steps is 56.

3 Communication Scheduling Algorithm

The proposed algorithm is named *Degree-Reduction (DR)* algorithm that consists of two phases: *degree reduction phase* and *coloring phase*. The main idea of *degree reduction* is to reduce $Degree_{max}$ in steps. DR schedules messages of processors with $Degree_{max}$ when $Degree_{max}$ is greater than two. The degree reduction is performed by the following processes.

Process 1: Sort vertices that with $Degree_{max}$ in a non-increasing order according to sum of its messages' size. Assume there are n nodes with $Degree_{max}$ and the sorted list be $S = \{v_1, v_2, ..., v_n\}$, where $S \subseteq V$.

Process 2: Let $d = Degree_{max}$. For all vertices $v \in S$, select the minimum message $m_j = \min\{m_1, m_2, ..., m_d\}$ into step d.

Process 3: Select other messages into step d. The selected messages in this process must satisfy two conditions: 1. smaller than the length of current scheduling step and 2. will not incur contention with those scheduled communications in previous Process. Schedule those messages into current step.

Process 4: Repeat *Processes* 1-3 if $Degree_{max} > 2$.

Given a bipartite graph $G = (V, E)$, let d be the maximum degree of vertices v, for all $v \in V$, a bipartite graph G' that with maximum degree 2 can be obtained after performing d-2 times degree-reduction iterations. This property denotes that the degree reduction technique reduces degree of nodes with $Degree_{max}$ in each reduction iteration.

Given a bipartite graph $G = (V, E)$ denotes the communication of irregular array redistribution. If the maximum degree of v is 2, there are $|V'| - 2$ vertices with degree 2 in each connected component $G' = (V', E')$, where $V' \subseteq V$, $E' \subseteq E$ and $|V'|$ denotes the number of vertices in G'. The coloring phase of DR employs an adjustable coloring mechanism which is used to schedule messages for the bipartite communications resulted from degree reduction phase. When $Degree_{max}$ is two, the left bipartite graph may consist of several connected bipartite sub-graphs. The coloring mechanism colors edges using two colors for each connected bipartite sub-graph. In order to reduce total length of the two communication steps, an adjustable method to exchange the colors is employed during the merging process among all connected components.

Let's demonstrate the example shown in Fig. 1 again using DR. In this example, $Degree_{max} = 3$, DR schedules messages into scheduling step 3 in degree reduction phase. Fig. 2(a) shows SP_4, SP_2 and DP_3 are candidate vertices that with $Degree_{max}$. According to Process 2, message m_8 and m_5 are scheduled into step 3 because of SP_4 and SP_2 have larger total message size than that of DP_3. DP_3 is then discarded because of the common link message with SP_4, m_8 has been scheduled and resulting $degree(DP_3) = 2$. After removing m_5 and m_8, DR schedules m_1 and m_{11} into step 3 according to Process 3. Fig. 2(b) illustrates this mechanism. There are four messages m_1, m_5, m_8 and m_{11} are scheduled in step 3.

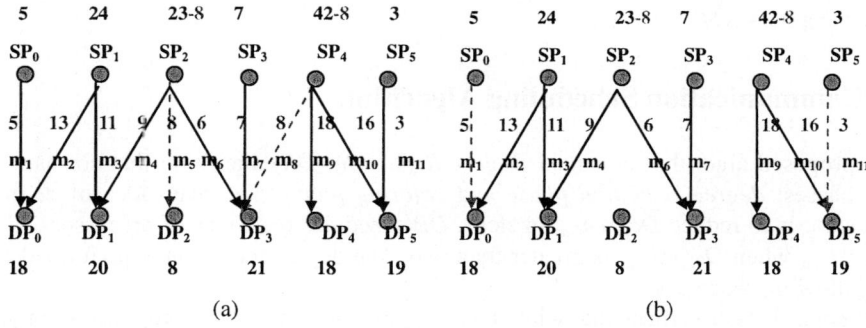

Fig. 2. Degree reduction scheduling processes. (a) State in Processes 1 and 2, messages m_8 and m_5 are scheduled in step 3, $Degree_{max}$ reduced to 2. (b) State in Processes 3, messages m_1 and m_{11} are scheduled in step 3.

There are two connected bipartite sub-graphs resulted after the completion of degree reduction phase as shown in Figure 3(a). The coloring phase is responsible to schedule the bipartite communications when maximum degree is not greater than 2. A simple coloring mechanism is to use two colors for the degree-2 coloring. Assume blue and red are colors for step-1 and step-2, respectively. Figure 3(a) shows this scenario. Messages m_2, m_4, m_7 and m_9 are colored blue and scheduled in step 1; messages m_3, m_6 and m_{10} are colored red and scheduled into step 2. The length of step 1 and 2 are 18 and 16, respectively. The scheduled result is shown in Figure 3(b) and the total length is 42.

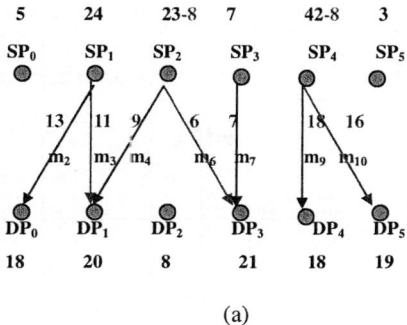

	Schedule
Step 1	m_2、m_4、m_7、m_9(18)
Step 2	m_3、m_6、m_{10}(16)
Step 3	m_1、m_5(8)、m_8(8)、m_{11}

(a)   (b)

Fig. 3. Coloring scheduling processes. (a) Edges are colored blue and red for step 1 and 2, respectively. (b) The complete schedule of *DR*. The length of step 1, 2 and 3 are 18, 16 and 8, respectively. The total length of scheduling steps is 42.

4 Performance Evaluation

Figure 4 shows the comparisons of these algorithms over 1000 random generated test samples. To simplify the presentation, *DR*, *LIST*, *COLOR*, *DC*1 and *DC*2 are denoted as the proposed algorithm, List scheduling algorithm [6], pure coloring scheduling mechanism and the two versions of Divide-and-Conquer scheduling algorithms [5], respectively. Algorithms are compared with each other and the results are compared by accumulating number of better, equal and worse cases. For example, there are 207 samples *DR* performs better than *LIST* over 1000 cases on 8 processors. Figure 4(a) summarizes the accumulating results on 8 processors. The term "Combined", is used to express the ratio of better, equal and worse compared to the other 4 algorithms. We observe that *DR* outperforms about 67% to 81% cases as shown in Figures 4(a) and (b). Although *LIST* performs better when number of processors is 8, *DR* can outperform *LIST* when number of processors is greater than 8. The *DR* scheduling algorithm uses a size-oriented policy in the degree reduction phase. Two optimizations are made in both phase in *DR* algorithm. In degree reduction phase, the *Process* 3 balances communication between different steps. This enables more flexible messages allocation. Second, the adjustable coloring scheme also reduces the length of total steps. Overall speaking, the *DR* scheduling method can avoid contention; schedules optimal steps and minimize length of total steps.

On the other hand, *DC*2 gives higher probability of reducing the length of total steps compare to *DC*1 because of that *DC*2 always schedules messages together if no contention. Both of them can schedule messages in minimal steps, but the merging phase limits the possibility of minimal length of total scheduling steps. *COLOR* can also schedule messages in minimal steps, but does not consider message size. This leads large length of total scheduling steps and performs worse in most cases in the simulation. *LIST* can efficiently reduce length of total steps. The simulations show *LIST* has good performance. However, *LIST* scheduling may cause more communication steps. In other words, number of scheduling steps of *LIST* is not guaranteed optimal. This might cause additional startup overheads.

Processor : 8		DR	LIST	DC1	DC2	Color	Combined
DR	better		207	856	669	957	67.225%
	equal		535	99	312	37	24.575%
	worse		258	45	19	6	8.2%
LIST	better	258		874	738	975	71.125%
	equal	535		101	165	4	20.125%
	worse	207		25	97	21	8.75%
DC1	better	45	25		243	755	26.7%
	equal	99	101		92	101	9.825%
	worse	856	874		665	144	63.475%
DC2	better	19	97	665		901	42.05%
	equal	312	165	92		39	15.2%
	worse	669	738	243		60	42.75%
Color	better	6	21	144	60		5.775%
	equal	37	4	101	39		4.525%
	worse	957	975	755	901		89.7%

(a)

Processor : 16		DR	LIST	DC1	DC2	Coloring	Combined
DR	better		331	985	931	998	81.125%
	equal		379	5	58	2	11.1%
	worse		290	10	11	0	7.775%
LIST	better	290		989	921	998	79.95%
	equal	379		4	25	0	10.2%
	worse	331		7	54	2	9.85%
DC1	better	10	7		179	774	24.25%
	equal	5	4		11	42	1.55%
	worse	985	989		810	184	74.2%
DC2	better	11	54	810		948	45.575%
	equal	58	25	11		7	2.525%
	worse	931	921	179		45	51.9%
Coloring	better	0	2	184	45		5.775%
	equal	2	0	42	7		1.275%
	worse	998	998	774	948		92.95%

(b)

Fig. 4. Performance comparisons of five algorithms. Figures (a) and (b) are results for 8 and 16 processors, respectively.

5 Conclusions

We have presented an irregular data redistribution scheduling technique, *DR*, in parallelizing compilers. *DR* is an efficient and practical algorithm. The simulation results show our algorithm outperforms other methods in most cases. The scheduling algorithm developed in this paper devoted to that the source and the destination processors are identical. In high performance Fortran, the irregular data redistribution is actually supported with arbitrary processor sets. We will improve *DR* for arbitrary processor sets. Besides, the issues of scheduling irregular problems on grid system and considering network communication latency in heterogeneous environments are also interesting and will be investigated.

References

1. Minyi Guo, "Communication Generation for Irregular Codes," *The Journal of Supercomputing*, vol. 25, no. 3, pp. 199-214, 2003.
2. Minyi Guo, Yi Pan and Zhen Liu, "Symbolic Communication Set Generation for Irregular Parallel Applications," *The Journal of Supercomputing*, vol. 25, pp. 199-214, 2003.
3. S. Lee, H. Yook, M. Koo and M. Park, "Processor reordering algorithms toward efficient GEN_BLOCK redistribution," *Proceedings of the ACM symposium on Applied computing*, 2001.
4. Hui Wang, Minyi Guo and Wenxi Chen, "An Efficient Algorithm for Irregular Redistribution in Parallelizing Compilers," *Proceedings of 2003 International Symposium on Parallel and Distributed Processing with Applications*, LNCS 2745, 2003.
5. Hui Wang, Minyi Guo and Daming Wei, "Divide-and-conquer Algorithm for Irregular Redistributions in Parallelizing Compilers", *The Journal of Supercomputing*, vol. 29, no. 2, 2004.
6. H.-G. Yook and Myung-Soon Park, "Scheduling GEN_BLOCK Array Redistribution," *Proceedings of the IASTED International Conference Parallel and Distributed Computing and Systems*, November, 1999.

A Chronological History-Based Execution Time Estimation Model for Embarrassingly Parallel Applications on Grids*

Chao-Tung Yang[1,†], Po-Chi Shih[1], Cheng-Fang Lin[1],
Ching-Hsien Hsu[2], and Kuan-Ching Li[3]

[1] High Performance Computing Laboratory,
Department of Computer Science and Information Engineering,
Tunghai University, Taichung 40704, Taiwan ROC
ctyang@thu.edu.tw
[2] Department of Computer Science and Information Engineering,
Chung Hua University, Hsinchu 300, Taiwan ROC
chh@chu.edu.tw
[3] Parallel and Distributed Processing Center,
Department of Computer Science and Information Management,
Providence University, Taichung 43301, Taiwan ROC,
kuancli@pu.edu.tw

Abstract. In order to identify and schedule jobs that are suitable for determined resources, an execution time estimation model is required. In this paper, it is described a Chronological history-based execution time estimation model to predict current execution time, according to the previous execution results. We built a heterogeneous computational Grid environment using Globus Toolkit, and our research is focused in Grid computing environments and to execute parallel jobs on multiple resources by measuring its accuracy. The experimental results shown that our model can accurately predict the execution time of embarrassingly parallel applications.

Keywords: Grid computing, time estimation model, embarrassingly parallelization, performance evaluation.

1 Introduction

One of the design goals of Grid computing technology is to solve large scale scientific problems. In Grid environments, problem can be divided to pieces or chunks, which can be distributed to many resources and execute them at the same time, to minimize overall execution time. The importance of this procedure is to retain the flexibility of work on multiple smaller problems. Grid computing involves sharing heterogeneous

---

* The authors would like to acknowledge the National Center for High-Performance Computing for sponsoring the Taiwan UniGrid project, under the national project, "Taiwan Knowledge Innovation National Grid".
† Corresponding author.

resources, which are based on different platforms, hardware, software, computer architecture, and computer languages, located in different places belonging to different administrative domains over a network using open standards [1, 2, 3].

It is easy to obtain static resource information of a Grid platform, such as CPU speed, memory capacity, network bandwidth, etc. But run-time resource information, such as CPU loading, free memory, and current network bandwidth, may change over time. In [5, 6], it is provided a general Grid scheduling algorithm that focuses the research in four aspects: static task scheduling, application-level scheduling, resource availability prediction, and economic methods in decentralized task scheduling system. These references served as base for the development of our estimation model. NASA Ames Research Center [4] provides performance models that parse the source code of parallel applications before its execution, in order to estimate the amount of CPU power and communication that are needed for execution.

In this paper, we use history-based model to find previous execution time records for similar applications, based on a number of parameters. The average execution time of previous execution result is computed within a tolerable error rate, and these data are used to estimate the execution time of current parallel application. By using empirical data analysis, it is hard to understand the behavior of performance generated by these applications. Therefore, we only consider the embarrassingly parallel jobs, which do not communicate with each other during execution. Our goal is to estimate the *Total Execution Time* (TET) executed on different sets of resources with different job sizes. In order to identify jobs that are suitable for specific resources, an execution time estimation model is required.

The main contribution of this paper is to describe a chronological history-based execution time estimation model, in order to predict the execution time of parallel application, according to previous execution results. This paper focuses on estimating execution time of embarrassingly parallel jobs. There are several factors, which might influence on overall performance of an application in the underlying heterogeneous Grid environment, such as processor power, network bandwidths or memory sizes. A set of applications were ran on a heterogeneous computational Grid environment we built using standard Grid middleware Globus Toolkit, and those experimental results show that our model can accurately predict the execution time of parallel applications.

2 Execution Time Estimation Model

Consider the problem of time estimation model. First, we have to know how many of variables will affect execution time when running a parallel job. Secondly, the amount of information we can obtain from historical data. In our model, there are three variables that might affect the estimated execution time, that are job size, quantity of processors and processor power. In our experimental computing environment, as the number of MPI jobs is divided by the number of processors, each processor will get coherent job sizes to execute. Load balancing can only be achieved by adding codes to MPI source code that cooperate with information service, since such cost is extremely high to users. We will leave this part of investigation for future research.

To meet the concept of heterogeneous environment, we propose the estimation model that considers the different processor power to formulate TET. We first define some terminologies that could affect the TET.

- T_mpi_{nop}: MPI start up time and Globus overhead of total *nop* processors,
- S_now: The total job size for current execution,
- Np_now: Number of processor for current execution,
- P_now_{pn}: Processor power for processor *pn*, $pn = 1 \sim Np\_now$,
- T_now: TET for current execution,
- N_pr: Number of previous result used for estimation,
- S_pre_{pr}: The total job size for previous *pr* times execution, *pr* from 1 to N_pr,
- Np_pre_{pr}: Number of processor for previous *pr* times execution, *pr* from 1 to N_pr,
- $P\_pre_{pn, pr}$: Processor power of processor *pn* for previous *pr* times execution, *pn* from 1 to Np_pre_{pr}, *pr* from 1 to N_pr,
- T_pre_{pr}: TET for previous *pr* times execution, *pr* from 1 to N_pr.

The part of jobs that every processor works on is calculated by:

$$Job\_pre = \frac{S\_pre_{pr}}{Np\_pre_{pr}}$$

The TET can be calculated by:

$$T\_pre = Max\left(\frac{Job\_pre}{P\_pre_1 \times \alpha}, \frac{Job\_pre}{P\_pre_2 \times \alpha}, ..., \frac{Job\_pre}{P\_pre_{Np\_pre} \times \alpha}\right) + T\_mpi_{nop}$$

$$= Job\_pre \times Max\left(\frac{1}{P\_pre_1 \times \alpha}, \frac{1}{P\_pre_2 \times \alpha}, ..., \frac{1}{P\_pre_{Np\_pre} \times \alpha}\right) + T\_mpi_{nop}$$

which can be simplified to

$$T\_pre = \frac{Job\_pre}{Min(P\_pre_1, P\_pre_2, ..., P\_pre_{Np\_pre}) \times \alpha} + T\_mpi_{nop}$$

This formula can be used to predict next execution time. This means that the slowest processor will slow down the progress of entire work. The TET is almost equivalent to the time that the slowest processor completing its job. Therefore, our estimation model is based on this particular idea. We must obtain the amount of work, so that it can be down per processor-power times TET (here we use the symbol α at previous result).

$$\alpha = Ave\left(\frac{Job\_pre_{pr}}{Min(P\_pre_{1,pr}, P\_pre_{2,pr}, ..., P\_pre_{Np\_pre,pr}) \times (T\_pre_{pr} - T\_mpi_{nop})}\right)$$

The function $Ave()$ is to calculate the average value of α. Finally, the estimated TET for current execution is:

$$T\_now = \frac{Job\_now}{Min(P\_now_1, P\_now_2, ..., P\_now_{Np\_now}) \times \alpha} + T\_mpi_{nop}$$

Our estimation model first gets rid of the influence of MPI and Globus overhead, in order to get actual processor execution time. Finally, we add this overhead according to how much processors is running. We will perform some experimental tests to obtain the table of overhead versus the number of processors.

3 Experimental Results

We built a computational Grid environment by using the Globus Toolkit 3.0.2 and MPICH library 1.2.6. The computing nodes are located in four different sites interconnected in TIGER project [8]. The average network bandwidth is about 30 Mbps over different sites. Table 1 shows the MPI and Globus overhead versus number of processors, that is, the real world value of T_mpi_{nop}. This variable is obtained by running hello world MPI program, which is almost the smallest program with no CPU power needed.

Table 1. MPI and Globus overhead vs. number of processors

N.O.P.	1	2	3	4	5	6	7	8	9	10
Time	1.10	12.56	12.40	14.47	14.15	15.73	16.23	16.93	16.97	16.86
N.O.P.	11	12	13	14	15	16	17	18	19	20
Time	17.31	17.64	18.88	20.86	23.59	26.62	26.51	26.93	27.01	27.84

During the test case, we chose three embarrassingly MPI parallel programs, which are CPI and prime number. These programs communicate at the start of execution, when master node communicates with slave nodes what parts of job which need to be handled and sent the results back to master node when execution is finish. We will describe the characteristics of each program and show the estimation result in following sections.

3.1 CPI Example

CPI is a program that calculates the π number accurately. It computes the value of π by numerical integration. Table 2 shows the calculated α value and estimated time in our model. We randomly execute CPI program on various numbers of processors with different CPU power. Up-left is the first execution result with 3 processors (N.O.P.). The second estimation is based on the first result; the third estimation is based on first and second result, and so on. This process continues until we have more then 5 newest previous results. The size in Table 2 is irrelevant because we can not change any parameter of this program. The value 100000 is just a proper value that makes α more readable. Figure 1 shows our model that can precisely estimate future values of execution time. In our experiments, the average error rate is 2.12% and the maximize error rate is 5.14%.

Table 2. Estimation results of CPI example

α	1.17683	1.18001	1.15143	1.16017	1.16946	1.16713	1.16509
Estimate		12.932	15.067	57.099	76.283	114.379	229.138
Time	30.174	12.897	15.420	57.555	76.130	114.423	229.248
Size	100000	100000	100000	100000	100000	100000	100000
N.O.P.	3	7	6	4	3	2	1
α	1.22250	1.21813	1.21436	1.16991	1.14709	1.14499	1.14963
Estimate	14.086	18.555	27.561	45.607	18.579	22.362	28.320
Time	13.397	17.926	26.973	46.680	19.404	23.327	29.041
Size	100000	100000	100000	100000	100000	100000	100000
N.O.P.	8	6	4	2	12	10	8

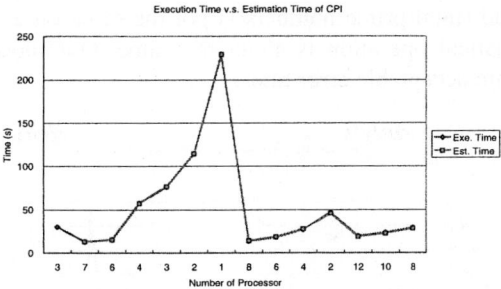

Fig. 1. Execution time vs. estimation time of CPI example

3.2 Prime Number Example

It is given a range of numbers where we want to find a list of prime numbers; for instance, between 1 and 20,000,000 (20 million). It proceeds to write code that initially runs on a master node and sends the task of testing 101-200 to node 1, and sends the task of testing 201-300 to node 2, and so on. Along with the testing task, there would also be an instruction to return prime numbers that a slave node discovered to the master node. When all nodes have completed their tasks, there will be a message to tell the amount of prime numbers is found and the biggest prime number. In this case, we still randomly execute prime number on various numbers of processors with various CPU power. Table 3 shows partial result of our estimation model. The size unit is million. Figure 2 shows our model that can still estimate the future execution time under an acceptable error. The average error rate is 28.82% and the maximize error rate is 57.84%.

Table 3. Estimation result of Prime number.

α	0.022972	0.018626	0.019046	0.017385	0.014597	0.012958
Estimate	26.184	47.537	39.309	59.605	107.777	176.815
Time	48.445	95.600	68.793	94.205	168.299	252.777
Size	50	80	80	100	150	200
NOP	12	12	8	8	8	8
α	0.011755	0.020827	0.015487	0.013007	0.007871	0.005814
Estimate	247.810	220.066	430.018	661.217	80.443	172.756
Time	348.315	160.061	430.503	768.894	151.321	409.746
Size	250	100	200	300	100	200
NOP	8	3	3	3	11	11

From the experiments, we can observe that, firstly, the estimation result of CPI is precise because there is no size variable, and the workload is equally distributed to each processor. Although the CPU power is different, our estimation model can handle it. Secondly, the prime number program owns almost the same characteristic with CPI, besides its size. The size here represents the total workload of program, which is linear increased. Although we cannot make sure that each processor will have equal workload (total prime numbers is not the same on each interval), but the amount of mathematical operation is about the same. Our model can estimate the execution time within acceptable error rate.

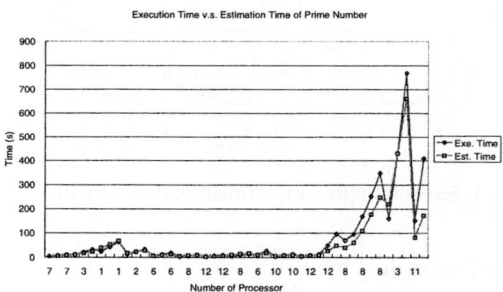

Fig. 2. Execution time vs. estimation time of Prime number

4 Conclusion

As Grid Computing is becoming a reality, there is a need for managing and monitoring the available resources worldwide, and require the prediction model to give users a general TET of his jobs or scheduling will be in job queue. This paper describes a historical based time estimation model that can predict TET within acceptable error rate which can be used for future job scheduling or users. We developed some small programs to get the variable needed for our model that would not cause any loading on the users. The experimental results shown that our model can accurately predict the execution time of embarrassingly parallel applications.

References

1. Global Grid Forum, http://www.ggf.org/
2. MPICH-G2, http://www.hpclab.niu.edu/mpi/
3. The Globus Project, http://www.Globus.org/
4. D.P. Spooner, S.A. Jarvis, J. Cao, S. Sainiz, and G.R. Nudd, "Local Grid Scheduling Techniques using Performance Prediction", *Computers and Digital Techniques, IEE Proceedings*, 150(2):87-96, May 2003,
5. K. Czajkowski, S. Fitzgerald, I. Foster, and C. Kesselman, "Grid Information Services for Distributed Resource Sharing", *Proc. of the Tenth IEEE International Symposium on High-Performance Distributed Computing*, IEEE Press, August 2001, available on http://www.globus.org/research/papers/MDS-HPDC.pdf
6. Introduction to Grid Computing with Globus, www.ibm.com/redbooks, 2002.
7. Yan Liu, "Survey on Grid Scheduling", available on http://www.cs.uiowa.edu/~yanliu/
8. C.T. Yang, K.C. Li, W.C. Chiang, and P.C. Shih, "Design and Implementation of TIGER Grid: an Integrated Metropolitan-Scale Grid Environment", *in Proc. of PDCAT 2005*.

Developing High-Performance Parallel Applications Using EPAS

Mohammad Mursalin Akon[1], Ajit Singh[1], Xuemin (Sherman) Shen[1], Dhrubajyoti Goswami[2], and Hon Fung Li[2]

[1] Department of Electrical and Computer Engineering,
University of Waterloo, Ontario, Canada
mmakon@ece.uwaterloo.ca, a.singh@ece.uwaterloo.ca,
xshen@bbcr.uwaterloo.ca
[2] Department of Computer Science,
Concordia University, Montreal, Canada
{goswami, hfli}@cs.concordia.ca

Abstract. In spite of the advent of high performance parallel computers and commodity clusters, complexity of parallel application development remains one of the major obstacles towards the mainstream adoption of parallel computing. Researchers are constantly investigating different approaches to reduce parallel application development time and increase productivity. As re-usable components, patterns have gained popularity in the sequential programming domain. Subsequently, several pattern-based parallel programming environments (PPEs) have been proposed to facilitate parallel application development procedure. Unfortunately, most of these PPEs lack the required flexibility in order to develop real-life parallel applications. In this paper, we describe the features of the EPAS (Extended Parallel Architectural Skeleton) PPE that enables development of complex parallel applications. We investigate and design the required patterns, and then use them to develop a parallel data cube computing application. Finally, we present the performance of the developed applications and discuss the results.

1 Introduction

Computer hardware has been getting inexpensive and faster. At the same time, scientists are investigating increasingly complex problems, requiring larger computing power, efficient algorithms and sophisticated software. Research in High Performance Computing (HPC) is exploring different aspects of available and foreseeable technology to realize those complex problems.

Design and development of parallel applications is complex. In this paper, we study a parallel programming environment (PPE) which is based on design patterns. In the domain of parallel computing, (parallel) design patterns specify recurring parallel computational problems with similar structural and behavioral components, and their solution strategies. Several parallel programming systems have been built with the intent to facilitate rapid development of parallel applications through the use of design patterns as reusable components. Some of these systems are *Enterprise* [1], *Tracs* [2], *DPnDP* [3], *COPS* [4], *PAS* [5], and *ASSIST* [6]. Most of the researches have focused on the algorithmic or behavioral aspects of patterns, popularly known as *algorithmic skeletons*. On the contrary, Parallel Architectural Skeletons (PAS) [7,5] focus on the architectural or structural aspects of message-passing parallel patterns. Each architectural skeleton in PAS encapsulates various structural attributes of a pattern in a generic (i.e., pattern- and application-independent) fashion.

Similar to the previous works, PAS was criticized due to the lack of supports to develop real-life parallel applications. EPAS [8], an extension of PAS, is a model which provides a high level abstraction to design parallel skeletons in a generic and platform independent way. We believe, this in turn expresses the ability to develop any form of parallel applications. In this paper, we demonstrate the use of EPAS to solve a real-life computational problem by developing a parallel data cube computing application.

The decision support system (DSS) needs analytical data to have a comprehensive view about the performance of the enterprise. Often queries for such analytical data are complex and require multi-dimensional view of the enterprise data. Codd et al. coined the term On-Line Analytical Processing (OLAP) which creates, manipulates, animates and synthesizes information from Enterprise Data Models (EDM) [9]. Usually relational databases are used to store and query about the enterprise data. Unfortunately, it is difficult to express those complex queries, required by the DSS, in SQL. The *CUBE* operation [10] was introduced to support multi-dimensional aggregates on OLAP databases. Later, multi-dimensional database system was proposed to provide a natural way to manage multi-dimensional aggregates.

An OLAP application usually analyzes a huge amount of data. On the contrary, a user would expect to have a real-time performance from the system. As a result, speed is a primary goal in this class of applications [9]. To make interactive analysis, OLAP databases usually pre-compute various aggregates on various combinations of attributes, often in the form of data cubes. However, speed is still a critical factor for this pre-computation as it affects how often the aggregates are revised. Several techniques have been proposed to speed up the data cube computational procedure [11,12]. Recent research efforts demonstrate that parallel computation of the data cube is the most effective solution [13,14].

While describing the design and development steps for the above application in EPAS, this paper illustrates different features and uses of this system. Throughout the paper, we answer the following questions:

– What is the EPAS model and how to map a parallel problem into this model?
– How to recognizing different parallel patterns, required to develop an application?
– How to design an EPAS parallel pattern which is not available in the repository?
– How to use the existing EPAS patterns (i.e., skeletons) to develop a parallel application?
– What is the performance implication of the applications developed using EPAS?

For the sake of clarity, we divide our discussion into the following sections. Section 2 section gives a brief introduction to the necessary preliminaries of PAS. Then we demonstrate the data cube application development procedure and explore different features of EPAS in section 3. Section 4 discusses the performance results and a detailed analysis. Finally, section 5 concludes our discussion and provides future research direction.

2 Preliminaries

Parallel Architectural Skeletons (PAS) [5, 7] generically encapsulate the structural/architectural attributes of message-passing parallel computing patterns. Each PAS skeleton is parameterized where each parameter is associated with some attributes. The value of a parameter is determined during the application development phase. A PAS skeleton with unbound parameters is called an *abstract skeleton*. An abstract skeleton becomes a *concrete skeleton*, when the parameters of the skeleton are bounded to actual values. A concrete skeleton is yet to be filled in with application-specific code. Filling a concrete skeleton with application-specific code results in a *code-complete parallel module* or simply a *module*. Various phases of an application development using PAS are roughly illustrated in Figure 1(a). The figure shows that different parameter bindings to the same abstract skeleton can result in different concrete skeletons.

Each abstract skeleton consists of the following set of attributes: (i) *Representative* of a skeleton represents the module in its action and interactions with other modules. The initial representative is empty and is subsequently filled with application-specific code during application development. (ii) The *back-end* of an abstract skeleton consists of a set of type-less abstract skeletons. The type

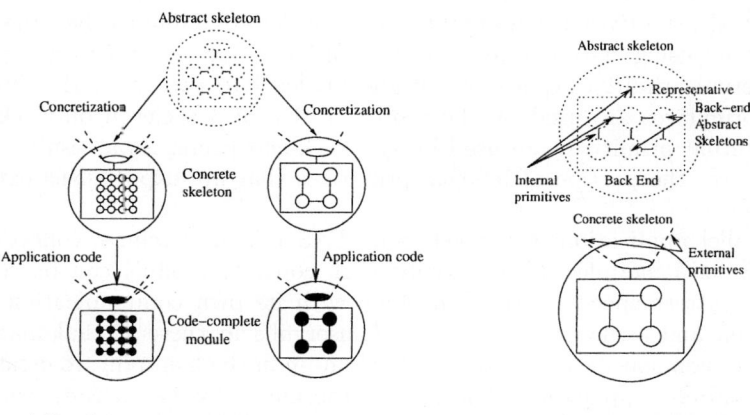

(a) Abstract skeleton, concrete skeleton and code complete module

(b) Different components of a skeleton

Fig. 1. PAS skeletons and their components

of each back-end skeleton is determined when the container abstract skeleton is concretized. Note that collection of concrete skeletons inside another concrete skeleton results in a (tree-structured) hierarchy. Consequently, each back-end skeleton has a *child-parent* relationship with its container skeleton. The children of a skeleton are *peers* of one another. In this paper, the children of a skeleton are also referred as *parallel entities* of the skeleton (or the associated pattern). (iii) *Topology* is the logical connectivity between the children as well as the connectivity between the children and the representative. (iv) *Internal primitives* are the pattern-specific communication, synchronization or structural primitives. Interactions among the various modules are performed using these primitives. The internal primitives are the inherent properties of a skeleton and capture the parallel computing model and topology of the associated pattern. Fig. 1(b) diagrammatically illustrates the attributes of an abstract and a concrete 2-D Data Parallel Mesh skeleton.

There are pattern-specific parameters associated with some of the previous attributes. For instance, if the topology is a Mesh, then the number of dimensions of the mesh is one parameter, and the nature of the connectivities among the nodes at the edges (i.e., toroidal or non-toroidal) is another parameter. Binding these parameters to actual values, based on the needs of an application, results in a concrete skeleton. A concrete skeleton becomes a code-complete module when: (i) the representative is filled in with application-specific code, and (ii) each child is code-complete.

All attributes of an abstract skeleton are inherited by the corresponding concrete skeleton and code-complete module. In addition, we define the term *external primitives* of a concrete skeleton or a code-complete module as the set of primitives using which the module (i.e. its representative) can interact with its parent (i.e. representative of the parent) and peers (i.e. representatives of the peers). Unlike internal primitives, which are inherent properties of a skeleton, external primitives are adaptable, i.e., a skeleton adapts to the context of its parent by using the internal primitives of its parent as its external primitives. Internal primitives of a skeleton are divided into two categories. *Private* internal primitives are used by the representative of a skeleton only whereas *Public* internal primitives are used by the back-end peers. As a result, public primitives are the portion of internal primitives that are exported as external primitives.

A parallel application developed using PAS is a hierarchical collection of (code-complete) modules. Conceptually, each concrete module can be considered as a pattern-specific virtual machine with its own communication, synchronization and structural primitives. A user fills in these virtual machines with application-specific code, starting bottom-up in the hierarchy, to create the complete parallel application. The root of the hierarchy, i.e., a code-complete module with no parent, represents a complete parallel application. Each non-root node of the hierarchy represents a partial parallel application. Each leaf of the hierarchy is called a *Singleton module* (and correspondingly, a *Singleton skeleton* for the abstract counterpart).

3 Developing the Data Cube Application

In this section, we describe different steps to develop a parallel data cube application using EPAS. We comprehend the discussion into the following sub-sections.

3.1 Problem Description

A data cube of raw data set R with d attributes (denoted as $D_1, D_2, \ldots D_d$) is composed of 2^d different views. Figure 2(a) shows a *lattice* of a data cube with attribute A, B, C and D. Both control parallel [15] and data parallel [13, 14] paradigm can be used to compute a data cube. In this paper, we consider a data parallel approach. Some hints about control parallel solution of the problem is discussed in sub-section 3.4.

In data parallel method, R is partitioned among p parallel computing entities (which are finally represented by p processes). Each entity computes all 2^d views considering only locally available data. A merge (reduction or gather) on the locally computed data cubes results in data cube, DC on entire R [14]. Here, we assume that $|D_1| \geq |D_2| \geq \ldots \geq |D_d|$, where $|D_i|$ is the cardinality of D_i. Denote D_i-*partition* as the set of views starting with D_i (refer to Fig. 2(b)). The computation of data cube can be expressed as,

```
for i = 1 to d do
   1. Partition the data on attribute D_i using Sample Sort
   2. Compute local D_i-partition
   3. Marge local D_i-partitions to compute global D_i-partition
```

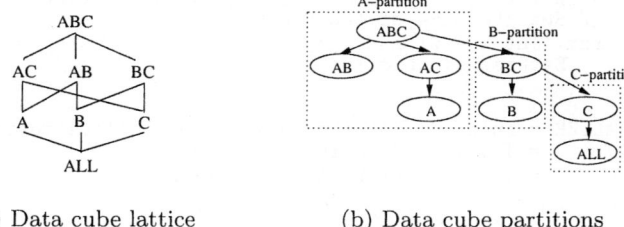

(a) Data cube lattice   (b) Data cube partitions

Fig. 2. Computing data cube

Chen et al. has proposed an Adaptive Sample Sort algorithm that partitions a data set, keeping load balancing in mind [14]. The algorithm sorts the initial data set $X_1, X_2, \ldots X_p$, distributed over processes $P_1, P_2, \ldots P_p$ to $X'_1, X'_2, \ldots X'_p$ which is globally sorted over the dimensions $D_i, D_{i+1}, \ldots D_d$ for D_i-partition. The algorithm chooses pivot points (for partitioning) through a collaborative regular (over) sampling procedure [16]. Computation of local D_i-partition by a process is a sequential operation without any collaboration. Finally, the merge operation is assigned to a dedicated process (P_0) so that other processes can go on with remaining computations.

3.2 Designing Phase

From the above discussion, developing a parallel data cube application should be easier with the use of a *Data Parallel* pattern. Along with many other skeletons, EPAS implements *Data Parallel* pattern as *DataParallel* skeleton (Fig. 3). However, for the sake of discussion, here, we consider that *DataParallel* skeleton does not exist in the skeleton repository and is required to be designed from the scratch.

A *Data Parallel* pattern represents the data parallel paradigm of parallel computing. It consists of a set of parallel entities where each parallel entity computes partial solution based on a subset of the input. Often the input data is partitioned into rows and/or columns (and/or at higher dimensions). A generic *Data Parallel* pattern has two parameters: (1) rank of the logical structure (denoted as *dim*) and (2) length of each of the dimensions (denoted as *length*). Fig. 3(b) shows an implementation of a *Data Parallel* pattern (i.e., *DataParallel* skeleton) in EPAS. The pattern is equipped with several public and private internal primitives. For example, an all-to-all communication is required by the parallel entities of the pattern to share some of their local data set (i.e., Sample Sort) and hence it is a private primitive. On the other hand, example of public primitive is that the representative gathers partial solutions from all the parallel entities (for the merge operation). After having those specifications, the design of the skeleton is straight forward. Following is the code of the skeleton, written using the Skeleton Description Language (SDL) of EPAS.

```
00 integer dim; // parameter: rank of the data parallel entities
01 integer length[dim]; // parameter: length of each dimension
02 pattern DataParallel(dim) { // Embedded into a dim dimensional VPG
03    LOCAL   = {
04       void init(void) { // The initialization function
05          // Set the size of the VPG space
06          for (int i = 0; i < dim; i++)
07             SetDimensionLimit(i, length[i]);
08       }
09    }
10    INITIALIZE = init; // Set the name of the initialization function
11    PRIVATE  = { ... }; // Private primitives
12    PUBLIC   = { ... }; // Public primitives
13 }
```

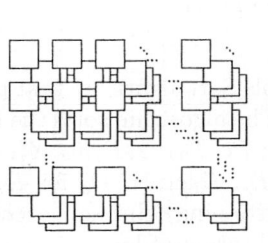
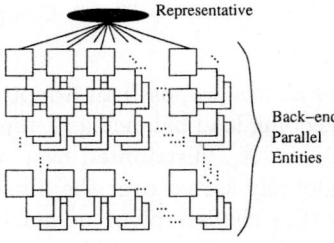

(a) Data parallel pattern   (b) DataParallel skeleton

Fig. 3. Designing required skeleton

An EPAS skeleton is designed on top of a set of virtual processor grids (VPG). Parallel entities of a *dim*-dimensional *DataParallel* skeleton can be easily mapped onto a *dim*-dimensional VPG. The size of the VPG is specified through the initialization function *init* (line 03 to 10). This function sets the length of dimension i to $length[i]$ (line 07). It may be worth mentioning that EPAS supports specification of a function $\mathcal{M} : L \to boolean$ which tells whether a location L of the VPG is part of the final skeleton. The existence of the representative and the support of $\mathcal{M}$ make the VPG model distinguished from the solid recti-linear Cartesian process model of MPI.

EPAS SDL supports a rich set of peer-to-peer and collective communication primitives as well as primitives to query about the structure of the underlying VPG. A skeleton designer develops the skeleton specific high level primitives on top of those built-in basic primitives. Some of the basic primitives can only be used to design either high level private or public primitives. For example, *AllToAllPeer* is a basic collective communication primitive to perform an all-to-all communication among back-end parallel entities. Hence, this primitive can be used to design public primitives only. However, *GetDimension* is a structural primitive to query about the rank of the associated VPG and can be used to design both public and private primitives. Following is a scratch of the primitives of the *DataParallel* skeleton.

```
integer dim; // rank of the data parallel entities
integer length(dim); // length of each dimensions
pattern DataParallel(dim) { // Embedded into a dim dimensional VPG
  PUBLIC     = { // Public primitives
    // primitive to do an all-to-all communication
    void AllToAllMesh(MsgVector msgSend, MsgVector msgRecv) {
      vector <Location> vl;
      ... // enumerates locations of all back-end entities in vl
      AllToAllPeer(vl, msgSend, msgRecv); // built-in primitive
    }
    ...
  }
  PRIVATE    = { // Private primitives
    // gather partial solutions from the back-end
    void GatherFromMesh(MsgVector msgRecv) {
      vector <Location> vl;
      ... // enumerates locations of all back-end entities in vl
      GatherChild(vl, msgRecv); // built-in primitive
    }
    ...
  }
}
```

The above SDL code uses several built-in objects. *Location* object represents a location in the VPG and *MsgVector* represents a vector of *Msg* object. Note that when a skeleton is used to develop an application, a developer can access only the high level primitives, designed into the skeleton. The basic primitives are completely hidden from the developer. Use of high level primitives, while developing an application, helps in reducing coding errors (provided that the designer ensures correctness of those primitives). As a result, skeletons provide a graceful way to develop parallel applications.

3.3 Development Phase

While using EPAS, an application developer needs to decide about the required skeletons. From sub-section 3.1, we know that the *DataParallel* skeleton is the perfect choice for developing the data cube application. The next step is to concretize the chosen skeleton. To concretize the *DataParallel* skeleton, the parameters are needed to be bounded with proper values. Parallel data cube application partitions data in columns, hence the parallel entities are of one dimension (i.e. *dim* is 1). We also need to specify the number of parallel entities by specifying proper value for *length*. Note that choice of this value is governed by the architecture of the application and the underlying platform.

To concretize *DataParallel* skeleton, we need to assign proper types for the back-end parallel entities. As each parallel entity of the application does a sequential computation, it is represented by a *DCSeq* skeleton, an instance of *Singleton*. Finally, the SDL code for concrete skeleton becomes as follow:

```
integer dim = 1; // 1 dimensional parallel entities
integer length(dim) = {4}; // which consists of 4 entries
pattern DataParallel(dim) { ... } // Embedded into a dim dimensional VPG
label { // mention the type of 4 parallel entities statically
  // in lexicographic order
  DCSeq{ }, DCSeq{ }, DCSeq{ }, DCSeq{ }
}
```

In stead of specifying the types of back-end entities statically, a developer can specify a function $\mathcal{L}: L \to A$ which labels a back-end entity of address L with an abstract skeleton A.

The developer can use the EPAS tools to generate C++ code for the designed skeleton hierarchy. The tools generate one file for each of the skeletons (i.e. for *DataParallel* and *DCSeq*). Finally, the developer needs to fill-up the skeletons with application specific code. For example, the role of the representative of the *DataParallel* skeleton is just to gather partial data cubes from all the *DCSeq* using the high level *GatherFromMesh* primitive and merge them into the final data cube.

3.4 Discussion

There are several ways to make the skeleton design and application development procedure more interesting. To make the *DataParallel* skeleton robust, the designer may introduce a third parameter to represent the choice of toroidal structure. In this way, the designer also needs to modify some of the primitives. The developer may want to combine control parallelism in this application by labelling the parallel entries of the *DataParallel* skeleton with proper control parallel skeleton(s), in stead of *DCSeq*.

4 Performance Related Issues

The usability studies of EPAS has been addressed in [8]. In this paper, we focus on the performance related issues. We developed our applications with the

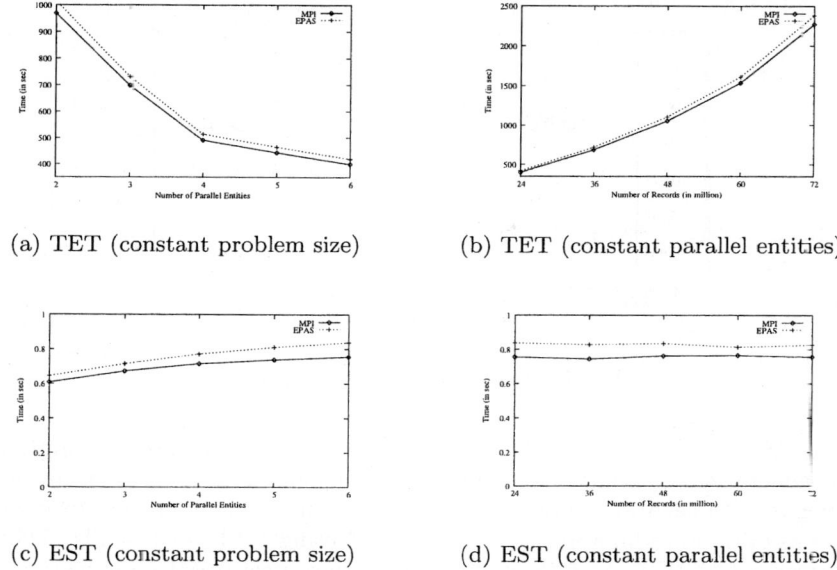

(a) TET (constant problem size)   (b) TET (constant parallel entities)

(c) EST (constant problem size)   (d) EST (constant parallel entities)

Fig. 4. Effects on performance

assumption that a parallel process can hold all its local data (consisting of 4 attributes) within the volatile memory. Chen et al. addressed the issue on performance where this assumption is not valid [14]. To run the application, we use a dedicated cluster with seven nodes. Each node is equipped with dual Pentium II 1 GHz processors, 512 MB memory, local SCSI hard drive and a connection to other nodes through a gigabits switch. We develop two sets of test cases: (1) variable number of parallel entities, keeping the input size fixed and (2) variable input size, keeping the number of parallel entities fixed. We develop the application using both MPI and EPAS to have a better understanding. For all the readings, we consider the average of five best runs out of fifteen.

Fig. 4(a) and Fig. 4(b) show the total execution time (TET) of the applications developed for both the test cases. It can be seen that EPAS applications are doing slightly poorer than the MPI applications. As the EPAS run-time system is developed on top of MPI-2 [17], this fact is very much expected. To have a better understanding, we divide TET into two segments: (1) environment setup time (EST) is the time to setup the parallel environment (for example, creating the processes, etc) and (2) actual computing time (ACT) is the time to compute the data cube. From Fig. 4(c) it can be seen that EST increments with the increasing number of parallel modules (as well as architecture of the application). This increment is faster in case of EPAS applications. Fig. 4(d) shows that with constant architecture of the parallel application, EST remains fairly constant (except the effect of the non-determinism). Note that EST takes place only once during the life-time of the application and hence, for an application with very long life-time, EST has almost negligible effect.

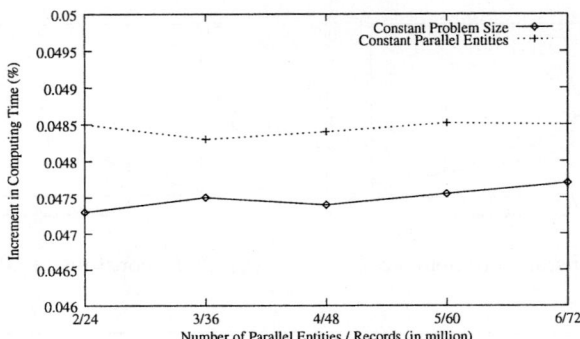

Fig. 5. Increment in computing time

The ACT of an EPAS application also faces a slowdown. This is mainly due to the generalized communication functions. Though EPAS tries to optimize the performance on each *Msg* object by using some rules, it may not produce result that is as optimal as an application, developed using MPI directly. Fig. 5 shows the increment of ACT of EPAS applications with respect to MPI applications for both the test cases. For this problem, both curves have very small slope and first test case produces steeper curve than the second (still all readings are less than 0.05%). Note that, increment of ACT depends on the behavior of the application as well as the way *Msg* objects are created.

5 Conclusion and Future Work

EPAS is an extensible parallel programming model and environment. It is implemented through a skeleton description language (SDL) which can be used by a skeleton designer to design new skeletons. The generic abstraction provided by the model as well as the SDL facilitates faster development of parallel applications. In this paper, we demonstrated that EPAS is a very attractive environment to develop real-life parallel applications without compromising performance.

We believe that EPAS now encompasses the core technical capabilities that are required in a flexible and extensible pattern-based parallel programming system whose repository of patterns would continue to evolve with time. Perhaps, the usability of the EPAS system could be further enhanced by designing a suitable graphical user interface for the system. Moreover, the associated subsystems for *performance modeling and profiling* need to be included into the system to provide a complete PPE. Currently we are investigating these aspects. A *synchronization skeleton* that extracts the communication-synchronization behavioral slice of a given parallel application is of particular interest. We are also working on the issues of *static and dynamic optimizations* and *fault tolerance* aspects of applications developed using EPAS, and these issues will be reported in our future works.

Acknowledgment

This research has been supported by grants from the Natural Sciences and Engineering Research Council (NSERC) of Canada.

References

1. Schaeffer, J., Szafron, D., Lobe, G., Parsons, I.: The enterprise model for developing distributed applications. IEEE Parallel and Distributed Technology: Systems and Applications **1** (1993) 85–96
2. Bartoli, A., Corsini, P., Dini, G., Prete, C.A.: Graphical design of distributed applications through reusable components. IEEE Parallel and Distributed Technology **3** (1995) 37–50
3. Siu, S., Singh, A.: Design patterns for parallel computing using a network of processors. In: 6th International Symposium on High Performance Distributed Computing (HPDC '97), Portland, OR (1997) 293–304
4. MacDonald S., Szafron, D., Schaffer, J., Bromling, S.: From patterns to frameworks to parallel programs. Parallel Computing **28** (2002) 1663–1683
5. Goswami, D., Singh, A., Preiss, B.R.: From design patterns to parallel architectural skeletons. Journal of Parallel and Distributed Computing **62** (2002) 669–695
6. Vanneschi, M.: The programming model of assist, an environment for parallel and distributed portable applications. Parallel Computing **28** (2002) 1709–1732
7. Goswami, D.: Parallel Architectural Skeletons: Re-Usable Building Blocks for Parallel Applications. PhD thesis, University of Waterloo, Canada (2001)
8. Akon, M.M., Goswami, D., Li, H.F.: A model for designing and implementing parallel applications using extensible architectural skeletons. In: The Eighth International Conference on Parallel Computing Technologies (to appear), Krasnoyarsk, Russia (2005)
9. Codd, E.F., Codd, S.B., Smalley, C.T.: Providing OLAP to user-analysts: An it mandate. Technical report, E. F. Codd and Associates, CA (1993)
10. Gray, J., Bosworth, A., Layman, A., Pirahesh, H.: Data cube: A relational operator generalizing group-by, tross-tab and sub-totals. In: The 12th International Conference on Data Engineering. (1996) 152–159
11. Agarwal, S., Agrawal, R., Deshpande, P.M., Gupta, A., Naughton, J.F., Ramakrishnan, R., Sarawagi, S.: On the computation of multidimensional aggregates. In: Proc. 22nd Int. Conf. Very Large Databases, VLDB. (1996) 506–521
12. Harinarayan, V., Rajaraman, A., Ullman, J.D.: Implementing data cube eddiciently. In: The 1996 ACM-SIGMOD Conference. (1996)
13. Goil, S., Choudhary, A.: High performance olap and data mining on parallel computers. Data Min. Knowl. Discov. **1** (1997) 391–417
14. Dehne, F., Eavis, T., Hambrusch, S., Rau-Chaplin, A.: Parallelizing the data cube. Parallel and Distributed Databases **15** (2004) 219–236
15. Dehne, F., Eavis, T., Hambrusch, S., Rau-Chaplin, A.: Parallelizing the data cube. Parallel and Distributed Databases **11** (2002) 181–201
16. Li, X., Lu, P., Schaeffer, J., Shillington, J., Wong, P.S., Shi, H.: On the versatility of parallel sorting by regular sampling. Parallel Computing **19** (1993) 1079–1103
17. Forum, M.: Message passing interface forum (2004)

On Utilization of the Grid Computing Technology for Video Conversion and 3D Rendering*

Chao-Tung Yang[1,*], Chuan-Lin Lai[1], Kuan-Ching Li[2],
Ching-Hsien Hsu[3], and William C. Chu[1]

[1] High Performance Computing Laboratory,
Department of Computer Science and Information Engineering,
Tunghai University, Taichung 40704, Taiwan ROC
ctyang@thu.edu.tw, chu@csie.thu.edu.tw
[2] Parallel and Distributed Processing Center,
Department of Computer Science and Information Management,
Providence University, Taichung 43301, Taiwan ROC
kuancli@pu.edu.tw
[3] Department of Computer Science and Information Engineering,
Chung Hua University, Hsinchu 300, Taiwan ROC
chh@chu.edu.tw

Abstract. In this paper, we investigate the recent popular computing technique called Grid Computing, and use video conversion and 3D rendering applications to demonstrate this technology's effectiveness and high performance. We also report on developing a resource broker called Phantom that runs on our grid computing testbed and whose main function is querying nodes in grid computing environments and showing their system information to aid in selecting the best nodes for job assignments to have the jobs executed in the least amount of time.

Keywords: Grid computing, Resource broker, Job submission, Video conversion, 3D rendering.

1 Introduction

Advances in media technology have made possible to store the content of complete DVDs on a single CD-ROM without noticeable loss of quality, which implies that expensive DVD burners with limited recording capacities are obsolete. To copy a video of up to 9 GB from a DVD to a CD-ROM, it is required large amounts of computing power and time, since the data volume must be reduced to about $1/12th$ of its original size to accommodate the limited 700 MB CD-ROM storage capacity. Data compression of this magnitude for digital video is only possible with the new MPEG-

---

* The authors would like to acknowledge the National Center for High-Performance Computing for sponsoring the Taiwan UniGrid project, under the national project "Taiwan Knowledge Innovation National Grid".
* Corresponding author.

4 video compression standard. Generally speaking, MPEG-4 is an extension of MPEG-2 technology, but MPEG-4 can be used more universally, with additional novel extensions [8, 9, 12, 13]. Converting a DVD title to MPEG-4 format on a single PC usually requires the steps shown in Figure 1.

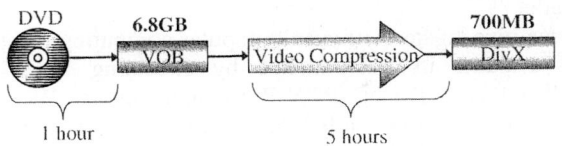

Fig. 1. Video conversion – single stream

It is hard to reduce the transfer time from the DVD to a storage device without upgrading to a SCSI transfer bus or using a RAID storage system. The video conversion time is the key to reducing the total time. One sequential processing machine needs 5 hours of compression time. However, if the video file is divided and the sub-files submitted to different compression computing nodes, it is possible to reduce the total video conversion time.

A grid computing resource broker can help users find available resources, to complete video conversion jobs. As each computing node completes its conversion job, it sends its results to the master node on the grid platform for combining. Thus, the process can save large amounts of time. The need for and a number of uses of this technology are explored in [1, 2, 3, 4, 5, 6, 7, 10, 11, 15, 16, 17]. Past studies on the video conversion testbed were based on local PCs, clusters, or supercomputers. However, there were problems with insufficient computing power and storage space. In this paper, the video conversion application was built to show a potentially practical use of the grid as well as to give a feel for the problems that may be encountered with data intensive applications. Video file conversions to be processed are simply submitted to the grid system, where the resource broker assigns them to the most suitable computing nodes in various sites. Use of our resource broker thus ensures that our goal of having submitted video conversion jobs concluded in the shortest possible time is achieved as shown in Figure 2.

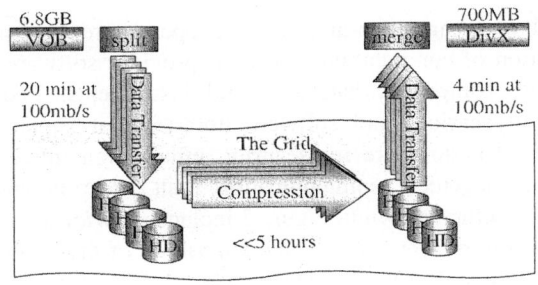

Fig. 2. Video conversion using Grid computing platform

Rendering refers to generating graphic images from mathematical models of two- and three-dimensional objects and scenes. Ray tracing, a common rendering technique, is used in computer graphics to create realistic images by calculating the paths taken by light rays entering the observer's eye at different angles. It is ideal for parallel processing since it involves many pixels with independent values that can be calculated in parallel [14].

In this paper, we investigate the recently popular computing technique called Grid Computing and evaluate its performance by executing video conversion and Persistence of Vision Ray Tracer (POV-Ray) applications. We also discuss the development of a resource broker called Phantom that runs on top of grid computing platforms. The Phantom resource broker's main job is to query computing nodes in Grid environments about their system information, and find one or more computing sites that best fit job-computing requirements provided by users and assign jobs for execution in the shortest time.

This paper is organized as follows. Background information on grid computing, the Globus Toolkit, video conversion and 3D rendering is given in Section 2. In Section 3, a grid platform used for experiments is introduced and some experimental results are discussed. Concluding remarks are presented and discussed in Section 4.

2 Background

2.1 Grid Computing

Grid computing enables the virtualization of distributed computing and data resources such as processing, network bandwidth, and storage capacity to create a single system image, granting users and applications seamless access to vast IT capabilities. Just as an Internet user views a unified instance of content via the Web, a grid user essentially sees a single, large virtual computer. At its core, grid computing is based on an open set of standards and protocols—Open Grid Services Architecture (OGSA)—that enable communication across heterogeneous, geographically dispersed environments. With Grid computing, organizations can optimize computing and data resources, pool them for large capacity workloads, share them across networks, and enable collaboration [1, 2, 3, 4, 5, 6, 7, 10, 11, 16].

2.2 Globus Toolkit

The Globus Toolkit is an open-architecture, open-source software toolkit that facilitates the creation of computational grids. It provides software tools that enable coupling of people, computers, databases and instruments. The Globus Toolkit consists of a set of services and software libraries that support grids and grid applications. Included is software for security, information infrastructure, resource management, data management, communication, fault detection, and portability. The layered Globus architecture shown in Figure 3 includes *fabric*, *connectivity*, *resource*, *collective* and *application* layers [16]. The composition of the Globus Toolkit can be pictured as three pillars: Resource Management, Information Services, and Data Management. Each pillar represents a primary component of the Globus Toolkit and makes use of a common foundation of security. The Globus Resource Allocation

Manager (GRAM) implements a resource management protocol, the Metacomputing Directory Service (MDS) implements an information services protocol, and GridFTP implements a data transfer protocol. They all use the GSI security protocol at the connection layer.

With Globus, jobs can be run on two or more high-performance parallel machines at the same time even though the machines might be located far apart and owned by different organizations. Globus software helps scientists deal with very large datasets and complex remote collaborations. Globus software is used for large distributed computational jobs, remote instrumentation, and remote data transfers.

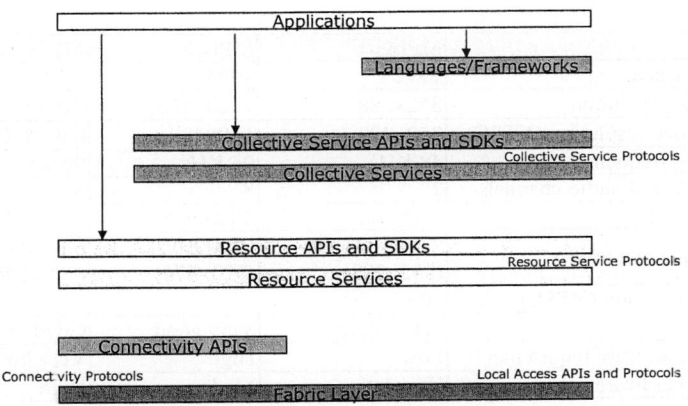

Fig. 3. The Globus Grid architecture, its protocols, services and APIs at each level

2.3 Video Format

Four choices are available for backing up DVD titles: VCD, MPEG4 (Divx), AVI, and video cassettes. Unfortunately, using AVI and video cassettes is impossible since raw AVI files are too large. Storing one minute of a raw AVI file requires about 207 MB of storage space. A DVD title has 135 minutes of playing time, and thus, backing it up requires some 27 GB of storage space. Video cassettes also have drawbacks. First, backing up a 135-minute DVD title requires 135 minutes (1:1 transfer ratio). Thus, backing up DVD titles on video cassettes is time-consuming. Second, video cassettes are about 2cm thick, where DVDs are 0.1cm thick. Thus, backing up DVDs on video cassettes is space-consuming.

The history of MPEG dates back to 1987. MPEG stands for Motion Pictures Expert Group, a worldwide organization that develops manufacturer- and platform-independent standards for video compression. Its first effort was introduced as MPEG-1 in 1992, and was the basis for the less-successful European Video-CD. Because its resolution is limited to 352×288 pixels, MPEG-1 is considered suitable only for home use, and its achievable video quality in relation to its data rate is rather low by today's standards. MPEG-2, based mainly on MPEG-1, was introduced in 1995. Its higher resolution—maximum 720×576 pixels—was a major improvement enabling significantly better video quality. MPEG-4 was released by the MPEG group in December 1999.

MPEG-1 features small files, but also has low quality; MPEG-2 has excellent video quality, but also large files. MPEG-4 thus has an advantage with "very good quality and small file sizes" [12]. See Table 1 for a comparison of the MPEG-1, MPEG-2, and MPEG-4 standards. Table 2 shows that after conversion, a 130-minute DVD (MPEG-2) or VCD (MPEG-1) will total 1.2GB (Divx) and 500MB (Divx), respectively.

Table 1. Comparison among MPEG-1, MPEG-2, and MPEG-4 standards

	MPEG-1	MPEG-2	MPEG-4
Available since	1992	1995	1999
Max. video resolution	352×288	1920×1152	720×576
Default video resolution (NTSC)	352×288	640×480	640×480
Max. audio frequency range	48 KHz	96 KHz	96 KHz
Max. number of audio channels	2	8	8
Max. data rate	3 Mb/sec	80 Mb/sec	5 to 10 Mb/sec
Regular data rate used	1380 Kb/sec (352×288)	6500 Kb/sec (720×576)	880 Kb/sec (720×576)
Frames per second (NTSC)	30	30	30
Video quality	Satisfactory	Very good	Good to very good
Encoding hardware requirements	Low	High	Very high
Decoding hardware requirements	Very low	Medium	High

Table 2. DVD and VCD converted file sizes

130 min. movie	Source file size	Destination file size
DVD (MPEG-2)	4.3GB (VOB)	1.2GB (Divx)
VCD (MPEG-1)	1.2GB (DAT)	500MB (Divx)

2.4 3D Rendering

Rendering refers to generating graphic images from mathematical models of two- and three-dimensional objects and scenes. Ray tracing, a common rendering technique, is used in computer graphics to create realistic images by calculating the paths taken by light rays entering the observer's eye at different angles. It is ideal for parallel processing since it involves many pixels with independent values that can be calculated in parallel.

The Persistence of Vision Ray Tracer (POV-Ray) is a 3-dimensional ray-tracing software package [14]. It takes input information and simulates the way light interacts with the objects defined to create 3D pictures and animations. Newer versions of POV-Ray can also use a variant of the process known as radiosity (sophisticated lighting) to add greater realism to scenes, particularly those with diffuse lighting, by simulating many atmospheric and volumetric effects, such as smoke and haze.

3 Experimental Results

3.1 Experimental Environments

We have built a grid computing testbed that includes four Linux PC clusters. Site 1 has 4 PCs with single Intel Celeron 1700 MHz processors, 256MB DDRAM, and 3Com 3c9051 interfaces. Site 2 has 4 PCs with Dual Intel Pentium3 866 MHz processors, 256MB SDRAM, and 3Com 3c9051 interfaces. Site 3 has 4 PCs with single Intel Pentium4 2.53GHz processors, 512MB DDRAM, and Intel PRO100 VE interfaces. Site 4 has 4 PCs with single Intel Pentium4 2.4GHz processors, 256MB DDRAM, and Accton EN-1216 interfaces.

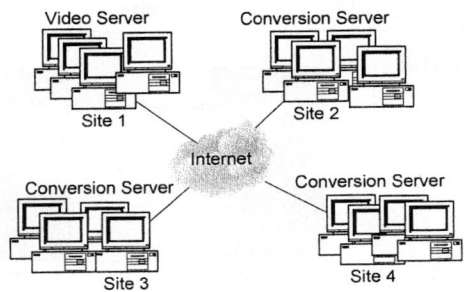

Fig. 4. Our grid computing testbed

Sites 1, 2, and 3 are located in various departments and laboratories at Tunghai University, Taiwan, while Site 4 is located at Taiwan's National Center for High-Performance Computing (NCHC). A general application was run to benchmark network traffic among sites. The results showed that the average network latency for Sites 1, 2, and 3 was 3ms, and the maximum transfer speed was 7600KB/s. Between Sites 1, 2, and 3 and Site4 the average network latency was 5ms and the maximum transfer speed was 2000KB/s.

3.2 Software for Video Compression

This section discusses DVD-to-DivX video conversion compression using grid technology. As shown in Figure 5, the first step is to split VOB files into as many chunks as the video conversion grid system has nodes. The sizes of divided files are based on information available in the MDS, as shown in Figure 6. Clients can gather useful information from the MDS, such as computational capacity, CPU loading, number of nodes, etc., and clients can submit jobs, represented by RSL, to remote servers using Globus GRAM. At present, divided VOB files are transferred to each conversion server's NFS via GridFTP. See Figures 6 and 7 for details. GRAM then submits the jobs to SGE for scheduling on clusters. As shown in Figure 7, SGE orders its nodes to compress the VOB file sections in its NFS, and as each node finishes compressing, it returns DivX files after conversion to the video server for merging.

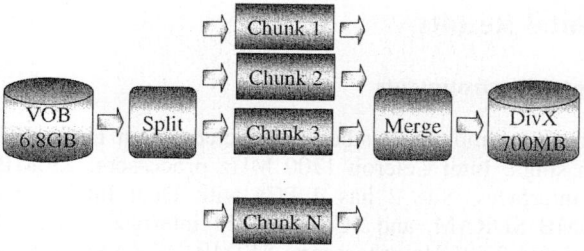

Fig. 5. Split and Merge video files

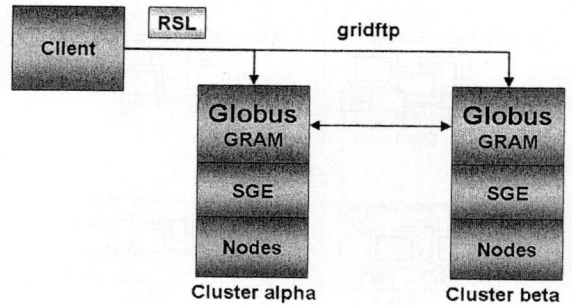

Fig. 6. System components

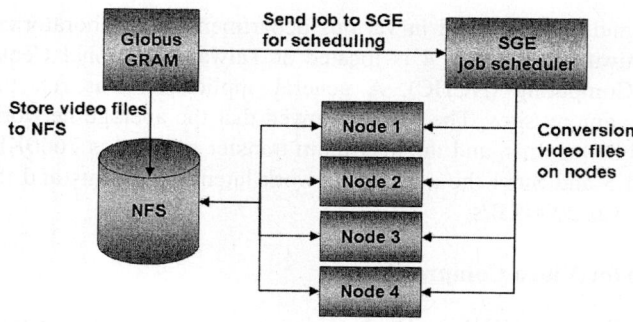

Fig. 7. Conversion server components

3.3 Phantom

We designed and implemented a Grid-Enabled Video converter broker called Phantom. This resource broker's implementation is based on Java CoG and Globus API, as shown in Figure 8. The use of Java technology means Phantom runs on various platforms and OSs, and can make use of Globus services, such as resource allocation information and data management services. Phantom gathers information on idle resources and storage space.

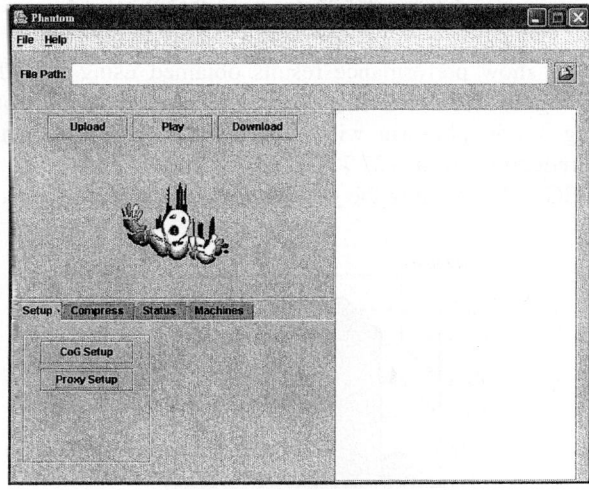

Fig. 8. Phantom resource broker main screen

Phantom can predict video transfer times, video conversion times, and storage system space by obtaining system information using MDS. After determining the best locations for video conversion, Phantom submits jobs to the master system. Figure 9 shows Phantom's input and output file formats.

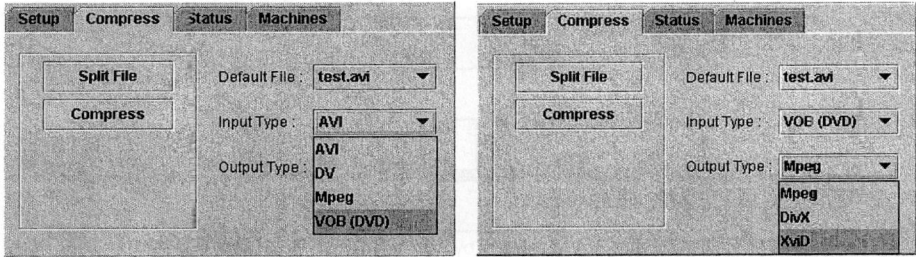

Fig. 9. Phantom resource broker's input and output files formats

The Phantom resource broker consists of the following major components.

1. **Information Monitor:** tracks system factors such as video transfer time, CPU type, storage system spaces; uses Globus MDS to gather needed information,
2. **Location Finder:** via the Information Monitor, evaluates and predicts where to find available systems,
3. **Data Transfer:** transfers files to destination nodes in specific system sites selected by the Location Finder; currently uses GridFTP for transfers,
4. **Executer:** uses Globus GRAM service to execute jobs on remote sites after file transfers to destination nodes.

3.4 Performance Results of Video Conversion

Figures 10 and 11 show performance results obtained using our Phantom broker, respectively. In Figure 10, conversion time is shown reduced from 2175.54s to 361.83s by using a grid platform with 8 processors. Figure 11 shows respective conversion time reductions from 127.73s to 29.75s, and 152.11s to 33.69s, for MPEG to XviD and MPEG to DviX using the grid platform with 8 processors.

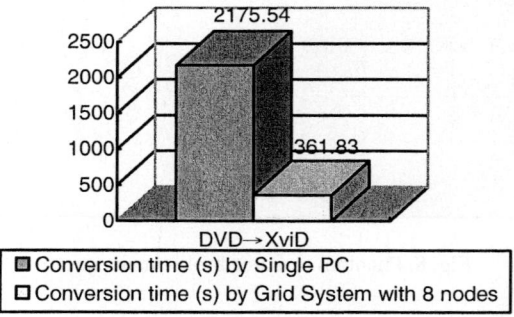

Fig. 10. Comparison of DVD and XviD conversion times using single PC and grid platform

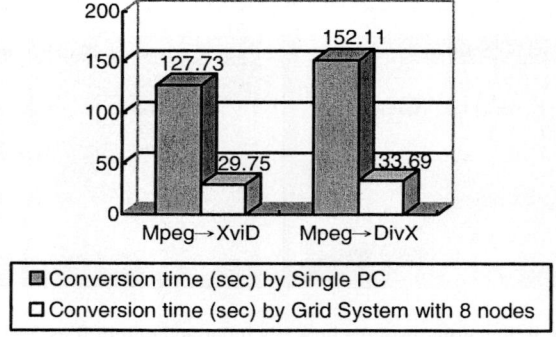

Fig. 11. Comparison of MPEG to XviD and MPEG to DivX conversion times using single PC and grid platform

3.5 Performance Results of 3D Rendering

MPI-Povray is used to demonstrate the performance of 3D rendering. MPI-Povray has the ability to distribute a rendering across multiple heterogeneous systems. Using the MPI code, there is one master and many slave tasks. The master has the responsibility of dividing the image up into small blocks, which are assigned to the slaves. When the slaves have finished rendering the blocks, they are sent back to the master, which combines them to form the final image. The code is designed to keep the available slaves busy, regardless of system loading and network bandwidth.

MPI-Povray consists of a patch to the Povray 3.1g raytracer that distributes work amongst a number of processing elements. Communication between the elements

Fig. 12. Images of three POV models

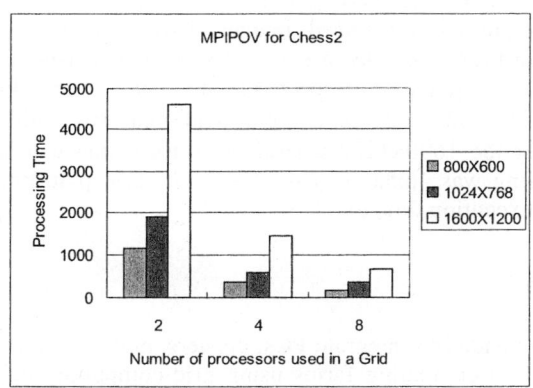

Fig. 13. Chess2.pov model processing times

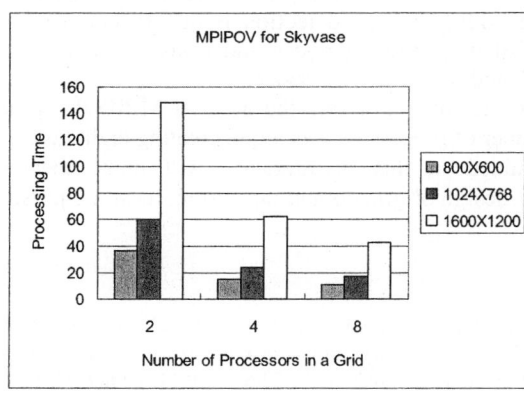

Fig. 14. Skyvase.pov model processing times

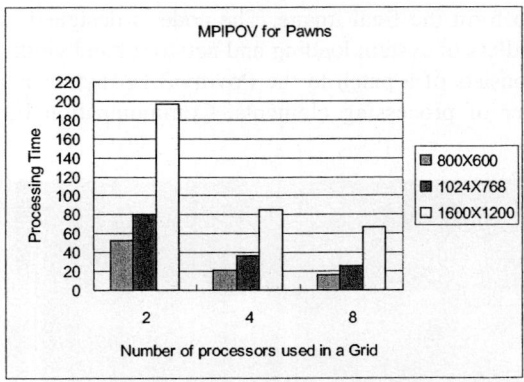

Fig. 15. Pawns.pov model processing times

achieved with MPI message passing [14]. MPI-Povray was executed on our grid platform to generate the ray-traced images shown in Figure 12. The POVray execution times for the Chess, Skyvase, and Pawns models using the grid platform are shown in Figures 13, 14, and 15, respectively. The greatest speedup was obtained for the 1600×1280 Chesss2 model using our grid platform with 8 processors. The rendering time for the 1600×1280 Chess2.pov model image using single-processor mode for processing was 4,652 seconds. Using the grid platform with 8 processors reduced the total execution time to 647 seconds.

4 Conclusion

This research is intended to integrate PCs, clusters, and SMP machines on campuses and the Internet into computing farms using grid-computing technology, as also to fully utilize available resources and idle cycles in these systems. We have developed the resource broker, called Phantom, to assist users in finding suitable resources for video conversion and 3D rendering in grid systems without wasting time. Our future work will include adding a fault-detection policy to enable the Phantom resource broker to detect failed computing nodes and re-assign their jobs to other available computing nodes listed by the MDS service.

Our experimental results show that the greatest MPIPOV speedups were obtained when the total number of processors was eight, creating eight tasks on the grid platform. The findings obtained in this investigation will make theoretical and technical contributions to the design of grid computing system message-passing applications.

References

1. W. Allcock, "GridFTP Protocol Specification", *Global Grid Forum Recommendation GFD.20*, April 2003, http://www.globus.org/alliance/publications/papers/GFD-R.0201.pdf
2. B. Allcock, J. Bester, J. Bresnahan, A. Chervenak, I. Foster, C. Kesselman, S. Meder, V. Nefedova, D. Quesnel, S. Tuecke, "Data Management and Transfer in High-Performance Computational Grid Environments," *Parallel Computing*, 28(5):749-771, May 2002.

3. K. Czajkowski, S. Fitzgerald, I. Foster and C. Kesselman, "Grid Information Services for Distributed Resource Sharing," *Proceedings of the Tenth IEEE International Symposium on High-Performance Distributed Computing (HPDC-10'01)*, pp. 181-194, August 2001.
4. K. Czajkowski, I. Foster, N. Karonis, C. Kesselman, S. Martin, W. Smith, and S. Tuecke, "A Resource Management Architecture for Metacomputing Systems", *Proc. IPPS/SPDP '98 Workshop on Job Scheduling Strategies for Parallel Processing*, pp. 62-82, 1998.
5. I. Foster, "The Grid: A New Infrastructure for 21st Century Science", *Physics Today*, 55(2):42-47, 2002.
6. I. Foster and C. Kesselman, eds., *The Grid 2: Blueprint for a New Computing Infrastructure*, Morgan Kaufmann; 2nd edition, 2004.
7. Global Grid Forum, http://www.ggf.org/
8. T.S. Gunawan and Cai Wen Tong, "Parallel motion estimation on SMP system and cluster of SMPs," *APCCAS '02. 2002 Asia-Pacific Conference on Circuits and Systems*, Vol. 2, pp. 467-472, Oct. 2002.
9. Yong He, Ishfaq Ahmad, and Ming L. Liou, "Real-Time Interactive MPEG-4 System Encoder Using a Cluster of Workstations," *IEEE Transactions on Multimedia*, 1(2):217-233, June 1999.
10. IBM Redbooks, *Introduction to Grid Computing with Globus*, http://www.redbooks.ibm.com/redbooks/pdfs/sg246895.pdf
11. IBM Redbooks, *Enabling Applications for Grid Computing with Globus*, http://www.redbooks.ibm.com/redbooks/pdfs/sg246936.pdf
12. Jack Y.B. Lee, "Parallel Video Servers: A Tutorial," *IEEE Multimedia*, 5(2):20-28, April-June 1998.
13. MPEG-4 - Copying a DVD Video to CD-ROM, http://www.tomshardware.com/video/20000913/
14. MPI-Povray, http://www.verrall.demon.co.uk/mpipov/
15. Sun N1 Grid Engine 6, http://wwws.sun.com/software/gridware/
16. The Globus Alliance, http://www.globus.org
17. X. Zhang, J. Freschl, and J. Schopf, "A Performance Study of Monitoring and Information Services for Distributed Systems", *Proceedings of 12th IEEE International Symposium on High Performance Distributed Computing (HPDC-12 '03)*, pp. 270-282, August 2003.

Communication-Free Data Alignment for Arrays with Exponential References Using Elementary Linear Algebra

Weng-Long Chang[1], Minyi Guo[2], Michael (Shan-Hui) Ho[1], and Sien-Tang Tsai[1]

[1] Department of Information Management,
Southern Taiwan University of Technology,
Tainan County, Taiwan
{changwl, tsai}@mail.stut.edu.tw, MHoInCerritos@yahoo.com
[2] Department of Computer Software,
The University of Aizu,
Aizu-Wakamatsu City, Fukushima 965-8580, Japan
minyi@u-aizu.ac.jp

Abstract. For array references with induction variables, after induction variable substitution for those induction variables is performed, those array references substituted are transformed as *nonlinear* expressions. The goal of data alignment is to intelligently map computations and data onto a set of virtual processors organized as a Cartesian grid with multi-dimensions (or a *template* in HPF term), and to provide data locality in a program so that the data access communication costs can be minimized. Most data alignment methods are mainly devised to align the arrays referenced using linear subscripts or quadratic subscripts with n loop index variables [Chang, 2004]. In this paper, we propose a new communication-free data alignment technique to align the arrays referenced using *exponential* subscripts with n loop index variables or other complex nonlinear expressions. The experimental results from our techniques on SPEC95FP Benchmarks point out that the techniques can be applied to improve the execution time of the subroutines in those benchmarks.

1 Introduction

For scientific and engineering applications, parallel systems based on distributed memory multicomputers have been increasingly applied [Guo 2003a and 2003b, Chang et al. 2004, Alex et al. 2004]. The main shortcoming of distributed memory multicomputers is the difficulty in programming because of without shared memory space [Michael 1996]. In such systems, the programmers (or compilers) must be responsible for distributing the computations and data in a program over processors and managing communications among tasks. Thus, carefully arranging the computations and data locality in a program can improve their throughput. This matter relates to determine which computations need to be distributed onto which processors and what data should be stored locally for the corresponding computations to access with little or no communication cost [Ramanujam et al. 1991, Chang et al. 2004].

Induction variable is one scalar integer variable, which is used in a loop to simulate do-variables: it is incremented or decremented by a constant amount through each iteration. Every induction variable can be replaced by a linear function or a nonlinear function in the form of do-variables. The transformation is called *induction variable substitution*. Consider do-loop shown in Figure 1(a). If induction variable substitution is performed for the induction variable K, the result after transformation can be shown in Figure 1(b). In Figure 1(b), each array reference contains 2 raised to the power of the outer loop index I. No existed data alignment method can be applied to solve the problem of communication-free data alignment for the case in Figure (1b). Therefore, an efficient and precise method for solving the problem of communication-free data alignment for arrays with *exponential* references is very important.

$K=2$	$K=2$
$DO\ I = 1, N, 1$	$DO\ I = 1, N, 1$
$DO\ J = 1, 2**I, 1$	$DO\ J = 1, 2**I, 1$
$\quad K = K + 1$	$\quad K = 2**I + J$
$S:\ X(K) = Y(K) * Z(K)$	$S:\ X(2**I + J) = Y(2**I + J) * Z(2**I + J)$
$\quad ENDDO$	$\quad ENDDO$
$ENDDO$	$ENDDO$

Fig. 1(a). A do loop   **Fig. 1(b).** After an induction variable induction variable substitution for the induction variable K

Fig. 1. A do-loop in a Fortran program

In this paper, we offer the alignment techniques to properly map the loop iteration space that implies the computation instances, and the array elements which are respectively referred using exponential subscripts with multiple loop index variables, onto the virtual processors so that no communication cost for data accesses is yielded. Based on operations of elementary linear algebra, our alignment methods reduce the mapping problem of the computations and array elements into the problem of determining a null space basis for a matrix. From solving the null space basis, the presented methods can readily figure out the desired mapping functions.

2 Background

The primary communication-free data alignment notion is described in subsection 2.1. Simultaneously, existed famous methods for solving the problem of communication-free data alignment are also shortly introduced in subsection 2.2.

2.1 Preliminary Data Alignment Notion

In general, the complete communication-free data alignment framework actually consists of three primary phases in terms of elementary linear algebra [Bau et al.]. The first phase is to figure out the constraints on the data mapping and computation.

In this phase, the data accesses in a program are inspected and formulated as a system of equations in which the unknowns can be utilized to compute the virtual processors for the computations and data to be mapped onto. Each equation in the system is actually equal to a constraint on the data mapping and computation. Any solution to the system figures out a so-called communication-free data alignment.

An alignment technique was offered from [Bau et al. 1994] and was applied to align arrays referenced using linear subscripts with one loop index variable in a communication-free manner. New communication-free alignment methods were proposed from [Chu et al. 1998, Chang et al. 2001] and were used to align the arrays referenced using linear subscripts with three loop index variables. For array references with *quadratic* subscripts or linear subscripts in a general n do loops, two new data alignment technologies were proposed from [Chang et al. 2004]. Our proposed techniques use to properly map the loop iteration space onto the virtual processors so that no communication cost for data accesses.

3 The Proposed Alignment Techniques

For referenced arrays, linear expressions with constant coefficients are the most common subscript patterns. [Peterson et al. 1996] pointed out that there are 5242 linear cases with *symbolic* coefficients, 6503 *nonlinear* cases and 4304 cases with references containing *arrays* in the analyzed Perfect Benchmarks, which were obtained in counting the number of feasible directions of the potential dependences. For data alignment, with our counting criteria for the number of *exponential* cases, which is the number of the nested loops including arrays with *exponential* references, it was found from [Reilly 1995] that several important loops in the TFFT2 programs in the SPEC95FP Benchmarks consist of arrays with exponential references after induction variable substitution and/or scalar expansion transformations and/or inlining substitutions. Those results mean that the number of the arrays with exponential subscripts might attain to certain extent.

3.1 Arrays with Exponential References

Assume that there exist q statements containing t arrays, each with one or more (say m) dimensions, referenced using exponential subscripts enclosed with a general n nested do loop. In order to align data elements for multi-dimensional arrays, a general approach is to use one dimension among others for each array as the alignment basis. The data alignment for multi-dimensional arrays is considered as the data alignment simply for the adopted dimension of the arrays in the following discussions. Assume that a reference function for the adopted dimension of an array A_e for $1 \leq e \leq t$ in this common loop is $R_{A_e} = a_{e,1} 2^{I_1} + \cdots + a_{e,n} 2^{I_n} + b_{e,1} I_1 + \cdots + b_{e,n} I_n + f_e$, where $I_1, I_2, \cdots, I_n$ are index variables of the general loop and $a_{e,1}, \cdots, a_{e,n}, b_{e,1}, \cdots, b_{e,n}$ are coefficients, which in general are integers or fractions in the exponential cases, and f_e is an integer constant. For treating the exponential references, we can extend an iteration vector **i** as $\mathbf{i} = [2^{i_1}, \cdots, 2^{i_n}, i_1, \cdots, i_n]^T$, i_v is an index value of I_v for $1 \leq v$

$\le n$ and T is the transposition operation) in the iteration space of this general n nested do loop, the alignment constraints require the processor performing iteration **i**, which stands for a computation instance, to own $A_e(R_{A_e})$. From our proposed methods, if there exist two or more *distinct* references (either read or write) to an array, each of the distinct references will be selected as the alignment constraints respectively for this array without considering their data dependences. Consider an example in Figure 1, where a statement containing three different one-dimensional arrays (i.e., $t = 3$ and $m = 1$). For an iteration vector **i** (**i** = $[2^i, 2^j, i, j]^T$), the alignment constraint demands that the processor performing iteration **i** must own $A(R_A)$, $B(R_B)$ and $D(R_D)$, where $R_A = 2^I + J$, $R_B = 2^I + J$ and $R_D = 2^I + J$.

```
DO I = 1, N, 1
    DO J = 1, 2 ** I, 1
        S1: A(2 ** I + J) = B(2 ** I + J) * D(2 ** I + J)
    ENDDO
ENDDO
```

Fig. 2. The Fortran do-loop extracted from TFFT2 programs in the SPEC95FP Benchmarks

Assume that C is the computation mapping function to map the loop iteration space onto virtual processors and D_{A_e} is the data mapping function to map the array elements of A_e onto virtual processors. The alignment problem can be formulated as: Find C and D_{A_e} such that $\forall$ **i** $\in$ iteration space of this loop, (Eq3-1): $C(\mathbf{i})=D_{A_e}(R_{A_e})$. In order to map the computations and array elements in a communication-free manner, our alignment methods consider the array subscript patterns that are generalized exponential subscripts here. Therefore, C and D_{A_e} will be formulated using our technique as follows: (Eq3-2),

$$[C' \ c_0]\begin{bmatrix}\mathbf{i}\\1\end{bmatrix} = [D'_{A_e} \ d_0]\begin{bmatrix}R'_{A_e} & f_e\\0 & 1\end{bmatrix}\begin{bmatrix}\mathbf{i}\\1\end{bmatrix}.$$ Let $C = [C' \ c_0]$, $D_{A_e} = [D'_{A_e} \ d_0]$,

$F_{A_e} = \begin{bmatrix}R'_{A_e} & f_e\\0 & 1\end{bmatrix}$ and $\mathbf{i}' = \begin{bmatrix}\mathbf{i}\\1\end{bmatrix}$, (Eq3-2) can be transformed into the following

equation, (Eq3-3): $C\mathbf{i}' = D_{A_e}F_{A_e}\mathbf{i}'$. From (Eq3-3), to determine C and D_{A_e} is to solve the equation $C = D_{A_e}F_{A_e}$ (or $C - D_{A_e}F_{A_e} = 0$) after $\mathbf{i}'$ is eliminated, where **0** is a zero matrix. Such an equation can be represented, without loss of generality, in block matrix form [Bau et al. 1994] as follows, (Eq3-4): $[C \ D_{A_e}]\begin{bmatrix}\mathbf{I}\\-F_{A_e}\end{bmatrix} = 0$. Here, **I** is an identity matrix, and **0** (zero matrix), C, D_{A_e} and F_{A_e} are square matrices with the same size as **I**. By expressing (Eq3-4) in the form of $UV = \mathbf{0}$ and determining a null space basis for V^T, the alignment problem is thus reduced to the standard linear algebra problem of determining a null space basis for a matrix. Using our technique, the above equations are reduced to the following equation:

$$\begin{bmatrix} c_{1,1} & c_{1,2} & c_{1,3} \\ c_{2,1} & c_{2,2} & c_{2,3} \\ c_{3,1} & c_{3,2} & c_{3,3} \end{bmatrix} \begin{bmatrix} 2^{i_1} \\ i_1 \\ 1 \end{bmatrix} = \begin{bmatrix} d_{1,1} & d_{1,2} & d_{1,3} \\ d_{2,1} & d_{2,2} & d_{2,3} \\ d_{3,1} & d_{3,2} & d_{3,3} \end{bmatrix} \begin{bmatrix} a_{e,1} & b_{e,1} & f_e \\ 0 & 0 & 1 \\ 1 & 1 & 1 \end{bmatrix} \begin{bmatrix} 2^{i_1} \\ i_1 \\ 1 \end{bmatrix}$$

Therefore, the alignment problem can be restated as: Find C and D_{A_e} such that $\forall\, \mathbf{i} \in$ iteration space of this loop: $C\mathbf{i}' = D_{A_e}F_{A_e}\mathbf{i}'$. Here, $\mathbf{i}' = [\mathbf{i}, 1]^T$, as mentioned. The above equation can be reduced to (Eq3-4) to determine C and D_{A_e}, as described. This requires the column vector $\mathbf{i}'$ on both sides of the equation to be eliminated to make $(C - D_{A_e}F_{A_e})$ equal to **0** for any $\mathbf{i}'$. To do this, we need the following lemma.

Lemma 3-1: Let P_i be a $p \times 1$ matrix for $1 \leq i \leq 2n$, $\mathbf{w}$ a p-elements column vector, **0** a p-elements zero vector and y_i a scalar variable for $1 \leq i \leq 2n$. Then,

$$\forall y_i \; [P_1 \cdots P_n \; P_{n+1} \cdots P_{2n} \; \mathbf{w}] \begin{bmatrix} 2^{y_1} \\ \vdots \\ 2^{y_n} \\ y_1 \\ \vdots \\ y_n \\ 1 \end{bmatrix} = \mathbf{0} \Leftrightarrow P_i = \mathbf{0} \text{ for } 1 \leq i \leq 2n, \text{ and } \mathbf{w} = \mathbf{0}$$

From Lemma 3–1, (Eq3-7) can actually be rewritten as: $C = D_{A_e}F_{A_e}$. (Eq3-9)

For $1 \leq e \leq t$, the equation system of (Eq3-9) can be converted into the following matrix equation (Eq3-10):

$$[C \; D_{A_1} \cdots D_{A_t}] \begin{bmatrix} I & I & \cdots & I \\ -F_{A_1} & 0 & \cdots & 0 \\ 0 & \ddots & & \vdots \\ \vdots & & \ddots & 0 \\ 0 & 0 & \cdots & -F_{A_t} \end{bmatrix} = [0 \cdots 0].$$

Here, **I** is a $(2n+1)\times(2n+1)$ identity matrix, **0** is a $(2n+1)\times(2n+1)$ zero matrix and $[0 \cdots 0]$ is a $(2n+1)\times((2n+1)\times t)$ zero matrix.

To solve the matrix equation $[U]_{s\times m}[V]_{m\times n}=[0]_{s\times n}$ in which $[U]_{s\times m}$ is unknown and $[V]_{m\times n}$ is known, we can first transform V into a 'rank-revealing' form by performing the required rank-preserving operations — elementary row and column operations. The notion behind this is to get a matrix into a form in which its rank can be determined by inspection [Edmonds 1967, Bau et al. 1994]. One way to achieve this is to perform integer preserving Gaussian elimination [Edmonds 1967, Luenberger 1984], whereby matrix rows or columns are systematically manipulated by elementary row or column operations to yield a matrix in echelon form, to enable us to obtain the following factorization (suppose that $V \in Z^{m\times n}$ and $rank(V) = r$):

$$[H]_{m\times m}[V]_{m\times n}[P]_{n\times n} = \begin{bmatrix} R_{1,1} & R_{1,2} \\ 0 & 0 \end{bmatrix}_{m\times n}.$$

Here, H is an $m\times m$ invertible matrix representing the row operations, P is an $n\times n$ unimodular matrix representing the column operations and $R_{1,1}$ is an $r\times r$ upper triangular invertible matrix. It is a property of this factorization that the transposition of the last $m-r$ rows of H spans the null space of V^T. Thus, we can then obtain the solution for $[U]_{s\times m}$ as follows: $U=H(r+1:m, 1:m)$. This means that only H, the composition of row operations, needs to be determined during the elimination.

We consider that in the example in Figure 2 the alignment constraint for the iteration space of this loop can be formally expressed as:

$$C\mathbf{i}' = \begin{bmatrix} c_{1,1} & c_{1,2} & c_{1,3} & c_{1,4} & c_{1,5} \\ c_{2,1} & c_{2,2} & c_{2,3} & c_{2,4} & c_{2,5} \\ c_{3,1} & c_{3,2} & c_{3,3} & c_{3,4} & c_{3,5} \\ c_{4,1} & c_{4,2} & c_{4,3} & c_{4,4} & c_{4,5} \\ c_{5,1} & c_{5,2} & c_{5,3} & c_{5,4} & c_{5,5} \end{bmatrix} \begin{bmatrix} 2^I \\ 2^J \\ I \\ J \\ 1 \end{bmatrix}.$$

The alignment constraints for arrays A, B and D can be respectively represented as:

$$D_A F_A \mathbf{i}' = \begin{bmatrix} x_{1,1} & x_{1,2} & x_{1,3} & x_{1,4} & x_{1,5} \\ x_{2,1} & x_{2,2} & x_{2,3} & x_{2,4} & x_{2,5} \\ x_{3,1} & x_{3,2} & x_{3,3} & x_{3,4} & x_{3,5} \\ x_{4,1} & x_{4,2} & x_{4,3} & x_{4,4} & x_{4,5} \\ x_{5,1} & x_{5,2} & x_{5,3} & x_{5,4} & x_{5,5} \end{bmatrix} \begin{bmatrix} 1 & 0 & 0 & 1 & 0 \\ 0 & 0 & 0 & 0 & 1 \\ 1 & 1 & 1 & 1 & 1 \\ 1 & 1 & 1 & 1 & 1 \\ 1 & 1 & 1 & 1 & 1 \end{bmatrix} \begin{bmatrix} 2^I \\ 2^J \\ I \\ J \\ 1 \end{bmatrix},$$

$$D_B F_B \mathbf{i}' = \begin{bmatrix} y_{1,1} & y_{1,2} & y_{1,3} & y_{1,4} & y_{1,5} \\ y_{2,1} & y_{2,2} & y_{2,3} & y_{2,4} & y_{2,5} \\ y_{3,1} & y_{3,2} & y_{3,3} & y_{3,4} & y_{3,5} \\ y_{4,1} & y_{4,2} & y_{4,3} & y_{4,4} & y_{4,5} \\ y_{5,1} & y_{5,2} & y_{5,3} & y_{5,4} & y_{5,5} \end{bmatrix} \begin{bmatrix} 1 & 0 & 0 & 1 & 0 \\ 0 & 0 & 0 & 0 & 1 \\ 1 & 1 & 1 & 1 & 1 \\ 1 & 1 & 1 & 1 & 1 \\ 1 & 1 & 1 & 1 & 1 \end{bmatrix} \begin{bmatrix} 2^I \\ 2^J \\ I \\ J \\ 1 \end{bmatrix}$$

and

$$D_D F_D \mathbf{i}' = \begin{bmatrix} z_{1,1} & z_{1,2} & z_{1,3} & z_{1,4} & z_{1,5} \\ z_{2,1} & z_{2,2} & z_{2,3} & z_{2,4} & z_{2,5} \\ z_{3,1} & z_{3,2} & z_{3,3} & z_{3,4} & z_{3,5} \\ z_{4,1} & z_{4,2} & z_{4,3} & z_{4,4} & z_{4,5} \\ z_{5,1} & z_{5,2} & z_{5,3} & z_{5,4} & z_{5,5} \end{bmatrix} \begin{bmatrix} 1 & 0 & 0 & 1 & 0 \\ 0 & 0 & 0 & 0 & 1 \\ 1 & 1 & 1 & 1 & 1 \\ 1 & 1 & 1 & 1 & 1 \\ 1 & 1 & 1 & 1 & 1 \end{bmatrix} \begin{bmatrix} 2^I \\ 2^J \\ I \\ J \\ 1 \end{bmatrix}.$$

According to the above lemma, a solution matrix is:

$$C = \begin{bmatrix} 1 & 0 & 0 & 1 & 0 \\ 0 & 0 & 0 & 0 & 1 \\ 1 & 1 & 1 & 1 & 1 \\ 1 & 1 & 1 & 1 & 1 \\ 1 & 1 & 1 & 1 & 1 \end{bmatrix}, D_A = \begin{bmatrix} 1 & 0 & 0 & 0 & 0 \\ 0 & 1 & 0 & 0 & 0 \\ 0 & 0 & 1 & 0 & 0 \\ 0 & 0 & 0 & 1 & 0 \\ 0 & 0 & 0 & 0 & 1 \end{bmatrix},$$

$$D_B = \begin{bmatrix} 1 & 0 & 0 & 0 & 0 \\ 0 & 1 & 0 & 0 & 0 \\ 0 & 0 & 1 & 0 & 0 \\ 0 & 0 & 0 & 1 & 0 \\ 0 & 0 & 0 & 0 & 1 \end{bmatrix} \text{ and } D_D = \begin{bmatrix} 1 & 0 & 0 & 0 & 0 \\ 0 & 1 & 0 & 0 & 0 \\ 0 & 0 & 1 & 0 & 0 \\ 0 & 0 & 0 & 1 & 0 \\ 0 & 0 & 0 & 0 & 1 \end{bmatrix}.$$

Therefore, using our alignment, iteration (I, J) is mapped onto virtual processor $(2^I + J)$ and the corresponding A, B and D array elements are mapped onto the same virtual processor. The **Align** statements adopted to describe the alignment relation for the array elements of among A, B and D are represented as follows: Align $A(2^I + J)$ with $T(2^I + J)$, Align $B(2^I + J)$ with $T(2^I + J)$ and Align $D(2^I + J)$ with $T(2^I + J)$. Here, the virtual processors are supposed to be organized as a one-dimensional template T. Because that no loop-carried output-dependences exist for array A and that the required data elements (the written data element of array A and the corresponding read data element of arrays B and D) for a computation are mapped onto the same template element, this nested loop can be executed in parallel without inter-processor communication.

3.2 Array Subscripts with $a_{e,1} * J * 2^{L-1} + a_{e,2} * 2^{L-2} + a_{e,3} * K + a_{e,4}$

Assume that there exist q statements containing t arrays of m-dimensions referenced using subscripts with the patterns $a_{e,1} * J * 2^{L-1} + a_{e,2} * 2^{L-2} + a_{e,3} * K + a_{e,4}$, where L, J ad K are loop index variables. Suppose that a reference function for the adopted dimension of an array A_e for $1 \le e \le t$ in a general loop is $R_{A_e} = a_{e,1} * J * 2^{L-1} + a_{e,2} * 2^{L-2} + a_{e,3} * K + a_{e,4}$, where L, J ad K are index variables of the general loop and $a_{e,1}$, $a_{e,2}$ and $a_{e,3}$ are coefficients, which in general are integers or fractions in the case and $a_{e,4}$ is an integer constant.

```
DO I = 0, 2**(M − 1)
  DO L = 1, (1 + M) / 2
    DO J = 0, 2**((1 + M − L) − 1)
      DO K = 1, 2**(L − 2)
        ...
        A(K + J * 2 ** (L − 1) + 2 ** (L − 2)) = &
                  B(K + J * 2 ** (L − 1) + 2 ** (L − 2))...
        ...
  ENDDO
  ENDDO
  ENDDO
ENDDO
```

Fig. 3. The Fortran do-loop extracted from TFFT2 programs in the SPEC95FP Benchmarks

The alignment constraint for the iteration space of this general loop can be formally expressed as follows, using our alignment technique:

$$C\vec{i}' = \begin{bmatrix} c_{1,1} & c_{1,2} & c_{1,3} & c_{1,4} \\ c_{2,1} & c_{2,2} & c_{2,3} & c_{2,4} \\ c_{3,1} & c_{3,2} & c_{3,3} & c_{3,4} \\ c_{4,1} & c_{4,2} & c_{4,3} & c_{4,4} \end{bmatrix} * \begin{bmatrix} J * 2^{(L-1)} \\ 2^{(L-2)} \\ K \\ 1 \end{bmatrix}.$$

The alignment constraint for an array A_e, $1 \le e \le t$, in the general loop can be represented as:

$$D_{A_e}F_{A_e}\mathbf{i}' = \begin{bmatrix} d_{1,1} & d_{1,2} & d_{1,3} & d_{1,4} \\ d_{2,1} & d_{2,2} & d_{2,3} & d_{2,4} \\ d_{3,1} & d_{3,2} & d_{3,3} & d_{3,4} \\ d_{4,1} & d_{4,2} & d_{4,3} & d_{4,4} \end{bmatrix} \begin{bmatrix} a_{e,1} & a_{e,2} & a_{e,3} & a_{e,4} \\ 0 & 0 & 0 & 1 \\ 1 & 1 & 1 & 1 \\ 1 & 1 & 1 & 1 \end{bmatrix} \begin{bmatrix} J*2^{(L-1)} \\ 2^{(L-2)} \\ K \\ 1 \end{bmatrix}.$$

Similar to the discussion in the previous subsection, the column vector $\mathbf{i}'$ on both sides of equation, $C\mathbf{i}' = D_{A_e}F_{A_e}\mathbf{i}'$, is required to be eliminated for any $\mathbf{i}'$. For this kind of loops, we need the following lemma.

Lemma 3-2: Let P_i be a 4×1 matrix for $1 \le i \le 3$, $\mathbf{w}$ be a four-elements column vector, $\mathbf{0}$ be a four-elements zero vector and y_z be a scalar variable for $1 \le z \le 4$. Then

$$\forall y_z \ [P_1 \ P_2 \ P_3 \ \mathbf{w}] \begin{bmatrix} y_3 * 2^{(y_2-1)} \\ 2^{(y_2-2)} \\ y_4 \\ 1 \end{bmatrix} = \mathbf{0} \Leftrightarrow P_i = \mathbf{0} \text{ for } 1 \le i \le 3, \text{ and } \mathbf{w} = \mathbf{0}.$$

In the example in Figure 3, the alignment constraint for the iteration space of this loop can be formally expressed as:

$$C\mathbf{i}' = \begin{bmatrix} c_{1,1} & c_{1,2} & c_{1,3} & c_{1,4} \\ c_{2,1} & c_{2,2} & c_{2,3} & c_{2,4} \\ c_{3,1} & c_{3,2} & c_{3,3} & c_{3,4} \\ c_{4,1} & c_{4,2} & c_{4,3} & c_{4,4} \end{bmatrix} \begin{bmatrix} y_3 * 2^{(y_2-1)} \\ 2^{(y_2-2)} \\ y_4 \\ 1 \end{bmatrix}.$$

The alignment constraints for arrays A and B can be respectively represented as:

$$D_A F_A \mathbf{i}' = \begin{bmatrix} x_{1,1} & x_{1,2} & x_{1,3} & x_{1,4} \\ x_{2,1} & x_{2,2} & x_{2,3} & x_{2,4} \\ x_{3,1} & x_{3,2} & x_{3,3} & x_{3,4} \\ x_{4,1} & x_{4,2} & x_{4,3} & x_{4,4} \end{bmatrix} \begin{bmatrix} 1 & 1 & 1 & 0 \\ 0 & 0 & 0 & 1 \\ 1 & 1 & 1 & 1 \\ 1 & 1 & 1 & 1 \end{bmatrix} \begin{bmatrix} y_3 * 2^{(y_2-1)} \\ 2^{(y_2-2)} \\ y_4 \\ 1 \end{bmatrix}$$

and

$$D_B F_B \mathbf{i}' = \begin{bmatrix} y_{1,1} & y_{1,2} & y_{1,3} & y_{1,4} \\ y_{2,1} & y_{2,2} & y_{2,3} & y_{2,4} \\ y_{3,1} & y_{3,2} & y_{3,3} & y_{3,4} \\ y_{4,1} & y_{4,2} & y_{4,3} & y_{4,4} \end{bmatrix} \begin{bmatrix} 1 & 1 & 1 & 0 \\ 0 & 0 & 0 & 1 \\ 1 & 1 & 1 & 1 \\ 1 & 1 & 1 & 1 \end{bmatrix} \begin{bmatrix} y_3 * 2^{(y_2-1)} \\ 2^{(y_2-2)} \\ y_4 \\ 1 \end{bmatrix}.$$

The alignment problem can be expressed as follows:

$$[C \quad D_A \quad D_B] = \begin{bmatrix} 1 & 1 & 1 & 0 & 1 & 0 & 0 & 0 & 1 & 0 & 0 & 0 \\ 0 & 0 & 0 & 1 & 0 & 1 & 0 & 0 & 0 & 1 & 0 & 0 \\ 1 & 1 & 1 & 1 & 0 & 0 & 1 & 0 & 0 & 0 & 1 & 0 \\ 1 & 1 & 1 & 1 & 0 & 0 & 0 & 1 & 0 & 0 & 0 & 1 \end{bmatrix}.$$

This gives us:

$$C = \begin{bmatrix} 1 & 1 & 1 & 0 \\ 0 & 0 & 0 & 1 \\ 1 & 1 & 1 & 1 \\ 1 & 1 & 1 & 1 \end{bmatrix}, D_A = \begin{bmatrix} 1 & 0 & 0 & 0 \\ 0 & 1 & 0 & 0 \\ 0 & 0 & 1 & 0 \\ 0 & 0 & 0 & 1 \end{bmatrix} \text{ and } D_B = \begin{bmatrix} 1 & 0 & 0 & 0 \\ 0 & 1 & 0 & 0 \\ 0 & 0 & 1 & 0 \\ 0 & 0 & 0 & 1 \end{bmatrix}.$$

We can obtain the mappings of computations and data as follows:

$$C\mathbf{i}' = \begin{bmatrix} 1 & 1 & 1 & 0 \\ 0 & 0 & 0 & 1 \\ 1 & 1 & 1 & 1 \\ 1 & 1 & 1 & 1 \end{bmatrix} \begin{bmatrix} J*2^{(L-1)} \\ 2^{(L-2)} \\ K \\ 1 \end{bmatrix} = \begin{bmatrix} J*2^{(L-1)} + 2^{(L-2)} + K \\ 1 \\ J*2^{(L-1)} + 2^{(L-2)} + K + 1 \\ J*2^{(L-1)} + 2^{(L-2)} + K + 1 \end{bmatrix},$$

$$D_A F_A \mathbf{i}' = \begin{bmatrix} 1 & 0 & 0 & 0 \\ 0 & 1 & 0 & 0 \\ 0 & 0 & 1 & 0 \\ 0 & 0 & 0 & 1 \end{bmatrix} \begin{bmatrix} 1 & 1 & 1 & 0 \\ 0 & 0 & 0 & 1 \\ 1 & 1 & 1 & 1 \\ 1 & 1 & 1 & 1 \end{bmatrix} \begin{bmatrix} J*2^{(L-1)} \\ 2^{(L-2)} \\ K \\ 1 \end{bmatrix} =$$

$$\begin{bmatrix} J*2^{(L-1)} + 2^{(L-2)} + K \\ 1 \\ J*2^{(L-1)} + 2^{(L-2)} + K + 1 \\ J*2^{(L-1)} + 2^{(L-2)} + K + 1 \end{bmatrix} \text{ and }$$

$$D_B F_B \mathbf{i}' = \begin{bmatrix} 1 & 0 & 0 & 0 \\ 0 & 1 & 0 & 0 \\ 0 & 0 & 1 & 0 \\ 0 & 0 & 0 & 1 \end{bmatrix} \begin{bmatrix} 1 & 1 & 1 & 0 \\ 0 & 0 & 0 & 1 \\ 1 & 1 & 1 & 1 \\ 1 & 1 & 1 & 1 \end{bmatrix} \begin{bmatrix} J*2^{(L-1)} \\ 2^{(L-2)} \\ K \\ 1 \end{bmatrix} =$$

$$\begin{bmatrix} J*2^{(L-1)} + 2^{(L-2)} + K \\ 1 \\ J*2^{(L-1)} + 2^{(L-2)} + K + 1 \\ J*2^{(L-1)} + 2^{(L-2)} + K + 1 \end{bmatrix}.$$

Hence, using our alignment, iteration (I, L, J, K) is mapped onto virtual processor $(J * 2 ** (L - 1) + 2 ** (L - 2) + K)$ and the corresponding A and B array elements are mapped onto the same virtual processor. The **Align** statements adopted to describe the alignment relation for the array elements of both A and B are represented as follows: Align $A(J * 2 ** (L - 1) + 2 ** (L - 2) + K)$ with $T(J * 2 ** (L - 1) + 2 ** (L - 2) + K)$ and Align $B(J * 2 ** (L - 1) + 2 ** (L - 2) + K)$ with $T(J * 2 ** (L - 1) + 2 ** (L - 2) + K)$. Here, the virtual processors are supposed to be organized as a one-dimensional template T.

4 Experimental Results

We have experimented with the proposed alignment techniques on some codes extracted from TFFT2 programs in the SPEC95FP Benchmarks in our PC-cluster environment. Our PC-cluster includes a master, a PC with one P4 (Pentium 4) 1.8 GHz CPU and 256 MB main memory, and 10 slaves, each a PC with one P4 1.5 GHz CPU and 128 MB main memory. The operation environment was the RedHat Linux 7.1 with the installed parallel software package– MPI-1.2.2.2. We hand-coded these extracted code segments in MPI (Message Passing Interface) with C language and executed them sequentially and in parallel in our MPI environment, respectively.

Table 1. The extracted code segment and the data alignments with our technique in 3.1

DO $P = 1, N, 1$
 ...
   DO $I = 1, M, 1$
     DO $J =1, 2^I, 1$
     ...
     S_1: $A(2 ** I + J) = r1 * s1 - r2 *$
                     $s2 + \text{COS}(ti)$
     S_2: $B(2 ** I + J) = r2 * s1 + r1 *$
                     $s2 + \text{SIN}(ti)$
     ...
     ENDDO
   ENDDO
 ...
 ENDDO
	Align $A(2 ** I + J)$ with $T(2 ** I + J)$.
	 Align $B(2 ** I + J)$ with $T(2 ** I + J)$.

The code segments extracted from TFFT2 programs in the SPEC95FP Benchmarks contain arrays referenced using exponential subscripts and other complex nonlinear subscripts, as shown respectively in Table 1 and Table 2. The code segment in Table 1 contains three do-loops. The first do-loop in Table 1 is only used to evaluate performance of every machine tested, so it is not considered to find alignment functions for those arrays in statements S_1 and S_2. Those arrays in statements S_1 and S_2 for the second do-loop and the third do-loop have no data dependence such that they can intrinsically be executed in parallel. Our proposed method in subsection 3.1 can align the arrays of this code segment in a communication-free manner that does not cause inter-processor communication.

The corresponding sequential and parallel run times for those code segments in Table 1 and Table 2 are shown, respectively, in Figures 4, 5, and 6. Figures 4 to 6 show that the difference between sequential and parallel run time is significant. This is because those code

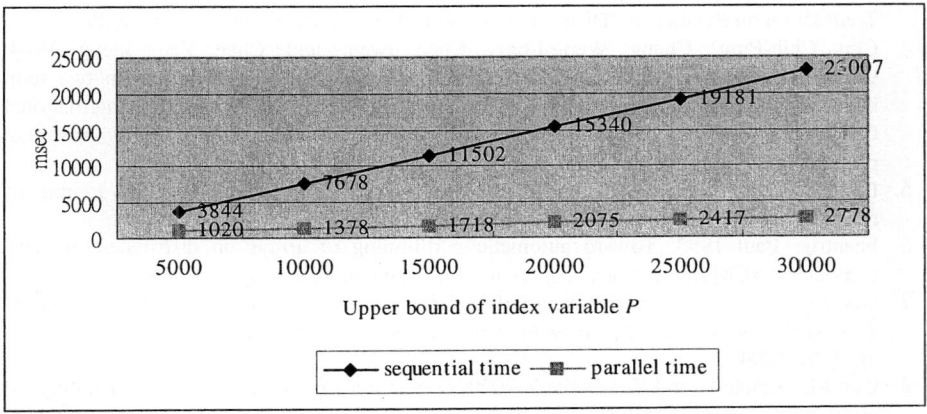

Fig. 4. The overall sequential and parallel run times for the extracted code segment in Table 1

5 Conclusions

For the referenced arrays, linear expressions appear the most frequency and most data alignment methods were used mainly to align the array references with linear subscripts. The number of the arrays with exponential subscripts or other complex non-linear subscripts might attain to certain extent. However, the data alignments for the arrays with exponential subscripts or other complex non-linear subscripts were scarcely discussed before. In this paper, we propose two alignment techniques to properly map, in a communication-free manner, computations and array references with exponential subscripts or complex other non-linear subscripts onto the virtual processors. Our alignment techniques, based on elementary linear algebra, reduce the alignment problem to the problem of determining a null space basis for a matrix. By simplifying solving the null space basis, the proposed techniques can easily determine the desired mapping functions. Obviously, many different mapping functions can be obtained by different linear combinations of the null space basis. Additionally, because dependent iterations with the properties described in Theorem 3–1 will be mapped onto the same template element, the proposed techniques are not one-to-one mappings.

References

1. Bau David, Kodukula Induprakas, Kotlyar Vladimir, Pingali Keshav, and Stodghill Paul 1994. Solving alignment using elementary linear algebra. In: Conference Record of the 7th Workshop on Languages and Compilers for Parallel Computing, pp. 46–60.
2. Chang Weng-Long, Chu Chih-Ping and Wu Jia-Hwa 2001. Communication-free alignment for array references with linear subscripts in three loop index variables or quadratic subscripts. The Journal of Supercomputing Vol. 20, Issue 1, pp. 67-83.
3. Chang Weng-Long, Huang Jih-Woei and Chu Chih-Ping 2004. Using elementary linear algebra to solve data alignment for arrays with linear or quadratic references. IEEE Transaction on Parallel and Distributed Systems, Volume 15, Number 1, pp. 28-39.
4. Chu Chih-Ping, Chang Weng-Long, Chen Iwen, and Chen Peng-Sheng 1998. Communication-free alignment for array references with linear subscripts in two loop index variables or quadratic subscripts. Proceedings of the Second IASTED International Conference on Parallel and Distributed Computing and Networks (PDCN'98), Australia, pp. 571-576.
5. Edmonds Jack 1967. Systems of distinct representative and linear algebra. Journal of research of national bureau of standards, Sect. B, Vol. 71, No. 4, pp. 241–245.
6. Feautrier Paul 1993. Toward automatic partitioning of arrays on distributed memory computers. ACM International Conference on Supercomputing, pp. 175-184.
7. Guo M., Yamashita Y., and Nakata I 1998. Efficient implementation of multi-dimensional array redistribution. *IEICE transactions on Information and Systems*, Vol. E81-D, No. 11, pp. 1195-1204.
8. Guo M., Nakata I., and Yamashita Y 2000. Contention-free communication scheduling for array redistribution. *Parallel Computing*, Vol. 26, No.8, pp. 1325-1343.
9. Guo M. and Nakata I 2001. A framework for efficient array redistribution on distributed memory multicomputers. The Journal of Supercomputing, Vol. 20, No. 3, pp. 243-265.
10. Guo M. 2003a. Efficient loop partitioning for parallel codes of irregular scientific computations. IEICE transactions on Information and Systems, Vol. E86-D, No. 9, pp. 1825-1834.
11. Guo M. 2003b. Communication generation for irregular codes. The Journal of Supercomputing, Vol. 25, No. 3, pp. 199-214.
12. Lam A. W. and Lam M. S. 1998. Maximizing parallelism and minimizing synchronization with affine partitions. Parallel Computing, Vol. 24, No. 3-4, pp. 445-475.
13. Lee PeiZong 1997. Efficient algorithms for data distribution on distributed memory parallel computers. IEEE Transactions on Parallel and Distributed Systems, Vol. 8, No. 8, pp. 825-839.
14. Paek Yunheung 1997. Compiling for distributed memory multiprocessors based on access region analysis. Ph.D. Thesis, Univ. of Illinois at Urbana-Champaign, Center for Supercomputing Res. & Dev.
15. Petersen M. Paul, and Padua A. David 1996. Static and dynamic evaluation of data dependence analysis techniques. IEEE Transactions on Parallel and Distributed Systems, Vol. 7, No. 11, pp. 1121-1132.

Parallel Unstructured Quadrilateral Mesh Generation

Jianjun Chen and Yao Zheng*

College of Computer Science, and Center for Engineering and Scientific Computation,
Zhejiang University, Hangzhou, 310027, P. R. China
`zdchenjj@yahoo.com.cn`, `yao.zheng@zju.edu.cn`

Abstract. In this paper we present our efforts to parallelize an unstructured quadrilateral mesh generator. Its serial version is based on the divider-and-conquer idea, and mainly includes two stages, i.e. geometry decomposition and mesh generation. Both stages are parallelized separately. A couple of parallel models are introduced and compared to parallelize the stage of geometry decomposition. A fine-grain level parallel algorithm proves preferable to that based on the task-dependency tree, with which the load imbalance brought by the improper utilization of the symmetry of the vertex pair matrix is removed nicely. Since the number of elements in sub-domains could be pre-computed before meshing, a simple static load balancing scheme is investigated, and the effect of granularity is also discussed briefly. Finally, experiments are designed to evaluate the performance of the parallel mesh generator in detail.

Keywords: mesh generation, parallel algorithm, quadrilateral elements, geometry decomposition.

1 Introduction

Mesh generation is one of important processes in applying the numerical methods for simulations. Many efficient serial mesh generation methods and corresponding research or commercial software have been developed in the past decades. However, when the ever larger problems arise in such areas as Computational Fluid Dynamics (CFD), Computational Electro Magnetics (CEM), a parallel simulation environment is required urgently, where the serial mesh generation process becomes a bottleneck in terms of both time and memory requirement. Close attention has been paid to parallelize it since the early 1990s [1-3].

Among the previous work in this field, much more attempts were made at parallelizing the problem rather than the algorithm for code-reusing and simplicity. The parallelization of the problem is usually geometry-based, where the complete domain is divided into a set of smaller sub-domains first, and then they are mapped to processors available with goals of load balancing and minimizing inter-processor communications. Two geometrical approaches are often adopted. One is to partition a coarse background mesh and subsequently to refine each partition independently [1, 4]. The other is to directly decompose the complete geometry described by CAD data in terms of vertices, edges, curves and surfaces [5]. It is noted that the second geometry ap-

---

* Corresponding author.

proach is also employed by many serial mesh algorithms. Therefore, for their parallel counterparts, the geometry approach is inherent to be considered as a tool for data decomposition.

Unstructured quadrilateral mesh generation approaches could be classified as direct and indirect ones. For indirect approaches, triangular elements are generated first, which are combined or split to form a quadrilateral or triangular/quadrilateral mixed mesh. The advancing front technique is successfully extended for direct quadrilateral mesh generation. However, it bears considerably heavy coding efforts. The quadtree method could also be applied in the quadrilateral mesh generation. The difficulties with it are the treatment with the complicated regional boundaries and the selection of the initial directions. Other than above approaches, Talbert et al [6] developed a so-called *looping algorithm* for meshing arbitrary planar domains with quadrilateral elements. In the algorithm, the problem domain is recursively bi-decomposed into sub-domains, where eleven six-node operators are employed to generate full quadrilateral elements, and finally, meshes of sub-domains are merged. Nowottny [7] and Chae et al [8] enhanced it by constructing much stronger operators. Sarrate et al [9] improved it with the adaptive capability and better density control with the help of the background mesh. However, the algorithm still has two drawbacks, i.e. the sub-domain definition being too stringent and the generation rule being too complex. We [10, 11] overcame both drawbacks by integrating the Pattern Module's Method (PMM) [12] into the stage of sub-domain mesh generation, and developed a fast, automatic and valid unstructured quadrilateral mesh generator for arbitrary planar domains.

In this paper, we focus on parallelizing the serial version of our enhanced unstructured quadrilateral mesh generator. Experimental data will be presented and analyzed to evaluate the performance of the algorithm.

2 Serial Quadrilateral Mesh Generation

In our algorithm, the geometry is represented by a piecewise linear curve. The multi-connected geometry is not discussed here as it could be easily converted into a single-connected one. Except coordinate values, each vertex has an attribute value to control element spacing at the location, obtained from a density function or a background mesh. The initial loop is recursively bi-decomposed, according to a weight function until all sub-domains meet some shape requirements. Each sub-domain will be recognized as "triangular type" or "quadrilateral type". A triangular sub-domain could be transformed into the combination of quadrilateral ones. Consequently, after geometry decomposition, the initial geometry could be considered as a combination of quadrilateral sub-domains, where the robust PMM [10] is applied to generate fully quadrilateral meshes. Meshes for sub-domains are eventually merged. Fig. 1 depicts the flowchart of our serial mesh generator.

A binary tree is designed to represent the algorithm. An example is given in Fig. 2, where three kinds of named entities, i.e. branches, leaves and splitting lines, are included. Their rules of nomenclature are as follows.

(1) Branches, leaves and splitting lines have an initial string 'B', 'L', and 'SL', respectively, after which two numbers i and j are connected by a separator '-'.

(2) For a branch or leave, i represents the level of the node in the tree, and j is determined by the recursive rule

$$\begin{cases} j = 1 & \text{for the root node} \\ j = 2 * parent\_j - 1 & \text{for the left node} \\ j = 2 * parent\_j & \text{for the right node} \end{cases}.$$

(3) For a splitting line, $SL\, i\text{-}j$ indicates that it bi-decomposes branch node $B\, i\text{-}j$.

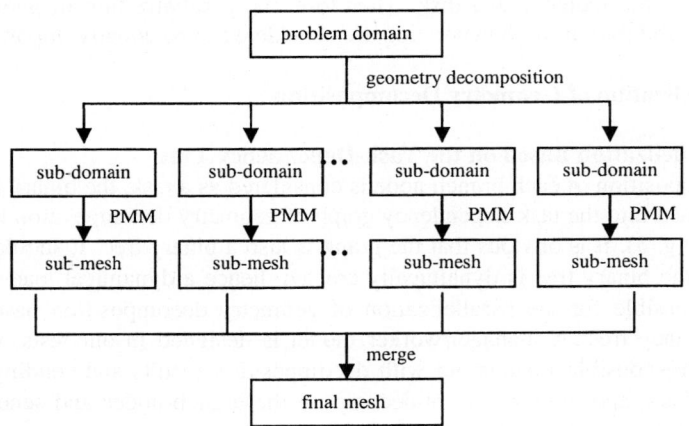

Fig. 1. The flowchart of the serial mesh generator

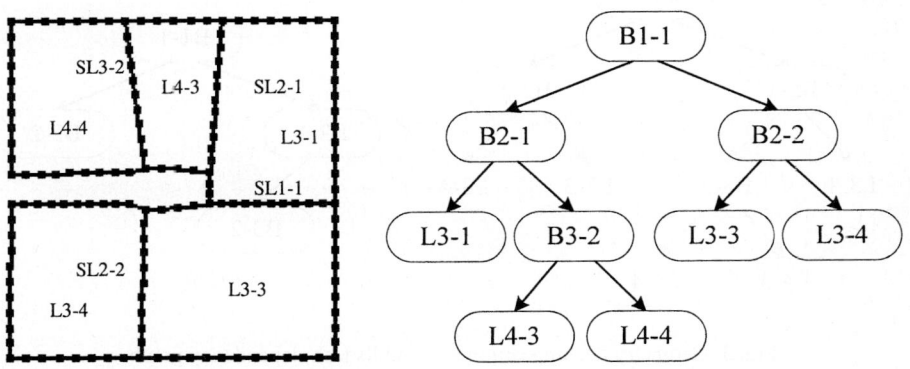

Fig. 2. An example to illustrate geometrical decomposition using the binary tree

3 Parallel Quadrilateral Mesh Generation

It is apparent that the serial mesh generator consists of two independent stages, i.e. geometry decomposition and mesh generation (including sub-domain mesh generation and merging of sub-meshes). Both stages are time-consuming. Moreover, the stage of mesh generation is intensively memory-consuming. If the initial loop of the geometry contains m vertices, and the number of elements of the final mesh is n, experiments show that the time complexities of geometry decomposition and mesh generation are $O(m^2)$ and $O(n)$, respectively. Time consumed by geometry decomposition is comparable with that consumed by mesh generation. It is observed that the former is even 3 times as much as the latter when only hundred thousands of elements are generated by the serial algorithm. Of course, when millions of elements are required, the latter increases much faster than the former due to the frequent and slow swap between the memory and disk. Therefore, the parallelization of geometry decomposition and that of mesh generation are considered to be equally important.

3.1 Parallelization of Geometry Decomposition

3.1.1 Parallelization Based on the Task-Dependency Tree

If the decomposition of each branch node is considered as a task, the binary tree could be transformed into the task-dependency graph of geometry decomposition by erasing all leaves (Fig. 3). It is obvious that the graph is also a binary tree. It should be mentioned that the binary tree is dynamically created, hence a dynamical load balancing scheme is feasible for the parallelization of geometry decomposition based on the task-dependency tree. A manager/worker model is designed in our tests, where the manager is responsible for dealing with decomposition results and sending tasks to hungry workers, and the workers bi-decompose the branch nodes and send back results. No communications exist between workers.

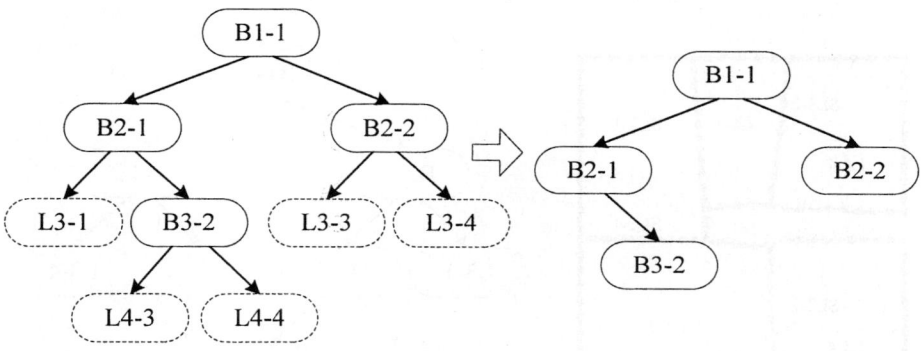

Fig. 3. Geometry decomposition tree and its task-dependency graph

Here, we present the pseudo-codes executed by the manager and workers, respectively. A list for backup tasks is maintained by each worker, which stores tasks created by the worker. All the requests for pending tasks are scheduled by the manager. A message MSG_IF_BACKUP_TASK_COULD_BE_DONE is sent from a hungry worker before the worker tries to do a backup task. It could synchronize the possible concurrent operations on the task by the manager and the worker.

```
Manager:
  decomposeRootAndGenInitTasks();
  while (!allWorkersAreHungryAndNoPendingTasks()) {
    MSG* msg = waitMessageFromWorkers();
    switch (msg->tag){
    case MSG_I_AM_HUNGRY:
      sendTaskToHungryWorker(msg); break;
    case MSG_TASK_FINISHED:
      receiveFinishedTask(msg); break;
    case MSG_IF_BACKUP_TASK_CAN_BE_DONE:
      tellWorkerIfBackupTaskCanBeDone(msg); break;
    }
  }
  sendExitMessages();

Worker:
  bool bExit = false;
  while (!bExit) {
    Task* pTask = NULL;
    while (!backupTasksIsEmpty()) {
      pTask = selectAndDetachBackupTask();
      if     (pTask    &&    askManagerCanIDoTask(pTask->unTaskId))
          break;
      pTask = NULL;
    }
    if (NULL == pTask) pTask = receiveTaskFromManager();
    if (pTask != NULL){
      doIt(pTask, &data);
      sendSubtasksAndBackupIt(pTask, &data);
    }
    bExit = pTask == NULL;
  }
```

3.1.2 Fine-Grain Level Parallelization

It costs almost all the time of geometry decomposition to find the optimal vertex pair, which are just the ending points of the splitting line bi-decomposing a domain. Assuming the decomposed domain is Ω_s, the vertex set included by the initial loop of the domain is V, $p,q \in V$, $\varepsilon := \overline{pq}$ is a line joining p and q, and $E := \{\varepsilon; \varepsilon \in \Omega_s\}$ is the set of all such lines inside the domain, then a weight function $f: R \rightarrow E$ could be defined. The line with minimal value f is called the optimal splitting line, and accordingly, the ending points of the line are called the optimal vertex pair.

For a loop with m vertices, $m*(m-3)$ candidate vertex pairs are required to be tested to find the optimal one. These pairs could be organized as a matrix with $m*(m-3)$ elements (Fig. 4). Each of its elements represents a vertex pair (i, j), where i and j are indices of both vertices of the pair, and i is equal to the index of the row the element belongs to. The traverse for the matrix could be implemented as a nest with two cycles, where all the matrix elements are accessed in the row-major order, and the time complexity for such an algorithm is at least $O(m^2)$.

Both vertices for a candidate optimal vertex pair are demanded to be visible with each other for a concave domain. As it costs $O(m)$ time to check if a couple of specified vertices are visible with each other, the time to find the optimal vertex pair will grow up to unpleasant $O(m^3)$ if the visibility check is delayed into the inner cycle. Therefore, an advance computation of visibility relations between vertex pairs is preferable. Its result is stored and accessed as necessary. It is not advisable to compute and store the visibility matrix for its terrible $O(m^2)$ memory requirement. It could be reduced to the much lower $O(m)$ by computing visibility relations of vertex pairs row by row. However, the computation could not cost more than $O(m)$ time to keep the integrated optimal $O(m^2)$ time complexity. Fortunately, a simple and eligible algorithm to attain this goal is recommended in literature [6].

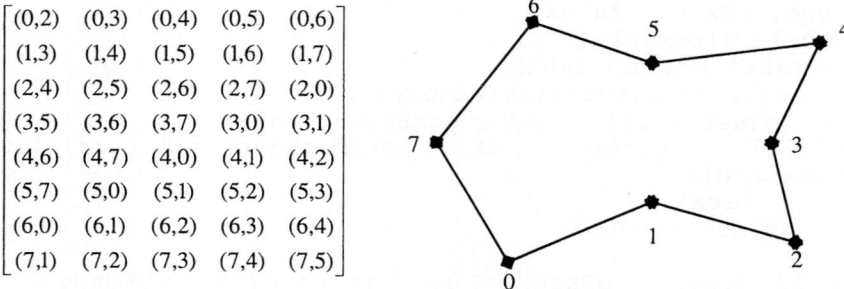

Fig. 4. A 8 * 5 vertex pairs matrix while $m = 8$

Obviously, (i, j) and (j, i) point to the same vertex pair. Taking into account this symmetry, only a half of the matrix elements are required to be accessed. However, there are many ways to get the half matrix. A direct way is

$$H = \{elem(r,c) \mid c \geq r+2, \; r = 0, \; 1, \; \cdots, \; m-3\}, \tag{1}$$

where r and c are the row and column indices, respectively, and $elem(r,c)$ is the corresponding element. Fig. 5(a) gives an example of H constructed in this way for the matrix shown in Fig. 4.

Consequently, the parallelization of geometry decomposition is reduced to the decomposition of H. Given $N = 2$ processors, for H shown in Fig. 5(a), its 20 elements could be decomposed into two parts, and each part has 10 elements (Fig. 6(a)). It is undesirable that the numbers of rows, which are also the iteration numbers of the outer cycle, are imbalanced for two processors. These are 2 and 4 for Processors 0 and 1 in this example, respectively.

As mentioned above, a visibility computation is placed between both cycles, the imbalance of the numbers of rows will bring the load imbalance among processors, which will become very huge while m increases up to more than thousands. Therefore, another rule is required to get the half matrix, which ought to well keep the balance of the numbers of rows among processors. A suggested one is

$$H = \{elem(r,c) \mid c \in [r+2, r+2+l], \ r = 0, 1, \cdots, m-1\}, \quad (2)$$

where l is defined as

$$l = \begin{cases} m/2 - 1 & r \text{ even}, r < m/2 \\ m/2 - 1 & r - m/2 \text{ odd}, m/2 < r < m, \\ m/2 - 2 & else \end{cases}$$

$$\begin{bmatrix} (0,2) & (0,3) & (0,4) & (0,5) & (0,6) \\ (1,3) & (1,4) & (1,5) & (1,6) & (1,7) \\ (2,4) & (2,5) & (2,6) & (2,7) & - \\ (3,5) & (3,6) & (3,7) & - & - \\ (4,6) & (4,7) & - & - & - \\ (5,7) & - & - & - & - \\ - & - & - & - & - \\ - & - & - & - & - \end{bmatrix} \quad \begin{bmatrix} (0,2) & (0,3) & (0,4) & - & - \\ (1,3) & (1,4) & - & - & - \\ (2,4) & (2,5) & (2,6) & - & - \\ (3,5) & (3,6) & - & - & - \\ (4,6) & (4,7) & - & - & - \\ (5,7) & (5,0) & (5,1) & - & - \\ (6,0) & (6,1) & - & - & - \\ (7,1) & (7,2) & (7,3) & - & - \end{bmatrix}$$

(a) half matrix constructed in Scheme 1 (b) half matrix constructed in Scheme 2

Fig. 5. Half matrices constructed in two different schemes

$$\begin{bmatrix} (0,2) & (0,3) & (0,4) & (0,5) & (0,6) \\ (1,3) & (1,4) & (1,5) & (1,6) & (1,7) \\ - & - & - & - & - \\ - & - & - & - & - \\ - & - & - & - & - \\ - & - & - & - & - \\ - & - & - & - & - \\ - & - & - & - & - \end{bmatrix} \quad \begin{bmatrix} - & - & - & - & - \\ - & - & - & - & - \\ (2,4) & (2,5) & (2,6) & (2,7) & - \\ (3,5) & (3,6) & (3,7) & - & - \\ (4,6) & (4,7) & - & - & - \\ (5,7) & - & - & - & - \\ - & - & - & - & - \\ - & - & - & - & - \end{bmatrix}$$

(a) decomposition result of the half matrix constructed in Scheme 1

$$\begin{bmatrix} (0,2) & (0,3) & (0,4) & - & - \\ (1,3) & (1,4) & - & - & - \\ (2,4) & (2,5) & (2,6) & - & - \\ (3,5) & (3,6) & - & - & - \\ - & - & - & - & - \\ - & - & - & - & - \\ - & - & - & - & - \\ - & - & - & - & - \end{bmatrix} \quad \begin{bmatrix} - & - & - & - & - \\ - & - & - & - & - \\ - & - & - & - & - \\ - & - & - & - & - \\ (4,6) & (4,7) & - & - & - \\ (5,7) & (5,0) & (5,1) & - & - \\ (6,0) & (6,1) & - & - & - \\ (7,1) & (7,2) & (7,3) & - & - \end{bmatrix}$$

(b) decomposition result of the half matrix constructed in Scheme 2

Fig. 6. Decomposition results of half matrices constructed in two different schemes ($N = 2$)

where m is an even number to ensure fully quadrilateral elements to be generated. Fig. 5(b) gives an example of H constructed in this way for the matrix shown in Fig. 4. Accordingly, given 2 processors, its decomposition result is shown in Fig. 6(b), where the above imbalance is nicely removed.

After all processors decompose a branch, an *MPI_Allgather* function is called to collect all locally minimal weight values for their locally optimal vertex pairs, and then the pair with the globally minimal weight value are found and broadcasted.

3.2 Parallelization of Mesh Generation

The domain is a combination of quadrilateral sub-domains after geometry decomposition. If a node denotes a sub-domain, and an edge exits between two sub-domains with shared interfaces, the domain could be identified as an undirected graph. Graph nodes and edges are both assigned weights which equal the numbers of elements and shared mesh edges between neighboring sub-domains, respectively. Given N processors, the problem of parallelizing the stage of mesh generation is equivalent to partition the graph into N parts with equal node weights and to minimize the inter-part edge weights as well. This famous graph partitioning problem was intensively investigated and will not be discussed here. A simple static load balancing scheme will be adopted in the present study. It will not consider how to minimize the inter-processor communications, which are deferred to future works.

3.2.1 Static Load Balancing

An advantage of the PMM is that the number of elements for a sub-domain could be pre-computed before meshing. So a simple static load balancing scheme could be nicely used to partition the domain. Given N processors, suppose the total number of elements in the domain is E_{tot}, the average elements E_{ave} for each processor is

$$E_{ave} = \frac{E_{tot}}{N}. \tag{3}$$

A traverse for the list of sub-domains is implemented to map sub-domains to processors. For Processor i, given a start sub-domain S (it is just the head of the list while $i = 0$), and then the sub-domains after S is accessed one by one. The number of elements to be generated for the accessed node is added to a float value E_{acc} (its initial value is zero). Let E_{acc} equals E_{bef} and E_{aft} before and after accessing a subdomain L, respectively. If

$$E_{bef} < E_{ave} < E_{aft}$$

holds, the access operation stops. Then check if

$$E_{ave} - E_{bef} > E_{aft} - E_{ave}$$

holds. If true, all the sub-domains from S to L are mapped to Processor i; otherwise L is excluded.

In practice, far less or more elements are allocated to the last processor than that to the others, which could be alleviated by dynamically changing E_{ave} as below.

$$E_{ave} = \frac{E_{tot} - E_{alloc}}{N - N_{alloc}}, \quad (4)$$

where E_{alloc} and N_{alloc} denote the numbers of allocated elements and processors before mapping sub-domains to the current processor, respectively.

3.2.2 Granularity

Whatever is selected for the load balancing schemes, the granularity of each sub-domain is an important factor. If many "large" sub-domains exist, the load imbalance will grow inevitably. Here the granularity of a sub-domain is measured by the number of elements inside. A maximal granularity is set by the user in our algorithm. If the granularity of a sub-domain exceeds the maximum, it's forced to be bi-decomposed continuously in despite it perhaps meets the shape requirements of the PMM.

The smaller is the maximal granularity, the more sub-domains are generated, which might slow the stage of geometry decomposition and degrade the mesh quality.

4 Experiments

All the experiments to be presented are performed on a Dawning PC Cluster at the Center for Engineering and Scientific Computation (CESC), ZheJiang University (ZJU), which consists of 24 dual-cpu nodes (2.4GHz, 1GB RAM).

The experimental geometry and its corresponding mesh are shown in Fig. 7. The number of vertices of the initial loop and that of elements inside are 88 and 358, respectively. All the following large examples are constructed from this geometry by refining the discretization of the initial loop.

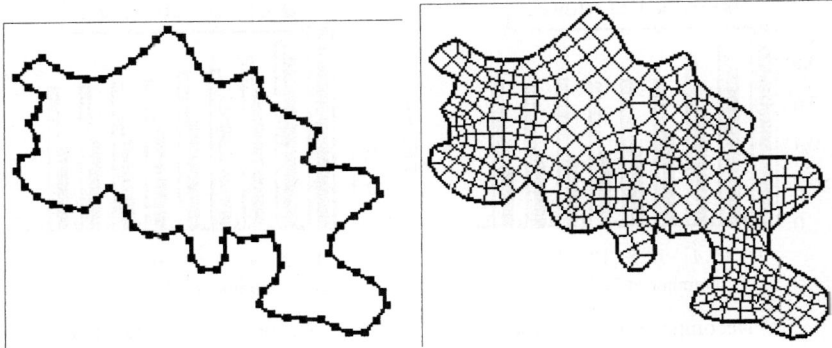

Fig. 7. The experimental geometry and its mesh

The geometry with 6,960 initial loop vertices is adopted to evaluate the parallelization of geometry decomposition based on the task-dependency tree (Section 3.1.1). The result shows that the wall-clock time changes slightly while the number of processors is greater than 5. An in-depth analysis tells that the low efficiencies mainly source from the inner restrictions of the parallel model based on the task-dependency tree. At the top of the tree, the tasks are heavy but their concurrencies are low. While searching down the tree, the concurrencies grow with task granularities diminishing even faster. For this example, the decomposition of the root node costs 88.08 seconds (more than 1/4 of the total time), while the concurrency is 1 (Table 1). After the decompositions of two children of the root performed on two processors separately, the totally elapsed time grows up to 137.72 seconds while the concurrency only grows to 2. It means that the maximal speedup for this example could not exceed 2.525(347.75/137.72).

Table 1. Experimental data for the parallelization of geometry decomposition based on the task-dependency tree

N	1	3	4	5	6	16
Time (s)	347.75	216.61	194.55	187.35	182.99	183.86
Speedup	1.0	1.61	1.79	1.86	1.90	1.89

Fig. 8 compares the efficiencies of the fine-grain level parallel geometry decomposition utilizing two different schemes to decompose H (Section 3.1.2). Schemes 1 and 2 represent schemes given in Equations 1 and 2, respectively. Figs. 8(a) and 8(b) provide data of the decomposition of the root and tree, respectively, and Scheme 2 is obviously preferable to Scheme 1. After balancing the numbers of rows among processors, the performance is enhanced largely. The remaining largest synchronization overhead for Scheme 2 is due to the imbalance of the numbers of visible vertex pairs among processors. However, it is shown that very high efficiencies (about 0.7) are still achieved for Scheme 2 with this kind of geometry-dependant overheads.

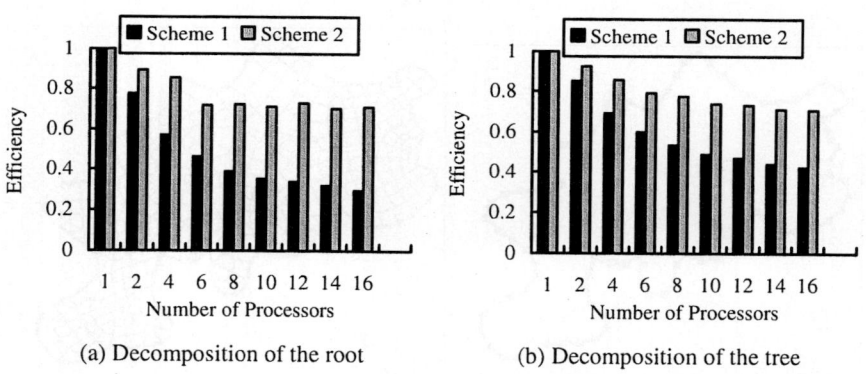

(a) Decomposition of the root   (b) Decomposition of the tree

Fig. 8. Comparison of efficiencies for two different schemes to decompose H

The simple static load balancing scheme is evaluated by an experiment with total 6,102,700 elements generated on 16 processors (Fig. 9). The maximal granularity value is 5,000, which means at most 5,000 elements are allowed to be generated in an individual sub-domain. It is seen that the number of elements on the last processor is clearly less than those on other processors while applying Equation 3. It produces a maximal 6.74% relative load imbalance between Processors 6 and 15. The value is reduced to 3.79% by applying Equation 4, which is between Processors 14 and 15.

The scalability of the parallel mesh generator in terms of problem size and the number of processors is very important. To show how the algorithm performs with increased problem size, seven meshes of various sizes (926,839~11,138,817 elements) are generated using 16 processors. Fig. 10(a) illustrates its timing performance against the mesh size. To determine performance figures as a function of the number of processors, a mesh with 1,598,213 elements is generated against different numbers of processors. Fig. 10(b) shows its timing performance. Of course, the preferable fine-grain level parallel scheme decomposing H using Equation 2 is employed to parallelize the stage of geometry decomposition.

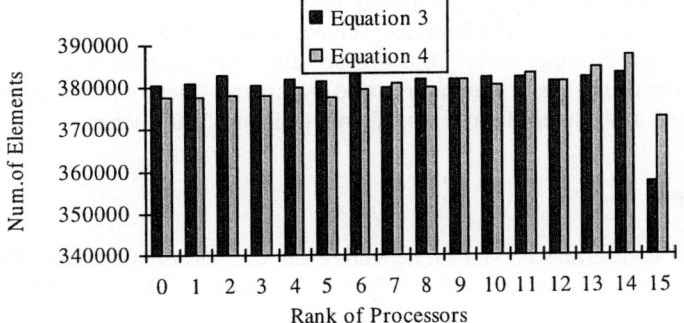

Fig. 9. Performance of the static load balancing scheme

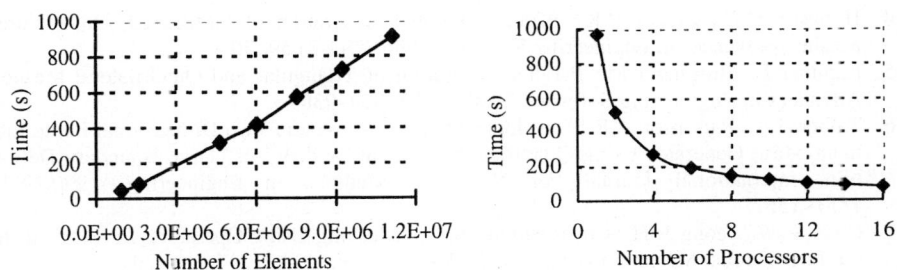

(a) timing performance against the mesh size

(b) timing performance against the number of processors

Fig. 10. Scalability of the parallel mesh generator

5 Conclusions and Future Works

The serial version of mesh generator consists of the stages of geometry decomposition and mesh generation. The stage of geometry decomposition is utilized for the data decomposition in the parallel mesh generator. As the load in sub-domains, measured by the number of elements inside, could be pre-computed accurately before meshing, a static load balancing scheme could be well performed to parallelize the stage of mesh generation. Furthermore, two parallel geometry decomposition algorithms are compared. The fine-grain level parallel strategy proves preferable to that based on the task-dependency tree, with which the load imbalance brought by the improper utilization of the symmetry of the vertex pair matrix is removed nicely. Experiments show that good scalability could be achieved for our parallel unstructured quadrilateral mesh generator.

The simple static load balancing scheme makes no attempt to minimize the numbers of share edges between neighboring processors. A graph partitioning algorithm might be employed to overcome the problem, and it is currently under investigation.

Acknowledgement. The authors would like to thank the National Natural Science Foundation of China, for the National Science Fund for Distinguished Young Scholars under grant Number 60225009. We are also very grateful to some parts of the serial version of the mesh generator coded by Ligang Chen, and the constructive discussions with Jifa Zhang, Bangti Jin, Zhongyi Lin and Wu Zhang.

References

1. Said R., Weatherill N.P., Morgan K., Verhoeven N.A.: Distributed Parallel Delaunay Mesh Generation. Computer Methods in Applied Mechanics and Engineering, 1999, 177(1-2):109~125.
2. Chrisochoides N., Nave D.: Parallel Delaunay Mesh Generation Kernel. International Journal for Numerical Methods in Engineering, 2003, 58(2):161~176.
3. Coupez T., Digonnet H., Ducloux R.: Parallel Meshing and Remeshing. Applied Mathematical Modelling, 2000, 25(2):153~175.
4. Hodgson D.C., Jimack P.K.: Efficient Parallel Generation of Partitioned, Unstructured Meshes. Advances in Engineering Software, 1996, 27(1-2):59~70.
5. Lämmer L., Burghardt M.: Parallel Generation of Triangular and Quadrilateral Meshes. Advances in Engineering Software, 2000, 31(12):929~936.
6. Talbert J.A., Parkinson A.R.: Development of An Automatic Two Dimensional Finite Element Mesh Generator Using Quadrilateral Elements and Bezier Curve Boundary Definition. International Journal For Numerical Methods in Engineering, 1990,29(7): 1551~1567.
7. Chae S.-W., Jeong J.-H.: Unstructured Surface Meshing Using Operators. In: Proc. of the 6th International Meshing Roundtable, Park City, Utah, USA, 1997. 281~291.
8. Nowottny D.: Quadrilateral Mesh Generation via Geometrically Optimized Domain Decomposition. In: Proc. of the 6th International Meshing Roundtable, Park City, Utah, USA, 1997. 309~320.
9. Sarrate J., Huerta A.: Efficient Unstructured Quadrilateral Mesh Generation. International Journal for Numerical Methods in Engineering, 2000, 49(10):1327~1350.
10. Chen J.J., Zheng Y.: A Robust and Quality Guaranteed Pattern Module Scheme for the Multi-subdomain Methods in Mesh Generation (in Chinese with English abstract). Journal of Computer-Aided Design and Computer Graphics, in press.
11. Chen J.J., Zheng Y., Chen L.G.: A New Quadrilateral Mesh Generation Method for Arbitrary Planar Domains (in Chinese with English abstract). Journal of Software, submitted.
12. Li H., Cheng G.D.: New Method for Graded Mesh Generation of Quadrilateral Finite Elements. Computers and Structures, 1996,59(5):823~829.

Container Problem in Burnt Pancake Graphs

N. Sawada, Y. Suzuki, and K. Kaneko

Tokyo University of Agriculture and Technology,
Koganei-shi, Tokyo 184-8588, Japan
s990032@cs.tuat.ac.jp, k1kaneko@cc.tuat.ac.jp

Abstract. In this paper, we propose an algorithm that solves the container problem in n-burnt pancake graphs in polynomial order time of n. Its correctness is proved and estimates of time complexity and sum of paths lengths are given. We also report the results of computer experiment conducted to measure the average performance of our algorithm.

Keywords: burnt pancake graphs, container problem, internally disjoint paths, polynomial time algorithm.

1 Introduction

Because a drastic improvement in sequential computation performance cannot be expected in future, research in parallel and distributed computation has become more significant. Extensive studies on so-called massively parallel machines have been also conducted recently, and many complex topologies of interconnection networks have been proposed[1, 6] and studied[2–5, 8, 9, 16] to replace simple networks such as a ring, a mesh, a torus and a hypercube[18]. A burnt pancake graph[10] provides one such new topology. It can provide interconnection networks that consist of different number of nodes from others such as a star graph, a pancake graph, a rotator graph, and so on.

Among the unsolved problems in burnt pancake graphs is the container problem, which is sometimes called the node-to-node disjoint paths problem or the internally-disjoint paths problem: Given a source node s and a destination node $d (\neq s)$ in a k-connected graph $G = (V, E)$, find k paths between s and d that are node-disjoint except for s and d. It is an important issue in parallel/distributed computation[7, 12, 15, 19], as is the node-to-set disjoint paths problem[11, 13, 14]. If these k paths are identified, the graph acquires some dependability[12, 17]; that is, at least one path can survive with $k - 1$ faulty components.

In general, internally disjoint paths can be obtained in polynomial order time of $|V|$ by making use of the maximum flow algorithm. However, in an n-burnt pancake graph, the number of nodes is equal to $n! \times 2^n$, so in this case the complexity of that algorithm is too large. In this paper, we propose an algorithm called N2N (node-to-node) which is of polynomial order of n instead of $n! \times 2^n$. The algorithm divides into three cases depending on the relative position between the source node and the destination node. The algorithm obtains n internally-disjoint paths between any pair of nodes where n is equal to the connectivity of an n-burnt pancake graph. We also present the results of an average performance evaluation.

The rest of this paper is organized as follows. Section 2 introduces burnt pancake graphs as well as other requisite definitions. Section 3 explains our algorithm in detail. Section 4 describes a proof of correctness and the theoretical complexities of our algorithm. Average performance results are reported in Section 5. Section 6 presents conclusions and ideas for future work.

2 Preliminaries

In this section, we introduce definitions of the signed permutation, the prefix reversal operation, burnt pancake graphs, and a simple routing algorithm in a burnt pancake graph.

Definition 1. *(signed permutation)* $\boldsymbol{u} = (u_1, u_2, \cdots, u_n)$ *is called a signed permutation of n integers $1, 2, \cdots, n$ if $\{|u_1|, |u_2|, \cdots, |u_n|\} = \{1, 2, \cdots, n\}$.*

Definition 2. *(prefix reversal operation) Let $\boldsymbol{u} = (u_1, u_2, \cdots, u_n)$ be a signed permutation of n integers $1, 2, \cdots, n$. Then the operation $\boldsymbol{u}^{(i)}$ ($1 \leq i \leq n$) is defined below:*
$$\boldsymbol{u}^{(i)} = (-u_i, -u_{i-1}, \cdots, -u_1, u_{i+1}, \cdots, u_n).$$
This operation is called the prefix reversal operation.

The successive applications of the prefix reversal operations $(\boldsymbol{u}^{(i_1, i_2, \cdots, i_{k-1})})^{(i_k)}$ are denoted by $\boldsymbol{u}^{(i_1, i_2, \cdots, i_{k-1}, i_k)}$. In the rest of this paper, we put the negative sign above expressions, $\overline{u}_1$, to save space.

Definition 3. *(n-burnt pancake graph or BP_n) A burnt pancake graph with degree n, or an n-burnt pancake graph, BP_n, is an undirected graph, which has $n! \times 2^n$ nodes. Each node has a unique label $\boldsymbol{u} = (u_1, u_2, \cdots, u_n)$ which is a signed permutation of n integers $1, 2, \cdots, n$. For two nodes $\boldsymbol{u}$ and $\boldsymbol{v}$, there exists an edge between them if and only if there exist i ($1 \leq i \leq n$) such that $\boldsymbol{u}^{(i)} = \boldsymbol{v}$.*

Figure 1 shows an example of BP_3. An n-burnt pancake graph BP_n includes $2n$ disjoint subgraphs BP_{n-1}. The nodes in each subgraph share a common integer, which we designate as k, for the final elements of their labels. Hence, each subgraph can be identified as $BP_{n-1}k$. Note that any edge $(\boldsymbol{u}, \boldsymbol{v})$ between two different subgraphs is given by the operation $\boldsymbol{v} = \boldsymbol{u}^{(n)}$ only.

Table 1 shows a comparison of characteristics of an n-burnt pancake graph BP_n with a pancake graph P_n, an n-rotator graph R_n, an n-star graph S_n, an n-cube Q_n, an (n, k)-de Bruijn graph $B_{n,k}$, and an (n, k)-Kautz graph $K_{n,k}$. If we define a performance metrics of interconnection networks by

$$\text{(Number of Nodes)} / \{\text{(Degree)} \times \text{(Diameter)}\},$$

BP_n is superior to P_n, R_n, S_n, $T_{n,k}$, $M_{n,k}$ and Q_n. Though $B_{n,k}$ and $K_{n,k}$ are superior to BP_n in the metrics, they do not have symmetry nor recursive structure, which are suitable for executing some parallel and distributed applications.

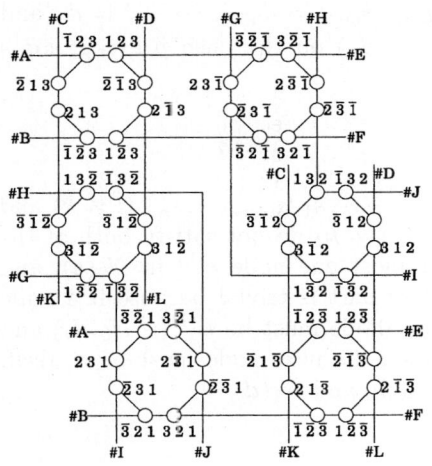

Fig. 1. An example of burnt pancake graph BP_3

```
procedure simple(s, d)
{Assume c = (c_1, ..., c_n) and
 d = (d_1, ..., d_n).}
begin
  c := s;  P := [c];
  for k := n to 1 step -1 do
    if c_k <> d_k then begin
      find h such that |c_h| = |d_k|;
      if h <> 1 then begin
        c := c^(h);
        P := P ++ [c] end;
      if k <> 1 and c_1 = d_k then
        begin
          c := c^(1);
          P := P ++ [c] end;
      c := c^(k);  P := P ++ [c] end
end;
```

Fig. 2. A simple routing algorithm simple

Table 1. Comparison of a burnt pancake graph with other topologies

	number of nodes	degree	connectivity	diameter
BP_n	$n! \times 2^n$	n	n	$\leq 2n+3$
P_n	$n!$	$n-1$	$n-1$	†
R_n	$n!$	$n-1$	$n-1$	$n-1$
S_n	$n!$	$n-1$	$n-1$	$\lfloor \frac{3(n-1)}{2} \rfloor$
Q_n	2^n	n	n	n
$B_{n,k}$	n^k	n	n	k
$K_{n,k}$	$n^k + n^{k-1}$	n	n	k

†: $\leq \lceil 5(n+1)/3 \rceil$ from [10].

For given source node s and destination node d in an BP_n, we use the routing algorithm simple shown in Figure 2 to obtain a path between s and d. We assume that the label of a node is represented by using a linear array and each element of the array consists of a word that can store the value n. Additionally, we assume that the labels represented by the arrays are all stored in memory to specify a path. Then this algorithm simple requires $O(n^2)$ time complexity and generates a path whose length is at most $3n - 2$.

For simple routing algorithm, the following lemma holds.

Lemma 1. *For an arbitrary node a, define $N_0(a)$ and $N_1(a)$ by $N_0(a) = \{a^{(i)} | i \in \{1, 2, \cdots, n\}\}$ and $N_1(a) = \{a^{(i,1)} | i \in \{2, \cdots, n\}\}$, respectively. Then for arbitrary two nodes s and d, the path p generated by simple(s, d) includes at most one node in each of $N_0(s)$, $N_1(s)$, $N_0(d)$, and $N_1(d)$.*

(Proof) Assume that $s_h \neq d_h$, $s_{h+1} = d_{h+1}$, $s_{h+2} = d_{h+2}$, $\cdots$, $s_n = d_n$ and $|s_k| = |d_h|$. Then any node $\boldsymbol{u} = (u_1, u_2, \cdots, u_n)$ on the path p except for $\boldsymbol{s}$ satisfies one of the following conditions:

- $|u_1| = |s_k|$, or
- $u_h = d_h$, $u_{h+1} = d_{h+1}$, $\cdots$, $u_n = d_n$.

On the other hand, any nodes $\boldsymbol{s}^{(i)} = (\overline{s}_i, \overline{s}_{i-1}, \cdots, \overline{s}_1, s_{i+1}, \cdots, s_n)$ $(i \neq k)$ and $\boldsymbol{s}^{(i,1)} = (s_i, \overline{s}_{i-1}, \cdots, \overline{s}_1, s_{i+1}, \cdots, s_n)$ $(i \geq 2, i \neq k)$ do not satisfy both of the above conditions. Then the path p has at most one node $\boldsymbol{s}^{(k)}$ in $N_0(\boldsymbol{s})$, and at most one node $\boldsymbol{s}^{(k,1)}$ in $N_1(\boldsymbol{s})$. The latter part is trivial because if a node $\boldsymbol{u}(\in N_1(\boldsymbol{d}))$ first appears on p, then the next node must be $\boldsymbol{u}^{(1)}(\in N_0(\boldsymbol{d}))$ and if a node $\boldsymbol{v}(\in N_0(\boldsymbol{d}))$ first appears on p, then the next node must be $\boldsymbol{d}$ itself. Hence p has at most one node in each of $N_0(\boldsymbol{d})$, and $N_1(\boldsymbol{d})$. $\square$

3 Algorithm N2N

Let the source node $\boldsymbol{s} = (s_1, s_2, \cdots, s_n)$ and the destination node $\boldsymbol{d} = (d_1, d_2, \cdots, d_n)$. If $n \leq 2$, the internally-disjoint paths problem is trivial. Hence, we assume that $n \geq 3$ in the rest of this paper. Then, our algorithm N2N to solve the container problem in burnt pancake graphs is described by the following three cases.

Case 1 $s_n = d_n$;
Case 2 $s_n = \overline{d}_n$; and
Case 3 $|s_n| \neq |d_n|$.

In the following sections, we represent an edge by $\rightarrow$ and a path generated by simple by $\rightsquigarrow$.

3.1 Case 1

This subsection presents Procedure 1 for the case that $s_n = d_n$, that is, $\boldsymbol{s}$ and $\boldsymbol{d}$ are both in $BP_{n-1}s_n$.

Step 1. In $BP_{n-1}s_n$, apply Algorithm N2N recursively and obtain $n-1$ internally disjoint paths from $\boldsymbol{s}$ to $\boldsymbol{d}$.
Step 2. If $s_1 \neq \overline{d}_1$, construct a path $\boldsymbol{s} \rightarrow \boldsymbol{s}^{(n)} \rightsquigarrow \boldsymbol{d}^{(n)} \rightarrow \boldsymbol{d}$. See Figure 3. Otherwise, construct a path $\boldsymbol{s} \rightarrow \boldsymbol{s}^{(n)} \rightarrow \boldsymbol{s}^{(n,1)} \rightsquigarrow \boldsymbol{d}^{(n)} \rightarrow \boldsymbol{d}$. Note that the path does not include the nodes inside $BP_{n-1}s_n$ except for $\boldsymbol{s}$ and $\boldsymbol{d}$. See Figure 4.

3.2 Case 2

This subsection presents Procedure 2 for the case that $s_n = \overline{d}_n$.

Step 1. From $\boldsymbol{s}$, construct n paths $p_1, p_2, \cdots, p_n$ as follows:
p_i's $(1 \leq i \leq n-1)$: Construct a path $\boldsymbol{s} \rightarrow \boldsymbol{s}^{(i)} \rightarrow \boldsymbol{s}^{(i,n)}$.

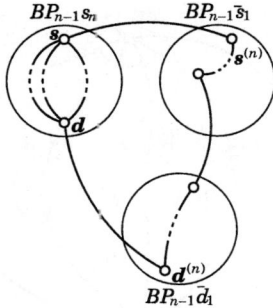
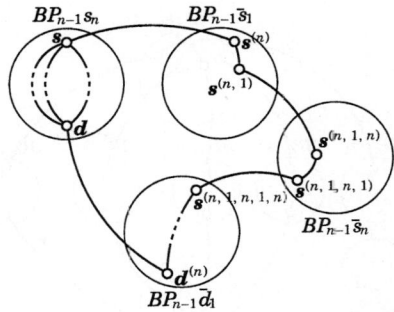

Fig. 3. Case 1, Step 2 ($s_1 \neq \overline{d}_1$)

Fig. 4. Case 1, Step 2 ($s_1 = \overline{d}_1$)

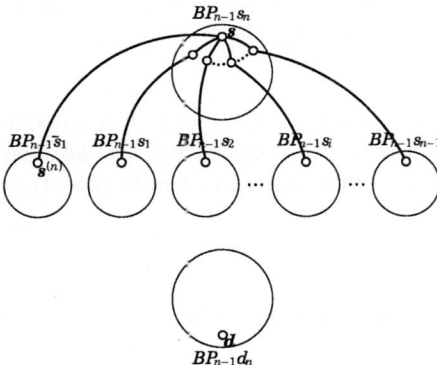
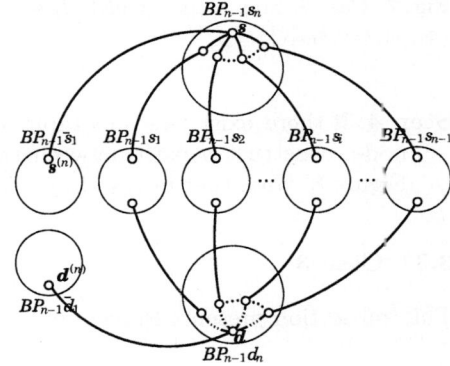

Fig. 5. Case 2, Step 1

Fig. 6. Case 2, Step 2 ($|s_1| \neq |d_1|$, $d_1 \in \{s_2, s_3, \cdots, s_{n-1}\}$)

p_n: Construct a path $s \to s^{(n)}$.

Note that each of n subgraphs $BP_{n-1}\overline{s}_1, BP_{n-1}s_1, BP_{n-1}s_2, \cdots, BP_{n-1}s_{n-1}$ has exactly one terminal node of p_i's. See Figure 5.

Step 2. From d, construct n paths $q_1, q_2, \cdots, q_n$ as follows:

q_1: Construct a path $d \to d^{(1)} \to d^{(1,n)}$.

q_j's ($2 \leq j \leq n-1$): We assume that $|d_j| = |s_i|$. If $d_j = s_i$, construct a path $d \to d^{(j)} \to d^{(j,n)}$. Otherwise, construct a path $d \to d^{(j)} \to d^{(j\,1)} \to d^{(j,1,n)}$.

q_n: Construct a path $d \to d^{(n)}$.

Note that each of n subgraphs $BP_{n-1}\overline{d}_1, BP_{n-1}s_1, BP_{n-1}s_2, \cdots, BP_{n-1}d_1, \cdots, BP_{n-1}s_{n-1}$ has exactly one terminal node of q_i's. The terminal nodes of p_i's and q_j's other than s and d are called anchor nodes. See Figure 6.

Step 3. In each subgraph, if it contains two anchor nodes of paths p_i and q_j, construct a path between these two nodes by `simple`. See Figure 7.

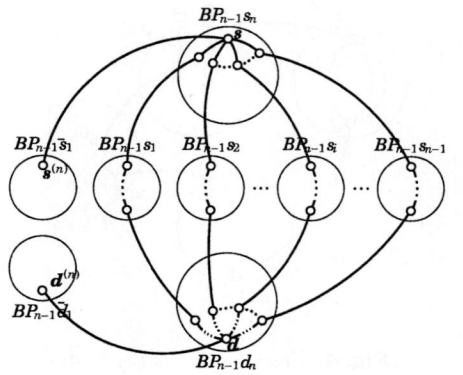

Fig. 7. Case 2, Step 3 ($|s_1| \neq |d_1|$, $d_1 \in \{s_2, s_3, \cdots, s_{n-1}\}$).

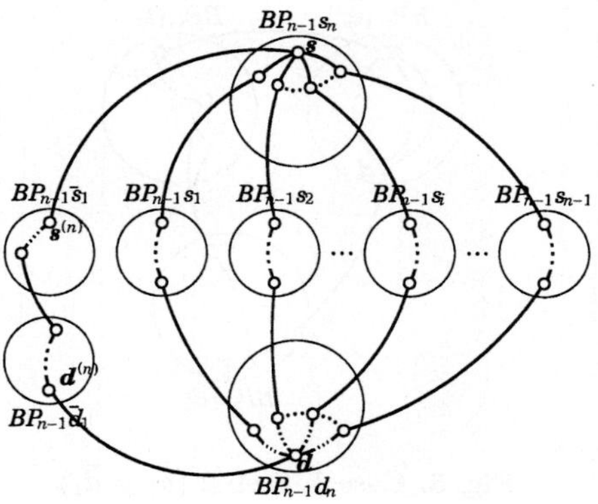

Fig. 8. Case 2, Step 4 ($|s_1| \neq |d_1|$, $d_1 \in \{s_2, s_3, \cdots, s_{n-1}\}$).

Step 4. If there exist two subgraphs each of which contains only one anchor node, construct a path between these two terminal nodes by simple. See Figure 8. Note that in case $|s_1| = |d_1|$, there is no need to execute this step.

3.3 Case 3

This subsection presents Procedure 3 for the case that $|s_n| \neq |d_n|$.

Step 1. By simple construct two paths p and q from s to d and from d to s, respectively. Let $s^{(k)}$ and $d^{(h)}$ be the neighbor nodes of s and d on q and p, respectively. See Figure 9 (a). If $s^{(k)} \in p$ then let $T = \{q\}$. See Figure 9 (b). Or, if $d^{(h)} \in q$ then let $T = \{p\}$. Otherwise, let $T = \{p, q\}$. See Figure 9 (c).

Step 2. From s, construct paths p_i's as follows:

p_1: If $s^{(1)}$ is not included in any path in T, construct a path $s \to s^{(1)} \to s^{(1,n)}$.

p_i's ($2 \leq i \leq n-1, i \neq k$): If $s^{(i)}$ is not included in any path in T, construct a path $s \to s^{(i)} \to s^{(i,n)}$.

p_n: If $s^{(n)}$ is not included in any path in T, construct a path $s \to s^{(n)}$.

Note that inclusion of $s^{(i)}$ in any path in T can be checked by comparing it with the neighbor node of s on the path. See Figure 10.

Step 3. From d, construct paths q_j's as follows:

q_1: If $d^{(1)}$ is not included in any path in T, construct a path $d \to d^{(1)} \to d^{(1,n)}$.

q_j's ($2 \leq j \leq n-1, j \neq h$): In case that $d^{(j)}$ is included in any path in T, do not construct a path. Otherwise, we assume that $|d_j| = |s_i|$. If $d_j = s_i$, construct a path $d \to d^{(j)} \to d^{(j,n)}$. If $d_j = \overline{s}_i$, construct a path $d \to d^{(j)} \to d^{(j,1)} \to d^{(j,1,n)}$.

q_n: If $d_1 \neq \overline{s}_n$, construct a path $d \to d^{(n)}$.

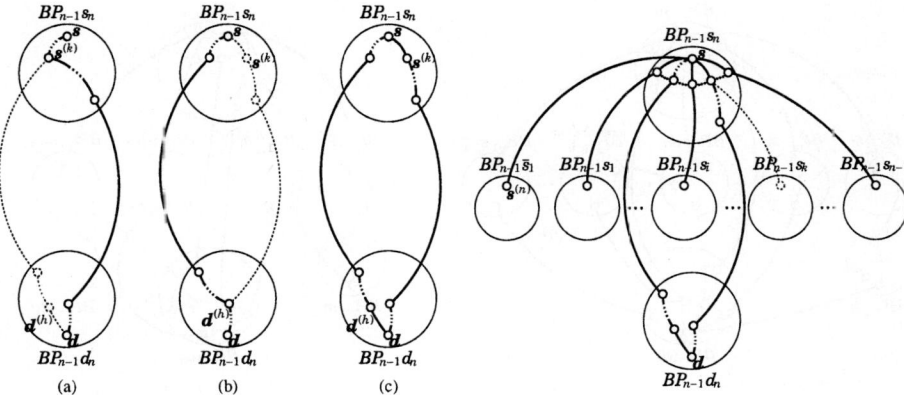

Fig. 9. Case 3, Step 1   **Fig. 10.** Case 3, Step 2

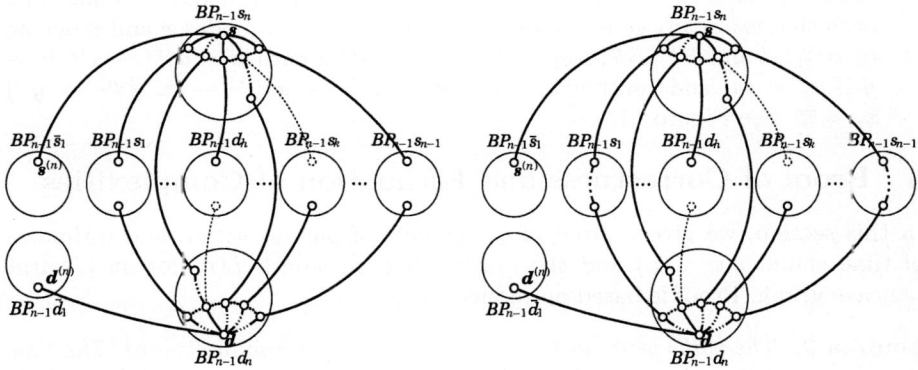

Fig. 11. Case 3, Step 3   **Fig. 12.** Case 3, Step 4

The terminal nodes of p_i's and q_j's other than s and d are called anchor nodes. See Figure 11.

Step 4. In each subgraph, if it contains two anchor nodes of paths p_i and q_j, construct a path between these two nodes by simple. See Figure 12.

Step 5. If there exist four subgraphs $BP_{n-1}l_1$, $BP_{n-1}l_2$, $BP_{n-1}l_3$, and $BP_{n-1}l_4$ such that $BP_{n-1}l_1$ and $BP_{n-1}l_2$ contain exactly one anchor node of p_i's and $BP_{n-1}l_3$ and $BP_{n-1}l_4$ contain exactly one anchor node of q_i's, then we can make two pairs of subgraphs so that for each pair $BP_{n-1}l_i$ and $BP_{n-1}l_j$, $i \in \{1,2\}$ and $j \in \{3,4\}$ and $l_i \neq \bar{l}_j$. For each pair of them, apply simple to connect the anchor nodes and terminate. See Figure 13.

Step 6. If there exist two subgraphs $BP_{n-1}l$ and $BP_{n-1}l'$ each of which contains only one anchor node and $|l| \neq |l'|$, construct a path between these two terminal nodes by simple. Otherwise, if there exist two subgraphs $BP_{n-1}l$ and $BP_{n-1}l'$ each of which contains only one anchor node and $l = \bar{l}'$, there

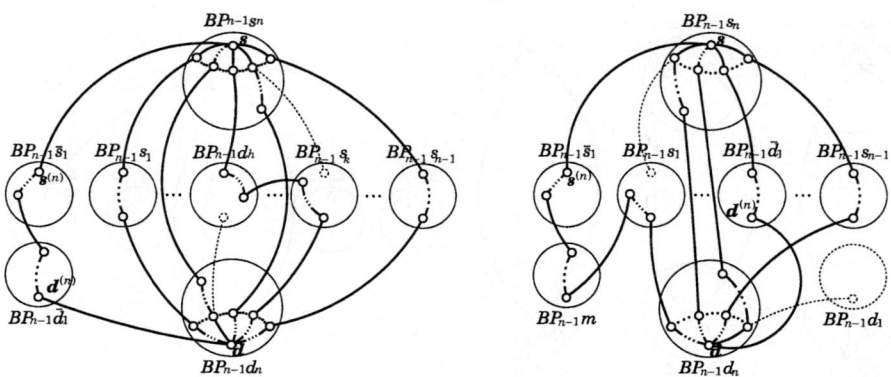

Fig. 13. Case 3, Step 5   **Fig. 14.** Case 3, Step 6

must exist at least one subgraph $BP_{n-1}m$ that does not include any node of a path that is already constructed. Assuming the anchor nodes x and y belong to $BP_{n-1}l$ and $BP_{n-1}l'$, respectively, construct a path $x \to x^{(r)} \to x^{(r,n)} \rightsquigarrow y$ if $x_r = m$, and construct a path $x \to x^{(r)} \to x^{(r,1)} \to x^{(r,1,n)} \rightsquigarrow y$ if $x_r = \overline{m}$. See Figure 14.

4 Proof of Correctness and Estimation of Complexities

In this section, we give a proof of correctness of our algorithm and estimates of time complexity $T(n)$ and the maximum path length $L(n)$ for an n-burnt pancake graph. Proof is based on induction on n.

Lemma 2. *The paths generated by Procedure 1 are internally disjoint. The time complexity of Procedure 1 is $T(n-1) + O(n^2)$ and the maximum length of the paths obtained is* $\max\{L(n-1), 3n-2\}$.

(Proof) Paths obtained in Step 1 are known to be internally disjoint by induction. The path obtained in Step 1 is outside of $BP_{n-1}s_n$ except for s and d. Hence, it is internally disjoint to the paths obtained in Step 1. Step 1 takes $T(n-1)$ time to generate paths, the maximum length of the paths is $L(n-1)$. Steps 2 takes $O(n^2)$ time and generate a path whose length is at most $3n-2$. Hence, the time complexity is $T(n-1) + O(n^2)$ and the maximum path length is $\max\{L(n-1), 3n-2\}$. □

Lemma 3. *The paths generated by Procedure 2 are internally disjoint. The time complexity Procedure 2 is $O(n^3)$ and the maximum length of the paths obtained is $3n+3$.*

(Proof) Paths selected in Steps 1 and 2 are trivially disjoint other than s and d. The paths generated in Step 3 are included in separate subgraphs. Hence they are disjoint each other and they are also disjoint with the paths p_i's and q_j's other than the anchor nodes. The path generated in Step 4 is included in two subgraphs each of which has exactly one anchor node. Hence, the path is disjoint with other paths generated in Steps 1 to 3 except for the anchor nodes. Therefore all the paths generated in Procedure 2 are internally disjoint. Step 1 requires $O(n^2)$ time and generates paths whose maximum length is 2. Step 2 takes $O(n^2)$ time and generates paths whose maximum length is 3. Step 3 takes $O(n^3)$ time and the length of each path generated in this step is at most $3n-5$. Step 4 requires $O(n^2)$ time and the maximum length of the path is $3n-2$. Hence, the time complexity is $O(n^3)$ and the maximum path length is $3n+3$. □

Lemma 4. *The paths generated by Procedure 3 are internally disjoint. The time complexity of Procedure 3 is $O(n^3)$ and the sum of lengths of paths obtained is $3n+4$.*

(Proof) The at most two paths selected in Step 1 are internally disjoint from Lemma 1. It can be proved in the similar manner to the proof of Lemma 3 that the paths generated in Steps 2 to 4 are internally disjoint. These paths are also disjoint with the paths selected in Step 1. The two paths established in Step 5, if any, are disjoint because their nodes other than s and d are included in their own subgraphs. It is also possible to prove in the similar manner to the proof of Lemma 3 that these two paths are disjoint with other paths generated in Steps 1 to 4. The path established in Step 6, if any, is disjoint with other paths because the subpath between the anchor nodes are established by using two subgraphs in which the anchor nodes are included as well as the subgraph that does not included another path's node at all. Therefore all the paths generated in Procedure 3 are internally disjoint. The paths generated in Steps 3 and 4 are internally disjoint to other paths because the paths that share some nodes are discarded in these steps. Step 1 takes $O(n^2)$ time and generates paths whose maximum length is $3n-2$. Step 2 requires $O(n^2)$ time to generate paths whose maximum length is 2. Step 3 takes $O(n^2)$ time and generate a path whose length is at most 3. Step 4 takes $O(n^3)$ times and the length of the path generated in this step is at most $3n-5$. Step 5 takes $O(n^2)$ times and the maximum length of the paths generated in this step is $3n-2$. Step 6 requires $O(n^2)$ time and the maximum length of the path is $3n$ because the first element of the label of $x^{(r,n)}$ and the final element of that of y are identical. Consequently, the time complexity is $O(n^3)$ and the maximum path length is $3n+4$. □

Theorem 1. *Paths generated by N2N are internally disjoint. For an n-burnt pancake graph, the time complexity $T(n)$ of N2N is $O(n^3)$ and the maximum length of paths $L(n)$ generated by N2N is $3n+4$.*

(Proof) From Lemmas 2 to 4 above, paths generated by N2N are proved to be internally disjoint and it also holds that $T(n) = \max\{T(n-1), O(n^3)\}$ and $L(n) = 3n+4$. Hence $T(n) = O(n^3)$. □

5 Performance Evaluation

To evaluate the average performance of algorithm N2N, we conducted a computer experiment by sampling the source node randomly as follows:

For each $n = 3, 4, \cdots, 80$, repeat the following steps 10,000 times.

1. Select the destination node randomly.
2. Select the source node s randomly other than d.
3. For s and d, apply algorithm N2N and measure the execution time and the maximum path length.

The algorithm was implemented using the functional programming language Haskell. The program was compiled with the Glasgow Haskell compiler ghc with -O and -fglasgow-exts options. The target machine is equipped with a Pentium III 700MHz CPU, 256MB main memory. The average execution time and the maximum path length obtained by this experiment are shown in Figures 15 and 16, respectively. From Figure 15, we can see that the average execution time is $O(n^{3.0})$. Also, from Figure 16, we can see that the maximum of path lengths is $3n + 4$.

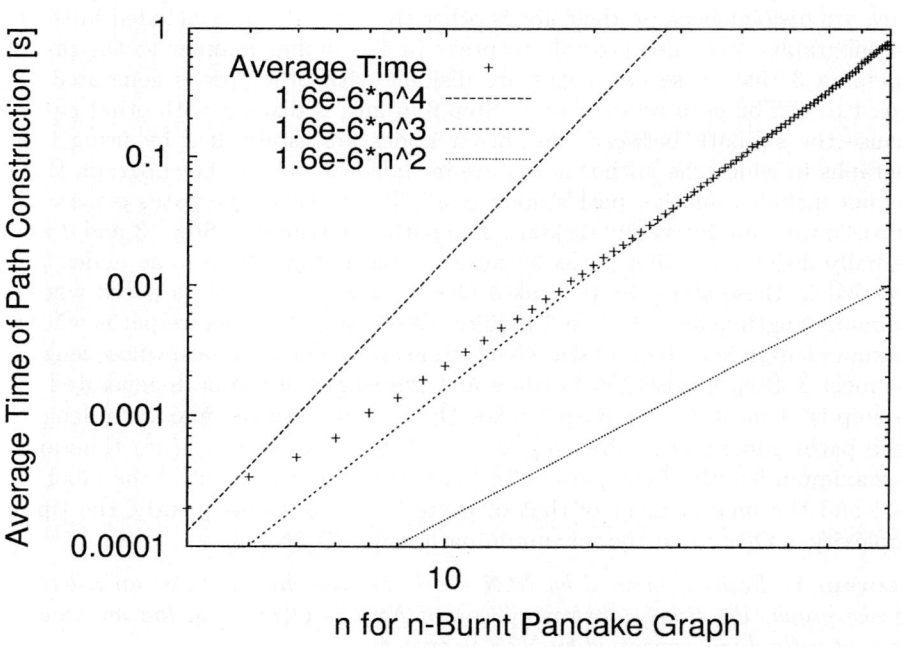

Fig. 15. Average execution time

6 Conclusions

In this paper, we proposed a polynomial algorithm for the container problem in n-burnt pancake graphs. Its time complexity is $O(n^3)$ and the maximum path

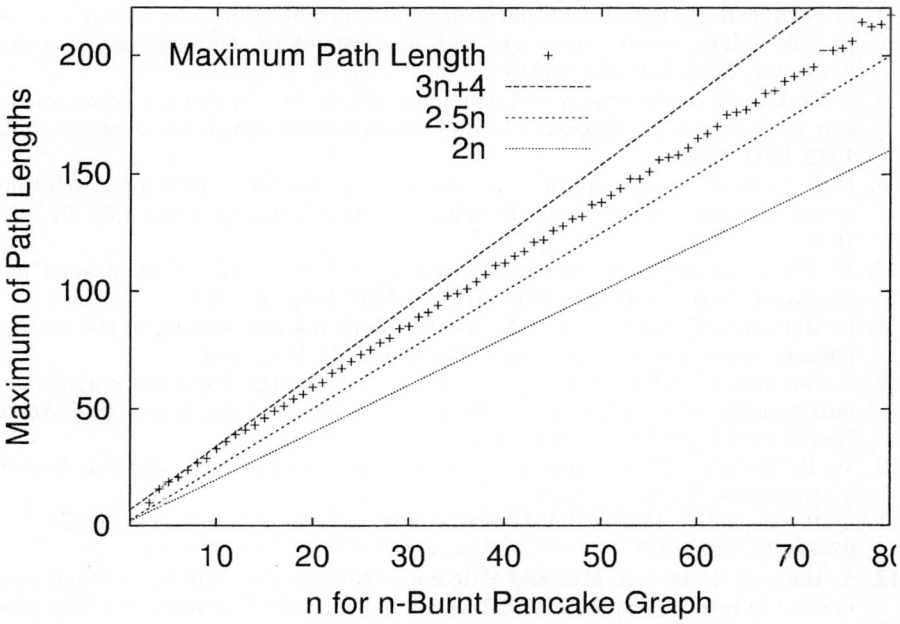

Fig. 16. Maximum length of paths.

length is $3n + 4$. We also conducted computer experimentation and showed that the average execution time and the practical maximum path length is $O(n^{3.0})$ and $3n + 4$, respectively. Future work will include an improvement of the algorithm to generate shorter paths in shorter execution time as well as application of our approach to other topologies of interconnection networks.

Acknowledgements

This study is was partly supported by a Grant-in-Aid for Scientific Research (C) of the Japan Society for the Promotion of Science under the Grant No. 16500015.

References

1. S. B. Akers, and B. Krishnamurthy: A group theoretic model for symmetric interconnection networks, IEEE Trans. Comput., 38(4), 555–566, 1989.
2. S. G. Akl and K. Qiu: Parallel minimum spanning forest algorithms on the star and pancake interconnection networks, Proc. of Joint Conf. Vector and Parallel Processing, 565–570, 1992.
3. S. G. Akl and K. Qiu: A novel routing scheme on the star and pancake interconnection networks and its applications, Parallel Computing, 19(1), 95–101, 1993.

4. S. G. Akl, K. Qiu, and I. Stojmenović: Fundamental algorithms for the star and pancake interconnection networks with applications to computational geometry, Networks, 23(4), 215–226, 1993.
5. P. Berthomé, A. Ferreira, and S. Perennes: Optimal information dissemination in star and pancake networks, IEEE Trans. Parallel and Distributed Systems, 7(12), 1292–1300, 1996.
6. P. F. Corbett: Rotator graphs: An efficient topology for point-to-point multiprocessor networks, IEEE Trans. Parallel and Distributed Systems, 3(5), 622–626, 1992.
7. M. Dietzfelbinger, S. Madhavapeddy and I. H. Sudborough: Three disjoint path paradigms in star networks, Proc. IEEE SPDP, 400–406, 1991.
8. L. Garfgano, U. Vaccaro, and A. Vozella: Fault tolerant routing in the star and pancake interconnection networks, IPL, 45(6), 315–320, 1993.
9. L. Gardner, Z. Miller, D. Pritikin, and I. H. Sudborough: Embedding hypercubes into pancake, cycle prefix and substring reversal networks, Proc. 28th Annual Hawaii Int'l Conf. System Sciences, 537–545, 1995.
10. W. H. Gates and H. Papadimitriou: Bounds for sorting by prefix reversal, Discrete Mathematics, 27, 47–57, 1979.
11. Q.-P. Gu and S. Peng, Node-to-set disjoint paths problem in star graphs, IPL, 62(4), 201–207, 1997.
12. Y. Hamada, F. Bao, A. Mei, and Y. Igarashi: Nonadaptive fault-tolerant file transmission in rotator graphs, IEICE Trans. Fundamentals, E79-A(4), 477–782, 1996.
13. K. Kaneko and Y. Suzuki: An algorithm for node-to-set disjoint paths problem in rotator graphs, IEICE Trans. Information and Systems, E84-D(9), 1155–1163, 2001.
14. K. Kaneko: An algorithm for node-to-set disjoint paths problem in burnt pancake graphs, IEICE Trans. Information and Systems, E86-D(12), 2588-2594, 2003.
15. S. Madhavapeddy and I. H. Sudborough: A topological property of hypercubes — node disjoint paths, Proc. IEEE SPDP, 532–539, 1990.
16. K. Qiu, H. Meijer, and S. G. Akl: Parallel routing and sorting on the pancake network, Proc. Int'l Conf. Computing and Information, 360–371, 1991.
17. M. O. Rabin: Efficient dispersal of information for security, load balancing, and fault tolerance, JACM, 36(2), 335–348, 1989.
18. C. L. Seitz: The cosmic cube, CACM, 28(7), 22–33, 1985.
19. Y. Suzuki and K. Kaneko: An algorithm for node-disjoint paths in pancake graphs, IEICE Trans. Information and Systems, E86-D(3), 610–615, 2003.

A Cost Optimal Parallel Quicksorting and Its Implementation on a Shared Memory Parallel Computer

Jie Liu, Clinton Knowles, and Adam Brian Davis

Department Of Computer Sciences,
Western Oregon University,
Monmouth, OR 97361
{liuj, cknwle, addavis}@wou.edu

Abstract. This paper discusses a parallel quicksort algorithm that is cost optimal, in average, using $O(n/\log(n))$ processors. The cost optimality is mainly due to a cost optimal partitioning algorithm that utilizes all the processors when partitioning the array. A temporary array of the same size as the original array is needed during the partitioning process. The prefix sums are used to determine where a processor can copy its data.

We will prove that the algorithm has an average case complexity $O(\log^2 n)$, where n is the size of the data array. We will also discuss the implementation of our algorithm on a shared memory parallel computer and demonstrate that it outperforms other $O(\log^2 n)$ parallel sorting algorithms. In addition, it outperforms the sequential quicksort algorithm starting with two processors.

1 Introduction

One of the common tasks performed by computers is sorting. Quicksort is a popular sequential sorting algorithm due to its average case efficiency and easy of implementation. Formally, given (1) a list of n elements a_0, a_1, ..., a_{n-1}, and (2) a predefined linear order such that for any two elements a_i and a_j, one and only one of the following can be true: $a_i < a_j$, $a_i = a_j$, or $a_i > a_j$, sorting is a problem of finding a permutation (p_0, p_1, ..., p_{n-1}) so that $a_{p_0} \leq a_{p_1} \leq ... a_{p_{n-1}}$.

In the rest of discussions, we assume that n elements are stored in a zero based array a[]. In addition, without losing generality, we assume these n elements are unique. If two elements a[i] = a[j] and i < j, we define the linear order to be a[i] < a[j]. Under these settings and for the clarity of later discussions, a sequential quicksort algorithm in its most basic form is presented in List 1. Most computations occur at step 2, which is the focus of this paper.

Developing parallel sorting algorithms are the research focus of many researchers. There are two major approaches: designing new algorithms, such as bitonic merge sort [4], or modifying existing sequential algorithms, such as parallel merge [13].

Both bitonic sort and parallel merge have a complexity of $\Theta(\log^2 n)$ using $\Theta(n)$ processors. Therefore, the cost of the algorithms is $\Theta(n \log^2 n)$, which is not optimal. In addition, since all processors are busy in the entire execution of the algorithms, reducing the number of processors results in increasing in complexity. Therefore, neither algorithm cannot be cost optimal even using fewer processors, which is a common way of achieving cost optimality for many parallel algorithms [10].

```
Step 1: Finding a pivot: find a pivot pv such that
```
$\min(a_0, a_1 \ldots a_{n-1}) \le pv \le \max(a_0, a_1 \ldots a_{n-1})$
```
Step 2: Partition: divide the array into two subarrays:
s1 and s2 such that s1 contains all elements less than
or equal to pv, and s2 contains all elements greater
than pv.
Step 3: Recursion: repeat step 1 and 2 on s1 and s2,
respectively, unless a subarray contains only one ele-
ment.
```

List 1. Outline of the quicksort algorithm

Muller and Preparata proposed an algorithm to sort n elements in a constant time on a nonstandard CRCW PRAM using n^2 already activated processors [2]. The algorithm is not cost optimal because it performs $O(n^2)$ comparisons. Several O(log n) parallel sorting algorithms were proposed by various researchers [5-7]. However, as pointed out by Leighton, the constant of proportionality of the algorithms is immense and, unless n is unrealistically large, these algorithms would be slower in practice than other parallel sorting algorithms [7].

Quicksort is a divide-and-conquer algorithm. The results of each "dividing" are two disjoint sub-problems with no further communication between them. Therefore, these two sub-problems can be resolved concurrently and recursively. A direct approach utilizing this characteristic is to start with a single partition running on a single processor. The result is assigned to two processors, then to four processors, and so on. The problem is that at the beginning, when the problem sizes are relatively large, only few processors participate in the partitioning phase of the sorting process. That greatly affects the utilization of processors and results in a maximum speedup of about 6 [8].

In situations where the number of processors is much smaller than the problem size, Francis and Pannan proposed a parallel partitioning approach, where the array was divided into several segment and partitioned in parallel [8]. This parallel step results in an almost partitioned array. The two ends of the array are partitioned. The middle section is not. The size of this unpartitioned middle section depends on data distributions in the original array and the section of the pivot. A sequential pass has to be introduced to partition the unpartitioned middle section. Since the size of this middle section cannot be determined, the performance of the approach is unpredictable.

Heideberger, Norton, and Robinson introduced a parallel quicksort algorithm that sorts n elements in $\Theta(\log n)$ time using n processors [9]. The algorithm assumes a CRCW PRAM with the capability of performing Fetch&Add as an atomic operation. The core of the algorithm is a parallelized partitioning as given in List 2. The do_parallel loop indicates that the iterations of the loop are carried out simultaneously. Array a[] holds the original data; array b[] holds the results of partitioning with the left side holding the elements smaller than the pivot pv, and the right side holding the rest.

```
do_parallel i = 1 to n
   t = a[i]
   if (t < pv)
       then b[F&A(L, 1)] = t;
       else b[F&A(R, -1)] = t;
end do_parallel
```

List 2. A parallel partitioning of array a[] using an atomic Fetch&Add given in [9]

Given that the iterations are carried out concurrently, the do_parallel loop has a time complexity of $\Theta(1)$. In addition, in an average case, the array can be partitioned to size of 1 in $O(\log n)$ time, the average time complexity of the algorithm is $\Theta(\log n)$ with the worst time complexity of $\Theta(n)$. Since simulating such a nonstandard CRCW PRAM processor using an EREW or CREW PRAM processor requires $\Theta(n)$ time, it is safe to state that, until we can build such a powerful CRCW parallel computer as proposed, this quicksort algorithm can still be improved on a weaker parallel computation model such as CREW PRAM. In addition, implementing such an algorithm on a real parallel computer and expecting good performance will not likely be feasible in the near future due to the special requirements on the processors.

Liu and He presented an approach of solving the partitioning problem using parallel prefix sums in two steps [14]. We will discuss Liu and He's approach in detail in the next section because our algorithm is based on Liu and He's approach.

2 The Liu and He's Parallel Quicksort

The basic approach of Liu and He's algorithm is to copy the elements smaller or equal to the pivot, i.e. s1, to the front of a temporary array concurrently, and then copy elements great than the pivot, i.e. s2, to the back of the temporary array concurrently. Let us consider the steps forming s1 first.

It first marks all elements that should be in s1 concurrently, and then uses parallel prefix sum algorithm to calculate, for each marked element a_i, the number of marked elements with an index value smaller than i. The result is the index of a_i in the temporary array. The formation of s2 is similar. The outline of Liu and He's approach is given in List 3.

In the steps listed in List 3, step 1 matches the step 1 of List 1, and step 9 matches the step 3 of List 1. Steps 2 to 8 partition the original array into two segments: s1 – a segment contains all elements that are greater than the pivot (steps 2 to 4), and s2 – another segment contains the rest (steps 6 to 8). That is, steps 2 to 8 accomplish the partitioning process and are carried out in parallel (except step 5).

List 4 is the prefix sum algorithm used in [14] based on the discussions in [10]. The loop structure ForAll indicates that all the processors specified perform the loop body concurrently. Other statements carry the same meanings as in most programming languages.

Figure 1 shows an example of running the algorithm given in List 4 for an array of eight elements. Initially, the array has a set of 0's and 1's. Let us assume that in Figure 1, a "1" in the initial stage indicates an element being greater than the pivot. The result of the prefix sum is that each array element indicates the number of elements with a smaller index that are also greater than the pivot. For example, a[6] has a final value of 4, indicating that there are three elements that have an index value less than 6 and are also greater than the pivot. This information is valuable because when we partition the array by extracting the elements greater than the pivot, we can just copy data element corresponding to a[6] into a temporary array's forth element. Know so for each element, all elements can be extracted in one step with enough processors.

```
Do_Sort(b, e)
   1.   Determine the pivot pv
   2.   If a[i] <= pv and b <= i < e, mark it by setting
        aux[i] to 1; otherwise, set aux[i] to 0.
   3.   Perform the prefix sum on array aux. If array
        element a[i] is marked, the result of aux[i] after
        the prefix sum is an integer indicating the number of
        elements with an index smaller and equal to i that
        are also marked.
   4.   Copy a[i] to temp[b + aux[i] -1] if a[i] <= pv.
   5.   Store aux[e -1] + b in variable m
   6.   If a[i] > pv and b <= i < e, mark it by setting
        aux[i] = 1; otherwise, set aux[i] to 0.
   7.   Perform the prefix sum on array aux. If array
        element a[i] is marked, the result of aux[i] after
        the prefix sum is an integer indicating the number of
        elements with an index smaller and equal to i that
        are also marked.
   8.   Copy a[i] to temp[m+ aux[i] -1].
   9.   Call Do_Sort(b, m) and Do_sort(m, e)
```

List 3. Outline of Liu and Hu's parallel quicksort

```
Parallel_prefixes(a[], b, e)
Local variable j
ForAll pi where b<= i <= e - 1 do
    for j from 0 to     -1
        if (i - 2j) >= 0 then
            a[i] = a[i - 2j] + a[i]
```

List 4. The paralle prefix sum algorithm

The complexity analysis of the sequential quicksort is a classical case of average time complexity of $O(n \log n)$ and worst time case of $O(n^2)$ [11]. Since all the steps in List 3 have a complexity of $O(\log n)$ or less, the function Do_Sort(b, e) has a complexity of $O(\log n)$, where $n = e - b + 1$. In average case, the function is called $O(\log n)$ times. Therefore, the algorithm has an average time complexity of $O(\log n * \log n)$. We will show later that, contrary to the claim in [14], the algorithm as presented is not cost optimal because the prefix sum algorithm is not cost optimal.

Initially	0 | 1 | 0 | 1 | 1 | 0 | 1 | 0
j = 0 a[1]=a[0]+a[1], a[2]=a[1]+a[2], etc.	0 | 1 | 1 | 1 | 2 | 1 | 1 | 1
j = 1 a[2]=a[0]+a[2], a[3]=a[1]+a[3], etc.	0 | 1 | 1 | 2 | 3 | 2 | 3 | 2
j = 2 a[4]=a[0]+a[4], a[5]=a[1]+a[5], etc.	0 | 1 | 1 | 2 | 3 | 3 | 4 | 4

Fig. 1. An example of carrying out the parallel prefix sum

3 Improving Partitioning of the Array

When performing on a real parallel computer, the number of processors p is much smaller than the problem size n. In such case, the partitioning takes at least $\Theta(n/p)$ time. As a result, it is not necessary to know the exact destination index for every element because not all element will be extracted at the same time, as presented in line 4 and line 8 of List 3. With that understanding, we propose the following approach of partitioning the array.

We divide the array into p chunks. To partition an array of size n, we first count, for each chunk, the total number of elements less than and equal to the pivot and the total number of elements greater than the pivot within the chunk. We then calculate the prefix sums using these values separately. The results of the prefix sum calculations provide, for each processor, the starting index for copying elements back to the data array during the partitioning process. By doing this, we only need one temporary array of size n and two other temporary arrays of size p. We will explain the partitioning process using an array of 12 elements, a[] = {5, 17, 42, 3, 32, 22, 51, 26, 15, 9, 19, 99}, on four processors. First, we select a pivot. Let a[5], which is has a value of 22, be the pivot. The next step is to divide the array into four, the number of processors, chunks as shown in Figure 2.

   5, 17, 42,   3, 9, 22,   51, 26, 15,   32, 19, 99

Fig. 2. Dividing the array into four chunks

Next, we count, for each chunk, the number of elements smaller than or equal to the pivot, and then the number of elements larger than the pivot, and transfer elements to a temporary array while counting. List 5 shows this process. Note that this same code segment is carried out by each processor. Therefore, each processor has a different values for variables `start`, `end`, and `id`. The `start` and `end` indicate the starting and ending point of the chuck a processor needs to work. The variable `id` is unique for each processor. Line 13 calculates the number of elements less than or equal to the pivot and places the value in an array nSmallerEqual[]. Line 14 calculates the number of elements greater than the pivot and place the value into temporary arrays nGreaterThan[]. In our example, the values in nSmallerEqual[] and nGreaterThan[] are {2, 3, 1, 1} and {1, 0, 2, 2} respectively.

```
1.  lesser = start;  //start is the 1st element's index
2.  greater = end;   //end is the 1st element's index
3.  for(i=start;i<=end;i++)
4.  {if(a[i] <= pivot)
5.         { temp[lesser] = a[i];
6.            lesser++;
7.         }
8.   else
9.         { temp[greater] = a[i];
10.           greater--;
11.        }
12. }
13. nSmallerEqual[id] = lesser - start;
14. nGreaterThan[id] = end - greater;
```

List 5. Count the elements <= pv, and elements > pv and copy them into a temporary array

The next step is to transfer the elements in temp[] back to the primary array a[] in their final partitioned form. To do this, we need to calculate where a processor can start placing the partitioned elements. This step can be accomplished by calculating the prefix sums of nSmallerEqual[] and nGreaterThan[], respectively, using the algorithm in List 4 (notice the array sizes of nSmallerEqual[] and nGreaterThan[] is p), which would have the same effect as the code segment given in List 6.

```
1.  count = 0;
2.  countb = 0;
3.  for(i=0;i<id;i++)
4.  {count += nSmallerEqual[i];
5.   countb += nGreaterThan[i];
6.  }
```

List 6. Calculating the prefix sums over nSmallerEqual[] and nGreaterThan[]

During partitioning, elements are copied back to the original array. If an element is less than or equal to the pivot, we place it toward the front of the array; otherwise, we place it toward the end of the array. Since each processor knows exactly how many elements the processors before it will copy back, it starts copying into the section assigned to it as indicated by variables count, and countb. The variable count starts from the front of the array, and the variable countb starts from the end of the array. This way, the copying process can be accomplished concurrently.

Figure 3 shows the values of count, and countb for each processor. It also shows the process of copying the elements back to the primary array. At this point, the partition is completed. Elements from a[0] to a[6] are smaller than or equal to the pivot, and element from a[7] to the last element a[11] are greater than the pivot. We can then recursively sort these two subarrays.

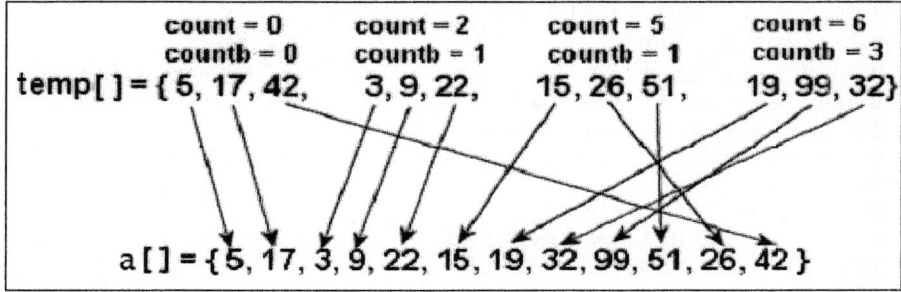

Fig. 3. The values of variables count, and countb, as well as the copying of elements from the temporary array back to the primary array

4 The Improved Algorithm Is Cost Optimal

In this section, we first outline the improved algorithm just discussed. We assume a shared memory parallel computer and the number of processors is much smaller than the problems size. We then prove that the algorithm sorts n elements in $O(\log^2 n)$ time using $O(n/\log n)$ processors, which means it is cost optimal.

List 7 shows the partitioning of an array with n elements over the pivot value pv. To save space, we omitted variable declarations. Each processor has its own value for the variable id. Lines 2 to 5 calculate the array section a processor is responsible. Variable l tracks the number of elements <= pv; Variable g tracks the number of elements > pv. The "for" loop from lines 8 to 14 moves the elements <= pv to the beginning of the array and moves the elements > pv to the end of the array. In addition, it counts the number of elements that are <= pv and > pv, respectively. Lines 15 and 16 copy the results of counting form the for loop to the corresponding arrays to prepare for the prefix sum calculation. Lines 17 to 20 calculate the prefix sums. Lines 21 to 26 determine the starting points for each processor to copy both the elements <= pv and the elements > pv, respectively. Lines 27 to 33 copy the element back to array a[]. What is returned at line 34 is the total number of elements <= pv.

Theorem 1: The complexity of partitioning n elements with p processors using the algorithm given in List 7 is $O(\max\{n/p, \log(p)\})$.

Proof: Let C be the cost of all statements not in any loop body, t_1 be the time of the "for" loop at line 8, t_2 be the time of the "for" loop at line 17, and t_3 be the time of the "for" loop at line 27. The total time of the function Partition $T = C + t_1 + t_2 + t_3$. By studying the code we have $t_1 = t_2 = O(n/p)$, and $t_3 = O(\log(p))$. As a result, the complexity of function Partition $T = O(n/p + \log(p)) = O(\max\{n/p, \log(p)\})$.

Corollary 1: Using $n/(\log n)$ processors, the time complexity of using the algorithm given in List 7 is $O(\log n)$.

Proof: By replacing p in Theorem 1 with n/(log n) we have
T= O(max{n/p, log(p)}) = O(max{n/(n/log (n)), log(n/log (n))}) = O(log n).

```
function partition(a[], n, pv)
1.     ForAll pid   where 0<= id < p do
2.         ws = ⌈n/p⌉
3.         b  = ws * id
4.         e = ws * (id+ 1)
5.         if e > n then e = n
6.         l = b
7.         g = e -1
8.         for i from b to e
9.             if a[i] <= pv then
10.                temp[l] = a[i]
11.                l = l +1
12.            else
13.                temp[g] = a[i]
14.                g = g - 1
15.        nSmEql[id] = l - b
16.        nGtTn[id] = e - g
17.        for j from 0 to ⌈log p⌉  -1
18.            if (id - 2ʲ) >= 0 then
19.                nSmEql [id] = nSmEql[id - 2j] + nSmEql[id]
20.                nGtTn [id] = nGtTn [id - 2j] + nGtTn [id]
21.        if id <> 0 then
22.            count = nSmEql [id -1]
23.            countb = nGtTn [id -1]
24.        else
25.            count = 0
26.            countb = 0
27.        for i from b to e
28.            if temp[i] <= pv then
29.                a[count] = temp[i]
30.                count = count + 1
31.            else
32.                a[e - countb] = temp[i]
33.                countb = countb - 1
34.    return nSmEql[p -1]
```

List 7. Partitioning array a[] of size n using p processors over pivot pv

Based on **Corollary 1**, since, in average, the number of steps of dividing in a quicksort is O(log n), a parallel quicksort algorithm using the algorithm given in List 7 to partition the array should have an average case complexity of $O(\log^2(n))$. The cost of the algorithm is then O(n *log(n)), which is cost optimal. We will use Brent's Theorem to prove the algorithm is this, starting with calculating the amount of operations performed by the prefix sum using p processors.

Lemma 1: The prefix sum algorithm given in List 4 takes O(p log(p)) operations using p processors.

Proof: The algorithm takes $p - 2^0$ operations the first iteration, $p - 2^1$ operations the second iteration, and $p - 2^j$ operations the jth iteration. With total of $\lceil \log p \rceil -1$ iterations, the total number of operations w is

$$w = \sum_{j=0}^{\lceil \log(p) \rceil - 1} p - 2^j = \sum_{j=0}^{\lceil \log(p) \rceil - 1} n - \sum_{j=0}^{\lceil \log(p) \rceil - 1} 2^j$$
$$= p\lceil \log(p) \rceil - 1 - 2^{(\lceil \log(p) \rceil - 1) + 1} / (1 - 2) \leq p(\log(p) + 1) - 2^{\log(p)} + 1$$
$$= p \log(p) + p - p + 1 = O(p \log(p))$$

Theorem 2: The number of operations performed by the algorithm given in List 7 is $O(n + p*\log(p))$ for an array of n elements using p processors.

Proof: The algorithm consists of two "for" loops each incurs $O(n/p*p) = O(n)$ operations. It also contains a "for" loop to perform the prefix sum, which should incurs $O(p \log(p))$ operation based on Lemma 1. Combining all the operations, it has $O(n + p*\log(p))$ operations.

List 8 is a simple parallel quicksort algorithm that utilizes partitioning algorithm presented early to sort a[] from b to e using p processors. Notice that we added the allocation of processors because we assume that the p << n. What omitted is the assignment of processors to subarrays because we believe that doing so only complicates the discussion of the algorithm without adding any value to our goal – to prove that the use of the algorithm given in List 7 to performing parallel quicksort using $O(n/\log n)$ processors is cost optimal. For now, we assume a simple method of allocating processors to tasks exists that each time the Do_Sort is called, at least one processor, or proportional to the number of elements, is allocated. In the event the number of subarrays is greater than the number of processors, we proposed to use the existing processors to simulate the processors needed. In actuality, we would likely to introduce some kinds of threshold to reduce the number of recursive calls incurred in quicksort.

```
Do_Sort(a[], b, e, p)
1.   if e> b then
2.       pv = a[(b + e)/2]
3.       m = Partition(a[b], e - b, pv) // of List 7
4.       pc = ⌈p*(m - b)/(e - b)⌉
5.       call Do_Sort(a[], b, m, pc)
6.       call Do_sort(a[], m, e, p - pc)
```

List 8. A quicksort algorithm using the cost optimal partitioning algorithm

One way of viewing this algorithm is that it forms a binary tree. Each internal node of the binary tree is a subarray containing unsorted elements. At stage i, we may have 2^i or less subarrays. We use k_i to represent the number of subarrays at stage i. The root is the original data array. Let s_{ij} be the jth subarray from the left at the ith stage. We assume that subarray s_{ij} has n_{ij} elements starting at b_{ij} and ending at e_{ij}.

Theorem 3: With the algorithm outlined in List 8, $O(n/\log(n))$ processors can partition the subarrays at a stage to form the subarrays of the next stage in $O(\log(n))$ time.

Proof: Let us consider stage i. Based on Corollary 1, if we have infinite number of processors, this step can be accomplished in $t_\infty = O(\max\{\log(_{ij}): 1 <= j <= k_i\})$. If we use n_{im} to represent the largest subarray of stage i, then $t_\infty = O(\log(n_{im})) < O(\log(n))$. Based on **Theorem 2**, the total number of operations m_{ij} performed to partition a given subarray s_{ij} with $n_{ij}/\log(n_{ij})$ processors, is

$O(n_{ij} + p_{ij} * \log(p_{ij})) = O(n_{ij} + n_{ij}/\log(n_{ij}) * \log(n_{ij}/\log(n_{ij})))$
$= O(n_{ij} + n_{ij}(1 - \log(\log(n_{ij}))/\log(n_{ij}))) = O(n_{ij})$

Accordingly, the total number of operations m performed to partition all subarrays at stage i is $O(n)$.

According to Brent's Theorem, the execution time T_i of partitioning the subarrays at stage i is $T_i = O(t_\infty + (m - t_\infty)/(n/\log(n)))$. Because $m = O(n)$ and $t_\infty < O(\log(n))$, we have $T_i < O(\log(n)) + \log(n) * \frac{n - \log(n)}{n}) = O(\log(n))$.

Based on Theorem 3, we can easily drive that the average execution time of the algorithm given in List 8 with $O(n/\log(n))$ processors is $O(\log^2(n))$ because, in average, the height of the binary tree (i.e., the number of stages) is $O(\log(n))$. Clearly, the algorithm is cost optimal because the cost is $O(n / \log(n) * \log^2(n)) = O(n \log(n))$, which is the same as the comparison based best sequential sorting algorithms.

5 Implementing the Algorithm on a Shared Memory Parallel Computer

We have access of a Sequent Symmetry with 12 processors. The two problems we faced during implementation are (1) the detecting of termination conditions, and (2) the inefficiency caused by sorting large number of small array segments. To resolve these two problems we introduce two stacks: Partitions and Chunks. The stack Partitions is intended to store the boundaries of array segments that need to be partitioned. Initially, it has one element, segment 0 to n -1, i.e., the entire data array.

The entire sorting process has two stages: partitioning and sorting. During the partitioning stage, one processor pops an unpartitioned array segment and all processors working together to partition it using the algorithm given in List 7. At the end of each partitioning, a partitioned segment is pushed into the stack Partitions if its size is greater than a pre-defined threshold k. If a partitioned segment's size is smaller than k, it is pushed into the stack Chunks. This process repeats until the stack Partitions is empty and no processors is working on partitioning, which are our termination conditions for partitioning. During the second stage, the unsorted chunks in stack Chunks are assigned to processors and individually sorted sequentially using insertion sort. Once the stack Chunks is empty, the array is sorted.

Figure 4 shows the execution times of four different sorting algorithms: the sequential quicksort running on one processor, the bitonic sort, the parallel merge sort as described in [10], and the sorting algorithm described in this paper marked as JieSort. All the parallel sorting algorithms, except bitonic sort, are switched to sequential quicksort at the threshold of 100. An array section that is less than or equal to 15 is sorted using insertion sort in all the algorithms except bitonic sort.

From Figure 4 we can see that the parallel quicksort algorithm introduced in this paper incurs some overhead comparing to the sequential quicksort. However, the overhead is far less than that of other parallel sorting algorithms of the same complexity. In addition, the newly introduced parallel quicksort starts outperforming the sequential quicksort with two processors, indicating that we have proposed a viable parallel sorting algorithm for real parallel computers.

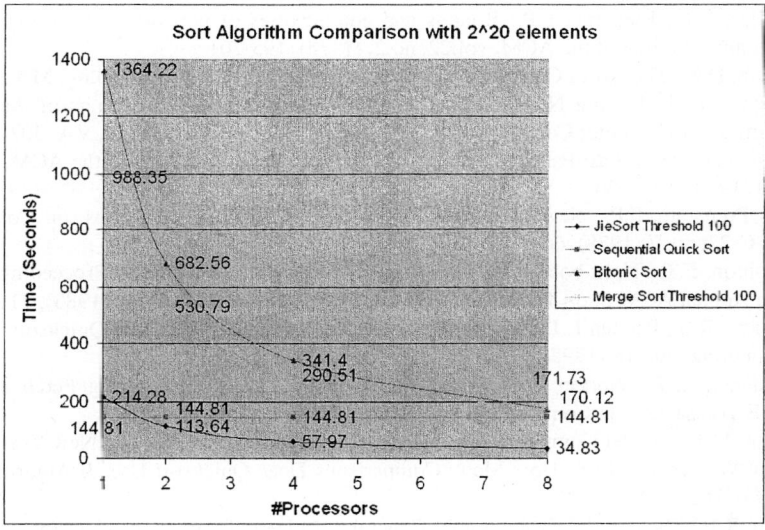

Fig. 4. Sorting an array of 2^{20} elements on a Sequent Symmetry with 12 processors

6 Conclusions and Future Works

We introduced some major improvements over the algorithm given in [14] and proved that the improved algorithm is cost optimal when executed using $O(n/\log(n))$ processors. We also presented the strategies we used to implement the algorithm on a shared memory parallel computer and showed that the modified algorithm is a viable parallel sorting algorithm, at least for shared memory parallel computers. It outperformed other well known $O(\log^2 n)$ parallel sorting algorithms. It also starts outperforming the sequential quicksort with two or more processors.

We plan to further study our implementation and to identify ways to improve the parallel quicksort algorithm proposed in this paper on a shared memory parallel computer. We are also working on porting the idea over to a Beowulf cluster with eight dual-processor nodes. We would also like to identify a shared memory parallel computer with more processors to test our algorithm.

Acknowledgments

We would like to thank Dr. Mike Quinn and Dr. Robert Broeg for their encouragement and productive discussions. We also would like to thank Western Oregon University and our division for supporting this research and publishing of this paper.

References

1. Akl, S.G.: Parallel Sorting Algorithms. Academic Press, Orlando, FL, 1985.
2. Muller, D.E., Preparata F.P.: Bounds and complexities of networks for sorting and for switching. Journal of the ACM, vol.22, no.2, (1975) 195-201
3. Knuth, D.E.: The Art of Computer Programming, Addison-Wesley, Reading, MA, (1973)
4. Batcher, K.E.: Sorting Networks and Their Applications. In Proceedings of the AFIPS Spring Joint Computer Conference, vol. 32 (1968), AFIPS Press, Reston, VA, 307-314
5. Hirschberg, D.S.: Fast Parallel Sorting Algorithms. Communications of the ACM, vol. 21, no.8 (1978), 657-666
6. 6. Preparata, F.P.: New Parallel Sorting Schemes, IEEE Transactions. on Computers, vol. C-27, no. 7 (1978), 669-673
7. Leighton, F.T.: Tight bounds on the complexity of parallel sorting. In Proceedings of the 16th Annual ACM S. on Theory of Computing, ACM, New York, May (1983), 71-80,
8. Francis, R.S., Pannan L.J.H.: A parallel partition for enhanced parallel Quicksort. Parallel Computing, vol. 18 (1992), 543-550
9. Heideberger, P., Norton A., . Robinson J.T.: Parallel Quicksort Using Fetch-and-Add. IEEE Transaction on Computer, vol. C39, no. 1 (1990), 133-138
10. Quinn M.J:. Parallel Computing Theory and Practice. McGraw-Hill, Inc, New York (1994)
11. Eddy W. Schervish M.: How Many Comparisons Does Quicksort Use, J. Algorithms, 19 (1995), 402--431
12. Brent R.P.: The parallel Evaluation of General Arithmetic Expressions. J. of the ACT, vol. 21. no 2 (1974), 201-206
13. Gibbons, A., Rytter W.: Efficient Parallel Algorithms. Cambridge U. Press, Cambridge, (1988)
14. Liu J., He J.: A Cost Optimal Parallel Quicksort On CREW PRAM, in the Proceedings of CATA 03, Honolulu, Hawaii, 13-16

Near Optimal Routing in a Small-World Network with Augmented Local Awareness

Jianyang Zeng[1], Wen-Jing Hsu[1], and Jiangdian Wang[2]

[1] Center for Advanced Information Systems,
Nanyang Technological University, Singapore
zengjy@gmail.com, hsu@ntu.edu.sg
[2] School of Electrical Electronic Engineering,
Nanyang Technological University, Singapore
wang0059@pmail.ntu.edu.sg

Abstract. In order to investigate the routing aspects of small-world networks, Kleinberg [13] proposes a network model based on a d-dimensional lattice with long-range links chosen at random according to the d-harmonic distribution. Kleinberg shows that the greedy routing algorithm by using only local information performs in $O(\lg^2 n)$ expected number of hops, where n denotes the number of nodes in the network. Martel and Nguyen [17] have found that the expected diameter of Kleinberg's small-world networks is $\Theta(\lg n)$. Thus a question arises naturally: Can we improve the routing algorithms to match the diameter of the networks while keeping the amount of information stored on each node as small as possible?

Existing approaches for improving the routing performance in the small-world networks include: (1) Increasing the number of long-range links [2, 15]; (2) Exploring more nodes before making routing decisions [14]; (3) Increasing the local awareness for each node [10, 17]. However, all these approaches can only achieve $O\big((\lg n)^{1+\epsilon}\big)$ expected number of hops, where $\epsilon > 0$ denotes a constant. We extend Kleinberg's model and add two augmented local links for each node, which are connected to nodes chosen randomly and uniformly within $\lg^2 n$ Mahattan distance. Our investigation shows that these augmented local connections can make small-world networks more navigable.

We show that if each node is aware of $O(\lg n)$ number of neighbors via the augmented local links, there exist both non-oblivious and oblivious algorithms that can route messages between any pair of nodes in $O(\lg n \lg \lg n)$ expected number of hops, which is a near optimal routing complexity and outperforms the other related results for routing in Kleinberg's small-world networks. Our schemes keep only $O(\lg^2 n)$ bits of routing information on each node, thus they are scalable with the network size. Our results imply that the awareness of $O(\lg n)$ nodes through augmented links is more efficient for routing than via the local links [10, 17].

Besides adding new light to the studies of social networks, our results may also find applications in the design of large-scale distributed networks, such as peer-to-peer systems, in the same spirit of Symphony [15].

1 Introduction

A well-known study by Milgram in 1967 [18] shows the *small-world phenomenon* [9], also called "six degree of separation", that any two people in the world can be connected by a chain of six (on the average) acquaintances, and people can deliver messages efficiently to an unknown target via their acquaintances. This study is repeated by Dodds, Muhamad, and Watts [8] recently, and the results show that it is still true for today's social network. The small-world phenomenon has also been shown to be pervasive in networks from nature and engineering systems, such as the World Wide Web [21,1], peer-to-peer systems [2,16,15,22], etc.

Recently, a number of network models have been proposed to study the small-world properties [19,21,13]. Watts and Strogatz [21] propose a random rewiring model whose diameter is a poly-logarithmic function of the size of the network. The model is constructed by adding a small number of random edges to nodes uniformly distributed on a ring, where nodes are connected densely with their near neighbors. A similar approach can also be found in Ballabás and Chung's earlier work [6], where the poly-logarithmic diameter of the random graph is achieved by adding a random matching to the nodes of a cycle. However, these models fail to capture the algorithmic aspects of a small-world network [13]. As commented by Kleinberg in [13], the poly-logarithmic diameter of some graphs does not imply the existence of efficient routing algorithms. For example, the random graph in [6] yields a logarithmic diameter, yet any routing using only local information requires at least $\sqrt{n}$ expected number of hops (where n is the size of the network) [13].

In order to incorporate routing or navigating properties into random graph models, Kleinberg [13] develops a new model based on a d-dimensional torus lattice with long-range links chosen randomly from the d-harmonic distribution, i.e., a long-range link between nodes u and v exists with probability proportional to $Dist(u,v)^{-d}$, where $Dist(u,v)$ denotes the Mahattan distance between nodes u and v. Based on this model, Kleinberg then shows that routing messages between any two nodes can be achieved in $O(\lg^2 n)$ expected number of hops by applying a simple greedy routing algorithm using only local information. This bound is tightened to $\Theta(\lg^2 n)$ later by Barrière et al. [3] and Martel et al. [17]. Further research [16,14,17,10] shows that in fact the $O(\lg^2 n)$ bound of the original greedy routing algorithm can be improved by putting some extra information in each message holder. Manku, Naor, and Wieder [16] show that if each message holder at a routing step takes its own neighbors' neighbors into account for making routing decisions, the bound of routing complexity can be improved to $O(\frac{\lg^2 n}{q \lg q})$, where q denotes the number of long-range contacts for each node. Lebhar and Schabanel [14] propose a routing algorithm for 1-dimensional Kleinberg's model, which visits $O(\frac{\lg^2 n}{\lg^2(1+q)})$ nodes on expectation before routing the message, and they show that a routing path with expected length of $O(\frac{\lg n(\lg \lg n)^2}{\lg^2(1+q)})$ can be found. Two research groups, Fraigniaud et al. [10], and Martel and Nguyen [17], independently report that if each node is aware of its $O(\lg n)$ closest local neighbors, the routing complexity in d-dimensional Kleinberg's small-world networks can be improved to $O(\lg n \lg^{1+1/d} n)$ expected number of hops. The difference is that [17] requires keeping additional state information, while [10] uses an oblivious greedy routing algorithm. Fraigniaud et al. [10] also show that $\Theta(\lg^2 n)$ bits of topological awareness per node is optimal for their oblivious routing scheme. In [17], Martel and Nguyen show that the expected diameter of a d-dimensional Kleinberg network is $\Theta(\lg n)$. As such, there is still some room for reducing the routing complexity, which motivates our work.

1.1 Our Contributions

We extend Kleinberg's structures of small-world models with slight change. Besides having long-range and local links on the grid lattice, each node is augmented with two extra links connected to nodes chosen randomly and uniformly within $\lg^2 n$ Mahattan distance. Based on this extended model, we present near optimal algorithms for decentralized routing with $O(\lg n)$ augmented awareness. We show that if each node is aware of $O(\lg n)$ number of nodes via the augmented neighborhood, there exist both non-oblivious and oblivious routing algorithms that perform in $O(\lg n \lg \lg n)$ expected number of hops (see Theorem 1 and Theorem 2). Our investigation constructively show that the augmented local connections can make small-world networks more navigable.

A comparison of our algorithm with the other existing schemes is shown in Table 1. Our decentralized routing algorithms assume that each node can compute a shortest path among a poly-logarithmic number of known nodes. Such an assumption is reasonable since each node in a computer network is normally a processor and can carry out such a simple computation. Our schemes keep $O(\lg^2 n)$ bits of routing information stored on each node, thus they are scalable with the increase of network size. Our investigation shows that the awareness of $O(\lg n)$ nodes through the augmented links is more efficient for routing than via the local links [10, 17].

Table 1. Comparisons of our decentralized routing algorithms with the other existing schemes. In the first three schemes (in [13, 2, 15, 16, 14]), we suppose that each node has q long-range contacts, while in the next three schemes (in [17, 10] and this paper), we suppose that each node has one long-range contact. A routing protocol is *oblivious* if the message holder makes routing decisions only by its local information and the target node, and independently of the previous routing history, otherwise, it is said to be *non-oblivious*.

Scheme	#bits of awareness	#steps expected	Oblivious or Non-oblivious?
Kleinberg's greedy [13, 2, 15]	$O(q \lg n)$	$O(\lg^2 n/q)$	Oblivious
NoN-greedy [16]	$O(q^2 \lg n)$	$O(\lg^2 n/(q \lg q))$	Non-oblivious
Decentralized algorithm in [14]	$O(\lg^2 n/\lg(1+q))$	$O((\lg n)^2/\lg^2(1+q))$	Non-oblivious
Decentralized algorithm [17]	$O(\lg^2 n)$	$O((\lg n)^{1+1/d})$	Non-oblivious
Indirect-greedy algorithm [10]	$O(\lg^2 n)$	$O((\lg n)^{1+1/d})$	Oblivious
Our algorithms for the model with augmented awareness	$O(\lg^2 n)$	$O(\lg n \lg \lg n)$	Both are provided

We note that besides adding new light to the studies of social networks such as Milgram's experiment [18], our results may also find applications in the design of large-scale distributed networks, such as peer-to-peer systems, in the same spirit of Symphony [15]. Since the links in our extended model are randomly constructed according to the probabilistic distribution, the network may be less vulnerable to adversarial attacks, and thus provide good fault tolerance.

1.2 Organization

The rest of the paper is organized as follows. Section 2 gives notations for Kleinberg's small-world model and its extended version with augmented local connections. Section 3 gives some preliminary notations for decentralized routing. In Section 4, we propose both non-oblivious and oblivious routing algorithms with near optimal routing complexity in our extended model. Section 5 briefly concludes the paper.

2 Definitions of Small-World Models

In this section, we will give the definition of Kleinberg's small-world model and its extended version in which each node has extra links. For simplicity, we only consider the one-dimensional model with *one* long-range contact for each node. In addition, we assume that all links are directed, which is consistent with the real-world observation, for example, person x knows person y, but y may not know x.

Definition 1. (Kleinberg's Small-World Network (KSWN) [13]) *A Kleinberg's Small-World Network, denoted as $\mathcal{K}$, is based on a one-dimensional torus (or ring) $[n] = [0, 1, \cdots, n]$. Each node u has a directed local link to its next neighbor $(u + 1)$ mod n on the ring. We refer to this local link as **Ring-link** (or **R-link** for short), and refer to node $(u + 1)$ mod n as the **R-neighbor** of node u. In addition, each node has one long-range link to another node chosen randomly according to the 1-harmonic distribution, that is, the probability that node u sends a long-range link to node v is $\Pr[u \to v] = \frac{1}{Z_u \cdot Dist(u,v)}$, where $Dist(u, v)$ denotes the ring distance [1] from u to v, and $Z_u = \sum_{z \neq u} \frac{1}{Dist(u,z)}$. We refer to this long-range link as the **Kleinberg-link** (or **K-link** for short), and refer to node v as a **K-neighbor** of node u if a K-link exists from u to v.*

Our extended structure introduces several extra links for each node. Its definition is given below.

Definition 2. (KSWN with Augmented Local Connections (KSWN*)) *A Kleinberg's Small-World Network with Augmented Local Connections, denoted as $\mathcal{K}^*$, has the same structure of KSWN, except that each node u in $\mathcal{K}^*$ has two*

---
[1] Or Mahattan distance for multi-dimensional models.

*extra links to nodes chosen randomly and uniformly from the interval $(u, u + \lg^2 n]$. We refer to these two links as the **augmented local links** (or **AL-links** for short), and refer to node v as a **AL-neighbor** of node u if an AL-link exists from u to v.*

There are in total four links for each node in a KSWN*: one R-link, one K-link, two AL-links. We refer to all nodes linked directly by node u as the **immediate neighbors** of u. Our extended structure retains the same $O(1)$ order of node degree as that of Kleinberg's original model.

3 Decentralized Routing Algorithms

Based on the original model, Kleinberg presents a class of decentralized routing algorithms, in which each node makes routing decisions by using local information and in a greedy fashion. In other words, the message holder forward the message to its immediate neighboring node, including its K-neighbor, which is closest to the destination in terms of the Mahattan distance. Kleinberg shows that such a simple greedy algorithm performs in $O(\lg^2 n)$ expected number of hops. The other existing decentralized routing algorithms [2, 15, 14, 10, 17, 16] mainly rely on three approaches to improve routing performance: (1) Increasing the number of long-range links [2, 15]; (2) Exploring more nodes before making routing decisions [14]; (3) Increasing the local awareness for each node [10, 17]. However, so far using these approaches can only achieve $O((\lg n)^{1+\epsilon})$ expected number of hops in routing, where $\epsilon > 0$. Although the scheme in [16], where each node makes routing decision by looking ahead its neighbors's neighbors, can achieve an optimal $O(\lg n / \lg \lg n)$ bound, their result depends on the fact that each node has at least $\Omega(\lg n)$ number of K-links.

There are normally two approaches for decentralized routing: oblivious and non-oblivious schemes [10]. A routing protocol is *oblivious* if the message holder makes routing decisions only by its local information and the target node, and independently of the previous routing history. On the other hand, if the message holder needs to consider certain information of the previous routing history to make routing decisions, the protocol is referred to as *non-oblivious*. The non-oblivious protocol is often implemented by adding a header segment to the message packet so that the downstream nodes can learn the routing decisions of upstream nodes by reading the message header information. The scheme in [10] is oblivious, while the schemes in [14] and [17] are non-oblivious.

We refer to the message holder as *the current node*. For the current node x, we define a sequence of node sets $T_0, T_1, \cdots, T_i, \cdots$, where $T_0 = \{x\}$, $T_1 = \{$ u's AL-neighbors, $\forall u \in T_0\}$, $T_2 = \{u$'s AL-neighbors, $\forall u \in T_1\}$, and so on. We refer to T_i as the set of nodes in *the ith level of AL neighborhood*, and let $H_i = \bigcup_{j \leq i} T_j$ denote the set of all nodes in *the first i levels of AL neighborhood*. At a certain level i of AL neighborhood, we may also refer to H_{i-1} as the set of *previously known nodes*. Let $L_i = T_i - H_{i-1}$ denote the set of *new* nodes discovered during the ith level of AL neighborhood. Let $A_x(k) = H_k$ denote the *augmented local awareness* (or *AL awareness* for short) of a given node in a KSWN*, where each node is aware of the first k levels of its AL neighborhood.

In Section 4, we will show that there exists a sufficiently large constant σ such that $|A_x(\lg\lg n)| \geq \lg n/\sigma$, based on which we propose both non-oblivious and oblivious routing algorithms running in $O(\lg n \lg\lg n)$ expected number of hops and requiring $O(\lg^2 n)$ bits of information on each node.

Our near optimal $O(\lg n \lg\lg n)$ bound on the routing complexity outperforms the other related results for Kleinberg's small-world networks. To our knowledge, our algorithms achieve the best expected routing complexity while requiring at most $O(\lg^2 n)$ bits of information stored on each node.

4 Near Optimal Routing with $O(\lg n)$ Awareness

4.1 Augmented Local Awareness of $O(\lg n)$

In this subsection, we will show that $|A_x(\lg\lg n)|$, the number of distinct nodes that node x is aware of via the first $\lg\lg n$ levels of AL neighborhood, is not less than $\lg n/\sigma$ for a constant σ, which, as will be shown in Lemma 3, is sufficiently large to guarantee that $A_x(\lg\lg n)$ contains a K-link that jumps over half distance (Suppose that the destination node is at a certain large distance from the current node). These results are useful for the subsequent analysis of our oblivious and non-oblivious routing schemes.

Lemma 1. *Let $A_x(\lg\lg n)$ denote the AL awareness of node x in a KSWN* $\mathcal{K}^*$, where each node is aware of $\lg\lg n$ levels of AL-neighbors. Then*

$$\Pr[\ |A_x(\lg\lg n)| \geq \frac{\lg n}{\sigma}\ ] > \psi,$$

where σ denotes a sufficiently large constant and ψ denotes a positive constant.

Proof: Throughout the proof, we assume that $|H_i| < \frac{\lg n}{\sigma}$ for all $1 \leq i \leq \lg\lg n$, otherwise, the lemma already holds, since $|A_x(\lg\lg n)| = |H_{\lg\lg n}| > \lg n/\sigma$. We will show that at each level of AL neighborhood, the probability that each AL-link points to previously known nodes is small so that a large number of distinct nodes will be found via the first $\lg\lg n$ levels of AL neighborhood.

Consider the construction of an AL-link for the current node x. By definition of KSWN*, each AL-link of x is connected to a node randomly and uniformly chosen from the interval $(x, x+\lg^2 n]$, that is, each AL-link of x points to a node in the interval $(x, x+\lg^2 n]$ with probability $(\lg n)^{-2}$. By assumption, there could be no more than $\lg n/\sigma$ previously known nodes in the interval $(x, x+\lg^2 n]$. Thus, the probability for an AL-link of a given node to point to a previously known node is at most $(\lg n/\sigma) \cdot (\lg n)^{-2} = (\sigma \lg n)^{-1}$. Thus, the probability for an AL-link of x to point to a new node is at least $1 - (\sigma \lg n)^{-1}$. There are in total at most $2 \cdot |H_{\lg\lg n}| \leq 2\lg n/\sigma$ number of AL-links, so the probability for all AL-links to point to new nodes is at least $(1 - (\sigma \lg n)^{-1})^{2\lg n/\sigma} \geq 1 - \frac{2}{\sigma^2}$ for sufficiently large n. Here we use the fact $(1+x)^a \geq 1 + ax$ for $x > -1$ and $a \geq 1$. When σ is a sufficiently large constant, we have $\Pr[\ |A_x| \geq \frac{\lg n}{\sigma}\ ] > \psi$ for a positive constant $\psi = 1 - \frac{2}{\sigma^2} > 0$. Thus, the proof of Lemma 1 is completed. ∎

4.2 Non-oblivious Decentralized Routing

Our non-oblivious routing algorithm is given as follows: Initially the source node s finds in its AL awareness $A_s(\lg \lg n)$ an intermediate node z that is closest to the destination, and then computes a shortest path π from s to z in $A_s(\lg \lg n)$. Before routing the message, s adds the information about shortest path τ to the message header. Once the message passes a node on the shortest path π, the next stop is read off the header stack. When the message reaches node z, node z can tell that it is an intermediate target by reading the message header and then route the message to its K-neighbor. Such processes are repeated until the message reaches a certain node close enough to the destination node. After that, Kleinberg's plain greedy algorithm can be used to route the message effectively to the target node. Given a message M, a source node s and a target node t in a KSWN* $\mathcal{K}^*$, the pseudocodes of our non-oblivious algorithm running on the current node x are given in Algorithm 1.

Algorithm 1.

Input: the source s, the target t and the message M.
Initialization:
  Current node $\leftarrow s$.
  Set the header stack of the message M to be empty.
while Distance between the current node and the destination $\geq (\lg n)^2 \lg \lg n$ **do**
  if the header stack of the message M is empty **then**
    Route the message M to x's K-neighbor y.
    Find an intermediate node z in $A_y(\lg \lg n)$ whose K-neighbor is closest to t (ties are broken arbitrarily).
    Compute a shortest path $\pi : x_0 = y, x_1, \cdots, x_t = z$ from y to z, and push the shortest path information π $x_1, \cdots, x_t = z$ into the header stack of the message M.
  else
    Pop up the first node x_i from the header stack and route the message M to node x_i.
  end if
end while
Final phase (Kleinberg's greedy algorithm):
  Route the message M to an immediate neighbor of x that is closest to the target t, until it reaches t.

Next we will analyze the performance of the Algorithm 1. We first give a basic lemma, which provide a lower bound and an upper bound on the probability of the existence of a K-link in Kleinberg's small-world networks. Its proof can be found in [23].

Lemma 2. *Let* $\Pr[u \xrightarrow{K} v]$ *denote the probability that node u sends a K-link to node v in a KSWN* $\mathcal{K}^*$. Suppose that $a \leq Dist(u,v) \leq b$, then $\frac{c_1}{b \lg n} \leq \Pr[u \xrightarrow{K} v] \leq \frac{c_2}{a \lg n}$, where c_1 and c_2 are constants independent of n.*

In Lemma 1, we have shown that $\Pr[\ |A_x(\lg \lg n)| \geq \lg n/\sigma\ ]$ is at least a positive constant for a sufficiently large constant σ. Based on this result, Lemma 3 shows that the probability for $A_x(\lg \lg n)$ to contain a K-link jumping over half distance is at least a positive constant.

Lemma 3. *Suppose that the distance between the current node x and the target node t in a KSWN* $\mathcal{K}^*$ is $Dist(x,t) \geq \lg^2 n \lg \lg n$. Then with probability at least a positive constant, node x's AL awareness $A_x(\lg \lg n)$ contains a K-neighbor within $Dist(x,t)/2$ distance to the target node t.*

Proof: Let $\mathcal{A}$ denote the event that $|A_x(\lg \lg n)| \geq \frac{\lg n}{\sigma}$. By Lemma 1, we have $\Pr[\mathcal{A}] > \psi$ for a constant $\psi > 0$.

Let $B_l(t)$ denote the set of all nodes within l ring distance to t. Let $\Pr[x \xrightarrow{K} B_l(t)]$ denote the probability that x's K-neighbor is inside the ball $B_l(t)$.

Let $m = Dist(x,t)$. By Lemma 2, the probability for a K-link to point to a given node inside the ball $B_{\frac{m}{2}}(t)$ is at least $\frac{c_1}{m \lg n}$, so we have

$$\Pr[x \xrightarrow{K} B_{\frac{m}{2}}(t)] \geq |B_{\frac{m}{2}}(t)| \cdot \frac{c_1}{m \lg n} = \frac{m}{2} \cdot \frac{c_1}{m \lg n} \geq \frac{c_3}{\lg n},$$

where c_3 is a constant.

Since $Dist(x,t) \geq \lg^2 n \lg \lg n$ and each AL-link spans a distance no more than $\lg^2 n$, the nodes in AL awareness $A_x(\lg \lg n)$ are all between the current node x and the target node t. Let $\Pr[A_x(\lg \lg n) \xrightarrow{K} B_{\frac{m}{2}}(t)]$ denote the probability that at least one node in $A_x(\lg \lg n)$ has a K-neighbor in $B_{\frac{m}{2}}(t)$. Then we have

$$\Pr[A_x(\lg \lg n) \xrightarrow{K} B_{\frac{m}{2}}(t)] \geq \Pr[A_x(\lg \lg n) \xrightarrow{K} B_{\frac{m}{2}}(t) \mid \mathcal{A}] \cdot \Pr[\mathcal{A}]$$
$$\geq \left(1 - \left(1 - \frac{c_3}{\lg n}\right)^{\frac{\lg n}{\sigma}}\right) \cdot \psi$$
$$\geq \psi(1 - e^{-\frac{c_3}{\sigma}}),$$

which is larger than a positive constant. At the last step, we obtain $(1 - \frac{c_3}{\lg n})^{\frac{\lg n}{\sigma}} \leq e^{-\frac{c_3}{\sigma}}$ by using the fact that $(1 + \frac{b}{x})^x \leq e^b$ for $b \in \mathbb{R}$ and $x > 0$. ∎

Lemma 4. *Suppose that the distance between the current node x and the target node t in a KSWN* $\mathcal{K}^*$ is $Dist(x,t) \geq \lg^2 n \lg \lg n$. Then after at most $O(\lg n \lg \lg n)$ expected number of hops, Algorithm 1 will reduce the distance to within $\lg^2 n \lg \lg n$.*

Proof: Since $Dist(x,t) \geq \lg^2 n \lg \lg n$, all known nodes in x's AL awareness $A_x(\lg \lg n)$ are between the current node x and the target node t. We can apply the result in Lemma 3 to analyze Algorithm 1.

We refer to the routing steps from a given node x to any node within $A_x(\lg \lg n)$ as an indirect phase. The routings in different indirect phases are independent from each other. By Lemma 3, the probability that node x's AL awareness $A_x(\lg \lg n)$ contains a K-neighbor within $Dist(x,t)/2$ distance to the target node t is at least a positive constant, so after at most $O(1)$ expected number of indirect phases, Algorithm 1 will find an intermediate node whose K-link jumps over half distance. Since each indirect phase takes at most $\lg \lg n$ hops and the maximum distance is n, after at most $O(\lg n \lg \lg n)$ expected number of hops, the message will reach a node within $\lg^2 n \lg \lg n$ distance to the target node t. ∎

Lemma 5. *Suppose that the distance between the current node x and the target node t in a *KSWN *$\mathcal{K}$ is $Dist(x,t) \leq \lg^2 n \lg \lg n$. Then using the final phase of Algorithm 1 (i.e. using Kleinberg's greedy algorithm) can route the message to the target node t in $O(\lg n)$ expected number of hops.*

Proof: When the distance $Dist(x,t) \leq \lg^2 n \lg \lg n$, the final phase in Algorithm 1 is executed. By Kleinberg's results in [13], after at most $O\big(\lg^2(\lg^2 n \lg \lg n)\big) = O(\lg n)$ expected number of steps, the message will be routed to the destination node. ∎

Combining the above lemmas, it is not difficult for us to obtain the routing complexity of Algorithm 1.

Theorem 1. *In a KSWN* $\mathcal{K}^*$, Algorithm 1 performs in $O(\lg n \lg \lg n)$ expected number of hops.*

4.3 Oblivious Decentralized Routing

In our oblivious scheme, when the distance is large, the current node x first finds in $A_x(\lg \lg n)$ whether there is an intermediate node z, which contains a K-neighbor within $Dist(x,t)/2$ distance to the target node, and is closest to node x in terms of AL-links (any possible tie is broken arbitrarily). Next, node x computes a shortest path π from x to z among the AL awareness $A_x(\lg \lg n)$, and then routes the message to its next AL-neighbor on the shortest path π. When the distance is small, Kleinberg's plain greedy algorithm is applied.

Given a message M, a source s and a target t in a KSWN* $\mathcal{K}^*$, the pseudocodes of our oblivious algorithm running on the current node x are given in Algorithm 2.

Algorithm 2.

Input: the source s, the target t and the message M.
Initialization:
  Current node $\leftarrow s$.
while Distance between the current node and the destination $\geq c(\lg n)^2 \lg \lg n$ **do**   (c is a sufficiently large constant and will be given later)
  $z \leftarrow$ a node in $A_x(\lg \lg n)$ that contains a K-neighbor within $Dist(x,t)/2$ distance to t, and is closest to node x in terms of AL-links (ties are broken arbitrarily).
  if node z does not exist **then**
    Route the message M to an immediate neighbor closest to node t.
  else
    Compute a shortest path π from x to z among $A_x(\lg \lg n)$.
    if π consists of only node x itself **then**
      Route the message M to the K-neighbor.
    else
      Route the message M to the next AL-neighbor on the shortest path π.
    end if
  end if
end while
Final phase (Kleinberg's greedy algorithm):
  Route the message M to an immediate neighbor of x that is closest to the target t, until it reaches t.

Based on Algorithm 2, we have the following theorem. Due to page limitation, its proof is not shown in this conference paper. The reader is referred to [23] for more details.

Theorem 2. *In a KSWN* K*, Algorithm 2 performs in $O(\lg n \lg \lg n)$ expected number of hops.*

5 Conclusion

We extend Kleinberg's small-world network with augmented local links, and show that if each node participating in routing is aware of $O(\lg n)$ neighbors via augmented links, there exist both non-oblivious and oblivious decentralized algorithms that can finish routing in $O(\lg n \lg \lg n)$ expected number of hops, which is a near optimal routing complexity. Our investigation shows that the awareness of $O(\lg n)$ nodes through the augmented links will be more efficient for routing than via the local links [10, 17].

Our extended model may provide an important supplement for the modelling of small-world phenomenon, and may better approximate the real-world observation. For example, each person in a human society is very likely to increase his/her activities randomly within some certain communities, and thus is aware of certain levels of "augmented" acquaintances. This augmented awareness would surely help delivery the message to an unknown target in the society.

Our results may also find applications in the design of large-scale distributed networks, such as distributed storage systems. Unlike most existing deterministic frameworks for distributed systems, our extended small-world networks may provide good fault tolerance, since the links in the networks are constructed probabilistically and less vulnerable to adversarial attacks.

References

1. R. Albert, H. Jeong, and A.-L. Barabasi. The diameter of the World Wide Web. *Nature*, 401(9):130–131, 1999.
2. J. Aspnes, Z. Diamadi, and G. Shah. Fault-tolerant routing in peer-to-peer systems. In *Proceedings of PODC'02*, pages 223–232, 2002.
3. L. Barriére, P. Fraigniaud, E. Kranakis, and D. Krizanc. Efficient routing in networks with long range contacts. In *Proceedings of the 15th International Symposium on Distributed Computing (DISC'01)*, pages 270–784, 2001.
4. I. Benjamini and N. Berger. The Diameter of Long-Range Percolation Clusters on Finite Cycles. *Random Structures and Algorithms*, 19(2):102–111, 2001.
5. M. Biskup. Graph diameter in long-range percolation. *Submitted to Electron. Comm. Probab*, 2004.
6. B. Bollobás and F.R.K. Chung. The Diameter of a cycle plus a random matching. *SIAM Journal on Discrete Mathematics*, 1(3):328–333, 1988.
7. D. Coppersmith, D. Gamarnik, and M. Sviridenko. The diameter of a long-range percolation graph. *Random Structures and Algorithms*, 21(1):1–13, 2002.
8. P. Dodds, R. Muhamad, and D. Watts. An experimental study of search in global social networks. *Science*, 301:827–829, 2003.

9. M. Kochen Ed. *The small world (Ablex, Norwood)*. 1989.
10. P. Fraigniaud, C. Gavoille, and C. Paul. Eclecticism shrinks even small worlds. In *PODC 2004*, pages 169–178, 2004.
11. C.M. Homan and G. Istrate. Small worlds, locality, and flooding on landscapes. Research Report TR-2003-796, Department of Computer Science, University of Rochester, USA, 2003.
12. D. Kemper, J. Kleinberg, and A. Demers. Spatial gossip and resource location protocols. In *Proceedings of STOC*, pages 163–172, 2001.
13. J. Kleinberg. The Small-World Phenomenon: An Algorithmic Perspective. In *Proceedings of the 32nd ACM Symposium on Theory of Computing*, pages 163–170, 2000.
14. E. Lebhar and N. Schabanel. Almost optimal decentralized routing in long-range contact networks. In *ICALP 2004*, pages 894–905, 2004.
15. G. S. Manku, M. Bawa, and P. Raghavan. Symphony: Distributed hashing in a small world. In *Proceedings of the 4th USENIX Symposium on Internet Technologies and Systems*, pages 127–140, 2003.
16. G.S. Manku, M. Naor, and U. Wieder. Know thy neighbor's neighbor: The power of lookahead in randomized p2p networks. In *Proceedings of STOC 2004*, pages 54–63, 2004.
17. C. Martel and V. Nguyen. Analyzing Kleinberg's (and other) small-world models. In *PODC 2004*, pages 179–188, 2004.
18. S. Milgram. The small world problem. *Psychology Today*, 61, 1967.
19. M.E.J. Newman. Models of the small world. *J. Stat. Phys.*, 101, 2000.
20. V. Nguyen and C. Martel. Analyzing and Characterizing Small-World Graphs. In *SODA 2005*, 2005.
21. D. Watts and S. Strogatz. Collective dynamics of small-world networks. *Nature*, 393:440–442, 1998.
22. H. Zhang, A. Goel, and R. Govindan. Using the small-world model to improve Freenet performance. In *Proceedings of IEEE INFOCOM 2002*, pages 1228–1237, 2002.
23. J. Zeng and W.-J. Hsu. Near Optimal Routing for Small-World Networks with Augmented Local Awareness. Available at http://www.cais.ntu.edu.sg/~zjy. 2005.

Systolic Routing in an Optical Fat Tree

Risto T. Honkanen

Department of Computer Science, University of Kuopio,
P.O. Box 1627, FIN-70211 Kuopio, Finland
rthonkan@cs.uku.fi

Abstract. In this paper we present an all-optical network architecture and a systolic routing protocol for it. An r-dimensional optical fat tree network ($\mathcal{OFT}$) consists of $2^r - 1$ routing nodes and $n = 2^r$ processing nodes deployed at the leaf nodes of the network. In our construction packets injected into the $\mathcal{OFT}$ carry no routing information. Routing is based on the use of a cyclic control bit sequence and scheduling. The systolic routing protocol ensures that no electro-optical conversion is needed in the intermediate routing nodes and all the packets injected into the routing machinery will reach their target without collisions. A work-optimal routing of an h-relation is achieved with a reasonable size of h.

Keywords: Optical fat tree, systolic routing, work-optimal routing.

1 Introduction

Optics offers a possibility to increase the bandwidth of intercommunication networks. Optical communication offers several advantages in comparison with its electronic counterpart, for example, a possibility to use broader bandwidth and insensitivity to external interferences. These advantages have been covered, e.g., by Saleh and Teich in their book [12].

Our work is motivated by another kind of communication problem, namely the emulation of shared memory with distributed memory modules [5]. If a parallel algorithm has enough parallel *slackness*, the implementation of shared memory can be reduced to efficient routing of an h-relation [13]. An h-relation is a routing problem where each processing node has at most h packets to send and it is the target of at most h packets [1]. An implementation of an h-relation is said to be *work-optimal* at *cost* c, if all the packets arrive at their targets in time ch. A precondition for work-optimality is that h is greater than the diameter $\Omega(\phi)$ of the network and the network can move $\Omega(n\phi)$ packets in each step, where n is the number of processors. Otherwise slackness cannot be used to "hide" latency influenced by the diameter [5]. For an r-dimensional optical fat tree $\mathcal{OFT}$ having $n = 2^r$ processing nodes, the diameter $\phi = r$ fulfills this condition when $h \in \Omega(n \log n)$.

Using the fat tree topology as an intercommunication network is a cost-effective way to connect a large number of processors. Congestion problems are avoided by providing more bandwidth in the higher levels of the tree. A number of intercommunication networks has been implemented by using fat tree topology. For example, the basic architecture of the Thinking Machine CM-5 data network is a fat tree [8]. High performance clusters typically use fat tree networks as well. For instance the InfiniBand architecture utilizes fat tree [9]. Recent implementations use packet switching as the routing strategy. A drawback of packet switching is that routing decisions must be done in an electronic form. For now we do not know any all-optical implementation of fat tree network architecture.

In this work we present an all-optical fat tree network architecture and a systolic routing protocol for it. The r-dimensional optical fat tree consists of $2^r - 1$ routing nodes and $n = 2^r$ processing nodes deployed at the leaf nodes of the network. Routing nodes are connected to each other by optical links. In this paper we present a novel packet routing protocol, called the *systolic routing protocol*.

Additionally, when a packet is injected into the routing machinery, neither electro-optic conversions are needed during its path from its source to the target processing node nor any collisions happen between two distinct packets. An r-dimensional $\mathcal{OFT}$ can route an h-relation in $\Theta(h)$ time, if $h \in \Omega(n \log n)$. Section 2 presents the structure of routing nodes and the structure of an $\mathcal{OFT}$ network. In Section 3 we introduce the systolic routing protocol. Section 4 presents the analysis of our construction. Section 5 sketches conclusions and future work.

2 Optical Fat Tree with Systolic Routers

We study the r-dimensional structure of an $\mathcal{OFT}$ of diameter $\phi = r$ and having $n = 2^r$ processing nodes. Section 2.1 represents the structure of routing nodes. In section 2.2 we introduce the construction of an $\mathcal{OFT}$. Section 2.3 discusses the feasibility of our construction.

2.1 Systolic Routers for $\mathcal{OFT}$

Routing nodes of an $\mathcal{OFT}$ at the level r' have $\frac{l}{2} = 2^{r'-1}$ outgoing links both to its left and right subtrees and $l = 2^{r'}$ incoming links from its parent node. The indegree of a routing node equals to the out-degree. Let $\mathcal{I} = \{i_0, i_1, \ldots, i_{l-1}\}$ denote the set of incoming links of a router at level r', and $\mathcal{O} = \{o_0, o_1, \ldots, o_{\frac{l}{2}-1}, o_{\frac{l}{2}}, \ldots, o_{l-1}\}$ denote the set of outgoing links of the router. A routing node can be in two states. When a routing node routes signals from inputs to outputs using mapping $i_s \to c_s$ for all $0 \leq s < l$ it is said to be in *drop* state. Respectively, when a routing node routes signals from inputs to outputs using mapping $i_s \to o_{(s+\frac{l}{2}) \bmod l}$ for all $0 \leq s < l$ it is called to be in *turn* state. An example of a routing node at level 2 in its two possible states is presented in Figure 1.

The basic component of routing nodes is the electrically controlled all-optical 2×2 switch. Switches can be implemented by $LiNbO_3$ technology [12]. We can construct a routing node of any level with edge-disjoint paths, e.g., by using the Beneš network structure [7]. The construction ensures that whatever state is applied, signals never collide.

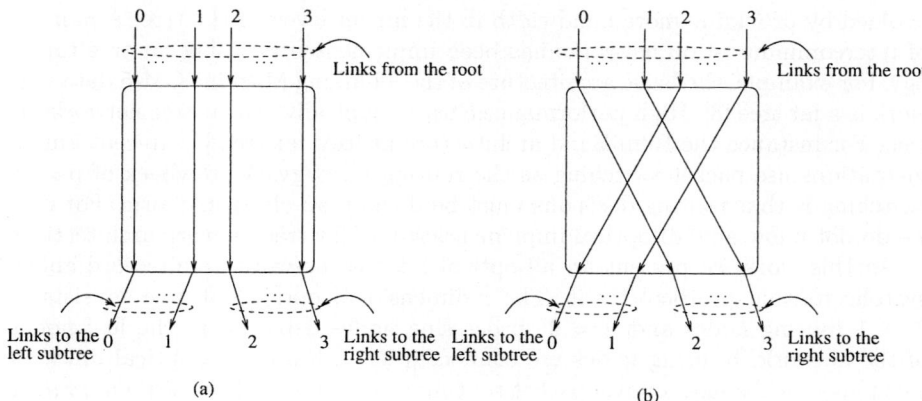

Fig. 1. A routing node at level 2: (a) in the drop state, and (b) in the turn state

2.2 Construction of an Optical Fat Tree

Construction of an $\mathcal{OFT}$ is recursive. A 1-dimensional $\mathcal{OFT}$ consists of $2^1 = 2$ processing nodes and a routing node of level 1 (R_{11}). Processing nodes are connected to the router as its left and right leaves by one outgoing link. Outputs of processing nodes are connected to inputs of the router. A 2-dimensional $\mathcal{OFT}$ can be constructed out of two 1-dimensional $\mathcal{OFT}$'s and a routing node of level 2 (R_{22}). Each processing node is relabelled by a unique r-bit binary string w. Two 1-dimensional $\mathcal{OFT}$'s are connected as left and right subtrees of the routing node R_{22} by using mapping $o_w \rightarrow P_w$ for all $0 \leq w < 2^r$. Outputs of processing nodes are connected to inputs of the routing node R_{22} by using mapping $P_w \rightarrow i_w$ for all $0 \leq w < 2^r$. An example of constructing of 2-dimensional $\mathcal{OFT}$ is presented in

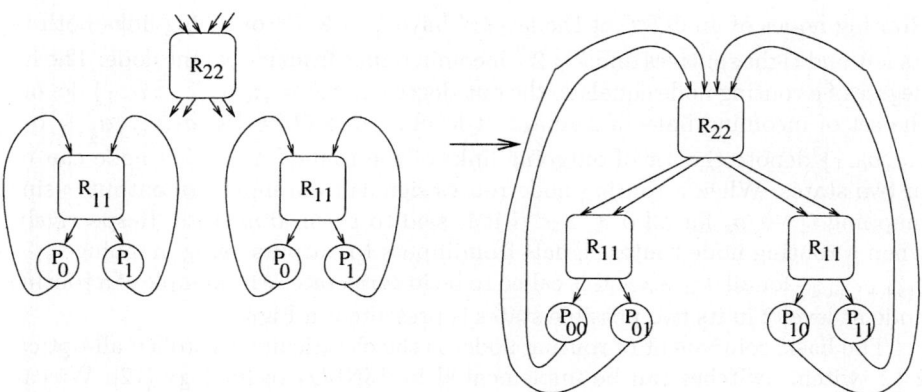

Fig. 2. Construction of 2-dimensional $\mathcal{OFT}$ out of two 1-dimensional $\mathcal{OFT}$'s and one routing node of level 2 with relabelling of processing nodes

Figure 2. In Figure 2, a rounded square indicates a routing node, a circle indicates a processing node, and an arrows between objects indicate unidirectional links.

Respectively, an r-dimensional $\mathcal{OFT}$ can be constructed by two $(r-1)$-dimensional $\mathcal{OFT}$'s and a routing node of level r. The bandwidth of the systems is divided in time slots, whose length t_p equals to the bypass time of a packet via a link between two consecutive routing nodes. We call the length of time slot t_p the *packet cycle*. A packet consists of data bits so that the overall length of the time slot measured in time units is t_p. Each processing node P_i is uniquely labelled by a bit sequence $x_0 x_1 \ldots x_{r-1}$, and it has $n = 2^r$ sending buffers $(b_{(i,0)}, b_{(i,1)}, \ldots, b_{(i,n-1)})$ that have an important role in routing.

The number of routing nodes at each level s' is $2^{(r-s')}$, where r is the dimension of $\mathcal{OFT}$. Respectively, the number of links can be calculated by $(r+1)2^r$. Because the number of processing nodes of an $\mathcal{OFT}$ is 2^r and the diameter r, we can conclude that the precondition for work-optimality is satisfied.

2.3 Feasibility of $\mathcal{OFT}$ with Systolic Routers

The switching time of LiNbO$_3$ switches lies in the range of 10–15 ps [12]. The length of packet (l_p) can be evaluated by equation $l_p = \frac{N_p \times v_c}{B \times r}$, where N_p is the size of the packet in bits, $v_c = 0.3$ m/ns is the speed of light in vacuum, $r = 1.5$ is the refraction index of fiber [12], and B is the link bandwidth. Assuming the bandwidth to be B=100 Gb/s, the length of a bit in a fiber is $\frac{v_c}{B \times r} = 2$ mm.

In order to estimate the feasibility of a 6-dimensional $\mathcal{OFT}$ (having 64 processing nodes) let us assume the link bandwidth to be $B = 100$ Gb/s, and the size of packets to be $N_p = 128$ b. The corresponding length of a packet in a fiber is $l_p \simeq 256$ mm and the length of time slot is $t_p \simeq 1.3$ ns. Assuming the length of clock cycle of processing nodes to be $t_{cc} = 1$ ns (corresponding the frequency of 1 GHz), it will take 1.3 clock cycles for a packet to travel between two adjacent routing nodes. The overall amount of fibers is $L_f \simeq 115$ m, and the routing time of packets is $t_r \simeq 8$ clock cycles for each packets. We consider the requested parameters to be reasonable and the architecture to be feasible to construct in the near future. A drawback of our construction is that the complexity of routers increases with respect to the dimension of $\mathcal{OFT}$.

3 Routing in Optical Fat Tree

We develop a routing algorithm for $\mathcal{OFT}$. The algorithm can be divided in two phases. During the initialization phase we first construct a control bit sequence that controls the system. Then the routing table is determined. The initialization phase must be executed only once when the system is set up. During the utilization of the $\mathcal{OFT}$ packets are injected into the network so that they are routed level by level to the destination. In section 3.1 we present properties of routing and transitions between subtrees. Section 3.2 introduces the initialization phase of the system. Section 3.3 introduces the routing algorithm for the optical fat tree.

3.1 Properties of Routing

According to our construction an r-dimensional $\mathcal{OFT}$ consists of 2^r processing nodes and r levels of routing nodes. Each routing node has an equal number of incoming and outgoing links. Let us consider a routing node at level s'. It has $2^{r-s'}$ incoming links from its parent node, $2^{r-s'-1}$ links leading to its left subtree, and $2^{r-s'-1}$ links leading to its right subtree. The incoming links can be divided in two groups. Let us denote g_l to be the group of $2^{r-s'-1}$ leftmost incoming links and g_r to be the group of $2^{r-s'-1}$ rightmost incoming links of the routing node. Clearly we can see that any packet reaching the routing node uses a link belonging to one of the incoming link groups and prefers a link leading to left or right subtree.

Let $a_0 a_1 \ldots a_{r-1}$ ($a_i \in \{0, 1\}$) be a bit sequence indicating the states of routing nodes used by a packet on its path from the source to the target in an r-dimensional $\mathcal{OFT}$. The value 1 in a bit position $\ldots a_{s'} \ldots$ indicates that at level $r - s'$ the packet using incoming link group g_l or g_r should be routed to the right or left subtree respectively. Correspondingly, the value 0 in a bit position $a_{s'}$ indicates that the packet using incoming link group g_l or g_r should be routed to the left or right subtree respectively. It is obvious that we can construct an r-ary routing bit sequence for any source/destination pair so that it leads the packet correctly through the $\mathcal{OFT}$. To notice this, let us assume that in a bit sequence $a_0 a_1 \ldots a_k \ldots a_{r-1}$, the k'th bit stands for the state leading to the wrong subtree. We just substitute the initial bit sequence by $a_0 a_1 \ldots \bar{a}_k \ldots a_{r-1}$, where $\bar{a}_k$ is the complement of a_k.

The routing information for packets can be evaluated by the bitwise XOR-operation $\oplus$. For example, if processor P_{011} (belonging to the leftmost group g_l of the root routing node of a 3-dimensional $\mathcal{OFT}$) has a packet destined to

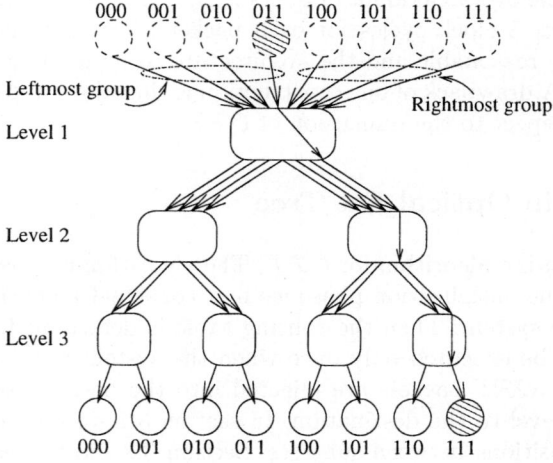

Fig. 3. Example of routing of a packet in an $\mathcal{OFT}$

Table 1. Correspondence between routing bit information, transitions between link groups and subtrees, and the required state of router

Routing information	Transition	Required state
0	$g_l \to$ Left	Drop
0	$g_r \to$ Right	Drop
1	$g_l \to$ Right	Turn
1	$g_r \to$ Left	Turn

processor P_{111}, the routing information can be expressed as $011 \oplus 111 = 100$. The meaning of this is that the packet from P_{011} to P_{111} must be routed from the leftmost incoming link group to the right subtree at the level 3 routing node, from the rightmost incoming link group to the right subtree at the level 2 routing node, and from the rightmost link to the right subtree at the level 1 routing node. Example of the routing is presented in Figure 3.

Routers can be considered to be an interface between incoming link groups and subtrees. Let us assume that a packet has the the bit $\ldots 1 \ldots$ in its ith bit position. The router responsible to route this packet (at the level $r - i$) receives the packet from the leftmost link group g_l or from the rightmost link group g_r. Regardless of the link group used the router node should be set in turn state. Correspondence between routing bit information, transitions between link groups and subtrees, and required states is presented in Table 1.

3.2 Initialization Phase

In our construction injected packets carry no routing information. When a packet reaches a routing node it is routed into the left or right subtree according to the state of the router. Anyway we are able to arrange a control system so that every packet injected into the $\mathcal{OFT}$ reaches its target. We will use a cyclic control bit sequence and timing of injections of packets.

Determining the Control Bit Sequence. An r-dimensional $\mathcal{OFT}$ has r levels of routing nodes. Packet routing in an r-dimensional $\mathcal{OFT}$ can be implemented by constructing a long control bit sequence $s_0 s_1 s_2 \ldots$, applying at time step t the state corresponding to the value of bit position s_t to all the routing nodes of the $\mathcal{OFT}$, and synchronizing injections of packets so that they reach every routing node in the correct state. Precondition of all-to-all routing is that the bit sequence includes (cyclically) all bit sequences of r bits. A naive solution would be to construct the control bit sequence of all r-ary bit combinations. The length of control cycle would be $r2^r$. The control sequence can be reduced to $T = 2^r$ by using *de Bruijn sequences* [3].

A de Bruijn sequence (in alphabet $\mathcal{A} = \{0, 1\}$) of length 2^r is a sequence of 2^r bits in which every subsequence of r bits appears once, including wraparound [7]. For $r = 4$, for example, $\xi = 0000111101100101$ is a de Bruijn sequence applicable for our purpose. All sixteen 4-bit sequences occur exactly once as subsequence of ξ.

Fredricksen has presented an algorithm to construct a de Bruijn sequence [2]. The algorithm is *Prefer one* and it can be presented as follows:

Algorithm Prefer one
   1: Write $l = r$ zeros;
   2: for the kth bit of the sequence, $k > l$, write a one;
      if the newly formed l-tuple has not previously appeared in
         the sequence then $k := k + 1$
      else
   3: for the kth bit of the sequence, write a zero;
      if the newly formed l-tuple has not previously appeared in
         the sequence then $k := k + 1$ and go to step 2
      else stop;

Bit positions of $\boldsymbol{\xi}$ present states of routers of $\mathcal{OFT}$. That is, let $\boldsymbol{\xi}_m$ denote the value the mth bit of de Bruijn sequence $\boldsymbol{\xi}$. At each time step t all the routing nodes are set in turn state if $\boldsymbol{\xi}_{t \bmod \|\boldsymbol{\xi}\|} = 1$, where $\|\boldsymbol{\xi}\|$ is the length of $\boldsymbol{\xi}$, and in drop state otherwise. Determining of the control sequence is necessary to do only once at the initialization phase of the $\mathcal{OFT}$.

Determining the Routing Table. The optical fat tree has a number of properties. Firstly, the structure of routing nodes and connections at each router level are uniform. Secondly, it is possible to determine a unique routing bit sequence for any packet from a source P_s to the destination P_d for any pair (s, d). Thirdly, determination of unique transitions between link groups and subtrees is possible as well because of uniformness of the construction of the $\mathcal{OFT}$ and uniqueness of the routing bit sequences. Forthly, the $\mathcal{OFT}$ is controlled by the static control bit sequence $\boldsymbol{\xi}$. For these reasons we are able to determine a routing table for every connection at the initialization phase.

Let us consider an r-dimensional $\mathcal{OFT}$ having $p = 2^r$ processors. For this construction the length of routing bit sequence is $\|w\| = r$ and the length of control sequence is $\|\boldsymbol{\xi}\| = 2^r$. A packet is routed correctly if it is injected into the network so that during the next r time steps holds $\tau_t = \boldsymbol{\xi}_{t \bmod \|\boldsymbol{\xi}\|}, t = 0 \ldots r - 1$.

At the initialization phase every processor P_i determines a routing table R having $\|\boldsymbol{\xi}\| = 2^r$ rows. Let R_i denote the value of i'th row of the routing table. The algorithm determining routing table is *Routing table* and it can be presented as follows:

Algorithm Routing table
   {Assuming s and d are the source and the destination processors,
   and $\boldsymbol{\xi}$ is the control sequence};
   1: $i = 0$;
   2: **repeat**
      In the i'th row of routing table R write the index
      value of destination processor for which
         $\tau_t = \boldsymbol{\xi}_{i+t+1 \bmod \|\boldsymbol{\xi}\|}, t = 0 \ldots r - 1; \; i := i + 1;$
   3: **until** $i = 2^r$;

Algorithm Routing table is necessary to do only once at the initialization phase of the $\mathcal{OBF}$.

3.3 Routing Algorithm for the Optical Fat Tree

At the initialization phase each processor determines the control sequence ξ and the routing table. This must be done when the system is set up. At the beginning of routing each processor of the $\mathcal{OFT}$ has a number of packets to send. In the preprocessing phase each processor P_s inserts packets destined to processor P_d into sending buffer $b_{(s,d)}$.

At each time step t each processor s picks up a packet from sending buffer $b_{(s,d')}$, where $d' = R_{t \bmod \|\xi\|}$ is the value of $(t \bmod \|\xi\|)$'th row in the routing table and inject it into the outgoing link. The r-tuple of bits starting at ξ_t then indicates successive drop and turn states that correctly route the packet to the target processor d.

4 Analysis of Systolic Routing

In the preprocessing phase, each of the h packets of a processing node P_s was inserted into sending buffer $b_{(s,d)}$, where P_d is the target of the packet. Clearly, all of the packets have been routed after time $O(Tn)$, where T is the maximum size of all buffers and $n = 2^r$ is the number of processing nodes. The result is poor if the packets have an odd distribution over targets. In this presentation we assume that packets have an even distribution over targets.

According to Mitzenmacher et al. [10], supposing that we throw n balls into n bins with each ball choosing a bin independently and uniformly at random, then the *maximum load* is approximately $\log n / \log \log n$ with high probability (whp)[1]. Maximum load means the largest number of balls in any bin. Correspondingly, if we have n packets to send and n sending buffers during a simulation step, then the maximum load of sending buffers is approximately $\log n / \log \log n$ whp. The overall routing time of those packets is $n \log n / \log \log n + \Theta(1)$ that is not work-optimal according to the definition of work-optimality.

If the size of h-relation is enlarged to $h \geq n \log n$, the maximum load is $\Theta(h/n)$ [11]. Assuming that $h = n \log n$ the maximum load is $\Theta(\log n)$, the corresponding routing time is $\Theta(n \log n)$. A work-optimal result is achieved according to the definition of work-optimality. Routing h packets in time $\Theta(h)$ implies work-optimality. Intuitively it is clear that the cost approaches to 1, when h/n grows.

We ran some experiments to get an idea about the cost. We ran 5 simulation rounds for each occurrence using a visualizator programmed with Java [6]. Packets were randomly created and put into output buffers and the average value of the routing time over all the 5 simulation rounds were evaluated. The results are only speculative because of a small number of evaluation rounds executed. The average cost was evaluated using equation $c_{ave} = \frac{t_r}{h}$, where t_r is the average routing time. Figure 4 gives support to the idea that h does not need to be extremely high to get a reasonable routing cost.

---

[1] We use *whp, with high probability* to mean with probability at least $1 - O(1/n^\alpha)$ for some constant α.

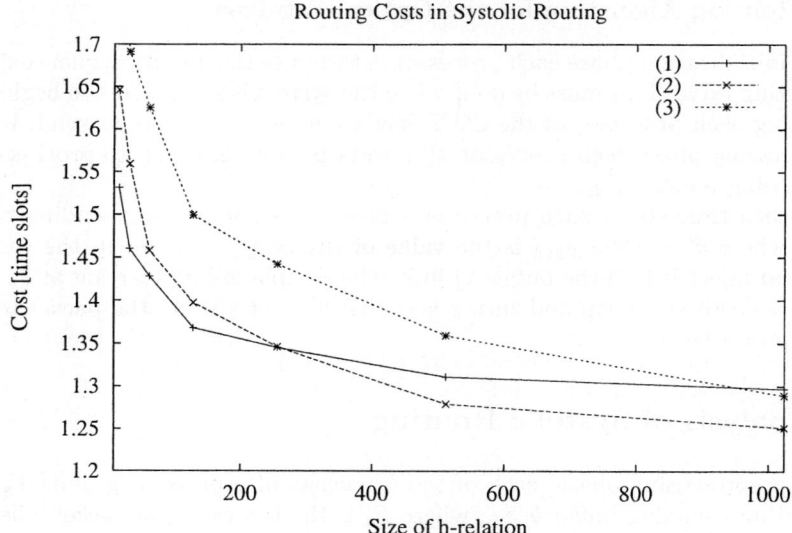

Fig. 4. Routing costs, when the size of h-relation varies. (1) $n = 4$, (2) $n = 8$, and (3) $n = 16$.

5 Conclusions and Future Work

We have presented the systolic routing protocol for optical fat tree. No electro-optical conversion is needed during the transfer and all the packets injected into the routing machinery are guaranteed to reach their destination. The simple structure presented and the systolic routing protocol are useful and realistic and offer work-optimal routing of h-relation if $h \in \Omega(n \log n)$.

An advantage of our construction is that the overall number of links is $\Theta(n \log n)$. We presented the systolic routing protocol for sparse optical torus ($\mathcal{SOT}$) in paper [4]. For $\mathcal{SOT}$, the number of links is $\Theta(n^2)$.

However, a couple of drawbacks arise, when the systems are scaled up. Firstly, the degree of root node the $\mathcal{OFT}$ increases with respect to the size of network. Secondly, putting M elements in the physical space requires at least a volume of size $\Omega(\sqrt[3]{M})$ [14, 15]. The length of wires between routing nodes increases with respect to the physical space required.

References

1. Adler, M., Byers, J.W., Karp, R.M.: Scheduling Parallel Communication, the h-Relation Problem. Proceedings of Mathematical Foundations of Computer Science, (MFCS). Prague Czech Republic (1995) 1–20
2. Fredricksen, H.: A Survey of Full Length Nonlinear Shift Register Cycle Algorithms. SIAM Review **24**,2 (1982) 195–221

3. Golomb, S.W.: Shift Register Sequences. Aegean Park Press, Laguna Hills California (1982)
4. Honkanen, R.T.: Systolic Routing in Sparse Optical Torus. Proceedings of the 8th Symposium on Programming Languages and Programming Tools (SPLST'03). Kuopio Finland (2003) 14–20
5. Honkanen, R., Leppänen, V., Penttonen, M., 2001: Hot-Potato routing Algorithms for Sparse Optical Torus. Proceedings of the 2001 ICPP Workshops. Valencia Spain (2001) 302–307
6. Koivistoinen, A., Pietarinen, K., Rantonen, A., Valo T.: Visualisator for OFT network. Programming project, University of Kuopio. Kuopio Finland URL: http://www.cs.uku.fi/~rthonkan/OFT/Laski.htm (March 30, 2005)
7. Leighton, F.T.: Introduction to parallel algorithms and architectures: arrays, trees, hypercubes. Morgan Kaufmann Publishers, Inc., California USA (1992)
8. Leiserson, C.E., et al.: The Network Architecture of the Connection Machine CM-5. Proc. 4th Ann. Symp. Parallel Algorithms and Architectures. New York USA (1992) 272–285
9. Mellanox Technologies Inc.: InfiniBand Clustering — Delivering Better Price/Performance than Ethernet. White paper, Mellanox Technologies Inc., Santa Clara California (2005)
10. Mitzenmacher, M., Richa, A.W., Sitaraman, R.: To appear in: Handbook of Randomized Algorithms. URL: http://www.eecs.harvard.edu/~michaelm/ (June 24, 2002)
11. Raab, M, Steger, A.: "Balls into Bins"—A Simple and Tight Analysis. Proceedings of 2nd Workshop on Randomize and Approximation Techniques on Computer Science (RANDOM'98). Barcelona Spain (1998) 159–170
12. Saleh, B.E.A., Teich, M.C.: Fundamentals of Photonics. John Wiley & Sons, Inc., New York USA (1991)
13. Valiant, L.G.: General Purpose Parallel Architectures. In: Algorithms and Complexity, Handbook of Theoretical Computer Science volume A (1990) 943–971
14. Vitányi, P.B.M.: Locality, Communication, and Interconnect Length in Multicomputers. SIAM Journal of Computing **17**,4 (1988) 659–672
15. Vitányi, P.B.M.: Multiprocessor Architectures and Physical Law. Proceedings of 2nd Workshop on Physics and Computation (PhysComp'94). Dallas Texas (1994) 24–29

Fast Total-Exchange Algorithm

Anssi Kautonen

University of Joensuu, Department of Computer Science,
P.O.Box 111, 80101 Joensuu, Finland
Anssi.Kautonen@cs.joensuu.fi

Abstract. Optical communication offers huge bandwidth and makes it possible to build communication networks of very high bandwidth and connectivity. We study routing of the h-relations in optical communication pararallel computer under so called *OCPC* or *1-collision* assumption. In an h-relation each processor is the origin and the destination of at most h-messages.

In this paper we study the case where h is much larger than the number of the processors. Our algorithm uses total-exchange primitive to route packets. Our algorithm routes random h-relations in a p-processor network using $\frac{h}{p}(1+o(1))+O(\sqrt{\frac{h}{p}\log p})$ total-exchange rounds with high probability. The algorithm attempts to balance the number of packets between origin-destination pairs. The experiments show that when h is large compared to the number of processors, the algorithm achieves simulation cost which is very close to 1. I.e. the h-relation is routed in the ch, where c is only little more than 1.

1 Introduction

We assume the OCPC (*Optical Communication Parallel Computer*) model (also known as *Local Memory PRAM*, *S*PRAM*, and *Optical Crossbar Parallel Computer*). The OCPC model was first introduced by Anderson and Miller [1], and has been studied in [4], [5], [6], [7], [9], [10], [11], [12], [13], [14], [16] and [17].

The memory of OCPC is divided into modules, one module per processor. Communication network is a complete network, thus distance between any pair on nodes is one and the degree of nodes is $p-1$. Processors communicate with each other by transmitting messages. A processor can transmit a message directly to any other processor and the transmission takes one time unit. At any time unit a processor can send at most one message. The message will succeed in reaching the processor, if it is the only message with that processor as its destination at that time step. If two or more processors attempt to send a message to the same processor, no transmission is successful and a retransmission must occur. This is called the *OCPC* or *1-collision* assumption.

In this paper we consider balanced communication patterns, called h-relations. Let p be the number of processors in a parallel computer. Let $K = (k_{ij})$ be a $p \times p$ matrix, where k_{ij} gives the number of messages originating at processor i and destined for processor j. If we let h be the maximum sum of any row or column of this matrix; then the matrix specifies an *h-relation*. The problem of solving this communication task is termed the *h-relation problem*.

The problem is motivated by implementation of the shared memory abstraction, for example the PRAM model [2] and the BSP model [17], and also by direct implementation of specific parallel algorithms. The value of h affects the latency parameter of the BSP model, and the effiency of the implementation of the h-relation affects the bandwidth parameter of the BSP model.

2 Routing Protocol

We have developed an algorithm to route messages in a complete optical network. The algorithm is collision-free, no special acknowledgement step is required. The algorithm is based on total-exchange [3] and it is indirect, thus some packets are sent to final destination via an intermediate destination(s).

In order to be efficient, total-exchange based algorithms require a large h/p-ratio. The problems in a simple total-exchange scheme are that the number of the messages between origin-destination pairs in not balanced, and routing two messages from processor P_i to processor P_j takes at least p routing steps.

Algorithm 1. Simple Total-exchange algorithm

1: **proc** Simple total-exhange(p, h)
2: **for** all processor P_i **par do**
3:    $t = (P_i + 1) \bmod p$
4:    **while** packets remain **do**
5:      **if** processor has a packet to send to processor t **then**
6:        Send that packet to processor t
7:      $t = (t + 1) \bmod p$
8:      **if** $t = P_i$ **then**
9:        $t = (t + 1) \bmod p$

The expected number of packets over any any origin-destination pair is h/p. However the number packets over all origin-destination pairs is not uniform. Some pairs have "excess" of packets and some pairs have "deficiency" of packets with respect to the average value. The standard deviation of the number of packets over all origin-destination pairs is $\Theta(\sqrt{h/p})$, thus to route all packets to their final destinations would require at least $h/p + \Omega(\sqrt{p/h})$ total-exchange rounds using the Algorithm 1 [3]. Especially the routing of the last packets takes many routing steps. The maximum number of messages between any origin-destination pair determines the number of routing steps required to route all messages to their final destinations.

We have developed an algorithm that balances the load so that the number of messages over all origin-destination is approximately equal. Routing is done using the total-exchange protocol. If the processor has no packet to send to the current target processor, then it checks to which processor it has most packets to send. Let m be the maximum number of messages to any other processors. Let $x_1, \ldots, x_n$ be a set of processors to which the current processors have m packets to send. If m is greater than one, then one of packets destined to one of processors $x_1, \ldots, x_n$ is chosen uniformly at random. If m is one, then the last packets to some destination are not sent because a packet may travel from intermediate destination to intermediate long before the packet arrives at its final destination.

Algorithm 2. Balance algorithm

1: **proc** Balance (p, h)
2: **for** all processors P_i **par do**
3:    $t = (P_i + 1) \bmod p$
4:    **while** packets left **do**
5:       **if** processor has a packet to send to processor t **then**
6:          Send that packet to processor t
7:       **else**
8:          Let m be the maximum number of packets left that the current
9:          processor has to send to any other processor
10:         **if** $m > 1$ **then**
11:            Let $x_1, \ldots, x_n$ be the set of processors for which
12:            the current processor has m packets to send
13:            Select uniformly at random one of packets targetted
14:            to some of processors $x_1, \ldots, x_n$.
15:            Send the selected packet to processor t
16:       $t = (t + 1) \bmod p$
17:       **if** $t = P_i$ **then**
18:          $t = (t + 1) \bmod p$

In order to analyse the algorithms we must estimate how many messages are sent between processors. In the Simple Total-Exchange (See Algorithm 1) the number of required routing steps depends on the maximum number of packets over all origin-destination pairs. We can estimate that number using the following theorem (Theorem 1) by Raab and Steger [15].

Theorem 1. *Let M be the random variable that counts the maximum number of balls in any bin, if we throw m balls independently and uniformly at random into n bins. Then $Pr[M > k_\alpha] = o(1)$ if $\alpha > 1$ and $Pr[M > k_\alpha] = 1 - o(1)$, if $0 < \alpha < 1$, where*

$$k_\alpha = \begin{cases} \frac{\log n}{\log \frac{n \log n}{m}} \left(1 + \alpha \frac{\log \log \frac{n \log n}{m}}{\log \frac{n \log n}{m}}\right), & \text{if } \frac{n}{\text{polylog(n)}} \leq m \ll n \log n \\ (d_c - 1 + \alpha) \log n, & \text{if } m = c * n \log n \text{ for some constant } c, \\ \frac{m}{n} + \alpha \sqrt{2 \frac{m}{n} \log n}, & \text{if } n \log n \ll m \leq n * \text{polylog}(n) \\ \frac{m}{n} + \sqrt{\frac{2m \log n}{n}} \left(1 - \frac{1}{\alpha} \frac{\log \log n}{2 \log n}\right), & \text{if } m \gg n(\log n)^3. \end{cases}$$

Here d_c is a suitable constant depending only on c.

Next we prove that the Balance algorithm is only a little worse than the Simple Total-Exchange algorithm in the worst case. In the Experimental results section we will show that the Balance algorithm is much better in practise.

We present following theorem

Theorem 2. *The Balance algorithm requires at most twice as many total-exchange rounds than the Simple Total-Exchange algorithm when routing the same packets to their final destinations.*

Proof. We construct a scenario where the Balance algorithm is as slow as possible in comparison with the Simple Total-Exchange algorithm. Assume that the machine has p processors. Then make following assumptions:

1. Each processor has m packets to send to every other processor, with the following exceptions
2. No processor has packets to send to processor P_x.
3. The number of packets that each processor has to send to processor P_y is $m + n$, $1 \leq n \leq m$.
4. Processor P_x has $m + n$ packets to send to every processor.
5. The number of packets that processor P_y has to processor P_z is also $m + n$.
6. Processor P_x, P_y and P_z are different processors

In this scenario the Simple Total-Exchange algorithm requires $m + n$ total exchange rounds. In the Balance algorithm, processor P_x has $(m + n) * (p - 1)$ packets in the beginning of the routing. During the first m total-exchange rounds processor P_x can send one packet at every time step. Processor P_x also receives a packet almost every step during the first m total-exchange rounds. Processor P_x is not the final destination for any of the packets it receives. It receives packets destined to processors P_y and P_z. The worst case is when processor P precedes processor P_y by one position. In this case processor P_x has received $m*(p-1)-1$ new packets. Depending on their order either P_y has still one packet left to send to P_z or P_z has one packet to send to P_y.

To send all packets that processor P_x had in the beginning of the routing, n more total-exchange rounds are required. After $m + n$ total exchange rounds processor P_x still has $m * (p - 1) - 1$ packets to send. Sending those packets to intermediate destination requires m total-exchange rounds. Sending packets to final destinations may require one additional total-exchange round. The total number of routing steps is $2 * m + n + 1 \leq 2 * (m + n)$. We can conlude that in the worst case the Balance algorithm requires twice as many total-exchange rounds as the Simple Total-Exchange algorithm.

Assume that $h >> p \log p$, then routing random h-relation then routing a random h-relation takes $\frac{h}{p}(1 + o(1)) + O(\sqrt{\frac{h}{p}} \log p)$ total-exchange rounds. Arbitrary h-relations can be routed about in twice that time, by routing messages first to random intermediate destinations and then to their final destinations as proposed by Valiant [17].

3 Experimental Results

We have compared four algorithms. The results of the experiments can be seen in the Table 1. In the leftmost column are the results of the Simple Total-Exchange algorithm. See the Algorithm 1. In next column are the results of Rao & al.'s algorithm [16]. In third column are results of Kautonen's Halving algorithm [9]. The last column contain the results of the Balance algorithm, Algorithm 2.

Table 1. Simulation results

p	h	direct	Rao & al.	Halving	Balance
64	p	5.65	n/a	2.14	2.12
	2p	4.07	n/a	1.77	1.63
	4p	3.06	2.00	1.54	1.37
	8p	2.41	1.54	1.37	1.22
	16p	1.96	1.31	1.25	1.14
	32p	1.67	1.19	1.18	1.09
256	p	7.14	n/a	1.88	2.07
	2p	5.02	n/a	1.62	1.62
	4p	3.65	2.00	1.41	1.36
	8p	2.77	1.61	1.29	1.22
	16p	2.19	1.32	1.20	1.15
	32p	1.82	1.19	1.14	1.09
1024	p	8.45	n/a	1.73	2.03
	2p	5.80	n/a	1.52	1.61
	4p	4.15	2.00	1.40	1.35
	8p	3.08	1.63	1.29	1.21
	16p	2.41	1.31	1.25	1.15
	32p	1.93	1.21	n/a	1.09

The results show that the Balance algorithm is much better than the Simple Total-Exchange and it is better than the Halving algorithm when $h > 8p$. In the Balance algorithm the simulation cost seems to depend on only on h/p-ratio and it is independent on h and p when $h > p$.

When comparing these results with the results of Rao & al. [16], we notice that our results were better in the all cases. However in their simulations they assumed that each processor had at most h packets to send, but it was not limited how many packets one processor receives. We routed true h-relations. If the number of packets that one processor receives is not limited to h, then the Balance algorithm gives results which are 1-2% worse than those mentioned in Table 1.

Acknowledgments

The author thanks professor Martti Penttonen for comments and for useful discussions.

References

1. Anderson, R.J, Miller, G.L.: Optical Communication for Pointer Based Algorithms. Technical Report CRI-88-14, Computer Science Department, University of Southern California, LA, (1988)
2. Fortune, S., Wyllie, J.: Parallelism in Random Access Machines. Proceedings of the 10th ACM Symposium on Theory of Computing, (1978), 114–118
3. Gerbessiotis, A. V., Valiant, L.G: Direct Bulk-Synchronous Parallel Algorithms. Journal of Parallel and Distributed Computing **22**(2), (1995), 251–267
4. Geréb-Graus, M., Tsantilas, T.: Efficient Optical Communication in Parallel Computers. Proceedings of the 4th Annual ACM Symposium on Parallel Algorithms and Architectures, (1992), 41–48
5. Goldberg, L A., Jerrum, M, Leighton, T., Rao, S.: A Doubly Logarithmic Communication Algorith for the Completely Connected Optical Communication Parallel Computer. SIAM Journal on Computing **26**(4), (1997), 1100–1119
6. Goldberg, L A., Jerrum, M., MacKenzie, P.D.: An $\Omega(h + \sqrt{\log \log n})$ Lower Bound for Routing in Optical Networks. SIAM Journal on Computing **27**(4), (1998), 1083–1098
7. Goldberg, L.A., Matias, Y, Rao, S.: An Optical Simulation of Shared Memory. SIAM Journal on Computing **28**(5),(1999), 1829–1847
8. Karp, R.K., Luby, M., Meyer auf der Heide, F.: Efficient PRAM Simulation on a Distributed Memory Machine. Algorithmica **16**(4/5), (1996), 517–542
9. Kautonen, A.: Collision Free OCPC Algorithm for $O(p)$-relations. Manuscript.
10. Kautonen, A., Leppänen, V., Penttonen, M.: Simulations of PRAM on Complete Optical Networks, Lecture Notes in Computer Science 1124, (1996), 307–310
11. Kautonen, A., Leppänen, V., Penttonen, M.: Constant Thinning Protocol for Routing h-Relations in Complete Networks. Lecture Notes in Computer Science 1470, (1998), 993–998
12. Kautonen, A., Leppänen, V., Penttonen, M.: Thinning Protocols for Routing h-Relations in Complete Networks. Proc. of International Workshop on Randomized Algorithms, (1998), 61–69
13. MacKenzie, P.D., Ramachandran, V.: ERCW PRAMs and Optical Communication. Theoretical Computer Science **196**(1–2), (1998), 153–180
14. Meyer auf der Heide, F., Schrder, K, Schwarze, F.: Routing on networks of optical crossbars. Theoretical Computer Science **196**(1–2),(1998), 181–200
15. Raab, M., Steger, A.: "Balls into Bins" – A Simple and Tight Analysis. Proceedins of 2nd Workshop on Randomization and Approximation Techniques in Computer Science, (1998), 159–170
16. Rao, S., Suel, T., Tsantilas, T., Goudreau. M.: Efficient Communication Using Total-Exchange. Proceedings of 9th IEEE International Parallel Processing Symposium, (1995), 544–555
17. Valiant, L.G.: General Purpose Parallel Architectures. Handbook of Theoretical Computer Science **1**, (1990)

MFLWQ: A Fair and Adaptive Queue Management Algorithm for Scavenger Service

Xiaofeng Chen, Lingdi Ping, Zheng Wan, and Jian Chen

College of Computer Science, Zhejiang University, Hangzhou, Zhejiang, P.R.C.
cxf_wz@hotmail.com, ldping@cs.zju.edu.cn,
zhengwan66@yahoo.com.cn

Abstract. This paper presents a MFLWQ Algorithm for Scavenger Service, which is a non-elevated QoS technique proposed by the Internet2 project. The algorithm balances the bandwidth distribution among Scavenger Service flows by a modified Flow Random Early Detection (FRED) algorithm; estimates active Scavenger Service flow number by the variable *nactive* in FRED and accordingly tunes the bandwidth allocation between SS flows and BE flows in a logarithmical way to reach better performance and robustness. Simulations show that the algorithm provides more appropriate bottom bandwidth guarantee for Scavenger Service flows when protecting Best-Effort flows well and extends the applicability of Scavenger service to no-adaptive traffic like UDP.

1 Introduction

The reason why Internet can expand to such an enormous scale today mostly contributes to the Best-Effort design principle in TCP/IP protocol stack. But as the fast expanding of Internet and the emerging of various new network services, the shortcoming that original network lacks QoS warranty becomes increasingly critical.

Traditional IP network QoS researches focus on the ways to improve the service of the 'important flows' and to guarantee that the packets of these flows get priority service over the packets of Best-Effort flows (called BE flows below) alone the path. Many framework standards (such as IntServ [1] and DiffServ [2] from IETF) and protocols (such as RSVP [3] and MPLS [4]) have been raised to achieve QoS, but these standards and protocols are never widely employed. This is because that the Internet today is enormous and to achieve QoS on the Internet and to give the 'important packets' better service, all the route devices along the flow path must recognize these different standards and protocols. Even one device at the bottleneck fails to do this will make QoS unfeasible. On the basis of the IETF drafts [5,6], the Internet2 project [7] proposed a reverse-thinking QoS technology: QBone Scavenger Service [8]. In brief, it is a network mechanism that users (or their applications) voluntarily mark packets of some 'unimportant flows' with a specific DSCP (Differentiated Service Code Point) value (001000B). The routers implemented with Scavenger Service forward packets of BE flows with priority. And if there is some unused network capacity available, they forward packets of Scavenger Service flows (we call them SS flows below). As we give the SS flows a downgrade service, the performance of BE flows is upgraded. But the routers implemented with Scavenger Service don't strictly forward packets by priority. They still guarantee SS flows a minimal departure rate to avoid connection time out and intolerable response delay of applications. All the unused network capacity can be used by SS flows if the whole capacity is more than BE flows require, so the resource won't be wasted. An outstanding advantage of Scavenger Service is that it doesn't need all routers' support along the flow path. Even some routers give same service to BE flows and SS flows, the other routers implemented with Scavenger Service function as throttle valves and the goal of Scavenger Service still can be realized. So, Scavenger Service is a special deployable technology in the current Internet environment. The Internet2 project deployed Scavenger Service on QBone, the QoS test bed of Internet2, and Abilene network. They also recommended several packets queuing mechanisms such as WRR, WFQ, MDDR [8]. References [9, 10] presented some router configuration examples and [10, 11, 12] did some tests on Scavenger Service and gave the results. IETF has defined those Lower-Effort QoS technology like Scavenger Service as a new DiffServ PDB (Per-Domain Behavior) and published the relevant RFC document [13].

2 Design Principles and Realization

2.1 Unsolved Problem

In IP network, the fairness of bandwidth distribution among flows is not guaranteed. Those no-adaptive flows and robust flows are likely to seize more network capacity than other flows. In Scavenger Service, because SS traffic is given a very small portion of whole network capacity when network is busy, i.e. extremely congested, the unfair distribution of bandwidth between individual flows inside SS traffic is much more critical. And more, by analyzing the available queue management algorithms such as WRR, WFQ, MDRR [14] dealing with Scavenger Service, it can be found that they are only able to allocate the minimum departure rate for Scavenger Service in a static way when BE flows are over subscribing network bandwidth. As the total network capacity allocated for SS traffic is very low and the capacity for each SS flow is in inverse proportion to the number of SS flows, the SS flows may likely experience starvation if there are too many SS flows. However, allocating more capacity for Scavenger Service leads to resource misusing when there are few SS flows.

2.2 Design Principle and Components of the Algorithm

The design principle of MFLWQ queuing management algorithm aims at the peculiarity of Scavenger Service. It forwards BE packets with priority and allocates the spare capacity for SS flows. When BE traffic is heavy, it gives SS traffic a small guaranteed share of whole capacity. Furthermore, the algorithm balances the bandwidth allocation inside SS aggregate flow by a modified FRED algorithm and estimates active SS flow number by the variable *nactive* in FRED to tune the bandwidth allocation between SS flows and BE flows accordingly.

MFLWQ has two queues: *queue_BE* and *queue_SS*. The algorithm classifies arrived packets by the DSCP tag and enqueues them to the relevant queue. The management algorithms of the two queues can be individual. When forwarding packets, MFLWQ chooses one queue by weighted round robin and send the head packet. So, MFLWQ is composed of three components: BE queue management, SS queue management and scheduling algorithm between the two queues. For that most applied Best-Effort networks are satisfying with common queue management algorithm and the relevant topics are widely discussed, this paper doesn't contain the algorithm used in BE queue. And more, whatever algorithm being used in BE queue doesn't affect the discussions in this paper. In the simulations in paper, a simple Drop-Tail algorithm is used for BE queue.

2.3 Queue Management Algorithm in SS Queue

RED (Random Early Detection)[15] is a widely used active queue management algorithm. It detects congestion by monitoring the average queue size *avg*, which is calculated through a low-pass filter. Average queue size is compared with two thresholds, *maxth* and *minth*, which usually equal to half buffer size and quarter buffer size respectively. When *avg* is less than *minth*, all arriving packets are accepted. And when *avg* is greater than *maxth*, all arriving packets are dropped. When the value of *avg* is between the two thresholds, each arriving packet is dropped by a probability *p*, which is positive proportional with the value *avg* exceeding *minth* and the number of packets accepted after last drop. FRED (Flow Random Early Detection)[16,17]is a modification to RED intending for fairness. The key idea of FRED is that balancing buffered packet number of each flow leads to balanced bandwidth allocation, for that every packet is forwarded from the head of the queue. FRED introduces the parameters *minq* and *maxq*, which are the minimum and maximum number of packets each flow should be allowed to buffer. FRED maintains *nactive*, the number of flows having packets buffered, and the average per-flow buffered packets number *avgcq*. For each buffered flow *I*, FRED maintains the buffered packet number *qlen[I]* and a counter *strike[I]*, which indicates the times the flow has met the condition to be non-adaptive. The expression *qlen[I] >= maxq* ||*(avg >= maxth && qlen[I] > 2*avgcq)* ||*(qlen[I] >= avgcq && strike[I] > 1)* is used to identify and punish non-adaptive flows. FRED adds *strike[I]* with 1 and drops current packet when the judge condition is meet. When flow *I* is identified non-adaptive with *strike[I]>1*, the random drop won't function any more. Regardless of average queue length *avg*, if buffered packet number *qlen[I]* reaches average per-flow buffered packets number *avgcq*, current packet is dropped immediately. And more, the *strike[I]* won't decrease in FRED algorithm until the state table item for flow *I* is deleted when it has no packet buffered in the queue. The detailed FRED pseudo code is presented in [16]. Restricted by volume, only the part relevant to identifying and managing non-adaptive flows is given below:

```
maxq = minth;
if (avg >= maxth)
   maxq = 2;
```
identify and manage non-adaptive flows:
```
if (qlen[I]>=maxq ||(avg>=maxth && qlen[I]>2*avgcq)
||(qlen[I] >= avgcq && strike[I] > 1)) {
  strike[I]++;
  drop packet P;
  return;
}
```

By experiments, we found that the way FRED identifies non-adaptive flows doesn't work well for SS traffic when BE traffic is busy. Because of the extreme congestion and the randomness of packet dropping, an adaptive TCP flow may be identified no-adaptive by mistake. The wrongly identified flow will then experience wrong punishment, until it has no packet in the queue. And more, because of the sudden change of dropping judgment condition before and after misidentify, a number of following packets of this flow may be dropped back to back. This likely leads to TCP timeout and forces the TCP flow into the slow-start phase, congestion window rising from 1 again. Upon that, we modified FRED algorithm and design a mistake correcting mechanism as follows. When the identify condition is meet, *strike* is added with a number N instead of 1. When *strike[I]* reaches M, the flow *I* is identified non-adaptive and is punished. When forwarding a packet of flow *I*, *strike[I]* is decreased by 1 if it isn't zero. So, when the judge expression is true with an adaptive TCP flow, the flow will experience a packet dropping but won't be punished immediately. The adaptive flow will respond to packet dropping and adjust the departure rate. After several packets of this flow are forwarded, *strike* value of this flow will return to 0. So, the mistake is corrected. As for a non-adaptive flow, such as UDP flow, because it doesn't respond to packet dropping, the speed *strike* value increasing by N when the judge expression is true is greater than decreasing by 1 when it's packets are forwarded, it still will be identified non-adaptive. By experiment, we found that when N=5 and M=20, the mechanism works well. We call the modified algorithm MFRED here. The modification to the code is shown as follows:

```
Maxq = minth;
if (avg>= maxth)
  maxq = 2;
identify and manage non-adaptive flows:
if (qlen[I]>=maxq || avg>=maxth && qlen[I]>2*avgcq
||(qlen[I]>=avgcq && strike[I]>20)) {
  strike[I]+=5;
  drop packet P;
  return;
}
Add the following code to the packet departing part:
if (strike[I]>0)
  strike[I]--;
```

2.4 Tuning Guaranteed Bottom Bandwidth for SS Traffic

To adjust the minimum guaranteed capacity for SS flows, the algorithm should first get the number of active SS flows. Generally, a queuing management algorithm that counts active flow number should maintain a flow state table to record the flow id and the arriving time of each packet and calculates the number of flows that have packets arrived recently. This usually makes it impractical by reason of the enormous cost brought by the huge state table when there are many flows. MFRED has maintained a parameter *nactive*, the number of flows having packets buffered, which indicates the number of SS flows without any additional computing. It is obvious that not all active flows have packets buffered at a given time and *nactive* has a theoretical upper limit, which is the size of buffer size. When flow number approaches or exceeds the buffer size, there will be a considerable error between *nactive* and actual SS flow number. But because of the characteristic of logarithmic functions used by MFLWQ, value rising very slowly when the independent variable goes up to a fairish value, the algorithm is insensitive with the error. And for the aim of MFLWQ, a little error of flow number is tolerated. Further more, to avoid impact on BE traffic, it is a reasonable choice that the bandwidth allocation for Scavenger Service not be increased any more when the active SS flow number rises excessively.

Having got the indicator of active flow number, the algorithm would adjust the guaranteed minimum aggregate capacity for SS flows. MFLWQ algorithm keeps the number of slices allocated for SS queue as 1 and reduces the number of whole round robin slices. The proportion between SS flows number growth and SS bandwidth increment is the key of the queuing management algorithm. Increasing excessively will affect BE flows and that increasing too little may plunge the SS flows in risk of starvation. MFLWQ uses logarithmic function $f(x)=log_a(x)$ to fix on the proportion. Its going up curve is appropriate to the peculiarity of Scavenger Service. Natural logarithm based on e, Euler's constant, is used to calculate in this paper.

Supposing $ln(flow\_count) \times tot\_slices = C$, total round robin slices number is

$$tot\_slices = \frac{C}{ln(flow\_count)} \quad (1)$$

In the equation, C is a chosen constant(it can also be translated into the base a, then the numerator is 1). Then, the share of BE flows and SS flows is

$$proportion\_vq\_be = \frac{tot\_slices - 1}{tot\_slices} = \frac{\frac{C}{ln(flow\_count)} - 1}{\frac{C}{ln(flow\_count)}} = 1 - \frac{ln(flow\_count)}{C} \quad (2)$$

$$proportion\_vq\_ss = \frac{1}{tot\_slices} = \frac{ln(flow\_count)}{C} \quad (3)$$

It is distinctly impractical that the routers do complicated logarithmic computing when running. We should calculate the reciprocal of natural logarithms in advance and multiply them by the chosen C to set up a table when algorithm starts. The routers access the table to get *tot_slices* after calculating *nactive* when running. A part of the table is shown as table 1.

The constant C determines the actual proportion of link capacity for Scavenger Service with a given SS flow number and may be chosen according to the application

Table 1. *nactive* and corresponding *total slices* in a cycle

flow_count	tot_slices	SS aggregate bandwidth (%)	SS average per-flow bandwidth (%)
1	100	1.00	1.00
2	66	1.52	0.76
3	42	2.38	0.79
4	33	3.03	0.76
5	28	3.57	0.71
6	26	3.85	0.64
7	24	4.17	0.60
8	22	4.55	0.57
9	21	4.76	0.53
10	20	5.00	0.50
……	……	……	……

circumstance. In this paper, we take $C=45.5$ here to make $tot\_slices=66$, i.e. SS aggregate flow given about 1.5% of whole link capacity when there are two active SS flows. Because $ln(1)=0$, we should deal with the case designedly. Here we make $tot\_slices=100$ when $flow\_count=1$.

MFLWQ uses a slice turn counter deq_turn in dequeuing algorithm. When $deq\_turn=0$, $queue\_SS$ is chosen. It can be seen that MFLWQ allocates network capacity to BE and SS traffic by number of packets instead of actual bandwidth. The actual bandwidth SS traffic attained is relevant to the size of packets and not so fixed. But as for the objective of Scavenger Service, it is more appropriate to give SS flows a bottom packet rate than a bit rate. The dequeuing algorithm is as follows:

```
Upon interface free and queue not empty:
if (deq_turn_>0) {
  if (queue_BE not empty){
    dequeue queue_BE;
    deq_turn++;
    if (deq_turn>=tot_slices){
      deq_turn_ = 0;
      tot_slices=lookup_table(nactive);
    }
  }
  else {
    dequeue queue_SS;
    deq_turn=1;
  }
}
else {
  deq_turn=1;
  if (queue_SS not empty)
    dequeue queue_SS;
  else
    dequeue queue_BE;
}
```

3 Simulations and Analysis

3.1 Tools and Environment

NS Version 2.26[18] was used to do all the simulations below and we realized MFLWQ algorithm by c++. The topology of simulated network is shown as Fig. 1. R1 and R2 are routers connected by a bi-directional link of 10Mbps bandwidth and 6ms latency. The MFLWQ algorithm is implemented in the interfaces of R1 and R2 connecting each other. The buffer for BE and SS flows is 256 packet-size each. Except this link, all other links are 4Mpbs capacity and 3ms latency with common Drop-Tail queue. S1 to Sn are Scavenger Service data sources communicating respectively with DS1 to DSn. B1 to Bm are Best-Effort data sources communicating respectively with DB1 to DBm. In each simulation, the appropriate values of n and m are variously chosen. All communications take FTP as data source and use TCP/Reno protocol with TCP window size of 20 and packet size of 1000bytes.

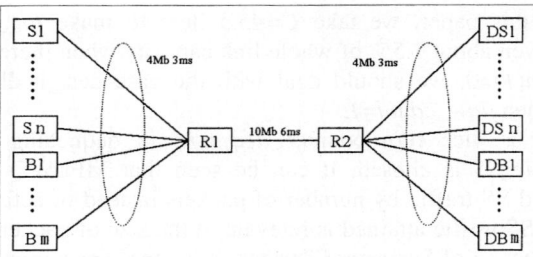

Fig. 1. Network topology

3.2 Realization of Scavenger Service

To validate the realization of Scavenger Service, we take 5 BE sources and 10 SS sources to run the simulation. BE source B1 starts at the beginning. At time of 2.0s, all 10 SS sources start one by one with 2s interval. At 22.0s, the left 3 BE sources start one by one with 4s interval. The simulation ends at 35.0s. In this simulation, we observed the aggregate bandwidth of two kinds of traffic. Simulation result is shown in Fig. 2.

The simulation result shows that SS flows fully utilize the spare network capacity when BE traffic load is light. The increment of SS flows number doesn't prevent the BE flow from reaching its utmost bandwidth. After B2 starts, SS flows begin to give up network capacity voluntarily till they only hold a tiny guaranteed capacity. The start of left BE sources doesn't prevent SS aggregate flow from getting its guaranteed bottom bandwidth. Scavenger Service is realized well.

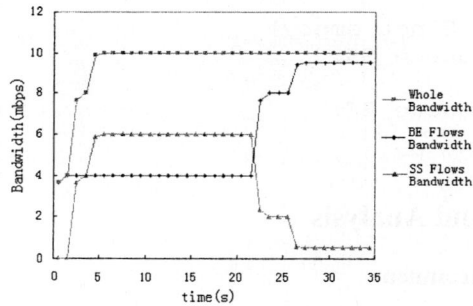

Fig. 2. Realization of Scavenger Service

3.3 Improvement of MFRED Contrasting to FRED

For better observation, the buffer for SS flows is reduced to 128 packet-size here and adaptation of SS bottom bandwidth is canceled. The guaranteed capacity allocated for SS aggregate flow is set to 5% of whole link capacity, i.e. 500 kbps. The simulation uses 5 BE source and 10 SS sources and runs the following scenario: all BE sources start at the beginning; at 1.0s all SS sources start one by one with 1s interval; simulation ends at 30.0s. *Strike* value of all SS flows is recorded each 10 ms. The result of MFRED and FRED is shown in fig. 3 and fig. 4.

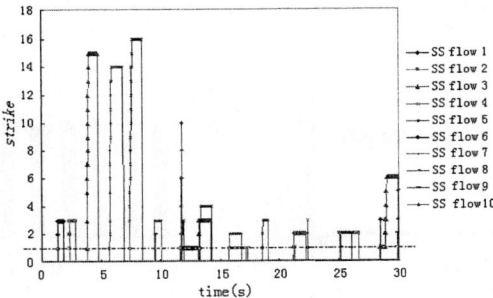

Fig. 3. *Strike* in FRED

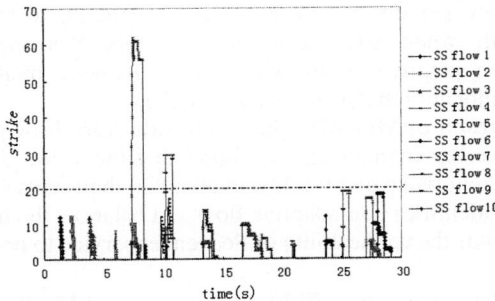

Fig. 4. *Strike* in MFRED

The number of misidentifications (*strike*>1) in fig. 3 adds up to 20 and the duration that each adaptive TCP flow is misidentified non-adaptive adds up to 13.7 seconds. All the right edges of the curves are smooth, meaning that the misidentifications are ended only when the flow has no packet buffered after being wrongly punished. Fig. 4 shows that there are only 2 misidentifications (*strike*>20) when flow number is increasing in the anterior segment of simulation and the duration adds up to only 1.3 seconds. Most right edges of the curves go down point by point, meaning that the possible misidentifications are corrected.

3.4 Balancing SS Flow Bandwidth

Here we take 5 BE sources and 10 SS sources to run the simulation. As an exception, the SS source S10 is a CBR type source with 400kbps rate using UDP protocol. For better observation, the guaranteed minimum bandwidth is also fixed to 5% of whole capacity. In the simulation, all 5 BE sources start at the beginning and all 10 SS sources start in a random order within the first second. To lessen the effect brought by randomness in packet dropping of the algorithms, the simulation is executed 5 times and the result is averaged. We focus on the average bandwidth each SS flow gets in the 100 seconds duration from 1.0s to 101.0s.

Fig. 5 shows the result of RED. The non-adaptive flow 10 seizes most capacity while the other adaptive flows are starved. This means that the bandwidth a

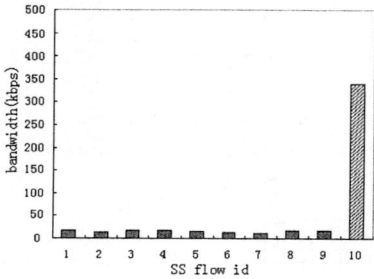
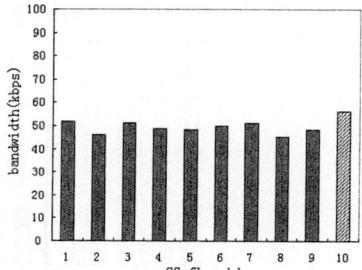

Fig. 5. Bandwidth distribution of RED   **Fig. 6.** Bandwidth distribution of MFRED

non-adaptive SS flow get doesn't decrease corresponding to the reduction of SS aggregate bandwidth when BE traffic is busy. So, Scavenger Service is not compatible with non-adaptive flows when using a queue management algorithm without bandwidth allocation balancing such as RED.

Fig. 6 shows the result of MFRED. The bandwidth every flow get is approximately equivalent. And more, by monitoring, we found that the value of *strike* of the non-adaptive SS flow 10 kept rising and reached to about 20 thousands in the end in all the 5 executions. MFRED identifies non-adaptive flow and balances the bandwidth allocation effectively. This extends the applicability of Scavenger service to no-adaptive flows.

3.5 Relationship Between Active SS Flow Number and Nactive

In this simulation, we focus on the relationship between factual active SS flow number and *nactive* value. We used 10 BE sources and 150 SS sources to run this simulation. The following simulation steps were executed: All 10 BE sources start at the beginning of simulation so as to make SS flows only able to attain the guaranteed bottom bandwidth. After 1s, all the SS sources start one by one with 1s interval. The simulation ends at 155.0s. Result is shown in Fig. 7.

It can be seen that when there are few SS flows, the error between SS flow number and *nactive* is little. *Nactive* indicates the actual flow number well. And the error rises while SS flow number increases. When the value of *nactive* approaches half of average queue size, it goes up very slowly.

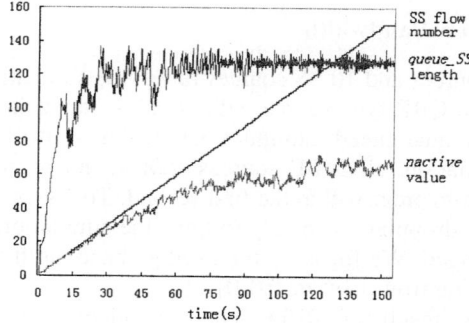

Fig. 7. *Nactive* value and active SS flow number

3.6 Reaction to SS Flows Number when BE Traffic is over Subscribing

Here 10 BE source and 100 SS source are chosen and the scenario is set as follows. All 10 BE sources start at the beginning of simulation. At time of 1.0s, all 100 SS sources start one by one with 1s interval. Simulation runs for 5s more after last SS source S100 starts at 100.0s. We focus on aggregate bandwidth of SS flows in this simulation.

To compare, we first choose a queue management algorithm that configures the SS traffic minimum departure rate in a static way to run the simulation. Fig. 8 is the result of WRR, which is one of the queuing disciplines recommended by Internet2 for Scavenger Service. SS traffic minimum departure rate is set to 5% of link capacity, i.e. 500Kpbs. For easy observation, the y-axis of the SS flow bandwidth curve is blown-up. It can be seen that as the active SS flows number rises from 1 to 100, the SS aggregate bandwidth remains constant.

The result of MFLWQ in Fig. 9 shows that the aggregate bandwidth attained by SS traffic went up approximately as a logarithmic curve. This meets the design aim. Compared with WRR in Fig. 8, MFLWQ adapts the aggregate minimum bandwidth of SS traffic to the number of active SS flows. When there are few SS flows, it allocates less guaranteed bandwidth to SS traffic in order to give the capacity to BE traffic at best. This will make BE flows perform better. When the number of active SS flows increases, it allocates more bandwidth to SS traffic in order to turn SS flows away from starvation. This gives SS flows more robustness.

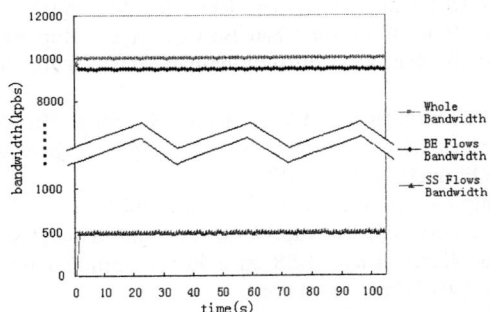

Fig. 8. Reaction of WRR

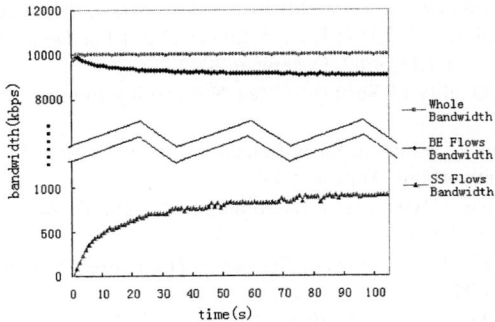

Fig. 9. Reaction of MFLWQ

4 Conclusions

This paper presents a MFLWQ Algorithm for Scavenger Service. The algorithm balances the bandwidth distribution among Scavenger Service flows by modified FRED. It estimates active Scavenger Service flow number by the variable *nactive* in FRED and accordingly tunes the bandwidth allocation between SS flows and BE flows in a logarithmical way to reach better performance and robustness. Simulations show that it provides more appropriate bottom bandwidth guarantee for Scavenger Service flows when protecting Best-Effort flows well and it extends the applicability of Scavenger service to no-adaptive traffic like UDP.

References

1. BRADEN R, CLARK D, SHENKER S. Integrated Services in the Internet Architecture: an Overview. RFC1633, June 1994.
2. BLAKE S, BLACK D, CARLSON M, et al. An Architecture for Differentiated Service. RFC2475, December 1998.
3. WROCLAWSKI J. The Use of RSVP with IETF Integrated Services. RFC 2210, September 1997.
4. LE FAUCHEUR F, WU L, DAVIE B, DAVARI S, et al. Multi-Protocol Label Switching (MPLS) Support of Differentiated Services. RFC3270, May 2002.
5. BLESS R, WEHRLE K. A Lower Than Best-Effort Per-Hop Behavior. http://quimby.gnus.org/internet-drafts/draft-bless-diffserv-lbe-phb-00.txt. Work in Progress, September 1999.
6. CAREPENTER B, NEICHOLS K. A Bulk Handling Per-Domain Behavior for Differentiated Services. http://www.ietf.org/proceedings/01aug/I-D/draft-ietf-diffserv-pdb-bh-02.txt. Work in Progress, January 2001.
7. Internet2-Home. http://www.internet2.edu/. January, 2001
8. QBone Scavenger Service (QBSS). http://QBone.internet2.edu/qbss/.
9. Stanislav Shalunov. Configuring QBSS on a Juniper. http://archives.internet2.edu/guest/archives/i2ss-dt/log200105/msg00024.html.
10. SLAC QBSS Testbed. http://www-iepm.slac.stanford.edu/monitoring/qbss/qbss.html.
11. Juniper QBSS experiment. http://www.transpac.org/qbss-html/.
12. SHALUNOV S. Testing QBSS config at Advanced.org:Good. http://archives.internet2.edu/guest/archives/i2ss-dt/log200105/msg00000.html
13. BLESS R, NICHOLS K, WEHRLE K. A Lower Effort Per-Domain Behavior (PDB) for Differentiated Services. RFC3662, December 2003.
14. VEGESNA S. IP Quality of Service (Cisco Networking Fundamentals). Cisco Press. 23 January, 2001
15. Floyd, S., Jacobson V. "Random Early Detection for Congestion Avoidance". IEEE/ACM Transactions on Networking. August 1993
16. D. Lin and R. Morris, "Dynamics of random early detection". ACM SIGCOMM, Cannes, France, Oct. 1997, 127-137.
17. H.J. Chao, Xiao-lei GUO, Quality of Service in High-speed Network. Beijing: Tsinghua University Press, 2004.
18. The Network Simulator - ns-2. http://www.isi.edu/nsnam/ns/index.html.

CBTM: A Trust Model with Uncertainty Quantification and Reasoning for Pervasive Computing

Rui He, Jianwei Niu, and Guangwei Zhang

Beijing University of Aeronautics and Astronautics,
Xueyuan Road 37, Beijing, China, 100083
{harry.he, niujianwei}@buaa.edu.cn, ezhang@263.net

Abstract. This paper presents a novel trust model in which we model trust based on an exotic uncertainty theory, namely cloud model. We regard trust between entities as a cloud that is called as trust cloud. Based on such a quantification model of trust, we further propose the algorithms to compute propagated trust relationships and aggregated trust relationships, which are needed for trust reasoning in pervasive computing environments. Finally, we compare the proposed trust model with other three typical models in simulation experiments, and the results shows the cloud-based trust model performs better in a total sense.

1 Introduction

Trust has been researched for more than teen years since Marsh's work [1]. Because trust mechanism is more flexible and extensible than traditional security approaches such as PKI[20], trust has been introduced into many other cyber fields, i.e. pervasive computing, peer-to-peer networks, etc. In such contexts, trust is always regarded as subjective, therefore, how to measure trust become very important. Till now many approaches have been proposed to quantify trust [1,2,3], which either use discrete numbers such as *-1, 0, 1*, etc. to indicate different trust levels, or use a real number interval, for instance *[0, 1]*. However, since trust is subjective, it is not enough to describe trust with deterministic values.

As we know, in human society, when we say we trust a person *very much*, actually we are not so sure about to what an accurate degree to trust him or her. On the other hand, we can trust two persons both *very much,* but we may trust one a little more than the other. The same can be applied to pervasive computing environments. Hence we declare that uncertainty is an important nature of trust, which means trust relationships between entities are fuzzy and stochastic. For example, for two completely unacquainted entities, they may trust each other to *a little* degree, so that they can begin to cooperate in a task. Meanwhile, two familiar entities can also trust one another to *a little* degree, which may result from their bad interaction history. From these two cases, we can see that, regarding the same trust description, say trust *a little*, the former is absolutely uncertain but the latter is quite assure. Therefore, we must incorporate uncertainty when modeling trust.

In this paper, we propose such an trust model, namely the cloud based trust model or CBTM. We will present an overview of the cloud model in section 2. And in section 3 we will delineate the cloud based trust model in detail. Then simulation experiments will be presented in section 4. Related work will be listed in section 5. Finally, we will summarize our work and point out our future work in section 6.

2 Cloud Theory Overview

The cloud model was firstly proposed as a model of the uncertainty transition between a linguistic term of a qualitative concept and its numerical representation [9]. Till now, the cloud model has been applied in many fields successfully, such as automatic control [11], knowledge discovery and data mining [10,12], etc

Formally, a cloud can be defined as follows [22].

DEFINITION 1: Let U be the set as the universe of discourse, f is a random function with a stable tendency $f : U \rightarrow [0,1]$, and g is also a random function with a stable tendency $g : U \rightarrow U$, He is an uncertain factor and $0 \leq He$, and

1) $u' = g(u, He), u \in U$.
2) $y = f(u', He)$.

Then (U, g, f, He) is a cloud, and (u', y) is a cloud drop.

In DEFINITION 1, the mapping f from U to the interval [0,1] is a one-point to multi-point transition, so the degree of membership of u is a probability distribution rather than a fixed value, which is the very place where the cloud theory is different from the fuzzy logic. For example, a one-dimension normal cloud can be formalized as follows.

$$\begin{aligned} nc &= (\mathbf{R}, g, f, He) \\ g &= \text{randn}(Ex, \text{randn}(d, He)) \\ x' &= g(x, He) \\ f &= e^{-\frac{(x'-Ex)^2}{2 \times \text{randn}(d, He)^2}} \end{aligned} \quad (1)$$

where $d, x \in \mathbf{R}$ (**R** is the set of real numbers) and randn(a, b) is a normally distributed random number generation function with a as the mean and b as the standard deviation.

For the purpose of simpliness, normal clouds defined by Formula (1) can be denoted by three digital characteristics [9], namely Expected Value (*Ex*), Entropy (*En*) and Hyper-Entropy (*He*). With these digital characteristics, the fuzziness and randomness of uncertain concepts can be integrated in a unified way. The expected value *Ex* points out the center of gravity of a normal cloud. The entropy *En* is a measure of the fuzziness of the concept over the universe of discourse. It shows the span of cloud drops distribution. The hyper entropy *He* is a measure of the uncertainty of the entropy *En*. And the greater *He* is, the more dispersedly the membership degrees are distributed. In the extreme case, both entropy *En* and hyper entropy *He* is equal to zero, namely (*Ex*, 0, 0), which presents the concept of a deterministic datum.

It is easy to see that the *He* in Formula (1) is the same as the *He* in DEFINITION 1. Furthermore, based on the normal cloud definition, and given three digital characteristics, say *Ex*, *En*, *He*, we can build a normal cloud with the so-called normal cloud generator, which is described by the following algorithm [9].

ALGORITHM 1: Given a normal cloud (*Ex, En, He*) and the number of the cloud drops *N*, a normal cloud can be computed following steps as follows.

1) Produce a normally distributed random number *En'* with the mean *En* and the standard deviation *He*;
2) Produce a normally distributed random number *x* with the mean *Ex* and the standard deviation *En'*;
3) Calculate $y = e^{-\frac{(x-Ex)^2}{2(En')^2}}$;
4) Point (*x, y*) is a cloud drop in the universe of discourse;
5) Repeat steps 1-4 until *N* cloud drops are generated.

Fig. 1 illustrates the normal cloud description of the term "10 miles around".

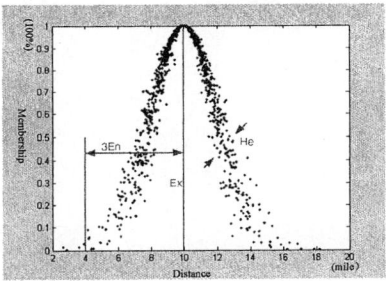

Fig. 1. Cloud shape and three digital characteristics of the linguistic term "10 miles around"

3 Cloud-Based Trust Model

Based on the cloud model, we research on uncertainty of trust and propose a novel cloud based trust model or CBTM, which will be described in this section in detail.

3.1 Trust Cloud

The trust cloud is the core concept of CBTM, which is defined as follows.

DEFINITION 2: A trust cloud is a normal cloud to quantify a trust relationship between two entities, indicating how much and how surely one is trusted by the other. Formally, the trust cloud held by an entity, i.e. *A*, about the other entity, i.e. *B*, can be denoted as:

$$tc_{AB} = nc(Ex, En, He)$$
$$0 \leq Ex \leq 1$$
$$0 \leq En \leq 1 \quad (2)$$
$$0 \leq He \leq 1$$

where $nc(Ex, En, He)$ is a normal cloud defined by Formula (1), and Ex is the trust expected value here, which indicates the basic trust degree of B for A. En reflects the uncertainty of the trust relationship. It also describes the scope of cloud drops which can be accepted by A, namely the fuzziness degree. And En shows the stochastic density of the cloud drops in the trust space, namely the randomness of the trust relationship. He is the trust hyper entropy here, which indicates the uncertainty of fuzziness degree of the trust relationship.

It should be pointed out that, when $En \neq 0$ and $He = 0$, the trust relationship of entity A to entity B is fuzzy, but the fuzziness degree is deterministic; and when $En = 0$ and $He = 0$, the trust relationship of entity A to entity B is deterministic and there is no uncertainty in the trust. For example, the entities belonging to an internal system or the same administrative domain could have deterministic trust relationships.

Fig. 2 illustrates some typical trust clouds.

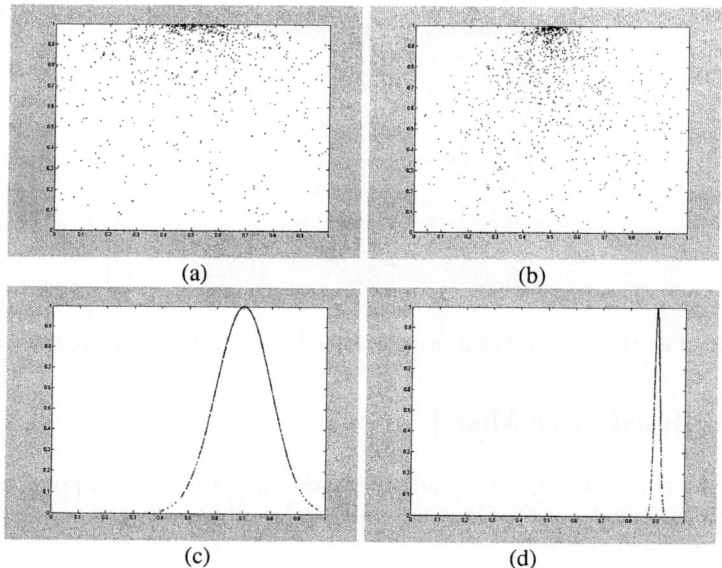

Fig. 2. Typical trust clouds. (a) tc (0.5, 0.1, 0.6). (b) tc (0.5,0.1,0.2). (c) tc (0.7,0.1,0). (d) tc(0.9,0.01,0).

From Fig.2 we can deduce that: (1) The greater Ex is, the closer a trust cloud approaches to the max trust value, namely 1; (2) The greater En is, the wider the span of a trust cloud is; (3) The greater He is the more dispersive the cloud drops of a trust cloud are.

3.2 Distrust and No trust

In trust modeling, distrust and no trust have different meanings. If entity A distrusts entity B, it means A knows B can not be trusted. On the contrary, if entity A has no trust about entity B, it means A does not know whether or how much B should be trusted. Traditionally, different values are used to distinguish distrust and no trust. For example, -1 indicates no trust, and 0 indicates distrust [13]. However, we declare that distrust and no trust are two different concepts describing trust from different viewpoints, namely trustworthiness viewpoint and uncertainty viewpoint. Therefore, more should be done rather than just assigning different values to them.

From the standpoint of the cloud model, distrust is used to describe trust relationships from the aspect of trustworthiness degree, and we can denote distrust with $Ex = 0$. And no trust is a concept describing trust relationships from the aspect of uncertainty of trust, and it can be indicated by setting $En = 1$ and $He = 1$. Therefore, we can see that distrust and no trust are two intercrossed concepts and in some cases both of them can even co-exist in one trust relationship. For example, entity A meets a stranger entity B, and then the trust relationship A established to B should be no trust. At the same time, A may also label the trust degree as distrust, because A is very cautious. On the contrary, if A is adventurous, A may set an average trust degree to the no trust relationship. In a word, distrust and no trust are not exclusive. This distinguishes CBTM from all other trust models.

Fig. 3 shows some examples of distrust clouds and no trust clouds.

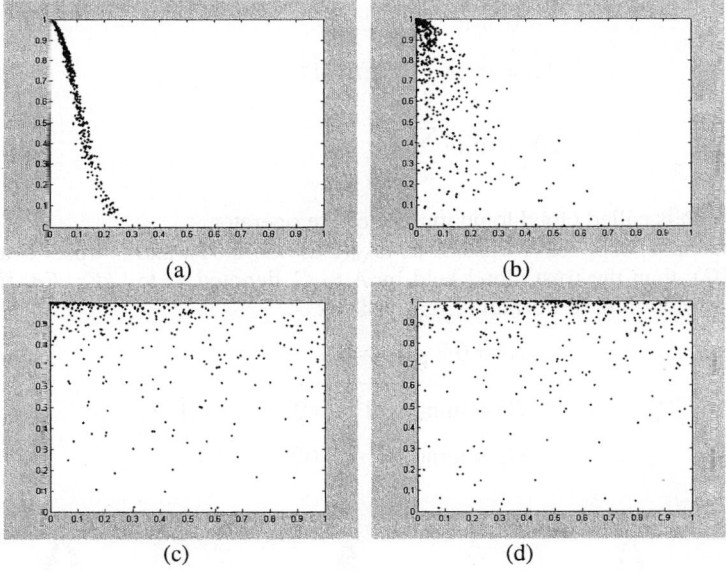

Fig. 3. Distrust and unknown trust clouds. (a) distrust cloud tc(0,0.1,0.01). (b) distrust cloud tc(0,0.1,0.1). (c) no trust and distrust cloud tc(0,1,1). (d) no trust cloud tc(0.5,1,1).

3.3 Trust Reasoning

In pervasive computing environments, unknown entities are always met. Before these strangers cooperate with each other, their trustworthiness should be determined. However, as strangers, their trust degrees can not be known by one another at present.

Therefore, it is necessary for any entity to derive a trust relationship to the stranger based on exiting trust relationships. Therefore algorithms of computing trust clouds are needed for trust reasoning.

In CBTM, trust cloud computation consists of two parts, namely computing a new trust cloud through trust propagation and combining many trust clouds into one unique trust cloud.

Propagating Trust Clouds

In pervasive computing environments, e.g. ad-hoc networks, entities always can not get trust recommendation of a stranger from their trusted neighbors directly, so trust cloud propagation is needed.

Supposing there are m entities, say $A_1, A_2, A_3, ..., A_m$, and the trust cloud from A_i to A_{i+1} ($1 \leq i \leq m-1$) is $tc_i(Ex_i, En_i, He_i)$, then the trust cloud of A_1 about A_m, denoted as $tc(Ex, En, He)$, can be computed as follows.

$$tc(Ex, En, He) = tc_1 \otimes tc_2 \otimes ... \otimes tc_m = \prod_{i=1}^{m} tc_i(Ex_i, En_i, He_i)$$

$$Ex = \prod_{i=1}^{m} Ex_i$$

$$En = \min(\sqrt{\sum_{i=1}^{m} En_i^2}, 1) \quad (3)$$

$$He = \min(\sum_{i=1}^{m} He_i, 1)$$

Where $\otimes$ is called cloud logic multiplicative operator.

For instance, suppose A trusts B as $tc_{AB}(0.8, 0.1, 0.01)$, and B trusts C as $tc_{BC}(0.5, 0.05, 0.02)$, then the trust cloud held by A to C, denoted as $tc_{AC}(Ex, En, He)$, can be computed according to Formula (3) as follows.

$$Ex = 0.8 \times 0.5 = 0.4$$

$$En = \min(\sqrt{0.1^2 + 0.05^2}, 1) \approx 0.112 .$$

$$He = \min(0.01 + 0.02, 1) = 0.03$$

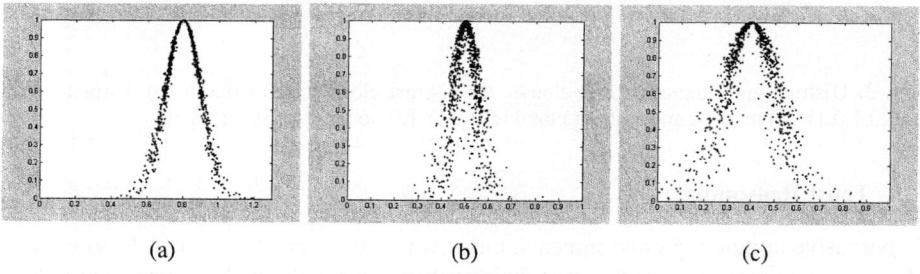

(a)   (b)   (c)

Fig. 4. Propagating trust cloud. (a) $tc_{AB}(0.8, 0.1, 0.01)$. (b) $tc_{BC}(0.5, 0.05, 0.02)$. (c) tc_{AC} (0.4, 0.112, 0.03).

We illustrate these three trust clouds in Fig. 4, from which it is easy to see that after propagation, the trust cloud becomes more dispersive and closer to 0. This means the trust degree is decreased and the uncertainty is increased. This accords with human experience

Aggregating Trust Clouds
In many cases, more than one trust clouds of a stranger entity can be computed, therefore, it is necessary for an entity to combine these trust clouds into a unique one.

Supposing there are m trust clouds, say tc_1, tc_2, tc_3, ..., tc_m, then these trust clouds can be combined into one trust cloud, say $tc(Ex, En, He)$, as follows.

$$tc(Ex, En, He) = tc_1 \oplus tc_2 \oplus ... \oplus tc_m = \sum_{i=1}^{m} nc_i(Ex_i, En_i, He_i)$$

$$Ex = \frac{1}{m} \sum_{i=1}^{m} Ex_i$$

$$En = \min(\frac{1}{m} \sum_{i=1}^{m} En_i, 1) \quad (4)$$

$$He = \min(\frac{1}{m} \sum_{i=1}^{m} He_i, 1)$$

Where $\oplus$ is the cloud logic additive operator.

For example, entity A gets two propagated trust clouds, i.e. $tc_1(0.4, 0.112, 0.03)$ and $tc_2(0.72, 0.2, 0.05)$, then the aggregated trust cloud $tc(Ex, En, He)$ can be computed according to Formula (4) like this.

$$Ex = (0.4 + 0.72)/2 = 0.56$$

$$En = \min((0.112 + 0.2)/2, 1) = 0.156$$

$$He = \min((0.03 + 0.05)/2, 1) = 0.04$$

These three trust clouds are illustrated in Fig.5, from which we can see the combined trust cloud is between the two operand trust clouds from both aspect of trust level and uncertainty. This also accords with our intuition.

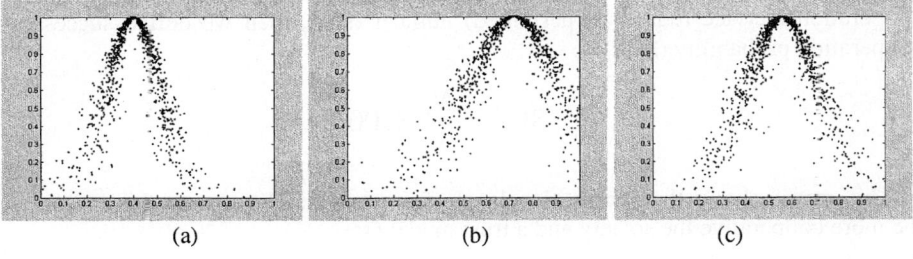

Fig. 5. Aggregated trust clouds. (a)$tc_1(0.4, 0.112, 0.03)$ (b)$tc_2(0.72, 0.2, 0.05)$ (c)tc (0.56, 0.156, 0.04).

4 Simulation Experiment

Since using cloud to model trust is absolutely exotic, it is necessary for us to prove the validation of CBTM in experiments. Therefore, we carried out a simulation experiment.

Our experiment is based upon a simulation platform RePast[19], which is popular in simulating agent-based systems. Over RePast, we developed CBTM. As comparison, we also implemented other three trust models, which are based on Depster-Shafer theory, probability theory, and Fuzzy logic respectively. These trust models are:

- Yu Trust Model (abbreviated as Y Model) [18]
- Beth Trust Model (abbreviated as B Model) [2]
- Tang Trust Model (abbreviated as T Model) [21]

In the experiment, our proposed trust model is abbreviated as C Model.

4.1 Metrics

To compare selected trust models quantitatively, we define some metrics first.

DEFINITION 3: Suppose $\mathbf{E} = \{A_i \mid 1 \leq i \leq N\}$ are the set of entities in a pervasive environment, and $\mathbf{Tr} = \{(A_i, A_j, tval_{ij}) \mid A_i, A_j \in \mathbf{E}, 0 \leq tval_{ij} \leq 1\}$ is the set of trust relationships between these entities, then we define average trust density (ATD) as

$$\mathrm{ATD} = \frac{\sum_{tval_{ij} \in \mathbf{Tr}} tval_{ij}}{\mathrm{P}_N^2} = \frac{\sum_{tval_{ij} \in \mathbf{Tr}} tval_{ij}}{N \times (N-1)}. \tag{5}$$

This metric represents the overall trust level of a network. If the ATD of a network is too low, it means the society formed by the network is fragile and it is easy to collapse. At the same time, the faster the ATD curve become horizontal, the better a trust model's convergence is.

DEFINITION 4: Suppose the total interaction (from service request to its being permitted or denied) number between entities in the network is N_t, and total successful cooperation (service request is permitted) number is N_s, then we define successful cooperation probability (SCP) as

$$\mathrm{SCP} = \frac{N_s}{N_t} \times 100\%. \tag{6}$$

This metric shows the cooperation level of a network. The greater this metric is, the more cooperative the society and a trust model are.

DEFINITION 5: Suppose the time an entity receives a request is t, and the time a trust model finishes evaluating the requester entity's trust is t', and the total number of interaction in the network is N, then we define average response delay (ARD) as

$$\text{ARD} = \frac{\sum_{i=1}^{N}(t_i - t_i')}{N} \tag{7}$$

This metric shows the complexity of a trust model. Since our simulation does not consider physical network delay, the delay time is due to trust model computation. So the bigger ARD is the more complex a trust model is. And the less complex a trust model is, the better it is.

4.2 Simulation Parameter Setting

In the experiment, we created a network with specific number of entities and the entities in it are reachable for one another. During initialization, each entity was assigned randomly the specific number of acquaintances, and the trust relationships between them were initialized randomly.

During the experiment, entities interacted with each other for specific times. In each interaction, the simulation system chose two entities randomly, and the first was requester and the other was server. The server computed the requester's trustworthiness using a trust model, and decided whether the request would be accepted not by comparing the evaluation result with the predefined cooperation threshold value. In each interaction, every trust model was used and concerned data were recorded.

The simulation system parameter setting is described in Table 1.

Table 1. Simulation system parameter setting

Parameter	Value
Initial Acquaintance.	5
Entity Number	100
Interaction Number	25×2500
Threshold Value	0.5

4.3 Experiment Results

The experiment results are illustrated in Fig. 9.

From Fig.9 (a), we can see that the proposed C model and Y model's NTD are very close and much higher than both B model and T model. But C model becomes convergent faster than Y model.

From Fig.9 (b), we can observe that our proposed C model has a much far better performance than all the other models in terms of successful cooperation probability. This indicates CBTM will provide entities more chances to cooperate with each other.

From Fig.9 (c), we can see that the ARD of C model is much lower than the other models, which indicates CBTM is much easier and will consume less CPU time.

Based on all the experiment results, we can tell that CBTM performs quite well in terms of convergence, cooperation, and complexity.

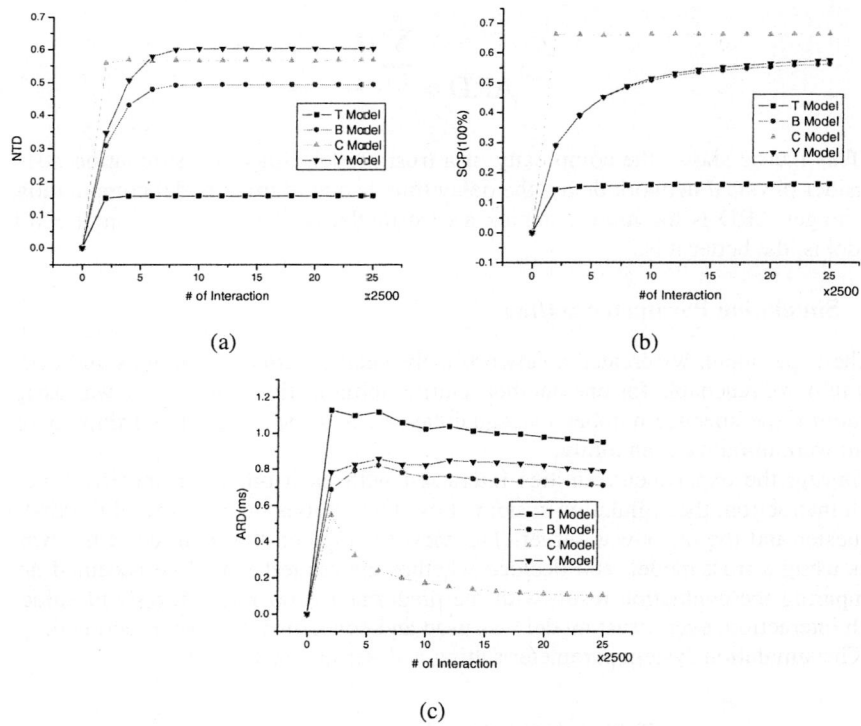

Fig. 9. Experiment results. (a) NTD (b) SCP (c) ARD.

5 Related Work

In the computer science literature, Marsh is among the first to study trust. In [1], he provided a clarification of trust and presented an implementable formalism for trust, and he applied his trust model in the distributed artificial intelligence (DAI) community to enable the agent to make trust-based decisions. Since his model attempted to integrate all the aspects of trust taken from sociology and psychology, it is rather complex.

At almost the same time, Beth et al. [2] also proposed a trust model for distributed networks. They considered trust in different classes, which are Per Se different functionalities in authentication protocols. Furthermore, they distinguished recommendation trust from direct trust and gave their formal representations, as well as rules to derive trust relationships and algorithms to compute trust values.

Another important trust model is proposed by Abdul-Rahman et al. [13]. They tried to give a model of generalized trust to be suited to trust relationships that are less formal, temporary or short-term. For this purpose, they classified trust relationships into two types, namely direct trust relationship and recommender trust relationship, which is quite different from recommendation trust in the model of Beth described above. Besides, they proposed a recommendation distribution protocol, as well as an algorithm to compute trust value of target for a single recommendation path.

Following these basic work, a lot of trust models [4, 5, 16, 6, 15, 14,17] were proposed to various systems, including multi-agent systems, peer-to-peer networks, as well as pervasive computing. Unfortunately, these models do not consider uncertainty of trust at all. C. Castelfranchi et al [7], H. Zhuang et al [8], and Tang [22] did consider uncertainty, more accurately, fuzziness, and they used fuzzy logic to deal with trust related problems. It is their work to inspire us to research the uncertainty of trust deeply.

6 Conclusion and Future Work

In this paper, we propose a novel trust model, namely the cloud based trust model or CBTM. Distinguished from previous trust models, CBTM takes uncertain of trust into account and describes the trust degree and trust uncertainty in a uniform form, namely cloud. In CBTM, we give the cloud description of trust as well as algorithms to compute propagated trust values and aggregated trust values. And our simulation experiment demonstrates the better performance of CBTM preliminarily.

As for our future work, we will continue to perfect CBTM. We will incorporate other factors into current model, such as risk, reputation, etc. In other words, we will work on a more complex model, which will be more practical to deal with trust issues in pervasive computing. Besides, we will consider cheating or vicious behaviors in pervasive computing environments and methods will be researched to detect such behaviors, and further reduce or even prevent them.

References

[1] S. P. Marsh. Formalising Trust as a Computational Concept. Ph.D. Thesis, University of Stirling, 1994.
[2] T. Beth, M. Borcherding, and B. Klein. Valuation of trust in open networks. In ESORICS 94. Brighton, UK, November 1994
[4] Bin Yu, Munindar P. Singh, An Evidential Model of Distributed Reputation Management, Proceedings of First International Joint Conference on Autonomous Agents sand Multi-Agent Systems, pages 294-301, 2002
[5] K. Aberer, Z. Despotovic. Managing Trust in a Peer-2-Peer Information System. In Proceedings of the 10th International Conference on Information and Knowledge Management (ACM CIKM), New York, USA, 2001.
[6] Huafei Zhu, Bao Feng, Robert H. Deng. Computing of Trust in Distributed Networks. http://venona.antioffline.com/2003/056.pdf
[7] Cristiano Castelfranchi, Rino Falcone, Giovanni Pezzulo. "Trust in Information Sources as a Source for Trust: A Fuzzy Approach". In Proceedings of the second international joint conference on Autonomous agents and multiagent systems, July 14-18, 2003. pp. 89-96
[8] Hanqi Zhuang, Songwut Wongsoontorn, Yuanhui Zhao. A Fuzzy-Logic Based Trust Model and its Optimization for e-Commerce. F Florida Conference on the Recent Advances in Robotics (FCRAR 2003).
[9] Deyi LI, Haijun MENG, Xuemei SHI. Membership clouds and membership clouds generator. Journal of Computer Research and Development, 42(8): 32-41, 1995.

[10] Deren Li, Shuliang Wang, Wenzhong Shi, Xinzhou Wang, 2001, On spatial data mining and knowledge discovery (SDMKD), Geomatics and Information Science of Wuhan University, 26(6):491-499
[11] Deyi Li. The Cloud Control Method and Balancing Patterns of Triple Link Inverted Pendulum Systems. Chinese Engineering Science. Vol 1, No 2, p41-46, Nov 1999.
[12] Deyi Li. Uncertaintyin Knowledge Representation. Chinese Engineering Science. Vol 2, No 10, p73-79, Oct 2000.
[13] A. Abdul-Rahman and S. Hailes. A Distributed Trust Model. New Security Paradigms Workshop 1997, ACM, 1997.
[14] Brian Shand, et al. Trust for Ubiquitous, Transparent Collaboration. IEEE Pervasive Computing and Communication 2003.
[15] L. Mui, M. Mohtashemi, A. Halberstadt. "A Computational Model of Trust and Reputation," 35th Hawaii International Conference on System Science (HICSS), 2002.
[16] R. Chen and W. Yeager, "Poblano: A Distributed Trust Model for Peer-to-Peer Networks", Sun Microsystems Technical Paper, 2000, http://www.sun.com/software/jxta/poblano.pdf
[17] M. Carbone, M. Nielsen and V. Sassone. A Formal Model for Trust in Dynamic Networks. Proceedings of IEEE International Conference on Software Engineering and Formal Methods (SEFM '03), 2003.
[18] Bin Yu, Munindar P. Singh, An Evidential Model of Distributed Reputation Management, Proceedings of First International Joint Conference on Autonomous Entities and Multi-Entity Systems, pages 294-301, 2002
[19] RePast WebSite: http://repast.sourceforge.net/
[20] IETF PKIX Working Group. http://www.ietf.org/html.charters/pkix-charter.html
[21] Wen Tang. The Research on Fuzzy Set Theory Based Trust Management. Beijing University. PhD Thesis. 2003.
[22] Deyi Li, Kaichang Di, Deren Li, and Xuemei Shi, Mining Association Rules with Linguistic Cloud Models, Proceedings of PAKDD98, Australia, 15-17 April, 1998, Springer-Verlag Heidelberg, P392-394.

An Authentication Protocol for Pervasive Computing*

Shiqun Li[1,2], Jianying Zhou[2], Xiangxue Li[1], and Kefei Chen[1]

[1] Department of Computer Science and Engineering,
Shanghai Jiao Tong University, Shanghai 200030, China
{sqli, xxli, chen-kf}@cs.sjtu.edu.cn
[2] Institute for Infocomm Research, 21 Heng Mui Keng Terrace, Singapore 119613
{stusqli, jyzhou}@i2r.a-star.edu.sg

Abstract. Authentication protocols are essential for security in many systems. However, authentication protocols are error-prone and difficult to design. In pervasive computing, the inherent characteristics such as mobility and restricted resources make it even harder to design suitable authentication protocols. In this paper we propose an authentication protocol to solve an open problem in pervasive computing, that is secure use of public information utilities without accessing a *trusted third party* (TTP). Our solution not only provides authentication, but also establishes a secure communication channel between the user and the service provider without the participation of TTP. The authentication protocol can be built with any secure symmetric and asymmetric cryptographic algorithm. We show the protocol can resist passive and active attacks. We also discuss how the protocol can be extended to an applicable scheme with payment support.

Keywords: Authentication, Pervasive Computing Security, Public Key Infrastructure, E-Commerce.

1 Introduction

Authentication protocols are essential for security in many systems. However, authentication protocols are error-prone and difficult to design in many settings. There are a lot of published protocols with flaws that have later been found in literatures [1, 2, 4].

In pervasive computing environments, devices and applications are as mobile as the users. Thus, the pervasive computing devices would often work in an unknown and untrusted environment which makes authentication more important and necessary. However, in the pervasive world devices and applications are constrained by many factors such as limited computation and communication

---

* This work is partially supported under NSFC 60273049, 60303026 and 60473020. The first author's work is done during his attachment to Institute for Infocomm Research under its sponsorship.

capability as well as resource restrictions. These limitations make it even harder to design suitable protocols [7, 16].

With the development and deployment of pervasive services, payment becomes an important component. But payment protocols are overlooked in many pervasive applications. In literatures, there are a number of proposed payment protocols for electronic commerce such as Millicent [13], CyberCash [9], First Virtual [11], DigiCash [10], and NetBill [8]. But due to lack of supporting infrastructure, those payment protocols are not deployed in reality.

1.1 Background and Motivation

In pervasive computing environment, communication and computation devices pervade all our surroundings, and the facilities provided by pervasive computing technology can be accessed and used easily and efficiently. But the convenience also brings security risks.

Fig. 1. A scenario of use of public printers

Let us consider an example introduced by Creese et al. [7] for using public information utilities as illustrated in Fig. 1. A user at an airport wants to print out confidential data in his PDA. There are a number of printers for him to use. The security requirement here is the data on the PDA should go to the specific printer chosen by the user and be printed out without leaking any confidential information to others. To satisfy the security requirement, the following constraints should be considered:

(1) *No pre-existent shared secret:* The user and the printer are definitely strangers to each other. There is no shared key between them.
(2) *Resource restraints:* The user may have no access to the Internet, so a *trusted third party* is not accessible in this scenario. Further, updating *certificate revocation list* (CRL) of a traditional *public key infrastructure* (PKI) is not applicable. Furthermore, the PDA probably has limited resource to store the certificate revocation list.

In [6], Balfanz et al. proposed a solution to the above problem. Their proposal for securing the PDA-to-printer wireless link uses a location-limited channel introduced by Stajano and Anderson [18]. In their solution, the location-limited channel requires the user to touch the objective printer with the PDA for pre-authentication. The secure wireless link is then created via the pre-authentication. The solution does not use any pre-existent authentication mechanisms. However, there is no entity authentication for the establishment of the secure channel. But we argue that security is limited without entity authentication. What if the printer is a fraudulent one?

The traditional PKI and certificate-based scheme may be a good solution for entity authentication. But it is not suitable to solve the above problem because the pervasive computing device is resource constrained - it may have no access to a TTP like a *certification authority* (CA). Without accessing the CA, it is difficult to check the status and validity of a certificate. Whereas in [6], Creese et al. suggested that verifying the location of the printer using GPS can be a characteristic for authentication. But the assumption of a secure GPS is too strong and is not easy to implement and access.

To the best of our knowledge, the secure use of public information utilities is still an open problem in the security of pervasive computing till now.

1.2 Our Contributions

The main contribution of the paper is to provide a suitable authentication protocol to solve the open problem of using public information facilities in pervasive computing. Our solution not only provides authentication, but also establishes a secure communication channel between the parties without accessing any TTP. By introducing a new PKI and a new signature scheme, we do not have to rely on the assumption of a secure GPS service. The authentication protocol can be built with any secure symmetric and asymmetric cryptographic algorithms and it can resist passive and active attacks provided the symmetric and asymmetric cryptographic algorithms are secure. Finally, we extend our authentication protocol to a more applicable scheme with payment support.

The remainder of the paper is organized as follows. The design goals and preliminaries for authentication protocol are described in Section 2. In Section 3, a concrete authentication protocol is proposed, and its security is analyzed informally. A payment protocol based on Millicent is also introduced in Section 3. Finally, conclusions are given in Section 4.

2 Design Goals and Preliminaries

2.1 Design Goals

For use of public utilities in pervasive computing environment, a good authentication protocol should provide the following necessary properties:

(1) *Entity Authentication*: The user should ensure which utility is exactly the one s/he interacts with, even without accessing an on-line TTP. In this scenario, we only consider the authentication of the printer to the user.

(2) *Data Confidentiality*: The user should make sure that the document s/he wants to print is encrypted in transmission. Neither passive attackers nor active attackers can reveal the contents.

In the considered scenario, we assume the authenticated service provider is trusted not to leave a copy of the document. This assumption is not very strong because the service provider will be responsible for the service it provides.

2.2 Notations

The following notations are used in the rest of this paper:

S:	Name of the public information utility service provider (e.g., name of an airport printer)
U:	Name of the user
PK_S:	The public key of S
SK_S:	The private key of S corresponding to PK_S
$Cert(S)$:	The certificate of S
K:	The symmetric session key between S and U
R_S, R_U:	Random numbers generated by S and U, respectively
$\{M\}_K$:	The symmetric encryption of M with session key K
$\{M\}_{PK_S}$:	The asymmetric encryption of M with public key PK_S
$H^i(r)$:	Recursive hash operation of the input r, i.e., $H^i(r) = H(H^{i-1}(r))$
D:	Starting valid date of a certificate
T:	Maximum lifetime of a certificate
L:	Time period for refreshing validity of a certificate
$SIGN_{CA}(M)$:	CA's signature on M
D_v:	Date for validating a certificate
j:	An integer, $j = T/L$

2.3 A New PKI

As mentioned above, the traditional PKI services relying on the access to an on-line CA would not work in this application. However we noticed in [19], Zhou proposed an efficient signature validation scheme without the CA's involvement for releasing the certificate revocation information based on a new PKI [20].

The new PKI is a CRL-free public key framework. In the new PKI, the lifetime of a certificate is divided into short periods and the certificate owner could control the expire of the certificate. The CA need not to release CRL [14] or provide OSCP service [17]. Thus the status of a public key certificate can be validated without the CA's participation.

Certificate Generation
To apply for a certificate, a user S takes the following steps:

(**S-1**) Generate a pair of keys PK_S and SK_S;
(**S-2**) Define parameters D, T, and L;
(**S-3**) Generate a random number r and calculate a one way hash chain $H^i(r) = H(H^{i-1}(r))$ $(i = 1, 2, ..., j)$;
(**S-4**) Send $(PK_S, D, H^j(r), j, L)$ to CA.

The CA issues a certificate to S as follows:

(**CA-1**) Authenticate S's request;
(**CA-2**) Generate a certificate $Cert(S) = SIGN_{CA}(S, PK_S, D, H^j(r), j, L)$;
(**CA-3**) Issue $Cert(S)$ to user S.

When S gets a certificate, it can use it to authenticate itself to others. It can also control the validation status of its certificate by releasing a proper hash value at a proper date (illustrated in Fig. 2).

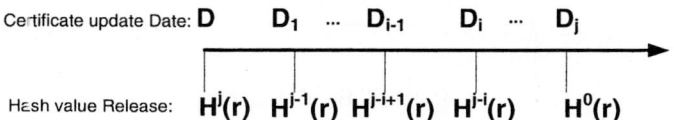

Fig. 2. Certificate validation status controlled by hash value releasing

As in Fig. 2, S must release a valid hash value $H^{j-i}(r)$ to ensure $Cert(S)$ is still valid at date D_i. If S wants to revoke $Cert(S)$ after date D_i, it can stop releasing $H^{j-i}(r)$ and any further hash value.

Certificate Validation
Based on the new PKI, a certificate can be validated without the CA's participation. Suppose the current date is D_v and the current hash value released by S is $H^{j-i}(r)$. The following steps can check the certificate status efficiently:

(1) Verify CA's signature on $Cert(S)$. This check can ensure the correctness of public key PK_S, date D, refreshing time period L, and hash chain $H^j(r)$;
(2) Check if $H^i(H^{j-i}(r)) = H^j(r)$ for $0 \leq i < j$. This check can make sure that the hash value provided by S is valid;
(3) Check if $D_v \leq D + i * L$. This check can make sure the certificate is valid now.

If the above checks pass, the verifier can be sure $Cert(S)$ is *currently* a valid certificate.

With the above new PKI solution, the public information utility service provider can then authenticate itself to the user, even if the user has no access to the CA.

3 The Proposed Authentication Protocol

In this section we propose an authentication protocol for secure use of public information utility in pervasive computing. The protocol consists of 5 steps, as illustrated in Fig. 3.

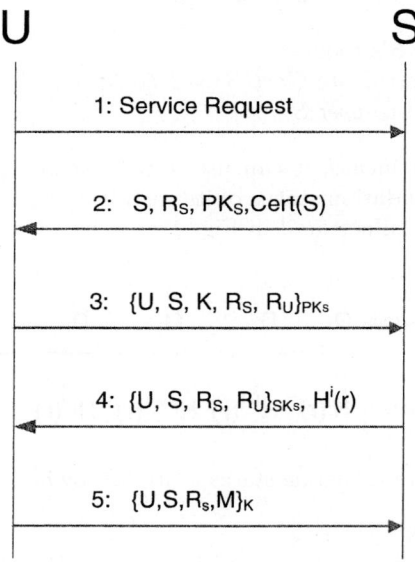

Fig. 3. The proposed authentication protocol

3.1 Protocol Description

At Step 1, when the user U wants to use service provided by the service provider S, U first submits its service request to S.

After receiving the service request, S generates a random number R_S, and sends $\{S, R_S, PK_S, Cert(S)\}$ to U at Step 2.

Upon receiving the message $\{S, R_S, PK_S, Cert(S)\}$, U parses the message into S, R_S, PK_S, and $Cert(S)$. Then U verifies $Cert(S)$ according to Section 2.3 [1] and checks the coherence of the name and public key with $Cert(S)$. If all

---

[1] We assume user U knows the CA's public key in advance.

the checks pass, U generates another random number R_U and a random session key K. Then U sends $\{U, S, K, R_S, R_U\}$ encrypted with PK_S to S at Step 3 [2].

Once obtaining the ciphertext from U, S decrypts $\{U, S, K, R_S, R_U\}$ with its private key, and uses R_S to check the freshness of this message. Then S sends its signature on $\{U, S, R_S, R_U\}$ along with the hash value $H^i(r)$ of the current time period to U at Step 4 [3].

When U receives message 4, U first uses $H^i(r)$ to check that $Cert(S)$ has not been revoked, and is still valid in the current time period. Then U verifies the signature of S with its public key PK_S, If both verifications are passed, U believes he is actually talking with S. By further checking that R_U is included in the signature of S, U also believes that S has received the session key K. Then U sends his document encrypted with the session key K for printing to S at Step 5.

3.2 Security Analysis

Before analyzing the protocol, we stress it is important for S to authenticate itself to U in this scenario. So the protocol is then designed to be secure in this sense.

Basically, attackers are divided into two categories: *passive adversaries* and *active adversaries*. The passive adversaries can only eavesdrop, whereas active adversaries have the power to control the communication channel to modify, add or drop messages. A secure authentication protocol should resist these attacks.

In order to design proper protocols and avoid the above attacks, various formalisms have been proposed for analyzing protocols. Bellare and Rogaway proposed a formal proof for a two party protocol [5]. Bellare, Canetti and Krawczyk proposed a modular approach for provable security [3]. This approach uses layers to treat authentication and key exchange.

Informally, Abadi et al. [1] analyzed several protocols and pointed out why they had such kind of weakness. They also set out 11 heuristic principles to guide designers to develop good protocols. Boyd et al. [4] investigated several well known protocols for mobile communication and discovered their weaknesses in some cases. Gollmann [12] pointed out successful proof indicates a new model to find further attacks. Based on these analysis and the known attacks, we examine our authentication protocol.

For the passive attacks, since the passive adversary can only see the encrypted message and then s/he will not get any information about the confidential data. Thus, the proposed authentication protocol is secure against passive attack provided the underlying symmetric and asymmetric algorithms are secure.

For the active adversaries, we should take more careful consideration. We briefly give the following analysis:

---

[2] The keys for signature/verification and encryption/decryption are usually different, so there may exist different certificates for S.

[3] If S suspects its private key has compromised, S can invalidate $Cert(S)$ by stopping release of $H^i(r)$.

- *Impersonation attack.* In Steps 3 to 5 of the protocol, identities of U and S are explicitly included. So it ensures to the user that the printer is exactly the one s/he chooses and avoids the impersonation attack.
- *Message reply attack.* In Steps 3 to 5 of the protocol, random numbers R_U and R_S are explicitly included. So it guarantees the freshness of the messages and avoids the message reply attack.
- *Parallel session attack & interleaving attack.* These attacks are a kind of man-in-the-middle attack and are not uncommon in mobile communication [4]. To avoid these attacks, the explicit identity binding and freshness of random number R_S and R_U are essential. Our protocol has considered these issues so it is immune to these attacks.

From the above analysis, we can conclude that our authentication protocol can resist the passive attack as well as known active attacks.

3.3 Extension with Payment Support

For the scenario of use of public information utilities, payment is another necessary requirement. Here we extend our authentication protocol with the payment support.

There are a number of payment protocols proposed for electronic commerce. Generally, the payment protocols can be divided into three categories [15]:

- Traditional money transaction protocol such as SET, PCT and iKP ect. These protocols use public key cryptology to encrypt a customer's credit card number. It is mainly used to deal with relatively high value transactions.
- Credit-debit payment protocols such as Millicent, Netcheque and UEPS. In these protocols, the customer maintains a positive balance that is debited when a debit transaction is processed.
- Digital currency methods such as DigiCash, NetCash and CAFE. In these methods, digital money is encoded and carried in a smart card or a computer disk. Users can make a payment to others by placing cards in a "digital wallet" that moves coins from one card to another without the TTP's participation.

Millicent [13] introduced the idea of script-based accounts. A piece of scrip represents an account the user has established with a vendor. At any given time, a vendor has outstanding scrip with the recently active users. The balance of the account is kept as the value of the scrip. When the customer makes a purchase with the scrip, the cost of the purchase is deducted from the scrip's value and a new scrip is returned as change. When the user has completed a series of transactions, s/he can "cash in" the remaining value of the scrip.

Brokers serve as accounting intermediaries between users and vendors. Customers enter into long-term relationships with brokers, in much the same way as they would enter into an agreement with a bank, a credit card company, or a service provider. Brokers buy and sell vendor scrip as a service to users and

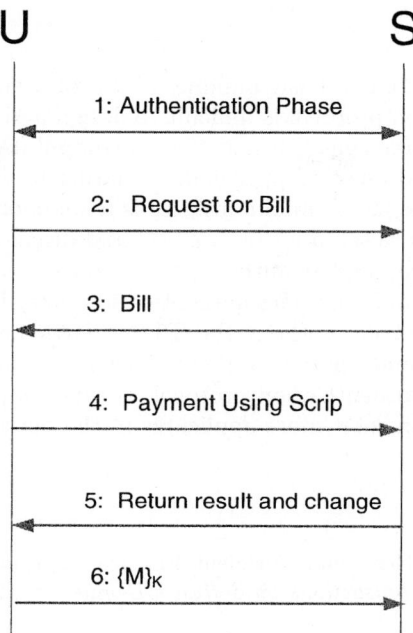

Fig. 4. A payment protocol

vendors. Broker scrip serves as a common currency for customers to use when buying vendor scrip, and for vendors to refund the unspent scrip.

Based on the Millicent protocol, we can extend our authentication protocol to support payment for a commercial application. Before a customer initiates transactions with a service provider, s/he should have got the broker scrip which can be used to buy the service provider's scrip directly.

Fig. 4 illustrates the payment protocol. For Step 2 through Step 5, all the messages are encrypted with the session key K established as in the previous authentication protocol. The protocol is described as follows:

(1) User and Service Provider complete authentication process and negotiate a session key K.
(2) User requests a bill from the Service Provider.
(3) Service Provider returns the bill it generated.
(4) User pays the bill using the scrip s/he has.
(5) Service Provider returns the result and change.
(6) User sends the encrypted data to Service Provider for printing.

The payment protocol is built on the authentication protocol. Its security then is ensured by the underlining symmetric and asymmetric cryptographic algorithms. We have proved the security of the authentication protocol in the previous section. Then the payment protocol provides a security model that is well suitable for profit-based public services in pervasive computing.

4 Conclusions

Authentication protocol is a basic building block for security in many systems. However authentication protocol is difficult to design and error-prone. In pervasive computing, resource constrains such as in computation capability, communication capability and power supply make it harder to design suitable authentication protocols. The use of public utilities is a common scenario in pervasive computing, and it has raised a lot of interests and discussion in literatures.

In this paper we proposed an authentication protocol to solve the above problem. Our solution not only provides authentication, but also establishes a secure channel for communication without the TTP's participation. The authentication protocol can be built on any secure symmetric and asymmetric algorithms. We also extend our authentication protocol to support payment based on the Millicent protocol to make it more applicable in the pervasive environment.

References

1. M. Abadi and R. Needham, "Prudent Engineering Practice for Cryptographic Protocols", *IEEE Transactions on Software Engineering*, 22(1), pp. 6-15, January 1996.
2. M. Burrows, M. Abadi, and R. Needham. "A Logic of Authentication", *ACM Transactions on Computer Systems*, 8(1), pp. 18-36, February 1990.
3. M. Bellare, R. Canette, and H. Krawczyk, "A Modular Approach to the Design and Analysis of Authentication and Key Exchange Protocols", *30th ACM Annual Symposium on the Theory of Computing*, pp. 412-428, 1998.
4. C. Boyd and A. Mathuria, "Key Establishment Protocols for Secure Mobile Communications: A Selective Survey", *ACISP'98*, LNCS 1438, pp. 344-355, Springer-Verlag, 1998.
5. M. Bellare and P. Rogaway, "Entity Authentication and Key Distribution", *Crypto'93*, LNCS 773, pp. 232-249, Springer-Verlag, 1994.
6. D. Balfanz, D. Smetters, P. Stewart, and H. Wong, "Talking to Strangers: Authentication in Ad-hoc Wireless Networks", *NDSS'02*, Available from: www.isoc.org/isoc/conferences/ ndss/02/proceedings/papers/balfan.pdf.
7. S. Creese, M. Goldsmith, B. Roscoe, and I. Zakiuddin, "Authentication for Pervasive Computing", *Security in Pervasive Computing 2003*, LNCS 2802, pp. 116-129, Springer-Verlag, 2004.
8. B. Cox, J.D. Tygar, and M. Sirbu, "Netbill Security and Transaction Protocol", *1st USENIX Workshop on Electronic Commerce*, 1995.
9. CyberCash, http://www.cybercash.com.
10. Digicash, http://www.digicash.com.
11. First Virtual Holdings Incorporated, http://www.fv.com.
12. D. Gollmann,"Analysing Security Protocols", *1st International Conference on Formal Aspects of Security*, LNCS 2629, pp.71 - 80, Springer-Verlag, 2003.
13. S. Glassman, M. Manasse, M. Abadi, P. Gauthier, and P. Sobalvarro, "The Millicent Protocol for Inexpensive Electronic Commerce", *4th WWW Conference*, pp. 603-618, December 1995.
14. R. Housley, W. Ford, W. Polk, and D. Solo, "Internet X.509 Public Key Infrastructure Certificate and CRL Profile", *RFC 2459*, January 1999.

15. P.Havinga, G Smit, and A. Helme, "Survey of Electronic Payment Methods and Systems", *Euromedia'96*, pp. 180-187, 1996.
16. D. Hutter, W. Stephan, and M. Ullmann, "Security and Privacy in Pervasive Computing State of the Art and Future Directions", *Security in Pervasive Computing 2003*, LNCS 2802, pp. 285-289, Springer-Verlag, 2004.
17. M. Myers, R. Ankney, A. Malpani, S. Galperin, and C. Adams, "X.509 Internet Public Key Infrastructure On-line Certificate Status Protocol (OCSP)", *RFC 2560*, June 1999.
18. F. Stajano and R. Anderson, "The Resurrecting Duckling: Security Issues for Ad-hoc Wireless Networks", *7th Security Protocols Workshop*, LNCS 1796, Springer-Verlag, UK.
19. J. Zhou, "Efficient Signature Validation Based on a New PKI", *EC-Web'03*, LNCS 2738, pp. 94-103, Springer-Verlag, 2003.
20. J. Zhou, F. Bao, and R. Deng, "Validating Digital Signatures without TTP's Time-Stamping and Certificate Revocation", *ISC'03*, LNCS 2851, pp. 96-110, Springer-Verlag, 2003.

A Hybrid Neural Network Approach to the Classification of Novel Attacks for Intrusion Detection

Wei Pan and Weihua Li

School of Computer Science, Northwestern Polytechnical University,
Shaanxi, Xi'an, 710072 China
panweihh@hotmail.com

Abstract. Intrusion Detection is an essential and critical component of network security systems. The key ideas are to discover useful patterns or features that describe user behavior on a system, and use the set of relevant features to build classifiers that can recognize anomalies and known intrusions, hopefully in real time. In this paper, a hybrid neural network technique is proposed, which consists of the self-organizing map (SOM) and the radial basis function (RBF) network, aiming at optimizing the performance of the recognition and classification of novel attacks for intrusion detection. The optimal network architecture of the RBF network is determined automatically by the improved SOM algorithm. The intrusion feature vectors are extracted from a benchmark dataset (the KDD-99) designed by DARPA. The experimental results demonstrate that the proposed approach performance especially in terms of both efficient and accuracy.

1 Introduction

With the increasing number of computers being connected to the Internet, the security of communication networks becomes more and more important. Particularly where sensitive and confidential information is stored or transmitted, there is a vital importance of security. Among various other techniques, intrusion detection systems (IDS) are needed to protect against attacks.

Currently, intrusion detection techniques can be categorized into misuse detection and anomaly detection. Misuse detection techniques usually recognize the signature of intrusion patterns that have been recognized and reported by experts. Anomaly detection techniques establish normal usage patterns. They can detect the unseen intrusions by investigating their deviation from the normal patterns. The current intrusion detection systems suffer a number of drawbacks that limited their efficacy in protecting against novel attacks. The crucial problems of intrusion detection systems are detection accuracy (false positive alarms and false negatives), real-time performance, new attack recognition, and scalability. The artificial neural networks provide a number of advantages in the detection of network intrusions [1, 3].

In this paper, we present an improved SOM-based RBF network approach for intrusion detection. The number of hidden neurons of the RBF networks is self-adjustable. The best possible network architecture is determined according to the input data by the proposed training algorithm. An improved SOM algorithm is used to automatically determine the centers and the number of hidden neurons. It does not require the many trial tests to determine the appropriate network architecture. This feature is user friendly for intrusion detection with large number of attack records. After completion of the training, the learned network is able to detect different types of attacks dramatically. Our obtained results indicate that the proposed neural network approach has significant advantages, such as the shorter training time, the easier choice of hidden neurons, the higher detection rate and the wider stable range.

The rest of the paper is organized as follows. In section 2, we give a brief overview of the relevant works and background of the application of artificial neural networks to intrusion detection. In Section 3, we briefly introduce the RBF network approach and discuss the improved SOM algorithm. In Session 4, the proposed neural network approach is implemented in intrusion detection process, and the experiments reveal the performance of the proposed approach. Finally, the summary and conclusions of our study are drawn in Section 5.

2 Related Works

An increasing amount of research has been conducted on the application of neural networks for detecting network novel attacks. The multilayer perceptron (MLP) was used in [4] for anomaly detection and in [5] for misuse detection based on attack-specific keywords. A cerebellar model articulation controller (CMAC) neural network [7] was applied in the detection of DoS attacks. A hybrid model of BP network and C4.5 was proposed in [6] for misuse detection. In that work, the model achieved a detection rate of 85% when it was tested on the KDD-99 dataset. The SOM was applied to perform the clustering of network traffic and to detect attacks in [16, 18]. The RBF network was also proposed in [8] for intrusion detection on sequences of system calls.

When neural-network-based AI approaches are used for practical applications, there are always problems in determining the appropriate network architecture. In our work, we propose an improved SOM-based RBF network model. As a result, we are able to establish the optimal network architecture without going through the laborious trial-and-error process. This will be proved to be extremely useful for intrusion detection.

3 Methodology

3.1 Structure of RBF Network

Radial Basis Function (RBF) networks consist of only one hidden layer with locally tuned neurons and are fully interconnected to the output layer. The structure of the RBF networks is illustrated in Fig. 1.

We assume data pairs $(x_i \in R^n, y_i \in R^m)$ of input and desired output. In intrusion detection, the attack features are the input vectors, and the attack types are the output vectors. The output of each RBF unit is as follows:

$$y_i(x) = \sum_{j=1}^{n_h} w_{ji} \varphi(\|x - c_j\|), \quad 1 \leq i \leq n_o \quad (1)$$

where n_i, n_h, and n_o are the numbers of neurons of the input, hidden, and output layers, respectively, c_j is the center of the neural network in the j th hidden neuron, w_{ij} is the weight between j th hidden neuron and i th output neuron. The nonlinear kernel function $\varphi(\bullet)$ has a radially symmetric shape. The Gaussian function is the most popular function by the following equation:

$$\varphi(r) = e^{-(r^2/2\sigma^2)}, \quad (\sigma > 0, r \in R) \quad (2)$$

where σ is the width of the radial basis function.

Usually, the RBF network is trained by first finding centers of the network, which are parameters of hidden neurons, and then finding the weights between the hidden and output layer by a linear optimization strategy. The usual procedure for training such a network consists of two consecutive phases:

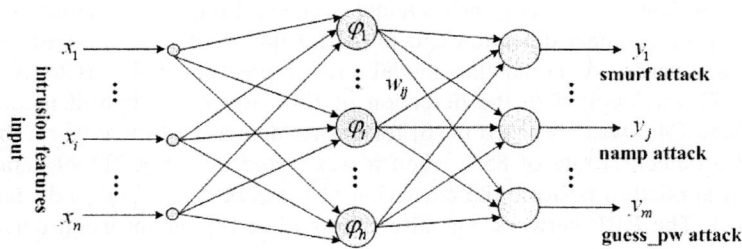

Fig. 1. Structure of RBF networks

(1) Unsupervised learning: The nearest center from the input vector is moved in its direction, such as k-mean clustering algorithm:

$$\tilde{k} = \arg(\min_k \| X(n) - C_k(n) \|)$$

$$C_k(n+1) = \begin{cases} C_k(n) + \mu[X(n) - C_k(n)] & \text{if } k = \tilde{k} \\ C_k(n) & \text{otherwise} \end{cases} \quad (3)$$

(2) Supervised learning: The output layer weights are updated with the LMS algorithm.

$$w_k(n+1) = w_k(n) + \mu[d(n) - Y(n)] \cdot e^{\frac{-\|X - C_k\|^2}{\sigma_k^2}} \quad (4)$$

3.2 The SOM-Based RBF Network

Although the described networks as before are reported to be computationally rather efficient, they have some important drawbacks. Estimating an appropriate number of units is very dilemmatic. And the k-means clustering algorithm might be not at all optimal in some case. Consider a classification problem with two classes in anomaly detection, where most of the data vectors lie in two well-separated clusters, but the remaining vectors of both classes are scattered in several small clusters which are pretty close to each other.

According to these, we employ a hybrid network architecture [9] which is composed of two kinds of networks such as a basic network and a cluster network. A RBF network and a Kohonen SOM [11] network are adopted as the basic network and cluster network, respectively, shown in Fig. 2. The input of the basic network is the same as the ones in SOM.

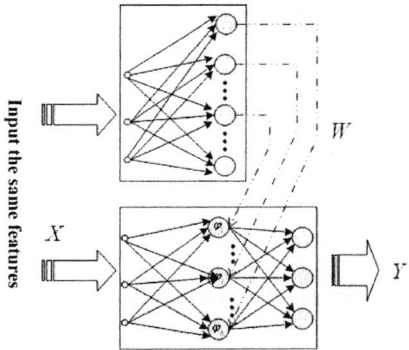

Fig. 2. The SOM-Based RBF network

SOM network performs unsupervised learning. It generates ordered mappings of the input data onto some low-dimensional topological structure. The relationship between the output nodes in SOM and the hidden nodes in the RBF network is one to one correspondence.

$$\bar{k} = \arg(\min_k \| X(n) - C_k(n) \|)$$
$$C_i(n+1) = C_i(n) + h_{\bar{k}i}[X(n) - C_i(n)] \quad \forall i \in \{1,...,n_o\} \quad (5)$$

The RBF network performs supervised training using delta rule [12]. The weight vector belonging to the output in SOM are transmitted to the hidden node in the RBF network as its center of RBF activation function.

3.3 Improved SOM

In practical applications, the main drawback of the conventional SOM is that one must predefine the map structure and the map size before commencement of the training process. Usually, one must rely on numerous trial tests in order to identify the appropriate network architecture. In intrusion detection, we need a convenient approach to recognizing and classifying novel attacks. Hence, we derive a new approach from an improved SOM algorithm named CSG [13].

During the processing in the CSG algorithm, the network itself determines the growth of new neurons according to the activation level. The weight adaptation in the CSG algorithm is adapted slightly within the winner neuron and its direct neighboring neurons. The learning rate is small and does not decrease to zero.

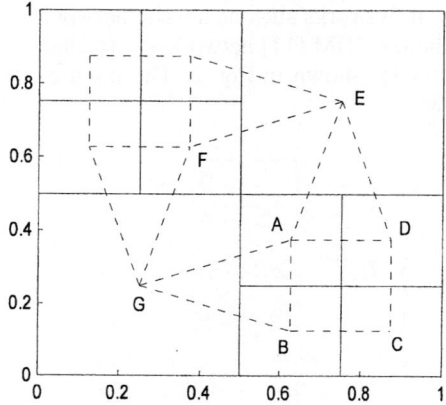

Fig. 3. A is the winner neuron, and B, C, D, E, F, and G are its direct neighboring neurons

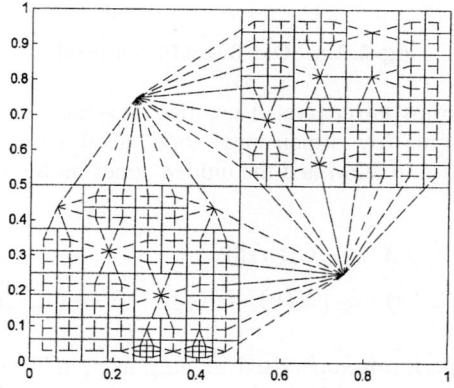

Fig. 4. Output map with connections of neighboring neurons

The CSG algorithm enables a 2-D representation on the output map confined in a square region and the neurons are distributed on the 2-D map according to the density distribution of the input data. The neurons representing the dense region of the input data are densely distributed on the 2-D map, whereas those lying in the sparse region of the input data are located on the sparse region of the 2-D output space. As a result, the nonuniform distribution of neurons on the output map is able to preserve the data distribution in the input space. The CSG output map is constrained in a square of unit length. All neurons are generated within the square. Each neuron corresponds to a square region with different size and neighboring neurons are connected to form neighboring relationships. A typical output map at a certain learning stage is shown in Fig. 3, 4, 5.

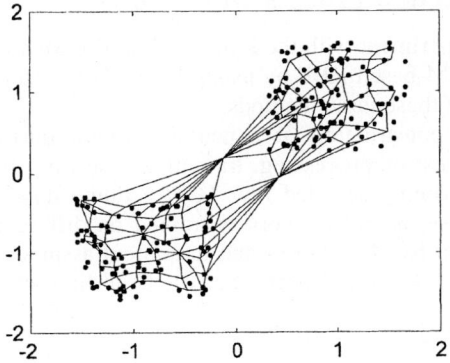

Fig. 5. Input space with connections

The algorithm of the whole process of the improved SOM-Based RBF network is outline as follows.

```
Input: X = {x₁,x₂,...,xₙ}; /* the input dataset */
Output: W = {w₁,w₂,...,wₘ}; /the weight vectors */
Begin
Initialize the improved SOM's structure;
Create a weighted connection wₖ from each RBF cell C to
the output unit i, (i∈{1,...,m}) in the RBF network;
Associate every cell in the RBF network with a Gaussian
function: φ(r) = e^{-(r²/2σ²)}.
while (classification error not low enough) do
begin
repeat
 • Choose I/O-pair from training data;
 • Determine best-match unit S;
 • Increase matching for S and its first neighbors in
improved SOM;
 • Compute activation for every cell;
 • Compute the vector of all output unit activations;
 • Perform one delta-rule learning step for the weights;
 • Add counter variable;
until λ times
```

```
    Determine cell q with maximum resource value;
    Insert a new cell r between q and the direct
neighbor f with maximum distance in input vector space;
    Give the new cell I an initial weight connecting to
the output in the RBF network;
end
End
```

4 Intrusion Detection Process and Results

In this section, we experiment with the k-means-Based RBF and the SOM-based RBF and the improved SOM-based RBF by using the KDD-99 data [14] respectively, and compare the results of these three methods.

In our study, the construction of a neural network intrusion detection system consists of three phases: preprocessing, training and testing. In preprocessing phase, we transform the randomly selected raw TCP/IP dump data into machine-readable form. In training phase, neural network is trained on different types of attacks and normal data. The input has 41 features and the output assumes different attack types. In testing phase, neural network is performed on the testing set.

4.1 Data Preprocess

The KDD-99 dataset was used for the Third International Knowledge Discovery and Data Mining Tools Competition. This dataset was acquired from the 1998 DARPA intrusion detection evaluation program. From the KDD-99 dataset, 132108 records

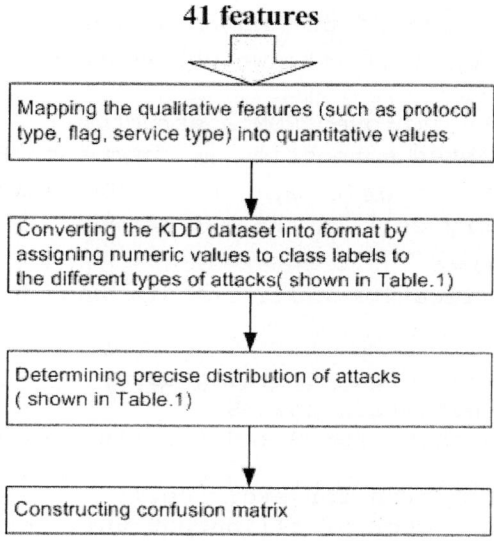

Fig. 6. The preprocess of dataset

Table 1. Distribution of Attacks

Class Label	Normal and Attacks	Training Data	Testing Data
1	normal	32278	40549
28	smurf	12079	26091
8	ipsweep	1247	2452
16	namp	1589	4633
24	rootkit	857	641
18	perl	1017	429
3	buffer overflow	2650	1176
5	guess passwd	1053	3367
Total	7 attacks	52770	79338

were chosen as our experimental data. The selected connections were further split into the training set and the test set, containing 52770 and 79338 connections respectively. We select 7 types of attacks in the training set and the testing set that are smurf attack, ipsweep attack, namp attack, rootkit attack, perl attack, buffer_overflow attack and guess_passwd attack in addition to normal dataset. The same data sets were respectively used in the experiments to evaluate the performance of the k-means-based RBF and the SOM-based RBF and the improved SOM-based RBF in the same environment. The preprocess of dataset is shown in Fig. 6.

4.2 Using the Neural Network

The Performance of the classification of novel attacks for intrusion detection is evaluated in terms of the false positive and detection rates, estimated as follows:

$$\text{False Positive Rate} = \frac{\text{The number of False Positives}}{\text{Total number of Normal Connections}} \quad (6)$$

$$\text{Detection Rate} = 1 - \frac{\text{The number of False Negatives}}{\text{Total number of Attack Connections}} \quad (7)$$

Where False Positive (Negative) Rate is the number of Normal (Attack) connections labeled as Attack (Normal).

In the training phase, we use initial training set of 52770 normalized I/O-pairs consisting of attack patterns, and normal user patterns. The training of the neural networks was conducted using the k-means-based RBF, the SOM-based RBF, and the improved SOM-based RBF network model respectively. Each network was set to train until the desired mean square error of 0.001 was met. Fig. 6 shows the training

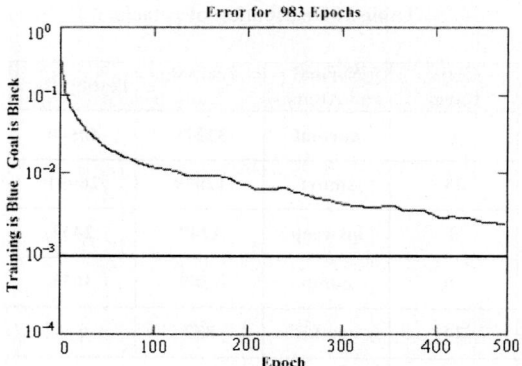

Fig. 7. The k-means-based RBF training on KDD-99 dataset

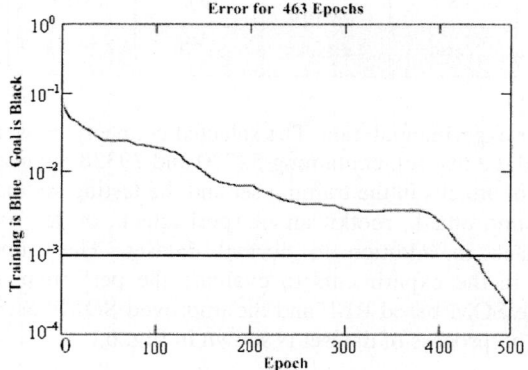

Fig. 8. The SOM-based RBF training on KDD-99 dataset

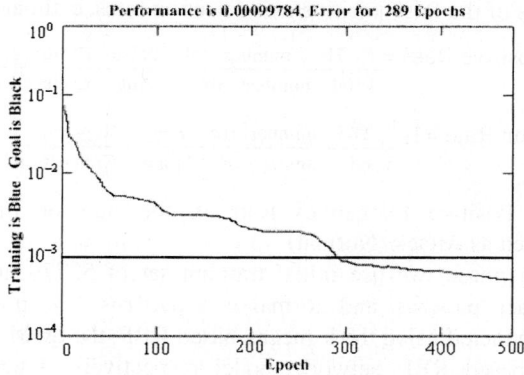

Fig. 9. The improved SOM-based RBF training on KDD-99 dataset

process. During the training process using the improved SOM-based RBF, the goal was met at 289 epochs with a performance of 0.00099784 by 43 hidden neurons in Fig. 9. In contrast, two other methods we tried took longer. The k-means-based RBF network converges in 983 epochs by 88 hidden neurons and the SOM-based RBF converges in 463 epochs by 51 hidden neurons, shown in Fig. 7, 8. As can be seen the number of epochs required by the improve SOM-based RBF is smaller than two other methods.

Table 2. Confusion Matrix obtained by the k-mean-based RBF

	normal	smurf	ipsweep	namp	rootkit	perl	buffer overflow	guess passwd	% correct
normal	40058	242	72	73	26	18	38	22	98.79
smurf	571	25157	88	121	34	10	27	14	96.42
ipsweep	196	17	2355	22	2	0	3	0	96.03
namp	87	20	31	4464	1	15	2	12	96.36
rootkit	64	22	9	21	510	12	14	19	79.66
perl	57	32	0	5	12	295	9	0	68.81
buffer overflow	95	21	43	22	8	7	959	38	81.58
guess passwd	339	61	22	19	0	0	89	2837	84.22
% correct	94.28	98.37	89.89	94.04	86.00	82.64	84.12	96.43	

Table 3. Confusion Matrix obtained by the SOM-based RBF

	normal	smurf	ipsweep	namp	rootkit	perl	buffer overflow	guess passwd	% correct
normal	40267	174	22	16	7	13	31	19	99.30
smurf	237	25673	49	56	12	4	27	33	98.39
ipsweep	47	34	2366	22	2	0	9	5	96.49
namp	22	41	31	4500	6	16	3	14	97.13
rootkit	32	7	3	12	543	1	15	28	84.71
perl	19	32	0	5	29	337	1	6	78.55
buffer overflow	26	11	13	23	5	15	1042	41	88.61
guess passwd	207	65	24	43	0	0	89	2939	87.29
% correct	96.69	98.60	94.34	96.22	89.90	87.31	85.62	95.27	

In the test phase, the testing set consists of 79338 connection records with 41 features. As before, we test each network (the k-means-based RBF, the SOM-based RBF, and the improved SOM-based RBF).The classified results, the false and detect rate are obtained in confusion matrix shown in the following Table 2,3,4.

Our obtained results indicate that the proposed neural network approach has significant advantages, such as the shorter training time, the easier choice of hidden neurons, the higher detection rate and the wider stable range. According to the tables, we can see the improved SOM-based the average detect rate of 95.80%, the false positive rate is 0.63%. In contrast with other methods, the proposed approach model performs remarkably in intrusion identification.

Table 4. Confusion Matrix obtained by the improved SOM-based RBF

	normal	smurf	ipsweep	namp	rootkit	perl	buffer overflow	guess passwd	% correct
normal	40415	65	0	38	7	13	0	11	99.67
smurf	114	25939	12	21	3	0	2	0	99.42
ipsweep	23	17	2518	19	0	0	7	0	99.09
namp	14	9	31	4565	6	0	5	1	98.53
rootkit	36	7	4	12	570	1	11	0	88.87
perl	21	13	0	0	19	372	0	4	86.74
buffer overflow	7	6	0	11	0	0	1140	8	96.98
guess passwd	42	23	0	4	0	0	28	3270	97.12
% correct	99.37	99.46	98.17	97.96	94.21	96.37	95.56	99.27	

5 Conclusion

In this paper, a new-style improved SOM-based RBF network is employed for the classification of novel attacks for intrusion detection. Our intensive experimental results on the KDD-99 dataset demonstrate that the proposed approach is able to deliver very high detection accuracy. The future work will address the remaining issues in the development of a complete intrusion detection system using the improved SOM-based RBF network.

Acknowledgments

This research was supported by the National High Technology Research and Development Program of China (863 Program) under agreement number 2003AA142060.

References

1. Hofmann, A., Schmitz, C., Sick, B.: Rule extraction from neural networks for intrusion detection in computer networks. Systems, Man and Cybernetics, 2003. IEEE International Conference on, Volume: 2, 5-8 Oct. 2003
2. Denning, E.D.: An intrusion detection model. Proceedings of the IEEE Symposium on Security and Privacy, 1986 S&P, 1986. 118-133
3. J. Cannady: Artificial neural networks for misuse detection. In Proceedings of the 1998 National Information Systems Security Conference (NISSC'98) October 5-8 1998. Arlington, VA., pages 443 – 456, 1998.
4. A. K. Ghosh, A. Schwartzbard: A study in using neural networks for anomaly and misuse detection. In Proceedings of USENIX Security Symposium, 1999.

5. R. P. Lippmann, R. K. Cunningham: Improving intrusion detection performance using keyword selection and neural networks. Computer Networks (Amsterdam, Netherlands:1999), 34(4):597 - 603, 1999.
6. Zhi-Song Pan, Song-Can Chen, Gen-Bao Hu, Dao-Qiang Zhang: Hybrid neural network and C4.5 for misuse detection. Machine Learning and Cybernetics, 2003 International Conference on , Volume: 4 , 2-5 Nov. 2003
7. Cannady, J.: Applying CMAC-based online learning to intrusion detection. Neural Networks, 2000. IJCNN 2000, Proceedings of the IEEE-INNS-ENNS International Joint Conference on , Volume: 5 , 24-27 July 2000
8. Rapaka. A., Novokhodko. A., Wunsch. D.: Intrusion detection using radial basis function network on sequences of system calls.Neural Networks, 2003. Proceedings of the International Joint Conference on , Volume: 3 , 2003
9. Qingyu Xiong, Hirasawa, K., Jinglu Hu, Murata, J.: Growing RBF structures using self-organizing maps. Robot and Human Interactive Communication, 2000. RO-MAN 2000. Proceedings. 9th IEEE International Workshop on , 27-29 Sept. Pages:107 – 111.2000
10. Ambwani, T.: Multi class support vector machine implementation to intrusion detection .Neural Networks, 2003. Proceedings of the International Joint Conference on , Volume: 3 , 20-24 July 2003
11. T. Kohonen: Self-Organizing Maps. Berlin, Germany, Springer-Verlag, 1997.
12. B. Fritzke: Growing cell structure: A self-organizing network for supervised and un-supervised learning. Neural Networks, vol. 7, Pages: 1441–1460, 1994.
13. Wu, S., Chow, T.W.S.: Induction machine fault detection using SOM-based RBF neural networks. Industrial Electronics, IEEE Transactions on , Volume: 51 , Issue: 1 , Pages:183 – 194, Feb. 2004
14. S. Hettich, S. D. Bay: The UCI KDD archive, 1999.[http://kdd.ics.uci.edu]. Irvine, CA: University of California, Department of Information and Computer Science.
15. Lee, S.C., Heinbuch, D.V.: Training a neural-network based intrusion detector to recognize novel attacks. IEEE Transactions on Systems, Man and Cybernetics, Part A, Vol 31 Issue: 4, Pages: 294 –299,July 2001.
16. M. Ramadas, S. Ostermann, B. Tjaden: Detecting anomalous network traffic with self-organizing maps. In Recent Advances in Intrusion Detection, 6th International Symposium, RAID 2003, pages 36–54, 2003.
17. Y. Guan, A. A. Ghorbani, N. Belacel: Y-means: A clustering method for intrusion detection. In IEEE Canadian
18. Conference on Electrical and Computer Engineering, proceeding, pages 1083–1086, 2003.
19. Lei, J.Z., Ghorbani, A.: Network intrusion detection using an improved competitive learning neural network. Communication Networks and Services Research, 2004. Proceedings. Second Annual Conference on , 19-21 May 2004 Pages:190 - 197
20. Sung, A.H., Mukkamala, S.: Identifying important features for intrusion detection using support vector machines and neural networks.Applications and the Internet, 2003. Proceedings. 2003 Symposium on , 27-31 Jan. 2003
21. Zhen Liu, Florez, G., Bridges, S.M.: A comparison of input representations in neural networks: a case study in intrusion detection. Neural Networks, 2002. IJCNN '02. Proceedings of the 2002 International Joint Conference on , Volume: 2 , 12-17 May 2002 Pages:1708 – 1713
22. Zhen Liu, Bridges, S.M., Vaughn, R.B.: Classification of anomalous traces of privileged and parallel programs by neural networks. Fuzzy Systems, 2003. FUZZ '03. The 12th IEEE International Conference on , Volume: 2 , Pages:1225 - 1230 ,25-28 May 2003

Efficient and Beneficial Defense Against DDoS Direct Attack and Reflector Attack*

Yanxiang He, Wei Chen, Wenling Peng, and Min Yang

Computer School, The State Key Lab of Software Engineering,
Wuhan University, Wuhan 430072, Hubei, China
{yxhe, chenwei, wlpeng, myang}@whu.edu.cn

Abstract. Distributed Denial-of-Service (DDoS) attacks misuse network resource and bring serious threats to the internet. Detecting DDoS at the source-end has many advantages over defense at the victim-end and intermediate-network. However, one of the main problems for source-end methods is the performance degradation brought by these methods and no direct benefit for Internet Service Provider(ISP), which discourages ISPs to deploy the defense system. We propose an efficient detection approach, which only requires limited fixed-length memory and low computation overhead but provides satisfying detection results. Our method is also beneficial because the method can not only detect direct DDoS attack for other ISPs, but also protect the ISP itself from reflector DDoS attack. The efficient and beneficial defense is practical and expected to attract more ISPs to join the cooperation. The experiments results show our approach is efficient and feasible for defense at the source-end.

1 Introduction

Distributed Denial-of-Service (DDoS) attacks misuse network resource and bring serious threats to the internet. There still is a lack of efficient defense mechanisms. Current TCP based DDoS attacks include direct DDoS attack and reflector DDoS attack [1], which exploit TCP three-way handshake [2]. The direct DDoS attack is launched by sending numerous SYN request packets towards victim server. The server reserves lots of half-open connection which will quickly deplete system resource, thus preventing the victim server from accepting legitimate user requests. The attackers perform TCP based reflector DDoS attack by utilizing the automatic message generating ability of reflectors. The reflector DDoS attacker sends SYN packets with the same spoofed source IP to some public servers, which are called reflectors. These reflectors will automatically send back reply traffic to victim host. The victim's recourse or bandwidth will be exhausted by congestion of replying packets.

According to the deployment location of defense systems, the current DDoS detection and prevention methods can be classified into three categories: defense

---

* This work is supported by the National Natural Science Foundation of China under Grant No. 90104005.

at the source-end, at victim-end or at intermediate-network. Compared to defense at the victim-end and intermediate methods, defense at the source-end has the following advantages:

- **Low overhead for monitoring traffic.** Detections at the victim-end or at intermediate-network have to monitor numerous traffic. Detection at the source brings low overhead to network infrastructure due to less traffic at the source-end
- **Little vulnerability to DDoS attack.** The burden of monitoring numerous attacking packets congesting at the victim side make the defense system itself vulnerable to DDoS attack. Defense at source-end will avoid this problem due to limited attack streams near source end. This enable the defense system itself has little risk of becoming potential target of DDoS attacks.
- **Efficient response.** As soon as attack is detected at the source, efficient response can be adopted to filter malicious traffic. Compared to response at the victim side, the overhead of performing response at the source is rather low. More complicate and sophistical methods can be applied at the source-end.

Unfortunately, one of the biggest problems for the source-end detections is a lack of motivation to deploy them. Source-end detection requires widely deployment among different Internet Service Providers(ISPs), for example, RFC2827 [3] requires to be implemented at all the ingress router. However, the ISPs can not get a direct benefit from the deployments. Furthermore, the deployment of source-end method will degrade the performance of network devices. The ISPs are poorly motivated to join cooperation.

On the one hand, we should design more space and computation efficient method, which does not evidently bring degradation. On the other hand, benefits should be provided to ISPs to attract more ISPs to participate the widely deployed source-end detection method. An efficient and beneficial method is presented in this paper.

To save memory storage and computation cost, the Bloom filter[4] method is modified and employed. The Bloom filter based method makes a tradeoff between state-method and stateless-method. Stateless-method, which does not need to record the states of each packet, can save storage and computation resource. But these efficiency is obtained at the sacrifice of accuracy. State-method, which monitors each packet behavior, is more accurate than the stateless-method. But monitoring each packet is expensive and infeasible on the high speed link network. The tradeoff method offers accurate detection results with little memory and low computation overhead requirement.

Based on the space-efficient and computation-efficient method, we propose a beneficial method, which can not only provide support for other ISPs against direct DDoS attack, but also enhance the security of its own domain against reflector DDoS attack. Thus it is expected to be adopted by more ISPs and provide more accurate and prompt detection results.

In order to defense against direct DDoS attacks and reflector DDoS attack at the source-end, we summarize the novel contributions made in this paper:

- A data structure with limited storage cost is proposed on the basis of Bloom filter. The fixed size memory is required, which avoids the potential DDoS attack threat for most dynamic memory allocation methods. The data structure is space-efficient, which can be acceptable by more ISPs to join widely-deployed source-end defense.
- A detection scheme with little computation overhead is presented to monitoring malicious packets. With proposed data structure, only addition and subtraction operations are required, which brings litter overhead to current computers.
- The proposed method provides direct benefits to the ISP who is willing to join the cooperation. Both direct attack against other ISPs and reflector attack against the ISP itself can be efficiently detected with our method.

The remainder of this paper is organized as follows. Section 2 introduces the related work in the area of DDoS attacks research. In Section 3, the space-efficient data structure is presented first. Then the detection schemes against both direct DDoS attack and reflector DDoS attack are proposed. Experimental results show that our approach can accurately detect a spoofed IP DDoS attack with little overhead, which will be presented in Section 4. Section 5 offers our conclusion.

2 The Related Work

According to the location of the detector, most of current spoofed IP DDoS attack detection and prevention schemes can be classified into three categories : the source-end, victim-end or intermediate-network. Detecting spoofed IP DDoS at the victim server side encourages researchers because the deployment of IDSs at the victim servers seems more practical. In [5] Wang detects the SYN flooding attacks near the server side and the detector is installed at leaf routers that connect end hosts to the Internet. Their method performs detection by monitoring abnormal SYN-FIN pairs behavior and a non-parameter CUSUM method is utilized to analyze these pairs. In Cheng's work [6], their approach utilizes the TTL in the IP header to estimate the Hop-Count of the each packets and detect attacks by the spoofed packets' Hop-Count deviation from normal ones. Syn cache and cookies method is evaluated in Lemon [7] work, the basic idea is to use cache or cookies to evaluate security of connection before establishing the real connection with protected server.

The detection at the source end has more advantages but has deployment difficulties. It is not easy to attract more ISPs to deploy source-end defense in their domains. For example the RFC2827 [3] is to filter spoofed packets at each ingress router. Before the router forwards one packet to destination, it will check the packet whether belongs to its routing domain. If not, it is probably a spoofed packet with malicious attempt and the router will drop it. However, it may degrade routing performance, which discourages the ISPs to participate defense. Mirkovic introduces D-WARD [8], a DDoS defense system at source-end. Attacks are detected by the constant monitoring of two-way traffic flows and periodic comparison with normal flow models.

Defense at intermediate-network mainly includes filtering [9, 10, 11], traceback [12, 13, 14, 15, 16], and pushback [17]. Attack source traceback attempts to identify the real location of the attacker. Most of the traceback schemes are to mark some packets along its routing path or send some special packets. In [14] the authors describe a series of marking algorithms starting from the simplest to the more sophistical ones including node append, node sample and edge sample. With the identification of real path of the spoofed packets, pushback technique can be applied to inform upstream ISP to perform specified filtering [17].

3 The Efficient and Beneficial Approach

To make defense at source-end more attractive, we propose an efficient and beneficial method. The proposed method has two main advantages: First, it can give satisfying results with little storage consumption and computation overhead. Second, it can provide protection for other ISPs as well as the ISP itself, who is willing to deploy the method.

In this section, the TCP handshakes for different scenarios are analyzed first. Then a space-efficient data structure, which is based on Bloom filter, is discussed. With this data structure, the detection schemes against direct DDoS attack and reflector DDoS attack are presented.

3.1 Analysis of TCP Handshakes

We first analyze the difference between normal traffic and attack traffic, including both direct DDoS attack and reflector DDoS attack. The different three-way handshake scenarios of normal TCP connection, direct SYN flooding attack and reflector TCP attack are compared.

The normal three-way handshake is shown in Figure 1(a). First the client C sends a SYN request to the server S. After receiving such request, server S replies with a packet, which contains both the acknowledgement ACK and the synchronization request SYN(denoted as ACK/SYN hereinafter). Then client C sends an ACK back to finish the building up of the connection. All the three-way handshake control packets will be observed at router R_c near the source-end.

In a direct DDoS attack, the three-way handshake will be modified. Figure 1(b) shows the difference. Direct attack usually uses the unreachable spoofed source IP in the attacking packets to improve attack efficiency [18]. These packets will not trigger the third round of handshake. The detector at the source-end will only observe the first round handshake, SYN, but never find the second and the third round handshake.

The reflector attack uses the victim IP as the source IP in the attacking packets and send these malicious packets to reflectors(Figure 1(c)). The reflector is an innocent third-party and sends the reply traffic to the victim according to spoofed IP address. Since the reflector does not need to be compromised before

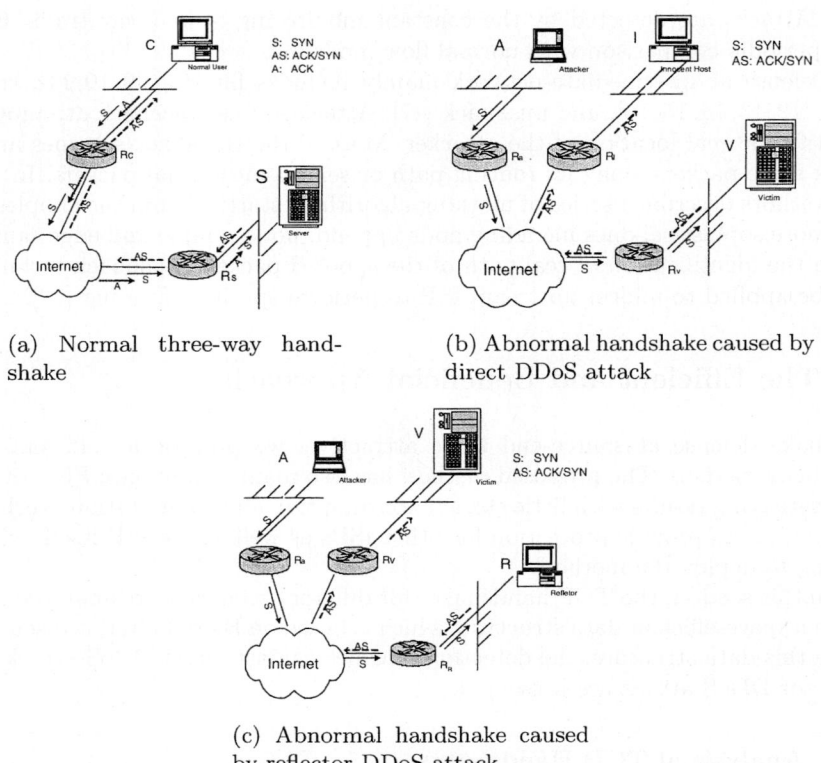

(a) Normal three-way handshake

(b) Abnormal handshake caused by direct DDoS attack

(c) Abnormal handshake caused by reflector DDoS attack

Fig. 1. Three-way handshake in a complete TCP connection and half-open connections caused by direct DDoS attack and reflector DDoS attack

attack, the attacker can use many public servers in the Internet as the available reflectors. If a host get an unknown ACK second round handshake packet, it will send back a RST packet back to reset the TCP connection.

Table 1 gives a comparison of different scenarios of TCP three-way handshakes.

Based on these difference, we deploy a detector near the side of attacking source to monitor the status of handshake. For each connection, each round of three-way handshake is monitored. If all the TCP control packets for a complete connection are observed, this connection is regarded as legal. Otherwise, the three-way handshake will be checked to find whether it matches some kind of DDoS attack.

Keeping handshakes records for each connection is infeasible due to numerous traffic on high link speed network. However, stateless method, which does not keep records for each connections, may have high potential false negatives. To make a tradeoff, a space-efficient data structure is proposed in the following subsection.

Table 1. TCP handshakes packets observed at the source-end for different scenarios

Scenario	SYN	ACK/SYN	ACK	RST
Normal	Y	Y	Y	N*
Direct DDoS	Y	N*	N	Seldom
Reflector DDoS	N	Y	N	Y

* Assume that there is no other network errors or congestion.
* Assume that the spoofed source IP does not belong to the same domain.

3.2 Space-Efficient Monitoring Table

Compared to stateless method, the state method exceeds in its accuracy. But it requires significant memory and computational resource. To save the storage cost and computation overhead, Bloom filter, a kind of space-efficient hash data structure, is applied in our method.

Bloom Filter. Bloom filter is first described by Burton Bloom [4] and originally used to reduce the disk access to differential files and other applications, e.g. spell checkers. Now it has been extended to defend against DDoS attack [15, 19, 20]. The idea of Bloom filter is to allocate a vector v of m bits, initially all set to 0, and then choose k independent hash functions, $h_1, h_2, \ldots, h_k$, each with range $\{1, \ldots, m\}$. For each element $a \in A$, the bits at positions $h_1(a), h_2(a), \ldots, h_k(a)$ in v are set to 1(Figure 2(a)). Note that a particular bit might be set to 1 multiple times which may cause potential false result. Given a query for b we check the bits at positions $h_1(b), h_2(b), \ldots, h_k(b)$. If any of them is 0, then certainly b is not in the set A. Otherwise we conjecture that b is in the set. However there is a certain probability that Bloom filter give false result, which is called a "false positive". The parameters k and m should be chosen such that the probability of a false positive is acceptable.

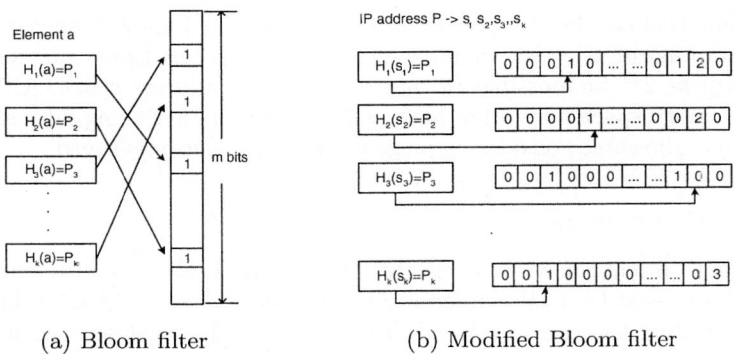

(a) Bloom filter   (b) Modified Bloom filter

Fig. 2. Bloom filter uses independent hash functions to map input into corresponding bits

Modified Monitoring Table. Considering numerous IP addresses in network traffic, using limited m bit array to record IP address is not sufficient and may bring high false positive. We make two main modifications to original Bloom filter as Figure 2(b) shown: First, we use an array of counts table to substitute m bit array. Second we split the IP address into several segments and hash them separately into hash table.

After using counts table to replace m bit array, all the counts are initially 0. When a key is inserted or deleted, the counts are incremented or decremented by 1 accordingly. When a count changes from 0 to 1, the corresponding bit is turned on. When a count changes from 1 to 0 the corresponding bit is turned off. The number in the count indicates the current statistic results of traffic.

The IP address is split into k segments and in our paper k is set to 4. Then each segment is an octet in IP address, which is convenient for process. Since the value range for each octet is from 0 to 255, the m is set to 256, i.e. each table contains 256 counts. If the IP address is directly hashed into monitoring table as [20] did, there will occur serious hash collision. The reason is the counts is rather limited compared to numerous values of IP addresses in the internet. When the IP address is separated into several segments, the value range for each segment is rather small for each segment.

In our defense method, both the source IP and destination IP are recorded in hash table. In the Bloom filter, k tables by m bins with k independent hash functions are used to record IP address of recent three-way handshakes. Although it is possible that some segments of two IP addresses are mapped into the same count in one table, the probability is rather little that all the segments of two different IP addresses are mapped to the same counts in all k tables.

When recording a segment of the IP address, the segment is mapped into a count according to the its value. For example, the IP address '202.114.64.2' is split into '202','114','64' and '2'. The segment '202' is recorded into the 202th count of the table, '114' into 114th count and so on. Our hash function does not require any cryptographic one-way properties, which is impossible to reconstruct the list of keys in a filter without doing an exhaustive search of the key space. A simply function can be straightforward to compute at high link speeds.

The advantage of using Bloom filter is to save storage cost from using memory of the complete 2^{32} for possible IP address to $k*m$ address space. Although reducing memory space may bring hash collision and further bring false alarms, the errors are allowable considering large volume of memory is saved.

3.3 Detection Scheme

To detect both direct DDoS and reflector DDoS attack, the source IP and destination IP are recorded in the different hash tables. Two sets of hash tables are used for recording the source IP and destination IP. To illustrate the method clearly, one set of hash tables is called destination IP table and denoted as H_d. The other is called source IP tables and denoted as H_s. When a SYN packet is captured from the outgoing traffic, the source IP and destination IP are hashed into the hash table H_d and H_s respectively. If the corresponding count is 0, the

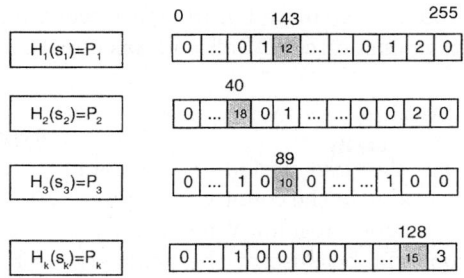

Fig. 3. The DDoS attack alarm will be announced when there is at least one count in each table beyond the threshold

corresponding count is turned on. If the count is already turned on, the count is incremented accordingly. When corresponding ACK/SYN packet for the second round of handshake is soon captured in the incoming traffic. Both the source IP and destination IP are hashed into the hash table again. The corresponding count is decremented by 1. When a count changes from 1 to 0 the corresponding bit is turned off. The count will keep unchanged if the first two rounds of three-way handshake are completely captured at the ingress and egress router at the source side. These counts are reset for every period t. The setting of parameter t will be discussed in Section 4.

When a direct DDoS attack happens, there is no any second round handshake packet ACK/SYN sent back to response previous SYN. Therefore, the count has no chance to be decremented by 1 for this handshake. It cannot recover to original value because it has been increased by 1. When a DDoS attack happens, an exceptional heavy volume of packets are sent toward to the victim. The value of the count is expected to increase dramatically. If the value of a count exceeds the predefined threshold during period t, this value is regarded as suspicious. In Figure 3, the suspicious value is filled with gray color. If there is at least one count in each table containing suspicious value, the DDoS attack alarm will be launched. In Figure 3, there is a suspicious value in each table. The counts IDs are 143, 40, 89, 128 and IP 143.40.89.128 is reconstructed. This reconstructed IP is called suspicious IP and it means there is suspicious traffic toward 143.40.89.128.

Detection scheme against reflector attack has the same philosophy as detection against direct one but uses different hash tables set. H_s is used for direct attack detection and H_d for reflector one. If there exists suspicious IP in H_s, direct DDoS attack alarm is announced and sent to the host with this IP. On the other hand, if there exists suspicious IP in H_d, It means there is suspicious reflector DDoS attack toward the this IP.

4 Experiments Results

Experiments are designed to evaluate the performance of our detection method. First we discuss how set the parameter of reset period t. Then the network simulator NS2 [21] is used to simulate DDoS attack scenarios. In NS2 simulation the detection schemes against direct DDoS and reflector DDoS will be evaluated.

4.1 Parameter t Setting

The parameter t defines the reset period of each count in the monitoring table. After each period t, the value in the count will be reset to 0. An appropriate value for t will improve the detection results. When there is no attack traffic, the value of count will keep constant because of the symmetric SYN and ACK/SYN packets in handshake. To get a suitable t value, we first only play normal traffic in simulation and observe the mean and the standard deviation of count values according to different t. The experiment results are listed in Table 2:

Table 2. The mean and standard deviation of count values for different parameters t

t(sec)	mean	standard deviation
0.3	-0.25	3.277
0.5	2.6075	2.1299
1	4.6418	1.6921
5	21.2667	4.5586
10	43.0	5.5976
15	63.4	5.8566

When the t is set a larger value, the mean grows larger because there are more unfinished handshakes during a larger t period. The unfinished handshake will increase the value of the count. The larger t may effect the accuracy of detection because it brings difficulty to decide whether the large value is caused by malicious traffic.

The smaller value for t ensures early detection against a DDoS attack and the mean value is approaching zero. The little value of count can distinguish the normal traffic from the attacking traffic. But the smallest value for t is not always the best choice. From the standard deviation column, we find the smaller value for t may cause larger deviation value, which means the value fluctuates more frequently for small t. It is because during the less t period for sampling handshakes will indicate the more deviation.

We should make a tradeoff between the less mean and less deviation to ensure the accuracy and stability of detection results. In the following experiments, the t is set to 1 second.

4.2 Detection Results

To evaluate the detection method against direct DDoS, three scenarios are designed: there is no attacking traffic, the total traffic contains 1% attacking traffic and the total traffic contains 5% attacking traffic. The network delay from the source to the victim server is set to 100ms and the bottleneck bandwidth for

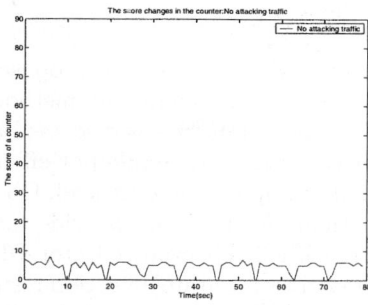 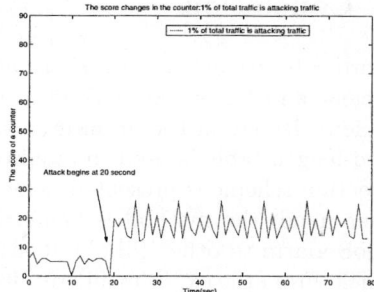

(a) There is no direct attacking traffic

(b) the total traffic contains 1% direct attacking traffic

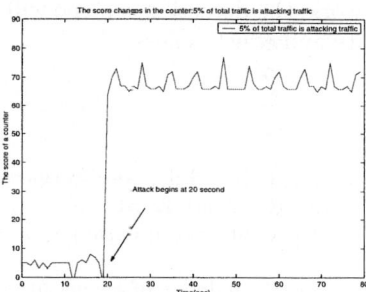 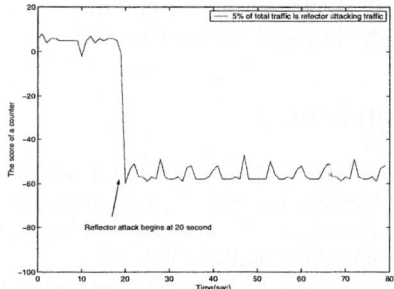

(c) the total traffic contains 5% direct attacking traffic

(d) the total traffic contains 5% reflector attacking traffic

Fig. 4. The value of a count increases when a direct DDoS attack begins and it decreases when a reflector DDoS attack happens

victim server is 10M. The attacking traffic begins the 20 second and the whole simulation last for 80 seconds. The detection results are shown in the Figure 4.

As the figure shown, when the attack begins, the score will increase and distinguish itself from normal score. When there is more attacking traffic, the score will be increased more dramatically. Figure 4(c) shows the 5% attacking traffic triggers a much larger score than 1% attacking traffic in Figure 4(b). Our method can accurately find the abnormal score caused by direct DDoS attack with fixed-length monitoring table.

Then the performance of reflector DDoS attack detection is evaluated. In reflector attack experiment, the parameter setting in NS2 is almost same as the direct one except that the spoofed source IP is filled with the victim's IP. Therefore, malicious traffic will be reflected to the victim by innocent reflectors. From Figure 4(d), we can see the value of count decreases evidently when a reflector DDoS attack is launched. The decrease is explained by the existence of numerous reflected ACK/SYN packets. These packets will decrement the value in the count while there are no previous corresponding SYN packets to increase the value. Thus the value will be reduced sharply.

5 Conclusion

In order to attract more ISPs to attend the source-end defense, we propose an efficient and beneficial method in this paper. On the one hand, the method is efficient. Based on Bloom filter, a space-efficient data structure is discussed and fixed-length table is used to monitor traffic at the source. A simple but efficient detection scheme is presented, which brings little computation overhead. On the other hand, the method is beneficial. the method can not only provide direct DDoS alarm to other ISPs, but also protect the ISP itself from reflector DDoS attack. From the experiments results our method gives accurate detection results.

The low resource requirement brings limited performance degradation to ISPs. It also provides benefits to ISP, which will motivate more ISPs to join the widely deployment of source-end defense. Our method is a more practical method than most of current source-end methods. In future work, the detection scheme will be applied to real internet to evaluate the feasibility and effectiveness.

References

1. Rocky.K.Chang: Defending against flooding-based distributed denial-of-service attacks: a tutorial. Communications Magazine, IEEE **40** (2002) 42–51
2. Postel, J.: Transmission Control Protocol : DARPA internet program protocol specification,RFC 793 (1981)
3. Ferguson, P., Senie, D.: Network ingress filtering: Defeating denial of service attacks which employ IP source address spoofing (2000)
4. Bloom, B.H.: Space/time trade-offs in hash coding with allowable errors. Communications of the ACM **13** (1970) 422–426
5. Wang, H., Zhang, D., Shin, K.G.: Detecting SYN flooding attacks. In: Proceedings of IEEE INFOCOM. Volume 3. (2002) 1530–1539
6. Jin, C., Wang, H.N., Shin, K.G.: Hop-count filtering: An effective defense against spoofed DDoS traffic. In: Proceedings of the 10th ACM conference on Computer and communication security(CCS), ACM Press (2003) 30–41
7. Lemon, J.: Resisting SYN flood DoS attacks with a SYN cache. In: In Proceedings of the BSDCon 2002 Conference. (2002)
8. Mirkovic, J., Prier, G.: Attacking DDoS at the source. In: In 10th Proceedings of the IEEE International Conference on Network Protocols, Paris, France. (2002)
9. Yaar, A., Perrig, A., Song, D.: SIFF: A stateless internet flow filter to mitigate DDoS flooding attacks. In: Proceedings. 2004 IEEE Symposium, Security and Privacy. (2004) 130–143
10. Tupakula, U., Varadharajan, V.: Counteracting DDoS attacks in multiple ISP domains using routing arbiter architecture. In: Networks ICON2003. The 11th IEEE International Conference. (2003) 455–460
11. Sung, M., Xu, J.: IP traceback-based intelligent packet filtering: A novel technique for defending against internet DDoS attacks. IEEE Transactions on Parallel and Distributed Systems **14** (2003) 861–872
12. Dean, D., Franklin, M., Stubblefield, A.: An algebraic approach to IP traceback. Information and System Security **5** (2002) 119–137
13. Park, K., Lee, H.: On the effectiveness of probabilistic packet marking for IP traceback under denial of service attack. In: INFOCOM. (2001) 338–347

14. Savage, S., Wetherall, D., Karlin, A., Anderson, T.: Practical network support for IP traceback. In: Proceedings of the ACM SIGCOMM Conference, ACM Press (2000) 295–306
15. Snoeren, A.C.: Hash-based IP traceback. In: Proceedings of the ACM SIGCOMM Conference, ACM Press (2001) 3–14
16. Song, D.X , Perrig, A.: Advanced and authenticated marking schemes for IP traceback. In: INFOCOM 2001. (2001) 878–886
17. Ioannidis, J., Bellovin, S.M.: Implementing pushback: Router-based defense against DDoS attacks. In: Proceedings of Network and Distributed System Security Symposium, Catamaran Resort Hotel San Diego, California, The Internet Society (2002)
18. Schuba, C.L., Krsul, I.V., Kuhn, M.G., Spafford, E.H., Sundaram, A., Zamboni, D.: Analysis of a denial of service attack on TCP. In: Proceedings of the 1997 IEEE Symposium on Security and Privacy, IEEE Computer Society, IEEE Computer Society Press (1997) 208–223
19. Abdelsayed, S., Glimsholt, D., Leckie, C., Ryan, S., Shami, S.: An efficient filter for denial-of-service bandwidth attacks. In: IEEE Global Telecommunications Conference, 2003. GLOBECOM '03. Volume 3. (2003) 1353–1357
20. Chan, E., Chan, H., Chan, K.M.and Chan, V.C.S., etc.: IDR: an intrusion detection router for defending against distributed denial-of-service(DDoS) attacks. In: Proceedings of the 7th International Symposium on Parallel Architectures, Algorithms and Networks 2004(ISPAN'04). (2004) 581–586
21. Network Simulator, NS2: (http://www.isi.edu/nsnam/ns/)

Study on Equipment Interoperation Chain Model in Grid Environment*

Yuexuan Wang and Cheng Wu

National CIMS Engineering Research Center, Department of Automation,
Tsinghua University, Beijing 100084, P.R. China
{wangyuexuan, wuc}@tsinghua.edu.cn

Abstract. Scientific collaboration has emerged as an important tool for getting forefront research results by interoperating geographically distributed scientific equipment to solve complicated scientific problems. Grid technologies offer effective strategies to achieve this ambitious goal. However, more capabilities are required in the context of Equipment Grid due to the complexity of collaboration between equipment resources. In this paper an interesting equipment interoperation chain model is proposed. Equipment resources are organized into equipment pools, based on which the interoperation chain of equipment is built. The performance is discussed by means of several theoretical tools like Petri Net and π-Calculus from the different viewpoint of users. The structure of interoperation chain is proven highly efficient and feasible. Finally we analyze the prospective direction and challenges in this field.

1 Introduction

With the development of scientific research and continuous emergency of cross-discipline studies, it becomes highly desirable to share related knowledge and equipment, especially those expensive or rare ones. However, due to different communication protocols and data formats, information cannot be easily integrated and understood by each other, making it difficult to achieve this ambitious goal and thus affecting the research severely [1]. Besides that, many scheduling and management problems remain unresolved in this context for large scale scientific applications.

Fortunately, grid technologies provide revolutionary ways to couple geographically distributed equipment resources and solve above problems in wide area networks [2][3][4][5][6]. The ultimate goal of grid is to build an information processing infrastrucrure by intergrating high-speed Internet, supercomputers, sensors, instruments, databases and people in the world together and make them be an organic macrocosm, providing nontrivial quality of services [3]. Meanwhile, there is no need to know the location of such services. Thus we can enjoy unprecedented super computing power just as if we are using electric power. This provides an advanced means for the remote sharing and cooperation of equipment and instruments.

---

* This paper is supported by China "211 project" "15" construct project: National Universities Equipment and Resource Sharing System and China Postdoctoral Science Foundation (No. 2003034155).

Equipment Grid provides an abstraction of equipments, then presents and publishes their functionalities in the form of grid service to some granularity. Each service clearly shows its processing flow and value. Users can conveniently utilize published services despite their intrinsic specific technologies. Any service conforming to the certain standards may become an element in a workflow, and any change from one participant will not affect its cooperative counterpart. In such way, the uniform operation and cooperative sharing of equipment can be achieved [7][8][9][10].

However, more capabilities are required in the context of Equipment Grid due to the complexity of collaboration between equipment resources. To accomplish a complicated task, equipment grid application often integrates with a large number of equipment to cooperate, which involves not only selecting appropriate equipment service, but also ensuring the optimization of service flow.

In this paper, a promising equipment interoperation chain model is proposed from the perspective of the grid users in the context of Equipment Grid. Interoperability means multiple equipment or equipment systems can provide and accept services between each other, so as to endow their ability of unified and effective operability. Such ability should satisfy corresponding criteria when exchanging control and/or data information. Interoperability involves several aspects of two levels: technical interoperability that equipments send information and utilize information among each other, and semantic interoperability that equipments have the same understanding of the same information with each other.

The rest of the paper is organized as follows. In Section 2, we examine some related work on equipment grid and equipment interoperation. In Section 3, we show the equipment resource organization model called equipment pool. It is precondition of equipment interoperation chain modeling. And Section 5 presents the equipment interoperation chain model and its performance analysis. In Section 5, we present the design of an equipment interoperation chain system based on the proposed model and show how the equipment interoperation chain works in equipment grid. Finally, Section 6 concludes this paper.

2 Related Work

E-Science is about global collaboration in key areas of science and the next generation of infrastructure that will enable it. It is important to share precious equipment such as satellites, Hubble Telescopes, etc [11][12]. NEESgrid is implemented as a national network-enabled collaboration for earthquake engineering research. Members of the earthquake engineering community will be able to interact with one another, access unique, next generation instruments and equipment, share data and computational resources, and retrieve information from digital libraries without regard to geographical location [13]. DataGrid is a project funded by European Union [5][6]. The objective is to build the next generation computing infrastructure providing intensive computation and analysis of shared large-scale databases, from hundreds of TeraBytes to PetaBytes, across widely distributed scientific communities. Our goal is to exploit a combination of advanced networking, middleware services, and remote instrumentation technologies to achieve interactive "better - than - being - there" capabilities for remote experiment planning, instrument operation, data acquisition, reduction and analysis. These capabilities are being deployed and evaluated at several X-ray crystallography facilities including the Advanced Light Source and the Indiana University Molecular Structure Center. China Education and Scientific Research Grid Project (ChinaGrid) is another grid program, aiming at constructing public service systems for education and research in China [14]. An education resources sharing grid (CersGrid) based on network was investigated and developed by Tsinghua University and it is expected to improve education equipment collaboration. However, to realize equipment interoperation in grid still has a long way to go.

Equipment interoperation chain is the "system of systems" coupled by grid technologies, which can realize interlink, interconnection and interoperation of all the equipment nodes, and improve the automation of information acquisition, processing, publishing and utilizing. By means of OGSA (Open Grid Service Architecture) [16][17], unified information presentation and consistent using manner can be set up for different systems, therefore correct understanding is formed, correct interoperating behavior is produced, and in this way interoperation is upgraded to cognitive domain. With unified platform, interfacing standard and interfacing flow, any information resource, equipment and so on. As long as they conform to the specification, they can provide or acquire information to and from the grid, automatically realize the interoperation with other equipments. With the technology of XML, information form can be normalized, differences in data management, storing form and searching manner of various information systems can be shielded. As a result, the problem that "some obtained data can not be used or can not be conveniently used" is resolved, and in unified semantics information interoperability, high-degree integration and sharing are achieved.

3 Equipment Resource Organization Model: Equipment Pool

Based on the current schemes of equipment management, equipment will be classified by a new criterion. A concept of "meta-equipment" is introduced and then a global uniform hierarchical equipment grid model called an equipment pool is build. The equipment pool consists of same kind of equipments and different kinds of equipment pools constitute an equipment pool alliance. Equipments of same kind will then logically be organized and managed in a dynamical equipment pool. Equipments distributed geographically will be connected with high-speed networks and agglutinated with technically designed middleware software. Through the Web interface, it receives the requests from scientific researchers here and there for experiments and dispatches them to a proper node. The equipment pool supports equipment joining and leaving dynamically. It extracts equipment resource parameters from the heterogeneous to from the basis of the uniform equipment resource presentation and avoids blindness for equipment resource choosing effectively. This will greatly improve the service quality and utilization rate and avoid the low efficiency and complexity caused by the distributed applications to meet the demand of practicability under present conditions. In this way, the whole system acts as a dynamical aggregate of different equipments, namely a dynamical equipment pool alliance. As Fig. 1 shown, different equipment and different equipment pools interconnect to form the interoperation chain of different equipments to provide high-level service to the users. In a word, integrally, the system presents a three-layer framework structure of "equipment- equipment pool- equipment pool alliance" to achieve layered management and then reduce the costs. The equipment pool is the equipment resource organization model and it provides precondition to the equipment interoperation chain.

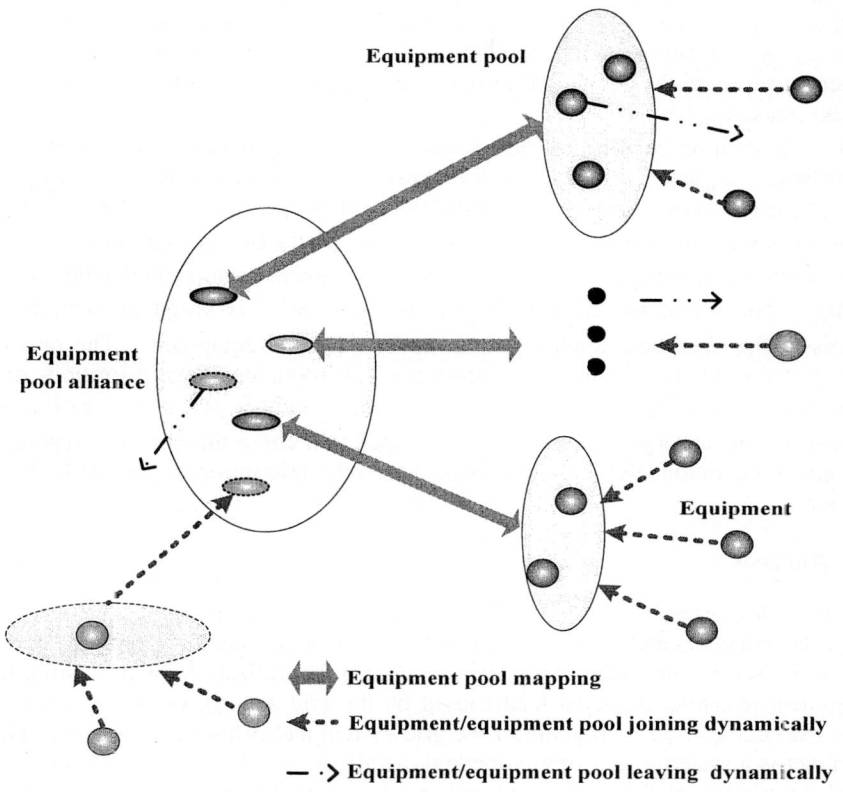

Fig. 1. Equipment pool

4 Equipment Interoperation Chain Modeling and Analysis

4.1 Equipment Grid and Its Interoperation Chain Model

Based on the equipment pool as shown in Section 3, an equipment grid can be regarded as a 4-tuple: $DIG = \{U, R, P, M_\Pi\}$.

U : Set of grid users, including the resource provider and the resource consumer and tagged $U_{\text{Pr}oS}$ and U_{ConS} respectively. $U = U_{\text{Pr}oS} \cup U_{ConS}$. For there might be some cases that a consumer is also a resource provider, we can see $U_{\text{Pr}oS} \cap U_{ConS} \neq \Phi$.

R : Resources in the system, including equipment resource set D and other assistant resource set A (such as network, etc.). The reason we divide the resources in the system as two parts is that we will emphasize the main entity in the system: the sharing mechanism of equipment resource research. $D = \{T; Op(t \in T, u \in U_{\Pr oS})\}$, T is type set of the equipment resources, u is subset of the resource provider, Op denotes the operation set offered by the t types of equipment resources provided by u. Following the trend of SOA (Service-Oriented Architecture) service architecture, each sharing operation of each resource will publish a service in the equipment grid system. Therefore, the equipment resource set D equals the set of operation, that's to say $D = \{Op(u \in U_{\Pr oS})\}$.

P : The sharing rule set of the resource set by the resource provider. It can be described as the following mathematical expression: $U_{\Pr oS} * U_{ConS} * OP \rightarrow \{yes, no, N/A\}$, The value will certain be N/A if a user who do not have the possession right $(U1, U2, op(t1, U1)) = N/A$, if $UI \neq U1$, as said above, it shows that $U1$ do not have the possession right of the equipment resource belonging to UI.

M_Π : The set of the equipment interoperation chain is based on workflow. It expresses the operation combination mode between the equipments. The operation interoperation model can be a combination of different functional operations of the same type of equipment or of different ones. So we can get $M_\Pi = \{op^+, op \in OP(t, u)\}$. It aims to record at large the equipment interoperation chain through the construct of equipment operations in the system using a flexible description to provide high-level service.

4.2 Analysis

Based on the definition of the 4-tuple equipment grid model discussed above, we will study the behaviors and features based on Petri Net and π-Calculus theory separately.

For the service providers, they mainly concern the utilization of the sharing local equipment resource, the local load caused by the grid actions, i.e. the effect on the local resource caused by running of the grid system and behaviors of the consumers. Petri Net is a systemic description method mainly droved by status, and is proper for static description of the component and service internal behaviors. Furthermore, the visual description of Petri Net makes the system description more intuitionistic. Because the scale of the local service system on one site is small, it is easy to rage the behavior situations. It is therefore feasible to model the running situation using the Petri Net method.

For service consumers, they care how to use the service in the grid system fast and better. They accentuate the pace and service quality, and this is mainly about the optimization of the service combination in the dynamical service composing, so it can be merge into the research work of a system layer. The exclusive work of this part is the deadlock and the verification of the reachability. Because the resource owners can set the access right of their shared equipment resources, each service selection at the dynamical service combination period must accord to the access right of the consumers on the resource when they visit the grid interoperation chain system.

For the system, the running situation of the overall grid environment, such as the feasibility and efficiency of the combination of different services, system wasting overall, etc., should be emphasized. The running of the whole grid system does not care the internal situation of each service. Service can be regard as an independent running entity. So we can give much concern about the interaction between behaviors visible outside and dynamical change between services. Moreover, the whole grid system is more complex than the partial local environment. What's more, the actions and behaviors of the system trend are incertitude and pluralistic. So π-Calculus is suitable for system action and behavior describing is mobile, it is easier and more suitable than Petri Net when describing the dynamic change between services. Concretely, on the premises $\{U;R;P\}$ is already defined, elements in $M_\Pi = \{op^+, op \in OP(t,u)\}$ will be validated about the deadlocking and reachability using π-Calculus and similar elements will be analyzed and compared using a equivalent comparison method to give the evidence for selecting and optimizing in dynamical service combination.

5 The Equipment Interoperation Chain System

Based on the equipment interoperation chain model proposed in Section 4, we designed an equipment interoperation chain system based on SOA service architecture, as Fig. 2 shown. The logical model "Information center" records all kinds of information. Information about the equipment and nodes in the system submits at the component of "equipment/node information warehouse" in the information center, and the content to submit includes portal information, deployment information, the equipment category and parameter attributes, the access and control information of the equipments, etc. The definition of the flow of the equipment resource interoperating workflow is recorded at the "workflow warehouse". In Fig. 2, a workflow definition example of "call the service 3 firstly, and then service 4" is shown, and this flow is named "workflow 1".

Certain nodes have their own local operating environment for equipment, and the basic functional interface of the equipment resource is published in services. The combination flow of multiple equipment resources in a node can be defined and saved beforehand, then released as a service to provide high-level function. In Fig. 2, the flow database of node A describes that the flow of service 4 calls service 1 first, and then service 2.

The data representation mode in the local operating environment of equipments may be specific. The high-level data in the object system should be mapped to the relevant local data, and this will be done by "object transform interface module". The model of "concrete implement environment" will take charge of a certain implement process of the equipment.

The logical module "job manager" or "resource agent" will accept the job request from users. When receiving a request, the job manager would query the flow definition of the work flow from the "workflow warehouse" in the information center; then for each operation, query "equipment/node information warehouse", select the resource according to users' demand for access right and matching conditions or scheduling rule made previously, transmit the operating request to the objective node, and continue the resource choosing and scheduling for the next operation. Fig. 2 shows a user's job flow for workflow 1: there are two operations in workflow1. The first one is service 3, and its result of dynamical choosing and scheduling is node B.

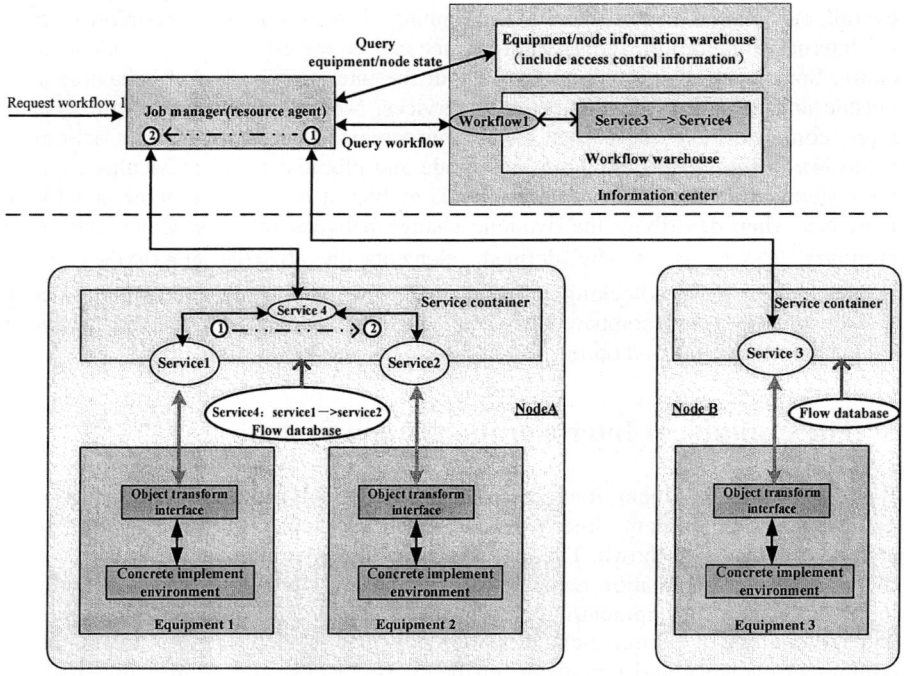

Fig. 2. The Equipment Interoperation Chain Architecture

The job manager sends the request to node B. when service 3 is finished it is the turn for the second operation of service 4 in workflow 1. Node A is selected this time. So the request and result from service 3 is transmitted to service 4 of Node A; service 4 is high-level service made up of service 1 and service 2. According to the flow setting in the flow database, service 1 and service 2 are called successively. Each non-combined service, such as service 1, service 2, service 3, corresponds to a basic operation provided by the concrete equipment respectively.

6 Conclusions and Future Work

Based on grid technologies and SOA service architecture, the equipment interoperation chain provides effective strategies to handle interoperation issues in the context of equipment grid. Equipment resources are organized into equipment tools according to some certain criterions. Accordingly, virtual equipments integrating equipment resources distributed across a machine room, institution, or the globe are created, which is used to perform interoperation and share services. The performance and characteristic of the equipment interoperation chain are also discussed by means of Petri Net and π-Calculus theories. The abstract model of target equipment grid is also brought forward.

Needless to say, achieving this vision requires us to overcome many challenges. We must learn how to research the problems that we want to solve the equipment resource services which are available to use and we need to discover the way to knit those equipment resources and interoperation chains into grid environments. What's more, how to validate and optimize interoperation chain models is the key to the equipment grid and it is an emergency to find an efficient solution. Anyway, with this challenge comes the opportunity, and as this rich, distributed environment enables us to tackle problems that would simply not be possible with today's technologies.

References

1. Jindong Wang, Hai Zhao, Guangjie Han, Jiyong Wang: Research of a SBDM model based on interoperable computing. Journal of China Institute of Communications (2004), 25 (4): 84 - 93
2. Foster I, Kesselman C.: The Grid: Blueprint for a future Computing Infrastructure. USA: Morgan Kaufmann (1999)
3. Foster, I., Kesselman, C., et al.: The Anatomy of the grid: Enabling scalable virtual organizations. International Journal of Supercomputer Applications (2001) 15(3): 200 - 222.
4. Zhihui Du, Yu Chen, Peng Liu: Grid Computing. Publishing House of Tsinghua University (2002)
5. Ian Foster, Carl Kesselman: The Grid: Blue print for a New Computing Infrastructure, 2nd Edition. USA: Morgan Kaufmann (2004).
6. Hai Jin, Pingpeng Yuan, Ke Sh:. Grid Copmuting 2. Publishing House of Electronics Industry (2004)
7. Yuexuan Wang, Lianchen Liu, Xixiang Hu, Cheng Wu: The Study on Simulation Grid Technology for Equipment Resource Sharing System. In Proceedings of the 5th World Congress on Intelligent Control and Automation (2004) 3235-3239
8. Yuexuan Wang, Cheng Wu, Xixiang Hu, Lianchen Liu: The Study of Equipment Grid Based on Simulation Modeling. Computer Integrated Manufacturing Systems (2004) 10(9): 1031-1035.
9. Yuexuan Wang, Lianchen Liu, Cheng Wu: Research on equipment resource scheduling in grids. The Third International Conference on Grid and Cooperative Computing (GCC 2004). wuhan, China (2004) 927 - 930.
10. Yuexuan Wang, Lianchen Liu, Cheng Wu. Research on Equipment Grid Platform for Resource Sharing. World Engineers Convention (WEC) Shanghai, (2004) 148-151.
11. Hey, A., and Trefethen, A. The UK e-Science Core Programme and the Grid. Future Generation Computer (2002) 18 (8): 1017-1031.
12. Hey, A., Trefethen A. The data deluge: An e-science perspective in Grid Computing: Making the Global Infrastructure a Reality. Wiley, New York (2003)
13. The NEES System Integration Team. NEESgrid TR-2004-13: Introduction to NEESgrid. August 23, (2004) http://it.nees.org/documentation/pdf/TR_2004_13.pdf.
14. China Education and Scientific Research Grid Work Group. China Education and Scientific Research Grid Support Platform Design. Publishing House of Tsinghua University (2004)
15. Foster, I., Kesselman, C., et al. The Philosophy of the Grid: An Open Grid Service Architecture for Distributed Systems. Global Grid Forum (2002)
16. Foster, I., Gannon, D., et al. Open Grid Services Architecture Use Cases Version 1.0. Global Grid Forum public documents (GFD-I.029). http://www.ggf.org/documents/final.htm. 2004.
17. Yolanda, G., Ewa, D., et al. Artificial Intelligence and Grids: Workflow Planning and Beyond. IEEE Intelligent Systems (2004) 19 (1): 26 - 33.

Grid Accounting Information Service with End-to-End User Identity

Beob Kyun Kim[1], Haeng Jin Jang[2], Tingting Li[1], Dong Un An[1], and Seung Jong Chung[1]

[1] Dept. of Computer Engineering, Chonbuk National University, South Korea
{kyun, duan, sjchung}@chonbuk.ac.kr, pekingltt@yahoo.com.cn
[2] Korea Institute of Science and Technology Information
hjjang@kisti.re.kr

Abstract. Grid computing virtualizes heterogeneous geographically disperse resources. Because of the characteristics of the grid environment, the concept of 'user' is different from that of traditional local computing environment. That mean, new resolution that providing the end-to-end user identity from grid user to local account is needed. In this paper, we design and implement an accounting information gathering and service (AIService) system. To resolve this problem, we designed a grid access control system, called PGAM. Usage Record of UR-WG in GGF is used as a common usage record. And we designed and implemented a grid service which provides the gathered accounting information.

1 Introduction

Grid computing represents the fundamental computing shift from a localized resource computing model to a fully-distributed virtual organization with shared resources [1][2][3][4]. Fueling the emergence of Grid computing is the ever-increasing cost of local information technology resources. With the Grid, companies achieve a cost efficient and effective mechanism for building and deploying applications across a wide spectrum of devices.

There are several commercial obstacles, most notably security and accounting, that have impeded the widespread adoption of the Grid. Several projects around security and authentication have begun both within and outside the Grid community, enabling companies to confidently use Grid services. Accounting for these services has until recently, been a sparsely-addressed problem, particularly in practice. The Grid community has yet to produce either framework or, better still, an implementation of Grid accounting [5][6].

We design and implement the accounting information gathering and service system. The gathering process is an implementation of monitoring block of GSAX (Grid Service Accounting Extension) framework [5] of RUS-WG (Resource Usage Service) in GGF. Grid accounting information service is named as "AIService" and is based on OGSA (Open Grid Service Architecture). It is included as a part of KMI [7] which is an integrated Grid middleware package.

To provide end-to-end user identity of accounting information on each resource, we use a Grid access control system, called PGAM [9]. This system works on heterogeneous resources and can be applied to the additional service development and its service. PGAM uses globus toolkit as its default middleware which is the most widely adopted Grid middleware in the world. PGAM tries to support site autonomy, a factor which encourages a site to get into the Grid environment, and provides template account mechanism.

And the schema of gathered and serviced accounting information is followed Usage Record - XML Format [10] of UR-WG (Usage Record) in GGF. The system comprises of several modules which work independently from each other. In addition, a portlet (AIService) to view the gathered accounting information has developed.

2 Related Works

The area of Grid accounting has also been investigated by others [5][10][11][12]. Some of these have provided guidance in outlining the accounting information gathering system architecture.

2.1 GSAX

GSAX [5] is an extensible OGSA accounting and logging framework. It is designed to provide a functionally modular accounting framework which can be expanded by adding or changing components, to allow use of accounting at many levels of application and user understanding, to provide information at different levels of granularity (from real-time information to data on a per-job basis), to integrate QoS and service-level agreements into the accounting framework, and at different levels, to be independent of any economic model, and to allow dynamic pricing stages. This framework is not tied to Grid or OGSA and can easily be adapted to scale with the growth in accountable web services.

The implementation of accounting information gathering process is an implementation of monitoring block of this framework. That means, this design gathers raw accounting information from each local site and produces grid-aware accounting information and may provide interfaces to communicate with metering block of this framework.

2.2 DGAS

DGAS (DataGrid Accounting System) model, developed by DataGrid Project [11], envisions a whole new economic Grid market, where supply and demand of Grid resources work in unison to strive towards equilibrium where all resources are fully utilized to the lowest possible price. The Home Location Register (HLR) acts as a local bank branch managing the fund status of a subset of Grid users and resources (one-bank-per-VO).

But, DataGrid employs a centralized resource broker intercepting all jobs within the Grid. Such centralized solutions are not in agreement with the decentralized nature of the Grid.

2.3 Usage Record (UR) and Resource Usage Service (RUS)

UR-WG in GGF provides information to the Grid community in the area of usage records and accounting. A UR defines a common format for exchanging basic accounting and usage data over the Grid. URs contain usage information which could potentially be collected at Grid sites, such as CPU-time, memory and network usage. A UR is an XML document whose structure is specified in a schema defined in terms of the XML schema Definition (XSD) [13] language. URs can be stored in a Resource Usage Service (RUS) [14], which is a Grid service for publishing and retrieving information about resource usage.

3 Design of Accounting Information Gathering System

Designed and implemented system uses the globus toolkit as its default middleware which is the most widely adopted grid middleware. But, the globus toolkit is lack of end-to-end user identity.

3.1 Identity in Globus Toolkit

Globus toolkit is one of the most widely adopted grid middleware in the world. Globus toolkit comprises a set of components that implement basic services for resource management, information service, data management, grid security, etc. GRAM (Grid Resource Allocation Manager) is responsible for access to remote resources, coallocation of distributed resources, and processing of heterogeneity of resource management. The gatekeeper is an extremely simple component that responds to a request by doing three things: performing mutual authentication of user and resource, determining a local user name for the remote user, and starting a job manager which executes as that local user and actually handles the request. Normally, when a request for access is received, the gatekeeper attempts to find the corresponding local username in the "grid-mapfile." This file lists pairs of certificate subjects (e.g.,

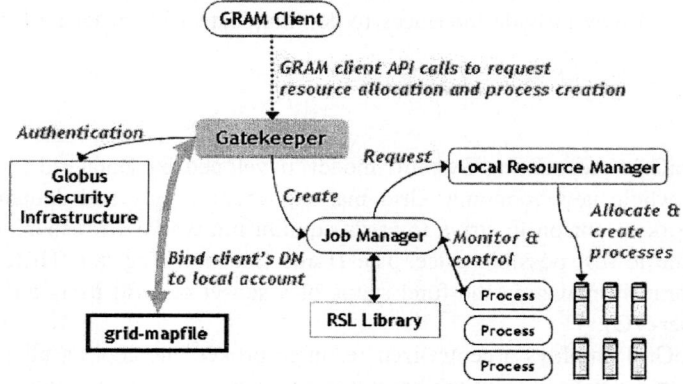

Fig. 1. Major components of the GRAM

```
"/O=Grid/O=Globus/OU=chonbuk.ac.kr/CN=hdg"   gw1
"/O=Grid/O=Globus/OU=chonbuk.ac.kr/CN=dgs"   gw2
"/O=Grid/O=Globus/OU=chonbuk.ac.kr/CN=kyun"  gw2
"/O=Grid/O=Globus/OU=chonbuk.ac.kr/CN=duan"  gw3
```

Fig. 2. An example of "grid-mapfile"

"/O=Grid/O=Globus/OU=chonbuk.ac.kr/CN=hdg") and usernames (e.g., gw1). If no line is found for the current subject, access request is denied.

In the original syntax of this file, several certificate subjects can be mapped to one local username. But, this mechanism cannot guarantee end-to-end user identity: who is the owner of local process or job, if there are several certificate subjects mapped to one local username. If the site administrator wants to trace the usage of local resource, he must deploy other monitoring or tracing tool which is implemented by kernel programming. For example, if there are process which is invoked by local account 'gw2' in fig. 2, who is responsible for these processes? Also, sharing of the same right to local files, directories and mails by multiple grid users can cause security problem, digging into privacy.

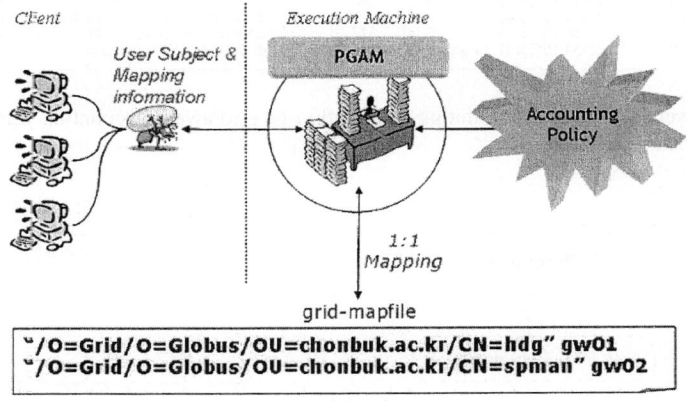

Fig. 3. Function of PGAM

3.2 PGAM

To guarantee end-to-end user identity, we adopted PGAM. It uses only 1-to-1 mapping of certificate subject and local username. But 1-to-1 mapping can cause a heavy load on the site administrator and local system. So, PGAM implements template account mechanism [15] to reduce the burden of administrator and local system.

When a grid user requests a right for access to local resource with his credential and personal information and job specification, PGAM creates new thread to process it. Each thread processes interaction from client, logs all the record during operation, enforce local resource management policies (e.g., pool of available local usernames, client host policy, stage policy, personal information policy, local resource's status policy). By using this system, we can get end-to-end user identity. In figure 4., PGAM provides mapped information to convert local accounting information to grid-aware accounting information.

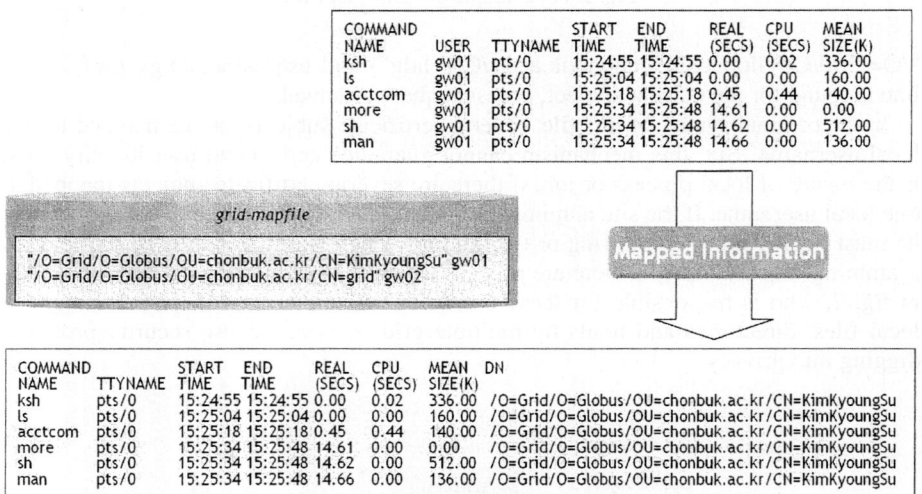

Fig. 4. Conversion of local accounting information to grid-aware accounting information by help of mapped information

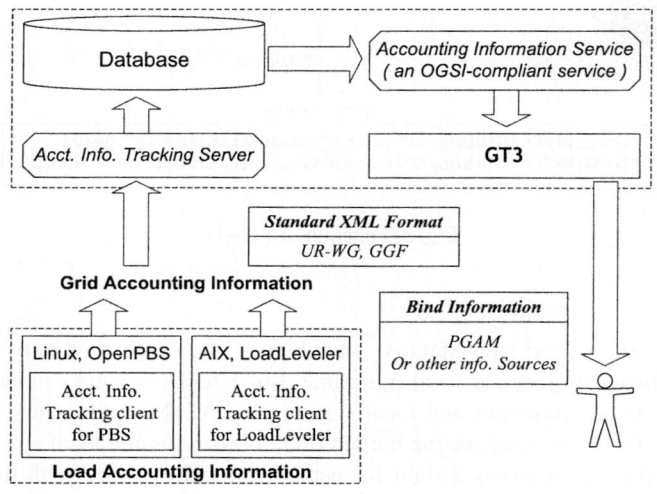

Fig. 5. System architecture with PGAM

3.3 System Architecture

Figure 5 shows a schematic view of this system. This system is divided into two major parts: accounting information gathering and accounting information service. Local accounting information, which has different format and meaning at each site, is transformed into a uniform grid accounting information with PGAM. And this system serves the requested information as an OGSI-compliant service if user or other authority requests accounting information.

3.4 Schema of Usage Record

Accounting in the grid environment is very different from that in the traditional computing environment, because the concept of the user is different from the traditional local user and the format of accounting data of each system is different from each other. Accounting information in the grid environment is not produced by the local user but by the grid user. The format and meaning of accounting information produced by OpenPBS is different from that produced by LoadLeveler. To build an accounting information service, which incorporates heterogeneous systems, each gathered accounting information must be transformed into a standard format.

In this paper, we choose Usage Record, suggested by UR-WG in GGF, as a standard format of the gathered accounting information. Usage Record is represented in an XML format and intended to be a common exchange format.

3.5 Gathering Accounting Information

We design the accounting information service system to be independent from any other services or resources and to follow the GSAX framework. Each resource gathers its raw accounting data and converts into the standard format and sends to accounting information tracking server.

Because of characteristics of the grid environment, most of grid programmers try to keep the autonomy of each site with minimum intrusion. Thus, the use of the output of the local accounting system is preferred to the use of intrusion into local system kernel. So, we decided to use the accounting log of each local scheduler. If local system uses fork as local scheduler on Linux, we will use the package 'psacct' which contains several utilities for monitoring process activities. If local system uses OpenPBS as local scheduler, we will use the accounting log produced by OpenPBS. If local system uses LoadLeveler, we will use the output of LoadLeveler.

Most of Unix operating systems provide utilities for monitoring process activities on each system. For the Linux, psacct package contains several utilities for monitoring process activities. The result of the process monitoring is saved into the file "pacct". The location of this file is different from each operating system and site. We use this file to extract process accounting information. This file contains information sufficient for Minimum Set of Usage Record. The extracted process accounting information from this file is sent to accounting information database in the Accounting Information Service. We tested it for IBM AIX 4.3.2, IBM AIX 5.1L, Linux 7.3, Linux 9.0.

Figure 6 shows the architecture for gathering process accounting information. If a machine is structured as a cluster, AITC is located in the front node only and creates

NodeController for each slave node. For each slave node, NodePacct collects process accounting information from the file "pact" and interacts with NodeController. AITC gathers process accounting information and converts into standard grid-aware accounting information with the information from PGAM and sends to accounting information tracking server.

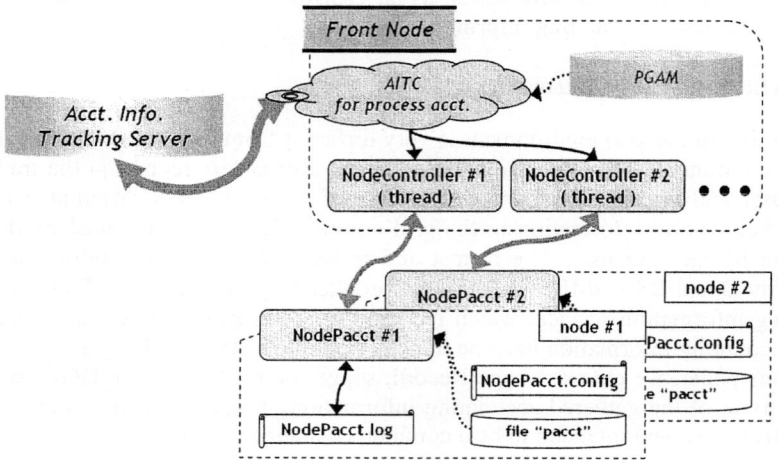

Fig. 6. Architecture for gathering process accounting information

Environments variables for this system is contained in "NodePacct.config" and check points for reading the file "pact" is contained in "NodePacct.log." PGAM provides the end-to-end user identity from grid user DN to local account. So, AITC collects only processes which are invoked by local accounts which is indicated by PGAM.

Figure 7 shows the architecture of gathering job accounting information produced by LoadLeveler. AITC gathers local job accounting information from LoadLeveler, converts into standard grid-aware accounting information with help of PGAM, and sends to accounting information tracking server. AITC in figure 7 is the almost same module in figure 6. AITC converts accounting information which is identified by local account into grid-aware accounting information which identified by grid user DN. Client for OpenPBS has similar architecture and operations to that for LoadLeveler.

In most cases, job scheduler has its own home directory and this directory is shared by each node. So, accounting information tracking client will be usually installed in the master or the front node of cluster. In Figure 7, 'LLUsageTracker.conf' is a configuration file that stores the LoadLeveler's home directory, the name of the file which contains LoadLeveler's slave nodes (LLNodes in Figure 7), and other related information.

Because the architecture of this tracking system is layered, extension to other job manager or other kind of platform is very easy. If new platform is planned to be included into the domain, all the need work is the development of the client for new platform and the registration on database server.

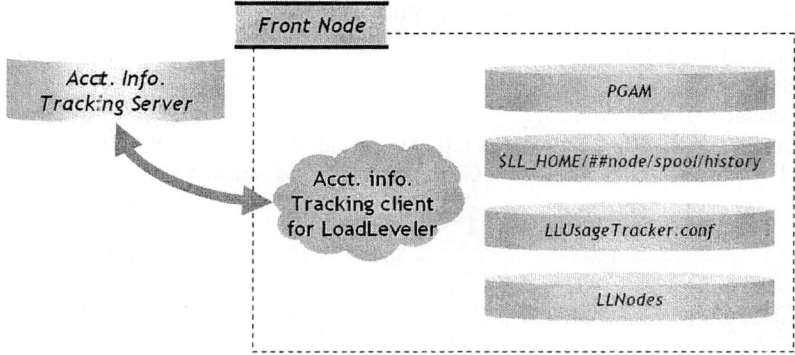

Fig. 7. Architecture of accounting information tracking client for LoadLeveler

3.6 Accounting Information Service

The gathered grid accounting information is served as an OGSI-compliant service. We named it as "AIService." To be an OGSI-compliant service, globus toolkit 3 must be installed in database server. Because multiple users can request his accounting information to one accounting information service simultaneously, this service must consider this relationship. We use GridSphere as our portal framework to build a client of this service. GridSphere provides a complete portal framework based upon the portlet API and a minimal set of core portlets.

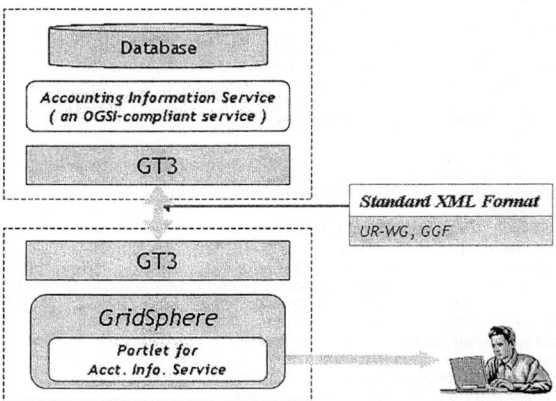

Fig. 8. Accounting information service using GridSphere

4 Implementation

We implemented this system in the following environments. For the portability of this system, Java is selected. We use MySQL for DBMS. But, for the service following OGSA, we would like to recommend the native XML database [16].

In the test the software conditions are given as follows:

Language : Java 1.4.2
DBMS : MySQL
OS : Redhat 8.0, 9.0 / AIX 5.1L
Job Manager : OpenPBS on Redhat 8.0, 9.0 / LoadLeveler on AIX 5.1L
Portal Framework & Middleware : GridSphere 2.0.2, Tomcat 5.0.28, GT 3.0.2

Fig. 9. An example of gathered process accounting information

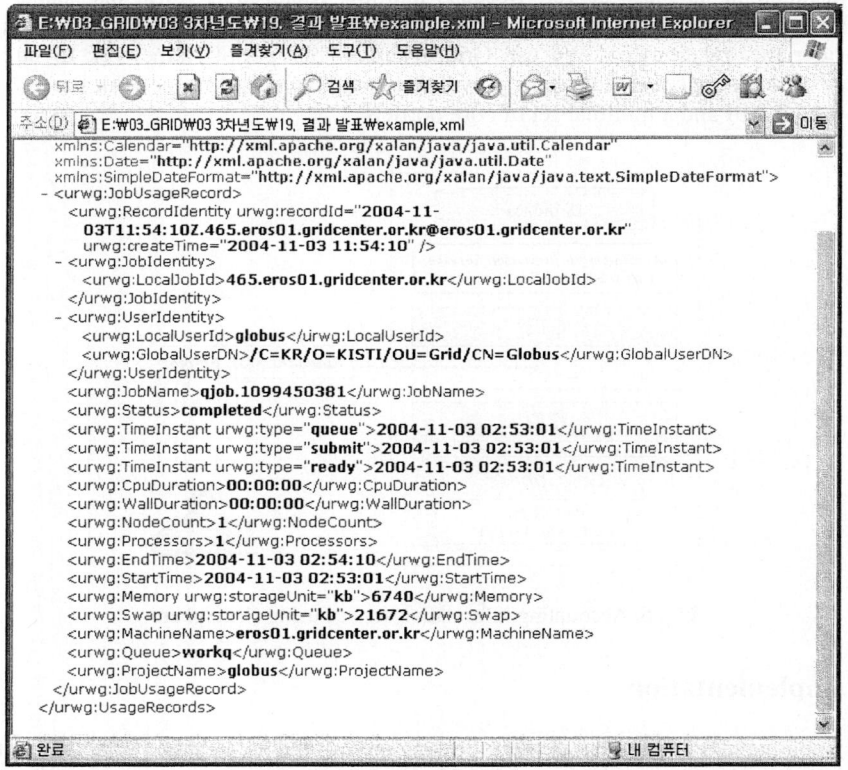

Fig. 10. A sample gathered grid accounting information

Figure 9 shows an example of gathered process accounting information. We can see all the required information without the grid user identity. To find the grid user who is responsible for these processes, utilities for access control in the grid environment is needed[9].

Figure 10 shows an example of gathered grid accounting information. This accounting information is expressed and stored as XML format [10]. By the operation of PGAM, the entity '<urwg:GlobalUserDN>' is included. Without this entity, we cannot identify which grid user is the real owner of this accounting information. With this information, we can identify the real grid user and we can create new service based on this accounting information.

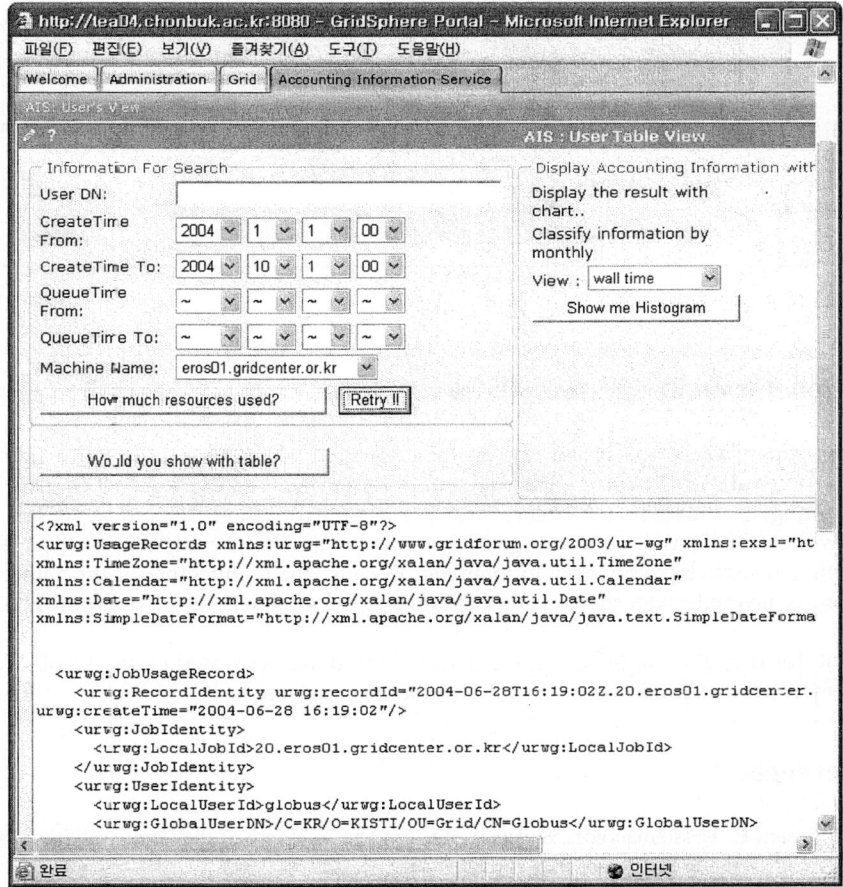

Fig. 11. AIService : a portlet for grid accounting information service

Figure 11 shows a view of the portlet for grid accounting information service. We developed this portlet to show the original grid accounting information in XML format and to show as table and to show a chart. Figure 12 shows table view of this grid accounting information. Other value added service can be easily developed based on this service.

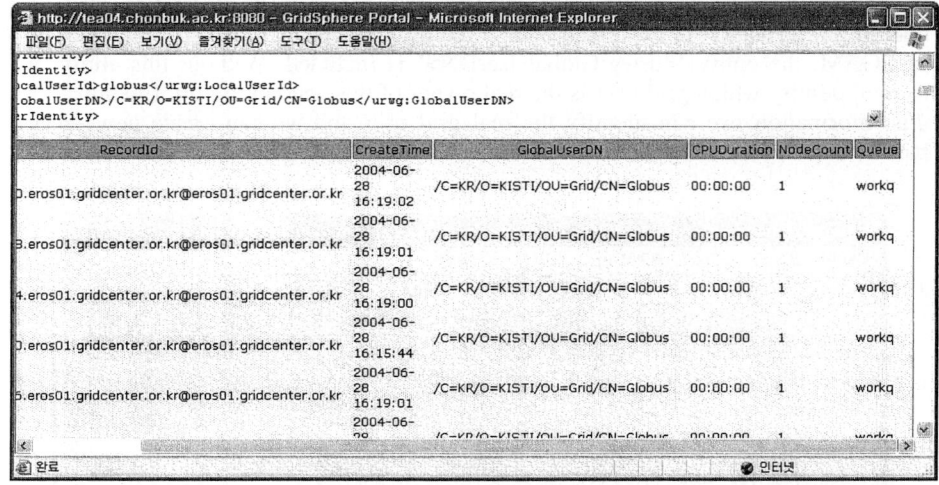

Fig. 12. AIService's table view

5 Conclusion and Future Works

In this paper, we designed and implemented the grid accounting information gathering system and its service. This system follows the GSAX framework and the accounting information is formatted so that it follows Usage Record suggested by UR-WG in GGF. And we developed its service as an OGSI-compliant service. This system and service is very easy to maintain. Because the architecture of the gathering system is layered, extension to other job manager or other kind of platform is very easy.

But, for the future application, the native XML database would be used as DBMS. And more various kind of Job Manager would be considered.

References

1. I. Foster, C. Kesselman(eds), S. Tuecke Q.25, "The Anatomy of the Grid:Enabling Scable Virtual Organizations", Intl. J. Supercomputer.
2. Global Grid Forum, http://www.ggf.org
3. The Globus Alliance, http://www.globus.org
4. Grid Forum Korea, http://www.gridforumkorea.org
5. A. Beardsmore et al, "GSAX(Grid Service Accounting Extensions)", (draft), GGF6, 2002
6. S. Mullen et al, "Grid Authentication, Authorization and Accounting Requirements Research Document", (draf), GGF8, 2003

7. KMI, http://kmi.moredream.org
8. Beob Kyun Kim et al, "Implementation of Access Control System for Site Autonomy in Grid Environment", Proceedings of The 30th KISS Fall Conference, KISS, 2003
9. Usage Record, http://forge.gridforum.org/projects/ur-wg
10. The DataGrid Project, http://eu-datagrid.web.cern.ch/eu-datagrid
11. Sebastian Ho, "GridX System Design Documentation", (draft), Bioinformatics Institute, 2002
12. W3C XML Schema, http://www.w3.org/XML/Schema
13. Resource Usage Service, http://forge.gridforum.org/projects/rus-wg
14. Thomas J. Hacker, Brian D. Athey, "Account Allocations on the Grid", Center for Parallel Computing University of Michigan, 2000
15. Apache Xindice, http://xml.apache.org/xindice
16. OpenPBS, http://www.openpbs.org

Performance Analysis and Prediction on VEGA Grid

Haijun Yang[1], Zhiwei Xu[1], Yuzhong Sun[1], Zheng Shen[2], and Changshu Liu[1]

[1] Institute of Computing Technology, Chinese Academy of Sciences,
100080 Beijing, P.R.China
{navy, zxu, yuzhongsun}@ict.ac.cn
[2] Beijing Institute of Technology, 100081 Beijing, P.R. China
{shengzheng}@software.ict.ac.cn

Abstract. With the dramatic development of grid technologies, performance analysis and prediction of grid systems is increasingly significant to develop a variety of new grid technologies. The VEGA grid, a new grid infrastructure developed by Institute of Computing Technology, CAS, views a grid as a distributed computer system. In this paper, we propose some new metrics to evaluate the performance of it. Moreover, we apply queueing system models to model the VEGA grid and predict the performance of it in terms of the mean queue length and mean service time, especially, in the equilibrium state. Hence, a real application, the Air booking service, is deployed on the VEGA grid as a benchmark to measure the performance via latency and throughput. Finally, we point out this method can be used on other homogeneous grid systems.

1 Introduction

As a novel computer technology, the grid has made a rapid progress in recent years. Meanwhile, the grid has evolved in the view of its architecture. From the initial layered architecture to the famous OGSA which is being exemplified in the OGSI[1-4], more recently, WSRF is employed as a new architecture to deeply support Web Services [5,6]. The grid assembles a set of geographically distributed, heterogeneous resources via the underlying networks to provide much more easier resource sharing and more efficient collaboration to users, which can be considered as a distributed system augmented with special grid features[1]. The grid possesses some attractive traits such as large-scale, wide-area resource sharing and powerful dynamic extensibility that become prominent as parallel and distributed computing, power-sharing mechanism and collaboration enhance continuously. In order to understand the traits of the grid more exactly and optimize its architecture design, the performance evaluation becomes a critical problem in the grid research field. The more its architecture and applications make progress, the more people pay attention on the performance evaluation of it. It is helpful to exactly distinguish between the advantages and disadvantages of the grid architecture designs for the advancing grid technologies. Not only in academy but also in industry, the performance analysis and evaluation of the grid are going to become increasingly important in the field[5-9].

The EUROGRID project employed the UNICORE system to establish the European grid, which highlighted the benefits of the grid technologies[10]. At the same time, UK e-Science grid program began in 2001. They built e-Science grid to solve some challenging scientific computing problems and integrate computing, data and visualization resources on a global scale. They promised to share the computing and information resources at many universities and research institutes. Furthermore, they have developed some applications with workflows on the e-Science. These applications have been applied by some famous pharmaceutical companies. Meanwhile, G. Fox and D. Walker pointed out some gaps of e-Science in their technical paper. In that paper, they analyzed e-Science and gave some advices to improve its architecture[11]. Zsolt et al. studied the performance evaluation of grid and pointed out that computing grid and conventional distributed computing system were different in performance evaluation. Parameters of performance evaluation and experiment environment must reflect the characteristics of the grid systems[12].

On the other side of the Atlantic, there are some grid middleware that have been developed to establish grids. As a grid middleware, Condor-G was born at the University of Wisconsin, which provided high throughput computing on distributed computing resources[13]. The GrADS was a grid middleware also. It supported different format earth science data to be accessed, manipulated, and visualized[14,15]. X. Liu et al. designed a grid simulator called MicroGrid at UCSD, which can be used to simulate a virtual grid environment[16]. Though some grid components have been used to monitor the grid performances, the above mentioned grids all neglected mathematical models to analyze and predict their performances. When monitoring any grid resources, one must want to foresee the grid performance at next time and want to know the maximum system workload. So, it is important to predict the grid performance in equilibrium.

In this paper, we will use queueing system to model and analyze the performance of the VEGA grid. The results can be used to predict the performances of it in equilibrium. To our best knowledge, this method is the first endeavor to model and analyze the grid performance by queueing system. These models and results can also be applied on other grids, for instance, e-Science and Condor-G.

The remainder of this paper is organized as follows. In section 2, we address the architecture of the VEGA grid. We employ the air booking service as a typical application and give some measuring metrics of performance analysis in section3. Then, queueing system models are taken as tools to analyze it in section 4. Section 5 presents some experiment results and their analysis. Section 6 summarizes this paper and gives some open issues.

2 The VEGA Grid

The goal of the VEGA grid is to develop and implement grid technologies. The VEGA grid can be considered as a service grid, which shows the fundamental architecture of distributed systems[17]. In the VEGA grid, all resources are encapsulated as services. The resources include computing abilities, storage mediums, programs and information resources called physical resources. If a physical resource can be used by end-users, it must be mapped into a virtual resource firstly. The end-users can only find and employ the virtual resources. Grid resource router is a key factor which takes charge of finding the appropriate resources for the end-users and supporting the links to the physical resources. The VEGA grid architecture is illustrated as Fig.1.

Each physical resource owns unique physical address. The end-user can not find and use any physical resources in the system. By a mapping policy, it maps physical resources to virtual resources. Every physical resource has a unique physical address. At the same time, each virtual resource owns a virtual address. But a virtual address is not unique. The shared virtual address takes advantages of the end-users. For example, a service provider has changed his physical address but not changed the service content. If virtual resources being applied, the end-user can complete his job without rewriting his program. Otherwise, he must replace the old physical address by a new one in his program. Moreover, the method can optimize the applications, because the same services with different physical addresses share the same virtual address.

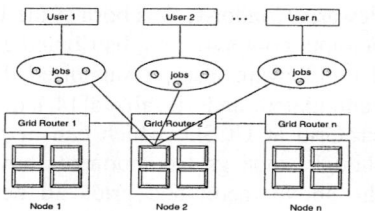

Fig. 1. The architecture of the VEGA grid

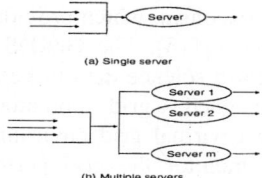

Fig. 2. The architecture of the VEGA grid

The VEGA grid is considered as a system platform being compliant with current computing technologies and providing diversified services. The platform supports services composition, services shared and services cooperation. A general grid will provide following three basic grid operations:(1) File transfer, (2) Remote deployment & execution of programs, and (3) Query & interaction of information.

3 The Application and Metrics of Performance Analysis

In this section, the air booking service is taken as a usage scenario of Web services on the VEGA grid. And then, some measures of performance evaluation are employed to depict it. These measures make performance evaluation of VEGA grid more exactly.

3.1 The Application of Performance Analysis

The air booking service is a typical application which reflects query & interaction of information in a grid. We assume that a grid is already running, and the air booking service exists as a physical service either. The administrator of air booking service applies a virtual address through a mapping policy providing by VEGA grid. Address translation allows a special device, the grid router, to act an agent between the virtual address and the physical address. For an end-user, it connects with the physical resource by the grid router. Then, the end-user transmits an air booking request to the service system. So, the air booking service and VEGA grid construct an object of performance evaluation in this paper.

3.2 The Metrics of Performance Analysis

The measure is an important component of the system performance evaluation, because different measure metrics determine the results of performance analysis. The experiment results can not be compared with each other on the condition that grid systems and their applications run on different hardware platforms. Even though grid is deployed on the same hardware platforms, different efficiency of hardware will affect the experiment results. So, we must clarify grid efficiency firstly. Efficiency of resource utilization comprises efficiency of CPU utilization, efficiency of memory utilization and efficiency of I/O utilization.

For above scenario in VEGA grid, the performances of end-users have little effect on the grid system. So, the servers are only considered in the system. We give some performance metrics as follows. Where, X_i' denotes latency which sample from X_i with 90% probability, n denotes the statistic times of latency.

Definition 1. 90th% Mean Latency

$$\overline{X}' = \sum_{i=1}^{n} X_i' / n \qquad (1)$$

Definition 2. 90th% Maximum Latency

$$X'_{max} = \max_{i=1}^{n}(X_i') \qquad (2)$$

Definition 3. 90th% Variance of Latency

$$V_x' = \frac{1}{n-1} \sum_{i=1}^{n} E(X_i' - \overline{X}')^2 \qquad (3)$$

4 Queueing System Models

In this section, we model the VEGA grid with two queueing models. Fig.2 describes the models with different service modes. One is single-server mode, another is multiple-servers mode. We assume that the input of the VEGA grid is a bulk input which forms a Poisson process. The bulk input is a random variable denoted as ξ, which can take on any positive integral value but less than $+\infty$. The expectation of variable ξ is denoted as $k = E(\xi)$, the deviation of ξ is σ_ξ^2. $F(t)$ is the probability distribution of ξ. $f(t)$ is probability density function of ξ.

4.1 Bulk Input and Single Service

In this subsection, we abstract the VEGA grid as a $M^\xi/G/1$ queueing system which is illustrated as Fig.2(a). We have no information about the VEGA grid before experiments. By assumption, the service-time distribution of the VEGA grid is arbitrary in this model. The arbitrary service-time distribution is denoted as G, the expected value of service-time is μ and its variance is denoted as σ^2. Some queueing system results will be given to depict the VEGA grid, such as mean queue length, and waiting time. In virtue of the experiment results in section 5, we will give the distribution of VEGA grid in next section.

For a Poisson bulk input Process and service-time distribution being arbitrary, we obtain the following proposition from the result of $M/G/1$ model[20-22]. For model $M^\xi/G/1$, Q_n is the number of tasks in the system when the nth task has been completed. T_n denotes the time that the nth task has spent in the system. R_n is the number of arrival tasks in T_n. Hence, we obtain formulae (4) and (5) in equilibrium for different situation in the system.

$$Q_n = Q_{n-1} + R_n - 1 \quad \text{where} \quad Q_{n-1} \geq 1,\ n \geq 2 \tag{4}$$

$$Q_n = R_n + \xi - 1 \quad \text{where} \quad Q_{n-1} = 0,\ n \geq 2 \tag{5}$$

A unification formula is given on the basic of formulae (4) and (5).

$$Q_n = Q_{n-1} + R_n - \delta(Q_{n-1}) + (\xi-1)\delta(1-Q_{n-1}) \tag{6}$$

Where, $\delta(x) = \begin{cases} 1 & x \geq 1 \\ 0 & x < 1 \end{cases}$, $n \geq 2$.

Proposition 1. $\{Q_n,\ n=1,2,...\}$ is a time-homogeneous Markov chain.

Proof: We first prove that $\{Q_n,\ n=1,2,...\}$ is a Markov chain. According to the definition of Markov chain, following formulae are derived.

$$\begin{aligned}
& P(Q_n = q_n | Q_{n-1} = q_{n-1}, Q_{n-2} = q_{n-2}, \cdots, Q_1 = q_1) \\
&= P(Q_{n-1} + R_n - \delta(Q_{n-1}) + (\xi-1)\delta(1-Q_{n-1}) = q_n | Q_{n-1} = q_{n-1}, Q_{n-2} = q_{n-2}, \cdots, Q_1 = q_1) \\
&= P(R_n = q_n - q_{n-1} + \delta(q_{n-1}) - (\xi-1)\delta(1-q_{n-1}) | Q_{n-1} = q_{n-1}, Q_{n-2} = q_{n-2}, \cdots, Q_1 = q_1) \\
&= \frac{P(R_n = q_n - q_{n-1} + \delta(q_{n-1}) - (\xi-1)\delta(1-q_{n-1}), Q_{n-1} = q_{n-1}, Q_{n-2} = q_{n-2}, \cdots, Q_1 = q_1)}{P(Q_{n-1} = q_{n-1}, Q_{n-2} = q_{n-2}, \cdots, Q_1 = q_1)} \\
&= P(R_n = q_n - q_{n-1} + \delta(q_{n-1}) - (\xi-1)\delta(1-q_{n-1})) \\
&= P(Q_{n-1} + R_n - \delta(Q_{n-1}) + (\xi-1)\delta(1-Q_{n-1}) = q_n | Q_{n-1} = q_{n-1}) \\
&= P(Q_n = q_n | Q_{n-1} = q_{n-1})
\end{aligned}$$

So, we have proved that $\{Q_n,\ n=1,2,...\}$ is a Markov chain. Then to prove Q_n is time-homogeneous. We calculate one-step transition probability firstly.

$\forall n \in N$, $P_{i,j}(n,n+1) = P(Q_{n+1} = j | Q_n = i) = P(R_{n+1} = Q_{n+1} - Q_n + \delta(Q_n) - (\xi-1)\delta(1-Q_n))$

$$= P(R_{n+1} = j - i + \delta(i) - (\xi-1)\delta(1-i)) \tag{7}$$

When $i = 0$, (7) can be written as, $P_{i,j}(n,n+1) = P(R_{n+1} = j - \xi + 1) \tag{8}$

When $i = 1$, (7) can be written as, $P_{i,j}(n,n+1) = P(R_{n+1} = j) \tag{9}$

When $j+1 \geq i > 1$, (7) can be written as, $P_{i,j}(n,n+1) = P(R_{n+1} = j-i+1) \tag{10}$

When $i > j+1$, (7) can be written as, $P_{i,j}(n,n+1) = P(R_{n+1} = j-i+1) = 0 \tag{11}$

Formulae (8), (9), (10) and (11) show that P_{ij} is independence with n, so $\{Q_n, n=1,2,...\}$ is a time-homogeneous Markov chain. #

The necessary and sufficient condition for ergodicity is $k \cdot \lambda < \mu$ in the time-homogeneous Markov chain Q_n [20]. On this condition, Q_n can converge to an equilibrium solution. And then, mean queue length and waiting time will be given

We first square equation(6), and calculate expected value, then take limit as $n \to \infty$, such that obtain equation(12).

$$2E(Q)(1-E(R)) = E(R^2) + E(\delta(Q)) + E((\xi-1)^2)E(\delta(1-Q)) \\ -2E(R)E(\delta(Q)) + 2E(R)E(\xi-1)E(\delta(1-Q)) \quad (12)$$

In order to obtain $E(Q)$, we must calculate $E(R^2)$ firstly.

$$E(R_n^2) = E(X^2(T_n)) \xrightarrow{n \to \infty} E(R^2) = E(X^2(T))$$

We define the z-transform for random variable R.

$$R(z) = E(z^R) = \sum_{i=0}^{\infty} P(R=i)z^i \quad (13)$$

$$R(z) = \sum_{i=0}^{\infty} \int \frac{(\lambda \xi x)^i}{i!} e^{-\lambda \xi} z^i f(x)dx = \int e^{-(\lambda \xi - \lambda z)x} f(x)dx \quad (14)$$

Applying the Laplace transform on above equation, the result as follow:

$$R(z) = B^*(\lambda - \lambda E(z^{\Sigma \xi_i}))$$
$$E(R^2) = R''(1) + R'(1)$$
$$= \frac{k^2 \lambda}{\mu} + (\frac{k\lambda}{\mu})^2 + k\lambda\sigma^2 + \frac{\lambda}{\mu}\sigma_\xi^2 \quad (15)$$

We take expectation of both sides of equation(6), then obtain equation(16),(17).

$$E(\delta(1-Q)) = P(Q=0) = \frac{\mu - k\lambda}{k\mu} \quad (16)$$

$$E(\delta(Q)) = P(Q>0) = 1 - P(Q=0) = 1 - \frac{\mu - k\lambda}{k\mu} = \frac{k\mu - \mu - k\lambda}{k\mu} \quad (17)$$

Applying (15), (16) and (17) to (12), we get the mean queue length.

$$2E(Q)(1-E(R)) = E(R^2) + E(\delta(Q)) + E((\xi-1)^2)E(\delta(1-Q)) \\ -2E(R)E(\delta(Q)) + 2E(R)E(\xi-1)E(\delta(1-Q))$$

$$E(Q) = \frac{k\lambda}{\mu} + \frac{1}{2k(\mu - k\lambda)}(\mu k^2 - \mu k + k^3\lambda^2/\mu + \mu\sigma_\xi^2 + \mu\lambda k^3\sigma^2) \quad (18)$$

Using Little theorem, we obtain equation(19). Where, waiting time is denoted as $E(W)$.

$$E(W) = E(Q)/k\lambda \quad (19)$$

If we have known some statistical value of VEGA grid by experiments, like expectation and deviation, then, we may obtain mean queue length by the formula(18) and service waiting time by formula(19). These values are keys of grid performance.

4.2 Bulk Input and Multiple Services

In order to make the model $M^\xi/G/m$ having an analytic solution, we give the following assumption.

Assumption 1. In the VEGA grid, the distribution of service time can be considered as exponential distribution.

In this subsection, we abstract the VEGA grid as a $M^\xi/G/m$ queueing model which is illustrated as Fig.2(b). Considering of assumption1, it can be rewritten as $M^\xi/M/m$. The service-time distribution is denoted as M, the expected value of service-time is μ. The model provides for a maximum of m services. Mean queue length and waiting time will be given to depict the VEGA grid. Some marks are given as following.

$$\lambda_i = \xi_i \lambda \qquad i = 0,1,2,\cdots, \qquad \mu_i = \min(i\mu, m\mu) = \begin{cases} i\mu & 0 \le i \le m \\ m\mu & i \ge m \end{cases}$$

$$E(\lambda_i) = k\lambda, \quad \rho_i = \frac{\lambda_i}{m\mu}, \quad E(\rho)_i = E(\frac{\lambda_i}{m\mu}) = \frac{k\lambda}{m\mu} = \rho$$

For bulk input being a Poisson Process and service-time distribution being a Poisson Process also, we obtain the following results[21].

The probability distribution of queue length P_i can be depicted as follows:

$$P_0 = 1/(1+\sum_{i=0}^{m-1}\frac{(m\rho_i)^i}{i!}+\sum_{i=m}^{\infty}\frac{(m\rho_i)^i}{m!}\frac{1}{m^{i-m}}) \tag{20}$$

$$P_i = \begin{cases} P_0 \dfrac{m^i \prod_{j=1}^{i}\rho_i}{i!} & 0 \le i \le m \\ P_0 \dfrac{m^m \prod_{j=1}^{i}\rho_i}{m!} & i \ge m \end{cases} \tag{21}$$

Thus, we obtain mean queue length $E(Q)$.

$$E(Q) = \sum_{i=0}^{\infty} i \cdot P_i = (\sum_{i=1}^{m-1}\frac{im^i \prod_{j=1}^{i}\rho_i}{i!}+\sum_{i=m}^{\infty}\frac{im^m \prod_{j=1}^{i}\rho_i}{m!})P_0$$

$$= (\sum_{i=1}^{m-1}\frac{(m\rho)^i}{(i-1)!}+\frac{(m\rho)^m(\rho+m(1-\rho))}{m!(1-\rho)^2})P_0 \tag{22}$$

Using Little theorem, we can write down equation(23). Where, waiting time is denoted as $E(W)$. $\qquad E(W) = E(Q)/k\lambda \qquad$ (23)

When $m \to +\infty$, model $M^\xi/M/m$ can be rewritten as $M^\xi/M/\infty$.

$$\lambda_i = \xi_i \lambda \quad i = 0,1,2,\cdots, \quad \mu_i = i\mu \quad i = 0,1,2,\cdots, \quad E(\lambda_i) = k\lambda,$$

$$P_i = P_0 \prod_{j=1}^{i-1} \frac{\lambda_j}{\mu_{j+1}} = P_0 \prod_{j=1}^{i-1} \frac{\xi_j \lambda}{(j+1)\mu} \tag{24}$$

$$E(Q) = k\lambda / \mu$$

Using Little theorem, we get equation (25). Where, waiting time is denoted as $E(W)$.

$$E(W) = E(Q)/k\lambda = \frac{1}{\mu} \tag{25}$$

For above two models, we have obtained the expressions of mean queue length and waiting time. But, we can not calculate the results before we obtain the parameters μ and σ^2. So, the following experiments will be used to get μ and σ^2.

5 Experiment Design and Results

In this section, experiment environment will be briefly shown. Then, the VEGA grid will be tested through a typical transaction oriented application, the air bocking service. At the same time, we will obtain some statistic value to predict its performance.

5.1 Experiment Environment

Air booking service is taken as a typical application to test the VEGA grid. In this experiment, client's browser and portal container share the subnet. Grid router1 and grid router2 lie on different subnet. In this paper, the grid router, grid service router, is different from network router. The grid operating system(GOS) is the kernel of the VEGA grid which runs on the grid node. Besides of tomcat, the GOS is deployed on the portal container. JSP pages get address of service by GOS when it connects local gird router without the register information in it. Air booking service is deployed on grid service container. The main performance parameters of machines and running environment are shown as below table.

Table 1. Experiment environment

	CPU(GHz)	Memory(M)	OS
Client	Celeron™ 1.3	512	Win 200C
GOS Router	4 Xeon™ 2.4	1024	Linux Redhat7.3
Grid Server	4 Xeon™ 2.4	1024	Linux Redhat7.3

In this experiment, we employ MYSQL as database. The data of database are practical data obtained from Air China Corporation. Although these data are not full-scale, they can reflect the characteristics of the application. In this experiment, the monitor is placed on the Browser end. We will record the four time points and calculate four time segments in the experiment. In the first time segment, the application invokes the VEGA API and establishes a service instance. In the second time segment, the application invokes the VEGA API to destroy the service instance. The application invokes a service interface of the VEGA API in the third time segment. The fourth time segment records the application running time.

Throughput and workload are two important measure values. In this paper, we measure them on VEGA server end.

5.2 Experiment Results and Analysis

A browser submits concurrent transactions to a portal container, firstly. Then, the portal delivers them to the air booking service through the VEGA grid. Finally, the air booking service sends the results to the browser. We employ threads to simulate concurrent transactions and change the number of concurrent transactions on client. The arrivals of concurrent transactions are Poisson distributions. In the below figures, we use data1 to note $10*\xi$ concurrence, data2 to note $20*\xi$ concurrence, data3 to note $30*\xi$ concurrence.

Fig.3 shows that the maximum GOS running time increase along with the increase of concurrent transactions. Specially, the increase is rapid form data2 to data3. This phenomenon implicates that the respond time of GOS increases very evidently. This is a critical message of system performance. Fig.4 illustrates the mean GOS running time at three different input conditions. These curves become smoother than Fig.3. But the changes among the three curves are consistent with Fig.3. We use deviation of GOS running time to depict stability of the VEGA grid by Fig.5. From this figure, we can learn that the data3 has a worst stability than the two others. This result is relation

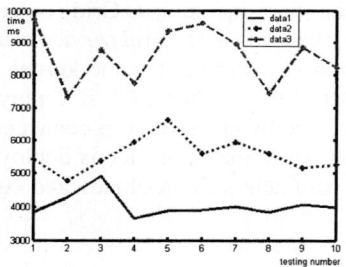

Fig. 3. The maximum VEGA running time

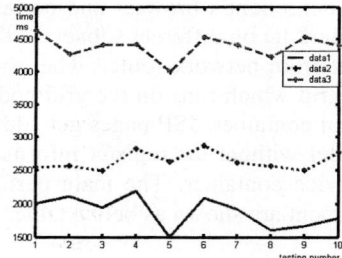

Fig. 4. The mean VEGA running time

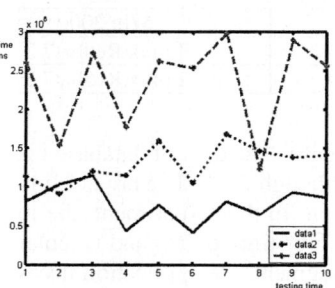

Fig. 5. The deviation of VEGA running time

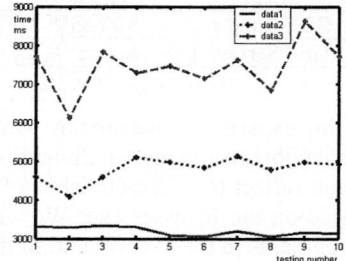

Fig. 6. The maximum $90th\%$ running time

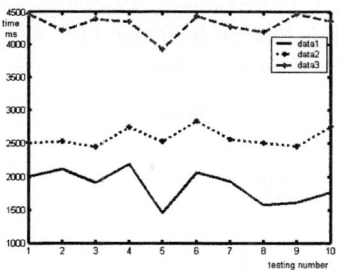 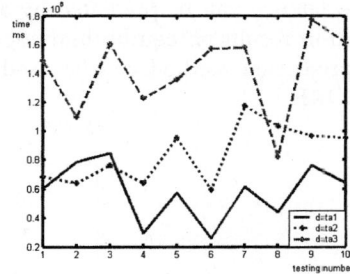

Fig.7. The mean of VEGA $90th\%$ running time

Fig. 8. The deviation of VEGA $90th\%$ running time

with the results of Fig.3. That is to say, the tested system is not stability enough under the current workload. This is an inevitable result when the system goes to equilibrium.

For air booking service, we propose $90th\%$ sample method to get rid of the influence of occasional factors. We present Fig.6, Fig.7 and Fig.8 as follows.

Comparing Fig.6, Fig.7, and Fig.8 with Fig.3, Fig.4, and Fig.5, we can learn that the new curves are smoother than the old ones. But, the new figures clarify the relation among data1, data2 and data3 more clearly, which is useful to deeply analyze the VEGA grid. These data can be used to predict the performance of the grid in equilibrium. On the other hand, we monitor the throughput of GOS server and efficiency of CPUs. These measure values can affect the VEGA grid directly. When the server has low throughput and high efficiency of CPU, the experiment results will be incredible. The monitoring results as below.

Fig.9 depicts the throughput curve of GOS server under three different conditions. We find the throughputs do not decrease when the data change from data1 to data2, and data3. This result shows that GOS only consumes a few resources. On the other hand, we learn that GOS only occupies a few CPU time through Fig.10. The mean CPU time is lower than 7%. Monitoring results tell us the GOS occupies a few server resources. The resources utilization of GOS hardly increases when the transactions have a rapid increase. This is a good character for the VEGA grid because it needs a very strong extensibility to large-scale. The above results illuminate that GOS server satisfies the needs of this experiment and the experiment results are credible.

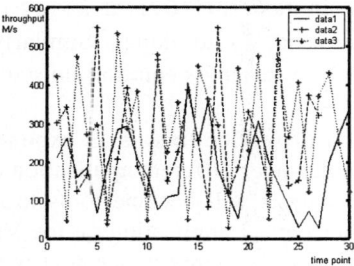 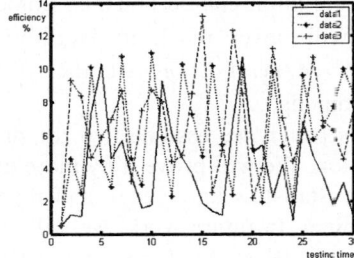

Fig. 9. Throughput of VEGA server

Fig. 10. Efficiency of CPU

The latency can be predicted by above results. For example, we can give some prediction results in equilibrium about model Fig.2(a) by formulae (18) and (19). This prediction method can be used on other grid system, like as e-Science and UNICORE.

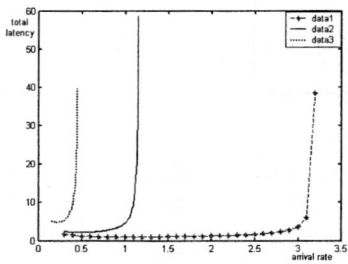

Fig. 11. Performance Prediction of VEG A

6 Discussion and Conclusion

Performance analysis is a fundamental challenge in the VEGA grid. To model this system exactly, choosing an appropriate mathematical tool is an important question. In this paper, we apply queueing system to model his system. Because, queueing system has been employed to analyze and evaluate computer system widely. There are many classical queueing models have been used in this field. But not all of them are suitable for the VEGA grid. We consider the distribution of arrival satisfies a Poisson distribution with bulk. The bulk Poisson process can exactly reflect the concurrent requires which can be found in Internet everywhere. And this form will become the main form in grid system. So, we give a simple model $M^s/G/1$ firstly. For a general model $M^s/G/m$, we can not obtain its analytic solution. Accounting for the characteristic of service respond, we give the assumption1 in section 4. So we predigest the general model $M^s/G/m$ to model $M^s/M/m$. And then, its analytic solution can be written as equations (22) and (23). For a service provider using the VEGA grid, he can use our results to adjust his setting. For example, he can choose an appropriate number of servers to satisfy the end-users and decrease its costs. Moreover, he also can use these results to predict the behaviors of the VEGA grid. The critical point can be obtained immediately. In model $M^s/G/1$, if $k\lambda/\mu \geq 1$, the system will never reach its equilibrium state and go to dump. Similarly, in model $M^s/M/m$, if $k\lambda/m\mu \geq 1$, the system will never reach its equilibrium state and go to dump also.

In this paper, we assume that the distribution of service time is an exponential distribution. We will prove it by more experiments under different application environment. Statistics knowledge and regression analysis will become tools to solve this problem. In future work, we will study other typical application on the VEGA grid, such as Blast. Modeling and analyzing the system deeply is our next focused work.

Acknowledgements

Supported in part by National "863" Program(No. 2002AA104310) and Theory Foundation of ICT(No. 20056130).

References

1. I. Foster and C. Kesselman. The Grid: Blueprint for a New Computing Infrastructure, second edition, Morgan Kaufmann, Amsterdam, 2004.
2. I. Foster, C. Kesselman and S. Tuecke. The Anatomy of the Grid: Enabling Scalable Virtual Organizations. International Journal of Supercomputer Applications, 15(3), (2001) 200-222
3. I. Foster, C. Kesselman , J. M. Nick, and S. Tuecke, Grid Services for Distributed System Integration, Computer, 35(6), (2002) 37-46
4. D. Talia. The Open Grid Services Architecture: where the grid meets the Web. IEEE Internet Computing, 6(6), (2002) 67-71
5. M. Baker and I. Foster, On recent changes in the grid community. Distributed Systems Online, IEEE, Volume: 5(2), (2004) 4/1 - 4/10
6. The Globus Project Team, Open Grid Services Architecture, available on-line at http://www.globus.org /ogsa/.
7. I. Foster, et. al, Modeling stateful Resources with Web Services V1.1, available on-line at http:// www.globus.org /research/papers.html.
8. T. Zhang, S. Subramanyam, and A.Sucharitakul. Optimizing Web Services Performance for Sun Java System Application Server. Sun Microsystems, Tech Rep.
9. H. Dail, F. Bern, and H. Casanova, A decoupled scheduling approach for Grid application development environments. International Journal Parallel & Contributed System vol63 (5), (2003) 505-524
10. Http://www.eurogrid.org.
11. G. Fox and D. Walker, e-Science Gap Analysis, available on-line at http://www.nesc.ac.uk/technical_papers/UKeS-2003-01/index.html.
12. Zsolt. Németh, G. Gombás, and Z. Balaton. Performance Evaluation on Grids: Directions, Issues, and Open Problems. In Proceedings of the Euromicro PDP 2004, A Coruna, Spain, IEEE Computer Society Press. (2004) 290-297
13. D. Thain, T. Tannenbaum, and M. Livny, Condor and the Grid Douglas, in Grid Computing: Making the Global Infrastructure a Reality. (2003) 299-335
14. F. Berman, A. Chien, et al., The GrADS Project: Software Support for High-Level Grid Application Development. International Journal of High Performance Computing Applications, (2001) 327-344
15. http://grads.iges.org/grads/grads.html
16. Xin Liu, Huaxia Xia, Andrew A.Chien, Validating and Scaling the MicroGrid: A Scientific Instrument for Grid Dynamics. The Journal of Grid Computing, vol(2), (2004) 141-161
17. Zhiwei Xu, et al., VEGA: A computer systems approach to grid computing Technology, The Journal of Grid Computing, vol(2), (2004) 109-120
18. Zhiwei Xu. et al. Architectural Guidelines of VEGA GOS 2.0 Institute of Computing Technology, Chinese Academy of Science, Tech Rep:VGD-8, (2004)
19. http://vega.ict.ac.cn/index.html
20. Kleinrock, L. Queueing Systems, Vol. 1: Theory. New York: Wiley. (1975)
21. Donald, G. and Carl, H.H. Fundamentals of Queueing Theory. Third edition. New York: John Wiley & Sons, Inc. (1998)
22. E. Modiano, J. E. Wieselthier and A. Ephremides, A simple analysis of average queueing delay in tree networks. IEEE transaction on information theory, Vol42 (2), (1995) 660-664

An Accounting Services Model for ShanghaiGrid*

Jiadi Yu, Qi Qian, and Minglu Li

Department of Computer Science and Engineering,
Shanghai Jiao Tong University, Shanghai 200030, P.R. China
{jdyu, qiqian, liml}@cs.sjtu.edu.cn

Abstract. The ShanghaiGrid, as a Grid Computing Environment, is an information Grid to serve the public in the city, and all resources are regarded as Grid Services in the Open Grid Services Architecture (OGSA). The primary goal of the ShanghaiGrid is to build a generally shared information grid platform. Charging and accounting are an important part of the grid computing system in the ShanghaiGrid. This paper discusses an accounting services model and accounting life cycle that will be used in the ShanghaiGrid. We will analyze the charging and accounting process in detail based on this model and cycle.

1 Introduction

Grid computing that is able to harness distributed resources to solve large-scale computationally intensive problems, has been widely accepted as a promising paradigm for large-scale distributed systems in recent years [1][2][3]. The main goal is to share large-scale resources and to accomplish collaborative tasks [2] in science, engineering, and commerce. In the past few years, the main application of grid computing was mostly academic or exploratory in nature. However, with the emergence of Web Services technologies and the Open Grid Services Architecture (OGSA) [4][5], Grid infrastructures have made significant inroads into a multi-institutional production scale and need infrastructure to support various services: security, uniform access, resource management, scheduling, application composition, computational economy, and accounting. Therefore information Grid has become increasingly important.

A charging and accounting service to be functional in a grid environment will have to manage the cost of usage and support the economic activities according to computational economy. It must be decentralized, scalable and flexible. A reliable accounting system must also be able to carry out the following functions: metering, data collection, pricing, charging and payment.

The problem of accounting for a computational resource can face many different problems. Different grids may have different accounting structure and

---

* This work is supported by a 973 project (No.2002CB312002) of China, a grand project (No.03dz15027) and a key project (No.025115033) of the Science and Technology Commission of Shanghai Municipality.

technologies to adapt to their own Grid Computing Environment. Charging and accounting for grid has been taken into account for some grid projects. DGAS [6] presented an accounting system for the European DataGrid project, which described a scheme based on the concept of Home Location Register (HLR). In this model, users pay in order to execute their job on the resources and resources earn credits by executing the user's jobs. GridBank[7] was introduced as a grid accounting services architecture for computational grids, which presents requirements of Grid accounting and different economic models within which it can operate and proposes a Grid Accounting Services Architecture to meet them. GGF proposes a Grid Economic Services Architecture (GESA) [8], which define the Chargeable Grid Service (CGS) and the Grid Banking Service (GBS) that may be integrated into OGSA. IBM's 'Extreme Blue' grid accounting project proposed a grid accounting framework GSAX [9] with dynamic pricing strategies independent of economic models. Although above charging and accounting approaches offered a range of valuable solutions, they lack extensibility, flexibility and a uniform accounting standard.

To make good use of local accounting systems at various organizations and to eliminate their performance bottleneck. In [10], We propose a hierarchical grid accounting services framework(HiGAF), which is based on a two-level architecture, and list its advantages over its previous counterpart. In the ShanghaiGrid, multiple virtual organizations (VO) will be integrated into a grid system. Therefore, this accounting structure of HiGAF is most suitable to the requirements of ShanghaiGrid project. In this paper, we focus on a practical accounting model specifically designed for the ShanghaiGrid. Not only will we have to consider the upper layer organization, but will also have to accommodate the lower layers in each VO in ShanghaiGrid. Furthermore, we will introduce accounting life cycle of the ShanghaiGrid and based on such cycles, the entire process of accounting is analysed.

The paper is organized as follows. In Section 2, we introduce background and overview of the ShanghaiGrid. Then, in Section 3, we propose a detailed architecture of ShanghaiGrid accounting model, and analyze the accounting processes in Section 4. In Section 5, we briefly describe the accounting and charging mechanism in the ShanghaiGrid. Finally, we present the conclusion of this paper.

2 An Overview of ShanghaiGrid

The ShanghaiGrid is an ongoing Grid Computing Environment based on the Grid Service standards and the Open Grid Services Architecture, which is funded by the Shanghai Science and Technology Development Foundation. ShanghaiGrid project is one of five top grand Grid projects in China. As a City Grid, the ShanghaiGrid is to provide a general shared information Grid platform for various Grids.

The primary aim of the ShanghaiGrid is to develop a set of system softwares for the information grid and to establish an infrastructure for grid-based applications [11]. By means of flexible, secure, open standards sharing and coordinating of computational resources, data information and dedicated services among virtual organizations, this project will build an information grid tailored for the characteristics of Shanghai and support the typical application of grid based traffic congestion control and guidance. The subjects to be researched in the project covers a wide range, including infrastructures, standard protocols, softwares, and collaboration platforms [12]. In [12],[13], the architecture of the ShanghaiGrid and potential services provided by ShanghaiGrid is shown. Although several initiatives are engaged in the development of ShanghaiGrid technologies, Grid accounting issues are yet to be addressed.

3 Accounting Model

Accounting model that we designed for ShanghaiGrid is based on Architecture of the ShanghaiGrid, which is able to support local accounting of resource and service usage in various organizations, and is generic enough to be used for resource trading.

3.1 Architecture

Fig. 1 shows accounting services architecture of ShanghaiGrid, which breaks down the centralized accounting system into two hierarchies: Global Accounting Manager (GAM) and Local Accounting Manager (LAM)[10]. GAS is located in central server in Grid, and coordinates accounting systems among various LASs; LAS exists in specific administrative organization, and manages local accounting services.

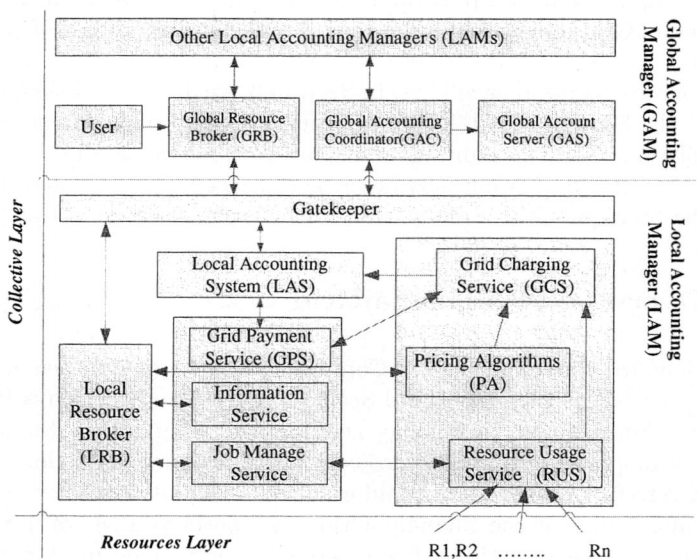

Fig. 1. ShanghaiGrid Accounting Services Architecture

Local Resource Broker (LRB) is a local mediator between the user and grid resources by using middleware services in specific administrative organization. It is responsible for discovers local resources, negotiates for service prices, performs local resource selection and so on.

Grid Payment Service (GPS) provides a service to a payment infrastructure. It can trade between Grid Resource Consumers and Grid Resource Providers, and include systems based around electronic cash, credit cards, pre-paid account, service tokens, etc.

Grid Charging Service (GCS) provides a basic infrastructure that has been enabled to support economic interaction.

RUS [14] [15] provides a basic infrastructure to support the auditing and monitoring capability for the resources consumed by OGSA services.

Pricing Algorithms (PA) define the prices that resource provider would like to charge users. In order to maximize profit, resource provider may follow various policies to user, and the pricing can also be driven by demand and supply.

Information Service provides a complete list of resources.

Job Manage Service deals with job submission to grid resource provider.

Local Accounting System (LAS) provides a local service to manage and maintains accounts and resource usage records in virtual organization.

Gatekeeper is the common interface provided by LAM to GAM. All the interactions between GAM and LAM are via this component.

Global Accounting Coordinator (GAC) coordinates various accounting systems in LAMs, and performs transfer in the same user distributed among various LAMs.

Global Resource Broker (GRB) is a Global mediator between various LAMs and GAM. It is responsible for discovers and select resources among various virtual organizations, and finally gathers results and hands them to the user.

Global Account Server (GAS) provides a global service to manage and maintains user accounts information, fund and the credit rating of the user in grid.

3.2 Global Account Server

Global Account Server was designed to store and manage user accounting information. When a job is done, accounting information of resources usage is sent to Global Account Server from Local Accounting System via gatekeeper, and store user total fund from various LAM accounts. Fig. 2 shows Global Account Server architecture.

- **API** provides a Global Account Server interface to other services.
- **Security Protocol** performs authentication and authorization of users.
- **Administration** provides basic account operation and management such as open account, update account, close account, deposit, transfer, etc.
- **DB** is a database that user accounting information.

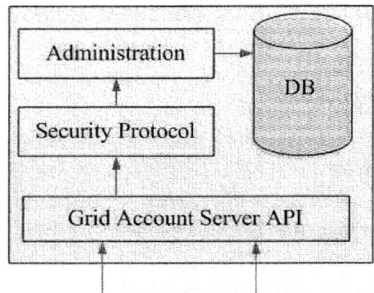

Fig. 2. Grid Account Server Architecture

An authorized manager creates user accounts, called initial account, at the Global Account Server. Total fund of various LAMs accounts and a credit value are stored to Global Account Server according to the credit rating of the user. When a user starts a request for an application, the server checks and charges the user's account for its application in order to determine whether the user can afford the job to be computed or not. In order to execute a submitted job, the user needs to have an account at Global Account Server with a positive amount of money.

Communication between user and Global Account Server must relate to security and access protection. User isn't able to change his identification, and isn't trusted to manipulate server's central storage. An authentication server should be implemented, which handles login and logout procedures. Once clients are authenticated, the client is authorized to establish a connection between client and server. Clients cannot send any requests if a connection is refused. Clients will be checked for their identification every time when they request an accounting service and communicate with server. Clients will be able to access only their own data, unless they have special administration privileges.

3.3 Accounting Protocols

Accounting protocols can be distinctive the following two types: Security Protocol and data Transfer Protocol.

Security Protocol: It is developed an architecture for authentication and authorization of clients. The architecture is client-server architecture. Authentication is based on Public Key Infrastructure (PKI) using X509v3 certificate [16], and certificates can be issued by certificate authority (CAs). The clients send authentication request to server, and server decides whether the user is authorized to use grid resources.

Data Transfer Protocol: TCP-based transfer protocols such as SMTP, FTP, or HTTP can be used to transfer information of payment and charge between user account and provider account. These protocols is reliable, efficient, and security.

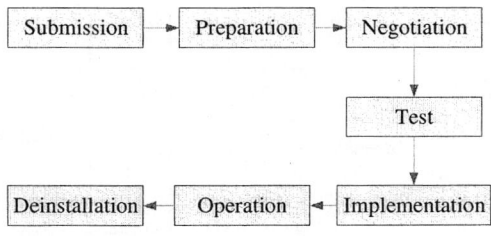

Fig. 3. Accounting Life Cycle

4 Accounting Process

4.1 Accounting Life Cycle

Fig. 3 shows an accounting life cycle, which is divided into the following phases: submission, preparation, negotiation, test, implementation, operation and deinstallation.

The accounting life cycle starts with the *submission* of application. User submits a job with specification of the needed functionality and possible QoS parameters. Then, in the *preparation* phase, suitable resources can be selected.

Afterwards, the provider and user start the *negotiation* phase. This phase deals with the process of service negotiation between provider and user, which contains detail about functionality, QoS, and pricing mechanism. The negotiation phase ends with signing an agreement.

The *test* phase estimates the application cost, and estimates if user have enough fund to pay.

During the *implementation* phase, the provider provides resources to user, and then the user job is executed, as well as meters the resources consumed.

The *operation* phase combines changing service functionality, which calculates total cost based on the resource usage and the resource price, and then user pays charge the user resource usage.

Finally, the accounting life cycle ends with the *deinstallation*. In this phase, the implementation's resources are released.

4.2 Analysis of Accounting Process

The accounting processes as a whole can be separated into several phases that already mentioned above. In order to realize an overall integrated accounting service system, we need to take processes of the accounting life cycle phases into account. In the following, we will give a description the relevant accounting processes along the accounting life cycle that are shown Fig. 4 (activity diagram of the accounting processes) and Fig. 5 (sequence interaction diagram of the accounting processes).

The submission phase: a detailed analysis of user requirement is done in this phase. The user submits their applications with some parameters including

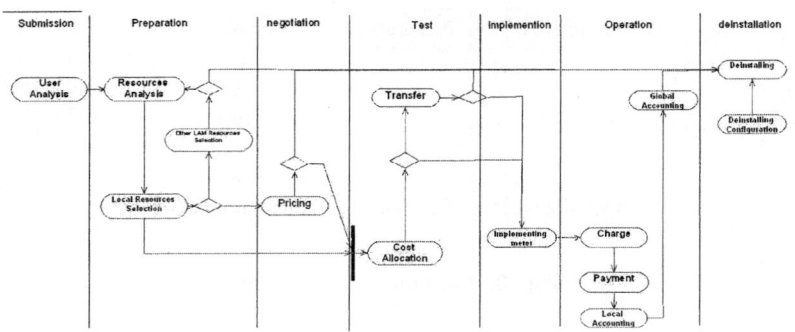

Fig. 4. Activity Diagram of the Accounting Processes

budget and deadline to GRB so that GRB may correctly choose resources, and estimation the application cost.

The preparation phase: GRB analyse user resources requirement, and then send this requirement to LRB in one LAM that belongs to a VO including user, in order to select local resources. The local Information Service provides a complete list of resources to LRB, and then LRB selects suitable resources according to different scheduling criteria. If local resources don't meet user requirement, local LRB notify GRB via gatekeeper to select other necessary resources from LAM of other VOs. In whole Grid environment, if user resources requirement can not be satisfied, the process terminates immediately.

The negotiation phase: LRB interacts with PA to consult acceptable price of services for both grid resource provider and user in every LAM that participate in resources supply. If they come to an acceptable price, PA informs GCS about accepted price. The LRB, having received the job description and select suitable resources for the given job. If resource provider and user can't come to an prices agreement, the process terminates.

The test phase: the overall cost of the job should be estimated , and verified whether user has enough Grid Credit to run his application. It will firstly try to get the user's deposit information from the LAM(i). If user holds enough credit in LAM(i), accounting processes enter into implementation phase. Or else LAM(i) have to perform transfer in some user account from other LAMs via GAC.If the sum of user's deposits is less than the estimated job cost, the process terminates.

The implementation phase: GRB submits user job to grid resource provider via LRB and Job Manage Service. Grid resource provider provides the service by executing the user job and RUS meters the resources consumed while processing the user job. After the job finished, RUS will obtain the usage statistics of the grid resources, and then generates a standard Resource Usage Record (RUR) [15].

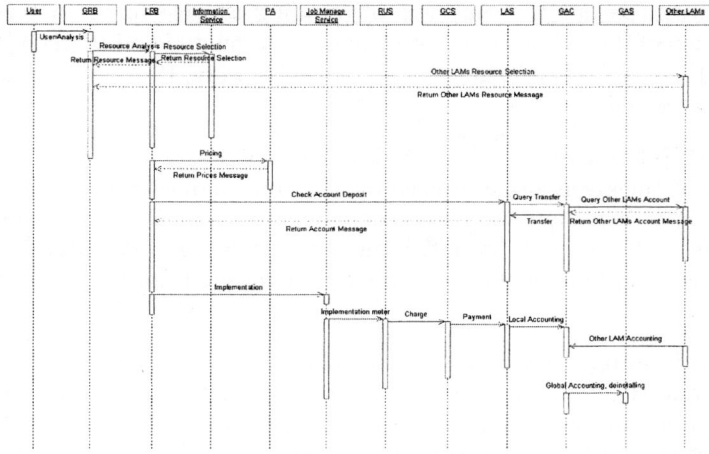

Fig. 5. Sequence Interaction Diagram of the Accounting Processes

The operation phase: GCS receives the price from PA, which negotiates with resource users, and the data from RUR. Then It calculates total cost based on the resource usage and pricing algorithms that the mutually agreed. GCS contacts GPS with a request to charge the user account. User will pay resource usage charge by using payment strategies of GPS. Afterward, GCS sent the total service cost and the resources usage statistics to LAS to implement local accounting. Finally, GAM collect local accounting information from LAMs that participate in resources supply, and then send it to GAS to record and store.

The deinstallation phase: GRB returns the results to the user, and resources are released.

we present typical accounting process of our accounting model, in order to explain the mechanisms of economic transaction. Our major aim is to develop an accounting architecture which is capable of managing the accounting process and local accounting system in ShanghaiGrid.

5 Accounting Mechanisms

The accounting mechanism describes the accounting policies, and determines the resources exchange rates during the performance of accounting, which maximize benefits of grid resource provider and consumer. The accounting mechanism should be simple enough to be understood by all resource providers and users.

Accounting Items: It is necessary to decide for which resource elements one should pay. Any services invocation will consume a wide range of resources. However, a services provider may only be interested in a relatively small subset of these resources for the purposes of deciding a price to use a service. The consumption of the following resources may be accounted and charged [14]: CPU, Memory, Disc, Wall Clock Time, Node Count, Network, Processors, Software and Libraries accessed.

Book and Estimate: After the job description was received and select suitable resources for the given job, user need book a portion of resources to execute job. Then, resource consumption should be estimated, which has two constituents: rate of consumption, and estimated maximum durations. The overall estimated resource consumption would then be (rate of consumption) × (expected duration).

Resource Pricing: Pricing schemes should base on the supply and demand for resources and the QoS requirements. GBR and LRB was requested to mediate resources price by grid resource producers and users. LBR sets firstly a price for a resource and then queries both producers and consumers whether or not accept that price. With time elapsing, LRB increases or decreases the price by a small amount after each negotiation, namely $P_t = p \pm \varepsilon \Delta t$, until producers and users come to an acceptable price.

Accounting Checking: The overall cost of the job is estimated by multiplying resource price with estimated resource consumption. The user's account is checked whether there is a positive amount of "money" to pay. If the estimated overall cost of the job exceeds the user's funds, the resource provider may provide a loan for user according to the credit rating of the user.

Accounting Policies: Account policies concern is how to charge for resource usage in some particular situations. We propose the following system policies: 1. If user job is cancelled during execution because of user action, resource provider will charge for resources already used; 2. If user job is suspended because of resource provider action, resource provider don't charge to the user; 3. If the resource usage expectations is underrated, resource provider provide a loan to user so as to complete whole job; 4. If the expected resource usage is overrated, the job is executed.

6 Conclusions and Further Work

ShanghaiGrid is an ongoing project aimed at constructing a metropolitan-area information service infrastructure. The development of services and applications includes a set of middlewares, high-level services, design tools, package tools, etc. Charging and accounting is an important part of ShanghaiGrid. In this paper, we presented an accounting services model for ShanghaiGrid, which is flexible, scalable and extensible. We also analysed grid resources accounting process along accounting life cycles and accounting mechanism in ShanghaiGrid. A prototype of the described architecture in this paper has been applied to the ShanghaiGrid project. We are planning to install an accounting management test bed based on the concepts presented in this paper in the near future.

References

1. Foster, I., Kesselman, C.(eds.).: The Grid: Blueprint for a New Computing Infrastructure. Morgan Kaufmann (1999)
2. Foster, I., Kesselman, C., Tuecke S.: The Anatomy of the Grid: Enabling Scalable Virtual Organizations. International Journal of High Performance Computing Application, 15(3) (2001) 200-222
3. Foster, I., Kesselman, C., Nick, J., Tuecke, S., The Physiology of the Grid: An Open Grid Services Architecture for Distributed Systems Integration.
4. Tuecke, S , Czajkowski, K.,Foster, I., Frey, J. Graham, S., Kesselman, C., Vanderbilt, P.: Grid Service Specification. Global Grid Forum (2003)
5. Globus Project - http://www.globus.org
6. C.Anglano, S.Barale, L.Gaido, A.Guarise, S.Lusso, A.Werbrouck.: An accounting system for the DataGrid project -Preliminary proposal. draft in discussion at Global Grid Forum 3, Frascati, Italy, October, 2001. Available: http://server11.infn.it/workload-grid/docs/DataGrid-01-TED-0115-3-0.pdf
7. Alexander, B., Rajkumar, B.: GridBank: A Grid Accounting Services Architecture (GASA) for distributed systems sharing and integration. In 17th Annual International Parallel and Distributed Processing Symposium (IPDPS 2003) Workshop on Internet Computing and E-Commerce, 2003
8. S. Newhouse: Grid Economic Services Draft, www.ggf.org, 2003.
9. Magowan, J.: Extreme Blue Grid Accounting Project (Grid Service Accounting Extensions-GSAX). GGF Resource Usage Service Working Group. 2003
10. Qi Qian, Minglu Li: HiGAF: A Hierarchical Grid Accounting Framework. Proceedings of International Workshop on Agents and Autonomic Computing and Grid Enabled Virtual Organizations (AAC-GEVO 2004) 650-657
11. Minglu Li, Hui Liu, Changjun Jiang, Weiqin Tong, Aoying Zhou, Yadong Gui, Hao Zhu Shui Jiang, Ruonan Rao, Jian Cao, Qianni Deng, Qi Qian and Wei Jin. ShanghaiGird in Action: the First Stage Projects. Proceedings of the Second International Workshop on Grid and Cooperative Computing, Shanghai. December, 2003. LNCS Volume 3032.
12. Ruonan Rao, Baiyan Li, Minglu Li, and Jinyuan You The Delivery and Accounting Middleware in the ShanghaiGrid, Proceedings of the Second International Workshop on Grid and Cooperative Computing, Shanghai. December, 2003. LNCS Volume 3032.
13. Minglu Li, Min-You Wu, Ying Li: ShanghaiGrid: A Grid Prototype for Metropolis Information Services. Proceedings of 7th Asia-Pacific Web Conference, Shanghai, China, March 29 - April 1, 2005(APWeb 2005) 1033-1036
14. Global Grid Forum, Gird Economic Services Architecture (GESA) http://www.gridforum.org/3-SRM/gesa.htm
15. Global Grid Forum, RUR - Resource Usage Record Working Group, http://www.gridforum.org/3-SRM/ur.htm
16. Foster, I., Kesselman, C., Tsudik, G., Tuecke, S., A Security Architecture for Computational Grids, Proceedings of the 5th ACM Conference on Computer and Communication Security, 1998.

An Agent-Based Grid Computing Infrastructure

Jia Tang and Minjie Zhang

School of Information Technology and Computer Science,
University of Wollongong, Wollongong NSW 2522, Australia
{jt989, minjie}@uow.edu.au

Abstract. The conventional computing grid has developed a service oriented computing architecture with a super-local, two commit scheduling strategy. This architecture is limited in modeling open systems with highly dynamic and autonomous computing resources due to its server-based computing model. The use of super-local scheduling strategy also limits the utilization of the computing resources. In this paper, we propose a multi-agent based grid computing infrastructure to tackle the above issues, while provide reasonable compatibility and interoperability with the conventional grid systems and clients. Compared with the existing grids, the new infrastructure is leveraged by the intelligent agents, and therefore is more efficient and flexible for open systems.

1 Introduction

Today, the shear numbers of desktop systems make the potential advantages of interoperability between desktops and servers into a single grid system quite compelling. However, these commodity systems have significantly different properties than the conventional server-based grid systems. They are usually highly autonomous and heterogeneous systems. And their availability varies from time to time. In other words, they are open systems in terms of autonomy, heterogeneity, and availability.

The conventional computing grid has developed a service oriented computing architecture with a super-local, two commit scheduling strategy. In this architecture, the functionalities of the grid are implemented as a variety of Web Services. These services are deployed to the service containers, which normally run on high-end workstations and servers.

The embrace of Web Services is important, as Web Services provide standard means for communications and object invocations between the clients and the service providers. The super-local scheduling strategy is also a success in high-end computational environments, because of the wide acceptance of the local schedulers such as Condor [1], PBS, and LSF, and the flexibility of the strategy when dealing with various local schedulers. But the circumstances are different when considering a grid made up of open systems. The service oriented architecture preserves the client/server computing model, and therefore is limited in modeling open systems with highly dynamic and autonomous computing resources. In addition, the use of super-local scheduling strategy limits the utilization of the computing resources.

This paper attempts to tackle the above issues by proposing a new job/service model and applying multi-agent technologies to the grid architecture. The rest of this paper is organized as follows. Section 2 reviews the architecture of Globus Tookit 4 [2] (the official implementation of most current grid standards), and discusses its defects in more detail. Section 3 proposes the S.M.A.R.T. (Service-oriented, Microkernel, Agent-based, Rational, and Transparent) grid infrastructure, demonstrates its new job/service model and core components. Section 4 details the scheduling strategy of S.M.A.R.T. using Colored Petri Nets [3] (CPNs). Section 5 probes into the compatibility and interoperability issues with the existing grid systems and clients. Section 6 concludes this paper.

2 Review of the Conventional Grid Architecture

To contrast our differences to the current grid architecture, it is necessary to revisit the service oriented architecture and the two commit scheduling strategy in Globus Toolkit 4 (GT4).

2.1 Service Oriented Architecture

GT4 fully adopts Web Services standards [4]. More specifically, it is a set of software components that implement Web Services mechanisms [2]. Nine predefined services are implemented to provide functionalities such as job management, monitoring and discovery, etc. In addition, a stateful resource framework for Web Services [5] was proposed to preserve the states between service invocations.

As discussed in Section 1, the embrace of service oriented architecture and Web Services standards increases the interoperability of the grid, and provides a message passing standard. However, the defects are fourfold:

1. The predefined services are essential to the proper functioning of the grid, and therefore require reliable service nodes with high availability. However, such nodes can not be guaranteed in open systems.
2. Services are not suitable to describe all applications. Some applications are more "job-like", and not suitable to be modeled as services.
3. Web Services are usually stateless. Although Web Services Resource Framework [5] (WSRF) was introduced to make Web Services "stateful", it is not efficient and effective enough, as the stateful information must be stored apart (as WS-Resources), and some states may be unable to be described with WSRF or even they could be yet too complicated.
4. The current service oriented architecture has poor adaptability in terms of performance, availability, and scalability, as services must be manually deployed to the service containers. The current grid has no facility that allows automatic deployment of services according to the clients' requests and the load of the grid.

2.2 Scheduling Strategy

In the Globus Toolkit, the scheduling functionality is provided by two services - Monitoring and Discovery Service (MDS) [6], and Grid Resource Allocation and Management (GRAM) [7].

MDS is responsible for gathering static and dynamic information from distributed information providers. GRAM on the other hand manages the submission and execution of the jobs. Globus uses a two commit scheduling strategy: the super scheduler schedules a job to a suitable local scheduler based on the job's requirements and the status of the resources in the grid; the local scheduler then schedules a job to a specific computing node. Figure 1 [2] depicts the scheduling strategy used in GT4. The dashed area indicates services hosts. The compute element consists of a local scheduler and computing nodes.

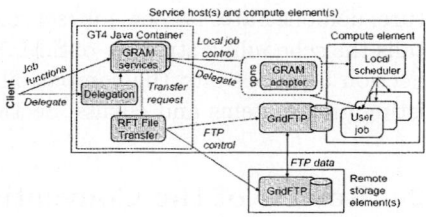

Fig. 1. The Two Commit Scheduling Strategy in GT4

Although the two commit scheduling strategy is very flexible in the face of different local schedulers, the disadvantages are threefold:

1. The super-local scheduling architecture limits the overall performance and the scalability of the grid.
2. It is infeasible to introduce local schedulers in open systems, as local schedulers require a relatively static and non-autonomous environment.
3. The dependency on local schedulers increases the complexity of application programming in the grid environment, as it is impossible to provide a uniform programming model that supports task decomposition, state persistence, and inter-task communications for various local schedulers.

3 Job/Service Model and Core Grid Components of S.M.A.R.T.

In this section, we propose S.M.A.R.T, a multi-agent [8] based grid infrastructure, and discuss its job/service model and core components.

3.1 Job/Service Model

S.M.A.R.T. has a services-oriented architecture regarding its clients, and conforms to the Web Services (WS) standards [4]. The adoption of Web Services gives S.M.A.R.T. good interoperability with the WS-compatible clients and other WS-compatible grids. However, due to the defects discussed in Section 2, S.M.A.R.T. uses *Task/Service (TS)* to describe jobs and services in the grid environment.

Fig. 2. The S.M.A.R.T. Task/Service

A TS comprises of the TS description, the executables, and the data. When being rescheduled (i.e. when a running task is suspended), the TS is serialized and suspended. Figure 2 shows the composition of a TS. TSs without serialization and checkpoints are called *Raw TSs (RTSs)*.

The TS Description (TSD) is described by the Task/Service Description Language (TSDL), which is a superset of the Web Service Description Language (WSDL) [9] and the WS-Resource [5]. In fact, a TS description has two sections, namely, the task section and the service section.

The task section of TSD includes three subsections. The dependencies subsection defines the dependencies of the runtime components (called bundles), and the dependencies of other services. The scheduling policies subsection defines the instance policies (the minimum number of active instances, the maximum number of active instances, the minimum number of standby instances, the maximum number of standby instances) (discussed in Section 4), the minimum hardware requirements (on machine type, processor type, the amount of cycles contributed, the amount of memory contributed, and the amount of storage contributed), the estimated amount of computation, the expected completion time, the priority level and the chaining policies (discussed in Section 4). The information subsection defines the information of the executables, the data, and the checkpoints. Figure 3 depicts the task/service description in S.M.A.R.T.

The service section of TSD uses the WSDL and WS-Resource specifications to define the service interfaces and the related stateful information.

The data of a TS is optional, and may come from multiple sources that are defined in the data information section of the TSD. The serialization is equivalent to the class serialization [10] of Java. It stores the runtime dynamics of any suspended TS. S.M.A.R.T. also supports checkpoints. As not all runtime states can be preserved through the serialization process, the checkpoint mechanism is provided to give the TS a chance to save its additional runtime states as checkpoints when the TS is suspended. When rescheduled, the TS is deserialized, and then resumed so that the TS is able to restore its states from previous checkpoints. Checkpoints are also useful if a TS wants to rollback to its previous states.

```
{Dependencies
  {Bundle dependencies
   Service dependencies}
 Scheduling policies
  {Instance policies
   Minimal hardware requirements
   Estimated computation amount
   Expecting completion time
   Priority level
   Chaining policies}
 Information
  {Executables information
   Data information
   Checkpoints information}}
```

Fig. 3. The Task Section of the Task/Service Description

3.2 Core Components

There are three kinds of entities in S.M.A.R.T: the clients, the trackers, and the computing nodes. Figure 4 depicts them.

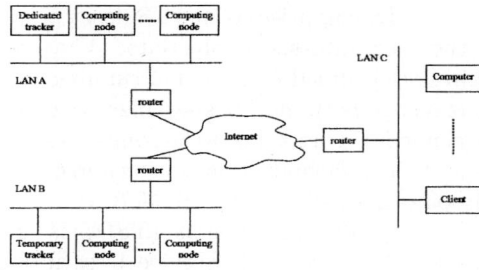

Fig. 4. The Entities in S.M.A.R.T.

A *client* is defined as a generic computing device that seeks services from the grid. It uses the Web Services standards to interact with the Grid. A *computing node* is the place where tasks are executed and computing occurs. A *tracker* is a computer which performs scheduling in its managed LAN. It is allowed for a client or a tracker to act as a computing node as well.

Each tracker has information about the computing resources available (called *profile*) on each managed node within the LAN, all tasks submitted to it (including the running tasks, and the tasks in the waiting queue), the overall load of its managed LAN, and the contacts of a limited number of other trackers. Multiple trackers may exist in a LAN for performance or fault-tolerance consideration.

Any computing device can be manually configured as a tracker (called *top-level tracker*), or can become a tracker by registering itself to an existing tracker (called the *portal* of the registering tracker). Any tracker therefore has at least one portal except the top level trackers. All top level trackers are dedicated trackers, which means that they are dedicated to the grid, and are not dynamic compared with the temporary trackers. A computing device can register itself to an existing dedicated tracker as a new dedicated tracker.

A temporary tracker comes into being through a selection process. The computing nodes and the clients only communicate with the trackers within the same LAN. If there is no tracker available in the LAN, a computing node or a client queries a default tracker for the best tracker, and

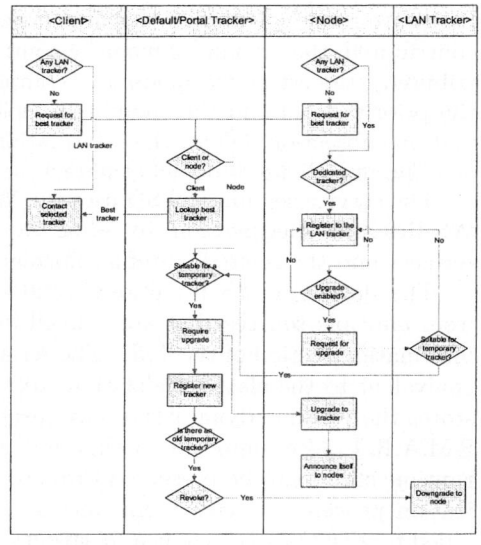

Fig. 5. The Self-organizing Process in S.M.A.R.T.

communicates with the resulting tracker. Further more, if a computing node is suitable to become a temporary tracker in its LAN, it upgrades to a temporary tracker until another more suitable computing node takes its place. This process is called *self-organizing*. Figure 5 demonstrates the process.

In S.M.A.R.T, each computing node and tracker runs a microkernel grid container, which serves as the runtime and managerial environment for jobs and services. The container consists of four components: the Runtime Environment (RT), the Management Agent (MA), the Profiling Agent (PA), and the Scheduling Agent (SA). Figure 6 depicts the architecture of the S.M.A.R.T. Grid Container.

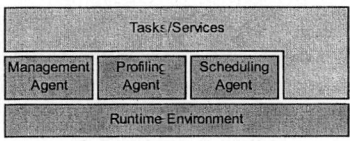

Fig. 6. The S.M.A.R.T. Grid Container

The Runtime Environment provides runtime libraries and software components for both the agents and the tasks/services. For example, the XML parsing libraries, and the implementations of some Web Services standards such as SOAP are included in the Runtime Environment. The Management Agent provides the service and managerial interface within the Grid and to the client. Policies and configurations are managed by the MA as well. The Profiling Agent gathers the status of the network, the trackers, the computing nodes, and the running tasks, and provides dynamic and optimized configurations for the scheduling agent. The Scheduling Agent is responsible for scheduling and management of tasks. It manages the lifecycle of tasks/services, and provides scheduling, fault-tolerance, and load balance services to the grid. Figure 7 depicts the agent interactions within a grid container.

The runtime environment and the agents are partially exposed to the TSs so that the TSs can utilize the underlying scheduling and management facilities.

4 Scheduling Strategy of S.M.A.R.T.

The scheduling process in S.M.A.R.T. is mainly involved in coordinating the agents' actions within and between the grid containers, and constructing a self-organized evolving computing network. More specifically, there are two separate processes, i.e. to schedule the TSs to the suitable computing nodes, and to balance the requests and schedule the corresponding TSs to the computing nodes to serve these requests.

It is consensus that CPN is one of the best ways to model agent interaction protocols [11,12]. In the CPN model of an agent interaction protocol, the protocol structure and the interaction policies are a net of components. The states of an agent interaction are represented by CPN places. Each place has an associated type determining what kind of data the place may contain. Data exchanged between agents are represented by tokens, whose colors indicate the value of the representing data. The interaction policies of a protocol are carried by CPN transitions and their associated arcs. A transition is enabled if all of its input places have tokens, and the colors of these tokens can satisfy the constraints that are specified on the arcs. A transition can be fired, which means the actions of this

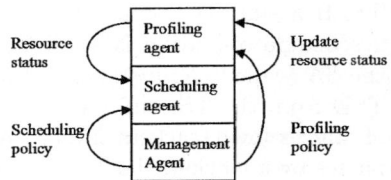

Fig. 7. The Agents Interactions in the S.M.A.R.T. Grid Container

transition can occur when this transition is enabled. When a transition occurs, it consumes the input tokens as the parameters, conducts the conversation policy and adds the new tokens into all of its output places. After a transition occurs, the state of a protocol is changed. A protocol is in its terminated state when there is no enabled or fired transition. The detailed principles of CPNs will be discussed together with its use in Subsection 4.2.

In the S.M.A.R.T's scheduling strategy, the TSs, the requests, and the profiles of the trackers and the computing nodes are represented as three kinds of tokens. The transition rules of these tokens are different when the tokens are placed at different places. The agents in S.M.A.R.T. are responsible for allocating the tokens and modifying them after the transitions are fired.

In the rest of this section, we discuss the lifecycle of the TS first, and then explain the TS-related and the request-related scheduling processes mentioned at the beginning of this section respectively. We use CPNs to describe the agent interaction protocols. We also describe the detailed algorithms used in these processes.

4.1 The Lifecycle of the TS

Figure 8 depicts the states of a TS in its lifecycle. When a Raw TS is submitted by a client via a tracker's MA, the MA checks the TS's validity. If the TS is valid, it enters the *SUBMITTED* state. A set of pre-schedule operations are then applied to the TS by the MA and the SA of the tracker. These operations include making a backup of the submitted TS, allocating and initializing the internal resources for scheduling purpose of that TS, etc. If all operations succeed, the TS enters the *READY* state.

The *READY* state means that the TS is ready to be scheduled. In this state, the SA of the tracker uses a "best-match" algorithm to determine whether the managed computing nodes of the tracker are suitable for the TS. If a suitable computing node is found, a schedule operation is applied. Otherwise, the SA (called *chaining source*) extracts the TSD from the TS, and passes it to the SAs of other known trackers. Every time the TSD passes by a tracker, the TTL (Time-to-Live) specified in the chaining policies of the TSD decreases by 1. If one of the trackers happens to be able to consume the TS according to the best-match algorithm, it contacts the source SA to transfer the TS to it. If the tracker is not able to consume the TS, it keeps passing on the TSD until the TTL equals 0. The above process is called *chaining*. After chaining, the TS remains in the *READY* state. Chaining is the core mechanism in S.M.A.R.T. to balance

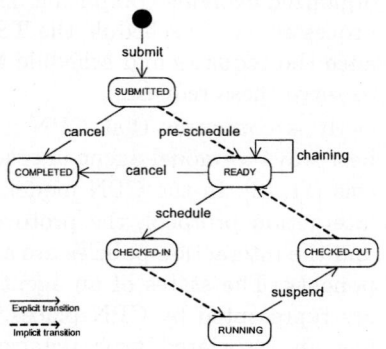

Fig. 8. The States of a S.M.A.R.T. Task/Service

the loads and requests globally. The detailed chaining and related protocols are discussed later.

The TS enters the *CHECKED-IN* state after the schedule operation, which means that the TS is scheduled to a computing node, the executables are resolved by the runtime environment of the computing node, and the runtime dynamics and the checkpoint have been restored for a suspended TS. The TS then automatically enters the *RUNNING* state until the suspend operation is applied, where the TS is serialized and suspended, and enters the *CHECKED-OUT* state. Following this, the TS is automatically transferred to the tracker where the computing node registers for rescheduling. One special situation is that if the TS exits, it fires the suspend operation itself and stores the computing result when being suspended.

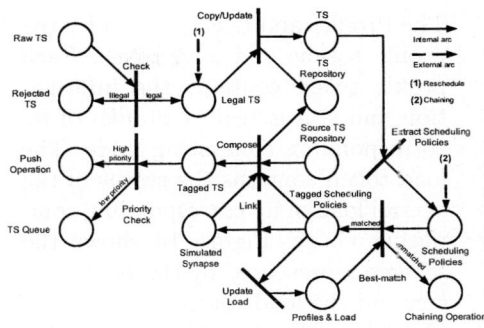

Fig. 9. The scheduling process within a Tracker

4.2 TS-Related Scheduling

The TS-related scheduling process in S.M.A.R.T. can be described as three sub processes: scheduling within a tracker, scheduling between the tracker and the computing nodes, and scheduling among the trackers.

Scheduling Within a Tracker. Figure 9 depicts the scheduling process with a tracker modeled by a CPN. There are four kinds of places defined in the CPN: the TS-related places, the operation places, the profile/load place, and the simulated synapse place. All of them are described as follows:

1. The Raw TS place holds the Raw TS token, which is received from the client.
2. The Rejected TS place holds the Raw TS tokens, which are rejected by the Check transition.
3. The Legal TS place holds the Raw TS token, which is asserted as legal by the Check transition. The legal Raw TS token may also come from the tracker itself due to a reschedule operation.
4. The TS Repository place holds the backup TS tokens. A backup TS token is removed when the corresponding TS exits or moves to another tracker through the chaining process. A backup TS token is updated when the corresponding TS is rescheduled.
5. The TS place holds the TS token which is produced by the Copy/Update transition.

6. The Scheduling Policies place holds the scheduling policies token, which is extracted from its corresponding TS token. The scheduling policies token may also come from another tracker through the chaining process.
7. The Profiles and Load place holds the profile tokens and load token. Each profile token contains the information and status (called *profile*) of its corresponding computing node. The load token contains the status of the overall load of its corresponding computing nodes. Figure 10 shows the scheme represented by the profile token and the load token.

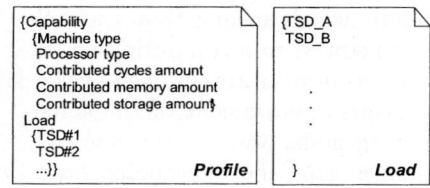

Fig. 10. The Profile and the Load

8. The Chaining Operation place holds the unmatched scheduling policies token, which is consumed by the chaining process.
9. The Tagged Scheduling Policies place holds the Tagged Scheduling Policies token, which is produced by the best-match transition. The tagged token has "winner" tags, which contain the identifiers of the best suitable nodes (the *winners*).
10. The Synapse place holds the syn-apse token, which represents the link between the destination and the source of a chaining process.
11. The Source TS Repository places holds the corresponding TS token of the scheduling policies token which is passed through the chaining process.
12. The Tagged TS place holds the Tagged TS token, which is composed from the TS token and the Tagged Scheduling Policies token.
13. The Push Operation place holds the Tagged TS token, which will be "pushed" to its corresponding computing node.
14. The TS Queue place holds the Tagged TS tokens, which will be "pulled" by any of the winner nodes.

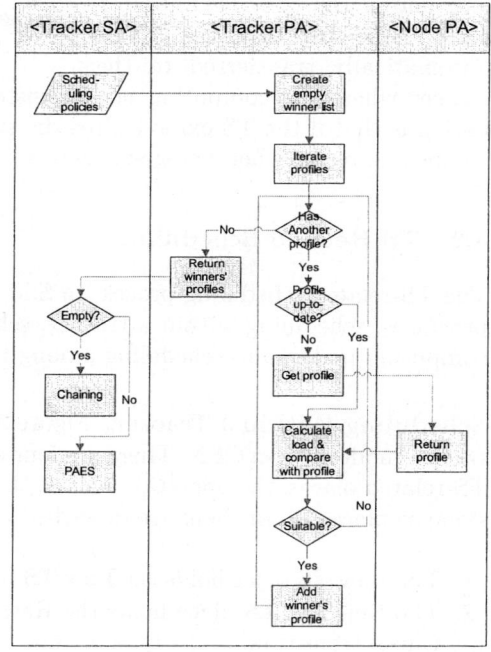

Fig. 11. The Best-match algorithm

There are eight transitions, which represent eight operations. They are described as follows:

1. The Check transition checks the syntax of the TSD of the Raw TS token. It also checks whether the dependent bundles and services exist, and whether the services defined by the Raw TS conflict with the existing services (e.g. conflict due to the same service name). In addition, the Check transition converts the Raw TS token into the TS token.
2. The Copy/Update transition either duplicates the TS token, or updates the TS token in the TS repository place.
3. The Extract Scheduling Policies transition extracts the scheduling policies from the TSD.
4. The Best-match transition performs the best-match algorithm. Figure 11 depicts the algorithm. PAES stands for Profile-Aware Eager Scheduling, which will be discussed later.
5. The Update Load transition converts the scheduling policies into the computing load, and adds the load to the overall load of the tracker.
6. The Link transition connects the two endpoints of a chaining process. Scheduling from one node to another node within the same LAN is a special case, as a tracker is always linked with itself.
7. The Compose transition transfers the TS token from the source TS repository, updates the local TS repository, and composes the Tagged TS token from the TS token and the tagged scheduling policies token.
8. The Priority Check transition compares the priority of the tagged TS token with the current loads of the winners to determine whether the token is "pushed" to its corresponding computing node, or stored in a queue for the "pull" operation.

Scheduling Between a Tracker and Its Nodes. S.M.A.R.T. uses a scheduling algorithm called *Profile-Aware Eager Scheduling (PAES)*, which is derived from eager scheduling, to schedule the TSs from the trackers to their managed computing nodes.

The eager scheduling algorithm was firstly introduced in Charlotte [13]. Its basic idea is that faster computing nodes will be allocated tasks more often, and if any task is left uncompleted by a slow node (failed node is infinitely slow), that task will be reassigned to a fast node. In other words, it uses a "keep the faster nodes busy" strategy. It also guarantees fault-tolerance by using a redundant task cache with a time out mechanism. The PAES algorithm takes the profiles of the computing nodes provided by the profile agent and the scheduling policies provided by the TSs into consideration when perform scheduling.

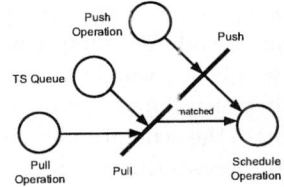

Fig. 12. The Push and Pull operations

In contrast to eager scheduling, it allows bidirectional scheduling operations, i.e. pull and push. Figure 12 depicts the two operations.

The Schedule Operation place holds the TS token which is scheduled to the corresponding computing node. The push operation is straightforward. The

Push transition represents the push operation, i.e. to assign the TS to one of the winners. The Pull Operation place holds the requests from the computing nodes. Whenever the scheduling agent of a node determines that it is able to run a new task, it sends a request to the tracker. The pull transition represents the pull operation, i.e. the scheduling agent matches the computing node requesting the TSs with the tagged TS tokens. If the node is the winner of the TS, the TS is assigned to the node.

Scheduling Among the Trackers. Trackers are linked by the chaining process, which is much of the scheduling process among the trackers.

Figure 13 depicts the basic chaining mechanism. The two places are defined exactly the same as those in Figure 9. However, in this case, they represent places in different trackers. The Check/Send transition checks the TTL in the scheduling policies token first. If it is greater than 0, the TTL decreases by 1, and the scheduling policies with the new TTL is sent to all known trackers. If the TTL equals 0, the scheduling policies token is discarded.

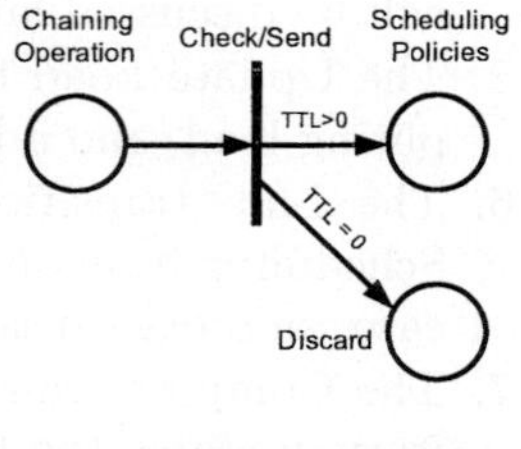

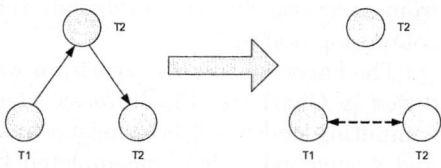

Fig. 13. The Basic Chaining Mechanism

Recalling Figure 9, there is a link transition, which makes two chained trackers (i.e. if tracker A successfully schedules the chained TS of tracker B, A and B are chained) learn, and preserve each other's information for future chaining processes. However, if the links exist permanently, the performance of the chaining process will gradually decrease as time goes by because of the explosive numbers of links. A link must therefore be able to be strengthened and weakened. Such a link is called a *simulated synapse*. Figure 14 depicts it.

The underlying algorithm used to strengthen and weaken the link can be defined in the chaining policies. One of the simplest algorithms is the *aging* algorithm. In the aging algorithm, every simulated synapse has an associated weight. A weight is a numerical value between 0 and 1, which is used to evaluate the strength of its associated chain (1 representing the most strong link, and 0 representing no link). Weight is calculated based on the frequency of communication occurring on its associated chain. When a simulated synapse is created, an initial weight is specified. Then for each interval I, the weight squares. If the resulting weight is less than the threshold θ, the simulated synapse is removed. On the other hand, each time the Link transition is fired, the square root of the weight is calculated.

Fig. 14. The Simulated Synapse

To take the advantage of the simulated synapse, the chaining process must take the strength of the simulated synapse into consideration. Figure 15 depicts an example of the advanced chaining mechanism.

4.3 Request-Related Scheduling

As the TSs are allowed to register services in S.M.A.R.T. One of the functions of scheduling is to balance the requests and schedule the corresponding TSs to the computing nodes to serve these requests. In fact, the only difference between TS-related scheduling and request-related scheduling is the objects that are actually scheduled. In the former case, the object is the TS or the scheduling policies extracted from the TS. In the later case, the object is the service request. As the requests have no common characteristic in terms of the potential load that they may bring in, it is hard for the scheduling components to make rational decisions. However, S.M.A.R.T. still provides two ways to help services achieve high throughputs.

Recalling the TSD, there is a subsection called instance policies, which defines the Minimum number of Active Instances (MINAI), the Maximum number of Active Instances (MAXAI), the Minimum number of Standby Instances (MINSI), and the Maximum number of Standby Instances (MAXSI). When a service TS (a TS that defines services) is scheduled, the instance policies are used to guide the scheduling components to keep a proper number of service instances.

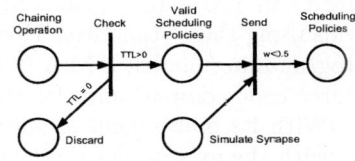

Fig. 15. An Example of the Advanced Chaining Mechanism

Then when a client attempts to invoke these services, it uses the Web Services standards to discover the service instances. It is at that time that the clients' requests are distributed to the pre-allocated services instances so that these requests are balanced.

Another way to balance service requests is to let the service provider itself manage the requests, as only they know about the internals of the requests and the best way to handle the requests. The multi-agent architecture of S.M.A.R.T. allows the service TSs to use the underlying APIs to provide their own scheduling strategies, and schedule the requests themselves.

5 Discussion

In this section, we discuss the compatibility and interoperability issues with the existing grid systems and clients, and how the new infrastructure can operate with the existing local schedulers.

Recalling the Task/Service model (see Section 3), it is easy to find that the TS model enables the modeling of both the conversional stateless services and stateful tasks. As it is undefined in the Web Services standards whether a service is stateless or not, both the stateful TSs and the stateless TSs can use TSDL, which is compatible with WSDL, to register its own interface to the clients. Therefore any WS-compatible client is capable of accessing these interfaces through S.M.A.R.T.

There are two means to maintain stateful information for a conversional service in S.M.A.R.T. The client and the service can use agreed methods, e.g. WS-Resource, to exchange the stateful information. S.M.A.R.T. supports the WS-Resource standards, hence a WS-Resource based client needs no modification to work with S.M.A.R.T. as long as the service interface is not changed. Another way to preserve the states throughout different service transactions is to dynamically create transaction-specific service tasks. In S.M.A.R.T., a TS can be transaction-specific (which is specified by the instance policies in the TSD). Whenever a request for such a TS is received, a TS instance will be created to serve that request. One variation of this method is that there is a main TS serving as a proxy. Whenever a request is received by that TS, it delegates the request to a service task, which is created by the main TS.

As S.M.A.R.T. conforms to the Web Services and WS-Resource standards, any TS in S.M.A.R.T. is able to operate on the services in other WS-compatible grids using these standards. However, being different in the architecture and the programming model, S.M.A.R.T. has neither the binary compatibility nor the source code compatibility for the programs running in the existing grids.

With its multi-agent architecture, S.M.A.R.T. has promising interoperability with the existing local schedulers. There are two approaches. A local scheduler specific agent can be deployed to the local scheduler. It keeps the same interface with S.M.A.R.T. and adapts itself to the scheduling and job management interface provided by the local scheduler. In the scheduling and job management process, it works as an intermedium or an adapter to interpret the scheduling and job management operations and data between S.M.A.R.T. and the local scheduler. This approach is straightforward, but different local schedulers need different adapter agents. In the second approach, a more generic design of the S.M.A.R.T's agents is required. Instead of hard coding a full version of the scheduling and management operations and protocols into the S.MA.R.T's agents, a set of predefined preliminary operations and protocols, which allow the construction of more complex and complete operations and protocols using a uniform scheme, are carefully selected and implemented into these agents. Hence, the scheduling and management operations and protocols of S.M.A.R.T. itself and the local schedulers can be represented by the schemes. These schemes are understandable and checkable for the S.M.A.R.T's agents. Once the agents are deployed, they read the schemes in, check them before any scheduling and management operation occurs, and then use them in the operations. A promising way to represent the scheme is to use CPN and the Matrix Equation Method [14], which allows the agents to check whether a scheme is understandable.

6 Conclusion

In this paper, we firstly analyzed the service-oriented architecture of the existing grid systems. By introducing a task/service model, we covered the deficiencies of the current grid standards. Secondly, we abandoned the conventional two commit scheduling strategy, and proposed a multi-agent based scheduling strategy. The intelligent agents in the system are able to make rational decisions and exhibit the flexibility in face of uncertain and changing factors. These advantages make the new architecture more efficient and flexible when dealing with open systems. Thirdly, we extended the eager scheduling algorithm to the profile-aware eager scheduling algorithm, and introduced the best-match algorithm and the chaining mechanism, which achieve local optima and global optima respectively in terms of load balance for both the TSs and the requests. The policy free best-match algorithm abstracts itself from decision making by extracting the scheduling policies from the user configurations (i.e. the TSD). This enables sophisticated scheduling and resource utilization. Finally, we clarified how S.M.A.R.T. preserves the compatibility with the WS-compatible clients, and discussed its promising interoperability with the existing grids and local schedulers.

Future work of this research includes proposing detailed algorithms and schemes that allow S.M.A.R.T. to collaborate with the existing grids and local schedulers, and testing and evaluating S.M.A.R.T. in real applications.

References

1. Epema, D.H.J., Livny, M., vanDantzig, R., Evers, X., Pruyne, J.: A worldwide flock of condors: Load sharing among workstation clusters. Future Generation Computer Systems **12** (1996) 53–65
2. Foster, I.: A Globus Toolkit Primer (An Early and Incomplete Draft). http://www-unix.globus.org/toolkit/docs/4.0/key/GT4_Primer_0.6.pdf (2005)
3. Jensen, K.: Colored Petri Nets - Basic Concepts, Analysis Methods and Practical Use. Volume 1. Springer-Verlag, Berlin (1992)
4. W3C: Web Services. http://www.w3.org/2002/ws/ (2002)
5. Foster, I., Czajkowski, K., Ferguson, D., Frey, J., Graham, S., Maguire, T., Snelling, D., Tuecke, S.: Modeling and managing state in distributed systems: the role of ogsi and wsrf. Proceedings of the IEEE **93** (2005) 604–612
6. Czajkowski, K., Fitzgerald, S., Foster, I., Kesselman, C.: Grid information services for distributed resource sharing. In: the 10th IEEE International Symposium on High-Performance Distributed Computing (HPDC-10), San Francisco, California, the United States, IEEE Press (2001) 181–194
7. Czajkowski, K., Foster, I., Karonis, N., Kesselman, C., Martin, S., Smith, W., Tuecke., S.: A resource management architecture for metacomputing systems. In: IPPS/SPDP '98 Workshop on Job Scheduling Strategies for Parallel Processing. (1998) 62–82
8. Lesser, V.: Cooperative multiagent systems: A personal view of the state of the art. IEEE Transactions on Knowledge and Data Engineering **11** (1999) 133–142
9. Christensen, E., Curbera, F., Meredith, G., Weerawarana, S.: Web Services Description Language (WSDL) 1.1. http://www.w3.org/TR/wsdl (2001)
10. Greanier, T.: Discover the secrets of the java serialization api. http://java.sun.com/developer/technicalArticles/Programming/serialization/ (2000)

11. Cost, R.S.: Modeling agent conversations with coloured petri nets. In: the Workshop on Specifying and Implementing Conversation Policies, Seattle, Washington, the United States (1999) 59–66
12. Cranefield, S., Purvis, M., Nowostawski, M., Hwang, P.: Ontology for interaction protocols. In: the 2nd International Workshop on Ontologies in Agent Systems (AAMAS'02), Bologna, Italy (2002)
13. Baratloo, A., Karaul, M., Kedem, Z., Wyckoff, P.: Charlotte: Metacomputing on the web. In: the 9th Conference of Parallel and Distributed Computing Systems, Dijon, France (1996)
14. Peterson, J.: Petri Net Theory and the Modeling of Systems. Prentice-Hall, Inc., N.J. (1981)

Dynamically Mining Frequent Patterns over Online Data Streams

Xuejun Liu[1,2], Hongbing Xu[1], Yisheng Dong[1], Yongli Wang[1], and Jiangbo Qian[1]

[1] Department of Computer Science and Technology, Southeast University,
Nanjing 210096, China
[2] College of Information Science and Engineering, Nanjing University of Technology,
Nanjing 210009, China
lxj-gd@vip.sina.com

Abstract. Data streams are massive unbounded sequence of data elements continuously generated at a rapid rate. Consequently, it is challenge to find frequent items over data streams in a dynamic environment. In this paper, a new novel algorithm was proposed, which can capture frequent items with any length online continuously. Furthermore, several optimization techniques are devised to minimize processing time as well as main memory usage. Compared with related algorithm, it is more suitable for the mining of long frequent items. Finally, the proposed method is analyzed by a series of experiments and the results show that this algorithm owns significantly better performance than before.

1 Introduction

In recent years, with the development of the Internet and sensor networks, Data streams process has become a new research issue[1,2]. To find the frequent items over data streams is one of the fundamental problems in this field. In many applications, such as network traffic measurements, data mining, web-server logs analysis, telecom call records analysis, and sensor network, we all hope to find the data items whose frequency exceed certain threshold.

According to the features of data streams, the FP-stream structure was proposed to solve the problem of mining the frequent itemsets over data streams [4]. When the average length of the transaction and frequent pattern are both very short, this algorithm is effective. On the contrary, the space cost and execution time increase dramatically and the efficiency of this algorithm declines quickly. The Lossy Counting [5] is a algorithm based on a well-known Apriori algorithm to mining all frequent itemsets over the entire history of the data streams and it is a representative method. Karp [6] and Charikar [7] study how to find a single frequent pattern. The work by Chang [8] emphasizes on finding the latest frequent pattern. The mining problem of sequential pattern is studied in [9]. Graham [10] and Tatsuya [11] study Hierarchical frequent pattern over data streams and the discovery of frequent pattern of semi-structural data streams respectively. Ruoming Jin and Gagan Agrawal[12] extends the work by Karp [6], which can cut down the number of itemsets needed to store. The approach in [13,14] is more applicable to the problem of single pattern or the pattern is fixed in advance and will not change.

This paper presents an effective frequent pattern-mining algorithm----FP-DS algorithm over data streams. The user can obtain current frequent itemsets online continuously without pattern-delay. Compared with the existing related algorithms, the FP-DS algorithm is especially suitable for the mining of long frequent items. It is unnecessary to enumerate every subset on transactions, nor produce a lot of frequent candidate items. In FP-DS algorithm, we propose a data structure, named FP-DS tree, to store the potential frequent itemsets. It does not need to store all subsets of itemsets independently. It reduces the storage capacity of itemsets and moreover, the itemsets are put in the order of the descending sequence of support of global 1-itemset. The more frequently the items appear, the closer to the root of the tree. Such a compression tree has a higher compression ratio, and by using FP-DS tree we can obtain all frequent itemsets efficiently.

This paper consists of five sections. Section 2 describes the fundamental problems and the FP-DS algorithm is presented in section 3. Section 4 is about performance analysis of the algorithm, and the last section concludes this paper.

2 Definitions and Description of the Problem

Definition 1. Suppose DS represents data streams, the number of transactions which include itemset X is called the support counts of itemset X and is marked as $f_{DS}(X)$. The support of itemset X is marked as X.sup, X.sup= $f_{DS}(X)/|DS|$, of which $|DS|$ is the number of transactions in DS.

Definition 2. Suppose a given support S and a permitted error ε, $|N|$ denotes the number of transactions in data streams up to now. For itemset X, if there is $f_{DS}(X) \geq (S-\varepsilon)|N|$(ie. X.sup$\geq$S-$\varepsilon$), we call X a frequent itemset; if $f_{DS}(X) > \varepsilon|N|$, we call X a subfrequent itemset; if $f_{DS}(X) \leq \varepsilon|N|$, we call X an infrequent itemset. If X is made up of k items, we call X a k-itemset.

Definition 3(FP-DS Tree).

a) It consists of one root labeled as 'null', a set of prefix subtrees as the children of the root, and a header table.

b) Every node in the prefix subtree is made up of seven fields: *data, f, reval, pnode, par, leftchild* and *rightchild*, where *data* is the item-name of this node, *f* denotes the count of the itemset which starts from the root node(excluding root node) to the current node, *reval* is a count to avoid the repetition of itemset insertion when re-constructing FP-DS tree, *pnode* is the pointer pointing to a node that has the same item-name or null when there is no such nodes, *par* is the pointer points to its parent node, *leftchild* is the point pointing to the first child node, and *rightchild,* the one pointing to its brother node.

c) Every tuple in the header table consists of two fields: item-name and head of *pnode* which points to the first node in the FP-DS tree bearing the same item-name.

Any tree that satisfies all the above conditions is called a FP-DS tree. A FP-DS tree is shown in figure 1 (the nodes of tree are only labeled with data, f and reval).

A FP-DS tree is similar to a FP-tree[3]. Compared with a FP-tree, its every node has one more *reval* field.

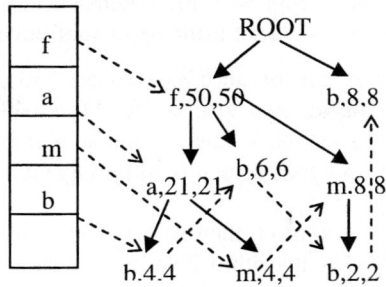

Fig. 1. FP-DS tree structure

Theorem 1. Divide DS into segments $N_1, N_2, \ldots, N_m, \ldots$, let $N = N_1 \cup N_2 \cup \ldots \cup N_k$, any itemset X, for given support S and error ε, if $f_{Ni}(X) \leq \varepsilon |N_i|$, $f_N(X) \geq S|N|$, $1 \leq i < k$, of which $|N_i|$ denotes the number of transactions of Segment i, then $f_{Nk}(X) \geq (S-\varepsilon)|N|$.

The proposition is easily proved. According to theorem 1, we can draw a conclusion that if delete current infrequent itemsets, even they become frequent itemsets in the futrue, its support error will not exceed ε at most, and this deletion will not affect the proper output of frequent itemsets. Thus, we only need to preserve all subfrequent itemsets.

3 FP-DS Algorithm

3.1 The Production and Reconstruction of Global Subfrequent 1-Itemset

Data streams are divided into segments $N_i (i=1, 2, \ldots)$, and the length of every segment is $|N_i| = \lceil 1/\varepsilon \rceil$ or $k*\lceil 1/\varepsilon \rceil$ $(k=1,2,\ldots)$. To make the description of this algorithm more clear, we suppose $|N_i| = \lceil 1/\varepsilon \rceil$. The f_list is made up of many 1-itemsets and every 1-itemset in the f_list is a structure with three fields: *data*, *f* and *del*, of which, *data* is the item-name of 1-itemset, *f* is counts of the 1-itemset, and *del* is the conditional-variable to indicate when to delete the 1-itemset. Following is the description of the algorithm.

```
Algorithm 1. Scands _ DB algorithm.
Input : data of Segment N_i; the f_list of Segment N_{i-1}. (In
        Segment N_1, the original f_list is empty)
Output : the f_list of Segment N_i.
(1) for every new arrived data stream element e_i ,
    if e_i ∈ f_list then
(2)     e_i.f= e_i.f+1, e_i.del= e_i.del+1;
(3) else insert e_i, let e_i.f= 1, let e_i.del= 1;
(4) sort f_list in the descending order of support;
(5) for each e_i ∈ f_list {
(6)     e_i.del= e_i.del-1;
(7)     if e_i.del=0 then delete e_i.}
```

Theorem 2. According to above approach, the 1-itemsets deleted from f_list must be infrequent itemset, and f_list is a data set made up of subfrequent 1-itemsets.

Proof. For any 1-itemset $a \in$ f_list, because $a.\text{del}=a.\text{del}-1$ in every segment, suppose until Segment N_i, negative is k, then $k \leq i$, while $a.f \leq a.\text{del}+k$, so $a.f \leq a.\text{del}+i$. The condition of deleting a in Segment N_i is $a.\text{del}=0$, and now, $a.f \leq i$, and another reason is $\varepsilon|N|=\varepsilon*i*|N_i|=\varepsilon*i*\lceil 1/\varepsilon \rceil \geq i$, so $a.f \leq \varepsilon|N|$, ie. a is an infrequent itemset, so f_list is a data set of subfrequent 1-itemsets.

If 1-itemset is an infrequent itemset, then its supersets must be infrequent itemsets too. Due to Theorem 2, in FP-DS algorithm, deleting 1-itemset from f_list will not lead to the loss of frequent items.

Theorem 3. The maximum storage space is $O(L/\varepsilon)$ in f_list. And L is the average length of the transaction.

In order to prove theorem 3, we give out theorem 4.

Theorem 4. Suppose a is a 1-itemset, $I(DS,\varepsilon)=\{f_{DS}(a)>\varepsilon|DS|\}$, then $|I(DS,\varepsilon)| \leq L*\lceil 1/\varepsilon \rceil$.

Proof. We use counter-proof. Because the supports of data items in $I(DS,\varepsilon)$ are all greater than $\varepsilon|DS|$, then $|I(DS,\varepsilon)|*\varepsilon|DS| \leq L*|DS|$, if $|I(DS,\varepsilon)|>L*\lceil 1/\varepsilon \rceil$ is true, then $|I(DS,\varepsilon)|*\varepsilon|DS| > L* \lceil 1/\varepsilon \rceil *\varepsilon|DS| \geq L*1/\varepsilon*\varepsilon|DS|=L*|DS|$, that is to say, $|I(DS,\varepsilon)|*\varepsilon|DS|>L*|DS|$, this is in contradiction with the conclusion we have got $|I(DS,\varepsilon)|*\varepsilon|DS| \leq L*|DS|$, the proposition is proved.

According to theorem 4, the number of items needed to be stored in f_list will not exceed $L*\lceil 1/\varepsilon \rceil$, that is to say, when error is ε, we need space $O(L/\varepsilon)$ at most to store all the 1-itemsets with the above approach. So theorem 3 is proved. Theorem 3 gives us the maximum space cost of f_list. The maximum storage space of f_list has nothing to do with the number of the transactions and the number of items. It is only related to ε and the average length of transaction. Therefore, even ε is very small, it does not need a huge storage space to store f_list.

3.2 The Production and Reconstruction of FP-DS Tree

Definition 4. All nodes in the path from the node e to the root in FP-DS tree constitute the itemset whose name is the pattern e. The set made up of all patterns e is called the pattern set of e.

FP-DS tree is used to compress and store global subfrequent itemsets. Every segment produces a new FP-DS tree and that of the last segment is removed at the same time. The production of FP-DS tree is similar to that of FP-tree. Firstly, establish the root and header table of the tree. Then insert a subfrequent itemset into the tree, and the first branch is formed. Only those items in f_list will be selected. The itemset is inserted in order of f_list. Next we add the second subfrequent itemset to the existing FP-DS. If there exists same prefix with the existing branch, the f of the nodes of the same prefix are added the count of second subfrequent itemset respectively. Otherwise, the exiting FP-DS is spread into a new branch. The above procedure iterates until all subfrequent itemsets are inserted. To speed up searching in the tree, we maintain a header table.

When producing FP-DS tree of Segment i, subfrequent itemsets include not only the subfrequent itemsets produced from FP-growth algorithm in this segment, but also the subfrequent itemsets stored in FP-DS tree of Segment N_{i-1}.

Algorithm 2. Reconstruction algorithm (To produce the FP-DS tree of Segment N_i).
Input : data of Segment N_i; the FP-DS tree of Segment N_{i-1} (when i>1); errorε.
Output : the FP-DS tree of Segment N_i.
(1) To produce the original FP-DS tree of Segment N_i including a header table and a root node. The header table is produced from the f_list of Segment N_i, and the root node is marked with 'null'.
(2) If (i>1) {
(3)   call insertconstruct function;   /*insert the subfrequent itemsets stored in the FP-DS tree of Segment N_{i-1} into the FP-DS tree of Segment N_i */
(4)   delete the FP-DS tree of Segment N_{i-1}; }
(5) With ε as the support, call FP-growth algorithm to produce subfrequent itemsets of this segment, sort every itemset in the order of that of f_list, delete those items don't exist in f_list, then insert the rest into the FP-DS tree of Segment N_i;
(6) release the storage space FP-growth algorithm occupies;

The description of *Insertconstruct* function is listed as follows:

(1) Take item e_i according to the inverted sequence of the header table in FP-DS tree of Segment N_{i-1};
(2) for each e_i {
(3)   we obtain the pattern set of e_i in FP-DS tree. The patterns are pattern e_{i1}, pattern e_{i2}, pattern e_{i3}, ...respectively
(4)   for each e_{ij}, if (e_{ij}.reval≠0) then {
(5)   if ($e_i \in$ f_list of Segment N_i)
(6)   { reorder all the items of pattern e_{ij} in the order of that of f_list in Segment N_i, and delete those items not included in f_list, then insert the rest into the FP-DS tree of Segment N_i }
(7)   every reval of all nodes in pattern e_{ij} minus e_{ij}.reval;
   } }

3.3 The Production and pruning of Frequent Itemsets

The production algorithm of frequent itemset is similar to *insertconstruct* function. The former handles the *f* of items and the latter handles the *reval* of items. Following are detailed description.

Algorithm 3. Ds_growth algorithm.
Input : FP-DS tree in Segment N_i; support S(suppose
         corresponding count as SF).
Output : frequent itemsets.
(1) Take item e_i in the order of converse sequence of header
    table of FP-DS tree in Segment N_i;
(2) for each e_i {
(3)   take the pattern set of e_i of FP-DS tree, whose patterns
       are pattern e_{i1}, pattern e_{i2}, pattern e_{i3}, respectively...
(4)   for each e_{ij} {
(5)   if (e_{ij}.f>SF)
(6)   put out pattern e_{ij} and its count;
(7)   if (e_{ij}.f≠0) then
(8)   the f of every node minus e_{ij}.f in pattern e_{ij}; } }

The pruning of FP-DS tree aims to delete the nodes as many as possible permitted by error ε, to reduce the storage space of data. Pruning should go from leaves to the root. For each leaf node, the cumulative counts of deleted leaf nodes bearing the same item name cannot exceed the difference between this item's *f* and *del* in f_list.

3.4 The FP-DS Algorithm

Following are the full description of FP-DS algorithm:

Algorithm 4. FP-DS algorithm.
Input: data streams DS; the minimum support threshold S;
         permitted error ε.
Output: the complete set of frequent itemsets.
Divide data streams into segments $N_i (i=1 \cdot 2 \cdot ...)$, the length
of every segment is $|N_i| = \lceil 1/\varepsilon \rceil$.
(1) for(i=1;i<=the number of segments; i++) {
(2)   call *Scands_DB*, produce f_list of Segment N_i;
(3)   call *Reconstruction*, produce FP-DS tree of Segment N_i;
(4)   every several segments, call pruning algorithm, to
       reduce the storage capacity of data;
(5)   call *Ds_growth*, put frequent itemsets out;   }

When the length of segments is the integer times of $\lceil 1/\varepsilon \rceil$ (suppose *n* times), then after scanning segment N_i once, every 1-itemset in f_list is e_j.del= e_j.del-n. when e_j.del=0, e_j is deleted. Other parts are the same as described above.

4 Performance Analysis and Experimental Research

Data streams adopted by this paper are the customer shopping data sets produced by IBM synthetic data generator. The experiments adopt three sets of data: T15I10D1000K, T15I6D1000K and T7I4D3000K Divide the incoming data streams into segments, and every segment contains 50000 transactions. Suppose support as S, let permissible error ε=0.1S. The experiment mainly studies time efficiency and space efficiency of the algorithm, and compares the experiments with other algorithms.

4.1 Performance Analysis of the Algorithm

Experiments environment are: Intel Celeron CPU 1GHz, Memory128MB, Redhat 9.0 operating system. Take data sets T15I10D1000K, of which 1K different items, support is 0.007、0.005 and 0.004 respectively. The main aim is to observe time efficiency and space efficiency of the algorithm.

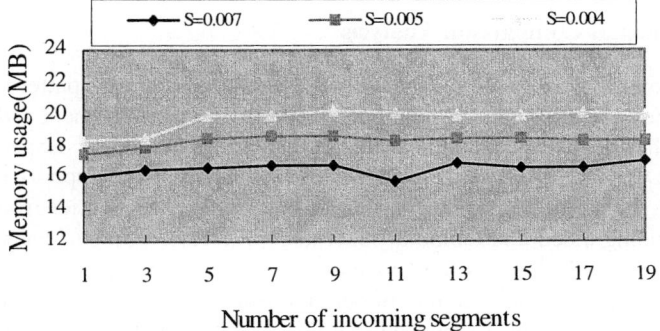

Fig. 2. Maximal memory usage in each segment

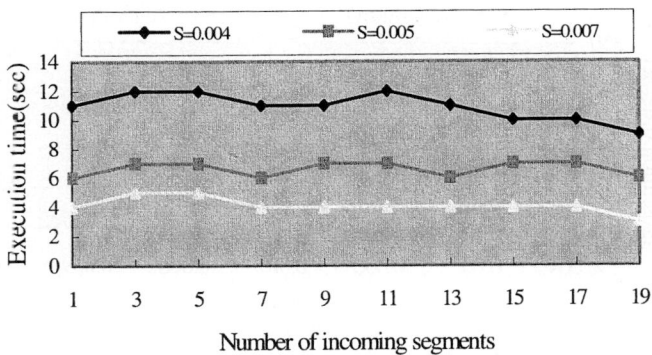

Fig. 3. Execution time in each segment

The maximum memory usage in the Figure 2 refers to the maximum memory space algorithm needs when dealing with every data segment (including aided memory and temporary memory too). Execution time in the Figure 3 refers to the execution time of every data segment. From Figure 2 and Figure 3 we can see that, with the decrease of support, the maximum memory space and execution time of every segment increase gradually. However, when the support is given, the maximum memory space and execution time of every segment tend to be steady. That is to say, it has nothing to do with the size of data sets. Consequently, we can apply this algorithm to data streams. When the support S is smaller, the effect of support change on execution time is obvious. The main reason is: the greatest time cost of the algorithm in every data segment is calling FP-growth algorithm to produce subfrequent itemsets. When using FP-growth algorithm to mine frequent pattern, it needs to produce conditional FP-tree gradually, and must produce one conditional FP- tree when producing one frequent pattern. When the support S is smaller, error ε is even smaller than it(letε=0.1S here), FP-growth algorithm produces subfrequent itemsets with a very small ε as support, and will produce a great number of frequent patterns. It will cost a lot of time to produce and release these condition FP-trees dynamically.

4.2 Experimental Comparison Analysis

The algorithm in [5] is a typical approach of mining frequent patterns over data streams. We test the algorithm with the same experimental environment and datasets as that of [5]. Then we compare and analyze the result with that of [5]. Experiments data set is T15I6D1000K, of which 10K different items. When the support ranges from 0.004 to 0.01, the maximum memory usage of FP-DS algorithm varies from 21.7 M to 17.8 M (including aided and temporary memory). Execution time of the algorithm in [5] will decrease with the growth of memory usage. We compare the execution time with a memory cost of 28M with that of our algorithm. The result is shown in figure 4. Algorithm I and Algorithm II represents FP-DS algorithm and the algorithm proposed in [5] respectively.

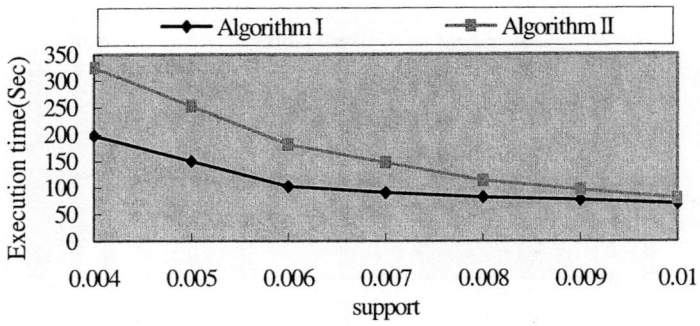

Fig. 4. Comparison of execution time

We can see that, even under the condition of space cost is smaller, the time efficiency of FP-DS algorithm is also much higher than that of algorithm proposed in [5]. The main time and space cost of FP-DS algorithm are the time cost and temporary space cost of calling FP-growth algorithm in every segment. We can improve the time and space efficiency of FP-DS algorithm further if we adopt an improved FP-growth algorithm.

FP-DS algorithm and the algorithm proposed in [4] are both based on FP-growth algorithm. So we compare and analyze the algorithm adopting the similar experimental environment. Take T7I4D3000K as test set, of which 1K different items. The data is divided into segments and the support is 0.05. The approach in [4] is more suitable for short itemsets. If the above test set is adopted, it can only handle about 180 transactions per second. Obviously, in the environment of high-speed data streams, this speed is not fast enough. In contrast, our approach can treat 30000 transactions per second. We also compare the maximum storage space of FP-stream tree and that of FP-DS tree in every segment. The maximum storage space of the FP-stream tree is about 2.5M, and that of FP-DS tree is about 0.9M. The reason is that FP-stream tree needs to store every subfrequent itemsets and all its subsets while FP-DS tree need not. When the average length of the frequent itemsets is larger, FP-DS tree saves more storage space than FP-stream does. According to above analysis, we can conclude that FP-DS algorithm has better time and space efficiency compared with approach in [4].

5 Conclusion

This paper proposes a new approach, which aims at the mining of frequent pattern s over data streams-----FP-DS algorithm. It solves the problem of mining frequent patterns with any length. Current frequent itemsets can be obtained online continuously, and the system need not store the whole data set. Compared with other existing related algorithms, there is no pattern delay, and the efficiency does not decrease dramatically with the growth in length of frequent patterns. Consequently, it is especially suitable for mining long frequent itemsets over data streams. Experiment results indicate that FP-DS algorithm has a good time and space efficiency.

References

1. B. Babcock, S.Babu and M.Datar. Model and Issues in Data streams Systems. PODS, 2002..
2. Jin CQ, Qian WN, Zhou AY. Analysis and management of streaming data: A survey. Journal of Software, 2004,15(8).
3. Jiawei Han, Jian Pei, Yiwen Yin. Mining frequent patterns without candidate generation. In Proc. 2000 ACM-SIGMOD Int. Conf. Management of Data (SIGMOD'00).
4. C. Giannella, J. Han, J. Pei, X. Yan, and PS Yu. Mining Frequent Patterns in Data Streams at Multiple Time Granularities. in H. Kargupta, A. Joshi, K. Sivakumar, and Y. Yesha (eds.), Next Generation Data Mining, AAAI/MIT,2003.
5. G.S. Manku and R. Motwani. Approximate Frequency Counts over Streaming Data. In Proc. of the 28th International Conference on Very Large Data Bases (VLDB 2002), August 2002.
6. Karp, R. M.; Papadimitriou, C. H.; and Shenker, S. A simple algorithm for _finding frequent elements in streams and bags. ACM Trans. Database Systems, 2003.
7. M. Charikar, K. Chen, and M. Farach-Colton. Finding frequent items in data streams. In Proceedings of 29th International Colloquium on Automata, Languages and Programming, 2002.
8. Joong Hyuk Chang , Won Suk Lee. Finding Recent Frequent Itemsets Adaptively over Online Data streams. The 9 th ACM SIGKDD International Conference on Knowledge Discovery and Data Mining (KDD 03), Washington, DC, August, 2003

9. Wei-Guang Teng, Ming-Syan Chen, Philip S. Yu. A Regression-Based Temporal Pattern Mining Scheme for Data streams. Proceedings of the International Conference on Very Large Data Bases, Berlin, Germany, Sept. 2003.
10. Graham Cormode, Flip Korn, S. Muthukrishnan, Divesh Srivastava. Finding Hierarchical Heavy Hitters in Data streams. In the International Conference on Very Large Data Bases (VLDB) 2003.
11. Tatsuya Asai, Hiroki Arimura, Kenji Abe, Shinji Kawasoe, Setsuo Arikawa. Online Algorithms for Mining Semi-structured Data streams. In the IEEE International Conf. Data Mining (ICDM) 2002.
12. Ruoming Jin, Gagan Agrawal. An Algorithm for In-Core Frequent Itemset Mining on Streaming Data. By submitted for publication 2004.
13. Graham Cormode, S. Muthukrishnan. What's Hot and What's Not: Tracking Most Frequent Items Dynamically. In the ACM Symposium on Principles of Database Systems (PODS) 2003.
14. Cheqing Jin, Weining Qian, Chaofeng Sha, Jeffrey X. Yu, Aoying Zhou. Dynamically Maintaining Frequent Items Over A Data streams. In the Conference on Information and Knowledge Management (CIKM) 2003.

Clustering Mixed Type Attributes in Large Dataset*

Jian Yin and Zhifang Tan

Department of Computer Science, Zhongshan University, Guangzhou 510275, China
issjyin@zsu.edu.cn

Abstract. Clustering is a widely used technique in data mining, now there exists many clustering algorithms, but most existing clustering algorithms either are limited to handle the single attribute or can handle both data types but are not efficient when clustering large data sets. Few algorithms can do both well. In this paper, we propose a clustering algorithm CFIKP that can handle large datasets with mixed type of attributes. We first use CF^*-tree to pre-cluster datasets. After the dense regions are stored in leaf nodes, then we look every dense region as a single point and use an improved k-prototype to cluster such dense regions. Experiments show that the CFIKP algorithm is very efficient in clustering large datasets with mixed type of attributes.

1 Introduction

Clustering is widely used in data mining, statistic, biology, machine learning and so on. It is a popular approach to implementing the partitioning operation. It partitions a set of objects into clusters such that objects in the same cluster are more similar to each other than objects in different clusters according to some defined criteria.

The most distinct characteristic of data mining is that it deals with very large and complex data sets. The data sets to be mined often contain millions of objects described by tens, hundreds or even thousands of various types of attributes or variables (interval, ratio, binary, ordinal, nominal, etc.). This requires the data mining operations and algorithms to be scalable and capable of dealing with different types of attributes. However, most algorithms currently used in data mining do not scale well when applied to very large data sets because they were initially developed for other applications than data mining that involve small data sets. In terms of clustering, we are interested in algorithms that can efficiently cluster large data sets containing both continuous and categorical values because such data sets are frequently encountered in data mining

---

* This work is supported by the National Natural Science Foundation of China (60205007), Natural Science Foundation of Guangdong Province (031558, 04300462), Research Foundation of National Science and Technology Plan Project (2004BA721A02), Research Foundation of Science and Technology Plan Project in Guangdong Province (2003C50118) and Research Foundation of Science and Technology Plan Project in Guangzhou City(2002Z3-E0017).

applications. Most existing clustering algorithms either can handle both data types but are not efficient when clustering large data sets or can handle large data sets efficiently but are limited to continuous attributes. Few algorithms can do both well.

K-means [1] clustering method put forward by MacQueen is the earliest and the most simply algorithm. However, it only works on numeric data and can not cluster categorical attributes and mixed attributes.

K-modes and k-prototype [2] is the extending of k-means. They can cluster categorical attributes and mixed attributes respectively. But it has such shortcomings as instability, randomicity and so on. And when clustering big data sets it has bad efficiency.

The data mining community has recently put a lot of efforts on developing fast algorithms for clustering very large data sets. Some popular ones include CLARANS [3], DBSCAN [4] and BIRCH [5]. These algorithms are often revisions of some existing clustering methods. By using some carefully designed search methods (e.g., randomised search in CLARANS), organising structures (e.g., CF-Tree in BIRCH) and indices (e.g., R-tree in DBSCAN), these algorithms have shown some significant performance improvements in clustering very large data sets. Again, these algorithms still target on numeric data and cannot be used to solve massive categorical data clustering problems.

In this paper we present a new algorithm CFIKP that can handle the large data sets with mixed type of attributes. We first use CF^*-tree [6] to pre-cluster datasets. After that the dense regions are stored in leaf nodes, then we look every dense region as a single point and use the improved k-prototype [7] to cluster such dense regions. Because the dense region is less than the all data sets, our clustering algorithm is very efficient.

2 An Improved k-Prototype Algorithm

2.1 Problems of k-Prototype Algorithm

k-prototype is the mutation of k-means, it has the advantage of k-means. But it is easy to get in local result and this result completely rely on the selection of preliminary clusters.

For example clustering the data sets of table 1.

If we initialize this data sets into C1{1,4,5}, C2{2,3,6,7,8} two clusters, then the prototype is z1{2,B,Y}; z2{3,B,Y}. Continue iterating we will find that record 1 is close to cluster 1 and record 2, 3 is close to cluster 2, then the prototype is invariability and iteration is over.

But the fact is the worth function of cluster C1{1,2,3},C2{4,5,6,7,8} is less than the worth function of cluster C1{1,4,5},C2{2,3,6,7,8}. So the clustering result above is not good enough.

The cause of this condition is that the amount of attributes value "A" and "X" in C-attribute is less. If we can't initialize well, it is easy to lose the attributes value. Whereas we put forward an improved algorithm making clustering result steady and reasonable and not be influenced by initialization and input order.

Table 1

ID	N-attribute	C-attribute1	C-attribute2
1	2	A	X
2	3	A	X
3	3	A	X
4	2	B	Y
5	2	B	Y
6	3	B	Y
7	3	B	Y
8	3	B	Y

Regard the categorical attributes with n different value as attributes with n-dimension, for example, look C-attribute1 has "A" and "B" two dimensions, C-attribute2 has "X" and "Y" two dimensions. When compute the prototype in iteration we should also do like this.

Come back to the above example again, if we initialize the data sets into C1{1,4,5},C2{2,3,6,7,8}, the prototype in the first iteration is:

$$z1\{2, \{1/3(A), 2/3(B)\}, \{1/3(X), 2/3(Y)\}\};$$

$$z2\{3, \{2/5(A), 3/5(B)\}, \{2/5(X), 3/5(Y)\}\}.$$

Continue iterating and we can get the reasonable result:

$$C1\{1,2,3\}, C2\{4,5,6,7,8\}.$$

We call the method above categorical attribute decomposed method. It can be applied in datasets with categorical and mixed attributes and has more stability and reliability than k-prototype.

2.2 An Improved k-Prototype Algorithm

Apply the above categorical attribute decomposed method into the original k-prototype and get the new k-prototype. The detailed algorithm is described below:

1. Decompose the categorical attributes in data set X with categorical attribute decomposed method
2. Initialize X, appoint the amount of the cluster k first, then select k records randomly as the centers of clusters, turn to (3), or group into k clusters arbitrarily
3. Allot each record in X to the closest cluster, update the center of cluster
4. Checkout the similarity between each record and the center of current cluster. If find the closest center to one record is not the current cluster center, allot this record to the closest cluster and update the center of all clusters
5. Repeat item.4. until no records changed.

3 Clustering Algorithm CFIKP

CFIKP algorithm is divided into two steps. In the first step, we use the CF^*-tree to pre-cluster datasets. After that the dense regions are stored in leaf nodes; in the second step, we look every dense region as a single point and use the improved k-prototype to cluster such dense regions. Because the dense region is less than the all data sets, our clustering algorithm will be very efficient.

3.1 Pre-clustering

We use the cluster feature CF^* which is resemble to cluster feature CF in BIRCH to pre-cluster the original data sets. Cluster feature is the statistic summary of child cluster, it summarizes the information of child cluster instead of storing all object.

The cluster feature CF^* of Cluster C_j is:

$$CF_j^* = (N_j, LS_{cj}, SS_{cj}, N_{cj})$$

where N_j is the number of data records in C_j, LS_{cj} is the sum of continuous attributes of the N_j data records, SS_{cj} is the sum of squared continuous attributes of the N_j data records, and $N_{dj} = (N_{dj1}, N_{dj2}, \ldots, N_{djp_d})$, given by $N_{djk} = (N_{jk1}, N_{jk2}, \ldots, N_{jkl})$, in which N_{jkl} is the number of data records in C_j whose k-th categorical attribute takes the l-th category.

When two clusters C_i and C_j are said to merge, it simply means that two corresponding sets of data points are gathered together to form a union. In this case, the $CF^* < i, j >$ for the merged cluster $C < i, j >$ can be calculated by simply adding the corresponding entries in CF_i and CF_j, that is:

$$CF^* < i, j > = \{N_i + N_j, S_{ci} + S_{cj}, SS_{ci} + SS_{cj}, N_{di} + N_{dj}\}$$

In the pre-clustering step, we will construct a modified CF-tree: CF^*-tree. With the insertion of records, CF^*-tree is built dynamically. When a data record is passing through a non-leaf node, it finds the closest entry in the node and travels to the next child node. This process continues recursively and data record descends along the CF^*-tree and until reaches a leaf-node. Upon reaching a leaf node, the data record finds the closest entry. The record is absorbed to its closest entry if distance of record and the closest entry is within a threshold value; otherwise it starts as a new leaf entry in the leaf node. If the CF^*-tree grows beyond the maximum size allowed, it is rebuilt by a larger threshold criterion. The new CF^*-tree is smaller and hence has more room for incoming records. The process continues until a complete data pass is finished.

3.2 Clustering

In this step, we will use the improved k-prototype algorithm to cluster the leaf-node of CF^*-tree. After the CF^*-tree is built in step one, a collection of dense region is identified and is stored in the leaf nodes of the tree. Since the number of dense region is usually far less than the number of data records in the dataset and summery statistics stored in the cluster feature are sufficient for calculating the distance and related criterion, so use CFIKP to cluster the big dataset will very efficient.

4 Experimental Results

In this section, we present the experiment evaluation of CFIKP algorithm and compare its performance with k-prototype algorithm.

4.1 Experimental Data

In this experiment, we have generated a serial of synthesize data. Continuous attributes in a cluster are generated from multivariate normal distribution. The means and covariance matrices of different clusters are used to control the separation of continuous attributes of the clusters; to generate categorical attributes in a cluster, we first choose a cluster center and then sample all attribute category combinations such that the center occurs most frequently. For any pair of clusters, the number of mismatched attributes of the two centers is used to control the separation of categorical attribute part of the clusters.

4.2 Scalability

Scalability of algorithm is very important for large dataset. We test the scalability of CFIKP algorithm by increasing the number of data records and the number of attributes. All experiments are run on a PC with a 733 Mhz Pentinum processor and 256MB RAM.

The left panel of Figure1 shows the relation between run time and number of records, while other factors fixed. For datasets with mixed attributes, there are 5 continuous attributes and 5 categorical attributes with 2, 3, 5, 8 and 12 categories

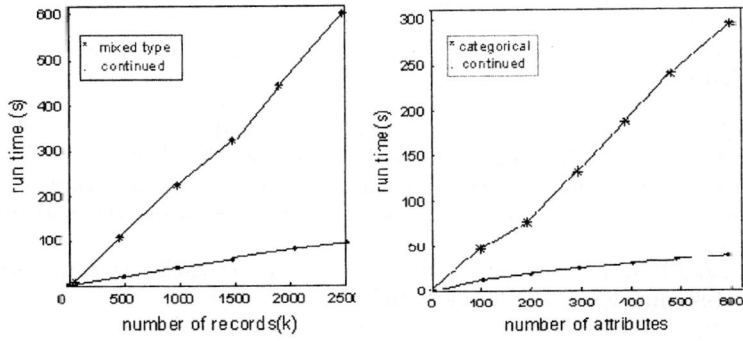

Fig. 1. Relation between run time and number of record and numberof attributes

respectively; other datasets have 5 continuous attributes only. The right panel of figure 1 shows the relation between run time and number of attributes, other factors fixed. All datasets have 8k records. All categorical attributes have 10 categories. From figure 1 we can see that CFIKP algorithm is highly scalable.

4.3 Comparisons with k-Prototype

We simulated 7 datasets, all of which have 5 continuous attributes and 5 categories with 5 categories respectively. The number of data records goes from 100K to 2500K. Table 2 gives Comparison between CFIKP and k-prototype in speed.

Table 2. Comparison between CFIKP and k-prototype in speed

Data Records	CFIKP(s)	K-prototype(s)
100k	26	27
200k	50	55
400k	97	100
500k	120	135
1000k	242	220
2000k	487	460
2500k	610	655

5 Conclusions

In this paper, we introduce a new clustering algorithm CFIKP that can handle large dataset with mixed attributes. It overcomes the shortcoming of traditional algorithms that can't deal with the mixed attributes in large datasets. CFIKP uses CF^*-tree to pre-cluster datasets and makes the dense regions be stored in leaf nodes, which improves the run efficiency of algorithm. Experiment shows CFIKP algorithm has strong scalability and can cluster the large datasets with mixed attributes quickly and efficiently.

References

1. J.MacQueen. Some methods for classification and analysis of multivariate observations. Pro.5th Berkeley Symp.Math.Statist, Pro.,1967, 1:128-297
2. Z. Huang. Extensions to the k-means algorithm for clustering large data sets with categorical values. Data Mining and Knowledge Discovering, 1998, 2:283-304
3. R.Ng and J.Han. Efficient and effective clustering method for spatial data mining. In Pro.1994 Int.Conf .Very Large Data Bases,1994, 144-155
4. M. Ester, H.-P.Kriegel, J.Sander, and X.Xu. A density-based algorithm for discovering clustering in large spatial database with noise. In Proc. 1996 Int. Conf. Knowledge Discovering and Data Mining.1996:266-231.

5. Zhang T., Ramakrishnan R. and Livny M. BIRCH: an efficient data clustering method for very large databases. In Proc. ACM-SIGKDD Int. Conf. Managament of Data, 1996, 103-114
6. T.Chiu, D.P.Fang, J.Chen and Y.W. A Robust and Scalable Clustering Algorithm for Mixed Type Attributes in Large Database Environment. In Proc. ACM-SIGKDD int.conf. Knowledge discovery and data mining (KDD'2001),2001 263-268
7. Peijun Chen, Yu Wang. An Efficient clustering algorithm for categorical and mixed typed attributes. Computer Engineering and Application. 2004(1): 190-191

Mining Association Rules from Multi-stream Time Series Data on Multiprocessor Systems

Biplab Kumer Sarker[1], Toshiya Hirata[2],
Kuniaki Uehara[2], and Virendra C. Bhavsar[1]

[1] Faculty of Computer Science, University of New Brunswick, Fredericton, Canada
{sarker, bhavsar}@unb.ca
[2] Graduate School of Science and Technology, Kobe University, Japan
{hito, uehara}@ai.cs.scitec.kobe-u.ac.jp

Abstract. Mining association rules from multi-stream data has received a lot of attention to the data mining community. It is quite effective and useful to discover such rules. However, it is a very time consuming and expensive task to mine the rules from these kinds of time ordered real valued continuous data sets with high dimensionality when they are enormous in size. This strongly motivates the need of efficient parallel processing techniques and algorithms. In this paper, we use parallel processing to discover dependency from the large amount of time series multi-stream data. We apply two parallel programming techniques (OpenMP and MPI) to implement this. The experimental results conducted in multiprocessor systems show the effectiveness of MPI over OpenMp.

1 Introduction

Discovery of dependencies in multi-stream time series data is an important problem with great significance. The stock price is a good example for such dependencies. Rise and fall of price on some stocks obviously cause price of other stocks to rise and fall. If we analyze the multi-stream of time series for some stock prices and can discover dependencies between all streams, these dependencies can help us to decide better time to buy stocks. These dependencies can also be expressed as association rules.

The task of finding all association rules can require a lot of computational and memory resources, especially when the data is enormous and high dimensional. It is crucial to leverage the aggregate computational power of multiple processors for fast response and scalability to find the association rules from the huge number of motion data. In this paper, we focus on human motion data deemed as high dimensional multi-stream time series data due to its features [8]. The correlations that are discovered from multi-stream of human motions data characterize a specific motion data. For example, association rule discovered from motion data about *'walking'* can be expressed as *"when right hand is up towards front then the left hand and left knee are down towards back"*. Furthermore, these correlations become basic elements that can be used to construct motion with combinations of themselves, just as phonemes of human voice do. These basic elements are called primitive motions. As a result, we can use these primitive motions as indices to retrieve and recognize motion, for example, for creating SFX movies, computer graphics and animations [8].

A good number of serial and parallel algorithms have been developed for mining association rules [1]-[5], [7], [9], [10]. The algorithms are basically proposed for mining so called basket (supermarket transactions) data and have been implemented on both shared memory [5], [9] and shared-nothing multiprocessor [1], [7] environments. Several researchers have applied data mining concepts on time series data to find patterns and rules from it [3], [4], [6], [10]. However, all the above-mentioned algorithms are sequential and data streams used for the purpose are one dimensional in nature. In this paper, we consider a real multi-stream data set e.g. human motion data which is three dimensional in nature. Further, we convert the large amount of three dimensional motion data in symbols of multi-stream to make the data in lower dimension viz. one dimension. Finally, we provide two pseudo-codes of the algorithm for discovering the association rules using OpenMP API and MPI programming paradigms from symbol streams onto Distributed Shared Memory (DSM) Multiprocessor platform and evaluate its performance.

2 Discovery of Association Rules from the Symbols of Multi-stream Data

The human motion data captured by a motion capturing system consists of various types of information of the body parts. The motion data captured by the system can be represented by the three dimensional time series stream considering various positions of different body joints (see Fig .1(a)). Moreover, body parts can be represented as tree structure as shown in Figure 1(a)[8].

In order to find motion association rules with an analysis of various occurrences and reduce the cost of the task, we convert the high dimension multi-stream motion data into sequence of symbols of one dimension. Each symbol represents a basic feature of motion data and such symbols can be expressed as a set of primitive motions. Finally, motion data is converted into symbol streams based on its content by using symbols that we call the sequence of symbols of multi-stream. The details of this process can be found in [8].

The dependency on data of various operations in motion data depends on operations performed in the past (we call it active operations) has a relation to affect on generating operations (passive operations) in the future. Such a dependency is called an association rule. In order to find active operations and passive operations, we set two windows W_a (active) and W_p (passive) with the fixed interval Int. The Int is the interval between the windows in order to discover the group of active operations and passive operations that appears in the fixed amount of time (see Fig. 1(b)).

We define the strength of association rules in motion data by using the probability of occurrence for two operations. The probability is calculated by the

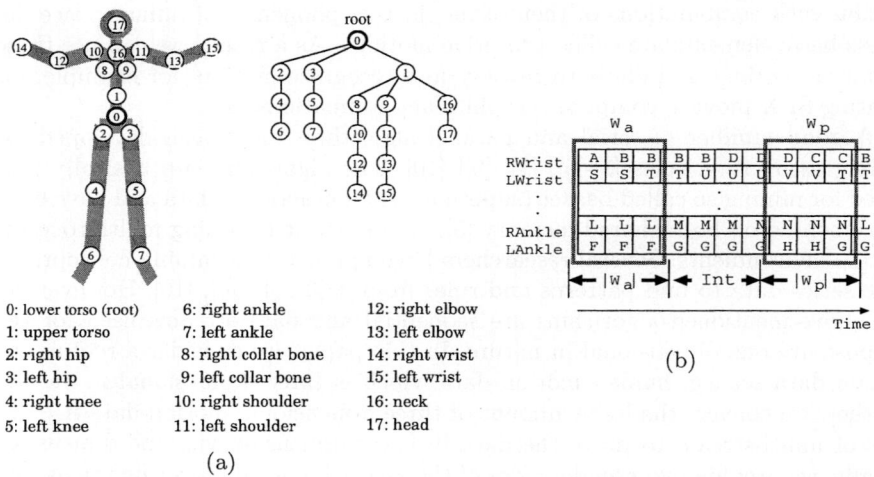

Fig. 1. (a) Body parts used for the experiments, (b) Discovery of association rules using W_a and W_p

following function where δ calculates the probability of occurrence for a pattern B which occurs after a pattern A in certain blocks of the interval. P_a and P_p are the occurrences of the active and passive operations respectively. $t(P_a \wedge P_p)$ represents the number of simultaneous occurrences of P_a and P_p. The significance of the association rules depends on the value of δ.

$$\delta = t(P_a \wedge P_p)/t(P_a) \tag{1}$$

3 Parallel Data Mining

In our case, the symbols of multi-stream data consist of the combinations of 17 body parts ($_{17}C_{17}$) and therefore, they are very large. Consequently, a lot of time is required to find out the associations among the body parts represented as symbols employing the technique described in Section 2. This motivates us to introduce parallel association mining algorithm based on rule mining algorithm *apriori* [1] for our time series multi-stream data.

3.1 The Algorithm for Mining Rules

The proposed algorithm consists of two parts. First, it generates a candidate set of symbols in parallel and further it determines the large set of symbols above a pre-determined minimum support value and finally generate the association rules from the symbols of multi-stream. For candidate generation purpose we consider a set of symbols of multi-stream of body parts G_k consisting of the 17 parts of the body as shown in the Fig. 1, where k represents the number of body

(a)
```
G₁ = {Total Body parts lists }
for (k=2; G_{k-1} ≠ 0; k++) in parallel do begin
  // Each processor P_i generates the C_k, another
    list of body parts using the complete list of
    body parts of G_{k-1} considering parts id.
  C_k = get_learning_stream ( );
  //Compare each two parts of the body from
    the C_k and try to find the dependency between
    them as association rule. And if found join it
    as an item set and compare with another part
    from the parts list C_k to search whether there
    exits any dependency.
  C_k = find_rules( ).
  //Find the rules from the parts list C_k according
    to the given confidence and minimum support.
    Initially found rules are kept in the list l. In
    this function, the technique of finding
    association rules by using the W_a and W_p are
    performed according to the description of sec. 2.
  forall the rules l ∈ ml in parallel do begin
    C_l = integrate_rules(C_k, l);
    // Copy rules from C_l into ml and check whether
      it exists in the ml. ml is the superset of the all
      the rules found during the operation. First copy
      the rules exists in l into the ml. Then check
      whether the rules are already exists or not in
      ml. If the rules are already exists in ml then
      increase the counter for the same rule. And if
      not in ml then register it as separate rule.
    forall rules num_cpl ∈ C_l do
      num_cpl.count++;
  end
  G_k = {num_cpl ∈ C_k | num_cpl ≥ minimum _support}
end
Answer = ∪_k G_k
```

(b)
```
G = {Total body parts}
// a processor is treated as parent
  whose ID = 0
// other processors are treated as
  children in the system
if = 0, then
  C_k = get_learning_stream();
  // Parent evenly distributes C_k
    to the children so that
    each processor gets same number of data C_l
  forall (n = 0; n < num_cpl; n++) in parallel do
    C_l = find_rules();
    // Each processor finds rules respectively
      and discard the same rules.
    Send the discovered rules R_l to the parent.
  barrier
end
rules_l = integrate_rules();
// Check for the same rules in the parent
  and take the unique rules.
if ID = 0, then
  forall rules_i num_cpl ∈ C_l do
    num_cpl.count++;
end
G_k {num_cpl ∈ C_k | num_cpl ≥
  minimum_support};
Answer = ∪ _l G_k
```

Fig. 2. Pseudo-code of the Algorithm ($_{17}C_k$) using: (a) OpenMp, (b) MPI

parts i.e. 1, 2, ..., 17. As a naive way we start with considering 2 body parts from the 17 parts of the body with $_{17}C_2$ combinations, i.e. finding the association rules between 2 parts of the body at a time. So, we compare all sets of two parts of the body from the list G_k considered as candidates of the parts list using parts ID. If a dependency is found then we apply the candidate generation step to check the dependency with the other parts upto a k number with the earlier found dependency between two body parts. In Fig. 2(a), we present a pseudo-code of the algorithm which is based on OpenMp for our case.

3.2 Experimental Results Using OpenMP API

All of the experiments were performed on a 64-node SGI Origin 3000 DSM system. Each node consists of 2 MIPS R10000 processors running at 500 MHz with a total of 8 processors in a node board. The database is stored on an attached 6 GB local disk. For the test data set, we consider 50 different kinds of performed motions such as walking, running, dancing, and pitching. The motions were performed 23 times in 6 different types, each of which lasts for about 6-12 seconds. In order to decrease the influence of the variation, we set the size of windows W_a and W_p to $|P_a|$ and $|P_p|$, and the interval of W_a and W_p to 'Int'. The values of P_a, P_p and Int can be determined flexibly according to suitability for the experiments. For our experiment, we set $W_a = 5$, $W_p = 5$ and $Int = 0$. The size of $W_a = 5$ ($W_p = 5$) is about 0.5 seconds long and can extract motion association rules in the scope of $(0.5 + 0.5 + 0) = 1.0$ second which we found appropriate to find different kinds of motion association rules using the parallel algorithm. As an example of such rule is $LeftAnkle(P) \Rightarrow LeftShoulder(I), LeftAnkel(Q); LeftAnkle(P), LeftHip(K) \Rightarrow RightElbow(Y)$ from the dance data set. It means that while performing dancing, Left Ankle represented by symbol P has associations with Left Shoulder and Left Ankle represented by symbols I and Q respectively.

3.3 MPI (Message Passing Interface) Based Mining Approach

From the results in Figure 3(a), it is evident that the parallelism using OpenMP API is not efficient for our algorithm in terms of scalability. To confirm these results, we conducted an experiment using the same OpenMP based algorithm in a SUN Fire 12K with 16 UltraSPARC-III processors, each running at 1050 MHz (total 8 node boards with 2 processors in each) with the same data set. We have obtained the similar results as reported in Fig. 3(a). Therefore, we made an attempt to use Message Passing Interface which is suitable for distributed shared memory processors. For this purpose, we modified the algorithm (see Fig. 2(b)). The algorithm basically uses a parent-child approach, i.e. processor treated as parent is responsible for reading all of the data evenly from the database and then it distributes the data to other processors treated as children. After that each processor including parent starts to find the rules from their part of data. When they finish finding rules, they send those rules to the parent. The results are given in Fig. 3(b) which show good scalability.

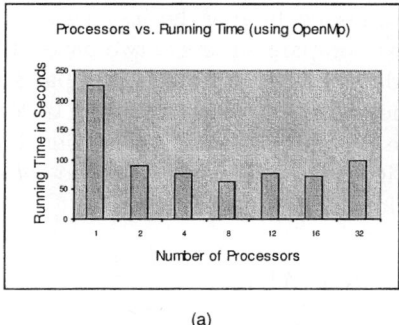
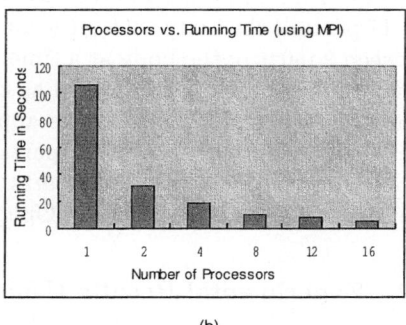

Fig. 3. Running time vs. number of processors using: (a) OpenMp, (b) MPI

In this case, the rules may appear in the corresponding part of the data in each processor. If the duplications are appeared, the procedure *find-rules()* compares them and count only the unique rules. Other rules are thus discarded. After employing these phases, each processor sends the part of discovered rules to the parent using barrier synchronization. Then, again duplications among the rules are counted from all the rules sent to the parent and finally the distinct rules are counted.

4 Conclusion

In this paper, we have considered the problem of mining association rules for multi-stream time series data on distributed shared memory multiprocessors systems. We have presented two parallel processing techniques for this purpose using OpenMP and MPI parallel programming paradigms. The experimental results show that the MPI based technique for our algorithm is superior for the problem of human motion data considered in this paper. In future, we plan to apply these techniques to other time series data applications and carry out performance analysis of implementation in cluster environments.

References

1. R. AGRAWAL, AND J. SHAFER, *Parallel mining of association rules*, IEEE Trans. Knowledge and Data Eng., 8 (1996), pp. 962–969.
2. R. AGRAWAL, AND R. SRIKANT, *Fast algorithms for mining associations rules*, Proc. 20th VLDB Conf., (1994), pp. 487–499.
3. G. DAS, K. LIN, H. MANNILA, G. RENGANATHAN, AND P. SMYTH, *Rule discovery from time series*, Proc. 4th Int. Conf. Knowledge Discovery and Data Mining, (1998), pp. 16–22.
4. H. MANNILA, H. TOIVONEN, AND A. VERKAMO, *Discovering frequent episodes in event sequences*, Journal of Data mining and Knowledge Discovery, 3(1) (1997), pp. 259–289.
5. J. S. PARK, M. S. CHEN, AND P. S. YU, *Efficient parallel data mining for association rules*, Proc. Int. Conf. Information and Knowledge Management, (1995), pp. 31–36.
6. J. F. RODDICK AND M. SPILIOPOULOU, *A survey of temporal knowledge discovery paradigms and methods*, IEEE Trans. on Knowledge and Data Engineering, 14(4) (2002), pp. 750–767.
7. T. SHINTANI AND M. KITSUREGAWA, *Mining algorithms for sequential patterns in parallel: hashed based approach*, Proc. 2nd Pacific-Asia Conf. on Knowledge Discovery and Data Mining, (1998), pp. 283–294.
8. M. SHIMADA, AND K. UEHARA, *Discovery of correlation from multi-stream of human motion*, Lecture Notes in Artificial Intelligence, (2000), pp. 290–294.
9. M. J. ZAKI, S. PARTHASARATHY, M. OHIGARA, AND W. LI, *New algorithms for fast discovery of association rules*, Proc. 1997 ACM-SIGMOD Int. Conf. Management of Data, (1997), pp. 255–264.
10. Y. ZHU, AND D. SHASHA, *StatStream: statistical monitoring of thousands of data streams in real time*, Proc. of the 28th VLDB Conf., (2002), pp. 358–369.

Mining Frequent Closed Itemsets Without Candidate Generation

Kai Chen

Southwest Jiaotong University,
School of Computer Science and Communication Engineering,
610031 Chengdu, China
chkv@sohu.com

Abstract. Mining frequent closed itemsets provides complete and non-redundant result for the analysis of frequent pattern. Most of the previous studies adopted the FP-tree based conditional FP-tree generation and candidate itemsets generation-and-test approaches. However, those techniques are still costly, especially when there exists prolific and/or long itemsets. This paper redesigns FP-tree structure and proposes a novel algorithm based on it. This algorithm not only avoids building conditional FP-tree but also can get frequent closed itemsets directly without candidate itemsets generation. The experimental results show the advantage and improvement of these strategies.

Keywords: data mining; association rule; frequent closed itemsets; stack.

1 Introduction

Association rule is a very important topic at data mining area. A fundamental problem for mining association rule is how to mine frequent itemsets efficiently. In a transaction database (*TDB*), if the support of every frequent itemset is found, the complete associational rule can be obtained straight from it. However, with dense database and low support threshold, the CPU and I/O bound limit the performance of mining, because too large itemsets should be generated and the burden is too high to reach. As an example, if there is one frequent itemset of length l, that implies the presence of 2^l-2 additional frequent itemsets as well. When l is too large, it is practically unfeasible to mine the set of all frequent itemsets.

There are two current solutions for the long frequent itemsets mining: maximal frequent itemsets and frequent closed itemsets. The first one, which generates minimal itemsets, can maximal help understanding the long itemsets in dense domain. But, unfortunately, it only presents that all its subsets are frequent and the support of each one is not less than the minimum support threshold. But the exact value of support is unknown. The second one is an interesting alternative, proposed by Pasquier [2]. The frequent closed itemsets is not only typically orders of magnitude fewer than frequent itemsets, but also contains all information about it.

FP-tree [4] has been shown to be one of the most efficient data structures to store compressed, crucial information about frequent itemsets in *TDB*. However, the former frequent closed itemsets mining algorithms based on FP-tree (such as CLOSET [5], CLOSET+ [6]) spend a lot of time to recursively build conditional FP-tree and memory space to keep it. Especially, although many techniques are used trying to mine FP-tree efficiently, the candidate itemsets generation-and-test step is still necessary. So, if the step of recursive building conditional FP-tree and candidate itemsets generation-and-test can be avoided, the performance of FP-tree based algorithms should be better. This paper presents a stack-based algorithm mining FP-tree, denoted as S-growth. S-growth algorithm successfully avoids the defects of former FP-tree based algorithms discussed above. For reaching this aim, this algorithm only keeps one global FP-tree in memory and uses stack structure to mine the FP-tree from bottom to up. The process of pushing stack is used to grow the length of suffix itemset. If current suffix itemset is frequent closed itemset, the process of popping stack is used to search next available suffix itemset orderly. For carrying out this thought, the variation of FP-tree data structure, denoted as FP-tree*, in combination with stack technique, has been adopted. The experimental results demonstrate the fact that S-growth is a robust and time-saving algorithm for mining frequent closed itemsets.

The remaining of this paper is organized as follow. Section 2 briefly revisits the framework of concepts and related works. Section 3 first introduces FP-tree* structure and then releases S-growth algorithm. A through performance study of S-growth is presented in Section 4. Section 5 summarizes the study.

2 Framework and Related Works

2.1 Framework for Concepts

A transaction database *TDB* is a set of transactions, where each transaction, denoted as a tuple $< tid, X >$, contains a set of items (*i.e.*, *X*) and attaches with a unique transaction identity *tid*. Let $I = \{i_1, i_2, ..., i_n\} | i_j \neq i_k, j \neq k; j, k \in [1, n]$ be a set of complete items appearing in *TDB*. And an itemset $S = \{s_1, s_2, ..., s_n\} | s_i \in I$ called **n-itemset**. A transaction $< tid, X >$ is said to contain itemset *Y*, if $Y \subseteq X$. The **support** of an itemset *S*, denoted as *sup(S)*, is the complete number of transactions containing *S* in *TDB*. *S* is **frequent itemset**, if *sup(S)* is no less than the given minimum support threshold ξ.

Definition 1. Let s_1 and s_2 ($s_1 \subset s_2$) be two itemsets, if every transaction containing s_1 also contains s_2 (i.e. $sup(s_1) = sup(s_2)$), then represents as $s_1 \angle s_2$.

Definition 2. Let *s* be an itemset. *s* is closed itemset, if and only if there is not $s', s \angle s'$ hold.

Roughly speaking, itemset *s* is **frequent closed itemset** if and only if it is frequent and there exists no superset of it with the same support at the *TDB*.

Lemma 1. Let *s* be a non-closed frequent itemset, then there must exit a frequent closed itemset s', while $s \angle s'$.

2.2 FP-Tree Data Structure

The FP-tree method had been proved a power method to store compressed, complete information of frequent itemsets of *TDB*. To construct the FP-tree need scan *TDB* two times. First finds all frequent items by an initial scan of the *TDB*, and then inserts these items into the header table in decreasing order of their support, denoted as *m_list*. In the next (the last) scan, the set of frequent items in every transaction is sorted according to *m_list* and inserted into the FP-tree as a branch. If an itemset shares a prefix with the itemsets already in the tree, the new itemset should share the prefix of the branch representing that itemset. In addition, the count of every node along the common prefix is increased by 1. Fig. 1 (a) shows an example of a *TDB* and Fig. 1 (b) the FP-tree for that *TDB*. The FP-tree contains all frequent information of the *TDB*. Thus mining *TDB* can become mining the corresponding FP-tree. Compression is achieved by building the tree in such a way that overlapping itemsets share the prefix of corresponding branch. To facilitate tree travel, a header table is built, so that the head of node-link of each item points to its occurrence in the tree via a chain of node-link.

TID	Set of Items	Ordered Frequent Items
100	a,c,f,m,p	f,c,a,m,p
200	a,c,d,f,m,p	f,c,a,m,p
300	a,b,c,f,g,m	f,c,a,b,m
400	b,f,i	f,b
500	b,c,n,p	c,b,p

Header Table	
Item	Head of node-link
f:4	
c:4	
a:3	
b:3	
m:3	
p:3	

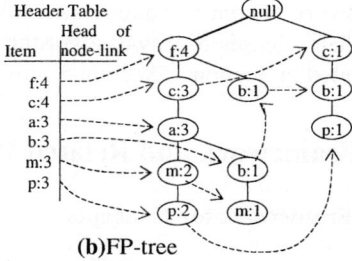

(a) A transaction database as run example   (b) FP-tree

Fig. 1. An Example FP-tree ($\xi = 2$)

Definition 3. Let i_m and i_n be two frequent item of *TDB*, if i_m is located before i_n in *m_list*, then presents as $i_n < i_m$.

Definition 4. If item α at the prefix subpath of suffix *s* is frequent, then α is a conditional frequent item of *s*.

Property 1. In every branch of FP-tree, the count of a node is no more than the count of nodes within higher layer.

Property 2. Each branch of FP-tree represents at lest one transaction information of *TDB*.

 1) The support of an itemset equals the sum of the count of the last frequent item in it, restricted to those branches that contain the itemset.

 2) The count of an item at the prefix subpath of a suffix is the count of the last item of the suffix.

Property 3. (Prefix path property)[4] To calculate the frequent itemsets for a node α_i in a path *p*, only the prefix subpath of node α_i in *p* need to be accumulated and the frequency count of every node in prefix path should carry the same count as node α_i.

2.3 CLOSET+ Algorithm

CLOSET+ is evolution of FP-growth algorithm [4] for frequent closed itemsets mining. The main difference between mining frequent closed itemsets and frequent itemsets among the two algorithms is that according to lemma 1, it is not necessary to build conditional FP-tree for every suffix. In despite of adopting many optimization approaches to eliminate generation of unnecessary suffix, CLOSET+ also need to 1) construct conditional FP-tree with suffix and keep it in memory until all frequent closed candidate itemsets with this suffix have been mined; 2) search frequent items carrying same support and item-name at the header table of different layer's conditional FP-tree for shrinking the search area of suffix; 3) generate and test candidate itemsets. Such the cost of time and space is nontrivial. So, how to avoid building conditional FP-tree and generating candidate itemsets is the key point to speed up the efficiency of FP-tree based algorithms for mining frequent closed itemsets.

3 Efficient Mining Frequent Closed Itemsets

According to property 3, a totally new data structure, denoted as Stack-table, has been designed instead of header table of original FP-tree, which can denote the count of every conditional frequent items and the relation in the condition of a certain suffix itemset. For carrying out the Stack-table, the structure of FP-tree should be reorganized. The variation of FP-tree is denoted as FP-tree*. S-growth algorithm mines frequent closed itemsets based on FP-tree* and using Stack-table structure, which avoids the defects of former FP-tree based algorithms.

3.1 FP-Tree*

If want to calculate the support of every item at the condition of certain suffix, according to property 3, we only interest in the prefix subpaths of the suffix. Based on this thought, the initial FP-tree is enough to identify the relation between the suffix and its conditional frequent items. But the count and the tree-node link should change under different suffix. The main contribution of Stack-table structure is that it separates count and tree-node link from relation among tree-nodes of FP-tree, which makes avoiding recursively building conditional FP-tree possible and only need one FP-tree in the memory during mining process without conditional FP-tree generation.

Comparing Fig. 2 (a) with Fig. 1 (b), FP-tree* is only a mild reorganization of original FP-tree. Stack-table replaces header table and, at the same time, the count and node-link of each tree-node are moved into it. Stack-table is a table of stack, in which each frequent item sorted in *m_list* and has a stack on his own. And the stack of every item has a slight difference with common stack structure, in which the value of the top element can be changed. The element α of Stack-table consists of three fields: *layer*, *support* and *node-array*, denoted as $\alpha.layer$, $\alpha.sup$ and $\alpha.parray$ respective. The *layer* has relation with the process of pushing and popping stack and it directly reflects the length of suffix *s* when the element of the stack has been pushed. The *support* registers the support of the item at the condition of *s*. Each element of *node-array* consists of two fields: *tree-node pointer* and *count*, where each tree-node pointer points to a tree-node carrying the same item-name with the item at the condition of *s* and the count represents the count of this tree-node. The node-array of every element in Stack-table can access all tree-nodes carrying same item-name without duplication at the condition of corresponding *s*.

The initialization process of FP-tree* also initializes every stack of frequent items of Stack-table ($s = \{\emptyset\}$), as shown in Fig. 2 (a). The stack element *(x: y)* denotes that the support of this item at layer *x* is *y*. For convenience of revelation, the node-array of *0* layer element of Stack-table in Fig. 2 (b) has been cut down.

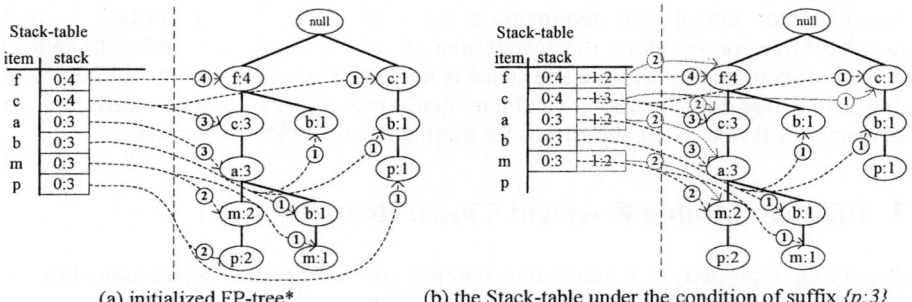

(a) initialized FP-tree*   (b) the Stack-table under the condition of suffix *{p:3}*

Fig. 2. FP-tree*

3.2 S-growth Algorithm

S-growth algorithm uses Stack-table structure to store conditional frequent items information of current suffix itemset apart from building conditional FP-tree to collect it. The process of pushing stack is used to grow the length of suffix itemset. If current suffix itemset contents the condition of frequent closed itemset, the process of popping stack is adopted to search next available suffix itemset orderly. And then the process of growing next suffix itemset begins. These processes run recursively until Stack-table is null. In the following, first we present theories and then give the pseudo code of the S-growth algorithm, which adopts these theories step by step.

FP-tree is a compressed representation of *TDB*. According to property 2, every branch of FP-tree represents at least one transaction. S-growth algorithm generates suffix itemsets in the reversed order of *m_list* and mines FP-tree from bottom to up. So, it is a way to check whether current suffix itemset is available for mining frequent closed itemsets that checking whether current suffix itemset is the subset of the mined suffix itemset with the same support.

Lemma 2. (Suffix check) Let $s = (s_1, s_2, ..., s_m) | s_i > s_j, i < j$ be current suffix, if there exists an item $s_n (s_n < s_m)$ that the counts of s_m and s_n are equal in each branch restricted to these branches that contain *s*, then *s* is not the available suffix for mining frequent closed itemsets.

Proof: Because of mining itemsets at the reverse order of *m_list*, there exits a suffix $\{s_1, s_2,..., s_m, s_{m+1},...\}$, which is mined before suffix $\{s_1, s_2,..., s_m\}$. If all branch contained s have an item $s_n (s_n < s_m)$ in which the counts of s_n and s_m are same in each branch, there must exist a mined itemset s', $s \angle s'$ hold. So s must be not the available suffix for mining frequent closed itemsets.

Corollary 2.1. If the sum of count of s_n, restricted to those branches that contain itemset s, is equal to the support of itemset s, then s is not the available suffix for mining frequent closed itemsets.

Proof: According to property 1, the count of s_n no more than s_m's. This corollary can be proved easy.

Corollary 2.2. If s is not the available suffix for mining frequent closed itemsets, then all supersets of s also are not.

Proof: Let $s' = \{s'_1,..., s'_m, s_1,..., s_m\}$ be an itemset of suffix s. The every branch contained s' also contain s. So the every branch contained s' has an item $s_n (s_n < s_m)$ in which the counts of s_n and s_m are same in each branch. So, according to lemma 6, we can draw the conclusion.

Lemma 3. (Suffix growth) Let s be current suffix, which has conditional frequent items. If at least one item's support among these is less than *s.sup* and other's equal to *s.sup*, then the next suffix is $s \cup \alpha$, in where α is the bottom item of Stack-table among the maximal layer (i.e. the conditional frequent item of s).

Proof: If the support of a (not all) conditional frequent item of s equal to *s.sup*, there must exit s', $s \angle s'$ hold. So, according to the definition of frequent closed itemsets, s is trivial suffix for frequent closed itemsets.

Lemma 4. Let s be current suffix, if all supports of conditional frequent items of it are less than *s.sup*, then s is frequent closed itemsets.

Proof: It is easy proved according to the definition of frequent closed itemsets.

Corollary 4.1. Let s be current suffix, if all conditional frequent items of it have same support with s, then $s \cup$ these items is frequent closed itemset.

Proof: If s has the same support with its all conditional frequent items, then s and those items share common transaction of *TDB* and no other items share with them. So, $s \cup$ these items is frequent closed itemset.

Lemma 5. (Layer absorb) Let α be a common frequent items in the condition of suffix s and s', $s \subset s'$ hold. If there exists $\sup(\{\alpha\} \cup s) = \sup(\{\alpha\} \cup s')$, then Stack-table only need to save the information of α at the layer of s'.

Proof: Since $s \subset s'$ and $\sup(\{\alpha\} \cup s) = \sup(\{\alpha\} \cup s')$, s and s' share the common transactions of *TDB*. So α can be saved at s' safely.

which shrink the search area of suffix for mining frequent closed itemsets.

Procedure: S-growth (Stack-table, s, ξ)
Input: Stack-stable, suffix itemset s, minimal support threshold ξ
Note that for initialization of s, the last item α of initial Stack-table should be popped and let $s = \{\alpha\}$, $s.sup = \alpha.sup$, $s.parray = \alpha.parray$, $s.layer = 1$.
Output: frequent closed itemset
{
    if not (isClose(Stack-table, s)) **then**
        nextSuffix (Stack-table, s)
    else
        max_sup = InsertStack(Stack-table, s, ξ)
        if *s.sup = max_sup* **then**
            if *the count of all conditional frequent items of s = s.sup* **then**
                pop these items, $s = s \cup$ *these items* is closed
        else   // *s.sup > max_sup*
            s is closed
            nextSuffix (Stack-Array, s)
    S-growth (Stack-Array, s, ξ);
}

Procedure: InsertStack (Stack-table, s, ξ)
Input: Stack-stable, suffix itemset s, minimal support threshold ξ
Output: pushing the conditional frequent items of s and return the maximal support among them
{
    Search every conditional frequent item α_i from bottom to up at FP-tree
    {
    If $\alpha_i.sup$ = *support of top element τ of the stack of α_i* **then**
        $\tau.layer = \alpha_i.layer$
    else create new element ε
        Let $\varepsilon.sup = \alpha_i.sup$, $\varepsilon.parray = \alpha_i.parray$, $\varepsilon.layer = \alpha_i.layer$
        Push ε into the stack of α_i
    }
    if there exit no conditional frequent items of s **then**
        return 0
    else return max($\alpha_i.sup$)
}

Procedure: isClose(Stack-table, s)
Input: Stack-table, suffix itemset s
Output: Whether s is the available suffix for mining frequent closed itemset
{
    if *no count among child items of s = s.sup* **then**
        return TRUE
    else return FALSE
}

Procedure: nextSuffix (Stack-table, s)
Input: Stack-table, suffix itemset s
Output: next suffix itemset
{
    if Stack-table is null **then**
        mining process finish
    else
        pop bottom element α of maximal layer in Stack-table
        keep first $\alpha.layer$ element of s
        $s = s \cup \alpha$, $s.sup = \alpha.sup$
        $s.layer = \alpha.layer+1$, $s.parray = \alpha.parray$
}

Fig. 3. S-growth Algorithm

Lemma 6. (Suffix rollback) Let s be current suffix, which has not any conditional frequent item, α be the bottom stack of Stack-table with the maximal layer, the next suffix is $\{\alpha\} \cup \{the\ first\ \alpha\ .layer\ items\ of\ s\}$.

Proof: At the track of generation of $s = \{s_1, s_2, ..., s_n\}$, the 0_layer elements of Stack-table are pushed at the condition of $\{\phi\}$, and the 1_layer elements at the condition of $\{s_1\}$,.... The maximal layer k of Stack-table denotes that there exists conditional frequent items at condition of $s' = \{s_1, s_2, ..., s_k\} \mid k < n$. So, the bottom element α of maximal layer of Stack-table is popped and the next suffix after s is $\{\alpha\} \cup s'$.

Algorithm Specification: S-growth algorithm mines FP-tree* at the reverse order of m_list. First, the algorithm gets an available suffix s for closed itemsets mining with suffix growth and check techniques (Lemma 2, 3 and their corollaries). And then, it pushes conditional frequent items of s into Stack-table with new layer in company with suffix absorb technique (Lemma 5). Whether s is frequent closed itemset can be judged by the supports of items with new layer (Lemma 4 and its corollary). And then search the next suffix (Lemma 6). Because the layer keeps the growth track information of current suffix, if there are no frequent items at the condition of s, s should rollback according to the maximal layer of FP-tree* and then start the next circle growth. If Stack-table is null, then the process of mining FP-tree* is over and obtains all frequent closed itemsets.

4   Experimental Evaluation and Performance Study

In this section, we present a performance comparison of S-growth with the classic mining frequent closed itemsets algorithm CLOSET+, which had been proved that its effect is more outstanding than other classic algorithms, such as CHARM[7], in synthetic performance.

All the experiments are performed on Intel(c) 1.7GHz PC with 256 megabytes main memory, running on Microsoft Windows XP. All the programs are written in Visual C++. The experimental datasets are two classic test datasets mushroom and connect which are used by lots of algorithms, such as [5], [6], [7], [8]. The characters of the two classic datasets are described in table 1. We first test the speed property of the two algorithms on the real datasets by changing the minimum support threshold. The results of the experiments are show in figure 4 and 5. S-growth is faster than CLOSET+ in the two datasets, especially in mushroom, because of avoiding the calculation time about generation of conditional FP-tree and candidate itemsets in mining process. Then we test the memory occupation property of the two algorithms by changing the minimum support threshold. Because the lower minimum support threshold is, the more frequent closed itemsets should be generated, which brings on more memory occupation. The curve of S-growth is smoother than CLOSET+ since this algorithm need not generate conditional FP-tree for frequent closed itemsets mining. From the above performance study, we can see that S-growth algorithm has good performance both in speed and memory occupation property.

Table 1. Datasets parameters

Dataset	Number of transaction	Total items	Maximal length of transaction
Mushroom	8124	120	23
Connect	67557	150	43

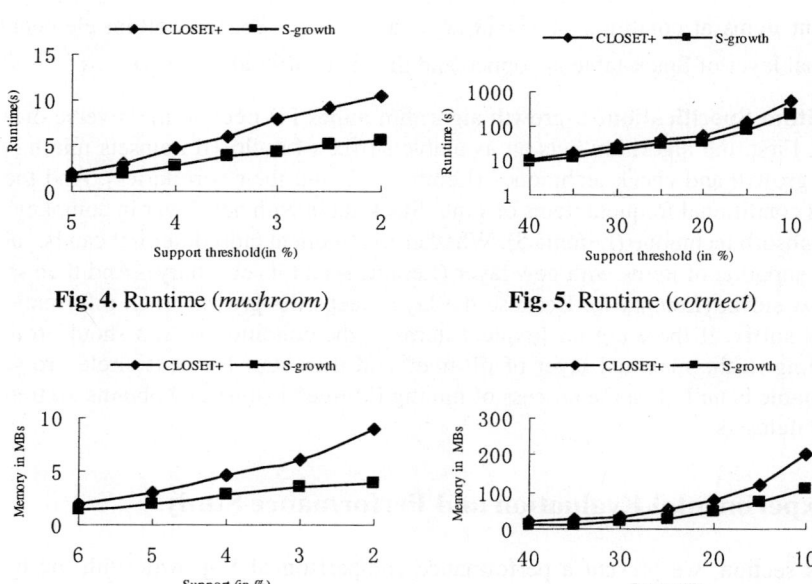

Fig. 4. Runtime (*mushroom*)   **Fig. 5.** Runtime (*connect*)

Fig. 6. Memory occupation (*mushroom*)   **Fig. 7.** Memory occupation (*connect*)

The good performance of S-growth algorithm comes from the following reasons. Firstly, S-growth adopts Stack-table structure to mine global FP-tree, pushing and popping stack processes on Stack-table instead of generation of conditional FP-tree. Then several optimization strategies have been adopted to shrink the search area and reduce the working of pushing and popping stack, which also reduce the process of traveling FP-tree. Finally, suffix checking technique has been used to detect the suffix whether it is available for closed itemsets mining without candidate generation. So, S-growth algorithm can save more CPU occupation about runtime and memory.

5 Conclusion

FP-tree is a power structure to compress the complete information of frequent itemsets of *TDB*. But most former FP-tree based mining frequent closed itemsets algorithms need to build conditional FP-tree recursively and keep it in the memory until traveling over above it, but they still cannot generate frequent closed itemsets directly. So, much time and memory space are wasted. How to avoid building conditional

FP-tree and generating closed itemsets directly become the key point to enhance the efficiency of FP-tree based mining frequent closed itemsets algorithms. This paper first proposes a new stack-based algorithm to solve these problems. The experiment evaluation and performance study on synthetic datasets show that the new algorithm has good performance both in runtime and memory occupation property.

Reference

1. R. Agrawal, and R. Srikant. Fast Algorithms for Mining Association Rules. In Proceeding of the *20th VLDB Conference*, Santiago, Chile, 1994.
2. N. Pasquier, Y. Bastide, R. Taouil, and L. Lakhal. Discovering frequent closed itemsets for association ruels. In 7th *International Conference on Database Theory*, Jan. 1999.
3. A. Silberschatz, and A. Tuzhilin. What Make Patterns Interesting in Knowledge Discovery Systems. In *IEEE Transaction on Knowledge and Data Engineering*, Dec. 1996.
4. J. Han, J. Pei, and Y. Yin. Mining Frequent Patterns without Candidate Generation. In Proceeding of *ACM SIGMOD'00*, May. 2000.
5. J. Pei, J. Han, and R. Mao. CLOSET: An Efficient Algorithms for Mining Frequent Closed Itemsets. In *DMKD'00*, May 2000.
6. J. Wang, J. Han, and J. Pei. CLOSET+: Searching for the Best Strategies for Mining Frequent Closed Itemsets. In Proceeding of *ACM SIGKDD'03*, Aug. 2003.
7. M. J. Zaki, and C. Hsiao. CHARM: An Efficient Alogrithm for Closed Itemset Mining. In *SDM'02*, Apr. 2002.
8. L. Li, D. Zhai, and F. Jin. GRG: An Efficient Method for Association Rules Mining on Frequent Closed Itemsets. In Proceeding of *the 2003 IEEE International Symposium on Intelligent Control*, Oct. 2003.

Distribution Design in Distributed Databases Using Clustering to Solve Large Instances

Joaquin Perez Ortega, Rodolfo A. Pazos Rangel,
Jose A. Martinez Florez, J. Javier Gonzalez Barbosa,
E. Alejandor Macias Diaz, and J. David Teran Villanueva

[1] Centro Nacional de Investigación y Desarrollo Tecnológico (CENIDET),
AP 5-164, Cuernavaca, Mor., 62490, México
{jperez, pazos}@cenidet.edu.mx
[2] Instituto Tecnológico de Ciudad Madero (ITCM),
hfraire@prodigy.net.mx, {jose_mtz, jgbarbosa, a_macias_diaz, david_teran}@hotmail.com

Abstract. In this paper we approach the solution of large instances of the distribution design problem. The traditional approaches do not consider that the size of the instances can significantly reduce the efficiency of the solution process, which only involves a model of the problem and a solution algorithm. We propose a new approach that incorporates multiple models and algorithms and mechanisms for instance compression, for increasing the scalability of the solution process. In order to validate the approach we tested it on a new model of the replicated version of the distribution design problem which incorporates generalized database objects, and a method for instance compression that uses clustering techniques. The experimental results, utilizing typical Internet usage loads, show that our approach permits to reduce at least 65% the computational resources needed for solving large instances, without significantly reducing the quality of its solution.

1 Introduction

The increasing popularity of the Internet and e-business has generated a great demand of applications of distributed databases (DDB's). These applications are developed using Distributed Database Management Systems (DDBMS's). Despite the advanced technology of DDBMS's, the design methodologies and tools have many limitations. Consequently, database administrators carry out the distribution design using empirical and informal approaches due to the problem complexity. In this paper a formal and systematic methodology is proposed aimed at overcoming the limitations.

The distribution design problem consists of determining data allocation so that the communication costs are minimized. Like many other real problems, it is a combinatorial NP-hard problem. The solution of large scale instances is usually carried out solving a simplified version of the problem or using approximate methods [1,2]. General purpose nondeterministic heuristic methods are at present the best tools for the approximate solution of this class of problems [3, 4]. In the balance these methods will be referred to as heuristic methods.

For several years we have worked on the distribution design problem and its solution with heuristic methods. In [5] we proposed an on-line method to set the control parameters of the Threshold Accepting algorithm. In [6] a mechanism for automatically obtaining some control parameter values for genetic algorithms is presented.

2 Related Work

The distribution design problem has been dealt with by many investigators [5, 7, 8, 9, 10, 11, 12]. The approach proposed in [5] has been the most successful in solving large scale instances of the problem. The main limitation of these approaches is that they do not consider that the size of the instances can significantly reduce the efficiency of the solution process, which only involves a model of the problem and a solution algorithm. Conversely, in [13] the relevance of instance compression is recognized, but the effect of compression on the solution quality is not considered; consequently, the compression methods proposed are inefficient and do not guarantee the scalability of the tools for automatic database design.

In order to overcome these limitations, we propose an approach that consists of instance compression and selection of algorithms and models. We tested it on a new model of the replicated version of the distribution design problem that incorporates generalized database objects, and a method for efficient instance compression that uses clustering techniques [14, 15].

3 Distribution Design Problem

This section describes the distribution design problem and the mathematical model used for validating the proposed approach.

3.1 Problem Description

The DDB distribution design problem consists of allocating DB-objects, such that the total cost of data transmission for processing all the applications is minimized. A DB-object (or simply object) is an entity of a database that requires to be allocated, which can be an attribute, a tuples set, a relation or a file. DB-objects are independent units that must be allocated at the sites of a network. A formal definition of the problem is the following:

Let us consider a set of DB-objects $O = \{o_1, o_2, \ldots, o_{no}\}$, a computer communication network that consists of a set of sites $S = \{s_1, s_2, \ldots, s_{ns}\}$, where a set of operations $Q = \{q_1, q_2, \ldots, q_{nq}\}$ are executed, the DB-objects required by each operation, an initial DB-object allocation schema, and the access frequencies of each operation from each site in a time period. The problem consists of obtaining a new allocation schema that adapts to a new database usage pattern

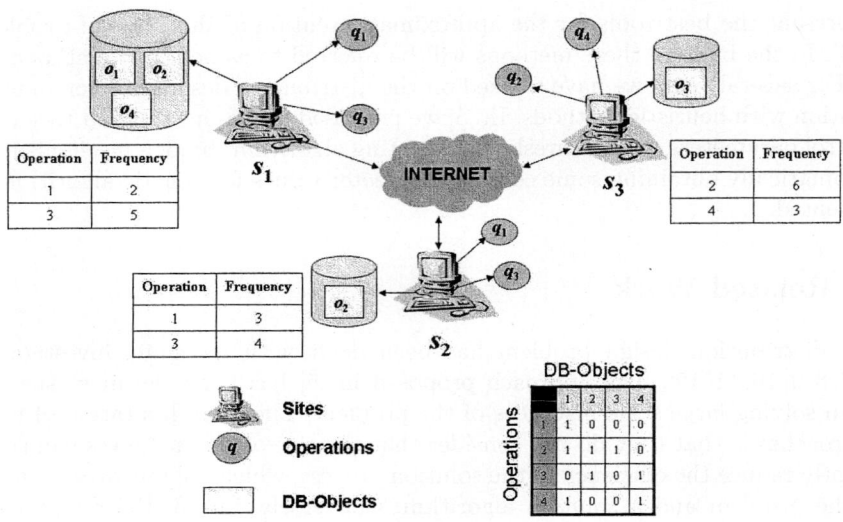

Fig. 1. Distribution design problem

and minimizes transmission costs. Fig. 1 depicts an instance of the problem with 4 DB-objects, 3 sites and 4 operations, as well as the emission frequency of the operations from each site and the usage matrix of DB-objects by operations.

3.2 Mathematical Model

Traditionally it has been considered that the DDB distribution design consists of two sequential phases. Contrary to this widespread belief, it has been shown that it is simpler to solve the problem using our approach which combines both phases. A key element of this approach is the formulation of a mathematical model that integrates both phases.

The mathematical model objective function 2 includes four terms: the first models the cost of processing read-only operations, the second models the cost of read-write operations, the third models the migration cost of the DB-objects, and the last one models the storage cost of DB-objects in the sites.

$$\min Z = \sum_k \sum_j f_{kj} \sum_m \sum_i q_{km} l_{km} c_{ji} w_{jmi} \qquad (1)$$
$$+ \sum_k \sum_j f'_{kj} \sum_m \sum_i q'_{km} l'_k c_{ji} x_{mi}$$
$$+ \sum_j \sum_m \sum_i w'_{jmi} c'_{ji} d_{mi} + \sum_m \sum_i CA_i b_m x_{mi}$$

The problem is modeled using binary integer linear programming. In Table 1 the elements used in the formulation are described. A solution to the model must satisfy a set of constraints that specify: the possible replication of DB-objects, their location, the access policy applied to the read and write operations, the conditions for DB-object migration, and the storage capacity of the sites. More details about the model can be found in [16, 17].

Table 1. Model elements

Element	Meaning
no	Number of DB-objects to be distributed.
ns	Number of sites in the network.
nq	Number of user operations.
b_m	Byte size of object m.
s_{km}	Selectivity of DB-object m from operation k.
PA	Byte size of the communication package.
P_k	Byte size of the write instruction from operation k.
F_{mi}	Usage frequency of DB-object m at site i.
f_{ki}	Frequency matrix of integer values that describes the emission frequency of read-only operation k from site i, in a given time interval.
q_{km}	Usage matrix. It indicates which DB-objects are used by the different read only-operations; $q_{km} = 1$ if read-only operation k uses DB-object m; $q_{km} = 0$ otherwise.
l_{km}	Communication packages required to send on the DB-object m needed by the read-only operation k. $l_{km} = (b_m \times s_{km})/PA$
f'_{ki}	Frequency matrix of integer values that describes the emission frequency of read-write operation k from site i, in a given time interval.
q'_{km}	Usage matrix. It indicates which DB-objects are used by the different read-write operations; $q'_{km} = 1$ if read-write operation k uses DB-object m; $q'_{km} = 0$ otherwise.
l'_k	Communication packages required to broadcast a write instruction. $l'_k = P_k/PA$.
d_{mi}	Communication packets required to create a DB-object m replica in site i.
CA_i	Byte storage cost per byte in site i.
CS_i	Byte storage capacity in bytes of site i.
c_{ij}	Communication cost between sites i and j.
A_{mi}	Initial allocation scheme.
x_{mi}	Binary variable. It indicates whether the DB-object m is allocated in site i ($x_{mi} = 1$) or not $x_{mi} = 0$.
w_{jmi}	Binary variable. It indicates whether the DB-object m, allocated in site i is required by a read-only operation issued at site j, ($w_{jmi} = 1$) or not ($w_{jmi} = 0$).
w'_{jmi}	Binary variable. It indicates whether the DB-object m, actually allocated at site j must be reallocated to site i, ($w'_{jmi} = 1$, with $j \neq i$) or not ($w'_{jmi} = 0$).

4 Proposed Solution Approach

4.1 General Description

This section describes the methodology proposed for the solution of large scale instances of the distribution design problem. Three strategies that can be used for the approximate solution of a large scale instance are: transforming the instance into another instance whose solution requires fewer resources, choosing the algorithm that has had the best performance on instances of the same type, or using a model that requires less computing cost. For solving a large scale instance, the main strategy of the methodology consists of applying approximation techniques of this type. The following definition formally describes this strategy.

Definition 1. *Solution strategy*

Given π : *distribution design problem,*
I : *instance set of* π,
R : *finite set of transformations of instances of* π,
M : *finite set of models of* π,
A : *finite set of solution algorithms for the models,*

if $s \in R \times A \times M$, then s *is a solution strategy of a given instance of* π (Fig. 2).

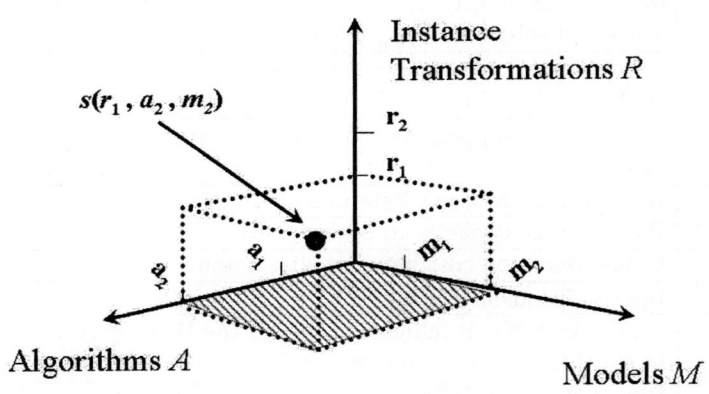

Fig. 2. Aspects (dimensions) of solution strategies

For a given instance $i \in I$, the purpose of the methodology is finding a strategy $s = (r_i, a_j, m_k)$ that permits solving the reduced instance of i resulting from transformation r_i, using algorithm a_j and model m_k.

A major difference from other approaches is the following: when a model and an algorithm are chosen they lie at a point on the dark plane of Fig. 2. In [18] a method to select algorithms is described. In our approach, the addition of a preprocessing dimension extends the possibilities beyond the dark plane. The transformation mechanisms must be devised in such a way that they permit solving larger instances with a given set of computing resources. The following section describes an instance transformation method that attains this design objective and shows the feasibility of this approach.

5 Instance Transformation Using Clustering

5.1 Description of the Transformation Method

Regarding the DDB distribution design problem, when an instance has repetitive operations it is possible to transform it into an instance with fewer operations, since repetitive operations are represented by similar rows in the access matrix. Therefore, such operations can be considered as a single operation that is issued with larger frequency. The reduction level that such transformation can yield is directly proportional to the proportion of repetitive operations. The instances reported in [13], characterized as typical on the Internet, are an example of instances that show this property. Such transformation is a relation on the problem instances set, which associates a given instance to a smaller instance. Fig. 3 depicts a transformation r of this type, where I is the instance set of the DDB distribution design problem, and i is an instance, and I' is a subset of I.

The binary vector that indicates from which sites a operation is issued is called access pattern. The access pattern matrix P_{ki} is constructed in such a way that, for every k and i, $P_{ki} = 1$ if and only if $f_{ki} \neq 0$. Fig. 4 shows the

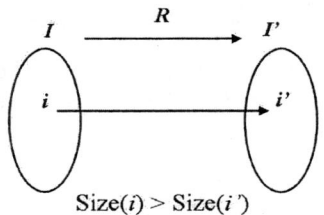

Fig. 3. Instance transformation

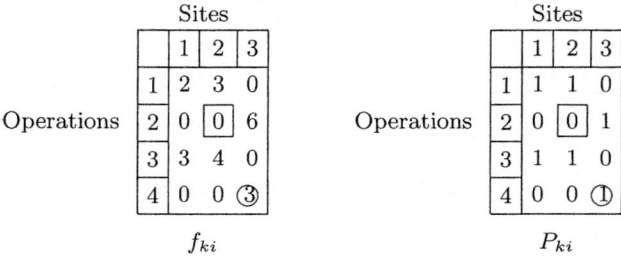

Fig. 4. Access pattern matrix P_{ki}

access frequency matrix f_{ki} of the operations involved in the example of Fig. 1 and the corresponding access pattern matrix P_{mi}. The marked cells show the way the process is carried out when the access frequency is zero (squares) and larger that zero (circles).

All the operations that have the same access pattern are considered as a single operation of the transformed instance. All the DB-objects needed by the grouped operations constitute a single DB-object of the transformed instance.

5.2 Adjustment of the Transformed Instance Formulation

Once the operation and DB-object groups are created, it is necessary to adjust the access frequencies to the groups, the operation selectivity to each group and the group sizes of the transformed instance. The adjustment process is carried out as follows.

Given the original instance i, matrix f_k, operation selectivities s_{km} and DB-object sizes b_m, then the access frequency of each grouped operation c at site i is given by:

$$f^\star_{ci} = \sum_{k \in OpCluster(c)} f_{ki} \qquad \forall\, c, i, k \qquad (2)$$

the size of DB-object group c is given by:

$$b^\star_c = \sum_{m \in DB\_ObjCluster(c)} b_m \qquad \forall\, c, m \qquad (3)$$

and the selectivity of operation k to DB-object group c is given by:

$$s^\star_{kc} = \frac{\sum_{m \in DB\_ObjCluster(c)} s_{km} \times b_m}{\sum_{m \in DB\_ObjCluster(c)} b_m} \qquad (4)$$

Fig. 5 describes the transformation process and the formulation adjustment, and shows the operation access f_{ki}, the access pattern P_{ki} and the grouped operation access $f^\star_{ci}$ matrices.

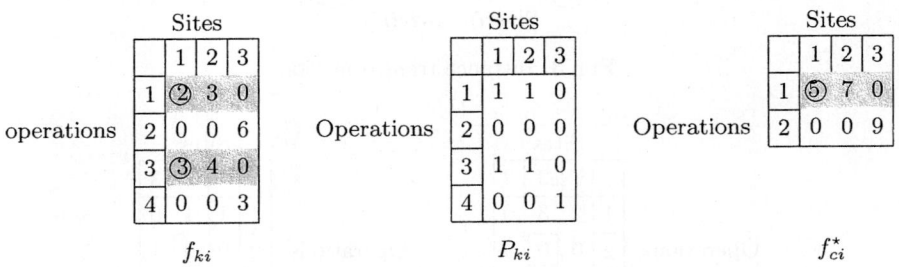

Fig. 5. Transformation Process

Since operations # 1 and # 3 have the same access pattern (dark rows in matrices f_{ki} and P_{ki}), they are integrated into operation # 1 (dark row in matrix $f_{ci}^{\star}$) of the transformed instance. Similarly operations # 2 and # 4 of the original instance are integrated into operation # 2 of the transformed instance. The sum of the two encircled frequencies, corresponding to operations # 1 and # 3, becomes the frequency of operation # 1 of the transformed instance, which is shown encircled. The rest of the frequencies of the transformed instance are calculated similarly.

5.3 Clustering Algorithm

The input to the algorithm is matrix f_{ki} and its output is matrix $f_{ci}^{\star}$. In the process each pattern is assigned a decimal code, which is used to identify the group to which the operation belongs.

```
For Each operation k of f_ki
    Code ←— 0
    For Each site i of f_ki
        If f_ki > 0 then
            Code ←— Code + 2^i
        End If
    End For
    Group_k ←— Code
    Card_Code ←— Card_Code + 1
End For
```

Fig. 6. Clustering algorithm

The algorithm complexity is $nq \times ns$. Table 2 describes the main elements used.

Table 2. Algorithm elements

Element	Dimensions	Objective
f_{ki}	$nq \times ns$	Emission frequency of operation k from site i.
$Group_k$	nq	Group to which operation k belongs.
$Card_l$	no	Cardinality of group l.
$Code$	2^{ns}	Decimal codification of the operation access pattern.

6 Experimental Results

In order to validate our approach, a set of experiments were conducted using instances of different sizes and characteristics, and configured for simulating typical access patterns on the Internet. For each experiment a test case was created with 100 randomly generated instances keeping unchanged the configuration of DB-objects, sites and operations. To simulate several access patterns of the users to

Table 3. Test cases used in the experiments

Test case	Characteristics				Q/S
	DB-Objects (O)	Sites (S)	Operations (Q)	Size in Bytes	
C_1	100	3	100	86,060	33
C_2	200	5	200	338,560	40
C_3	500	7	500	2,062,252	71
C_4	1,200	15	1,200	11,823,420	80
C_5	1,000	10	1,000	8,172,480	100

the sites, test cases with 10, 20, 30 and 40% access probability of the operations to the sites were generated. For each instance of a particular experiment, the clustering method was applied to compress it. Once the compression was performed, the original instance i and the compressed instance i' were solved using an exact method, and compared the costs of both solutions.

Table 3 shows the characteristics of a representative sample of test cases used in the experiments. The table includes a test case identifier (C_i), the numbers of DB-objects (O), sites (S), and operations (Q) of the included instances in the test case, the size in bytes ($Size$) of the test case, and the operations to sites ratio (Q/S). For each test case the instance sizes and the optimal solution values were accumulated, and the global reduction and the error generated by the compression were calculated. All the instances generated for a particular experiment have the same size, since the instances have the same number of objects, sites and operations; a similar situation occurs with all the compressed instances of a particular experiment.

Figure 7 shows the reduction levels observed in the experiments. Notice that, for instances with access probability of 10% and 20%, the compression yields a reduction of at least 65% in the amount of resources needed for solving the instances. The minimal and maximal reduction levels are 65% and 99%, which constitute a considerable reduction of resources.

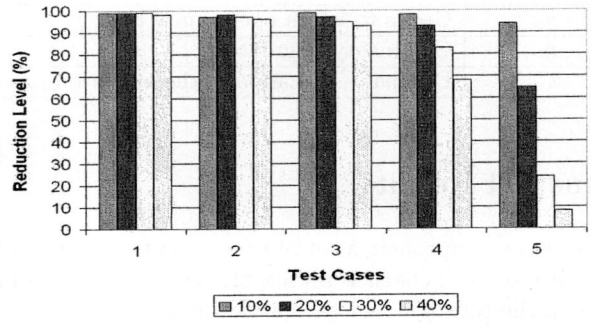

Fig. 7. Reduction level

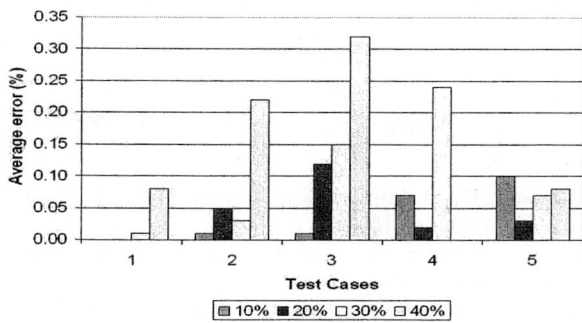

Fig. 8. Impact of compression on solution quality

Figure 8 shows the impact of the compression process on the solution quality. The error percentage varies in the range from 0.10% to 3.20%, which shows that the degradation is relatively small. Therefore, under the established conditions and assumptions, this shows the feasibility of reducing the resources required for solving large scale instances at the expense of a reasonable reduction in solution quality.

7 Conclusions and Future Work

This paper shows the feasibility of the proposed approach to solve large scale instances of the distribution design problem. The general strategy includes, unlike other approaches, an additional dimension for compressing the instance to be solved. The compression method consists of the application of a transformation of the original instance into a new instance that requires fewer resources to solve it than the original. The goal of the transformation is to obtain a reduction in the amount of resources needed to solve the original instance, without significantly reducing the quality of its solution. In order to preserve the solution quality, the transformation *summarizes the access pattern* of the original instance, using clustering techniques.

A set of experiments, using instances generated with typical access patterns found on the Internet, were conducted for evaluating quantitatively the size reduction that can be achieved and its effect on the solution quality. The transformation yields at least a 65% reduction in the amount of resources needed, without significantly reducing the quality of its solution. This shows that, given a set of computing resources, it is now possible to solve instances larger than those previously solvable.

Given the encouraging results, at the moment we are working on the design and implementation of efficient compression methods using other data mining techniques.

Acknowledgments

We thank the financial support of the following institutions: Consejo Nacional de Ciencia y Tecnología (CONACYT), Consejo Tamaulipeco de Ciencia y Tecnología (COTACYT), Consejo del Sistema Nacional de Educación Tecnológica (COSNET), and Dirección General de Educación Superior Tecnológica (DGEST).

References

1. Garey, M., Johnson, D.: Computer and Intractability: A guide to the theory of NP-Completeness. Freeman (1979)
2. Papadimitriou, C., Steiglitz, K.: Combinatorial Optimization: Algorithms and Complexity. Dover Publications (1998)
3. Barr, R., Golden, B., Kelly, J., Steward, W., Resende, M.: Guidelines for designing and reporting on computational experiments with heuristic methods. In: Proceedings of International Conference on Metaheuristics for Optimization, Kluwer Publishing (2001) 1–17
4. Michalewicz, Z., Fogel, D.: How to Solve It: Modern Heuristics. Springer Verlag (1999)
5. Pérez, J., Pazos, R., Frausto, J., Romero, D., Cruz, L.: Vertical fragmentation and allocation in distributed databases with site capacity restrictions using the threshold accepting algorithm. Lectures Notes in Computer Science. Springer-Verlag **1793** (2000) 75–81
6. Pérez, J., Pazos, R., Frausto, J., Rodríguez, G., Cruz, L., Mora, G., Fraire, H.: Self-tuning mechanism for genetic algorithms parameters, an application to data-object allocation in the web. Lectures Notes in Computer Science. Springer Verlag, Berlin Heidelberg New York **3046** (2004) 77–86
7. Ceri, S., Navathe, S., Wiederhold, G.: Distribution design of logical database schemes. In: IEEE Transactions on Software Engineering. Volume SE-9. (1983) 487 – 503
8. Navathe, S., Ceri, S., Wiederhold, G., Dou, J.: Vertical partitioning algorithms for database design. Volume 9. (1984) 680–710
9. Apers, P.: Data allocation in distributed database systems. Volume 13. (1988) 263–304
10. Johansson, J., March, S., Naumann, J.: The effects of parallel processing on update response time in distributed database design. In: Proceedings of the 21st International Conference On Information Systems. (2000) 187–196
11. Visinescu, C.: Incremental data distibution on internet-based distributed systems: A spring system approach. Master's thesis, University of Waterloo, Ontario, Canada (2003)
12. Baiao, F., Mattoso, M., Zaverucha, G.: A distribution design methodology for objects dbms. Distributed and Parallel Databases. Kluwer Academic Publishers **16** (2004) 45–90
13. Zilio, D., Rao, J., Lightstone, S., Lohman, G., Storm, A., Garcia-Arellano, C., Fadden, S.: Db2 design advisor: Integrated automatic physical database design. In: Proceedings of the Thirtieth International Conference on Very Large Data Bases 2004, Toronto, Canada (2004) 1087–1097
14. Halkidi, M., Batistakis, Y., Vazirgiannis, M.: On clustering validation techniques. In: Journal of Intelligent Information Systems. Volume 17., Kluwer Academic Publishers (2001) 107–145
15. Berkhin, P.: Survey of clustering data mining techniques. Technical report, Accrue Software (2002) http://www.accrue.com/products/rp_cluster_review.pdf.

16. Pérez, J.: Integración de la Fragmentación Vertical y Ubicación en el Diseño Adaptativo de Bases de Datos Distribuidas. PhD thesis, ITESM, Morelos, México (1999)
17. Fraire, H.: Una Metodología para el Diseño de la Fragmentación y Ubicación en Grandes Bases de Datos Distribuidas. PhD thesis, CENIDET, Cuernavaca, Morelos, México (2005)
18. Cruz, L.: Clasificación de Algoritmos Heurísticos Para la Solución de Problemas de Bin Packing. PhD thesis, Centro Nacional de Investigación y Desarrollo Tecnológico (CENIDET), Cuernavaca, México (2004)

Modeling Real-Time Wormhole Networks by Queuing Theory

Lichen Zhang and Yuliang Zhang

Faculty of Computer Science and Technology,
Guangdong University of Technology, 510090 Guangzhou, China
zhanglichen1962@163.com

Abstract. This paper discuses a new approach that models the single node of general real-time wormhole networks, and analyzes this new model with queuing theory. Since the wormhole network's node is too complicated to analyze generally, a multi-vision solution is applied to analyzing the wormhole network's node. The wormhole network single-node model is decomposed into three sub-models, and each of them can be analyzed with queuing theory separately. Lastly, a simulation model is made with this solution, and several simulation results are presented to illustrate the performance of real-time wormhole scheduling in single-node.

1 Introduction

Nowadays, most Massively Parallel Processors (MPP) adopt wormhole networks as their communication subsystems, on which a wormhole routing strategy runs. As presented in [1], a message is divided into flits (flow information units), which are the smallest units of information that a queue or a channel can handle. When the header flits of a message are received by a node, the node decides the next node the message should be routed based on the destination information contained in the message header. As the header flits are forwarded to the next node, the subsequent flits follow flit-by-flit in a cut-through fashion. If the header flits of a message are blocked at one node as the outgoing channel required is occupied, the message is buffered in the on-line flit buffers at each node along the path up to the current node, and then blocks other messages until it is able to make forward progress.

Accordingly, Dally [2] proposed Virtual Channel (VC), which is multiplexed over physical channels on demand, to reduce wormhole network contention and to improve physical link utilization. The virtual channels of a physical link require extra flit buffers and an arbitration scheme to share the link bandwidth among buffers. Therefore, the blocked flits will not always occupy the physical link, and the network latency is mostly insensitive to the distance between the source node and the destination node [3]. The benefits of wormhole networks with virtual channels, which include small buffer sizes, low network latency and low network contention, make them attractive for running real-time applications on large-scale parallel systems.

The two sections of a real-time flow control scheme in wormhole networks that manage two types of resources—virtual channels and the bandwidth of physical links—are the virtual channel assignment strategy and the arbitration function of physical link respectively.

Based on the two parts presented above, this paper firstly introduces six basic assumptions and issues for modeling real-time wormhole networks in the single-node case with queuing theory. Then, a single-node queuing model is proposed with a multi-vision solution. Furthermore, some simulation experiments are performed according to this solution. The last section presents some conclusions and future work.

2 Basic Assumptions and Issues

A single-node queuing model of wormhole networks running many typical wormhole routing schemes can be illustrated abstractly in Fig.1. A single-node queuing model in multi-vision is constructed based on this framework. For modeling, we make the following assumptions and issues.

A1: The number of servers and the relationship to the queues. There are three kinds of basic queuing models in general: single server, multi-server and multiple single-server. All of them are depicted in Fig.2, Fig.3 and Fig.4 respectively. The number of servers is denoted by N.

A2: Population size (K). When the number of customers' sources is at least 5 to 10 times the capacity of the system, infinite source assumption is reasonable [4]. For an infinite source model, there is assumed to be a Poisson arrival (M) with a

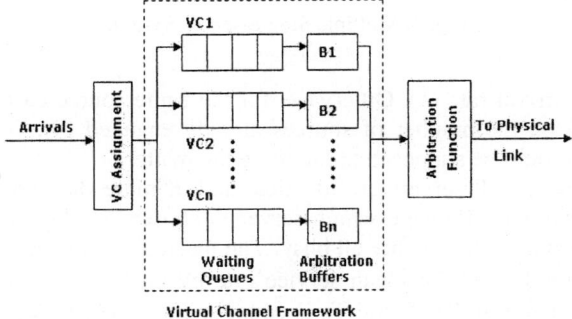

Fig. 1. Virtual Channel Framework in Single-node of Wormhole Networks

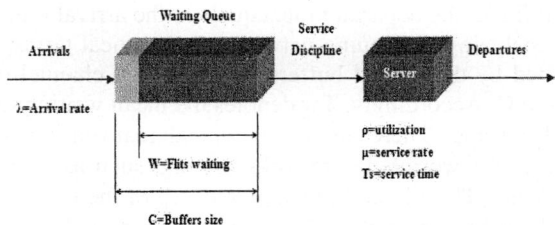

Fig. 2. Single Server System

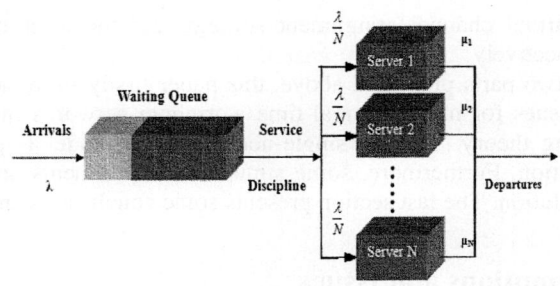

Fig. 3. Multi-server System

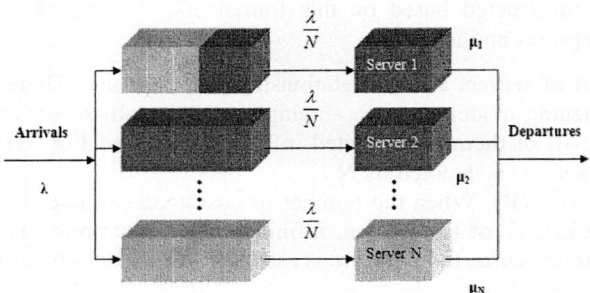

Fig. 4. Multiple Single-server System

fixed mean arrival rate (λ). Otherwise, for the finite source case, the arrival rate will depend on the number of sources already engaged [4]. Generally, infinite population should be supposed to facilitate the matters.

A3: It's assumed that all servers are identical and, if more than one server is available, it makes no difference which server is chosen for the customer. A queue does not form until servers are all busy. The mean service time for each customer is denoted by Ts and the mean service rate by μ, thus Ts=1/μ. σ_{Ts} denotes the standard deviation of Ts. If σ_{Ts}/Ts is equal to zero, the service time distribution is deterministic, namely constant service time (D). If σ_{Ts}/ Ts ≈1, the service time distribution is exponential (M), namely the service times are essentially random.

A4: Let w denote mean number of customers waiting to be served. If the length of the queue is infinite, the departure rate equals to the arrival rate. This assumption is helpful to analyzing in queuing networks. In practical terms, the length of the queue is limited by the size of buffers in one virtual channel (C). So, w is less than or equal to C. Accordingly, Tw denotes the mean waiting time.

A5: Flow control scheme. There are many typical real-time virtual channel flow control schemes for wormhole networks routing, such as Source-Link, Source-VC, PPCS-RT and Throttle-and-preempt, etc. All of them are based on real-time scheduling algorithms executed on a uniprocessor such as First-Come-First-Served, Earliest-Deadline-First, Least-Laxity- First and Rate-Monotonic-

Scheduling, etc. Applying queuing theory to schemes modeling directly is difficult. We have to abstract their essential characteristics, as shown in Fig.1. Most real-time flow control schemes differ in their virtual channel assignment strategies that decide which arrival flits can use the virtual channels and, arbitration functions that choose the next flits to be sent on the physical link. There are two typical arbitration functions, one is round-robin fashion and the other is priority-based fashion. However, the VC assignment strategies are determined by the concrete scheduling algorithms.

A6: If priority-based fashion is applied to the arbitrator of a physical link, there are two basic classes of priority policies: preemptive-resume policy and non-preemptive priority policy. Under a non- preemptive priority policy, the difference with preemptive-resume policy is that class 1 customers are not allowed to interrupt the service of class 2 customers who have lower priority until the service ends. As far as data transmission system are concerned, non-preemptive priority policy is more desirable.

According to six assumptions presented above, a single-node queuing model of wormhole networks can be easily constructed with multi-vision solution. And what is multi-vision? That means if a paradigm is too complex to analyze or model, multiple views should be made to decompose it into several logical components. Each component can be modeled easily with queuing theory.

3 Basic Sub-models

This virtual channel framework illustrated in Fig.1 can be split into 3 close coupled components, each of them can be specified by the elementary queuing models presented in A1, and shown in Fig.2, Fig.3 and Fig.4 respectively. To make further discussion easier, a shorthand notation called Kendall Notation in the form A/S/m/B/K/SD should be introduced, where A is the inter-arrival time distribution, S is the service time distribution, N is the number of servers, B is the number of buffers, namely the maximum length of the queue, K is the population size, SD is the service discipline. In addition, we denote several shorthand symbols. FCFS means First Come First Served, RR means Round-Robin, PR means Preemptive-Resume and, NP means Non- Preemptive.

Besides, we make the following assumptions. Each flit can be considered as fixed size unit, and each buffer unit can only store one flit. Similarly, each arbitration buffer can only store one flit. The three Sub-models are specified as follows.

3.1 Model One

We regard the arbitration buffers as a queue, arbitrator of a physical link as a server, those make up model 1.

A1: The number of servers N=1. Single server systems.
A2: It is convenient to guarantee that the number of VC buffers is much larger than the number of arbitration buffers (5 to 10 times), that is, the population size (Flits of messages) is unlimited ($K=\infty$). Therefore, in heavy traffic conditions, inter-

arrival times can be easily supposed to be exponentially distributed (Poisson Stream). Each arbitration buffer has its respective source from corresponding VC, that is, they have respective arrival rates λ_i. As viewed from the structure, flits do not join the queue in a FIFO fashion, but in a "jump the queue" fashion. Actually, the queue has no structural head, but logical one that is determined by the arbitration discipline. This model approximates to the polling systems (Fig.5) in a way, where all N queues can accommodate only one customer (flit, C=1).

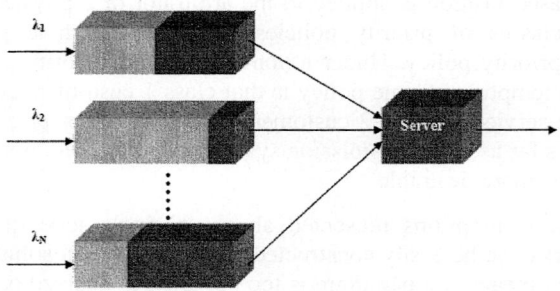

Fig. 5. Schematic of a Polling System

A3: Since the arbitration time and transmission time of flits are deterministic (provided that the next node is available), the service time (Ts) and the service rate (μ) are constant.

A4: Since there are only N arbitration buffers, the mean length of the queue w is not larger than N.

A5: The most commonly used service disciplines, namely arbitration functions here, are RR, PR and NP. As discussed in A2, if the arbitrator of a physical link polls its arbitration buffers in a round-robin fashion, then the buffers queue is always saturated in heavy traffic conditions. Under these circumstances, RR fashion approximates to FCFS fashion for a sufficiently long period of time.

A6: In polling systems [5], there are two service types appropriate for our model: one is Single Service, where only a single customer is served per queue before the server proceeds to the next queue; the other is Exhaustive Service, where a queue is serviced until it is empty. Thus, as viewed from this sub-model only, Single Service is adopted and, PR discipline is similar to NP discipline due to the slight sizes of flits. However, in view of the whole system, all flits in one message have the same priority, and they must be sent continuously flit by flit. Because all routing information is contained in the message header—if a message is split into two parts due to preemption, the first part will have lost its tail and the second part will not have a header to guide it to its destination.

Therefore, PR discipline differs from NP discipline. Generally, we choose NP.

Finally, a primitive sub-model 1 can be derived from the 6 assumptions addressed above. As presented in A2 and A5, heavy traffic conditions and RR discipline can guarantee that the sub-model is in a FCFS fashion in a steady state. Thus

$\lambda = \sum_{i=1}^{N} \lambda i$ and it has multiple sources. In this paper, model 1 can be reduced to M/D/1/N/∞/RR or M/D/1/N/∞/NP.

3.2 Model Two

Each VC is referred to as a queue, while each arbitration buffer as a server. That is model 2 as illustrated in Fig.4.

A1: In this multiple single-server system, there are N servers and N corresponding queues. In general, the header flit in each VC buffer can only enter respective arbitration buffer (VCi→Bi). However, it has no constraint on special routing design.

A2: Population size K = ∞, and Poisson distribution. Assume that each source has its arrival rate λ_i, then the whole rate $\lambda = \sum \lambda_i$. Under certain priority disciplines [3], a message can request to be allocated any VC number that is lower than its priority. Thus, the higher the priority of a message, the larger number of VCs from which a message can request an allocation. That is, the probability of meeting tight deadlines for messages is increased. In this situation, i is not more than N.

A3: Obviously, each server (arbitration buffer) is independent and identically distributed, provided that RR discipline is adopted in model 1. But if priority discipline is adopted in model 1, servers in model 2 are not independent. Further more, the service times of servers vary with priorities they own. Service discipline in model 1 will have effect on the mean service time $1/\mu$ of each server in model 2. That is, if RR discipline is applied to model 1, and the mean service time is $1/\mu$, then the mean service time N/μ will be provided by each server in model 2 under heavy traffic conditions; If priority discipline is applied to model 1, the mean service time in model 2 become complex. As addressed in A2, each VC and its arbitration buffer have respective priority. Besides, suppose that Exhaustive Service is running in model 1 as presented in A6 of model 1. So, under NP discipline, all the flits except header flit in a message with highest priority have the same service time $1/\mu$. And the header flit may have a longer service time L/μ, where L denotes the length of another message with lower priority. Similarly, all the flits except header flits in any messages with other lower priorities have the same service time $1/\mu$, because of the NP discipline. But the service time of header flits differ in their priorities. The header flits with second highest priority may have the service time L/μ or $2L/\mu$ (provided that there are no continuous messages with same priorities), the third one may have L/μ or $2L/\mu$ or $3L/\mu$, etc.

A4: Obviously, the mean lengths of queues (Wi) in VCs are not larger than the capacity (Ci) of respective VCs. For analysis as a whole, we can derive the mean length of queues from calculating the formula $\overline{w} = \sum^{N} wi/N$

A5: As presented in A1 and A2, if VCs are specified by their priorities, the service discipline is only FCFS. Otherwise, if the VCs are identical with flits of different priorities in each of them, and the priorities of arbitration buffers are distinguishable (e.g. $B_1 > B_2 > \cdots > B_N$), then there is a multiple-to-multiple mapping from VCs to arbitration buffers ($N_{VC} \to N_B$), and the service discipline is in priority fashion. This is distinguished from the pattern presented in A3.

A6: In this model, NP discipline may be the most commonly used fashion. After deliberating on this model, services are not simultaneous, because the servers (arbitration buffers) have common exit--the physical link. However, as viewed from the VCs, entering the arbitration buffers means the service starts, though the flits have to take a slight period of time to wait for sending. In other words, the servers have different service time from one another. Hence, servers are not independent. It's difficult to use pure queuing theory directly for this model. For simplification, a heavy traffic condition [6] can be introduced to this model. Thus, we can denote this sub-model by M/D/N/N*C/∞, where C stands for the capacity of each VC. If each VC has distinguishable priority with the same arrival rate, this sub-model can even be split into N single server systems for further study, each of which can be denoted by M/D/1/C /∞/FCFS.

3.3 Model Three

Each VC is considered as a server, while no queue is formed when the servers are all busy. That means there is no waiting queue in Fig.3. The service provided by VCs is the available space for buffering the flits waiting for forwarding. That is, the servers are busy if all the buffers of VCs are saturated, and the flits blocked are waiting in previous node for repeatedly and continuously attempts to gain service[1]. In contrast, the servers are idle if there are available buffers in VCs.

A1: The number of servers is equivalent to the number of VCs. This sub-model is a type of multi-server systems.
A2: Population size K=∞, and Poisson distribution. $\lambda=\Sigma \lambda i$, where 'i' denotes the number of customer sources.
A3: Assume that the VCs are equivalent. In heavy traffic conditions, the mean service time is equivalent to the mean service time $1/\mu$ in model 1, no matter which arbitration discipline is running, because the flit arriving can be received as soon as one buffer is available in VCs. If there is more than one buffer available in VCs at any given time, contrary to heavy traffic conditions, the mean service time is determined by the sum of executing time of VC assignment strategy and the placing time of flits. Similarly, if VCs are distinguished by their priorities, the mean service time of the whole system is also $1/\mu$ in heavy traffic conditions. Nevertheless, the mean service times are different as viewed from various sources with different priorities.
A4: There is no queuing room for blocking flits. Thus, w=0.
A5: This sub-model is applying VC assignment strategy to its service discipline, so that the service discipline varies from strategy to strategy. A polling manner can be used, similar to RR discipline. We can assign flits to the VC who has the shortest queuing length in it, or the shortest emptying time. Also, we can constrain the flits to use given VCs according to their timing properties.
A6: There is no preemption issue for the special discipline.

---

[1] When all the servers are busy, the customer arriving is blocked. There're 3 manners to handle these blocked customers [4], where Lost Calls Delayed—customer blocked can be placed in a queue awaiting a free server—is the most commonly used manner, and Lost Calls Held—repeatedly and continuously attempts to gain service—is used in this paper.

By the analysis above, model 3 can be denoted as M/D/N/N, which is called Loss Queuing System in some theses. In order to work out the probability of blocking state, that is, all the VCs are busy, Erlang's loss formula [7] can be proposed. Parameters λ and μ are defined as arrival rate and service rate of each server, respectively. $\pi(i)$ is defined as the d.f. of the number of customers in the system in steady-state. We consider a heavy traffic condition, so that each VC has only two states, saturated or one buffer available. In this case, $\pi(i)$ can also be denoted as the number of busy servers. Hence, this sub-system can be modeled as a birth and death process with birth rate

$$\lambda_i = \begin{cases} \lambda, i=0,1,\cdots,N-1 \\ 0, i \geq N \end{cases}$$

and death rate $\mu_i = i \times \mu (i=1,2,\cdots,N)$. And then, a formula can be deduced from balance equations[2] of a birth and death process. That is $\pi(i) = \pi(0) \times \dfrac{\rho^i}{i!}$, for i=0,1,...,N, $\pi(i)$=0 for i>N, where $\pi(0) = \left[\sum_{i=0}^{N} \dfrac{\rho^i}{i!} \right]^{-1}$.

In particular, $\pi(N)$ gives the probability of blocked flits, it's given by

$$\pi(N) = \dfrac{\dfrac{\rho^N}{N!}}{\sum_{i=0}^{N} \dfrac{\rho^i}{i!}}.$$

4 Simulation Results

With multi-vision solution introduced, a simulator can be implemented easily to study the performance of real-time wormhole systems in single-node based on a primitive queuing model [8]. Because of the dynamic nature of discrete-event simulation models, a next-event time mechanism is introduced to construct our model. First of all, a simulation clock should be made to advance simulated time from one event time to another nearest event time. Second, there are two events, arrival and departure. Both of them can be implemented by independent event routines. Lastly, according to multi-vision solution, VC assignment strategy and physical link arbitration can be implemented in corresponding functions, and the whole simulated system can be assembled with these two components easily. Besides, priority mapping function should be made to generate priority of messages which reflect the timing properties.

After the simulator running, several typical results are extracted from huge data to illustrate some problems. In order to assess the performance of the model, several evaluation parameters should be included, average delays, deadline missed rate, loss rate and server utilization.

As showed in Fig.6, flits' loss rate exponentially increases as the service time increases. Under the same conditions, deadline missed rate is not like the loss rate does (Fig.7). With the population size getting larger and larger, the curves become steady. Hence, most study is based on heavy traffic conditions. As presented above, Erlang's

---

[2] Equilibrium equation—the probability flow out of a state = the probability flow in that state.

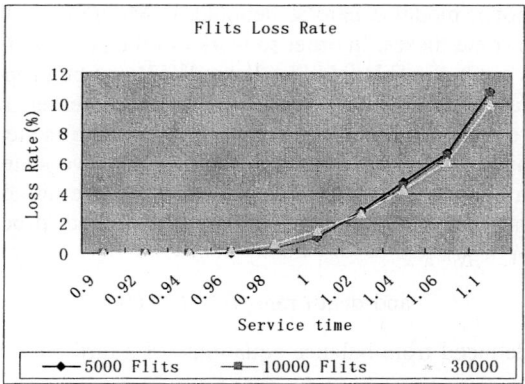

Fig. 6. Flits loss rate

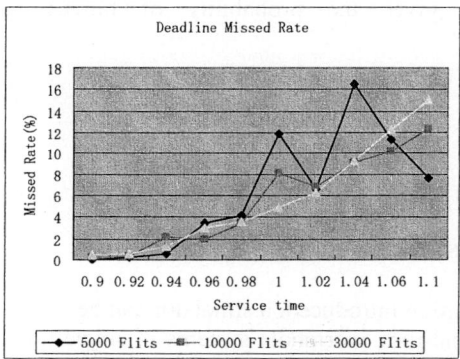

Fig. 7. Deadline missed rate

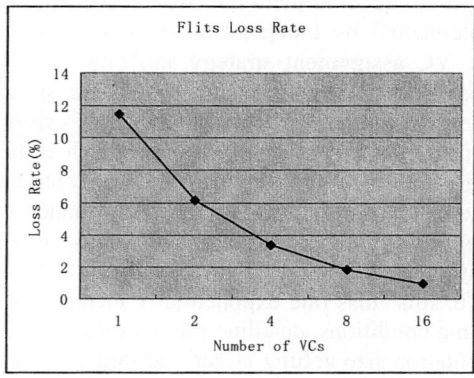

Fig. 8. Loss rate with the number of VCs

loss formula most likely conforms to the curve showed in Fig.8. Therefore, the increment of VCs will reduce the network contention.

Not only can the performance results be made, but also any algorithms or strategies on real-time wormhole networks can be involved in this simulator with multi-vision solution. This method facilitates the simulation experiments with many alterable factors.

5 Conclusion

Since real-time wormhole networks with VC technology are complicated systems, a multi-vision solution is proposed to decompose the queuing model of single-node, so that the sub-models can be studied easily.

Although the queuing models studied in this paper ignore important aspects of real systems, the work is a first step in the development of analytic methods for real-time wormhole networks. However, the attraction of the solution proposed in this paper is that it maybe opens up a new research topic that can be pursued by us or other researchers.

Finally, our future work possibly includes (1) incorporating typical real-time wormhole routing strategies in our models and making performance evaluation, (2) quantitative analysis with queuing theory or queuing network theory, (3) more popular and stronger simulator to our models.

Acknowledgements

This work is partly supported by the National Natural Science Foundation of China under Grant No.60474072 and No.60174050; the Natural Science Foundation of Guangdong Province of China under Grant No.04009465, the Natural Science Foundation of Guangdong Education Department under Grant No. Z03024.

References

1. Lionel M. Ni, Philip K. McKinley. A survey of wormhole routing technique in direct networks. *Computer* 26, 2 (1993), 62–76.
2. Dally, W.J. Virtual-channel flow control. IEEE Trans. Parallel Distrib. System 3, 2 (Mar. 1992), 194-205
3. Jong-pyng li and Matt W. Mutka, Real-Time Virtual Channel Flow Control. Journal of Parallel and Distributed Computing 32, 49–65 (1996) Article NO. 0004
4. William Stallings. Queuing Analysis. http://www.WilliamStallings.com/StudentSupport.html, 2004-11.
5. Andreas Willig. Performance Evaluation Techniques. Hasso-Plattner-Institut, University Potsdam, June 2004.
6. Shu-Ngai Yeung, John Lehoczky. End-to-end Delay Analysis for Real-Time Networks. Proceedings of the 22nd IEEE Real-Time Systems Symposium, 0-7695-1420-0/01, 2001.
7. Philippe Nain. Basic Elements of Queueing Theory: Application to the Modeling of Computer Systems. USA: University of Massachusetts, Jan 1998.
8. Averill M.Law and W.David Kelton. Simulation Modeling and Analysis [Third Edition] . McGraw-Hill series in industrial engineering and management science. Singapore, 2000.1.

9. Frode B.Nilsen. Queuing system: Modeling, analysis and simulation. Department of Informatics, University of OSLO, April 1998.
10. Ivo Adan, Jacques Resing. Queueing Theory. The Netherlands: Department of Mathematics and Computing Science of Eindhoven, University of Technology, Feb 2001.
11. Oleg ZaiKin, Przemyslaw Korytkowski, Przemyslaw Rozewski. Queuing Systems. Poland: Technical University of Szczecin, 2004.
12. Sunggu Lee. Real-Time Wormhole Channel. J. Parallel Distrib. Comput. 63 (2003) 299–311.
13. John P.Lehoczky. Scheduling Communication Networks Carrying Real-Time Traffic. IEEE 0-08186-9212- X/98, 1998..Oleg ZaiKin, Przemyslaw Korytkowski, Przemyslaw Rozewski. Queuing Systems. Poland: Technical University of Szczecin, 2004.

A Discrete Event System Model for Simulating Mobile Agent[*]

Xuhui Li[1,2], Jiannong Cao[2], Yanxiang He[1], and Jingyang Zhou[2,3]

[1] State Key Lab of Software Engineering,
Wuhan University, Wuhan, Hubei, China
{lixuhui, yxhe}@whu.edu.cn
[2] Department of Computing, Hong Kong Polytechnic University,
Kowloon, Hong Kong, China
csjcao@comp.polyu.edu.hk
[3] Department of Computer Science and Technology,
Nanjing University, Nanjing, Jiangsu, China
zhoujingyang@hotmail.com

Abstract. Simulation has been proved to be a practical approach for performance evaluation of mobile agents. However, the lack of a standard for the execution of mobile agents makes the semantics ambiguous. Thus, the simulation of mobile agents is not feasible or reasonable without an explicitly defined execution model of agents. In this paper, we propose an execution model of mobile agents called SMA. Based on the SMA model, the discrete event models describing the SMA agents and hosts, called SMA-DEVS, are presented using the modelling approach of DEVS and DSDE. We implement a simulation environment based on SMA-DEVS and test the environment with certain mobile agent-based algorithms.

1 Introduction

As a novel network computing technology, mobile agent has been widely adopted in solving various parallel and distributed problems, ranging from information searching and retrieval to distributed coordination and synchronization. A lot of mobile agent algorithms have been proposed to find new solutions for those problems to improve performance in circumstances where the systems exhibit heavy network traffic, large amount of transferring data, and unbalanced workload among nodes. Naturally, performance evaluation of those algorithms becomes essential to discover the performance and scalability bottlenecks and optimize the application design.

However, performance evaluation of mobile agent algorithms remains a complex task. The solutions for performance evaluation of conventional distributed algorithms, such as theoretical analysis and live deployment, seldom fit for mobile

---

[*] This research is partially supported by the University Grant Council of Hong Kong under the CERG Grant B-Q518 and the Hubei Nature Science Fund under contract No. 2005ABA235.

agent algorithm due to its features of mobility and reactivity [8]. Alternatively, simulation has been proposed as a valuable method for analyzing the complex nature of the dynamic aspects of parallel and distributed systems. In [8], we have proposed a direct execution simulation approach to efficiently evaluating the performance of some mobile agent algorithm. The prototype built following the approach worked well for simple algorithms under simple circumstances. But the simulation results deviate from anticipation once the number of agents or the complexity of the algorithms increases.

With a deep exploration to the algorithm and the prototype, we found that different mechanisms of agents to handle message and migrate are adopted by the designer and the system respectively. This difference thus results in the divergence of agent semantics, which made our previous simulation model not fit for concrete agent systems. Further, different mobile agent systems deploy different implementation mechanisms, so we have to resort to a platform independent semantical description of mobile agent behaviors to simulate mobile agent, which makes its performance unambiguous. Based on such a consistent description, a discrete event system model of mobile agents should be built as the fundamental work of simulation.

Through the work of implementing mobile agent algorithms and understanding the architecture of concrete systems, we propose a common execution model for describing mobile agent semantics. The model, called SMA standing for Simple Mobile Agent, adopts common concepts of mobile agent behaviors and its semantics get the idea originating form concrete mobile agent systems such has IBM Aglets[1]. Based on the SMA model, we utilize the discrete event system modelling approach to build a theoretical model called SMA-DEVS for mobile agent simulation. The model has been deployed in practical simulation environment and proved to be generic and effective for mobile agent algorithms. In this paper, we would introduce the ideas and features of the two models.

The rest of the paper is organized as follows. In Section 2, we describe related works on mobile agent systems, discrete event systems and simulation of mobile agents. In Section 3, we introduce the SMA model with the explanation of SMA agent semantics. In Section 4, the discrete event system model SMA-DEVS for simulating the execution of mobile agents is presented in detail. A direct execution simulation prototype adopting the SMA-DEVS model is briefly introduced in Section 5. Finally, Section 6 concludes the paper and discusses our future works.

2 Related Works

Kinds of mobile agent systems have been designed and implemented. Among them were Agent TCL by Dartmouth College, Concordia by Mitsubishi Electric Information Technology Center, Mole by University of Stuttgart, Voyager by ObjectSpace Company and Aglets by IBM Research [1]. Early mobile agent systems were often developed in certain script languages such as TCL. Later, when Java was developed and became popular, most mobile agent systems adopted it as implementation language because it is pure object-oriented and supports object serialization. Though these systems differ in their goals, motivations and implementations, they all provide common functionalities that support the migration of agents, the communication between agents, various programming languages and various forms of security. However, the difference among the implementations of the functionalities, mainly on migration and communication, results in different simulation model for agents. For instance, most mobile agent systems adopt the weak migration scheme where only the values of agent variables are maintained during migration, whereas some early systems support the strong one where the execution states would also be maintained. As to agent communication, in some systems agent handles the messages one by one, whereas in other systems messages are handled concurrently. In some deliberately designed agent systems such as Aglets, options are provided for the agent to handle the messages sequentially or concurrently, which makes the agent algorithm more difficult to be designed and understood.

Discrete event system (DEVS) is a formal model introduced by Zeigler [13] to describe the actions and state transitions of a system caused by input or time elapse. The DEVS model introduce some elements representing time, event and input/output functions into conventional state machine, enabling the model efficiently describing the state transitions of an actual system. DEVS model has been adopted as a standard modelling approach in simulation, and many extensions to DEVS model have been proposed to describe various complicated systems behaviors. These extensions include: the Coupled DEVS model proposed by Zeigler to describe the coupled system in a hierarchy schema [14]; the Parallel DEVS model proposed in [4] to describe parallel and distributed systems; and Dynamic Structure DEVS model proposed by Barros in [2] to describe the systems with dynamic structures, which fits modelling mobile agent system.

Some studies have been done to model and simulate mobile agent. Works can be found in literatures on modelling mobile agents with the canonical stochastic analytic approach [7] or simulating mobile agent applications [10][12], but these efforts are usually devoted to evaluating different, application-specific mobile agent programs under different system assumptions. Few works have been taken to establish the practical generic simulation model for mobile agents. J.Kim [6] once built a model to describe the mobility of agents with a Coupled-DEVS with dynamic structures, but the model ignores the internal execution model of the agents and thus not strong enough to simulate concrete agents. The solid simulation model must be built on the explicitly described model of mobile agent execution, so we introduce the SMA model to standardize agent execution.

3 SMA: An Execution Model for Mobile Agents

SMA is a model designed for specifying mobile agent execution. It adopts common concepts of mobile agent such as creation, communication, migration etc. We also propose a script language called SMAL to specify SMA agent programs. The details on syntax and semantics of SMAL can refer to [9].

In SMA a mobile agent is a program consisting of a *Declaration* section declaring agent state variables and three statement block sections, *Initialization*, *MigrationRecovery* and *Messages*, containing pseudo codes and primitives specifying agent behaviors. The primitives are deeply related with agent threads' execution and interaction. Variables can also be declared in the *BlockDeclaration* subsection in each statement block, but only the state variables in *Declaration* would be retained during migration because of the weak migration scheme adopted by SMA.

SMA drives a set of threads to execute the statement blocks. That is, *Initialization*, *MigrationRecovery*, and each *Message* statement block would be executed by a separate thread. SMA adopts the message-driven model. Generally, a manager thread and a set of message threads are involved in message handling. Manager thread runs in background and schedules message threads. Each message block defines how to handle a certain kind of messages and is executed by a message thread under the control of the manager thread once a message is received. SMA assumes that the messages are sent in an asynchronous way. Incoming messages are transferred by the agent platform and forwarded to manager threads. Manager thread manages two message queues, a *processing* queue and a *waiting* queue, to accommodate the messages being handled or not currently. Designers can manage the threads with four primitives, *blockmessage*, *unblockmessage*, *regainmessage* and *removemessage*, in the statement blocks. *Blockmessage* and *unblockmessage* are used to signify whether to process the message, *regainmessage* moves the messages in the *waiting* queue to the *processing* queue, and *removemessage* removes the current message from the *waiting* queue. The messages can be handled as the designer prefers to by properly using the four message primitives.

In the statement blocks, some primitives are provided for common agent behaviors. They are *sendmessage*, *createagent*, *migrateto*, and *dispose*. The semantics of the primitives are apparent. Another two primitives, *lock* and *unlock*, are associated with special lock variables being declared in *Declaration* and only serving as signs of critical sections. Once a lock statement, e.g., *lock(r)*, is executed by one thread, representing it would require the control of a lock variable *r*, the other threads would be suspended if they encounter a *lock(r)* until the statement *unlock(r)* is executed by the thread who have acquired the control of *r*. Providing the *lock* and *unlock* primitives, SMA model gives designers full control over thread's execution whereas leaves them the problem of concurrently accessing the agent's shared area.

A simple example of SMA agent is described with a SMAL program as below:

```
Agent sample Body Declaration
     a: Int;
     r: Lock;
Initialization
    BlockBegin
        a = 0;
        unblockmessage();
```

```
        BlockEnd
MigrationRecovery
    BlockBegin
        a = 0;
        regainmessage();
        unblockmessage();
    BlockEnd
On Message m1 With b: Int Do
    BlockBegin
        lock(r);
        a = b;
        sendmessage("sample2", m2, 3);
        removemessage();
        unlock(r);
    BlockEnd
On Message m2 With c: Int Do
    BlockBegin
        lock(r);
        createagent("sample3", sample, "host2");
        migrateto(host2);
        unlock(r);
    BlockEnd
BodyEnd
```

In the example, a statement *createagent("sample1", sample, "host1")* would create an agent instance *sample1* of agent type *sample* at a host named *host1*, the name *sample1* and *host1* are passed to the predefined variables *AgentName* and *HostName*. During the agent's lifetime, the name *sample1* would be used as the unique identification of this agent, but the *HostName* variable would change its value when the agent migrates to another host. When the agent is created, it would handle two kinds of messages: the message *m1* would incur sending a message to another agent named *sample2*, and the message *m2* would cause the agent to create a new agent named *sample3* in *host2* and then migrate to there. However, only one of the worker threads can do its job at a time because each worker thread would encounter a *lock(r)* statement once it begins to handle the message.

SMA presents a simple scheme to specify mobile agent algorithm based on asynchronous message passing. It explicitly describes the internal behaviors of the agent and lays a foundation for building a simulation model for mobile agents. In the next section, we will introduce the DEVS model for simulating mobile agents based on SMA.

4 SMA-DEVS: Discrete Event System for SMA

SMA enables us to build a DEVS model that can explore state transition during agent execution. As to the mobile agent systems based on the SMA model, the whole environment can be set into four layers: system, hosts, agents, and threads, which form a 4-layer simulation architecture as shown in the left part of Fig.1. In SMA an agent is regarded as some shared data manipulated with a set of threads including a manager thread and some message threads (here we can treat the *initialization* thread and *recovery* thread as special message threads). Our simulation system is supposed to be built with the direct execution simulation approach in which the thread is the basic running element to be scheduled. Naturally we would regard the thread as the atomic system representing both logic process and physical process. Further, the host and the agents in it can be combined to be one system in simulation because the agent is always treated as a subset of the threads contained in the host. Therefore, we can define the SMA-DEVS model with a 3-layer architecture: SMA-System, SMA-Host, and SMA-Thread, as the right part of Fig.1 shows.

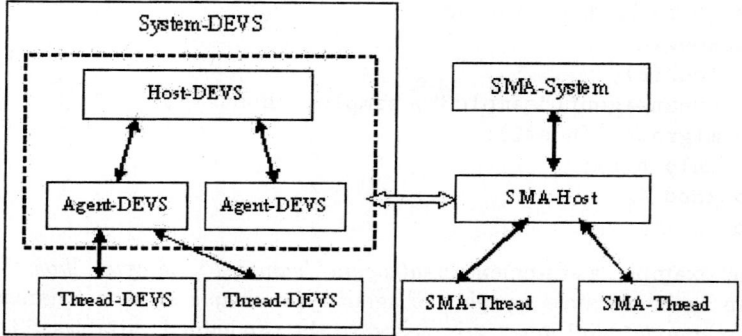

Fig. 1. Simulation architecture for mobile agent system

SMA-Thread mainly behaves as the event source involving the interactions both between the threads and between the hosts. In process simulations, the discrete code segments involving no interaction and thus executing sequentially are often called local code blocks. During its lifetime a thread is usually in one of two kinds of states: executing a local code block and taking an interactive action. Those actions, tightly associated with agents' behaviors, are usually determined by the thread's execution model. Based on the primitives indicating the behaviors (interactive actions) of the SMA threads, it is easy to define a concrete SMA thread's DEVS model.

Definition 1. *A* **SMA-Thread** *is a standard basic DEVS defined as follows:*

$$\text{SMA-Thread} = < X, Y, S, \delta_{int}, \delta_{ext}, \lambda, \text{ta} > \text{ where}$$

– X *and* Y *are the input and the output value set.* X *is defined by an enumerated set* $X_T = \{\text{notify, stop}\}$. Y *is the output value set defined by a set* $Y_T = \{(\text{create\_agent}, h, an, agent), (\text{migrate\_agent}, h, an, agent), (\text{send\_message},$

an, msg), (block_message, an), (unblock_message, an), (regain_message, an), (remove_message, an), (pick, an, msg), (lock, an, r, t), (unlock, an, r, t), (dispose, an) | h∈HN, msg∈MSG, r∈Lock}, *where* HN *represents the set of host names,* MSG *represents the set of messages,* Lock *represents the set of lock variables in the owner agent the thread belongs to,* agent *represents the instance of the agent program,* an *represents the name of the owner agent, and* t *represents the thread itself.*
- S *is the state set with the form of* {(si, st) | si∈SI, st∈{running, waiting, stopped}} *where* SI *represents the set of the thread's execution states.*
- δ_{int}, δ_{ext}, λ, ta *are common DEVS functions. The rule to define them would be introduced later.*

SMA-Thread simplifies the execution of a thread as a set of states with certain transition rules and input and output values. The input values in X_T show that the thread could be notified to resume the execution and be stopped to abort the execution. The output value set is composed of the interactive actions that are specified as primitives in SMA and *(pick, an, msg)*. The latter one is sent out by an agent's message manager thread when a message named *msg* in the waiting queue is picked up to handle. For facility, we treat all these interactive actions as primitives.

SMA-Thread only presents a rough sketch of the DEVS model for the threads. Those transition functions are not described accurately because they are related to the semantics of the concrete thread. However, our purpose is not to simulate a concrete agent program but to build a generic simulation environment based on direct execution simulation. Therefore, instead of using the common basic DEVS models to describe agent threads, we define a template for generating various concrete SMA-Thread models from agent execution. To facilitate the representation, we can use something of a thread's state transition sequence as the input of the template.

Definition 2. *A* **Thread-ST** *is a tuple defined as follows:*

$$\text{Thread-ST} = < \text{SI, Act, Tr} > \text{ where}$$

- SI *represents the states set of the program's execution. The elements of* SI *adopt a 2-tuple form as* (st, sc) *where* st *stands for the states of the thread variables and* sc *stands for the states of the common variables shared by the threads in an agent.*
- Act = Instruction ∪τ∪ Primitive *is the set of actions executed by the thread. Instructions consists of actions executed thread's local code block;* τ *is a special notation indicating an external action that would affect the agent's shared variables.*
- Tr ⊂ U* *is the set of the thread's state transition sequences. Here* U = SI×Act×SI *is the domain of state transition indicating the semantics of the program. For a state sequence* $\delta \in$ Tr, $\delta = (u_1, u_2, \ldots, u_n)$ *where* $\forall 1 \leq i < n$, $u_i = (s_i, a_i, s_{i+1})$.

Thread-ST presents a simple way to describe threads' state transitions during the execution. It is practical from Thread-ST to build the template for threads' simulation with the direct execution simulation approach. Usually a Thread-ST model corresponds to a thread. We denote the set of the Thread-ST models as **ST** and denote the set of the SMA-Thread models as **Thread**.

Definition 3. *A* **SMA-Temp**: **ST**→**Thread** *is a function: for a* st = (SI, Act, Tr)∈**ST**, SMA-Temp(st) = (X, Y, S, δ_{int}, δ_{ext}, λ, ta), *where*

- X, Y, *and* S *are defined as Def.1 shows;*
- δ_{int}: S → S *is the internal state transition function. For a* (s_1, a, s_2) ∈ Tr: δ_{int}((s_1, running)) = (s_2, running), *if* a ∈ Instruction ∪ {τ} ∪ (Primitive-{Lock}); δ_{int}((s_1, running)) = (s_2, waiting), *if* a = Lock; δ_{int}((s_1, waiting)) = (s_2, waiting), *if* a = τ.
- δ_{ext}: S × X → S *is the external state transition function. For a* (s_1, running) ∈ S, δ_{ext}((s_1, running), stop) = (s_1, stopped); *for a* (s_1, waiting) *in* S, δ_{ext}((s_1, waiting), notify) = ((s_1, running), δ_{ext}((s_1, waiting), stop) =(s_1, stopped).
- λ: S → Y *is the output value function. For a* (s_1, a, s_2) ∈ Tr, a ∈ Primitive: $\lambda(s_1)$ = output(a) *where* output *is a wrapper function to transform the primitive actions into the output value defined in* Y_T.
- ta: S → R *is the time advance function.*

In Def.3, *ta* is the sole function whose definition depends on the SMA-Temp. That is, each SMA-Temp would define a template for generating a concrete *ta* function for a *Thread-ST* model.

Direct execution simulation approach has been successfully used in many simulation systems, especially the distributed computing systems. However, literatures mainly focus on the implementation detail and seldom dwell on its formal model and its relation with DEVS model. Here we use SMA-Temp to associate thread's state transitions with its simulation model, formally illustrating the essence of the direct execution simulation as a function generating a simulation of the thread with its concrete execution.

It is hard to describe host's dynamic structure with the conventional DEVS models, because the agents would migrate or die and the threads handling the messages would be stopped or finish its work. Fortunately, Barros has proposed a dynamic structure discrete event model called DSDE [2] that exactly fits the case here. Adopting the features of the dynamic structure models, we use the model of the executive in DSDE to describe the agent hosts as follows.

Definition 4. *A* **SMA-Host** *is an 8-tuple:*

$$\text{SMA-Host} = < X_h, Y_h, S_h, \gamma, \Sigma^*, \delta_{int,\ h}, \delta_{ext,\ h}, ta_h > where$$

- X_h *and* Y_h *are input and output value sets.* $X_h = X_{int} \cup X_{ext}$, $Y_h = Y_{int} \cup Y_{ext}$, *where* $X_{ext} = Y_{ext}$ = {(create_agent, h', agent, agentname), (migrate_agent, h', an, agent), (send_message, an, msg) | h'∈ HN}, X_{int}

= {(block_message, an), (unblock_message, an), (regain_message, an), (remove_message, an), (pick, an, msg), (lock, an, r, t), (unlock, an, r, t), (dispose, an) | msg MSG, r Lock, t ∈ Th}, Y_{int} = {(notify, t), (stop, t) | t ∈ Th}. *Here HN is the host name set, MSG is the message set, Lock is the lock variable set, Th is the thread set.*

- S_h *is host's state set.* S_h = {(T_h, C_h, TV)}, *where* T_h *is the thread set,* C_h *is common state set, TV represents temporary values for output. The element of* T_h *is denoted as a triple:* (an, type, seqno), *indicating the owner agent name, the thread type, e.g. initializing thread with* init *type, migrate recovery thread with* migrate *type, message manager thread with* manager *type, and message handler thread with the message name as the type, and the sequence number of the thread once it is an message handler thread. The element of* C_h *is denoted as a tuple:* (an, MQ_w, MQ_p, b, {(r, ts) | r∈L_{an}, ts∈ T_h*}), *indicating the agent's message waiting queue and processing queue, the message block flag, and the lock variables with the queue of the threads waiting for the control of the lock.*

- γ: $S_h \rightarrow \Sigma^*$ *is the structure function and* Σ^* *is the set of the structures of the threads in the host. For a* $s_{j,h}$ = $(T_{j,h}, C_{j,h})$∈S_h, *a structure* Σ_j = $\gamma(s_{j,h})$ ∈ Σ^* *is defined as* Σ_j = $(T_{j,h}, \{M_{i,j}\}, \{I_{i,j}\}, \{Z_{i,j}\})$, *where* $M_{i,j}$ *is the SMA-Thread model of the thread* i *for all* i ∈ $T_{j,h}$, $I_{i,j}$ *is the set of component influencers of* i *for all* i ∈ $T_{j,h}$∪ {h}, $Z_{i,j}$ *is the input function of component* i *for all* i∈ $T_{j,h}$∪{h}. *For all* i∈$T_{j,h}$, $I_{i,j}$ = {h}, *and for* i=h, $I_{i,j}$ = $T_{j,h}$. *The function* $Z_{i,j}$: $Y_{k,j} \rightarrow X_{i,j}$ (k∈$I_{i,j}$) *is defined as follows:*

  - ∀ i ∈ $T_{j,h}$, ∀ y ∈ Y_h, *and* k=h *holds: if* y=(notify,i), *then* $Z_{i,j}(y)$ = notify; *if* y=(stop,i), *then* $Z_{i,j}(y)$= stop; *otherwise,* $Z_{i,j}(y)$ *is undefined.*
  - *if* i=h, *then* ∀ y∈$Y_{k,j}$, $Z_{i,j}(y)$=y.

- δ_{int}: $S_h \rightarrow S_h$ *is the internal transition function;* λ_h: $S_h \rightarrow Y_h^b$ *is the output function;* ta: $S_h \rightarrow R_0^+$ *is the time advance function. For a state* s_h = (T_h, C_h, tv): *if* tv ∈ Y_h^b *and* tv ≠ ϕ, *then* $\delta_{int}(s_h)$ = (T_h, C_h, ϕ), $\lambda_h(s_h)$ = tv, $ta_h(s_h)$=0; *otherwise, their values are not defined.*

- δ_{ext}: $S_h \times R \times X_h^b \rightarrow S_h$ *is the external transition function.* δ_{ext} *is defined in a recursive way with a function* **sort** *whose purpose is to transform the input value set as an ordered value list:*
  $\delta_{ext}(s_h,e,x)$=$\delta_{ext1}(s_h,e,\text{sort}(x))$=$\delta_{ext1}(\delta_{ext2}(s_h,e,\text{fst}(\text{sort}(x)),e,\text{snd}(\text{sort}(x))))$
  The auxiliary function δ_{ext2} *defines actual state transition to each input value. Here list part of its definition with certain input values:*

  - $\delta_{ext2}((T_h, C_h, tv), e, (\text{create\_agent}, h, an, agent))$ = $((T_h \cup \{(an,\text{manager},-)\}, (an,\text{init})\}, C_h$ {(an,ε,ε, true, {(r, ε) | r∈ agent.Lock})}, tv)
  - $\delta_{ext2}((T_h, C_h, tv), e, (\text{migrate\_agent}, h', an, agent))$ = $((T_h -\{(an,*)\}, C_h-\{(an, *)\}, tv\cup\{(\text{stop}, (an, *))\}\cup\{(\text{migrate\_agent}, h', an, agent)\})$
  - $\delta_{ext2}((T_h, C_h, tv), e, (\text{send\_message}, an, msg))$ = $((T_h, C_h[(an. -, (MQ_w, msg), -)/(an, -, MQ_w, -)], tv)$, if (an, manager,-)∈$T_h$
  - $\delta_{ext2}((T_h, C_h, tv), e, (\text{pick}, an, msg))$ = $(T_h\cup\{(an, msg, seqno)\}, C_h[(an, (MQ_p, msg), MQ_w-\{msg\}, -)/(an, MQ_p, MQ_w,-)], tv)$

- $\delta_{ext2}((T_h, C_h, tv), e, (lock, an, r, t)) = (T_h, C_h[(an, -, \{(r, (t)),-\})/(an, -, \{(r,),-\})], tv \{(notify, t)\})$

SMA-System is composed of the hosts with the function specifying the delay time to transfer the information between them; the definition can be easily presented as:

Definition 5. *A* **SMA-System** *is a tuple:*

$$\text{SMA-System} = < H, M_H, T_{i,j} > where$$

- H *is the set of hosts;*
- M_H *is the SMA-Host models for those hosts in* H*;*
- $T_{i,j}$: R $\rightarrow$ R, i,j $\in$ H. *The time function to calculate the time for transferring information between two hosts.*

SMA-DEVS models behaviors of the mobile agents and their hosts based on the execution model defined by SMA. Under the guideline of establishing the abstract simulators with the DEVS and DSDE model, we can build the simulation model and, further, the simulation environment of mobile agents for its performance evaluation.

5 SimulAgent: A Simulation Environment Prototype

Based on the SMA-DEVS model presented above, we have built a generic simulation environment prototype with the direct execution approach. The prototype called SimulAgent is implemented with JDK 1.4 and the concrete mobile agent system is IBM Aglets 2.0. Although IBM Aglets has a similar execution model as SMA, they are different in some facets. For example, the common Aglet handles the message one by one. Therefore, we modify the Aglets accordingly to make the runtime layer capable of supporting the standard Aglets meanwhile adopting the SMA model during agent's execution. The basic interface is shown in Fig.2.

To verify the function of SimulAgent, we implemented some mobile agent algorithms and tested their performance in SimulAgent. Here we present the experiment of a classical distributed problem-distributed mutual exclusion problem solved by mobile agent. The details of the algorithm can be referred to [5]. The algorithm involves a number of migrations and message exchange, making it a good case to testify our prototype.

We implement the algorithm with SimulAgent's API, and simulate its execution in SimulAgent. The experiment environment is set up with 5 PCs in a fast LAN, the hardware configuration of machine is PIII 900M / 256M / 20GB, the operating system is Windows 2000, and the version of Java VM is JDK1.4. We simulate the execution of the system composed of the nodes whose number ranges from 4 to 40, and make the performance evaluation based on the simulation results. Figure 3 show the diagram of the performance metrics including average time for a node to enter the critical region and average traffic cost for a node.

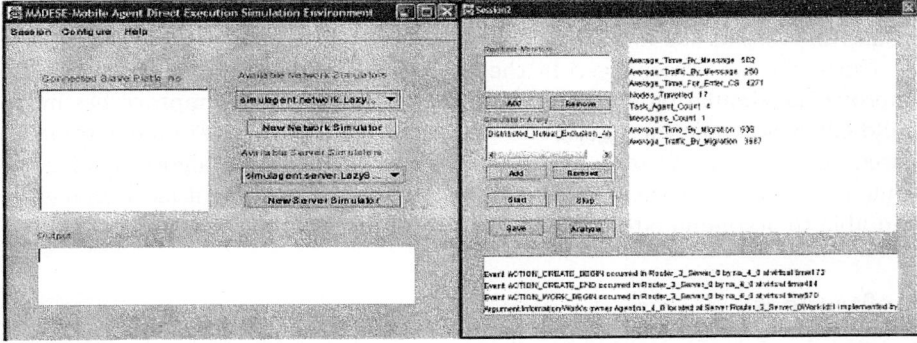

Fig. 2. User interface of SimulAgent

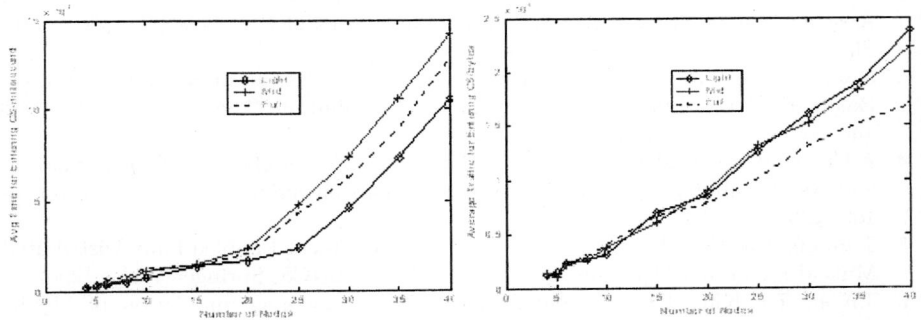

Fig. 3. Simulation results of MA-DME algorithm from SimulAgent

Figure 3 depicts the performance of the algorithm under full load, middle load, and light load respectively. From the analysis of the algorithm in [5] and the following works, we know that the average cost such as the traffic and waiting time in heavy load would be smaller than it is in middle load, which is the major advantage of the algorithm. The simulation results got from SimulAgent explicitly confirmed the proposition.

From the results we got from the experiments, we found that the SimulAgent can correctly simulate the mobile agent algorithms in complicated environment, which proves the validity of the SMA-DEVS model.

6 Conclusion

The lack of a standard execution model for mobile agents make its modelling and simulation ambiguous and thus hinder its performance evaluation. In this paper, we establish a model called SMA to specify mobile agent execution, and then establish a discrete event system model SMA-DEVS for simulating mobile agents based on SMA. A direct execution simulation environment prototype based on

SMA-DEVS is implemented in Java based on IBM Aglets, and the experiment results shows that the models and the simulation environment are valid.

Currently, we are engaged in the work of looking for better approaches to improve the simulation environment. The major aspects to improve lies in: to build efficient simulation model and architecture for the simulation environment based on SMA-DEVS; to design prompt parallel simulation algorithms for the simulator; to improve the structure of the SimulAgent, making it more extensible and able to accommodate different simulation algorithm.

References

1. Ariv Aridor and Mitsuru Oshima. Infrastructure for Mobile Agents: Requirements and Design. In Proc. of MA'98, Springer Verlag, September 1998.
2. F.J.Barros. Dynamic Structure Discrete Event System Specification: Formalism, Abstract Simulators and Applications. Transactions of the Society for Computer Simulation, Vol.13, pp.35-46, 1996.
3. Jiannong Cao, Graeme Bennett, Kang Zhang. Direct Execution Simulation of Load Balancing Algorithms with Real Workload Distribution. The Journal of Systems and Software, Vol.54, pp.227-237, 2000.
4. A.Chow. Parallel DEVS: a Parallel, Hierarchical, Modular Modeling Formalism and Its Distributed Simulator. SCS Transactions on Simulation Vol.13(2), pp.55-102, 1996.
5. Jiannong Cao, Xianbing Wang, Jie Wu, A Mobile Agent Enabled Fully Distributed Mutual Exclusion Algorithm. In Proc. of MA'02, LNCS, Springer-Verlag, 2002.
6. J.Kim, T.G.Kim. DEVS-Based Framework for Modeling/Simulation of Mobile Agent Systems. Simulation Vol.76, No.6, pp.345-357, 2001.
7. Seong-Hwan Kim, Thmas G.Robertazzi. Mobile Agent Modeling. Technical Report, University at Stony Brook, College of Engineering and Applied Science, No. 786, November 2000
8. Xuhui Li, Jiannong Cao, Yanxiang He. A Direct Execution Approach to Simulating Mobile Agent Algorithms. The Journal of Supercomputing, Vol.29, No.2, pp.171-184, 2004.
9. Xuhui Li, Zhiyong Peng, Jiannong Cao. A Practical Approach to Specifying and Verifying Mobile Agent Algorithms. Journal of Pervasive Computing and Communications, Vol.1, No.2, pp.113-121, 2005.
10. Anselm Lingnau, Oswald Drobink. Simulating Mobile Agent Systems with Swarm. In Proc. of First International Symposium on Agent Systems and Applications Third International Symposium on Mobile Agents, October, 1999
11. M.C.Seong, T.G.Kim. Realtime DEVS Simulation: Concurrent, Time-Selective Execution of Combined RT-DEVS Model and Interactive Environment. In Proc. of SCSC-98, pp.410-415, Reno, 1998.
12. Adelinde M. Uhrmacher, Petra Tyschler, Dirk Tyschler. Modeling and Simulation of Mobile Agents. Future Generation Computer Systems, pp. 107-118, 2000.
13. B.P.Zeigler. Theory of Modeling and Simulation. Wiley Interscience, 1976.
14. B.P.Zeigler. Multifaceted Modeling and Discrete Event Simulation. Academic Press, London, 1984.

A Holistic Approach to Survivable Distributed Information System for Critical Applications

H.Q. Wang, D.X. Liu, D. Xu, Y.Y. Lan, X.Y. Li, and Q. Zhao

College of Computer Science and Technology,
Harbin Engineering University, Harbin 150001, China
wanghuiqiang@hrbeu.edu.cn

Abstract. In this paper, a holistic approach to realize survivability of distributed information network systems for critical applications(DISCA) based on three basic states, processed, stored, and transmitted, of information (called a PST-based system model), is proposed and its evaluation method and some experiment results are given as an example of its application. A PST-based system model brings all three parts together and coordinates them through the services supported by them, in which whole system's survivability is embodied by system services and their interdependency relations. With this model, a multi-layer survivability framework based on the information states is formed and the complexity of a DISCA system in implementation and evaluation can be conquered in the most prevalent approach—"divide and conquer" approach.

Keywords: DISCA, Survivability, Evaluation, PST-based model.

1 Introduction

Modern society increasingly depends on distributed network systems to conduct business, government, and defense. Yet Distributed Information System for Critical Applications (DISCA) is the most important one of them because it is widely used in the national defense, military information system and other key departments of the state. Survivability of these systems is very crucial and is receiving increasing attention as a key property of thus critical systems. Survivability is the capability of a system to fulfill its mission in the presence of attacks, failures, or accidents, and recover full service in a timely manner.

Survivability is the sum of the parts of a system, not some of the parts [3], but capturing the survivability of an entire system as a whole unit is a very complex issue in itself [4]. The complexity and size of today distributed systems, with increasing complicated environment, makes developing and demonstrating the system's survivability remain an important and unattained research goal [5]. In this sense, the most prevalent approach—"divide and conquer" approach should be used to conquer a DISCA system complexity. From the information system security model [1] [2], within any system and for any given moment, information is found in one or more of the three states: processed, stored, or transmitted. In a DISCA setting, the processing state is corresponding to system services (functions in the point of users' view) and their support components and configurations; the storage state is corresponding to the data storage being processed and transited by the system, which can be viewed as one of the supports of system services; the transmission state is corresponding to the system communication infrastructure which is in turn viewed as another support of system services. So the whole system's survivability depends on those of all three parts and their interdependencies. Should the solutions to the survivability of each of them be reached and should interdependencies between them be figured out, it is easy for us to approach to a holistic solution to that of the whole system.

The reminder of the paper is organized as follows: Section 2 presents an information state-based system model and each of three parts is described. Section 3 introduces a method of survivability performance evaluations for such system model. Section 4 gives experiments and analyzing results and Section 5 discusses related works. We close with conclusions in Section 6.

2 Architecture Descriptions

2.1 A PST-Based Survivable System Model

An overview of a PST-based system model is shown in Fig. 1 and a PST abstract model in Fig.2. As we have known that within any system and at any given moment, information is found in one or more of the three states: processed, stored, and transmitted. In this context, any computer-based system including DISCA can be considered as composing of triple-components: processing, storage and transmission, each of whom supports a set of services, called P-Services, S-Services and T-Services respectively. A PST-based system model brings them together and coordinates the three components through the services supported by them, in which the whole system's survivability is embodied by P-Services that in turn depend on the survivability of S-services and T-Services. With this model, a multi-layer survivability framework based on information states is formed and a DISCA system complexity can be conquered in the most prevalent approach—"divide and conquer" approach. The design and evaluation of the whole system's survivability are decomposed into three subsystems or three sets of services and the smaller problems can be solved independently. Once the smaller ones are solved, the subsystem solutions can then be integrated into a global one. In our system, the end users can only perceive the P-services, whose survivability is as our final goal over other two sets of services.

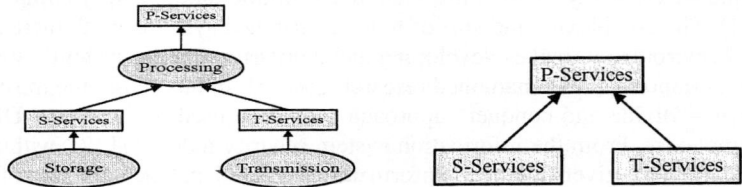

Fig. 1. A PST-based survivable system model   **Fig. 2.** A PST abstract model

We discuss each of their constructs briefly, including ABRAR [6] for P-Services, FDRD [7] for S-Services and FTLAN [8]] for T-Services and motivate them in the following subsections. It is important to recognize that a PST-based system model is designed in a modular fashion, so each of these components can be adopted or discarded according to the survivability requirements of the services being offered. Furthermore, we can integrate other similar modules as they become available.

2.2 P-Services Survivability

It's extremely important for a mission-critical distributed system to ensure the reliable and continuous running through all time, especially in a crisis state. The reasons why a system is failed to run stem probably from two aspects. One is the blow of external strength, such as war destruction, malicious intrusion. The other is the natural damage of some part of functions in the system, such as the hardware malfunction. The former belongs to the survivability of the system, while the later belongs to the reliability of the system. The two problems can come down to the survivability and availability of the system services. And they can be settled by the ABRAR [6] methods offering automatic backup, reconfiguration and recovery of the services.

The design and implementation of a system functional backup, reconfiguration and recovery are mainly related to the associated technical keys: design requirements, backup strategies, detecting mechanism and graded implementation, etc. The design requirements include the reconfiguration and recovery time, the maintenance of essential functions after function backup, the performance and quality assurance and the mastering of recovery opportunity.

There are two basic backup modes known as hardware backup and software backup for backup strategies. The widely adopted mode now is the union of hardware and software backup, that is, using a little proportion of hardware cooperated with appropriate software constructs a system with higher reliability and usability. Furthermore, in generally the probability of simultaneous damage of the key parts in a system is little (if any). So, when there are faults, we can use software to adjust and recombine the hardware and implement dynamically the mutual backup between the key parts or between the non-key parts and the key parts, which is called software-hardware hybrid mode. Here, we name it system function backup.

Understandably, each running step of a system with function backup is showed in Fig.3. Obviously, the key here is having a detecting mechanism with low system overhead and accurate site failure and recovery. Associated with the characters of network communication protocols, we advance four detecting algorithms according

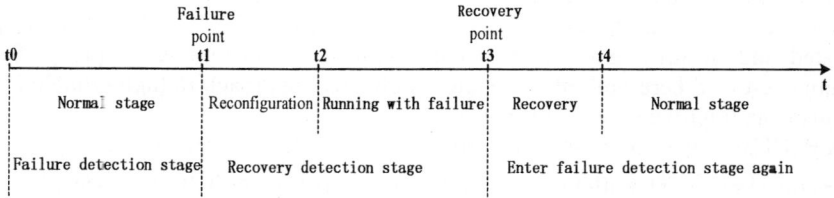

Fig. 3. Each step of the system running

to different communication modes between sites. The former two, Piggyback detection and Timed detection, are used for failure detection and the latter two, Calling/Interception detection and Active report, for recovery detection.

The graded implementation is mainly treated differently according to the service types and key degrees offered by system.

2.3 S-Services Survivability

The survivable S-Services are supported by FDRD [7] system based on concepts of DRD [9]. A survivable storage system would securely store critical information, ensuring that it persists, is continuously accessible, cannot be destroyed, and is kept confidential over time despite of malicious compromises and of storage node subsets [10].

A DRD system is a collection of several disks subsystems that have independent functions and are attached to network servers. It seems as a single server disk subsystem of network servers to NOS.

A DRD system is obviously a multi-server network system. These servers work cooperatively and realize a DRD system together. As a result, the key here is how to clearly tell the two concepts—individual physical servers and the disk accessing services provided by them apart. What the network users and user programs need is to read/write data on a high capacity, survivable and rapid server disk subsystem, and they do not mind the specific styles, number and architectures of servers. Of course, the responses to data r/w (read /write) requests would still be put on a group of physical servers which work cooperatively, and the tasks are performed by all of them together. To an end user, what he can see is only a single network server. We call it a logical server or a virtual server, which is called server transparency: the invisibility or irrelevancy of the server topology, styles and number involved in a given service.

A FDRD (Full DRD) means that each of its station can be used as both a client and a server, and their functions are fully distributed among them. A FDRD system has two technical features: (1) Server and transmission transparency; (2) Distribution transparency.

2.4 T-Services Survivability

The main goal of survivable T-Services is to provide high reliability and connection performance transmission with redundant channels. In our system, P_FTLAN [8] thesis is assumed. A P_FTLAN can be constructed by introducing double off-shelf transmission media and connection components along with carefully designed and dedicated network layer protocols and software. Under normal state of the system, data are transmitted in parallel on the two subnets. When one of two subnets gets failed, the system can be reconstructed automatically by itself and the failed one is isolated and meanwhile the system can continue to run without stopping. So the scheme assumed here not only provides an effective approach to high reliable LANs, but also can improve their performance greatly.

A P_FTLAN has three function modes and functions as following:

→Basic mode→Parallel mode→Failure-switching mode→ Basic mode……

P_FTLAN has yet two technical characters: (1) Protocol transparency; (2) Topology and medium independency.

The three function modes and two technical characters given above are all provided by P_FTLAN's network layer, called Parallel and Fault-Tolerant Network Layer or PFTNL, which is our major work to do and is particularly added to P_FTLAN.

3 Service Survivability Evaluations

To analyze and demonstrate the survivability of the whole system based on services and their interdependency relations, Meadow's theorem on dataset aggregates and service-configuration-component model are adopted [11]. First, some definitions are given. Then, the expressions of survivability with and without redundancy are described. Finally, the evaluation results suggest that the survivability of service with redundancy configurations is higher than that of service without redundancy configurations.

3.1 Definitions

Definition 1 (Service): The functions that can be seen by users. We use S_P, S_S and S_T to express P-Services, S-Services and T-Services.

Definition 2 (Configuration): Sets of components supporting service. We use C_P, C_S and C_T to express Configuration supporting P, Configuration supporting S and Configuration supporting T.

Definition 3 (Component): The combination of hardware and software that can implement some functions in the configurations. We use N_S, N_T to express component S and T.

Definition 4 (Dependency): If some configurations (or components) support some services (or configurations), then the latter depends on the former. The relationship can be expressed by "$\leq$".

Definition 5 (Redundancy): The system G is considered as an undirected graph. So G is a connected undirected graph without loop, i.e. a tree, of which the components are leaf nodes whose degree is 1.

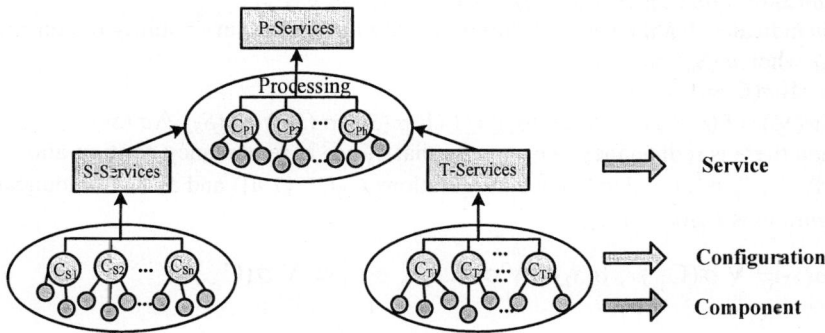

Fig. 4. Service-configuration-component model

3.2 The Expressions of Survivability

The expressions of survivability can be divided into two classes:

1. Non-redundancy configuration

Suppose the configurations and services depended on S respectively are $C_1, C_2 \ldots C_h$ and $S_1, S_2 \ldots S_n$. So, their survivabilities are: $\sigma(C_1), \sigma(C_2), \ldots, \sigma(C_h)$ and $\sigma(S_1), \sigma(S_2) \ldots \sigma(S_n)$. Then the survivability of S is:

$$\sigma(S) = f(\sigma(C_1), \sigma(C_2), \ldots, \sigma(C_h), \sigma(S_1), \sigma(S_2)\ldots\sigma(S_n))$$
$$= \sigma(C_1) \wedge \sigma(C_2) \wedge \ldots \wedge \sigma(C_h) \wedge \sigma(S_1) \wedge \sigma(S2) \wedge \ldots \wedge \sigma(S_n) \quad (1)$$

2. Redundancy configurations

Suppose the configurations and services depended on S respectively have h redundancy configurations $C_k (k \in [1,h])$ and n services $S_j (j \in [1,n])$, in which each service S_j has m redundancy configurations: S_{jci} ($j \in [1,n]$, $i \in [1,m]$). Their survivabilities are $\sigma(C_k)$ ($k \in [1,h]$), $\sigma(S_j)$ ($j \in [1,n]$) and $\sigma(S_{jci})$ ($j \in [1,n]$, $i \in [1,m]$).

So the survivability of S is:

$$\sigma(S) = f(\sigma(C_1), \sigma(C_2), \ldots, \sigma(C_h), \sigma(S_1), \sigma(S2)\ldots\sigma(S_n))$$
$$= (\bigwedge_{k=1}^{h} C_k) \wedge (\bigwedge_{j=1}^{n} \bigvee_{i=1}^{m} S_{jci}) \quad (2)$$

From the example in the figure we can simplify (1) (2) to a general formula.

Because S_P depends on C_P, S_S and S_T, there are some function relations between $\sigma(S_P)$ and $\sigma(C_P), \sigma(S_S), \sigma(S_T)$, that is:

$$\sigma(S_P) = f(\sigma(C_P), \sigma(S_S), \sigma(S_T)) = \sigma(C_P) \wedge \sigma(S_S) \wedge \sigma(S_T)$$

Survivability σ are mapped to probability space, and the values are arbitrary real numbers between [0, 1].

When $\sigma(s) = 0$, the survival probability of s is 0;
When $\sigma(s) = 1$, the survival probability of s is 1.
With a view to facilitate the research, we discuss the problem in two conditions:

1. If $\sigma(S_S) = \sigma(S_T) = 1$

Then $\sigma(S_P) = f(\sigma(C_P), \sigma(S_S), \sigma(S_T)) = f(\sigma(C_P), 1, 1) = \sigma(C_P)$

This indicates that the survivability of S_P only lies on the survivability of configuration C_P when $\sigma(S_S) = \sigma(S_T) = 1$.

2. If $\sigma(C_P) = 1$,

Then $\sigma(S_P) = f(\sigma(C_P), \sigma(S_S), \sigma(S_T)) = f(1, \sigma(S_S), \sigma(S_T)) = \sigma(S_S) \wedge \sigma(S_T)$

When there is redundancy, we suppose that S_S has m redundancy configurations C_{Si} ($i \in [1,m]$), S_T has n redundancy configurations $C_{Tj} (j \in [1,n])$ and S_P has l redundancy configurations $C_{Pk} (k \in [1, l])$

$$\sigma(S_S) = \bigvee_{i=1}^{m} \sigma(C_{S_i}) , \quad \sigma(S_T) = \bigvee_{j=1}^{n} \sigma(C_{T_j}) , \quad \sigma(C_P) = \bigvee_{k=1}^{l} \sigma(C_{P_k}) \circ$$

Then $\sigma(S_P) = f(\sigma(C_P), \sigma(S_S), \sigma(S_T)) = \bigvee_{k=1}^{l} \sigma(C_{P_k}) \wedge \bigvee_{i=1}^{m} \sigma(C_{S_i}) \wedge \bigvee_{j=1}^{n} \sigma(C_{T_j})$

With a view to facilitate the research, we also discuss the problem in two conditions:
1. When $\sigma(S_S)=\sigma(S_T)=1, \sigma(S_P)=\sigma(C_P)= \overset{1}{\underset{k=1}{V}} \sigma(C_{P_k})$;
2. When $\sigma(C_P)=1, \sigma(S_P)= \sigma(S_S) \wedge \sigma(S_T)=[\overset{m}{\underset{i=1}{V}} \sigma(C_{S_i})] \wedge [\overset{n}{\underset{j=1}{V}} \sigma(C_{T_j})]$ 。

3.3 The Survivability Evaluation of Service with Redundancy Configurations

In a unit of time we suppose that service S has n redundancy configurations. and the failure rate of service of each configuration is p_i ($i \in [1, n]$) , $p_i \in [0, 1]$, and $p_1 > p_2 > p_3 > ... > p_n$, in which the minimal one is:

$$P_1 = p_n \text{ and } \because p_i < 1 \quad \therefore P_n = \prod_{i=1}^{n} p_i < p_n = P_1$$

∵ Low failure rate indicates high survivability
∴ The survivability of the service with redundancy configurations is higher than that of the service without redundancy configurations.

1. When $\sigma(S_S) = \sigma(S_T) = 1$,

   Without redundancy: $\sigma(S_P) = \sigma(C_P)$

   With redundancy: $\sigma'(S_P) = \overset{1}{\underset{k=1}{V}} \sigma(C_{P_k})$

   From the proof above, we know: $\sigma(S_P) < \sigma'(S_P)$

2. When $\sigma(C_P) = 1$,

   Without redundancy: $\sigma(S_P) = \sigma(C_{S_i}) \wedge \sigma(C_{T_j})$

   With redundancy: $\sigma'(S_P) = [\overset{m}{\underset{i=1}{V}} \sigma(C_{S_i})] \wedge [\overset{n}{\underset{j=1}{V}} \sigma(C_{T_j})]$

   From the proof above, we know: $\sigma(C_{S_i}) < [\overset{m}{\underset{i=1}{V}} \sigma(C_{S_i})]$

   And $\sigma(C_{T_j}) < [\overset{n}{\underset{j=1}{V}} \sigma(C_{T_j})]$, then $\sigma(S_P) < \sigma'(S_P)$

3. From 1, 2 we know $\sigma(S_P) < \sigma'(S_P)$, that is:

The survivability of the service with redundancy configurations is higher than that of the service without redundancy configurations.

4 Experiments and Numeral Analyzing Results

4.1 Service Survivability

High survivability and availability can be used to characterize a distributed system. To attain this goal, however, many efforts need to be made and many techniques need to be solved. In conjunction with the design and implementation of a distributed C^2 system on warships, we have constructed a simulating system environment. Some concrete technical problems are solved and engineering methods are examined. It is experimentally testified that with the approach presented in this paper, the P-Services of the system can still fully function well even if it loses its devices up to 50 per cent and run without stopping when up to 70 per cent, and meanwhile the degraded system can be automatically recovered in any failed grade, which, therefore, illustrates that our approach presented here is correct, feasible and effective.

4.2 System Availability and Bit Error Rate

1. System availability

The main measures of S-services' survivability are availability and BER, which are analyzed the availability of the system from the point of view on the assumption that the transmission be not failed, that is, $\sigma(S_T)=1$.

Suppose n-servers consist of the multi-severs system, and the k of them are used to store data information, the r of them are used to storage redundancy information ($n=k+r$), this system allows the less or equal of r servers occur disk failure. Suppose B_i is an event, and it denotes that there are I-servers of server system are failed at random time t. Suppose the availability of single sever is A_d, then the availability of system $A_s(t)$ is:

$$A_s(t) = \sum_{i=0}^{r} \binom{n}{i} A_d^{n-i} \cdot (1-A_d)^i = A_d^n + nA_d^{n-1}(1-A_d) + O\left((1-A_d)^2\right)$$

$$= nA_d^{n-1} - (n-1)A_d^n + O\left((1-A_d)^2\right) \quad (3)$$

So, we can conclude the normal formula of computing the availability of system, when $n=3$, $r=1$, suppose that $MTBF=10000$ hours, $MTTR=1$ hour, then

$$A_d = 10000/(10000+1) \approx 99.99\%$$

$$A_s(t) = 3A_d^2 - 2A_d^3 = 99.99999\%$$

2. Bit error rate

Suppose B denotes the event that there is no server failed, C denotes the event that there is only one server failed. Since the failure can be repaired quickly, so we can consider that there are no more than two servers are failed at the same time, and data are not failed in the course of transmission. Thus event B and C accord with following probability relation:

$$P(C)=1-P(B) \quad (4)$$

Suppose A is the event that there are error codes when reading data, there are $n-r$ bits in n bits according with the definition and the format of conditional probability, averagely the probability of every bit is:

$$P_r = P(A)/(n-r) = (P(AB)+P(AC))/(n-r)$$
$$= (P(B) \cdot P(A|B) + P(C) \cdot P(A|C))/(n-r) \quad (5)$$

And suppose that the probability of making a mistake when servers read data is P_e, we can conclude that:

$$P_r = \frac{1}{n-1}(A_s(t) \cdot P(A|B) + (1 - A_s(t)) \cdot P(A|C)) \qquad (6)$$

In addition n=3, r=1, $A_d = 99.99\%$, $P_e = 10^{-9}$, then $P_r \approx 1.26 \times 10^{-16}$.

4.3 Transmission Reliability and Performance

4.3.1 Reliability Analysis
Suppose our network transmission system adopts multi-links redundancy, namely there are more than two passageways between every two nodes (such as double-subnets-interconnected LAN or double-bridged LAN), parallel running and redundancy passageways standby mutually. Failure mode is divided into two cases: maintainable failure and un-maintainable failure.

1. Un-maintainable failure analyses

For the architecture of n shunt-wound multi-links redundancy, suppose the reliability of each link is $R_1, R_2, \cdots, R_N$, the failure of each link is independent. Suppose the probability of the failure of each link is $\lambda_i (i = 1, 2, \cdots, N)$, and R_i is the exponential function of λ_i. So when N=2, if $\lambda_1 = \lambda_2 = \lambda$, then $m_p = 3/2\lambda$

So we can see that MTTF prolongs 1.5 times contrast with N=1.
Normally, if $\lambda_1 = \lambda_2 = \cdots \lambda_N = \lambda$, then MTTF is

$$m_p = 1/\lambda + 1/2\lambda + \cdots + 1/N\lambda \qquad (7)$$

So, the influence of increasing the number of parallel connections is not obvious.

2. Maintainable failure analyses

To be convenient, we assume the model of a parallel connection system with double-links. Suppose the probability of the maintainable failure of each link is μ. Since the reliability of the maintainable failure of the parallel connection system is $3/2\lambda$ and $\mu/2\lambda^2$ is the reliability of the increased part that comes from the system that is maintained. The distribution of the un-maintainable failure and the maintainable failure is based on the probability, then suppose them as p_1, p_2 ($p_1 + p_2 = 1$), the reliability of the double links is:

$$m'_p = p_1 \cdot (3/2\lambda) + p_2 \cdot (3/2\lambda + u/2\lambda^2) = 3/2\lambda + p_2 \cdot u/2\lambda^2 \qquad (8)$$

4.3.2 Total Performance Analysis
From M/D/1 model we can get the average diagram's time delay of the network as follows:

$$T = (1/uc_1) + (1/2uc_2(1-\rho)) \qquad (9)$$

Where $1/U$ is a frame's length, C_1 is media rate, C_2 is the network channel capacity, ρ is the channel intensity.

In equation (9) the first item is a datagram's transmission time.

In P_FTLAN, the introduced two subnets do not change either of the media's communication rate, so the first item's value is equal to the single networks. Now we analyze the second item, which is a datagram's average waiting time and the time value to evaluate network's collisions. In the case of the system with two identical communication subnetworks, and the network's total channel capacity C_2 will be doubled. Keep ρ constant we can make file's average waiting time reduce 50%, and from following equation shown in equation (10), when ρ is constant, N will also be doubled because of C_2's doubling.

$$\rho = N/uc_2 \qquad (10)$$

N is the average number of the arrived files.

According to the above description, in the dual subnet system we could not only double the average arrived file number but also reduce the average file waiting time by 50%, which will in turn make the possibility of the network collision reduce 50%.

4.3.3 The Analysis of Individual Station Communication Rate

We define that Parallel Degree H is the ratio between the time of two NIC simultaneously sending data and the whole period, where the period is the time from the moment the system begins to send any two diagrams through the dual subnetworks to the moment when system begins to send next two datagrams, shown in Fig. 5, so

$$H = t_p/(t_p + 3t_s) \qquad (11)$$

Where t_s is the switching time between the two subnetworks, whose size depends on memory operation time (fetching time refreshing time) once and times for each datagram.

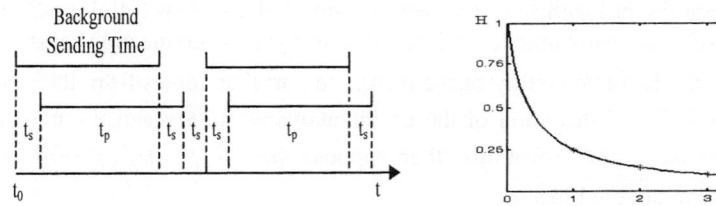

Fig. 5. Time-space diagram for parallel communication   **Fig. 6.** The relation of H and t_s/t_p

The relation of H and t_s/t_p is given in Fig. 6. Generally, the network transmission rates are among 10 Mb/s, 100Mb/s or 1000 Mb/s, and we get the system's Parallel Degree H is between 0.7 and 0.5. So the parallel communication rate is between 1.7 and 1.5 times of that of the single network.

5 Related Works

Our early work related to the proposed approach can be found in [6] [7] [8] [9]. Other related work includes studying the survivability of storage systems [10], services [12] and networks [13] separately. General network information system survivability at a high level has been studied extensively, e.g. in [14], [15], [13], [16], [17]. Conceptually, however, survivability covers a wide spectrum of issues at many different levels of abstraction [19] and applications [18]. So some researches are more directly related to multi-layered surviving systems. In [20], Critical applications are referred to as critical infrastructure applications and their depended underlying information systems as critical information systems, but only the survivability of information system is dealt with. Services survivability and network survivability are considered differently in [4] and the former is sometimes called system survivability or disaster avoidance.

Multi-layered strategy has traditionally been used to implement fault tolerance, or security, or both of them, but different multi-layered techniques have also been used to increase a whole system's survivability. For example, a multi-layer framework is used as a unified approach to both address the survivability of a fragile infrastructure and defend against malicious attacks [3]. In the general case three layers are defined: (1) application layer; (2) traffic layer; and (3) physical layer. The emphasis of their research is to provide survivability to networked systems by developing a coherent and integrated approach across the three layers of the network model and implement into the coordination of different restoration techniques. Multi-Layered Network Survivability Models [13] provide similar three layers: the top ('application/service') layer, the middle layer ('switched network layer'), the bottom ('physical') layer. In this work, the emphasis is to address survivability to network design and management procedures towards minimizing the impact of failures on multi-networks.

However, to the best of our knowledge there is still no project having explored the use of information-states-based techniques in survivability. We believe our ideas of putting this philosophy at work are truly unprecedented.

6 Conclusions and Future Work

Survivability is very important, but a composed and complex issue both in realization and evaluation. This paper has presented a holistic approach to realize and evaluate survivability for a DISCA system. The triple-states model makes the system's architecture more clarity and less complexity. The services-oriented survivability strategy makes system implementation flexible and feasible and provides us with an easier method to demonstrate survivability and other performances quantifiably.

Our future work is to make the approach more autonomic, that is, to pursuit Autonomic Survivability using the philosophy of Autonomic Computing [21], and an integrated and composed measure model to unify survivability, performance, reliability and security evaluation of a system also needs to be developed.

References

1. McCumber, John: Information Systems Security: A Comprehensive Model. Proceedings 14th National Computer Security Conference. National Institute of Standards and Technology, Baltimore, MD. (1991) 328-337
2. Maconachy Victor, Corey Schou, Daniel Ragsdale, etc.: "A Model for Information Assurance: An Integrated Approach". Proc. of the 2001 IEEE Workshop on Information Assurance and Security. U.S. Military Academy, West Point, N.Y. (2001) 306-310
3. William Yurcik , David Doss: A Survivability-Over-Security (SOS) Approach to Holistic Cyber-Ecosystem Assurance. Proc. of the 2002 IEEE Workshop on Information Assurance United States Military Academy. West Point, N.Y. (2002)
4. S. V. Kartalopoulos: Surviving a Disaster. IEEE Comm. Mag. (2002).6:124-126
5. J. Voas, G. McGraw, A. Ghosh: Reducing uncertainty about survivability. In Proceedings of the 1997 Information Survivability Workshop (1997)
6. Wang, HQ: An Approach to Designing and Implementing Function Back-up, Reconfiguration and Recovery for Distributed Fir Control System on Warship. Fire Control & Command Control(in Chinese), 21(2),(1996) 64-68
7. Wang, HQ: Research on a Full Distributed Redundant Disk System. Proc. of 1997 IEEE ICIPS. Beijing (1997)
8. Wang, HQ: A Parallel and Fault-tolerant LAN with Dual Communication Subnetworks. Proc. of pAs'97,(Fukushima/JAPAN) , IEEE Comp. Soc. Press (1997)
9. Wang, HQ: Distributed Redundant Disks: A new Approach to Reliably Sharing Network-based Storage System. System Eng'r and Electronics (in Chinese) 19(4),(1997) 58-61
10. J. Wylie, M. Bigrigg, J. Strunk, etc.: Survivable Information Storage Systems. IEEE Computer. 33(8), (2000) 61-68
11. JK Millen June. Survivability Measure. www.csl.sri.com/users/millen/papers/ measure.ps (2000)
12. A. D. Keromytis, J. Parekh, P. N. Gross, etc.: A Holistic Approach to Service Survivability. In: Proc. of the ACM Survivable and Self-Regenerative Systems Workshop (2003) 11-22
13. D. Medhi , D. Tipper: Multi-Layered Network Survivability – Models, Analysis, Architecture, Framework and Implementation–An Overview. Proc. of DISCEX'2000. IEEE Computer Society Press, Hilton Head, SC (2000)
14. T. Bowen, D. Chee, M. Segal, etc.: Building Survivable Systems: An Integrated Approach Based on Intrusion Detection and Damage Containment. Proc. Of DISCEX'OO. Vol. 2, Hilton Head Island, South Carolina (2000) 84-99
15. E. Ellison, L. Linger, M. Longstaff: Survivable Network Systems: An Emerging Discipline. Technical Report CMU/SEI-97-TR-013, Carnegie Mellon University, Pittsburgh (1997)
16. D. Fisher: Emergent Algorithms: A New Method for Enhancing Survivability in Unbounded Systems. IEEE Proceedings of the Hawaii International Conference on Systems Sciences. IEEE Computer Society Press, New York (1999)
17. J. Knight, R. Lubinsky, J. McHugh,etc.: Architectural Approaches to Information Survivability. Technical Report: CS-97-25, University of Virginia ,Charlottsville (1997)
18. J. Knight, etc.: Topics in Survivable Systems. Computer Science Report. No. CS-98-22, University of Virginia (1998)
19. P. Neumann: Practical Architectures for Survivable Systems and Networks, (Phase-Two Final Report). Computer Science Laboratory, SRI International (2000)
20. J. C. Knight, K. J. Sullivan, M. C. Elder, etc.: Survivability Architectures: Issues and Approaches. DISCEX 2000. Hilton Head, South Carolina, Vol. 2, (2000) 1157-1171
21. A. G. Ganek , T. A. Corbi: The dawning of the autonomic computing. IBM SYSTEMS JOURNAL. 42(1), (2003) 5-18

A Personalized and Scalable Service Broker for the Global Computing Environment

Kyung-Lang Park[1], Chang-Soon Kim[1], Oh-Young Kwon[2],
Hyoung-Woo Park[3], and Shin-Dug Kim[1]

[1] Department of Computer Science, Yonsei University,
134 Shinchon-Dong, Seodaemun-Ku, Seoul 120-749, Korea
{lanx, flsoon, sdkim}@yonsei.ac.kr
[2] Dept. of Computer Engineering, Korea University of Technology and Education,
P.O. BOX 55, Chonan, 330-600, Korea
oykwon@kut.ac.kr
[3] Korea Institute of Science and Technology Information,
P.O. BOX 122, Yusong, Taejun, 305-806, Korea
hwpark@kisti.re.kr

Abstract. Service broker is a software component that maps user's request to proper services. By using the broker, users can access various services without any knowledge of the services. However, design of the service broker for GCE (Global Computing Environment) is quite difficult because a broker cannot cope with all the information of services which are spread over the world. Thus, we need to build new architectural foundations for global service brokering. In this paper, we propose a scalable broker system for GCE based on the federation of personalized brokers. In our broker system, every user can have a service broker. The broker maintains the information of services related to the user and exchanges the information with neighboring brokers if necessary. As a result, the broker can provide proper services to users faster and a burden of brokers can also be decreased. Experimental results show that the proposed service broker can reduce the average service discovery time and the average operation overhead of each broker comparing to other brokering architectures.

1 Introduction

Today's computing infrastructure is gradually being integrated and abstracted. All functions, data, and many types of resources are interconnected physically and logically, and they tend to be represented in a uniform interface, named *services*. Thus, users can access many different kinds of distributed services via this uniform interface. Software architects have made efforts to design such a global infrastructure and suggested several standards on services and architectures [8, 12, 14]. However, design of the service broker for global computing environments (GCE) is quite difficult because a broker cannot cope with all the information of services which are spread over the world. It is generally assumed that there are a huge number of services in GCE. Thus, the broker should be designed to operate properly without any performance degradation even if the number of services increases rapidly. In addition, GCE should consider various types of users, so that the service broker should be able to reflect their preference for providing services more efficiently. Recently, numerous brokers have been developed, but there is no one that suits for global service brokering. Most systems are still based on the centralized architecture [2, 4, 10]. However, this centralized approach cannot reflect personal preference and also the system performance is not guaranteed when the number of services increases. Some advanced systems use multi-brokering mechanism with peer-to-peer architecture [1, 3, 5]. The peer-to-peer architecture considers the scalability, but it is not sufficient for designing the broker for GCE. There are many other issues that should be addressed to make a scalable and personalized broker system.

In this paper, we propose a PnS (Personalized and Scalable) broker system for GCE. Our architecture is based on peer-to-peer and supplements some features to make the broker more efficient. Each broker maintains a real-time data structure named PSR (Personal Service Registry) which contains a portion of service interfaces related to the user. Thus, the user can quickly discover any particular service or services related to the user and annotate useful information about services. Also, brokers can maintain relationships among neighboring brokers and neighbors can exchange information in the PSR. It can also support fast discovery of services. Experimental results show that the proposed broker system can reduce discovery time up to 50% and reduce the overhead of broker up to 30% comparing to general peer-to-peer systems. Rest of the paper is organized as follows: In Section 2, we introduce background of the research and related works. Section 3 describes the proposed broker system in detail and Section 4 demonstrates the effectiveness of our system. Finally, we conclude in Section 5.

2 Background

In this section, we frame the global brokering problem into several pieces and some related work will be discussed.

2.1 Global Brokering Problem

First of all, well-defined brokering architecture is required to solve the global brokering problem. Brokering architecture for the GCE can be categorized in three types. The first one is global broker approach. As shown in Figure 1-(a), all services are registered to a central broker and it handles all requests from users. Because of its simplicity, many brokers are based on this architecture. However, it is not applicable to the GCE because of its inherited inscalability. The second one is broker federation approach. Several brokers join together to perform a role of a global broker. In this approach, the user sends a request to an accessible broker and the broker returns a service interface by cooperating with other brokers. This approach is separated into hierarchical architecture and peer-to-peer architecture as shown in Figure 1-(b) and 1-(c). In the hierarchical architecture, services are registered to lower-level brokers and lower-level brokers are registered to higher-level brokers. Thus, users only need to know some higher-level brokers. It is comparatively scalable and requires reasonable maintenance cost. However, it is rather static and sensitive to faults. In peer-to-peer architecture, all brokers are composed as a network by communicating to each other at equal positional level. Thus, users only need to know one broker to access any broker in the network. It is dynamic and applicable to very large system, but the algorithm can be complex, requiring high network utilization. Considering the scale and characteristics of GCE, peer-to-peer approach is very plausible. The last one is user-centric approach. It is similar to broker federation approach with peer-to-peer architecture. But, in this approach, every user has own broker and the broker can maintain user's preference and history. Thus it acts like a personal agent, whereas other approaches treat brokers as the manager of a system.

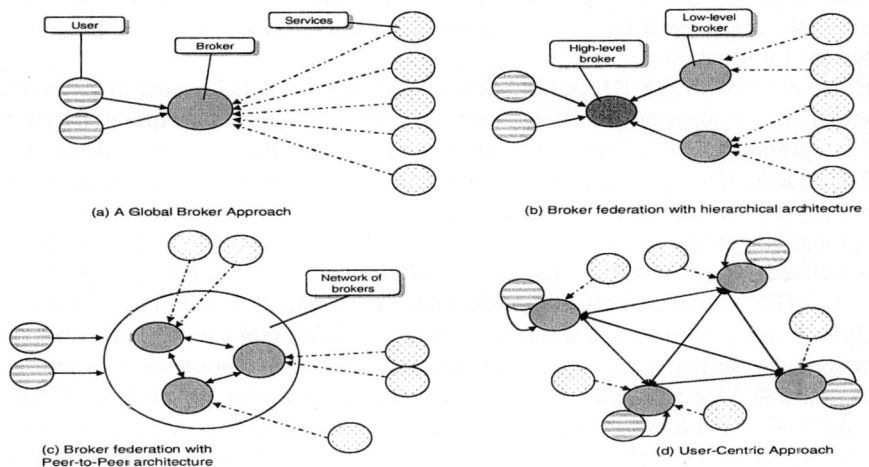

Fig. 1. Various architectures for global brokering

Next problem is how brokers aggregate information of services. The fundamental solution is that services are registered to pre-defined broker(s) and they update soft-state information periodically. Specifically, brokers maintain index and data structures to store the information of services. Such index and data structures may affect the performance in discovering services significantly. UDDI (Universal Description, Discovery and Integration) suggest well-defined data structures to store the information of services [6].

The last one is the service discovery. Assuming the broker has sufficient information of services, the next step is to find proper services corresponding to the user's request. It can be divided into two procedures, i.e., matchmaking and service selection. Matchmaking is the procedure that the broker can determine whether the service satisfies user's request or not. There can be more than one matched services in many cases. If so, we must choose efficient one among them, which is service selection procedure.

2.2 Related Work

There are a number of researches that attempt to address the global brokering problem or to introduce advanced service brokering architecture. Many researchers of Grid and

Web Services have been interested in the global brokering problem. Early researches focus on finding efficient resources and services. They provide efficient services or resource discovery methods with an assumption that information services provide all the necessary information to the broker system. However, as mentioned before, information gathering and maintenance are also important parts of brokering problem. Efficient brokering algorithms can be worthless according to the performance of information service. Thus, these kinds of researches always have to accompany with the research of the scaling information service. S. Venugopal et al. provides a well-defined brokering architecture and an efficient discovery algorithm [11]. However, it is basically based on a centralized architecture and assumes that GIS provides all necessary information.

Emergency of OGSA (Open Grid Service Architecture) [12] results in the convergence of Grid computing and Web services. UDDI (Universal Description, Discovery and Integration) [6] is a standard Web Services registry having service descriptions and interfaces. It provides a well-defined index structure for finding a certain service. However, it is fundamentally a centralized architecture, so that it is hard to apply it to the global computing infrastructure. Also, it does not offer dynamic data model and personalized information. Several researches attempt to supplement additional features to UDDI to make an efficient brokering architecture. S. Miles et al. introduces a method to use personalized metadata, their UDDI-M system can associate metadata with services, so that users can utilize several useful information such as price for accessing a service and reliability of the service by retrieving metadata in UDDI-M [2]. Also, K. Sycara et al. introduce usefulness of semantic information in service discovery. These researches partially suggest personalized brokering architecture, but do not get out of the centralized nature, so that it does not exploit scalability.

InfoSlueth [1] is also an agent-based brokering system. Like Condor system, brokering in InfoSlueth is a matchmaking process. It provides a service ontology for users and service providers to make subscriptions and advertisements easily. Additionally, it addresses many issues of the service broker such as collaboration of multi-brokering, management of brokers, and maintaining connectivity. As a consequence, it provides a scalable service brokering mechanism. However, it rather overlooks performance improvement by exploiting personalization and locality caused by user's pattern and preference. Also, it does not seem to consider the global infrastructure. Thus the concept of brokering is needed to be modified partially. In addition to above projects and systems, there are several research papers focused on global brokering and service discovery. Recently, most of them are based on peer-to-peer architecture rather than centralized and hierarchical architecture to exploit scalability [1, 2, 4, 12]. They supplement the peer-to-peer architecture to improve performance, to reduce overhead, and to reflect personal preferences and requirements. Our research holds the same view with those approaches.

3 Personalized and Scalable Service Broker System

Service broker needed to be designed as scalable and personalized in order to be applicable to the GCE, and both characteristics are our design objectives. In this section, the proposed PnS broker system is described in detail.

3.1 Architecture Overview

Our broker system is built on peer-to-peer architecture because of its scalable nature. Also, several features are considered to exploit both scalability and personalization. In our broker system, every broker stores a portion of interfaces into its memory. We call this portion as the *tablet* of services and the memory as the *PSR* (Personal Service Registry) of the broker. Whole interface are stored in a file system which is called the *repository*. Brokers have a list of brokers which it can communicate with. These communicable brokers are defined as neighbors. The system consists of three kinds of participants, namely brokers, services, and users. Every user has his broker to help the user to discover and use services. Brokering is performed by following six operations among these participants.

The first one is *registration*. A service has to be registered to at least one broker. At the first, the whole interface of the service is transferred to the broker. Then, the broker makes the tablet of the interface and stores it into its PSR. The original interface is stored in the repository. Once the service is registered to the broker, only the changed information is updated to the broker periodically. The second one is *exchange*. This operation is only allowed between neighbors. Every broker has a neighbor list. A broker sends updates of the PSR to the neighbors and also receives neighbor's updates. The next is *request*. A user can send a request to his broker. The request includes the name of service and some conditions to discover proper services. The fourth one is *discovery* operation which means a broker obtains the interface of services. When the broker receives user's request, it searches the PSR and reads the interface in its repository or receives the interface from one of its neighbors. If the discovery is failed, the broker performs the flooding operation. The fifth one is *flooding* operation which is a well-known discovery method used in peer-to-peer systems. If the broker fails to find a proper service on its PSR, the broker broadcasts the request to its neighbors. The message is passed on along the neighbors and the interface of service is returned to the broker if an appropriate service is found [8]. The last one is *invocation*. Once the broker obtains an interface of the service, the user can invoke the service or the broker can invoke the service and the result is returned to the user.

Based on these six operations, users can find and use services efficiently. The conceptual architecture of PnS broker system is shown in Figure 2. User *C0* has a broker named *B0* and all his requests are sent to B0. Similarly, *C1, C2, C3, C4, C5*, and *C6* are the owners of the brokers *B1, B2, B3, B4, B5*, and *B6* respectively. The broker *B0* has the interface of *S0* in the repository and the tablet of *S0* in the PSR because *S0* is registered to *B0*. Thus, *B0* can return the interface of *S0* immediately when the user *C0* requests *S0*. Also, the brokers *B1, B2, B3*, and *B4* are neighbors of *B0*. Thus, the broker *B0* can exchange information in its PSR with those brokers periodically. Since the *B0* exchanges the information in its PSR with the neighbors, *B0* has information of services which are not registered to *B0* directly. Assume that a user want to use the service *S3*. The broker can find S3 in its PSR because *B0* exchanges the PSR with *B2* to which *S3* is registered. Then, *B0* can send a discovery message to *B2* and receive the interface of *S3*. If the broker cannot find the service in the PSR, it means that the broker and even its neighbor do not have the information of the services. Therefore, the broker has to perform the flooding operation to find the service. For example, *B0* can find the *S8* only by the flooding operation.

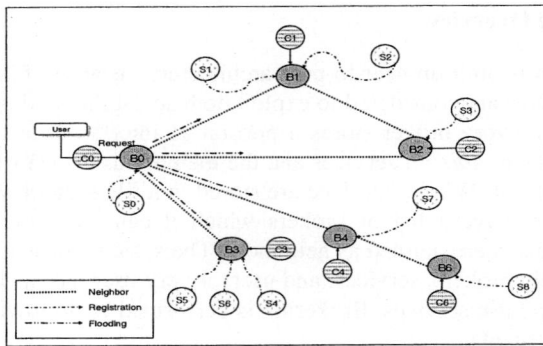

Fig. 2. The architecture of PnS broker system

3.2 Information Management

In this section, we describe how an individual broker maintains the information of services and how brokers exchange the information to each other. Such information management is highly associated with performance and scalability of the broker system. Each PnS broker maintains a PSR and a repository to manage the information of services efficiently. The PSR is a real-time volatile memory space in the broker and the repository is non-volatile large memory space out of the broker. Figure 3 shows the structures of the PSR and the repository. The PSR consists of a list of the broker's neighbors and a list of tablets. The neighbor list includes the broker itself and its all neighbors. An element of the neighbor list includes the name of the broker and its contact point. When the broker wants to connect a certain neighbor broker, it uses the contact point in the neighbor list. As mentioned before, a tablet is a part of each service interface. It includes a service name, an interface name, and several conditions for the broker to discover a certain service. Because it only includes a small portion of the service interface, the broker can ensure whether the appropriate services exist or not very quickly by scanning the list of tablets in the PSR. Additionally, the user can annotate useful information to each tablet. A tablet for a particular service interface contains more useful information for several purposes such as personal preference and privacy. For example, assume that a service is always overburdened at 2 P.M. This information cannot be treated in service interfaces, but a user can add this information to the tablet of the service in his broker. Thus, it can be used in the discovery stage.

The tablet list includes not only the services that are registered to the broker, but also the services that are registered to its neighbors because brokers exchange its information in PSR to each other. Thus, when the broker scans the list from the head of the list to the end, it can find any service that is registered to both itself and its neighbors. Also, the neighbor list and the tablet list are correlated. Each tablet has a pointer to a neighbor, which means that the service corresponding to the tablet is registered to the pointed neighbor. Thus, when the broker finds a proper tablet corresponding to the service that the user wants, it will come to know what broker has the interface of the service. The repository is a simple file system which contains full interfaces of services. After the broker finds the service on the PSR, the broker retrieves an interface of the service from the repository.

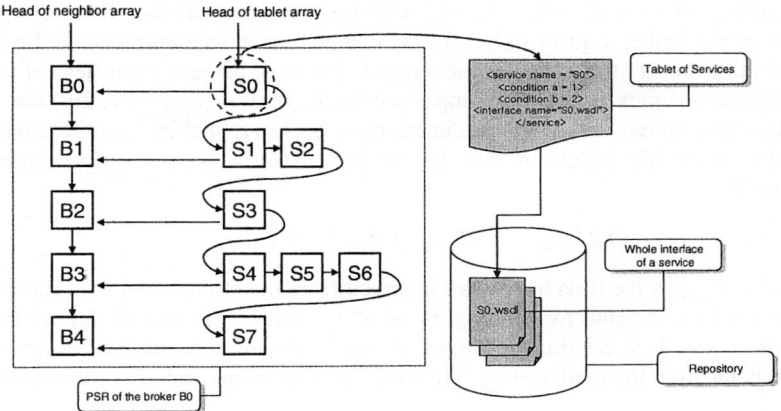

Fig. 3. Data structures in a PnS broker

4 Experimental Result

In this section, we analyze the performance of the proposed broker system and describe several experimental results. We focus on two metrics, average service discovery time (ASD) and operation overhead per broker (OPB). In Section 5.1, we analyze these metrics in the PnS broker system. In Section 5.2, we simulate a large-scale system which comprises thousands of brokers and thousands of service providers and compare ASD and OPB of the PnS broker system to other brokering architectures.

4.1 Performance Analysis of the PnS Broker

The average service discovery time is expressed as equation (1):

$$ASD = \frac{\sum_{i}^{n_r} T_{Di}}{n_r}, \qquad (1)$$

where T_{Di} is the service discovery time for request i, and the number of requests is nr. Here, the service discovery time can be separated into the time to scan a certain service in some index structure like the PSR in PnS brokers and the time to retrieve an interface from some storage like the repository. Thus, T_D can be expressed as equation (2):

$$T_D = T_{SCAN} + T_{RETRIEVE} \qquad (2)$$

T_{SCAN} also can be expanded as equation (3):

$$T_{SCAN} = n \times T_{UNIT-SCAN} + 2 \times L(1), \qquad (3)$$

where the n is the number of elements for a given index structure, $T_{UNIT-SCAN}$ is the time to scan one element of the index, and $L(m)$ is message transfer function. to the load m size of message. In equation (3), $2 \times L(1)$ represents the time to send a query for scanning index and to receive the response showing whether the index has the service or not. Either a query or a response can be treated as a unit load. If the index is located in the broker that receives the request, $L(m)$ can be zero regardless of m. Thus, the location of index is the most important factor in T_{SCAN}. Specifically, the time to scan the index stored in the memory in the main broker is shorter than the time to scan the index in the file system in the other brokers. Also, $T_{RETRIEVE}$ can be expressed as equation (4):

$$T_{RETRIEVE} = T_{READ} + L(1) + L(s), \qquad (4)$$

where the T_{READ} is the time to read an interface from the storage and $L(1)$ represent the time to send a command for sending the interface and $L(s)$ is time to deliver the interface whose size is s. Sending a command and delivering the interface occur only the storage is far from the main broker. Therefore, T_D can be expanded as the equation (5):

$$T_D = n \times T_{UNIT-SCAN} + T_{READ} + 3 \times L(1) + L(s), \qquad (5)$$

We can apply the equation (5) to several brokering architectures. For example, suppose that a centralized system with a well-defined index in its memory stores the interfaces in a file system. Then discovery time can be equation (6) because both $L(1)$ and $L(s)$ are zero:

$$T_D = n \times t_{index\_memory} + t_{int\,erface\_file}, \qquad (6)$$

where t_{index_memory} is time to scan one index from memory and $t_{interface\_file}$ is time to read one interface from the files system. Thus, it is natural that developers focus on building an efficient index structure and scanning algorithms to reduce t_{index_memory}. However, it cannot be applicable in the global system as we mentioned before because the number of services is extremely large and all services are registered to the centralized broker. In this case, n will be too large for the broker to store the entire index in its real time memory. Otherwise, general peer-to-peer architecture can reduce n, the number of elements for an index structure. T_D can be modified as equation (7) in peer-to-peer architecture:

$$T_D = n_p \times t_{index\_memory} + t_{int\,erface\_file} + 3 \times L(1) + L(s), \qquad (7)$$

where n_p is the number of elements in an index structure in a peer. Because n_p is relatively small, T_D is dominated not by t_{index_memory}, but by $L(s)$, i.e., the message transfer function. Therefore, developers of peer-to-peer architecture do not focus on the index structure, but on the selection of proper peer to reduce $L(1)$ and $L(s)$. Now, we will expand the equation (5) to be applied in PnS broker system. According to the architecture of the PnS broker system, the interface can be stored in the main broker, neighbors, or other brokers. Let p_{main} be the probability of the case that the interface is located in the main broker and $p_{neighbor}$ be the probability of the case the interface is located in a neighbor. Also, p_{repeat} is the probability of the case that the original interface is stored in a neighbor of main broker, but the main broker retrieved the interface and still holds the interface in his repository. Also, p_{repeat} is a subset of $p_{neighbor}$. The main broker can maintain the interface to be valid by exchanging operations. Then, the equation (5) can be expanded as equation (8):

$$T_D = n_{pns} \times t_{cache} + (1 - p_{main} - p_{neighbor})(n_{pns} \times t_{cache} + 2 \times L(1))$$
$$+ t_{interface\_file} + (1 - p_{main} - p_{repeat})(L(1) + L(s)),\quad (8)$$

Because the PSR includes the information of neighbors, n_{pns} is larger than n_p, so that T_D of PnS broker can be higher than other architectures represented as equation (6) and (7). However, t_{PSR} is extremely smaller than other operations such as $t_{interface\_file}$ and the message transmissions $L(s)$, and such operations occurs with lower probabilities, so that the average service discovery time of the PnS broker system can be lower than others. Table 3 shows the several operation times of PnS broker. To measure the operation times, we run a couple of PnS brokers on Pentium 4 machines in our campus and use 6KB WSDL file as an interface. t_{PSR} is extremely small and $n_{pns} \times t_{PSR}$ is not more than 10ms even though the PSR has 500 tablets.

Now, let us consider OPB (Operation overhead Per Broker). It can be expressed as equation (9):

$$OPB = \frac{\sum_{i}^{n_b} O_{bi}}{n_b}, \quad (9)$$

where O_{bi} is the operation overhead of ith broker, and nb is the number of brokers. OB means the number of operations that a broker has to do for a given period. It includes many kinds of operations that we introduced in Section 3 such as service registration, service request, service discovery, and exchange. Therefore, O_b can be expressed as equation (10):

$$O_b = O_{REGISTRATION} + O_{REQUEST} + O_{EXCHANGE} + O_{DISCOVERY}, \quad (10)$$

We assume all other operations have a unit operation overhead except the $O_{DISCOVERY}$. In the discovery operation, sub-operations such as scanning PSR and reading a file are considered as a unit operation overhead. Namely, when a service is registered to a broker, the Ob of the broker is increased by one, and when a broker performs service discovery operation, the Ob of the broker is increased by the number of sub-operations. In equation (9), $O_{REGSTRATION}$ is directly proportional to the ratio of services per a broker and $O_{REQUEST}$ is also directly proportional to the ratio of requests per broker. Thus, the centralized broker systems cannot cope with $O_{REGSTRATION}$ and $O_{REQUEST}$ when the numbers of services and requests are large, whereas the other brokering system based on the peer-to-peer does not suffer from the overhead because the brokers share the overhead with other peers. $O_{EXCHANGE}$ only exists in the PnS broker system, which is related to the number of neighbors. Therefore, we cannot increase the number of neighbors thoughtlessly to improve the T_D. $O_{EXCHANGE}$ can increase the OPB of PnS broker system, but $O_{DISCOVERY}$ of PnS broker system is smaller than that of peer-to-peer architectures because the flooding operation is used only in restrictive situation. Thus OPB of PnS is less than that of peer-to-peer architecture. Next section describes ASD and OPB in detail with several experimental results.

4.2 Simulation-Based Experiments

Based on the analysis described in the previous section, we also perform several simulation-based experiments to evaluate the performance of PnS broker system. Our objective is to simulate behaviors of the PnS broker system over Internet-like wide area network environments. To achieve this goal, we generate a physical network topology of 1000 nodes by using BRITE topology generation software [11]. We assume links have constant latency and infinite capacity. Next, we generate PnS brokers and services, map them with the nodes in the generated topology, and make relations between brokers and services. Then, configuration of an environment is finished. Finally, we generate scenarios which consist of requests for services and run them on the generated environment. All generations are performed randomly. We repeat experiments with changing the environment enough to guarantee the confidence. Namely, we regenerate brokers, services, and their relations and repeat the same experiment to obtain a mean value for the experiment. As we mentioned before, evaluation metrics are ASD and OPB. With changing parameters such as the number of brokers and the number of services, we observe ASD and OPB and compare them to those of other architectures. First of all, to show the scaling properties of PnS broker system, we fix other parameters as constants while varying the number of services from 10 to 10000. Figure 5 shows the ASDs and OPBs when the number of brokers is 100 and the number of neighbor for each broker is 10. Four bars in each histogram show four brokering architectures, i.e., centralized architecture, peer-to-peer architecture, peer-to-peer architecture with no index, and the proposed PnS broker system. Centralized architecture shows the best ASD if it can load and scan 10,000 elements of index on the memory efficiently. However, the centralized architecture cannot be used as a global brokering system because OPB is too high. Also, peer-to-peer with no index architecture cannot be used in the global system because the increase of services results in high scanning time.

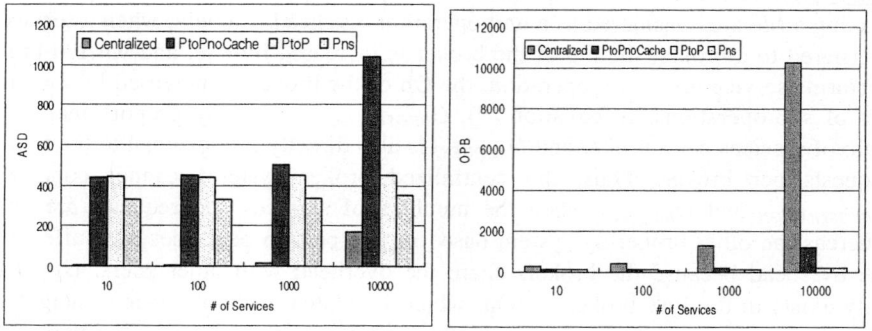

Fig. 4. Average service discovery time and operation overhead per broker (the number of broker is 100 and the number of neighbors is 10)

Figure 4 also shows the rapid rise of ASD and OPB of peer-to-peer with no index architecture when the number of services is close to 10,000. Peer-to-peer architecture relatively reveals scaling properties. Both of ASD and OPB of peer-to-peer architecture are stable and not degraded even if the number of services increases to 10,000. However, the ASD and OPB are still high, which can be caused by using flooding operation too many times. PnS broker system overcomes such a problem by using the concept of PSR and neighbors. The PSR of the PnS broker includes not only services that are registered to the main broker, but also the services that are registered to neighbors. Thus, the flooding operation is used restrictively. The experimental result shows the ASD is decreased by 20% and the OPB is reduced by 30% compared to the peer-to-peer architecture.

Performance improvement is related to the number of neighbors. Increasing the number of neighbors also results in the increase of the probability of the case that the services are found in the PSR. Thus, high neighbor ratio improves ASD and OPB. However, high neighbor ratio also causes the increase of $O_{EXCHNGE}$, the overhead to exchange the PSR contents with neighbors. Thus, we should maintain proper number of neighbors to exploit both ASD and OPB. Figure 5 shows the change of ASD and OPB according to the ratio of neighbors.

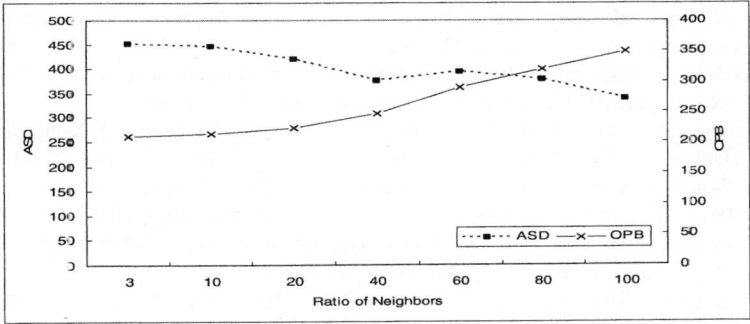

Fig. 5. Change of ASD and OPB according to the ratio of neighbors (# of broker = 100, # of service = 10000)

5 Conclusion

Designing an algorithm to find a service from the unrealistic space that has information of all services in the world is not a good start in building an efficient global service brokering system. Several foundations have to be predefined. In this paper, we propose an efficient service brokering method for the global infrastructure based on the well-defined architecture. Proposed PnS broker system is stable even though the numbers of brokers and services increase rapidly and shows better performance than other brokering architectures. Experimental results show that it can reduce the average service discovery time and operation overhead per broker. Also, we consider personalization as much as scalability. In our system, every user can maintain his own broker and manage its data structures such as the PSR, so that the personal preferences are reflected in the PSR of the broker. Considering the future computing infrastructure is getting intelligent, personalized data will be used for various purposes. Therefore, we expect that our research can be a primitive to build a future brokering system.

References

1. M. Nodine, A. Ngu, A. Cassandra, and W. Bohrer.: Scalable Semantic Brokering over Dynamic Heterogeneous Data Sources in InforSleuth. IEEE Transactions on Knowledge and Data Engineering. Vol. 15. No. 5. (2003).
2. S. Miles, J. Papay, V. Dialani, M. Luck, K. Decker, T. Payne and L, Moreau.: Personalized Grid Service Discovery. IEEE Proceedings of Software. Vol. 150. No. 4. (2003).
3. K. Sycara, M, Paolucci, J. Soudry, and N. Srinivansan.: Dynamic Discovery and Coordination of Agent-based Semantic Web Services. IEEE Internet Computing (2004)
4. C. Schmidt and M.Parashar.: A Peer-to-Peer Approach to Web Service Discovery. World Wide Web Journal. Vol. 7. Issue 2. (2004) 211-229.
5. Universal Description, Discovery ad Integration of business of the Web. http://www.uddi.org, (2001).
6. Web Services Description Language (WSDL). Online at http://www.w3.org/TR/wsdl. (2001).
7. The Gnutella protocol specification v4.0. http://dss.clip2.com/GnutellaProtocol04.pdf.
8. Matei Ripeanu, Ian Foster, and Adriana Iamnitchi.: Mapping the Gnutella network: Properties of large-scale peer-to-peer systems and implications for system design. IEEE Internet Computing. Vol. 6. No. 1. (2002) 50-57.
9. A. Medina, I. Matta, and J. Byers.: BRITE: A Flexible Generator of Internet Topologies. Techinical Report BU-CS-TR-2000-005. Boston University. (2000).
10. S. Venugopal, R. Buyya, and L. Winton.: A Grid Service Broker for Scheduling Distributed Data-oriented Applications on Global Grids. In Proceedings of the 2nd International Workshop on Middleware for Grid Computing. ACM Press. (2004).
11. I. Foster, C. Kesselman, J. Nick, and S. Tuecke.: The Physiology of the Grid: An Open Grid Services Architecture for Distributed Systems Integration. Globus Project. Online at http://www.globus.org/research/papers/ogsa.pdf. (2002).
12. K. Czajkowski, S.Fitzgerlad, I. Foster, and C.Kesselman.: Grid Information Services for Distributed Resource Sharing. In Proceedings of 10th IEEE HPDC. (2001).
13. Web Service Architecture. online at http://www.w3c.org/TR/ws-arch/

Distributed Network Computing on Transient Stability Analysis and Control

Chenrong Huang[1] and Mingxue Chen[2]

[1] Nanjing Institute of technology, Jiangsu Nanjing, China 210013
HuangCR@njit.edu.cn
[2] Nanjing University of Posts and Telecommunications, Jiangsu Nanjing, China 210003
MXChen@njit.edu.cn

Abstract. In this paper, we introduce graph theory into transient stability analysis in power system. In the weighted graph, Vertex weight represents node's parallel computing workload and edge weight represents serial computing workload on the border of regions, which reflects the degree of parallelism of computing and improves speed-up ration of system. In order to reduce communication time wastage induced by CSMA protocol in TCP/IP based LAN, asynchronous message passing is used in our method. Simulation results show that it achieves better performance.

1 Introduction

In power system, real-time transient stability simulation according to "online budget, real-time matching" principle is the preconditions to protect power system against the disturbances. Single computer can't satisfy the requirements of power system transient stability simulation because it is time critical and involves a large amount of data and solving of complicated non-linear equation. Parallel machine can meet the requirements but it's costly. For the relative cheap price of PC cluster, parallel computing technology based on PC cluster was introduced into power system transient stability simulation. So far, the parallel algorithms have applied to the computation of tidal current, transient stability analysis and static security evaluation[1-3], etc.

Coarse granularity parallel-in-space algorithms are usually used for transient stability analysis in distributed network. Current granularity partition algorithms are largely based on selection of dominant nodes or random optimization or factorization tree, which emphasize the mathematical essence of the problem. In the real environment, power system is partitioned to several regions. It often lacks recognition that there are less links among the regions and there is unbalanced electric power in local region and some regions have more power than others. The goal of task allocation is limited to the parallel solution of network equation, which can't reflect the overall computing workload, especially the serial computing workload on the border of regions. It causes more serial computing workload and more unnecessary computation and communication so that it can't meet the requirements of real-time transient stability simulation.

We introduce weighted graph including vertex weight and edge weight into transient stability analysis in power system. Vertex weight represents node's parallel computing workload and edge weight represents the serial computation workload on the border of regions. It reduces the serial computation workload and improves speed-up ratio consequently. In our simulation, the results show that it achieves better performance.

2 Discussion of Parallel Algorithm of Transient Stability Analysis

The dynamic network model for an interconnected power system can be completely described by a set of differentiated equation as (1) and (2). Equation (1) describes dynamic properties of component in power system and equation (2) describes static properties of network[4-5]

$$X = f(x,V) = Ax + Bu(x,V) \quad (1)$$
$$g(x,V) = I - \gamma(x)V = 0 \quad (2)$$

where x is state vector of dynamic component, V is node's voltage vector. u is the input of network, which is a function of x and V. is admittance matrix related to x.

Parallel computing of transient stability analysis involves solving a large-scale sparse linear equation. According to features of electric power grid, the effective method to get solutions of transient stability in PC cluster is to build node's admittance matrix of each region and cutting-branch impedance matrix into a matrix of BBDF (Bordered Block Diagonal Form) [6-8]. Given the linear network equation Ax=b, the matrix A can be arranged into BBDF. Bordered block (A_{ci}) links diagonal block (A_i) and bordered common block (A_c). A_{ci}, A_i, A_c are allocated to each region. Fig. 1 shows the network partition of BBDF.

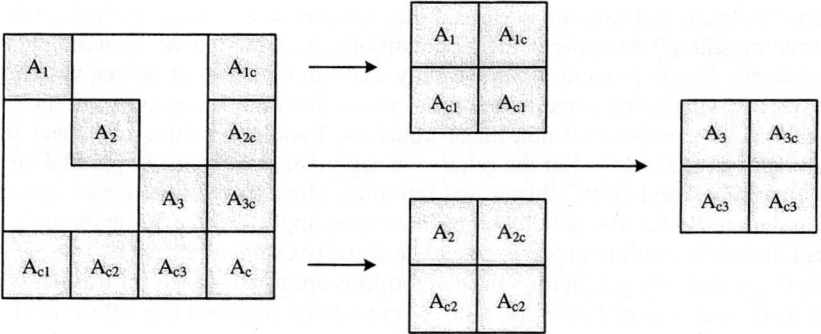

Fig. 1. Partition of BBDF

Fig. 2 shows the process of parallel solving of power system transient stability simulation. The partitioned region can be solved simultaneously, but the bordered block of each region needs to compute serially and communicate with all regions.

Define speed-up ratio as: $Sp = T_s / T_P$, where Ts is the time taken to solve the problem using serial algorithm and T_P is the time using parallel algorithm.

$T_P = T_{PS} + T_{PA} + T_{PC}$,

where T_{PS} is the max computation time among all regions. T_{PA} is the extra workload due to algorithm parallelization such as the solution of differentiated equation, which

Sub network 1~n: event handling, solving of differentiated network equation, computing of injected current vector, judgment of local network convergence, vector revising and matrix computation.	Parallel computing
Inter-communication: coordinated system collects the computing results from all regions; Verification of global convergence (if the convergence conditions satisfied, then jump outside the iterative loop and set the convergent flag); Coordinated system start to compute; Inter-communication: distribute the computing results of coordinated system or global convergence information and the new event to all nodes;	Serial computing
Sub network 1~n: local judgment of convergence, voltage computing, output the computing results	Parallel computing
Output the computing results and export data to real-time database; Accept new events from external system.	Serial computing

Fig. 2. Parallel processing of transient stability simulation in power system

is dependent on conditions of the border. T_{PC} is the communication overhead caused by the exchange of border information[9]. In order to increase the speed-up ratio, we should decrease T_P by effectively partitioning network to decrease $T_{PS}+T_{PA}$, or decreasing T_{PC} by using asynchronous communication to reduce communication traffic.

Traditional partition method can't reflect serial computing workload related to T_{PA} so that there are unnecessary computing workload and more communication time if inappropriate partition. We optimize parallel computing of power system transient stability from the aspect of partition strategy and communication mechanism.

3 Partition of Regions of Transient Stability Analysis

3.1 Partition Strategy

The network model of power system in China is a 4 hierarchical model: district, province, region and power plant, which feature the regional property of electric power grid. The components and equipments in power plant can't be partitioned for their strong electric coupling. Moreover, power plant level network model is large enough to reflect the correlation property of system and satisfies the requirement of coarse granularity parallel algorithm of transient stability. So power plant is used as the finest level of network model rather than the computing node in power plant.

The three steps of network partition is as follows: 1) Mapping electric power grid into a graph. 2) Partition of the graph. 3) Adjustment of partition. The first step transforms hierarchical model into small-scale condensed graph, and the parallel computing workload of transient stability of each region is mapped into vertex's weight while the serial computing workload on the border of regions is mapped into edge's weight. The second step is to partition the weighted graph into several parts and searches the optimal solution with layered refinement. Finally, the partition results are mapped on the original network and the quality of partition may be improved by further adjustment.

According to above partition strategy, partition algorithm with the regional property can identify the weak correlation of network and solve the optimal combination problem of multiple regions. Layered refinement offers more freedom of partition and improves the balance degree of partition.

3.2 The Solution of the Overall Computing Workload

We introduce the concept of vertex weight and edge weight into the original condensed graph to reflect the overall workload of serial and parallel computation and transform the condensed graph into a weighted graph Gw=(V, E, W_V, W_E), where W_V is the vertex weight set of the condensed graph, W_E is the edge weight set of the condensed graph. Define the partition of condensed graph as follows:

Given k, the number of partitioned region, and |V| = n, partition weighted graph Gw into k subsets S_{V1}, S_{V2}, ...and S_{Vk}, which satisfied the following conditions:

$a. S_{Vi} \cap S_{Vj} = \phi, \forall i, j \in (1,2,\cdots k), i \neq j;$

$b. S_{V1} \cup S_{V2} \cup ..... \cup S_{Vk} = V;$

$c. \sum W_{VS_{Vi}} \approx \sum W_{VV} / k, i = 1,2,....k;$

$d. \min \sum W_{EC}$, where C is the cutting-edge set caused by partitioning, and

$C = \{(V_m, V_n) \in E \mid \exists V_m \in S_{Vi}; V_n \in S_{Vj}; i, j \in (1,2,.....k); i \neq j\}.$

1) Vertex weight represents computing workload of condensed network and dynamic components, which is the workload of solving the network equation and components computing. The number of path between the state variables in dynamic component model and interface variables in topology is used to measure the workload of solving dynamic component equation approximately. The number of non-zero elements of the admittance matrix of network equation is used to measure the workload of solving network equation. The approximation can match the relative computing workload of each condensed network by using global dynamic node numbering. So, the vertex weight of vertex Vi can be described as:

$$W_{V_i} = N_n + 2N_{bc} + \sum_{D_i} P(D_i)$$

where N_n is the number of nodes of condensed network; N_{bc} is the number of correlated edges of condensed network, which is the number of non-zero elements of upper triangular block or lower triangular block in network admittance matrix; $P(D_i)$ is the path of dynamic components variables.

2) Edge weight is used to measure the computing workload induced by cutting edges in condensed network. Under circumstance that exploits strategy based on node's branch, it is the number of computing nodes after cutting edges rather than the number of cutting-edges itself that determines the computing workload of border blocks. Given the edge which links node N_p and N_q in the original network, $E_i =(V_i, V_j)$, define the edge weight before partitioning as:

$$W_{E_i} = 1/D_E(N_p) + 1/D_E(N_q)$$

where $D_E(N_p)$ and $D_E(N_q)$ are out-degrees of node N_p and N_q.

3) Fig. 3 shows that our partition method has the advantage over traditional partition method.

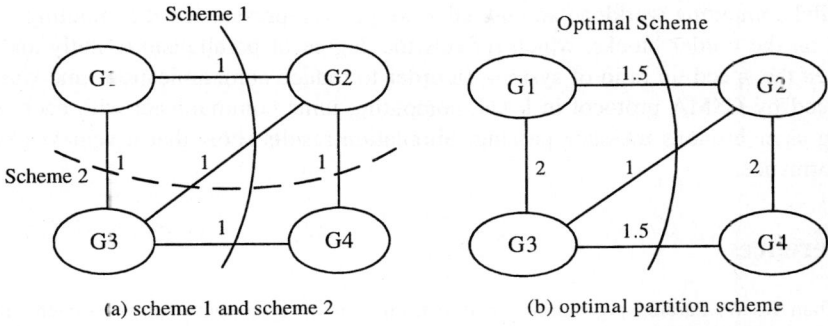

Fig. 3. Definition of condensed edge weight based on node's out degree

As seen from Fig. 3, node G1, G2, G3 and G4 are partitioned to 2 parts. Fig. 3 (a) shows traditional definition of condensed edge weight in which 5 edges have the same edge weight. Both scheme 1 and scheme 2 are reasonable partition, but the scale of their coordinate system are not the same, which the number of nodes of coordinate system is 4 in scheme 1 and 6 in scheme 2. Fig. 3 (b) describes an optimal partition scheme based on our definition of edge weight. Our method takes coordinate system into account and achieves the optimal partition. In conclusion, our partition method defines vertex weight and edge weight to build a weighted condensed graph. The computing task allocation of transient stability is transformed into the partition of weighted condense graph.

4 Message Passing Mechanism

As described in section 1, communication time T_{PC} is one of the parameters to influence speed-up ratio. It is often negligible compared to T_{PA}. But in our implementation, T_{PC} can't be ignored sometimes when using synchronous communication. The reason is that Ethernet is a bus-based LAN, which is based on TCP/IP protocol and adopts CSMA (Carrier Sense Multiple Access) technology. The goal of synchronous parallel computing is load balancing. Multiple processors exchange and evaluate their information before starting the computing until every processor has arrived at the same barrier. Synchronous communication will cause communication bottleneck and the exchanged messages will congest the communication. In the contrary, asynchronous communication makes it possible, which processors can compute and communicate simultaneously. So we use asynchronous message passing in our method.

5 Conclusion

In this paper, we analyze the parallel algorithms of transient stability analysis and study the partition strategy of BBDF suitable for distributed PC cluster and its parallel computing process. To reflect the overall workload of parallel and serial computing, we introduce graph theory into power system transient stability analysis according to properties of power system. In our scheme, we use vertex weight to represent node's parallel computing workload and use edge weight to represent serial computing workload on the border blocks, which reflects the degree of parallelism roundly and improves the speed-up ratio of system. In order to reduce communication time wastage induced by CSMA protocol in LAN, computing units communicate with each other using asynchronous message passing. Simulation results show that it achieves better performance.

References

1. Chan K. W. Parallel algorithms for direct solution of large sparse power system matrix equations [J]. IEEE Proceeding-C; Generation, Transmission and Distribution, 2001, 148 (6): 615-622.
2. Zhu Ning,Bose,Anjan, A dynamic partitioning scheme for parallel transient stability analysis[J], IEEE Transactions on Power Systems,vol.7,No.2,pp:940-946,May 1992.
3. Yong Jie Fang, Yusheng Xue. An on-line pre-decision based transient stability control system for the Ertan power system[C]. International Conference on PowerCon 2000. IEEE Vol.1, pp:287-292, Dec. 2000.
4. Hong Chao. Implementation of parallel-in-time Newton method for transient stability analysis on a message passing multicomputer[C]. International Conference on PowerCon 2002. IEEE Vol.2, pp:1239-1243,Oct.2002.
5. Iavernaro, F. La Scala, M. Mazzia, F. Boundary values methods for time-domain simulation of power system dynamic behavior[J]. IEEE Transactions on Circuits and Systems, vol.45, No.1, pp50-63, Jan.1998.
6. LI Ya-lou, et al. Personal Computer Cluster based Parallel Algorithms for Power System Electromechanical Transient Stability Simulation. Power System Technology, vol. 27, No. 11, 2003.
7. HONG Chao, C. M. Shen. A Parallel-in-space algorithm for Power System Transient Stability Simulation. Power System Technology, 2000, 24 (5): 20-24.
8. Decker I. C, Falcao D. M, Kaszkurewicz E. Conjugate gradient methods for power system dynamic simulation on parallel computers [J]. IEEE Transactions on Power Systems, 1996, 11 (3): 1218-1227.
9. Feng Tu,Flueck,A.J. A message-passing distributed-memory parallel power flow algorithm[J]. IEEE Vol.1, pp:211-216,Jan 2002.

A Distributed Power-Efficient Data Gathering and Aggregation Protocol for Wireless Sensor Networks

Ming Liu[1,2], Jiannong Cao[1], Hai-gang Gong[2], Li-jun Chen[2], and Xie Li [2]

[1] Department of Computing, Hong Kong Polytechnic University,
Hung Hom, Kowloon, Hong Kong
[2] State Key Laboratory for Novel Software Technology,
Nanjing University, Nanjing 210093, China

Abstract. In this paper, we propose a distributed power-efficient data gathering and aggregation algorithm (DPEG), in which a node, according to its residual energy and the strength of signal received from its neighboring nodes, independently makes its decision to compete for becoming a cluster head. In addition, assume that the inter-cluster communication data is, in a multi-hop manner, sent to the designated node, which then sends the data gathered by the whole network to the base station. DPEG also proposes a simple approach to solve the cluster coverage problem. With the increase in node density, this approach lets sensor network lifetime be linear in the number of nodes. Our experimental results have proved that DPEG algorithm, in the best case, lets sensor network lifetime be respectively increased by 1800% and 300% as compared with another two data gathering and aggregation protocols--- LEACH and PEGASIS.

1 Introduction

With the development of the sensor technology, the embedding technology and the technology of wireless communication with low power consumption, it has become possible to produce the micro wireless sensors for sensing, wireless communication and processing information. These inexpensive and power-efficient sensor nodes work together to form a wireless sensor network, which, through the cooperation of sensor nodes, delivers various kinds of monitored and sensed environment information (e.g. temperature, humidity, etc.) to the base station, which processes the report messages it receives. Wireless sensor networks (WSNs) enjoy a wide-range of applications, including military surveillance, disaster prediction, environment monitoring, etc. Since WSNs have great application value, they have been paid closest attention to in the fields of military, industry and academy in many countries. Actually, a lot of research efforts have been made on WSNs. Recently, wireless sensor networks, composed of micro sensor nodes, have already been developed into an important computing platform [1][2]. Wireless sensor networks, different from mobile ad hoc networks (MANETs), globally have comparatively high node density and weak node mobility (usually the sensor nodes do not move any more after they are deployed). Meanwhile, for the reasons of cost and volume, etc, the wireless sensor node resource is insufficient in terms of processing capability, wireless bandwidth and battery power, etc. Especially, since in many applications sensor nodes are intended to work in hostile or inaccessible environments, e.g., the enemy-occupied areas, node energy fails to be recharged, and thus how to prolong sensor network lifetime has become one of the crucial problems needed to be considered in designing [3][4][5][6][7]. This paper, from the point of view of communication protocol, proposes a distributed power-efficient data gathering and aggregation algorithm, DPEG.

2 Related Work

The main task of a sensor network is to forward the data gathered by sensor nodes to the base station. One simple approach to the fulfillment of this task is direct data transmission, i.e., each node in the network directly sends gathered data to the base station. However, if the base station is remote from the sensor node, the node will soon die for suffering excessive energy consumption for delivering data. To solve this problem, some algorithms that are aimed to save energy have been proposed one after another [9][10][11][12][13].

In the literature [9], Wendi and others proposed LEACH algorithm. LEACH is a kind of distributed self-configuring protocol, the fundamental concept of which focuses on energy efficiency by reducing the number of the nodes that can directly communicate with the base station. LEACH protocol involves round-operation. Each round includes two phases: setup and steady. In the phase of setup, first some sensor nodes, in a self-configuring manner, are randomly selected as the cluster heads, and then these selected cluster heads are broadcast. Which cluster head a regular node decides to join depends on the strength of the radio signal it receives. The phase of steady begins after clustering. In the phase of steady, the regular nodes first deliver gathered data to the cluster head, and then the cluster head fuses the data received and the data gathered by itself together. After that the cluster head delivers the fused data to the base station. In LEACH protocol, each round gets involved in the reselection of cluster heads. In this way, uniform energy consumption for all the nodes can be guaranteed. Compared with DIRECT protocol, LEACH protocol, by reducing the number of the nodes that directly communicate with the base station and using data fusion technology, can make sensor network lifetime (until the first node dies) be increased by 800% or so. Although LEACH algorithm can prolong sensor network lifetime by a wide margin compared with DIRECT protocol, it fails to consider the following issues: 1) To optimize the number of cluster heads; in LEACH algorithm, for any node, the probability of being a cluster head is p, so the number of cluster heads is proportional to the quantity of sensor nodes; 2) To reduce energy consumption of cluster heads; in LEACH protocol, all the cluster heads directly communicate with the base station; since the nodes selected as cluster heads, remote from the base station, have to receive data delivered by all the member nodes, they will suffer a faster energy consumption; and when the number of cluster heads in network is large enough, the global energy consumption of the network will have to increase; 3) To guarantee optimal cluster head distribution; since the cluster heads are randomly selected, LEACH algorithm does not guarantee good cluster head distribution, but the cluster head distribution determines the energy consumption of sensor network in the round.

In the literature [10], the authors notice that for a node, within a range of some distance, the energy consumed for receiving or sending circuits is higher than that consumed for amplifying circuits. In order to reduce the energy consumption of sensor nodes, the authors propose PEGASIS protocol, which uses GREED algorithm to form all the sensor nodes in the system into a link. The sum of the side length of the link is close to the minimum. Each side of the link receives and sends data only once. Specifically speaking, in each round, any node receives data from one neighboring node in the link, and fuses the data received and the data gathered by itself together, and then delivers the fused data to the other neighboring node in the link. The work of delivering and fusing data begins with the node at one end of the link, and continues till the data is sent to the designated node, which is in charge of delivering the final fused data to the base station. Compared with LEACH protocol, PEGASIS protocol lets the energy consumption in each round be remarkably reduced because it allows a smaller number of nodes that can directly communicate with the base station and a better data fusion. The result is particularly notable when the base station is remote from the working area of the sensor network. According to the simulation experiments, sensor network lifetime in PEGASIS protocol can be increased by 100% to 300% compared with that in LEACH protocol. However, PEGASIS algorithm's contribution to prolong sensor network lifetime is made on the basis of the assumption that all the nodes know the global information of sensor networks. We argue this assumption fails to take the following problems into account: 1) It is very difficult for a single node to store the global information of the sensor network because the number of sensor nodes in the network is very large while both the node's processing capability and its memory capacity are quite limited; 2) Since in many applications sensor nodes are deployed in hostile or inaccessible environments, there exist other reasons for node failures in addition to energy depletion; so it has to pay a considerably high price for maintaining the storage of correct global information; 3) PEGASIS algorithm forms all the nodes in the sensor network into a link, but if some node in the link dies, the data gathered by all the nodes between the end of the link and the location of the node itself cannot be delivered to the base station; 4) Since the length of the link has much to do with the number of nodes and the quantity of sensor nodes in the network is considerably large, there exists much delay for transmitting gathering data to base station.

3 System Model and Problem Statement

The clustering algorithm DPEG proposed in this paper, like the other clustering algorithms in [9][10][11][12], also involves round-operation. Each round is divided into three phases: clustering, forming spanning tree and gathering data, respectively denoted by $T_{cluster}$, T_{tree} and T_{data}. T_{data} refers to the phase of data gathering, in which the data gathered by sensor nodes are delivered to the base station for processing. In order to guarantee the useful (data gathering) working time of the network, the algorithm has to satisfy the condition: $T_{data} \gg T_{cluster} + T_{tree}$.

3.1 Network Model

This paper assumes that N sensor nodes are randomly deployed in a square field A, and the sensor network has the following properties:

1) Sensor nodes in the network do not move any more after they are deployed.
2) There exists only one base station, which is deployed at a fixed place outside A.
3) The deployed network does not need to be maintained by people.
4) All the nodes share equal significance and similar capabilities (processing/communication).
5) Sensor nodes in the network are not equipped with GPS, i.e. Nodes are location-unaware.
6) The radio power can be controlled, i.e., a node can control its transmission power level according to the distance.

The first four properties are typical setting in ordinary sensor networks. The fifth property makes it clear that DPEG algorithm proposed in this paper, like LEACH protocol, does not need to use location information of sensor nodes. We argue that for the approach to determine the location of sensor nodes through exchanging information, the increase in the number of nodes brings such rapid increase in the amount of exchanged information that the network efficiency degrades and the scalability of the system is immediately affected. Moreover, the energy consumption for exchanging information will also affect the lifetime of the sensor network. Considering energy efficiency a goal, the sixth property mainly deals with the definition of different power levels for intra-cluster and inter-cluster communications. In this way, the node energy consumption can be remarkably reduced so as to further prolong sensor network lifetime.

3.2 Radio Model

In the recent years, great deals of research efforts have been made on low-energy wireless communication. This paper uses the same radio model as in the literature [14]. This model provides a threshold d_0 (d_0 is a constant, which is decided by the application environment). When the value of distance from sender to the node receiver falls below d_0, the energy consumption for sending data is proportional to the second power of the distance; otherwise it is proportional to the fourth power of the distance. These two energy attenuation models are respectively called free space model and multi-path fading model. Therefore, according to the distance of receiver, the node that sends data can use one of the above two models to calculate the energy consumption for its sending data. For example, the node a, which sends k-byte data to the node b (the distance from a to b is d), can uses the following formula to calculate its energy consumption:

$$E_{tr}(k,d) = E_{elec}(k) + E_{amp}(k,d)$$
$$= \begin{cases} kE_{elec} + k\varepsilon_{fs} d^2 \\ kE_{elec} + k\varepsilon_{amp} d^4 \end{cases} \quad (1)$$

When b receives the message sent by a, the energy consumption of its wireless devices can be calculated through Formula 2:

$$E_{Rx}(k) = kE_{elec} \quad (2)$$

In the above two formulae, E_{elec} denotes the energy consumption of the wireless circuit for sending and receiving data. The energy consumption of the amplifier is denoted by E_{amp}, which is decided by the distance from the sender to the receiver as well as the acceptable bit error rate. In addition, most protocols and algorithms prefer to use data fusion technology to reduce the amount of the data transferred in network so as to save energy. DPEG algorithm also adopts data fusion technology to reduce energy consumption. DPEG algorithm, like PEGASIS, assumes the ability of data fusion to be: $Nk = k$, where N denotes the number of nodes in the sensor network and k refers to the length of data packet. The energy consumption for fusing data is denoted by $E_{\_fusion}$.

3.3 Problem Statement

In essence, all approaches that involve round-operation and aim to prolong sensor network lifetime want not only uniform energy consumption for every node but also the minimization of the total energy consumption in every round. For the clustering algorithm, the formation of cluster will decide the amount of energy consumed in every round. Assume that N nodes are dispersed in the field A at random. Then we argue that the clustering algorithm, in order to reduce energy consumption in every round and guarantee energy consumption is uniformly distributed in every node, has to satisfy the following conditions:

1) It should be a complete distributed and self-configuring algorithm in which a node uses only the local information to decide its own status. Before the phase of $T_{cluster}$ ends, every node has to elect to become a cluster head or a member node of one cluster.
2) The energy consumption for communication between nodes should, to the largest extent, satisfy free space model. In other words, both intra-cluster and inter-cluster communications have to satisfy free space model. However, LEACH algorithm fails to guarantee good cluster distribution. In this case, there may be more energy consumption, for the intra-cluster communication fails to satisfy free space model.
3) The intra-cluster and inter-cluster communications use different power levels. When the node density is high enough, the power level for the inter-cluster communication should guarantee the communication range is over twice of the cluster range. In this case, the connectivity of the clustered network can be guaranteed.
4) The cluster head distribution should be optimized. When free space model is satisfied, the inter-cluster communication should, to the largest extent, guarantee that the distance between any two cluster heads is larger than the cluster range r_c. In this paper, r_c denotes cluster size. Only those nodes located within the range r_c of one cluster head are allowed to join the cluster. There exists signal interference in the wireless channel, and the signal inference will be worsened if a cluster head falls within the range of another cluster head. In this case, the data will be retransmitted so as to cause extra energy consumption.

4 Description of DPEG Protocol

DPEG protocol involves round-operation. Each round includes three phases: $T_{cluster}$, T_{tree} and T_{data}.

4.1 Clustering Algorithm

Our clustering algorithm based on the algorithm proposed in [13]. In DPEG algorithm the cluster range is fixed, i.e., $r_c < d_0/2$. The communication range of a cluster head is denoted by R_{ch}, and we define $R_{ch} = 2.5r_c$. The distance between two neighboring cluster head nodes, denoted by d, satisfies the formula: $r_c < d <= R_{ch}$, which will guarantee good distribution of cluster heads in sensor networks. Since the cluster range is fixed and the relationship between clusters is bound to the above formula, the number of clusters covering A, a monitored field, is directly related to the size of A as well as the cluster range r_c. [15] presents a formula to calculate the minimum number of nodes needed to cover the field A, where n denotes the minimum number of nodes, as follows:

$$n\pi r^2 / A_{area} = 2\pi / \sqrt{27} \qquad (3)$$

According to Formula 3, for each node S_i (1< i < N), we define its initial probability of becoming a cluster head as:

$$p_{init} = 2A_{area} / \sqrt{27} N r_c^2 \qquad (4)$$

The initial probability is defined to control the number of initial candidate cluster heads. As to the number of final cluster heads, obviously, we have $N_c \geq N p_{init}$. With the execution of DPEG protocol, one node's probability of becoming a cluster head (denoted by p_{ch}) has to be related to its energy in order to guarantee that energy consumption is uniformly distributed in every node:

$$p_{ch} = p_{init} \times \frac{E_{current}}{E_{max}} \qquad (5)$$

Where $E_{current}$ denotes the current residual energy in the node and E_{max} denotes its initial energy. When a node's residual energy is lower than the threshold E_{min}, the node will no longer join the competition for becoming a cluster head. Since the energy consumption for sending, receiving and aggregating data can be calculated, E_{min} may be computed through the following formula:

$$E_{min} = cycle \times l \times \left(C_{degree} \times (E_{elec} + E_{DA}) + l \times E_{DA} + l \times \varepsilon_{fs} \times d_0^2 \right) \qquad (6)$$

Where cycle denotes the frequency of data gathering in each round, and C_{degree} is the mean of the number of member nodes in the cluster, and l refers to the length of data packet.

Any node S_i, in the phase of $T_{cluster}$ in each round, needs to execute the clustering algorithm. The clustering process requires a number of iterations. The number of iterations is related to $E_{current}$, the current residual energy in the node. Every step takes time t, which should be long enough to guarantee that the node S_i can receive the message sent by any node within the range r_c of S_i. We note that when a node is competing for cluster head, its residual energy is not the only parameter necessary to be considered in an attempt to prolong sensor network lifetime.

Before the iteration begins, S_i broadcasts itself within the range r_c and receives the broadcast messages sent by all the neighboring nodes within the range r_c. According to the strength of signal received, let $PRI = \sum_{n=1}^{m} RadioStr \bigg/ m$, where m is the number of S_i' s neighbor within the range r_c. The higher PRI is, the lower energy the cluster, with S_i as its cluster head, consumes. Thus, PRI will be considered as the priority of a node to compete for cluster head. In static sensor networks the normal death of a node (for energy depletion) can be calculated. If the node fault rate is lower, the neighbor set of every node does not change very frequently. Moreover, DPEG protocol distributes uniform energy consumption in every node and thus extends the lifetime of all the nodes in the sensor network, which adds to the stability of the neighbor set. As illustrated in Line 3-6, Figure 1, in DPEG protocol, PRI is computed through broadcast in every count-round, and the assumed value of count is related to the node fault rate in the network.

```
1.   If  round = 1
2.      Bs_str = Receive_Str(msg form BS)    // radio strength
3.   If  round%count = 0
4.      Broadcast(S_i->ID)
5.      Receive_Str(msg from neighbor in s_i's cluster range )
6.      PRI = Avr_Str(all neighbor in the cluster range of s_i)
7.   p = max(p_ch, p_min)           //p_min = p_init*(E_min/E_max)
8.   is_CH = false

9.   while(p > 1)
10.     If  New_CH != empty
11.        Add(CH_Set, New_CH)
12.     If  CH_Set = empty and p != 1
13.        If  random(0,1) <= p
14.           Broadcast(S_i->ID, temp, PRI)
15.     Else If  CH_SET = empty and p = 1
16.        Broadcast(S_i->ID, CH, PRI)
17.        is_CH = true
18.     Else If  CH_Set != empty
19.        cluster_head = Max_PRI(all nodes in CH_Set)
20.        If  S_i ∈  CH_Set and S_i has highest PRI in CH_Set
21.           If  p = 1
22.              Broadcast(S_i->ID, CH, PRI)
23.              is_CH = true
24.           Else
25.              Broadcast(S_i->ID, temp, PRI)
26.     p = min(2*p, 1)

27.  If  is_CH = true
28.     Broadcast(S_i->ID, CH, PRI)
29.  Else
30.     If  CH_Set = empty
31.        Broadcast(S_i->ID, CH, PRI)
32.     Else
33.        join_cluster(cluster_head, S_i->ID)
```

Fig. 1. Clustering pseudo-code

As each iteration starts, S_i first judges whether there is any new cluster head announcement. If yes, let the new cluster head join the tentative set of candidate cluster heads, denoted by CH_Set. If CH_Set is not empty nor does include the node S_i itself, S_i will lose the chance of being selected as a cluster head. But if the iteration ends with no candidate cluster head announcing itself to be a state cluster head, S_i will consider itself uncovered, and then announces itself to be a final cluster head. If S_i is a candidate cluster head ($S_i \in CH\_Set$), then it is needed to judge whether the priority of S_i PRI is the highest. If its priority is the highest, when the iteration ends, S_i broadcasts itself to be a final cluster head; otherwise, when the iteration ends, S_i will join the final cluster head some candidate node announces to be. If when the iteration ends, CH_Set is still empty, i.e., S_i is not covered by any cluster, S_i will broadcast itself to be a final cluster head. Note that in process of competing for becoming the cluster head, the node's broadcasting range is r_c, and the algorithm is illustrated in Figure 1.

4.2 Formation of Approximate Minimum Spanning Tree

After clustering, the cluster heads in the sensor network begin to compete for becoming the CH_b node. We define each cluster head's probability of becoming candidate CH_b as follows:

$$p_b = BS\_str \times E_{current} / BS\_str_{max} \times E_{max} \qquad (7)$$

where BS_str denotes the strength of radio signal received from the base station, and BS_str_{max} is the maximal strength of the signal received from the base station within the field A. Obviously, the smaller the distance from a cluster head to the base station is and the higher its power is, the larger the cluster head's probability of becoming the candidate CH_b is. The candidate CH_b node broadcasts to its neighboring cluster heads within its broadcasting range R_{ch} the message, which includes node_ ID and p_b. The neighboring cluster heads transmit the broadcast message they receive to its neighbor so that all the cluster heads receive the message broadcast by the candidate CH_b. The candidate cluster head with the largest p_b will be selected as the CH_b node (if there are two or more candidate cluster heads that have the same p_b, the one with higher ID value becomes the CH_b node). Note that in the later period of network lifetime, a large quantity of nodes die, so the node density in the field A fails to guarantee the cluster head connectivity. In this case, if a cluster head does not receive the message broadcast by the candidate CH_b within a given time, it then automatically becomes the CH_b node.

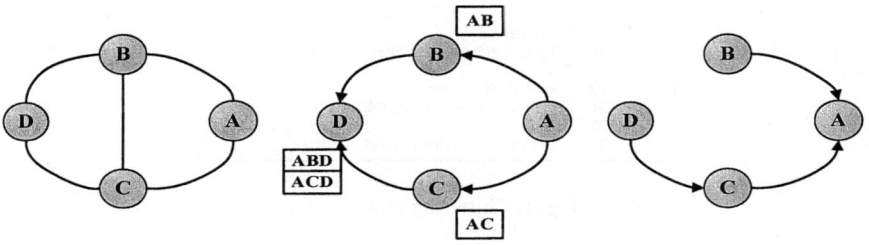

Fig. 2. (2a, 2b, 2c): Illustration of the algorithm for producing approximate minimum spanning tree

The routing tree is formed with the selected CH_b node as its root. First, the CH_b node broadcasts the message including its own node_ID to all the neighboring cluster heads within its broadcasting range R_{ch}. Then the neighboring cluster heads add the routing information from the CH_b node to the local cluster heads to the message they receive and transmit the join message in a way similar to flooding algorithm till all the cluster heads receive the routing information from the local cluster heads to the CH_b node. In order to reduce the degree of complexity in exchanging routing information and save limited resources in the node, the longer routing information will be dropped in the process of flooding. When the broadcast ends, each node reserves all the messages that travel the smallest number of hops from the CH_b node to the local node, and then selects the closest node on the upper channel as its parent node (according to the strength of signal received) and sends child message to it. For example, Figure 2a illustrates the relationship between neighboring cluster heads. In this figure, A is the selected CH_b node from which the broadcast starts. After receiving the message from A, Node B, C broadcast the messages{ A, B} and { A, C} to all the neighboring nodes within the range R_{ch}. Since the message{ A, B} travels a larger number of hops than the message{ A} , it is dropped by Node C; similarly, Node B drop the message{ A, C} . For Node D, the number of hops the message{ A, B} from Node B travels is as large as that the message{ A, C} from Node C travels, so both{ A, B} and{ A, C} will be reserved. The routes reserved by the nodes after broadcasting are illustrated in Figure 2b. Assume that the strength of signal Node D receives from Node C is greater than that it receives from Node B. In this case, Node D sends the child message to Node C. The final spanning tree is illustrated in Figure 2c.

4.3 Cluster Coverage

For the random deployment, it is impossible to guarantee that the deployed nodes can cover the whole area. Therefore, we hope to solve the following problems: how many sensor nodes with the sensing range r_s are needed to be randomly deployed in the monitored area C with the range R so as to guarantee that the covered sections in the whole area are as large as what they are expected to be.

Definition 1. Neighborhood. For any point $(x, y) \in C$, its neighborhood is defined as:

$$\aleph(x, y) = \{(x', y') \in C\} | \forall((x'-x)^2 + (y'-y)^2 \le r_s^2) \tag{8}$$

Definition 2. The area C'. For the area C', have $C' \subset C$. And for any point $(x, y) \in C'$, satisfy the following formula:

$$x^2 + y^2 <= (R - r_s)^2 \tag{9}$$

For any point $(x, y) \in C$, if there exists at least one node in its neighborhood, it is covered. Since sensor nodes in the area C are uniformly distributed, the probability that a node falls within the neighborhood of the point (x, y) is $p = \aleph(x, y)_{area} / C_{area}$. Assume that m nodes are deployed in the area C. Then the probability that the point (x, y) is covered is

$$p_{coverage} = C_m^1 p(1-p)^{m-1} + C_m^2 p^2(1-p)^{m-2} + \cdots\cdots + C_m^m p^m \qquad (10)$$

For $\forall (x, y) \in C'$, the area of its neighborhood $\aleph(x, y)_{area} = \pi r_s^2$. Thus, the probability that a single node falls within the neighborhood $p = \aleph(x, y)_{area} / C_{area} = \pi r_s^2 / \pi R^2$. According to Formula 10, if m nodes are randomly deployed in the area C, the probability that the point $\forall (x, y) \in C'$ is covered is

$$P_{cover} = \sum_{n=1}^{m} C_m^n \left(\frac{r_s}{R}\right)^{2n} \left(1 - \frac{r_s^2}{R^2}\right)^{m-n} \qquad (11)$$

If the node density is high enough, the clusters formed in the phase of $T_{cluster}$ in each round will cover the whole monitored field A. Theoretically, the area of a cluster is πr_c^2, but there exist overlapping parts between neighboring clusters in order to cover A, i.e., the practical area of the cluster is smaller than πr_c^2. Therefore, m the number of nodes needed to cover the designated area can be approximately computed through Formula 11, where p_{cover}, according to the application, is determined. In order to save energy, a cluster head randomly selects m nodes from its member nodes as the active nodes and lets other nodes sleep. The cluster head's arrangement of its member nodes is completed by the intra-cluster broadcast of TDMA schedule.

5 Performance Evaluation

5.1 Simulation Parameter

We use GlomoSim as the simulation platform with various parameters in the simulation experiments shown in Table 1. In the simulation experiments, sensor

Table 1. Simulation parameter

parameter	value
Network size	(100X100), (150x150), (200X200), (250X250), (300X300), (350X350), (400X400)
Sink position	(50, 175), (50, 200), (20, 215), (50, 230), (50, 245), (50, 260), (50, 275), (50, 300), (50, 400)
Node number	100, 150, 200, 250, 300, 350, 400, 450, 500, 1000
Threshold distance (d_0)	75m
Cluster radius (r_c)	30m
Coverage radius (r_s)	12m
E_{elec}	50nJ/bit
e_{-fs}	13pJ/bit/m^2
e_{-mp}	0.0013pJ/bit/m^4
E_{fusion}	5nJ/bit
Data packet size	500 bytes
Broad packet size	25 bytes
Packet header size	25 bytes
round	5 TDMA frames
Initial energy	2J

network lifetime involves three kinds of definitions, which differ in terms of the time when sensor network terminates, i.e. sensor network terminates until the first node dies or half the nodes die or the last node dies. In addition, in the simulation experiments to verify DPEG protocol (DPEG-1 does not use the cluster algorithmic approach), we define the sensing range of each node as $r_s = 12m$, and a node is considered dead if its residual energy is lower than E_{min} (0.0025J).

With an attempt to make a comprehensive caparison among the four protocols, i.e., DIRECT, LEACH, PEGASIS and DPEG, through the simulation experiments we respectively observe how the performance of each protocol varies with the changes in the size of the monitored area, the location of the base station and the number of the nodes. The experimental results and the analysis of them are illustrated in Section 5.3, in which DPEG protocol includes DPEG-1 and DPEG-2 (using the cluster coverage method).

5.3 Experimental Results And Analysis

Figure 3 and Figure 4 respectively illustrate the relationship between the location of the base station and network lifetime of the above three definitions. As shown in Figure 3, in DPEG protocol, with the increase in the distance from the base station to the monitored area A network lifetime defined according to the death time of the first node decreases more slowly. The experimental results have shown that when the location of the base station is shifted from (50, 175) to (50, 300), network lifetime decreases by less than 18% from 892 rounds to 732 rounds. In this case, DPEG protocol is superior to PEGASIS and LEACH protocols. Meanwhile, it can be seen that there is the least alteration in the graphs that illustrate DPEG protocol in the two figures. This means that for the sensor network that executes DPEG protocol, there is no remarkable difference among the three definitions mentioned earlier in terms of sensor network lifetime.

In the simulation experiments we consider that the change in the size of the monitored field A will influence the performance of various protocols. From Figure 5 and Figure 6, it can be seen that DPEG protocol still performs very well with the monitored field enlarged. This is because that DPEG protocol can guarantee that there is good cluster distribution and the data are forwarded to the base station in a multi-hop manner. Therefore, the performance of DPEG is, on the same condition, better than that of LEACH and PEGASIS.

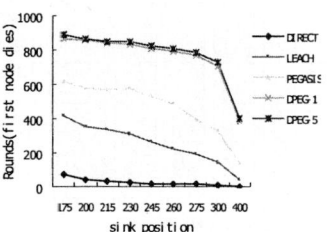

Fig. 3. Network lifetime as sink travels farther (FND)

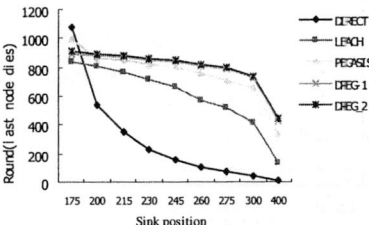

Fig. 4. Network lifetime as sink travels farther (LND)

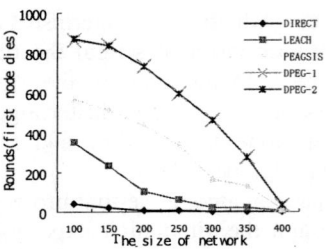
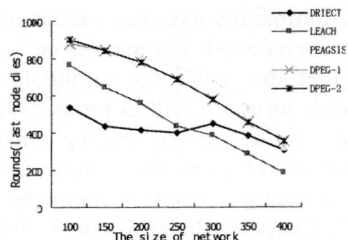

Fig. 5. Network size vs. network lifetime (FND)

Fig. 6. Network size vs. network lifetime (LND)

Figure 7 illustrates the relationship between the number of nodes and network lifetime. It is worth to note that as the number of nodes increases the above four protocols fail to prolong network lifetime (with the exception of DPEG-2). This is because that these algorithms do not take the coverage problem into account. When the node density is high enough, only a certain number of nodes are needed to cover the whole field A. Thus, it is necessary to let the surplus nodes sleep so as to reduce the energy consumption in these nodes and further prolong network lifetime. However, in the above four protocols that leave the coverage problem out of consideration, all the nodes are active nodes in each round so that the increase in the number of nodes cannot lead to the obviously increase in network lifetime. Meanwhile, the number of the member nodes in the cluster in DPEG-1 will increase as the number of nodes increases, since the number of cluster heads formed in DPEG algorithm is only related to the size of the monitored field A and the cluster range r_c. In this case, there will be more energy consumption in the cluster head so as to make the first node die at an earlier time. It can be seen in Figure 7 that when the number of nodes is 100, the first node dies in the 890th round. As the number of nodes reaches 500, the first node dies as early as in the 831st round. DPEG-2 uses the cluster coverage algorithm in which if the number of member nodes in a cluster is larger than is needed (according to the application requirements), the cluster head will inform the redundant nodes to fall asleep in this round. The experimental results have proved that in DPEG-2 the increase in network lifetime is linear with the number of nodes.

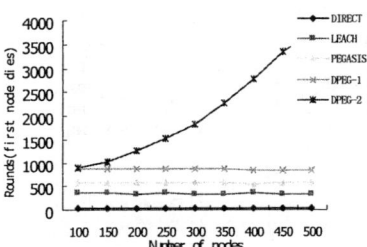
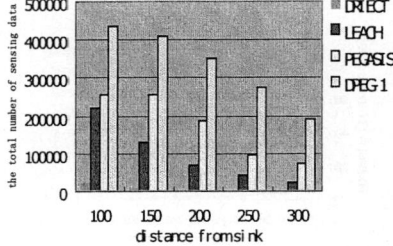

Fig. 7. Network lifetime as the number of nodes increased (FND)

Fig. 8. The total number of sensing data gathered by all nodes in the network (FND)

In protocols that involve round-operation, for all the nodes, the frequency of gathering data in each round is uniform (in the simulation experiments we define that the frequency of gathering data by the node is 5 times in each round). So, the performance of the protocol can be assessed on the basis of the total frequency of gathering data by all the nodes in the sensor network. As shown in Figure 8, according to the variation in the distance from the base station to the monitored field A, we respectively calculate the total frequency of gathering data in the above four protocols before the network lifetime terminates. Obviously, the total frequency of gathering data in DPEG-1 is far higher than that in the other three protocols. So this means DPEG protocol is superior to the other three protocols in terms of the monitoring quality.

6 Conclusion

In this paper, we propose a distributed power-efficient data gathering and aggregation protocol for sensor networks, in which a node, according to its own residual energy and the strength of signal received from its neighboring nodes, independently makes its decision to compete for cluster head. After the selection of the cluster heads, the regular nodes choose to join the closest cluster head to form the cluster. In order to further reduce energy consumption, the cluster head remote from the base station sends the gathered data, in a multi-hop way, to the base station. Moreover, in DPEG protocol the execution of a simple cluster coverage algorithm helps to prolong network lifetime with the increase in node density. The experimental results have proved that DPEG protocol can prolong network lifetime by a wide margin and make the information monitored by the sensor network more reliable for all the nodes have to die within the last 40 rounds (the last node die) in DPEG.

Acknowledgement

This research is supported in part by Hong Kong Polytechnic University under the ICRG grant A-PF77 and the China National 973 Program Grant 2002CB312002

References

1. D. Estrin, L. Girod, G. Pottie, and M. Srivastava, "Instrumenting the World with Wireless Sensor Networks," in International Conference on Acoustics, Speech, and Signal Processing (ICASSP2001), Salt Lake City, Utah, May 2001.
2. G. J. Pottie and W. J. Kaiser, "Wireless Integrated Newtork Sensors," *Communications of the ACM*, vol. 43, no. 5, pp. 51–58, May 2000.
3. W. Ye, J. Heidenmann, and D. Estrin, "An Energy-Efficient MAC Protocol for Wireless Sensor Networks," in *Proceedings of IEEE INFOCOM*, New York, NY, June 2002.
4. K. Sohrabi, J. Gao, V. Ailawadhi, and G. J. Pottie, "Protocols for Self-Organization of a Wireless Sensor Network," *IEEE Personal Comm. Mag.*, vol. 7, no. 5, Oct. 2000

5. J. Kulik, W. R. Heinzelman, and H. Balakrishnan, "Negotiation-Based Protocols for Disseminating Information in Wireless Sensor Networks," *ACM Wireless Networks*, vol. 8, no. 2-3, pp. 169–185, 2002.
6. A. Cerpa and D. Estrin, "ASCENT: Adaptive Self-Configuring Sensor Networks Topologies," in *Proceedings of IEEE INFOCOM*, New York, NY, June 2002.
7. V. Kawadia and P. R. Kumar, "Power Control and Clustering in Ad Hoc Networks," in *Proceedings of IEEE INFOCOM*, April 2003.
8. D. Estrin, et al. Next Century Challenges: Scalable Coordination in Sensor Networks. In Proc. of MobiCOM '99, August 1999
9. W. R. Heinzelman, J. Kulik, and H. Balakrishnan. Adaptive Protocols for Information Dissemination in Wireless Sensor Networks. In *Proc. 5th Ann. Intl. Conf. on Mobile Computing and Networking*, pages 174–185, Seattle, WA, August 2001. ACM.
10. S. Lindsey and C. S. Raghavendra, "Pegasis: Power-efficient gathering in sensor information systems," in *IEEE Aerospace Conference*, March 2002.
11. Huseyin Ozgur Tan, et al. Power Efficient Data Gathering and Aggregation in Wireless Sensor Networks. SIGMOD Record, Vol. 32, No. 4, December 2003
12. S. Bandyopadhyay and E. Coyle, "An Energy-Efficient Hierarchical Clustering Algorithm for Wireless Sensor Networks," in *Proceedings of IEEE INFOCOM*, April 2003.
13. O. Younis and S. Fahmy, "Distributed Clustering in Ad-hoc Sensor Networks: A Hybrid, Energy-Efficient Approach," in *Proceedings of IEEE INFOCOM*, March 2004.
14. W. R. Heinzelman, et al. An Application -Specific Protocol Architecture for Wireless Microsensor Networks. IEEE Transactions on Wireless Communications, vol. 1, no. 4, Oct. 2002
15. R. Williams, "The geometrical foundation of natural structure: A source book of design," Dover Pub. Inc., New York, pp. 51-52, 1979.
16. S. Tilak, N. Abu-Ghazaleh, and W. Heinzelman. Infrastructure tradeo.s for sensor networks. In *Proceedings of First International Workshop on Wireless Sensor Networks and Applications (WSNA'02)*, pp 49−57. Atlanta, USA, September 2002.

A Key Management Scheme for Cross-Layering Designs in Wireless Sensor Networks

Bo Yu, Haiguang Chen, Min Yang, Dilin Mao, and Chuanshan Gao

Department of Computer Science and Engineering,
Fudan University, 200433, P. R. China
{bcyu, hgchen, m_yang, dlmao, cgao}@fudan.edu.cn

Abstract. The current wireless sensor network designs are largely based on a layered approach. The suboptimality and inflexibility of this paradigm result in poor performance, due to constraints of power, communication, and computational capabilities. Key management plays an important role in wireless sensor networks, because it not only takes charge of securing link-layer communications between nodes, but also has great effects on other protocol layers, e.g. routing and IDS (Intrusion Detection System). However, no existing key management protocols have attached enough importance to cross-layering designs. In this paper, we propose a cross-layering key management scheme, which can provide other protocol layers with a nice trust-level metric. The trust-level metric is generated during the pairwise key establishment phase, and it varies as system conditions change. This metric describes the security level between two neighboring nodes and helps other protocol layers to make decisions. We also present simulations and analysis to show the superior characteristics of our scheme against both passive attacks and active attacks.

1 Introduction

Recent advance in nano-technology makes it possible to develop low-power battery operated sensor nodes which are tiny and cheap, and could be deployed in a wide area. Many sensor systems are deployed in unattended and possibly adversarial environments. Hence, security mechanisms that provide confidentiality and authentication are critical for the operations of many sensor applications. However, individual sensor nodes have limited power, computation, memory, and communication capabilities, which make it infeasible to use traditional public-key cryptosystem.

Due to constraints of limited computational and communication capabilities, key management is a challenging problem in wireless sensor networks. It not only takes charge of securing link-layer communications between nodes, but also has great effects on other protocol layers, e.g. routing, MAC and IDS (Intrusion Detection System). A number of key management schemes for wireless sensor networks have been proposed recently [5,6,8,9,10,13,14]. However, none of the existing key management protocols has attached enough importance to cross-layering designs. We will introduce more about these schemes in section 2. These schemes are especially vulnerable to active attacks, especially fabrication attacks. Suppose that a number of sensor nodes are compromised, and all secret information stored in their memory is exposed to the adversary. Then the adversary can fabricate to be a legal node and make a successful shake-hand with any other nodes in the network. Thus, the adversary can inject any messages into the network at will. The existing key management schemes cannot distinguish between malicious shake-hands and friendly ones as long as the previous compromised nodes are not detected. We think that since key management takes charge of setting up and maintaining a secure communication link between two neighboring nodes, it can provide some important information about the communication link. This information could be very valuable for other protocol layers to make decisions, e.g. routing and IDS (Intrusion Detection System). In this way, even if the adversary could make a successful shake-hand, the activities of the adversary will be quite limited by other protocol layers.

The current wireless sensor networks are largely based on a layered approach. The suboptimality and inflexibility of this paradigm result in poor performance [2], due to constraints of power, communication, and computational capabilities. The existing key management schemes have done a quite good job on the link-layer security problems [3,5,6,8,9,10,13,14]. Once a session key is created for a communication link, it's hard for a passive attacker to eavesdrop and apply cryptanalysis. But the existing schemes are quite vulnerable to active and smart attackers. So now the challenge is how to intensify the network's strength against active attacks, especially fabrication attacks. We believe that a cross-layering design [2] will help resolve the problem, in which different protocol layers, e.g. key management, routing and IDS (Intrusion Detection System), cooperate with each other to make the sensor system more efficient and more robust.

In this paper, we present a key management scheme for cross-layering designs in wireless sensor networks. The scheme provides a nice trust-level metric, which can dynamically evaluate the trust relationship between two neighboring nodes and help other protocol layers, such as MAC, routing, IDS, to make decisions. It could be utilized locally or globally in the network. For instance, if one node finds that one of its neighbors is not so reliable, it could change its routing table and avoid forwarding packets to the neighbor. What's more, if all the network-wide trust-level metrics are collected, the IDS (Intrusion Detection System) could use the information to find out which nodes are the most suspicious nodes and which parts of the network are the most vulnerable parts. Our scheme is based on Zhu's scheme [10]. We extend his scheme and adapt it to cross-layering designs. To the best of our knowledge, our scheme is a first attempt to design a cross-layering oriented key management scheme.

The main contributions of this paper are as follows:

1. Trust-level metric that helps the sensor system to make cross-layering decisions.
2. Strengthened pairwise keys that make the network stronger against the compromise.
3. Theoretical analysis and simulations of different key management schemes.

The remainder of this paper is organized as follows. We first review some other related work in adhoc network security problems, in section 2. In section 3, we describe our key management scheme in detail. Section 4 presents the analysis and simulations of our scheme in security, communication and computation. Finally, we provide some concluding remarks in Section 5.

2 Related Work

We first review the work to establish shared keys in mobile ad-hoc network, and then review several key management schemes in wireless sensor network.

Zhou and Hass [1] present a distributed public-key management scheme for ad hoc networks. Zhu et al [10] present an approach for establishing a pairwise key that is exclusively known to a pair of nodes with overwhelming probability. His scheme is based on the combination of probabilistic key sharing and (threshold) secret sharing.

Eschenauer and Gligor [9] present a key management scheme for sensor networks based on probabilistic key pre-deployment. Chan et al [8] extend this scheme and present three new mechanisms for key establishment based on the framework of probabilistic key predeployment. Wenliang Du et al. [14] proposed a method to improve the Eschenauer-Gligor scheme using a priori deployment knowledge. And later, he proposed a matrix-computation-based key pre-distribution scheme [13]. The scheme exhibits a threshold property that when the number of compromised nodes is less than the threshold, the probability that any other nodes are affected is close to zero. Zhu et al. [11] propose LEAP, a key management protocol for large-scale distributed sensor networks. In his scheme, keys for secure communication are divided into four types: individual key, group key, cluster key, and pairwise shared key.

3 Key Management Scheme

In this section, we first describe our assumptions and then present our scheme in detail.

3.1 Assumptions

We assume that sensor nodes are static once they are deployed. The network links are bidirectional, i.e., if node A can hear node B, B can also hear A. The resources of a node, such as power, computation, communication capacity, are relatively constrained. The sensor nodes are similar in their computational, communication capabilities and power resources. We assume that every node has space for storing up to hundreds of bytes of keying material. Deployment knowledge of nodes will not be known in advance, i.e., sensor nodes do not know their neighboring nodes until deployed. We also assume that an adversary can eavesdrop on all traffic, inject packets or replay older messages. If a node is compromised, all the information it holds will also be compromised. The adversary may launch fabrication attacks by manipulating the compromised secret keys.

3.2 Detailed Key Management Scheme

Motivation
Current wireless sensor network protocol designs are largely based on a layer approach. However, a crossing-layer design can help different layers, including security layer, to cooperate with each other efficiently. For example, if a sensor node finds that one of his neighbors is not so reliable, its routing layer could avoid forwarding

packets to this neighbor. For another example, a node could attach some reliability evaluation at the end of the packets being forwarded. It finally helps the base station to recognize the fabricated data injected by the adversary.

The existing key management protocols in sensor networks [5,6,8,9,10,11], didn't attach enough importance to crossing-layer designs. After all the secure communication links over the network were set up, these protocols can do little, even when the adversary is launching an attack. We believe that key management protocol should cooperate with other protocol layers, such as, IDS (Intrusion Detection System). The key management protocol takes charge of setting up secure links between nodes, so it could also provide IDS with some suggestions, e.g. how secure some communication links are, or how suspicious some nodes behave. In our scheme, we provide a trust-level metric to help the key management scheme to cooperate with other protocol layers.

In our scheme, key management consists of four phases, namely key pre-distribution, logical path establishment, pairwise key establishment, and key maintenance.

Key Pre-distribution

During *key pre-distribution phase*, for each node, we select k random keys from a large key pool and store them in the node's memory. The key pool size is P. This phase occurs before the deployment of the network. The key pre-distribution scheme enables every pair of nodes to share one or more keys with a chosen probability.

Logical Path Establishment

The *logical path establishment phase* occurs when a node wants to securely exchange with other nodes in the network. We say there are logical paths between two nodes when (i) the two nodes share one or more keys. We call such paths *direct paths*. (ii) the two nodes do not share any keys, but through other intermediate nodes they can exchange messages securely. We call such paths *indirect paths* and call the involved intermediate nodes *proxies*. We have the same logical path establishment method as Zhu's [10]. So for detailed description, please read Zhu's [10].

Pairwise Key Establishment

After the sensor nodes are deployed, a *pairwise key establishment phase* begins. Two neighboring nodes need to set up a session key to communicate securely. Suppose that node u and v wish to communicate securely. Node u and v may already share one or more keys from the pool of keys after the key pre-distribution phase, but the shared key(s) is not known exclusively to u and v, it is also loaded in many other nodes during the key pre-distribution phase. So it is important for node u and v to set up a session key, which is known exclusively to node u and v. To establish session key, node u first generates a random number as its session key with node v, and then node u divides sk into n shares and sends these n shares to node v through different paths. If a (k,n) threshold algorithm is used, node v needs to get at least k shares to reconstruct the session key. Then node v could use this exclusive session key to communicate with node u.

More specifically, the pairwise key establishment phase is as follows:

$$S_u \xrightarrow{broadcast} \text{id}_{S_u} \parallel \{\text{id}_{key}\} \tag{i1}$$

First, each node broads its node id and the key id list which are stored in its memory during the key pre-distribution phase. After this, nodes get to know who their neighbors are. We can also use a challenge method [9] to hide the key-sharing patterns among nodes from the adversary, who might be a smart attacker and chooses an optimal set of nodes to compromise.

Suppose that node u hears node v's broadcast. Node u generates a random number as a secret key ks, then divides ks into n shares $ks_1, ks_2, ..., ks_n$, using a (k,n) threshold algorithm. Note that the secret key ks is not the final session key. Then node u saves ks and the n shares in its memory, and send them to node v through different logical paths.

$$S_u \xrightarrow{\text{Logical Path}} S_v \quad \{ks \parallel \text{id}_{ks}\} \tag{i2}$$

Node v need to successfully get at least k shares from different logical paths to recompute ks. When node v regain the secret key ks, it uses the following equation to generate the session key sk with node u.

$$sk = ks \oplus ks_{i_1} \oplus ks_{i_2} \oplus \cdots ks_{i_m} \quad m \geq k \tag{i3}$$

$\oplus$ is an XOR operation. $ks_{i1}, ks_{i2}, ..., ks_{im}$ are the secret key shares which node v successfully gets from node u through different logical paths. Then node v sends the key id list of $ks_{i1}, ks_{i2}, ..., ks_{im}$ to node u directly, i.e., not through any logical paths.

$$S_v \longrightarrow S_u \quad \{\text{id}_{ks}\} \tag{i4}$$

After node u gets the id list of keys which node v successfully gets, node u can also generate the session key sk using equation (i3).

$$S_u \longleftrightarrow S_v \quad E_{sk}(data) \tag{i5}$$

Once the session key sk is set up, node u and node v can communicate securely. This session key sk is exclusively known to node u and node v. The security analysis about the pairwise session key establishment will be described in section 4.

Trust-level Metric

In our scheme, we propose a *trust-level metric*, which is established during the pairwise key establishment phase. For each link between a node and its neighbors, there is a trust-level tuple which is stored in the node's memory, i.e. if a node have 5 neighboring nodes, it have 5 tuples stored in its memory, one for each. The tuples describe the security state of the communication links between a node and its neighbors.

We define the trust-level metric as a tuple (m,t,B). In the tuple, m is the same in equation (i3), which is the number of secret shares which a node could get through logical paths, and t means secure time, i.e. how long have past since two neighboring nodes set up a secure link, B means behavior, i.e. how some neighboring node is behaving recently, e.g. traffic. The parameter m could helps to evaluate the secure level of the communication link. Larger m means securer links, for if m is larger, the adversary has to compromise more nodes in the logical paths.

We think that the more actual definitions of m, t, B are application specific. Different application purposes and different deployment environments make different requirements. So it's hard to provide a general compute method for these parameters. But we do provide a possible evaluation function f to evaluate the secure state of a communication link.

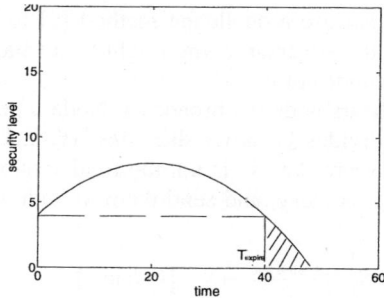

Fig. 1. Trust-level evaluation function

$$f(m,t,A) = \alpha(t - \frac{T_{expire}}{2})^2 + \beta m - \gamma B \tag{16}$$

In the equation, α, β, γ are some constants which we could adjust according specific application, T_{expire} is the expire time when re-keying should start, and m, t and B are the same as the ones in the trust-level tuple.

We can see a nice sample of function f in Fig. 1. The x axe is time since pairwise session key is established, and the y axe is the security-level evaluation of some communication link. The function f initially starts at a *base security level*, which is decided by parameter m. Then as time is going, if the neighbor doesn't show any abnormal behavior, the curve goes up. After the acme is reached, the curve goes down. And when the curve enters the shadowed area, i.e. the life time of session key expires, a re-keying operation must be taken. The parameter B is presumed to be zero in figure 1. If parameter B is considered, some vibrations will appear on the curve. If the range of the vibration is so large that the curve falls below the base security level, we consider that the communication link is in a dangerous state and a re-keying operation must be taken to ensure the neighbor is still a legal node. Many causes would lead to the vibrations of the curve, e.g. a routing message received from this neighbor is quite different from the ones from the other neighbors, a bust of traffic is injected by this neighbor in a short time, etc. So the behavior parameter B is application specific. We could assign definite meaning to the parameter B according definite deployment requirements.

The trust-level metric makes our key management scheme a dynamic scheme. The trust-level tuple provides an instant evaluation of the current network security state, and crossing-layer designs could make adaptive decisions on the fly.

Key Maintenance

After the nodes set up a session key with their neighbors, the network moves into a *key maintenance phase*. Key maintenance operations consist of three tasks: *reporting*, *re-keying*, and *revocation*. The trust-level metric is helpful for the sensor system to make key maintenance decisions. Nodes periodically report its trust-level metrics to the base station. If the base station finds some abnormal situations, e.g., attacks or abnormal sensor readings, the base station may send out revocation commands to let the nodes to revoke the compromised keys. Even if no attacks occur, re-keying is also necessary after the life-time of pairwise keys expires in case of cryptanalyzing.

4 Simulations and Analysis

We use simulations to investigate the characteristics of our key management scheme. The simulations assume a network of 1000 nodes, which are deployed within a square area of 1000m x 1000m. The communication range of nodes is 50m, which also means that a node have 24 neighbors in average when deployed in the simulation area. The key pool size P is 10000, and each node is loaded with 75 random keys from the key pool.

4.1 Security Analysis

We mainly focus on the security problems about node compromise. Suppose that a number of nodes in the network are compromised by the adversary, the secret keys stored in the nodes' memory are also uncovered, and what's more, the compromise operations of the adversary might not be detected within a period of time. The adversary can launch two kinds of attacks: *passive attacks* and *active attacks*. Passive attacks include communication-link eavesdropping, traffic analysis, key pre-distribution pattern analysis, etc. Active attacks include injecting fake information, e.g. fake routing information and fake sensor readings, fabricating new sensor nodes, flooding and DOS[7] attacks, etc. Passive attacks can be effectively prevented by using session keys and re-keying, but active attacks are harder to prevent. The adversary can use the compromised secret keys to pretend to be a legal node to take a successful shake hand with any sensor node in the network. We call this type of shake-hands *malicious shake-hands*, for after shake-hands the adversary could inject the network with all kinds of messages at will. Malicious shake-hands are hard to prevent, as long as the compromise operations are not detected. Wireless sensor networks are usually deployed in an unattended environment, sometimes it's impossible to give every node a physical check to make sure the node is still not compromised. The existing key management schemes [5,6,8,9,10,13,14] could do little to prevent these active attacks, especially malicious shake-hands. It's hard for these schemes to distinguish malicious shake-hands from friendly ones. We conclude Table 1 by taking some simple deductions and analysis for Eschenauer's scheme [9], Chan's q-composite scheme [8], and Zhu's scheme [10]. From Table 1, we find that in Eschenauer's scheme, if a node is compromised, the adversary can take a successful shake-hand with 99.68% of nodes in the network, as long as the compromise is not detected. The percent value is the same as the connectivity probability of the network, but from another point of view, we can also regard it as a malicious shake-hand percent. The conclusion of Table 1 is based on the simulation configurations described in the head of this section, and for Chan's q-composite scheme, we suppose $p_{connect} \geq 0.33$, please refer to Chan's [8] for detail.

Table 1. Fraction of malicious shake hand

Scheme	Fraction of malicious shake hand
Eschenauer's	1. 0.9968
Chan's q-composite	2. 0.9372
Zhu's	3. 0.9968

Our scheme cannot distinguish malicious shake-hands from friendly ones too, as long as the compromise is not reported. But we provide a trust-level metric to reduce the effects of possible malicious attacks. The trust-level metric provide the security state information between a node and its neighbors. It is a cross-layering metric, which could help other sensor layers to make decisions. For example, the routing layer could avoid forwarding packets to a new neighbor no matter whether it is friendly or malicious. The metric is a tuple, which contains three parts: m,t,B. m is the number of logical paths which were used to set up a session key. t is time since the session key has been set up. B is behavior, e.g. traffic. These parameters could be taken into account by other sensor protocol layers. Fig. 2 is a typical application of the trust-level metric. We call Fig. 2 a *security map*. In the map, (x,y) are the physical position of a node, axis z is the value of the evaluation function f which is introduced in section 4. We compute the value of the evaluation function f for every node, and then a security map forms. From the map, we can find the security weak area of the network. The protuberant area in the map is more secure than the concave ones. If the concave areas are below some pre-defined security level limit, the base station must send commands to let the nodes in that area to take re-keying, key revocation or other security mechanisms to strengthen the security level.

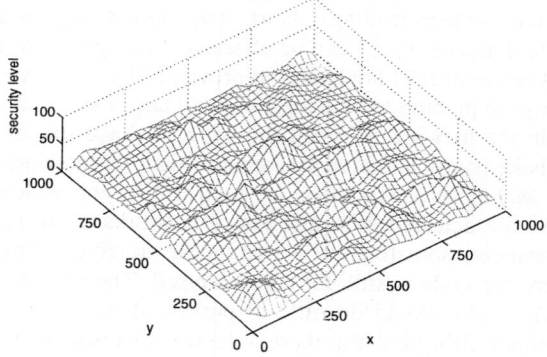

Fig. 2. Security map

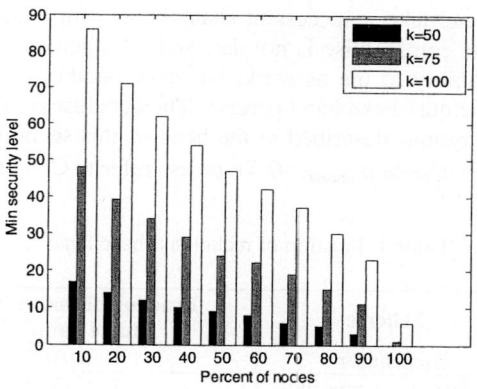

Fig. 3. Security level distribution

The security map can be generated by a base station. When sensor nodes report their readings to the base station, the trust-level metrics could be attached in the packet. The security map is also a dynamic map. If the adversary takes malicious shake-hands with any nodes in the network, a new concave area will appear in the map. So we can pay more attention to the area and avoid some activities in the area, e.g. forwarding packets to the area.

Fig. 3 shows the security level distribution among nodes. k is the number of secret keys each node loads before deployment. We vary k from 50 to 100. The y axis is also the value of the evaluation function f. When k is set to 100, we can find 100% nodes have a minimal security level of 7, and 90% nodes have a minimal security level of 25. This figure can help us to choose a pre-defined security level limit. We believe this security limit is an application specific value, and it can be adjusted to meet specific requirements.

In the following, we discuss the characteristics of our scheme against passive attacks. Passive attacks include communication-link eavesdropping, traffic analysis, key pre-distribution pattern analysis, etc. Usually session key, re-keying, key revocation, etc. are used to prevent passive attacks [8,9,10]. One of the most important metrics to evaluate a key management scheme is the fraction of communications compromised when the adversary has captured some set of w nodes. This metric is also discussed by [8,10]. Our scheme is based on Zhu's scheme, but Zhu's analysis doesn't take the (k,n) threshold algorithm into account. So in the following, we will extend Zhu's analysis.

Note that we only consider the communication links secured by a pairwise session key during the pairwise key establishment phase. So if the adversary begins to eavesdrop the link after the session key has been set up, it would be very hard to decrypt the session key, which is exclusively known to the two neighboring nodes. But in our analysis, we suppose that the most terrible situation appears that a number of nodes are compromised at the very beginning, the adversary eavesdrops all the later processes of pairwise key establishment.

Given that w nodes have been captured in the very beginning, P is the size of the key pool, k is the number of random keys each node has. The probability p_c that any key is contained in the union of the key sets of the w nodes is

$$p_c = 1-(1-\frac{k}{P})^w$$

Suppose that node u hears node v's request, then node u generates a random number as a secret key ks, then divides ks into n shares $ks_1, ks_2, ..., ks_n$, using a (k,n) threshold algorithm. In the n shares, $z1$ shares are delivered through direct paths and $z2$ shares are delivered through indirect paths. For simplicity, we suppose the indirect paths are one-proxy paths. Finally, node v successfully gets only z_{10} shares from the z_1 ones and z_{20} share s from the z_2 ones, and node v must have $k \leq z_{10} + z_{20} \leq z_1 + z_2$ to recompute the secret key ks. We suppose that there are z_{10} direct paths and z_{20} indirect paths compromised by the adversary. Thus, for Zhu's scheme, the security of the pairwise key is

$$p_w = (1-(1-\frac{k}{P})^w)^{z_{10}} \binom{z_1}{z_{10}} \times (1-(1-\frac{k}{P})^{2w})^{z_{20}} \binom{z_2}{z_{20}}$$

But for our scheme, the security of the pairwise is

$$p'_w = (1-(1-\frac{k}{P})^w)^{z_{10}} \times (1-(1-\frac{k}{P})^{2w})^{z_{20}}$$

So, we have $p_w \geq p'_w$. This is because in Zhu's scheme, the adversary need have any combination of z_1 shares taken z_{10} and any combination of z_2 shares taken z_{20} to recompute the secret key ks. But in our scheme, the adversary must have capture the exact z_{10} shares and the exact z_{20} shares, which are the same as node v gets, because node v makes the secret key ks XOR with the $z_{10}+z_{20}$ shares to generate the final session key sk. So, compared with Zhu's scheme, our scheme would have a less fraction of total communication links that are compromised by a capture of x nodes.

Fig. 4 shows the simulation results of the fraction of communications compromised when x nodes have been captured by the adversary. Eschenauer's scheme [9], Chan's q-composite [8], Zhu's scheme [10] and ours are tested in the simulation. The figure shows that our scheme has nice strength against small-scale attacks. In our scheme, when the number of compromised nodes is 130, just about 1% of the total communication links are in danger. In the simulation, for Chan's and our scheme, we use a (k,n) threshold algorithm where $k=n-4$.

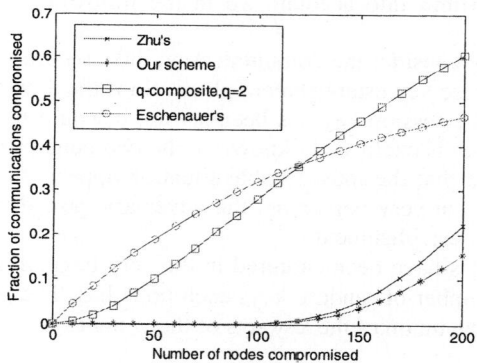

Fig. 4. Fraction of communications compromised when x nodes have been captured by the adversary

4.2 Computation Analysis

The computation cost consists of two parts: pairwise key establishment cost and securing communication links cost. Once a session key is established during the pairwise key establishment phase, communication links can be secured by inexpensive link-layer symmetric key operations. So the main computation cost of our scheme is the cost during the pairwise key establishment phase. Suppose that node u divides a secret key into n shares and deliver them to node v through logical paths. During the phase, the computation includes threshold algorithm and symmetric encryptions and decryptions for logical paths. The threshold algorithm is based on polynomial interpolation. Many efficient $O(n \log^2 n)$ algorithms are fast enough for the sensor's key management system [15]. In the worst case when all the n shares are delivered through one-proxy logical paths, the number of encryptions and decryptions is 4n.

5 Conclusions

Due to constrains of power, communication, and computational capabilities, protocol layers of a sensor should cooperate with each other to work more efficiently. In this paper, we present a key management scheme for cross-layering designs in wireless sensor networks. To the best of our knowledge, our scheme is a first attempt to design a cross-layering key management protocol which can provide other sensor protocol layers with dynamic security information. Our approach is also scalable and flexible. We provide simulations and analysis which indicate that our scheme has superior characteristics of resilience against both passive attacks and active attacks.

In our future work, we are going to design secure routing layer and IDS (Intrusion Detection System) for wireless sensor networks, which can cooperate with our key management scheme.

References

1. Lidong Zhou and Zygmunt J. Haas. Securing Adhoc Networks. IEEE Network Magazine, 13(6):24-30, November/December 1999.
2. I. F. Akyildiz and I. H. Kasimoglu, Wireless sensor and actor networks: research challenges, Ad hoc networks 2 (2004), pp351-367, May 2004.
3. C. Karlof, N. Sastry and D. Wagner, TinySec: A Link Layer Security Architecture for Wireless Sensor Networks, Second ACM Conference on Embedded Networked Sensor Systems (SensSys 2004) 2004.
4. I. Akyildiz. W. Su, Y. Sankarasubramaniam and E. Cayirci "Wireless sensor networks: a survey," Computer Networks 2002.
5. A. Wadaa, S. Olariu, L. Wilson, M. Eltoweissy, Scalable cryptographic key management in wireless sensor networks, Distributed Computing Systems Workshops, 2004. Proceedings. 24th International Conference on , 23-24 Mar. 2004 Pages:796 – 802
6. G. Jolly, M.C Kuscu., P. Kokate, M Younis., A low-energy key management protocol for wireless sensor networks, Computers and Communication, 2003. (ISCC 2003). Proceedings. Eighth IEEE International Symposium on , 30 June-3 July 2003 Pages:335 - 340 vol.1
7. A. D. Wood and J. A. Stankovic, Denial of Service in sensor network, IEEE Computer Magazine, October 2002
8. Haowen Chan, Perrig A., Song D., Random key predistribution schemes for sensor networks, Security and Privacy, 2003. Proceedings. 2003 Symposium on , 11-14 May 2003 Pages:197 – 213.
9. L. Eschenauer and V. Gligor, A Key-Management Scheme for Distributed Sensor Networks. In Proc. Of ACM CCS 2002.

10. Sencun Zhu, Shouhuai Xu, Sanjeev Setia, and Sushil Jajodia. Establishing Pair-wise Keys For Secure Communication in Ad Hoc Networks: A Probabilistic Approach. In Proc. of the 11th IEEE International Conference on Network Protocols (ICNP'03), Atlanta, Georgia, November 4-7, 2003.
11. Sencun Zhu, S. Setia and S. Jajodia. LEAP: Efficient Security Mechanisms for Large-Scale Distributed Sensor Networks. the 10th ACM Conference on Computer and Communications Security (CCS'03), Washington D.C., October, 2003.
13. Wenliang Du, Jing Deng, Yunghsiang S. Han, and Pramod Varshney. A Pairwise Key Predistribution Scheme for Wireless Sensor Networks. In Proceedings of the 10th ACM Conference on Computer and Communications Security (CCS), Washington DC, October 27-31, 2003.
14. Wenliang Du, Jing Deng, Yunghsiang S. Han, Shigang Chen and Pramod Varshney. A Key Management Scheme for Wireless Sensor Networks Using Deployment Knowledge. In Proceedings of the IEEE INFOCOM'04, March 7-11, 2004, Hongkong. Pages 586-597.
15. A. Shamir. How to share a secret. Comm. ACM, 22(11):612-613,1979.

A Clustering Mechanism with Various Cluster Sizes for the Sensor Network

Yujin Lim[1] and Sanghyun Ahn[2,*,**]

[1] Department of Information Media,
University of Suwon, Suwon, Korea
yujin@suwon.ac.kr
[2] School of Computer Science,
University of Seoul, Seoul, Korea
ahn@venus.uos.ac.kr

Abstract. One of the most important issues on the sensor network with resource-limited sensor nodes is prolonging the network lifetime by effectively utilizing the limited node energy. The most representative mechanism to achieve a long-lived sensor network is the clustering mechanism which can be further classified into the single-hop mode and the multi-hop mode. In the single-hop mode, all sensor nodes in a cluster communicate directly with the cluster head (CH) via single hop, so the contention-less MAC protocol is preferred. In the multi-hop mode, sensor nodes communicate with the CH with the help of other intermediate nodes and the contention-less MAC protocol is not required. One of the most critical factors that impact on the performance of the existing multi-hop clustering mechanism (in which the cluster size is fixed to some value, so we call this the fixed-size mechanism) is the cluster size and, without the assumption on the uniform node distribution, finding out the best cluster size is intractable. Since sensor nodes in a real sensor network are distributed non-uniformly, the fixed-size mechanism may not work best for real sensor networks. Therefore, in this paper, we propose a new dynamic-size multi-hop clustering mechanism in which the cluster size is adjusted according to the information on the load and the residual energy of a CH and that of other nodes near to the CH. We show that our proposed scheme outperforms other clustering mechanisms by carrying out simulations.

1 Introduction

The wireless sensor network is the network composed of wireless sensor nodes distributed over a specific area to monitor the current condition within that area.

---

* This research was supported by the MIC(Ministry of Information and Communication), Korea, under the Chung-Ang University HNRC-ITRC (Home Network Research Center) support program supervised by the IITA (Institute of Information Technology Assessment).
** This work was supported by grant No. R01-2004-10372-0 from the Basic Research Program of the Korea Science & Engineering Foundation.

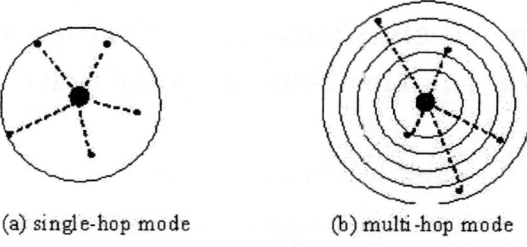

(a) single-hop mode (b) multi-hop mode

Fig. 1. Communication modes within a cluster

Sensor nodes recognize and measure some requested phenomena, and send the sensed data to the sink via the wireless channel. The sink collects and analyzes data from sensor nodes. The sensor network is different from the mobile ad hoc network in the sense that sensor nodes have lower mobility and more restricted energy and denser distribution.

One of the most important issues in the sensor network is to prolong the network lifetime. In general, the network lifetime is defined as the time when for the first time any sensor node experiences energy depletion. Major part of node energy consumption comes from the radio communication. For example, the amount of the energy consumed for the delivery of 1 bit to a place located 100m apart is almost the same as the energy required for the execution of 3000 commands [1].

In the sensor network, there are two categories of approaches to reducing the node energy consumption. The first approach is to turn off the radio of a node which does not need to send or receive data at the MAC and the network layers. In the mechanisms like [2] [3] [4], only those nodes belonging to the network backbone turn on their radio and other nodes save their energy by turning it off and entering into the sleep mode. And, in the mechanisms like [5] and [6], each node tries to increase the network capacity by adjusting their transmission power.

The second approach is using the data aggregation to reduce the amount of the transmitted data for the reduction of the communication cost. The most representative mechanism belonging to this approach is the clustering mechanism. The clustering mechanism is very useful for those applications requiring scalability to efficiently handle several hundreds to thousands of sensor nodes. In the clustering mechanism, sensor nodes form a number of clusters and send their sensed data to the cluster heads (CHs) of the clusters that they belong to instead of sending them to the sink. Each CH aggregates collected data and sends the aggregated data to the sink in lieu of sensor nodes in its cluster.

The clustering mechanism can be further classified into the single-hop and the multi-hop clustering mechanisms according to the communication mode within a cluster [7]. In the single-hop mode, as shown in figure 1.(a), all the sensor nodes in a cluster communicate with the CH via single hop and, in this case, data is not relayed from sensor nodes to the CH by other intermediate sensor nodes. Because the communication between sensor nodes and the CH is direct, sensor nodes are not allowed to transmit data to the CH simultaneously and, therefore, the contention-less MAC protocol (such as TDMA) is preferred and each sensor node is required to send a join message to the corresponding CH.

On this other hand, in the multi-hop clustering, as shown in figure 1.(b), sensor nodes communicate with the CH via multiple hops and intermediate sensor nodes relay data to the CH, so there is no requirement on the contention-less MAC protocol. However, sensor nodes near the CH may suffer from extra overhead of relaying data between the CH and other sensor nodes.

Another aspect that we have to consider is the node distribution within a sensor network. Since there is no guarantee on the uniform distribution of sensor nodes, the node density within a cluster may be different from that within other clusters, so in the single-hop mode some specific CHs may get overloaded. On the other hand, the multi-hop mode can control the overhead imposed on a CH by determining the best cluster size. However, since the node distribution within a real sensor network is not uniform, it is almost infeasible to find out the best cluster size for a real sensor network.

Therefore, in this paper, we propose a clustering mechanism which can prolong the entire network lifetime by controlling the load on each CH with adjusting the size of each cluster according to the information on the load and the residual energy of the CH. The rest of this paper is organized as follows: in section 2, we introduce the representative clustering mechanisms supporting the single-hop and the multi-hop modes, respectively. In section 3, our proposed dynamic-size multi-hop clustering mechanism is described in detail, and section 4 gives the performance comparison between the proposed mechanism and others by carrying out simulations. Section 5 concludes this paper.

2 Related Work

LEACH [8] and HEED [9] are the most representative clustering mechanisms using the single-hop mode. LEACH [8] is the mechanism whose goal is to balance the load on each CH by allowing each sensor node to become a CH in a round-robin fashion by applying Eq.1. P is the probability of a sensor node being elected as a CH (ex. P = 0.05), r indicates the number of the current round, and G is the set of nodes not elected as CHs for $\frac{1}{P}$ rounds. The node elected as a CH announces itself as a newly elected CH by broadcasting an advertisement message. Each non-CH sensor node receiving advertisement messages decides a cluster that it is going to join and sends a message notifying its join to the corresponding CH. This procedure is called the set-up stage and, once all sensor nodes join clusters, they enter into the steady-state. In the steady-state, each sensor node transmits its sensed data to the CH of the cluster that it belongs to instead of directly sending them to the sink. The CH receiving data from sensor nodes reduces the amount of the transmitted data by aggregating the collected data, and sends the aggregated data to the sink. A round is composed of the set-up and the steady-state stages and, for each round, a new CH is elected.

$$T(n) = \begin{cases} \frac{P}{1-P\times(r\,mod\frac{1}{P})} & \text{if } n \in G \\ 0 & \text{otherwise} \end{cases} \quad (1)$$

HEED [9] tries to increase the network lifetime by assigning the same probability of being a CH to each node and electing the node with the largest amount of available energy as a CH using Eq.2. $E_{residual}$ is the amount of available energy and E_{max} is the initial node energy.

$$CH_{prob} = CH_{prob} \times \frac{E_{residual}}{E_{max}} \quad (2)$$

S. Bandyopadhyay [10] has proposed a multi-hop clustering mechanism in which a sensor node elected as a CH with probability p broadcasts an advertisement message of its becoming a CH and other nodes relay this message up to k hops (which is the cluster size). A sensor node receiving more than one advertisement messages decides which cluster it is going to join, and transmits a join message to the corresponding CH. In this case, the most critical factor that affects the performance is the cluster size and the best cluster size has been calculated with assuming the uniform distribution of sensor nodes. However, in the real network environment, it is almost impossible to distribute sensor nodes uniformly and, with non-uniform distribution of sensor nodes, it is not feasible to compute the best cluster size. Therefore, in this, paper, we propose a multi-hop clustering mechanism that dynamically adjusts the cluster size based on the information on the node density and the available energy of a CH.

3 The Dynamic-Size Multi-hop Clustering Mechanism

We assume a contention-based MAC protocol and the multi-hop mode for our proposed mechanism. The multi-hop mode is adopted since it gives a higher probability of aggregation than the single-hop mode since usually the single-hop mode requires more CHs.

The existing multi-hop clustering mechanism assumes all clusters have the same size (we call this the fixed-size mechanism) and tries to compute the best cluster size with assuming the uniform node distribution. However, the node distribution in most real sensor networks is non-uniform (i.e., each cluster may have different node density) making the fixed-size mechanism less efficient in improving the network lifetime. Hence, if the size of a cluster is decided according to the node density and the available energy of the corresponding CH, the overhead imposed on the CH can be controlled according to the current condition of the CH and, ultimately, the non-uniform node distribution problem can be resolved. Therefore, our proposed clustering mechanism, the dynamic-size multi-hop clustering mechanism, adopts the concept of adjusting the cluster size according to the information on the node density within a cluster and the available energy of the corresponding CH. The operation of the proposed mechanism is as follows.

If a node is elected as a CH by applying either Eq.1 or Eq.2 (i.e., the CH election mechanism of either LEACH or HEAD) (in this paper, we do not focus

```
compute CH_prob ← CH_prob × E_residual/E_max
TTL ← any_default_value       // TTL means cluster size
if (CH_prob ≥ Random(0,1)) { // I am a Cluster Head
        my_status ← Cluster_Head
        compute CL_CH ← Σ_{j=0}^{n} E_RX,j + E_TX,sink
        if ( CL_CH/E_residual ≤ min(load of near-by nodes))
                TTL ← TTL + 1
        else if ( CL_CH/E_residual ≥ max(load of near-by nodes))
                TTL ← TTL - 1
        broadcast an advertisement msg with CL_CH/E_residual & TTL
}
else {          // I am a regular node
        my_status ← Non_Cluster_Head
        if (received any advertisement msg) {
                save the CL_CH/E_residual of the advertisement msg
                if (received one or more advertisement msg.s)
                        my_cluster_head ← sender of max(TTL of advertisement msg)
                if (updated TTL ≠ 0)
                        forward the advertisement msg
        }
        else  // not received any advertisement msg within a specific time interval
                my_status ← Cluster_Head
}
```

Fig. 2. Operation of the set-up stage of the dynamic-size multi-hop clustering

on how to elect a CH, but on the way of adjusting the cluster size to prolong the network lifetime), the CH broadcasts an advertisement message with TTL being set to the size of the corresponding cluster. The initial cluster size is set to a default value and, after that, the cluster size is increased or decreased according to the load condition of the CH. The load on a CH comes from the processing load PL_{CH} and the communication load CL_{CH}.

$$L_{CH} = f(PL_{CH}, CL_{CH}) \qquad (3)$$

CL_{CH} is the load receiving sensed data from other nodes within the cluster and transmitting the aggregated data to the sink.

$$CL_{CH} = \sum_{j=0}^{n} E_{RX,j} + E_{TX,sink} \qquad (4)$$

The load information on a CH, $\frac{CL_{CH}}{E_{residual}}$ (where CL_{CH} is obtained from Eq.4), is included in an advertisement message. Each sensor node receiving this message stores the information and, when it becomes a CH, it compares its own load information with that of other nodes. If its own load information is less than that of others, it increases its cluster size (i.e., increases TTL by 1) and, if its load information is greater than that of others, it decreases its cluster size (i.e., decreases TTL by 1). The algorithm for the set-up stage is described in figure 2.

A sensor node receiving advertisement messages decides the cluster that it is going to join, but it does not need to send a join message to the corresponding CH since the contention-based MAC protocol is used (i.e., the CH does not have to maintain the list of nodes within the cluster). A sensor node not receiving any advertisement message within a specific time interval becomes a CH, and a sensor node receiving more than one advertisement messages selects the CH which seems to be the nearest to itself (the TTL value within an advertisement message can be used for this purpose).

Once a cluster is formed, sensor nodes within the cluster send data to the CH and the CH aggregates the collected data and transmits the aggregated data to the sink.

4 Performance Evaluation

In order to evaluate the performance of the proposed dynamic-size multi-hop clustering mechanism, we have used the NS-2 simulator [11] and the sensor network extension package of NRL [12]. Simulations are performed for the range of 1000m × 1000m with randomly distributed 50 ~ 120 nodes. The initial energy for each sensor node is set to 5 J (Joule) and each sensor node can store up to 50 packets. If the available energy of a sensor node is less than or equal to 10^{-4} J, the node is assumed to be dead. The transmission range of a sensor node is 200 m and the packet length is 100 bytes. The event that triggers a sensor node to send sensed data occurs at every second, and the location of the event is randomly selected. The simulation parameters are shown in table 1.

The performance of the proposed dynamic-size multi-hop clustering mechanism is compared with the single-hop mode and the multi-hop mode, and the CH selection rules of LEACH and HEED are both applied. The performance

Table 1. Simulation parameters

Parameter	Value
Network grid	1000×1000m
Initial energy	5J
Tx/Rx power of a node	160mW
Max. transmission range of a sensor	200m
Message size	100bytes
Pulse rate of a target phenomenon	1 packet/sec
CH re-election interval	5×pulse rate

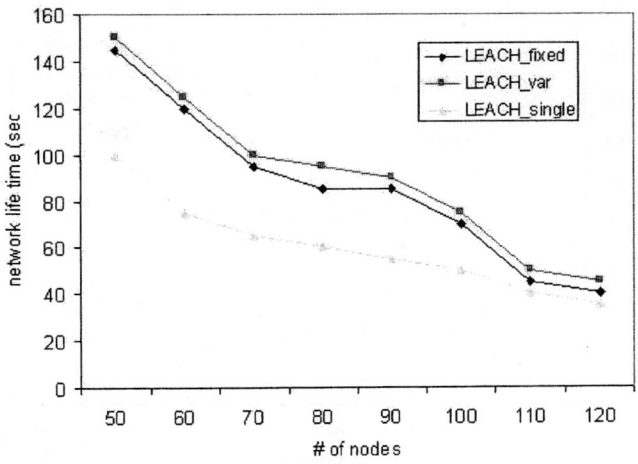

Fig. 3. Network lifetime of the single-hop and the multi-hop modes (with using LEACH as the CH selection mechanism)

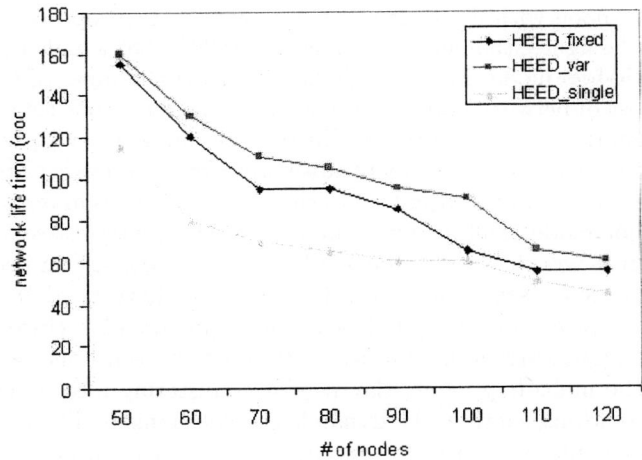

Fig. 4. Network lifetime of the single-hop and the multi-hop modes (with using HEAD as the CH selection mechanism)

evaluation factors considered for the simulation are the network lifetime, the variance of the available energy of each node, and the size of clusters.

Figure 3, figure 4 and figure 5 show the network lifetime with varying the number of nodes. figure 3 is the result obtained by using LEACH as the CH selection mechanism, and LEACH_single represents the single-hop mode case and LEACH_fixed the multi-hop mode with fixed-size clusters and LEACH_var

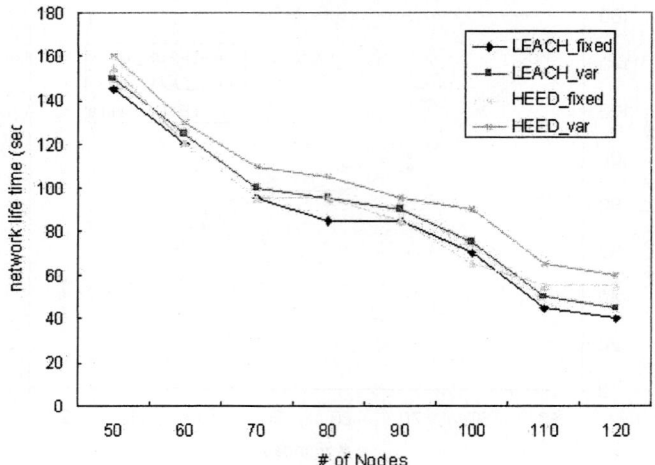

Fig. 5. Network lifetime of the fixed-size and the dynamic-size multi-hop modes (with using either LEACH or HEED as the CH selection mechanism)

the multi-hop mode with dynamic-size clusters (i.e., our proposed mechanism). As shown in the figure, the multi-hop mode gives 30 ∼ 50 % higher performance than the single-hop mode. In the single-hop mode, the number of CHs required to include most of network nodes within clusters is almost four times more than that of the multi-hop mode with the cluster size being 3. Thus, in the single-hop mode, because of more CHs, more advertisement messages are broadcast and more aggregated data are transmitted to the sink, so it yields lower performance. In the multi-hop mode, if all the sensor nodes receiving an advertisement message forward the message, the overhead caused by the forwarding can become severe especially in a dense sensor network. Therefore, we have tried to reduce this overhead by allowing nodes located near the boundary of a cluster (by using the Received Signal Strength Indicator (RSSI)) to forward the advertisement message. In the multi-hop mode, the fixed-size clustering mechanism shows 10 ∼ 15 % less performance than the dynamic-size mechanism. The reason for this is that the dynamic-size clustering mechanism controls the amount of energy consumption of a CH by adjusting the cluster size with increasing or decreasing it according to the load on the CH which is affected by the node density within the cluster.

Figure 4 shows the network lifetime when HEED is used for the election of CHs. Overall, HEED gives longer lifetime than LEACH. This shows that HEED considering the available energy of a node is more effective in prolonging lifetime than LEACH making all nodes become CHs in a round-robin fashion. Also, we can see that the dynamic-size multi-hop mode improves the performance by 10 ∼ 15 % compared with the fixed-size multi-hop mode as shown in figure 3.

Figure 5 shows the network lifetime of the fixed-size clustering mechanism and that of the dynamic-size mechanism with varying the number of nodes.

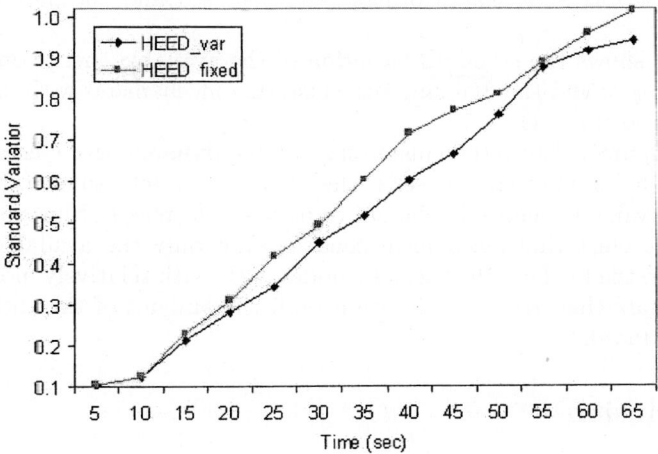

Fig. 6. Standard variation of the amount of available energy of each sensor node for the fixed-size and the dynamic-size multi-hop clustering mechanisms (with using HEED as the CH selection mechanism)

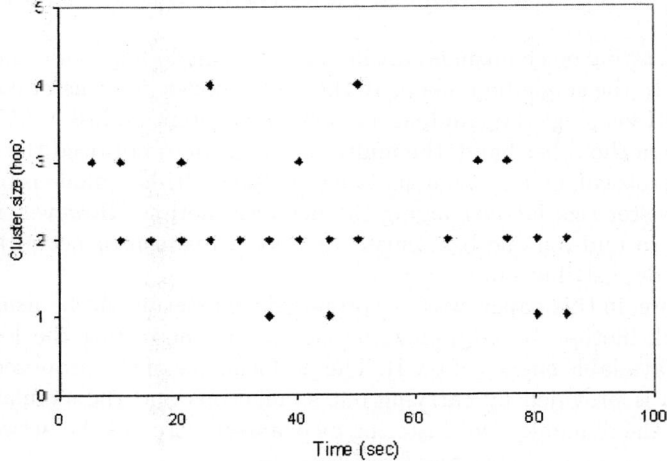

Fig. 7. Cluster size vs. simulation time

Overall, HEED gives better performance than LEACH and the dynamic-size clustering mechanism than the fixed-size one. This is due to the fact that the fixed-size clustering mechanism forms fixed-size clusters without considering the load of a CH. That is, if a node located in an area with higher node density becomes a CH, it has to receive and process that many number of messages from the cluster members and, as a result, the difference between the available energy of the CH and that of others gets increased and the network lifetime decreases.

Figure 6 shows the standard variation of the available energy on each node for the fixed-size and the dynamic-size clustering mechanisms with using HEED as the CH selection rule.

Lastly, figure 7 shows the cluster size for the dynamic-size clustering mechanism. As the simulation proceeds, the cluster size gets smaller because the amount of available energy in the entire network decreases. However, since the dynamic-size clustering mechanism considers not only the available energy of CHs but also the load of other near-by nodes, CHs with relatively more available energy increase their own cluster size even if the amount of the entire network energy is reduced.

5 Conclusion

One of the most important issues on the sensor network with resource-limited sensor nodes is prolonging the network lifetime by effectively utilizing the given energy. The most representative mechanism to prolong the network lifetime is the clustering mechanism. In the clustering mechanism, sensor nodes are formed into clusters and the cluster head (CH) of a cluster collects data from sensors noticing a specific phenomenon and aggregates the collected data and sends it to the sink.

The clustering mechanism is classified into the single-hop mode and the multi-hop mode. In the single-hop mode, all the sensor nodes in a cluster communicate with the CH via single hop and, as a result, the contention-less MAC protocol is preferred. On the other hand, the multi-hop mode does not need the contention-less MAC protocol. One of the main issues on the multi-hop mode is to determine the best cluster size for prolonging the network lifetime. However, it is almost impossible to find out the best cluster size for a real sensor network with non-uniform node distribution.

Therefore, in this paper, we have proposed a clustering mechanism to prolong the network lifetime by adjusting the cluster size according the load and the amount of available energy of a CH. The performance of the proposed clustering mechanism is provided by carrying out simulations and the simulation results imply that the dynamic-size clustering mechanism increases the network lifetime by 10~15 % compared with the fixed-size one.

References

1. G. J. Pottie and W. J. Kaiser, "Wireless integrated network sensors", Communications of the ACM, vol 43, no 5, pp51-58, May 2000.
2. W. Ye, J. Heidemann, and D. Estrin, "An energy-efficient mac protocol for wireless sensor networks", IEEE Infocom, pp1567-1576, June 2002.
3. A. Cerpa and D. Estrin, "ACENT: Adaptive self-configuring sensor networks topologies", IEEE Infocom, pp1278-1287, June 2002.

4. B. Chen, K. Jamieson, H. Balakrishnan, and R. Morris, "SPAN: An energy-efficient coordination algorithm for topology maintenance in ad hoc wireless networks", ACM/IEEE Mobicom, pp85-96, July 2001.
5. V. Kawadia and P. R. Kumar, "Power control and clustering in ad hoc networks", IEEE Infocom, pp459-469, April 2003.
6. S. Narayanaswamy, V. Kawadia, R. S. Sreenivas, and P. R. Kumar, "Power control in ad-hoc networks: Theory, architecture, algorithm and implementation of the COMPOW protocol", European wireless, pp156-162, Feb. 2002.
7. V. Mhatre and C. Rosenberg, "Design guidelines for wireless sensor networks: communication, clustering and aggregation", Ad-hoc networks journal, Elsevier science, vol. 2, pp45-63, 2004.
8. W. R. Heinzelman, A. Chandrakasan, and H. Balakrishnan, "Energy-efficient communication protocol for wireless microsensor networks", IEEE Hawaii international conference on system sciences, January 2000.
9. O. Younis and S. Fahmy, "Distributed Clustering in Ad-hoc Sensor Networks: A hybrid, energy-efficient approach", IEEE Infocom, pp629-640, March 2004.
10. S. Bandyopadhyay and E. J. Coyle, "An energy efficient hierarchical clustering algorithm for wireless sensor networks", IEEE Infocom, pp1713-1723, April 2003.
11. The network simulator, ns-2, http://www.isi.edu/nsnam/ns/
12. NRL's sensor network extension to ns-2, http://nrlsensorsim.pf.itd.nrl.navy.mil/

Percentage Coverage Configuration in Wireless Sensor Networks

Hongxing Bai[1], Xi Chen[1], Yu-Chi Ho[1,2], and Xiaohong Guan[1,3]

[1] Center for Intelligent and Networked Systems (CFINS),
Tsinghua University, Beijing 100084, China
hongxing99@mails.tsinghua.edu.cn,
bjchenxi@mail.tsinghua.edu.cn, xhguan@tsinghua.edu.cn
[2] Division of Engineering and Applied Sciences,
Harvard University, Cambridge, MA 02138 USA
ho@hrl.harvard.edu
[3] Systems Engineering Institute and SKLMS Lab,
Xian Jiatong University, Xi'an 710049, China

Abstract. Recent researches on energy efficient coverage configuration in wireless sensor networks mainly address the goal of 100% or near 100% coverage preserving. However, we find that a small percentage of loss of coverage, which is acceptable in many applications, can result in dramatic increase in energy savings. Therefore, in this paper percentage coverage rather than complete coverage is selected as the design goal, and a location-based Percentage Coverage Configuration Protocol (PCCP) is developed to assure that the proportion of the sensing area after configuration to the original sensing area is no less than a desired percentage. Numerical testing results show that PCCP can not only guarantee the desired coverage percentage but also generate more energy efficient configuration in comparison with the existing schemes so that the system lifespan is extended significantly.

1 Introduction

Energy consumption (or system lifespan, accordingly) is one of the most important issues in wireless sensor networks (WSN). Since significant energy conservation can be achieved by appropriately scheduling the sensors between ACTIVE and OFF states, where in OFF state, a sensor node consumes very little energy, coverage configuration becomes a key issue in order to assure the coverage quality.

Recent study on coverage configuration concentrates on the goal of *coverage preserving*, which means the sensing area within the Area of Interest (AoI) even with some sensors scheduled OFF should be exactly the same as the original sensing area without any loss of coverage. The work of Tian and Georganas [6,7], Wang et al. [8] and Jiang and Dou [4], etc., belongs to this category.

However, complete coverage is unnecessary in many applications, and a percentage of sensing loss below a certain threshold is acceptable. This has been noticed by many researchers as seen from the definitions of system lifetime. For example, Ye et al. [9] define coverage lifetime as the time that coverage drops below a threshold and never comes back again. Wang et al. [8] define the overall system lifetime as the continuous operational time of the system before the coverage drops below a specified threshold. Zhang and Hou [13] define the sensor network lifetime as the entire interval in which at least α portion of the AoI is covered by at least one sensor node.

Relaxing the requirement from complete coverage to a percentage of coverage can result in dramatic increase in energy savings. In [13], Zhang and Hou have derived that the upper bound of the lifetime can increase by 15% for 99%-coverage and over 20% for 95%-coverage. An intuitive explanation is: when many disks are used to cover a convex region completely, there must be much overlap of the disks; while if certain uncovered areas (sensing loss) are acceptable, the overlap can be reduced significantly.

In this paper the *percentage coverage preserving* is proposed as a new design goal for coverage configuration such that the sensing area within the AoI with some sensors scheduled OFF should be no less than a certain percentage of the original sensing area. A location-based Percentage Coverage Configuration Protocol (PCCP) is developed to achieve this goal with assurance. Numerical testing results show that PCCP can not only guarantee the desired coverage percentage but also generate more energy efficient configuration in comparison with the existing schemes under the same circumstances so that the system lifespan is extended significantly.

The rest of the paper is organized as follows. In the next section, we review the related work in the literature. In section 3, the problem is formulated and the PCCP is described in details. Simulation experiments and numerical testing results with PCCP are presented in Section 4 and are compared with the existing work. The concluding remarks are given in Section 5.

2 Related Work

Energy-efficient coverage problem has attracted the interests of many researchers. Cardei and Wu [2] and Sahni and Xu [5] have given a detailed survey of the existing contributions in this area respectively. Here we only review those distributed algorithms since they are scalable and more suitable for WSN.

Ye et al. [9,10] proposed a node scheduling algorithm called PEAS. In PEAS, active sensors remain working until their energy is used up, and off sensors turn active randomly. Once an off sensor become active, it checks whether there are active sensors within its probing range. If so, it turns off again; otherwise, it stays active and remains working. Though there may be sensing loss, the proportion of sensing loss is not quantified in PEAS.

Tian and Georganas [6] presented a scheme to maintain complete coverage. Their scheme divides the lifetime of WSN into rounds. At the beginning of each round, every sensor will check whether its neighbors can help it to monitor its whole sensing area. If so, it will turn off. After them, Hsin and Liu [3] and Jiang and Dou [4] have developed this scheme.

Wang et al. [8] proved a sufficient condition for satisfying multi-degree of complete coverage and presented a coverage configuration protocol (CCP) based on the sufficient condition. CCP can dynamically configure the network to get coverage and connectivity at the same time. Different from their work, here we only consider coverage issue, because for many off-the-shelf wireless sensors, sensing module is independent of radio module. Therefore, a coverage configuration algorithm will not affect the connectivity of the network.

Zhang and Hou [11] presented a density control algorithm called OGDC, which works in rounds. In each round, with a random starting sensor, other sensors will decide whether to be active or not according to locations of themselves and the sensors which become active before them.

All above work cannot afford flexible coverage percentage requirement.

Tian and Georganas also proposed three location-free schemes in [7], including nearest-neighbor-based, neighbor-number-based and probability-based schemes. All of them work in rounds, and each sensor determines its own OFF-duty eligibility according to whether the nearest neighbor's distance, the minimal neighbor number or a randomly generated number is more than a threshold D, K or p respectively. The parameter choosing of D, K or p is based on a statistical calculation (also based on the assumption that sensors are uniformly randomly deployed in the AoI) given a desired coverage percentage loss. At the first sight, their design goal is very similar to ours. However, in their work, the coverage percentage is a statistical concept and cannot be guaranteed above a desired threshold always. This is the fundamental difference between PCCP and their schemes. In fact, since location information are not used, these location-free schemes will suffer from either bad efficiency (turn on much more sensors than PCCP) or bad coverage quality (cannot assure the coverage percentage above the desired threshold), which will be shown in section 4.1.

3 Percentage Coverage Configuration

3.1 Basic Assumptions and Concepts

We have the following assumptions and concepts:

1. All sensors are homogeneous.
2. All sensors are time-synchronized. Time synchronization methods in WSN can be found in [14, 15].
3. Each sensor knows its own position. It is not impractical, since many researchers have addressed node localization problems in WSN, such as in [16, 17].
4. Each sensor's sensing region is a disk centered at the sensor's location with a fixed radius R_s.
5. The communication radius is larger than two times of the sensing radius.

Definition 1 (Neighbor). For any two sensors A and B, if the distance between them is less than or equal to $2*R_s$, then sensor A and B are neighbors.

Definition 2 (Coverage Percentage). Suppose the original sensing area is A, the sensing area within the AoI after coverage configuration is B. The ratio of B to A is called coverage percentage.

In this paper, we denote the desired coverage percentage threshold as p^*.

Another important concept used in PCCP is Voronoi diagram. Suppose there are N sensor nodes in a two dimensional plane, if we partition the plane into N convex polygons such that each polygon contains exactly one node and every point in a given polygon is closer to the node in this polygon than to any other node, then we get a Voronoi diagram [1].

In a Voronoi diagram, each polygon is called a Voronoi cell. Particularly, we call a sensor node's Voronoi cell as its *Occupation Area* (OA) in this paper. If two OAs share a common edge, the owner sensors of the two OAs are called *Voronoi neighbors*.

3.2 Description of PCCP

The basic idea of our protocol is Divide and Conquer. Since all OAs constitute the AoI without overlap, we can divide the AoI into regions based on the concept of OA. More precisely, each region is a collection of several OAs in the AoI. After that, the percentage coverage configuration will be done in each region.

The following is the detailed description of PCCP.

In PCCP, the network lifetime is divided into a sequence of working rounds. Each round begins with a node scheduling phase, followed by a sensing phase. At the beginning of each round, all sensors turn on and enter the node scheduling phase. After deciding its state, the ACTIVE-duty sensors enter the sensing phase starting working (sensing) and the OFF-duty sensors turn off. Then each sensor stays in its state until the next round starts.

The node scheduling procedure consists of two sub-phases: occupation area obtaining sub-phase and Percentage Coverage Configuration (PCC) sub-phase.

In the occupation area obtaining sub-phase, each sensor broadcasts its ID and location with radio radius $2*R_s$ and records the ID and location information of its neighbors when hearing their messages. To avoid collision, each sensor should generate a random back-off (bounded by the length of this phase) time T_b and only broadcast when T_b expires. At the end of this phase, each sensor knows the location information of its neighbors. Then by calculating its own OA and the original sensing area within its OA (denoted by S_{OA}), it finishes its task in this sub-phase. The OA and S_{OA} calculation algorithm will be described in section 3.2.1 and 3.2.2.

In the percentage coverage configuration sub-phase, for each sensor, there are three possible statuses: Waiting Sensor for broadcasting Start Sensing Message (SSM), Percentage Coverage Configuration Head (PCC Head) and Percentage Coverage Configuration Member (PCC Member). All sensors start with the status of a waiting sensor at the beginning of percentage coverage configuration sub-phase. Then each sensor will negotiate with its neighbors and changes its status accordingly as described in the below.

For a Waiting Sensor:

Each sensor of this status first generates a random delay time T_d. When a waiting sensor's T_d expires, it will broadcast a Start Sensing Message (SSM), turn on its sensing module and assume itself a PCC head. If a waiting sensor receives an SSM from one of its neighbors before its own T_d expires, it will stop the timer for T_d, assume itself a PCC member of the SSM sender, and ignore any other SSM when it is a PCC member.

For a PCC Member:

A PCC member O will calculate the area of the part in sensor O's OA which is covered by its neighbors which are PCC heads (denoted by S_c). Then this sensor sends

S_{OA} and S_c to its PCC head. After that, this sensor will listen to the channel until it receives an OFF-duty Eligible Neighbors Message (OENM) from its PCC head. When this sensor receives the OENM, it will check whether its ID is contained in the OENM. If so, it will turn off itself; otherwise, it will generate a random delay time T_d once more and then become a waiting sensor again.

What need to be pointed out is, since there are usually many PCC members sharing a common PCC head, to avoid collision, each PCC member should send its S_c and S_{OA} with a random back-off time. The maximal back-off time should be bounded by a predetermined time T_h in order to let the PCC head make sure all members have sent their messages.

For a PCC Head:

A PCC head will listen to the channel during the T_h time interval to collect the S_{OA} and S_c information of its PCC members. When T_h expires, this sensor will execute an OFF-duty Eligible Neighbor Choosing Algorithm (as described in section 3.2.3) to judge which members can be turned off. Then it will broadcast an OENM which includes the OFF-duty eligible sensors' IDs. After that, it will remain ACTIVE until the next round comes.

Either PCC head or PCC member is a temporary role for a sensor. The relationship between head and member will disappear after the PCC head sends the OENM.

Remark 1. To minimize the energy consumption overhead in percentage coverage configuration, the length of each round should be long enough compared to the configuration time, but it should be much smaller than the sensors' average continuous working time.

Remark 2. If the sensors have no IDs, they can use their locations as their IDs since they can distinguish each other according to their locations.

3.2.1 OA Calculation Algorithm

In general, suppose the AoI can be described as the solution of J inequalities: $a_j x + b_j y + c_j \leq 0$, $j=1,2,...,J$. Suppose there are totally N sensors in the AoI with locations (x_i, y_i), $i=1,2,...,N$ respectively. Then any point (x, y) in the kth sensor's OA should satisfy the following inequalities:

$$\begin{cases} \sqrt{(x-x_k)^2 + (y-y_k)^2} \leq \sqrt{(x-x_i)^2 + (y-y_i)^2}, i=1,2,...,N \\ a_j x + b_j y + c_j \leq 0, j=1,2,...,J \end{cases} \quad (1)$$

Though there are $N+J$ inequalities above, no more than $L+J$ of them are active constraints where L is the number of the kth sensor's Voronoi neighbors. As any sensor's Voronoi neighbors are usually near the sensor, in this paper we use the neighbors' locations to calculate any sensor's OA. We name the neighbor-based calculation result as the sensor's Neighbor-based OA (NOA).

For an arbitrary sensor node O, denote its own location as (x_0, y_0). Suppose sensor O has totally M neighbors with locations (z_i, w_i), $i=1,2,...,M$ respectively. Then we describe sensor O's NOA by the $J+M$ inequalities

$$a_j x + b_j y + c_j \leq 0, j=1,2,\ldots,J+M \qquad (2)$$

where $a_{J+i} = 2(z_i - x_0)$, $b_{J+i} = 2(w_i - y_0)$ and $c_{J+i} = (x_0^2 + y_0^2) - (z_i^2 + w_i^2)$ (for $i=1,2,\ldots,M$) are come from the first part of (1).

We assume the AoI is a convex polygon. Thus an NOA (or OA) is also a convex polygon, which can be determined by its vertices. Therefore, sensor O only needs to calculate and record the vertices of an NOA, where a vertex is an intersection of two lines $a_j x + b_j y + c_j = 0$ and $a_k x + b_k y + c_k = 0$ ($j,k=1,2,\ldots, J+M$ and $j \neq k$) which is a feasible solution of (2). Thus we can calculate all the $(J+M)(J+M-1)/2$ intersections and select those satisfying all the inequalities in (2).

According to the definition of "neighbor" we presented in section 3.1, an arbitrary sensor O's Voronoi neighbors may not be contained in sensor O's neighbors. As the number of constraints in (2) is less than those in (1), sensor O's NOA may be the same as its OA, or larger than its OA. However, when a sensor uses NOA instead of OA to calculate S_{OA} and S_c, the sensor will get the right values of S_{OA} and S_c. This will be proved in section 3.2.2.

3.2.2 S_{OA} and S_c Calculation Algorithm

To calculate S_{CA}, we give the following theorems in advance.

Theorem 1. For an arbitrary sensor O, if some point P in sensor O's OA is in the original sensing area, then P is covered by sensor O's sensing disk.

Proof. As point P is in sensor O' OA, for any sensor Q in the AoI, we have $d_{PO} \leq d_{PQ}$ according to the definition of OA, where d_{AB} denotes the distance between point A and point B. If $d_{PO} > R_s$, P cannot be covered by any sensor's sensing disk. Therefore, if P is in the original sensing area, P must be within sensor O's sensing range. □

From Theorem 1 we know that a sensor O's S_{OA} can be calculated as the area in sensor O's OA covered by its own sensing disk.

Theorem 2. For any point P within sensor O's sensing disk, if P is in sensor O's NOA, P is also in sensor O's OA, and vice versa.

Proof. For any point P in sensor O's sensing disk, for any sensor Q which is more than $2*R_s$ far away from sensor O, Q cannot be P's nearest sensor, since $d_{PO} \leq R_s$ and $d_{PQ} > R_s$. That means, the nearest sensor to P is either sensor O or one of sensor O's neighbors. Therefore, it is sufficient to assure sensor O is P's nearest sensor, given $d_{PO} \leq d_{PU}$ for any U which is a neighbor of sensor O. Thus if P is in sensor O's NOA, P is also in sensor O's OA, and vice versa. □

According to Theorem 2, we propose in PCCP that any sensor obtains its S_{OA} by calculating the area in its NOA covered by its own sensing disk.

In PCCP, another important value is S_c, i.e., the part of area in a sensor's OA that is covered by its neighbors which are PCC heads. Next we show how to calculate S_c.

Theorem 3. For any sensor O, if some point P in sensor O's NOA is covered by the sensing disk of one of sensor O's neighbors, then P is in sensor O's OA.

Proof. *For any point P' within sensor O's NOA but outside sensor O's sensing disk, P' cannot be covered by the sensing disk of any of sensor O's neighbors, because sensor O is nearer to P' than to sensor O's neighbors, and $d_{P'O} > R_s$. Since P is covered by one sensor O's neighbor's sensing disk, P is within sensor O's sensing disk. According to Theorem 2, P is in sensor O's OA.* □

By Theorem 3, a sensor's S_c calculated in its NOA is no more than the real S_c (calculated in its OA). Since a sensor's NOA is always no smaller than its OA, a sensor's real S_c is no more than the S_c calculated in its NOA. So a sensor's real S_c is equal to its S_c calculated in its NOA. Thus we can calculate S_c based on NOA.

Since a PCC member O may be OFF-duty ineligible informed by a PCC head U and then become a waiting sensor again, sensor O may become a PCC member of another PCC head V. In this case, we use an iterative way to calculate sensor O's S_c. Limited by the length of the paper, here we only give an example as an illustration. Suppose sensor O's OA is the pentagon $p_1p_2p_3p_4p_5$ as in Fig. 1(a). When one of sensor O's neighbors U becomes a PCC head, sensor O becomes a PCC member of sensor U. Then sensor O will calculate S_c as the area of the pentagon $p_1p_6p_7p_4p_5$.

Suppose sensor U has not chosen sensor O as an OFF-duty eligible neighbor, sensor O becomes a waiting sensor again. After that, sensor O hears another neighbor V broadcasting an SSM. In this case, sensor O calculates its S_c as the last-time S_c (recorded in sensor O's memory) plus the area of the quadrangle $p_3p_7p_8p_9$. See Fig. 1(b).

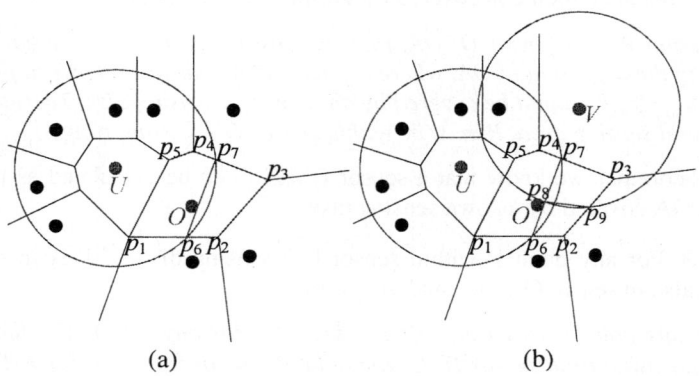

Fig. 1. An illustration of S_c calculation

3.2.3 OFF-Duty Eligible Neighbor Choosing Algorithm

When a sensor becomes a PCC head, it may have many PCC members. But there may be only a part of them can be turned off to guarantee a certain coverage percentage. If there are K PCC members, the number of possible solutions is 2^K. To select the optimal set of OFF-duty eligible PCC members is a NP-hard problem. Therefore, in PCCP, we only use a two-step heuristic choosing algorithm as described below:

1. For those PCC members whose $S_c/S_{OA} \geq p^*$, add them into the OFF-duty Eligible Neighbors Message (OENM).

2. For those members whose $S_c/S_{OA}<p^*$, first sort them according to their values of S_c/S_{OA} descendingly (for those members with equal S_c/S_{OA}, sort them according to their distances to the PCC head). Then following the sorted order, add as many as possible PCC members into the OENM until the cumulated S_c/S_{OA} (including the PCC head itself) is smaller than p^*, i.e., when $\sum S_c / \sum S_{OA} < p^*$, eliminate the last selected PCC members from the OENM and end the choosing algorithm.

In each working round, PCCP in fact divides the AoI into H pieces of regions without overlap, where H is the number of PCC heads and each region consists of the OAs of one PCC head and its OFF-duty eligible PCC members. If for any sensor the proportion of its S_{OA} to the area of its OA is no smaller than p^*, according to the heuristic algorithm above, by using PCCP, the coverage percentage in any piece of the divided region is no less than p^*. Therefore, the coverage percentage of the total AoI is no less than p^*, too.

In fact, as the S_c calculation is conservative, the real coverage percentage is usually much larger than p^*. This fact can be seen in the experimental results in section 4.

4 Experimental Results

In this section, performance evaluation of PCCP and comparison between PCCP and others' work are shown via simulation experiments. In the simulation, N sensors are uniformly randomly deployed (distributed) in a 50×50 square field (the AoI). The sensing radius R_s is set as 10. To calculate coverage percentage in each round, we divide the AoI into 0.1×0.1 unit cells. Since in the experiment, the original sensing area is the same as the area of the AoI in most replications and very near to the area of the AoI in other replications, we use the ratio of the number of cells whose centre is covered by at least one ACTIVE sensor to the total number of cells (250,000) as the coverage percentage.

4.1 Comparison with Location-Free Algorithms

In this section we compare PCCP with three location-free algorithms proposed in [7]. We set $p^*=80\%$, $N=100$, $R_c=2*R_s$, and implement PCCP and the three location-free schemes in 100 rounds. As suggested in [7], when $p^*=80\%$, the parameters setting in the three location-free algorithms are: the nearest neighbor distance $D=0.315*R_s$, the minimal neighbor number $K=6$, and probability p is calculated in terms of D and N). In the experiment, the coverage percentage and active sensor number in each round are recorded. We repeat the experiment in several replications, where in each replication we randomly generate one topology of the WSN. We find the results are similar in all replications, so we here only give the result in one replication as illustrated in Fig. 2.

Fig. 2(a) shows the coverage percentage got by each algorithm in each round. We can see that PCCP can guarantee the coverage percentage above 80% all through the 100 rounds, as well as the nearest-neighbor-based and probability-based schemes. However, the neighbor-number-based scheme provides a less than 80% coverage percentage in many rounds.

Fig. 2(b) illustrates the active sensor number in each round. We can see that active sensor number in PCCP is far less than the others. The nearest-neighbor-based and probability-based schemes even cost 3-5 times ACTIVE sensors than PCCP. Therefore, PCCP is much more energy efficient than these location-free schemes.

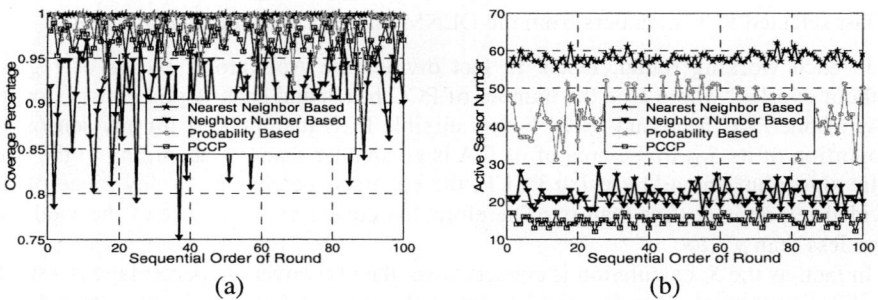

Fig. 2. Comparison PCCP with three location-free schemes

From the experimental results we can see that the location-free schemes suffer from either bad coverage quality (cannot assure the coverage percentage above a threshold all the time) or bad efficiency (turn off much less sensors than PCCP). It is reasonable, since PCCP makes use of the location information of each sensor, while these location-free schemes only use statistical calculation.

4.2 Comparison with CCP

This section will illustrate the further improvement obtained by percentage coverage compared with complete coverage. We use the performance obtained by CCP [8] as a reference, because CCP provides a better performance than the other coverage preserving algorithms, such as in [4,6,9] (this can be seen from the experimental results in their papers). In the experiments, we choose N from 50 to 300 with an increment of 50. Under each value of N, 100 replications are implemented where in different replication sensors are uniformly randomly deployed in the AoI with different network topology. Since the random delay time will affect the configuration result in CCP and PCCP, in each replication, we run CCP in 5 rounds and run PCCP in 5 rounds at each value of p^*=0.5, 0.6, 0.7, 0.8, 0.9 separately. The coverage percentage and active sensor number are shown in Fig. 3. Both metrics are measured after the coverage configuration process is finished. Each point in Fig. 3 represents the mean value of 100 replications times 5 rounds.

From Fig. 3 we can see that PCCP can not only provide desired coverage percentage, but also let more sensors turn off. In general, the active sensor number in PCCP is less than the active sensor number in CCP multiplied by p^*. This shows the energy efficiency of PCCP. Notice that when N=50, the AoI is not completely covered when all sensors are ACTIVE. In this case, PCCP performs a little bad (also because the calculation error of S_c is large due to the large OA when N is small).

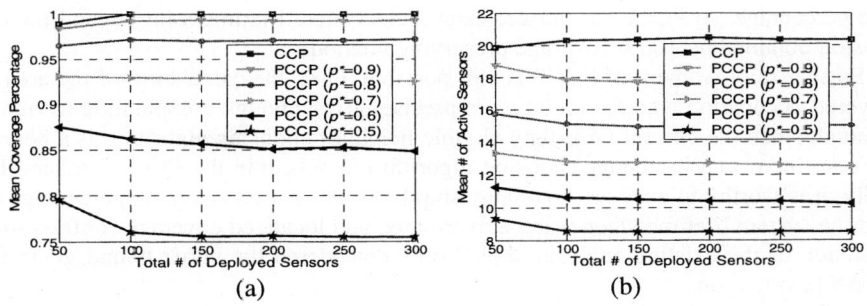

Fig. 3. Comparison PCCP with CCP on Coverage Percentage and Active Sensor Number

Here we introduce the concept of *system lifetime upper bound* to show the effect of active sensor number on network lifetime. Assume the working round is long enough so that the over head of coverage configuration can be ignored. If the average continuous working time of one sensor is T_s, then the system lifetime upper bound is T_s multiplied by the total number of sensors divided by the mean active sensor number in a round. We plot the system lifetime upper bound obtained by CCP and PCCP under different p^* in Fig. 4, which shows that the system lifetime upper bound is further extended obviously by PCCP. For example, when $N=300$, CCP extends the system lifetime (the upper bound) by about 15 times, while PCCP with $p^*=0.5$ (the average real-time coverage percentage is more than 75% which can be see from Fig. 3(a)) can extend the system lifetime (the upper bound) by more than 35 times!

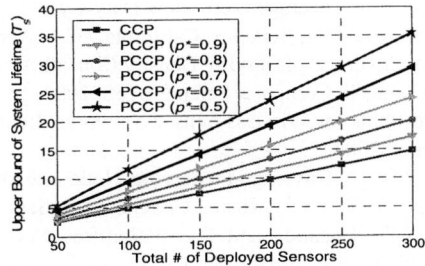

Fig. 4. Comparison PCCP with CCP on system lifetime upper bound

5 Conclusions and Future Work

In this paper we have investigated the energy efficient coverage configuration problem in WSN. Instead of pursuing the complete coverage preserving, we have designed the Percentage Coverage Configuration Protocol (PCCP) for scheduling the sensors to maintain the coverage percentage above a desired threshold. Simulation experiments show that PCCP can turn off much more sensors than the existing location-free algorithms, while the desired coverage percentage is guaranteed. Comparison with CCP also shows that PCCP makes good trade off between active sensor number and coverage percentage, so PCCP can further extend the system lifetime a lot beyond the extension obtained by 100% coverage preserving methods.

Further improvement of PCCP is still possible. First, the calculation of the area of covered occupation area S_c can be more precise, given enough computation resource. Second, since the current OFF-duty eligible neighbor choosing algorithm is a heuristic one, there may be better choosing algorithm to schedule the PCC members. Finally, it is worthy to analyze the relationship between desired coverage percentage p^* and the system lifetime when using a distributed and localized coverage configuration protocol, as the existing analysis in [13] only considered the upper bound given the global information.

Acknowledgements. The research presented in this paper is supported in part by the National Outstanding Young Investigator Grant (6970025), National Natural Science Foundation (60243001) of China. The work of the third author is supported in part by ARO contract DAAD19-01-1-0610, AFOSR contract F49620-01-1-0288 and NSF grant ECS-0323685.

References

1. Aurenhammer, F.: Voronoi Diagrams – A Survey of a Fundamental Geometric Data Structure. ACM Computing Surveys, Vol. 23 (3), 1991, pp. 345-405.
2. Cardei, M., Wu, J.: Energy-Efficient Coverage Problems in Wireless Ad Hoc Sensor Networks. Accepted to appear in Special Issue of the Journal of Computer Communications on Sensor Networks. (This paper can be got from the following link: http://polaris.cse.fau.edu/~jie/research/publications/Publication_files/coverage.pdf).
3. Hsin, C. and Liu M.: Network Coverage Using Low Duty-Cycled Sensors: Random & Coordinated Sleep Algorithms. IPSN'04, Berkeley, California, USA, April, 2004, pp. 433-442.
4. Jiang, J., Dou, W.H.: A Coverage-preserving Density Control Algorithm for Wireless Sensor Networks. Lecture Notes in Computer Science 3158, 2004, pp. 42-55.
5. Sahni, S., Xu, X.: Algorithms for Wireless Sensor Networks, International Journal on Distributed Sensor Networks, 2004.
6. Tian, D., Georganas, N.D.: A Coverage-Preserving Node Scheduling Scheme for Large Wireless Sensor Networt. WSNA'02, Atlanta, Geogia, USA, September, 2002.
7. Tian, D., Georganas, N.D.: Location and Calculation-free Node-scheduling Schemes in Large Wireless Sensor Networks. Ad Hoc Networks, Vol. 2, 2004, pp. 65-85.
8. Wang, X., Xing, G., Zhang, Y., Lu, C., Pless, R. Gill, C.: Integrated Coverage and Connectivity Configuration in Wireless Sensor Networks. ACM SenSys'03, Los Angeles, CA, USA, November 2003.
9. Ye, F., Zhong, G., Lu, S., Zhang, L.: Energy Efficient Robust Sensing Coverage in Large Sensor Networks. Technical Report, 2002.
10. Ye, F., Zhong, G., Lu, S., Zhang, L.: PEAS: A Robust Energy Conserving Protocol for Long-Lived Sensor Networks. ICNP'02, Paris, France, November, 2002, pp. 200-201.
11. Zhang, H., Hou, J.C.: Maintaining Sensing Coverage and Connectivity in Large Sensor Networks. Technical Report. UIUCDCS-R-200302351.
12. Zhang, H., Hou, J.C.: Maintaining Coverage and Connectivity in Large Sensor Networks. The Wireless Ad Hoc and Sensor Networks: An International Journal, 2005.

13. Zhang, H., Hou, J.C.: On Deriving the Upper Bound of alpha-Lifetime for Large Sensor Networks. MobiHoc'04, Roppongi, Japan, May, 2004, pp.121-132
14. Ganeriwal, S., Kumar, R., Srivastava, M.B.: Timing-sync protocol for sensor networks. ACM SenSys'03, Los Angeles, CA, USA, November 2003.
15. Li, Q., Rus, D.: Global Clock Synchronization in Sensor Networks. Infocom'04, Hong Kong, China, March, 2004.
16. Savvides, A., Han, C.C., Srivastava, M.B.: Dynamic Fine-Grained Localization in Ad-Hoc Networks of Sensors. MobiCom'01, Rome, Italy, July, 2001, pp.166-179
17. He, T., Huang, C., Blum, B.M., Stankovic, J.A., Abdelzaher, T.: Range-Free Localization Schemes for Large Scale Sensor Networks. MobiCom '03, San Diego, California, USA, September, 2003.

A Fault-Tolerant Content Addressable Network[*]

Daisuke Takemoto, Shigeaki Tagashira, and Satoshi Fujita

Department of Information Engineering,
Graduate School of Engineering, Hiroshima University
{strategist, shigeaki, fujita}@se.hiroshima-u.ac.jp

Abstract. In this paper, we propose a new method to enhance the fault-tolerance of the Content Addressable Network (CAN), which is known as a typical pure P2P system based on the notion of Distributed Hash Table (DHT). The basic idea of the proposed method is to introduce a redundancy to the management of index information distributed over the nodes in the network, by allowing each index to be assigned to several nodes, which was restricted to be one in the original CAN system. To keep the consistency among several copies of indices, we propose an efficient synchronization scheme based on the notion of labels assigned to each copy in a distinct manner. The performance of the proposed scheme is evaluated by simulation. The result of simulations indicates that the proposed scheme really enhances the fault-tolerance of the CAN system.

Keywords: Peer-to-peer system, fault-tolerance, distributed hash table, content addressable network.

1 Introduction

According to the recent advancement of network technologies, it emerges an increasingly strong requirement for the high quality communications over the large-scale interconnection networks. In fact, as the number of web sites serving real-time contents increases, the number and the size of data flows exchanged among remote hosts also increase, and in addition, it significantly increases the complexity of server procedures to keep (or often to improve) the quality of such data streams to be satisfactory. In general, a high complexity of server procedures will limit the scalability of distributed systems under the conventional server-client model, which motivates the study of *fully distributed systems* such as grid computers and peer-to-peer (P2P) systems. A P2P system consists of a collection of host computers called nodes or peers, and those nodes are connected with each other by an interconnection network such as the Internet. In recent years, a lot of important services such as shared file systems and Domain Name Systems (DNS) have been constructed over the P2P model, and they have been used in many application fields, such as electronic bulletin broad system, network auction systems, and so on.

---

[*] This research was partially supported by the Grant-in-Aid for Scientific Research.

By their logical structure, P2P systems could be classified into two categories, i.e., hybrid type or pure type. In hybrid P2P systems, retrieval of objects will be realized by sending an inquiry message to a dedicated server who maintains a set of indices to the objects in a centralized manner, while the actual contents of the objects will be maintained by each node in a distributed manner. On the other hand, pure P2P systems do not rely on servers, and the retrieval of contents will be realized by peer nodes in a distributed manner. Examples of pure P2P systems include Gnutella [3] and FreeNet [2], where in Gnutella, indices of objects will be retrieved by using collective communications (i.e., flooding) over all nodes in the system, which severely limits the scalability of the overall system.

Distributed Hash Table (DHT) is a common technique to overcome such a low scalability of the flooding-based indexing schemes, and it has been applied to many pure P2P systems such as Tapestry [8], Chord [6], P-Grid [1], and Content-Addressable Network (CAN) [5]. In particular, in the CAN system proposed by Ratnasamy *et al.*, indices to the objects that are distributed over the physical network will be maintained by those nodes in the system in a fully distributed manner. More concretely, CAN assumes a virtual d-dimensional coordinate space, and each index to be stored and retrieved is mapped onto a point in the space by an appropriate uniform hash function. At any point in time, the entire coordinate space is dynamically partitioned among all nodes in the system, in such a way that every node "owns" its individual portion within the overall space called "zone," and thus, the store and the retrieval of an index will be realized by routing an inquiry message to the corresponding point, i.e., to the node who owns the point. Since each node in CAN is associated with its own zone, an unexpected leave of a node due to node or link failures would cause a fatal damage to the overall system, since the zone owned by a leaving node becomes invisible to the other nodes. To overcome such a critical problem, the basic design of the CAN system took an approach such that each node keeps a copy of its neighboring zones in addition to its own zone, and uses it to recover from unexpected leave of its neighbors. Unfortunately however, such a sharing of copies among nearby nodes is not sufficient in actual P2P environments, which may contain several mobile hosts that could easily be disconnected due to the physical mobility of the participating nodes, and may contain several nodes that are likely to be simultaneously disappeared without any notifications (e.g., imagine nodes settled in an isolated island).

In this paper, we propose a new method to enhance the fault-tolerance of the CAN system. The basic idea of the proposed method is to introduce an additional redundancy to the management of DHT by allowing each zone to be assigned to several nodes, which was restricted to be one in the original CAN system. To keep the consistency among several copies of a zone, we propose an efficient synchronization scheme based on the notion of labels assigned to each copy in a distinct manner. The performance of the proposed scheme is evaluated by simulation. The result of simulations indicates that the proposed scheme really enhances the fault-tolerance of the CAN system. Although it causes an increase of the maintenance cost, the maintenance cost will be dominated by the recovery cost if the number of nodes participating to the CAN system is sufficiently large.

The remainder of this paper is organized as follows. After describing the basic notion of the CAN in Section 2, we propose a method to enhance the fault-tolerance of the CAN in Section 3. The performance of the proposed method is evaluated in Section 4. Finally, Section 5 concludes the paper with future works.

2 Content Addressable Network

2.1 Design

In this section, we describe the basic design of CAN, with several techniques to enhance the fault-tolerance.

CAN [5] provides a mechanism for managing and retrieving objects distributed over the network, in a fully distributed manner. The design of CAN is based on a virtual d-dimensional Cartesian coordinate space on d-torus. In the following exposition, we fix d to two for simplicity. Note that this coordinate space is completely logical, and bears no relation to any physical coordinate system. At any point in time, the entire coordinate space is dynamically partitioned among all nodes in the system in such a way that every node "owns" its individual, distinct space within the overall space. In the following, we refer to a distinct space owned by each node as a **zone**. Figure 1 illustrates an overview of CAN. Each node in the system learns and maintains the IP addresses of those nodes that own coordinate zones adjacent with its corresponding zone. This set of neighboring nodes in the coordinate space serves as a coordinate routing table that enables routing between arbitrary points in this space. For example, nodes A and B in the figure are assigned to the zones, which are adjacent with each other in the coordinate space, and connected by a logical link in such a way that they know their IP addresses with each other.

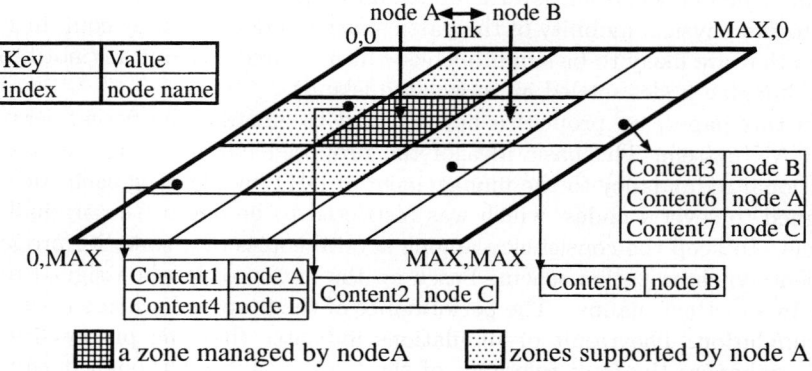

Fig. 1. Overview of CAN

Consider an object held by a node in the system. To realize an efficient management of objects, CAN stores a key-value pair (K_1, V_1) to the virtual coordinate space, where K_1 is the name of an object and V_1 is the name of a node who holds the contents of the object. The management scheme first maps key K_1 onto a point in the coordinate space in a deterministic manner by using a uniform hash function. It then stores the corresponding pair at the node that "owns" the zone within which the point lies. (see Figure 1 again for illustration). The retrieval of a stored pair could be done in a similar manner; that is, to retrieve an object corresponding to key K_1, any node can apply the same deterministic hash function to map the key onto the target point and then retrieve the corresponding value from the point.

If the calculated target point is owned by the requesting node or an immediate neighbor of him, the value associated to the given key can easily be obtained by using a local communication. However, if it is not the case, the request must be *routed* through the CAN infrastructure until it reaches the node who owns the zone containing the target point.

2.2 Join Operation

In the CAN system, the entire coordinate space is divided into zones, and those zones are assigned to the nodes currently in the system in a one-to-one manner. Thus, to allow the CAN to grow incrementally, a new node joining the system must be assigned its own portion of the coordinate space, by splitting a zone owned by an existing node to several subzones and by taking over one of them to the new node. More concretely, such an assignment is conducted as follows:

procedure JOIN

1. First, the new node u locates a node v in the CAN by using an appropriate locating mechanism, and sends a join message to v.
2. Upon receiving the message, node v splits his zone into two halves by using an appropriate coordinate, and sends back one half to node u.
3. After receiving it, u becomes the owner of the zone assigned by v, and notifies the fact to all neighbors to keep the consistency of the routing table.

In the method shown in the original paper [5], the locating of node v in the first step is conducted in a random manner. More concretely, it randomly chooses a point in the coordinate space and sends a join request destined for the point, which will eventually be received by the node who owns that point. Recently, we proposed several methods to locate a target zone to be split into several subzones, which could realize a load balancing on the number of inquiries received from the other nodes in the system [7].

2.3 Leave Operation

Before leaving the system, a leaving node must take over its zone to the other node to keep the consistency of the coordinate space; i.e., in such a way that the

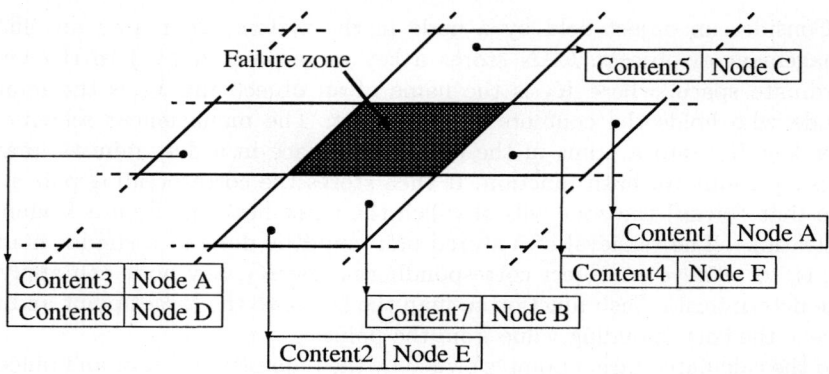

Fig. 2. Lost zone

coordinate space is covered by zones owned by the existing nodes. In addition, it must keep the consistency of the routing table, and if possible, it should balance the size of zones owned by those nodes as much as possible. A concrete procedure for the leaving is described as follows:

procedure LEAVE

1. Let α be a zone owned by the leaving node u. Node u selects a node v with a smallest zone among all neighbors of u, and sends a leave message to node v to take over α to v.
2. Upon receiving the message, node v examines if α could be merged with a zone owned by v, say β; i.e., examines if $\alpha \cup \beta$ is a tetragon or not.
3. If it could be merged, v merges them, and becomes an owner of the new zone $\alpha \cup \beta$; otherwise, it becomes the owner of α in addition to β. After that, it notifies the result to all neighbors of u and v.
4. If node u still owns a zone, then go to Step 1; otherwise, terminate.

2.4 Fault-Tolerance Problem

If a node in CAN fails by an accident, or leaves the system without executing the ordinary procedure described in the last subsection, the zone(s) owned by the node will be "lost," i.e., it becomes invisible from the other nodes (see Figure 2 for illustration, where a lost zone is painted black). In addition, it causes an inconsistency in routing tables maintained by the neighboring nodes, which violates an efficient message routing conducted by the remaining nodes. In the following, we refer to the zone owned by such a disappeared node as the **lost zone**, and will discuss about several methods to recover it.

In the design of the (original) CAN system, the problem of lost zones was tried to be fixed by sharing copies of a zone by its neighboring nodes. Suppose that a node leaves the system without notifications. In CAN, such an unexpected leave of a node could be detected by its neighboring nodes either by periodically sending hello messages or when forwarding a message to the leaved node. In both cases, it must execute a recovery procedure before going back to a normal state; i.e., a neighbor must become a new owner of the lost zone and it must notify the fact to the other neighboring nodes. Such a recovery procedure generally takes a long time compared with the normal message routing, and in addition, such a local sharing of copies among nearby nodes is not sufficient in actual P2P environments, since it may occur critical situations in which all nodes around a zone are simultaneously damaged. Hence, in order to improve the availability of the CAN system, we have to develop a new method such that the amount of redundancy could be controlled by adjusting an appropriate parameter and the time required for the recovery could be bounded as small as possible.

In the next section, we propose a new method to enhance the fault-tolerance of CAN which allows each zone to be assigned to several nodes besides neighbors. Although it has already been pointed out that the recovery time against an accident could significantly be reduced by assigning each zone to several nodes [5], to the authors' best knowledge, there have not been proposed any concrete schemes to realize the maintenance of those copies with a reasonably small cost.

3 Proposed Architecture

3.1 Overview

In this section, we propose a new method to enhance the fault-tolerance of the CAN system, which will be referred to as Multiple Management CAN (MM-CAN) in what follows. The basic idea of MM-CAN is to associate nodes to zones in such a way that: 1) each node owns several zones, and 2) each zone is shared by several nodes. The shape of each zone in the coordinate space is restricted to be a tetragon, which could be changed dynamically by applying split and merge operations as in the original CAN.

Let $V = \{v_1, v_2, \ldots, v_{|V|}\}$ be the set of nodes participating to the system, and $Z = \{z_1, z_2, \ldots, z_{|Z|}\}$ be the current set of zones. Let P_j denote the number of nodes sharing zone $z_j \in Z$, and Q_i denote the number of zones owned by node $v_i \in V$. In the proposed method, we define an upper limit on P_j, denoted by $P_{\max}$, to control the trade-off between the fault-tolerance and the efficiency of the underlying resource management scheme. That is, a larger $P_{\max}$ increases the fault-tolerance because it increases the number of copies stored in the system, whereas it degrades the efficiency because it causes a larger overhead due to the maintenance of those copies.

3.2 Join Procedure

Let u be a node who wants to join the system. In the join procedure of the proposed method, a zone owned by a node will be "copied" or "taken over" to u without splitting, as long as it does not violate a predetermined condition. In the procedure, node u first locates a zone z_j by using an appropriate locating scheme, and it will be assigned (a copy of) a different portion of the coordinate space around z_j, depending on the number of nodes sharing z_j.

procedure MM_JOIN

Let $z_j \in Z$ be a zone located by u. Let P_j be the number of nodes sharing zone z_j. If $P_j = P_{\max}$ then go to Case 1; if $0 \leq P_j \leq P_{\max}/2$ then go to Case 2; and if $P_{\max}/2 < P_j < P_{\max}$ then go to Case 3.

Case 1: Let S_j be the set of nodes sharing z_j. If z_j has a neighbor z_i such that $P_i < P_{\max}$, then go to Case 2 or 3 by letting z_i as a new located zone; otherwise, 1) split z_j into two subzones z_j^1 and z_j^2 by using an appropriate coordinate, 2) partition $S_j \cup \{u\}$ into two subsets S_j^1 and S_j^2 of an equal size, and 3) (re)assign zone z_j^k to all nodes in S_j^k for $k = 1, 2$. After that, it notifies the fact to all nodes owing a neighbor of z_j to keep the consistency of the routing table.

Case 2: A copy of z_j is assigned to u, and after that, u notifies the fact to all nodes owning z_j or its neighbor.

Case 3: Let v_i be a node in S_j such that $Q_i = \max_{v_k \in S_j}\{Q_k\}$. If $Q_i = 1$, then split z_j into two subzones, and (re)assign them to the corresponding nodes as in Case 1; otherwise, the set of zones owned by v_i into two halves, and a half of them is taken over to u.

3.3 Leave Procedure

Let u be a node who wants to leave the system. In the leave procedure of the proposed method, a leaving node first examines neighboring zones for each zone owned by the node, and tries to merge them with zones owned by u.

procedure MM_LEAVE

For each zone z_j owned by a leaving node u, execute the following operation in a concurrent manner. If $P_j = 1$ then go to Case 1; if $1 < P_j \leq P_{\max}/2$ then go to Case 2; and if $P_j > P_{\max}/2$ then go to Case 3.

Case 1: Node u first selects an appropriate neighbor $\tilde{z}$ of z_j that could be merged with z_j. If there are no such neighbors, go to Case 2 to take over z_j to an appropriate neighboring node w. Otherwise, u sends a merge message to the owner v of $\tilde{z}$. Upon receiving that, v merges z_j with $\tilde{z}$, and notifies the fact to all nodes sharing $\tilde{z}$ to replace the shared zone with the merged one.

Case 2: Node u finds a node w with the smallest Q_i among its all neighbors, and sends a message to take over z_j to w. Upon receiving the message, w becomes a new owner of (a copy of) zone z_j.

Case 3: Node u simply sends a leave message to all nodes sharing the same zone.

3.4 Maintenance of Indices

Next, we describe the mechanism adopted in the proposed method to keep the consistency among copies of the same zone. Note that to realize a transparent access to the indices held by the nodes distributed over the network, a modification of indices stored in a zone must be reflected to all copies of the zone, as well as the change of the shape of zones due to split and merge operations.

In general, there is a trade-off between the accuracy and the efficiency on the consistency holding mechanism; i.e., we could increase the accuracy by increasing the frequency of synchronizations, and we could increase the efficiency by decreasing the frequency. In the proposed method, we introduce the notion of **label**, which will be associated with each copy of a zone in a distinct manner, to improve the efficiency without degrading the accuracy. More concretely, in the proposed method, each copy of a zone is associated with a label drawn from set $\mathcal{P} \stackrel{\text{def}}{=} \{0, 1, \ldots, P_{\max} - 1\}$ in an injective manner (i.e., in such a way that any two copies are associated with distinct labels), and for each index to be retrieved, a node with a *most appropriate* label will be selected as the **leader** of those nodes sharing the zone containing the index, and will be given a privilege to control the other nodes.

The appropriateness of a label with respect to the given index is determined as follows: Let f be an appropriate hash function from the set of indices to set $\mathcal{P}$. We first apply f to the given index i, and examine if a node with label $f(i) \in \mathcal{P}$ exists or not. If it exists, the node with label $f(i)$ is selected as the leader with respect to index i; otherwise, it examines labels $f(i)+1, f(i)+2, \ldots$ in this order, and selects the firstly found one as the leader, where all additions is conducted with modulo $P_{\max}$. By using the notion of leader, the management of copies is conducted as follows: 1) An update of a zone is notified only to the leader of the zone with respect to the given index, which will be forwarded to the other nodes from the leader, and 2) an inquiry destined for a zone will be received only by the leader with respect to the inquiry, which is given a responsibility to adequately reply to the inquiry.

4 Evaluation

4.1 Simulation Environment

Let V be the set of nodes to be considered in the simulation. In this paper, we consider a situation in which: 1) the CAN system initially contains a single node in V called an **anchor**, and 2) the other nodes in V repeat join and leave operations in a dynamic and concurrent manner. In addition, each node participating with the system repeatedly tries to access an object stored in the system, and issues an inquiry message to find the index of the object accordingly.

More concretely, a node who is not contained in the system issues a join message according to a Poisson distribution with mean $\lambda_{\text{join}} = 150$ [sec], and the time duration before issuing a leave message follows an exponential distribution with mean $\lambda_{\text{hold}} = 200$ [sec]. A node who is participating with the system issues an inquiry message according to a Poisson distribution with mean $\lambda_{\text{access}} = 8$ [sec]. In addition, we assume that the message transmission between any pair of nodes takes 1 sec, and the transaction of an inquiry takes 1 sec on any node.

Table 1. The number of invocations of initialization

P_{max}	64	128	256	512	1024	2048	4096	8192	16384
1	0	0	5	5	5	16	31	43	72
3	0	0	1	1	1	0	5	2	16
4	0	0	0	0	0	0	0	0	0
5	0	0	0	0	0	0	0	0	0
6	0	0	0	0	0	0	0	0	0

We use a hash function with range 1024 × 1024. In addition, the number of nodes who repeat join and leave operations (i.e., the cardinality of set V) is varied from 64 ($= 2^6$) to 16384 ($= 2^{14}$), and we examine several characteristics including the fault-tolerance and the maintenance cost by varying P_{max} as 1, 3, 4, 5, and 6 and by fixing the maximum number of zones that could be owned by each node by three. Note that the case of "$P_{max} = 1$" coincides with the original CAN. Finally, upon detecting an inconsistency of the coordinate space that could not be recovered by the underlying resource management scheme, each node invokes an "initialization" to reconstruct the entire coordinate space from scratch in the worst case. Thus, the frequency of initializations represents the fault-tolerance of the resource management scheme, which significantly affects to the overall performance of the underlying scheme.

4.2 Results

(a) Frequency of Initializations. At first, we evaluate the fault-tolerance of the proposed scheme by measuring the number of initializations invoked during the simulation time. Table 1 summarizes the result. As is shown in the table, although it causes no initializations for sufficiently large P_{max} (i.e., when $P_{max} \geq 4$), when P_{max} is relatively small (i.e., when $P_{max} \leq 3$), it causes several initializations and its frequency will be increased as increasing the number of nodes participating to the system. In addition, the number of initializations reduces to about 20% by increasing P_{max} from 1 to 3. By those observations, we can conclude that an increase of P_{max} is really effective to enhance the fault-tolerance of the underlying resource management system.

(b) Average Number of Hops. Next, we evaluate the impact of the proposed scheme to the efficiency of the underlying message routing schemes. An increase of the value of P_{max} would reduce the number of resultant zones, since it reduces the frequency of splitting a zone into two halves. Thus, it is strongly expected that an increase of P_{max} reduces the number of hops before reaching to the destination for each message. To verify this intuition, we examine the average number of hops destined for randomly generated points in the coordinate space by varying P_{max} from 1 to 6. Figure 3 illustrates the result, where the horizontal axis is the number of nodes. As is shown in the figure, the average number of hops monotonically decreases as increasing the value of P_{max}, which monotonically increases as increasing the cardinality of V. In particular, the average number of hops reduces to about 50% by increasing $P_{\max}$ from 1 to 6. Thus, we can conclude from this result that, as a side effect, an increase of $P_{\max}$ really improves the performance of the underlying routing scheme.

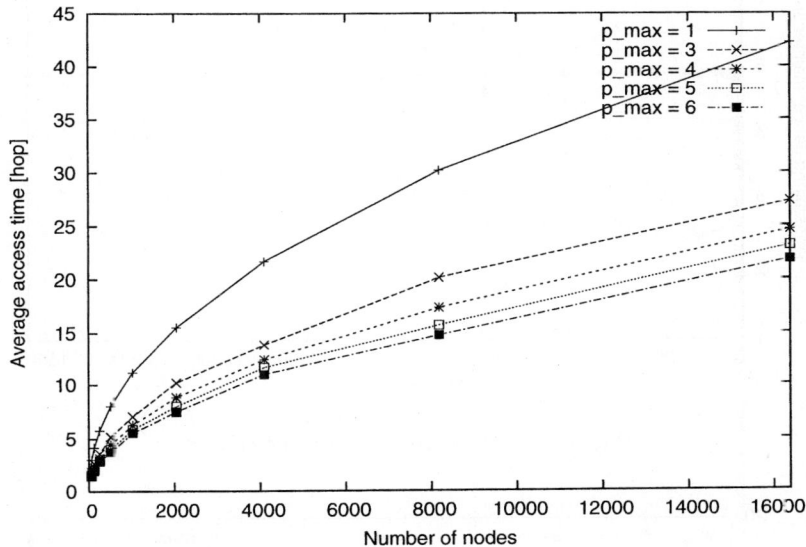

Fig. 3. Average number of hops to the target node

(c) Total Data Size. Although there are several advantages as examined previously, an increase of $P_{\max}$ causes an increase of the maintenance cost, which would degrade the performance of the overall system. To clarify that point, we evaluate the maintenance cost of the proposed scheme by measuring the total amount of data exchanged among nodes in the system, which includes the data required for the ordinary operations in addition to the overhead due to the redundancy having been introduced to the proposed scheme. Figure 4 summarizes the result, where the horizontal axis is the number of nodes, as before. As is shown in the figure, although it keeps a constant value regardless of the number of nodes for sufficiently large $P_{\max}$ (i.e., when $P_{\max} \geq 4$), the amount of exchanged data is significantly affected by the number of nodes if $P_{\max}$ is smaller than or equal to three. More concretely, the amount of exchanged data monotonically increases as increasing the cardinality of V, which corresponds to the increase of the number of initializations observed in Table 1. In addition, the amount of exchanged data monotonically increases as increasing $P_{\max}$ for small number of nodes, which would correspond to the increase of the maintenance cost due to the increase of the number of copies in the proposed scheme.

To examine the effect of the maintenance cost in more detail, we finally evaluate the average number of neighbors in the proposed scheme. Figure 5 illustrates

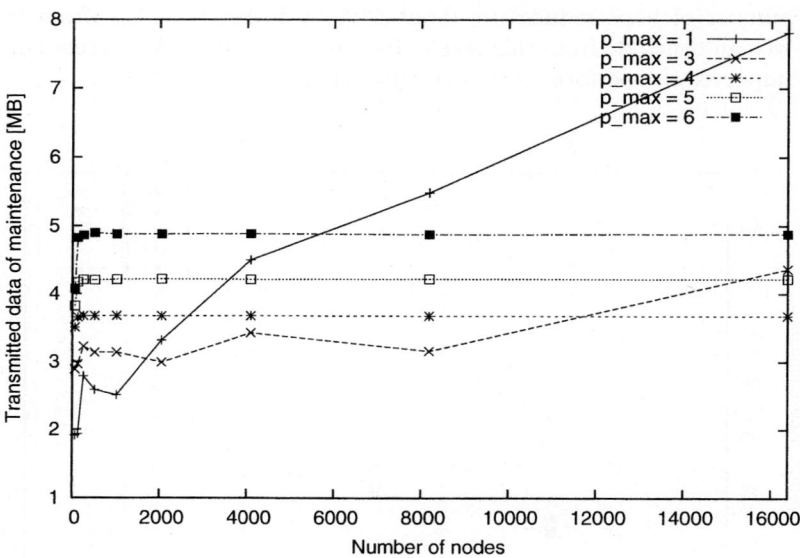

Fig. 4. The total size of maintenance cost

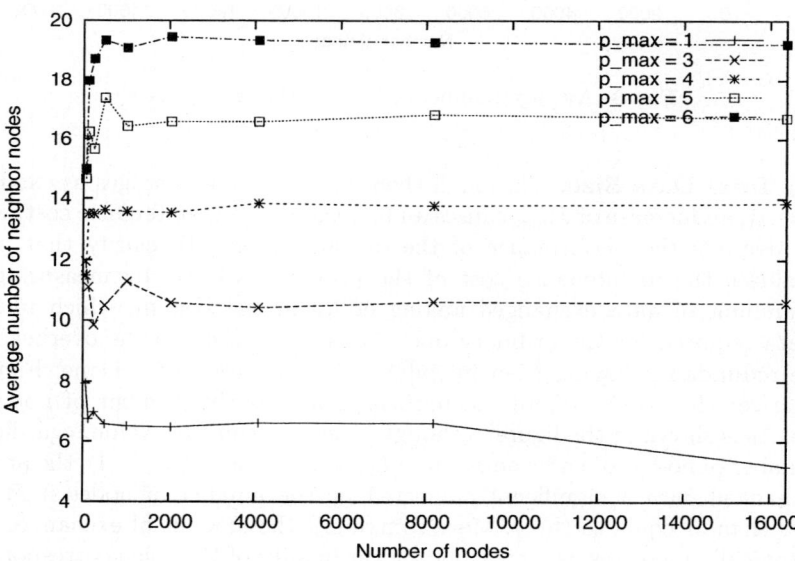

Fig. 5. Average number of neighboring nodes of each node.

the result. As is shown in the figure, the number of neighbors increases as increasing $P_{\max}$, which is very similar to the increase of the amount of exchanged data observed in Figure 4. Although it is not clear why it rapidly changes by varying the cardinality of V from 64 to 256, we could conclude from those results that the maintenance cost of the proposed scheme really increases as increasing $P_{\max}$, which will be dominated by the initialization cost that could be frequently incurred for small $P_{\max}$'s.

5 Concluding Remarks

In this paper, we proposed a new method to enhance the fault-tolerance of the CAN system that is known as a typical pure P2P system. The basic idea of the proposed method is to introduce a redundancy to the management of indices distributed over the P2P network, and to keep the consistency among copies of such indices, we proposed an efficient synchronization scheme based on the notion of labels assigned to each copy in a distinct manner. The performance of the proposed scheme was experimentally evaluated by simulation. The result of simulations indicates that the proposed scheme really enhances the fault-tolerance of the CAN system.

We have left several important issues as future problems, such as the examination of the proposed scheme under a realistic environment and an application of the scheme to the other DHT-based systems.

References

1. K. Aberer, P. Cudé-Mauroux, A. Datta, Z. Despotovic, M. Hauswirth, M. Punceva, and R. Schmidt. P-Grid: A Self-Organizing Access Stricture for P2P Information Systems. *ACM SIGMOD Record*, pp. 29–33 (Sept. 2003).
2. I. Clarke, O. Sandberg, B. Wiley, and T.W.Hong. Freenet: A distributed anonymous information storage and retrieval system. In *Workshop on Design Issues in Anonymity and Unobservability*, pp. 46–66 (July 2000).
3. Gnutella. http://gnutella.wego.com (2001).
4. L. Gong. ProjectJXTA : A Technology Overview. Sun Microsystems Inc. (Apr. 2001).
5. S. Ratnasamy, P. Francis, M. Handley, R. Karp, and S. Shenker. A Scalable Content-Addressable Network. In *Proc. ACM SIGCOMM 2001*, pp. 161–172, (Aug. 2001).
6. I. Stoica, R. Morris, D. Karger, M. Frans Kaashoek, and H. Balakrishnan. Chord: A scalable peer-to-peer lookup service for internet applications. In *Proc. ACM SIGCOMM 2001*, pp. 149–160 (Aug. 2001).
7. D. Takemoto, S. Tagashira, and S. Fujita. Distributed Algorithms for Balanced Zone Partitioning in Content-Addressable Networks. In *Proc. ICPADS 2004*, pp. 377–384 (July 2004).
8. B. Y. Zhao, J. D. Kubiatowicz, and A. D. Joseph. Tapestry: An Infrastructure for Fault-tolerant Wide-area Location and Routing. Tech. Rep. UCB/ CSD-01-1141 (Apr. 2000).

Effective Resource Allocation in a JXTA-Based Grid Computing Platform JXTPIA

Kenichi Sumitomo[1], Takato Izaiku[1], Yoshihiro Saitoh[1],
Hui Wang[1], Minyi Guo[1,2], and Jie Huang[1]

[1] Department of Computer Software,
University of Aizu, Aizu-Wakamatsu, Fukushima 965-8580, Japan
[2] State Key Laboratory for Novel Software Technology,
Nanjing University, Nanjing 210093, P.R. China

Abstract. To extend a Peer-to-Peer (P2P) network system with the mechanisms of distributed/Grid computing, we developed a flexible JXTA-based P2P network interface and architecture, JXTPIA. The JXTPIA system provides the basic functionalities for Grid computing, such as resources allocation and sharing, task scheduling and assignment, network structure constructing and maintenance, etc. One of the main challenges in developing the JXTPIA system is efficient allocation of resources. We developed and evaluated algorithms for resource allocation to improve the efficiency of the JXTPIA system. The experimental results show that the efficiency of the JXTPIA system differs depending on the adopted algorithms. It indicates that scheduling based on limited information about peers has effects on the performance of the entire system. Though the adopted algorithms are specialized for the JXTPIA system only, the principle of the algorithms can be widely used on similar systems.

Keywords: JXTPIA system, resource allocation, Grid computing, network structures.

1 Introduction

Grid computing is an emerging technology that enables the sharing, selection, and aggregation of geographically distributed "autonomous" resources dynamically at runtime depending on their availability, capability, performance, cost, and users' quality-of-service requirements [1]. Especially, PC Grid, a type of Grid Computing like SETI@HOME [2] and UD Cancer Research [3], has become popular to ordinary people as the most familiar type of grid computing and has gathered millions of participants. In order to develop a PC Grid platform that can provide more general computing services, we launched a project named "JXTa-based Peer-to-peer Interface and Architecture," or JXTPIA [4].

Grid computing system are distributed system connected within a physical network, such as the Internet. The distributed components in a Grid computing system must distribute and search resources dynamically. It is quite frequent, and naturally not in a balanced way, to transfer and search for resources in a Grid computing system. So the resource distributed processing becomes congested. Communication between all devices on the network causes network traffics, which is one of bottlenecks in PC Grid computing. So one of the objectives in developing the JXTPIA system is to efficiently allocate resources to reduce the network traffics. In this paper, we seek the more suitable resource allocation methods adapted to the nature of JXTPIA.

This paper is organized as follows. Section 2 describes related work on resource allocation in distributed/Grid computing environment. In Section 3, the overview of the JXTPIA system is presented. In Section 4, we present the resource allocation algorithms and Section 5 evaluates their performance. Section 6 illustrates experiments on resource allocation, and conclusions are in Section 7.

2 Related Work

There are many papers on resource allocation under Grid computing environments. Grid resource allocation and control have been studied in Ref. [5] by using a model called G-commerce. In G-commerce model, users and Grid-aware applications are resource consumers, while resource producers are the sellers. The GridSim toolkit [6] provides some tools to model and simulate some main entities in Grid computing, such as users, applications, resources, and resource brokers etc. In Ref. [7], resource allocation using reinforcement learning is studied in a simplified Grid-like environment. Java Market project [8] treats resources and tasks as goods in markets. Nimrod [9], and Compute Power Market (CPM) [10] are also market based resource management and scheduling systems.

JNGI [11] is a distributed computing framework based on JXTA [12][13] that users can use it to submit jobs to JXTA groups. These jobs can be split and distributed among several peers. A Personal Power Plant (P3) [14] is a middleware on pure P2P facilities provided by JXTA for distributed computing using volatile personal computers.

Since resource allocation is very important in Grid computing systems, they must be implemented efficiently within Grid computing systems. Globus [15][16] architecture is a *de facto* standard for computational grid [17]. Globus Toolkit provides the basic system to achieve Grid computing, and it is very close to satisfy the demand of Grid computing. In Globus architecture, GRAM service supports submission, monitoring, and control of jobs on computers. GRAM provides interfaces which can integrate with other traditional resource allocation systems, such as Portable Batch System (PBS) [18], Platform LSF [19], Condor [20]. In our experience, using Globus Toolkit is only a small part of cost on developing a Grid computing program. Globus requires programmers an additional overload and much stress. Of course, Globus has the value which offsets these costs. It is a trade-off between working cost and effectiveness.

3 JXTPIA System Overview

The JXTPIA system contains four main modules: JXTPIA network module, JXTPIA Homework Distribution module (JHD), JXTPIA Trigger Distribution

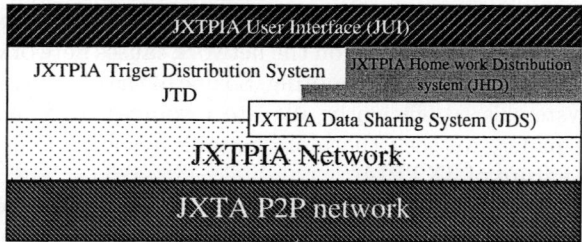

Fig. 1. Layers in the JXTPIA System

module (JTD), and JXTPIA Data Sharing module (JDS). The relationships of these modules are illustrated in Figure 1. JXTPIA network layer, built upon JXTA [12][13] P2P network, supports the core of system layers, such as JTD, JHD, and JDS, where JTD distributes task information to peers and gets feedback from peers, JHD provides users distribute JHD tasks to JXTPIA network via the JXTPIA user interface, and JDS keeps the data communication among these system layers.

There are two principal types of peers in the JXTPIA system, *leader peer* and *worker peer*. A worker peer is an ordinary peer which handles practical work. A leader peer is responsible for managing the information of worker peers in a *worker ring*. Leader peers are also connected roundly to make a *leader ring*. Since the network is organized on JXTA, JXTPIA has an advanced network transparency such as connecting across NAT, or connecting in the condition where only HTTP protocol works.

To get the system scalability, a *message-listener* model is adopted in the JXTPIA system. The message-listener model can handle large numbers of clients / connections, spread across multiple machines. It can minimize what needs to be stored in memory, and make it possible for multiple classes to reuse instances of event handlers and events.

The ring-based network structure in the JXTPIA system keeps its scalability and solid [4]. JXTPIA network has construction methods for fast building the network and also self-recovering methods to avoid the collapse. JXTPIA network treats the leader loss and the worker peer loss in different ways to reduce the communication time and messages.

4 Resource Allocation in JXTPIA

Two principal elements in the JXTPIA system are *task* and *resource (or data)*. One task commonly has a large number of data as its targets. For example, in the case of matrix multiplication, the task is the program which describes the algorithm of matrix multiplication, and the resources are two matrices being targets of the matrix multiplication. In JXTPIA, the task is expressed as JAR archives named *homework set* (HWS), and the resources are expressed as common files named *target data*. An HWS is an ordinary JAR archive apart from

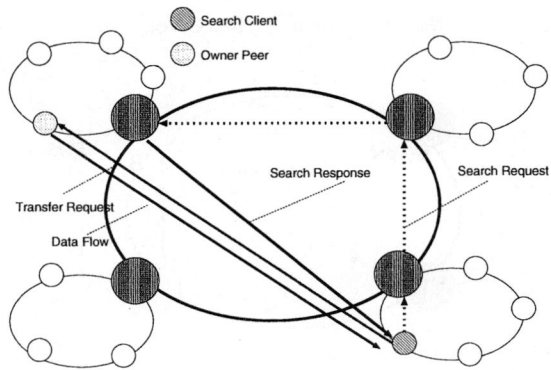

Fig. 2. Task searching algorithm. Details can be found in Section ??

including the class file inside which implements a particular interface and whose name is the same as the HWS. Also, target data can be any types of resources such as a plain text file and/or a binary file storing serialized objects. If a peer wants to issue a task, all it has to do is to outfit an HWS and the target data associated with it.

The JDS module searches for the resources within the network, and/or transfers the resource to the client peer. After transferring the tasks and arguments to the peer, the JTD module executes the task and receives the results. To distribute many tasks in a short time, it is necessary to reduce network loads and the searching response time when deploying and searching resources. In this section, we will describe algorithms used for resources allocation.

Resource allocation includes resource searching and resource distribution. Figure 2 shows the outline of the resource searching algorithm. Since in the

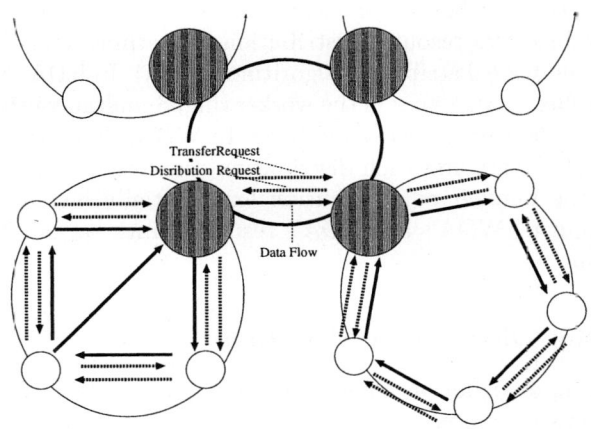

Fig. 3. Message flow in the ring distribution algorithm

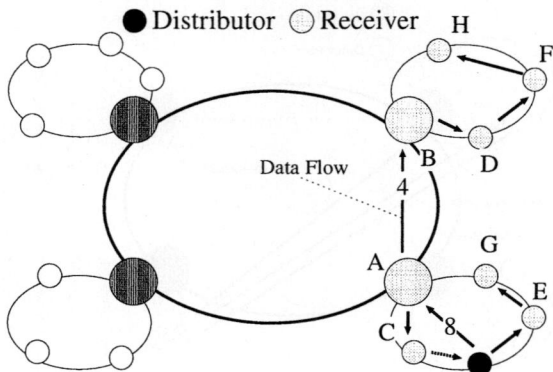

Fig. 4. Data flow in the ring distribution algorithm

JXTPIA system, the leader peer knows the resources in each worker peer within the same group, the resource can be found by asking the leader peer only. A resource searching client peer creates the search entry and requests its leader peer to search for the specific resource. The leader peer sends a request to its neighbor leader peer for the resource location. After finding it, the leader peer will inform the client peer the resource location. If the leader peer can not know find the location, the leader peer keeps asking its neighbor leader peer. When the searching client peer receives information from the owner peer, it will request the owner peer to transfer the resource directly. Then, the searching client peer informs its leader peer to update its list of resources, and then delete the searching entry.

Resource distribution processes include sending/receiving messages and then sending/receiving resources based on the response to the request message. Since the JXTPIA system is built upon the ring-based network structure, one of our main concerns is how to efficiently use it to reduce the network traffics. Here we introduce two resource distribution algorithms: ring distribution algorithm (RDA) and wide distribution algorithm (WDA). In RDA, data are distributed to the neighbor worker peer in the worker ring. Simultaneously, data are distributed to the leader peers in the leader ring. In WDA, data are distributed to peers in each worker ring, and each distribution source search for two destination peer. Hence, the number of distribution exponentially increases like tree structure. By computing WDA's and RDA's response time, we can find the more effective algorithm.

4.1 Ring Distribution Algorithm

In the ring distribution algorithm (RDA), a peer first sends out requests to its neighbor worker peer and its leader peer. Then both peer send the request to its neighbor which hasn't received the request, while the leader peer sends the request to the neighbor leader peer in the leader ring. In the meantime, the leader peer decreases the rest number of distribution by the number of the worker peer in its leader ring. The message flow and data flow of RDA are illustrated in Figures 3 and 4, respectively. In Figure 3, transfer-request messages are sent to its neighbor peers, including the leader peer, then the leader peer forward the request to other leader groups. Simultaneously, distribution requests are sent out in the inverse direction. In Figure 4, we show an example of the data flow in RDA. Data are distributed from Distributor to eight Receivers A, B, C, D, E, F, G, and H. Here we suppose each peer can send out only two copies of data simultaneously. The distributor first sends out data to both leader peer A and worker peer E. Then the worker peer E sends data inside the ring, while peer A sends data to the next leader peer B and worker peer C. Peer H receives data from the distribution inside the ring supervised by leader peer B. So data are distributed in peer group A and peer group B.

The distribution time of RDA becomes large because data are distributed to only its neighbor worker peers and/or its neighbor leader peer.

4.2 Wide Distribution Algorithm

In the wide distribution algorithm (WDA), a peer first sends requests to its leader peer. The leader peer sends the request to other leader peers, and then each leader peer sends request to the worker peers in its worker ring. The message flow and data flow of WDA are illustrated in Figures 5 and 6, respectively. In Figure 5, a client peer asks its leader peer to request two destination peers which are not in the same worker ring. The processes are repeated by the destination peers on the basis of remaining storage amount. The receiving peer distributes and transfers data until the number of distribution becomes zero. We show an example of data flow of WDA in Figure 6. Data are distributed from the distributor to eight receivers A, B, C, D, E, F, G, and H. As done in RDA, we assume that each peer can send out only two copies of data simultaneously. The distributor first sends out data to peer A and peer B. Then peer B sends data

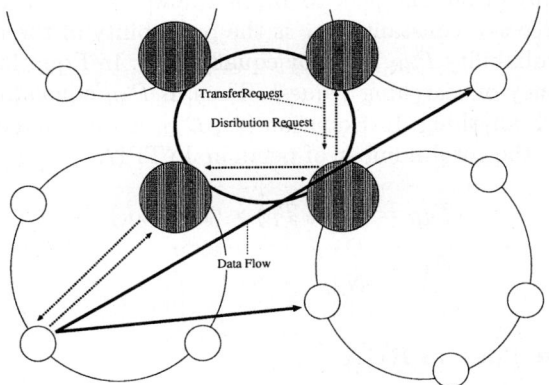

Fig. 5. Message flow in the wide distribution algorithm

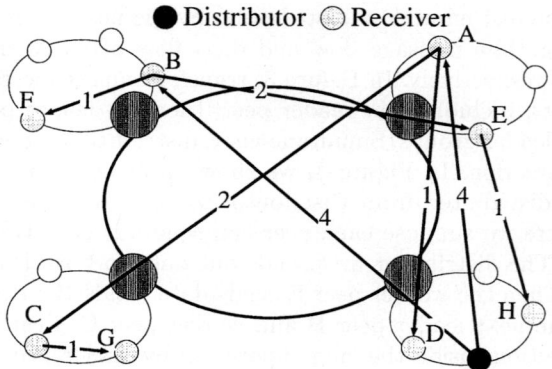

Fig. 6. Data flow in the wide distribution algorithm

to peer E and peer F, while peer A sends data to peer C and peer D. Finally, peer C sends data to peer G, and peer E sends data to peer H.

WDA can quickly find resources because resources are widely distributed to rings, but the distribution costs much time because the time to search for the destination peer is quite long.

5 Performance Evaluation

The average search response time is the time that a peer receives the specific resource from other peers. Equation (1) shows the average resource search response time. An average resource search response time, T_{SR}, is expressed by an average time to discover a peer, T_S, and an average time for transferring resource, T_T. T_S is used to find the peer which has the required resources and then get the peer's identification which is like IP address. T_T is the time for transferring resource from one peer to another, and the time is a constant if the size of the resource is a constant. P_{All} is the probability of the resource located in a peer. The probability P_{All} is led by equation (2). In Equation (2), $(1 - P_{All})$ shows the frequency of searching request. Thus, If P_{All} equals to 1, a peer does not need to search anything. In Equation (2), D_{All} is the number of distributed resources. N_{All} is the total number of peers in JXTPIA.

$$T_{SR} = (T_S + T_T) \times (1 - P_{All}) \qquad (1)$$

$$P_{All} = \frac{D_{All}}{N_{All}} \qquad (2)$$

5.1 Allocation Time in RDA

The average search time, T_S, in Equation (1), can be expressed as in Equation (3),

$$T_S(N_L, P_L) = \sum_{H=1}^{N_L}(H \times T_{enq} \times (1 - P_L)^H) \quad (3)$$

where, H is the number of hop counts, and N_L and P_L are the total number of peers and the probability of the resource located in a peer in the worker peer group L, respectively. T_{enq} shows an enquiry time to inquire whether a leader has the resources, and normally it is a constant. $(1 - P_L)^H$ shows the rate of occurring search request to the peer at a distance of n hops. This Equation shows P_L has much effect on T_S.

$$D_L = \frac{D_{All}}{N_W} \quad (4)$$

$$P_L = \frac{D_L}{N_L} = \frac{D_{All}}{(N_L \times N_W)} \quad (5)$$

In RDA, D_L can be decided by D_{All} and N_W, the number of worker peers in a worker ring. The value of P_L alters when using different algorithms. When using RDA, P_L can be obtained from Equation (5).

$$T_D = \begin{cases} (D_L + N_W) \times T_T, & if(D_{All} \geq N_W) \\ D_{All} \times T_T, & if(D_{All} < N_W) \end{cases} \quad (6)$$

When using RDA, the distribution time can be figured out by Equation (6). In Equation (6), $(D_L + N_W)$ is the number of hop counts to the most deep peer. If D_{All} is smaller than N_W, the resource is distributed in the leader ring.

5.2 Allocation Time in WDA

The average discover time in the wide distribution algorithm (WDA), T_S in Equation (1), can also be expressed as in Equation (3) but with different parameters.

In WDA, D_L is the minimum of D_L and D_{All}, shown in Equation (8). P_L in Equation (8) is different from the one used in the ring distributed algorithm. It shows that P_L increases in using WDA more than RDA. It also shows that T_S is exponentially reduced in using WDA.

$$D_L = \begin{cases} D_L, & if(D_{All} \geq D_L) \\ D_{All}, & if(D_{All} < D_L) \end{cases} \quad (7)$$

$$P_L = \frac{D_{All}}{N_L} \quad (8)$$

Equation (9) presents the distribution time, T_D when using WDA. When distributing resources, WDA needs to decide which peer receives the resource. ($T_T + T_M$) is the time to transfer resource in one step, where T_M is the management time to assign the resource to a suitable peer, which includes looking up leader's resource information list, sending the request, and getting the response. If D_{All} is small, T_D becomes smaller with RDA than WDA. On the contrary, if D_{All} is large, T_D becomes smaller with WDA than RDA.

$$T_D = 2 \times (T_T + T_M) \times \log_2(D_{All} - 1) \quad (9)$$

6 Experimental Results and Discussion

The experimental environments and execution times are shown in Table 1. The JXTPIA system is tested on network with more than 200 Sun Blade 150 workstations. Each Sun Blade workstation has a 550 MHz CPU and a 512 MB Memory running with the Solaris 8 operating system. The parameters such as the task file size, transferring time, management time, sending message time are set to constants as in Table 1, if not be further specified.

Figure 7 shows the effects of the file size to the distribution times of both Ring Distribution Algorithm and Wide Distribution Algorithm. In the experiment, the management time is set to 0.001 ms, but the transferring time is changed from 1 ms to 8 ms. The distribution times of both RDA and WDA increase linearly when the file size becomes larger. For small transferring time, for example, 1 ms or 2 ms, the distribution time of WDA is larger than that of RDA. For large

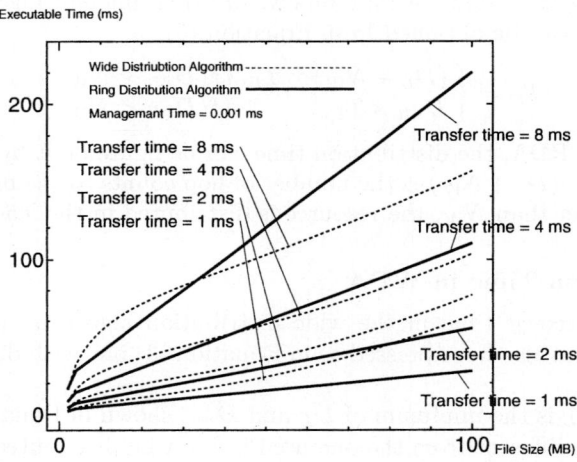

Fig. 7. Effects of the file size to the distribution times of both the Ring Distribution Algorithm and the Wide Distribution Algorithm

Table 1. Environments

Machine	Sun Blade150
CPU	UltraSPARC-IIe 550MHz
Memory	512 MB
OS	Solaris 8
A task file size	30 MB
Transferring time	1.0 ms
Management time	0.012 ms
Sending message time	0.01 ms

transferring time, say, 4 ms or 8 ms, the distribution time of WDA is larger than that of RDA if the file size is smaller than 30 MB, but smaller if the file size is larger than 30 MB. Further detailed experiments will be conducted soon.

Figure 8 shows the effects of the distribution number to the distribution times of both RDA and WDA. Same as the previous experiment, the management time is set to 0.001 ms, and the transferring time is changed from 1 ms to 8 ms. When the distribution number increases, the distribution time of RDA increases linearly, but the distribution time of WDA increases much more quickly. It indicates that RDA has better performance on distributing a large number of resources. The transferring time, the number of distribution resources, and the resource size affect on distribution time dominantly. It is effective to use RDA if the transferring time is small. WDA is more effective only if both the resource size and the transferring time are large. To treat a large number of distributions, RDA is chosen since its character of linearly increasing with the distribution number.

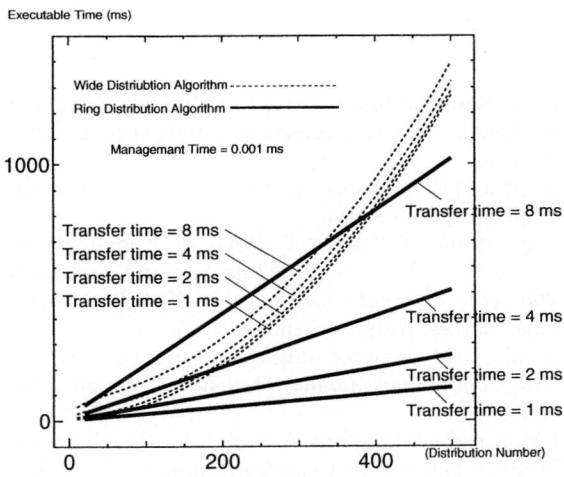

Fig. 8. Effects of the distribution number to the distribution times of both Ring Distribution Algorithm and Wide Distribution Algorithm

7 Conclusions

We developed an extended Peer-to-Peer (or P2P) network system with the mechanisms of cluster computing and Grid computing, JXTPIA system. It provides the basic facilities for Grid computing, such as resources allocation and sharing, task scheduling, task assignment, network structure constructing and maintenance, etc. One of main challenges in developing Grid computing system are network traffics.

In this paper, we proposed some efficient algorithms for the JXTPIA system to efficiently allocate of resources. We devise, test, and evaluate new algorithms for resource allocation in the JXTPIA system. The experimental results show that it is effective to reduce network load and search response time by using these algorithms. Transferring time and the number of distributions affects the executable time largely. The efficiency of the JXTPIA system differs depending on the adopted algorithms. The results indicate that scheduling based on limited information about peers has some effects on the performance of the entire system. Though the adopted algorithms are specialized for the JXTPIA system only, the principle of the algorithms can be widely used on systems similar to the JXTPIA system.

The JXTPIA system is still under development. No existence of security system is a fatal defect. The implementation of a security system into JXTPIA also will affect the algorithms and performances of resource allocation. Also, more experimental results will be committed to improve the reliability of the JXTPIA system.

References

1. R. Buyya. Grid Computing Info Centre. *http://www.gridcomputing.com/*.
2. SETI@HOME. Search for Extraterrestrial Intelligence at home. *http:// setiathome.ssl.berkeley.edu/*.
3. United Devices. Runs grid.org projects for large-scale, non-profit research projects. see *http://www.grid.org/home.htm*.
4. Y. Saitoh, K. Sumitomo, T. Izaiku, T. Oono, K. Yagyu, H. Wang, and M. Guo. JXTPIA: A JXTA-Based P2P Network Interface and Architecture for Grid Computing. *The 2005 International Conference on High Performance Computing and Communications*, Naples, Italy, September, 2005.
5. R. Wolski, et al. Grid resource allocation and control using computational economies. *Grid Computing: Making The Global Infrastructure a Reality*, John Wiley & Sons, 2003.
6. R. Buyya and M. Murshed. GridSim: A Toolkit for the Modeling and Simulation of Distributed Resource Management and Scheduling for Grid Computing. *The Journal of Concurrency and Computation: Practice and Experience (CCPE)*, Volume 14, Issue 13-15, Wiley Press, Nov.-Dec., 2002.
7. A. Galstyan, et al. Resource Allocation in the Grid Using Reinforcement Learning. *AAMAS'04*, July 19-23, 2004, New York, New York, USA.
8. Y. Amir, B. Awerbuch and R. S. Borgstrom. The Java Market: Transforming the internet into a Metacomputer. *Technical Report CNDS-98-1, Johns Hopkins University*, 1998.
9. Nimrod Project. *http://www.csse.monash.edu.au/ davida/nimrod/*.
10. Compute Power Market Project. *http://grid.cs.usm.my/cpm.htm*.
11. JNGI Project. *http://jngi.jxta.org/*
12. JXTA Project. *http://platform.jxta.org*.
13. L. Gong. JXTA: A Network Programming Environment. *IEEE internet Computing*, 5(3):88–95, May/June 2001;
    Bernard Traversat. Project JXTA 2.0 Super-Peer Virtual Network. *http://www.jxta.org/ project/www/docs/ JXTA2.0protocols1.pdf*.

14. Personal Power Plant (P3) Project. *http://p-three.sourceforge.net/*.
15. Globus 2.4. *http:// www.globus.org/gt2.4/*, 2004.
16. I. Foster, et al. The Anatomy of the Grid: Enabling Scalable Virtual Organizations, *International J. Supercomputer Applications*, 15(3), 2001;
    I. Foster, et al. A Metacomputing Infrastructure Toolkit. *International J. Supercomputer Applications*, 11(2):115-128, 1997;
    J. Nabrzyski, J.M. Schopf, J. Weglarz (Eds). Grid Resource Management. *Kluwer Publishing.* Fall 2003.
17. I. Foster, C. Kesselman. The Grid: Blueprint for a New Computing Infrastructure. *Morgan Kaufmann Publisher*, 1998.
18. Portable Batch System. *http://www.fysik.dtu.dk/CAMP/pbs.html*.
19. Platform LSF. *http://www.platform.com/products/LSF/*.
20. Condor. Overview of the Condor High Throughput Computing System. *http:// www.cs.wisc.edu/ condor/overview/*, 2004.
21. J. Verbeke, N. Nadgir, G. Ruetsch and I. Sharpov. Framework for Peer-to-Peer Distributed Computing in a Heterogeneous, Decentralized Environment. *http://www.jxta.org/ project/www/docs/ mdejxta-paper.pdf* .

A Generic Approach to Make Structured Peer-to-Peer Systems Topology-Aware

Tongqing Qiu, Fan Wu, and Guihai Chen

State Key Laboratory of Novel Software Technology, Nanjing University, China
{qtq, wufan}@dislab.nju.edu.cn, gchen@nju.edu.cn

Abstract. With the help of distributed hash tables, the structured peer-to-peer system has a short routing path and good extensibility. However, the mismatch between the overlay and physical network is the barrier to build an effective peer-to-peer system in the large-scale environment. In this paper, we propose a generic approach to solve this problem, which is quite different from other protocol-dependent methods. We reserve the structure of system and break the coupling between the node and its identifier by swap operations. We also propose several policies to reduce the traffic overhead. The policies include adaptive probing and shadow scheme. The experiment shows that our approach can greatly reduce the average latency of overlay networks and the overhead is controllable.

Keywords: peer-to-peer, overlay network, topology-aware, stretch.

1 Introduction

Several recent peer-to-peer (P2P) systems (CAN [1], Chord [2], Pastry [3], etc.) provide a self-organizing substrate for large-scale P2P applications. These structured P2P systems can be viewed as providing a scalable, fault-tolerant distributed hash table (DHT). Any item (content) can be located with in a bounded number of hops, using a small per-node routing table. However, as a node is hashed to a random identifier (node ID), the mismatch between physical topologies and logical overlays is a major factor that delays the lookup response time. In this situation, "hop" is no longer a reasonable metric to measure the delay. We usually call it *mismatching* or *topology-aware* problem. There are several methods to solve the problem. Most of methods solve it in two basic steps [4]: 1) to gather some information about network proximity, and 2) to construct or repair the overlay network using information above. In order to show the limitations of recent work, we will discuss these two steps in the following two subsections.

1.1 Collect Proximity Information

To solve the mismatching problem, some sort of proximity information of the underlying network is needed. There are two general ways which have been proposed – *landmark clustering* and *flooding or heuristic-based search*. Landmark clustering is based on the intuition that nodes close to each other are likely to have similar distances to a few landmark nodes. S. Ratnasamy et al [5] utilize this idea to optimize CAN system. The main limitation of this solution is that it is a coarse method to discover the proximity of different nodes. Besides, the landmarks are like servers in the system, introducing some *single-point failure* problems [6]. Flooding or heuristic-based search is another choice to get proximity information. It is like searching method in a P2P system. Instead of getting contents, it tries to get delay information. In this way, we can gather more detailed knowledge about the physical network than landmark method. However, uncontrollable searching will be too expensive for topology matching. So the challenge is to make tradeoff between effectiveness and probing cost.

1.2 Utilize Proximity Information

When we have got some knowledge about the proximity, the next step is to utilize the proximity information to construct or repair the structured peer-to-peer system. Three basic approaches have been suggested for exploiting proximity in DHT protocols [7] – *proximity routing, proximity neighbor selection* and *geographic layout*. There are several systems which use one of these three policies. Topologically-Aware CAN [5] is an example with geographic layout. This approach unfortunately creates uneven distribution of nodes on the overlay. Pastry uses proximity neighbor selection to construct the routing table [8]. However, the ID prefix of Pastry is a constraint to limit the selection range. As a matter of fact, all of these have a common limitation – *protocol-dependent*. For instance, geographic layout ensures that nodes that are close in the network topology are close in the node ID space, which is only suitable for the system like CAN [9]. Because in CAN, the nearness in node ID means less hops in routing. In systems like Pastry or Tapestry, we have some degree of freedom to choose nodes in the routing table. But in Chord or CAN, the entries in routing table are deterministic. Proximity routing also has the requirement that there must be more than one choice for next hop, which is not suitable for systems like Chord.

The further problem is the dynamism in peer-to-peer systems. As nodes arrive or depart, the existing routing tables need to be repaired. Without timely repairing, the structure of overlay will digress from optimal condition as inefficient routes gradually accumulate in routing tables. So an effective overlay should be adaptive to the system's dynamic change.

In order to solve all problems mentioned above, we propose a novel method to make the structured P2P system topology-aware. This method periodically adjusts the node ID and preserves the structure of P2P systems. By iteratively reducing the average logical link latency, the overlay trends to match the physical network. This method is protocol-independent and easy to be built on any structured P2P systems. Through our experiment based on Chord, we find that this approach can greatly reduce average logical/physical link latency. Besides, the overhead of adjustment is very low when using adaptive policies.

This paper is organized as follows. In section 2 we describe our approach in detail, including basic policy and several overhead-reducing mechanisms. In section 3, we illustrate the results of our experiment and give some explanations.

Other related work is introduced in section 4. Finally, in section 5 we conclude the paper and point out some future work.

2 Variable Node ID

2.1 Basic Method

We propose a novel solution to the mismatching problem of distributed hash table, which is based on *variable node ID*. As we know, in a DHT system, one node is hashed into a unique identifier which is called node ID. Usually, the node ID will not change during the node's lifetime. The advantage of this scheme is obvious. It is very easy to manage a large-area system using these identifiers. Besides, the hashing process is totally random. In other words, each peer in the system is anonymous. The disadvantage of invariable node ID is also apparent. There are many constraints of routing and some constraints are unreasonable. "Mismatching problem" is an example. Figure 1 gives a mismatching situation. If node A wants to route a message to B in structure (b), the cost is 12 ($A \rightarrow C \rightarrow B$) or 14 ($A \rightarrow D \rightarrow B$), both larger than routing in (a). The essential cause of mismatching is that each node is always combined with an identifier. When one node joins into the system, its position is unchangeable. We consider whether it is possible to make the node ID more flexible, without weakening the power of DHT scheme. There are several *guidelines* we should follow when making some kind of node ID varying. First, the change of node ID should not change the structure of a P2P system. As we mentioned in section 1, the common limitation of most recent methods is that they rely on the specific protocols. If our change breaks the original structure, we can not reconstruct it without specific protocol information. In other words, it will also be protocol-dependent. Second, this change should not be arbitrary. As we know, one of the basic characteristics of the P2P system is its anonymity. If the node ID can be changed discretionarily, the system will become fragile and easily attacked by hackers. Last, the overhead of changing should be controllable. If the overhead is too expensive, the method can not achieve good performance.

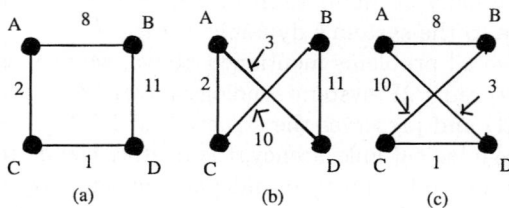

Fig. 1. A mismatching example. (a) is the physical topology with four nodes, and the latencies are marked with integer numbers. (b), (c) are both overlay structures on that physical topology. We assume that neighbors' latencies in overlay are the shortest paths between them. For example, the latency of $A \rightarrow D$ in (b) is calculate as the path $A \rightarrow C \rightarrow D$ in (a). So it equals to 3.

Table 1. The notation table

Notation	Meaning
t_0	the time before nodes a and b swap
t_1	the time after nodes a and b swap
$N_{t_i}(a)$	the neighbor set of node a at time t_i
$d(ij)$	latency between nodes i and j
L_{t_i}	the accumulated latency value of overlay at t_i

We explain our method as follows. In a structured P2P system, each item is hashed into a unique identifier. All of these identifiers constitute a "ID space" At the same time, each node also has one identifier. We call the set of these identifiers "node ID space". It is a subset of ID space. Regardless of peers' dynamism, node ID space is relatively invariable. In our method, each node can not arbitrarily choose an identifier in id space. However, each one has the freedom to choose a *better* identifier in the node ID space. In this way, the logical structure which is built on node ID space will not be broken (following guideline one). In addition, as the identifiers in node ID space is totally random, the anonymity will be preserved (following guideline two). To achieve this kind of node ID re-assignment, the basic operation is *swap*: swap the node ID, and exchange the corresponding routing tables. For example, if we want to adjust the identifiers in figure 1(b) or 1(c), we will just swap node B's id and D's or swap C's and D's correspondingly. After the adjustment, the overlay will totally match the physical network.

Figure 1 just illustrates a simple and ideal case. In a real P2P system, things are more difficult. Table 1 gives several useful notations for our expression. We assume there is a swapping try between nodes a and b. Node a is the *counterpart* of b, and vice versa. Two different situations t_0 and t_1 represent the time before and after a swap. In fact, t_1 is not actually the time after the swap, but the *hypothetical* time if we make the swap. In addition, $N_{t_i}(a)$ represents the neighbor set of node a at time t_i. It is worth to emphasize the fact that neighbors of one node N are not just the entries in its routing table. The nodes which point to node N should be also included. At the beginning, nodes a and b will exchange their neighbors' addresses. Then both of them probe the counterpart's neighbors and measure these latencies $d(ij)$. Node a calculates the accumulated latency of its current neighbors $\sum_{i \in N_{t_0}(a)} d(ai)$ and the one if the swap is done $\sum_{i \in N_{t_1}(a)} d(ai)$. The similar results are calculated by node b. The difference between before and after swap is shown in equation 1.

$$Diff = \sum_{i \in N_{t_0}(a)} d(ai) + \sum_{j \in N_{t_0}(b)} d(bj) - \sum_{i \in N_{t_1}(a)} d(ai) - \sum_{j \in N_{t_1}(b)} d(bj) \quad (1)$$

If $Diff > 0$, nodes a and b will exchange their identifiers and routing tables. Unfortunately, in many structured P2P systems, it is not enough to change the state of these two nodes. The reason is that the routing in most systems is unidirectional[1]. As a result, the change of any node N will impact the nodes which have an entry $E = N$ in their routing tables. However, the unidirectional property will not complicate the implementation of our approach. Because the change of each node can be realized using *leave()* and *join()* procedures, which are already implemented in any P2P system. Until now, we just illustrate a single swap operation. In a distributed environment, every node will periodically contact a random node. The TTL-packet is used to realize this contact. At the beginning, we set $TTL = k$. When TTL becomes zero, the target node is located. Given that the method is totally distributed, each node tries to make a swap at a fixed interval. If a swap can improve the match degree, many swaps at the same time will achieve accumulated effect. In the next subsection, we will try to explain the effectiveness of node swap.

2.2 Effectiveness of Node Swap

To explain the effectiveness of node swap, we make several definitions and explain the meaning of notations first. We define *stretch* as the ratio of the average logical link latency over the average physical link latency. Stretch is a common parameter to quantify the topology match degree. *Average latency (AL)* is a basic parameter to quantify the property of a network. If there are n nodes in a network, and accumulated latency of any two nodes is $Acc(n)$, then[2]

$$AL = Acc(n)/n^2 \qquad (2)$$

We analyze the change of average latency after a swap between nodes a and b. Supposing that the number of nodes is invariable during $t_0 \to t_1$, so the *accumulated latency* (L_{t_i}) is analyzed instead. Next two equations show this change:

$$L_{t_0} = C + \sum_{i \in N_{t_0}(a)} \alpha_i d(ai) + \sum_{j \in N_{t_0}(b)} \beta_j d(bj) \qquad (3)$$

$$L_{t_1} = C + \sum_{i \in N_{t_1}(b)} \gamma_i d(bi) + \sum_{j \in N_{t_1}(a)} \delta_j d(aj) \qquad (4)$$

In equation 3 and 4, C represents the invariable part before and after one swap operation. The coefficients of the summations $\alpha, \beta, \gamma, \delta$ represent the times each neighbor link used. We notice that nodes a and b just exchange their neighbors, so $N_{t_1}(b) = N_{t_0}(a)$ and $N_{t_0}(b) = N_{t_1}(a)$. Besides, assuming that each link has the same probability to be visited, then $\alpha_i \approx \gamma_i$ and $\beta_j \approx \delta_j$. To calculate the variation by (3) − (4), we get that if $Diff > 0$ then $L_{t_0} > L_{t_1}$, which implies that a swap makes the stretch reduced. It is worth to mention that it is an approximate analysis. In fact, when the positions of the nodes changed, the times each neighbor link visited are variable. In other words, those coefficients are different, that is why not all swaps can reduce the average latency. We will see that in our experiment.

---
[1] CAN is an exception. Its routing is bidirectional.
[2] We assume the latency between one node and itself is zero.

2.3 Controllable Overhead

In section 2.1, we have given three guidelines to change node ID. However, we have not given the method to control the overhead yet. The overhead of our approach includes four aspects: (1) the probing of neighbors, (2) the probing of random nodes, (3) exchanges of the routing tables, and (4) exchanges of the contents. We believe that the cost (1) is limited as it can be realized as a piggyback process when constructing the P2P system. So we just give solutions to reduce cost of (2-4).

Adaptive Probing. Cost (2) and (3) are relative to swap times. In our basic method, we do probing periodically at a fixed interval. However, as the system trends to be steady, this periodic adjustment becomes costly and not necessary. The ideal time to stop the periodic adjustment is when the system's average latency doesn't change obviously. Due to the limitation of distributed systems, we can only make decisions based on the local information. So we propose an *adaptive policy* to reduce the operations of probing and swapping. From a local view, every node lives in an *environment* consisting of its neighbors. If neighbors of one node change continually, this node lives in an *unstable* environment. So it will try to do probing and make swapping. Oppositely, if the node's neighbors do not change at a relatively long interval, we can believe that this node is *stable*. To realize this idea, a parameter *activity* is used as the description of node's state and the criterion of periodic probing. At the beginning, the activity parameter is set as an initial number. If one node makes a swap operation, it will move to a new environment, so this parameter will increase to make probing continue. Besides, it will also notify its neighbors to increase activity number. As the fixed intervals pass, the activity number will be reduced. Algorithm 1 is the pseudo code of adaptive probing. Tow parameters – initial number and threshold both have an effect on the number of probing operations. Appropriate value of the two parameters will make the system achieve a better performance. In our experiment, both of them are zero. The results show that this adaptive method greatly reduce the number of the nodes' probing and swap operations without sacrificing the effectiveness of stretch reduction too much.

Shadow Scheme. In a real P2P system, all contents reside on different nodes. In other words, each node owns one part of id space. After exchanging the identifiers of nodes a and b, the contents that they owns should be exchanged respectively. This process may be most expensive one among four aspects mentioned above. Inspired by Baumann et al's work in mobile agent area [10], we propose a *shadow scheme* to reduce the overhead. We view the nodes a and b as mobile agents. After they swap their identifiers, they will not exchange the contents immediately. Instead, both of them own their counterpart's *shadow*, which records the specific lifetime of the shadow and the address information of their counterpart. So before the lifetime becomes zero, the content queries will be forwarded by the counterpart to the correct destination. When the nodes become *stable* and the lifetime is over, the contents will be exchanged. The value

Algorithm 1. Adaptive probing of each node

$activity = initial\ number$
while $activity \geq threshold$ **do**
  probe one node
  if swap is necessary **then**
    exchange the node ID and routing tables
    $activity = activity + 1$
    notify neighbors to increase activity
  end if
  $activity = activity - 1$
  wait for an fixed interval
end while

---

of the lifetime is related to the state of a node which we describe above. Utilizing shadow scheme, the content distribution times are reduced. Obviously, it will take a longer path to locate the content. So it's necessary to consider the tradeoff between the query latency and the distribution overhead in a real P2P application. As the content distribution is relative to specific applications, we propose a generic scheme here and will not consider it in our experiments.

3 Performance Evaluation

3.1 Simulation Methodology

We use the GT-ITM topology generator [11] to generate transit-stub models of the physical network. In fact, we generate two different kinds of topologies. The first topology, *ts-large* has 70 transit domains, 5 transit nodes per transit domain, 3 stub domains attached to each transit node and 2 nodes in each stub domain. The second one, *ts-small*, differs from ts-large in that it has only 11 transit domains, but there are 15 nodes in each sub domain. Intuitively, ts-large has a larger backbone and sparser edge network than ts-small. Except in the experiment of physical topology, we always choose ts-large to represent a situation in which the overlay consists of nodes scattered in the entire Internet and only very few nodes from the same edge network join the overlay. We also assign latencies of 5, 20 and 100ms to stub-stub, stub-transit and transit-transit links respectively. Then, several nodes are selected from the topology as overlay nodes, with the node number $n = \{300, 600, 1200\}$. Chord is chosen as the platform of our simulation because the limitation of Chord makes it unsuitable for many mismatching solutions. We have discussed the limitation in section 1.

3.2 Effectiveness of Swap

The *stretch* is used to characterize the match degree of the overlay to the physical topology. The time interval is fixed as one minute. Figure 2 shows the impact of the TTL scale on stretch. We choose node number $n = 600$ and four typical scenes of probing node. In a centric scene, we can just choose a random node as

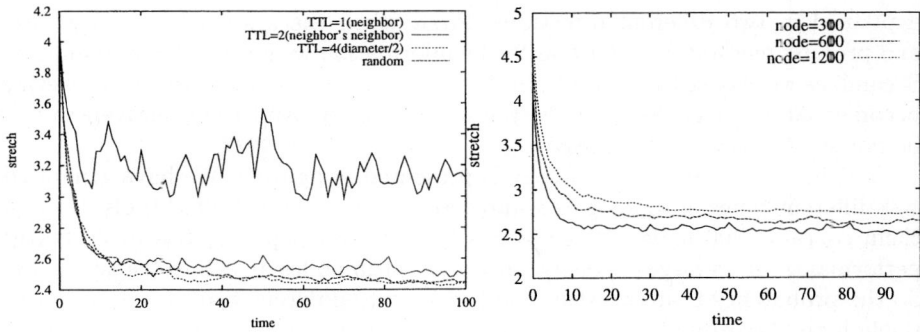

Fig. 2. Varying the TTL scale   **Fig. 3.** Varying the system size

the probing target. In a distributed system, we use $TTL = \{1, 2, 4\}$. $TTL = 1$ means probing neighbors; $TTL = 2$ means probing neighbors' neighbors and $TTL = 4$ means probing the node half of diameter away from the original node[3]. We can find that neighbors' swap is not suitable as it can't greatly reduce the stretch, while other three different ways have nearly the same impact on stretch reduction. The reason is obvious, as $TTL = 1$ gets only neighbor information which is too limited. Given that random probing is not practical in a distributed system, only when $TTL \geq 2$ can achieve a good performance in a P2P system. In order to minimize cost, $TTL = 2$ may be a better choice, and it will be used in next several experiments. In figure 2, we can also discover that the stretch is not reduced all the time, which is consistent with our approximate analysis in section 2.2.

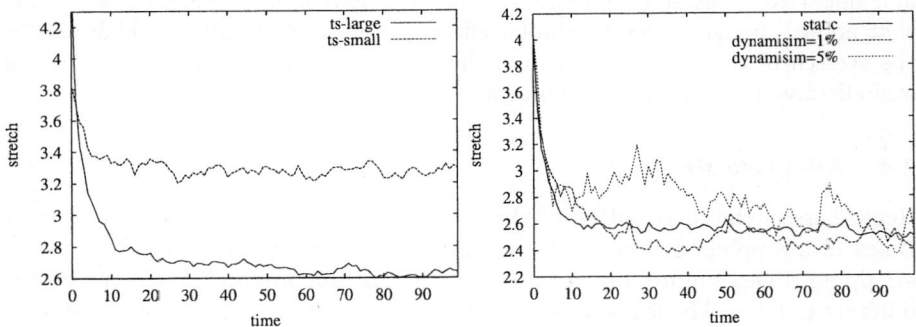

Fig. 4. Varying the physical topology   **Fig. 5.** The stretch in dynamical environment

Figure 3 illustrates the impact of system size. We choose $n = 300, 600, 1200$. The effectiveness is reduced as the size becomes larger. This situation can be

---

[3] As node number is 600, we suppose that the diameter $d = \log_2 n \approx 8$.

explained in two different directions. First, when the system has a large size and probing method fixes TTL as 2, the information we get is relatively limited. Second, as we choose the nodes from the same physical network, when the overlay becomes larger, it is closer to the physical topology. And the effectiveness will be not so obvious.

The impact of physical topology is presented in figure 4. We have generated two different types of topologies *ts-large* and *ts-small* by GT-ITM tools. Both of them contain 2200 nodes. It is obvious that ts-large topology has much better performance. In ts-large topology, only a few stub nodes attach to transit nodes. So the probability that two stub nodes belong to different transit nodes is relatively high. Accordingly, the probability that these nodes exchange is also great. It means that two *far* nodes make adjustment to match the physical topology with a high probability. This kind of swap will greatly improve the performance of the system. As we mentioned above, ts-large topology is much like the Internet, so our method will significantly improve performance in a real large-scale system.

3.3 Dynamic Environment

Dynamism is a very important property in P2P systems. In this part, we try to discover the impact of dynamism on our approach. Although people do several searches about dynamism of the P2P system [12], there is not a standard model to describe it. In our simulation, we just set a very simple dynamic environment. There are δ percent of nodes join and δ percent of nodes leave at a time interval t. $\delta = \{0, 1, 5\}$ and $t = 1min$. Figure 5 shows the results. It is obvious that stretch fluctuates greatly when the system is under a dynamic situation in which 5 percent of nodes change per minute. However, we can see that nodes' arrival and departure may not lead the system to a poor match degree. It's possible that nodes' changes have the similar effect as our swap operation which reduces the stretch of the system. Although there is a fluctuation, our method can be still effective in dynamic environment.

3.4 Adaptive Probing

Regardless of the distribution of the content, the largest overhead is related to times of swapping. In section 2, we introduce an adaptive method to reduce swapping times. Figure 6 illustrates the effect of this method. We compare two different policies. The first one is to probe at a fixed interval, while the second one is to probe with an additional parameter – *activity*. Initial number and threshold are both zero. In this figure, x axis represents stretch and y axis represents the swap times. One point records the swap times in one minute and the stretch value after these swap operations. The adaptive method significantly reduces the swap times. At the same time, it sacrifices the effectiveness of stretch reduction. The points at the high-stretch interval of fixed method are less than adaptive one. However, it is not as significant as the reduction of swap operation. So we choose the adaptive method to reduce the overhead.

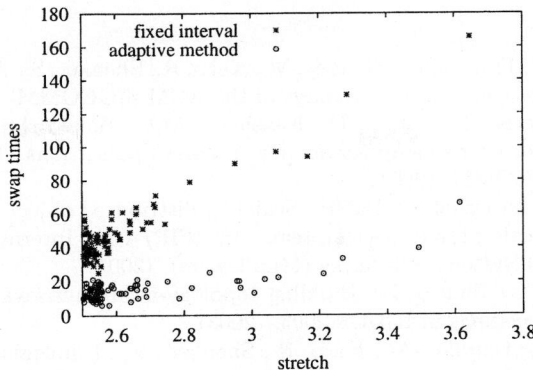

Fig. 6. Tradeoff between swap and stretch

4 Related Work

There are several methods that try to solve the mismatching problem. The most related one to our work is a method called "SAT-Match" [13]. The basic operation in this system is *jump*. When one node discovers several nearby nodes by flooding, it will jump to the nearest node in the nearby area. In fact, it is one kind of variable node ID. However, this method has several limitations. First, the node ID space changes after jumping. So the original overlay structure is broken. Arbitrary change of ID also violates the anonymity of the P2P system. One node which is controlled by a hacker can easily jump to a specific area. Second, although author mentioned the impact of the dynamism, we can not find detail evaluation in different dynamic environments. Last, with respect to the overhead, SAT-Match didn't give a solution to reduce the cost of the content movement.

5 Conclusion

This paper proposes a novel method to solve the mismatching problem in structured P2P systems. This method is totally protocol-independent, which can be easily used on any P2P system based on DHT. Besides, we propose a series of solutions to minimize the overhead cost, including adaptive probing and shadow scheme. Our experiment has shown that node swap greatly reduces the stretch of overlay networks, and the number of swap operations is also greatly reduced when using adaptive probing. In the near further, we will try to combine our method with other different solutions like *proximity neighbor selection* (PNS) together to achieve better performance.

Acknowledgement. This work is supported by the China NSF grant, the China Jiangsu Provincial NSF grant (BK2005208), the China 973 project (2002CB312002) and TRAPOYT award of China Ministry of Education.

References

1. Ratnasamy, S., Francis, P., Handley, M., Karp, R., Shenker, S.: A scalable content-addressable network. In: Proceedings of the ACM SIGCOMM. (2001)
2. Stoica, I., Morris, R., Karger, D., Kaashoek, M.F., Balakrishnan, H.: Chord: A scalable peer-to-peer lookup service for internet applications. In: Proceedings of the ACM SIGCOMM. (2001)
3. Rowstron, A., Druschel, P.: Pastry: Scalable, distributed object location and routing for large-scale peer-to-peer systems. In: IFIP/ACM International Conference on Distributed Systems Platforms (Middleware). (2001)
4. Xu, Z., Tang, C., Zhang., Z.: Building topology-aware overlays using global soft-state. In: Proceedings of ICDCS 2003. (2003)
5. Ratnasamy, S., Handley, M., Karp, R., Shenker., S.: Topologically-aware overlay construction and server selection. In: Proceedings of INFOCOM 2002. (2002)
6. Winter, R., Zahn, T., Schiller, J.: Random landmarking in mobile, topology-aware peer-to-peer networks. In: Proceedings of the 10th IEEE International Workshop on Future Trends of Distributed Computing Systems (FTDCS04). (2004)
7. Ratnasamy, S., Shenker, S., Stoica., I.: Routing algorithms for DHTs: Some open questions. In: 1st International workshop on P2P Systems(IPTPS02). (2002)
8. Castro, M., Druschel, P., Hu, Y., Rowstron, A.: Exploiting network proximity in distributed hash tables. In: Proceedings of FuDiCo 2002. (2002)
9. Waldvogel, M., Rinaldi., R.: Efficient topology-aware overlay network. In: Proceedings of HotNets-I. (2002)
10. Baumann, J., Hohl, F., Rothermel, K., StraBer, M.: Mole – concepts of a mobile agent system. In: Proceedings of World Wide Web. (1996)
11. Zegura, E.W., Calvert, K.L., Bhattacharjee., S.: How to model an internetwork. In: Proceedings of INFOCOM. (1996)
12. Ge, Z., Figueiredo, D.R., Jaiswal, S., Kurose, J., Towsley, D.: Modeling peer-to-peer file sharing systems. In: Proceedings of IEEE INFOCOM. (2003)
13. Ren, S., Guo, L., Jiang, S., Zhang, X.: SAT-Match: A self-adaptive topology matching method to achieve low lookup latency in structured P2P overlay networks. In: Proceedings of the 18th International Parallel and Distributed Processing Symposium (IPDPS04). (2004)

A Workflow Management Mechanism for Peer-to-Peer Computing Platforms

Hong Wang[1], Hiroyuki Takizawa[1], and Hiroaki Kobayashi[2]

[1] Graduate School of Information Sciences, Tohoku University,
6-3 Aramaki-Aza-Aoba, Aoba-ku, Sendai 980-8578 Japan
wangh@sc.isc.tohoku.ac.jp, tacky@isc.tohoku.ac.jp
[2] Information Synergy Center, Tohoku University,
6-3 Aramaki-Aza-Aoba, Aoba-ku, Sendai 980-8578 Japan
koba@isc.tohoku.ac.jp

Abstract. This paper proposes a workflow management mechanism to address a neglected aspect of existing P2P computing platforms - the lack of support for various computational models. In the workflow management mechanism, a workflow description file is used to define the workflow diagram of the target application. We develop a prototype system, and evaluate it using a test program to demonstrate how the workflow management mechanism effectively works.

1 Introduction

The aim of P2P computing [4] is to use the Internet-connected individual computers to solve computing problems. Existing P2P computing platforms includes SETI@home [1], XtremWeb [2], and JNGI [3]. SETI@home currently provides a processing rate of more than 60 Teraflops. Anderson mentioned that SETI@home's 1 million computers represent a tiny fraction of the approximately 150 million Internet-connected PCs, and the latter number is projected to grow to 1 billion by 2015 [5]. Thus it has the potential to provide many Petaflops of computing power.

Embarrassingly parallel computation is best suited for the existing P2P computing platforms. However, it is only minority of all the computational problems. Since many computational problems cannot be divided into independent tasks, support for task dependency handling is crucial for P2P computing platforms.

To our knowledge, no workflow management mechanism exists for P2P computing platforms. In the field of grid workflow management, WebFlow [6] is a visual programming paradigm to develop high performance distributed computing applications. Bivens has defined a grid workflow specification [9] in XML. GridFlow [7] is a two-layer workflow management system for grid computing, including global job workflow management and local sub-workflow scheduling. GridAnt [10] extends the vocabulary of Apache Ant to support workflow management in grid. The key issue that differentiates this work from the related studies for grid is that the dynamic management of P2P computing is the main concern, because the P2P computing platforms consist of much more volatile peers. In the previous work related to grid computing, the optimized scheduling/mapping of tasks to resource is mainly discussed, without considering the unstable behavior of computing platforms.

In this paper, a workflow management mechanism with redundant task dispatching is proposed to solve various computational problems that can be described with a set of tasks and their dependency. Implemented with Java and XML, the mechanism can be applied to heterogeneous environments that are common for P2P systems. To achieve a simple and low-overhead implementation, we develop a prototype system on one of the representative P2P platforms - JNGI [3].

2   A P2P Computing Platform

Using the master-worker model, existing P2P computing platforms usually consist of two kinds of peers: master peers and worker peers. For most existing platforms, the master peer is a specified server. Worker peers are volatile peers.

Here, we use JNGI as an example P2P platform. JNGI is a P2P computing platform based on JXTA [8]. A job of JNGI consists of independent tasks. A computational job is processed by JNGI in the following four steps.

1. A job submitter submits a job to a monitor group (the portal server). The monitor group decides the destination worker group for this job
2. A task dispatcher (master peer) in the worker group dispatches independent tasks of the job to workers.
3. A worker sends back the results of task to the task dispatcher after the task is processed.
4. While all results of tasks in the job are received, the master peer sends back the results to the job submitter.

Without any process sequence control, the task dispatcher simply dispatches an un-dispatched task in the task list when a worker peer inquires for a task. Since existing P2P computing platforms are basically designed based on this architecture, their applicable areas are limited to embarrassingly parallel problems.

3   Workflow Management Mechanism

To control the job's process sequence, we propose a *workflow management mechanism* for P2P computing platforms. The functions of this mechanism include *task dependency check in workflow, task dispatch*, and *redundant task dispatch*. All these functions will be included in a *workflow management module*. With the workflow management module, we name a task dispatcher of JNGI a *job manager*.

To describe a workflow, we define a vocabulary of the workflow markup language in XML. A *workflow parser* is designed to parse the *workflow description*

A Workflow Management Mechanism for Peer-to-Peer Computing Platforms

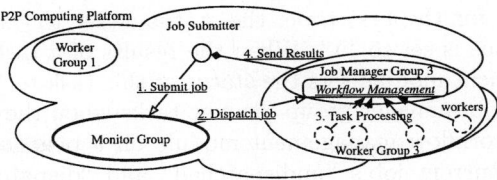

Fig. 1. Overview of the proposed P2P computing platform

file in the markup language into a workflow DAG (*directed acyclic graph*). Each task has its own status in a workflow DAG.

As shown in Figure 1, when a job (a set of tasks and a workflow description file) is submitted to a monitor group, the monitor group forwards it to a worker group. Then the task distribution of this job is controlled by the workflow management module of the job manager with the workflow description file.

We introduce a *redundant task dispatching* mechanism to handle the dynamic nature of P2P systems. By processing the same task on different peers, this mechanism can provide a higher probability that the dispatched tasks will be finished without failure. When workflow is blocked, there will be some workers that keep waiting for tasks. Redundant task dispatching uses these workers for redundant execution of the dispatched tasks. Suppose the failure probability of each worker is $1/f$, then the failure probability of a task that is processed by x workers is $1/f^x$. Without redundant task dispatching, a failed task is only re-dispatched after the worker failure is noticed. Therefore, a P2P computing platform with frequent peer failure will have a serious performance loss. Redundant task dispatching can save lots of time from re-dispatching of failed tasks. Thus the performance can be improved. On the other hand, unlimited redundant task dispatching may result in a performance loss because too much computing power is wasted for the processing of same task. Therefore, when the workflow passes a blocked status, there will be many available tasks while few workers can start processing in a short time. This situation may also results in a performance loss. To have a trade-off between re-process time of failed tasks and performance loss for redundant task dispatching, we define i as the acceptable redundancy rate for one task. The "redundancy" value ("redundancy"$\leq i$) of task status records how many workers are processing this task at the same time.

The overview of the workflow management module is shown in Figure 2. The initial status of each task is "undispatched" and "redundancy"=0. When the

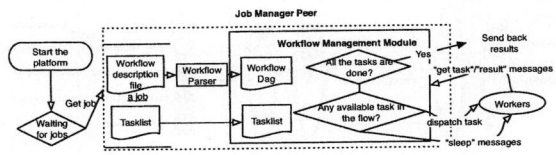

Fig. 2. Process diagram of workflow management module

task is dispatched for the first time, the status is set to "dispatched," and a "redundancy" status is set to "1". When the results of a task are received, the workflow management module sets the status of this task to "finished." Worker peers inquire the job manager group for new tasks when they are idle or finish their tasks. The workflow management module on a peer in the job manager group checks the current job's "undispatched" and "dispatched" tasks in the task list, and analyzes the task dependency in the workflow DAG. If all the tasks that the next task depends on are "finished," the module updates the arguments of the next task with the results of "finished" tasks following the definition in the workflow DAG. Then the next task is dispatched to the worker. If there is any "dispatched" task whose results are needed to launch subsequent tasks, the workflow is blocked and redundant task dispatching mechanism is used. Status of "dispatched" tasks is checked to find a task with the least "redundancy" value. This task is dispatched again and the "redundancy" is incremented. If there is no such task, which means the "dispatched" tasks already have a low failure probability, the workflow will be blocked and the worker will wait for the next inquiring time. When all the tasks are "finished," the workflow management module returns the results back to the job submitter.

4 Evaluation

We implemented a JNGI-based prototype system with the proposed mechanism on 10 PCs. Both the monitor group and job manager group have one peer each. These two peers are running on two PCs each equipped with an Intel Celeron 2.2GHz CPU. The worker group has eight workers. Each worker peer is a PC with an AMD Athlon 64 3400+ CPU.

A test program for performance evaluation consists of two parts. The first part checks large integers to find prime numbers. It is a computation-intensive

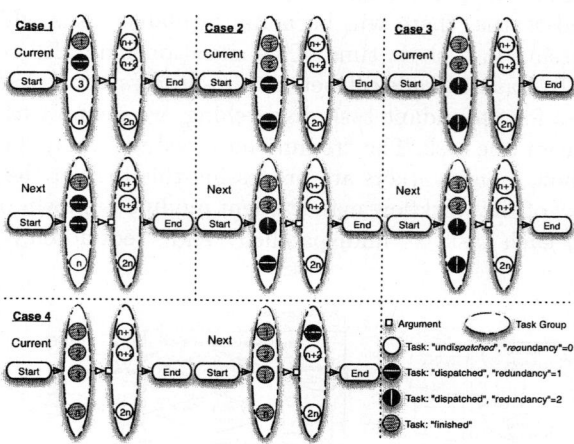

Fig. 3. Four cases of workflow DAG status.

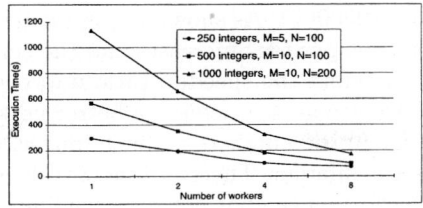

Fig. 4. Execution time

problem. The second part simply adds the non-prime numbers together. Each task checks and adds the same number of integers. The acceptable redundancy rate is 2 ($i=2$). As the later part depends on the former one, the workflow management is required to perform this job, even though the original JNGI cannot execute it due to the task dependency. Accordingly, it is clear that the workflow management can extend the applicable area of P2P computing.

The workflow description file is presented as follows:

```
<Workflow>
  <Group id=1>
    <TaskList first="1" last="n" />
    <Description>Prime Checking</Description>
  </Group>
  <Group id=2>
    <TaskList first="n+1" last="2n" />
    <Dependency groupID="1" arg="1" />
    <Description>Summation</Description>
  </Group>
</Workflow>
```

Figure 3 shows all the following four possible cases of workflow DAG status.

Case 1: If the next task has no dependency, it is dispatched, and its status is changed.

Case 2: If the tasks that the next task depends on are not "finished," and there is a task "a" with the status "dispatched" and "redundancy"=1, then the workflow management module dispatches a redundant task of the task "a" and sets the "redundancy"=2.

Case 3: If the tasks that the next task depends on are not "finished," and "redundancy" of all the "dispatched" tasks is 2, then the workflow management module stalls the workflow.

Case 4: If all the tasks that the next task depends on are "finished," it is dispatched and its status is changed.

We also discuss the computational efficiency. Let N be the number of tasks and M be the number of integers that are checked or added in one task. The integer range starts from 10000001. As shown in Figure 4, while M increases, the maximum computation time per task increases and the communication time per task does not change, therefore the speedup ratio improves. While the number of workers is increased, we can always achieve a better performance. However, as the computation time for prime numbers is much longer, the task computation times of different tasks are different. Therefore the workloads of different workers are different, and the performance does not improve linearly.

5 Conclusions

We have designed and implemented the workflow management mechanism for P2P computing platforms. We describe how task dependency is actually described, translated and performed in the experiment. The experimental results indicate that this workflow management mechanism works well. For our future work, internal message passing within worker groups will be designed and implemented to extend the capability of the mechanism.

Acknowledgment

The authors would like to thank NTT East Corporation for providing computing facilities for this work.

References

1. SETI@home. http://setiathome.ssl.berkeley.edu
2. Gilles Fedak, Cécile Germain, Vincent Néri, and Franck Cappello: XtremWeb: A Generic Global Computing System. In Proc. CCGRID 2001.
3. Jerome Verbeke, Neelakanth Nadgir, Greg Ruetsch, Ilya Sharapov: Framework for Peer-to-Peer Distributed Computing in a Heterogeneous, Decentralized Environment. In Proc. GRID 2002.
4. David P. Anderson: BOINC: A System for Public-Resource Computing and Storage. In Proc. GRID 2004.
5. David P. Anderson: Public Computing: Reconnecting People to Science. In Conference on Shared Knowledge and the Web, Madrid, 2003.
6. D. Bhatia, V. Burzevski, M. Camuseva, G. Fox, W. Furmanski, and G. Premchandran: WebFlow - a Visual Programming Paradigm for Web/Java Based Coarse Grain Distributed Computing. Concurrency: Practice and Experience, Vol. 9, No. 6, 1997.
7. Junwei Cao, Stephen A. Jarvis, Subhash Saini and Graham R. Nudd: GridFlow: Workflow Management for Grid Computing. In Proc. CCGRID 2003.
8. Project JXTA, http://www.jxta.org
9. Hugh P. Bivens: Grid Workflow. Grid Computing Environments Working Group, Global Grid Forum, 2001.
10. Kaizar Amin, Gregor von Laszewski, Mihael Hategan, Nestor J. Zaluzec, Shawn Hampton, and Albert Rossi: GridAnt: A Client-Controllable Grid Workflow System. In Proc. HICSS 2004.

DDSQP: A WSRF-Based Distributed Data Stream Query System

Jia-jin Le and Jian-wei Liu

College of Computer Science and Technology,
DongHua University, Shanghai, 200051, China
lejiajin@dhu.edu.cn,
liujw@mail.dhu.edu.cn

Abstract. Today many current and emerging applications require support for on-line analysis of rapidly changing data streams. Limitations of traditional DBMSs in supporting streaming applications have been recognized, prompting research to augment existing technologies and build new systems to manage streaming data. Stream-oriented systems are inherently geographically distributed and because distribution offers scalable load management and higher availability, future stream processing systems will operate in a distributed fashion. Moreover, service-based approaches have gained considerable attention recently for supporting distributed application development in e-business and e-science. In this paper, we present our innovative work to build a large scale distributed query processing over streaming data, this system has been designed as a WSRF-compliant application built on top of standard Web services technologies. Our distributed data stream Queries are written and evaluated over distributed resources discovered and accessed using emerging the WS-Resource Framework specifications. The data stream query processor has been designed and implemented as a collection of cooperating services, using the facilities of the WSRF to dynamically discover, access and use computational resources to support query compilation and evaluation.

1 Introduction

Today many applications routinely generate large quantities of data. The data often takes the form of a stream -- an ordered sequence of records. Traditional DBMS need to store the data before they can handle it. However, many application domains would benefit from on-line analysis and immediate indication of results. Therefore, we focus our attention on a new emerging DBMS technology called Data Stream Management Systems (DSMSs). In contrast to traditional DBMSs, DSMSs can execute continuous queries over continuous data streams that enter and leave the system in real-time, i.e., data is only stored in main memory for processing. Analysis of this data requires stream-processing techniques, which differ in significant ways from what current database query languages and statistical analysis tools support today. These applications are characterized by the need to process high-volume data streams in a timely and responsive fashion. It is impossible to control the order in which items arrive, nor is it feasible to locally store a stream in its entirety. Likewise, queries over streams run continuously over a period of time and incrementally return new results as new data arrive. A technique for querying such data is so called continuous queries, these are known as long-running, continuous, standing and persistent queries [1]. Motivating applications include:

(i) Networking traffic engineering, network monitoring and intrusion detection.
(ii) Fraud detection and data mining in telecommunications.
(iii) Financial monitoring, financial Tickers, clickstream analysis and personalization service in e-commerce.
(iv) Sensor networks, location-tracking services, fabrication line management.

These applications have spawned a considerable and growing body of research into data stream processing [2], ranging from algorithms for data streams to full-fledged data stream systems such as Aurora and Medusa [3], STREAM [4], TelegraphCQ [5], Gigascope [6], Hancock [7], Niagara [8], Tangram [9, 10], Tapestry [11], Tribeca [12], and others. For the most part, research in data stream systems has hitherto focused on devising novel system architectures, defining query languages, and designing space-efficient algorithms, and so on. Important components of systems research that have received less attention to date are architectural issues facing the design of large-scale distributed data stream query processing system.

In this paper we focus on architectural aspect of large-scale distributed data stream query processing (DDSQP). A WSRF-enabled architecture of DDSQP systems comprising a collection of distributed Web services is presented [13,14,15]. The distributed service architecture increases the portability by isolating platform dependent services to appropriate sites accessible using a well-defined API, facilitates the overall maintenance of the system, and enables light-weight clients, which are easy to install and manage. Moreover, it decouples the clients from the system, allowing users to move, share, and access the services from different locations.

We base DDSQP system on WSRF and build it as a Web service for the following two aspect reasons: on the one hand, utilization of parallel and distributed environment facilitates distributed resources dynamic, scalable sharing and coordination in dynamic, heterogeneous, multi-institutional environments. Specifically, (i) The volume of data produced is too large to fit in a single main-memory, and therefore suggests data to be distributed among clusters of main-memories. (ii) The very high data flow rate requires very high performance of insert, delete and data processing operations. (iii) The Web service also provide an ideal substrate in an environment where different number of data streams are used over time or the source streams have varying incoming rates. (iv) The Web service allows the query optimizer to choose from multiple providers, and to spawn multiple copies of a query-algebraic operator to exploit parallelism.

On the other hand, WSRF convention address the constructs used to enable Web services to access state in a consistent and interoperable manner. It identifies and standardizes the patterns by which state is represented and manipulated, so as to facilitate the construction and use of interoperable services.

The remainder of this paper is structured as follows: The next section gives an overview of the WSRF-based distributed data stream queries system. Sections 3 describe the basic components of the system. Section 4 discusses WSRF Implementation Mechanism of system. Section 5 contains conclusions and summarizes open problems for future research.

2 System Architecture Overview

This section describes a distributed data stream query processing framework in which query compilation, optimization and evaluation are viewed and implemented as invocations of WSRF-compliant Web service having an association with a stateful resource.

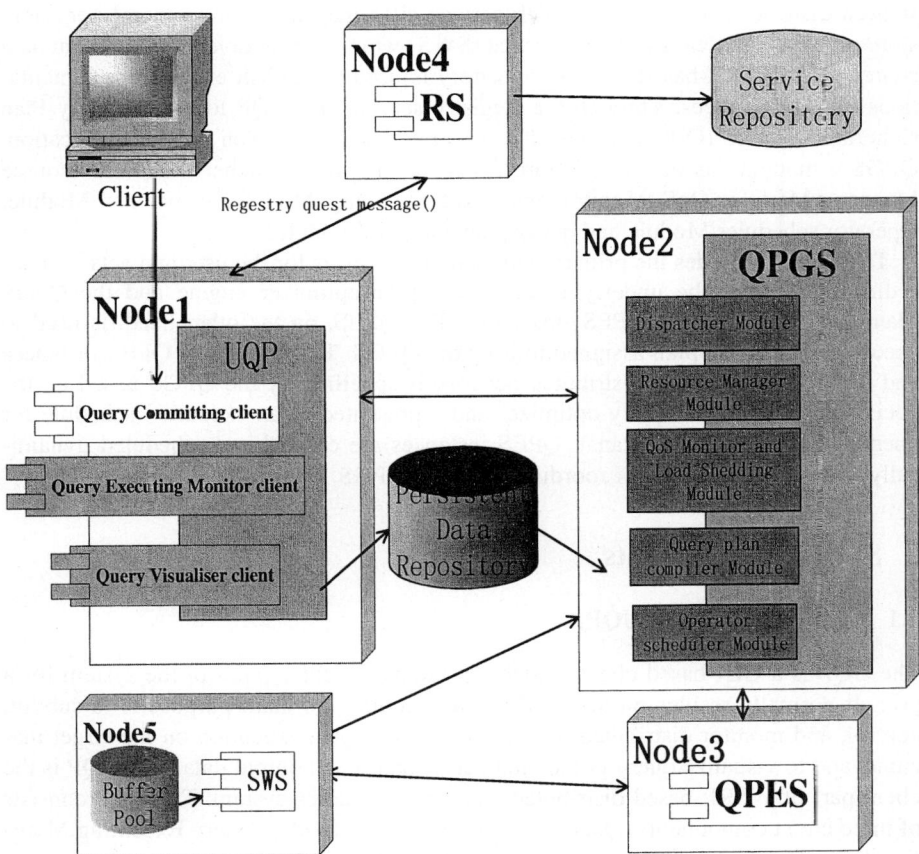

Fig. 1. Distributed data stream queries WSRF-based architecture

A Web service site is a host that can be accessed over the Internet. A WSRF-compliant WS-Resource is an application that runs on a Web service site and can be remotely invoked through a well-defined interface. In this system, a Web service site can elect to provide services and it can also access services provided by other Web service sites. It serves as an internal server or client in each context respectively. Services are usually partitioned, replicated, aggregated, and then delivered to external clients. The Web service site may cluster nodes when the target applications produce very large streams that cannot be managed through a single node.

The goal of the architecture design for WSRF-based DDSQP system is to propose a simple, flexible yet efficient query model in aggregating and replicating Web services with frequently updated persistent data stream. The model has to be simple enough to shield application programmers from the complexities of data replication, service discovery, load balancing, failure detection and recovery.

This DDSQP system is designed as a WSRF-compliant architecture, depicted in Fig. 1, consisting of several distinct Web services, for which arbitrarily many instances distributed over several Web service sites may exist, and several persistent store repository. Stream wrapper service (SWS) wraps a great diversity of stream data sources. The UDDI-based service repository is used to publish existing implementations of Web services. Through the Registry service, the UQP locates a Query Plan Generator Service (QPGS) to which it generates the query plan of user application. QPGS is modular, as shown in Figure 1, compositing of dispatcher Module, Resource Manager Module, QoS Monitor and Load Shedding Module, dispatcher Module, Operator scheduler Module and query plan compiler module.

The QPGS provides the primary interaction interfaces for the user and acts as a coordinator between the underlying query compiler/optimizer engine and the Query Plan Executing Service (QPES) instances. The QPES, on the other hand, is used to execute a query sub-plan assigned to it by the QPGS. The number of QPES instances and their location on the distributed network is specified by the QPGS based on the decisions made by the query optimizer and represented as an execution schedule for query partitions (i.e. sub-plans). QPES instances are created and scheduled dynamically, and their interaction is coordinated by the QPGS.

3 System Components

3.1 User Query Portal (UQP)

The UQP is a GUI-based client, which represents the entry point of the system for a user. It normally resides on the user's local machine. Its main purpose is to submit, control, and monitor distributed data stream queries plan execution on the target machine, and to visualize query processing performance and output data. The UQP is the client part of WSRF-based distributed data stream queries system. The UQP consists of three client components: Query Committing client (QMC), Query Executing Monitor client (QEMC), and Query Visualiser client (QVC). UQP supports a declarative query language using an extended version of SQL.

3.2 Registry Service (RS)

All Web services register with a Registry Service, thus making themselves publicly available. The Registry service is a persistent service which maintains an updated list of endpoint reference that contain URLs to the WSDL files of registered Web service instances and Reference Properties components that may contain an XML serialization of a stateful resource identifier, as understood by the Web service addressed by the endpoint reference.

We use the UDDI-based Service Repository to store (static) information about Web service implementations only, and not about Web service instances. Instead, Web service instances are published within this registry service.

There can be an arbitrary number of RS services in the system. A WS-Resource factory may convey the reference to the new WS-Resource through means such as placing the WS-Resource-qualified endpoint reference into a registry for later retrieval.

RS follows the lease mechanism. The RS grants leases to services for a certain period of time. If a service does not, renew its lease before the lease expires, the RS deletes the service from its list. Leasing is a very effective and efficient way to cope with network failures and to ensure network resilience. WS-Notification mechanism is used to inform the clients (i.e. the UQP) about new services that registered with the RS and about existing services that failed to renew their lease. Thereby, clients are always provided with a dynamically updated view of the Web service environment.

The registry would range over a Virtual Organization (VO) known to the client, and would be identified by a WS-Addressing endpoint reference. The UQP implemented for DDSQP system provides a dialog where it is possible to enter the WS-Addressing qualified endpoint references of a registry and inspect its content. A Web service registers itself with at least one, but potentially multiple, registries when it is initialized.

The new operator, schema, or stream registers entity-name in RS. To find the definition of an entity given its name, or the location where a data stream is available or a piece of a query is executing, we define two types of catalogs of UDDI service repository in our distributed infrastructure: intra-VO and inter-VO catalogs. Within a VO, the catalog contains definitions of operators, schemas, streams, and queries. For streams, the catalog also holds information on the physical locations where entities are being made available. Indeed, streams may be partitioned across several nodes for load balancing. For queries, the catalog holds information on the content and location of each running piece of the query. Inter-VO catalogs includes the list, description, and current location of pieces of queries running at each service instance that collaborate and offer services that cross their boundaries, this catalogs must be made globally available. The catalog may be centralized or distributed. Each participant that provides query capabilities holds a part of the shared catalog.

3.3 Query Plan Generator Service (QPGS)

The QPGS resides on the S-site and uses the query request document committed by client via UQP to generate appropriate QPGS instances. The distributed query execution plans are generated on the local S-site. Query plans execution can be copied to a target E-site or deleted if no longer needed.

Our QPGS is modular. There are five types of modules:

Dispatcher Module: the dispatcher generates the dispatcher's local view of the load situation of the service hosts by means of Resource Manager Module. The dispatcher looks for the service instance running on the least loaded service host and forwards the query operator message to it. A dispatcher service can act as a proxy for arbitrary services and a general coordination of DDSQP system. Using this dispatcher service, it is possible to enhance many existing services or develop new services with load balancing and high availability features without having to consider these features during their development. All kinds of services are supported as long as concurrency control mechanisms are used, e.g. by using a database as back-end. The concurrency control mechanisms ensure a consistent view and consistent modifications of the data shared between all service instances. The standard operation mode of the dispatcher is forward, other modes are buffer or reject.

Resource Manager Module: The modules can measure the average CPU, disc I/O and memory load on service hosts and on hosts running database management systems and collect to the load situation archive which stores aggregated load information. It also does provide a high-level Index Service, to enable collecting, caching and aggregating of computational resource metadata.

QoS Monitor and Load Shedding Module: A QoS specification is a function of some performance, result precision, or reliability related characteristic of an output stream that produces a utility value to the corresponding application. The operational goal of DDSQP is to maximize the perceived aggregate QoS delivered to the client applications. A user can specify quality constraints on the query execution itself to fulfill QoS-aware query execution algorithms. These constraints can be separated in three different dimensions: result, cost and time. QoS constraints will be treated during all the phases of query processing. DDSQP system must constantly monitor the QoS of output tuples, this information is important since it drives the QPGS in its decision-making, and it also informs the Load Shedder when and where it is appropriate to discard tuples in order to shed load. Load shedding is one technique employed by DDSQP system to improve the QoS delivered to applications.

Query Plan Compiler Module: This module follows the two-step optimization paradigm, which is popular for both parallel and distributed database systems [16]. In the first phase, the single node optimizer produces a query plan as if it was to run on one processor. In the second phase, the sequential query plan is divided into several partitions i.e. subplans which are allocated QPESs by the QPGS.

Operator Scheduler Module: The module encapsulates adaptive flow control, tuple routing and inter-service communication. Operator level load balancing is provided via online repartitioning of the input stream and the corresponding internal state of operators and employs buffering and reordering mechanisms to smoothly repartition operator state across service instances with minimal impact to ongoing processing. It also fulfill fault-tolerance for dataflows by leveraging these state movement mechanisms to replicate an operator's internal state and in-flight data. Operator scheduler Module decides whether or not and how partition and schedule operator and data when executed on multiple service instances and whether data needs to be exchanged among the service instances. Currently, data distribution policy supported by DDSQP system includes round rubin, hash distribution and range partitioning. The Operator can be composed into multi-step dataflows, exchanging records via this module that can support communication via either asynchronous push or synchronous pull modalities. This module also supports to constructs a query plan that contains adaptive routing function, which are able to re-optimize the query plan on a continuous basis while a query is running and adaptively decide how to route data to other query operators on a tuple-by-tuple basis. Moreover, these modules can serve to partitioning/replication of dataflows across multiple service instances and reconsider and revise these decisions while a query is in flight.

The QPGS service type implements two port types from DataService (DS) portType and DataTransport (DT) portType. To these, it adds a Distributed Query (DQ) port type that allows source schemas to be imported. Note that this provides a context over which global models can be specified. The Distributed Query (DQ) port type that is extended from OGSI-DAI specification is composed of five portType, i.e. Dispatcher portType, Resource Manager portType, QoS Monitor and Load Shedding portType, Query plan compiler portType, Operator scheduler portType, which is respectively associated with one stateful resource property document that act as a view on, or projection of the actual state of WS-Resouce of every module. Client can use QueryResourceProperties, QueryResourcePropertiesResponse, GetMultiple Resource Properties, SetResourcePropertiesResponse operations to query and modify via Web service message exchange[14,15].

DS portType allows the QPGS to import logical and physical schemas of the participating data sources as well as information about computational resources into the resource property document used by the query compiler and optimizer.

3.4 Query Plan Executing Service (QPES)

Each QPES instance is an execution node and is dynamically created by the QPGS on the node it is scheduled to run. The QPES execute query plan on the target machine called E-site (Which could coincide with the S-site). The QPES enables compilation and execution control of query plan. Upon completion, the QPES optionally stores the query result's output into the Persistent Data Repository (PDR) or dispatch the partial results to other QPESs. UQP can access the PDR concurrently for post-mortem performance analysis, load shedding and visualization. Evaluator functionality is exposed via QPES instances that implement the DS and DT port types.

The QPGS receives the request and compiles it into a distributed query plan, each partition of which is assigned to one or more execution nodes. Each execution node corresponds to a QPES instance, which is created by the QPGS, Each plan partition to its designated QPES instance. Upon receiving its plan partitions, each QPES instance initiates its evaluation The overall behavior of a QPES instance is a data flow computation using an iterator model of Graefe [17,18], with each operator implementing an {open(), next(),close()}interface.

Note that each operator is implemented as a function, instead of a thread due to the fact that (i) the context switch cost from one thread to another is much higher than a function call. (ii) it is much easier to control a function through scheduling and to manage resource for a function than a thread.

3.5 Stream Wrapper Service (SWS)

A data stream is a continuous sequence of attribute-value tuples that all conform to some pre-defined schema (sequence of typed attributes). Operators are functions that transform one or more input streams into one or more output streams. A loop-free, directed graph of operators is called a query network and all queries are continuous, because they continuously processes tuples pushed on their input streams.

A stream data source can be associated with many SWSs. SWSs is responsible for interfacing with external data sources and act as wrappers, such as an HTML/XML screen scraper, a proxy for fetching data from popular peer-to-peer networks, and a local file reader. SWSs may also cache data locally to hide network delays. In addition more sophisticated function can be built that can also send messages back to the network. For example a sensor proxy may send control messages to adjust the sample rate of a sensor network based on the queries that are currently being processed. Similarly, SWSs are also able to pass bindings into remote websites to perform lookups.

4 WSRF Implementation Mechanism

When a user sends a request message to a Web service that WS-Addressing-related conventions used in the implied resource pattern. An endpoint reference is returned to the requestor in response to some request sent to the Web service. This processing of the request resulted in the creation of the stateful resource that has a WS-Resource-qualified endpoint reference which contains an XML serialization of a stateful resource identifier. Specifically, the Web service represents an explicit WS-Resource factory.

In WSRF, a specific resource's state may be implemented as an actual XML document that is stored in memory, in the file system, in a database, or in some XML Repository, also as active programmatic entity abstraction. In this abstraction, the WS-Resource can be thought of as a piece of code being executed by a thread of control separate from the web service. The execution context provided to the web service allows the web service to communicate with this code, parameterize it, access its state or invoke functions that it exposes. This WS-Resource abstraction also allows legacy code to be used as a WS-Resource. The five modules of QPGS use this resource' state characteristic to fulfill functionality described in 4.3.

In the implementation of our system, Elements of WS-Resource properties document of SWS, QPES, RS, QPGS and QPES serves two purposes in our system. First, some WS-Resource properties elements are used to dynamically control the behavior of service instance in DDSQP system. For example, the amount of memory used by a QPES instance can be controlled by updating the value of Memory element in its WS-Resource properties document of Resource Manager Module. Second, some WS-Resource properties elements are used to collect statistics about service instance behavior. For example, the number of tuples that have passed through a queue q stored in SWS. These statistics are available for resource management and for user-level system monitoring. It is a simple matter to add new WS-Resource properties elements to WS-Resource properties document as needs arise, offering convenient extensibility.

Note that WSDL 1.2 has introduced the notion of multiple portType extension. Web services allow us to construct a new interface from several existing interfaces via a process of composition. It is absolutely essential for our system implementation. Use it, We may aggregate the WS Resource properties defined in the WS-Resource properties documents of the various constituent portTypes to yield the final, complete WS-Resource property document declared with the final composed portType. This WS-Resource properties document composition may be accomplished by adding additional XML element declarations. WS-Resource properties document of the

QPGS follows this methods to construct its assembled interface from DS, DT, DQ, Dispatcher portType, Resource Manager portType, QoS Monitor and Load Shedding portType, Query plan compiler portType, Operator scheduler portType.

DDSQP system also support normal operations of WSRF on resource properties, such as QueryResourceProperties, QueryResourcePropertiesResponse, SetResource PropertiesResponse,GetMultipleResourceProperties, GetMultipleResourceProperties Response, WS-information operation and WS-ResourceLifetime resource operaties operations[14,15].

The data sources have to be identified by the SWSs WS-Addressing endpoint reference that wraps those data sources. The query service has to be identified by URLs, which point to the WSDL documents describing those services. Both the endpoint reference and the WSDL URLs have to be structured as a list inside an XML document.

The DS allows clients to access information about its state, including information on the data resources to which it provides access, and the operations upon these data resources, which it supports. This access is provided via the DS's GetMultipleResourceProperties operation. The DS supports a document-oriented interface for database requests in which clients to specify operations use DS Perform documents. These documents contain the statement text and delivery instructions.

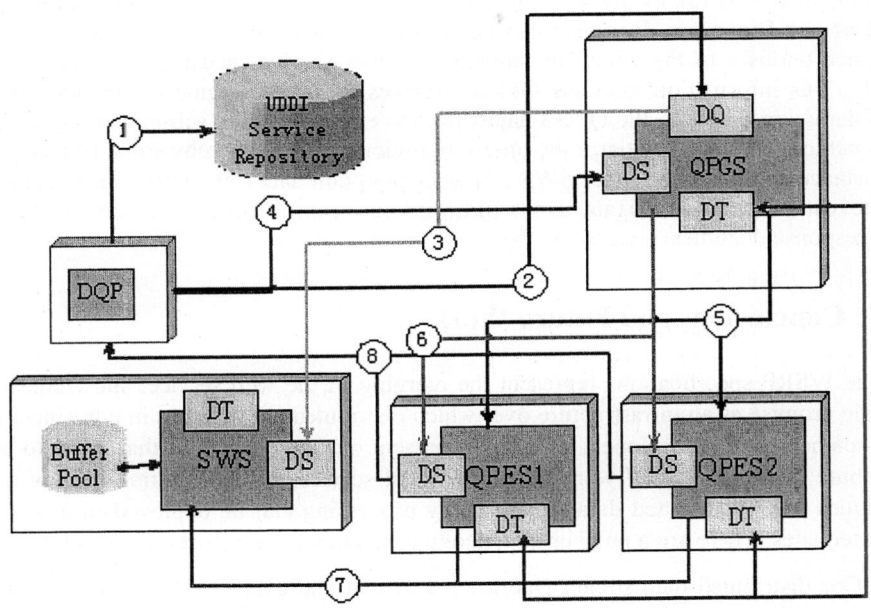

Fig. 2. An overview of interactions of query implementation process

The QPGS allows clients to access information about its state, including information on the data resources to which it provides access, and the operations (activities) upon these data resources, which it supports. This access is provided in the form of

WS Resource Properties document via the DataService::FindServiceData operation. Since QPGS implements DS port type most of the WS Resource Properties elements defined by that port type are supported.

Fig.2 illustrates a walkthrough of the interactions that take place when client submit a query to DDSQP system. The Solid arrows labeled by sequence numbers denote interactions that take place.

We are assumed that all persistent service in DDSQP system has registered themselves to registry service repository via registry service. The interactions process is described as follow:

Client locates the QPGS by querying the Registry service repository. In the response message, client obtains the endpoint reference content of the QPGS and SWS. Message that client send a query also causes to create QPGS and SWS instance(Interaction 1).Then the client calls the importSchema operation on the DQ port type of QPGS instance and provides a list of resources (interaction 2). The QPGS then interacts with the specified DS portType of SWS to obtain the schemas of the databses they wrap (interactions 3). The QPGS also creates DS instances so that the QPES can access data during query execution. The QPGS accepts query submissions in the form of SQL queries via the DS port type of QPGS instance (interactions 4). The query is embedded within an XML document called a DS perform Resource Properties document that is used to compile and optimize into a distributed query execution plan, whose partitions are scheduled for execution at different QPESs. The perform Resource Properties document can be configured such that the results are delivered synchronously to the client, or streamed another service instance. The QPGS then uses this information to create QPES instances on their designated execution nodes (interaction 5). Next, the QPGS hands over to each QPES the sub-plan assigned to it (interaction 6). This initiates the query execution process whereby some of the QPES instances interact with other SWS instances to obtain data (interaction 7). Eventually, the results start to propagate across QPES instances and, ultimately, reach the client as a response document (interaction 8).

5 Conclusions and Future Work

The WSRF specifications represent the merging of the web service, show considerable promise as an infrastructure over which distributed applications in e-business and e-science can be developed. This paper present our ongoing work that seeks to contribute to the corpus of work on higher-level services by demonstrating how techniques from distributed data stream query processing can be deployed in a service-based sites. There are a number of concrete contributions to report on at this point:

(i)Our distributed data stream Queries are written and evaluated over distributed resources discovered and accessed using emerging the WS-Resource Framework specifications.
(ii)The data stream query processor has been designed and implemented as a collection of cooperating services, using the facilities of the WSRF to dynamically discover, access and use computational resources to support query compilation and evaluation.

We plan to extend our DDSQP system in a number of areas. Firstly, extend our system to operate with resources grid-enabled using Globus 4.0[19] via cross-platform web services interface. Secondly, we are working on support for caching with communication between query plan execution. Thirdly, we plan to support utility-based resource allocation policies driven by economic, quality of services, and service-level agreements. Fourthly, we are investigating strategies for supporting to minimal transaction support. Finally, we plan to provide d topic hierarchy approach for publish/subscribe-based notification, which is a common model followed in large-scale, distributed event management.

References

1. L. Liu, C. Pu, W. Tang.: Continual Queries for Internet-Scale Event-Driven Information Delivery. In IEEE Trans. Knowledge and Data Eng., (1999) 11(4): 610–628.
2. B. Babcock., S. Babu., M. Datar., R. Motwani., J. Widom.,: Models and Issues in Data Stream Systems. In Proc. of the 2002 ACM Symp. on Principles of Database Systems, (June 2002).
3. D. Carney., U. Cetintemel., M. Cherniack., C. Convey., S. Lee, G. Seidman., M. Stonebraker., N. Tatbul., S. Zdonik.: Monitoring Streams: A New Class of Data Management Applications. In Proc. 28th Intl. Conf. on Very Large Data Bases(August 2002).
4. Stanford Stream Data Management (STREAM) Project, http://www-db.stanford.edu/stream.
5. J.M. Hellerstein., M.J. Franklin., Sirish Chandrasekaran., Amol Deshpande., Kris Hildrum., Sam Madden., Vijayshankar Raman., Mehul A. Shah.: Adaptive Query Processing: Technology in Evolution. IEEE Data Engineering Bulletin (June 2000) 23(2):7-18.
6. T. Johnson., C. Cranor., O. Spatsheck., V. Shkapenyuk.: Gigascope: A Stream Database for Network Applications. In Proc. of the 2003 ACM SIGMOD Intl. Conf. on Management of Data (June 2003).
7. C. Cortes., K. Fisher., D. Pregibon., A. Rogers., F. Smith.: Hancock: A Language for Extracting Signatures from Data Streams. In Proc. of the 2000 ACM SIGKDD Intl. Conf. on Knowledge Discovery and Data Mining (August 2000) pages 9-17.
8. Niagara Project. http://www.cs.wisc.edu/niagara/
9. D. S. Parker, R. R. Muntz., H. L. Chau.: The Tangram Stream Query Processing System. In Proc. of the 1989 Intl. Conf. on Data Engineering (February 1989) pages 556-563.
10. D. S. Parker., E. Simon., P. Valduriez.: SVP: A Model Capturing Sets, Lists, Streams, and Parallelism. In Proc. of the 1992 Intl. Conf. on Very Large Data Bases (August 1992) pages 115-126.
11. D.B. Terry., D. Goldberg., D. Nichols., B.M. Oki.: Continuous Queries over Append-only Databases. SIGMOD Conference (1992): 321-330.
12. M. Sullivan : Tribeca: A Stream Database Manager for Network Traffic Analysis. In Proc. of the of the 1992 ACM SIGMOD Intl. Conf. on Management of Data, June (1992) pages 321-330.
13. Foster, I., Frey, J., Graham, S., Tuecke, S., Czajkowski, K., Ferguson, D., Leymann, F., Nally, M., Storey, T., and Weerawarana, S.: Modeling Stateful Resources with Web Services. Available at http://www-106.ibm.com/developerworks/library/wsresource/ws-modelingresources.pdf (2004).
14. www-106.ibm.com/developerworks/webservices/ library/ws-resource/
15. http://www.ibm.com/developerworks/webservices/library/ws-add/

16. D. Kossmann.: The State of The Art in Distributed Query Processing. ACM Computing Surveys, (2000) 32(4):422-469.
17. G. Graefe.: Encapsulation of Parallelism in The Volcano Query Processing System. In ACM SIGMOD,1990(102-111)
18. G. Graefe.: Query Evaluation Techniques for large databases. ACM Computing Surveys, (June1993) 25(4):73-170.
19. Globus Project. 2004. Argonne National Labs. http://www.globus.org

Quantitative Analysis of Zipf's Law on Web Cache

Lei Shi[1,2], Zhimin Gu[1], Lin Wei[2], and Yun Shi[3]

[1] Department of Computer Science and Engineering, Beijing Institute of Technology,
Beijing 100081, China
shilei@zzu.edu.cn, zmgu@x263.net
[2] College of Information Engineering, Zhengzhou University, Zhengzhou 450052, China
weilin@shengda.edu.cn
[3] Department of Information Technology, State Post Bureau, Beijing 100808, China
shiyun@postmail.com.cn

Abstract. Many studies have shown that Zipf's law governs many features of the WWW and can be used to describe the popularity of the Web objects. Based upon Zipf's law, we analyze quantitatively the relationship between the hit ratio and the size of Web cache, present approximate formulae to calculate the size of Web cache when the hit ratio is given under the condition of basic Zipf's law and Zipf-like law, determine the critical value n in the top-n prefetching algorithm by studying the effect of parameter α on the hot Web documents. Zipf's law plays an important role in solving the Internet latency, and holds the promise of more effective design and use of Web cache resources.

Keywords: Zipf's law, Web Cache, Web Prefetching, Top-N.

1 Introduction

The WWW latency problem is a critical problem in Quality of Service (QoS) of network. It depends on several factors such as network bandwidth, propagation time, queuing latency and speed of server and client computers. Currently, Web caching and prefetching are the two main solutions to reduce the Web latency and to improve QoS. The hit ratio of caching is usually below 50%, while prefetching can improve it up to 60% or even more. It is certain that there are close relationships between the characteristics of Web access pattern, especially the distribution of Web objects access popularity and the caching and prefetching policy the Web system adopted. Zipf's law has been proven that it can be employed to describe the phenomena [1][3].

Recent studies [2][3][4] have shown that Zipf's law (basic Zipf's law) and Zipf-like law govern many features of the WWW such as Web objects access distribution, the number of pages within a site, the number of links to a page, the number of visits to a site, the number of people in the Usenet discussion group, the access pattern in VOD system. Some studies, for example, the work of Glassman's [2] where Zipf's law was first employed to describe the Web object access distribution argued that Web access pattern satisfies Zipf's law quite well, but more studies such as Breslau [3] gave the evidence that Web access pattern follows Zipf-like law. How to make use of the law has been discussed these recent years [5][6][7][8], but most of which are based on the Zipf's law with one parameter or two parameters with fixed α [7].

The modeling method above has some limitations due to the influence of the diversity of a group of users' surfing interests on parameter α. This paper considers the general form of the Zipf's law. In Web caching research area, one of the key points in designing Web cache systems is to analyze the close relationship between the hit ratio and the size of Web cache quantitatively. In Web prefetching, it is important to study the attributes of hot Web objects in Web prefetching algorithms and how to determine the critical value n in the top-n prefetching approach is the essence of the algorithm, which is still under discussion to our knowledge. These motivate the problems solved herein.

The rest of this paper is organized as follows. Section 2 introduces the backgrounds of Zipf's law. Section 3 discusses the relationship between the size and the hit ratio of the Web cache, and gives the method to calculate the sizes of the caches required to achieve high cache hit ratio under the condition of basic Zipf's law and Zipf-like law. Section 4 studies the effect of parameter α on the hot Web documents, and determines the critical value n in the top-n prefetching algorithm. Section 5 contains the summary and conclusions.

2 Backgrounds

Zipf's law was originally applied to the relationship between words in a text and their frequency of use. The probability of occurrence of words or other items starts high and tapers off. Thus, a few occur very often while many others occur rarely. The frequency P_i of the i'th most frequent item satisfies the formula below:

$$P_i = \frac{C}{i} \qquad (1)$$

where C is a constant. Formula (1) is called basic Zipf's law or Zipf's law with one parameter. At most circumstances, Zipf's law is usually used to refer to the basic law. Apparently Zipf's law predicts that the probability of access for an object is a function of its popularity.

A more generalized form of Zipf's law may be stated mathematically as:

$$P_i = \frac{C}{i^a} \qquad (2)$$

where C is also a constant, α a positive parameter and $0 < \alpha \leq 1$. Formula (2) can be called Zipf-like law or Zipf's law with two parameters. It's in the form of power law. Obviously basic Zipf's law is the special form of Zipf-like law.

Considering the facts that Internet object requests follow a Zipf-like distribution, this paper assumes that the client requests Req is a series of independent events and $Req = <R_0, R_1, ...R_{|Req|}>$ where |Req| is the length of Req.

Let N stand for a set of N possible objects such as Web pages. The popularity of a Web object can be measured, and refers to the access probability of the object, and for any object O_i, i represents the i'th popularity. S is a set of N objects, where S={O_i|1<=i<=N}. It will be accessed by a group of users during a time interval t_i. The time interval of the Web objects is long enough, which will be described in the definition of stability below. The harmonic number of order n of α is defined as $H_\alpha(n)$.

Most of the reported estimates of α lie in the range between 0.6 and 1.0. Studies [3][4] have revealed that the value of parameter α is ranged between 0.75 and 0.85 for the Web servers, 0.64 and 0.83 for the Web proxies.

Definition 1. The Web object popularity model can be set up based on the redefinition of the Zipf's law as follows:

$$P_i = \frac{C}{i^a}, \quad \alpha \in [0.5, 1] \tag{3}$$

where the meaning of parameter C and i are the same as in (2), P_i is the probability of the i'th Web object O_i.

3 Web Cache Size and Web Caching Hit Ratio

The harmonic number of order n of α can be written as:

$$H_\alpha(n) = \frac{1}{1} + \frac{1}{2^a} + \ldots + \frac{1}{i^a} + \ldots \frac{1}{n^a} = \sum_{i=1}^{n} \frac{1}{i^a} \tag{4}$$

If $\alpha \leq 1$, while $n \to \infty$, the harmonic series does not converge. Actually the sum is the Riemann zeta function. When $n \in [1, \infty)$, we can calculate the approximate value of $H_\alpha(n)$ as follows:

$$H_\alpha(n) = \sum_{i=1}^{n} \frac{1}{i^a} \approx \int_{\leq i \leq n} \frac{1}{i^a} di = \frac{n^{1-\alpha}}{1-\alpha}, \alpha \neq 1 \tag{5}$$

Since the sum of all probabilities is equal to 1, then:

$$\sum_{i=1}^{N} P_i = 1 \tag{6}$$

Thus C can be calculated as:

$$C = \left(\sum_{i=1}^{N} \frac{1}{i^a} \right)^{-1} \approx \frac{1-\alpha}{N^{1-\alpha}}, \alpha \neq 1 \tag{7}$$

Let Φ(k,α) be the cumulative probability of the k most popular Web objects, then

$$\Phi(k,\alpha) = \sum_{i=1}^{k} \frac{C}{i^a} = C \times H_a(k) \approx \frac{Ck^{1-\alpha}}{1-\alpha} = (\frac{k}{N})^{1-\alpha} \tag{8}$$

So the number of accesses of the k most popular objects $O_1, O_2, O_3 \ldots O_k$ can be computed as follows. As any object O_j, 1≤i≤N, will be accessed $P_i \times N_W$ times (where

N_W is the number of accesses and large enough), the total number of accesses to the k most popular Web objects will be:

$$\sum_{i=1}^{k} N_W \times P_i = N_W \times \sum_{i=1}^{k} P_i = N_W \times \Phi(k,\alpha) \qquad (9)$$

If the system caches the k most popular objects, then it is likely to get a high hit ratio. Considering the ideal situation when the cache is large enough, if the k most popular objects are cached, then the cache hit ratio is:

$$h = \frac{\sum_{i=1}^{k} N_W \times P_i}{N_W} = \Phi(k,\alpha) \qquad (10)$$

For different value of α, There are two typical cases:

Case 1: If $\alpha \neq 1$, the situation is corresponding to the Zipf-like distribution. From formula (8) and (10), under the assumption of a given hit ratio h, the number of objects in the cache k can be expressed as:

$$k = N \times h^{\frac{1}{1-\alpha}} \qquad (11)$$

Case 2: If $\alpha = 1$, corresponding to the basic Zipf distribution, then,

$$H_n = \ln n + \gamma + \varepsilon_n \approx \ln n \qquad (12)$$

where γ is the Euler's constant 0.5772156649…, when n is large enough, $\lim_{n \to \infty} \varepsilon_n = 0$.

Constant C can be calculated as the following equation:

$$C = \left(\sum_{i=1}^{N} \frac{1}{i}\right)^{-1} = H_n^{-1} \qquad (13)$$

Thus, the basic Zipf's law can be written as:

$$P_i = \frac{C}{i} = \frac{1}{H_n \times i} \approx \frac{1}{\ln N \times i} \qquad (14)$$

And formula (8) can be changed to the following form:

$$\Phi(k,1) = \sum_{i=1}^{k} \frac{C}{i} = C \times H_k = \frac{H_k}{H_N} \approx \frac{\ln k}{\ln N} \qquad (15)$$

From formula (10) and (15), the number of objects k in the cache, under the assumption of a given hit ratio h and the basic Zipf's law, can be calculated as:

$$\ln k = h \times H_N \Rightarrow k \approx e^{h \times \ln N} \quad (16)$$

(11) and (16) reveal the relationship between the size and the hit ratio of the Web cache under the condition of the basic Zipf's law ($\alpha = 1$) and Zipf-like ($\alpha \neq 1$) law.

4 The Parameter α and Hot Web Objects

Now let's turn to the study of the impact of α on the hot Web objects. Since $\frac{k}{N} < 1$, formula (8) shows the close relationship between Φ(k,α) and α: The larger parameter α is, the higher Φ(k,α) will be. Thus comes to the conclusion: A larger α increases Φ(k,α), which means more requests are concentrated on a few hot Web objects such as Web pages.

Furthermore, Formula (3) implies: if i=1, P_1=C, C is actually the probability of the first Web object; if i=2, comparing P_1 and P_2, we can find that P_1 and P_2 increase as α increases, and P_1 increases quicker than P_2; P_2 and P_3 have the same property. But when i goes up to some extent, P_i will increase incipiently and then decrease afterwards along with α, as shown in Figure 1. Assuming n is the critical point, now we can determine the critical value n in a mathematical analysis method.

Calculate the one order derivative of formula (3), we have:

$$\frac{dP_i}{d\alpha} = \frac{d(\frac{C}{i^\alpha})}{d\alpha} = \frac{dC}{d\alpha} \times \frac{1}{i^\alpha} + C \times \frac{1}{i^\alpha} \times \ln i \quad (17)$$

Let the above expression equal to 0, then
$\frac{dC}{d\alpha} \times \frac{1}{i^\alpha} - C \times \frac{1}{i^\alpha} \times \ln i = 0$ Thus,

$$\ln i = -\frac{C'}{C} \Rightarrow n = i = [e^{-(\frac{C'}{C})}] \quad (18)$$

owing to $C = \left(\sum_{i=1}^{N} \frac{1}{i^a} \right)^{-1}$,

$$C' = -C^2 \sum_{i=1}^{N} \frac{\ln i}{i^\alpha} \quad (19)$$

Then,

$$n = e^{-(\frac{C'}{C})} = e^{C \sum_{i=1}^{N} \frac{\ln i}{i^\alpha}} \quad (20)$$

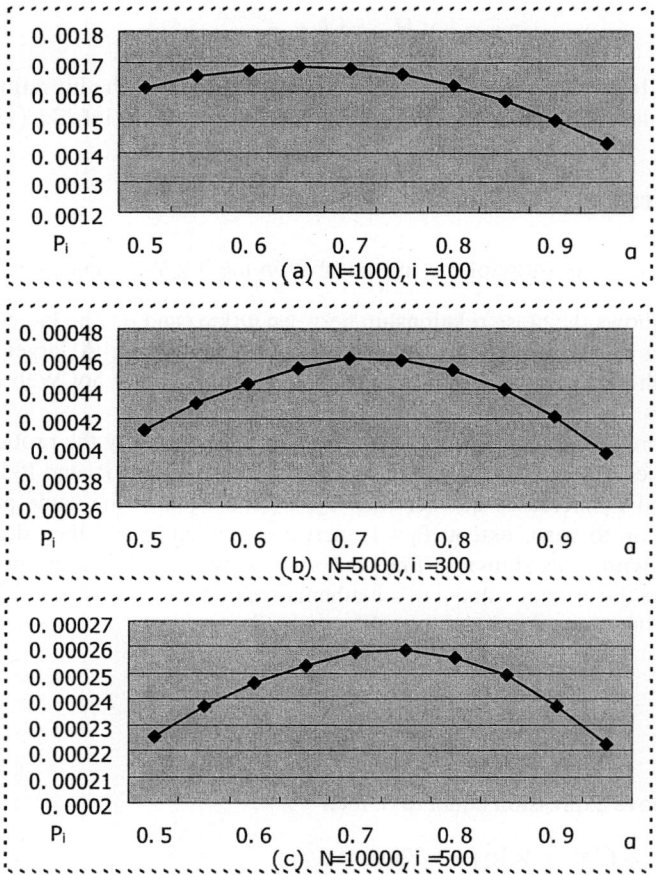

Fig. 1. Diagram of P_i versus α when (a)N=1000, i=100; (b)N=5000, i=300; (c)N=10000, i=500

Figure 2 shows that n is a function of N and α in terms of formula (20). Each curve refers to the critical n over N with a different α. when α goes up , n goes down; when α goes down, n goes up. They develop in an opposite way.

Among the Web prefetching algorithms, top-10 approach is an effective way [10]. The algorithm predicts the 10 most popular Web documents and stores them in the local Web cache. If N is relatively big, based upon the analysis above, the hit ratio of the Web cache will be quite low. For instance, if N=10000, even if a quite high value of α, say 0.9 is used, it's difficult for the hit ratio of top-10 exceeding 40%. In contrast, if we modify top-10 approach to top-n approach, where the value of n is determined by formula (20), since n is a critical value and according to the principle of locality, the system can enhance the hit ratio to a relative high degree if the top-n popular Web objects are cached. Under the same circumstance, when N=10000, α=0.9, the ideal hit ratio of top-n algorithm can reach 66% approximately. Table 1 shows the N, n and $\Phi(k, \alpha)$ relationship when α=0.9.

Apparently, the theoretical result discussed above can be used to guide the design of simple and effective top-n prefetching algorithm.

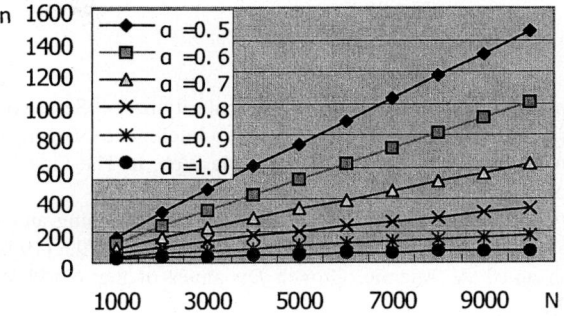

Fig. 2. Diagram of n versus N based on formula (20)

Table 1. n and $\Phi(k,\alpha)$ over N(α=0.9)

N	1000	2000	3000	4000	5000	6000	7000	8000	9000	10000
n	38	58	76	91	105	118	131	142	154	164
$\Phi(k,\alpha)$	72%	70%	69%	68%	68%	68%	67%	67%	67%	66%

5 Conclusions

One of the most important problems in the application of Web caching is how to manage Web cache efficiently, studying the Web access characteristics is the foundation of managing Web cache efficiently and also plays an important role in the design of Web site. Zipf's law has been proven that it can be used to describe the popularity of the Web objects.

Based on the Zipf's law, this paper analyzes quantitatively and discusses in two aspects: (1) the relationship between the hit ratio and the Web cache size, where approximate calculation formulae are presented. (2) the effect of parameter α on the hot Web documents where the value n in top-n algorithm is determined.

The effective use of Zipf's law will be an important component of effective Web caching and Web prefetching. Zipf's law holds the promise of more effective design and use of Web cache resources.

Acknowledgements

This work was partially supported by the National Natural Science Foundation of China (Grant No.50207005), the National Fund for Studying Abroad (Grant

No.21307D05) and the Research Foundation of Beijing Institute of Technology (Grant No. 0301F18). We would like to thank Professor Jun Zou of Tsinghua University for the helpful and constructive comments.

References

1. Lei Shi, Zhimin Gu, Lin Wei, Yun Shi. Popularity-based Selective Markov Model. IEEE/WIC/ACM International Conference on Web Intelligence, Beijing (2004) 504-507.
2. S. Glassman. A caching relay for the World Wide Web. In The First International World Wide Web Conference, Geneva, Switzerland, (1994).
3. L. Breslau, P. Cao, L. Fan, G. Phillips, S. Shenker. Web caching and Zipf-like distributions: evidence and implications. In Proceedings of INFOCOM '99, (1999) 126-134.
4. B.A. Huberman and L.A. Adamic, Growth Dynamics of the World Wide Web, Nature 401:131. (1999).
5. A. Mahanti, C. Williamson, D. Eager. Traffic Analysis of a Web Proxy Caching Hierarchy. IEEE Network, (2000) 16-23.
6. T. Kelly, D. Reeves, Optimal Web cache sizing: scalable methods for exact solutions. Computer Communications, Vol.24 (2), (2000) 163-173.
7. D.N. Serpanos, G. Karakostas, Proof for effective and efficient Web caching. Electronics Letters, Vol.38 (10), (2002) 490–492.
8. P. Cao, S. Irani, Cost Aware www proxy caching algorithms. In Proceedings of the 1997 USENIX Symposium on Internet Technology and Systems. (1997) 193-206.
9. X. Chen, X. Zhang, A Popularity-based Prediction Model for Web Prefetching, Computer, Vol.36 (3), (2003) 63-70.
10. E. P. Marcatos, C.E. Chronaki A Top-10 Approach to Prefetching the Web. The Eighth Annual Conference of the Internet Society(INET'98),Geneva.Switzerland. (1998).
11. Lei Shi, Zhimin Gu, Yunxia Pei, Lin Wei. A PPM Prediction Model Based on Web Objects' Popularity. Lecture Notes in Artificial Intelligence 3614, (2005) 110-119.

An Adaptive Web Caching Method Based on the Heterogeneity of Web Object

Yun Ji Na[1], Il Seok Ko[2], and Gun Heui Han[3]

[1] Dept. of Internet Software, Honam University, 59-1 Seobon-Dong,
Gwangsan-Gu, Gwangju, 506-714, S. Korea
yjna@honam.ac.kr
[2] Dept. of e-Business, Chungbuk Provincial University of Science & Technology,
40 Gumgu-ri, Okchon-eup, Okchon-gun, Chungbuk, 373-807, S. Korea
isko@ctech.ac.kr
[3] School of Information Communication, Cheonan University, 115 Anseo-dong,
Chonan, 330-704, S. Korea
hankh@cheonan.ac.kr

Abstract. Heterogeneity of Web objects is the important causes of the decrease the performance of web caching algorithms. To increase the throughput of web caching process and to improve service availability, we may consider heterogeneity of web object adaptively. In this study, we proposed the new web-caching algorithm. A heterogeneity variation of an object can be reduced as the proposed method dividedly managing. Web objects and a cache scope with heterogeneity, and it is adaptively reflecting a variation of object reference characteristics with the flowing of time. In the experiments, we verified that the performance of the proposed method was more improved than existing algorithms through the two experiment models, which considered heterogeneity of an object.

1 Introduction

With the progress of network technology and advancement of production technology of digital contents, the heterogeneity of Web objects has gradually increased and has gradually had many influences to Web efficiency [1,2]. The heterogeneity increase of objects more frequently substitutes Web objects, but traditional substitute techniques cannot reflect enough these characteristics. Also, the reference locality [5,6] and other reference characteristics vary depending on the flow of time, and are major factors decreasing the performance of previous caching techniques [3,4]. This study proposed Adaptive Caching Algorithm with Size Heterogeneity, which is a Web caching technique that adaptively reflects the heterogeneity of Web objects. The proposed method approached Web caching problems as follows.

• The heterogeneity of Web objects has a close relationship with size variation, and the identification of objects according to heterogeneity is able to divide objects according to object size.
• The SIZE technique and LRUMIN algorithm can decrease the cases in which a big size object eliminates many small size objects from the storage domain.

• By managing objects by unit size, the variation of object size in each storage domain can be decreased compared to management by one unit. We can reduce the number of small size objects needed to substitute a big size object with the decrease of size variation.
• The reference characteristics of objects is very variable, and the variation of heterogeneity also is variable. An adaptive caching technique needs to reflect variable reference characteristics.

So, to increase the throughput of caching process and to improve service availability, we may consider heterogeneity of web object adaptively. Also, to evaluate the performance, this study presented two kinds of object use models which reflected the heterogeneity of objects: it analyzed the hitting ratio and response time of objects, and the profit ratio by comparing a developed substitute technique with pervious substitute techniques (LRU, LRUMIN, SIZE). By these experimental results, the developed substitute technique could confirm a greater improvement of performance than the previous substitute techniques.

2 Proposed Method

We divide the storage space of a Web cache into two kinds of domain according to object size. Then the following points are considered:

• It is best to store web objects as often as possible in a Web cache and to save small-sized web objects in the cache with this perspective.
• As above research, the replacement of a big-sized object generates the replacement of many small-sized ones at same time. This largely decreases the performance of a cache. The absence of a cache for a big-sized object highly increases network traffic and reduces the performance of a system. Finally, to save a big-sized object in a cache is better with respect to the network.

According to the analysis of web object reference characteristics in prior research, we can identify a large amount of difference between the total transmission quantity and the number of frequency references based on a 10K size object. Therefore, ACASH manages web objects by dividing LARGE (over 10K in object size) from SMALL (below 10K in object size). Then, the reference characteristics of web objects gain the adaptability according to time flow by managing the division rate of each available cache domain. If there is an object requested by a client, a cache manager checks the existence of the object in the division domain constituted by object size. Generating a cache hit, it thereby provides the object service for a client request, and the cache manager updates the used time record for which this object receives a high priority in a LRUMIN replacement. (See Figure 1)

After generating a cache miss, the cache manager receives the transmission of the object by requesting service from the URL Internet server that generated the cache miss. The transmitted object then divides the object on the basis of object size. The cache manager then checks the storage space to save this object in the cache domain in the proper object level. If there is space to save it, the object is stored in the cache, and if there is no space to save it, the object is assigned to free space by LRUMIN and is saved in the cache. The web object saved in each space level can be placed between same level objects, and high priority is assigned by saving the time record of the newly stored object. At this time, because the proposed method manages the storage space of object by dividing object size into SMALL and LARGE, it has a relatively smaller variation of web object size compared with LRU, LRUMIN and SIZE. Therefore, compared with the previous algorithm, the number of small-sized objects generated by a big size object can be reduced.

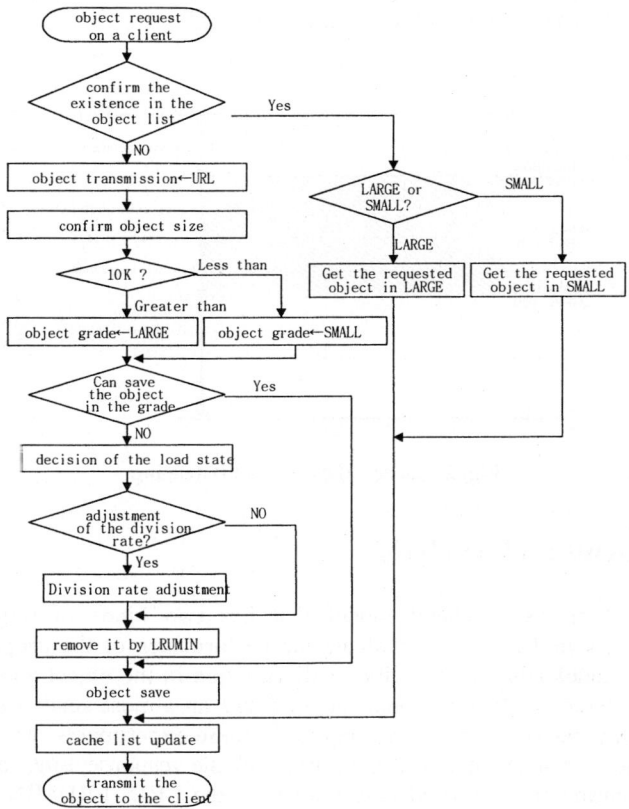

Fig. 1. Flow Chart

Also, the proposed method adaptively reflects change according to the reference characteristics time of a web object. In order to do this, we use Cache Adaptor as follows in Figure 2.

1) Each domain is divided into a lightly loaded state, lightly overloaded state, and an overloaded state. The basis rate of a load state (SMALL and LARGE domains) reflects the variation of object size, these difference are presented in Figure 2.

2) The load state of each domain increases according to the reference object for each division domain. This is first divided into 5:5.

3) According to the time flow, each divided ADAPTOR load state is changed by reflecting the reference characteristics of an object. If the load state of a domain arrives at an overloaded state, ADAPTOR checks the load state of different domain.

3-1) If the load state of other domains is smaller than the overloaded state, the total cache division rate for overload state is increased by 5%.

3-2) If the load state of another domain is in a slightly overload state; the total cache division rate operates without an adjustment to the division rate.

4) The rate of one domain cannot be over 70% in a division rate adjustment. In other words, the maximum rate of division is 7:3 or 3:7.

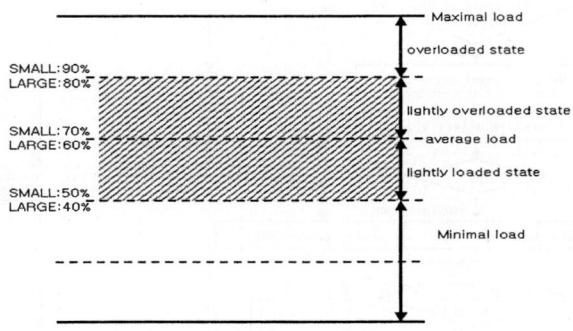

Fig. 2. Cache Adaptor Load Balancing

3 Experiments and Analysis

We established an experimental model that has two kinds of object reference characteristics, as in Table 1, to evaluate the performance of the proposed method. Experimental model 1 has a generally small variation in the object and many small-sized object references. Experimental model 2 has an almost small variation in the object and many big-sized object references. In these experiments, we measured the object-hit ratio, the average object-hit ratio, and the response time, and evaluated them by comparing the proposed algorithm with the LRU, LRUMIN and SIZE of previous algorithm.

To reflect the physical environment of the network, we have to consider factors influencing traffic. Of various factors influencing traffic, object size is a factor of the objects themselves. Hence, we can reflect the size factor of web object. An average object size hit ratio in equation (1) reflects the factor of object size to object-hit ratio. An average object-hit ratio indicates an average value of the object size and object-hit ratio of the requested object.

$$\sqrt{\frac{\sum_{j=0}^{k}(OB_{hit(j)} \times SO_{hit(j)})}{\sum_{i=1}^{n}(OB_{req(i)} \times SO_{req(i)})}}$$

OBreq(i) : the requested object
SOreq(i) : size of the requested object
OBhit(i) : the hit object
OBhit(i) : size of the hit object

In light of the experiment results of the object-hit ratio, MODEL 1 resulted in more of a decrease than did the previous algorithm in the object hit-ratio. This is because the object characteristics of MODEL 1 generate frequent object requests for small-sized objects, and the size decrease in the small domain due to the division of large domain is why the new algorithm is better than was the previous algorithm not using the division domain. In the experiment we considered object size as Figure 3, and the new algorithm indicates an average better performance improvement of 15% against the previous algorithm due to the increase in the object-hit ratio for big-sized objects.

Table 1. Characteristics of Experimental Model

Division	Reference Characteristics	Variation
MODEL1	Includes a high quantity of text object	small
MODEL2	High ratio of big-sized objects such as MPEG	large

The object-hit ratio for MODEL 2 has more of an increase than it does for MODEL 1. This is because the average value of the object-hit ratio is raised by many requests for big-sized objects. However, we can ascertain that the object-hit ratio has little decrease or is much the same as the previous algorithm for the same reasons as the experiment results for MODEL 1. The new algorithm indicates an average 30% more than the previous algorithms do, as per the experiment results in Figure 4 showing the improvement of the object-hit ratio for big-sized objects. The difference however of the object hit ratio between the proposed method and the previous algorithms will decrease with the increase in use of a cache exclusive server and cache capacity.

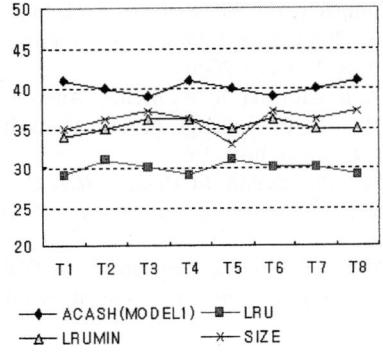

Fig. 3. Object Size Hit Ratio in MODEL1

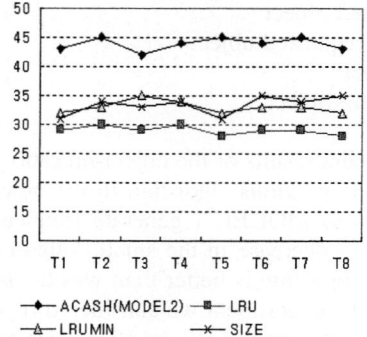

Fig. 4. Object Size Hit Ratio in MODEL2

4 Conclusion

The proposed method reflected this heterogeneity based on object reference characteristics and indicated user reference characteristics within the flow of time. According to the experiment results, the proposed method verified the improvement of performance in the scale in which considered object size for the previous replacement algorithms is considered. The proposed method, as proposed by this study, is a replacement algorithm reflecting object reference characteristics based on a key. In future research, an algorithm reflecting the transmission expense on the network and the heterogeneity of web objects need to be developed by studying the mixed form algorithm based on key and expense.

References

[1] G. Barish, K. Obraczka, World Wide Web Caching: Trends and Techniques. IEEE Communications, Internet Technology Series, May 2000.
[2] H. Bahn, S. Noh, S. L. Min, and K. Koh, "Efficient Replacement of Nonuniform Objects in Web Caches," IEEE Computer, Vol.35, No.6, pp.65-73, June 2002.
[3] L. Rizzo, L. Vicisano, "Replacement Polices for a Proxy Cache," IEEE/ACM Trans. Networking, vol.8, no.2, pp.158-170, 2000.
[4] C. D. Murta, Virgilio A. F. Almeida, Jr. W. Meira, "Analyzing Performance of Partitioned Caches for the WWW," In Proceedings of the Third International WWW Caching Workshop, Manchester, England, June, 1998.
[5] Annie P Foong, Yu-Hen Hu, Dennis M Heisey, Web Caching: Locality of References Revisited, IEEE International Conference on Networks (ICON'00), Singapore, September 05-08, 2000.
[6] E. Cohen and H. Kaplan, "Exploiting Regularities in Web Traffic Patterns for Cache Replacement," In Proceedings of the 31st Annual ACM Symposium on Theory of Computing, ACM, 1999.

Supporting Wireless Web Page Access in Mobile Environments Using Mobile Agents*

HaiYang Hu[1], JiDong Ge[1], Ping Lu[1], XianPing Tao[1], and Jian Lu[1]

[1] State Key Laboratory for Novel Software Technology,
Nanjing University, 210093, China
{hhy, gjd, luping, txp}@ics.nju.edu.cn, lj@nju.edu.cn

Abstract. Because of the limited bandwidth, wireless communication in mobile environments is much more expensive than the communication cost in wired network Thus, to save the cost of wireless communication, during the process of wireless Web page access, mobile unit usually prefetches some Web pages into its local cache and then disconnect itself from the network, so that updates are performed in its local cache and propagated back to Web server upon reconnection again. In this paper, after discussing the design rationale of a new Web page access mechanism, the performance of this mechanism is analyzed theoretically and experimentally. The results show that the efficiency of update propagation is improved and the burden of Web server is decreased.

1 Introduction

The rapidly expanding technology of cellular communication, wireless LANs, and satellite services will make information accessible anywhere and at any time [1]. People equipped with mobile devices can access Web page along wireless links everywhere. Recently, as real-time Web applications being more popular, supporting disconnected write operation in mobile environments becomes necessary. However, for the limited hardware capability of mobile unit (MU) and the high cost of wireless communication, MU can't connect with Web server continuously during the process of Web access. Usually in hoarding phrase, it prefetches some web pages into its local cache and then disconnects from the web server. During disconnection, the write operations to these Web pages performed by MU are recorded into a log. After a certain period, MU reconnects to networks and sends the log to Web server for reintegration. During this reintegration process, the conflicts of updates performed by other users need to be resolved. As the cost of hoarding is usually fixed, how to reduce the total cost of wireless communication in reintegration phrase becomes important.

Until now, different mechanisms proposed in [2], [4], [5], [6], [7] support disconnected Web access in wireless environments in the above three phases. Most existing schemes just support read-only Web page access during disconnection. However, with the rapidly increasing of distributed web authoring and form-based electronic commerce web applications [7], supporting to write operations is needed. Work re-

---

* Funded by NNSFC (60233010, 60273034, 60403014), 973 Program of China (2002CB 312002), NSFC of Jiangsu Province(BK2002203, BK2002409), 863 Program of China.

ported in [11] proposes the concepts of lock and version. Each PUT request indicates the original version of the web page from which its new revision is derived. If the web page has already been updated by other applications, the update request of the client is denied. The client can then fetch the new version of the page and lock the web page to ensure there is no update for the page from other clients at the same time. The client can lock multiple web pages on the same web server to ensure an atomic update be done on these web pages. [5] uses a cache manager named Venus on the client-side. During disconnection, all updates to the Web pages made by the client are recorded into an operation log. Upon reintegration, the Venus resynchronizes its local cache with the server. If Venus detects a divergence, an application specific resolver (ASR) is invoked to resolve the difference. If the ASR fails to resolve the difference, then a manual repair tool running on the client side is invoked. [14] integrates the concept of coherency interval of supporting disconnected Web browsing proposed in [9] with the concept of versioning and locking as proposed in [16] to support disconnected write operations for wireless Web access, and presents three update propagation algorithms. The goal of it is to identify the length of the disconnected period so that to minimize the total communication costs during the reintegration phrase.

However, in reintegration phrase, all of the above works directly propagate their updated Web page to Web server. If some of the Web pages have already been updated by other applications, then these updated Web pages will be rejected by Web server. Thus, transferring these pages along wireless link becomes unnecessary to MU and the correlated communication cost is wasted. On the other hand, during the reintegration phrase, MU has to communicate with Web server many times for conflicts resolving and forced updating, thus, the burdens of Web server are increased. This paper presents a new reintegration protocol based on mobile agents to improve the efficiency of update propagation and decrease the burdens of Web server. The motivation of our scheme is inspired by [17], [19], [20] and [21]. Also the mobile agents help us to implement a fault-tolerant Web page access progress, as they can be used to facilitate seamless logging of access activities for the future recovery from failure. The related content is out scope of this paper, and we have presented it in [22].

This paper is organized as follows. Section 2 gives the analysis for update propagation of Web pages in MU's reintegration phrase. Section 3 presents our reintegration protocols based on mobile agents. Performance analysis of the protocols compared with other protocols is given in section 4. Finally, Section 5 concludes the paper.

2 Protocol Design

Suppose that MU has prefetched Web page i in hoarding phrase, then in reintegration phrase, there exist four possible states for this page (shown in Table 1).

If the Web page has both been updated by MU and some other applications, then the update propagation performed by MU becomes unnecessary and will be rejected by Web server. In this scenario, MU has to receive the update-to-date version of the page and perform operations for resolving conflict based on the data of the page. So we can see that, if MU has the capability to know the state of the page in advance, its unnecessary propagation action can be avoided, so that to decrease the cost of wireless communication.

Table 1. Four possible states for a Web page prefetched by MU

In disconnected phrase, whether MU has updated it	In disconnected phrase, whether other applications have updated it	In reintegration phrase, the following operations that MU will have to perform
Yes	Yes	Resolving conflicts
Yes	No	Update propagation
No	Yes	Force update
No	No	Force update

If the Web page has only been updated by MU, it can perform update propagation smoothly without worrying about the rejection from Web server.

If the Web page has only been updated by other applications, MU also has to perform force update operations depending on the latest version of the page and then propagate its updated page.

If the Web page has not been updated by MU or other applications, MU must perform a *forced update* to the page (because of the real-time requirements of online Web applications).

From the above analysis, we can see that if MU has the ability to know the states of the Web pages in advance, it can pay less for the cost the wireless communication and improves the efficiency of update propagation. Inspired by [17], [19], [20], [21], we use mobile agent as the broker of MU on base station to pre-detect the state of the Web pages that MU has prefetched and tell MU the following operations that it has to perform. This agent called MuAg is responsible for a certain MU. In this way, MU doesn't communicate with Web server directly. All the messages and data sent from one part are first transmitted to MuAg, and it sends them to the other. Before the incoming reintegration phrase, MU inquires Web server about the state information of the Web pages which MU has prefetched in hoarding phrase and locks all these Web pages to ensure that there is no update for these pages from other applications when MU perform its update propagation. If such a Web page has already been updated by other applications, Web server sends the data of the new Web page to MuAg In reintegration phrase, MU first sends MuAg an inquiry message containing the states of the Web pages as which pages have already been updated. Depending on this message and the table 1, MU tells MU the following operations which it will perform. This process is shown in Fig.1.

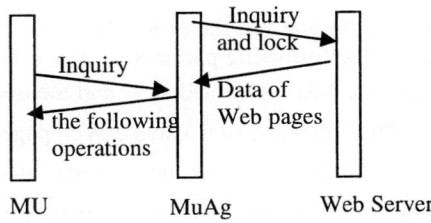

Fig. 1. MU's "pre-detecting" the states of Web pages

Depending on table 1, there are four different kinds of following operations that MU will perform. Here, we give three protocols to cope with the four kinds of following operations.

Protocol 1: For the Web page *i* already updated by MU, if it has not been updated by other users, then MuAg sends MU a message informing MU to propagate the modified Web page to Web server. MU propagates the updates to MuAg. MuAg puts them to Web server and release the lock (shown in Fig.2).

Protocol 2: Shown in fig.3, for the Web page *i* cached by MU, if some other user has also already updated it when MU is in disconnection phrase, then MuAg sends the differences of the Web page to MU. Based on the new version received, MU applies a merge algorithm to resolve the update conflict and sends a data packet carrying the differences of the updated Web page to MuAg. MuAg propagates the updates to Web server and releases the lock.

Protocol 3: For the Web pages *i* cached by MU, if there are no updates to it during disconnection phrase, MU must perform a *forced update* on the page (because of the real-time requirements of online Web applications) when it reconnects with network again. Thus, after receiving a reply message indicating *forced update* from MuAg, MU performs forced updates and propagates the updates to MuAg. After MuAg propagates the updated Web page sent by MU to Web server, MuAg releases the lock.

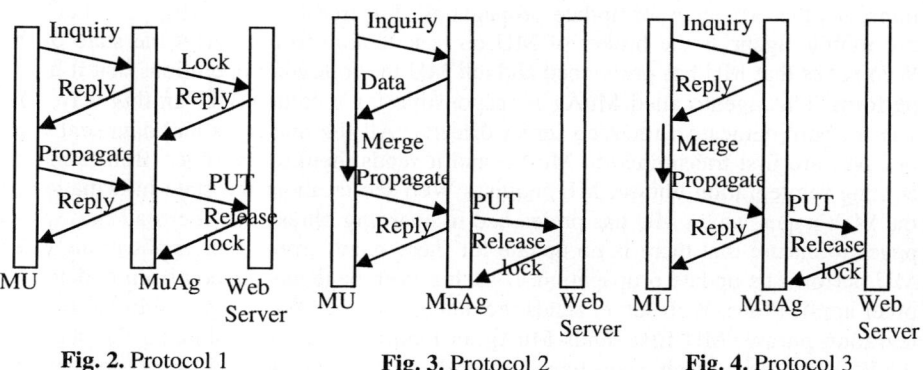

Fig. 2. Protocol 1   **Fig. 3.** Protocol 2   **Fig. 4.** Protocol 3

3 Wireless Web Page Update Propagation

The same as in [14], [22], to analyze the protocols of Web page update propagation quantitatively, we define the following parameters. For a Web page *i* cached by MU, the update rate done to it by MU is denoted as λ_i^m and the update rate done by all other users is denoted as λ_i^o. Thus, for read-only cached Web pages, its λ_i =0. There are two general cost parameters, C_m and C_w. C_m is the average one-way communication cost of transmitting a simple message over the wired network; C_w is the average one-way communication cost of transmitting a data packet carrying a Web page over the wired network. α is denoted as the ratio of the bandwidth of wired network to the bandwidth of wireless network. Then the average cost of transmitting a message from base station to MU is denoted as αC_m, and the average cost of transmitting a data packet over wireless network is αC_w. C_{rm} is the cost of resolving Web page conflicts performed by MU, and we also denote C_{rm} as the cost of force update.

At the time of L_x- mnC_w (here, n is the number of Web pages cached by MU, m is the number of static nodes between the base station and Web server), MuAg inquires Web server about the up-to-date versions of the Web pages which MU has prefetched in hoarding phrase and applies to Web server for locking all these Web pages.

Supposing that updates to Web page i arrive at the system as an exponential distribution and the length of disconnection period is Lx, then Pi, the probability that updates to page i performed by other users during MU's disconnected phrase, is given as

$$p_i = 1 - e^{-\lambda_i^o (Lx - mnC_w)} \qquad (1)$$

Also, q_i, the probability that Web page i has been updated by MU during the period of L_x, is as follows

$$q_i = 1 - e^{-\lambda_i^m Lx} \qquad (2)$$

Based on the above, we now present and analyze the wireless Web page propagation process in our scheme quantitatively. Supposing that MU propagates only one modified Web page to Web server during reintegration phrase, there are two cases as follows:

1. In disconnection phrase, MU has updated the page i and restored it in local cache. After the period of L_x, MU propagates the updates to MuAg. With the probability p_i that the update request is rejected, the overall communication cost is $2\alpha C_m + 2\alpha C_w + C_{rm}$; The cost is $3\alpha C_m + \alpha C_w$ with the probability $1 - p_i$ that the update request is accepted.

2. In disconnection phrase, MU has not updated the page i. When it reconnects to the network again, MU has to perform forced update propagation. The communication cost is $2\alpha C_m + 2\alpha C_w + C_{rm}$ with the probability p_i that other users have already updated the page, or the cost is $3\alpha C_m + \alpha C_w + C_{rm}$ with the probability $1 - p_i$ that no other user has updated the page during L_x.

Summarizing 1) and 2), the average communication cost of MU propagating the updates of one Web page i to MuAg upon reconnection, is as follows:

$$C_{s1(i)} = q_i (p_i (2\alpha C_m + 2\alpha C_w + C_{rm}) + (1 - p_i)(3\alpha C_m + \alpha C_w)) + (1 - q_i)$$
$$(p_i (2\alpha C_m + 2\alpha C_w + C_{rm}) + (1 - p_i)(3\alpha C_m + \alpha C_w + C_{rm})) \qquad (3)$$

The minimized value of $C_{s1(i)}$ is obtained as a solution of

$$\frac{\partial C_s}{\partial L_x} = 0 \quad \text{and} \quad \frac{\partial^2 C_s}{(\partial L_x)^2} > 0 \qquad (4)$$

And this means that both the following formulas hold at the same time:

$$L_x = (\ln(C_{rm}(\lambda_i^m + \lambda_i^o))) - \ln((\alpha C_w + C_{rm} - \alpha C_m)\lambda_i^o)) / \lambda_i^m + mnC_w \text{ and}$$
$$L_x < (\ln(C_{rm}(\lambda_i^m + \lambda_i^o)^2) - \ln(\lambda_i^{o2}(\alpha C_w + C_{rm} - \alpha C_m))) / \lambda_i^m + mnC_w$$

Now suppose that MU prefetches a set of Web pages in local cache in hoarding phrase. Then in reintegration phrase, MU propagates multiple modified Web pages to Web server. MU can send one updated Web page to MuAg each time or send all the updated Web pages in batch to MuAg. In the first case, the overall communication cost of propagating n updated Web pages is as follows:

$$C_{s2} = \sum_{i=1}^{n} c_{s1(i)} \qquad (5)$$

In the second case, MU sends all the updated Web pages in batch to MuAg. The protocol is shown below:

1. MU sends an inquiry message to base station indicating which pages it has already updated.
2. After receiving the message, MuAg sends MU a data packet carrying new version of the pages already received from Web server and a message indicating the following operations that MU will have to perform. The communication cost is $\sum_{i=1}^{n} p_i \alpha C_w$.
3. When MU receives the data packet sent by MuAg, it knows immediately which pages can be accepted by Web server. MU sends them to MuAg. The cost is $\sum_{i=1}^{n} q_i(1-p_i)\alpha C_w$.
4. Depending on the data packet received, MU performs forced updates for the pages that could have been rejected by Web server, including 1) pages updated by MU and also by other users; 2) pages not updated by MU but updated by other users; 3) pages not updated by MU and also not by other users. Then, MU propagates these updated pages to MuAg. The overall communication cost needed is as follows:

$$\sum_{i=1}^{n}(1-q_i)(1-p_i)(\alpha C_w + C_{rm}) + \sum_{i=1}^{n} q_i p_i(\alpha C_w + C_{rm}) + \sum_{i=1}^{n}(1-q_i)p_i(\alpha C_w + C_{rm})$$

5. MuAg receives the updated Web pages and sends an ACK message to MU.
6. MuAg propagates the updated Web pages to Web server and release the lock.

Thus, the overall communication cost of multiple Web page update propagating is as follows:

$$C_{s1} = 3\alpha C_m + \sum_{i=1}^{n} p_i \alpha C_w + \sum_{i=1}^{n} q_i(1-p_i)\alpha C_w + \sum_{i=1}^{n}(1-q_i)(1-p_i)(\alpha C_w + C_{rm})$$
$$\sum_{i=1}^{n} q_i p_i(\alpha C_w + C_{rm}) + \sum_{i=1}^{n}(1-q_i)p_i(\alpha C_w + C_{rm}) \qquad (5)'$$

Comparing (5) with (5)', the difference is $\sum_{i=1}^{n}(3\alpha - \alpha P_i)C_m - 3\alpha C_m$. Since $C_m \approx 0$, (5) $\approx$ (5)' for a not large value n.

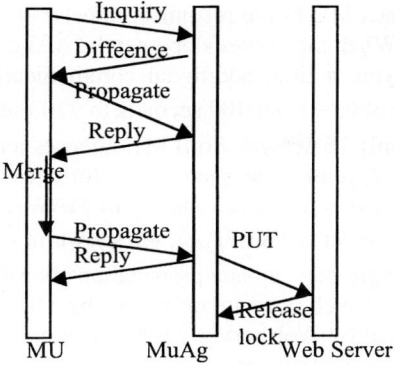

Fig. 5. Multiple Web pages update propagation

4 Performance Analysis

We compare our mechanism with SPUPA (single page update propagation algorithm), MPUPA-1 (multiple-page update propagation algorithm 1), and MPUPA-2 (multiple-page update propagation algorithm 2) that are proposed in [14]. This section tests the effects of different parameters (λ_i^o, λ_i^m, C_{rm}, C_w) on them. Table 2 lists the input parameters needed. The values of these parameters come from [14], [16] and [20].

Table 2. The values of input parameters

Input Parameter	Value
Wireless network factor α	10
Update rate for web page i λ_i $(= \lambda_i^o + \lambda_i^m)$	(0,15)updates/hour
Average cost of transferring a message over wired network C_m	0.01 second
Average cost of transferring a web page over wired network C_w	(0.5, 5) second
Average cost of resolving update conflicts C_{rm}	(30, 180)second
Average cost of transferring a MuAg C_{Ag}	0.1 second
Bandwidth of a wireless channel	9.6 K/S

We use MAWA-1 to denote the single-page update propagation protocol in our scheme and use MAWA-2 to denote the multiple-page update propagation protocol in our scheme.

To demonstrate the effect of (λ_i^o, λ_i^m) on the two different single-page update propagation algorithms (MAWA-1 vs. SPUPA), we fix C_{rm}=100 seconds, C_w=1.5 second, λ_i=10 updates/hour, C_m=0.01second. The value of λ_i^m / λ_i varies from 0.2 to 1.0. Figs.6-8 shows the results. Observed from the figures 6 and 7, the minimized cost of update propagation in reintegration phrase with the value of L_x is in the range of (200,600). But this requires MU to reconnect to network more frequently. And in this way for every 400 seconds MU has to reconnect to network to do update reintegration for about 110 seconds. When the curves slope gently, MU can get a longer disconnection period just for paying a little additional communication cost. For instance as $\lambda_i^m / \lambda_i = 0.6$, when L_x prolongs from 400 seconds to 3200 seconds, the additional cost paid by MU increases only 25 second. So if MU chooses an appropriate L_x during the period when curves slope gently, the overall cost for network connection can be reduced. From Figs.7, the average cost consumed in MAWA-1 decreases about 14.7% than that of SPUPA. However, when $\lambda_i^m / \lambda_i =1$ (shown in Fig.8), there is little difference between the two single-page update propagation algorithms. The reason is that in this case all the updates to Web page are only done by MU, and all the updates propagated by MU are accepted by Web server. So MU can prolong L_x freely without worrying about performing forced updates.

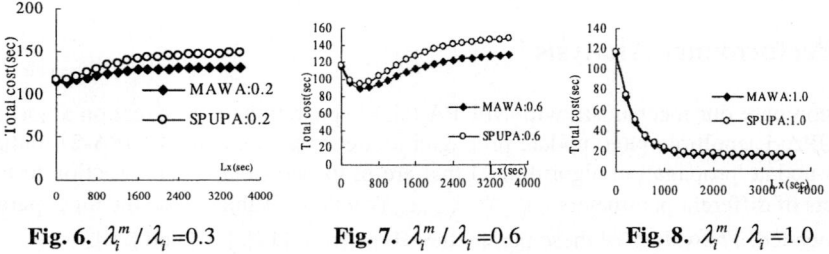

Fig. 6. $\lambda_i^m / \lambda_i =0.3$ **Fig. 7.** $\lambda_i^m / \lambda_i =0.6$ **Fig. 8.** $\lambda_i^m / \lambda_i =1.0$

Fig. 6-8. Effect of update rate on the two single-page update propagation algorithms

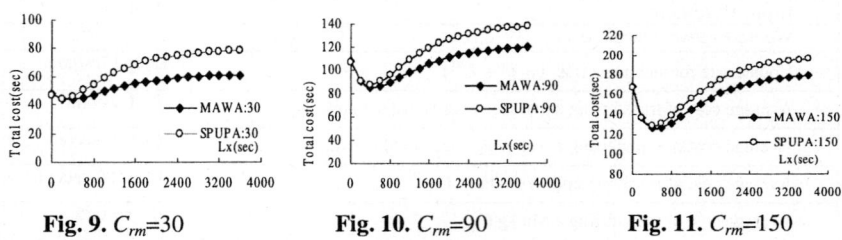

Fig. 9. $C_{rm}=30$ **Fig. 10.** $C_{rm}=90$ **Fig. 11.** $C_{rm}=150$

Fig. 9-11. Effect of C_{rm} on the two single-page update propagation algorithms

Fig.9-11 shows the effect of parameter C_{rm} on the two single-page update propagation algorithms. We fix $\lambda_i^m / \lambda_i =0.6$, $\lambda_i =10$ updates/hour, $C_w =1.5$ second, $C_m =0.01$ second, and C_{rm} varies in the range of [30, 150]. Seen from the figures, the curves in two algorithms both get deeper with C_{rm} increased. The means that MU has to pay more cost for resolving update conflicts. When $C_{rm} =30$, the average cost of MAWA-1 is about 26.7% lower than that of SPUPA. As C_{rm} increases, the efficiency of MAWA-1 decreases. However, even for C_{rm} increase up to 150, the average cost of MAWA-1 is still 9.4% lower than that of SPUPA. And this is because MU in our scheme first sends MuAg a message to inquire the state of the cached Web pages. Thus, some unnecessary page update propagation performed by MU is avoided.

Figs.12-14 shows the effect of C_w on the two single-page update propagation algorithms. We fix λ_i^m / λ_i =0.6, λ_i =10 updates/hour, C_{rm} =100 seconds, and C_m =0.01second. The value of C_w varies from 1 to 5 seconds. The communication cost increases when the value of C_w increased. Indicated by the figures, when C_w =1, the cost of MAWA-1 is only 6% lower than that of SPUPA. However, when C_w increases up to 5, the cost of MAWA-1 is nearly 25% lower than that of SPUPA. We can see that as the cost of transferring the data packet of Web pages increases, MAWA-1 shows an obvious advantage than SPUPA.

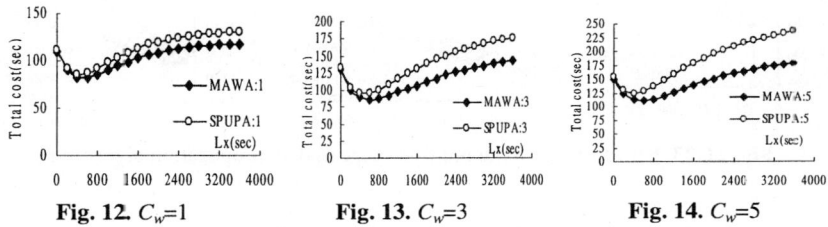

Fig. 12. C_w=1   Fig. 13. C_w=3   Fig. 14. C_w=5

Fig. 12-14. Effect of C_w on the two single-page update propagation algorithms

The multiple-page update propagation algorithms MPUPA-1, MPUPA-2 and MAWA-2 are compared in Figs.15-23, under the effect of the different parameters λ_i^m, C_{rm} and C_w. In this case MU is assumed to updates ten Web pages each time and the updated rate λ_i of each Web page i is selected in the range of [0,15] randomly. Observed from the figures, MAWA-2 is distinctly more effective than MPUPA-1, and is slightly more effective than MPUPA-2. The reason is that in MPUPA-2, MU also sends an inquiry message to Web server to avoid unnecessary updates propagation. The distinction between them is that in MAWA-2 all the differences of Web pages are sent to MU by MuAg, while in MPUPA-2 they are sent by Web server. So if there is a long distance from Web server to the base station, MU in MAWA-2 can save more communication cost. And Figs.24 shows this case, the average cost of MAWA-2 is about 15.7% lower than that of MPUPA-2 when the data sent by Web server has to be transmitted over four other physical nodes to the base station in the wired network.

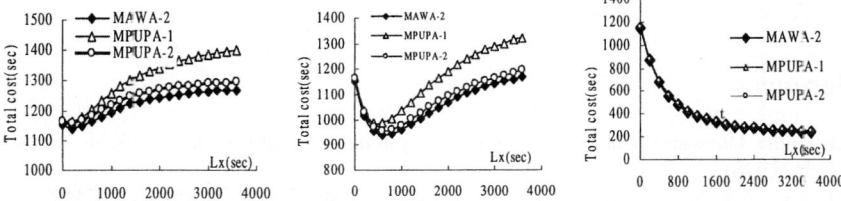

Fig. 15-17. Effect of update rate on the multiple-page update propagation algorithms

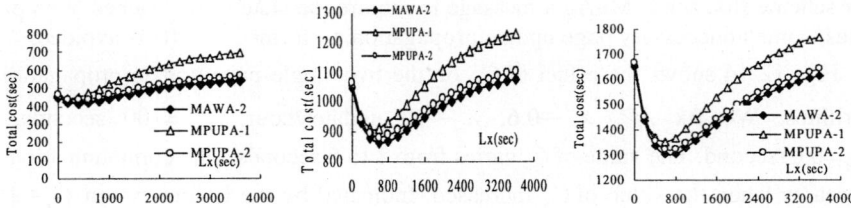

Fig. 18-20. Effect of C_{rm} on the multiple-page update propagation algorithms

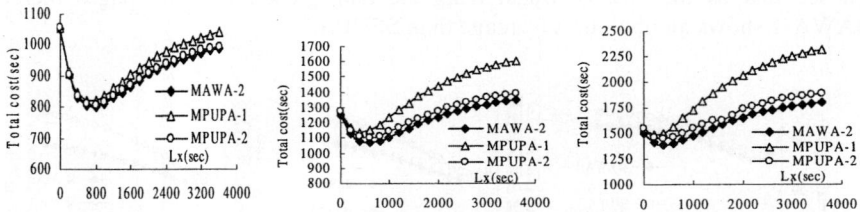

Fig. 21-23. Effect of C_w on the multiple-page update propagation algorithms

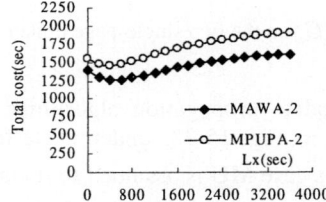

Fig. 24. Comparing MAWA with MPUPA-2

5 Conclusion

This paper presents a set of new Web page access protocols based on mobile agents which help MU implement its update propagation in reintegration phrase. In the scheme, mobile agent is used as the broker of MU on base station to pre-detect the state of the Web pages that MU has prefetched in advance and tells MU the following operations that it has to perform. As a result, the efficiency of update propagation has been improved and the burdens of Web server have been decreased. Compared with other protocols, our mechanism shows its efficient behavior.

References

1. Chander Dhawan.: Mobile Computing: A systems Integrator's Handbook.Mc Graw Hill, USA(1998)
2. J. Jing, A.S. Helal.: Client-Server Computing in Mobile Environments. *ACM Computin Survey*, vol. 31(2).(1999) 117-157

3. E. Pitoura and G. Samaras.: Data Management for Mobile Computing. Kluwer Ac-ademic Publishers(1998)
4. H. Chang.: Web Browsing in a Wireless Environment:Disconnected and Asynchronous Operation in ARTour Web Express. *Proc. Third ACM/IEEE Conf. Mobile Computing and Networking*, (1997) 260-269
5. J.J. Kistler, Satyanarayanan.:Disconnected Operation in the Coda File System *ACM Trans. Computer Systems*, vol. 10(1). (1992)3-25
6. Z. Jiang, L. Kleinrock.:Web Prefetching in a Mobile Environment, *IEEE Personal Comm.* vol. 5(5).(1998) 25-34
7. M.S. Mazer, C.L. Brooks.:Writing the Web while Disconnected, *IEEE Personal Comm.* vol. 5(5),(1998) 35-41.
8. A. Joshi, S. Weerawarana, E. Houstis.:On Disconnected Browsing of Distributed Information. *Proceeding of the 7th IEEE Workshop on Research Issues in Data Engineering RIDE*, (1997) 101-107
9. R. Floyd, R. Housel, C. Tait.:Mobile web access using eNetwork Web Express.*IEEE Personal Communications*, Vol. 5(5). (1998) 47-52
10. M. Liljeberg, T. Alanko, M. Kojo, H. Laamanen, K. Raatikainen. Optimizing World Wide Web for weakly connected mobile workstations: An indirect approach. *Proceeing of the 2nd International Workshop on Services in Distributed and Networked Environments*, (1995) 153-161
11. E.J. Whitehead Jr, M.Wiggins. WEBDAV: IEIF Standard for Collaborative Authoring on the Web. *IEEE Internet Computing*, Vol.2(5) (1998) 34-40
12. M.S. Mazer,C.L. Brooks. Writing the web while disconnected. *IEEE Personal Communications*, Vol. 5(5), (1998) 35-41
13. M.F. Kaashoek, T. Pinckney, J.A. Tauber. Dynamic documents: mobile wireless access to the WWW. *IEEE Workshop on Mobile Computing Systems and applications*,Santa Cruz, CA, Dec. (1994) 179-184
14. Ing-Ray Chen, Ngoc Anh Phan, I-Ling Yen. Algorithms for Supporting Disconnected Write Operations for wireless Web Access in Mobile Client-Server Environments. *IEEE Transactions on mobile computing*, VoL.1(1) (2002) 46-58
15. Debra VanderMeer, Anindya Datata, Kaushik Dutta. Mobile User Recovery in the context of Internet Transactions. *IEEE Transactions on Mobile Computing*, Vol.2(2). (2003) 132-146
16. Taesoon Park, Namyoon Woo, Heon Y. Yeon. An Efficient Recovery Scheme for Mobile Computing Environments. *Proceedings of the Eighth International Conference on Parallel and Distributed Systems*. (2001) 53-60
17. Cris Pedregal-Martin, Krithi Ramamritham. "Support for recovery in mobile System. *IEEE Transactions on Computers*. Vol.51(10).(2002) 1219-1224
18. Z.jiang and L.Kleinrock. Web Prefetching in a Mobile Environment. *IEEE Personal Communication*, Vol.5(5). (1998) 25-34
19. Mohammad A.H., Mitsuji M. MAMI: Mobile Agent based System for mobile Internet. *Proceedings of the IEEE/WIC/ACM International Conference on Web Intelligence(WI'04)*.(2004) 241-250
20. Sashidhar G., Vijay, K. Recovery in the Mobile Wireless Environment Using Mobile Agents. *IEEE Transactions on Mobile Computing*, Vol.3(2). (2004) 180-191
21. Paolo B., Antonio Corradi., Cesare S. Mobile Agent middleware for mobile computing. *IEEE Computer*. Vol.34(3). (2001) 73-81
22. HaiYang Hu, XianPing Tao, JiDong Ge, Jian Lu. An Efficient Scheme for Fault-tolerant Web Page Access in Wireless Mobile Environments Based on Mobile Agents. *Proceedings of The International Conference on High Performance Computing and Communications*.(2005)(to appear)

TCP and ICMP in Network Measurement: An Experimental Evaluation

Wenwei Li[1], Dafang Zhang[2], Gaogang Xie[3], and Jinmin Yang[2]

[1] College of Computer & Communication, Hunan University,
Changsha, 410082, China
liww@hnu.cn
[2] School of Software, Hunan University, Changsha, 410082, China
{dfzhang, rj_jmyang}@hnu.cn
[3] Network Research Division, Institute of Computing Technology,
Chinese Academy of Science, Beijing, 100080, China
xie@ict.ac.cn

Abstract. Both TCP and ICMP are applied in network measurement, while investigating differences between the measured results of them is important but has been less addressed. To compare the differences between TCP and ICMP when they are used in measuring host connectivity, RTT, and packet loss rate, we designed two groups of comparison programs, after careful evaluating of the program parameters, we executed a lot of experiments on the Internet. The experimental results shows, there are significant differences between the host connectivity measured using TCP or ICMP; in general, the accuracy of TCP is 20%-30% higher than that of ICMP. The case of RTT and packet loss rate is complicated, which are related to path loads and destination host loads. While commonly, the RTT and packet loss rate measured using TCP or ICMP are very close. We also give some advices on protocol selection for conducting accurate network measurements.

1 Introduction

Network measurement is an important research area and a hot topic in network community. It is an effective method to investigate network performance and behavior characteristics. It also gives straightforward guidance to the evolution of the Internet infrastructure and the enhancement of protocols [1,2,3].

There are mainly two ways to measure the network: active and passive. Active measurement means that the user injects probe packets into the network from a probe host, and observes the response of the network to the probe packets at the probe host or destination host, to get knowledge about network performance. Active measurement is the primary method of network measurement. For example, the ping and traceroute programs are the most frequently used active measurement tools. In active measurement, the probe packets injected into the network usually are IP packets in which encapsulated with ICMP message. But ICMP is not designed for data transmitting, and it can be easily imposed by network attack activities. Accompanying with the popularization of Internet, in considering of the security and efficiency of network, many routers and end hosts have rate limited or even blocked ICMP packets, which may lead to obtain wrong measuring results or the measurement cannot be conducted at all [6]. Therefore recently, researchers proposed to measure network using the three-way handshake process of TCP [5,7].

Replace ICMP with TCP, when measuring network performance, an accompanied question is: Do there have any differences between the measured results of TCP and ICMP? The significance of research on this problem is manifold. First, researchers and operators have accumulated lots of history data about network performance; most of them were collected with ICMP. While after replacing ICMP with TCP in network measurement, we need understand the difference of measurement results of the two protocols. Secondly, some researches, e.g. [18,19], have analyzed and concluded network performance characteristics from measurement done with TCP or ICMP separately. Whether these conclusions truly reflect the network performance, it also needs we understand the differences of measurement results of the two protocols. Still other researches assume that there is no difference in the results of the two protocols, for example, the authors of [8] use the RTT and packet loss rate measured by ping (ICMP) to calculate and predict TCP throughput. To validate these researches, we must check this assumption. At last, in [4], the authors are aware of that; the same performance metric may have different measurement results, if it is measured using different protocols, and advise that, when discussing the measurement results, the protocol used in measuring must be pointed out. However this approach unnecessarily increases the amount of measurement, and augments the difficulty of result analysis, for people just wants to know the networks performance while not cares about protocols.

To investigate the differences in the measurement results of some network performance metrics such as host connectivity, RTT, and loss rate measured using TCP and ICMP, we designed two groups of comparison programs, and after carefully evaluate the values of the program parameters, we conducted lots of comparison experiments on the Internet.

The paper is organized as follows. We summarize the related work in section 2. In section 3, we describe the design of test programs and two groups of comparison experiments for finding out the protocol differences. We analyze the results differences of TCP and ICMP based on the experimental results in section 4. Finally, we conclude and discuss some future works in section 5.

2 Related Works

To the best of our knowledge, there has been no prior work that focused on comparing the network performance measured using TCP against which measured using ICMP. In [9], the authors proposed a high precision active measurement method, and compared the delays measured using the proposed method against passive measurement. The authors of [12] proposed a TCP-based RTT passive measurement method and compared the measured RTTs with ping. In [10], the authors compared active and passive measurement methods on packet loss rate. The authors of [11] compared two different measurement implementations of one way delay and one way loss rate metrics, which both are based on UDP. These researches mainly focus on comparison of active and passive measurement methods or implementations, they do not deal with the comparison of results measured using TCP or ICMP.

In the appendix of [13], the authors compared the path minimum delays measured using TCP or ICMP, and found that they are highly correlative. The authors of [14] compared the packet loss rate measured using ping against real loss rate in the bottleneck router under TCP flow, the experiments are conducted under a single router connected mini IP network which is built by the authors. Although these researches are partially related to comparison of the results measured using TCP or ICMP, they only involve a single metric or are experimented on a single router.

3 Experiments Design

For comparing the difference of TCP and ICMP in network measurement, we designed two groups of comparison programs: host connectivity comparison program and RTT, loss rate comparison program. The experiments are mainly completed with four PCs which all located at a same LAN in the campus network of Hunan University, these four PCs have the same configuration with P4 1.4GHz CPU, 256 MB memory, and RED HAT LINUX7.2 operating system. We denote them as source host HNU1, to HNU4 in this paper. The probe packets size is 64 bytes. All experiments had been done from Jun. 18, 2004 to Sept. 14.

In addition, to validate whether the experimental results are related to the location of source hosts, we also select a PC located at the Institute of Software of the Chinese Academy of Science, to execute some experiment. We denote this PC as IOS1 in this paper. The results from HNU1- HNU4 and IOS1 show that the locations of source hosts have no effect on results, so we do not select more source hosts from the Internet to execute our experiments.

3.1 Measurement Progress

One of the most frequent used network measurement tools using ICMP is ping program, it measures based on ICMP Echo request/reply mechanism. The measuring process is shown in Figure 1. We denote the method that measures using ICMP Echo request/reply as Iping.

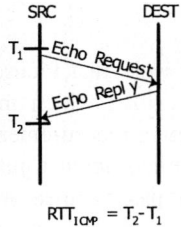
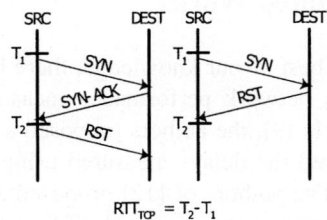

Fig. 1. The measurement process of ICMP   **Fig. 2.** The measurement process of TCP

In [5,7], the authors proposed another measurement method which based on TCP SYN/ACK, it makes use of the three-way handshake process of TCP. The measuring process is shown in Figure 2. One thing must be noted is that, when the source receives a SYN-ACK packet, it must send a RST packet to the destination to break down the established connection, to void continuous measurement process has been treated as a SYN-Flood attack by the destination, and refuses to respond the probe packet. We denote the method that measures using TCP SYN/ACK as Tping.

3.2 Connectivity Measurement Comparison Program

The processes of the program comparing connectivity results of TCP and ICMP are as follows: To a certain destination, the program first measures the host connectivity using Tping, then waits for a while, and measures the host connectivity using Iping. We use the connection rate calculated after measuring a lot of destination hosts to compare the differences of Tping versus Iping in connectivity measurement

3.2.1 Destination Host Sets Selection

The selection of destination hosts may affect the accuracy of comparison experiment. To find out the real difference of Iping and Tping in connectivity measurement, we build two destination host sets. One set is the top 500 websites from [15]. This set presents the difference of Tping and Iping in probing connectivity of web servers, and we denote it as TOP500 in this paper.

Beside the web servers, there still are a large number of other servers and clients on the Internet. To make the experiment more commonly, we need experiment more amounts and more types destination hosts. Then we collect 50,000 IP addresses or host names using the approach mentioned in [17] for comparison experiment, and we denote this host set as LARGE in this paper.

The experiment of LARGE set, if is executed by a single host, will persist 90 hours. The consumed time makes the experiment difficult. So we divide the LARGE set into four sub-sets, and execute one sub-set experiment on HUN1-HUN4 separately, to reduce the time needed for LARGE set experiment.

3.2.2 Setup of Test Parameters

Several parameters of the test program also may have effect on the experiment accuracy. The first parameter is the wait time t_{wait} between Iping and Tping probing. For network status keeps stable on the time scale of minutes [16], we set t_{wait} to 1 second. One similar parameter of the test program is the wait time between the probing of two different destination hosts, for the same reason, we set it to 1 second too.

Another parameter may affect the experiment accuracy is t_{out}, which means the duration the source wait for response after it send a Tping or Iping probe packet. To set a proper t_{out}, we first set t_{out} to 5 second, and measure the RTT of hosts in TOP500, most hosts have RTT no more than 2 second, so we set t_{out} to 3 second.

The last parameter may affect the experiment accuracy is c_{re}, the repeat probing times when the source received no answer. Analysis of results of RTT experiment discussed later show that, in the normal network status, the frequency of three continuous packets lost is tiny, so we set c_{re} to 3.

3.3 RTT and Loss Measurement Comparison Program

The processes of the program comparing RTT and loss rate results of TCP and ICMP are as follows: To a certian destination, the program first measures RTT using Tping, then waits for a while, and measures RTT using Iping, we denote the two probing as a probe packet pair; at last, the program waits 3 second and repeats the above process. If the source host gets no response after sending probe packet in a certain period, then it judges it detects a loss event.

4 Results Analysis

4.1 The Differences in Connectivity Measurement

4.1.1 Data Collection

We repeat connectivity comparison experiment many times. In every test, we record destination hosts count(h_{dest}), actually probed hosts count (h_{prb}), the amount of hosts which respond to both Tping and Iping(h_{both}), the amount of hosts only respond to Tping(h_{tcp}), the amount of hosts only respond to Iping(h_{icmp}), and the amount of hosts respond to none(h_{none}). We compare the difference of connectivity results measured using Tping and Iping by calculateting host connection rate of Tping and Iping. If we don't care about whether the hosts respond to neither Tping nor Iping are really inaccessible, the connection rate of Tping or Iping can be computed using formula (1) or formula (2), and we denote them as nominal connection rate.

$$R_{TCP} = (h_{both} + h_{tcp})/h_{prb} \times 100\% \tag{1}$$

$$R_{ICMP} = (h_{both} + h_{icmp})/h_{prb} \times 100\% \tag{2}$$

The nominal connection rate ascribes causes of hosts respond to neither Tping nor Iping to the protocols can't probe the host connection, this may underestimates the connection probing capability of Tping or Iping. In fact, these hosts are unaccessible even using web browser, i.e. these hosts real have connection problems, while it is not the protocols do not probe their connectivity. Reasonable comparison of the results must be based on the connectible hosts, So we must calculate the connection rate after exclude the really inaccessible hosts, using formula (3) or formula (4), we denote them as real connection rate.

$$TR_{TCP} = (h_{both} + h_{tcp})/(h_{prb} - h_{none}) \times 100\% \tag{3}$$

$$TR_{ICMP} = (h_{both} + h_{icmp})/(h_{prb} - h_{none}) \times 100\% \tag{4}$$

As discussed in section 3.2.2, the program parameters t_{out} and c_{re} may have effect on the results, we compound three parameters cases with different values of t_{out} and c_{re}, and repeat experiments under each case, to find out the proper parameters set for final comparison. The detailed compounding of parameters are as follows: Case 1 set

t_{out} to 3 second and c_{re} to 1; Case 2 set t_{out} to 3 second and c_{re} to 3; Case 3 set t_{out} to 5 second and c_{re} to 3.

4.1.2 The Effect of Test Parameters

Table 1 lists the real connection rate of TOP500 at HNU2 under different parameters cases; other source hosts have similar results. As can be seen from it, all the statistics of real connection rate measured under case 1 are lower than that measured under case 2 and case 3. In addition, the results measured under case 2 and case 3 are more stable than which measured under case 1. This indicates that small c_{re} actually makes the experiment results unstable and lower than the real conditions.

Furthermore, we also noticed that the results measured under case 2 and case 3 almost have no difference. This shows that, to do experiments under case 2 gets stable and accurate results and saves experiment time. So we only select the results measured under case 2 to analyze the differences of TCP and ICMP in the connectivity measurement on TOP500, and only do experiment under case 2 for LARGE set.

Table 1. The real connection rate measured on HNU2 for TOP500 under different parameter cases

Case	Test count	Mean TR_{TCP}	Max. TR_{TCP}	Min. TR_{TCP}	Mean TR_{ICMP}	Max. TR_{ICMP}	Min. TR_{ICMP}
Case 1	13	94.6	98.7	91.3	63.1	65.7	59.1
Case 2	17	99.0	99.8	98.0	65.0	66.0	63.7
Case 3	12	99.0	99.6	98.1	65.1	66.0	63.8

4.1.3 The Differences in Connectivity Measurement

Table 2 lists the final results of connection rate of TOP500, which measured under case 2. The actually probed hosts count (h_{prb}) is smaller than destination hosts count(h_{dest}), it is because some host name in the TOP500 can not been resolved by the DNS. The TR_{TCP} is about 99%, while TR_{ICMP} is only 65% around. This means that the connectivity measured using TCP is far more accurate than which measured using ICMP, For the TOP500 host set, the difference of them is 35% approximately. Even the nominal connection rate, which ascribes cause of hosts respond to neither Tping nor Iping to the protocols can't probe the host connection, Tping's is still upwards of 90%, which higher than Iping's with 30% nearly.

Table 2. The connection rate results for TOP500 set

Src host	h_{dest}	h_{prb}	Response				Connection rate (%)			
			h_{both}	h_{tcp}	h_{icmp}	h_{none}	R_{TCP}	R_{ICMP}	TR_{TCP}	TR_{ICMP}
HNU1	500	485	285	160	3	37	91.8	59.9	99.3	64.3
HNU2	500	486	285	156	6	39	90.7	59.9	99.0	65.0
HNU3	500	483	283	155	4	42	90.5	59.3	99.1	64.9
HNU4	500	484	287	158	4	35	91.9	60.1	99.1	64.8
IOS1	500	491	290	160	3	38	91.6	59.7	99.3	64.7

We also seen from Table 2 that, both the source hosts HNU1-HNU4 which locate at the same LAN and the host IOS1, have similar results, i.e. the experiment results are not related to the location of source hosts. Therefore, although the experiments are mainly completed at one place on the Internet, the conclusions are universal.

Table 3. The connection rate results for LARGE set

Test num.	h_{dest}	h_{prb}	Response				Connection rate (%)			
			h_{both}	h_{tcp}	h_{icmp}	h_{none}	R_{TCP}	R_{ICMP}	TR_{TCP}	TR_{ICMP}
1	50000	49104	36829	9034	231	3010	93.4	75.5	99.5	80.4
2	50000	49066	37446	8725	139	2756	94.1	76.6	99.7	81.2
3	50000	49125	36764	8774	276	3311	92.7	75.4	99.4	80.9
4	50000	49094	37324	8971	233	2566	94.3	76.5	99.5	80.7

The experiments of LARGE set repeat four times on source hosts HNU1-HNU4, the results are shown in Table 3. The connection rate of both TCP and ICMP increased more or less. But the connection rate of TCP is still higher than ICMP with 20% for TR_{TCP} and with 18% for R_{TCP}.

4.2 The Differences in RTT Measurement

4.2.1 Data Collection

In general, the mean RTT is a token of the performance baseline of a path at regular load. To find out the difference of RTT and loss rate measured using TCP or ICMP under different path conditions and host statuses, according to the RTTs of TOP500, and based on the subjective judgment, we divide the mean RTT into five levels, to present five kinds of typical path packet transmitting performance separately. Then, based on mean RTT to the host, we select two destination hosts for each level from TOP500 to measure their RTT and loss rate. The division of path performance level is shown in Table 4, the last row of it present the notations used for selected hosts at each level.

Table 4. Path performance level divisions

Performance Level	LEVEL1	LEVEL2	LEVEL3	LEVEL4	LEVEL5
RTT range	<30ms	30~100ms	100~900ms	0.9~1.5s	1.5~3.0s
Evaluation	Excellent	Good	Moderate	Bad	Poor
Host notation	L1A, L1B	L2A, L2B	L3A, L3B	L4A, L4B	L5A, L5B

The hosts in TOP500 usually have high load, to make the experiment general, we need some light loaded hosts in experiment. But it is not so easy to find such hosts on the Internet, through measuring, the mean RTT of the path from HNU1-HNU4 to IOS1 is about 246 ms, then we select IOS1 as a light loaded hosts at level 3. However, there are no light loaded hosts at the other performance levels, this may have some effects on the final comparison of RTT and loss rate measured using TCP and ICMP.

4.2.2 The Difference in RTT Measurement

We use measured mean RTT to compare the quantitive difference of RTTs measured using TCP and ICMP, the results are shown in Table 5. For small delay paths, the mean RTTs measured using Tping have no significant difference compared with which measured using Iping, but the IOS1 is an exception, with mean RTTs of Iping is larger than that of Tping with several millisecond. While for large delay paths, the mean RTTs measured using TCP is larger than which measured using Iping with tens of millisecond. The other statistics of measured RTT such as median, 25 percentile, 75 percentile etc. have similar characteristics, although the minimum RTTs of Tping and Iping are basically equal, as shown in Table 6, also with the exception of IOS1.

Table 5. Mean RTTs measured using Tping and Iping (ms)

Host	Tping	Iping	Host	Tping	Iping
L1A	7.4	8.1	L1B	22.1	22.5
L2A	37.8	37.3	L2B	66.9	67.5
L3A	274.1	273.6	L3B	255.4	255.9
L4A	1423.1	1262.5	L4B	1030.1	1014.8
L5A	2072.1	2051.9	L5B	2244.5	2222.5
IOS1	237.6	243.4			

Table 6. Minimum RTTs measured using Tping and Iping (ms)

Host	Tping	Iping	Host	Tping	Iping
L1A	2.74	2.78	L1B	3.43	3.41
L2A	26.59	26.71	L2B	29.57	29.53
L3A	48.6	48.5	L3B	33.9	34.2
L4A	23.77	23.79	L4B	37.65	37.32
L5A	27.61	27.55	L5B	57.43	57.52
IOS1	223.4	225.1			

The minimum RTT comprises of the fixed delays of the path, which presents the static performance of the path; while the mean RTT include the effects of the path loads and host loads at statistical meaning, which presents the dynamic performance of the path. The ratio of them can reflect the effect of path loads and host loads have on measured RTT in the rough, we define the ratio as RTT expanding ratio α as in formula (5).

$$\alpha = RTT_{mean} / RTT_{min} \tag{5}$$

Table 7 lists the α of every host for Tping and Iping. We can see from it, that small delay path has small α, while large delay path has α exceed 20.

Table 7. The RTT expanding ratio for the paths to destination hosts

	L1A	L1B	L2A	L2B	IOS1	L3B	L3A	L4B	L4A	L5B	L5A
Tping	2.7	6.4	1.4	2.3	1.1	7.5	5.6	27.4	59.9	39.1	75.0
Iping	2.9	6.6	1.4	2.3	1.1	7.5	5.6	27.2	53.1	38.6	74.5

Therefore, for the large delay path in experiment, the loads of path and destination host may have large effect on RTT measurement. In general, the routers give TCP packet higher transmitting priority, the effect of path on RTT measured using TCP should less than which measured using ICMP. While for the large delay path in experiment, the RTT measured using Tping is larger than which measured using Iping, it may because of that, the loads of destination host reach or exceed its process capability. In this situation, due to the process of TCP packet is more complicated than ICMP packet, the response of destination host to TCP packet will be slower than to ICMP packet. For the small delay paths in experiment, the loads of destination host are although high, while are still in the process ability of it, so there is little difference in the mean RTT measured using TCP and ICMP.

Based on Table 5-7, we can conclude that, for the path destined to light loaded host, the RTT measured using TCP will smaller than which measured using ICMP. While for the path to high loaded host, the quantitative relation of RTT measured using TCP and ICMP is determined by the RTT expand coefficient α, when α is smaller than 20, the RTT measured using TCP and ICMP are basically the same; if α is larger than 20, the RTT measured using TCP may larger than which measured using ICMP. For accurately measuring the path RTT, we can select the measuring protocols according to α, for the path have α smaller than 20, using TCP, when α is larger than 20, using ICMP.

4.2.3 Similarity in Statistics

Figure 3 shows the Tping and Iping RTT time series of the path to host L2A in 24 hours. The time serieses of RTT measured using Tping and Iing are very similar. In fact, this characteristic appears for almost all hosts in experiment, including IOS1, i.e. in the most case, Tping and Iping can measure the same RTT time series trend.

But this is not true for the path to host L4A. Figure 4 shows the Tping and Iping RTT time series of the path to host L4A in 24 hours. The RTT measured using Tping varied sharply along with time line; while the RTT measured using Iping are far more stable. We find that the path to L4A has large loss rate, for Tping, to 32%, Iping, 42%. This means that the path is very congested, however, the loss rate of the path to the last

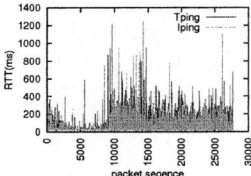

Fig. 3. One RTT time series for the path to L2A

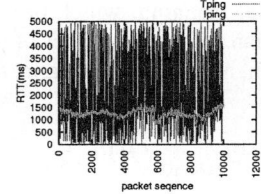

Fig. 4. One RTT time series for the path to L4A

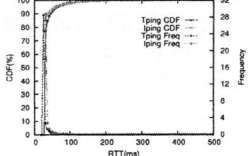

Fig. 5. The RTT CDF and frequency distribution of the path to L2A

router in the route to L4A, is only 7%. Then the high loss rate is due to that L4A host is overloaded. In the host, the process of TCP packet is more complicated than ICMP packet; when the host is overloaded, the response time of it to TCP packet varied sharply, while to ICMP packet keep relative stable, although with high loss rate.

The cumulate distribution function (CDF) and frequency distribution of RTT measured using Tping and Iping are also very similar, as an example, we show the RTT distributions of one measurement of the path to L2A in Figure 5. The CDF and frequency distribution curves of RTT measured using Tping and Iping are nearly superposed. All the other hosts, except L4A, have such characteristic too, i.e. at the normal case, Tping and Iping can measure very similar RTT distribution characteristics.

4.2.4 The Correlation Between RTT Values

To inspect whether the RTT measured using Tping and Iping in a packet pair is correlated, we also draw the scatter plot of the RTTs for consecutive Tping and Iping, and also calculate the correlation coefficient of them. Figure 6 is the RTT scatter plot of the measurement corresponding to Figure 3. It shows that the RTTs measured using TCP and ICMP in a packet pair are nearly not correlative. In fact, the correlation coefficient of RTT measured using Tping and Iping is only 0.034. Although the time series, CDF and frequency distribution are very similar for RTTs measured using Tping and Iping, they are not correlative in a packet pair.

To find out the cause of the lack of correlation between Tping and Iping in a packet pair, we slightly modified the test program, made it sends two TCP packets or two ICMP packets in a probe packet pair. Figure 7 shows the scatter plot of the case that both the packets in a probe packet pair are ICMP packets; the correlation coefficient of them is 0.041. The case of TCP has similar results. Therefore, the lack of correlation shown in Figure 6 occurs for the measurement method, and is not due to the protocols used in the measurement method.

While the minimum RTTs measured using Tping and Iping are strongly correlative. In Table 8, we list the correlation coefficient of minimum RTT measured using Tping and Iping in one-minute interval for all hosts we experimented.

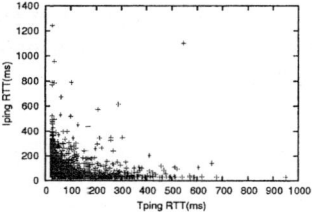 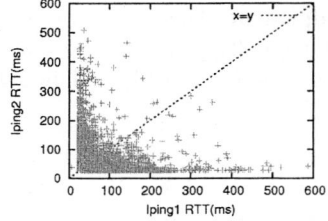

Fig. 6. The scatter plot of Tping RTT versus Iping RTT

Fig. 7. The scatter plot of RTT in an ICMP packet pair

Table 8. The correlation coefficient for minimum RTT measured using TCP and ICMP in a minute

	L1A	L1B	L2A	L2B	IOS1	L3A	L3B	L4A	L4B	L5A	L5B
R	0.74	0.81	0.78	0.76	0.85	0.81	1.0	0.60	0.67	0.71	0.74

4.3 The Difference in Loss Rate Measurement

The packet loss rate measured using Tping and Iping for all experimented hosts are listed in Table 9. For most destination hosts, the loss rate measured using Tping is very close to which measured using Iping. For the high loaded hosts with small path RTT, the loss rate measured using Tping is larger than which measured using Iping slightly; while if the path RTT is large, then the Tping measured loss rate is smaller than Iping measured slightly. But for the hosts have light loads, such as IOS1, although the RTT is relative small, the Iping measured loss rate is still larger than Tping measured with about 2%.

Table 9. Packet loss rate (%) measured using TCP and ICMP

	L1A	L1B	L2A	L2B	IOS1	L3B	L3A	L4B	L4A	L5B	L5A
Tping	0.56	2.58	1.22	0.59	1.67	0.76	2.43	4.21	31.6	3.75	10.2
Iping	0.52	2.56	0.92	0.53	3.02	0.95	2.65	4.87	42.9	3.96	10.6

5 Conclusions and Future Works

For quantitatively investigating the differences of network performance measured using TCP and ICMP, we have designed two groups of comparison tests, and done a large amount of experiments on the Internet, to find out the differences of TCP and ICMP when used to measure some basic network performance metrics such as host connectivity, RTT and packet loss rate. The experiment results show that, there really has difference, when using TCP or ICMP in network measurement.

The probe packet size is only set to be 64 bytes in our experiments, as the next steps, we will repeat the experiment with more packet sizes to find out whether the packet length has effect on the difference of TCP and ICMP when using in network measurement. We also plan to experiment more metrics on this problem.

Acknowledgement. This work was supported by National Natural Science Foundation of China under grant 60273070 and 60403031, it also was granted support from China Postdoctoral Science Foundation under grant 2005037114.

References

[1] V. Padmanabhan, J. Mogul: Improving HTTP latency. Computer Networks and ISDN Systems, 28(12): 25–35, 1995
[2] S. Floyd, M. Handley, J. Padhye: Equation-based congestion control for unicast applications. In Proceedings of ACM SIGCOMM '00, September 2000
[3] L. Breslau, P. Cao, L. Fan: Web caching and Zipf-like distributions: Evidence and implications. In Proceedings of IEEE INFOCOM '99, March 1999
[4] V. Paxson, G. Almes, J. Mathi: Framework for IP Performance metrics. RFC2330
[5] S. Savage: Sting: A tool for measuring one-way packet loss. In Proceedings of INFOCOM2000

[6] W. Matthews, L. Cottrel: The PingER project: Active Internet performance monitoring for the HENP community. IEEE Communications, 38(5):130--136, 2000
[7] M. Horneffer: Assessing Internet Performance Metrics Using Large-Scale TCP-syn Based Measurements. In Proceedings of Passive & Active Measurement Workshop (PAM'00), 2000
[8] M. Mathis: The Macroscopic Behavior of the TCP Congestion Avoidance Algorithm. Computer Communication Review, 27(3):44-57, 1997
[9] A. Pasztor. D. Veitch: A precision infrastructure for active probing. In Proceedings of Passive & Active Measurement Workshop (PAM'01), 2001
[10] Barford, Paul, Sommers: Comparing Probe- and Router-based Methods for Measuring Packet Loss. IEEE Internet Computing - Special issue on Measuring the Internet, Sept/Oct, 2004
[11] S. Kalidindi, M. Zekauskas, H. Uijterwaal: Comparing two Implementations of the IETF IPPM One-way Delay and Loss Metrics. In Proceedings of Passive & Active Measurement Workshop (PAM'00), 2000
[12] H. Jiang, C. Dovrolis: Passive Estimation of TCP Round-Trip Times. Computer Communication Review, 32(3):67-79, 2002
[13] Z. Wang. A. Zeitoun, S. Jamin: Challenges and Lessons Learned in Measuring Path RTT for Proximity-based Applications. In Proceedings of Passive & Active Measurement Workshop (PAM'03), 2003.
[14] S. Y. Wang:On comparing the real and probed packet drop rates of a bottleneck router: the TCP traffic case. Computer Communications, 26(6): 591-602, 2003
[15] http://www.alexa.com/
[16] Y. Zhang, N. Duffield, V. Paxson, S. Shenker: On the Constancy of Internet Path Properties. In Proceedings of Internet Measurement Workshop (IMW'2001), November 2001
[17] B. Krishnamurthy, J. Wang: On Network-Aware Clustering of Web Clients. In Proceedings of ACM SIGCOMM 2000, pp.97–110, Aug. 2000
[18] A. Acharya, J. Saltz: A study of internet round-trip delay. Univ of Maryland, Tech Rep. CS-TR-3736, 1996
[19] M. Allman, V. Paxson: On Estimating End-to-End Network Path Properties. In Proceedings of ACM SIGCOMM 1999, pp.263-274, 1999

Fuzzy Congestion Avoidance in Communication Networks

F. Habibipour, M. Khajepour, and M. Galily

Iran Telecommunication Research Center, Tehran, Iran
roudsari@itrc.ac.ir

Abstract. As an enhancement mechanism for the end-to-end congestion control, Active Queue Management (AQM) can keep smaller queuing delay and higher throughput by proposing fully dropping the packets at the intermediate nodes. comparing with RED algorithm, although PI controller for AQM designed by Hollot improves the stability, it seems other methods to design of robust controllers may lead to better results. Morover, the transient performance of PI controller is not perfect, such as the regulating time is so long. In order to overcome to this drawback, in this paper, a novel adaptive fuzzy logic based controller is designed for Active Queue Management (AQM) in TCP/AQM networks. From control point of view, it is rational to regard AQM as a typical regulation system. Recently many AQM algorithms have been proposed to address performance degradations of end-to-end congestion control. However, these AQM algorithms show weaknesses to detect and control congestion under dynamically changing network situations. A simulation study over a wide range of IP traffic conditions shows the effectiveness of the proposed controller in terms of the queue length dynamics, the packet loss rates, and the link utilization.

1 Introduction

A typical information exchange over the Internet is guaranteed by several intermediate nodes (routers) which direct packets originated by the sender to the receiver over links with limited bandwidths. Each router has a finite buffer for storing packets exceeding the total capacity of the link. When the packet net flow exceeds the buffer size the link becomes congested causing a so-called packet drop to occur. Namely, the packet is lost and the sender required to transmit it again.

TCP congestion control mechanism, while necessary and powerful, are not sufficient to provide good service in all circumstances, specially with the rapid growth in size and the strong requirements to Quality of Service (QoS) support, because there is a limit to how much control can be accomplished at end system. It is needed to implement some measures in the intermediate nodes to complement the end system congestion avoidance mechanisms. Active Queue Management (AQM), as one class of packet dropping/marking mechanism in the router queue, has been recently proposed to support the end-to-end congestion control in the Internet [1-5]. It has been a very active research area in the Internet community. The goals of AQM are (1) reduce the average length of queue in routers and thereby decrease the end-to-end delay experimented by packets, and (2) ensure the network resources to be used efficiently by reducing the packet loss that occurs when queues overflow. AQM highlights the tradeoff between delay and throughput. By keeping the average queue size small, AQM will have the ability to provide greater capacity to accommodate nature-occurring burst without dropping packets, at the same time, reduce the delays seen by flow, this is very particularly important for real-time interactive applications. RED [6,7] was originally proposed to achieve fairness among sources with different burst attributes and to control queue length, which just meets the requirements of AQM. However, many subsequent studies verified that RED is unstable and too sensitive to parameter configuration, and tuning of RED has been proved to be a difficult job [8-10].

Fuzzy logic controllers have been developed and applied to nonlinear system for the last two decades [11]. The most attractive feature of fuzzy logic control is that the expert knowledge can be easily incorporated into the control laws [12].

The intuition and heuristic design is not always scientific and reasonable under any conditions. Of course, since Internet is a rather complex huge system, it is very difficult to have a full-scale and systematic comprehension, but importance has been considerably noted. The mathematical modeling of the Internet is the first step to have an in-depth understanding, and the algorithms designed based on the rational model should be more reliable than one original from intuition. In some of the references, the nonlinear dynamic model for TCP flow control has been utilized and some controllers like PI and Adaptive Virtual Queue Algorithm have been designed for that [13-17]. In the research, we will apply a fuzzy controller to design the AQM system for congestion avoidance. The simulation results show the superior performance of the proposed controller in comparison with classic PI controller.

2 TCP Flow Control Model

In [13], a nonlinear dynamic model for TCP flow control has been developed based on fluid-flow theory. This model can be stated as follows

$$\frac{dW(t)}{dt} = \frac{1}{R(t)} - \frac{W(t)W(t-R(t))}{2R(t)} p(t-R(t)); \quad \frac{dq(t)}{dt} = \frac{N(t)}{R(t)} W(t) - C(t) \quad (1)$$

The definition of the parameters can be found in [2,13].

We believe that the AQM controller designed with the simplified and inaccurate linear constant model should not be optimal, because the actual network is very changeful; the state parameters are hardly kept at a constant value for a long time. Moreover, the equations (1) only take consideration into the fast retransmission and fast recovery, but ignore the timeout mechanism caused by lacking of enough duplicated ACK, which is very usual in burst and short-lived services.

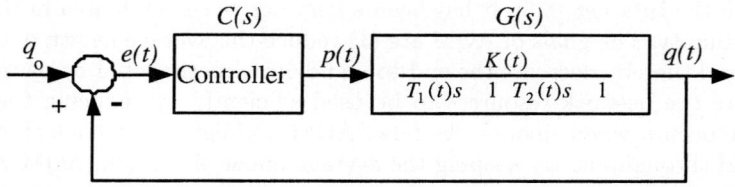

Fig. 1. Block diagram of AQM control system

In addition to, there are many non-respective UDP flows besides TCP connections in networks; they are also not included in equations (1). These mismatches in model will have negative impact on the performance of controller designed with the approach depending with the accurate model. For the changeable network, the robust control should be an appropriate choice to design controller for AQM. The above nonlinear and time-varying system was approximated as a linear constant system by small-signal linearization about an operating point [2,5,13] (Fig. 1), where

$$K(t) = \frac{[R(t)C(t)]^3}{[2N(t)]^2}; T_1(t) = R(t); T_2(t) = \frac{R^2(t)C(t)}{2N(t)} \quad (2)$$

To describe the system in state space form, suppose that $x_1 = e; x_2 = \frac{de}{dt}$, so the plant depicted in Fig. 1 is described by a second order system as

$$\frac{dx_1}{dt} = x_2; \quad \frac{dx_2}{dt} = -a_1 x_1 - a_2 x_2 - b + F \quad (3)$$

where

$$a_1 = \frac{1}{T_1 T_2}; a_2 = \frac{T_1 + T_2}{T_1 T_2}; b = \frac{K}{T_1 T_2}; F = \frac{d^2 q_0}{dt^2} + \frac{T_1 + T_2}{T_1 T_2}\frac{dq_0}{dt} + \frac{q_0}{T_1 T_2} \quad (4)$$

3 Design of Fuzzy Controller

Fuzzy logic control (FLC) has been demonstrated to solve some practical problems that have been beyond the reach of conventional control techniques. Fuzzy logic control is a knowledge-based control that uses fuzzy set theory, fuzzy reasoning and fuzzy logic for knowledge representation and inference [11,12]. The apparent success of FLC can be attributed to its ability to incorporate expert information and generate control surfaces whose shape can be individually manipulated for different regions of the state space with virtually no effects on neighboring regions.

In this paper, a fuzzy system consisting of a fuzzifier, a knowledge base (rule base), a fuzzy inference engine and defuzzifier will be considered. The knowledge base of the fuzzy system is a collection of fuzzy IF-THEN rules. Fuzzy logic control is ideal for the AQM problem, since there is no complete mathematical

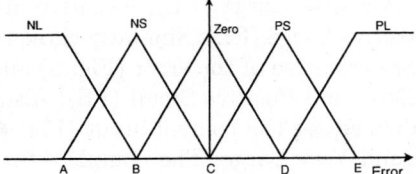

Fig. 2. Error membership function

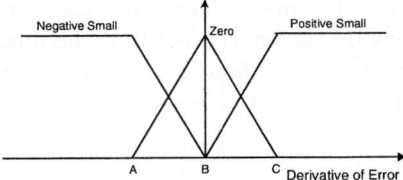

Fig. 3. Membership function for the derivative of Error

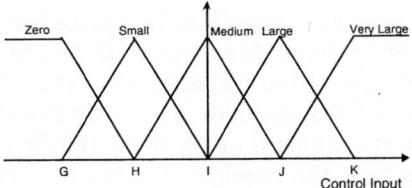

Fig. 4. Control input membership function

$\dot{e}$ \ e	NS	ZERO	PS
NL	ZERO	ZERO	ZERO
NS	SMALL	SMALL	SMALL
ZERO	ZERO	ZERO	ZERO
PS	SMALL	LARGE	MEDIUM
PL	MEDIUM	VERY LARGE	LARGE

Fig. 5. Fuzzy rules

model. However, human experience and experimental results can be used in the control system, design.

The controller has two inputs, the error (e) and its derivative ($\dot{e}$) and the control input (p). Five triangular membership functions are defined for speed error (Fig. 2), namely, Negative Large (NL), Negative Small (NS), Zero, Positive Small (PS), and Positive Large (PL). Similarly three triangular membership functions are defined for derivative of the error (Fig. 3) and there are as follows, Negative Small (NS), Zero, and Positive Small (PS). Also five triangular membership functions are defined for the control input (Fig. 4) and there are Zero, Small, Medium, Large and Very Large. The complete fuzzy rules are shown in Fig. 5. The first rule is outlined below

Rule 1: If (e) is PL AND $(\dot{x})$ is $Zero$, THEN (p) is $Large$.

The rest of the rules are derived similarly. The label names used here give an intuitive sense of how the rules apply. Through experimentation and tuning of the membership functions it was determined that the number of rules was sufficient to encompass all realistic combinations of inputs and outputs. This fuzzy logic controller is implemented using product inference and a center-average defuzzifier.

4 Simulation Results

The network topology used for simulation, is depicted in Fig. 6 [2,5]. The only bottleneck link lies between node A and node B. the buffer size of node A is 200 packets, and default size of the packet is 350 bytes. All sources are classed into three groups. The first one includes N_1 greedy sustained FTP application sources, the second one is composed of N_2 burst HTTP connections, each connection has 10 sessions, and the number of pages per session is 3. The thirds one has N_3 UDP sources, which follow the exponential service model, the idle and burst time are 10000msec and 1000msec, respectively, and the sending rate during "on" duration is 40kbps. We introduced short-lived HTTP flows and non-responsive UDP services into the router in order to generate a more realistic scenario, because it is very important for a perfect AQM scheme to achieve full bandwidth utilization in the presence of noise and disturbance introduced by these flows. The links between node A and all sources have the same capacity and propagation delay pair (L_1, τ_1) . The pair (L_2, τ_2) and (L_3, τ_3) define the parameter of links AB and BC, respectively.

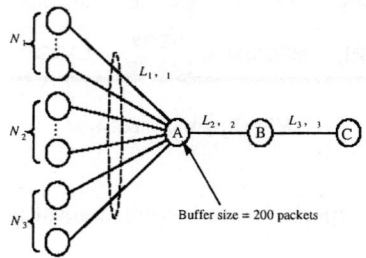

Fig. 6. The simulation network topology

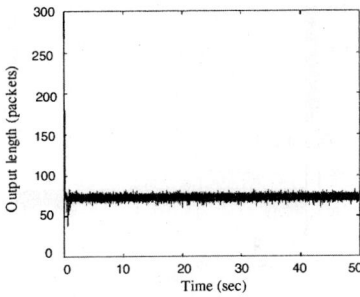

Fig. 7. Queue evaluation (FLC)

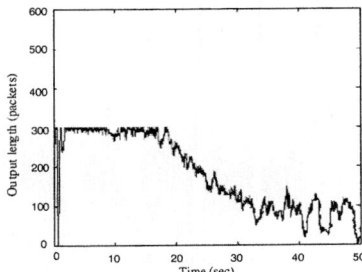

Fig. 8. Queue evaluation (PI)

In the first study, we will use the most general network configuration to testify whether the proposed Adaptive Fuzzy Logic Controller (FLC) can reach the goals of AQM, and freely control the queue length to stabilize at the arbitrary expected value. Therefore, given that $(L_1, \tau_1) = (10Mbps, 15ms)$, $(L_2, \tau_2) = (15Mbps, 15ms)$, $(L_3, \tau_3) = (45Mbps, 15ms)$, $N_1 = 270$, and $N_2 = N_3 = 0$. Let the expected queue length equal to 75 packets. The instantaneous queue length using the proposed FLC is depicted in Fig. 7. After a very short regulating process, the queue settles down its stable operating point. RED algorithm is unable to accurately control the queue length to the desired value [7,9]. The queue length varies with network loads. The load is heavier the queue length is longer. Attempting to control queue length through decreasing the interval between high and law thresholds, then it is likely to lead queue oscillation. To investigate the performance of the proposed FLC, we will compare the results with that of PI controller designed in [13]. The queue evaluation using PI controller is shown in Fig. 8. As it can be seen FLC acts much better that PI one.

Finally, we evaluate the integrated performance of the the proposed controller using one relatively real scenario, i.e., the number of active flows is changeable, which has 270 FTP flows, 400 HTTP connections and 30 UDP flows. Figs. 9 and 10 show the evaluation of queue controlled by FLC and PI controllers, respectively. It is clear that the integrated performance of FLC controller, namely

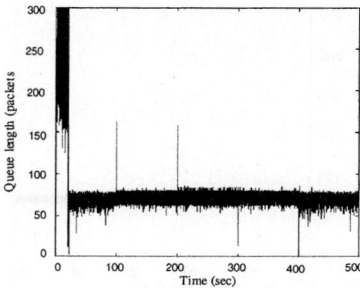

Fig. 9. Queue evaluation (FLC) for (FTP+UDP+HTTP) queue

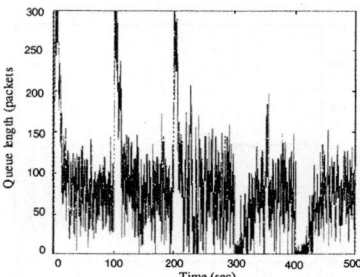

Fig. 10. Queue evaluation (PI) for (FTP+UDP+HTTP) queue

transient and steady state responses is superior to that of PI controller. The FLC controller is always keeping the queue length at the reference value, even if the network loads abruptly change, but PI controller has the inferior adaptability. In other words, the former is more powerful, robust and adaptive than the later one, which is in the favor of achievement to the objectives of the AQM policy.

5 Conclusion

In this paper, an adaptive fuzzy logic based controller was applied to TCP/AQM networks for the objective of queue management and congestion avoidance. For this purpose, a linearized model of the TCP flow was considered. We took a complete comparison between performance of the proposed FLC and classical PI controller under various scenarios. The conclusion was that the integrated performance of FLC was superior to that of PI one.

References

1. Barden, B. et al., Recommendation on queue management and congestion avoidance in the internet, REC2309, 1998.
2. Jalili-Kharaajoo, M., Application of robust fuzzy adaptive second-order sliding-mode control to active queue management, LNCS, 2957, 109-119, 2004.

3. S. Ryu, C. Rump and C. Qiao, A Predictive and Robust Active Queue Management for Internet Congestion Control, in Proc. ISCC'03, 2003.
4. S. Ryu, C. Rump, and C. Qiao. Advances in Internet congestion control. IEEE Communication Survey and Tutorial, 2002.
5. R. Fengyuan, et al., A Robust AQM algorithm based on Sliding Mode Variable Structure Control. in Proc. INFOCOM'2002, 21, 13-20, 2002.
6. Floyd, S. and Jacobson, V., Random early detection gateway for congestion avoidance, IEEE/ACM Trans. Networking, 1993.
7. C. V. Hollot, V. Misra, D. Towsley, and W. Gong. A control theoretic analysis of RED. in Proc. of INFOCOM'2001, 1510-1519, 2001.
8. Firoiu, V. and Borden, M., A study of active queue management for congestion control, in Proc. INFOCOM, 2000.
9. May, M., Bonald, T. and Bolot, T., Analytic evaluation of RED performance, in Proc. INFOCOM, 2000.
10. S. Floyd and V. Paxson. Difficulties in simulating the Internet, IEEE/ACM Transactions on Networking, 9(4), 392-403, 2001.
11. Zadeh, L.A., Fuzzy sets, Inf. Control (1965), 338-353.
12. Jalili-Kharaajoo, M., Improvement of second order sliding mode control applied to position control of induction motors using fuzzy logic, LNAI, 2715, 2003.
13. Misra, V., Gong, W.B. and Towsley, D., Fluid-based analysis of network of AQM routers supporting TCP flows with an application to RED, in Proc. ACM/SIGCOMM, 2000.
14. Hollot, C., Misra, V., Towsley, D. and Gong, W.B., On designing improved controllers for AQM routers supporting TCP flows, in Proc. INFOCOM, 2001.
15. Misra, V., Gong, W.B. and Towsley, D., Analysis and design an adaptive virtual queue (AVQ) algorithm for active queue management, in Proc. ACM/SIGCOMM, 2001.
16. Kelly, F.P., Maulloo, A. and Tan, D., Rate control in communication networks, Journal of the Operation Research Society, 49, 237-252, 1998.
17. Athuraliya, S., Lapsley, D.E. and Low, S.H., Random early marking for internet congestion control, in Proc. Globecom, 1999.

A New Method of Network Data Link Troubleshooting

Qian-Mu Li[1,2], Yong Qi[1], Man-Wu Xu[2], and Feng-Yu Liu[1]

[1] Nanjing University of Science and Technology, Computer Science Department,
210094 Nanjing, China
{liqianmu, houxiaozhu, liu.fengyu }@126.com
[2] Nanjing University, Computer Science Department,
210093 Nanjing, China
liqianmu@126.com,
liu.fengyu@263.net

Abstract. On the basis of analyzing the evolution and drawbacks of current network fault diagnosis methods, a novel network data link troubleshooting system (NDTS) based on fuzzy neural network is proposed. NDTS tightly combines neural network and rough sets, so that it can be used to fit the smooth curves perfectly. Let the membership function as the base, an rule scavenging method is put forward in NDTS, which is the variable-precision modal, and the notion of variable-precision be founded on the measurement of dependent degree. Furthermore, NDTS is adopted to deal with the mapping relation, categorizing the network faults. The experiment system implemented by this method shows the proposed system is an open and efficient troubleshooting engine.

1 Introduction

Due to the rapid growth in computer networks and the fast evolution in technology, the need for a more efficient and effective network management approach becomes more urgent. Today's networks are commonly put together by integrating equipment from multiple vendors. Consequently, management of such networks is becoming a more important and more difficult task. Due to various reasons, the network, or a portion of the network, can become disabled, or its performance can be degraded to an unacceptable level. In applications, when end-to-end network performance is guaranteed, many network entities need to be managed simultaneously. With larger networks, network management cannot be managed by human efforts alone. The complexity of such a network requires the use of automated network management tools. A considerable effort has been made to standardize network management protocols and develop network management systems, such as the Simple Network Management Protocol and the Common Management Information Protocol. However, there is much to be done towards formally specifying problems in network management and developing formal techniques to solve these problems. Many neural network applications can be found in network troubleshooting, most of which adopt 3-layer back propagation neural network (BPN) [1-4]. Those complicated BPNs contain severe localization. The more complicated of those models are, the weaker the generalization is, and at the same time the real-time computing ability also will descend. The representative causations are as follows:

- The convergence speed of these algorithms is too slow to fit on-line diagnosis;
- There are local optimization problems in most of the circumstances;
- The structural of the network is so indeterminate that we are difficult to get hold of the ideal model.

So, more effective analysis and solution techniques are needed. Leading the rough-fuzzy neural network into network data link troubleshooting, this paper proposed a novel method: NDTS. NDTS is good at solving indetermination problem and self-study ability.

2 The Network Troubleshooting Strategy

Network data link state can be classified: adding attribution, multiply attribution and min-max attribution. For some section of network P$(E_1, E_2, \cdots, E_{s-1})$, in which E be the states of network entities, if $e_{i,i+1} \in E_i$ (i=1,2,... S-1), define the j property of $e_{i,i+1}$ as $f_{i,i+1}^j$, and define the j property of the whole net-segment P as f_p^j, we get hold of the definitions as follows:

(1) adding attribution: If $f_p^j = \sum_{i=1}^{s-1} f_{i,i+1}^j$, name the j property of P a adding attribution, such as receive-datagram number, send-datagram number, jump number, delay time, delay tingle, cost, etc.

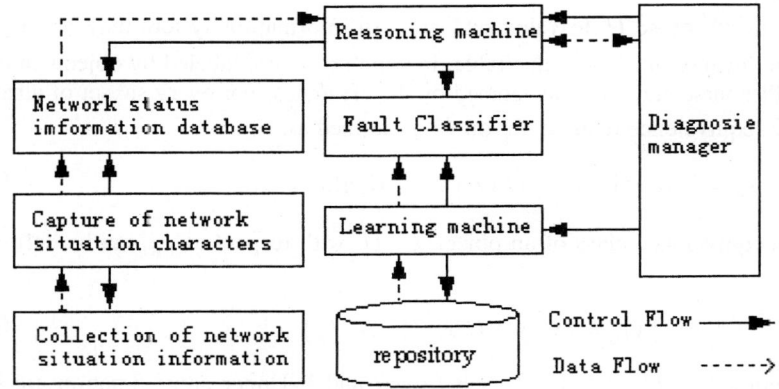

Fig. 1. The architecture of NDTS: (1) Collection of network situation information: Catch the attributed-values of network entities. (2) Capture of network situation characters: Without uniform form, network information needs to take the pretreatment, which maps original data to cognizable disperse state that is the capture operation of network situation characters. (3) Network status information database: The data in it can be used for data mining, and get some new potential fault modes. (4) Learning machine: Through training, the system gets neural network classifier for fault classification. (5) Fault classifier: the core unit of the system. (6) Reasoning machine: It is mostly used for assorting with (3) and (4). (7) Diagnosis manager: It provides interface with responsibility for the whole troubleshooting system.

(2) multiply attribution. If $f_p^j = \prod_{i=1}^{s-1} f_{i,i+1}^j$, name the j property of P a multiply attribution, such as error rate, losing rate, node utilization rate, etc.

(3) min-max attribution. If $f_p^j = \min_{i=1,2,...,s-1} \{f_{i,i+1}^j\}$, name the j property of P a min attribution, such as fluff rate, fee, etc. If $f_p^j = \max_{i=1,2,...,s-1} \{f_{i,i+1}^j\}$, we name it a max attribution, such as port utilization rate, flux, bandwidth, etc.

The essence of network data link troubleshooting is to capture a set of situation information on network entities, and deduce the fault reason or fault equipments. So that fault diagnosis is a kind of mapping from the situation information to the type of fault.

NDTS is composed by the building of normal situation database and detection. The process is shown by figure1.

2.1 Rule Scavenging

In network fault circumstance we can only get some sample data, but no rules. As rules are the foundation of constructing NDTS, how to acquire rules becomes the focus. This chapter tries to solve this problem using a novel approach.

Let an information system $K = (U, C, D)$ be an fault decision system, where U is a non-empty finite set, called the domain of discourse, C is a non-empty set that contains condition attributes, and D is a non-empty set which consists of decision attributes. Let $A = C \cup D$, attribute a ($a \in A$) can be regarded as a function from the domain of discourse U to value set Val_a. An information system may be represented in the form of attribute-value table, in which rows are labeled by objects in the domain of discourse and columns labeled by the attributes. For every subset of attributes $B \subseteq C$, equivalence relation I_B on U is defined as:

$$I_B = \{(x, y) \mid (x, y \in U) \wedge (\forall a \in B, a(x) = a(y))\} \quad (1)$$

Then the equivalence class of an object $x \in U$ with respect to I_B can be defined as:

$$[x]_B = \{y \mid y \in U \wedge (x, y) \in I_B\} \quad (2)$$

Given subset $X \subseteq U$, $B \subseteq C$, X's B-Lower and B-Upper approximation are be defined as:

$$\underline{B}(X) = \{x \mid x \in U \wedge [x]_B \subseteq X\}; \overline{B}(X) = \{x \mid x \in U \wedge [x]_B \cap X \neq \Phi\} \quad (3)$$

Suppose U is partition into m classes $\{x_1, x_2, ..., x_m\}$ by equivalence relation defined on D. Given any class $x \in \{x_1, x_2, ..., x_m\}$, all objects belonging to and not belonging to it are numbered with subscripts $i(i = 1, 2, ..., \gamma)$ and $j(j = 1, 2, ..., \rho)$, respectively. The decision matrix $M(K)=(M_{ij})$ of K is defined as a $\gamma \times \rho$ matrix ($(M_{ij})=\{(a_l,a_l(x_i))\mid a_l \in C \wedge a_l(x_i) \neq a_l(x_j)\}$), whose entry at position (i,j) is a set of attribute-value pair. To a given object $i(i=1,2,...,\gamma)$ belong to class $x \in \{x_1,x_2,...,x_m\}$; we can compute its minimal-length decision rule: $\mid B_i \mid = \bigcap_j \bigcup M_{ij}$. Here $\bigcap$ and $\bigcup$ are generalized interaction and union operator. So for the given class $x \in \{x_1,x_2,...,x_m\}$, its decision rule set can be represents as: $RUL = \bigcup \mid B_i \mid, (i=1,2,...,\gamma)$.

There is no problem when extract decision rules from consistent information table using the method described above. However, when the information table is inconsistent, how can we extract rules? To solve the problem, we first give two definitions:

Definition 1: Certain Decision Matrix of Concept c. Label the element in $\underline{B}(c)$ with i ($i=1,2,...,n$), and the element not in $\underline{B}(c)$ with j ($j=1,2,...,m$). Then the certain decision matrix of concept c in K is $M_c^{certain}(k)=(M_{ij}^{certain})$. The value in cell (i,j) is an attribute-value pair, defined as follows:

$$M_{ij}^{certain} = \{(a_l, a_l(x_i)) \mid a_l \in C \wedge a_l(x_i) \neq a_l(x_j)\} \tag{4}$$

Definition 2: Possible Decision Matrix of Concept c. Label the element in $\overline{B}(c)$ with i ($i=1,2,...,p$), and the element not in $\overline{B}(c)$ with j ($j=1,2,...,q$). Then the possible decision matrix of concept c in K is $M_c^{possible}(k)=(M_{ij}^{possible})$. The value in cell (i,j) is an attribute-value pair, defined as follows:

$$M_{ij}^{possible} = \{(a_l, a_l(x_i)) \mid a_l \in C \wedge a_l(x_i) \neq a_l(x_j)\} \tag{5}$$

From definition 1 and 2, we can extract certain and possible rules from inconsistent rules as follows:
(1) Rules extracted from certain decision rules of c are certain rules:

$$RUL_{certain}^c = \bigcup_i \mid B_i^c \mid_{certain}, (i=1,2,...,n) \tag{6}$$

(2) Rules extracted from possible decision rules of c are certain rules:

$$RUL_{possible}^c = \bigcup_i \mid B_i^c \mid_{possible}, (i=1,2,...,p) \tag{7}$$

2.2 Neural Network Model of NDTS

A lot of literature has proceeded with the research of fuzzy logical neuron model [8]-[10], especially in 2001 Glorennec put forward the concept of weak T/ S norm, which looses the constraint of associative law in T norm in order to make some controllable operation combination with simple form as and/or operation. He also constructed a kind of neuron model based on weak T/ S norm cluster. We improve his model, so that it could realize not only weak T/ S norm cluster, but also both equivalence operation and sequential average operation, which meet the requirement of data link fault prediction. Let $A'_1 \otimes A'_2 \otimes \cdots \otimes A'_n (u_1, u_2, u_n) = \bigwedge_{i=1}^{n} g_i(A'_i(u_i))$, in which g_i content $g_i(1) = 1$ in [0, 1]. The elasticity of every rule: $g_1, g_2, \cdots, g_n$ is set on through its importance. Let $(u_{1k}, u_{2k}, \cdots, u_{nk}) \in U_1 \times U_2 \times \cdots \times U_n$, where $u_{ik} \in U_i, k = 1, 2, \cdots, L$, $|U_1 \times U_2 \times \cdots \times U_n| = L$. The neuron model is shown in Fig. 2.

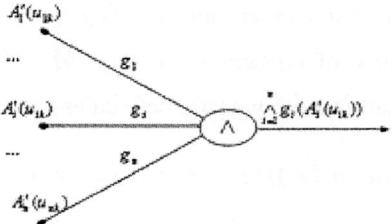

Fig. 2. The basic neuron of $A'_1 \otimes A'_2 \otimes \cdots \otimes A'_n (u_{1k}, u_{2k}, u_{nk}) = \bigwedge_{i=1}^{n} g_i(A'_i(u_{ik}))$

In order to make rendering neural network chart easier, we take fig. 3 to replace fig. 2 as a simple form.

$$A'_1(u_{1k}), \cdots, A'_n(u_{nk}) \bullet \!\!\!-\!\!\!-\!\!\!-\!\!\!-\!\!\!-\!\!\!-\!\!\!- \bigcirc g$$

Fig. 3. The simple form of the neuron

We design the neural network shown as figure 4.

Suppose $R_{(k)(j)} = R(\bigwedge_{i=1}^{n} g_i(A_i(u_{ik})), B(v_j))$, based on fig.4, we get

$$B'(v) = \bigvee_{(u_{1k}, \cdots, u_{nk})} \{p_1(v)[\bigwedge_{i=1}^{n} g_i(A'_i(u_{ik})) \wedge R(\bigwedge_{i=1}^{n} g_i(A_i(u_{ik})), B(v))] + p_2(v)[\bigwedge_{i=1}^{n} g_i(A'_i(u_{ik})) \vee R(\bigwedge_{i=1}^{n} g_i(A_i(u_{ik})), B(v))]\}, \text{ where } v \in V.$$

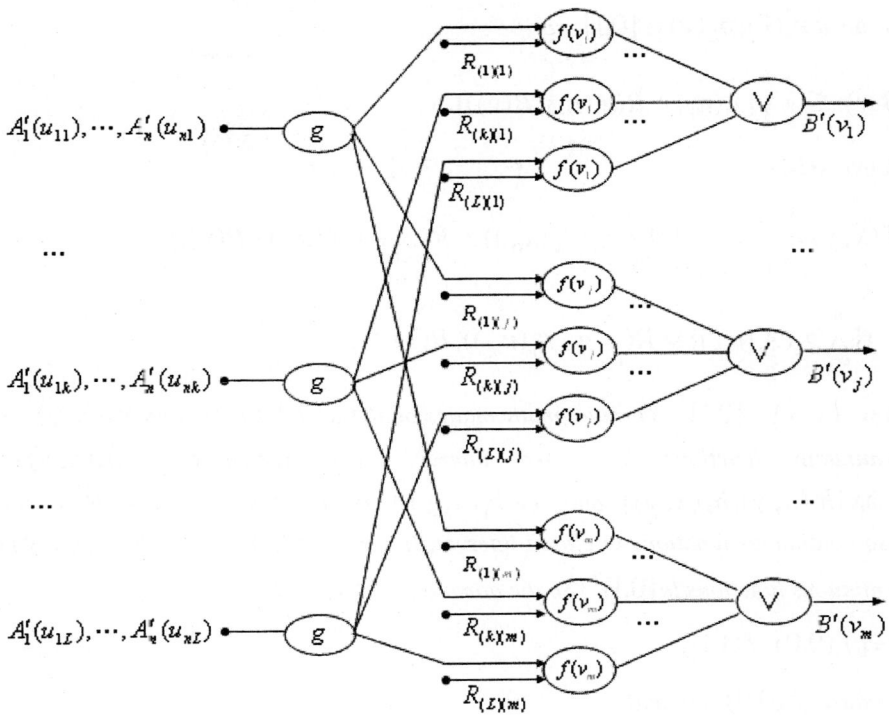

Fig. 4. Neural network structure for network data link fault prediction

Let $p_1(v) = 1$ $p_2(v) = 0$ $g_i(A_i(u_{ik})) = A_i(u_{ik})$, then
$$B'(v) = \bigvee_{(u_{1k},\cdots,u_{nk})} [\bigwedge_{i=1}^{n} A'_i(u_{ik}) \wedge R(\bigwedge_{i=1}^{n} A_i(u_{ik}), B(v))].$$
Distinctly, above is the CRI form of Zadeh now.

Consistency of consequence

Let $A_1 \otimes A_2 \otimes \cdots \otimes A_n \to B$ be a known rule, $R(A, B)$ be discretional implication relation. When training the neural network in fig4, always be $p_1, p_2 \in F(V)$, if $A'_i = A_i$, then $\forall v \in V$, $B' = B$ iff
$$B(v) \leq \bigvee_{(u_{1k},\cdots,u_{nk})} [\bigwedge_{i=1}^{n} g_i(\ (A_i(\ u_{ik})) + R(\bigwedge_{i=1}^{n} g_i(A_i(u_{ik})), B(v))].$$

Proof First, if $A'_i = A_i$, $\exists\ p_1, p_2 \in F(V)$, which makes $B' = B$. That is,
$$B(v) = \bigvee_{i=1}^{n} \{p_1(v)[A(u_i) \wedge R(A(u_i), B(v))] + p_2(v)(A(u_i) \vee R(A(u_i), B(v))]\}.$$

Because $p_1(v), p_2(v) \in [0,1]$, so

$$B(v) \leq \bigvee_{i=1}^{n}[A(u_i) + R(A(u_i), B(v))].$$

Conversely,

$$f(x,y) = \bigvee_{(u_{1k},\cdots,u_{nk})} \{x[\bigwedge_{i=1}^{n} g_i(A_i(u_{ik})) \wedge R(\bigwedge_{i=1}^{n} g_i(A_i(u_{ik})), B(v))]$$

$$+ y[\bigwedge_{i=1}^{n} g_i(A_i(u_{ik})) \vee R(\bigwedge_{i=1}^{n} g_i(A_i(u_{ik})), B(v))]\}.$$

Now, $(x,y) \in [0,1]^2$. Through mathematics analysis: if $h_1(x,y)$ and $h_2(x,y)$ are continuous functions in closed interval, then $\min\{h_1(x,y), h_2(x,y)\}$, $\max\{h_1(x,y), h_2(x,y)\}$ and $a \times h_1(x,y) + b \times h_2(x,y)$ ($a, b \in R$) are also continuous functions in closed interval. It is not difficult to find that $f(x,y)$ is continuous functions in $[0,1]^2$. So the domain of $f(x,y)$ be:

$H = [f(0,0), f(1,1)]$.

Because $f(0,0) = 0$, and

$$f(1,1) = \bigvee_{(u_{1k},\cdots,u_{nk})} \{[\bigwedge_{i=1}^{n} g_i(A_i(u_{ik})) \wedge R(\bigwedge_{i=1}^{n} g_i(A_i(u_{ik})), B(v))]$$

$$+ [\bigwedge_{i=1}^{n} g_i(A_i(u_{ik})) \vee R(\bigwedge_{i=1}^{n} g_i(A_i(u_{ik})), B(v))]\}$$

$$= \bigvee_{(u_{1k},\cdots,u_{nk})} [\bigwedge_{i=1}^{n} g_i((A_i(u_{ik})) + R(\bigwedge_{i=1}^{n} g_i(A_i(u_{ik})), B(v))]$$

So if $0 \leq B(v) \leq \bigvee_{(u_{1k},\cdots,u_{nk})} [\bigwedge_{i=1}^{n} g_i((A_i(u_{ik})) + R(\bigwedge_{i=1}^{n} g_i(A_i(u_{ik})), B(v))]$, obeying continuous function interpose-value theorem $\exists$ (p_1', p_2') leads to $f(p_1', p_2') = B(v)$, then let $p_1(v) = p_1'$, $p_2(v) = p_2'$. For the randomicity of v, it always $\exists$ $p_1(v)$ and $p_2(v)$, which hold reasoning results $B' = B$, when $A_i' = A_i$.

2.3 Network Data Link Fault Prediction

Using NDTS to single-step forecast, we choose the structure with two inputs and one output. Carve inputs variable into seven fuzzy subsets: {NL, NM, NS, ZO, PS,

PM, PL}, which express negative large, negative middle, negative small, zero, positive small, positive middle and positive large respectively.

Original partition is shown as figure 5. The value of x is disposed through normalization. So we get hold of 49 fuzzy rules, marking R:

R1: if x1 is NL, x2 is NL, then y1= $C_0^1 + C_1^1 x_1 + C_2^1 x_2$

R2: if x1 is NL, x2 is NM, then y2= $C_0^2 + C_1^2 x_1 + C_2^2 x_2$

...

R49: if x1 is PL, x2 is PL, then y49= $C_0^{49} + C_1^{49} x_1 + C_2^{49} x_2$

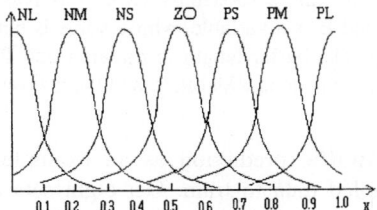

Fig. 5. Subjection function before training: x1 and x2 mean the node loading of the former two time segments (Ti-2, Ti-1) (Ti-1, Ti) at time of Ti. Let the network desired output be B^d, then output error be $J = \frac{1}{2}(B^d - B)^2$.

3 Simulation and Analysis

According to Gabarit approximation [6-7], data flow could be represented by continuum condition discrete time AR Markov model. If we let $\lambda(n)$ express the bit rate of No.n packets, then one rank AR Markov equation is shown as follows by the using of recursion relation:

$$\lambda(n-1) = l \cdot \lambda(n) + m \cdot \varpi(n) \tag{8}$$

l and m are influence genes. Following experience, we can evaluate l =0.8781, m =0.1108. $\varpi(n)$ is the independence gauss white noise sequence, and its mean is 0.572, its variance is 1[5]. Every node loading could be expressed by the formula:

$$L = \sqrt{\sum_{i=1}^{n}(k_i a_i^2)} \tag{9}$$

In the formula, L represents the loading value of local node; $a_1, a_2, ..., a_n$, are loading targets; $k_1, k_2, ..., k_n$, are weights.

The simulation environment in this paper is NS2. Figure 6 presents the network topology of simulation experiment.

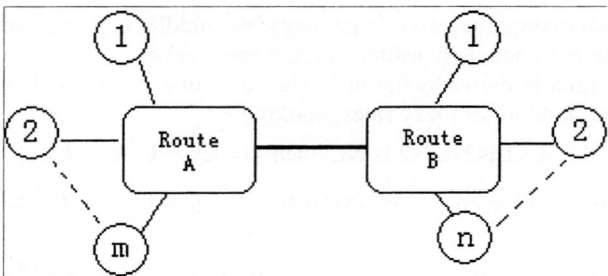

Fig. 6. Simulation network topology: Design a share bottleneck connection A and B in the topology, and the bandwidth of link is 100Mbit/s. Other link bandwidths are all 5Mbit/s. The link delay between node A and B is a variable, whose value is between 10ms and 300ms. Let packets length be 1024bytes. The buffer length in router A and B are all 40M. m=n=40. The send-velocity minimum of every node is 300kbits/s, and the maximum is 1500kbits/s.

We choose data link traffic prediction as an example. Set sampling cycle be 40ms, and get 400s sampled data to train. Get eight sets at random once more. In each sets, 320s data is to test. Based upon these hypothesis and parameter, the result of training is shown as figure 7. The figure 8 exhibits the subjection function curve after training.

The results of comparing BPN with the neural network of NDTS are shown in table 1. The first row represents TSE (total squared error), and the second and the third row represent iteration degree, when BPN or the neural network of NDTS reach corresponding TSE. We also can hold MSE (mean square error, MSE=TSE/400). From table 1, we can find that convergence rate of the neural network of NDTS is more quickly than BPN in evidence, and the neural network of NDTS could gain wee TSE and MSE in tolerable iteration degree.

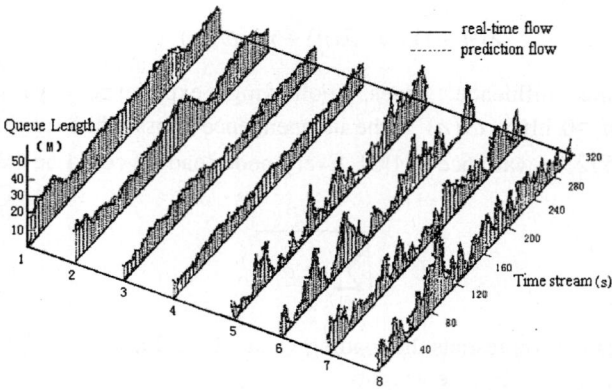

Fig. 7. Prediction result of node data flow

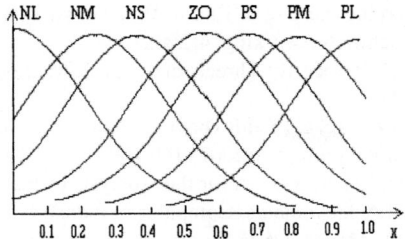

Fig. 8. The subjection function after training

Table 1. Iteration degrees of BPN and the neural network of NDTS

TSE	BPN	the neural network of NDTS
2.43	238	58
2.23	633	69
2.03	13232	81
1.83		95
1.63		118

4 Conclusion

The network troubleshooting with NDTS is provided with several advantages as follows:

(1) It is not necessary to establish accurate mathematical model. Making use of its powerful self-learning function, it is able to obtain features by rule and line with appropriate training.

(2) The parallel-distributed frame of neural network is fit for multi-info amalgamation and multimedia technique. It may integrate the fixed and qualitative information robustly.

(3) Neural network is easy to be implemented by VLSI hardware or software simulation. Once succeeding in training, the network would attain high response velocity, which is fit for the real-time requirement of high-speed net.

NDTS is combined by neural network and rough-fuzzy logic. This strategy is propitious to catch the flow features with mutative time exactly. Because the weight of network is adjustable, this strategy can satisfy the consistency requirement of fuzzy consequence for any implication relation $R(A, B)$. The experiment shows that it is effective to the adjustment of network rate and the of loss rate reduction. The strategy could show extensive adaptability with the adjustment of weight.

References

1. Jacobson V.: Data Link Fault Avoidance and Control. IEEE/ACM Transaction Networking, 3 (1998) 314–329
2. Caserri C, Meo M.: A New Approach to Model the Stationary Behavior of TCP Connections. In: Tel Aviv. (eds.): IEEE Computer Society, Proc IEEE INFOCOM2000, Israel, CA(2000) 245–251

3. Floyd S, Fall K.: Promoting the Use of End-to-End Network Troubleshooting in the Internet. IEEE/ACM Transaction Networking, 4(2002) 458–472
4. Harris B, Hunt R.: TCP/IP Security Threats and Attack Methods. Computer Communications, 10(2002) 885–897
5. Skoundrianos E N, Tzafestas S G.: Fault Diagnosis via Local Neural Networks. Mathematics and Computers in Simulation , 60 (2002) 169–180
6. Bullell P, Inman D.: An Expert System for the Analysis of Faults in an Electricity Supply Network: Problems and Achievements. Computer in Industry, 37 (1998) 113–123
7. Tagliaferri R, Eleuteri A, Meneganti M, Barone F.: Fuzzy Min-Max Neural Network: from Classification to Regression. Soft Computing, 5 (2001) 69–76
8. Gavalas D, Greenwood D, Ghanbari M.: Advanced Network Monitoring Applications Based on Mobile/Intelligent Agent Technology. Computer Communications, 23 (2002) 720–730
9. Li Q M, Qi Y, Zhang H, Liu F Y.: New Network Fault Diagnosis Method Based on RS-Neural Network. Computer Research and Development, 10(2004) 1696–1702
10. Li Q M, You J, Zhang H, Liu F Y.: Research and Design of a Data link User's Safeguard Strategy. Journal of Beijing University of Aeronautics and Astronautics, 11(2004) 1029–1032

Ethernet as a Lossless Deadlock Free System Area Network

Sven-Arne Reinemo and Tor Skeie

Simula Research Laboratory, P.O.Box 134, N-1325 Lysaker, Norway
`{svenar, tskeie}@simula.no`

Abstract. The way conventional Ethernet is used today differs in two aspects from how dedicated system area networks are used. Firstly, dedicated system area networks are lossless and only drop frames when bit errors occur, while conventional Ethernet drop frames whenever congestion occur. Secondly, these networks are either deadlock free or use mechanisms which avoids deadlock situations, while still using all available links. Ethernet avoids deadlocks by using a spanning tree protocol which turns any topology into a tree. A drawback of this approach is that we are left with a lot of unused links and thus wasting resources.

In this paper we describe how to obtain a lossless deadlock free network with the best possible performance, while adhering to the current Ethernet standard and using off-the-shelf Ethernet equipment. We achieve this by introducing flow control in all network nodes and by taking control over the routing algorithm. Also, we use TCP to illustrate the effect of flow control on higher layer protocols.

Through simulations we verify the following tree improvements. Firstly, the activation of flow control turns Ethernet into a lossless network. Secondly, taking control over the routing algorithm allows us to build any topology without the limitations of the spanning tree protocol. And thirdly, an overall improvement in throughput is achieved by combining these enhancements.

1 Introduction

For a long time Ethernet has been the dominating local area network standard. The introduction of 1 Gigabit Ethernet has further strengthened this position, while the recent introduction of 10 Gigabit Ethernet has made it more attractive in system and wide area networking. Furthermore, the recent effort for Backplane Ethernet will allow Ethernet to be used in server and I/O backplanes in the future. Ethernet has also gained popularity in the automation world [1–3], and wireless Ethernet has in a short time become the technology of choice for mobile computing. All things considered, Ethernet is truly on its way to become omnipresent. Still, there are some fields that have not yet fully embraced Ethernet, fields such as high performance computing, cluster computing and system area networks [4, 5]. These areas are still using a variety of technologies such as Fibre Channel [6], InfiniBand [7], Myrinet [8], and Scalable Coherent Interface [9]. These technologies are all niche products compared to Ethernet, something which makes them more expensive to produce, acquire and maintain. If Ethernet could be used in these environments huge savings would be possible with regards to both acquirement and maintenance costs.

The way conventional Ethernet is used today differs in two aspects from how dedicated system area networks are used. Firstly, dedicated system area networks are lossless and only drop frames when bit errors occur. Conventional Ethernet drop frames whenever congestion occurs. Secondly, these networks are either deadlock free or use mechanisms which avoid deadlock situations, while still using all available links. As conventional Ethernet allows frame dropping deadlock has not been a problem traditionally.

In Ethernet technology the issue of lossless networking was solved with an extension to the standard in 1997. This extension adds control frames and on/off type flow control to Ethernet [10], making lossless Ethernet a reality. Several contributions have studied the effect of Ethernet flow control on TCP congestion control and how TCP benefits from link layer flow control [11–14]. Furthermore, W. Noureddine et al. have proposed several improvements to the current mechanism by increasing the flow control granularity from port based to source/destination based [13, 15]. Common for all of the above studies is that they only consider simple scenarios with one or two switches.

The second problem with conventional Ethernet is how to handle deadlocks. When we introduce flow control and disallow frame dropping the possibility for deadlock appears in topologies with loops [16, 17]. Ethernet solves this by using a spanning tree protocol which turns any topology into a tree. This is done by disabling links until we are left with a tree, and since a tree contains no loops we have no deadlock potential. A drawback of this approach is that we are left with a lot of unused links and thus wasting resources. In many local area networks this might not be a severe problem, but with system area networks we want efficient topologies and we want to use every link to achieve the best performance possible. Then the spanning tree protocol is no longer a valid solution. A lot of research has been done on deadlock avoidance in general [16, 17] , but few of these techniques can be applied to Ethernet. And deadlock avoidance in Ethernet itself has received little attention. The only work we are aware of is by M. Karol et al., where they suggests a deadlock prevention scheme for Ethernet [18]. They have a novel approach, but with the drawback of changing the semantics of the Ethernet pause frame and adding extra housekeeping to the switches. This makes it incompatible with current off-the-shelf Ethernet equipment.

Several other contributions have studied Gigabit Ethernet as a cluster technology and compared it with technologies such as Myrinet. These contributions have shown Ethernet to be a feasible alternative as long as a suitable messaging system is used [19–22]. But none of these contributions have considered how to use Ethernet as a lossless and deadlock free architecture in a topology independent manner. Furthermore, most of these studies are limited to only a handful of nodes connected through one or two switches.

The objective of this paper is to show how to obtain a lossless deadlock free network with the best possible performance, while adhering to the current Ethernet standard and using off-the-shelf Ethernet equipment. We achieve this by introducing flow control in all network nodes and by taking control over the routing algorithm. Flow control puts the congestion control into the network allowing the network to signal end nodes when congestion occurs. This in turn makes the network lossless. Taking control over the routing algorithm lets us avoid deadlock and leverage the performance increase that regular topologies such as meshes and tori allows. Furthermore, we also model TCP to illustrate the effect of flow control on reliable transport protocols.

In Sect. 2 we discuss flow control in general and Ethernet flow control in particular. In Sect. 3 we review some deadlock prevention techniques and deadlock free routing schemes. In Sect. 4 we combine these two building blocks to a scheme capable of supporting high performance Ethernet in system area networks. We continue with a brief description of our simulation environment in Sect. 5 and an evaluation of our results in Sect. 6. Finally, in Sect. 7, we conclude.

2 Flow Control

In a system area network (SAN) environment the loss of frames is unacceptable in most situations. And Ethernet without flow control is unable to satisfy this requirement as Fig. 3(a) clearly shows. There is a large increase in frame loss as network load increase. At an injection rate of 300 Mb/s almost 90% of all frames are dropped. To remove frame loss we need to make sure that the sender never swamps the receiver with more frames than it can buffer. We achieve this with the use of flow control. Flow control puts the control of network congestion back into the network by letting the network itself signal the end nodes whenever congestion occurs. This stands in contrast to the way most link layer technologies in the Internet works, where the end nodes themselves, in the form of TCP, must be well-behaved and try to detect and avoid congestion.

2.1 On/Off Flow Control

To achieve flow control we need a way to inform the upstream nodes about our buffer situation. In on/off flow control this is done by simple on/off messages. When the downstream node have available buffer space it sends an *on* message to the upstream node telling it to start sending frames if any are available. As the transmission proceeds and the downstream node runs out of buffer space it sends an *off* message telling the upstream node to halt frame transmission. For this scheme to work we must make sure that these messages are sent in a timely manner. When the downstream node sends an off message it must do it at a point in time where it has enough space to buffer frames received while it waits for the off message to take effect. There will be a delay between the transmission and the activation of the off message due to the propagation and processing delay for the off message. According to [16] the buffer requirements and trigger values can be calculated as follows[1]:

$$F \geq F_{\text{on}} + \frac{t_{\text{rt}}b}{L_{\text{f}}} \geq F_{\text{off}} + \frac{t_{\text{rt}}b}{L_{\text{f}}} \geq \frac{2t_{\text{rt}}b}{L_{\text{f}}} \tag{1}$$

Here F is the total buffer space, F_{on} the number of buffers triggering the on message, F_{off} the number of buffers triggering the off message, t_{rt} the propagation and processing delay for a frame, b the link bandwidth, and L_{f} the frame size. The minimum number

---

[1] The formula shown is for frames while the original is for flits. The end result is the same as mentioned in [16] Sect. 13.3 page 245.

Table 1. Minimum buffer requirements for Gigabit Ethernet flow control

Allotment	Bits
Frame on transit	12,336
Frame on receive	12,176
Pause frame	512
Pause frame decode	1024
Propagation delay (10m UTP)	114

of buffers needed to allow full speed operation is $2t_{rt}b$. We need $t_{rt}b$ bytes to make sure we have buffers available to receive data sent after the off message was sent, but before it was received and processed at the other end. We need another $t_{rt}b$ bytes to make sure we have data to send while we wait for an on message to be received and processed at the other end. If we want to further reduce the number of on/off messages sent at the cost of more buffers, we can increase the number of buffers used for F, F_{on} and F_{off} according to the formula.

2.2 Ethernet Flow Control

When flow control was added to Ethernet the concept of *control frames* was introduced for the first time in Ethernet technology. Currently, there is only one flow control scheme specified and this is an on/off approach similar to the one described in the previous section. Here a *pause frame* is used to communicate the on/off messages. A pause frame is a special instance of the control frame shown in Fig. 1. According to the standard a pause frame must have the MAC control opcode set to 0x0001 and a MAC control parameter consisting of a 2 byte field called the *pause time*. The pause time P means the time the upstream node must wait before sending the next frame. This time is measured in 512 *bit-time* increments, where the bit-time B is the time it takes to send a single bit. For Gigabit Ethernet B equals 1 ns which gives P a range of 0–33.6 ms in 512 ns increments. A pause time P with a value of zero equals an *on* message and overrides any earlier pause times. A P between 1 and 255 equals an *off* message lasting $P \times B$ bit-times. As time passes the pause time will eventually expire, this is a safety measure to avoid permanently pausing a link if the on message should be lost. If the situation persists, however, we must refresh the pause by sending another pause frame.

As the exact algorithm to trigger the pause frame mechanism is unspecified, it is up to the individual vendors to find their own solutions. In our approach we use a threshold function to trigger the transmission of pause frames and a timer to check if the pause should be refreshed. This timer is a countdown to the expiration of the last pause frame transmitted. If the timer reaches zero and the current port is still congested, we have to resend the pause frame telling the upstream node to extend its pause time.

The threshold function is tightly connected to the minimum buffer space we need to avoid dropping frames and to keep the link running at full speed as described in (1). With the numbers from Table 1 we get the following buffer requirements when we replace $\frac{t_{rt}b}{L_f}$, F_{on} and F_{off} with 4566 bytes:

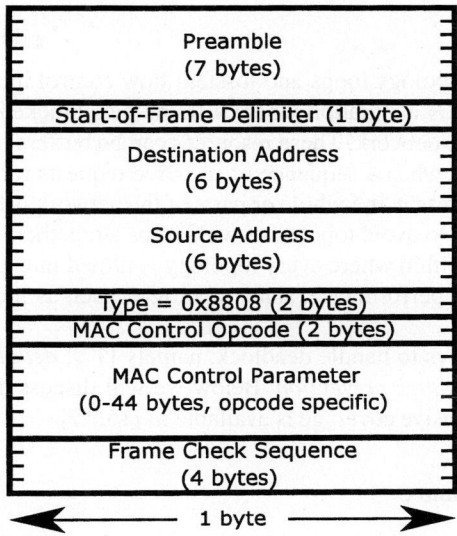

Fig. 1. MAC control frame format

$$F \geq 2 \times 4566 \tag{2}$$

These 4566 bytes consist of the fields in Table 1 described as follows: *Frame on transit* is a frame that has just been flushed for transmission when flow control has been activated on the sender side. This frame must be completed before we can send the pause frame. *Frame on receive* is a frame that has just been flushed for transmission when we have decoded the pause frame on the receiver side. We must finish transmission of this frame before we pause the link. *Pause frame* and *pause frame decode* is the time it takes to send and decode a pause frame respectively. The *propagation delay* is the delay over 10 meters of unshielded twisted pair for Gigabit Ethernet. All together this makes up 3270 bytes, but since we only buffer complete frames we round this upwards to three maximum-length Ethernet frames which equals 4566 bytes. Thus, the minimum buffer space necessary for full speed operation becomes:

$$F \geq 9132 \text{ bytes} \tag{3}$$

As we try to minimise buffer space we set $F_{\text{on}} = F_{\text{off}}$. This gives us a total of 9132 bytes for each port and a pause frame trigger at 4566 bytes.

The granularity of Ethernet flow control is per port, thus the upstream node can be told to stop frame transmission when the downstream node runs out of buffer space without affecting traffic on any other ports. The effect of increasing and decreasing flow control granularity is studied in [13]. The main conclusion being that increasing flow control granularity to act on source/destination pairs further improves performance. In this paper we assume port based flow control as this is the level of flow control that is supported by the Ethernet standard.

3 Deadlock

The combination of topology loops and lossless flow control introduce a potential for deadlock. A deadlock is a situation where a frame gets blocked forever because of a resource conflict in the network. These resources can be buffers or links in the network and a deadlock occurs when a sequence of resource requests form a cycle. When this happens forward progress in the whole or parts of the network is halted. To avoid deadlocks we could choose to avoid topologies with loops altogether, which is the case with the spanning tree algorithm where every topology is turned into a tree. But this is a bad option with regards to performance, since topologies such as meshes and tori contain lots of loops.

There are three ways to handle deadlock, namely [17]: *deadlock avoidance*, *deadlock recovery* and *deadlock prevention*. Below we will discuss deadlock avoidance in Ethernet. A more extensive coverage is available in [16, 17].

3.1 Deadlock Avoidance

Deadlock has been thoroughly studied in other network architectures where the use of flow control is the default practise [23, 16, 17]. One popular way of achieving deadlock avoidance is through the use of deadlock free routing algorithms. Such algorithms are either topology *dependent* or topology *agnostic*. Topology dependent algorithms are used for regular topologies where the regularity is exploited to improve the routing efficiency, while topology agnostic algorithms make no assumptions about the topology. They can be used for both regular and irregular networks. Topology dependent algorithms gives the best results with regards to performance, but they are more sensitive to topology changes. A faulty switch in a regular topology will degrade it into an irregular topology and then a topology dependent algorithm will fail. Topology agnostic algorithms will not have this problem.

One of the most well known topology agnostic routing algorithms is *Up*/down** [24]. Up*/down* can be used with any topology and it does not require virtual channels. This makes it suitable for a wide range of network technologies, including Ethernet. Up*/down* is a spanning three based routing algorithm that works in two steps. First it creates a breadth-first spanning tree of the topology to be used. Next it assigns either an *up* or *down* direction to each link in the topology. For host-to-switch links the *up* end is the switch end and for switch-to-switch links the *up* end is the end closest to the spanning tree root. Now packets can be routed deadlock free as long as we follow the up*/down* rule [24]: "a packet may never traverse a link in the *up* direction after having traversed one in the *down* direction."

For topology dependent routing one of the simplest and most popular options is *dimension-order* routing [17]. This algorithm is applicable to n-dimensional meshes and hypercubes, and works by crossing dimensions in strictly increasing order. E.g. in a 2-D mesh we would first route along the x-dimension until we reach the correct x-coordinate, then we would route along the y-dimension until we reach the destination.

More efficient routing algorithms exist, but as we limit ourselves to algorithms that can be used with the current Ethernet standard we cannot use algorithms that require functionality such as virtual channels. We end up with a deadlock avoidance scheme consisting of up*/down* and dimension-order routing. Both these algorithms allow us to use all available links in a network, compared to only a small subset (a tree) of links with the STP. Both up*/down* and dimension-order routing outperform STP, and when combined with flow control we have a high performance lossless network architecture.

Up*/down* and dimension-order routing can be used with most of the *managed* Ethernet switches available today. There are only two requirements, the switch must allow manual configuration of the MAC address table and it must support address entries which consider both destination and input port when forwarding frames[2].

In [18] Karol et al. propose a lossless deadlock avoidance scheme using advanced buffer management. Their scheme has a novel approach where the deadlock avoidance mechanisms is independent of the routing algorithm. The drawback is that it changes the semantics of the Ethernet pause frame and requires additional control logic for buffer handling. This makes it incompatible with current off-the-self Ethernet equipment.

4 Switch Architecture

Every switch needs an internal interconnect to allow the external connections to communicate with each other through the switch. This *switching fabric* can be designed in many ways. Three alternatives widely used in commercial switches are shared bus, shared memory and crossbars [25]. The switch model used in our evaluation has a shared memory architecture using store and forward switching.

4.1 Switch Organisation

We have modelled our switch as a shared memory architecture. Shared memory was chosen because it reduces the effect of head of line blocking. In a crossbar approach this must be dealt with specifically. Shared memory is also the most deployed switch architecture in current equipment [25].

Our switch model is shown in Fig. 2. It has a shared memory used to exchange frames between ports, and each port have a dedicated lookup engine to allow for distributed address lookup. The output port lookup is completed before the frame is stored in shared memory, but it would also be possible to store the frame before or in parallel with the lookup. Then the frame could be updated with the output port information when the lookup is complete. On the output side each output port has a FIFO queue for outgoing frames. This queue is implemented as pointer table to the corresponding frames in the shared memory. When an output queue is ready to transmit a frame it follows the pointer at the front of the queue, transmits the frame and frees the memory previously occupied by the frame. In order delivery is ensured by using links among packets received through the same input port.

4.2 Buffer Organisation

To combine our shared memory architecture with flow control we have divided our memory in global and local partitions. The global partition is common for all ports

---
[2] With dimension-order routing only the destination address is needed so even a wider range of equipment can be used.

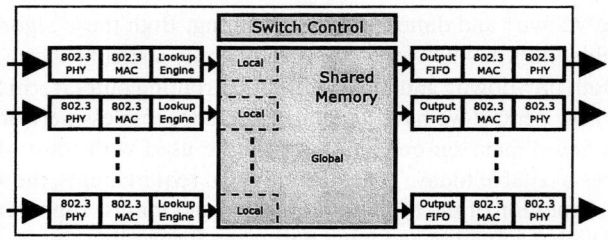

Fig. 2. Switch Architecture

(*global memory*), while the local partition (*local memory*) is dedicated to a single port (Fig. 2). The global memory is where frames are stored when there is no severe congestion in the switch. If short term congestion occurs the amount of global memory will be able to handle this without activating flow control, i.e. global memory is not subject to flow control. In case of long term congestion the global memory will be filled by frames destined for the congested port. As this happens additional frames destined for the congested port must use the local memory that belongs to the input port of the frame. Furthermore, as the local memory fills up flow control will be activated on this port. This scheme allows ports without frames destined for a congested port to continue operation as normal. To a certain extent it also removes head of line blocking from the ports with frames destined for a congested port, but as the local memory is filled no more progress can be made on this port until congestion resolves. This could be avoided if we, for each input port, had a local memory for each output port.

Flow control is triggered by the use of local memory as described in Sect. 2.2. As the local memory is filled a threshold function triggers the transmission of pause frames according to (3). With the current Ethernet standard per port flow control is the highest granularity allow. Improved performance is possible by increasing the flow control granularity to act on source address. This has been studied in [13].

5 Simulation

We have built our own Ethernet simulator in the JSim environment. JSim is a Java based environment for development of network simulation models [26]. Our simulator implements a shared memory architecture and Ethernet flow control as described in previous sections.

We have studied both regular and irregular topologies where each switch has a total of eight Gigabit Ethernet ports. The first four ports are used for host connections and the last four ports are used for network connections. Furthermore, each switch has a total of 146112 bytes of memory. Where the first half (73056 bytes) is global memory and the other half is local memory. The local memory is divided equally on the 8 ports for a total of 9132 bytes for each port.

We have evaluated networks with 16 and 32 switches, which amounts to 64 and 128 nodes respectively. The irregular topologies consist of 16 randomly generated topologies, while the regular topologies consist of one 4x4 mesh, one 8x4 mesh, one 4x4 tori and one 8x4 tori. Due to lack of space only results from topologies with 32 switches are presented here.

Our traffic model have a Poisson arrival rate with an increasing average rate and a fixed frame size of 1522 bytes. We use a traffic pattern with a uniform destination addresses distribution. Each simulation is run for 5 seconds of real time on each topology with 12 load levels increasing from 5%–100% load. The average throughput and latency is then calculated from the observed results.

6 Evaluation

Our evaluation consists of three routing schemes on both regular and irregular topologies with the major performance properties being throughput, latency and frame loss. We also consider TCP throughput and latency as a means to evaluate the effect of flow control on reliable transport protocols.

6.1 Throughput

For Ethernet performance we ran the spanning tree protocol (STP) and up*/down* (UD) routing on a set of irregular topologies. And for regular topologies we ran UD and dimension order routing (DOR) on a 8x4 torus and a 8x4 mesh respectively. We have also studied TCP performance in combination with UD routing, DOR and flow control. TCP in combination with STP was left out due to the poor performance of STP. The results for irregular topologies are presented in Fig. 3(a) and 3(b). The x-axis show the amount of traffic that each node is trying to send in Mbit/s, the left y-axis shows the average per node receive rate in Mbit/s, and the right y-axis shows the frame loss in Mbit/s. The frame loss for TCP is left out as the actual loss is negligible due to TCP's built in congestion avoidance mechanism. The actual packet loss with TCP when flow control is disabled (not shown) is in the order of tens of kilobytes while for Ethernet it is several megabytes (Fig. 3(a)).

Fig. 3(a) shows us that UD enabled Ethernet achieves more than tree times the throughput of conventional Ethernet when flow control is disabled. UD gives a per node throughput of 131 Mbit/s compared to 39 Mbit/s for STP. These data rates, however, are only of theoretical interest since the frame loss is so high. Figure 3(a) shows that an injection rate of 300 Mbit/s results in a 60% frame loss for UD and 88% frame loss for conventional Ethernet. Few applications are usable under such conditions, something the TCP results in Fig. 3(b) shows. Here the achieved throughput when running TCP over Ethernet without flow control is only 55 Mbit/s, which is less than half the throughput we measured on Ethernet with UD routing. This decrease in throughput happens because TCP use sliding windows and retransmissions to achieve a reliable service with in order delivery of packets. And it is a good example of the retransmission penalty that any application requiring a reliable transport layer will run into when trying to use Ethernet without flow control as in the UD scenario above. Even if we are allowed to inject a lot of frames most of them are wasted since they will either be dropped or retransmitted. The benefits of reducing retransmissions are larger than the benefits of blindly increasing the injection rate as we shall see below.

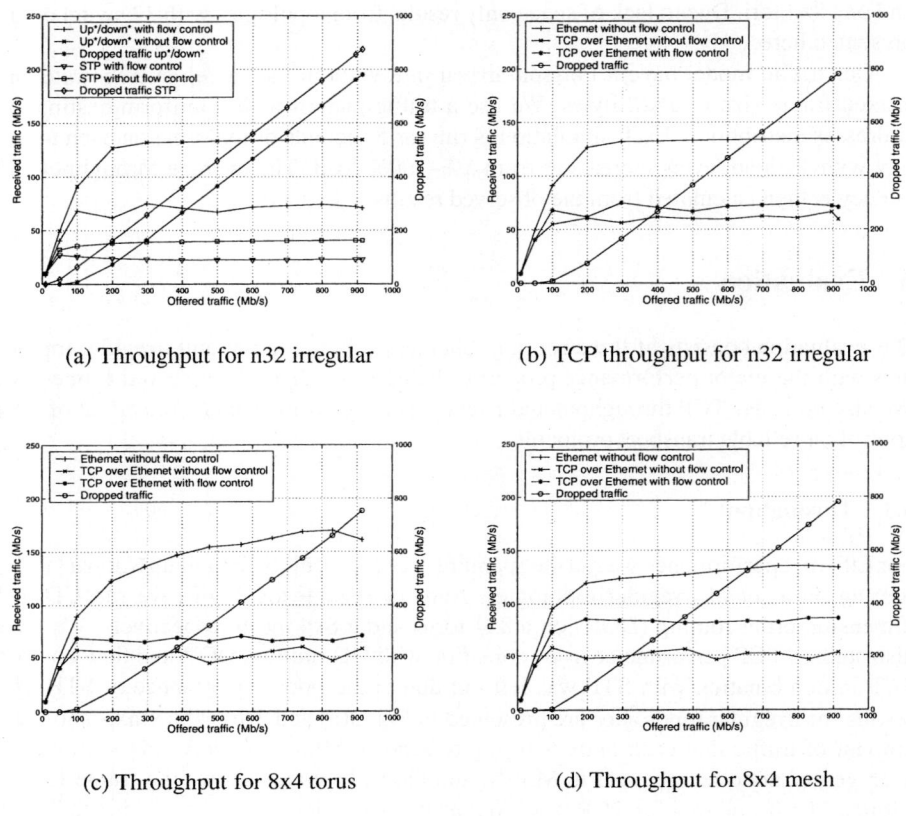

Fig. 3. Throughput

To improve performance we enable flow control. The new achieved throughput, now with zero frame loss, is 65 Mbit/s for UD and 21 Mbit/s for STP (Fig. 3(a)). When the network saturates, the end nodes are throttled since the switches in the network run out of buffer space. Throttling is achieved by pausing links in the network as described in Sect. 2.2. Thus, as more links in the network enters a paused state, the pause state propagates to the end nodes and reduced the number of frames injected into the network. The achieved throughput for TCP is now 65 Mbit/s compared to 55 Mbit/s without flow control. Which shows that the introduction of flow control has improved TCP throughput by 18% even if the Ethernet throughput has been reduced from 131 Mbit/s to 65 Mbit/s (Fig. 3(a)). TCP throughput is increased since we no longer drop frames, meaning that the TCP congestion mechanism is never activated. Every frame we inject arrives at its destination and there is never need for any retransmissions, this leads to increased throughput from the applications point of view even if the Ethernet injection rate has been reduced. With flow control we inject less frames, but every frame is useful. Without flow control we inject a lot of frames, but only a few of them are useful.

For regular topologies we obtain even better results, when we introduce flow control, compared to irregular topologies. With TCP the throughput is about 50 Mbit/s on both the torus and the mesh without flow control. When we enable flow control the TCP throughput increase by 30 % to 65 Mbit/s on the torus and by 60 % to 80 Mbit/s for the mesh. Again we see an increase in TCP performance even if the Ethernet injection rate is reduced. The 8x4 torus with UD routing and no flow control achieves a throughput of 160 Mbit/s, when we enable flow control this is reduced to 65 Mbit/s (Fig. 3(c)). For the 8x4 mesh with dimension-order routing throughput is slightly lower with 130 Mbit/s and when flow control is enabled this is reduced to 80 Mbit/s (Fig. 3(d)). It is easy to be seduced by these seemingly good numbers for Ethernet without flow control, but the truth is that the frame loss and the resulting retransmission rate leads to very poor performance for applications, something the TCP numbers confirms.

The large difference between the torus and mesh is due the different routing algorithms. The UD algorithm is unable to utilise the extra connectivity that is present in the torus due to its vulnerable to congestion around the root of the UD tree when flow control is enabled. This weakness of the UD algorithm is studied in [27]. DOR on the other hand is tailored to exploit the regularity of the mesh topology and handles the situation much better. The improvement in TCP follows from the reduction in packet loss as discussed earlier. In addition to the removal of frame loss TCP also benefits from the improvement in the routing algorithm. DOR is known to be better than UD routing, as can be seen in the differences between the torus and the mesh (Fig. 3(c) and 3(d)).

6.2 Latency

We present latency results for both Ethernet and TCP simulations to see how they differ when flow control is enabled and disabled. For irregular networks latency is increased with a factor of 2.5, from $1000\,\mu s$ to $2500\,\mu s$, when flow control is enabled and STP is used (Fig. 4(a)). For UD routing latency is just about doubled, from $700\,\mu s$ to $1300\,\mu s$, when flow control is enabled. The use of UD routing gives lower latency and higher throughput since it can use all links in the network.

The increase in latency that we observe when flow control is enabled is expected, and is due to the back pressure created by the pause frame mechanism. When links are paused data frames must wait in buffers along the path from source to destination, where they, in case of no flow control, would have been dropped. It is this waiting that causes the growth in latency. The worst case scenario is that a frame will wait at every hop towards its destination, resulting in a large increased in latency.

If we compare latency at the Ethernet and TCP level we see that there is almost no difference when flow control is enabled, and a large difference when flow control is disabled. When flow control is enabled TCP latency is only slightly higher than Ethernet latency because the only difference is the protocol overhead in the end nodes[3]. When we disable flow control we see an increase in TCP latency compared to Ethernet

---

[3] The latency introduced by the protocol stack in the end node can be large. As we are concentrating on the features of the network infrastructure the end node complexity has not been studied in detail. For more information on this topic please refer to [2, 19, 20, 21]

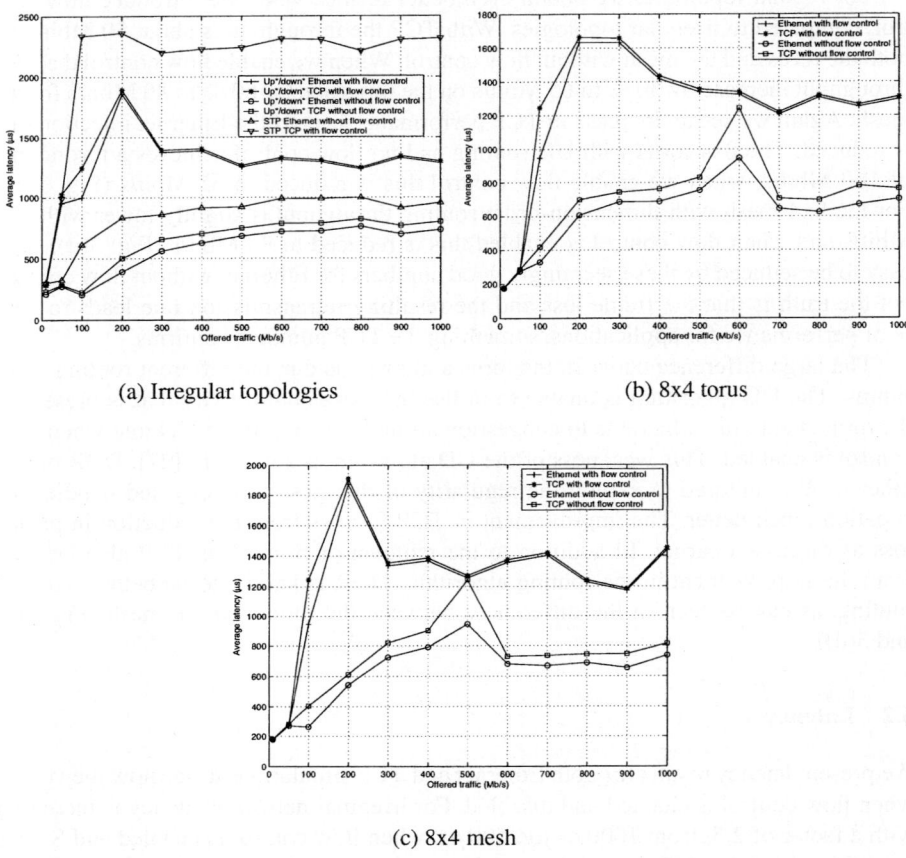

Fig. 4. Latency

latency. This increase is caused packet loss. Packet loss triggers the TCP retransmission mechanisms and this affects latency in the same way we saw it affect throughput in the previous section. Thus, the introduction of flow control increase throughput, but at the cost of also increasing latency.

The behaviour for regular topologies is very similar to that of regular topologies. When we enable flow control both the 8x4 torus and the 8x4 mesh see a doubling of latency from $750\,\mu s$ to $1400\,\mu s$ (Fig. 4(b) and 4(c)). The results are very similar even though the torus has a higher connectivity than the mesh. This is again due to DOR and its ability to exploit the regularity of the mesh topology better than UD routing is able to exploit the torus. When we consider TCP latency we see the same differences between TCP and Ethernet latency as for irregular topologies.

For applications where low latency is important further actions must be taken to improve latency. Possible solutions are admission control and Ethernet priorities combined with DiffServ, which have been effective with other technologies [28, 29].

7 Conclusion

We have shown how it is possible to use Gigabit Ethernet as a topology independent, lossless and deadlock free network architecture, while still being compatible with current off-the-shelf Ethernet equipment.

We have reviewed how conventional use of Ethernet has severe performance limitations and we have illustrated this through the use of TCP as a higher layer protocol. Furthermore, we have shown how to solve this by activating flow control and taking control over the routing algorithm. This has resulted in the following improvements. Firstly, the activation of flow control turns Ethernet into a lossless network. Secondly, taking control over the routing algorithm allows us to use any topology without the limitations of the spanning tree protocol. And thirdly, the combination of these enhancements issues results in a an overall improvement in throughput.

Acknowledgements

The authors would like to acknowledge Professor Olav Lysne and Dr. Jose Flich for useful input during the preparation of this paper.

References

1. Jaspernite, J., Neumann, P.: Switched ethernet for factory communication. In: Proceedings of 8th IEEE International Conference on Emerging Technologies and Factory Automation. (2001) 205–212
2. Skeie, T., Johannessen, J., Holmeide, .: The road to an end-to-end deterministic ethernet. In: Proceedings of 4th IEEE International Workshop on Factory Communication Systems. (2002)
3. Øyvind Holmeide, Apneseth, C., Løkstad, T.: Time distribution in switched ethernet for substation automation applications. IEEE Trans. on Control Systems Technology (2000)
4. Aggarwal, V., Maennel, O., Mogul, J., Romanow, A.: Workshop on network-i/o convergence: Experience, lessons, implications. ACM SIGCOMM Computer Communications Review 33 (2003) 75–80
5. john Recio, R.: Server i/o networks past, present, and future. In: Proceedings of the ACM SIGCOMM 2003 workshops. (2003) 163–178
6. ANSI: ANSI X3T9.3. Fiber Channel - Physical and Signaling Interface (FC-PH). 4.2 edn. (1993)
7. InfiniBand Trade Association: Infiniband architecture specification. 1.0a edn. (2001)
8. Boden, N.J., Cohen, D., Felderman, R.E., Kulawik, A.E., Seitz, C.L., Seizovic, J.N., Su, W.K.: Myrinet – a gigabit-per-second lan. IEEE MICRO (1995)
9. Hellwagner, H.: The sci standard and applications of sci. In: SCI: Scalable Coherent Interface, Architecture and Software for High-Performance Compute Clusters, Springer-Verlag (1999) 3–37
10. Seifert, R.: Gigabit Ethernet. Addison Wesley Pub Co. (1998)
11. Feuser, O., Wenzel, A.: On the effects of the ieee 802.3x flow control in full-duplex ethernet lans. In: Proceedings of the 24th Conference on Local Computer Networks. (1999)
12. Jing-Fei, R., Landry, R.: Flow control and congestion avoidance in switched ethernet lans. In: IEEE International Conference on Communications. Volume 1. (1997) 508–512

13. Noureddine, W., Tobagi, F.: Selective back-pressure in switched ethernet lans. In: Proceedings of GLOBECOMM. (1999)
14. Wechta, J., Eberlein, A., Halsall, F.: The interaction of the TCP flow control procedure in end nodes on the proposed flow control mechanism for use in IEEE 802.3 switches. In: HPN. (1998) 515–534
15. Noureddine, W.K.: Improving the performance of TCP applications using network-assisted methods. PhD thesis, Standford university (2002)
16. Dally, W.J., Towles, B.: Principles and practices of interconnection networks. Morgan Kaufman (2004)
17. Duato, J., Yalamanchili, S., Ni, L.: Interconnection Networks an Engineering Approach. IEEE Computer Society (1997)
18. Karol, M., Golestani, S.J., Lee, D.: Prevention of deadlocks and livelocks in lossless backpressured packet networks. IEEE/ACM Transactions on Networking **11** (2003) 923–934
19. Chen, H., Wyckoff, P.: Simulation studies of gigabit ethernet versus myrinet using real application cores. In: Communication, Architecture, and Applications for Network-Based Parallel Computing. (2000) 130–144
20. Ciaccio, G., Chiola, G.: Gamma and mpi/gamma on gigabit ethernet. In: Proceedings of the 7th European PVM/MPI Users' Group Meeting on Recent Advances in Parallel Virtual Machine and Message Passing Interface, Springer-Verlag (2000) 129–136
21. Ciaccio, G., Ehlert, M., Schnor, B.: Exploiting gigabit ethernet capacity for cluster applications. In: Proceedings of the 27th Annual IEEE Conference on Local Computer Networks (LCN'02). (2002) 669–679
22. Loeser, J., Haertig, H.: Low-latency hard real-time communication over switched ethernet. In: Proceedings of the 16th Euromicro Conference on Real-Time Systems (ECRTS 04). (2004) 13–22
23. Dally, W.J., Seitz, C.L.: Deadlock-free message routing in multiprocessor interconnection networks. IEEE Transaction on Computers **C-36** (1987) 547–543
24. Schroeder, M.D., Birrell, A.D., Burrows, M., Murray, H., Needham, R.M., Rodeheffer, T.L.: Autonet: a high-speed, self-configuring local area network using point-to-point links. IEEE Journal on Selected Areas in Communications **9** (1991)
25. Seifert, R.: The Switch Book: The Complete Guide to LAN Switching Technology. John Wiley & Sons, Inc. (2000)
26. ying Tyan, H.: Design, Realization, and Evaluation of Component-Based Compsitional Software Architecture for Network Simulation. PhD thesis, Ohio State University (2002)
27. Lysne, O., Skeie, T.: Load balancing of irregular system area networks through multiple roots. In: Proceedings of the International Conference on Communication in Computing. (2001) 165–171
28. Reinemo, S.A., Sem-Jacobsen, F.O., Skeie, T., Lysne, O.: Admission control for diffserv based quality of service in cut-through networks. In: Proceedings of the 10th International Conference on High Performance Computing. (2003) 118–128
29. Sem-Jacobsen, F.O., Reinemo, S.A., Skeie, T., Lysne, O.: Achieving flow level qos in cut-through networks through admission control and diffserv. In Arabnia, H.R., ed.: Proceedings of the 2004 International Conference on Parallel and Distributed Processing Techniques and Applications. Volume 3. (2004) 1084–1090

An Anycast-Based Geocasting Protocol for Mobile Ad Hoc Networks*

Jipeng Zhou

Department of Computer Science, Jinan University,
Guang Zhou 510632, P.R. China
jpzhoucn@sohu.com

Abstract. The goal of geocasting protocols is to deliver data packets to a group of nodes that are within a specified geographical area, i.e., the geocast region. In an ad hoc environment, there are numerous scenarios which benefit from geocast communication. In this paper, the network is divided into grids, we propose a new routing protocol for geocasting, which combines anycast and flood. The proposed protocol utilizes the location information to route messages in grid-by-grid manner. The routing path by using proposed protocol is the shortest route between hosts in grids. The grid structure is successfully used to eliminate redundant transmission of geocasting messages. The time complexity of route discovery and the routing overhead are reduced.

1 Introduction

A mobile ad hoc network(MANET) is a network, which consists of a set of mobile hosts that communicate with each other without the assistance of base stations. Due to considerations such as radio power limitation, power consumption, and channel utilization, a mobile host may not be able to communicate directly with other hosts in a single-hop. In this case, a multi-hop scenario occurs, where the packets sent by the source host are relayed by several intermediate hosts before reaching the destination host. Routes between two hosts in a MANET may consist of hops through other hosts in the network. The ability to establish an ad hoc network without using a fixed infrastructure makes them useful in many scenarios, including disaster recovery, search-and-rescue in remote areas, and home networking application. Application of MAENTs occurs in situations like battlefields or major disaster area, where networks need to be deployed immediately but base stations or fixed network infrastructure are not available. The advancement in wireless communication and economical, portable computing devices has made the design of mobile ad hoc network possible.

Since a MANET is likely to operate in a physical area, it is very natural to apply location information of mobile hosts on such an environment. We call this property location awareness, this means that a mobile host may know its

---

* This work is supported by GDNSF(04300769), the Ministry of Education Study Abroad Returnees Startup Fund and JNU Grant(640581).

own physical location and the physical location of some other mobiles. One way for a mobile host to know its current location is through a GPS(global positioning system) receiver connected to the host [6][13]. Location-aware or context-aware applications will be an important domain in mobile computing, such as navigation systems, telematic systems to facilitate communication with moving vehicles, geocasting, and tour guide system. The location information of destination nodes is used to reduce the overhead of route discovery and assist broadcasting in a MANET.

A MANET is a peer-to-peer network that allows direct communication between any two nodes, when adequate radio propagation conditions exist between the two nodes and are subject to transmission power limitations of the nodes. If there is no direct link between the source and the destination nodes, multi-hop routing is used. Of course, appropriate routing protocols are necessary to discover routes between the source and destination, or even to determine the presence or absence of a path to the destination node. Because of the lack of central elements, distributed protocols have to be used.

The main challenge in the design and operation of the MANETs, compared to more traditional wireless networks, stems from the lack of a centralized entity, the potential for rapid node movement, and the fact that all communication is carried over the wireless medium. In standard cellular wireless networks, there are a number of centralized entities(e.g., the basestation, the Mobile Switching Centers, the Home Location Register(HLR) and the visitor Location Register(VLR)), which perform the function of coordination. In ad-hoc networks, there is no preexisting infrastructure. The lack of these entities in the MANETs requires distributed algorithms to perform these functions. In particular, the traditional algorithms for mobility management, which rely on a centralized HLR/VLR, and the medium access control schemes by using the base-station/MSC support, become inappropriate in the MANETs.

Because of the possibly rapid movement of the nodes and variable propagation conditions, network information, such as a route table, become absolutely quick. Frequent network reconfiguration may trigger frequent exchanges of control information to reflect the current state of the network. However, the short lifetime of this information means that a large portion of this information never be used. Thus, the bandwidth used for distribution of the routing update information is wasted.

A node in an ad hoc network is in charge of routing information between its neighbors, thus it contributes to and maintains connectivity of the network. Many unicast routing protocols have been proposed for ad hoc networks. A review of unicast routing protocols appears in [19]. To do multicasting, some way is needed to define multicast groups. In wireless ad hoc environments, two approaches can be used for multicasting: multicast flooding or multicast tree-based approach. Tree-based multicast may not work well in mobile ad hoc networks as dynamic movement of group members can cause the frequent tree reconfiguration with excessive channel overhead and loss of datagrams [4][9]. Since the task of keeping the tree structure up-to-date in the multicast tree-based approach is nontrivial, sometimes, multicast flooding may be considered as an alternative approach in MANET [18]. The Location-based multicast schemes [9] attempt to decrease delivery overhead of geocasting packets by reducing the forwarding space for mutlicast packets, as compared to multicast flooding.

Geocasting, a variant of the conventional multicasting problem, delivers data packets to a group of nodes that are within a specified geographical area, i.e., the geocasting region. The concept of geocast was first proposed in [8][13] in the context of the Internet. In their scheme also, group members are defined as all nodes within a certain region. To support location-dependent services such as geographically-targeted advertising, they suggested three methods: Geographic Routing Method(i.e., georouting with location aware routers), Geographic Multicast Routing Method(i.e., geo-multicasting modifying IP multicast), and Domain Name Service Method(i.e., an application layer solution using extended domain name service).

GPS application in geographic messaging is presented in [16], which describes how to send packets to users who are located on a wired network within a particular polygon or circle defined by latitude and longitude. We will refer to the specified area as the "geocast region"–set of nodes in the geocast region forms the geocast group. If a host resides within the geocst region at a given time, it automatically becomes a member of the corresponding geocast group at that time. To determine group membership, each node is required to know its own physical location, i.e., its precise geographic coordinates, which may be obtained by using the Global Positioning System(GPS)[7]. It is assumed that each node has available its own location by deploying GPS in user terminals, and whenever a node in the geocast region receives a geocast packet, it will flood the geocast message to all its neighbors within the geocast region.

The geocast protocols are classified into two categories: data-transmission oriented protocols and routing creation oriented protocols in [20]. Since all the nodes in the geocast region share information among each other by flooding, the difference between these two categories is how they transmit information from a source to one or more nodes in the geocast region. Data-transmission oriented protocols use flooding or a variant of flooding to forward geocast packets from the source to the geocast region, such as LBM [9], GeoGrid [15] and others [11]. Routing-creation oriented protocols create routes from the source to the geocast via control packets, such as GeoTORA [10] and mesh-based Geocast routing protocol [2][3]. As mentioned in [15], flooding data packets may cause a storing effect giving serious redundancy, contention and collision. Routing-creation oriented protocols create route to transmit data from the source to the geocast region, one advantage of this kind of protocol is the reduced overhead in the transmission of data packets, as compared to data-transmission oriented protocols. One disadvantage of this kind of protocol is that it requires more latency and control overhead to create routes.

GeoGrid protocol [15] partitions the geographic area of the MANET into 2D logical grids. Each grid is a square of size $d \times d$. There are trade-off in choosing a good value of d, as discussed in the details of [15]. In GeoGrid protocol, the forwarding zone is defined by the location of the source and the geocast region, a gateway node is selected within each grid to transmit data to a forward zone. There are two suggestions on how to send geocast packets by GeoGrid in [15]: flooding-based GeoGrid and Ticket-based GeoGrid. In Flooding-based GeoGrid, only gateways in every grid within the forwarding zone will rebroadcast the received geocast packets. Overhead is the big problem of flooding scheme. In Ticket-based GeoGrid, the geocast packets are still forwarded by gateway nodes, but not all the gateways in the forwarding zone will forward each geocast packet. In this GeoGrid protocol, $m + n$ tickets are created by the source if the geocast region is a rectangle of $m \times n$ grids. The source then evenly distributes the $m+n$ tickets to the neighboring gateway nodes in the forwarding zone that are closer to the geocast region than the source. A gateway node that receives X tickets follows the same procedure as the one defined for the source.

The next two geocast routing protocols are route-based protocols, which create one or more routes to transmit geocast data between the source and the geocast region. GeoTORA [10] use a unicast routing protocol TORA(Temporally Ordered Routing Algorithm) to provide geocast communication. TORA is a distributed routing protocol based on a "link reversal" algorithm. It attempts to provide multiple routes to a destination with minimal communication overhead. TORA uses the notion of heights to determine the direction of each link. It attempts to maintain a destination-oriented directed acyclic graph such that each node can reach the destination. In GeoTORA, a source node essentially performs an anycast to any geocast group member via TORA. When a node in the geocast region receives the geocast packet, it floods the packet such that the flooding is limited to the geocast region.

MGRP(Mesh-based Geocast Routing Protocol) [2] is another route-based protocol. Unlike GeoTORA, this protocol establishes multiple paths via a mesh to send geocast packets. Mesh-based multicasting approach has been developed in order to avoid week performance with source tree-based and core-based multicasting protocols in ad hoc networks [5][14]. A mesh is a subset of the network topology that provides multiple paths between multicast senders and receivers. In the creation of the mesh, the protocol floods JOINT-REQUEST packets to a forwarding zone until it reaches a node within the geocast region. The node in a geocast region unicasts a JOIN-TABLE packet back to the source following the reverse route taken by the JOIN-REQUEST packet. Once the first JOIN-TABLE packet is received by the source, data packets can be sent to the nodes in geocast regions.

In this paper, the network is divided into grids, we combine data-transmission oriented protocols with routing creation oriented protocols. First, an anycast is used to rout packet from source to a node in the geocast region, then packet is flooded to any member in the geocast region. We propose a new routing protocol for geocasting, which utilizes the location information to select the host in each grid. The routing path by using proposed protocol is the shortest route between hosts in grids. The grid structure is successfully used to eliminate redundant transmission of geocasting messages. The time complexity of route discovery

Table 1. The comparison of geocast routing protocols

Protocol	Flood-based or route-based	Data Travels to Geocast region via
LBM [9]	Flood	Multiple routes
GeoGrid [15]	Flood	Multiple routes
GeoTORA [10]	Route	One route
MGRP[2]	Route	Multiple routes
GAMER[3]	Route	Multiple routes
Our Protocol	Route and flood	One route

and the routing overhead are reduced. Our geocast routing protocol is compared to others as shown in Table 1.

This paper is organized as follows. Section 2 presents the scheme of construction and label assignment of 2D grid; Section 3 gives an anycast-based geocasting protocol; In Section 4, Our anycast-based geocasting protocol is compared with other geocasting protocols; Section 5 concludes the paper and proposes further works.

2 Construction and Label Assignment of 2D Grid

The geographic area of the MANET is partitioned into 2D logical grids as shown in Fig. 1, in which each square is called a grid zone. Each grid is a square of size $d \times d$, where d is side length of grids. Let r be the transmission of a radio signal. The smaller value of d means more number of gateways in the network, which will in turn implies a higher overhead of delivering packet and more broadcast storm. If d is too large, the radio signal of a gateway host will have difficulty in reaching places outside of the grid, and thus a gateway-to-gateway communication is unlikely to succeed. Selection of d is related to r and routing protocol. In this paper, we define the relation of d and r as $r = \frac{3\sqrt{2}}{2}d$ as shown in Fig. 2, which

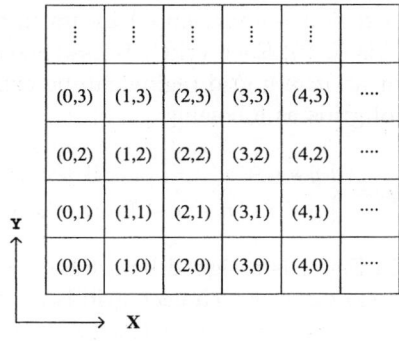

Fig. 1. Logical grid to partition a physical area

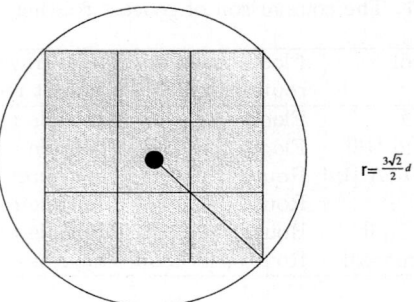

Fig. 2. The relation of transmission of radio signal r with side length d of a grid

24	25	26	27	28	29
23	22	21	20	19	18
12	13	14	15	16	17
11	10	9	8	7	6
0	1	2	3	4	5

Y ↑
→ X

Fig. 3. 6 × 5 grid network with label

guarantees a host in a grid to reach any host in its eight neighbor grids. This is convenient for selection of gateway in the grid.

In this section, we will propose a label assignment scheme for grid topology and prove that this assignment scheme will provide the shortest routing path in grid hops for any given pair of source and destination nodes. Suppose the address of a grid in 2D region is represented by its integer coordinate (x, y), where the lower left grid is $(0, 0)$. Each grid u is assigned a label $l(u)$. The label assignment function l for an $m \times n$ grid region can be expressed in terms of the $x-$ and $y-$coordinates of grids as following:

$$l(x,y) = \begin{cases} y*n + x & \text{if } y \text{ is even,} \\ y*n + n - x - 1 & \text{if } y \text{ is odd} \end{cases}$$

Each logical grid u in Fig. 1 is assigned by a label $l(u)$. Fig. 3 shows such a labeling in an 6 × 5 grid region, in which each grid is represented by an integer. We assume that every grid can communicate with its eight neighbors directly, the labeling effectively divides the grid network into two kinds of sub-networks. The *high-channel subnetwork* can be used to communicate from lower-labeled

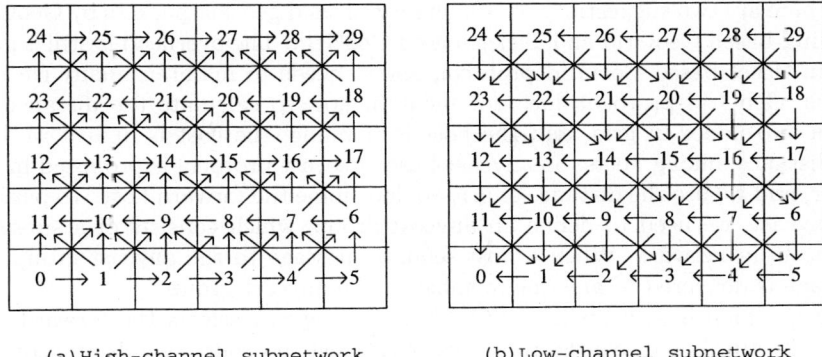

Fig. 4. The high-channel and low-channel subnetwork in 6 × 5 grid network

grids(gateways) to higher-labeled grids (gateways), for an example in Fig. 4(a); the *low-channel subnetwork* can be used to pass message from higher-labeled grids(gateways) to lower-labeled grids(gateways), such as in Fig. 4(b). Anycast communication will use the labeling for message routing. If the label of the destination zone is greater than the label of the source zone, the anycast routing always takes place in the high-channel subnetwork, otherwise, it will take the low-channel subnetwork.

3 An Anycast-Based Geocasting Protocol

Due to consideration such as radio power limitation, power consumption, and channel utilization, a mobile host may not be able to communicate directly with other hosts in a single-hop fashion. In this case, a multi-hop scenario occurs, where the packets sent by the source host are relayed by several intermediate hosts before reaching the destination host. In this paper, we combine data-transmission oriented protocols with routing creation oriented protocols. First, an anycast routing is used to rout packet from source to a node in geocast region; second, a multicast routing sends packets from one node in geocast region to all grid zones of geocast region; then packet is flooded to any member in each zone of geocast region. We describe the proposed protocol using 2D logical grid location information as shown in [15], and a gateway node is selected within each grid to transmit data to a forward zone. The forward zone is only determined by the current grid and the geocast region, and the optimal geocast routing path on grid level will be obtained.

In the location-unaware protocols, the route discovery is done by a blind flooding, it easily leads to cause broadcast storm problem, which is pointed out in [17]. Location-based multicast schemes in [9] use forwarding zones to avoid network-wide flooding, since its forwarding zones are too large, there may still exist a lot of unnecessary flooding packets within a forwarding zone and it does not give solution how to select the relay host, when source cannot reach the destination. This problem will be solved in this paper.

There are two suggestions in [15] on how to send geocast packets by GeoGrid: flooding-based GeoGrid and Ticket-based GeoGrid. The overhead is still a problem in ticket-based GeoGrid protocol, and it needs to maintain many $(m \times n)$ routes. GeoGrid protocol does not mention how to calculate the distance between two nodes in grid, and the host is roaming, the cost is high if we keep the distance among hosts. So anycast-based geocast protocol is proposed in this paper, and we use the distance of grid to determine the forward host. To perform an anycast, we need to define an anycast group, which consists of a subset of the hosts in network. When a host sends a message to the anycast group, the message is delivered to any one member of the anycast group.

In the following, we will describe how the anycast selects the forward zone in our protocol. To save the route discovery cost, no route search procedure is performed, instead, a source node will forward the packet to the neighbor node that is closest to the destination node. The location of source and geocast region is used to confine the forwarding range. The same procedure is repeated until the destination node is reached.

In our protocol, routing is performed in a grid-by-grid manner through grid gateways, which is the same as in [15]. If a gateway leaves its original grid, a behavior similar to the 'hand off' procedure in cellular systems will take place. In this case, the gateway passes its routing table to the next gateway. Each gateway only keeps the destination information, the intermediate node must keep a routing table to determine which node to forward packet to. The three major issues of a routing protocol should be considered in designing a routing protocol, that is route discovery, packet relay, and route maintenance. In route discovery, the location information is used to determine the quality of a route. A node in the ad hoc network obtains its location from a system such as the Global Positioning System(GPS). Some work in geocasting has considered how to integrate geographic coordinates into Internet protocol[8] . The only local information, instead of global information, is used to find the next host to forward the packet. We will consider two issues in our protocol design, one is that as less as possible nodes are searched in the each step of route discovery. Another is that the route path is as short as possible.

In order to reduce propagation of the flood, the route to a forwarding zone is determined by the location of the sender and coordinates of the geocast region. We define the distance between two grids $u = (x_1, y_1)$ and $v = (x_2, y_2)$ as $d(u,v) = max\{|x_1 - x_2|, |y_1 - y_2|\}$, the forwarding grid is selected by computing distance between the neighbor of current grid and destination, then select the grid with minimum distance to destination as forwarding grid.

Let V be the gateway node set in the grid. Finding a deadlock-free anycast algorithm for the 2D grid is to define a routing function $R_1 : V \times V \to V$ that uses the two subnetworks in such a way to avoid cycle routing. Here two grids (i_0, j_0) and (i_1, j_1) are neighbors, which denotes 8-neighbors ,i.e., $max\{|i_0 - i_1|, |j_0 - j_1|\} = 1$. One such routing function, for a source node in u and destination node in v, is defined as $R_1(u,v) = w$, such that w is in a neighboring grid of u, and if $l(u) < l(v)$, then we have the following equation:

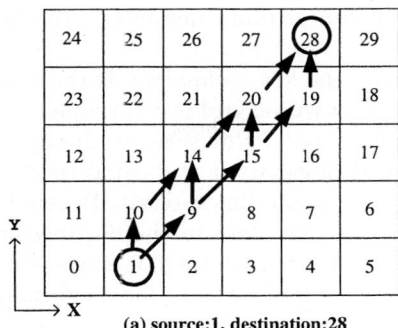 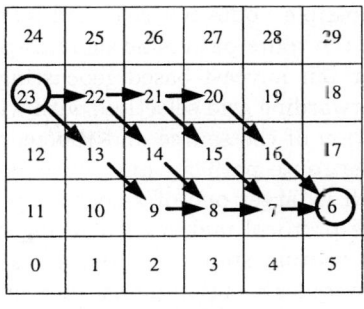

(a) source:1, destination:28   (b) source:23, destination:6

Fig. 5. Anycast Routing in the high-channel and low-channel subnetwork of 6 × 5 grid

$$d(w,v) = min\{d(z,v) : l(z) \leq l(v) \text{ and z is a neighboring node of u}\},$$

or if $l(u) > l(v)$, then we have the following equation:

$$d(w,v) = min\{d(z,v) : l(z) \geq l(v) \text{ and z is a neighboring node of u}\}.$$

If more hosts satisfy the condition, we only select anyone of them.

Anycast examples in high-channel subnetwork and low-channel subnetwork is shown in Fig. 5. All possible routes from source host in grid s ($l(s) = 1$) to destination host in grid $d(l(d) = 28)$ in high-channel subnetwork is shown in Fig. 5(a), where all routes are only from hosts in low label grid to hosts in high label grid; All possible routes from source host in grid s ($l(s) = 23$) to destination host in grid $d(l(d) = 6)$ in low-channel subnetwork is shown in Fig. 5(b), where all routes are only from hosts in high label grid to hosts in low label grid. The packet is forwarded one hop closer to its destination at each step and the route is along the shortest path between source and its destination in grid level.

4 The Anycast-Based Geocasting Protocol vs. Other Geocasting Protocols

In this paper, we propose an anycast-based geocasting protocol, a grid-by-grid routing protocol, the goal is to reduce the overhead of transmission of geocast packets, each gateway only keeps the destination and its neighbor grid information, which is used to determine which node to forward packet to. In the anycast-based geocasting protocol, a source node essentially performs an anycast to any geocast group host. The advantage of this strategy is that routes are adaptable to the dynamically changing environment of MANETs, since each host can update its routing table when it receives fresher topology information. In route discovery, the location information is used to determine a route and to improve the performance(i.e., low overhead) of a unicast routing. only local information, instead of global information, is used to find the next host to forward the packet. We will consider two issues in our protocol design, one is that as less as possible nodes are searched in the each step of route discovery. Another is that the route path is as short as possible.

In our anycast-based geocasting protocol, the key technology is the scheme of forwarding grid selection, with which the forwarding grid is determined by the location of the source and the geocast region. Under this scheme, the distance of the route path for any source node u and destination v is equal to $d(u,v)$, which is larger one of x-coordinate offset and y-coordinate offset. Because our route protocol makes the routing message one hop close to the destination at each routing step. The routing is the shortest path routing. It can establish routes quickly and minimize communication overhead by using local information only.

Our anycast-based geocasting protocol has some advantages in comparison with other geocast protocols. In the ticket-based GeoGrid approach [15], GeoGrid uses location information to define the forwarding zone and to elects special host for forwarding the geocast packets. But the forwarding zone in GeoGrid incurs unnecessary packet transmission, which will select its three neighbors that closer to the destination, and sends the ticket to these three neighbors. The disadvantage of Ticket-based GeoGrid is that some gateways will receive and transmit the geocast packet more than one times. This will cost more bandwidth and communication time. In comparison, our protocol does not provide redundant path from a source to a multicast group of nodes and has less searched nodes in the each step of route discovery. So it is less costly to provide routing path from a source to a geocast region than to provide the redundant paths from a source to a multicast group of nodes in a geocast region. It further reduces overhead (the number of nodes that forward geocast packet) in the transmission of data packets as compared to Ticket-Based GeoGrid protocol.

In GeoTORA protocol [10], creating routes from sources to the destination corresponds to establishing a sequence of directed links from each source to the geocast group. This is accomplished by maintaining a directed acyclic graph(DAG) rooted at each geocast group. The disadvantage of GeoTORA is that the algorithm may produce temporary invalid routes and it needs to maintain a directed acyclic graph(DAG) rooted at each destination geocast group.

MGRP [2] and GAMER [3] are mesh-based protocol for geocast routing. A mesh is used establish multiple paths between a source node and the geocast region. Unlike GeoTORA, these protocols establish multiple paths(via a mesh) to send geocast packets. For example, GAMER dynamically chooses one of three different forwarding approaches to forward packets to the geocast region. They reduce the control overhead by reducing forwarding zone, when forwarding zone is restrained to a small region, only a few mobile nodes are available to forward packets which reduces control overhead. In addition, fewer forwarding mobile nodes create a sparse mesh, which compared to a large forwarding zone and denser mesh, reduce transmission accuracy. Here forwarding region is determined by source node and geocast region, so it needs more setup time for each routing.

5 Conclusion

In this paper, a new geocasting protocol for MANETs is presented. The grid structure is successfully used to eliminate redundant transmission of geocasting messages. This is achieved by only one gateway in each grid. The time complexity of route discovery and the routing overhead are reduced. However further evaluation of the protocol is needed, for example, how can the protocol effectively divide the network into grids? what is an effective gateway election procedure? how can the protocol provide the high level of reliability? the further research is needed to answer these question, further analysis and simulation to compare with other geocasting protocols are needed.

References

1. Abolhasan, M., Wysocki, T., Dutkiewicz, E.: A review of routing protocols for mobile ad hoc networks. *Ad Hoc Network* , 2(2004), 1-22.
2. Boleng, J , Camp, T., Tolety, V.: mesh-based geocast routing protocols in ad hoc network. *Proc. of the International Workshop on Parallel and Distributed Computing Issues in Wireless Networks and Mobile Computing,*(2001),184-193.
3. Camp, T., Liu, Y.: An adadptive meshed-based protocol for geocst routing, *Journal of Parallel and Distributed Computing: Specical Issue on Mobile Ad-hoc Networking and Computing,*(2002),196-213.
4. Chiang, C., Gerla, M., Zhang, L.: Shared tree wireless network multicast. *Proc. of 6th International Conference on Computer Communications and Networks,*(1997),28-33.
5. Garcia-Luna-Aceves, J.J., Madrga, E.L.: A multicat routing protocol for ad-hoc network. *Proc. of the Annual Joint Conference of the IEEE Computer and Communication Societies(INFOCOM 1999),*784-792.
6. Jones, A.: Mobile computing to go, *IEEE Concurreny*, 7(2):20:23, April-June, 1999.
7. Hofmann-Wellenhof, B., Lichtenegger, H., Collins, J.: Global Positioning System: Theory and Practice, 4th ed. (1997) Springer-Verlag, New York.
8. Imielinski, T., Navas, J.C.: GPS-based geographic addressing, routing, and resource discovery, *Communications of the ACM 42(4)(1999)86-92.*
9. Ko, Y., Vaidya, N.H.: Geocasting in mobile as hoc networks: Location-based multicast algorithms. *Proc. of the 2nd IEEE Workshop on Mobile Computing Systems and Application,*(1999).
10. Ko, Y., Vaidya, N.H.: GeoTORA: A protocol for geocasting in mobile ad hoc networks. *Proc. of 8th International Conference on Network Protocols,*(2000).
11. Ko, Y., Vaidya, N.H.: Flooding-based geocasting protocols for mobile ad hoc networks, *Mobile Networks and Applications* 7, (2002)471-480.
12. Ko, Y., Vaidya, N.H.: Anycasting-based protocol for geocast service in mobile ad hoc networks, *Computer Networks* 41(2003)743-760.
13. Krikelis, A.: Location-dependent multimedia momputing, *IEEE Concurrency*, 7(2):13-15, April-June, 1999.
14. Lee, S.J., Gerla, M., Chiang, C.C.: On-demand multicast routing protocol. *Proc. of IEEE Wireless Communication and Networking Conference (WCNC'99)* , (1999).
15. Liao, W.H., Tseng, Y.C., Lo, K.L., Sheu, J.P.: GeoGrid: A geocasting protocol for mobile ad hoc networks based on grid. *Journal of Internet technology*, 1(2)(2000), 23-32.

16. Navas, J.C., Imielinski, T.: Geographic addressing and routing. *Pro. of the Third ACM/IEEE International Conference on Mobile Computing and Netwoking (MobiCom'97), Budapest, Hungary, September 26-30, 1997.*
17. Ni, S.Y., Tseng, Y.C., Chen, Y.S., Shen, J.P.: The broadcast storm problemmin a mobile ad hoc network. *Proc. of the fifth ACM/IEEE Intenational Conference on Mobile Computing and Networking(MobileCom'99)* , August, 1999.
18. Obraczka, K., Tsudik, G.: Multicast routing issues in ad hoc networks. *IEEE ICUPC, Otc. 1998.*
19. Royer, E., Toh, C.K.: A review of current routing protocols for ad hoc mobile wireless networks. *IEEE Personal communication maganize*,4(1999), 46-55.
20. Xia Jinag and Tracy Camp: A review of geocasting protocols for a mobile ad hoc network, in Proc. of Grace Hopper Celebration(2002).

A Mesh Based Anycast Routing Protocol for Ad Hoc Networks

Shui Yu and Wanlei Zhou

School of Information Technology, Deakin University,
221, Burwood HWY, Burwood, VIC 3125, Australia
{syu, wanlei}@deakin.edu.au

Abstract. Ad hoc networks became a hot topic recently, but the routing algorithm of anycast in the ad hoc networks has not yet been much explored. In this paper, we propose a mesh-based anycast routing algorithm (MARP) for ad hoc networks. The proposed routing model is robust and reliable, which can solve the unsteady topology problem in ad hoc networks. The future work is discussed at the end of this paper.

1 Introduction

Ad hoc networks have no fixed routers or gateways, and all the nodes are capable of movement and can be connected dynamically in an arbitrary manner, furthermore, each node can act as a router to provide the routing service for the others. Ad hoc networks have wide applications and the routing foundation is totally different in ad hoc networks, therefore new routing protocols should be designed explicitly for unicast, multicast and anycast. It is essential that the designed routing algorithm is simple and has minimum control message exchanging.

Mesh-based routing methods have been proposed for unicast and multicast in ad hoc network environments [7] [11] [12]. It is a reliable method in the wireless networks, because the mesh offers the sources more routes to the receivers, and the mesh has a strong recovery capability of local link failures. Mesh based routing method is very suitable for routing service in ad hoc network, however, to the best of our knowledge, it is not yet applied to anycast routing issue in ad hoc networks.

In this paper, we propose a mesh based anycast routing protocol (MARP in short), which provide reliable and efficient anycast routing service in ad hoc networks. The mesh architecture makes the routing service reliable; moreover, the proposed protocol can prevent the traffic storm in the network, and deduct the bandwidth consumption by reducing the control packets delivery.

The rest of this paper is organized as follows. Section 2 presents the related work of routing algorithms in wireless networks. A new mesh based anycast routing protocol is proposed in Section 3. Finally, Section 4 concludes the paper and discusses the future work.

2 Related Work

[16] reviewed the routing algorithms for ad hoc mobile wireless networks, and classified them into two categories: table-driven and source-initiated (demand-driven).

Table-driven ad hoc routing algorithms include Destination-Sequenced Distance-Vector (DSDV) routing [14] and Wireless Routing Protocol (WRP) [13]. The Clusterhead Gateway Switch Routing (CGSR) protocol [3] is derived from DSDV. All the table-driven algorithms try to maintain consistent, up-to-date routing information for every node in the network. Source-initiated on-demand algorithms have four protocols: the Ad hoc On-demand Distance Vector (AODV) [15], Dynamic Source Routing (DSR) [9], Temporally Ordered Routing Algorithm (TORA) [PAR97] which is similar to the Lightweight Mobile Routing (LMR) [4], Associativity-Based Routing (ABR) [17], and the Signal Stability Routing (SSR) [6] which was derived from the ABR. Source-initiated on-demand protocols create routes only when it is desired by a source node. Some papers [2] [5] [10] have shown that the source-initiated on-demand algorithms outperform the table-driven ad hoc routing algorithms.

[8] made simple extensions to the three existing routing algorithms for mobile ad hoc networks: Dynamic Source Routing (DSR), Ad-hoc On-demand Distance Vector (AODV) Routing and Temporally Ordered Routing Algorithm (TORA). All the updates locate at the sinks, for this reason, the modifications are very limited. In the mobile ad hoc environment, robustness of routing is a critical issue. Flooding is a reliable routing method in ad hoc networks, such as, the research in [18].

[7] [11] [12] researched on mesh-based multicast protocols, which provide alternative paths and a link failure does not trigger a recomputation of a mesh. All the multicast sources, receivers, forwarding nodes and the links establish a mesh, and the one hop away neighbours of the mesh nodes are the group neighbours. The multicast source submits a local request packet to maintain the mesh, and only the mesh nodes and the group neighbours deliver the packet. Once a request packet arrives at a receiver, the receiver responds with a reply packet back to the source along the reversal path, therefore a route is created between the source and the receiver.

3 An Anycast Routing Protocol in Ad Hoc Networks

Because of the ever changing ad hoc network topology, robustness is a critical issue that the routing service has to deal with. For this reason, we propose a mesh-based anycast routing protocol (MARP) for ad hoc networks. In the context of this paper, anycast source and source are exchangeable, and the same for anycast receiver, anycast server and receiver.

3.1 An Overview of MARP

The mesh-based anycast routing protocol is a robust and efficient protocol. Generally speaking, the mesh-based protocols are not as efficient as that of the tree-based protocols in terms of performance, but they are robust against topology changes [7] [12]. In the proposed MARP, some related hosts establish a mesh, and the anycast routing service depends on the mesh.

At the initial state of an anycast service, an anycast source uses broadcasting to flood mesh-establishing messages (flooding route discovery), once an anycast server receives the mesh-establishing message, it will respond an acknowledgement message, a route between the source and the receiver will then be established. After that, an on-mesh route discovery procedure is employed for the mesh refreshment and link failure recovery. The on-mesh route discovery packet is only delivered by the mesh nodes and the group neighbour nodes (which will be defined in section 3.2). This can prevent the mesh maintenance packets broadcast unnecessarily in the ad hoc network. The previous research [1] has proven that most link failure recoveries can be localized to a small region along a previous route, therefore, the method is feasible for on-mesh link failure recovery.

Because of the ever changing topology of ad hoc networks, MARP performs flooding route discovery occasionally, which can refresh the whole mesh and make sure its correctness. Flooding route discovery can also deal with the network partition issue. The flooding route discovery is expensive in terms of network bandwidth.

3.2 Anycast Mesh Creation

When an anycast source tries to join an anycast group, it initially broadcasts a JOIN_REQ packet, the JOIN_REQ packet has an *upstream node* field. When an intermediate node caches the JOIN_REQ packet, it updates the *upstream node* field with its own address, and then forwards (broadcasts) the updated packet to the next nodes. When an anycast server receives the JOIN_REQ packet, it responds a MESH_ACK packet back to the node from which it received the JOIN_REQ packet. Once the upstream node receives the MESH_ACK packet, it adds an entry for the anycast group to its routing table, and then it forwards the MESH_ACK packet to its own upstream node. This procedure continues until the MESH_ACK packet gets to the anycast source. And then an anycast route is established between the source and the receiver. The intermediate nodes that relay the MESH_ACK packet become *forwarding nodes*. An anycast mesh of an anycast group consists of anycast sources, anycast receivers, forwarding nodes, and links connecting them. All the nodes in an anycast mesh are called *mesh nodes*.

Figure 1 shows an ad hoc network as an example. In the ad hoc network, there are 29 nodes in total, includes two anycast sources (node 5 and node 20) and two anycast servers (node 7 and node 16). The link between any two nodes means that there is a network connection for the two nodes.

Figure 1 also demonstrates how an anycast mesh is established. In the initial state, node 7 and node 16 belong to an anycast group, we express it as $G(A) = \{7,16\}$. We assume that node 5 is a new anycast source as an example, and it broadcasts the JOIN_REQ packet, which includes the ID of node 5 and a broadcasting sequence number. When the JOIN_REQ packet arrives at node 6, node 6 updates the *upstream node* field of the packet with its own address and forwards the packet to its neighbours. Once node 7, an anycast server receives the packet, it sends a MESH_ACK packet back to node 6 which is the upstream node of node 7. Then node 6 realises that it is on the anycast mesh, it updates its routing table and relays the MESH_ACK to its upstream node, node 5. After this procedure, a route between the anycast source and one of the anycast servers is established. Similarly, there is a route between node 5 and node 16, which is another server of the anycast group.

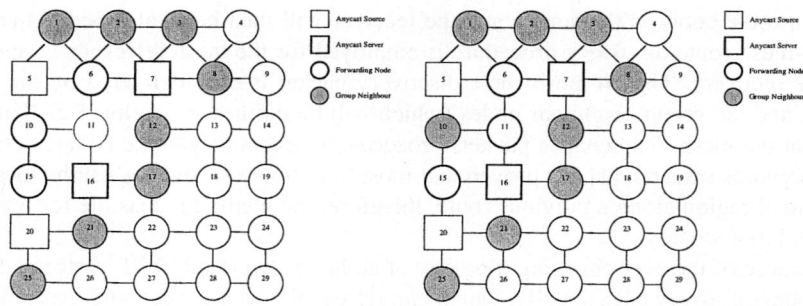

Fig. 1. The Ad Hoc Network after Mesh Creation

Fig. 2. The Network after Link Failure Recovery

MARP prefers a path that contains more existing forwarding nodes for route efficiency and maintenance reasons. Figure 1 shows the result after the anycast mesh is established. Once the anycast mesh is created, an anycast source holds all the routes to the anycast group members, respectively, therefore a "best" server can be chosen based on given metrics. For example, if we choose the "best" server based on the shortest path, then the anycast server node 7 is chosen for the source node 5 on path $P\{5,6,7\}$; and the anycast server node 16 is chosen for the source node 20 on path $P\{20,15,16\}$. When there are packet deliveries in the anycast group, the packets are only transported by the forwarding nodes among the sources and the receivers.

Anycast *Group Neighbour* nodes are defined as the nodes that are directly connected to at least one anycast mesh node. In Figure 1, nodes 1, 2, 3, 8, 10, 12, 17 and 25 are the group neighbour nodes. Group neighbour nodes are defined for the on-mesh broadcasting. In MARP, only the mesh nodes and group neighbour nodes forward the on-mesh broadcasting packets, while the other nodes do not forward the on-mesh broadcasting packets. Therefore MARP can effectively prevent the potential traffic storm and therefore reduce the network load.

3.3 Anycast Mesh Maintenance

In order to provide the up-to-date information of network topology in ad hoc networks, the route information has to be updated in time, and kept consistent with the instant practical network status. Anycast mesh maintenance includes two parts: on-mesh route discovery and flooding route discovery.

A. On-mesh Route Discovery

Each anycast source periodically broadcasts a MESH_REQ packet, and only the mesh nodes and the group neighbour nodes forward the packet. Similar to the JOIN_REQ packet for mesh creation, a mesh node or a group neighbour node updates the *upstream node* field of the received MESH_REQ packets with its own address and forwards the modified packets to the next nodes. When the MESH_REQ packet arrives at an anycast receiver, a MESH_ACK packet is sent back to the anycast source along the path from which the MESH_REQ packet came. After the on-mesh route discovery procedure, the updated mesh is established, and the forwarding nodes and the group neighbor nodes are refreshed as well.

Based on the rule of MARP, the nodes more than two hops away from the mesh can not receive the MESH_REQ. This mechanism can efficiently save the valuable network bandwidth in mobile ad hoc networks, and prevent the potential traffic storms. For example, in Figure 1, there are nearly ¼ nodes (node 14, 19, 23, 24, 27, 28, and 29) are not involved in the MESH_REQ packet broadcasting.

More importantly, on-mesh route discovery procedure can repair most link failures caused by node movements in ad hoc networks. For example, we assume that the mobile node 11 in Figure 1 is power off, then there are three link failures occur, namely link (6, 11), link (10, 11) and link (11, 16), when the anycast source node 5 submits the MESH_REQ packet, node 10 will deliver it to node 15, and further to node 16, then a path $P\{5,10,15,16\}$ is established. Figure 2 shows the ad hoc network after the link failure recovery.

Previous research [1] has shown that most of the on-mesh link failures can be repaired by on-mesh route discovery, but it can not solve all the possible link failures and network partitions. For example, if there are two link failures of link (5, 10) and link (12, 17) in Figure 2, the original mesh is then divided into two parts, and it can not be repaired by the on-mesh route discovery.

The on-mesh route discovery procedure tries to keep all the sources and receivers connected with each other by the mesh. This is important to provide a reliable anycast service in ad hoc networks. For example, to the source node 5 in Figure 2, if the "best" receiver node 7 is not reachable, then there is an alternative receiver node 16, which can provide the same service.

B. Flooding Route Discovery

Flooding route discovery is an important procedure to maintain an anycast mesh, although it is expensive in terms of network bandwidth. When a node initiates the flooding route discovery procedure, the JOIN_REQ packet is broadcasted to all its neighbors, and every node in the ad hoc network will forward the packet. The JOIN_REQ packet will cover all nodes of the ad hoc network, therefore, it brings an up-to-date view of the network topology and the anycast mesh. MARP does not perform flooding route discovery frequently, because of the expensive network bandwidth consumption. It happens in several cases, such as a new anycast source joins the group or a network partition happens.

5 Conclusions and Future Work

We proposed a mesh based anycast routing protocol (MARP) for the ad hoc networks. The proposed algorithm improves the robustness for routing in dynamic ad hoc mobile networks. Moreover, it also reduces the bandwidth consumption caused by control packets. We discussed the routing mechanism in details. The examples show that the proposed model does possess advantages in robustness and link failure recovery. A performance analysis based on queueing theory and evaluating the performance of MARP through simulations is the topics for future work.

References

1. G. Aggelou and R. Tafazolli, "RDMAR: A Bandwidth-Efficient Routing Protocol for Mobile Ad Hoc Networks," Proc. of the WoWMoM'99, Seattle, Washington, Aug. 1999.
2. J. Broch, D. A. Maltz, D. B. Johnson, Y. Hu, and J. Jetcheva, "A Performance Comparison of Multi-Hop Wireless Ad Hoc Network Routing Protocols," Proc. of the 4th Annual ACM/IEEE Inter. Conf. on Mobile Computing and Networking, ACM, Dallas, TX, Oct. 1998.
3. C. E. Chiang, "Routing in Clusterhead Multihop, Mobile Wireless Networks with Fading Channel," Proceedings of IEEE SICON'97, April 1997, pp.197-211.
4. M. S. Corson and A. Ephremids, "A Distributed Routing Algorithm for Mobile Wireless Networks," ACM/Baltzer Wireless Networks J., vol. 1, no. 1, Feb. 1995, pp.61-81.
5. S. Corson and J. Macker, "Mobile Ad Hoc Networking (MANET) : Routing Protocol Performance Issues and Evaluation Considerations," RFC 2501, IETF, Jan. 1999.
6. R. Dube et al., "Signal Stability Based Adaptive Routing for Ad Hoc Mobile Networks," IEEE Personal Communications, Feb. 1997, pp36-45.
7. J. J. Garcia-Luna-Aceves, and E. L. Madruga, "The Core-Assisted Mesh Protocol," IEEE Journal on Selected Area in Communications, Special Issue on Ad Hoc Networks, Vol. 17, No. 8, August 1999.
8. Vivek Gulati, Aman Garg and Nitin Vaidya, "Anycast in Mobile Ad Hoc Networks," Technical Report, Texas A&M University, April 2001.
9. D. B. Johnson and D. A. Maltz, "Dynamic Source Routing in Ad-Hoc Wireless Networks," Mobile Computing, T. Imielinski and H. Korth, Eds., Kluwer, 1996, pp. 153-181.
10. P. Johansson, T. Larsson, N. Hedman, B. Mielczarek, and M. Degermark, "Scenario-Based Performance Analysis of Routing Protocols for Mobile Ad-Hoc Networks," MobiCom'99, Aug. 1999.
11. S. Lee, W. Su, and M. Gerla, "Ad Hoc Wireless Multicast with Mobility Prediction," IEEE ICCCN'99, Boston, MA, Oct. 1999.
12. S. Lee and C. Kim, "Neighbor Supporting Ad Hoc Multicast Routing Protocol," IEEE VTC'2000, August 2000.
13. S. Murthy and J. J. Garcia-Luna-Aceves, "An Efficient Routing Protocol for Wireless Networks," ACM Mobile Networks and App. J., Special Issue on Routing in Mobile Communication Networks, Oct. 1996, pp.183-197.
14. C. E. Perkins and P. Bhagwat, "Highly Dynamic Destination-Sequenced Distance-Vector Routing (DSDV) for Mobile Computers," Computer Communication Review, October, 1994, pp. 234-244.
15. C. E. Perkins and E. M. Royer, "Ad-hoc On-Demand Distance Vector Routing," Proc. 2nd IEEE Workshop on Mobile Comp. Sys. and Apps., Feb. 1999, pp.90-100.
16. Elizabeth M. Royer, Chai-Keong Toh, "A review of current Routing Protocols for Ad Hoc Mobile Wireless Networks," IEEE Personal Communications, April 1999.
17. C-K. Toh, "A Novel Distributed Routing Protocol to Support Ad-Hoc Mobile Computing," Proc. IEEE 15th Annual Int'l. Phoenix Conf. Comp. and Commun., Mar. 1996, pp.480-486.
18. Jie Wu and Fei Dai, "Broadcasting in Ad Hoc Networks Based on Self-Pruning," IEEE INFOCOM 2003, 2003.

Research of Power-Aware Dynamic Adaptive Replica Allocation Algorithm in Mobile Ad Hoc Networks

Yijie Wang and Kan Yang

National Laboratory for Parallel and Distributed Processing, Institute of Computer,
National University of Defense Technology, Changsha, China, 410073
wwyyjj1971@vip.sina.com

Abstract. Power conservation is a critical issue in mobile ad hoc networks, as the nodes are powered by batteries only. In this paper, according to the mobility of nodes, the power-aware dynamic adaptive replica allocation algorithm is proposed. In the power-aware dynamic adaptive replica allocation algorithm, based on the locality of data access, the replica allocation scheme is adjusted regularly in order to reduce the power consumption, and thus extend the survival time of network. The relation between mobility models and efficiency of power-aware dynamic adaptive replica allocation algorithm is studied. The results of performance evaluation show that the power-aware dynamic adaptive replica allocation algorithm can reduce the total power consumption of network greatly.

1 Introduction

Recent advances in computer and wireless communication technologies have led to an increasing interest in mobile ad hoc networks (MANET) which are constructed by only mobile nodes.

A traditional mobile network consists of a fixed network of servers and clients, with a collection of mobile clients that move throughout the geographic area of the network. Within the mobile network, servers have unlimited power and communicate with mobile nodes over a wireless connection. Mobile clients may only communicate among themselves through a server.

In contrast, a MANET consists of a collection of wireless nodes without a fixed infrastructure. All nodes are wireless, mobile and battery powered [1]. The topology can change frequently. The nodes organize themselves automatically, and can be a standalone network or attached to a larger network, including the Internet. All nodes can freely communicate with every other node. Even if the source and the destination mobile nodes are not in the communication range of each other, each node in the network forwards packets for its peer nodes, data packets are forwarded to the destination mobile node by relaying transmission through other mobile nodes. In addition to the issues associated with a mobile network, the power consumption and mobility of the server(s) must also be considered in a MANET.

Data replication is an important way to improve the system performance and reliability, which is broadly used in database system, files system, operation system, and distributed system. In mobile ad hoc networks, wireless communication bandwidth is limited, disconnections occur frequently, and this causes frequent network division. While data replication is very effective for improving the data availability, mobile nodes generally have poor resources and it is impossible for mobile nodes to have replicas of all data items in the network. Therefore, data replication in such a dynamic resource-limited environment is a significant challenge.

At present, several algorithms are proposed for replica allocation in mobile ad hoc networks. Most of the existing algorithms are focused on the data availability during the network division, the power consumption of nodes is not considered sufficiently. The algorithms SAF[2], DAFN[3] and DCG[4] are proposed by Takahiro Hara in Osaka University. In these three algorithms, the access frequency from mobile nodes to each data item and the status of the network connection are taken into account to improve the data availability during the network division. The collection of global information of data access frequency will bring about vast communication cost, especially while the network topology changes frequently. The algorithm [5] proposed by Karen H. Wang in Toronto University, the algorithm [6] proposed by Jiun Long Huang in National Taiwan University and the algorithm [7] proposed by Kai Chen in Illinois University are all aimed at the group mobility model, and the replica allocation is decided by the prediction of network division.

In order to maximize the total battery life of mobile ad hoc networks, the power consumption of the entire network must be minimized. In this paper, in view of the power consumption and mobility of nodes, a power-aware dynamic adaptive replica allocation algorithm (PADARA) is proposed. Section 2 states the problem and our motivation. Section 3 describes the power-aware dynamic adaptive replica allocation algorithm. Section 4 presents the results of performance evaluation. Section 5 provides a summary of our research work.

2 Model and Statement of the Problem

2.1 The Power Consumption Model

Received signal power is smaller than the transmit power due to losses that occur due to several reasons. These path losses can be divided into large scale path loss, and small scale path loss. Large scale path loss models are used to predict the mean signal power for any transmitter-receiver separation. Small scale path loss models characterize the rapid fluctuations of the received signal strength over very short travel distances [8]. There are several models for large scale path loss, according to the log-distance path loss model, the transmit power falls as $1/d^n$, $n \geq 2$, so relaying information between nodes may result in lower power transmission than communicating over large distances.

The power consumption of a data transmission between node s and r includes transmit power, receive power and computation power. The transmit power is $P_t(s,r) = Kd(s,r)^n$, K is a constant, d(s, r) is the distance between s and r. When a node receives a signal from other node, it needs consume some power to receive, store and then process that signal. This additional power consumed at the receiver node is referred as the receive power. Typically, every node consumes the same receive power due to the nature of its operations. Hereafter, we will denote such power by a constant c. Notice that additional power will also be consumed when running the routing algorithm. In the design of modern processors, however, the power consumption required for such processing and computation can be made negligible compared to the transmit power and receive power. Therefore, the power consumption of a data transmission between node s and r is $P(s,r) = Kd(s,r)^n + c$.

2.2 Power Control

In the mobile ad hoc networks, nodes communicate with each other either through a single-hop transmission if the receiver node is within the transmission range of sender, or through multi-hop wireless links by using intermediate nodes to relay the message. In other words, each node in the network also acts as a router, forwarding data packets for other nodes. The transmission by a node can be received by all nodes within its transmission range. There are two models of the transmission range of all nodes: either all nodes have the same transmission power, or each node can adjust its transmission power independently according to its neighborhood information to possibly reduce the power consumption. In this paper, we assume that each mobile node can adjust the transmission power accordingly, and that the nodes are deployed in a two dimensional area, where no two nodes are in the same physical location. Minimizing power consumption has been a major design goal for mobile ad hoc networks. According to the power consumption model, even a node r is within the transmission range of another node s, it may be power efficient to use another node to relay the signal sent from s to r [9,10,11,12,13].

We assume that each mobile node typically has a portable set with transmission and reception processing capabilities, and that each node has a low-power GPS receiver, which provides the position information of the node itself, within at least 5 meters of accuracy [14].

Definition 1. Relay Region
The relay region of a node r for a node s is defined as

$$R(s,r) = \{x | P(s,r) + P(r,x) < P(s,x)\}.$$

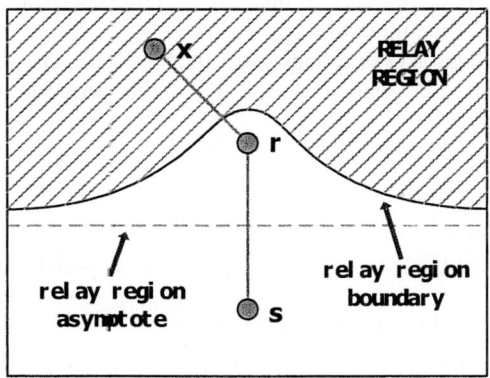 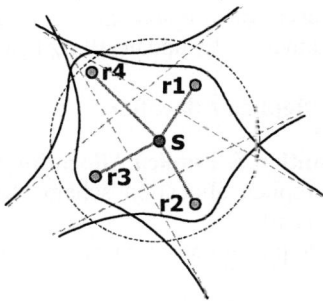

Fig. 1. Relay region of relay node r for transmit node s   **Fig. 2.** Neighbors of transmit node s

$P(s,x)$ is the power incurred if node s directly transmits signal to node x, and $P(s,r)+P(r,x)$ is the power incurred if node s uses the node r as the relay node for transmission from s to node x. Thus, given node s and node r, the locus of all node x, such that relaying through node r consumes less power than directly transmitting from s to x, is called the relay region of r for s. Fig. 1 illustrates a typical relay region in a propagation environment with $1/d^4$ transmit power rolloff.

Definition 2. Enclosure Region
The enclosure region of a node s is defined as
$$E(s) = \bigcap_{r \in T(s)} E(s,r).$$
The region $E(s,r)$ is called the enclosure region of node s by node r, it is the complement of region $R(s,r)$. $T(s)$ is the set of nodes lying within the transmission range of node s.

Definition 3. Neighbors
The neighbors of a node s is defined as
$$N(s) = \{y | y \in T(s), y \in E(s)\}.$$
The nodes that lie in the enclosure region of s is called the neighbors of s (Fig. 2), and they are the only nodes to which s will maintain communication links for power-efficient transmission. The other nodes lie in the relay regions of the neighbors of s, so it is not power-efficient to transmit directly to these nodes, it may be power efficient to use neighbors to relay the signal sent from s to these nodes.

While node transmits data, it can adjust the transmission power to the minimum power enough for the neighbor node to receive the data.

2.3 Data Access

Definition 4. Read-Write Pattern
The read-write pattern for an object O is the number of data access requests (read and write) to O generated by each node in a time interval t.

In this paper, we assume that the data access requests are independent. The read requests are implemented by access the replica node, the write requests are implemented by update all replica nodes.

2.4 Replica Allocation

Definition 5. Replica Allocation Scheme
The replica allocation scheme for an object O is the set of nodes at which O is replicated.

The power consumption of a single read request by node s is
$$P_{read}(s,O) = P(s,\ldots,r_v) = P(s,n_1) + \sum_{i=1}^{u-1} P(n_i, n_{i+1}) + P(n_u, r_v).$$

r_v is the replica node of object O, which is chosen for read request. n_i (i = 1, 2, ..., u) is the relay nodes between s and r_v.

The power consumption of a single write request by node s is

$$P_{write}(s,O) = P(s,...,r_v) + \sum_{r_i \in r\_set(O)} P(r_v,...,r_i).$$

r_v is the replica node of object O, which is chosen for write request. $r\_set(O)$ is the set of replica nodes of object O. $P(s,...,r_v)$ is the power consumption of update operation on r_v, $\sum_{r_i \in r\_set(O)} P(r_v,...,r_i)$ is the power consumption of update operations on other replica nodes in $r\_set(O)$.

The total power consumption of data access to object O in a time interval t is

$$POWER(O) = \sum_{s \in N}(\operatorname{Re}ad(s,O) \times P_{read}(s,O) + Write(s,O) \times P_{write}(s,O)).$$

$\operatorname{Re}ad(s,O)$ is the number of read requests to O in a time interval t, $Write(s,O)$ is the number of write requests to O in a time interval t.

For an optimal replica allocation scheme for object O, the total power consumption of data access to object O in a time interval t is minimum, but the problem of finding an optimal replica allocation scheme has been proved to be NP-complete for different power consumption models [15]. In this paper, based on the heuristic algorithm, a power-aware dynamic adaptive replica allocation algorithm is proposed to find a suboptimal replica allocation scheme.

3 Replica Allocation Considering Power Consumption

In the power-aware dynamic adaptive replica allocation algorithm, based on the local information of access requests collected from the neighbors by each replica node, replica expansion, replica switch and replica contraction are done in order to reduce the power consumption, and thus extend the survival time of network.

PADARA is executed periodically and independently in each replica node, the execution cycle is set according to the change of network topology and read-write pattern.

PADARA includes expansion test, switch test and contraction test. The description of PADARA is as follows:

//for object O, m∈ r_set(O)
Calculate the neighbors of replica node rn, which is denoted as N(rn).
for (u∈ N(m) , u∉ r_set(O))
{ // expansion test is done for each neighbor of m, which is not replica node of object O
    if (the expansion condition is satisfied)
    { // replica expansion
        r_set(O) = r_set(O) + {u} ;
        return;
    }
}

```
       for ( u∈ N(m) , u∉ r_set(O) )
       { // expansion test is done for each neighbor of m, which is not replica node of
object O
           if ( the switch condition is satisfied )
           { // replica switch
               r_set(O) = r_set(O) - {m} + {u} ;
               return;
           }
       }
       for ( m )
       { // contraction test is done for m
           if ( the contraction condition is satisfied )
           { // replica contraction
               r_set(O) = r_set(O) - {m};
               return;
           }
       }
```

For replica expansion, the number of replicas is increased, the power consumption of read operations for some nodes is decreased, but the power consumption of write operations on new replica should be considered. For replica switch, the power consumption of some nodes maybe decreased, but the power consumption of other nodes maybe increased. For replica contraction, the number of replicas is decreased, the power consumption of some write operations is avoided, but the power consumption of read requests on some nodes maybe increased. In PADARA, local information is utilized, so it is not guaranteed that each replica adjustment will reduce the power consumption, but the total power consumption of network will be decreased continuously.

3.1 Expansion Test

There are two extreme situations for expansion test (Fig.3).

In Fig.3(a), each shortest path between u and replicas of object O will pass through m. While the replica is expanded to u, the read requests forwarded by u to other replicas will be processed just by u, the power consumption of data transmission between u and m will be avoided; in order to maintain the consistency of replicas, the write requests will be propagated to all replicas including the new replica u, so the power consumption of the write requests will be increased. Therefore, the expansion condition is as follows:

$$\Delta E = \sum_{r \in r\_set(O)} write(r) \times P(r,...,u) + (num\_r\_set(O)-1) \times write(u) \times P(u,m) - read(u) \times P(u,m) < 0 \quad (1)$$

$write(r)$ is the number of write requests on object O received by r in the time interval t, $read(u)$ is the number of read requests on object O received by u in the time interval t. $num\_r\_set(O)$ is the number of replicas in $r\_set(O)$.

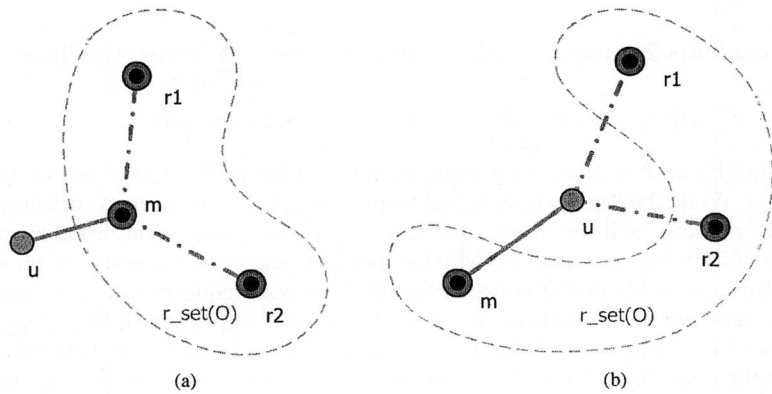

Fig. 3. Two extreme situations for expansion test and switch test

In Fig.3(b), each shortest path between m and other replicas of object O will pass through u. While the replica is expanded to u, the read requests forwarded by u to other replicas will be processed just by u, the power consumption of data transmission between u and m will be avoided; in order to maintain the consistency of replicas, the write requests will be propagated to all replicas including the new replica u, the power consumption of the write requests received by u will be decreased, the power consumption of the write requests to other replicas will be increased. Therefore, the expansion condition is as follows:

$$\Delta E = \sum_{r \in r\_set(O)} write(r) \times P(r,...,u) - (num\_r\_set(O)-1) \times write(u) \times P(u,m) - read(u) \times P(u,m) < 0 \quad (2)$$

The expansion condition (1) may be too strict to miss some expansions. The expansion condition (2) may be too loose to make wrong expansions. Therefore, the compromised expansion condition is as follows:

$$\Delta E = \sum_{r \in r\_set(O)} write(r) \times P(r,...,u) - (read(u) + write(u)) \times P(u,m) < 0 \quad (3)$$

3.2 Switch Test

There are two extreme situations for switch test (Fig.3).

In Fig.3(a), each shortest path between u and replicas of object O will pass through m. While the replica is switched from m to u, the read requests forwarded by u to other replicas will be processed just by u, the power consumption of data transmission between u and m will be avoided; the read requests to m will be forwarded to u, so the power consumption of these read requests will be increased; in order to maintain the consistency of replicas, the write requests will be propagated to all replicas including the new replica u, so the power consumption of the write requests will be increased. Therefore, the switch condition is as follows:

$$\Delta E = \left(read(m) + 2 \times (num\_r\_set(O) - 1) \times write(m) + \sum_{r \in r\_set(O)} write(r) \right) \times P(u, m) \quad (4)$$
$$+ (num\_r\_set(O) - 1) \times write(u) \times P(u, m) - read(u) \times P(u, m) < 0$$

In Fig.3(b), each shortest path between m and other replicas of object O will pass through u. While the replica is switched from m to u, the read requests forwarded by u to other replicas will be processed just by u, the power consumption of data transmission between u and m will be avoided; the read requests to m will be forwarded to u, so the power consumption of these read requests will be increased; in order to maintain the consistency of replicas, the write requests will be propagated to all replicas including the new replica u, because each shortest path between m and other replicas of object O will pass through u, the power consumption of the write requests will be decreased. Therefore, the switch condition is as follows:

$$\Delta E = \left(read(m) - (num\_r\_set(O) - 1) \times write(m) - \sum_{r \in r\_set(O)} write(r) \right) \times P(u, m) \quad (5)$$
$$- num\_r\_set(O) \times write(u) \times P(u, m) - read(u) \times P(u, m) < 0$$

The switch condition (4) may be too strict to miss some switch. The switch condition (5) may be too loose to make wrong switch. Therefore, the compromised switch condition is as follows:

$$\Delta E = (read(m) + write(m)) \times P(u, m) - (2 \times write(u) + read(u)) \times P(u, m) < 0 \quad (6)$$

3.3 Contraction Test

There are two extreme situations for contraction test (Fig.4).

In Fig.4(a), each shortest path between u and other replicas of object O will pass through m. While the replica u is deleted, the read requests to u will be forwarded to m, the power consumption of data transmission between u and m will be increased; the write requests to u will be forwarded to m, because each shortest path between u and other replicas of object O will pass through m, the power consumption of these write requests will be decreased; in order to maintain the consistency of replicas, the write requests will be propagated to all replicas, because the replica u is deleted, so the power consumption of the write requests to other replicas will be decreased. Therefore, the contraction condition is as follows:

$$\Delta E = (read(u) - (num\_r\_set(O) - 2) \times write(u)) \times P(u, m) - \sum_{r \in r\_set(O)} write(r) \times P(r, ..., u) < 0 \quad (7)$$

In Fig.3(b), each shortest path between m and other replicas of object O will pass through u. While the replica u is deleted, the read requests to u will be forwarded to m, the power consumption of data transmission between u and m will be increased; the write requests to u will be forwarded to m, because each shortest path between m and other replicas of object O will pass through u, the power consumption of these write requests will be increased; in order to maintain the consistency of replicas, the write requests will be propagated to all replicas, because the replica u is deleted, so the power consumption of the write requests to other replicas will be decreased. Therefore, the contraction condition is as follows:

$$\Delta E = (read(u) + (num\_r\_set(O) - 2) \times write(u)) \times P(u,m) - \sum_{r \in r\_set(O)} write(r) \times P(r,...,u) < 0 \quad (8)$$

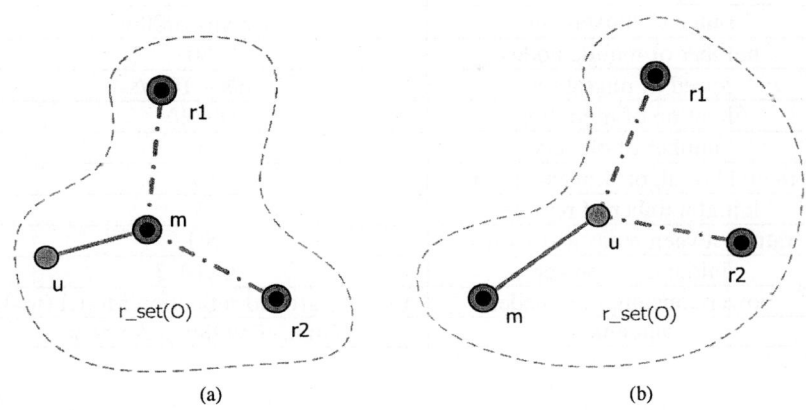

Fig. 4. Two extreme situations for contraction test

The contraction condition (7) may be too loose to make wrong contractions. The contraction condition (8) may be too strict to miss some contractions. Therefore, the compromised contraction condition is as follows:

$$\Delta E = (read(u) + write(u)) \times P(u,m) - \sum_{r \in r\_set(O)} write(r) \times P(r,...,u) < 0 \quad (9)$$

4 Performance Evaluation

In this section, the performance of power-aware dynamic adaptive replica allocation algorithm is analyzed.

4.1 Influence of Mobility of Nodes on Efficiency of Power-Aware Dynamic Adaptive Replica Allocation Algorithm

The parameters of test environment are shown in Table 1. We compare PADARA and algorithm ADR-G [16]. In ADR-G, the spanning tree is build to organize replicas. The mobility model of nodes is Random Waypoint Mobility Model [17].

In Fig.5, the total mobile node power decreased gradually. Compared with ADR_G, the mean power consumption in PADARA is 35.7% less. In ADR_G, the write requests are propagated among replica nodes along spanning tree, and the replicas are located in nodes adjacent to each other. While nodes move, the network topology changes, and the replica nodes are no longer adjacent physically, so the power consumption in ADR_G increases rapidly. In PADARA, the replica allocation scheme is adjusted according to power consumption, so the power consumption is reduced greatly, and the survival time of network is extended.

Table 1. Parameters of test environment

parameter	default value
range of movement	1000m×1000m
number of mobile nodes	50
speed of migration	0m/s ~ 10m/s
direction of migration	$0 \sim 2\delta$
number of objects	1
interval of algorithm execution	10s
initial number of replica	5
ratio between reads and writes	5:1
initial node power	10×10^3 J
power consumption model	two-ray ground reflection Model (n=4)
antenna	Omni-directional Antenna

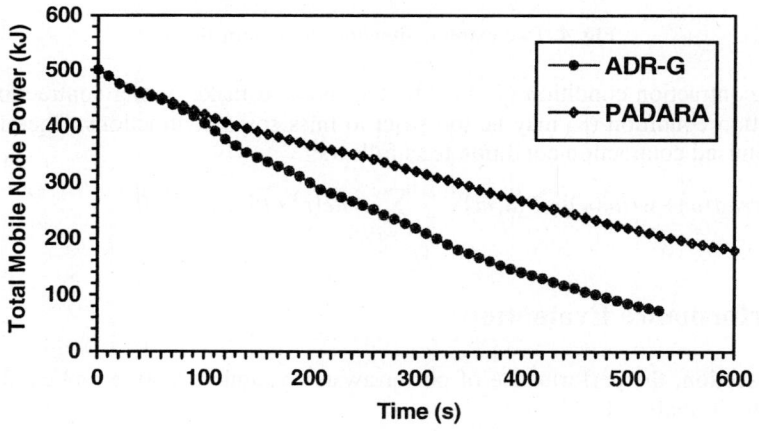

Fig. 5. Mobility of nodes

4.2 Relation Between Mobility Models and Efficiency of Power-Aware Dynamic Adaptive Replica Allocation Algorithm

Three typical mobility models [17] are selected to investigate the relation between mobility models and efficiency of PADARA. Three mobility models are Random Waypoint Mobility Model, Random Gauss-Markov Mobility Model and Reference Point Group Mobility Model, which are denoted as RW, GM and RPG respectively. The parameters of test environment are shown in Table 1. We observe the influence of different mobility models with different speed of migration on efficiency of PADARA.

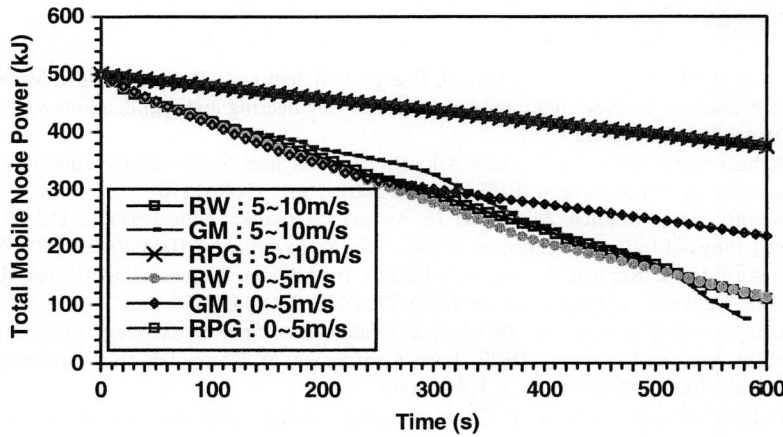

Fig. 6. Mobility models

In Random Waypoint Mobility Model (Fig.6), the power consumption difference between different speeds of migration is little. The movement of nodes is concentrated in the center of moving area, thus the replica allocation scheme is relatively stable.

In Random Gauss-Markov Mobility Model (Fig.6), the speed of migration influences the power consumption obviously. For high speed of migration, the power consumption changes greatly; for low speed of migration, the power consumption changes calmly; compared with the low speed of migration, the mean power consumption for high speed of migration is 53.4% more. The speed of migration is higher, network topology changed more frequently, if the replica allocation scheme is not adjusted in time, the power consumption will be increased more greatly.

In Reference Point Group Mobility Model (Fig.6), only one group is selected, the relative movement between nodes is little, the network topology is relatively stable, thus the replica allocation scheme can be adjusted in time, so the power consumption will not increased greatly.

5 Conclusion

Compared with the traditional mobile network, the power consumption and mobility of nodes are significant characteristic of mobile ad hoc network. In the power-aware dynamic adaptive replica allocation algorithm, according to the power consumption of nodes, the replica allocation scheme is adjusted regularly, thus the survival time of network is extended. The results of performance evaluation show that the power-aware dynamic adaptive replica allocation algorithm can reduce the total power consumption of network greatly. The relation between mobility models and efficiency of power-aware dynamic adaptive replica allocation algorithm is studied In the future research, the power-aware dynamic adaptive replica allocation algorithm will be improved in view of the feature of different mobility models.

References

1. Gruenwald, L., Javed, M., and Gu, M. Energy-Efficient Data Broadcasting in Mobile Ad-Hoc Networks. In Proc. International Database Engineering and Applications Symposium (IDEAS '02), July, 2002.
2. Takahiro Hara. Effective Replica Allocation in Ad hoc Networks for Improving Data Accessibility. Proceeding of IEEE Infocom 2001, 2001, 1568~1576
3. Takahiro Hara. Replica Allocation in Ad hoc Networks with Periodic Data Update. Proceedings of Int'l Conference on Mobile Data Management (MDM 2002), 2002, 79~86
4. Takahiro Hara. Replica Allocation Methods in Ad Hoc Networks with Data Update. Mobile Networks and Applications, MONET, 2003, 8(4):343~354
5. Karen H Wang, Baochun Li. Efficient and Guaranteed Service Coverage in Partitionable Mobile Ad-hoc Networks. IEEE Joint Conference of Computer and Communication Societies (INFOCOM'02), 2002, 1089~1098
6. Jiun-Long Huang, Ming-Syan Chen, Wen-Chih Peng. Exploring Group Mobility for Replica Data Allocation in a Mobile Environment, Proceedings of the 12th International Conference on Information and Knowledge Management, Database Session 3: Data Management in Mobile Environments, 2003, 161~168
7. Kai Chen, Klara Nahrstedt. An Integrated Data Lookup and Replication Scheme in Mobile Ad Hoc Networks. Proceedings of SPIE International Symposium on the Convergence of Information Technologies and Communications (ITCom 2001), 2001, 1~8
8. Theodore S Rappaport . Wireless Communications : Principles and Practice . New Jersey : Prentice Hall, 1996
9. L. Li and J. Halpern. Minimum energy mobile wireless networks revisited. In IEEE International Conference on Communications (ICC), June 2001.
10. P.-J.Wan, G. Calinescu, X.-Y. Li, and O. Frieder. Minimum energy broadcast routing in static ad hoc wireless networks. In IEEE Infocom, 2001.
11. J.-H. Chang and L. Tassiulas. Energy conserving routing in wireless ad-hoc networks. In Infocom, 2000.
12. V Rodoplu , T H Meng . Minimum Energy Mobile Wireless Networks . Selected Areas in Communications , IEEE Journal , 1999 , 17(8):1333~1344
13. V Rodoplu , T H Meng . Minimum Energy Mobile Wireless Networks . Proc. of the IEEE International Conference on Communication , 1998 , 3:1633~1693
14. Arvin R Shahani , Derek K Schaeffer , and Thomas H Lee . A 12mW Wide Dynamic Range CMOS Front-End for a Portable GPS Receiver . IEEE International Solid-State Circuits Conference , 1997 , 40:368~369
15. S.A Cook, J.K Pachl, and I.S Pressman, "The Optimal Location of Replicas in A Network Using A Read-One-Write- All Policy", Distribute Computing, vol.15, no.1, 2002, pp.7-17.
16. O Wolfson , S Jajodia , Y Huang . An Adaptive Data Replication Algorithm . ACM Transactions on Database System , 1997 , 22(4):255~314
17. T Camp , J Boleng , and V Davies . A Survey of Mobility Models for Ad Hoc Network Research . Wireless Communication & Mobile Computing (WCMC) , Special Issue on Mobile Ad Hoc Networking , 2002 , 2(5):483~502

GCPM: A Model for Efficient Call Admission Control in Wireless Cellular Networks

Lanlan Cong[1,2], Beihong Jin[1], Donglei Cao[1,2], and Jiannong Cao[3]

[1] Institute of Software, Chinese Academy of Sciences, Beijing, China
{lanlan, jbh, caodl}@otcaix.iscas.ac.cn
[2] Graduate School of the Chinese Academy of Sciences, Beijing, China
[3] Department of Computing, Hong Kong Polytechnic University, Hung Hom, Hong Kong
csjcao@comp.polyu.edu.hk

Abstract. Call Admission Control (CAC) is crucial for assuring the quality of service (QoS) of communication in wireless cellular networks. In this paper, we propose a model, called Guard Channel Prediction Model (GCPM), for efficient call admission control satisfying the QoS requirements. A predictive value of the appropriate number of guard channels can be calculated based on this model by using statistical properties of new and handoff call arrival rates and mean call residency time, as well as the total capacity of a specific cell. Simulation studies are carried out to evaluate the performance in comparison with an existing adaptive algorithm under variable traffic loads and mobility patterns. Simulation results show that our proposed GCPM, using the static and fractional Guard Channel policy to process both types of incoming calls based on the predictive values, has gained better QoS with less blocking probabilities of both types of calls and meanwhile, larger network utilizations.

Keywords: Call Admission Control, Guard Channel, Guard Channel Prediction Model (GCPM), Quality of Service (QoS), Wireless/Mobile Cellular Networks.

1 Introduction

Call Admission Control (CAC) policy is an important research issue in wireless/mobile cellular networks, which comprise a wired backbone network and a large number of fixed base stations (BSs) interconnected together through the backbone. The geographical area covered by a BS is referred to as a cell. A mobile, while needing to communicate with another party (a node on the wired network or another mobile), first tries to obtain a free channel from the BS of the cell it is located in to make a wireless connection. Since the number of channels allocated to each BS is limited, when there is no channel available, the call request will be blocked. There are two kinds of blocking in cellular networks: *new call blocking*, the refusal of a new call request, and *handoff call blocking*, the refusal of a handoff call request, which occurs while an ongoing call moving in from an adjacent cell. The quality of service (QoS) provided by wireless cellular network carriers will be determined by the probabilities of these two types of blocking, while the latter is usually given higher priority because an unsuccessful handoff which results in an abrupt, premature termination of an on-going conversation will definitely upset the caller more than a rejection of the call in the first place [1].

Handoff is referred to as the action of switching a call in progress in order to maintain the continuity and the required quality of service (QoS) of the call. It is one of the most important aspects of mobile computing since it allows for the uninterrupted movement of mobile users [2]. Handoff relies on the underlying call admission control (CAC) policies. CAC has been studied by many researchers during the last two decades and many schemes have been proposed for it [1, 3 -14].

The Guard Channel Scheme is a well-known and efficient CAC policy which was first introduced by Hong et al. in the mid-80s [3]. In this policy, a set of channels called the guard channels are permanently and exclusively reserved for handoff calls [3] to give priority to handoff calls over new calls. Ramjee et al. introduced the Fractional Guard Channel Policy [4], which effectively reserves a non-integral number of guard channels for handoff calls by rejecting new calls with some probability that depends on the current channel occupancy. A Dynamic Channel Reservation Scheme (DCRS) [5] was proposed by Kim et al., which is based on the notion of guard channels. The number of guard channels is static in that proposal, but they can also be used for new calls according to the mobility of calls and status of the network. A scheme for dynamically adjusting the number of guard channels [1] was proposed by Zhang et al. They developed an adaptive algorithm for CAC in wireless networks, which can automatically search the optimal number of guard channels to be reserved at each base station [1].

However, the setting of the threshold number of guard channels in DCRS and the adjusting algorithm from Zhang et al. are mainly derived from experience, lacking the support of a mathematical model. The reliance on experience may cause unstable performance in practice and be lack of the ability to adapt to changes. That means an improper setting of the threshold in DCRS will become a severe restriction to this scheme, as the threshold of guard channels' number is an upper bound for adjustment and cannot be exceeded according to DCRS procedure. Moreover, the adjusting algorithm [1] from Zhang et al. lacks the consideration of potential changes of network load and users' mobility, which will cause unstable QoS under different traffic patterns due to fluctuation of traffic load and calls' mobility.

In this paper, we propose a model, called Guard Channel Prediction Model (GCPM), for efficient call admission control. GCPM is based on the statistical properties of both types of calls in wireless/mobile cellular networks. It takes into consideration the relationships among cell's capacity, traffic load, users' mobility and the reserved number of guard channels, by which rational predictive values for the number of guard channels under different traffic patterns can be easily obtained. Using these predictive values, desired QoS can be achieved as shown in our simulations.

The remaining part of this paper is organized as follows. In Section 2, we will describe the GCPM model in detail. Simulations and evaluations will be presented in Section 3, with the discussion of the performance comparison with the adaptive adjusting algorithm [1]. Finally, Section 4 provides the conclusions and describes our future work.

2 The GCPM Model

2.1 Assumptions

Considering a mobile communication network with a cellular wireless infrastructure, there are a total number of C channels (in the form of frequencies, time slots or codes depending on the radio technology used) in each cell and each ongoing call is allocated a channel. When the number of mobile users is much larger than the total number of channels in the cell, call arrivals may approximate to a Poisson process [5]. We assume that new and handoff calls arrive according to Poisson processes with rates λ_n and λ_h respectively. Each accepted call (either new or handoff) will reside in the cell for an exponentially distributed time with mean $1/\mu$. When a call is completed in the cell or a user moves to an adjacent cell while his/her call is still in progress, a channel in this cell will be released. Such assumptions were also used in existing studies [1, 12].

In this paper, we will not consider the following issues: multiple services with different QoS requirements and traffic characteristics in the network, soft capacity and bandwidth degradation in Code Division Multiple Access (CDMA) systems, soft handoff in CDMA systems, in which a mobile can communicate with two base stations simultaneously, and delay-insensitive applications, which can tolerate long handoff time delay when there is momentarily insufficient bandwidth [6, 7]. Based on the above assumptions, the handoff queuing scheme [8] also will not be considered.

2.2 Mathematical Model

As mentioned before, GCPM is based on the statistical properties of both types of calls in wireless/mobile cellular networks. It takes into consideration and models the relationships among cell's capacity, traffic load, users' mobility and the reserved number of guard channels, by which rational predictive values for the number of guard channels under different traffic patterns can be easily obtained.

We assume that, after a long period of time for adjustment, the whole system will step into a steady state, during which the number of guard channels will be stabilized at a specific value, denoted by GC. In that case, new call blocking rate and handoff call blocking rate will also be stabilized at R_n and R_h respectively. Considering any time t in this steady state, the number of ongoing calls at t is approximately equal to the number of those calls which were admitted during the time period from $t - \dfrac{1}{\mu}$ to t, based on the assumption that call residency time of both types of calls follows an exponential distribution with mean $1/\mu$.

Therefore, we get:

$$ongoingCalls(t) = \frac{1}{\mu}[\lambda_n \cdot (1-R_n) + \lambda_h \cdot (1-R_h)] \cdot \qquad (1)$$

And the number of free channels in time t will be:

$$freeChannels(t) = C - ongoingCalls(t) = C - \frac{1}{\mu}[\lambda_n \cdot (1-R_n) + \lambda_h \cdot (1-R_h)] \qquad (2)$$

Then, we consider the process of call completions and call arrivals during a time period from t to $t+\Delta t$, with any time interval Δt. The number of calls that will complete during this time period approximates to those admitted from time $t - \dfrac{1}{\mu}$ to

$t - \frac{1}{\mu} + \Delta t$, that is: $\Delta t \cdot \lambda_n \cdot (1 - R_n)$ new calls and $\Delta t \cdot \lambda_h \cdot (1 - R_h)$ handoff calls will be completed during this time interval. Based on the stabilized new call blocking rate and handoff call blocking rate in the stable state, there will also be $\Delta t \cdot \lambda_n \cdot (1 - R_n)$ new calls and $\Delta t \cdot \lambda_h \cdot (1 - R_h)$ handoff calls admitted during this time period. Therefore, the system will be steady with invariable number of both types of ongoing calls in theory.

To make the maximum utilization of network resources, the free channels of each cell should be optimized to zero in the steady state. Based on eq. (2), we can get:

$$C - \frac{1}{\mu}[\lambda_n \cdot (1 - R_n) + \lambda_h \cdot (1 - R_h)] = 0 \cdot \quad (3)$$

To satisfy $R_h \leq T_H$, where T_H is an upper bound for handoff call blocking probability and specified as QoS requirement, we get the lower bound of new call blocking rate as follows:

$$C - \frac{1}{\mu}[\lambda_n \cdot (1 - R_n) + \lambda_h \cdot (1 - R_h)] = 0$$

$$\Rightarrow R_n = 1 - \frac{C \cdot \mu - \lambda_h \cdot (1 - R_h)}{\lambda_n} \quad (4)$$

$$\Rightarrow R_n \geq 1 - \frac{C \cdot \mu - \lambda_h \cdot (1 - T_H)}{\lambda_n} \quad \text{where } R_h \leq T_H.$$

Considering $R_n \in [0,1]$, if $1 - \frac{C \cdot \mu - \lambda_h \cdot (1 - T_H)}{\lambda_n} > 1$, $R_h \leq T_H$ can not be satisfied in theory. Meanwhile, if $1 - \frac{C \cdot \mu - \lambda_h \cdot (1 - T_H)}{\lambda_n} < 0$, the minimum upper bound of R_h will be reduced to $1 - \frac{C \cdot \mu - \lambda_n}{\lambda_h}$, which is smaller than T_H.

As a result, we get

$$\begin{cases} R_h \leq 1 - \frac{C \cdot \mu - \lambda_n}{\lambda_h} < T_H, R_n \geq 0 & 1 - \frac{C \cdot \mu - \lambda_h \cdot (1 - T_H)}{\lambda_n} < 0, \\ R_h \leq T_H, R_n \geq 1 - \frac{C \cdot \mu - \lambda_h \cdot (1 - T_H)}{\lambda_n} & \text{if} \quad 0 \leq 1 - \frac{C \cdot \mu - \lambda_h \cdot (1 - T_H)}{\lambda_n} \leq 1, \\ R_h \geq 1 - \frac{C \cdot \mu}{\lambda_h} > T_H, R_n \leq 1 & 1 - \frac{C \cdot \mu - \lambda_h \cdot (1 - T_H)}{\lambda_n} > 1. \end{cases} \quad (5)$$

Based on inequations (5), the appropriate values of R_h and R_n can be acquired by reducing R_h to satisfy $R_h \leq T_H$ if possible, and meanwhile minimizing the value of R_n as QoS requires. Using the appropriate values of R_h and R_n, we can obtain the predictable number of guard channels GC in the steady state. As discussed above, we know that the number of either type of ongoing calls will be stabilized in theory. As a result, we assume that there will be x new calls and $(C-x)$ handoff calls in the steady state.

To admit x new calls, there should be $x \cdot \frac{1}{1-R_n}$ new calls arrived. With the ratio $\lambda_n : \lambda_h$ of the arrival rates for new calls and handoff calls, $x \cdot \frac{1}{1-R_n} \cdot \frac{\lambda_h}{\lambda_n}$ handoff calls were accompanied to arrive, among which only $x \cdot \frac{1}{1-R_n} \cdot \frac{\lambda_h}{\lambda_n} \cdot (1-R_h)$ were admitted, based on the steady handoff call blocking probability R_h. So, we can get eq. (6):

$$C - x = x \cdot \frac{1}{1-R_n} \cdot \frac{\lambda_h}{\lambda_n} \cdot (1-R_h)$$
$$\Rightarrow x = \frac{C \cdot \lambda_n \cdot (1-R_n)}{\lambda_n \cdot (1-R_n) + \lambda_h \cdot (1-R_h)}. \tag{6}$$

It means that $\frac{C \cdot \lambda_n \cdot (1-R_n)}{\lambda_n \cdot (1-R_n) + \lambda_h \cdot (1-R_h)}$ new calls and $\frac{C \cdot \lambda_h \cdot (1-R_h)}{\lambda_n \cdot (1-R_n) + \lambda_h \cdot (1-R_h)}$ handoff calls are located in the steady system. While R_n is not equal to R_h, the allocated numbers of new calls and handoff calls are not in accord with the ratio of their arrival rates $\lambda_n : \lambda_h$. This is caused by the existence of guard channels, in which only handoff calls can be accepted exclusively.

Additional number of allocated handoff calls A_h due to the existence of available guard channels in the steady state can be calculated as follows:

$$A_h = \frac{C \cdot \lambda_h \cdot (1-R_h)}{\lambda_n \cdot (1-R_n) + \lambda_h \cdot (1-R_h)} - \frac{C \cdot \lambda_n \cdot (1-R_n)}{\lambda_n \cdot (1-R_n) + \lambda_h \cdot (1-R_h)} \cdot \frac{\lambda_h}{\lambda_n}$$
$$= \frac{C \cdot \lambda_h \cdot (R_n - R_h)}{\lambda_n \cdot (1-R_n) + \lambda_h \cdot (1-R_h)} \tag{7}$$
$$= \frac{1}{\mu} \cdot \lambda_h \cdot (R_n - R_h) \qquad \text{based on (3)}.$$

The steady value of guard channels' number GC should be proportional to A_h with a coefficient k due to the distribution rules and the mobility of allocated channels in practice. k is an important design parameter in our model and chosen as $1/3$. In addition, we assign a lower bound GC_{min} to GC for ensuring the priority of handoff calls even if the traffic load or calls' mobility is very light. And here, we set $GC_{min} = 1.0$.

Thus, we obtain the predictive number of guard channels as follows:

$$GC = \max\{GC_{min}, k \cdot A_h\}$$
$$= \max\left\{GC_{min}, k \cdot \frac{1}{\mu} \cdot \lambda_h \cdot (R_n - R_h)\right\} \quad \text{where} \quad GC_{min} = 1.0, k = \frac{1}{3}. \quad (8)$$

Based on equation (8), using reasonable blocking rates for both types of calls calculated from (5) with the statistical properties of new and handoff call arrival rates and mean call residency time in a specific cell obtained from historical records, we can predict an appropriate value of the number of guard channels. This value will facilitate the system to step into a steady state, maintaining the blocking rate of handoff calls as low as QoS requires, and meanwhile reducing the blocking probability of new calls as much as possible. The computational complexity of GCPM is so low that not much overhead will be imposed on the CAC procedure, which makes the prediction model feasible in practice.

3 Simulations

We have carried out simulations to study the performance of the proposed GCPM model. In this section, we describe the setup of the simulation environment and discuss the simulation results for performance evaluation in comparison with an existing algorithm, namely Zhang et al.'s adaptive adjusting algorithm [1].

3.1 Simulation Environments

Based on the predictive value of guard channels' number obtained from GCPM, we adopt the Limited Fractional Guard Channel Policy [4] to process the incoming calls in a cell. We set the threshold T in Ramjee et al.'s policy [4] as $C - \lceil GC \rceil$ and the new call accepting probability β in state T as $\lceil GC \rceil - GC$.

We consider a cell with total number of $C = 60$ channels, new call and handoff call arrivals are both modeled by Poisson processes with mean λ_n and λ_h respectively. Call residency time of both types of calls in the specific cell is assumed to follow an exponential distribution with mean $1/\mu = 180$ *seconds*. Following notations denote traffic parameters and performance metrics used to evaluate the performance of GCPM:

- ρ : offered load, a measurement of the traffic load in a cell, is defined as follows:
$$\rho = \frac{\lambda_n + \lambda_h}{C \cdot \mu};$$
- α : mobility of ongoing calls, a measurement of the terminal mobility, is defined as the ratio of handoff call arrival rate to new call arrival rate. That is: $\alpha = \frac{\lambda_h}{\lambda_n}$;
- P_n : new call blocking probability;

- P_h : handoff call blocking probability;
- T_H : threshold for handoff call blocking rate and a measurement for QoS, which is commonly chosen as 0.01; and
- CF : cost function, a weighted sum of the two blocking probabilities and another measurement for QoS, is defined as $CF = \omega P_n + (1-\omega)P_h$, where $\omega \in [0,1]$. We choose $\omega = \frac{1}{11}$, and such that $\omega/(1-\omega) = 1/10$ to give higher priority to handoff calls over new calls as QoS requires.

Similar parameters and performance metrics are also seen in [5, 9]. Based on the definitions of ρ and α, new call arrival rate and handoff call arrival rate can be represented respectively as eq. (9).

$$\begin{cases} \lambda_n = \dfrac{C \cdot \mu \cdot \rho}{1+\alpha}, \\ \lambda_h = \dfrac{C \cdot \mu \cdot \rho \cdot \alpha}{1+\alpha}. \end{cases} \quad (9)$$

3.2 Experimental Results

Predictive values of the number of guard channels obtained from GCPM are listed in Table 1 and Table 2, with variable offered loads and terminal mobility patterns respectively.

Table 1. Predictive number of guard channels with variable offered load ρ and stable terminal mobility $\alpha = 0.8$

ρ	α	λ_n	λ_h	GC
0.8	0.8	8.89	7.11	1.0
1.0	0.8	11.11	8.89	1.0
1.2	0.8	13.33	10.67	3.008
1.4	0.8	15.56	12.44	6.176
1.6	0.8	17.78	14.22	9.344
1.8	0.8	20	16	12.512
2.0	0.8	22.22	17.78	15.68
2.2	0.8	24.44	19.56	18.848

Table 2. Predictive number of guard channels with variable terminal mobility α and stable offered load $\rho = 1.4$

α	ρ	λ_n	λ_h	GC
0.2	1.4	23.33	4.67	1.544
0.4	1.4	20	8	3.088
0.6	1.4	17.5	10.5	4.632
0.8	1.4	15.56	12.44	6.176
1.0	1.4	14	14	7.72
1.2	1.4	12.73	15.27	9.264
1.4	1.4	11.67	16.33	10.808
1.6	1.4	10.77	17.23	12.352
1.8	1.4	10	18	13.896
2.0	1.4	9.33	18.67	15.44

The results of simulations based on the predictive values of guard channels' number listed in Table 1 and Table 2 are described below.

Figure 1 shows the handoff call blocking rate, new call blocking rate, cost function and network utilization as functions of offered load ρ for stable mobility $\alpha = 0.8$ of GCPM and Zhang et al.'s adaptive algorithm [1]. As shown in Fig. 1, we can observe that GCPM can achieve much less handoff blocking rates than Zhang's algorithm while keeping the new call blocking rates approximately at the same level. Meanwhile, GCPM can keep handoff call blocking rates under the threshold $T_H = 0.01$ as QoS requires with normal offered load (i.e. load less than 1.8, offered load larger than 2.0 with mobility 0.8 may be too heavy to adjust no matter what methods) while the handoff blocking rates based on Zhang's algorithm are so easy to exceed this threshold though the offered load is not very heavy.

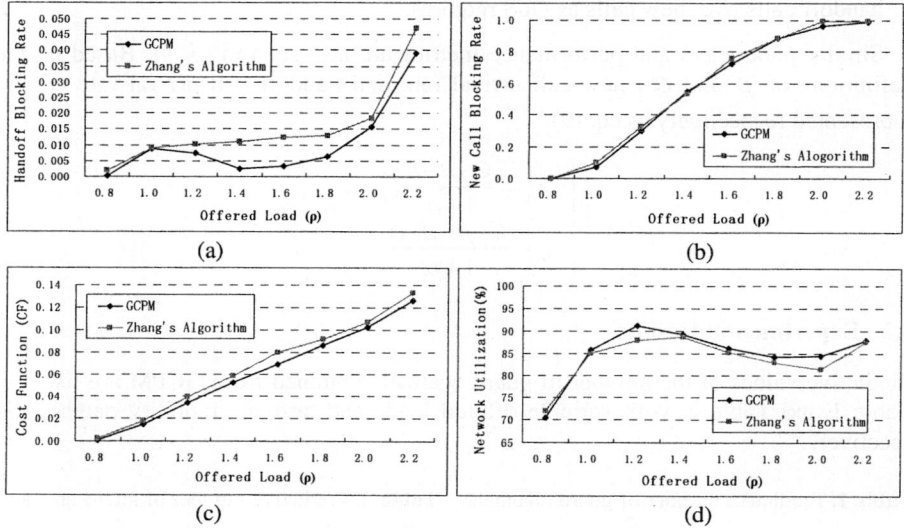

Fig. 1. Comparisons of handoff call blocking rate (a), new call blocking rate (b), cost function (c) and network utilization (d) of GCPM and Zhang et al.'s algorithm [1] under different offered loads ρ and stable mobility of calls $\alpha = 0.8$

Cost functions and network utilizations based on these two methods show similar changing trends when the offered load increases as shown in Fig. 1 (c) and (d). GCPM has obtained smaller values of cost functions with average 0.0604 compared to 0.0661 of Zhang's algorithm, and meanwhile obtained larger network utilizations with average 84.896% compared to 83.800% of Zhang's algorithm.

In Figure 2 (a)~(d), handoff call blocking rate, new call blocking rate, cost function and network utilization according to the variation of mobility patterns are presented respectively. As shown in Fig. 2 (a) and (b), GCPM achieves much less handoff call blocking rates than Zhang's algorithm and meanwhile keeps a slower increasing rate of new call blocking probabilities with a similar starting point compared to Zhang's algorithm when the mobility of calls increases. For example, when terminal mobility increases to 1.6, the new call blocking rate achieved by GCPM is a little more than 0.8, while that obtained from Zhang's algorithm is very close to 1.0, which means approximately no admission to new call requests. Moreover, similar to that shown in Figure 1, under normal level of terminal mobility (i.e. mobility less than 1.6, terminal mobility larger than 1.6 with offered load 1.4 may be too heavy to adjust no matter what methods), GCPM can keep the blocking rate of handoff calls lower than the threshold $T_H = 0.01$ while it's probably impossible for Zhang's algorithm as Fig. 2 (a) shows.

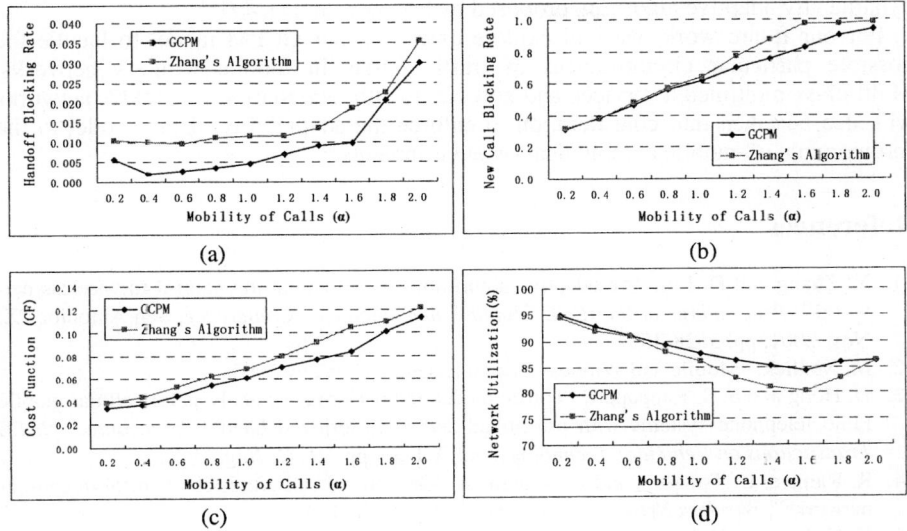

Fig. 2. Comparisons of handoff call blocking rate (a), new call blocking rate (b), cost function (c) and network utilization (d) of GCPM and Zhang et al.'s algorithm [1] under different terminal mobility patterns α and stable offered load $\rho = 1.4$

Cost functions and network utilizations comparison results shown in Fig. 2 (c) and (d) are similar to those shown in Fig. 1. Smaller values of cost functions and larger network utilizations have been obtained by GCPM with average 0.0675 and 88.390% respectively, compared to 0.0773 and 86.433% of Zhang's algorithm. Furthermore, most network utilizations obtained by GCPM are larger than 85% while the minimum network utilization from Zhang's algorithm approximates to 80% under the stable offered load $\rho = 1.4$ as it is shown in Fig. 2 (d).

From above results, we can see that our proposed GCPM has gained very good performance in simulations, with restricted and much smaller handoff call blocking rates, smaller new call blocking rates and cost functions, and larger network utilizations in comparison with Zhang et al.'s adaptive algorithm [1].

4 Conclusions and Future Work

In this paper, we have proposed a Guard Channel Prediction Model (GCPM) for efficient call admission control in wireless/mobile cellular networks. The proposed model is applicable to predict appropriate values of the number of guard channels based on statistical properties of new and handoff call arrival rates, mean call residency time and the total capacity of a specific cell. Different predictive values will be derived from different traffic loads and terminal mobility patterns; as a result, our model is adaptive to the changes of traffic properties. Based on the predictive values obtained from GCPM, we have gained satisfied QoS in our simulations with lower blocking probabilities of both types of calls and larger network utilizations in comparison with the dynamically adaptive algorithm proposed by Zhang et al. [1].

For our future work, we will explore extending our GCPM model to handle the possible particular circumstances of traffic bursts in mobile wireless networks. Multi-class multimedia services and soft bandwidth degradation in CDMA networks will also be taken into consideration to enforce the adaptability of our model to the forthcoming 3G mobile communication environments.

References

1. Y. Zhang and D. Liu, "An adaptive algorithm for call admission control in wireless networks", *Proceedings of the IEEE Global Communications Conference*, San Antonio, TX, Nov. 2001, pp. 3628-3632.
2. M. Mallick, "Mobile and Wireless Design Essentials", Wiley 2003.
3. D. Hong and S. S. Rappaport, "Traffic model and performance analysis for cellular mobile radio telephone systems with prioritized and nonprioritized handoff procedures", *IEEE Transactions on Vehicular Technology*, vol. VT-35, pp. 77-92, Aug. 1986.
4. R. Ramjee, D. Towsley, and R. Nagarajan, "On optimal call admission control in cellular networks", *Wireless Networks*, vol. 3, no. 2, pp. 29-41, 1997.
5. Y. C. Kim, D. E. Lee, B. J. Lee, Y. S. Kim and B. Mukherjee, "Dynamic Channel Reservation Based on Mobility in Wireless ATM Networks", *IEEE Communications Magazine*, Nov. 1999, pp.47-51.
6. F. Yu and V. Leung, "Mobility-Based Predictive Call Admission Control and Bandwidth Reservation in Wireless Cellular Networks", *Elsevier Computer Networks*, vol. 38, no. 5, pp. 577-589, Apr. 2002.
7. S. Choi and K. G. Shin, "Predictive and Adaptive Bandwidth Reservation for Hand-Offs in QoS-Sensitive Cellular Networks", *in Proceedings of ACM SIGCOMM'98*, pp. 155-166, Vancouver, British Columbia, September 2-4, 1998.
8. S. Tekinay and B. Jabbari, "A Measurement-Based Prioritization Scheme for Handovers in Mobile Cellular Networks", *IEEE JSAC*, vol.10, no.8, Oct. 1992, pp. 1343-1350.
9. M. Mandjes and K. Tutschku, "Efficient call handling procedures in cellular mobile networks", Forschungsbericht, Preprint-Reihe Nr. 144, Universität Würzburg, Institut für Informatik, July 1996.
10. H. G. Perros and K. M. Elsayed, "Call Admission Control Schemes: A Review", *IEEE Commun. Mag.*, vol. 34, pp. 82-91, Nov. 1996.
11. Y. C. Kim, D. E. Lee, B. J. Lee, Y. S. Kim and B. Mukherjee, "Dynamic Channel Reservation Based on Mobility in Wireless ATM", *IEEE wmATM'99*, June. 1999, pp. 100-106.
12. G. P. Basharin and V. E. Merkulov, "Blocking Probability Analysis of New and Handover Calls in Cellular Mobile Networks with Repeated Attempts", *7th International Conference on Telecommunications*, June 2003.
13. Y. Xiao, C. L. Philip Chen, and Y. Wang, "An Optimal Distributed Call Admission Control for Adaptive Multimedia in Wireless/Mobile Networks", *Proc. of MASCOTS 2000*, pp. 477-482.
14. C. Lindemann, M. Lohmann, and A. Thummler, "Adaptive Call Admission Control for QoS/Revenue Optimization in CDMA Cellular Networks", *ACM J. Wireless Networks (WINET)*, vol. 10, pp. 457-472, 2004.

Cross-Layer Flow Control Based on Path Capacity Prediction for Multi-hop Ad Hoc Network

Yongqiang Liu, Wei Yan, and Yafei Dai

Computer Networks and Distributed Systems Laboratory, Peking University.
Room 1716, Science Building No.1, Peking University, Beijing, China
{lyq, yanwei, dyf}@net.pku.edu.cn

Abstract. In this paper, we first present a simple and effective path capacity predicting method to model the complex interaction between medium access mechanism and routing scheme. Based on the predicting model, an end-to-end cross-layer flow control architecture is proposed. The key issues about flowing control are discussed deeply. As we designed, whenever the path length changes, the applications adaptively modify their sending rate with the pre-computed optimal value. Simulation evaluation has demonstrated that this technique can greatly improve the performance of end-to-end transmission in ad hoc network: the throughput of the long path is improved by up to 40%.

1 Introduction

Ad hoc network is formed and functioning without any established infrastructure. It consists of nodes that use a wireless interface to communicate with each other. These nodes serve as both hosts and routers, so they can forward packets to each other. Hence, they are able to communicate beyond their transmission range by supporting multi-hop communication. Ad hoc network has been proposed for use in military, disaster relief, emergency operations and sensor networks.

The most commonly used MAC protocol in MANET today is the IEEE 802.11 Distributed Coordination Function (DCF) [1]. Many studies have been conducted on 802.11 DCF and there are some concerns about its dysfunction in an ad hoc context. Among the most widely recognized problems, we can cite the hidden terminal problem [2], the gray zone problem [3] and the serious performance decrease due to the interaction between the medium access mechanism and routing scheme [4].

In this paper, we present a novel cross-layer flow control architecture based on the path capacity prediction. Firstly, a simple and effective path capacity predicting model is proposed. For the given path length, it can pre-calculate the maximum throughput (namely capacity) and optimal sending rate of the source node. Different from previously proposed node-oriented analysis models in [5-8], our model is based on path-orientation and focuses on end-to-end transmission time, so the complexity level normally encountered is reduced in this model by such standpoint turnaround. Furthermore, it considers a more realistic scenario. For example, it takes the hidden terminal problem into account and doesn't assume that every node must send packet at every moment.

A series of cross-layer optimization approaches have been developed in recent years. These approaches exhibit a distinct interaction between entities of different layers and include various transmission strategies such as MAC layer variable-rate according to SINR in [9], network layer multiple paths routing in [10] and PHY layer power control in [11]. Similar end-to-end flow control mechanism involving application layer is also researched in [12], but that main idea behind it is that the optimal sending-rates are got by simulation experiments and stored in the applications. Based on the analytical algorithm that allows applications to pre-compute optimal sending-rate, our flow control technique can be more accurate and flexible in the complicated situations. For example, the density of the network is time-varying because of topology changes.

The remainder of this paper is organized as follows. Section 2 describes the path capacity predicting model in detail. Section 3 introduces key issues of the end-to-end flow control based on the model. Section4 applies simulations and statistical analysis to evaluate the performance of the flow control. Finally, Section 5 presents the conclusions.

2 Path Capacity Predicting Model for MANET

We first briefly summarize the 802.11 DCF. For a more complete and detailed description, you can refer to the 802.11 standard [1].

A station with a new packet to transmit monitors the channel activity. If the channel is idle for a period of time equal to a distributed inter-frame space (DIFS), the station transmits. Otherwise, if the channel is sensed busy (either immediately or during the DIFS), the station persists to monitor the channel until it is measured idle for a DIFS. At this point, to minimize the probability of collision with packets being transmitted by other stations, the station generates a random back-off interval before transmitting (this is the Collision Avoidance feature of the protocol). In addition, to avoid channel capture, a station must wait a random back-off time between two consecutive packet transmissions, even if the medium is sensed idle in the DIFS time. For efficiency reasons, DCF employs a discrete-time back-off scale. The time immediately following an idle DIFS is slotted, and a station is allowed to transmit only at the beginning of each slot time. The slot time size σ is set to the time needed by other station to detect the transmission of a packet.

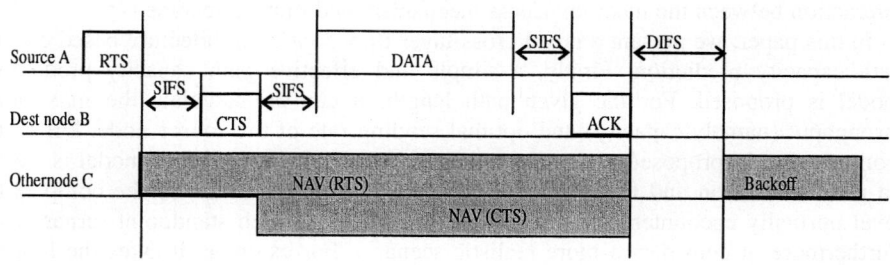

Fig. 1. RTS/CTS Access Mechanism

There is much work focused on the performance analysis of wireless LANS and ad hoc networks [5-8]. The model proposed in [5] is a classic one that depicts the performance of 802.11 DCF by employing a two dimensional Markov chain analysis. Based on [5], we propose a path-oriented model for predicting path capacity in MANET. The analysis currently assumes that the nodes keep stationary when packets are being transmitted and the data packets are generated only by the source node. Moreover, no other paths interference is considered now (A more delicate model considering path coupling and mobility is our future research work). The notations used in the model are defined in Table-1 and system parameters in simulations to validate the model are outlined in Table-2.

Table 1. Required notation in the model

Notation	Meaning
Thr_P^{max}	Available maximum throughput (capacity) of the path in MANET
$E[P]$	Average length of payload
N_P	Number of nodes (hops) along routing path (Except the destination.)
N_R	Possible number of nodes in the carrier sense range. (Values may be 3, 4, 5. it depends on the density of the network)
N_{hid}	Number of nodes along the path affected by the hidden terminal problem
T_{suc}	The average time of successfully transmitting a packet between two hops
T_{PDT}^{agv}	The average Path Delay Time caused by the hidden terminal problem

Table 2. Parameter values in simulation

Parameter	Value	
$E[P]$	4256	bits
CWmin	32	
MAC header	272	bits
PHY header	192	bits
CTS_Timeout	162	us
ACK	304	bits
SIFS	10	us
DIFS	50	us
RTS	352	bits
CTS	352	bits
Channel Bit Rate	1M	bit/s
Slot Time	20	us
Carrier sense range	550	m
Transmission range	250	m

2.1 Path Transmission Time Analysis

The key feature of the model is path-oriented. From the observation of the whole path, when there is no packet being transmitted along the path, any nodes attempting to transmit contend equally regardless of their previous transmitting. Once a node captures the path, the other nodes in its *carrier sense range* in the path must keep silent until the packet is received by its next hop. From the observation, we noted the packet transmission delay from source to the destination (or packet-arriving intervals at destination) should be multiple of a unit - T_{suc}, just like a pipeline. This is illustrated by Fig.2. T_{suc} consists of the node-waiting time from DCF, the back-off time because of RTS collision and the time of frames transmission. According to Fig 1, T_{suc} can be expressed as:

$$T_{Suc} = DIFS + T_{RTS} + T_{CTS} + 3 \times SIFS + T_{DATA} + T_{ACK} + \overline{W} \quad (1)$$

Where T_{RTS} and T_{CTS} indicate the time required to transmit the RTS and CTS frames respectively, T_{DATA} is the time required to transmit a MAC data frame including the PHY header, MAC header, and payload, and T_{ACK} is the time required to transmit an ACK frame including the PHY_{hdr} and MAC_{hdr}. The values of DIFS and SIFS are determined by PHY layer (DSSS or FSSS), $\overline{W}$ is the average waiting and back-off time. Note that when the density of the networks changes, for T_{suc}, only waiting time and back-off time needs re-computing.

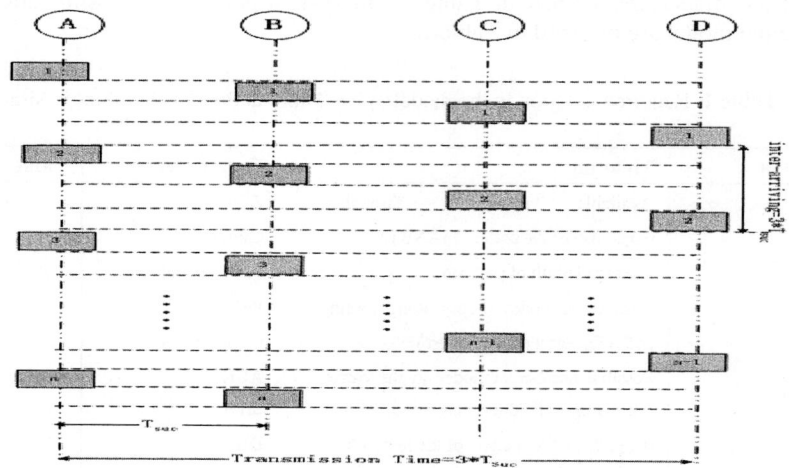

Fig. 2. Example of packet transmission along a path like a pipeline

2.2 Path Delay Time Analysis

RTS/CTS exchange can guarantee successful packet delivery in WLAN. Unfortunately, *the hidden terminal problem* still occurs in multi-hop ad hoc network because *carrier sense range* is larger than *transmission range*. Considering a chain of nodes depicted in Fig 3, r is the node A's *transmission range* in which nodes can successfully receive packets from A. R is the *carrier sense range* of D in which other nodes even can not receive D's packet correctly but can sense the channel busy and keep silent.

As illustrated in Fig.3, assuming node A wants to send data to B and at the same time D is forwarding data packet to E. Because be outside *the carrier sense range* of D, A does not overhear D's transmission and sends RTS to B. But being in *the carrier sense range* of D, B either receives corrupted RTS or is unable to send CTS after receiving RTS. When A waits for a CTS timeout, A will enter the back-off stage and then send RTS again after back-off time. However, because the data packet transmission time is long, collision occurs again at B. A thus repeats above back-off stage until CTS is received or transmission is cancelled. It can be noted in Fig.3 that there is an interval from the time the DATA arrives at E to the time that A's current back-off stage ends. No packet is transmitted along the path in the interval. From the view of the path transmission efficiency, the interval is wasted. We refer to this wasted interval as Path Delay Time (PDT). As shown in the next section, the PDT is generated by the hidden terminal problem and affects the end-to-end throughput of the path. The approximate computation of T_{PDT}^{agv} is given in appendix.

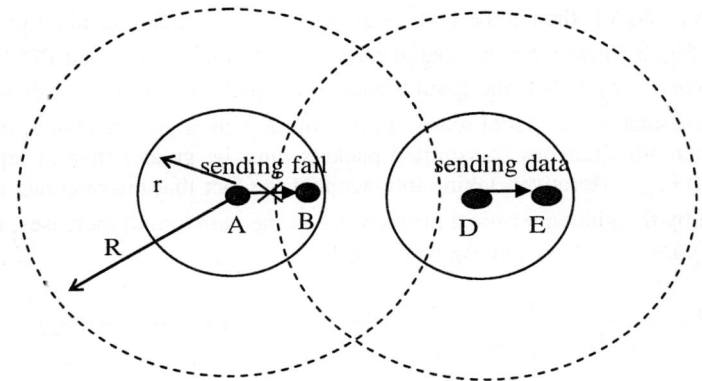

Fig. 3. Path Delay Time caused by the hidden terminal problem

2.3 Path Capacity Calculation

We first analyze the capacity of *the short path* in which all intermediate nodes are in the carrier sense range of the source node (namely $N_P \leq N_R$). As illustrated in Fig 4, scenarios (a),(b),(c) all belong to *short path* and corresponding N_R is 3,4,5 respectively.

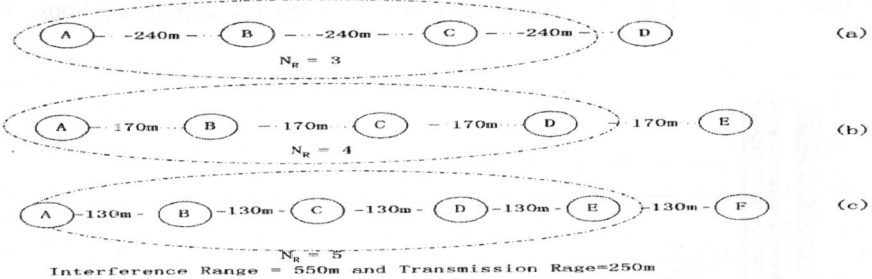

Fig. 4. Different scenarios of short path

Based on the RTS/CTS scheme, it is understood that when a pair of nodes are communicating with each other over a multi-hop short path, the spatial reuse of the path is 1. The path spatial reuse is defined as that approximately in one T_{s4c} slot, how many packets can be transmitted simultaneously along the path. So the minimal packet transmission time of the *short path* should be $T_{trans}^{min} = N_P \times T_{suc}$ and the capacity can be defined as:

$$Thr_P^{max} = \frac{E[P]}{N_P \times T_{Suc}} \qquad (2)$$

When $N_P = N_R + 1$, the source node is affected by the hidden terminal problem (As node A in Fig. 3 shows). So the spatial reuse of the path is still 1 and PDT should be counted. When $N_P > N_R + 1$, the spatial reuse of the path may be greater than 1. Therefore, it is true that if the spatial reuse of the routing path is greater than 1, the interval time between simultaneous transmitted packets must be greater than or equal to the time $(N_R + 1) \times T_{suc}$. Moreover, taking into account the fact that intermediate nodes will be affected by the hidden terminal problem when the path length increases, the capacity of *long path* ($N_P \geq N_R + 1$) can be defined as:

$$Thr_P^{max} = \frac{E[P]}{(N_R + 1) \times T_{Suc} + N_{hid} \times T_{PDT}^{agv}} \quad \text{where } N_{hid} \approx \min(N_P - N_R - 1, N_R) \qquad (3)$$

According to (2) and (3), the general equation of path capacity (maximum throughput) can be expressed as ($p_{hid} = N_{hid} / (N_P - N_R)$):

$$Thr_P^{max} = \frac{E[P]}{\{\min(N_P - 1, N_R) + 1\} \times T_{Suc} + p_{hid} \times \max(N_P - N_R, 0) \times T_{PDT}^{agv}} \qquad (4)$$

We simulated in ns-2[13] to validate the predicting model. Physical ratio and other parameter values are outlined in Table-2. The topology in simulations contains a chain of stationary nodes which are distributed uniformly. Considering a more realistic condition, the *carrier sense range* is set 550 m. The CBR traffic is generated only by the source nodes and we logged the maximum throughput at the destination when the path length (namely the route hops) increased from 1 hop to 10 hops. The

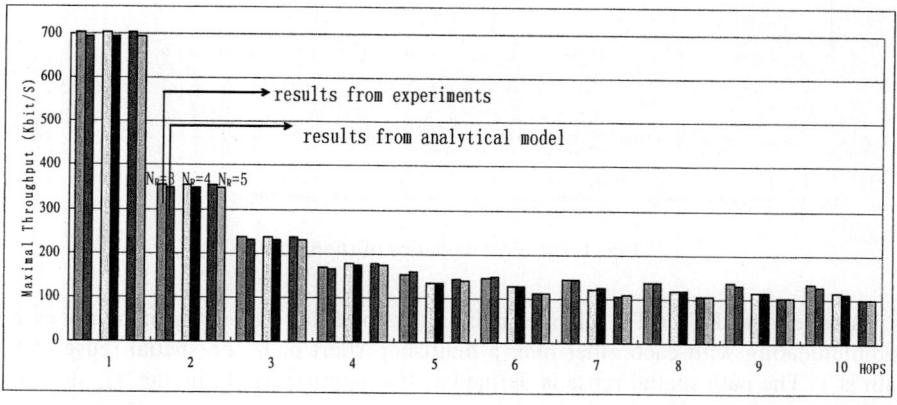

Fig. 5. Maximum Throughput vs Path length (simulation results and analytical results)

experimental results for three different scenarios (corresponding to N_R =3,4,5 respectively) and the analytical values calculated by the model are presented in Figure 6. Statistical analysis shows that the simulation results almost consistent with analytical ones with a 95% confidence level. So the model is accurate in predicting the path capacity of MANET.

3 Cross-Layer End-to-End Flow Control

3.1 The Effect of over Sending-Rate at the Source

The throughput calculated by equation (4) is the maximum value. In fact, the throughput actually degrades from its maximum value when the sending rate increases beyond an optimal point. To more concretely describe the phenomenon, we fixed N_R =3 and the path length (hops), then vary the source node sending-packet intervals from 48ms to 10ms (corresponding sending rate is from low to high). The available throughput at the destination for CBR is presented in Fig.7.

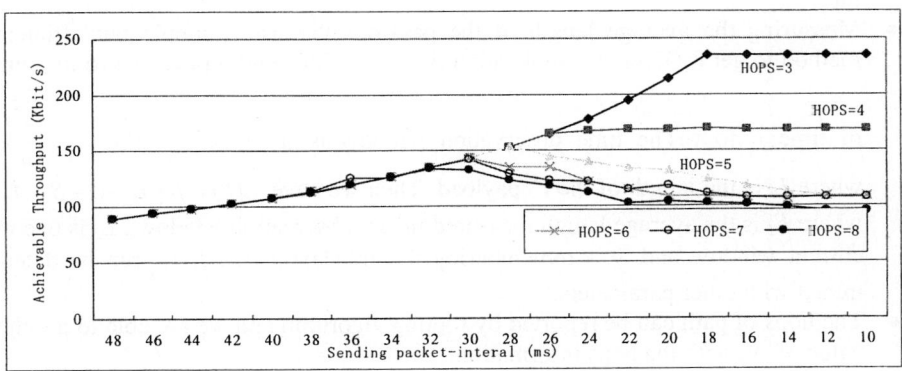

Fig. 6. Available throughput vs Sending rate

In Fig.7, for the path lengths of 3,4 hops, the throughput is gradually increasing to a certain point as sending rate growing and then stays flat. However, for the path lengths of more than 4 hops, a decrease by up to 30% of the maximum throughput is experienced! The result can be explained by our model: when the path length is less than 4 hops, intermediate nodes in the paths do not suffer from the hidden terminal problem because the carrier sense range is usually about 2.2 times of the transmission range. Nodes overhear another's transmission and almost no *data collisions* occur (Note that RTS frame collision has been accounted into T_{suc} as discussed in 2.1). The extra packets by higher sending rates are discarded by the source node and such source-drops only added PDT to the whole path transmission time. But when the path length exceeds 4 hops, the hidden terminal problem will reduce intermediate nodes' probability of catching the path. This leads to that the input packets sent to an intermediate node are more than output packets forwarded from it. Therefore, the excessive input packets may overflow the intermediate node's buffer and be dropped. From the standpoint of path-orientation, such intermediate-drops greatly undermine the efficiency of the path transmission because the time used to transmit those intermediate-dropped packets is actually wasted.Therefore, this suggests that there is opportunity for achieving higher throughput by employing a flow-control routing technique.

3.2 Key Issues About the Flow Control

The key issues related to predict optimal sending rate by the module are:
- Determining the PHY layer characteristic, which includes PHY channel rate, the size of RTS, CTS, ACK frames, the size of PHY header, the values of slot time(σ) and CW_{min}. All these parameters are used to compute $\overline{W}$ and T_{suc}.
- Estimating the approximate distance between adjacent nodes in the path. This parameter is used when calculating N_R in equation (4). There are some methods to estimate the distance in the literature. We assume the wireless channel radio-propagation model is TwoWayGround and the height and the gain of the antenna are fixed. Then the *range estimation algorithm* in Ref[14] is used in our architecture.
- Measuring the average length of the payload. We use a simple but efficient method to get it:Given the application is observed to send n payloads from point of time t_1 to t_2.The time observation window is $\Delta t = t_2 - t_1$. Define $L = \frac{\sum_{i=1}^{n} L_i}{n}$ where L_i is the length of the ith payload. Then we have $E[P] = \beta \times L_1 + (1-\beta) \times L_2$ where L_1 is the average length measured in last observation window , L_2 is one in current window and β is remembering factor. Having $E[P]$, T_{suc} can be determined with other parameters.
- The hops of path can be reported by routing algorithm and we are able to get the value of N_p with the hops information.

The predicting module is performed at the routing layer and the parameters estimation resorts to already proposed methods or the new ones designed by us at different layers. An application that is interested to achieve the maximum throughput should adaptively modify its sending rate according to the information provided by the predicting model. Such applications register a callback function at the underlying routing layer. The function is invoked by the module whenever the path length changes, for example, as a new route discovered. On accepting the notification, the application sets the new sending rate based on the pre-computed optimal packet-sending interval. The flow control method can be achieved by Leaky Bucket Queue Algorithm.

4 Performance Evaluation

We compare the performance of the cross-layer flow control with that of usual CBR with a fixed sending rate. PHY characteristics and topology are the same with the simulations in section 2 and the fixed sending-packet interval of CBR traffic is 6ms.

We refer to the version of CBR with flow control as CF-CBR and the other as CM-CBR in the following discussion.

In Fig. 7, we execute simulations in the sparse network (the distance between nodes is long enough to make $N_R = 3$). The bars represent the available throughput at destination when the path length gradually increases. It can be seen that the throughputs of both CBRs are almost equal in the path length from 2 to 4 hops and CF-CBR outperforms CM-CBR when the path length is more than 4. This is an expected result as discussed in section 3, because when the path is long, the flow control can reduce the intermediate-drops and improve the efficiency of the path transmission. Furthermore, we find that the larger the size of average payload is, the higher the improvement of CF-CBR. For example, in Fig.7, the average improvement of throughput is nearly 40% with $E[P]=512$bytes and about 58% with $E[P]=1000$bytes. The reason is that dropping larger packets at intermediate nodes wastes more time.

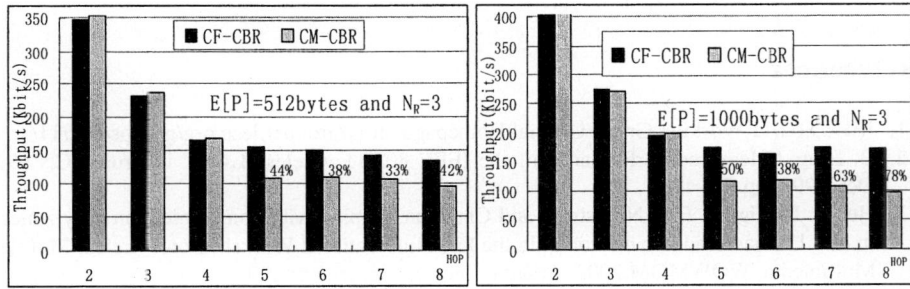

Fig. 7. Available Throughput of CF-CBR vs CM-CBR in the sparse network

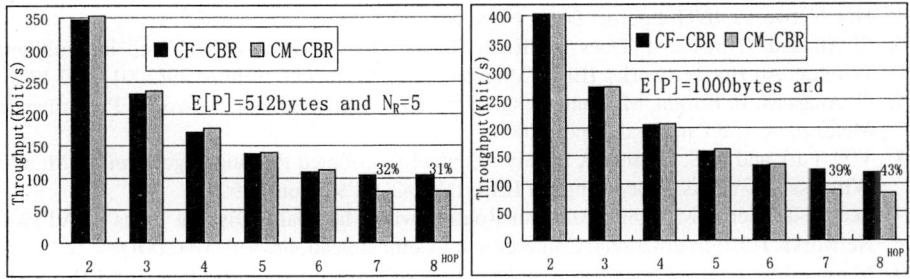

Fig. 8. Achievable Throughput of CF-CBR vs CM-CBR in the dense network

We then repeat the simulations in the dense network (namely $N_R = 5$) and the results are similar. As presented in Fig.8, the available throughput can be improved when $N_P > N_R + 1$ and the improvement is higher when $E[P]$ is larger. Moreover, it can be observed that the improvement in the dense network is lower than that in the sparse network (Improvements are 30% and 40% respectively). This is because fewer nodes are affected by the hidden terminal problem in dense network given the same path length.

5 Conclusions

The performance of 802.11DCF-based ad hoc networks deeply relies on the complex interaction between medium access mechanism and routing scheme. In this paper, we model the interaction and present the method for computing for optimal sending-rate a given path in the ad hoc networks. Different from the previous researches, we work with a more realistic scenario: the packet is scheduled arbitrarily and the carrier sense range of a node is longer than its transmission range. The effect of the over sending-rate is analyzed and the issues about flowing control are discussed deeply. Simulations has shown that our technique outperform usual CBR with fixed sending rate by improving throughput by up to 40%

References

1. IEEE 802.11 Working Group Official Homepage http://grouper.ieee.org/groups/802/11/
2. B. Bing, "Measured performance of the IEEE 802.11 wireless LAN," in Proc. LCN'99, Oct. 1999, pp. 34–42.
3. Henrik Lundgren, Erik Nordstron, and Christian. Coping with communication gray zones in 802.11b based ad hoc networks. In the Fifth International Workshop on Wireless Mobile Multimedia, WOWMOM 2002. Atlanta, Georgia, September 2002.
4. S. Xu and T. Saadawi, "Does the IEEE 802.11 MAC protocol Work Well in Multihop Wireless Ad Hoc Networks?", IEEE Communication Magazine, Volume 39,N. 6, June 2001, pp. 130-137.
5. Wakikawa R., Malinen J., Perkins C., Nilsson A: Global Connectivity for IPv6 Mobile Ad Hoc Networks, IETF Internet Draft, November 2001.Work in progress.
6. S. Xu and T. Saadawi: Does the IEEE 802.11 MAC protocol Work Well in Multihop Wireless Ad Hoc Networks. IEEE Communication Magazine, Volume 39(2001) 130-137.
7. G. Anastasi, E. Borgia, M. Conti, E. Gregori: IEEE 802.11Ad Hoc Networks: Performance Measurement. IIT Internal Report(2003)
8. V.D. Park and M.S. Corson: A Highly Adaptive Distributed Routing Algorithm for Mobile Wireless Net-works. Proceedings of IEEE INFOCOM'97 Conf (1997)
9. Lee, S.-J., Gerla, M: Split Multipath Routing with Maximally Disjoint Paths in Ad Hoc Networks. IEEE International Conference on Communications, Vol. 10 (2001)
10. Marina, M.K., Das, S.R.: On-demand Multipath Distance Vector Routing in Ad Hoc Networks. Proceedings of the International Conference for Network Protocols (2001)
11. Ye, Z., Krishnamurthy, S.V., Tripathi, S.K.: A Framework for Reliable Routing in Mobile Ad Hoc Networks. IEEE INFOCOM (2003)
12. K. Fall: The ns Manual. http://www.isi.edu/ ns/nsdocumentation.htm(2002)

Appendix: Computation process and result of T_{PDT}^{agv}

We first define variant T_c=DIFS+T_{RTS}+T_{CTS_OUT}, which is the collision time of the node. Equation (10) is the expression to calculate PDT derived from 802.11 DCF specification. $Xi \in (0, 2^i \times CW_{min}]$

$$T_{PDT} = T_c + X1 \times \sigma + T_c + X2 \times \sigma + \cdots + T_c + Xi \times \sigma - T_{Suc} = N \times T_c + \sigma \times \sum_{i=1}^{N} X_i - T_{Suc} \quad (5)$$

Because Xi and N are all random variants, and N is dependent on Xi and T_{suc}, it is very difficult to calculate the expectation of T_{PDT}. But we can get the bounds of it. it is easily understood that

- When the time the DATA arrives at E and the time A's current back-off stage ends are the same time, T_{PDT} gets the minimal value: $T_{PDT}^{min} = 0$.
- When the time the DATA arrives at E and the time of A's new back-off stage starts are the same time, T_{PDT} gets the maximum value: $T_{PDT}^{max} = 2^{i-1} \times CW_{min} \times \sigma$, when $(i-1) \times T_c + \sum_{j=1}^{i-1} Xj \times \sigma = T_{Suc}$

We approximately use T_{PDT}^{agv} as the average value of PDT in the model and it is defined as:

$$T_{PDT}^{agv} = \frac{T_{PDT}^{min} + T_{PDT}^{max}}{2} = 2^{i-2} \times CW_{min} \times \sigma \text{ where i satisfies}$$
$$(i-1) \times T_c + \sum_{j=1}^{i-1} 2^j \times CW \min \times \sigma > T_{Suc} \quad (6)$$

Constructing the Robust and Efficient Small World Overlay Network for P2P Systems*

Guofu Feng, Ying-chi Mao, and Dao-xu Chen

Department of Computer Science and Technology, Nanjing University,
The State Key Lab. for Novel Software Technology, Nanjing University,
Nanjing, Jiangsu, China, 210093
fgfmail@dislab.nju.edu.cn

Abstract. The current P2P application protocols are usually constructed over the application-level overlay network. However, because the users in the P2P systems always follow a very dynamic mode, the overlay network with poor performance will leads to the problem of connectivity---the departures of peers often break the network into plenty of small parts, and results in the resource islands. Although increasing the links between peers can enhance the performance of connectivity by information redundancy. But it will lead to the severe cost of maintenance. Then there is an urgent need to integrate the online peers as a "giant component" as large as possible, so that the resources online can be shared completely; at the same time to guarantee the cost of maintenance as little as possible. And due to the prevalence and significance of small world in reality and theory, in this paper we analyzed the correlation between the shortcuts density and the connectivity, as well as the impact of shortcuts density to robustness over the popular WS Small World model. At last, numerical simulation was done to confirm our analytic results.

1 Introduction

The peer-to-peer (P2P) computing model offers a radically different and appealing alternative to the traditional client-server model for many large-scale applications in distributed environment. The users in P2P model shares resources in a peer style, potentially acting as both client and server. The P2P approach removes central points of failure and associated performance bottlenecks and balances the load. It also releases the network from the hard traffic load by providing the service locally. P2P is gaining an increasing attention from both the academe and the Internet user community.

In current general approaches, the P2P applications firstly integrate the end-users into one overlay network, and then construct the application protocols over the overlay network. Theoretically, the topology of the overlay network can be organized as any type, i.e. any regular structured network or irregular unstructured. However, for the P2P system is mostly composed of a mass of peers with less power, designing scalable P2P application level protocols is not straightforward and remains an active

---

* This work is partially supported by the National Natural Science Foundation of China under Grant No.60402027, the National High-Tech Research and Development Program of China (863) under Grant No.2001AA113050.

area of research. The users in the P2P systems always follow a very dynamic mode, and always keep a very limited time online. Therefore, the overlay network with poor performance may be broken into pieces and pieces when some peers leave, resulting in the information islands. Most of the structured P2P reconnect the topology as soon as the peers leave in a real time manner. But it will consume too many messages, and sometimes it is not feasible, for many peers depart without any warnings. Although increasing the links between peers can enhance the performance of connectivity by the information redundancy, however which will lead to the waste of storage and the severe cost of maintenance. In addition, to avoid the real time maintenance of the peers' departure, the redundancy of appropriate links and replicas is another effective approach. Then there is an urgent need to integrate the online peers as a "giant component" as large as possible, so that the resources online can be shared completely; at the same time to guarantee the cost of maintenance as little as possible. In other words,

the largest cluster interconnected by the online peers should scale linearly with the system size when given the proportion of the online peers to all the peers.

This is because: if the rate is under the linear scale, the online peers will be broken into smaller and smaller clusters with the expansion of system; conversely if the rate is over the linear scale, the online peers will be ultimately integrated as one super large scale "giant component" with the extension of the whole network, which is beyond the "critical value" of link redundancy, resulting in much waste of storage and cost of maintenance.

And due to the prevalence and significance of small world model in reality and theory, in this paper we analyzed the correlation between the shortcuts density and the connectivity over WS small world model, as well as the impact of shortcuts density to the robustness of the overlay network based on the popular WS small world model. In addition, numerical simulation was done to confirm our analytic results.

2 Small World Model

The experiment of six-degree separation in 1976 proves that by simply forwarding mail among acquaintances, it only takes a chain of five to seven mails to reach a specific mail user unknown by the original mailer. This reveals the prevalent existence of short paths between individuals in a large social network. And the publication of [1] revives people's attention to the small world, and then the small world model is extensively introduced into their respective research fields [2,6,7]. The phenomenon of small world is embodied in the complex networks of a wide range of systems in nature and society, including the cell, a network of chemicals linked by chemical reactions, or the Internet, a network of routers and computers connected by physical links [2]. Some P2P applications also have proven the existence of small world in the networks composed of the active nodes [3,4]. [4,5,8] have designed P2P systems under the notion of small world and achieved not bad performance. Therefore, the research of fault-tolerance based on small world model is necessary and significant. Our work in this paper aims at the construction of the robust and efficient small world overlay network for the P2P systems.

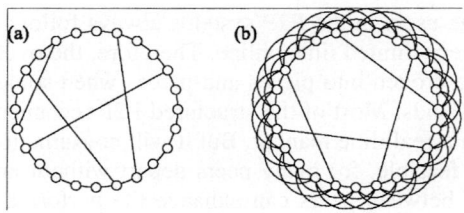

Fig. 1. (a) An example of a small-world graph with $L=24$, $k=1$ and 4 shortcuts (b) An example with $k=3$

The original small-world model suggested by Watts and Strogatz (WS) is defined as follows [6]. Take a one-dimensional lattice of L nodes with links between nearest neighbors and periodic boundary conditions (the lattice is a ring). Then go through each of the link in turn and independently with some probability Φ "rewire" it. The rewired links are referred to as "shortcuts". The Watts-Strogatz model embodies clustering property and a small average path length between any two individuals.

For the purposes of analytic treatment the Watts and Strogatz made a slight modification over the model above. In the variant version of the small world model Add shortcuts between pairs of nodes chosen uniformly at random with probability Φ but do not remove any links from the regular lattice. Fig. 1(a) shows one realization of the model for $L = 24$.

To simulate the more out-degree in real social networks, Watts and Strogatz [1] proposed adding links to next-nearest or further neighbors on the underlying one-dimensional lattice up to some fixed range, which we will call k. Fig. 1(b) shows one realization for $L= 24$, $k=3$. Watts and Strogatz found that the model displays many of the characteristics of true random graphs even for $\Phi<<1$, and it seems to be in this regime that the model's properties are most like those of real world social networks [1]. Our main interest in this paper is the influence of the shortcut probability Φ on the connectivity of the whole small world overlay network.

3 Constructing the Robust Small World Overlay Network

Considering a one-dimensional small world model as described above, it is standard to define the parameter Φ to be the average number of shortcuts per link on the underlying lattice. For large sites number L, the probability that two randomly chosen nodes have a shortcut is then

$$\varphi = 2k\Phi/L \qquad (1)$$

Define the parameter p to be the average online probability of a peer. Online peers are connected together by the near-neighbor links on the underlying lattice and the shortcuts. Offline peers disconnect some links, resulting in some isolated local clusters. Let's firstly ignore the shortcuts. For $k=1$, the average number of local clusters, the discrete clusters, of size i then is

$$N_i=(1-p^2)p^iL \qquad (2)$$

For general $k \geq 1$, $\quad N_i=(1-p)^{2k}p(1-(1-p)^k)^{i-1}L$ (3)

Now we build a connected larger cluster by the local clusters as follows. Let's start with an original cluster, one particular local cluster. We can get a new original cluster if we add other local clusters that can be reached by traveling along a single shortcut to it. Then we add local clusters, which can be reached from those new ones by traveling along a single shortcut step by step, and so forth until all the clusters that can reach from the first original local cluster are added. Let us define a vector $V_i[v_1,v_2,v_3...v_i...]$ at each step in this process, whose components v_j are equal to the probability that a local cluster of size j have been added to the overall connected original cluster in step i. Then $\sum v_j$, $v_j \in V_i$ equal to the number of clusters added in step i.

Define a matrix M,

$$M_{ij}=N_j(1-(1-\varphi)^{ij})$$ (4)

Here N_j is the number of local clusters of size j, and $1-(1-\varphi)^{ij}$ is the probability of a shortcut between two clusters respectively with size i and size j. And then M_{ij} stands for the number of clusters with size j that connect to a given cluster with size i. Then

$$V_{i+1}[v_1,v_2,v_3...v_i...]= V_i[v_1,v_2,v_3...v_i...]\,M$$ (5)

If Φ is held constant, then φ tends to zero as $L \rightarrow \infty$, so for large L we can approximately get

$$1-(1-\varphi)^{ij}=ij\varphi$$ (6)

$$M_{ij}=ij\varphi N_j$$ (7)

Then matrix M is the product of two vector $I=[...i\varphi...]^T$ and $J=[...jN_j...]$. Then Eq. (5) can be transformed to

$$V_{i+1}=V_i M=V_i IJ, \text{ i.e. } v_i=iN_i\sum v_i k\varphi v_k,\, v_i \in V_{i+1},\, v_k \in V_i$$ (8)

Let vector x is the eigenvector of matrix M corresponding to the eigenvalue λ,

$$Mx= \lambda x$$ (9)

And according to Eq. (9)

$$V_{i+1}= \lambda V_i$$ (10)

Therefore, if $\lambda <1$ and i is larger, $\sum v_i$, $v_i \in V_i$ tends to zero, namely, the number of new clusters added in step i is less and less until $\sum v_i$, $v_i \in V_i$ equals to zero, and then the largest "giant component" will not augment with the increase of i and the system scale, which cant answer for the issue described in section one. On the contrary, if $\lambda >1$, $\sum v_i$, $v_i \in V_i$ will grows until the size of the cluster becomes limited by the size of the whole system, which cannot be coincident with our target also, for the purpose of link maintenance. Therefore, our expected critical value p occurs at the point $\lambda =1$.

Consider Eq. (10), and according to Eq. (8)

$$\lambda i V_i = \sum_{vi} k\varphi v_k [\ldots i^2 N_i \ldots], v_k \in V_i \quad (11)$$

Sum the left and right side respectively,

$$\lambda \sum_{vi} k v_k = \varphi \sum_{vi} k v_k \sum_{vi} i^2 N_i, \quad \lambda = \varphi \sum_{vi} i^2 N_i \quad (12)$$

For $k=1$,

$$\lambda = \varphi(1-p)^2 L \sum i^2 p^i \quad (13)$$

$$\lambda = \varphi p L(1+p)/(1-p) = 2\Phi p(1+p)/(1-p) \quad (14)$$

Setting $\lambda =1$ yields the correlation between the shortcut density Φ and the critical value p for a resilient and efficient small world overlay network

$$\Phi = (1-p)/2p(1+p) \quad (15)$$

For general k, we have

$$\lambda = 2k\Phi p(2-(1-p)^k)/(1-p)^k \quad (16)$$

Setting $\lambda =1$, we also have the correlation equation on p and Φ

$$\Phi = (1-p)/2k p(2-(1-p)^k) \quad (17)$$

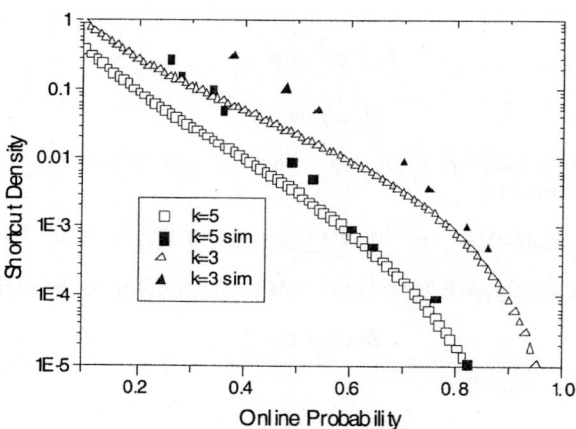

Fig. 2. The shortcut density as a function of online rate to preserve the overlay network having a good connectivity for a small world graph of $L=10,000$ with $k=3$(triangles) and 5(squares), where the consecutive curve is our results and the discrete point is the experimental results.

4 Numerical Calculations

We have performed computer simulations on small world networks as a check on our analytic results. In the experiment, there are initially zero online peers. And then the offline peers are randomly selected and wakened at a step of ten peers until all the peers are online. And a BFS (Breadth First Search) from every peer is used to find the largest cluster.

Fig. 2 shows the shortcut density as a function of the peers' online rate to preserve the overlay network having a good connectivity for a system of size L=10,000. As the figure shows the agreement between simulation and theory is good although there are some differences. The results fail to agree for lower online rate--- higher shortcut density. This is because Eq. (6) is not a correct expression for the larger Φ.

5 Conclusions

We have derived exact analytic expressions on the shortcut density and the proportion of online peers to preserve the robustness of small world overlay network, which can be considered the guidance when to construct the practicable applications based on small world overlay network. We also have performed numerical simulations and confirmed our conjecture and the analytic result.

References

1. D. J. Wattz, S. H. Strogatz. Collective dynamics of small world networks. Nature 393, 1998.
2. Reka Albert, Albert Laszlo Barabasi. Statistical Mechanics of Complex Networks. Reviews of Modern Physics 74, 47 (2002)
3. Adriana Iamnitchi, Matei Ripeanu, Ian Foster, Small-World File-Sharing Communities. Infocom 2004, Hong Kong, March 2004
4. A. Iamnitch:, M. Ripeanu and I. Foster, "Locating Data in (Small-World) Peer-to-Peer Scientific Collaborations", 1st International Workshop on Peer-to-Peer Systems (IPTPS'02), Cambridge, MA, March 2002.
5. Ian Clarke, Oskar Sandberg, Brandon Wiley, Theodore W. Hong. Freenet: A Distributed Anonymous Information Storage and Retrieval System, Lecture Notes in Computer Science.2000
6. M. E. J. Newman and D. J. Watts. Scaling and percolation in the small-world network model. Physical Review E, 60, 7332-7342 (1999).
7. C. Moore and MEJ Newman, Epidemics and percolation in small-world networks, Phys. Rev. E (2000).
8. G. S. Manku, M. Bawa, and P. Raghavan. Symphony: Distributed hashing in a small world. In 4th USENIX Symposium on Internet Technologies and Systems, USITS, 2003.

Transparent Java Threads Migration Protocol over Peer2Peer

Edgardo Ambrosi[1], Marco Bianchi[2], Carlo Gaibisso[3], Giorgio Gambosi[4], and Flavio Lombardi[5]

[1] Department of Computer Science University of Florence, Florence, Italy
ambrosi@dsi.unifi.it
[2] Department of Computer Science University of L'Aquila, L'Aquila, Italy
bianchi@dsi.unifi.it
[3] IASI-CNR, Roma, Italy gaibisso@iasi.rm.cnr.it
[4] Department of Computer Science University of Rome Tor Vergata, Rome, Italy
gambosi@mat.uniroma2.it
[5] CNR National Research Council, Rome, Italy flavio.lombardi@cnr.it

Abstract. The Java Virtual Machine computing model implements a multi-threading paradigm but its computing model does not define and does not verify the distribution paradigm of the threads over set of JVM instances. Without a distribution paradigm the Java Virtual Machine computing model cannot get any advantage from the theory of parallel Turing Machines. This work formally specifies and verifies the JVM computing model distribution paradigm. An intrinsic transparent thread distribution mechanism over many JVMs relying on different communication technology such as Peer to Peer is an important outcome of the presented solution. Other consequences, such as distributed JVM run-time location, aggregation and reachability, are achieved. Moreover the creation of Virtual Farms of JVMs for Multi-threading applications computing is made possible.

1 Introduction

The widespread diffusion of large scale systems has brought many researchers to propose distributed software solutions capable of "moving" the computation among networked physical computing machines. What is considered computable depends on the execution environment such as the JVM execution context where threads are computable. The problem of natively moving the computation among software computing machines such as instances of JVMs is our focus. Natively, the Java language allows expressing the parallel execution through *threads* and natively JVM performs parallel execution of threads inside the same execution context holding the same java application. What the JVM natively does not perform is the distribution of threads over external JVM execution contexts.

As an example, moving the computation among distributed machines [1] can be done for: code components (e.g. Sun Microsystems' Java Applets and Microsoft's ActiveX); data objects (e.g. IBM's Aglets [2] and Concordia [3]); processes (e.g. Esmerald [4], Sprite [5] and Charlotte [6]). All this kind of distributed computing requires specific operating system software component integration, implementing appropriate remote execution mechanisms. But if the execution context is not a physical machine but a virtual one, different problems arise.

In this paper we:

- formally extend the JVM computational model defining a native JVM distribution paradigm. We adopt the Abstract State Machine notation [7]. More precisely, the Java Virtual Machine formal description presented in [8] is extended.
- specify a formalized *Transparent Java Thread Migration Protocol* (JTTMP);
- show some aspects af the prototyping activity about our solution, to verify the extention of the JVM computational model and to verify the JTTMP, based on a Peer To Peer paradigm (JTTMPoP2P). The peer to peer thread migration protocol is then presented by means of a mapping between the Thread Migration Protocol and the JXTA Peer to Peer (P2P) primitives [9]. The choice of P2P as the communication paradigm among the DJVM nodes is motivated: it offers an intuitive approach to resource discovery and sharing, often without the need for a central authority [10]. The adoption of P2P makes it possible to enable dynamic discovery and automatic aggregation of computing farms belonging to different organizations.

1.1 JVM Computational Model

The analysis of the sound and complete mathematical formalization of the JVM [8] has been a great inspiration for this work. It has been the starting point of the project for extending the JVM computational model. In particular the Evolving Algebra (EA) paradigm [7] used as a formal method for specifing and verifing JVMs has attracted our attention, giving us the possibility to formally prove our idea. The limit of the JVM computational model lies with the absence of mechanisms for moving the computation over instances of JVMs. We argue that this problem is well expressed by the following : *A JVM is local to the main thread of a java application, whereas all the other instances with respect to the same application are remote, either if they are running on the same physical machine or if they are running on other physical machines.* The JVM computational model does not describe any aspect concerning the java threads lifecycle, about migration and synchronization among multiple local and remote JVMs. As a consenquence no advantages are taken from the distribution computation paradigm applied to the JVM computational model.

In this paper we focus our attention on the JVM ASM [8] model, because each extension can be formally verified. The verification process can be done through code development or formal verification. On the other hand the JVM ASM uses a metacomputing environment that simulates the execution environment for Abstract State Machines. The environment is a programming system called AsmGofer [11], an extension to the functional programming environment Gofer. The JVM ASM has been developed in this environment so that our computational model extension can be applied and verified. In particular in developing our idea we want to focus on the abstraction process [12] that we have adopted to create the intrinsic distribution model for JVM. The process has been focused on analysing the properties of JVM's thread control, trying to understand how the structure of computation could be manipulated for migrating and delegating thread mechanisms, and then considering these properties in isolation from the experimental JVMs. The abstraction process is followed by a reconstructive generalization using the EA formalism. The reconstructive generalization has produced the *Signatures Set* i.e. the new operators used to specify the distribution model. In this paper our attention has been focused on the communication model for moving the computation among JVM instances. The effectiveness of the model has been shown through informal analisys of a useful implementation of the JTTMP over P2P paradigm.

2 Java Thread Transparent Migration

Our idea has been developed by extending the mathematical structures *execJavaThread* and *execJava$_T$* defined in [8]. No change about the java thread statement specifications has been made. From a user point of view the JVM thread has the same behaviour and the same lifecycle of the original computational model. On the other hand, from a JVM point of view the thread controller method specifications have been extended in a way that particularly affects the lifecycle states and the synchronization phase. It is important to note that the dynamic semantic of the *execJavaThread* structure has been extended in order to support the execution of the threads migration tasks. We considered the JVM mechanisms for thread management, expecially those for synchronization, waiting and notification introduced for an effective transfer of control between JVMs. Such mechanisms define the *delegating* new phrase, and mechanisms for notification and waiting used for defining the *migrating* new phrase. Our solution focuses on three main aspects: i) modification of the mechanisms controlling the thread lifecycle states; ii) extension of the local scheduling process to the remote scheduling; iii) definition of the JVM communication protocol to support thread distribution.

In this paper we limit the description to the dynamic semantics of the support to migration and delegation, without proving the invariance of properties, proved in [8] for threads. We focus on the third point, showing an approach for embedding into a JVM the comunication framework for moving the computation. In particular we believe that an embedded distributed extension of java virtual machine mechanisms to perform migration and to invoke remote scheduling, is an important addition for the JVM, that does not have influence on the language specifications. First we define the protocol and then we give an implementation of it.

The actors. Two roles are defined in such a protocol: JVMConsole and JVMWorker. Moreover the JTTMP defines both a Thread Manager (TM) and a Migration Manager (MM) actors defined for the mentioned roles. TM and MM are thread daemons that let a JVM keep running independently of a java multithreaded application (*jmta*) execution. Moreover the MM and TM embed normal java threads specifications, but their methods are reserved to execJavaThread control. MM and TM are synchronized on the threads that can be migrated. When a new thread is created, its mode has to be initialised, and its locks stack and wait set have to be initialised to empty. Considering our extension, the migration stack is set to empty and its delegating stack, under certain conditions, is set to *TM*. Since *MM* and *TM* are initialised as any other thread, then the normal thread initialisation phase is not discussed in detail in the present work, because many entailments would have to be considered. Here we just discuss about some activity that are charged on the two actors. A *MM* is responsible for: discovering the network topology; collecting and maintaining the cluster nodes' load status information; applying the thread migration policy; selecting the unloaded nodes as migration targets; selecting the threads to migrate; selecting an unloaded node from which to subtract a previously migrated thread. A Thread Manager is responsible for creating a context for the migrated thread; destroying the context for the migrated thread; synchronising active remote threads in execution on the local node; scheduling the migrated thread.

Intuitively speaking, given a *jmta* to run, all JVM instances running on distributed resources start cooperating. The main goal of each JVM instance is to aggregate itself to a farm of JVMs. JTTMP provides rules for roles and actors, defining the behaviour of the Migration Manager (whose aim is the control of direct/inverse migration), as well as for defining the behaviour of the Thread Manager (whose tasks are status delegation and remote scheduling). Any computational resource can play both roles, but for the sake of simplicity and without loss of generality we consider a DJVM with a single JVMConsole. When a *jmta* is executed on a resource, the latter becomes the JVMConsole for that *jmta*, see the previous 1.1. All other nodes will behave as an extension to the computational and memory resources available on the Console, and will act as JVMWorkers with respect to the *jmta*. In order to show the protocol and behaviour of *TM* and *MM*, a natural language description and a reference to the formal funtional opearators are used. The reader can find in round brackets, the number of the referenced function.

Protocol Workflow. Obviously the first phase is the **opening of a communication channel**. Any JVM, independently from its role, defines a migration channel *CHM* (12) and a communication channel *CHC* (11). When a *jmta* is started on a JVM, the latter plays the role of JVMConsole by creating CHC_is towards the JVMWorkers. It will also create *CHM*s towards those JVMWorkers where to migrate threads. As a main difference between those two channel types, the latter requires larger bandwidth. All JVMs other than the Console will act as JVMWorkers and will define a communication (11) and a migration (12) channel towards the JVMConsole. Furthermore, by relaxing the requirement of the uniqueness of the JVMConsole, in a scenario where any resource can start a *jmta*, each JVM would have $(n-1)$ channels at its disposal. We will later discuss threads migration from a communication channel point of view. In the following two sections we discuss on the protocol workflows with respect to the formal definition of the list of functions involved in the protocol. The protocol first phase is followed by the **Discovery Information Request**. When running a *JVMConsole* on a resource, the *MM* looks for other *MM*s on JVMWorkers running on other resources. In this way it collects informations on the topology of distributed JVM instances (1). The **Load Information Request** is performed when the *jmta* start running, and the *MM*, in order to balance the load on the JVMConsole, sends the load request to every other resource to retrieve the load information of any other *JVMWorker* (3). Each JVMWorker handles the request according to its own load information, that is evaluated following the request (4). At this point the JVMConsole enter the next phase, where the **Evaluation of remote load information** is performed. The load status information of remote nodes is received, evaluated and compared in order to select a worker (5). Then the migration can be started towards that worker by using the function for direct migration. The most important phase is the **Direct Migration**. The *TM* on the JVMConsole selects the thread whereas the *MM* on the JVMConsole selects the JVMWorker to migrate to. The first thread to be evaluated is the currently executing thread. If the current thread can not be migrated, then the JVMConsole examines the other ones (9). A thread can migrate if it has a correct type (8) i.e. : i) it must not be a daemon thread; ii) it must be a local thread (i.e. it cannot be an immigrated (i.e. previously migrated there) thread); iii) it must not be the main thread. Once a thread is chosen, the JVMConsole instructs the selected JVMWorker to prepare the execution context for the migrating thread (10). At this point, the JVMWorker sets up the migration channel (12) where the migration will take place. It then informs the JVMConsole that the *CHM* and the execution context have been set up. The JVMWorker instructs the JVMConsole to prepare for sending the sequence of frames the thread is composed of (13) and requests sending the frames (17). The JVMConsole creates, a thread clone to send (14), and a migration channels (12). The JVMConsole splits the execution context Δ of the thread to send into ordered numbered fragments (15) called δ_{frame} and sends them (16), indicating the number of fragments and the total dimension of Δ.

As soon as the JVMWorker has collected the complete Δ, the latter is ordered in a machine-compatible format (17) and is executed (18). A request for re-sending a single δ_{frame} or the entire Δ (19) can be performed. Such a continuous control passing between JVMConsole and JVMWorker continues until the complete delta set has been received. At the end of the migration, the various *TM*s on the JVMWorker take care of migrated threads. The JVMConsole keeps listening for machine-dependent requests coming from migrated thread via the JVMWorker. There are four types of such requests (20): i) for synchronisation; ii) for acquiring a lock on a shared object; iii) for releasing a lock on a pre-acquired object; iv) for discovering who owns a certain lock. During the execution of the *jmta*, the *TM* requests informations on the status of the threads that have been migrated to a JVMWorker (21). The *TM* will take care of such requests (22). Furthermore, the JVMConsole might want to synchronise its knowledge on what has been migrated on JVMWorkers. It does so by requesting informations (23). Moreover, dynamic loading for some remote library can be necessary as well (24), or requesting the allocation of more memory (26). The dual phase of the previous one, is the **Inverse Migration**. The inverse migration may be invoked on a JVMWorker that is: i) the more heavily loaded, ii) the one that has finished executing a thread, iii) the one which is unable to satisfy the machine-dependent requests coming from a previously migrated thread (7). During the inverse migration process, after individuating the departure node (5), the JVMConsole starts the migration process (7). The JVMConsole is not responsible for choosing which thread must be retrieved back. The selected JVMWorker chooses among the higher priority threads, the first "retreat-able thread" (8), i.e. an active remote thread that does not contain machine-dependent code instructions. If such thread is found, the JVMConsole is required to prepare for receiving a modified thread execution context (19). After splitting and ordering the execution context Δ (17), the JVMWorker starts sending every δ_{frame} (16), also specifying the number and total size of Δ. A retransmission can be requested for the single δ_{frame} or the entire Δ (19) in case of partial or total reception failure.

For of a good understanding, we do not describe more phases of the protocol, but in the following we focus, on the dynamic semantic of the extensions introduced in the JVM model, that should explain the behaviour of roles and actors mentioned.

3 JTTMP Transitions

A jvm is started with a couple of initial threads MM and TM that are runnable and active, then the main thread of a jmta is started. The rule *execJava$_T$*, defined in [8], starts the MM and TM thread. MM or TM never dies, then the JVMConsole is forced to keep being alive. After a first phase for local synchronization, both MM and TM go upon normal execution of their protected statement. Alternatively the MM and the TM becomes the current thread in the execJavaThread. For both, methods are defined through which *execJava$_T$* can control their status as was mentioned above. *Definition: For all threads two simulated states are defined that are delegating and migrating. The delegating state is composed by the waiting and the notified states, the migrating state is composed by the waiting and the synchronizing states.* The first responsibility of a MM, started on a JVMConsole is to attempt to collect information about other MMs on the JVMs neighborhood. If some JVMWorker is available and answers, then the JVM-Console grabs load information and tries to define a DJVM. The MM keeps checking its own workload and the JVMWorker workload and it decides about the migration, or uses workload information for inverse migration later, in order to balance the load over

Table 1. jvmConsole and jvmWorker are the main transition of the protocol for clustering remote JVM

execJavaThreadConsole =
–**if** $\nexists$ DJVM **then**
——**choose** DJVM **in** createDJVM
–**choose** SELFLOAD **with** *request$_{Load}$*(..) **in** directMigrate(q)
–**choose** SELFLOAD **with** *request$_{Load}$*(..) **in** inverseMigrate(q)
–*request$_{sincroThread}$*(..)
–*status$_{migratedThread}$*(..)
–*request$_{sincroNode}$*(..)
–**if** dependency **then**
——*prepare$_{loadLib}$*(..)
——*prepare$_{allocateMem}$*(..)

execJavaThreadWorker=
–*prepare$_{toSend}$*(..)
–*executeW$_{\delta_{frame}}$*(..)

the DJVM. A MM on a JVMWorker that has been aggregated into a DJVM keeps listening for thread migration and execution requests. In the following we show the modified formal main transition rules of ASM for JVM [8, pg.99]:

A structure containing load information about JVMWorker nodes participating in a DJVM is thus created and maintained by the JVMConsole. As regards the migration policy, whose description is here simplifyed, in order to choose the targeting JVM-Worker for thread migration, the JVMConsole must know the load information about them. The choosing policy for each resource consist in a comparative analysis between its own load status and the load status of the other Workers.

At this point it is important to show the set of new function name introduced for the definition of the new actions that JVM and thread can performe. The set of functions describing the protocol operations is reported below. In the following by $[\![f]\!]$ we mean, with abuse of notation, the generation of a set obtained by the evaluation of the function f.

Table 2. looksUpJVM, createDJVM, and directMigrate are the transitions of the protocol for discovering remote JVM, for creating a cluster of JVM, and for starting a thread migration progress

---

1) createDJVM =
–*forall* WORKER ∈ DJVM
——-looksUpJVM
——-storeLoadInfoWorker

2) directMigrate(q) =
-**forall** WORKER
–**if** q ∉ {$DAEMON \wedge LOCAL \wedge notMAIN$)} **then**
——**if** loadratioD(WORKER)≤SELFLOAD *then*
————**if** $directMigration_{Thread}(..)$ *then*
——————$prepare_{toReceive}(..)$ **(preparing context of execution)**

3) inverseMigrate(q)=
–**if** (loadratioI(WORKER) ≤ SELFLOAD)
vee (exec(q) ∈ {$Dead \vee Machine - dep$}) **then**
——**if** $inverseMigration_{Thread}(WORKER)$ **then**
————$prepare_{toReceive}(..)$ **(preparing context of execution)**

4) looksUpJVM = **if** $discovery_{info}(..)$ **then** WORKER:=WKPROFILE

Table 3. Transitions of the protocol for evaluating the workload of remote JVMs

---

5) storeLoadInfoWorker : WORKER → LOAD **storing function worload of WORKER**

6) loadratioD : CONSOLE → LOAD **computing function ratio workload of JVMConsole**
7) loadratioI : WORKER → LOAD **computing function ratio workload of JVMWorker**

1. $discovery_{info}(WORKERQUERY) \rightarrow [\ [\![response_{info}(..)]\!]\ ]$.
2. $response_{info}(WORKERRESPONSE) \rightarrow [\langle WORKER, WKPROFILE \rangle]$.
3. $request_{load}(WORKER, LOADINFO) \rightarrow [\ [\![evaluate_{load}(..)]\!]\ ]$.
4. $evaluate_{load}(SELF) \rightarrow [\langle SUCCESS, LOAD \rangle, FAILED]$.
5. $select_{worker}(\ [\![request_{load}(..)]\!]\ ) \rightarrow [true, false, undef]$.
6. $directMigration_{Thread}(\ [\![select_{worker}(..)]\!]\ ) \rightarrow [SUCCESS, FAILED]$.
7. $inverseMigration_{Thread}(\ [\![select_{worker}(..)]\!]\ ) \rightarrow [SUCCESS, FAILED]$.
8. $request_{typeThread}(APOThread) \rightarrow [TID]$[1]
9. $select_{Thread}(\ [\![request_{typeThread}(..)]\!]\ ) \rightarrow [true, false, undef]$.
10. $prepare_{toReceive}(\ [\![select_{Thread}(..)]\!], MIGRATE) \rightarrow [\ [\![prepare_{toSend}(..)]\!]\ ]$
11. $createComm_{channel}() \rightarrow [CHC]$
12. $createMig_{channel}() \rightarrow [CHM]$
13. $prepare_{toSend}(\ [\![createMig_{channel}(..)]\!], CONT, READY) \rightarrow [\ [\![send_{\delta_{frame}}(..)]\!]\ ]$
14. $create_{cloneThread}(TID) \rightarrow [\ ]$
15. $sort_{\delta_{frame}}() \rightarrow [\Delta]$
16. $send_{\delta_{frame}}(\ [\![sort_{\delta_{frame}}(..)]\!], FRAME, FRAMESIZE) \rightarrow [\ ]$
17. $sort_{\delta_{frame}}() \rightarrow [\Delta]$
18. $executeW_{\delta_{frame}}(\ [\![sort_{\delta_{frame}}(..)]\!]\ ) \rightarrow [MORE, FAILED]$
19. $prepare_{toReceive}(\ [\![select_{Thread}(..)]\!], RETREAT) \rightarrow [\ [\![prepare_{toSend}(..)]\!]\ ]$
20. $request_{sincroThread}(TID) \rightarrow [LOCK, UNLOCK, GETLOCKHOLDER]$
21. $status_{migratedThread}(STATE, TID) \rightarrow [\ [\![evaluate_{threadStatus}(..)]\!]\ ]$
22. $evaluate_{threadStatus}(..) \rightarrow [WAITING, RUNNING, STOPPED, FINISHED]$
23. $request_{sincroNode}(MBARRIERSYNC, BARRIERID) \rightarrow [\ ]$
24. $prepare_{loadLib}(LIBLOAD, LIBSIZE) \rightarrow [\ [\![send_{lib}(..)]\!]\ ]$
25. $send_{lib}(lib) \rightarrow [\ ]$
26. $prepare_{allocateMem}(REMOTEMALLOC, MEMSIZE) \rightarrow [\ [\![prepared_{allocatedMem}(..)]\!]\ ]$
27. $prepared_{allocatedMem}(MCONT, MEMPOINTER) \rightarrow [\ ]$

---

[1] TID=Thread Identifier

4 JTTMP Binding to P2P

In this section we briefly describe the JXTA protocol we make use of when modeling JTTMP. In the following sections we will informally describe the usage we make of the JXTA protocol, with respect to the transitions described in the JTTMP protocol. All actors participating in the P2P protocol are interconnected nodes P (peers). Such nodes can be generally considered as service providers. In a DJVM context, they are the *TM*s and *MM*s. Every peer operates independently and asynchronously with respect to all others, and it is univoquely identified by an *ID*.

In a peer to peer network four kind of peers coexist: i)*minimum Peer*: can send and receive messages, but cannot store messages or route messages created by other peers. Essentially it is a limited resource peer. ii)*full Peer*: can send, receive and store messages, but cannot route messages created by other peers. iii)*rendezvous Peer*: can send, receive and store messages (advertisements). It can also route messages created by other peers. iiii)*Peer relay*: Gives a client/server mechanism that allows communicating with unaccessible peers (i.e. those behind NAT/firewalls). In a DJVM, the peerJVMConsoles implement the second, third and fourth kind of peer, whereas the peerJVMWorker only the second one. Peers aggregate themselves in *Peer Groups* where a set of peers can share the same "interest area" and can establish, independently from others, its own network membership policy. Peers can, as an example, belong to more than one group at the same time. Peers create logical regions on the net and access to these regions is given only to group members. These regions must not necessarily reflect the structure and physical links of the underlying network. The goal of a DJVM on a Peer to Peer network is that of creating peerGroupDJVMs. The protocols we make use of for implementing the JTTMP protocol are the following: *Peer Discovery Protocol (PDP)*: peers can use it for publishing their resources and the services they can offer, and for discovering other peers' resources; every resource is described and published via advertisements. *Peer Information Protocol(PIP)*: peers can use it to obtain information from other peers. *Pipe Binding Protocol(PBP)*: peers can use it to establish a virtual communication channel, called pipe, among two or more peers. *Rendezvous Protocol(RVP)*: this mechanism allows peers to subscribe to the Propagation Service. In fact, in a peer group, peers can be rendezvous peers or peers that listen to rendezvous peers.

The main consideration is about the **Peer Discovery Protocol implementing JTTMP**. A jmta instance on a JVMConsole starts the peerGroupDJVM process by publishing the related group advertisement. The peerJVMConsole implements the Membership, Rendezvous and Resolver services. The peerGroupDJVM consists of a virtual cluster composed of a number of peerJVMWorker whose advertisement specifies the *Java bytecode computation* service and the set of libraries they possess.

The creation of a peerGroupDJVM consist in dynamically searching for the peerJVM-Workers (transitions-1) that are able to offer a service or that possess some required libraries. The *Peer Discovery Protocol* (PDP) has been adopted since it has been specifically designed to allow performing the publishing and search operations on a Peer to Peer network. In particular: i) the peerJVMConsole sends a *Discovery Query* message via the MM component, to find a bytecode-execution-capable service. ii) All peer-

JVMWorker's MMs respond by sending its own profile, i.e. its *peerJVMWorker advertisement*, or the profile of specific libraries that are available on that Worker via the *Module Class Advertisement*; they also return the availability time of the JVM itself. iii) The MMs on every peerJVMWorker create and send a *pipe advertisement* specifying the *CHC* used to reach them (transitions-8), i.e. it contains the information on which peer offers the communication channel *startpoint*. iiii) The peerJVMConsole saves the collected MM advertisements inside its local cache; after having collected the peerJVMWorker's advertisements and the pipe advertisement for every CHC_i the peerGroupDJVM is active (transitions-2) and can proceed to publishing the group profile.

The peerJVMConsole apart from the peerJVMWorker or peerGroupDJVM characteristics, can decide the virtual cluster size and specify the number of advertisements to be returned from peerRandevouzs. We assume at the moment to run non-interactive jmtas that massively use computing resources. As a consequence, the peerJVMConsole will try to aggregate as many peerJVMWorkers as possible. The response received by the peerJVMConsole will come from a peerRandevouz or from a peerJVMWorker or from another peerJVMConsole with its own group advertisement. The number of potential peerJVMWorkers or peerJVMConsoles, and the remaining availability time of the service offered are essential information allowing the peerJVMConsole to decide the topology of the DJVM. The knowledge of a service length in time is particularly important during the direct and inverse thread migration phases, since the peerJVMConsole must be aware of the DJVM evolution over time.

To retrive updated information about the other JVM instances the **Peer Information Protocol is applied to the Thread Migration Protocol** The peerJVMConsole, after having stored in its local cache the result of its Discovery Query, collects information on the peerJVMWorkers' load. Such information is required in order to choose the scarcely loaded peerJVMWorkers to migrate threads to and those overloaded to retrieve back threads from. The information is collected using the Peer Information Protocol (transition-3). The peerJVMConsole sends to its peerGroupDJVM a *PeerInfoQueryMessage*, where a load request is specified. Every peerJVMWorker replies with a *PeerInfoResponseMessage*.

The creation of the CHM_i (transition-8) is particularly important and the **Endpoint Routing Protocol and Pipe Binding Protocol** are useful for the effective and efficient communication among JVM. In fact migration paths have to be optimized by the peerJVMConsole, in terms of bandwidth, availability, etc. We adopt the *Endpoint Routing Protocol* to manage such channels towards all peerGroupDJVM members. ERP is used by peerJVMConsole to find routes (paths) to DJVM members. Route information includes an ordered sequence of relay peer IDs that can be used to send a message to the destination. After defining the best available path, the peerJVMConsole uses PBP. The MM on the peerJVMConsole creates the communication channels with the MMs on the peerJVMWorkers. The PBP allows creating virtual communication channels between peers. Such channels are called pipes. The PBP takes care of specifying the virtual communication medium between peers, while the physical channel is taken care of by the Endpoint Routing Protocol. Every pipe has two endpoints, the InputPipe, for reception, and the OutputPipe, for sending. Every peerJVMWorker associates a listener to every

InputPipe in order to synchronize the migration. The listener is awakened every time a message is received. Last but not least are the consideration about the **Rendezvous Protocol implementing JTTMP**. Rendezvous Peers are particular peers that can route and propagate messages on the network. A peerJVMConsole implements the Peer to Peer protocol and creates the peerGroupJVM (transition-2). The discovery of a peerRandevouz allows a peerJVMConsole to exploit isolated peerJVMWorkers, whereas the discovery of another peerJVMConsole will allow to aggregate other peerGroupDJVMs.

5 Related Work

The research field on Distributing JVMs is valuable for high-performance computing [13]. Several prototypes have been presented such as [14],[15],[16],[17], each one implementing a different kind of computational moving over instances of JVM. The main of them consist in capturing the current execution state of the thread (mainly the thread stack) and then transferring such state to a target node on which execution is restored. The capturing activity mainly is charged on JVM external controller that performes surveillance of the local JVM and interacts with it. Moreover most of them are able to use operating system communication channel and for this kind of DJVM it is assumed that they are effective into a cluster machine. A consequence of these approach is that a DJVM supports the parallel execution of a multithreaded Java application on networked virtual machines as if it were executed on a single machine. Some DJVMs do not require any modification to the underlying operating system and expose the standard Java APIs. Furthermore, current DJVM prototypes usage is limited by some deficiencies affecting the thread migration subsystem. These problems regard the discovery, reachability and aggregation of distributed JVMs. In fact, present DJVM implementations do not care about firewalls, NATs and VPNs. This prevents their deployment over large area networks and, as a consequence, it prevents aggregating computing farms belonging to different organizations. Furthermore, existing DJVMs have to be statically aggregated and a priori configuration of the resources participating in a DJVM is needed. Such configurations have to be replicated and made consistent on every DJVM node. In this way the set of resources is not dynamically configurable and its management is difficult.

6 Conclusion

We have proposed an extension of the JVM computational model of JVM and in particular an implementation analysis of a *Transparent migration protocol for Java threads* over a Peer to Peer (P2P) infrastructure. The idea provides distributed JVM run-time location, aggregation and reachability. Moreover, it allows distributing threads effectively over wide area networks. Last but not least, it provides a mechanism for aggregating JVMs into Virtual Farms for Java Multi-threaded applications computing. In the future we will proof the formal correctness of the extentended model and the protocol and we will produce experimental result. Further in the future we will try the binding with other distribution framework such as Nexus [18].

References

1. Bouchenak, S., Hagimont, S.: Zero overhead java thread migration. Technical Report 0261, INRIA (2002)
2. Clemments Papaioannou, T., Edwards, J.: Aglets: Enabling the virtual enterprise. In: Proceedings of the Managing Enterprises - Stakeholders, Engineering, Logistics, and Achievement. (1997)
3. Wong, D., Paciorek, N., Walsh, T., DiCelie, J., Young, M., Peet, B.: Concordia: An infrastructure for collaborating mobile agents. In: Mobile Agents: Proceedings of the First International Workshop. (1997)
4. Jul, E., Steensgaard, B.: Object and native code thread mobility among heterogeneous computers. In: Proceedings of the 15th Symposium on Operating System Principles. (1995)
5. Douglis, F., Ousterhout, J.K.: Transparent process migration: Design alternatives and the sprite implementation. Software - Practice and Experience **21**(8) (1991) 757–785
6. Artsy, Y., Finkel, R.: Designing a process migration facility: The charlotte experience. Computer **22**(9) (1989) 47–56
7. Gurevich, Y.: Evolving algebras: An attempt to discover semantics. Current Trends in Theoretical Computer Science (1993) 266–292
8. Stark, R.F., Borger, E., Shmid, J.: Java and the Java Virtual Machine: Definition, Verification, Validation. Springer-Verlag (2001)
9. Gong, L.: Project jxta: a technology overview. http://www.jxta.org/ (2002)
10. Moro, G., Ouksel, A., Sartori, C.: Agents and Peer-to-Peer Computing: A Promising Combination of Paradigms. Volume 2530. (2003)
11. Cavarra, A., Riccobene, E., Scandurra, P.: A framework to simulate uml models: moving from a semi-formal to a formal environment. In: SAC '04: Proceedings of the 2004 ACM symposium on Applied computing, New York, NY, USA, ACM Press (2004) 1519–1523
12. Harel, G..T.: The general, the abstract, and the generic in advanced mathematics. For the Learning of Mathematics, 11(1), 38-42 (2001)
13. Zhu, W., Fang, W., Wang, C.L., Lau, F.C.: High Performance Computing on Clusters : The Distributed JVM Approach. John Wiley and Sons, Inc. (2004)
14. Aridor, Y., Factor, M., Teperman, A.: cjvm: a single system image of a jvm on a cluster. In: Proceedings of the International Conference on Parallel Processing. (1999)
15. Ma, M., Wang, C., Lau, F., Xu, Z.: Jessica: Java-enabled single-system-image computing architecture. In: International Conference on Parallel and Distributed Processing Techniques and Applications. (1999)
16. Antoniu, G., Boug, L., Hatcher, P., MacBeth, M., McGuigan, K., Namyst, R.: The hyperion system: Compiling multithreaded java bytecode for distributed execution. In: Parallel Computing. (2001)
17. Yu, W., Cox, A.: Java/dsm: A platform for heterogeneous computing. In: Concurrency - Practice and Experience. (1997)
18. Ian Foster, Carl Kesselman, S.T.: The nexus approach to integrating multithreading and communication. (1996)

Analytic Performance Modeling of a Fully Adaptive Routing Algorithm in the Torus

Mostafa Rezazad[1] and Hamid Sarbazi-azad[2]

[1] IPM School of Computer Science, Niavaran Bldg, Niavaran Square, Tehran, Iran
[2] Sharif University of Technology, Azadi Street, Tehran, Iran
{rezazad, azad}@ipm.ir,
azad@sharif.edu

Abstract. Over the past decade, many fully adaptive routing algorithms have been proposed in the literature, of which Duato's routing algorithm has gained considerable attention for analytical modeling. In this study we propose an analytical model to predict message latency in wormhole routed 2-dimensional torus networks in which fully adaptive routing, based on Linder-Harden's methodology [10], is employed. This methodology presents a framework in which adaptive routing algorithms can be developed for the k-ary n-cube network. Simulation experiments reveal that the latency results predicted by the proposed analytical model are in good agreement with those provided by simulation experiments.

1 Introduction

Most current multicomputers employ *k*-ary *n*-cubes for low-latency and high-bandwidth inter-processor communication. The two most popular instances of *k*-ary *n*-cubes are the hypercube (where *k* = 2) and the Torus (where *n* = 2) [7]. The former has been used in early multicomputers such as the cosmic cube, N-cube and iPSC/2.

The latest generations of multicomputers have widely used wormhole switching due to its low buffering requirements and, more importantly, it makes latency almost independent of the message distance in the absence of blocking [7].

Fully adaptive routing has often been suggested to improve network performance by enabling messages to explore all available paths. Several authors like Linder-Harden [10], Duato [6, 7], and Lin et al [9] have proposed fully adaptive routing algorithms that can achieve deadlock freedom with a minimal requirement for hardware resources.

Many studies have proposed analytical models for the performance evaluation of different interconnection networks [1-5,8,11-13] using results from combinatorial theory and/or queuing theory.

In this paper, a new analytical model for computing the mean message latency in 2-D torus with Linder-Harden's fully adaptive routing algorithm is proposed. Results from simulation experiments reveal that the present model exhibits a good degree of accuracy under light, moderate, as well as heavy traffic regions.

2 The Analytical Model

The proposed model here uses assumptions that are widely used in the literature [1-5,8,11-13]: (a) Nodes generate traffic independently of each other, and which follows a Poisson process with a mean rate of λ messages per cycle, (b) The arrival process at a given channel is approximated by an independent Poisson process, (c) Message destinations are uniformly distributed across network nodes, (d) Message length is fixed and equal to M flits each of which is transmitted in one cycle from one router to the next, (e) The local queue at the injection channel in the source node has infinite capacity, (f) 6 virtual channels are used per physical channel in dimension X and the number of virtual channels used in dimension Y is 3 virtual channels per physical channel. With $\overline{S}$ being the mean network latency, $\overline{W}_s$ being the mean waiting time seen by a message in the source node to be injected into the network, and $\overline{V}$ being average degree of virtual channels multiplexing, the mean message latency can be written as

$$\text{Latency} = (\overline{S} + \overline{W}_s)\overline{V} \tag{1}$$

With $\overline{d}$ being the average number of hops that a message makes across the network, the rate of messages received by each channel can then be computed as [11]

$$\lambda_c = \lambda \overline{d} / 4 \tag{2}$$

Since the torus is symmetric averaging the network latencies seen by the messages generated by only one node for all other nodes gives the mean message latency in the network. Let $S = (s_x, s_y)$ be the source node and $D = (d_x, d_y)$ denotes a destination node such that $D \equiv G - \{S\}$ where G is the set of all nodes in the network. Let us define the set $H = \{h_x, h_y\}$, where h_x and h_y denotes the number of hops that the message makes along X and Y dimensions, respectively, i.e. $(s_x + h_x) \bmod k = d_x$ and $(s_y + h_y) \bmod k = d_y$. The network latency, S_H, seen by the message crossing from node S to node D consists of two parts: one is the delay due to the actual message transmission time, and the other is due to the blocking time in the network. Therefore, S_H can be written as

$$S_H = (M + |H|)t_c + \sum_{j=1}^{|H|} B_j \tag{3}$$

where M is the message length, $|H|$ the distance (in terms of the number of hops made by the message) between the source and the destination node, t_c is the channel cycle time, and B_j the blocking time seen by a message on its j th hop. The terms $|H|$ and B_j are given by

$$|H| = h_x + h_y, \tag{4}$$

$$B_j = \begin{cases} P_{block_j} W_C, & \text{if } j < |H| \\ W_{ejection}, & \text{if } j = |H| \end{cases} \tag{5}$$

with P_{block_j} being the probability that a message is blocked on its j-th hop during its journey; W_c is the mean waiting time to acquire a channel in the event of blocking, and also $W_{ejection}$ is that for an ejection channel. Let us now calculate the blocking probability $P_{block j}$. Let $N_0^H(j)$ define the number of ways that j hops can be distributed over two dimensions such that the number of hops made in dimension X and Y be at most the h_x and h_y. The calculation of $N_0^H(j)$ can be determined as

$$N_0^H(j) = |Q_{H,j}| \tag{6}$$

$$Q_{H,j} = \{(x,y) \mid x+y = j, \ 0 \le x \le h_x, \ 0 \le y \le h_y\} \tag{7}$$

So, the probability that a message has entirely crossed dimension X and Y on its j-th hop is respectively given by

$$Pass_j^x = \frac{N_0^{\{0,h_y-1\}}(j-h_x)}{N_0^H(j)}, \qquad Pass_j^y = \frac{N_0^{\{h_x-1,0\}}(j-h_y)}{N_0^H(j)} \tag{8}$$

A message is blocked at a given channel when the virtual channels in both dimensions (to be traversed) are busy. The virtual channels that a message can utilize in each dimension, depends on the virtual network and level in which the message resides. Let P_{Dx} be the probability of the virtual channel used by a message in dimension X being busy, and P_{Dy} be the probability of dimension Y (messages in dimension X can move in both directions but they can move only in one direction in dimension Y depending on the virtual network). So the number of virtual channels in dimension X is two times greater than the number of virtual channels in dimension Y. The probability of blocking depends on the number of output channels (and thus on the virtual channels) that a message can use at its next hop. When a message has not entirely passed any dimension it can select each of two dimensions that has free virtual channel, but when a message has entirely crossed a dimension it should select virtual channels of the other dimension to make its next hop. A message is blocked at its j-th hop, if all the virtual channels that it can choose for its next hop, are busy. The probability of blocking, P_{block_j}, can therefore be written as

$$P_{block_j} = Pass_j^x P_{D_y} + Pass_j^y P_{D_x} + (1 - Pass_j^x Pass_j^y) P_{D_x} P_{D_y} \tag{9}$$

where P_{Dx} and P_{Dy} can be computed as follows

$$P_{D_x} = \sum_{i=1}^{6} \frac{\binom{5}{i-1}}{\binom{6}{i}} P_{x,i} \quad \text{and} \quad P_{D_y} = \sum_{i=1}^{3} \frac{\binom{2}{i-1}}{\binom{3}{i}} P_{y,i} \tag{10}$$

To determine the mean waiting time, W_c, to acquire a virtual channel a physical channel is treated as an M/G/1 queue with a mean waiting time of [13]

$$W_c = \frac{\rho \overline{S}(1+C_S^2)}{2(1-\rho)}, \qquad \rho = \lambda_c \overline{S}, \qquad C_S^2 = \frac{\sigma_S^2}{\overline{S}^2} \tag{11}$$

where λ_c is the traffic rate on the channel, $\overline{S}$ is its service time, and σ_S^2 the variance of the service time distribution. While λ_c is given above by Eq. (4), the quantities $\overline{S}$ and σ_S^2 are computed as follows. As adaptive routing distributes traffic evenly among all channels, the mean service time at each channel is the same regardless of its position, and is equal to the mean network latency, $\overline{S}$. Eq. (5) gives the network latency, S_H, seen by a message to cross from the source node S to the destination node D. Averaging over the $(N-1)$ possible destination nodes in the network yields the mean network latency as

$$\overline{S} = \frac{1}{k^2 - 1} \sum_{D \in G - \{S\}} S_H . \tag{12}$$

Since the minimum service time at a channel is equal to the message length, M, following a suggestion proposed in [5], the variance of the service time distribution can be approximated as $\sigma_{\overline{S}}^2 = (\overline{S} - M t_c)^2$. Hence, the mean waiting time becomes

$$W_C = \frac{\lambda_c \overline{S}^2 (1 + (\overline{S} - M t_c)^2 / \overline{S}^2)}{2(1 - \lambda_c \overline{S})} . \tag{13}$$

A message originating from a given source node sees a network latency of $\overline{S}$. Modeling the local queue in the source node as an M/G/1 queue, with the mean arrival rate $\lambda/6$ (recalling that a message in the source node can enter the network through any of the 6 virtual channels) and service time $\overline{S}$ with an approximated variance $(\overline{S} - M t_c)^2$ yields the mean waiting time seen by a message at source node as [13]

$$\overline{W}_s = \frac{\frac{\lambda}{6} \overline{S}^2 (1 + (\overline{S} - M t_c)^2 / \overline{S}^2)}{2(1 - \frac{\lambda}{6} \overline{S})} . \tag{14}$$

The waiting time at the ejection channel for a message arrived in the destination node can be approximated using an M/D/1 queue with arrival rate λ, service time M, to be

$$W_{ejection} = \frac{\lambda (M t_c)^2}{2(1 - \lambda t_c)} \tag{15}$$

The probability, $P_{x,v}$, that v virtual channels are busy at a physical channel in dimension X, and $P_{y,v}$, that v virtual channels are busy at a physical channel in dimension Y can be respectively determined as [13]

$$P_{x,v} = \begin{cases} (\lambda_c \overline{S})^v, & 0 \le v \le 5, \\ \frac{(\lambda_c \overline{S})^6}{1 - \lambda_c \overline{S}}, & v = 6, \end{cases} \qquad P_{y,v} = \begin{cases} (\lambda_c \overline{S})^v, & 0 \le v \le 2, \\ \frac{(\lambda_c \overline{S})^3}{1 - \lambda_c \overline{S}}, & v = 3, \end{cases} \tag{16}$$

When multiple virtual channels are used per physical channel in dimension X, they share the bandwidth in a time multiplexed manner. The average degree of multiplexing of virtual channels, that takes place at a given physical channel in dimension X, can be estimated by [12,13]

$$\overline{V_x} = \frac{\sum_{v=1}^{6} v^2 P_{x,v}}{\sum_{v=1}^{6} v P_{x,v}}. \tag{17}$$

Similarly the average degree of multiplexing of virtual channels, that takes place at a given physical channel in dimension Y, can be estimated by

$$\overline{V_y} = \frac{\sum_{v=1}^{3} v^2 P_{y,v}}{\sum_{v=1}^{3} v P_{y,v}}. \tag{18}$$

The average virtual channel multiplexing degree can be then approximated by

$$\overline{V} = \frac{\overline{V_x} + \overline{V_x}}{2}. \tag{19}$$

3 Simulation Experiments

The proposed analytical model above has been validated through comparison with the results obtained from a discrete-event simulator that mimics the behavior of Linder-Harden fully adaptive routing in the 2-D torus at the flit level. In each simulation experiment, a total of 100K messages are delivered. Statistics gathering was inhibited for the first 10K messages to avoid distortions due to the initial start-up conditions.

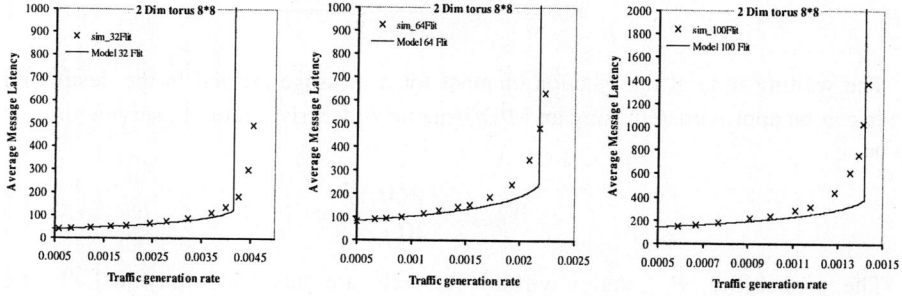

Fig. 1. Average message latency predicted by the model against simulation results

Numerous validation experiments have been performed for different network sizes and message lengths. However, for the sake of specific illustration, Fig. 1 shows latency results predicted by the proposed model plotted against those provided by the simulator for 8×8 torus networks, and for different message lengths $M = 32$, 64 and 100 flits. The horizontal axis in the figures shows the traffic generation rate at each node (λ) while the vertical axis shows the mean message latency.

The figure reveals that in all cases, the analytical model predicts the mean message latency with a good degree of accuracy in the steady-state regions. Moreover, the model predictions are still good even when the network operates in the heavy traffic region, and when it starts to approach the saturation region.

4 Conclusions

An analytical model to compute the mean message latency in wormhole-routed torus networks with Linder-Harden's fully adaptive routing algorithm has been proposed in this paper. Simulation experiments have revealed that the latency results predicted by the analytical model are in good agreement with those obtained through simulation. The proposed model achieves a good degree of accuracy under different operating conditions because it computes the exact expression for the probability of message blocking at a given router. Furthermore, it manages to achieve this good degree of accuracy while maintaining simplicity, making it a practical evaluation tool that can be used to gain insight into the performance behavior of Linder-Harden's fully adaptive routing in wormhole-routed torus interconnection networks.

References

1. Agarwal: Limits on interconnection network performance, IEEE TPDS 2 (4) (1991) 398–412.
2. Ciciani, B., M., Colajanni, Paolucci, C.: Performance evaluation of deterministic wormhole routing in k-ary n-cubes, Parallel Computing 24 (1998) 2053–2075.
3. Colajanni, M., Ciciani, B., Quaglia, F.: Performance analysis of wormhole switching with adaptive routing in two-dimensional torus, in: Proceedings of the EuroPar'99, Toulouse, France, August 31–September 3, 1999.
4. Dally, W.J.: Performance analysis of k-ary n-cubes interconnection networks, IEEE TC.C39 (6) (1990) 775–785.
5. Draper, J.T., Ghosh, J.: A comprehensive analytical model for wormhole routing in multicomputer systems, JPDC 32 (1994) 202–214.
6. Duato, J.: A new theory of deadlock-free adaptive routing in wormhole routing networks, IEEE TPDS 4(12)(1993) 320–1331.
7. Duato, J., Yalamanchili, S., Ni, L.: Interconnection Networks: An Engineering Approach, IEEE Computer Society Press, Silver Spring, MD, 1997.
8. Greenberg, R., Guan, L.: Modelling and comparison of wormhole routed mesh and torus networks, in: Proceedings of the Ninth IASTED International Conference on Parallel and Distributed Computing and Systems, 1997.
9. Lin, X., Mckinley, P.K., Lin, L.M.: The message flow model for routing in wormhole-routed networks, in: Proceedings of the International Conference on Parallel Processing, 1993, pp. 294–297.
10. Linder, D.H., Harden, J.C.: An adaptive and fault tolerant wormhole routing strategy for k-ary n-cubes, IEEE TC C40(1) (1991) 2–12.
11. Loucif, S., Ould-Khaoua, M., Mackenzie, L.M.: Analysis of fully-adaptive routing in wormhole-routed tori, Parallel Comput. 25 (1999) 1477–1487.
12. Ould-Khaoua, M.: A performance model of Duato's adaptive routing algorithm in k-ary n-cubes, IEEE TC 48(1999) 1297–1304.
13. Sarbazi-Azad, H., Ould-Khaoua, M., Mackenzi, L.M.: An accurate model of adaptive wormhole routing in k-ary n- cubes interconnection networks, Performance Evaluation, 43(2001) 165-179.

Redundancy Schemes for High Availability in DHTs

Fan Wu, Tongqing Qiu, Yuequan Chen, and Guihai Chen

State Key Laboratory of Novel Software Technology,
Nanjing University, China

Abstract. High availability in peer-to-peer DHTs requires data redundancy. This paper takes user download behavior into account to evaluate redundancy schemes in data storage and share systems. Furthermore, we propose a hybrid redundancy scheme of replication and erasure coding. Experiment results show that replication scheme saves more bandwidth than erasure coding scheme, although it requires more storage space, when average node availability is higher than 48%. Our hybrid scheme saves more maintenance bandwidth with acceptable redundancy factor.

Keywords: Peer-to-Peer, Distributed Hash Table, Replication, Erasure Coding.

1 Introduction

The last several years have seen the emergence of a class of structured peer-to-peer systems that provide a distributed hash table (DHT) abstraction [13, 16, 18]. DHTs propose a determined object locating service, and already are used in many applications [6, 7, 10, 17]. However, to provide high data availability in the DHT, when the peers that are storing them are not 100% available, needs some form of data redundancy. Peer-to-peer DHTs have proposed two different redundancy schemes: replication [6, 17] and erasure coding [7, 10].

Some comparisons [2, 7, 19] argued that erasure coding is the clear winner, due to huge storage and bandwidth savings for the same availability levels (or conversely, huge availability gains for the same storage space). The other comparisons [3, 15] argued that coding is an clear winner only when peer availability is low; the benefits of coding are so limited in some cases that they can easily be outweighed by some disadvantages such as extra complexity, download latency and lack of ability of keyword searching.

This paper argues that sharing user downloaded files for subsequent accesses (replication) and meanwhile utilizing erasure coding to maintain files' availability will achieve better performance: saving more bandwidth with acceptable redundancy factor. There are two talking points. First, in current peer-to-peer file sharing communities, popular files are automatically kept at high availability level, due to thousands of times of user downloads. Second, current hardware deployment suggests that idle bandwidth is the limiting resource that volunteers contribute, not idle disk space. Further, since disk space grows much faster than access point bandwidth, bandwidth is likely to become even scarcer relative to disk space.

This paper makes the following contributions: First, to our best knowledge, this paper is the first to take user download behavior into account — sharing user downloaded files for subsequent accesses — to evaluate redundancy schemes in data storage and share systems. Second, this paper demonstrates that replication saves more bandwidth than erasure coding, although it requires more storage space, when average peer availability is higher than 48%. Finally, this paper shows that the hybrid redundancy scheme of replication and erasure coding can achieve better overall performance: saving more bandwidth with redundancy factor less than 9.4 for three nines (99.9%) of per-file availability.

The rest of the paper is organized as follows. Section 2 formulates and describes three schemes for high availability: replication, erasure coding and the combination of them. Section 3 evaluates these three schemes by two sets of experiments. Finally, we conclude the paper and point out future work in Section 4.

2 Redundancy Schemes

This section presents three redundancy schemes for high availability: replication, erasure coding and a hybrid scheme which shares user downloaded files for subsequent accesses (replication) and utilizes erasure coding to adjust files' availability. All of them work upon consistent hashing [9], as used by storage systems such as CFS [6].

First, several key terminologies should be introduced. For simplicity, each file is identified by a unique identifier d, which is consistent hash of the file name. The peer that keeps location indexes for file copies or fragments is named *indexer*. Besides, a dualistic hash function should be declared: $h(d, n)$, where $n \geq 1$ is the sequence number of each indexer. $h(\bullet, \bullet)$ is the allocation function, typically based on the hash function shared by all peers. The allocation function might be defined as follows: $h(d, n) = H(d \parallel n)$, where $H(\bullet)$ is the hash function which is used in the DHTs and $\parallel$ is a concatenation.

All schemes consist of three parts with some difference due to their particularity: register, request and maintenance.

- Register: Each peer periodically registers the unique IDs of the files it holds and/or fragments in its cache in M distributed and independent indexers. The logical location of M indexes is determined by the hash function defined above: $h(d, n), n \in [1, M]$. If the peer pointed by $h(d, n)$ is not alive, its successor takes over its role. The indexer associates each item in the index with a timer. A copy of file or a fragment will be recognized as unavailable and removed from the index if its timer runs out.
- Request: When requesting a file d, a peer randomly refers to one or more indexers responsible for d. If the checked indexers do not provide enough whole file or fragment location information, the peer will turn to other indexers. If all M distributed indexers fail to provide enough location information, the peer will wait a period of time and do the procedure as stated above again, until maximum lookup time expires. This balances the load of directory service and reduces the chance of getting incomplete location index. Then the peer downloads the file or enough fragments to reconstruct the original file from peers registered in location index.
- Maintenance: Periodically, each indexer estimates the availability of files and/or fragments registered on it, and attempts to increase the availability of ones that is not yet at target availability.

2.1 Replication Scheme

Replication is the simplest redundancy scheme. Here r identical copies of each file are kept at each instant by peers. The value of r must be set appropriately depending on the desired object availability a (i.e., a has some "number of nines"), and on the average peer availability p. Throughout the analysis, it is assumed that the peer availability is independent and identically distributed. The needed number of copies can be determined by:

$$a = 1 - (1-p)^r \qquad (1)$$

which upon solving for r yields

$$r = \frac{\log(1-a)}{\log(1-p)} \qquad (2)$$

Each peer periodically registers shared and cached files in M distributed and independent indexes. When requesting a file d, a peer lookups a random index responsible for d. If the referred indexer fails, the peer will turn to another indexer. If all M indexers fail, the peer will wait a period of time and do the lookup procedure again, until maximum lookup time is reached. Then the peer accesses the file from a random peer registered in location index. The already downloaded file is automatically treated as a shared file for subsequent accesses. Finally, each indexer periodically adjust the availability of its indexed files by scheduling necessary number of file transfers from the whole file holder to randomly chosen peers to reach the desired availability of file d.

2.2 Erasure Coding Scheme

Erasure codes (e.g., Reed-Solomon [14] or Tornado [5]) divide an object into m fragments and recode them into n fragments, where $n > m$. This means that the effective redundancy factor is $r = n/m$. The common property of erasure codes is that the original object can be reconstructed from any m fragments (where the combined size of m fragments is approximately equal to the original object size).

We assume that we place one encoded fragment per file per peer and there is no duplicate fragments. File availability can be calculated by the probability of at least m out of n fragments are available:

$$a = \sum_{i=m}^{n} \binom{n}{i} p^i (1-p)^{n-i} \qquad (3)$$

where p is the average peer availability.

The number of files per host follows a Poisson distribution. Because it is difficult to directly evaluate the Poisson distribution, we use the normal approximation to the Poisson distribution. With the normal approximation, if we perform random placement of files on hosts then the number of files per host follows a normal distribution. Using algebraic simplifications and the normal approximation to the binomial distribution (see [1]), we get the following formula for the erasure coding redundancy factor:

$$r = \frac{n}{m} = \left(\frac{\sigma_a \sqrt{\frac{p(1-p)}{m}} + \sqrt{\frac{\sigma_a^2 p(1-p)}{m} + 4p}}{2p} \right)^2 \qquad (4)$$

where σ_a is the value of standard deviations in a normal distribution for the required level of availability. Table 1 shows the standard deviations in a normal distribution for different values of availability a. These results are standard for any normal distribution. For instance, $\sigma_a = 3.1$ corresponds to three nines of availability.

Table 1. Standard deviations that follows a normal distribution for the given level of availability

a	σ_a
0.800	0.84
0.900	1.28
0.990	2.48
0.995	2.81
0.998	2.88
0.999	3.10

When erasure coding is used, an indexer that generates new fragments to adjust availability must have access to the whole file. It is unscalable to download enough fragments to reconstruct the file and then generate new fragments, since it is likely that m fragments need to be downloaded to regenerate merely a new fragment. Thus the amount of file that needs to be transferred is m times as much as the amount of redundancy lost. An alternative is to associate the peer whose identifier is closest to the consistent hash of the file name as the *home peer* for that file. The home peer stores a permanent copy of the file and manages its fragment generation. If the home peer fails, the next closest peer in the identifier space automatically becomes the new home peer. This is reasonable because the peer that takes responsibility of a file restores a complete copy, generates and pushes new fragments to targets in need. This corresponds to increasing the redundancy factor by 1.

However, erasure coding scheme does not share the whole user downloaded files. All shared objects in the system are erasure coded fragments stored in caches. Each peer periodically registers all fragments it keeps in M distributed and independent indexes. When requesting a file d, a peer lookups a random indexer responsible for d's fragments. If the referred indexer can not provide enough fragment location information, the peer will turn to another indexer. If all M indexers fail, the peer will wait a period of time and do the lockup procedure again, until maximum lookup time is reached. Then it downloads enough number of fragments and resembles the original file, and tries to regenerate and leave a fragment in cache. Finally, each indexer periodically adjusts the availability of its indexed fragments. For a file whose availability is below target level, the indexer consigns the home peer of the file to generate and push necessary number of fragments to randomly selected peers.

2.3 Hybrid Scheme

The replication scheme shares user downloaded files for subsequent accesses to save maintenance bandwidth. It saves more maintenance bandwidth than the erasure coding scheme when average peer availability is high, but requires much larger redundancy factor. The erasure coding scheme requires much less storage space than the replication to reach the availability level with the same average peer availability, and saves more maintenance bandwidth in highly dynamic environment, but still unscalable when average peer availability is low. This paper proposes a hybrid scheme which combines replication and erasure coding to achieve to better overall bandwidth saving with acceptable redundancy factor.

The hybrid scheme shares user downloaded files for subsequent accesses (replication) and utilizes erasure coding to maintain files' availability. It automatically treats a downloaded file as shared file for subsequent accesses as the replication scheme. When adjusting file availability, it consigns a whole file holder to generate and push necessary number of fragments to other peers, instead of transferring whole copy of file. On one hand, the hybrid scheme utilizes file copies already downloaded on network for subsequent downloads to reduce maintenance bandwidth overhead as the replication scheme. On the other hand, the hybrid scheme uses erasure coding to achieve less bandwidth overhead than replication for the same increment of availability level.

We now exhibit the analogue of Equation (1) and (3) for the case of hybrid scheme. We assume that we do not place files and fragments with the same ID on the same peer, and there is no duplicate fragments. File availability a, can be calculated by the probability of at least a whole copy or at least m out of n fragments are available. So a is estimated as 1 minus the probability that all whole copies of a file are simultaneously unavailable and there are not enough (at least m out of n) fragments available to reconstruct the original file:

$$a = 1 - (1-p)^h \left(1 - \sum_{i=m}^{n} \binom{n}{i} p^i (1-p)^{n-i}\right) \quad (5)$$

where h is number of file copies.

The hybrid scheme's redundancy factor can be calculated by adding redundancy factor of replication and erasure coding:

$$r = h + \frac{n}{m} = h + \left(\frac{\sigma_a(h)\sqrt{\frac{p(1-p)}{m}} + \sqrt{\frac{\sigma_a^2(h)p(1-p)}{m} + 4p}}{2p}\right)^2 \quad (6)$$

where $\sigma_a(h)$ is a function of h, and its value corresponds to the availability level (see Table 1) a' that erasure coding has to obtain. a' is derived from Equation (5) as follows:

$$a' = \sum_{i=m}^{n} \binom{n}{i} p^i (1-p)^{n-i} = 1 - \frac{1-a}{(1-p)^h} \quad (7)$$

Figure 1 captures the theoretical redundancy factor for the replication, erasure coding and hybrid schemes determined by Equation (2), (4) and (6) to achieve three nines of per-file availability. The redundancy factor of the hybrid scheme is determined by two factors: average peer availability p and number of file copies h. With any fixed h, there is a corresponding line. Intuitively, erasure coding requires less storage space to reach the availability level than the other two with the same average peer availability.

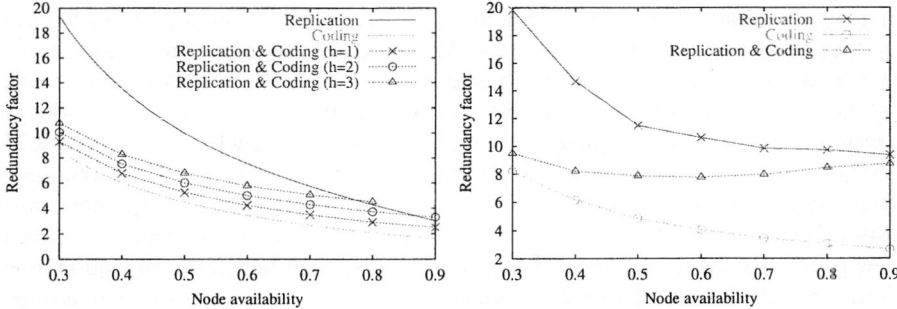

Fig. 1. Required redundancy factor for three nines of per-file availability, as a function of average peer availability, for the replication, coding and hybrid schemes as determined by Equation (2), (4) and (6)

Fig. 2. Required redundancy factor for three nines of per-file availability, as a function of average peer availability, for the replication, coding and hybrid schemes in simulation.

The hybrid scheme's redundancy factor is slightly larger than erasure coding, and saves more storage space than replication except when average peer availability is extremely high.

Each peer periodically registers shared files and cached fragments in M distributed and independent indexes. A peer locates a file with two kinds of indexes: whole file location index and fragment location index. When requesting a file d, a peer randomly refers to one or more indexers responsible for d. If the checked indexers do not provide enough whole file or fragment location information, the peer will turn to other indexers. If all M distributed indexers fail to provide enough location information, the peer will wait a period of time and do the above procedure again, until the maximum lookup time is reached. If the peer can not find a whole file living in system, it turns to gather enough fragments to resemble the original file. The downloaded and resembled files are regarded as shared.

Each indexer periodically adjusts the availability of its indexed files. For file d whose availability is below target level, the indexer consigns a peer holding file d to increase its availability by generating and pushing necessary number of fragments to randomly selected peers. For those files without a complete copy, the adjustment will be either delayed until a user download event happen, or performed as downloading enough fragments to reconstruct original file and issue fragments by the indexer itself when maximum waiting time is reached. Here, it is not necessary to use the mechanism as erasure coding scheme to maintain a complete file in system, because almost all the files have at least one copy in the system. Such, the hybrid scheme saves the bandwidth on maintaining a copy of file on home peer.

3 Evaluation

We implemented the three schemes for high availability in a discrete-event packet level simulator, p2psim [8]. The simulated network consists of 1024 peers. Each peer alternately crashes and re-joins the network; the interval between successive events for each peer is exponentially distributed with a mean of given time. When a peer crashes, all files, fragments and indexes on it are discarded. Each time a peer joins, it uses a different IP address and DHT identifier. There are 1000 same sized files in the system. Distribution of requests follows Zipf-like distribution, in which relative probability of requests for the i'th most popular file is proportional to $1/i^\alpha$, where α is set as 0.74 (average of six traces shown in [11]). We did two sets of experiments: different peer availability and different lookup rate. In different peer availability, average peer availability ranges from 30% to 90%. In different lookup rate, average number of lookups during peer's live time ranges from 2 to 20. Each simulation runs for a simulation time of 6 hours; statistics are collected only during the second half of the simulation time. We use $m = 7$, which is the number of fragments to reconstruct original object as used in CFS [6]. The target file availability is set to 99.9% which is the availability that end users might expect from today's web services [12]. Finally, each data point in our plots represents the average over 5 trials.

We evaluate three redundancy schemes using two primary metrics:

1. *Redundancy factor* is the total storage used to achieve target availability divided by storage needed to store one copy of the whole file.
2. *Bandwidth ratio* is the total maintenance bandwidth incurred due to (1) maintaining file availability, and (2) maintaining a copy of each file on home peer for erasure coding scheme, divided by total bandwidth due to serving file requests. Bandwidth on maintaining routing table and looking up is neglectable relative to maintenance bandwidth (1) and (2). A bandwidth ratio of 0.1 implies that the bandwidth overhead of maintaining availability is 10% as much as the system must consume for normal operations.

Bandwidth ratio is regarded as more important factor in this paper, since idle bandwidth is scarcer relative to idle disk space.

3.1 Redundancy Factor

In Figure 2, each line corresponds to a particular scheme for high availability. Figure 2 demonstrates that the erasure coding scheme's line goes generally the same as predicted in Figure 1, but the replication scheme's does not, especially when peer availability goes beyond 60%. While the erasure coding scheme makes the least use of user downloaded files, leaving only a fragment in cache, the replication scheme shares the whole user downloaded file. Meanwhile, the higher average peer availability is, the less copy loss rate is. The replication scheme's redundancy factor remains high with high average peer availability, due to too many copies of popular files living in system.

Figure 2 also shows that although average peer availability varies from 30% to 90%, the hybrid scheme's redundancy factor changes not obviously, between 8.5 and 9.4. When peer's churn rate is intensive, the hybrid scheme takes the advantage of erasure coding to save required storage space. When peer's average availability is high, the hybrid scheme's redundancy factor does not continue falling, and even increase instead. Its reason is the same as the replication scheme: too many copies of popular files living in system. This extra redundancy is harmless. Useless copies can be discarded by user or replacement function.

3.2 Bandwidth Ratio

Figure 3 shows that the replication scheme saves more bandwidth than the erasure coding scheme when average peer availability is higher than 48%, and the erasure coding scheme performs better than the replication scheme in the other case. The replication scheme shares user download files to reduce the time and transfer load on maintenance. The replication scheme is effective in communities with high average peer availability, because most files are kept at desired availability level by user downloads. But in highly dynamic communities, due to frequent peer joining and leaving, user downloads do not compensate for the loss of copies. In this case, the erasure coding scheme shows its advantage in achieving higher availability increment than replication does with the same bandwidth consumption; or conversely, requiring less bandwidth for the same increment of availability level.

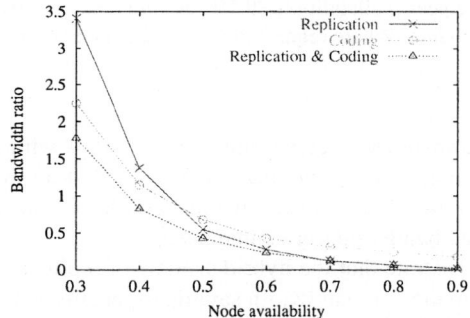

Fig. 3. Bandwidth ratio for three nines of per-file availability, as a function of average peer availability, for replication, coding and replication+coding

The highlight of Figure 3 is that the hybrid scheme of replication and coding achieves the best overall performance on bandwidth ratio. The hybrid scheme makes use of user download files as replication scheme, and maintains availability using erasure coding. When average peer availability is higher than 70%, the replication and the hybrid scheme consume approximately the same bandwidth on maintenance, because almost all of files' availability is high enough. When average peer availability is lower than 70%, the hybrid scheme's advantage is obvious. The hybrid scheme shares user downloaded files for subsequent accesses to save maintenance bandwidth. Another reason why the hybrid scheme saves more maintenance bandwidth than the erasure coding scheme is that the hybrid scheme do not need extra mechanism to maintain a copy of the file on home peer.

Figure 4(a) shows the situation which we might expect to see in a corporate or university environment with average peer availability is 80.7% [4]. It demonstrates that the more intensive request rate is, the less bandwidth ratio requires. While bandwidth ratio is a relative criterion, the absolute bandwidth overhead should also be paid attention to as shown in Figure 4(b). Figure 4(b) shows that while the replication and the hybrid

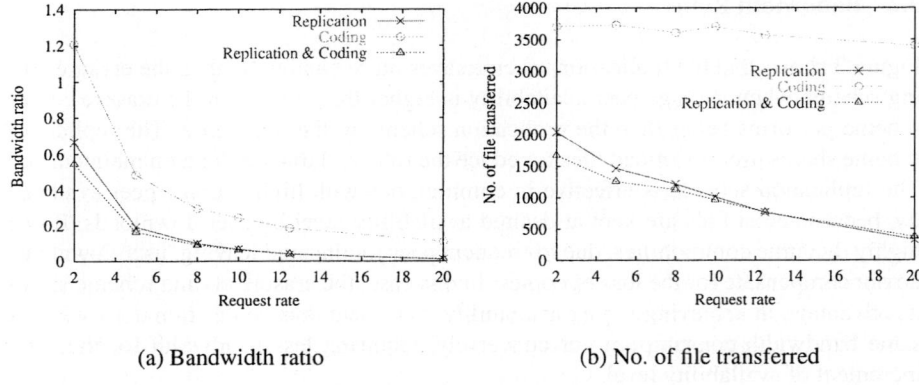

(a) Bandwidth ratio (b) No. of file transferred

Fig. 4. Bandwidth ratio and number of file transferred on maintenance for three nines of per-file availability when average peer availability is 80.7%, as a function of lookup rate, for replication, coding and replication+coding. Where request rate is average number of requests issued during a peer's lifetime.

scheme's number of transferred files on maintenance[1] falls with increment of request rate, erasure coding scheme's absolute maintenance bandwidth overhead decreases not obviously. This proves that sharing user downloaded files for subsequent accesses will considerably reduce the bandwidth on maintenance.

Figure 4 also demonstrate that the hybrid scheme of replication and erasure coding achieves better performance on bandwidth saving, especially when user request rate is low. When request rate is larger than 10, the replication and hybrid scheme's bandwidth ratio are extremely adjacent and close to x-axis. File or fragment transfer is rarely performed, because most of files' availability is maintained at desired level by abundant user downloaded files.

4   Conclusion and Future Work

This paper takes user download behavior into account to evaluate redundancy schemes in data storage and share systems. Experiment results show that unlike previous comparisons argued: the replication scheme saves more bandwidth than the erasure coding scheme, although it requires more storage space, when average peer availability is higher than 48%. When average peer availability is higher than 70%, the replication scheme consumes approximately the same bandwidth on maintenance as the hybrid scheme. Besides, the replication scheme introduces less complexity into system than the other two. So the replication scheme is a good choice, in high peer availability environments, e.g. university environment.

---

[1] Bandwidth overhead of the erasure coding scheme and the hybrid scheme is measured in terms of fragments. For comparison, their transferred number of fragments should be converted to number of files.

The erasure coding scheme requires less storage space to reach the availability level than replication with the same average peer availability, and consumes less maintenance bandwidth in highly dynamic environment. But it suffers from heavier maintenance bandwidth overhead than the replication, when average peer availability is higher than 48%, and introduces complexity into the system: not only encoding and decoding of fragments, but also entire system design complexity.

The highlight of this paper is that sharing user downloaded files for subsequent accesses (replication) and meanwhile utilizing erasure coding to maintain files' availability will achieve better performance: saving more bandwidth with acceptable redundancy factor (less than 9.4). The superiority of the hybrid scheme on saving maintenance bandwidth is obviously shown when average peer availability is lower than 70%. The experiment results also show that the hybrid scheme saves more bandwidth than the other two, when user request rate is low relative to peer churn rate. The hybrid scheme not only performs well in environments with high peer availability, but also demonstrates its advantages in highly dynamic communities. The disadvantage of the hybrid scheme is that it introduces complexity into the system.

The hybrid scheme achieve the best bandwidth saving, but in highly dynamic peer communities where average peer availability is lower than 0.5, its bandwidth ratio is still high, making the storage system suffer from poor scalability. Noting that bandwidth is scarcer relative to idle disk space, the future work should focus on saving bandwidth. Designing new coding algorithms and making further use of file copies already downloaded on network may be good for bandwidth saving. However, we leave these as issues for future work. This paper did not consider the storage limitations of the peers, we will consider it with some replacement strategies in the future.

Acknowledgements

This work is supported by the China NSF grant, the China Jiangsu Provincial NSF grant (BK2005208), the China 973 project (2002CB312002) and TRAPOYT award of China Ministry of Education.

References

1. R. Bhagwan, S. Savage, and G. Voelker. Replication strategies for highly available peer-to-peer storage systems. Technical Report CS2002-0726, UCSD, 2002.
2. R. Bhagwan, K. Tati, Y. Cheng, S. Savage, and G. Voelker. Total recall: System support for automated availability management. In *Proc. NSDI*, 2004.
3. C. Blake and R. Rodrigues. High availability, scalable storage, dynamic peer networks: Pick two. In *Proc. HotOS*, 2003.
4. W. J. Bolosky, J. R. Douceur, D. Ely, and M. Theimer. Feasibility of a serverless distributed file system deployed on an existing set of desktop PCs. In *Proc. SIGMETRICS*, 2000.
5. J. W. Byers, M. Luby, M. Mitzenmacher, and A. Rege. A digital fountain approach to reliable distribution of bulk data. In *Proc. ACM SIGCOMM*, 1998.
6. F. Dabek, M. F. Kaashoek, D. Karger, R. Morris, and I. Stoica. Wide-area cooperative storage with CFS. In *Proc. ACM SOSP*, 2001.

7. F. Dabek, J. Li, E. Sit, J. Robertson, F. Kaashoek, and R. Morris. Designing a DHT for low latency and high throughput. In *Proc. NSDI*, 2004.
8. T. Gil, F. Kaashoek, J. Li, R. Morris, and J. Stribling. p2psim: A simulator for peer-to-peer protocols. *http://www.pdos.lcs.mit.edu/p2psim/*.
9. D. Karger, E. Lehman, F. Leighton, M. Levine, D. Lewin, and R. Panigrahy. Consistent hashing and random trees: Distributed caching protocols for relieving hot spots on the world wide web. In *Proc. STC*, 1997.
10. J. Kubiatowicz, D. Bindel, Y. Chen, S. Czerwinski, P. Eaton, D. Geels, R. Gummadi, S. Rhea, H. Weatherspoon, W. Weimer, C. Wells, and B. Zhao. Oceanstore: An architecture for globalscale persistent storage. In *Proc. ASPLOS*, 2000.
11. L.Breslau, P. Cao, L. Fan, G. Phillips, and S. Schenker. Web-caching and zipf-like distributions: Evidence and implications. In *Proc. IEEE INFOCOM*, 1999.
12. M. Merzbacher and D. Patterson. Measuring end-user availability on the web: Practical experience. In *Proc. IPDS*, 2002.
13. S. Ratnasamy, P. Francis, M. Handley, R. Karp, and S. Shenker. A scalable content-addressable network. In *Proc. ACM SIGCOMM*, 2001.
14. S. Reed and G. Solomon. Polynomial codes over certain finite fields. In *J. SIAM*, 1960.
15. Rodrigo Rodrigues and Barbara Liskov. High availability in DHTs: Erasure coding vs. replication. In *Proc. IPTPS*, 2005.
16. A. Rowstron and P. Druschel. Pastry: Scalable, distributed object location and routing for large-scale peer-to-peer systems. In *Proc. Middleware*, 2001.
17. A. Rowstron and P. Druschel. Storage management and caching in PAST, a large-scale, persistent peer-to-peer storage utility. In *Proc. SOSP*, 2001.
18. I. Stoica, R. Morris, D. Karger, M. F. Kaashoek, and H. Balakrishnan. Chord: A scalable peer-to-peer lookup service for internet applications. In *Proc. ACM SIGCOMM*, 2001.
19. H. Weatherspoon and J. Kubiatowicz. Erasure coding vs. replication: A quantitative comparison. In *Proc. IPTPS*, 2002.

VIP: A P2P Communication Platform for NAT Traversal*

Xugang Wang and Qianni Deng

Grid Computing Center, Department of Computer Science,
Shanghai Jiao Tong University, China 200030
shakespeare119@sjtu.edu.cn,
deng-qn@cs.sjtu.edu.cn

Abstract. Nowadays, the Internet architecture is complicated and IP addresses are limited in IPV4 context. Many users located behind different kinds of NATs or Firewalls can hardly get a public unique IP. So the hosts behind the NAT can not be accessed by the hosts behind the other NATs. Some P2P systems can partially solve such kind of problems, but unfortunately, these systems just focus the specific self-contained applications such as Skype and BitTorrent whose P2P architectures and NAT traversal mechanisms can not be re-used by other applications directly. In this paper we present a solution by setting up a Virtual Intranet Platform (VIP) which use the public DHT service -OpenDHT as the distributed address/port information rendezvous. Without changing the configuration of the NAT, all the network and distributed application service behind the NAT can make use of the VIP to communicate with the corresponding peer services outside the NAT. The performance of the bandwidth, data lost and delay problems are much better than the existing traditional C-S framework platforms, more general than specific P2P applications. The P2P Communication Platform for NAT Traversal-VIP, is robust and scalable because there are no single failure points in the platform, the structure is in distributed, and majority of the traffic data between two hosts behind the NAT can be transfer directly without relaying.

1 Introduction

Nowadays, lots of" middleboxes" are used, such as network address translators(NAT)[1], driven primarily by the ongoing depletion of the IPv4 address space, to connect the different parts of Internet together. However, these" middleboxes" have created unique problems for peer-to-peer applications and protocols, such as teleconferencing and multiplayer on-line gaming application [2]. These problems are mostly to persist even into the IPv6 Network, where NAT is often used as an IPv4 compatibility mechanism [NAT-PT], and firewalls will still become commonplace even after NAT is no longer required.

---

* This paper is supported by National Natural Science Foundation of China(60403034) and Shanghai Technology and Science Committee Municipality (03dz15026, 03dz15027).

Some excellent P2P systems such as Skype [3] have solved NAT Traversal problem. But most solutions are just focus on the specific applications and can't be easily re-used by other application. For example, the NAT Traversal solution of Skype can't be used by other P2P applications. The ideal goal is to find out a general solution of NAT Traversal, which can easily be co-used by many P2P applications. That is the reason that we design and implement the Virtual Intranet Platform. Virtual Intranet Platform (VIP) can help the data traffic of upper level applications access through the NAT and successfully arrives at the destination hosts. Users behind the NAT can use this VIP platform to set up any p2p application services such as VOIP, Chat, Internet game and allow the outside users can find out these services and then connect to these NAT inside P2P communicate services. The host which has installed the VIP but had a public IP address takes the role to relay traffic data for the communication between the hosts behind the NAT if necessary. To make the whole platform scalable and robust we integrate a public DHT service-OpenDHT [4] and NAT Traversal solution similar with in ICE [5]. OpenDHT serves as a distributed rendezvous can store and publish the address and port information of all VIP hosts to helps users finding and connecting to their buddy users. ICE is a general solution for NAT Traversal, which both uses STUN [6] and TURN [7] methods synthetically to find out the best way of NAT traversal.

2 Related Works

The existing NAT Traversal solutions have different kinds of disadvantages.

- STUN is Simple Traversal of User Datagram Protocol (UDP) Through Network Address Translators (NATs). IETF, firstly, gave a standard NAT Traversal protocol and defined the three kinds of NAT which are cone NAT, address-restricted NAT and port-restricted NAT. STUN is in Client-server architecture. The STUN clients, by using STUN protocol and connecting to STUN server, map the private IP address into the public IP address and ports of the NATs behind. Then the source IP address of the data package sent by the STUN client will be changed into the NAT address and corresponding NAT port to get through NAT. After the connection is established, the media data is directly transmitted from NAT to NAT. It doesn't need to use public server node to relay the data. But STUN can't solve all kinds of NAT Traversal problems. When the type of the NAT is symmetric, we can't use STUN protocol to access through NAT. That is fatal disadvantage of STUN.
- Traversal Using Relay NAT (TURN), which is similar to STUN, uses TURN servers to relay all the traffic data to access through NAT. Although this method can solve all kinds of NAT traversal problems, it has performance problems. With the increasing of the users, more and more computers will be behind the NAT and more and more traffic data has to be relayed by the central TURN servers. The data delay and packet lost problems can't be radically solved by TURN.
- Application Layer Gateway (ALG) [8] and Middle box Communications (MIDCOM) [9] and other solutions for NAT Traversal are all the classic

NAT traversal solution. But these methods work by changing the NAT configuration more or less to get through NAT. But generally speaking, ordinary users behind the NAT have no right to change NAT configuration. So these NAT Traversal solutions are not suitable for the general p2p communication applications.
– Interactive Connecting Establishment (ICE) is a methodology for Network Address Translator (NAT) Traversal for Multimedia Session Establishment protocols. ICE synthesizes the STUN and TURN to get through all kinds of NAT. ICE first tries STUN to get through NAT (because STUN method doesn't need middle nodes to relay media data). When a host is behind symmetric NAT, another another host is behind the other NAT, traffic data transmitted between two hosts has to be relayed by middle nodes which only use TURN solution to get through. All the "ICE connecting check processes" [5] are set up from the NAT inside to avoid the anonymous connecting request to be blocked and dropped by NAT.

OpenDHT is a publicly accessible distributed hash table (DHT) service. In contrast to the usual DHT model, clients of Open DHT do not need to run a DHT node in order to use the service. Instead, they can issue put and get operations to any DHT node, which processes the operations on their behalf. No credentials or accounts are required to use the service, and the available storage is fairly shared across all active clients. OpenDHT are used to store the user's ID and IP address lists of the user's host which is shown in Table 1. Then the other buddy users can get this information which includes user ID, IP address list and type of NAT which it is behind from OpenDHT and finally judge the way to connect to that user. The detail process and contents is illustrated in section 4.

3 Components of VIP

To build a robust and scalable platform to make the different peer to peer communications get through the different types of NAT, the least VIP should has three components.

– NAT traversal: Because the P2P application services behind the NAT can not be seen or accessed by outside Internet users. VIP should adopt some ways and means to allow the outside hosts are able to get through NAT and access to the inside service. VIP uses the similar way with in ICE.
– Service Register and Discovery: NAT assigns the port numbers for inside applications services randomly , but these ports must be made known to the outside users to get through NAT and send packet to the inside services. So before the outside hosts set up the communication with the inside host it must know the ports number and kind of application services it want to connect. For example, NAT assigns port number 9999 for inside teleconference application service for outside users connecting in. But outside users don't know port 9999 is opening for teleconference application and even don't know

his friend has already set up this service. So VIP makes use of OpenDHT to store the user's ID and IP address lists of the user's host.
- Traffic Data Relay: Not all kinds of NAT support point to point media data transmitting. In some situations, media data has to be relayed by other nodes to get through NAT if the NAT is a symmetric NAT . The host which has installed the VIP but had a public IP address takes the role to relay traffic data for the communication between the hosts behind the NAT if necessary. How to find an available public node as a proxy to relay these media data and how to ensure the high quality and stable connection at the risk of the proxy would be crashed.

4 Design and Realization of VIP

4.1 Overview of VIP Architecture

As the Figure 1 shown, OpenDHT serves as a distributed rendezvous which can store and publish the address and port information of all VIP hosts. The hosts behind the NATs we call them VIP hosts. The hosts which have installed the VIP but had public IP addresses we call them VIP hosts/proxies, and they take the role to relay traffic data for the communication between the hosts behind the NAT if necessary. When any user is online and sets up any p2p communication service, the VIP daemon running in the host will judge the type of the NAT it behind and get the relative NAT address and port. Then VIP will put this information onto the openDHT nodes which is closest to it. When the other buddy users get online and want to connect with this user, the VIP daemon running on their hosts will get this information from OpenDHT. Depending on the type of the NAT it behind, VIP will choose the suitable way to get connected. The media data may be directly transferred from NAT to NAT or may have to be relayed by the proxy nodes on the Internet. The detail NAT Traversal algorithm will introduced in section 4.2. P2P communication service register and discovery process will be showed in section 4.3. Data Relay Traffic cases will be specified in section 4.4.

VIP has three components which are NAT Traversal (NATT), Service Register and Discovery (SRD) and Data Traffic Relay (DTR). NATT helps services behind the NAT punch hole on the NAT to let the data get through NAT easily. This function is not visible for upper layer application. SRD will register the NAT address, corresponding port and upper layer application type of the NAT-inside services onto the OpenDHT node. Other buddy users who want to connect to that user, are able to get this information down from OpenDHT. Except functions of NATT and SRD, VIP has another important function which is called Data Traffic Relay (DTR). When we deploy VIP platform onto the nodes which have public IP address, the modular DTR of VIP have responsibility to relay media data for other behind NAT users connecting. These relaying nodes are called proxy.

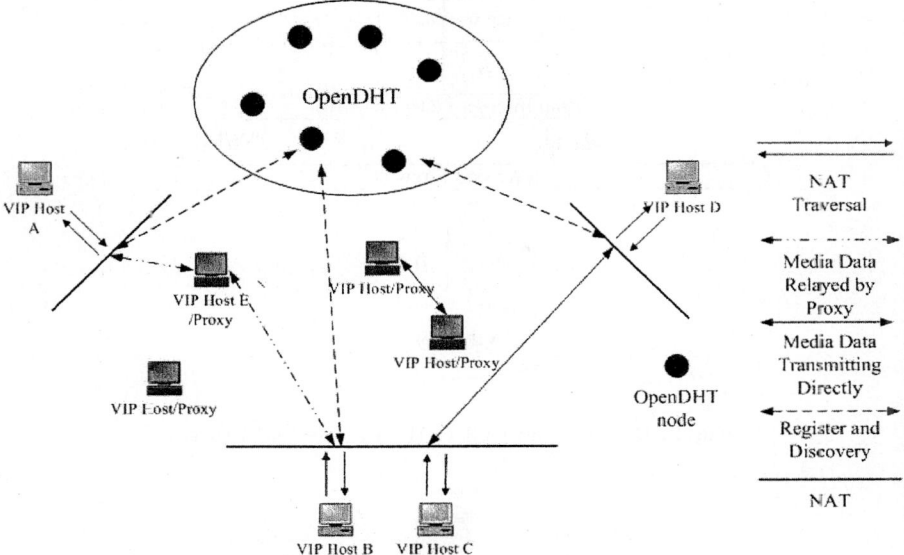

Fig. 1. VIP Platform Network

4.2 NAT Traversal

We use the algorithm similar with in ICE to get through NAT and punch hole on NAT for application services behind the NAT. So other users on the Internet could use the punched hole and NAT IP address to connecting to the P2P application. VIP will register two ports on NAT for the upper layer P2P application and stores IP and port mapping between local and NAT. VIP behind NAT can not know which port is assigned for this application, because NAT assigns port randomly. So VIP has to find the way to get the assigned port information. The Internet VIP nodes with public IP address which is called proxy will help behind VIP get this assigned port information. Proxy plays an important role in VIP network which helps behind NAT VIP judge the NAT type. If necessary, proxy also relays media data for other behind users connecting. The detail NAT Traversal procedure is showed in Figure 2.

In Figure 2 step 1, a local user sets up application service in local computer with private IP 192.168.42.210 which stays behind a NAT whose public IP address is 202.120.7.98. In step2, the VIP finds that there is a application with local IP address and port 3333 running up. In Step 3, VIP use port 3333 to send packets to outside VIP proxy, when the packet with source address-192.168.42.210:3333 through NAT, the packet source address will be changed to 202.120.7.98:45678 (supposing NAT assigns port 45678 for this connecting session.) in step 4. When the packets arrive at proxy whose IP address is 202.108.9.12 and port 8899 in step 4. The proxy will send back an ACK packet to VIP with NAT assigned port information-45678 in step 5. During step 6 to

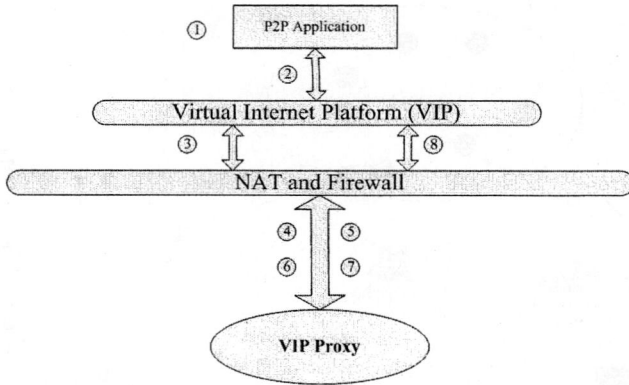

Fig. 2. Register and Collect IP Address List Process

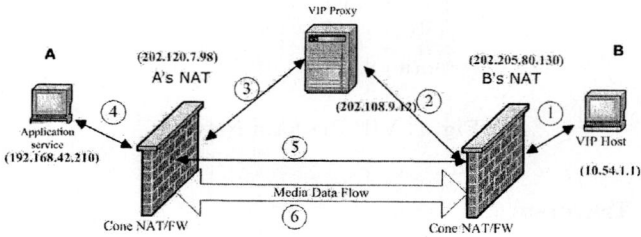

Fig. 3. Connection Establishment and Media Transmitting Process of Two Hosts(A and B) behind NAT VIP users A and B

7, VIP will get NAT assigned port information for proxy-DTR (Modular DTR is to relay media data for other behind users connecting. Supposing the port is 56789). At last VIP stores these two couples IP & Port mapping information into the local cache table for latter other users connecting. After the above process, the application has two registered ports on NAT 45678 and 56789 (If this NAT kind is cone-NAT, these two assigned ports have the same value. when this NAT is kind of Symmetric NAT, these two assigned ports will have the different value.). Till now, the inside p2p application has a unique IP and port on NAT 202.120.7.98:45678, all the media data from outside internet arriving at NAT 202.120.7.98:45678 will get through NAT and arrive at the 192.168.42.210:3333. Because of different kinds of NAT and Firewalls restriction, all the anonymous connecting requests will be blocked and drop at the NAT. So all the beginning connecting session should be set up from inside VIP firstly. Figure 3 is the connecting process between two VIP users. When the buddy host B in NAT 202.205.80.130 with local IP 10.54 1.1 wants to connect to this application service AAA, B firstly sends connecting request to A's NAT- 202.120.7.98:45678, this request will be dropped by NAT. So host B has to use A's proxy to relay this connecting request to application service AAA during step 1 to step 4. When

VIP receives the connecting request from host B, VIP will send Invite message to host B. A and B will transfer media data flow point to point. But in case of symmetric NAT, VIP can't build the directly connecting for A and B, All the media data from or out of A will be relayed by A's proxy.

4.3 Service Register and Discovery

Another problem appears when the NAT Traversal problem is solved. How to find whether my friends are online? What kinds of application are set up by my friends behind NAT and how to find the NAT address and port information of the application service? All the above problems could be resolved by VIP-SRD. In P2P environment, there is no center control application services to record which user is on line and which kind of application service is running. We use VIP to put such kind of information onto the OpenDHT nodes. Other buddy users could get the information from OpenDHT nodes and get the on line buddy lists, application types and location information. The information includes:

- User Unique ID: User should use a unique ID to let other buddies find him correctly. We use user email address as a unique ID.
- P2P application ID: There are many Internet applications. We should name every application a unique ID to distinguish.
- NAT Type: when the value is 0, that means the resided host has a public IP address and port. Value is 1 means the host is behind a Cone-NAT and value 2 means the host is behind a Symmetric-NAT. If the host is behind Symmetric-NAT, a proxy is to be used to relay the media data flow which will be introduced in section 4.4.
- NAT Address list: It stores the registered NAT IP address and port of the p2p application behind NAT.

For example:
User: Jacky whose email address is shak@sjtu.edu.cn, sets up a Counter-Strike Internet Game service and FTP service with local IP address on Computer A in Figure above. The Counter-Strike Internet Game has a unique ID AAA. The FTP service has a unique ID BBB. The network topology is shown in Figure 3 above. When the services are set up correctly, VIP will starts processes shown in Figure 2 processes and generate the following information as Table 1 shows. The following information will be put onto OpenDHT nodes. When Jacky's friend Frank wants to know whether Jacky is online and what kinds of services has already been set up by Jacky. He can search the Jacky information from OpenDHT bye Jacky's unique ID-shak@sjtu.edu.cn. When Frank wants to join in Jacky's Counter-Strike Game, he could send connecting request to Jacky. The connecting establishment process is showed in Figure 3.

4.4 Traffic Data Relay

Not all the media data can be transmitted directly. In some cases, when a host is behind a symmetric NAT, another host is behind a NAT, the media data has to be relayed.

Table 1. Information putted onto the Open DHT nodes

User Unique ID	Application Type ID	NAT Type	NAT Address list		On Line time
shak@sjtu.edu.cn	AAA	1	NAT IP/port	202.120.7.98:45678	13:56/2005/5/24
			Proxy IP/port	202.108.9.12	
	BBB	1	NAT IP/port	202.120.7.98:8888	13:59/2005/5/24
			Proxy IP/port	202.108.9.12	

Different kinds of topology affect the media data packets routing paths. Totally there are four kinds of topology graphs in VIP network.

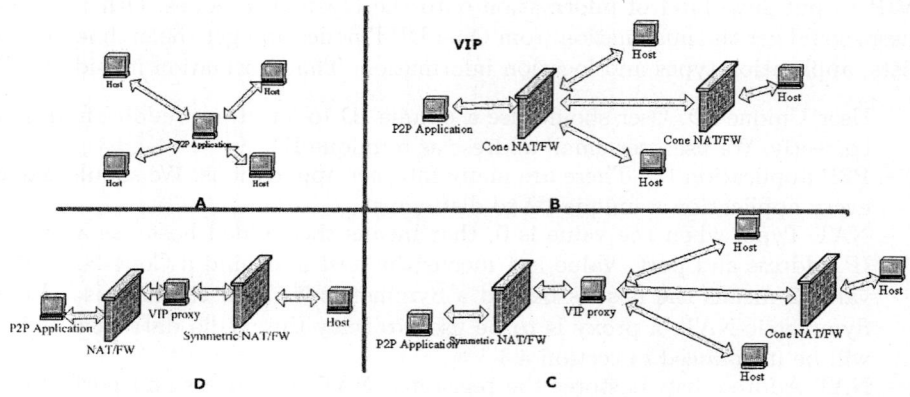

Fig. 4. Four Kinds of Topology and Media Flow Path

- The residing host of the application service has a public IP address. Other hosts can directly connect to the application service without using VIP. It shows in Figure 4 part A.
- The residing host of the application service is behind a Cone-NAT. Application service is able to use VIP platform to let outside hosts connecting to it directly. No matter hosts have a public IP or is behind a Cone-NAT. The media data packet flow will directly send to the host from the application service. It is shown in Figure 4 part B.
- The residing host of the application service is behind a Symmetric NAT. All the media data will be relayed by a VIP proxy. It shows in Figure 4 part C.
- The residing host of the application service is behind a NAT and the residing host of his buddy is behind a Symmetric-NAT. In this kind of situation, data flow of the buddy host will be relayed by VIP proxy. It is shown in Figure 4 part D.

In general situation, media data transfers from host to host directly, such as part A and B. But when two hosts are both behind NAT and one of them is behind symmetric NAT, Media data flow will be relayed by a VIP proxy. Any VIP host who has public IP address will be responsible for relaying media data flow. So no matter the point to point connecting or data relayed connecting, the performance of communication will be ensured.

4.5 VIP Working Process

VIP is composed by NAT Traversal, Service Register and Discovery, Data Relay. The Figure 5 shows the whole processes. After step 1 and 2, application service and hosts check the NAT type, collecting and registering IP addresses. In step 3 and 4. All the buddy hosts using Open DHT API- put()and get() [10] to put set up the application service and their IP address information onto the Open DHT nodes. When other hosts find his buddy's application service was set up, it will set up ICE checking connecting process and find the path to transmit media data flow. If there is no Symmetric-NAT exists, the media data packets are been transmitted point to point in step 9, if one side is behind Symmetric-NAT, the media data packets will be relayed by random VIP nodes around the Internet in step 6 and 7.

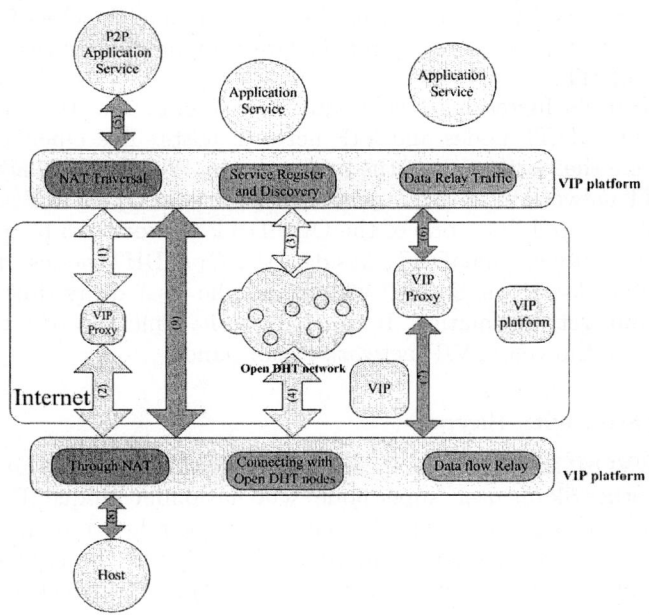

Fig. 5. VIP Working Process

5 Limitation and Optimistic Consideration of VIP

Within the VIP network, there is no specific servers arranged and if necessary, the media data is relayed by the nodes with public IP address for other behind NAT users. So the less nodes have public IP address, behind NAT users connecting has the worse performance.

To ensure the stability and scalability of VIP network, we make some optimistic consideration.

1. The hosts who are behind NAT keep a heart beat process with their proxies. When a proxy is offline without any notification, the heart beat process will notify the host to get another available proxy from OpenDHT. When a host is offline without any notification, the proxy can't get any heart beat from the host for a while, it will update itself to OpenDHT. Then when other new online hosts want to need a proxy, this proxy can be used again.
2. No matter with/without used, every proxy information will be stored into OpenDHT. Much more overdue useless proxy information is also stored in OpenDHT. So a new online host who needs proxy has to need more and more time to find an available proxy. To solve this problem, we set a time stamp to proxy information. When the information is time up, it will be deleted from OpenDHT and the updated information is put into OpenDHT.
3. Because hosts may change their proxies during online time . The host connecting information is always overdue. We also set a time stamp on the host information. Hosts will update their information onto the OpenDHT time to time. So other buddy users can get the latest application service information from OpenDHT.
4. With the hosts increasing, the frequent intercommunication will happens between OpenDHT nodes and VIP network hosts. The OpenDHT latency will become the bottleneck of the performance. We use the characteristic of OpenDHT network to solve this problem. Because in OpenDHT network, any information stored in a node of the OpenDHT network can be get out from any other nodes in OpenDHT, besides, the OpenDHT nodes are deployed into different locations. So VIP will choose the least delay time OpenDHT node to put/get information. It can reduce the time lost of modular SRD and enhance the whole VIP network performance.

5.1 Compared with Skype

Skype is P2P VOIP software. The media data from Skype users behind NAT will is relayed by other Skype user (super node) who has public unique IP address. No matter the type of NAT, all the media data has to be relayed by its super node. But in VIP, only just media data from users behind Symmetric-NAT will have to be relayed by other VIP users which have public unique IP address. Furthermore, Symmetric-NAT is not be widely used by Internet users. So the used bandwidth is less than Skype, at least equal to Skype. Another important advantage is that, VIP is a P2P middleware. All the other application can use this platform to communicate with each other rightly without changing or redeveloping. For example, users behind NAT use VIP to set up a FTP service which can be accessed by out side Internet users without changing the NAT configuration. But Skype and its Skype network only is able to be used to its VOIP applications which can not be used by FTP functions.

6 Conclusion

Using VIP platform, behind NAT users can set up P2P communication software easily. All the users can connect to each other and enjoy the communication application such as teleconferencing and multiplayer on-line gaming application without caring the limitation of NAT. VIP helps p2p communication software to get through NAT and register the p2p service function types and corresponding connecting information onto the OpenDHT network. Other peer p2p software users can get this connecting information from OpenDHT. With the modular NATT of VIP's help, multiusers can set up P2P connecting easily. In some cases, hosts with public IP address who is called proxy take the role of data relay for other behind NAT users connecting. The more hosts with public IP address exists on the Internet, the more proxies will be available for other behind NAT user connecting. VIP reduces the data relay bandwidth using. Besides some above optimistic consideration, VIP has better stability and scalability. VIP is much better than C-S framework platform on bandwidth, data delay/lost problems and more general and better performance than Skype. The source code of VIP refers to http://grid.sjtu.edu.cn/resource2.jsp.

References

1. J Rosenberg. Examples of network address translation (nat) and firewall traversal for the session initiation protocol (sip). *draft-rosenberg-sipping-nat-scenarios-01*.
2. Bryan Ford, Pyda Srisuresh, and Dan Kegel. Peer-to-peer communication across network address translators. In *USENIX Annual Technical Conference,*, Anaheim, CA, April 2005.
3. Salman A. Baset and Henning Schulzrinne. An analysis of the skype peer-to-peer internet telephony protocol. Technical report, Department of Computer Science Columbia University, 2004.
4. Brad Karp John Kubiatowicz Sylvia Ratnasamy Scott Shenker Icn Stoica Sean Rhea, Brighten Godfrey and Harlan Yu. Opendht: A public dht service and its uses. In *Proceedings of ACM SIGCOMM 2005*, August 2005.
5. J. Rosenberg. Interactive connectivity establishment (ice): A methodology for nettwork address translator (nat) traversal for the session initiation protocol (sip). draft-rosenberg-sipping-ice-01.
6. Weinberger J. Huitema C. Rosenberg, J. and R. Mahy. Stun - simple traversal of user datagram protocol (udp) through network address translators (nats). *RFC 3489*, March 2003.
7. J. Rosenberg. Traversal using relay nat (turn). draft-rosenberg-midcom-turn-02, October 2003.
8. D. Raz, J. Schoenwaelder, and B. Sugla. An snmp application level gateway for payload address translation. *RFC2962*, October 2000.
9. P. Sijben S. Brim R. P. Swale, P. A. Mart and M. Shore. Middlebox communications (midcom) protocol requirements. Frc 3304, August 2002.
10. http://opendht.org/users guide.html. *Using Open DHT*. PLANETLAB.

Hyper-Erlang Based Model for Network Traffic Approximation*

Junfeng Wang[1], Hongxia Zhou[2], Fanjiang Xu[1], and Lei Li[1]

[1] National Key Laboratory of Integrated Information System Technology,
Institute of Software, Chinese Academy of Sciences, Beijing 100080, P.R. China
[2] Chongqing Communication Institute, Chongqing 400035, P.R. China
`mailwangjf@yahoo.com.cn`

Abstract. The long-tailed distribution characterizes many properties of Internet traffic. The property is often modeled by Lognormal distribution, Weibull or Pareto distribution theoretically. However, it hinders us in traffic analysis and evaluation studies directly from these models due to their complex representations and theoretical properties. This paper proposes a Hyper-Erlang Model (Mixed Erlang distribution) for such long-tailed network traffic approximation. It fits network traffic with long-tailed characteristic into a mixed Erlang distribution *directly* to facilitate our further analysis. Compared with the well-known hyperexponential based method, the mixed Erlang model is more accurate in fitting the tail behavior and also computationally efficient.

1 Introduction

The self-similarity and long-range dependence nature of network traffic have been significant discoveries in the Internet during the past decade [1–6]. Such traffic pattern challenges the theoretical analysis and leads to difficulties in network equipment designing and system planning[7]. Traditionally, these characteristics are modeled by long-tailed (or heavy-tailed/fat-tailed) distributions[7, 8, 9, 10]. These stochastic models are mainly devoted to the expression of the tail behavior and still difficult for analytical or numerical studies due to their complex representations and theoretical properties. For example, the Pareto distribution (an instance of power-tailed distributions) does not have analytic Laplace transform, and Weibull and Lognormal do not have closed-form Laplace transforms. This makes Laplace transform based queueing analysis difficult[11].

An alternative way to overcome above disadvantages is to model the long-tailed network traffic by Markovian Arrival Process (MAP) or the Batch Markovian Arrival Process (BMAP). Hyperexponential distribution, a special case of Phase-type (PH) distributions, is widely used for such purpose. The merits of Exponential distributions and the existence of MAP/BMAP analytical framework result in the elaborate studies for fitting long-tailed traffic pattern by hyperexponential distributions [12–15]. The essence of such fitting methodology is to

---

* This project was granted financial support from China Postdoctoral Science Foundation under grant 2005037114.

approximate one distribution or (empirical) probability density function (pdf) by another. Though hyperexponential-based modeling makes performance modelling easier and tractable, Feldmann pointed out that the original pdf with complete monotonicity should be a prior condition for accurate approximation[12].

In the paper, we propose the Hyper-Erlang (HE) distribution based algorithm for long-tailed data set approximation. As a special case of PH distributions, HE distribution not only captures the tail behavior well for the complete monotone pdfs, but also achieves accurate fitting for non-monotone pdfs.

The rest of the paper is organized as follows. Section 2 reviews previous works related to the long-tailed network traffic approximation. Then the long-tailed distributions and the Hyper-Erlang model are introduced in Section 3 as a preliminary for further analysis. In Section 4, an Expectation Maximization (EM) based algorithm is derived for fitting data set directly by Hyper-Erlang distribution. Section 5 compares the fitting performance with the hyperexponential model from several dimensions for several popular long-tailed distributions and real network traffic as well. We conclude the paper in the last section.

2 Related Works

Replacing one distribution accurately by another, especially the *phase-type distribution* denoted by PH has been studied in many works. For the long-tailed network traffic approximation, the hyperexponential distribution based fitting is widely used. Feldmann summarized its advantages as that performance models tend to be easier to analyze when component distributions in the model are hyperexponential[12].

As to the fitting methodologies, [12] also developed a heuristic and recursive fitting algorithm that fits complete monotone pdf into hyperexponential distributions, which is referred to as Feldmann-Whitt (FW) algorithm. The FW algorithm first fits the rightmost part of the tail by a single exponential distribution, and then calculates the residual distribution for the next round of fitting. This procedure continues recursively until the parameters of all phases are determined. In practice, the FW algorithm will encounter several drawbacks when applied to real network traffic approximation.

- The FW algorithm is initially designed to fit the continuous distribution functions like Pareto and Weibull rather than data set. Therefore, it will need an additional step to describe the data set by such distributions, which may unavoidably introduce extra errors to the fitting procedure. For data sets, which can not modeled well by monotone pdfs, the errors introduced by such preprocess will be even larger.
- Another drawback of FW algorithm is that the performance is sensitive to the initial value of the algorithm parameters. How to choose the initial values is still an open problem.

The above disadvantages motivated the works of fitting data sets *directly* into hyperexponential distributions. Khayari proposed an Expectation Maximization

(EM) based algorithm denoted by KSH algorithm for such purpose[13]. The EM algorithm is a general solution of finding the maximum likelihood estimation of the parameters of an underlying distribution from a given data set[16]. As the nature of EM algorithm is to search the *global* optimal solution from parameter space, such algorithm may fail to capture the tail part accurately.

Riska applied the popular EM algorithm in a *divide-and-conquer* fashion, and proposed the D&C-EM algorithm. The algorithm splits the continuous data histogram (CDH) built from the data set into partitions and then employs the EM algorithm for each part. In this manner, the algorithm benefits from the strengths of the EM algorithm and reduces the effects of its known weaknesses at the same time[14]. As mentioned previously, the D&C-EM algorithm is also faced the monotone requirement for a precise fitting.

Therefore, an algorithm which can deal with non-monotone pdfs and maintains the fitting accuracy and efficiency is strongly needed. In the paper, we develop a Hyper-Erlang fitting algorithm (HE) for long-tailed network traffic to meet with the non-monotone pdfs requirement. To facilitate our discussion, we first introduce several popular long-tailed distributions used in network traffic modeling and present the Hyper-Erlang model in the next section.

3 Long-Tailed Distributions and the Hyper-Erlang Model

3.1 Long-Tailed Distributions

Let F be a cumulative distribution function (CDF) and its complementary CDF be $F^c(t) = 1 - F(t)$ denoted by CCDF. Network traffic with long-tail characteristic is generally defined as that the F^c decays more slowly than the nonnegative exponential distribution, i.e.,

$$\lim_{t \to \infty} \exp(\gamma t) F^c(t) \to \infty, \quad \gamma > 0 \tag{1}$$

Three well-known long-tailed distributions are Pareto, Weibull and the Lognormal distributions. For the convenience of following illustration, we list their pdfs, CDFs explicitly here as:

- Pareto distribution (denoted by Pareto(α, β))

$$f(x) = \frac{\alpha \beta^\alpha}{x^{\alpha+1}} \quad \text{and} \quad F(x) = 1 - (\frac{\beta}{x})^\alpha,$$

where $\alpha > 0$, $\beta > 0$ and $x \geq \beta$.
- Weibull distribution (denoted by Weibull(α, β))

$$f(x) = \alpha \beta^{-\alpha} x^{\alpha-1} \exp\{-(\frac{x}{\beta})^\alpha\} \quad \text{and} \quad F(x) = 1 - e^{-(\frac{x}{\beta})^\alpha},$$

where $\alpha > 0$, $\beta > 0$ and $x > 0$, $\Gamma(\cdot)$ is the *gamma function*.
- Lognormal distribution (denoted by LN(μ, σ^2))

$$f(x) = \frac{1}{\sqrt{2\pi}\sigma x} \exp\{-\frac{1}{2}[\frac{\ln(x) - \mu}{\sigma}]^2\} \quad \text{and} \quad F(x) = \frac{1}{2}\{1 + \text{erf}[\frac{\ln(x) - \mu}{\sqrt{2}\sigma}]\},$$

where $\mu > 0$, $\sigma > 0$ and $x > 0$, erf$(\cdot)$ is the *error function*.

3.2 Hyper-Erlang Model

A random variable X is said to be the Hyper-Erlang distribution if X is with probability α_i an Erlang random variable X_i with scale parameter λ_i. In this case, an *I-phase, C-order* Hyper-Erlang distribution can be seen as a probabilistic choice between I C-order Erlang distributions. For such random variable, we denote it by notation $\text{HE}_{I,C}(\alpha_1, \cdots, \alpha_I; \lambda_1, \cdots, \lambda_I)$, or simply $\text{HE}(I, C)$. The pdf is given by Equation (2):

$$f(x) = \sum_{i=1}^{I} \frac{\alpha_i \lambda_i^C}{\Gamma(C)} x^{C-1} e^{-\lambda_i x}, \ x \geq 0, \ \lambda_i > 0, \ \alpha_i \geq 0 \text{ and } \sum_{i=1}^{I} \alpha_i = 1. \quad (2)$$

From Equation (2), the CDF and the nth moment of $\text{HE}(I,C)$ can be derived as:

$$F(x) = 1 - \sum_{i=1}^{I} \alpha_i e^{-\lambda_i x} \sum_{j=0}^{C-1} \frac{(\lambda_i x)^j}{\Gamma(j+1)} \quad \text{and} \quad E(X^n) = \sum_{i=1}^{I} \alpha_i \lambda_i^{-n} \frac{\Gamma(C+n)}{\Gamma(C)}.$$

Define $\mathcal{H}$ be set:

$$\mathcal{H} = \left\{ f(x) \mid f(x) = \sum_{i=1}^{I} \frac{\alpha_i \lambda_i^C}{\Gamma(C)} x^{C-1} e^{-\lambda_i x}, C \geq I > 0, \ \lambda_i \geq 0, \ \sum_{i=1}^{I} \alpha_i = 1 \right\}. \quad (3)$$

Clearly, set $\mathcal{H}$ is basically the set of all Hyper-Erlang distribution models with fixed orders, it contains the exponential distribution, Erlang distribution and the hyperexponential distribution.

Theorem 1. *Let $\mathcal{F}$ denote the set of all pdfs of continuous nonnegative random variables, then any element can be approximated by Hyper-Erlang distributions in $\mathcal{H}$.*

Proof. Let $G(x)$ be the CDF of a continuous nonnegative random variable X. Then it is possible to choose a sequence of CDF $G_m(x)$, each of which corresponds to a Hyper-Erlang distributions, so that $\lim_{m \to \infty} G_m(x) = G(x)$, $x \geq 0$. Then, by constructing $G_m(x)$ as

$$G_m(x) = \lim_{C \to \infty} \sum_{k=1}^{C} \frac{k}{C} \left[G(\frac{k}{m}) - G(\frac{k-1}{m}) \right] G_m^C(x) \quad (4)$$

where $G_m^C(x)$ is the CDF of a C-order Erlang random variable X_m with mean $\frac{C}{m}$ and variance $\frac{C}{m^2}$, we get $E(X) = E(X_i)$. Thus, $G_m(x)$ shown in Equation (4) is also an approximation of $G(x)$ [17](see pp.77–80).

Let $g_m(x)$ denote the pdf of $G_m(x)$ and $g_m^C(x)$ be the pdf of $G_m^C(x)$, then we have

$$g_m(x) = \lim_{C \to \infty} \sum_{k=1}^{C} \frac{k}{C} \left[G(\frac{k}{m}) - G(\frac{k-1}{m}) \right] g_m^C(x) \quad (5)$$

It indicates that the $g_m(x)$ is a Hyper-Erlang distribution. □

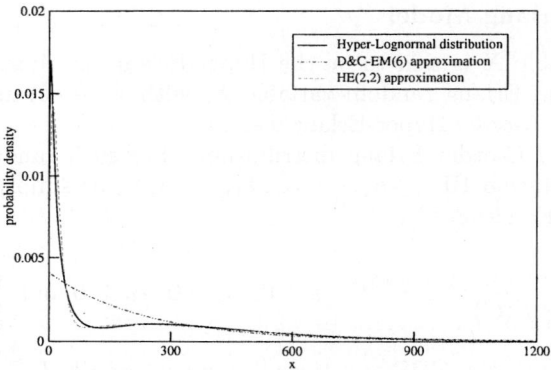

Fig. 1. Fitting a bimodal pdf by the HE model and the hyperexponential distribution

From Equation (5), we can use a finite number of phases to approximate an objective CDF under a controllable accuracy. In this case, it results in the CDF fitting by the *I-phase* and *C-order* Hyper-Erlang distribution ($I \leq C$).

To show the power of fitting non-monotone pdfs, Fig. 1 illustrates the fitted pdfs by HE model and hyperexponential distribution (denoted by D&C-EM, for the result is calculated by D&C-EM algorithm) to a bimodal distribution. The objective pdf is generated by a Hyper-Lognormal distribution, i.e., $f_X(t) = 0.5 f_{X_1}(t) + 0.5 f_{X_2}(t)$ where $X_1 \sim LN(3.0, 1.2^2)$ and $X_2 \sim LN(6.0, 0.6^2)$. From the figure, the HE model may fit the $f(t)$ well only with two phases of *2-order* Erlang distribution (there are five parameters including the order C in sum), while the hyperexponential pdf can not capture the non-monotone pdf soundly.

4 Expectation Maximization (EM) Fitting Algorithm

4.1 Basic EM Algorithm for Hyper-Erlang Model

The EM algorithm implements maximum likelihood estimation to fit data set into a given distribution by operating in an iterative manner. The mixture-density parameter estimation is probably one of the most widely used applications of the EM algorithm[16, 18].

Consider the scenario in which we have a pdf $f(x|\Theta)$ governed by the set of parameters $\Theta = (\underline{P}, \underline{\Lambda})$ where $\underline{P} = (\alpha_1, \alpha_2, \cdots, \alpha_I)$ and $\underline{\Lambda} = (\lambda_1, \lambda_2, \cdots, \lambda_I)$. A data set of size N is drawn from this distribution, i.e., $\mathcal{X} = (x_1, x_2, \cdots, x_N)$. We assume that the samples are independent and identically distributed (i.i.d) with the pdf f. Then the likelihood function for the data set is

$$f(\mathcal{X}|\Theta) = \prod_{n=1}^{N} \sum_{i=1}^{I} \alpha_i \, f(x_n|\lambda_i) = \mathcal{L}(\Theta|\mathcal{X}),$$

where $f(x|\lambda_i)$ is a *C-order* Erlang pdf with parameter λ_i. Thus the goal is to find the Θ that maximizes function $\mathcal{L}$, i.e., we want to search $\hat{\Theta} = (\hat{\underline{P}}, \hat{\underline{\Lambda}})$ where

$$\hat{\Theta} = \text{argmax}_\Theta \log \mathcal{L}(\Theta|\mathcal{X}) \tag{6}$$

By introducing a hidden variable $y, y \in \{1, 2, \cdots, I\}$ and its pdf $\delta(y)$, Equation (6) is transformed into Equation (7) to find $\hat{\Theta}$ that maximizes function $Q(\Theta, \hat{\Theta})$.

$$Q(\Theta, \hat{\Theta}) = \sum_{n=1}^{N} \sum_{i=1}^{I} \delta(i|x_n, \lambda_i) \log\left(\alpha_i f(x_n|\Theta)\delta(i|x_n, \Theta)\right) \tag{7}$$

where $\delta(y|x_n, \lambda_y) = \frac{\alpha_y f(x_n|\lambda_y)}{f(x_n|\Theta)}$.

As EM algorithm works iteratively, assuming in the round k, we obtain an estimation Θ^k of Θ, then Θ^k is used as the initial value for Θ^{k+1} calculation. With auxiliary condition $\sum_{i=1}^{I} \alpha_i^{k+1} = 1$, then α_i^{k+1} is given by

$$\frac{\partial Q}{\partial \alpha_i^{k+1}} = 0 \Rightarrow \alpha_i^{k+1} = \frac{1}{N} \sum_{n=1}^{N} \frac{\alpha_i^k f(x_n|\lambda_i^k)}{f(x_n|\Theta^k)}, \quad i = 1, \cdots, I. \tag{8}$$

Similarly, by substituting the function $f(x_n|\Theta)\delta(i|x_n, \Theta)$ in Equation (7) with Equation (2) and taking derivative of Equation (7) against λ_i^{k+1}, it gives

$$\sum_{n=1}^{N} \left\{ \delta(i|x_n, \lambda_i^k) \frac{\partial}{\partial \lambda_i^{k+1}} \left[\log\left(\alpha_i^k \frac{(\lambda_i^{k+1})^C}{\Gamma(C)} x_n^{C-1} e^{-\lambda_i^{k+1} x_n} \right) \right] \right\} = 0$$

$$\Rightarrow \sum_{n=1}^{N} \delta(i|x_n, \lambda_i^k)\left(\frac{C}{\lambda_i^{k+1}} - x_n\right) = 0$$

$$\Rightarrow \lambda_i^{k+1} = \frac{C \sum_{n=1}^{N} \delta(i|x_n, \lambda_i^k)}{\sum_{n=1}^{N} \delta(i|x_n, \lambda_i^k) x_n}, \quad i = 1, \cdots, I \tag{9}$$

From above discussions, the EM algorithm to estimate the parameter Θ with Hyper-Erlang model is summarized as follows:

procedure EM: **in**$(\mathcal{X}, K, I)$, **out**(Θ)
   initialize Θ and let $\Theta^0 = \Theta$
   for$(k = 1; k \leq K; k++)$
   for$(i = 1; i \leq I; i++)$
    $f(x_n|\Theta^{k-1}) = \sum_{j=1}^{I} \alpha_j^{k-1} f(x_n|\lambda_j^{k-1}); \quad \delta(i|x_n, \lambda_i^{k-1}) = \frac{\alpha_i^{k-1} f(x_n|\lambda_i^{k-1})}{f(x_n|\Theta^{k-1})}$
    $\alpha_i^k = \frac{1}{N} \sum_{n=1}^{N} \delta(i|x_n, \lambda_i^{k-1}); \quad \lambda_i^k = \frac{C \sum_{n=1}^{N} \delta(i|x_n, \lambda_i^{k-1})}{\sum_{n=1}^{N} \delta(i|x_n, \lambda_i^{k-1}) x_n}$
   end // end for i
   end // end for k
   return Θ^K
end // end for procedure

As to the initialization of the EM algorithm input parameters, [13] presented guidelines to choose the iteration K and Θ^0. The computational complexity of the EM algorithm is $O(NKI)$, where $N = |\mathcal{X}|$.

4.2 Divide-and-Conquer EM Algorithm for Data Set Approximation

For the principle of searching the global optimal solution, employing EM algorithm to fit long-tailed data set directly may not capture the tail behavior accurately. A natural way is to split the empirical pdf of data set into partitions, and apply the EM algorithm to each partition. This is the primary idea behind Riska's D&C-EM algorithm(divide-and-conquer EM algorithm). The D&C-EM algorithm works as following steps [14]:

- Build the continuous data histogram (CDH), i.e., empirical pdf from the data set.
- Split the CDH into partitions, such that the coefficient of variation (CoV) of samples in each partition bellows a given threshold CoV_{max}.
- Apply the EM algorithm to fit partition j into I-phase hyperexponential distribution, and obtain α_i^j and λ_i^j, $i = 1, \cdots, I$.
- Generate the final result. For each partition, let $\alpha_i^j = \alpha_i^j w_j$, $i = 1, \cdots, I$, where w_j is the weight of partition j.

Since each partition has reduced variability, D&C-EM algorithm can model the tail behavior considerably accurate than the EM algorithm. In the paper, this divide and conquer working mechanism is employed by replacing the above step 3 with applying the EM algorithm to fit each partition into I-phase and C-order Hyper-Erlang distribution. This will further improve the accuracy and efficiency of our Hyper-Erlang model to fit long-tailed data set.

5 Experimental Validation

Let the notation D&C-EM(I) indicate fitting a data set with I-phase D&C-EM algorithm, FW(I) be fitting a given pdf with I-phase Feldmann-Whitt (FW) algorithm and HE(I,C) illustrate the approximation with I-phase and C-order Hyper-Erlang model. As the D&C-EM algorithm and the EM algorithm developed in [13] all intend to fitting data set with hyperexponential distribution, thus the EM algorithm is excluded for our performance comparisons.

5.1 Data Sets Description for Performance Comparisons

In order to evaluate the performance of the above three fitting algorithms, we apply them to four highly variable data sets as shown in Table 1. The first three data sets are artificially generated by the three well-known long-tailed analytical models. Trace 4 consists of one month's valid HTTP requests to the NASA Kennedy Space Center WWW server from July 1, 1995 to July 31, 1995 [19].

5.2 Statistical Comparisons

In the paper, as we are concentrated on the fitting of long-tailed behavior, therefore algorithm performance are compared by checking the matching degree of the moments and the fitting of CCFDs as that in [12,13,14].

Table 1. Statistical metrics of the four data sets

trace	analytic model	entries	mean	CoV
1	Pareto(1.2, 1.0)	25000	5.19	448.97
2	Weibull(0.4, 9.2)	25000	30.76	301.11
3	LN(7.0, 1.5^2)	25000	3314.38	2.83
4	NASA http log	1732371	22337.0	3.59

Table 2 illustrates the matching from the first to fifth order moment. For the high-order moment, the long tail may contribute much to the whole moment, Thus it can present us an enlarged view of the moment matching performance among different algorithms.

Table 2. Moments matching performance of different fitting algorithms for the four traces

algorithm	1–5 order relative moments $\frac{E_A(X^n)}{E(X^n)}$				
	1	2	3	4	5
(a) Pareto(1.2, 1.0) trace					
FW(9)	1.20	$> 10^5$	$> 10^{11}$	$> 10^{17}$	$> 10^{24}$
D&C-EM(4)	1.01	1.49	2.95	7.01	20.04
HE(4,25)	1.01	1.00	1.00	1.03	1.09
(b) Weibull(0.4, 9.2) trace					
FW(4)	1.12	1.14	1.56	2.75	7.03
D&C-EM(4)	1.00	1.15	1.32	2.00	4.00
HE(2,2)	1.00	1.03	1.08	1.18	1.33
(c) LN(7.0, 1.5^2) trace					
FW(4)	1.04	1.15	2.49	11.65	79.61
D&C-EM(4)	1.00	1.27	1.81	3.56	8.68
HE(4,5)	1.00	1.01	1.02	1.08	1.20
(d) NASA http log trace					
D&C-EM(4)	1.95	0.55	0.09	0.01	0.001
HE(4,6)	1.00	0.92	0.89	1.06	1.85

In Table 2, the moment matching performance is shown by relative value, which is defined as the estimated moment $E_A(X^n)$ by a fitting algorithm A, i.e., the D&C-EM, FW and HE algorithms relative to the calculated moment $E(X^n)$ from trace. For the first 3 traces, FW algorithm fits their corresponding analytical models into hyperexponential distributions, for the trace 4, comparison are made only between HE algorithm and D&C-EM algorithm (the FW algorithm can not generate reasonable results for this web trace). From Table 2, though the FW algorithm could matching the first-order moment reasonable, the matching performance deteriorates considerably for high-order moments, especially for the first trace which means worse tail behavior is fitted (i.e., overestimated) by the algorithm. Performance of the D&C-EM algorithm overcomes the FW's, but it overestimates the high-order moments of 1–3 traces and underestimates for the

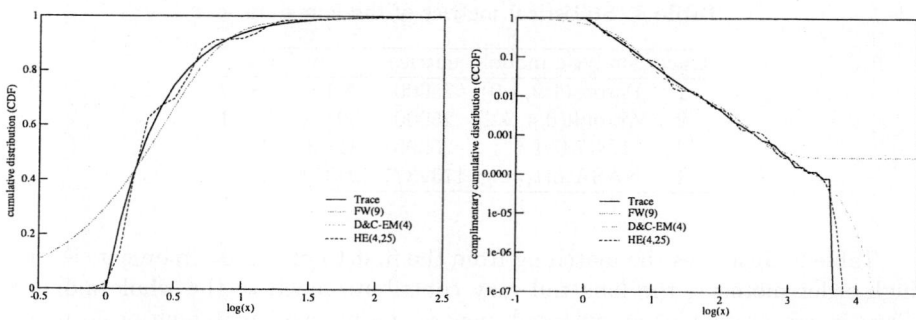

Fig. 2. CDFs and CCDFs for the Pareto trace

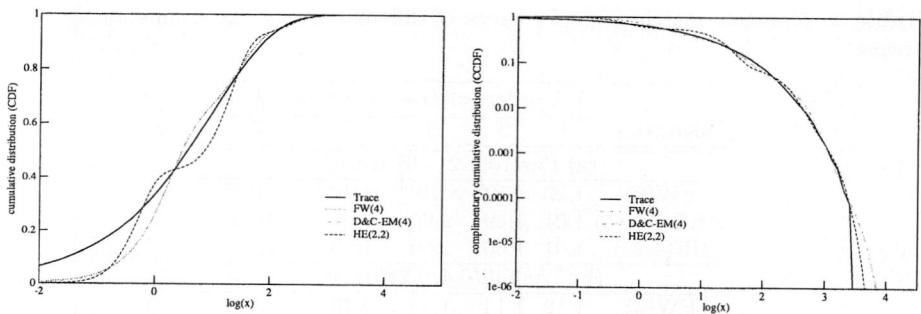

Fig. 3. CDFs and CCDFs for the Weibull trace

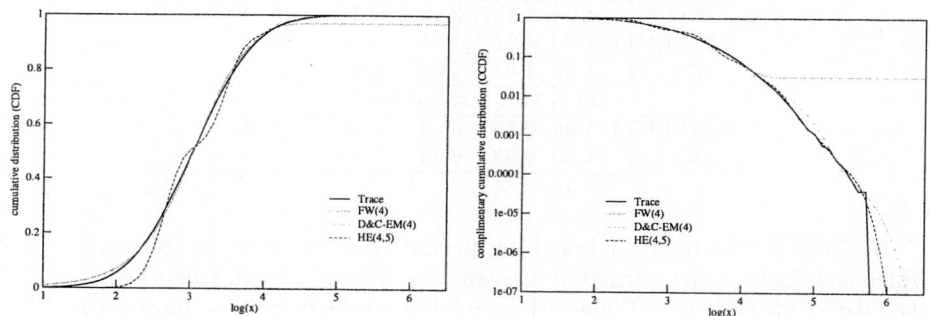

Fig. 4. CDFs and CCDFs for the Lognormal trace

NASA http trace. The HE algorithm is superior in the moment matching to the FW and D&C-EM algorithms. It provides more accurate and stable moment estimation for all traces whether for the highly variable analytical distributions or for the collected real network traffic.

The Cumulative Distribution functions (CDFs), Complimentary Cumulative Distribution functions (CCDFs) of the four traces and their counterparts fitted

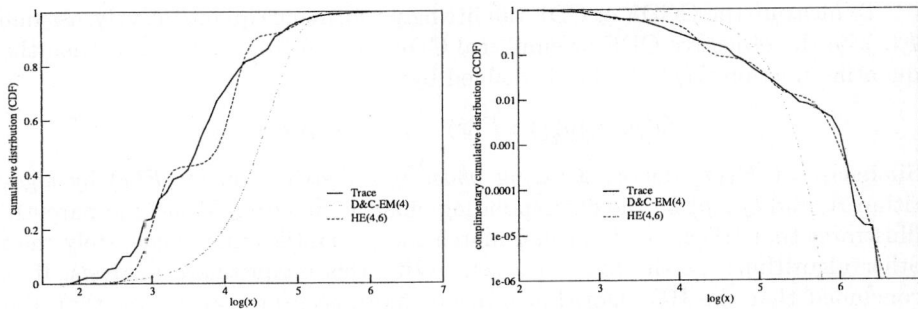

Fig. 5. CDFs and CCDFs for the NASA http trace

Table 3. Quantiles matching performance of different fitting algorithms for the four traces

algorithm	\multicolumn{6}{c}{relative p quantile $Q_A(p)/Q(p)$}					
	0.99	0.999	0.9999	0.99999	0.999999	0.9999999
(a) Pareto(1.2, 1.0) trace						
FW(9)	1.02	1.00	1.16	$>10^6$	–	–
D&C-EM(4)	1.02	1.00	0.94	1.7	–	–
HE(4,25)	1.00	1.02	0.98	1.37	–	–
(b) Weibull(0.4, 9.2) trace						
FW(4)	1.21	0.98	0.96	1.58	–	–
D&C-EM(4)	1.21	0.98	0.96	1.58	–	–
HE(2,2)	1.02	1.06	0.96	1.19	–	–
(c) LN(7.0, 1.5^2) trace						
FW(4)	$>10^7$	$>10^6$	$>10^6$	$>10^6$	–	–
D&C-EM(4)	1.19	1.25	0.89	1.39	–	–
HE(4,5)	1.09	1.03	1.06	1.04	–	–
(d) NASA http log trace						
D&C-EM(4)	0.67	0.27	0.32	0.17	0.19	0.10
HE(4,6)	1.33	0.85	1.27	0.87	1.15	1.28

by different algorithms are plotted in Fig 2–Fig 5. It shows that the FW algorithm has similar performance as the D&C-EM algorithm in fitting the main body of CDF. The two algorithms can not capture the main body of CDF well especially for the first two highly variable traces. The Hyper-Erlang model has more attractive performance on fitting the CDF with higher Erlang order C (see Fig 2). Even with lower Erlang order, the CDF derived by Hyper-Erlang model still tells the evolution trend of the objective CDF (see Fig 3–Fig 5, Fig 5 illustrates this ability more distinctly) and its performance also overcomes that of the FW and D&C-EM algorithm. Extra experiments with higher Erlang order indicate that the main body of CDF can be fitting more accurately as that in Fig 2 which does not shown in the paper.

To measure the CCDF or CDF tail fitting performance quantitatively, assume $F(x)$ be the objective CDF or empirical CDF derived from a data set, then the quantile function $Q(p)$ of $F(x)$ is defined by

$$Q(p) = \inf\{x : F(x) \geq p\},\ 0 < p < 1.$$

Similarly, let $F_A(x)$ denote a fitting *phase-type* distribution for $F(x)$ by algorithm A, and $Q_A(p)$ be the corresponding quantile function. Table 3 apparently illustrates that HE algorithm could match the p quantiles more accurately than other algorithms for the four data sets. With this quantitative analysis, It is concluded that the HE algorithm provides more accurate tail fitting than the FW and D&C-EM algorithms'.

6 Conclusions

In this paper, we propose the Hyper-Erlang model for long-tailed network traffic approximation for the first time. By applying the new model in a *divide-and-conquer* fashion, experiments on three well-known long-tailed analytical distributions and a real network traffic indicate that the new algorithm provides more robust and accurate moments matching performance than previously proposed algorithms provided. With this new model, it overcomes the complete monotone pdf limitation of hyperexponential distributions. Therefore, as a general fitting model, it possesses the ability to fit any continuous (empirical) pdfs, e.g., multimodal pdfs under controllable accuracy and efficiency.

References

1. Will Leland, Murad Taqqu, Walter Willinger, *et al.* On the Self-Similar Nature of Ethernet Traffic (Extended Version). *IEEE/ACM Transactions on Networking.* Vol.2, No.1, pp.1–15, February 1994.
2. Vern Paxson, Sally Floyd. Wide-Area Traffic: The Failure of Poission Modeling. *IEEE/ACM Transactions on Networking.* Vol.3, No.3, pp.226–244, June 1995.
3. Mark E. Crovella, Azer Bestavros. Self-Similarity in World Wide Web Traffic: Evidence and Possible Causes. *IEEE/ACM Transactions on Networking.* Vol.5, No.6, pp.835–846, December 1997.
4. Martin Arlitt, Tai Jin. A workload characterization study of the 1998 World Cup Web site. *IEEE Network (Special Issue on Web Performance),* Vol.14, No.3, pp.30–37, May–June, 2000.
5. Anirban Mahanti, Carey Williamson, Derek Eager. Traffic Analysis of a Web Proxy Caching Hierarchy. *IEEE Network (Special Issue on Web Performance),* Vol.14, No.3, pp.16–23, May–June 2000.
6. Shivkumar Kalyanaraman, Bobby Vandalore, Raj Jain, *et al.* Performance of TCP over ABR with Long-Range Dependent VBR Background Traffic over Terrestrial and Satellite ATM Networks. *In Proceedings of 23rd Annual Conference on Local Computer Networks, (LCN 1998),* Lowell, MA, pp.70–78, October 1998.
7. S. Ata, M. Murata, H. Miyahara. Analysis of Network Traffic and Its Application to Design of High-speed Routers. *IEICE Transactions on Information and Systems,* Vol.E83-D, No.5, pp.988–995, May 2000.

8. Takuya ASAKA, Katsunori ORI, Hiroshi YAMAMOTO. Method of Estimating Flow Duration Distribution Using Active Measurements. *IEICE Transactions on Communications*, Vol.E86-B, No.10, pp.3030–3037, October 2003.
9. A. B. Downey. Evidence for Long-tailed Distributions in the Internet. *In Proceedings of ACM SIGCOMM Internet Measurement Workshop 2001*, San Diego, CA, USA, November 2001.
10. Michael Greiner, Manfred Jobmann, Lester Lipsky. The Importance of Power-tail Distributions for Modeling Queueing Systems. *Operations Research*, Vol.47, No.2, March–April 1999.
11. John F. Shortle, Martin J. Fischer, Donald Gross, et al. Using the Transform Approximation Method to Analyzed Queues with Heavy-Tailed Service. *Journal of Probability and Statistical Science*, Vol.1, No.1, pp.15–27, 2003.
12. Anja Feldamann, Ward Whitt. Fitting Mixtures of Exponentials to Long-tailed Distributions to Analyze Network Performance Models. *Performance Evaluation*, Vol.31, No.3–4, pp.245–279, 1998.
13. Rachid E. Abdouni Khayari, Ramin Sadre, Boudewijn R. Haverkort. Fitting Worldwide Web Request Traces with the EM-algorithm. *Performance Evaluation*, Vol.52, No.2–3, pp.175–191, 2003.
14. Alma Riska, Vesselin Diev, Evgenia Smirni. An EM-based technique for approximating long-tailed data sets with PH distributions. *Performance Evaluation*, Vol.55, No.1–2, pp.147–164, 2004.
15. David Starobinski, Moshe Sidi. Modeling and Analysis of Power-Tail Distributions via Classical Teletraffic Methods. *Queueing Systems*, Vol.36, No.1-3, pp.243–267, 2000.
16. Jeff A. Bilmes. A Gentle Tutorial of the EM Algorithm and its Application to Parameter Estimation for Gaussian Mixutre and Hidden Markov Models. *Technical Report, TR-97-021*, International Computer Science Institue, Berkeley CA, April 1998.
17. Frank Kelly. Reversibility and Stochastic Networks. *New York, Wiley*, http://www.statslab.cam.ac.uk/ frank/rsn.html, June 2004.
18. Alexander Klemm, Christoph Lindemann, Marco Lohmann. *Modeling IP Traffic Using the Batch Markovian Arrival Process*.
19. NASA HTTP traces, http://ita.ee.lbl.gov/html/contrib/NASA-HTTP.html, May 2004.

Prediction-Based Multicast Mobility Management in Mobile Internet

Guojun Wang[1,2], Zhongshan Gao[1], Lifan Zhang[1], and Jiannong Cao[2]

[1] School of Information Science and Engineering, Central South University,
Changsha, Hunan Province, P. R. China, 410083
[2] Department of Computing, Hong Kong Polytechnic University,
Hung Hom, Kowloon, Hong Kong

Abstract. Multicast mobility management poses a great challenge in mobile Internet. This paper proposes a novel multicast mobility management algorithm using our proposed RingNet hierarchy, which takes advantage of our designed four states for mobility management: Not-in-the-group, PassiveReservation, QuasiReservation, and ActiveReservation, and two kinds of ranges which are closely related to a Mobile Host (MH)'s attached device called the Access Proxy (AP): TransmissionRange and ReservationRange. By judging the state of the AP and the distance between the AP and its attaching MH, operations of mobility management can be implemented. The introduction of prediction algorithm greatly decreases the blindness of resource reservation, and avoids the unnecessary waste of bandwidth. Furthermore, the introduction of resource reservation makes the smooth handoff highly probable.

1 Introduction

With the convergence of wired Internet and all kinds of wireless networks such as wireless LANs, cellular networks and satellite networks, mobile Internet becomes more and more popular in recent years. Mobility management is important to support roaming users with mobile terminals to enjoy their services in progress in mobile Internet.

Multicast is an efficient service that provides delivery of data from one source to a group of receivers. It reduces transmission overhead and network bandwidth. By combining the concept of *Multicast Communication* and *Mobility Management*, we propose a concept of "Multicast Mobility Management (MMM)". Simply stated, MMM is a set of schemes, algorithms and protocols, which are used to adapt to the location changes of group members and to ensure the efficiency of multicast communication in mobile and wireless network environment.

In this paper, we propose a novel multicast mobility management algorithm using our proposed RingNet hierarchy, which makes use of the location information got from our prediction algorithm to guide the resource reservation in order to realize smooth handoff.

The remainder of the paper is organized as follows. Section 2 introduces some related works about multicast mobility management in mobile Internet. In section 3, we introduce our proposed RingNet hierarchy. In section 4, we describe the multicast mobility management algorithm using this hierarchy. The final section concludes the paper.

2 Related Works

The two-tier Host-View protocol [8] provides a scalable mechanism for multicast communication in mobile Internet. The basic idea is to associate a Host-View with each group. The Host-View consists of a set of Mobile Support Stations (MSSs), which represents the aggregate location information of the group. Through tracking a set of MSSs other than each individual member MH, it only needs to send a copy of the message to those MSSs in the group's Host-View in order to deliver a multicast message to a group of MHs. In addition, through moving most functions from MHs to MSSs, the MHs are relieved from heavy tasks. However, this protocol does not allow dynamic joins or leaves, and does not specify a method for the creation or deletion of a multicast group. In particular, the global updates necessary with every "significant move" make it inefficient and may cause lengthy breaks in service to the MHs.

To deal with problems, a three-tier Reliable Multicast (RelM) protocol is proposed [9]. The bottom tier consists of the MHs which roam between cells. The middle tier consists of MSSs which provide the MHs with connectivity to the underlying network. The top tier consists of groups of MSSs. Each group of MSSs is controlled by an assigned supervisor machine called the Supervisor Host (SH). Since the SH is part of the wired network, it can handle most of the protocol details for MHs such as maintaining connections for MHs, and collecting acknowledgement messages for reliable communication. Simulation results show that the RelM protocol uses fewer buffers in virtually any system configuration in comparison with the Host-View protocol. However, the advantage of moving most functions from MSSs to SHs will also become its disadvantage. Since the SHs have to do so many tasks, the RelM protocol does not scale well when the number of group members becomes very large.

Another three-tier reliable multicast protocol with MHs, MSSs and Coordinators is proposed in [10]. In this protocol, each MSS maintains a data structure called *local* that identifies the set of MHs in its cell. In this way, the movements of MHs do not trigger any message transmission in the wired network as no notion of handoff is used in the wired network. As a consequence, it is potentially more scalable than the RelM protocol.

Besides the above two/three-tier protocols, another related work is logical ring-based reliable multicast protocol in mobile Internet [11]. A logical ring is maintained among all the Base Stations (BSs) to handle the multicast traffic of the same multicast group. A token passing protocol enforces a consistent view among all the BSs with respect to the messages that are considered to have been delivered to all the MHs. Furthermore, a handoff protocol is designed to handle the interaction of reliable multicast and handoff events of the MHs. Since all the control information has to be transferred along the logical ring, it may lead to large latency and require large buffers when the logical ring becomes large. Each logical ring within our proposed RingNet hierarchy [12] functions in a similar way, but it deals with only a local scope of the whole group. In this way, our proposed protocol can be as simple as this logical ring-based protocol, but our protocol can scale better than this logical ring-based protocol because our protocol uses a hierarchy of logical rings.

3 The RingNet Hierarchy

Researchers proposed many mobile Internet architectures, such as wireless overlay networking architecture [13], all-IP wireless/mobile network architecture [14], and Always Best Connected (ABC) architecture [15]. Based on them, we proposed a RingNet hierarchy for multicast mobility management shown in Fig. 1 (also see [12]).

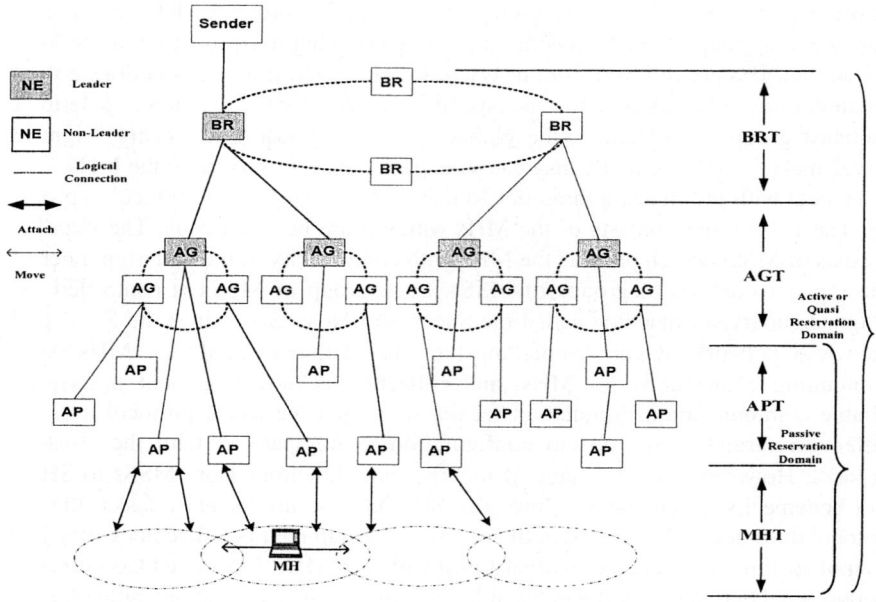

Fig. 1. The RingNet Hierarchy for Multicast Mobility Management

The four tiers of the RingNet hierarchy are Border Router Tier (BRT), Access Gateway Tier (AGT), Access Proxy Tier (APT), and Mobile Host Tier (MHT). The higher two tiers are dynamically organized into logical rings. Each logical ring has a leader node, which is also responsible for interacting with upper tiers. Access Proxies (APs) are the Network Entities (NEs) that communicate directly with the Mobile Hosts (MHs). Access Gateways (AGs) are the NEs that communicate either between different wireless networks or between one wireless network and one wired network. Border Routers (BRs) are the NEs that communicate among administrative domains. Notice that only those NEs that are configured to run the proposed protocol will be involved in the hierarchy.

Multicast communication using the RingNet hierarchy is simple [12]: Multicast Senders (MSs) send multicast messages to any of the BRs at the top logical ring. Then the multicast messages are transmitted along each logical ring, and downward to all the children nodes. Finally the MHs receive multicast messages from their attached APs. Thus the multicast data are delivered to all the MHs efficiently.

4 The Multicast Mobility Management Algorithm

In this section, we first overview the proposed algorithm and give some basic assumptions. We then design the corresponding data structures and operations for the algorithm. Finally we describe the proposed algorithm in detail.

4.1 Overview of the Proposed Algorithm

We use RingNet (RN)-based prediction algorithm to provide necessary information for advance resource reservation, and propose a novel multicast mobility management algorithm based on prediction and RSVP [16]. The algorithm makes use of four states: Not-in-the-group, PassiveReservation, QuasiReservation, and ActiveReservation, and two kinds of range which are closely related to the AP: TransmissionRange and ReservationRange. By judging the state of the AP and the distance between the AP and the MH, operations of mobility management can be implemented. Notice that the well-known MRSVP [17] algorithm uses only two states, i.e., PassiveReservation and ActiveReservation, which is not flexible compared with our proposed algorithm.

The multicast mobility algorithm can be divided into three procedures in Fig. 2. We define six types of messages, through which the system communicates with other procedures.

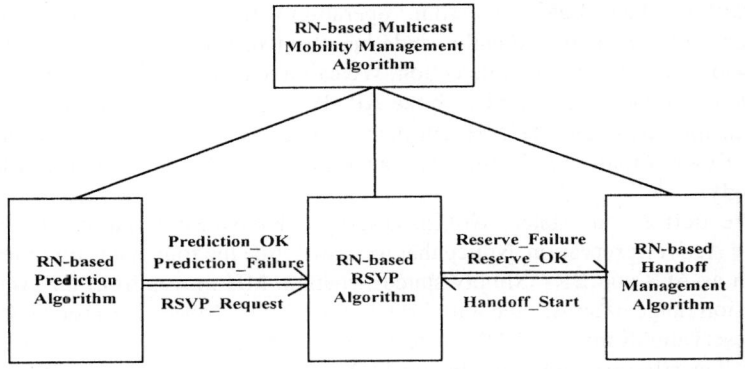

Fig. 2. The Framework of Multicast Mobility Management Algorithm

- RSVP_Request Message: MH sends the message to most likely reached AP for making resource reservation.
- Prediction_OK Message: MH sends the message to most likely reached AP in the case of accurate prediction.
- Prediction_Failure Message: MH sends the message to most likely reached AP in the case of inaccurate prediction.
- Handoff_Start Message: MH sends the message to most likely reached AP to start the handoff processing.

- Reserve_Failure Message: AP sends the message to MH in the case of the failure of resource reservation.
- Reserve_OK Message: AP sends the message to MH in the case of the success of resource reservation.

Firstly the *initialization* procedure runs to initiate the state of MH and other network entities. Then the three procedures run in a parallel and distributed way. The *RN-based prediction* procedure runs to predict the next location after a predefined time period, and the *RN-based RSVP* procedure runs to make advance resource reservation for the forthcoming handoff. Then the *handoff* procedure will be conducted using the reserved resources.

4.2 Basic Assumptions

The following assumptions are made for our proposed algorithm:

(1) For the AP tier, APs may be access points in WLANs, base stations in cellular networks, and satellites in satellite networks.

(2) We suppose that, at any specific time, at most one AP is selected as an MH's current AP, though the MH can simultaneously communicate with one or more APs at the same time.

(3) When an MH first moves into the range of an AP, there should be a "Join the Group" operation with Join_Group messages. When it leaves out of the range of the AP, there should be a "Leave the Group" operation with Leave_Group messages.

(4) For each AP, it periodically sends heartbeat messages to the MHs within its transmission range for mobility detection. We call it a heartbeat protocol. For each AP, we define two ranges associated with the AP: TransmissionRange, which denotes the signal transmission range (the MH within this range can receive signals transmitted by the AP); ReservationRange, within this range the AP will make resource reservation accordingly.

(5) We define four states: Not-in-the-group, PassiveReservation, QuasiReservation, and ActiveReservation. Notice that we also define the four states for other related NEs such as AGs and BRs. Simply stated, when an MH moves from far away to the transmission range of an AP, the initial state of the AP is "Not-in-the-group". If it is not in the ReservationRange, the AP's state becomes "PassiveReservation"; otherwise, it becomes "QuasiReservation", and its parent AG's state and the state of AG's parent BR also become "QuasiReservation". When the MH handoffs to a new AP and begins the handoff, the new AP's state becomes "ActiveReservation" and the states of its parent AG and BR also change to "ActiveReservation". Then it moves out of this AP's ReservationRange; the AP's state becomes "PassiveReservation". Finally it moves out of the AP's TransmissionRange, the states of all NEs associated with the MH become "Not-in-the-group". The four-states transition can be seen in Fig. 3.

As to the states of "ActiveReservation" and "QuasiReservation", they have both similarities and differences. They both require the changes of states of corresponding NEs. For example, when an AP's state is "ActiveReservation" or "QuasiReservation", other NEs also require making such changes. There is actual data transportation when the state of an AP is "ActiveReservation", while no real data transportation when the state of the AP is "QuasiReservation".

When the AP's state is "PassiveReservation", reservation is only made between the AP and the MH. While the AP's state is "ActiveReservation" or "QuasiReservation", reservation is made among the whole hierarchy.

(6) For each MH, it periodically sends back heartbeat messages to those APs from where it received the heartbeat messages with a list of records of its "location (x, y, z)", "velocity", and "direction". We suppose the location, velocity and direction information can be got from a GPS system or some location estimation techniques.

(7) For each AP, when it received the above information, it will use a prediction algorithm to predict its new location with a predefined time period as a parameter. If the new location is within the AP's ReservationRange, then the AP's state will become "QuasiReservation" when its original state is either "Not-in-the-group" or "PassiveReservation".

(8) As to multicast data transportation, we suppose that the multicast sender is fixed, and that there is only one multicast sender.

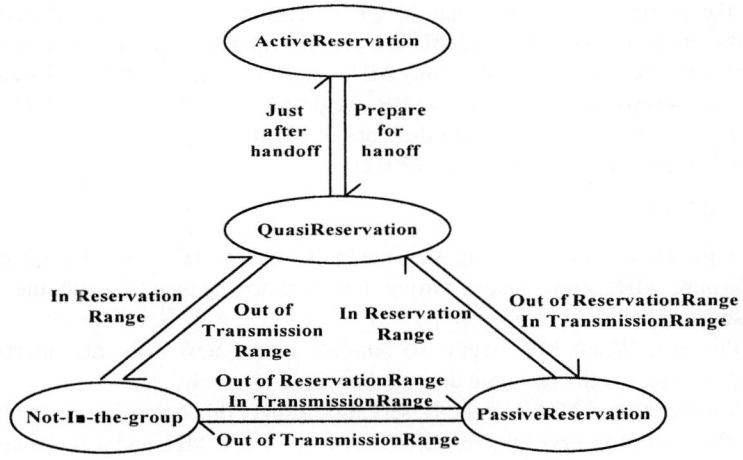

Fig. 3. Four-States Transition

4.3 Data Structures and Operations

Data Structure of MH:

- GID: GroupID. Group identity of some group addressing scheme, e.g. Class D address in IP Multicast.
- AP: NodeID. Node identity of the attached AP.
- GUID, LUID: UniqueID. Globally/locally unique identity of MH from some unique identity scheme, e.g. Mobile IP Home Address/Care-of Address.
- Dist(MH, AP): the distance between MH and AP, the value of which can be computed by MH, and the location information of which can be got from a GPS system or some location estimation techniques.

- SI(MH, AP): the Signal Intensity (SI) that MH receives from an AP.
- Reserve: the success or failure of resource reservation, with TRUE for the former case and FALSE for the latter case.
- Predict: the accuracy and inaccuracy of prediction, with TRUE for the former case and FALSE for the latter case.

Data Structure of NE (AP/AG/BR):

- GID: GroupID. Same as GID used by the MH.
- Current, Leader, Previous, Next, Parent, Children[]: NodeID. Node identities of this node, leader, previous, next, parent, and children nodes, respectively. Notice that Children[] consists of a list of node identities, each of which stands for one child node.
- PreviousOK, NextOK, ParentOK, ChildrenOK[]: Boolean. States of the previous, next, parent, and children nodes, respectively. Notice that ChildrenOK[] consists of a list of sub-items, each of which describes the state of one child node.
- State(MH, AP), State(AP, AG), State(AG, BR): NE has four kinds of states: Not-in-the-group, PassiveReservation, QuasiReservation and ActiveReservation. Since the states of AP, AG, and BR are closely related to the lower level of the hierarchy, for example, possibly many MHs attach to one AP, many APs attach to one AG, and many AGs attach to one BR, we define the state of AP state(MH, AP), the state of AG state(AP, AG), and the state of BR state(AG, BR). The value of the four states can be 1, 2, 3, and 4, respectively.

Basic Operations:

- JoinGroup: MH sends Join_Group message to the sender, and the sender processes it.
- LeaveGroup: MH sends Leave_Group message to the sender, and the sender processes it.
- ActiveReserve: When MH begins to handoff into a new AP, this operation is invoked. It reserves the resource among the whole hierarchy.
- QuasiReserve: When MH is in the ReservationRange, this operation is invoked.
- PassiveReserve: It reserves the resource between AP and MH, and it is not involved in the upper tiers of the hierarchy.

4.4 RN-Based Prediction Algorithm

We assume to use the random waypoint mobility model [18] which is natural and realistic to characterize the movement of MHs in a 2-dimensional space. The movement of MHs consists of a sequence of mobility epochs with random length between neighboring epochs. The speed V and direction θ of an MH keep constant during mobility epochs, and vary randomly from epoch to epoch, here $V \geq 0$ and $\theta \geq 0$. In addition, we assume that the acceleration γ of the same direction of previous speed exists in a very short time, because of the inertia effect.

Each MH detects the change of its speed and moving direction. When a new epoch starts, it records its current 2-dimentional coordinate (x, y), speed V and direction θ, the changing duration time Δ, and current time t'. Then the time interval T between two neighboring epochs can be got by $T_i = t'_{i+1} - t'_i$, the acceleration γ_i can be got by

$(v_{i+1} - v_i)/\Delta$, where $1 \leq i \leq P$. Here P is the number of sampling points. We call this recording process as *sampling*, and the recording place as *sampling point*. The number P of sampling points each MH recorded is determined by itself based on the degree of mobility. As the MH moves faster, P becomes larger.

Interpolation is used in the situation that function $f(x)$ is known at $a \leq x \leq b$, while we compute the value of $f(x)$ when $x<a$ or $x>b$. The extrapolation method is used to predict the location after a predefined time period. Extrapolation is not always very accurate, but it is relatively simple. Since the extrapolation in low-power multinomial is more accurate than that in high-power multinomial [19], we will use Subsection Low-power Interpolation method to get an approximate function.

Theorem 1: The predicted coordinate.
Given a quaternion (P, v_x, v_y, T), v_x and v_y denote the speed of MH in the direction of X-axis and Y-axis, got by $v_x = V\cos(\theta)$ and $v_y = V\sin(\theta)$. Suppose v_x', v_y', T', γ' denote the predicted values, and suppose current coordinate is (x_p, y_p), and current speed is (v_{xp}, v_{yp}), then the predicted coordinate (x', y') at time t can be attained by Formulae 4.1 and 4.2, respectively.

$$x' = f_x(t) = \frac{v_x' + v_{xp}}{2} \frac{v_x' - v_{xp}}{\gamma'} + v_x'\left(t - \frac{v_x' - v_{xp}}{\gamma'}\right) = v_x't - \frac{(v_x' - v_{xp})^2}{2\gamma'} \quad \ldots (4.1)$$

$$y' = f_y(t) = \frac{v_y' + v_{yp}}{2} \frac{v_y' - v_{yp}}{\gamma'} + v_y'\left(t - \frac{v_y' - v_{yp}}{\gamma'}\right) = v_y't - \frac{(v_y' - v_{yp})^2}{2\gamma'} \quad \ldots (4.2)$$

Proof: The function value of $v_{xk} = f_x(t_k)$ at the time $t_k = t_0 + \sum_{i=0}^{k} T_i$ $(k=0,1,2,\ldots,P-1)$ is known by sampling. We use Lagrange Multinomial to do secondary power interpolation at each section consisting of three points: (v_{xr0}, T_{r0}), (v_{xr1}, T_{r1}), (v_{xr2}, T_{r2}), where r is the section number and $0<r<P/3$, and $t_{rk} = t_{r0} + \sum_{i=0}^{k} T_{ri}$ $(k=0,1,2)$. At each section, we get approximate sub-function from Formula 4.3:

$$v_x = f_x'(t) = v_{xr0}\frac{(t-t_{r1})(t-t_{r2})}{(t_{r0}-t_{r1})(t_{r0}-t_{r2})} + v_{xr1}\frac{(t-t_{r0})(t-t_{r2})}{(t_{r1}-t_{r0})(t_{r1}-t_{r2})} + v_{xr2}\frac{(t-t_{r0})(t-t_{r1})}{(t_{r2}-t_{r0})(t_{r2}-t_{r1})} \quad \ldots (4.3)$$

Suppose v_x' is the value got from the latest subsetion's function. Then the value of v_y', T', and γ' can be got through the same method. So the predicted coordinate (x', y') at the time t can be attained by Formulae 4.1 and 4.2. Furthermore, we predict those parameters not only based on the latest subsection's function, but also considering the varying rule of the whole function $v_x = f_x(t)$ if the movement regularity of MH can be seen easily.

Theorem 2: The distance between MH and AP.
Suppose the coordinate of AP is (X_{AP}, Y_{AP}), and the coordinate of MH is (x, y), then the distance between AP and MH can be got by Formula 4.4:

$$Dist(MH, AP) = \sqrt{(X_{AP} - x)^2 + (Y_{AP} - y)^2} \quad \ldots (4.4)$$

Proof: According to the distance between two points in right-angle coordinates, it can be induced easily.

We define an AccuracyRange variable, which is decided by the difference between MH's actual position and predicted position in the usual case, to denote the degree of accuracy. If the prediction result is in the AccuracyRange, then the prediction is accurate; otherwise, the prediction is inaccurate. And we also define a t_threshold variable, which describes that MH predicts the new location after t_threshold time and can be tuned according to continuous system test. The proposed RN-based prediction algorithm is shown in Fig. 4.

Algorithm. RN-based prediction
Given an MH's speed $\vec{r}$ and direction θ at time t_0, and location coordinate (x_0, y_0);
While TRUE **Do** {
   Do
      Sampling;
   While the speed or direction changes;
   If a prediction event is triggered **Then**
      Get the predicted coordinate (x_i', y_i') at t_threshold value of time;
   Start the timer;
   Compute which AP the MH is in its transmission range;
   Send RSVP_Request message to AP;
   On the timer event:
      If the prediction is in the AccuracyRange **Then** {
      Send Prediction_OK message to the AP;
      MH.Predict=TRUE;
   }
      Else {
      Send Prediction_Failure message to the AP;
      MH.Predict=FALSE.
   }
}
Remark: The random length between mobility epochs should be larger than t_threshold, since we predicted the location after t_threshold value of time.

Fig. 4. RN-based Prediction Algorithm

4.5 RN-Based RSVP Algorithm

This algorithm mainly executes in the APs. Every AP constantly listens to the message from MHs, which makes the possible state changes of the AP and all the corresponding NEs. Finally the AP makes resource reservation according to different states. The proposed RN-based RSVP algorithm is shown in Fig. 5.

4.6 RN-Based Multicast Handoff Management Algorithm

We define a SI_threshold variable, which describes the state an MH begins to trigger a handoff when the signal intensity that the MH receives from its attached AP comes to the SI_threshold value. This variable can be tuned according to continuous system test. When the signal intensity that the MH receives is larger than SI_threshold, the MH triggers the handoff, the states of all the corresponding NEs become "ActiveReservation", and it begins to transmit multicast data accordingly. The proposed RN-based multicast handoff management algorithm is shown in Fig. 6.

```
Algorithm. RN-based RSVP
Initiate AP, AG, and BR, and make the states of NEs Not-in-the-group;
While TRUE Do {
    On Receiving RSVP_Request message:
      If MH.Dist(MH, AP)>AP.TransmissionRange Then
          Tear down old resource reservation (if exists);
      Else If MH.Dist(MH, AP)>AP.ReservationRange Then {
                AP.state(MH, AP)=PassiveReservation;
                Do PassiveReserve;
    }
         Else {
                AP.state(MH, AP)=QuasiReservation;
             AG.state(AP, AG)=QuasiReservation;
             BR.state(AG, BR)=QuasiReservation;
             Do QuasiReserve;
    }
    On Receiving Prediction_Failure message:
    Tear down old resource reservation if exists;
    If MH.Dist(MH, AP)>AP.TransmissionRange Then {
         AP.state(MH, AP)=Not-in-the-group;
         AG.state(AP, AG)= Not-in-the-group;
         BR.state(AG, BR)= Not-in-the-group;
    }
    On Receiving Prediction_OK message:
    If MH.Dist(MH, AP)>AP.TransmissionRange Then {
         AP.state(MH, AP)=Not-in-the-group;
         AG.state(AP, AG)= Not-in-the-group;
         BR.state(AG, BR)= Not-in-the-group;
    }
    On Receiving Handoff_Start message:
         AP.state(MH, AP)=ActiveReservation;
      AG.state(AP, AG)=ActiveReservation;
      BR.state(AG, BR)=ActiveReservation;
      Do ActiveReserve;
      If the required resource is not available Then
          Send Reserve_Failure message to MH;
      Else
             Send Reserve_OK message to MH.
}
```

Fig. 5. RN-based RSVP Algorithm

```
Algorithm. RN-based Handoff Management
While TRUE Do {
   On Receiving the signal from AP:
       If MH.Dist(MH,AP) < AP.TransmissionRange &&
          MH.AP.state(MH, AP)==Not-in-the-group Then
       Do JoinGroup;
       If MH.Dist(MH,AP) > AP.TransmissionRange &&
          MH.AP.state(MH, AP)==Not-in-the-group Then
       Do LeaveGroup;
   If MH.SI(MH, AP)>SI_threshold Then {
       If MH.Reserve==TRUE && MH.Predict==TRUE
       || MH.Predict==FALSE && the resource is available at the same time Then {
          Send Handoff_Start message to AP;
             Establish new connection;
          Tear down old connection;
       }
       Else {
             Start a timer and wait a certain period of time until the resource is
                available;
          Send Handoff_Start message to AP;
             Establish new connection;
          Tear down old connection;
       }
   }
   On Receiving Reserve_OK message:
      MH.Reserve=TRUE;
   On Receiving Reserve_Failure message:
      MH.Reserve=FALSE.
}
   Remark: If MH receives the signal from more than one AP at the same time, then the first
one that reaches the SI_threshold value triggers the handoff.
```

Fig. 6. RN-based Multicast Handoff Management Algorithm

5 Conclucsions

In this paper, we proposed a novel multicast mobility management algorithm, which combines advance prediction information and resource reservation. The prediction procedure sends three kinds of messages to RSVP procedure, which makes the latter one more efficient and straightforward, and the handoff procedure makes smooth handoff highly possible because of prediction and RSVP. As our future work, simulation is needed to evaluate the performance of our multicast mobility algorithm.

Acknowledgment

This work is supported in part by the Hunan Provincial Natural Science Foundation of China (No. 05JJ30118, Secure group communications in large-scale mobile ad-hoc networks), and in part by the University Grant Council of Hong Kong under the CERG Grant PolyU 5170/03E.

References

1. C. Perkins, "IP Mobility Support," *IETF RFC 2002*, Oct. 1996.
2. S. Deering and D.R. Cheriton, "Multicast Routing in Datagram Internetworks and Extended LANs," *ACM Transactions on Computer Systems*, Vol. 8, No. 2, pp. 85-110, May 1990.
3. T.G. Harrison, C.L. Williamson, W.L. Mackrell, and R.B. Bunt, "Mobile Multicast (MoM) Protocol: Multicast Support for Mobile Hosts," *ACM International Conference on Mobile Computing and Networking (MobiCom 1997)*, pp. 151-160, Sept. 1997.
4. C.L. Tan and S. Pink, "MobiCast: A Multicast Scheme for Wireless Networks," *ACM/Kluwer Mobile Networks and Applications*, Vol. 5, No. 4, pp. 259-271, Dec. 2000.
5. Y. Wang and W. Chen, "Supporting IP Multicast for Mobile Hosts," *ACM/Kluwer Mobile Networks and Applications*, Vol. 6, pp. 57-66, 2001.
6. Y.-J. Suh, H.-S. Shin, and D.-H. Kwon, "An Efficient Multicast Routing Protocol in Wireless Mobile Networks," *ACM/Kluwer Wireless Networks*, Vol. 7, No. 5, pp. 443-453, Sept. 2001.
7. C.R. Lin and K.-M. Wang, "Scalable Multicast Protocol in IP-based Mobile Networks," *ACM/Kluwer Wireless Networks*, Vol. 8, pp. 27-36, 2002.
8. A. Acharya and B.R. Badrinath, "A Framework for Delivering Multicast Messages in Networks with Mobile Hosts," *ACM/Kluwer Mobile Networks and Applications*, Vol. 1, Issue 2, pp. 199-219, Oct. 1996.
9. K. Brown and S. Singh, "RelM: Reliable Multicast for Mobile Networks," *Computer Communications (Elsevier Science)*, Vol. 21, Issue 16, pp. 1379-1400, Oct. 1998.
10. G. Anastasi, A. Bartoli, and F. Spadoni, "A Reliable Multicast Protocol for Distributed Mobile Systems: Design and Evaluation," *IEEE Transactions on Parallel and Distributed Systems*, Vol. 12, Issue 10, pp. 1009-1022, Oct. 2001.
11. I. Nikolaidis and J.J. Harms, "A Logical Ring Reliable Multicast Protocol for Mobile Nodes," *Proceedings of the Seventh International Conference on Network Protocols (ICNP 1999)*, pp. 106-113, Oct.-Nov. 1999.
12. G. Wang, J. Cao, and K.C.C. Chan, "A Reliable Totally-Ordered Group Multicast Protocol for Mobile Internet," *Proceedings of the IEEE 33rd International Conference on Parallel Processing Workshops (ICPPW 2004)*, Montreal, Quebec, Canada, pp. 108-115, Aug. 2004.
13. E.A. Brewer, R.H. Katz, Y. Chawathe, S.D. Gribble, T. Hodes, G. Nguyen, M. Stemm, T. Henderson, E. Amir, H. Balakrishnan, A. Fox, V.N. Padmanabhan, and S. Seshan, "A Network Architecture for Heterogeneous Mobile Computing," *IEEE Personal Communications*, Vol. 5, Issue 5, pp. 8-24, Oct. 1998.
14. T.B. Zahariadis, K.G. Vaxevanakis, C.P. Tsantilas, N.A. Zervos, N.A. Nikolaou, "Global Roaming in Next-Generation Networks," *IEEE Communications Magazine*, Vol. 40, Issue 2, pp. 145-151, 2002.
15. E. Gustafsson and A. Jonsson, "Always Best Connected," *IEEE Wireless Communications*, Vol. 10, Issue 1, pp. 49-55, Feb. 2003.
16. L. Zhang, S. Deering, D. Estrin, S. Shenker, and D. Zappala, "RSVP: A new resource ReSerVation Protocol," *IEEE Network*, Vol. 7, Issue 5, pp. 8-18, Sept. 1993.
17. A.K.Talukdar, B.R. Badrinath, and A. Acharya, "MRSVP: A Resource Reservation Protocol for an Integrated Services Network with Mobile Hosts," *ACM/Kluwer Wireless Networks*, Vol. 7, Issue 1, pp. 5-19, 2001.
18. J. Broch, D.A. Maltz, D.B. Johnson, Y.-C. Hu, J. Jetcheva, "A performance comparison of multihop wireless ad hoc network routing protocols," *Proceedings of the 4th International Conference on Mobile Computing and Networking (ACM MOBICOM'98)*, October 1998; pp. 85–97.
19. R.W. Hornbeck, "Numerical Methods," *Quantum publishers Inc*, 1975.

A Rule-Based Workflow Approach for Service Composition*

Lin Chen, Minglu Li, and Jian Cao

School of Computer Science and Engineering,
Shanghai Jiao Tong University, Shanghai, 200030, P.R. China
chen.lin@sjtu.edu.cn, {li-ml, cao-jian }@cs.sjtu.edu.cn

Abstract. With the frequent changes in recent business and scientific environment, more efficient and effective workflow infrastructure is required. Besides, with increasing emphasis on Service-oriented architecture, service composition becomes a hot topic in workflow research. This paper proposes a novel approach of using ECA rules to realize the workflow modeling and implementation for service composition. First of all, the concept and formalization of ECA rule-based Workflow is presented. Second, an automatic event composition algorithm is developed to ensure the correctness and validness of service composition at design time. Finally, the proposed ECA rule-based approach for service composition is illustrated through a prototype system.

1 Introduction

Workflow technology is increasingly used to manage complex processes in scientific and business field. The main characteristics of workflow approach are the clear separation of application program code from the overall process logic and the integration of automated and manual activities. Hence, it has been widely adopted as a core technology to support long-term application processes in heterogeneous and distributed environments. Meanwhile, with increasing emphasis on Service-oriented architecture, service composition becomes a hot topic in workflow research. Through the workflow approach, various customized services can be provided through the coordinated use of numerous distributed and heterogeneous services.

In this paper, we propose an approach of applying ECA rules to control workflow process as well as realize service composition. Compared with other workflow management system, the workflow model based on ECA rules can represent complicated business logic and provides more flexible support to the running of business. We give the formalization of the ECA rule-based workflow model for service composi-

---

* This paper is supported by 973 project (No.2002CB312002) of China, grand project (No.03dz15027) and key project (No.025115033) of the Science and Technology Commission of Shanghai Municipality. This work is also partly supported by "SEC E-Institute: Shanghai High Institutions Grid", Chinese high technology development plan (No.2004AA104340), Chinese Semantic Grid project (No.2003CB317005) and Chinese NSF project (No.60473092).

tion, where special activities and data structures are customized for the purpose of service composition. When modeling complicated ECA rule-based workflow, it's inevitable that the events composition occurs. If let user specify the event, it's error-prone and troublesome. Thus, this paper proposes an event composition algorithm to automate the event processing as well as ensure the validness of service composition at design time. Since the rules is an internal representation and difficult for user to understand, we visualize the meaning of the rules through a graphical process-modeling tool for human user to grasp the actual process and compose new ones conveniently. The workflow design tool transforms the graphical model into a set of ECA rules, so that the workflow execution engine is capable of controlling its execution automatically.

The remainder of this paper is structured as follows. Related work is addressed in Section 2. Then, we will present the formalization of ECA rule-based Workflow for service composition in Section 3. After that, we will introduce one algorithm with the automatic event composition to realize ECA rule-based modeling. In section 5, we will present a workflow prototype system based on ECA rules. Finally, Section 6 closes this paper with some brief concluding remarks and future research directions.

2 Related Work

There are quite a few works related to workflow system for service composition that have been proposed and used by researchers. The Business Process Execution Language for Web Services (BPEL4WS) is one of the leading candidates for business process modeling [4]. BPEL4WS supports business process coordination among multiple parties and enables modeling of long-running interactions between business processes [5] [6] [7]. However, BPEL only supports static binding and reference of Web Services, that is, every service partner has to be bound in design time. Besides, it doesn't address the composition of Grid Services [8], which becomes more and more important nowadays.

As to other workflow process modeling approaches, some workflow systems adopt the Directed Acyclic Graphs (DAG) [9] [10] [11]. However, DAG has no cycle circuits in its model; it's not applicable to explicitly express loops. Another modeling approach, Petri Nets, is frequently used in workflow systems [12] [13] [14]. They use Petri Net modeling method to describe user tools and depict the characteristics of a workflow process. However, Petri-net based workflow is hard to model uncertainty, thus it is not adaptive to the un-deterministic situations which usually appears in service composition.

There are also a lot of works related to ECA rule-based workflow systems. [1] proposes a systematic method of reducing an ECA rule-based process into a simple form. [15] reports the use of ECA rules to support workflows in product development. A rule-based workflow engine is implemented in [16]. However, they are limited to traditional applications. None of them address the issues of Web Service or Grid Service composition.

3 Formalization of ECA Rule-Based Workflow Modeling for Service Composition

3.1 The ECA Rules

ECA rule is originally used in active database systems [2] [3]. An ECA rule consists essentially three parts: an event, a condition, and an action. As shown in Figure 1, when the active DBMS detects that an event has occurred, it evaluates the condition, if the condition is satisfied, it executes the action. Events can be classified into primitive events and composite events. Primitive events refer to elementary occurrences that are predefined in the system, such as the state change of an activity, simple operation and time event. A composite event is a set of primitive events or composite events related by defined event operators. The condition is a logical expression that must be satisfied in order to activate the action part. The action involves the activity that needs to be executed or the Event needs to be triggered.

RULE <RuleName> [(Parameter list)]
WHEN <Event Expression>
IF <Condition 1> THEN <Action1>
...
IF <Condition n> THEN <Action n>
END RULE

Fig. 1. ECA Rules

There are many attempts in applying ECA rules to workflow management. The characteristic of ECA rule-based workflow, such as strong expressive power, flexible exception handling mechanism and automatic control of workflow process has entitled it a perfect candidate for solving complicated business logic and scientific problems. However, it's not easy to visualize the meaning of the rules, and also it's very difficult for user to construct and manage the rules. This is in fact the main reason why the ECA rule-based approach has not been a popular choice among commercial WFMSs [1]. Therefore, we propose a modeling approach combining graphical process representation and ECA rules. During modeling, we transform the graphical model into a set of ECA rules, so that our workflow execution engine is able to control its execution automatically. To adapt to new context of Web Service and Grid Service composition, special activities and data structures are customized for it. This leads to a new formalization of ECA rule-based workflow for service composition.

3.2 Formalization of ECA Rule-Based Workflow

In this section, we give a formal definition of ECA rule-based Workflow. This definition is based on the traditional process model and extended according to new features in service composition domain.

Definition 1. (ECA rule-based workflow) An ECA rule-based workflow model is an eight-tuple $(E, A, C, R, LC, TC, F, D)$:

- E is a finite set of events,
- A is a finite set of activities,
- C is a finite set of conditions,
- R is a finite set of rules, $R \subseteq E \times C \times A$,
- LC is a finite set of logical connectors,
- $TC \in LC \rightarrow \{\langle In, Out \rangle | In, Out \in \{AND, OR\}\}$ is a function, which maps each logic connector onto a connector type. In the connector type expression $\langle In, Out \rangle$, "In" represents the incoming flow logic whereas "Out" represents the outgoing flow logic.
- $F \subseteq (A \times LC) \cup (LC \times A) \cup (LC \times LC) \cup (A \times A)$ is a set of flows.
- D is a finite set of data structures' definition used in workflow model.

Definition 2. (F_C, F_D) F is divided into control flow (F_C) and data flow (F_D). And $F = F_C \cup F_D, F_C \cap F_D = \phi, F_C \subseteq (A \times LC) \cup (LC \times A) \cup (LC \times LC), F_D \subseteq (A \times A)$.

This definition denotes that data flow can only be connected from activity to activity. However the control flow can be connected from activity to logic connector, from logic connector to activity or from logic connector to another logic connector.

Definition 3. ($lc_{in}, lc_{out}, a_{in}, a_{out}$) Let LC be a set of logical connectors and F be the set of flow. For each logical connector $lc \in LC$, we define the set of its ingoing flows $lc_{in} = \{(x, lc) | (\exists x \in A \lor \exists x \in LC) \land (x, lc) \in F\}$, and we define the set of its outgoing flows $lc_{out} = \{(lc, y) | (\exists y \in A \lor \exists y \in LC) \land (lc, y) \in F\}$. Similarly, we get a_{in}, a_{out} for activities.

Definition 4. ($A_s, A_e, A_{WS}, A_{GS}, A_{APP}, A_{TX}, A_{SV}, A_{SW}, A_{CA}$) An ECA rule-based workflow for service composition may have nine kinds of activities as follows:

- A_s and A_e are start and end activity set. There are one start activity and one end activity, for $a \in A_s, b \in A_e$, $|a_{in}| = 0$ and $|b_{out}| = 0$.
- A_{WS} refers to the set of activities responsible for the invocation of Web Services whereas A_{GS} is utilized to invoke Grid Services. A_{APP} represents the activity set for legacy application, such as Java class, EJB, CORBA applications etc.
- The activity set of A_{TX} is utilized to execute the transformation of XML document by XSLT while the activities in A_{SV} are responsible for the value assignment of variables.
- A_{SW} refers to the set of activity which specify a sub workflow by referencing the name of an already existing workflow model. A_{CA} represents the set of

composite activity which divide a complicate activity into a serial of primitive activities.
- A_{SW} and A_{CA} allow the recursive composition of services and facilitate reuse of workflow models. All the activities are customized to new situations in service composition. It can be applied to most circumstance.

Definition 5. (PE, CE) Events in the workflow model are divided into primitive events (PE) and composite events (CE):

- There are six kinds of primitive events for each activity. $PE \subseteq \{e | \forall a \in A, e \in \{Initialize\ d(a), Started\ (a), EndOf\ (a), Overtime(a), Aborted(a), Error(a)\}$ The six primitive event types denote the different execution state of an activity.
- CE is a set of primitive events or composite events related by defined event operators. We define two operators: AND, OR. e_1 AND e_2 means that both e_1 and e_2 has to happen. e_1 OR e_2 denotes that at least e_1 or e_2 should happen.

Definition 6. (DO) There are four categories of data object (DO) definitions for the control and exchange of data in ECA rule-based workflow model for service composition:

- *Inherent Variable* is basic data type, such as Boolean, integer, string etc. It can be utilized to set guarding condition or act as a decision point.
- *XML Objects* are XML schema based data and generally used to represent the input and output messages of services.
- *Object Variable* is data item extracted from *XML Object* or *Other Document Object*. It is usually used to assign values from one field of XML Object to another.
- *Other Document Object* is an abstract representation of documents formats data except XML document, such as word, PDF, rtf and so on.

Through this definition, our workflow modeling supports various data formats that can be exchanged between different services.

Definition 7. $\forall f \in F_D$, f has following attributes (E, DO, Right). E refer to the triggering event of dataflow, it may be a primitive event or composite event. DO denote the data object set that sends from one activity to another. Right is utilized to differentiate target activity's access right to the data object.

Definition 8. $\forall lc \in LC, lc$ has following attributes (E, C, A). E refers to the triggering event of the control flow. Triggering event is a composite event related by "In" operator of the logical connector, if the $|lc_{in}| > 1$; otherwise, triggering event is a primitive event or null.

For example, if $\exists lc \in LC, TC(lc) = <AND, OR>$, and $\exists f_1, f_2 \in \{f \mid f \in A \times \{lc\} \cup LC \times \{lc\}\}$ suppose that the triggering event of f_1, f_2 is respectively e_1 and e_2, then the triggering event of lc is $e_1 AND e_2$. It is equal to the AND-JOIN workflow pattern in Petri-Net. Similarly, if there are two outgoing control flow to activities, the execution pattern is in accordance with the "Out" operator, in this case OR for parallel execution of activities. This is equal to the OR-SPLIT workflow pattern in Petri-Net.

Definition 9. (Reachability) A directed path p from a logic connector lc_1 to a logic connector lc_k is a sequence $\langle lc_1, lc_2, ..., lc_k \rangle$, so that $\langle lc_i, lc_{i+1} \rangle \in F_C$, for $1 \leq i \leq k-1$, if the "Out" operator of lc_i is AND, we call the triggering event of logic connector lc_1 is reachable to the logic connector of lc_k.

Triggering event of a logical connector is transitive in ECA rule-based workflow model when the "Out" operator is AND and the following node is also a logical connector. However, if the "Out" operator is "OR", it may induce another branch and be executed only if the condition is satisfied, so the triggering event is not transitive in this case.

4 Event Composition Algorithm

When modeling complicated ECA rule-based workflow for service composition, it's inevitable that the events composition appear. If let user specify the event, it's error-prone and troublesome. Thus, this paper proposes one event composition algorithm that can be utilized to automate the event processing as well as ensure the validness of manual activities composition at design time.

When developing the algorithm, there are two principles need to keep in mind. First one is that when encountering the logic connector whose "Out" operator is AND, the triggering event of the logic connector has to be passed to the following nodes. Second one is that each logic connector has a triggering event, if there are two ingoing flows connecting to the logic connector, a composite event needs to be created. Listed below is the notation used in the algorithm.

- input_event_list: the set of input events coming from ingoing flows of a logic connector.
- InOperator(lc): the "In" operator of a logic connector.
- OutOperator(lc): the "Out" operator of a logic connector.
- triEvent(lc): the triggering event of a logical connector.
- (InOperator(lc))(input_event_list): the triggering event of logical connector composed by all the input events.
- lc_{NEXT}: the set of logic connectors which directly follows lc.

In case of event composition, the algorithm first saves the former triggering event of the logical connector at which the event composition happens and then adds the new event to the input event list of this logical connector. After that, the algorithm detects the number of former ingoing flows and processes the events accordingly. If the number is zero, the triggering event is the new event; if the number is one, a composite event has to be composed by the former input event and the new event, also the triggering event is the newly created composite event; if the number is two or more, the triggering event is already a composite event, the only thing needs to be done is to refresh the triggering event to compose the new event. Finally, this algorithm checks the set of logical connectors that is reachable by the triggering event. If the set is not null, the changed triggering event has to be passed to the following logical nodes until a logical connector whose "Out" operator is OR appears.

PROCEDURE Event_Composition (Event e, LogicConnector lc) {
    formerTriEvent := (InOperator(lc))(input_event_list);
    add e to input_event_list;
    if ($|lc_{in}| == 0$) **then** triEvent(lc) := e;
    else if ($|lc_{in}| == 1$) **then** {
        // create a new composite event and add to event set.
        ce := (InOperator(lc))(input_event_list);
        add ce to CE;
        triEvent(lc) := ce;
    } **else if**($|lc_{in}| >= 2$) **then**
        // refresh the triggering event
        triEvent(lc) := (InOperator(lc))(input_event_list);
    if (OutOperator(lc)=="OR") **then return**;
    else {
    //pass triggering event to reachable logical connector
        for(all $lc_x \in lc_{NEX}$)**do**
            if ($|lc_{in}| == 0$) **then Event_Composition**(e, lc_x);
            else if ($|lc_{in}| == 1$) **then PassEventChange**(formerTriEvent, triEvent(lc), lc_x);
    }
}

PROCEDURE PassEventChange (Event formerInputEvent, Event e, LC lc){
    formerTriEvent := ((InOperator(lc))(input_event_list);
    if ($|lc_{in}| == 1$) **then** {
        triEvent(lc) := e;
        let e be the only element in input_event_list
    }**else if** ($|lc_{in}| >= 2$) **then** {
        // replace the former input event with new event

```
        remove formerInputEvent from input_event_list
        add e to input_event_list;
        triEvent(lc):= (InOperator(lc))(input_event_list);
    }
    if (OutOperator(lc)=="OR") then return;
    else{
        for(all $lc_x \in lc_{NEX}$)do
            if ($|lc_{in}| == 1$) then PassEventChange(formerTriEvent, triEvent(lc), $lc_x$);
    }
}
```

Event decomposition is the reverse process of event composition. When users design a workflow model, this algorithm can be utilized to automate the event processing. It greatly simplifies the process of modeling and ensures the validness of service composition at design time.

5 Rule-Based Workflow Prototype System for Service Composition

Based on above workflow model definition and algorithm, we develop an ECA rule-based workflow system for service composition. This system includes following parts: a graph-based workflow modeling tool to provide a GUI environment, which assists users quickly, and easily to create new workflow model from scratch or compose more complicated workflow based on legacy workflows [3] [17]; a workflow execution engine which responsible for the execution of workflow model; and web-based portal for user to submit the workflow to the workflow engine for running.

A workflow model contains different kinds of components. Fig.2 shows the class view of all the main components and their relationships. Generally speaking, a workflow model can be divided into four categories of components, that is, activity, link, logic node and data object. This components are in accordance with the definition in Section 3.

In the workflow-modeling tool as illustrated in Figure 3, we provide a graphical process representation for human user to design actual process conveniently Meanwhile, we transform the graphical model into a set of ECA rules during modeling, so that our workflow execution engine is able to control its execution automatically. Each activity is associated with six possible events in our workflow modeling tool, that is, Initialized, Started, EndOf, Overtime, Aborted, Error. Through Overtime, Aborted, Error event of an activity, the system can automatically trigger additional failure handling when some exception event or situation of interest occurs. It's very convenient to define exception flow separately from "routine" steps of the workflow and enable the system to be more easily modified or extended to react to events that were not anticipated. Data flow enables user to specify the access right and triggering event of data objects, which makes the fine-grained control of data flowing between different services a possibility.

Our workflow system currently supports three categories of services: Web Services, Grid Services and legacy applications. A service repository containing the

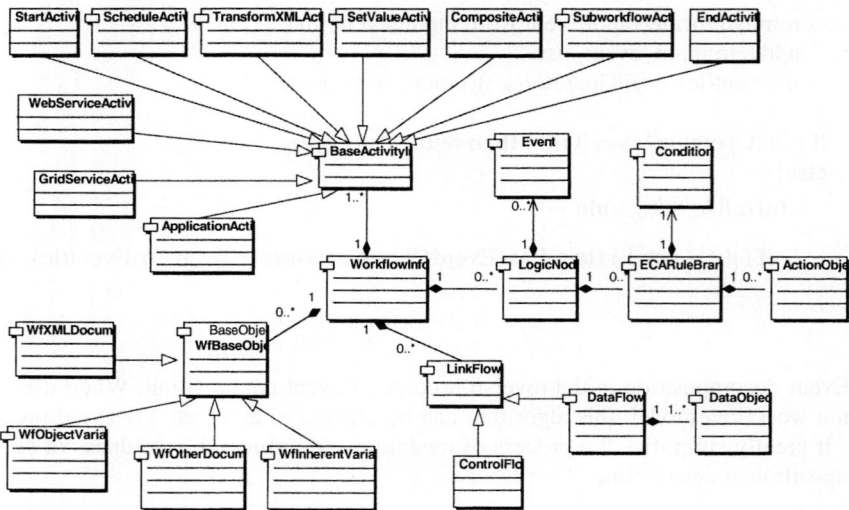

Fig. 2 Class view of the components of ECA rule-based Workflow

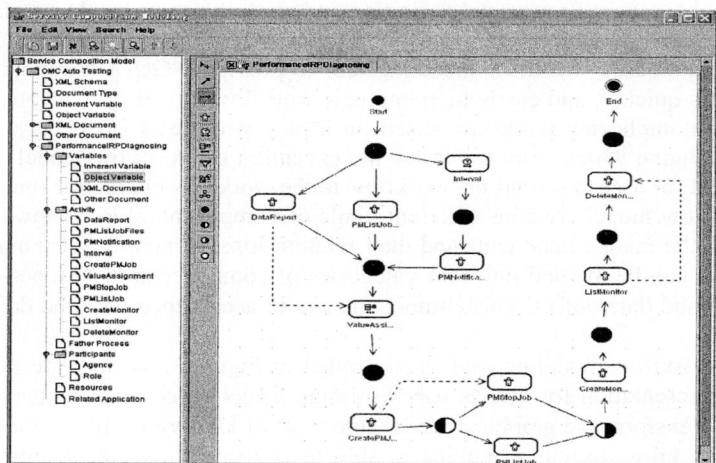

Fig. 3. A screenshot of the Workflow Modeling Tool. This Tool includes a menu bar and tool bar (*top*), a navigation tree to show the hierarchical structure of all the entities in the workflow (*left*), an element tool bar for drawing different workflow nodes and links (*middle*), and a composition panel for ECA rules based workflows (*right*). This Tool supports drag and drop to introduce new components to the workflow model.

available services' metadata exists. When user plan to create an activity invoking service, a service selection panel appears, this loads all the available services definition from the service repository and allows user to select proper services. However, when no suitable service exists in the service repository, user can resort to integration adapters to locate new services. There are three kinds of integration adapter presented to facilitate the composition of those three categories of possible services. Web Service adapter, for example, user can input a service WSDL Documents links or set a default UDDI registry, then the adapter explore the WSDL document, extract services, port types, input/output message's schemas and save them within the service repository for facilitating share and reuse of available services. Other integration adapters work in similar way.

Workflow model can be submitted through user portal to the workflow engine for running. Fig 4 shows the ECA rule-based workflow engine. It's supposed to deploy and start model service and process service firstly, which make preparations for the execution of forthcoming workflow request. When the workflow request is coming, workflow engine obtains a copy of the workflow model from database and then takes charge of the specific invocation and routing according to ECA rules.

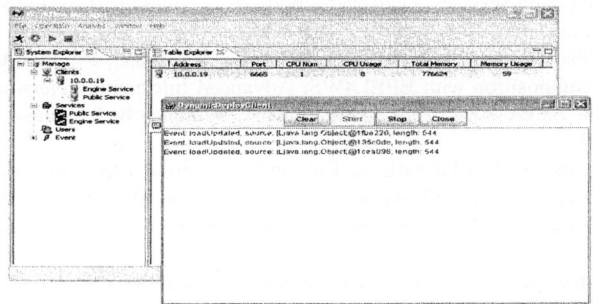

Fig. 4. ECA rule-based Workflow Engine

This ECA rule-based workflow-modeling tool together with the workflow engine has already been a vital part of Shanghai Grid and utilized frequently. The workflow model based on ECA rules can represent complicated business logic and provides a more flexible support to the running of business. It proves to be very flexible and powerful, which can satisfy the disparate need of both business and scientific domain.

6 Conclusions and Future Work

This paper describes an ECA rule-based workflow management system for service composition. The goal is to solve the complicated business logic or scientific application problems where the interaction between services and composition of new workflow out of existing ones needed. The formalization of ECA rule-based workflow for service composition is presented and an algorithm for event composition and decomposition is proposed to automate the event processing. The design principle and implementation details are also given in this paper.

In the future, we plan to apply agent technologies responsible for the dynamical discovery of suitable services at run time so that the process can be more flexible, conduct research on transaction based exception-handling mechanism. Additionally, the ongoing work focuses on providing support for automatic workflow generation by the aid of artificial intelligence planning technologies.

References

1. Joonsoo B, Hyerim B, and etc. Automatic Control of Workflow Processes Using ECA Rules, IEEE transactions on knowledge and data engineering, vol. 16, No.8, pp. 1010-1023, August 2004
2. N.W. Paton, Active Rules in Database Systems. Springer-Verlag, 1998.
3. C.W. Tan and A. Goh, "Implementing ECA Rules in an Active Database", Knowledge-Based Systems, vol. 12, no. 4, pp. 137-144, Aug. 1999.
4. T. Andrews et al., Business Process Execution Language for Web Services, IBM, version 1.1, 2nd public draft release, May 2003
5. Ranganathan, A.; McFaddin, S.; Using workflows to coordinate web services in pervasive computing environments; Web Services,2004.Proceedings.IEEE International Conference,6-9 July 2004 Pages:288 – 295
6. Staab, S. et al; Web services: been there, done that? Intelligent Systems, IEEE, Volume: 18 , Issue: 1 , Jan.-Feb. 2003 Pages:72 - 85
7. Kuo-Ming Chao; Younas, M.; Griffiths, N.; Awan, I.; Anane, R.; Tsai, C.F.; Analysis of grid service composition with BPEL4WS; Advanced Information Networking and Applications, 2004. AINA 2004. 18th International Conference on , Volume: 1 , 2004 Pages: 284 - 289 Vol.1
8. D.J.Mandell, and S. A. McIlraith; A Bottom-Up Approach to Automating Web Service Discovery Customization and Semantic Translation; The Proceedings of the Twelfth International World Wide Web Conference Workshop on E-Services and the Semantic Web, Budapest, 2003
9. Shields, Matthew and Ian Taylor, "Programming Scientific and Distributed Workflow with Triana Services", In Proceedings of Workflow in Grid Systems Workshop in GGF10, at Berlin, Germany, March, 2004.
10. Lorch, Markus and Dennis Kafura, "Symphony - A Java-based Composition and Manipulation Framework for Computational Grids", In Proceedings of 2nd IEEE/ACM International Symposium on Cluster Computing and the Grid (CCGrid 2002), at Berlin,Germany, May 21-24, 2002.
11. Altintas, Ilkay, Chad Berkley, Efrat Jaeger, Matthew Jones, Bertram Ludaescher, and Steve Mock, "Kepler: Towards a Grid-Enabled System for Scientific Workflows", InProceedings of Workflow in Grid Systems Workshop in GGF10, at Berlin, Germany, March, 2004.
12. Hoheisel, Andreas, "User Tools and Languages for Graph-based Grid Workflows", In Proceedings of Workflow in Grid Systems Workshop in GGF10, at Berlin, Germany, March 2004.
13. Zhang, Shaohua, Ning Gu, and Saihan Li, "Grid workflow based on dynamic modeling and scheduling", In Proceedings of International Conference on information Technology: Coding and Computing (ITCC2004), Vol. 2, at Las Vegas, Nevada, April 5-7, 2004, pp.35-9.
14. Grid-Flow: A Grid-Enabled Scientific Workflow System with a Petri Net-Based Interface
15. A.Goh, Y.K. Koh, and D.S. Domazet, "ECA rule-based Support for Workflows," Artificial Intelligence in Eng., vol. 15, no. 1, pp. 37-46, 2001.
16. A. Geppert, D. Tombros, and K. R. Dittrich, "Defining the Semantics of Reactive Components in Event-Driven Workflow Execution with Event Histories," Information Systems, vol. 23, pp. 235-252, May 1998.
17. L. Chen, M. Li, J. Cao, Y. Wang, "An ECA Rule-based Workflow Design Tool for ShanghaiGrid " Proceedings of Services Computing, 2005 IEEE International Conference on SCC 2004, July 2005.

Manage Distributed Ontologies on the Semantic Web*

Peng Wang[1], Baowen Xu[1,2], Jianjiang Lu[1,2,3], Dazhou Kang[1], and Yanhui Li[1]

[1] Department of Computer Science and Engineering, Southeast University,
Nanjing 210096, China
[2] Jiangsu Institute of Software Quality, Nanjing 210096, China
[3] PLA University of Science and Technology, Nanjing, 210007, China
Bwxu@seu.edu.cn

Abstract. Managing distributed ontologies is a challenging issue in the Semantic Web area. Different to most current distributed ontologies management researches, which focus on ontologies maintenance, evolutions, and versioning, this paper proposes a new distributed ontologies management framework based on the function-oriented perspective, and its goal is to bring multiple distributed ontologies together to provide more powerful capabilities. Ontology mapping is the key factor for manage distributed ontologies. This management framework also proposes a novel approach to eliminate the redundancies and errors of mappings in distributed ontologies.

1 Introduction

An ontology is a formal, explicit specification of a shared conceptualization [1]. Ontology plays critical role for dealing with heterogeneous and computer-oriented huge amount data, and has been used popularly in many fields. Especially in recent years, the rapid development of Semantic Web [2], which aims at providing high quality intelligent services on the Web, promotes the researches and applications of ontology greatly.

Usually, the ontologies are distributed, and produced by different community. These reasons cause ontologies are frequently heterogeneous, that has been the major difficulty to develop distributed applications based on ontologies. Integration and mapping are the two popular methods to solve these problems. Whereas, integrating ontologies is not only time-consuming and laborious, but lacks of automatic approach to support. It is difficult to keep consistent with changes of ontologies. Therefore, integration is unsuitable for handling distributed and dynamic ontology-based applications. Mapping just realizes the ontology interoperability by finding communication rules between ontologies. However, the number of mappings between distributed

---

* This work was supported in part by the NSFC (60373066, 60425206, 90412003, 60403016), National Grand Fundamental Research 973 Program of China (2002CB312000), National Research Foundation for the Doctoral Program of Higher Education of China (20020286004), Excellent Ph.D. Thesis Fund of Southeast University, and Advanced Armament Research Project (51406020105JB8103).

ontologies may be large, and their forms may be complex too. It faces the problem of how to organize mappings reasonably. Managing distributed ontologies reconciles multiple ontologies through collecting useful ontologies and organizing mappings between ontologies. Additionally, when mappings are introduced into distributed ontologies, the semantic balances in each original ontology would be destroyed meanwhile. Unexpected redundancies and clashes may appear in the whole distributed ontologies. So it is very necessary to refine redundancies and clashes to keep distributed ontologies sound and simple.

This paper presents a distributed ontologies management framework: FOMOM. Different to most existing works, which focus on evolutions and versioning [3-4], FOMOM focuses on how to exploiting the potential power of multiple ontologies. Additionally, FOMOM also can refine the mappings between distributed ontologies.

The paper is organized as follows: Section 2 presents the management framework. Section 3 discusses refinement method in distributed ontologies. Conclusions are given in Section 4.

2 A Framework for Managing Distributed Ontologies

Usually, traditional ontology managements are two-layer: ontology repository layer and application layer. Such architecture is too coarse for multiple ontologies managements, and the functions provided by multiple ontologies are embedded into the concrete applications. We designed a distributed ontologies management framework FOMOM with five-layer architecture as shown in Fig. 1. Through organizing mappings, the framework reconciles multiple ontologies soundly, and provides flexible and powerful services for applications.

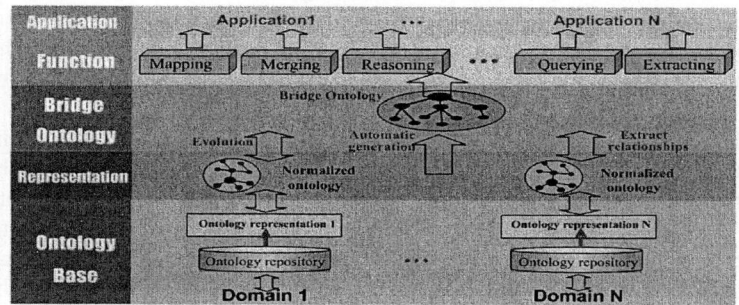

Fig. 1. The architecture of FOMOM

Ontology repository layer. This layer collects and stores the ontologies harvested from different ways.

Ontology representation layer. There are many different Ontology languages on the Web, such as OWL, DAML+OIL and Ontolingua. Besides the different in syntax, ontology languages may be based on different logic model, such as Frame Logic and

Description Logic. Translating ontologies into a unified internal representation is necessary.

Definition 1. An ontology is a six-tuple $O=(C,A^C,R,A^R,H,X)$, where C is a set of concepts; A^C is a attribute sets about concepts; R is a set of relationships; A^R is a collection of attribute sets about relationships; H represents a concept hierarchy; and X is the set of axioms.

Bridge ontology layer. To use the distributed ontologies efficiently and to avoid the ontology integration, we use bridge ontology to describe the communications between multiple ontologies. Bridge ontology is a special ontology, and can represent 12 kinds of mappings about the concepts and relations between ontologies [5]. The bridges between concepts include nine kinds: *Cequal, Cdiffer, Cisa, Cinstanceof, Coverlap, Chasa, Ccover, Copposed* and *Cconnect*. The bridges between relations include *Rsubsume, Rinverse* and *Rcompose*. In this layer, we use the methods in [6-7] to generate mappings between ontologies.

Multiple ontologies function layer. Distributed ontologies management should provide some general functions. First, bridges in bridge ontology should provide many simple and complex ontology mappings. Secondly, it should provide reasoning services across different ontologies. Thirdly, it should provide the services including the transformation and rewriting of querying expressions. Fourth, the services that integrating multiple ontologies and extracting the required sub ontology from multiple ontologies should be provided [8].

Multiple ontologies application layer. We use multiple ontologies to provide more detailed semantic data for the Semantic Web applications, and the method can avoid the problems of finding right ontology or building new one [9].

3 Refining Distributed Ontologies

3.1 Analyzing and Dividing the Refining Problems

Seven kinds of mapping: *Cequal, Cias, Cinstanceof, Chasa, Ccover, Rsubsume,* and *Rsubsume* are transitive relationships. Other kinds of mappings are not transitive and cannot cause reasoning failure and semantic redundancies. Because *Cinstanceof* is reverse to *Cias*, and can be translated to the *Cias* mappings, so the operation about the *Cinstanceof* mappings is similar to the *Cisa* mappings'. We can use the similar method of refining *Cisa* to deal with *Chas*. The way to solve relation mappings is similar to the concepts', and *Rsubsume* is similar to *Cisa*. We only focus on *Cequal, Cisa, Ccover* mappings, which is suit to other mappings too.

3.2 Mathematical Model

We use a graph to represent the concept direct inherited relations of an ontology. To keep the semantic integrity of the multi-ontologies graph, we add a global concept *Thing*, and every top concept in original ontology is the direct child of *Thing*.

Definition 2. The multi-ontologies direct inherited graph is denoted with $G=(C,E)$, where C is the set of concepts; E is set of direct inherited edges. If $(c_1,c_2)\in E$, c_1 is the direct child of c_2.

A matrix $U_{n\times n}$ is used to describe all edges of graph G, where $n=|C|$. All concepts in C are numbered form c_1 to c_n. The values of U_{ij} is:

$$U_{ij} = \begin{cases} 1 & (i,j)\in E \\ 0 & (i,j)\notin E \end{cases}$$

Before any mapping is imported, U only has the direct inherited relations in every original ontology, as Fig. 2 (a) shown, where $[O_i]$ denotes all direct inherited relations in the i-th ontology.

1) *Importing global concept Thing*

Every top concept in ontologies is the direct child of *Thing*, and the intersections of the top concepts and *Thing* in U are filled with 1. Matrix U becomes $(n+1)\times(n+1)$ as Fig. 2. (b).

2) *Importing the Ccover mappings*

The *Ccover* mappings will cause some new concepts added to the graph G.

Given a mapping $B_{cover}((a_1,a_2,...,a_m),(b_1,b_2,...,b_n))$, where $1\leq m \leq |C|$ and $1\leq n \leq |C|$, we will discuss four different processes according to different values of m and n as follows.

(1) $m=n=1$. The *Ccover* mapping degenerates to *Cias* mapping.

(2) $m=1$, $n\geq 2$. We add a new concept c_p in C, and its semantic meaning is $\bigcup_{1\leq i\leq n} b_i$. Meanwhile, new edges $\forall 1\leq i\leq n$, $(b_i,c_p)\in E$ and $(c_p,a_1)\in E$ are added to G.

(3) $m\geq 2$, $n=1$. We add a new concept c_q in C, its semantic meaning is $\bigcup_{1\leq i\leq m} a_i$. Meanwhile, new edges $\forall 1\leq i\leq m$, $(a_i,c_q)\in E$, $(b_1,c_q)\in E$ and $(c_q,Thing)\in E$ are added.

(4) $m\geq 2$, $n\geq 2$. We add two new concepts c_p and c_q to graph G, and add the new edge $(c_p,c_q)\in E$ and all new edges in the situation (2) and (3) to graph G as well.

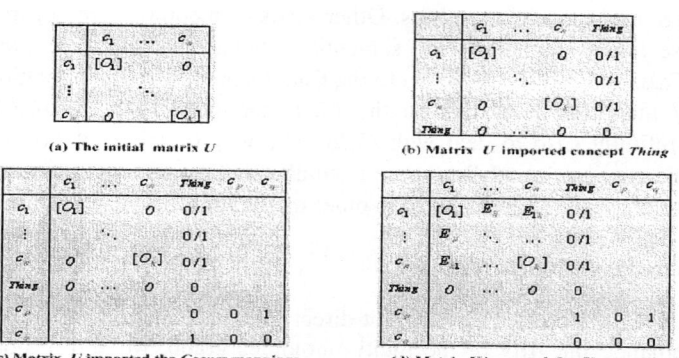

Fig. 2. The changes of matrix U in the introduction of mappings

3) *Importing the Cias mappings*

Cias mappings do not change the concepts, but add the direct inherited edges to graph G. We use E_{ij} to denote all direct inherited concept relations as Fig. 2. (d).

4) *Importing the Cequal mappings*

A *Cequal* mapping declares two concepts is synonym. Two concepts in a *Cequal* mapping should be removed one. In Algorithm 1, all semantic information of c_l is transferred to c_k.

Algorithm 1. Reducing synonym concepts

For each mapping *Cequal*(c_k, c_l), c_k and c_l is corresponding to the *k-th* and *l-th* row and column of matrix U respectively.

Step1. $U_{ki}=U_{ki}+U_{li}$, where $1 \leq i \leq |U|$, if the result $U_{ki} > 0$, let $U_{ki}=1$. Delete the *l-th* row.

Step2. $U_{ik}=U_{ik}+U_{il}$, where $1 \leq i \leq |U|$, if the result $U_{ik} > 0$, let $U_{ik}=1$. Delete *l-th* column.

Next mapping

3.3 Semantic Checking

Graph G should keep semantic consistency. If the cycles appear in graph G, the reasons may be the following two. (1) *Healthy cycles*. The concepts or relations in cycle are equal. We can use Algorithm 1 to delete redundant ones. (2) *Ill cycles*. The semantic conflicts may exist in the original ontology and bring about semantic error cycles. No algorithm can judge whether cycles are ill or healthy. Therefore, the manual interactions are needed.

3.4 Semantic Refinement

We should assure that every direct inherited relation in graph cannot be inferred from other direct inherited relations, that assures the graph is semantic irredundant. Our aim is refining graph G after mappings are introduced, which must satisfy two goals: (1) The graph G is irredundant; (2) The refining operations do not change the connectivity of graph G.

Definition 3. Minimal graph is denoted with $G_{min}=(C, E_{min})$, for $\forall (c_x, c_y) \in E_{min}$, there not exist a directed path $p_{xy}=(c_x, a_1, ..., a_s, c_y)$, where $s > 0$, $1 \leq i \leq s-1$, $(c_x, a_1), (a_s, c_y), (a_i, a_{i+1}) \in E$.

If path $p_{xy}=(c_x, a_1, ..., a_s, c_y)$ exists, we call it the substitute path of edge (c_x, c_y).

Definition 4. $G'=(C, E')$ is the equivalent connective graph of $G=(C,E)$, iff $\forall c_x, c_y \in C$, if G has a directed path $p_{xy}=(c_x, ..., c_y)$, then G' must has a directed path from c_x to c_y too.

Definition 5. If $G'_{min}=(C, E'_{min})$ is minimal graph, and is equivalent connective graph, we call $G'_{min}=(C, E'_{min})$ is minimal equivalent connective graph of $G=(C,E)$.

The goal of the refinement is to seek for the graph $G'_{min}=(C, E'_{min})$.

From the Definition 3, 4 and 5, we have the following three obvious conclusions:

Conclusion 1. Deleting all edges having substitute paths in G can get $G_{min} = (C, E_{min})$.

Conclusion 2. For a edge $(c_x, c_y) \in E$ in $G=(C,E)$, if it has a substitute path $p_{xy} = (c_x, a_1, ..., a_s, c_y)$, we can infer there is more than one directed path from c_x to c_y.

Conclusion 3. Delete all direct inherited edges having more than one directed path from c_x to c_y in $G=(C,E)$, we can get the minimal graph $G_{min} = (C, E_{min})$.

Then we discuss methods of finding all edges having substitute paths in graph as follows.

Let matrix U denotes all edges in G, and $U^n = U^{n-1} \times U$, where $n \geq 2$ and $U^1 = U$.

Theorem 1. $\forall c_i, c_j \in C$, U_{ij}^k denotes that the number of paths with k length from c_i to c_j.

According to Theorem 1, $U^1, ..., U^n$ denote the number of paths, whose length is $1, 2, ..., n$.

Let matrix $W = \sum_{k=2}^{n} U^k$, we compare W with U. According to Conclusion 2, if (c_i, c_j) have substitute paths, that equal to $U_{ij} = 1$ and $W_{ij} \geq 1$.

Definition 6. If a direct inherited edge has substitute paths, we call it deleting edge. All deleting edges compose the deleting edge set E_d, $E_d = \{(c_i, c_j) \mid (c_i, c_j) \in E \text{ and } W_{ij} \geq 1\}$.

Definition 7. If (c_m, c_k) has substitute path $p_{mk} = (c_m, a_1, ..., a_p, c_x, c_y, b_1, ..., b_q, c_k)$, where $p > 0$ or $q > 0$, $(c_m, a_1), (a_p, c_x), (c_y, b_1), (b_q, c_k) \in E$, and for $1 \leq i \leq p-1$, have $(a_i, a_{i+1}) \in E$, for $1 \leq j \leq q-1$, have $(b_j, b_{j+1}) \in E$. Meanwhile, (c_x, c_y) is a part of p_{mk}, denote with $(c_x, c_y) \prec (c_m, c_k)$.

Theorem 2. Relation $\prec$ is irreflexive, asymmetric and transitive.

Definition 8. E_b is the bottom edges set in E_d, $E_b = \{(c_i, c_j) \mid (c_i, c_j) \in E_d, \neg \exists (c_x, c_y) \in E_d, \text{and } (c_x, c_y) \prec (c_i, c_j)\}$. $E_x = E_d - E_b$ is the unbottom edges set in E_d under the relation $\prec$.

Obviously, $p_{xy} = (c_x, a_1, ..., a_s, c_y)$ is composed by the set:
$E_p = \{(c_x, a_1) \bigcup_{i=1}^{s-1} \{(a_i, a_{i+1})\} \cup (a_s, c_y)\}$.

Theorem 3. If $(c_x, c_y) \in E_d$, must have a substitute path $p_{xy} = (c_x, a_1, ..., a_s, c_y)$, where $s > 0$, $1 \leq i \leq s-1$, and every edge in the path $\notin E_d$.

Proof:
(1) $(c_x, c_y) \in E_b$, the theorem is valid obviously.
(2) $(c_x, c_y) \in E_x$, it must has a substitute path $p_{xy} = (c_x, a_1, ..., a_s, c_y)$, E_p is the set of edges in the path. Algorithm 2 constructs such a substitute path. p_{xy} must exist.
From (1) and (2), theorem 3 is proved. ◆

Algorithm 2. Construct the substitute path

Input: p_{xy} and its composing edges E_p, edges in E_p are stored in turn from c_x to c_y.

Step1. **For** each edge e_i in p_{xy}

Step2. **If** $e_i \in E_b$, must has a substitute path P_l, all edges in $P_l \notin E_d$, use the edges of P_l to substitute e_i in turn, go to Step 5.

Step3. **If** $e_i \in E_x$, must has a substitute path P_m, using the edges of P_m to substitute e_i in turn. Return to Step2.

Step4. **If** $e_i \notin E_b$ and $e_i \notin E_x$, go on to Step 5.

Step5. **Next** edge

Output: In the new substitute path p'_{xy}, all edges $\notin E_d$.

Theorem 4. After delete all edges in E_d, $G' = (C, E')$ is the equivalent connective graph of the original graph $G = (C, E)$.

According to the Conclusion 3 and Theorem 4, we can conclude that: after delete all edges E_d in $G' = (C, E')$, it is the $G'_{min} = (C, E'_{min})$ of $G = (C, E)$.

We complete the semantic refinement for multi-ontologies with mapping ontology. All the steps in our methods have constant time complexity obviously. So our method has high efficiency and is feasible.

4 Conclusions

Managing distributed ontologies is a challenging issue. This paper proposed the FOMOM framework for managing distributed ontologies to bring these ontologies together for providing more powerful capabilities. The framework also proposes a novel approach to eliminate the redundancies and errors of mappings in distributed ontologies.

References

1. Gruber, T.R.: A Translation Approach to Portable Ontology Specifications. Knowledge Acquisition, Vol. 5. (1993) 199-220
2. Berners-Lee, T., Hendler, J., O.Lassila: The semantic web. Scientific American. Vol. 284. (2001) 34-43

3. Noy, N.F., Musen, M.A.: Ontology versioning in an ontology-management framework. IEEE Intelligent Systems, Vol. 19. (2004) 6-13
4. Maedche, A., Motik, B., Stojanovic, L.: Managing multiple and distributed ontologies on the Semantic Web. The VLDB Journal, Vol. 12. (2000) 286-302
5. Wang, P., Xu, B.W., Lu, J.J., Li, Y.H., Kang D.Z. Using Bridge Ontology for Detailed Semantic Annotation Based on Multi-ontologies. Journal of Electronics and Computer Science, Vol. 6. (2004) 19-29
6. Wang, P., Xu, B.W., Lu, J.J., Li, Y.H., Kang, D.Z.: Theory and Semi-automatic Generation of Bridge Ontology in Multi-ontologies Environment. Proceedings of OTM 2004 Workshop on Ontologies, Semantics and E-learning, Lecture Notes in Computer Science (LNCS), Vol. 3292. (2004) 763-767
7. Lu, J.J., Xu, B.W., Kang, D.Z., Li, Y.H., and Wang, P. Approximations of concept based on Multielement Bounds. In Proceedings of 16th International Conference on Database and Expert Systems Applications, Copenhagen, Denmark, Aug. 2005.
8. Kang, D.Z., Xu, B.W., Lu, J.J., Wang, P., Li, Y.H.: Extracting Sub-Ontology from Multiple Ontologies. Proceedings of OTM 2004 Workshop on Ontologies, Semantics and E-learning. Lecture Notes in Computer Science (LNCS), Vol. 3292. (2004) 731-740
9. Xu, B.W., Wang, P., Lu, J.J., Li, Y.H., Kang D.Z.: Bridge ontology and its role in semantic annotation. Proceedings of the 2004 IEEE International Conference on CyberWorlds, (2004)

Next Generation Networks Architecture and Layered End-to-End QoS Control*

Weijia Jia, Bo Han, Ji Shen, and Haohuan Fu

Department of Computer Science, City University of Hong Kong,
83 Tat Chee Avenue, Kowloon, Hong Kong
wjia@cs.cityu.edu.hk

Abstract. Next-generation network (NGN) is a new concept and becoming more and more important for future telecommunication networks. This paper illustrates five function layers of NGN architecture and discusses some end-to-end QoS (quality of service) issues for NGN (called NGNQoS). The five function layers are: (1) Application Layer that supports SIP protocol; (2) Network Control Layer that aims at overcoming the bottleneck problems at edge nodes or servers for end-to-end admission control; (3) Adaptation Layer that supports different network configurations and network mobility; (4) Network Transmission Layer that provides end-to-end QoS control for real-time communications through integrating Differentiated Service (DiffServ) and Multi-Protocol Label Switching (MPLS) and (5) Management Layer that provides Web-based GUI browser for data presentation, monitoring, modification and decision making in NGN.

1 Introduction

Next-generation network is a new concept commonly used by network designers to depict their vision of future telecommunication networks. Various views on NGN have been expressed by network operators, manufacturers and service providers. NGN seamlessly blends the end-to-end QoS into the public switched telephone network (PSTN) and the public switched data network (PSDN), creating a single multi-service network, rather than a large, centralized and proprietary infrastructure. Next-generation network architecture pushes central functionality to the edge of the network. The result is a distributed network infrastructure that leverages new, open technologies to reduce the cost of market entry dramatically, increase operational flexibility, and accommodate both circuit-switched voice and packet-switched data services. The integrated services will bring communication market billions of incomes, however, the R&D for NGN still lack behind the actual demands of the society [1]. On the other hand, the architecture of the Internet and IP-based networks is rapidly evolving towards one where service-enablement, reliability and scalability become paramount.

Dynamic IP routing supported by routing protocols such as OSPF, IS-IS and BGP provides the basic internetworking function while confronting the dual challenges of larger scale and faster convergence. Many providers are looking to a converged

---

* The work is supported by CityU Strategic grant nos. 7001587 and 7001709.

packet switching network (PSN) based on IP/MPLS. The transport layer protocols including TCP and SCTP continue to be an area of active research as developers seek optimal application throughput and resilience. IP QoS defined by IntServ and DiffServ continues to evolve and interesting efforts are underway to enhance QoS signaling for both wired and wireless networks.

The challenges and opportunities associated with a fundamental transformation of current networks toward a multi-service ubiquitous infrastructure with a unified control and management architecture have been discussed in [2], which presented the outline of the fundamental reasons why neither the control infrastructure of the PSTN nor that of the present-day Internet is adequate to support the myriad of new services in NGN. Although NGN will inherit heavily from both the Internet and the PSTN, its control and management architecture is likely to be radically different from both, and will be anchored on a clean separation between a QoS-enabled transport/network domain and an object-oriented service/application domain, with a distributed processing environment that glues things together and universally addresses issues of distribution, redundancy, and concurrency control for all applications.

This paper presents NGN architecture and discusses the layered end-to-end QoS control for NGN. In Section 2, a survey for NGN is given and the five function layers of NGN are illustrated in Section 3. Some end-to-end QoS issues in NGN are described in Section 4 and we conclude in the final section.

2 Survey of NGN: Research and Development

Telcordia Technologies in NJ, USA proposed next generation networks that support a variety of communication services (data, video, and voice) seamlessly [4]. Customers will demand that these networks be highly reliable as there will be more and more traffic and services. Because of the historically exceptional reliability of wireline voice telephony, the reliability of voice services supported by NGN necessitates special attention in order to achieve the customer satisfaction of the service.

In South Koera, KT is considering the installation of NGN backbone network. QoS discussions on whether the IP router satisfies the forthcoming NGN customers who use basic application of NGN still remain. QoS values as packet delay, packet loss and jitter are measured and analyzed at the KT-NGN test bed, and are compared with the ITU-T QoS recommendation values [5].

Some German companies discuss QoS from a somewhat unconventional point of view and argue that high availability is a key ingredient in QoS perceived by the user. High availability with extremely short interruptions in case of failure is needed for acceptable QoS in real-time dialog services such as telephony or video conferencing and an even distribution of the traffic load over the network is essential to ensure the efficient network utilization given that some kind of admission control for QoS traffic has to be in place for overload avoidance [9].

Alcatel (France) proposes the NGN multimedia network structure and its business model with four players involved in charging: access provider, connection provider, telecommunication service provider, and value-added service provider. Often charging components must be correlated to create a clear postpaid bill and ensure correct treatment of prepaid accounts, as well as settlement between the providers involved. If charging is to remain a prime competitive tool in next-generation networks, it must be functionally intelligent and flexible, and able to optimize network operator and service provider revenues while providing a fair policy toward the end users [10].

In UK, next generation IP-based networks that offering QoS guarantees by deploying technologies such as DiffServ and MPLS for traffic engineering and network-wide resource management have been proposed. An ongoing work towards inter-domain QoS provisioning is presented [16].

The basic issue of NGN trials on Russian public networks is interoperability testing of foreign equipments that are adapted to Russian network, domestic NGN system SAPFIR. Results of these NGN trials will be used for the development of the "NGN Evolution Concept" for Russian public networks [17].

3 Overall NGN Architecture

NGNQoS can be described from five function layers: (1) Application layer that contains the typical middleware for authorization, accounting, directory, search and navigation for millions of users; (2) Network control layer aims at overcoming the bottleneck problems at edge nodes or servers and it is composed of a series of control

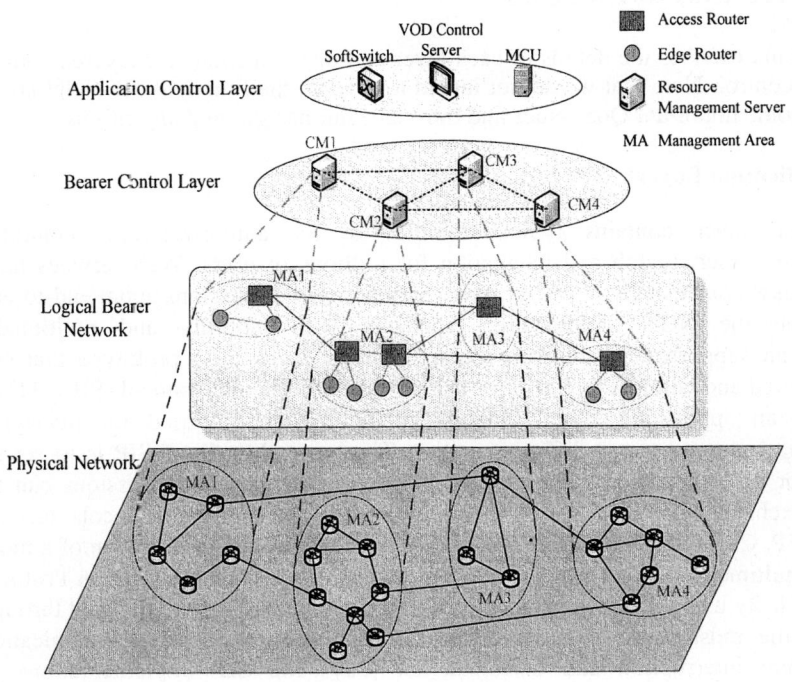

Fig. 1. NGN Network Architectures

agents for admission control, call setup and end-to-end QoS control through available bandwidth detection, local information control, class priority and intelligent scheduling. Multicast and anycast group managements will be implemented to leverage the load for admission control or service/message distributions; (3) Adaptation layer that supports different network configurations and network mobility. This layer can provide soft switching between different networks on different levels such as IPv4, IPv6, ATM, Ethernet, WLAN, WMAN and 3G networks. It supports both packet and circuit switching and provides interconnection between the two switching networks; (4) Network Transmission Layer that provides the effective end-to-end QoS control for real-time requests and flows through integration of parameterized QoS control and class priority control. This is particularly important to resolve the bottleneck problems such as multi-path routing that enables the multiple choices for the path and anycast routing that enables the selection from different (replicated) servers and (5) Management layer that provides Web-based GUI browser and wireless connection information such as the data access using XML and Web-based visualization for data presentation, monitoring, modification and decision making in NGN. The IP telecommunication network architecture and software layer architecture are shown in Fig. 1 (see http://www.huawei.com) in which Bearer Control Layer and Logical Bearer Network perform network control together.

4 Layered End-to-End QoS

This section describes the details of each layer and their functions for layered end-to-end QoS control. Note that we do not intend to give all the functions for NGN layers but give some important QoS issues and introduce our designs and algorithms.

4.1 Application Layer: SIP

Application layer contains typical middleware for authorization, accounting, directory, browser, search and navigation for millions of users. Web services have been discussed extensively; however, there are not many discussions about end-to-end service on the NGN architecture, especially with mobility and multimedia transmission supported. In this subsection, we only focus on a prototype that can provide wired and wireless QoS service using Session Initiation Protocol (SIP) [11].

SIP is an application layer signaling protocol which is used for managing multimedia sessions among different parties. The principle role of SIP is to set up sessions or associations between two or more end users. Initiated Sessions can be used to exchange various types of media data using appropriate protocols such as RTP, RSTP. Currently, SIP is able to set up a call carrying the information of a more detailed multimedia session using protocols such as the Session Description Protocol (SDP) [21]. By using adaptive protocol, the selection mechanism is achieved through applying the most suitable protocol for end user devices during communication without any interruption and disconnection [22]. The SIP implementations in application layer may integrate both wired and wireless networks based on NGN architecture.

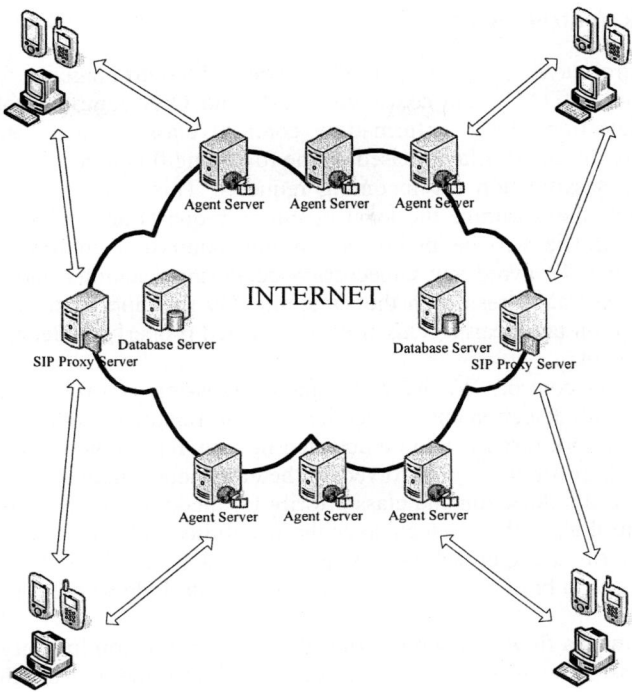

Fig. 2. SIP based end-to-end multimedia transmission system

Little work is done to enable end-to-end QoS multimedia transmission over hybrid of wired and wireless networks with SIP. Based on SIP, we have implemented an end-to-end multimedia transmission system, called AnyServer, for real time and non-real time video/audio communications, as shown in Fig. 2. To achieve SIP based end-to-end multimedia transmission, SIP is not only used for call setup signaling, but also carries information for session establishment in adaptive protocol selection mechanism. SIP carries an SDP packet describing an audio or video session, indicating supported communication protocols and end terminals' capabilities. To select the most suitable protocol for adapting different situations intelligently during a communication, data buffering service is also provided. In this way, end users can communicate with the others at their best acceptable QoS level. Currently, we are integrating AnyServer with NGN to provide multi-point end-to-end QoS applications such as video conferencing. QoS requirements of applications and session IDs are used for user identification of multi-parties communication in video-conferencing. Four major functional components of the current system are User Agent in client device, SIP Proxy Server, Database Server and Agent Server to form the heterogeneous wireless and Internet services [15, 22].

4.2 Network Control Layer

Network control layer is composed of a series of control agents for distributed admission control (DAC), call setup and end-to-end QoS control through available bandwidth detection, local information control, class priority and intelligent scheduling. We discuss this layer based on the following functions:

(1) Traffic classification for incoming requests: This function is performed by scheduler agents that examine the legal incoming requests and make classifications. The classified traffic will be processed through admission control agents (or the admission nodes). To avoid any unnecessary delay, the scheduler and the admission control agents normally reside on the same site. By this approach, the Internet and telecommunication tasks can be classified and treated properly as detailed in the end-to-end QoS design.

(2) Admission control: We have designed admission control algorithms which perform bandwidth detection and connection control. Bandwidth detection enables the approximate network resources to be detected in case that the networks are managed by different administrators or involved in heterogeneous networks. Based on the available bandwidth detection and class priority for incoming requests, our distributed admission control algorithms can enhance the scalability and admission probability. A cooperative distributed approach can be implemented at some board NGN admission nodes and we give a brief discussion of admission control algorithm for anycast flows [6] below.

Anycast flow is a flow which may connect to any destination in a target group. We consider anycast flow as a general flow concept because the anycast flow may be a unicast flow if the group only has one destination or multicast flows when the flow must be sent to every destination in the group. We first consider the destination selection issue. Destination selection determines which destination the anycast flow should be sent to. A good selection will bring a better chance for the flow to be admitted. We propose several weight assignment algorithms based on available information such as route distance and available bandwidth. Different status information surely impacts differently on the network performance in terms of admission probability, overhead, and compatibility as illustrated below:

(1) Weighted destination selection based on the static route distance information [6, 20]: The admission control routers/servers may apply even weight assignments for the destination selection if none of the information is available. The length of the route may be easily obtained via current routing protocols [18, 19]. The differences of route distances reflect the different resource consumption by the anycast flow. Intuitively, the flow to destinations with shorter distances will consume less bandwidth and fewer resources. Hence a smart destination selection algorithm should prefer destinations with short route distances.

(2) Weight assignment based on local admission history: The local admission history may be defined as a log that records the successfulness of selecting individual destinations in admission control. Let Hi record the number of the continual failures in the most recent admission history. For example, $Hi = 3$ implies that for the last three times when destination i was selected in admission control process, there was insufficient bandwidth and resource reservation. We proposed a destination selection algorithm to combine both route distance and local admission history information and the admission probability is expected to be higher than that of some static algorithm.

(3) Weighted Assignment based on available bandwidth: Local admission history may not accurately reflect the network dynamic status. We may also use available bandwidth detection for admission control. Resource Reservation can be made by some standard protocols such as RSVP [12] or by checking the availability of link bandwidth along the route based on the approach illustrated before. We have extended our anycast admission control protocol [3, 6] to include the available bandwidth information.

4.3 Adaptation Layer

This layer provides soft-switching between different networks on different levels such as IPv4, IPv6, ATM, Ethernet, WLAN, WMAN or 3G networks which support both packet and circuit switching. The layer can be divided into the following major functions:

(1) Soft switching between IPv4 and IPv6 using tunneling techniques carried out by edge routers of the subnet between the networks.

(2) ATM convergence sub-layer merges the ATM cells to IP packets (which may be used by WLAN and WMAN networks).

(3) Soft switching between ITU H.323/H.324 protocols to handle the circuit/packet switching.

We have efficiently implemented the 3G-324M protocol stack for 3G wireless communications [7]. Fast transformation between circuit switching networks to packet switching networks is under development. We are currently designing some new algorithms for the connections of heterogeneous wireless networks such as WLAN, WMAN and 3G networks.

4.4 Network Transmission Layer

In this layer, we focus on the discussions of Differentiated Service and Multi-Protocol Label Switching and the related end-to-end QoS issues.

Differentiated service. Differentiated Service architecture achieves scalability by aggregating traffic classification state. Packets are classified and marked to receive a particular per-hop forwarding behavior on nodes along their path. Sophisticated classification, marking, policing, and shaping operations only need to be implemented at network boundaries or hosts. The major advantage of DiffServ is that the Internet flows can be differentiated from the telecommunication flows by the board routers that may deal them with different QoS requirements. This is particularly useful for NGNQoS. We designed some special devices called network mapping (NM) that maps user's QoS requirement into service level agreements contract between customer and Internet service provider (ISP). The admission control can also be integrated with DiffServ architecture for the end-to-end QoS solutions. Fig. 3 shows the block diagram of a classifier and traffic conditioner. Note that a traffic conditioner may not necessarily contain all the four elements. For example, in the case where no traffic profile is in effect, packets may only pass through a classifier and a marker.

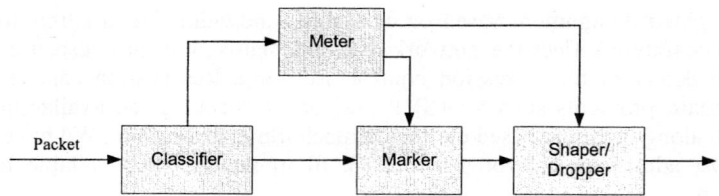

Fig. 3. Logical View of a Packet Classifier and Traffic Conditioner

To achieve the scalability and QoS for the DiffServ flows, we have designed a generalized regulator to provide an adaptive traffic control mechanism for very high rate real-time aggregated flows, especially, for those traffic that have been marked as red. Normally, three classes of traffic flows (green, yellow and red) in DiffServ network are defined in [13, 14] and we are interested in the deterministic delay bound for the real-time flows which may be marked as red/yellow but have stringent delay requirements. The generalized regulator, based on the extended network calculus, is developed for the purpose of effective control of high rate flows with QoS requirements as detailed in [8].

Multi-Protocol Label Switching (MPLS). In MPLS, packets are encapsulated at ingress points. The local significant labels, which have short fixed-length, are used in the headers of encapsulated packets. The packets are forwarded via Label Switching Routers (LSRs) by label swapping. An explicit path for each connection is called Label Switched Path (LSP). A reservation protocol is required to establish a LSP through a network. MPLS networks provide QoS guaranteed services with a lower computational complexity and operational costs, compared with IP networks using ATM connectivity structure. The most important advantage of MPLS networks is that they can perform the traffic engineering for load balancing, which is able to improve the network performance in a long run. Traffic engineering (TE) is in general the process of specifying the manner in which traffic is treated within a given network. Users usually expect certain performance from the network, which in turn should attempt to satisfy these expectations. The expected performance depends on the type of traffic the network carries, and is specified in the service level agreement contract between customer and ISP. The network operator, on the other hand, should attempt to satisfy the user traffic requirements. Hence, the target is to accommodate as many traffic requests as possible by optimally using the available network resources.

4.5 Management Layer

This layer provides Web-based GUI browser and wireless connection information such as the data access using XML. Web-based visualization presentation is critical for the management of NGNQoS for data presentation, monitoring, modification and decision making. Network management is an indispensable building block in our proposed NGN architecture. Effective management of the NGN is becoming the key to the successful competition and continued growth. NGN management layer contains the management functions relating to QoS, security and network management. There are five levels in NGN Management Layer defined as (1) fault-management level, (2) configuration level, (3) accounting level, (4) performance level and (5) security level.

Based on a modular concept of element management and domain management, we have designed the NGN Management Layer that fully supports day-to-day operation, administration and maintenance tasks, network configuration and service provisioning (including mass deployment for China Mobile in FoShan). We also plan to integrate NGN Management Layer into cross-domain management systems and the business processes of the network operators.

5 Conclusions

We have discussed some important design issues for the next generation architecture and different layers for end-to-end QoS control. The issues of NGNQoS presented in this paper are not exhaustive; however, the most functions presented are drawn from our design and implementation experiences. We are currently focusing on the implementation of cross layer platform of packet switching and circuit switching for 3G wireless networks. The future work will tackle with the cross layer protocols that can harness the heterogeneous networks across Internet, telecommunication and wireless networks.

References

1. Cochennec, J.-Y.: Activities on next-generation networks under Global Information Infrastructure in ITU-T, IEEE Communications Magazines, 40(7), July 2002, pp.98–101.
2. Modarressi, A.R. and Mohan, S.: Control and management in next-generation networks: challenges and opportunities, IEEE Communications Magazine, Oct. 2000, 38(10), pp. 94 – 102.
3. Jia, W., Xuan D. and Zhao, W.: Integrated Routing Algorithms for Anycast Messages, IEEE Communications Magazine, Jan. 2000.
4. Bennett, J.M.: Voice over packet reliability issues for next generation networks, Proc. of ICC 2001, June 2001, pp.142 – 145.
5. Lee, K.O., Kim, S.Y., and Park, K.C.: QoS evaluation of KT-NGN, 9th Asia-Pacific Conference on Communications, Proc. of APCC 2003, pp.900–903.
6. Jia, W., Xuan, D., Tu, W., Lin L. and Zhao, W.: Distributed Admission Control for Anycast Flows, IEEE Transactions on Parallel And Distributed Systems, 15(8), August 2004, pp. 673–686.
7. Jia, W., Han, B. Fu, H., Shen J. and Yuen M.-C.: Efficient Implementation of 3G-324M Protocol Stack for Multimedia Communication", Proc. of IEEE ICPADS 2005.
8. Jia W., Wang H., Tang M. and Zhao W.: Effective delay control for high rate heterogeneous real-time flows, Proc. of IEEE ICDCS 2003, pp. 367–375.
9. Schollmeier, G. and Winkler, C.: Providing sustainable QoS in next-generation networks, IEEE Communications Magazine, 42 (6), June 2004, pp. 102–107.
10. Ghys, F. and Vaaraniemi, A.: Component-based charging in a next-generation multimedia network, IEEE Communications Magazine, Jan. 2003, 41(1), pp.99–102.
11. Handley M., Schulzrinne H., Schrooler E. and Rosenberg J.: Session Initiation Protocol, RFC 2543, IETF., March 1999.
12. Zhang, L., Deering, S., Estrin, D., Shenker S. and Zappala, D.: RSVP: a new resource reservation protocol, IEEE Networks Magazine, vol. 31, No. 9, September 1993, pp. 8–18.
13. Heinanen J. and Guerin, R.: A Single Rate Three Color Marker, RFC 2697, Sept. 1999.

14. Heinanen J. and Guerin, R.: A Two Rate Three Color Marker, RFC 2698, Sept. 1999.
15. Cheng, L., Au, P., and Jia, W.: Wireless AnyServer –A Mobile ad hoc web-based learning system, LNCS 2783, 2003, pp. 37–45.
16. Pavlou, G.: Traffic engineering and quality of service management for IP-based next generation networks, IEEE/IFIP Network Operations and Management Symposium, 19–23 April 2004.
17. Koucheryavy, A.E., Fedosecv, A.P., Nesterenko, V.D., Gilchenok, L.Z., Pyattaev, V.O.: NGN trials on Russian public networks, The 6th International Conference on Advanced Communication Technology, 2004. pp.123–125.
18. Hedrick, C.: Routing Information Protocol, RFC 1058, June 1988.
19. Moy, J.: OSPF Version 2, RFC 1583, March 1994.
20. Xuan, D., Jia W. and Zhao, W.: Routing Protocols for Anycast Messages, IEEE Transactions on Parallel & Distributed Systems, 11(6), June 2000, pp. 571–588.
21. Handly M. and Jacobson V.: SDP: session description protocol, RFC 2327, IETF, April 1998.
22. Yuen M.-C., Cheng L., Au P.-O. and Jia W.: Adaptive Generic Communications for Integrated Mobile and Internet Web-Services, The 5th International Conference on Web-Age Information Mangement, 2004.

FairOM: Enforcing Proportional Contributions among Peers in Internet-Scale Distributed Systems

Yijun Lu[1], Hong Jiang[1], and Dan Feng[2]

[1] Department of Computer Science and Engineering,
University of Nebraska–Lincoln, Lincoln, NE 68588, USA
{yijlu,jiang}@cse.unl.edu
[2] Department of Computer Science and Engineering,
Huazhong University of Science and Technology, Wuhan, 430074, China
dfeng@hust.edu.cn

Abstract. The viability of overlay multicasting has been established by previous research. However, in order to apply overlay multicast to Internet-scale distributed systems, such as the Grid and Peer-to-Peer systems, the issue of effectively enforcing fairness among peers so as to optimize overall performance remains as a challenge. This paper argues that simply applying a multiple-tree scheme does not provide sufficient fairness, in terms of performance. Instead, we believe that a better way to define fairness, for performance's sake, is to factor in peers' proportional contributions as it provides the opportunity to support many simultaneous multicasting sessions. This paper then presents a protocol, called FairOM (Fair Overlay Multicast), to enforce proportional contributions among peers in Internet-scale distributed systems. By exploiting the notion of staged spare capacity group and deploying a two-phase multicast forest construction process, FairOM enforces proportional contributions among peers, which enables more simultaneous multicasting sessions and alleviates potential hot-spots. The simulation results of a large multicast group with 1000 members show that FairOM achieves the goal of enforcing proportional contributions among peers and does not overwhelm the peers, including the multicast source. FairOM also achieves low delay penalty for peers and high path diversity.

1 Introduction

In Internet-scale distributed systems, such as the Grid and Peer-to-Peer (P2P) computing, reliable and efficient data dissemination plays a very important role, with examples ranging from the massive data delivery in data Grid to multimedia delivery in P2P environment. In these systems, overlay multicasting [4, 5, 11] is a better choice than IP level multicast for several reasons. First, overlay multicasting does not need the support from the network infrastructure. Second, it can be configured on top of the application level, thus providing opportunities to capture the semantics of the applications. And finally, it is easy to use and configure in practice.

The biggest challenge in applying overlay multicasting to an Internet-scale environment, such as the Grid and P2P environment, is to meet the peers' requirement of fairness [3], which stems from the equal status of peers in the distributed systems (in

Grid environment, different sites can be treated as equal status peers; in P2P environment, each node can be treated as a peer). In these environments, no one is supposed to contribute dramatically more or less than others.

The conventional single-multicast-tree structure does not satisfy the fairness requirement as the leaves in the tree have no contribution to the multicast effort while the interior nodes contribute all the forwarding bandwidth [3]. To tackle this problem, the notion of multicast forest, or multiple multicast-trees, has been explored in several studies [3, 9]. A good example of these systems is SplitStream [3], which builds a multicast forest and ensures that each peer only serves as an interior node once (as a contributor in one tree) on average and is a receiver in all other trees.

In this paper we revisit the issue of fairness requirement by asking the question of how to properly define fairness so as to increase overall performance. Even if we have a multicast forest in which each peer contributes some (by being an interior node in one multicast tree, for example) and no peer is overwhelmed, is there any chance that the multicast is still unfair in the sense that it results in relatively poor performance?

We argue that simply letting each peer contribute once and satisfying each peer's outgoing bandwidth constraint is not enough for enforcing fairness for the sake of performance. A better way to define fairness, we believe, is to enforce that peers' contributions are proportional to their total available outgoing bandwidths, which is analogous to taxation or donation. In taxation or donation, it is desirable for people to give the same percentage of their available capital as their contributions to the society (here, we assume all the people are in the same tax bracket).

Performance-wise, enforcing proportional contribution provides an environment to support multiple simultaneous multicasting sessions that may not otherwise be achievable by simply asking every peer to contribute *arbitrarily*. Consider the following example in which peers A and B are both going to multicast a movie and each multicast will span all the peers in the network. Suppose that A builds its multicast forest first and one peer, C, is assigned to contribute 90% of its outgoing bandwidth to it. Then when B tries to establish its multicast forest, chances are that C just does not have enough bandwidth to support it because it has contributed too much to the first multicast session. In this case, the construction of a forest for B becomes either infeasible or, barely feasible by saturating C's outgoing bandwidth and making C a hotspot/bottleneck. In this case, if we instead let each peer contribute roughly the same percentage of its outgoing bandwidth, say 20%, then C has a chance to support the two multicasting sessions simultaneously.

Moreover, as alluded to in the previous paragraph, enforcing proportional contribution among peers can reduce the probability of hot-spots. Using the same example, if multiple multicasting sessions are forced upon C when it barely has enough bandwidth, then C will become a hot-spot of the system and packets will be delayed, or worse yet, lost.

We present a protocol, called FairOM (Fair Overly Multicast), to enforce proportional contributions among peers through a two-phase forest construction process, with the assumption that all peers play by the rules. The case where peers may not be trustworthy is beyond the scope of this paper and will not be considered any further except for a brief discussion in Section 3.7.

The performance of FairOM is evaluated in a large size multicast group with 1,000 members through simulations. Simulation results demonstrate that FairOM achieves the goal of enforcing proportional contributions among peers, does not overwhelm peers, including the source, has low delay penalty, and achieves high path diversity.

Before we move on to the next section, it is noteworthy that, in terms of bandwidth constraint, we only concern about the outgoing bandwidth for two reasons. First, current broadband technologies, such as ADSL, have limited outgoing bandwidth and larger incoming bandwidth. Second, each peer should have enough incoming bandwidth to accept all the stripes otherwise it cannot benefit from the multicast system.

We also recognize that, if the network bandwidth is so constrained that all the bandwidth is needed, there is no need to concern about the proportionality. However, with the proliferation of wireless-enabled laptops and high-speed Internet connections, we believe that there will be certain amount of excessive bandwidth available within Internet-scale distributed systems in the near future that should be effectively exploited to benefit the overall performance.

The rest of the paper is organized as follows. Section 2 formulates the problem and section 3 discusses the design of FairOM. The evaluation of FairOM is discussed in section 4 and related work is discussed in section 5. Finally, section 6 concludes this paper and discusses future work.

2 Problem Formulation

We represent each peer's total outgoing bandwidth as its total contribution capacity. Because of the design goal of minimizing the standard deviation of contribution proportions, we make the following three assumptions:

- Each data package to be multicast is encoded into n equal sized stripes and each peer has enough incoming bandwidth to absorb all the n stripes. This is essential to successfully build a multicast forest because otherwise the receiver cannot receive all the stripes no matter what multicast scheme is used.
- The total available outgoing bandwidth of peers is sufficient to build a forest to multicast data to the peers. Again, this assumption is to make the forest building feasible.
- There is excessive outgoing bandwidth in this multicast group. While this assumption is not essential to the correctness of the protocol, it provides the opportunity to show its advantages. If there is little excessive bandwidth left, all peers will have to contribute almost all their capacities, thus reducing to a special case of this protocol and making it identical or similar to other schemes.

Before we state our design goal, let us first formally define several terms with the assumption that there are a total of n peers in this multicast group.

- **Ti:** Total available outgoing bandwidth for each peer i, or, the maximum number of stripes it is capable of forwarding.
- **Ci:** The forwarding load of peer i, in term of the number of stripes it is assigned to handle.
- **Ri:** defined as Ci/Ti, is the contribution ratio of peer i.
- **$StdR$:** The standard deviation of the contribution ratios (R) of all the n peers. That is,

$$StdR = \sqrt{\frac{1}{n}\sum_{i=1}^{n}(R_i - \overline{R})^2}$$

A complete multicast forest must satisfy the following two conditions:

- Multicast satisfaction: each peer should receive all the n stripes.
- Bandwidth limitation: the forwarding load of each peer i should be less than or equal to its total available outgoing bandwidth, or $Ci \le Ti$.

The design goal is to minimize the standard deviation of all the peers' contribution ratio *StdR* in a complete multicast forest.

Goal: minimize *StdR*.

3 Design of FairOM

The basic idea of FairOM is to build a multicast forest in two phases. In the first phase, the peers join the multicast group and establish the neighborhood by a pair-wise neighborhood establishment procedure and use this neighborhood information to build an initial multicast forest that may not be complete. In the second phase, a peer contacts the source to ask for any missing stripes to make the forest complete.

FairOM assumes that a new peer knows at least one other member in the current multicast group when it joins, implying that FairOM does not directly deal with bootstrap mechanism. Further, FairOM assumes that all the peers know when the forest construction starts and the number of trees they need to join. In practice, the source and the peers can exchange this information through web page announcements or emails. As well, a peer can learn this information from its neighbors.

3.1 Establishment of Neighborhood

After joining the multicast group, a new peer will eventually establish its neighbor list by running a periodical neighborhood establishment procedure. In each round of this procedure, the peer contacts its neighbors (there is at least one bootstrap neighbor by assumption) and checks this neighbor's neighbor list. If its neighbor's neighbors do not appear in this peer's own neighbor list, it acts as follows. When its neighbor list is not full (each peer defines its length of neighbor list), it puts the new peers into its neighbor list. Otherwise, it compares the new peers with the ones already in its neighbor list according to the routing latency between the peers and itself. If a new peer has smaller latency, this peer replaces a current neighbor by the new one with a certain probability (currently we use 0.8) to prevent hot spot. If this peer adds a new peer to its neighbor list, it sends a notice to this new peer about this. While not immediately clear here, the purpose of this operation will become obvious later when we discuss the staged quota relaxation next.

In this way, each peer will establish its own neighbor list after a certain number of rounds. After that, this periodical process servers as a way to adjust peers' neighbor lists and maintain the neighborhood among peers.

3.2 Staged Spare Capacity Group

Staged spare capacity group is a key data structure in FairOM to enforce proportional contributions. Suppose that the spare capacity group has five stages, where each stage represents a percentage range of the capacity (e.g., stage 1 represents [0%, 20%], stage 2 (20, -40%], etc), then the source will put each of the registered peers into an appropriate stage. To illustrate this concept, we consider a simple example as illustrated in Figure 1.

In Figure 1, suppose that peer A has a total outgoing bandwidth of 20 (i.e., it can forward 20 stripes of data) and has already contributed 3 units of the total, then its current contribution is 15% (3/20). Because A's contribution is less or equal to 20%, it is put into stage 1. B is put into stage 2 because its contribution is in the range (20%, 40%]. Follow the same criteria, C and D are put in stage 1 and 5, respectively.

It is worth noting that the source maintains an independent staged capacity group for each stripe. So if a peer has contribution for more than one stripe, it needs to register the contribution information for each stripe independently.

stage 5	D
stage 4	
stage 3	
stage 2	B
stage 1	A, C

Fig. 1. Layout of the staged spare capacity group for A, B, C and D while the contributions of them are 15%, 25%, 10% and 82%, respectively

3.3 Phase I: Initial Forest Construction

Now we illustrate the first phase of the multicast forest construction among all the peers. The purpose of the initial forest construction is by no means to build a complete forest. Instead, it servers as a good start and provides a skeleton on which the second phase can improve. Because this is a quota-driven system, the system has a predefined initial quota. Each peer is willing to contribute as much as it can within this predefined quota.

More specifically, the source first sends all the stripes out, which are then forwarded to different neighbors to achieve path diversity. For each peer that receives a stripe, it forwards the stripe to as many neighbors as it can within the predefined quota. If a peer receives multiple transmissions of the same stripe, it picks one and rejects others. At this stage, let us assume that a peer picks the parent that notices it first.

When a multicast relationship between a parent and a child has been established (the parent picks the child and the child accepts it), the parent and the child both record this relationship locally. Then both of them start to run a heartbeat checking procedure to detect any failure.

For each peer, when it receives a stripe and has gotten all the responses from the children candidates it picked, it calculates its contribution and registers it to the staged spare capacity group by sending a message to the multicast source.

There is no clear line between the first phase and the second one in a global scale. Instead, it is each peer's own decision on when to start the second phase that we describe next.

3.4 Phase II: Making the Forest Complete

After the forest building process starts, each peer checks with those peers that treat it as a neighbor (recall that a peer sends a notice to its neighbor after the neighbor is added to its neighbor list in the establishment of neighborhood procedure). If all peers it contacts have already gotten some stripes and did not choose it as a child in the initial forest construction, it will seek help from the source. Moreover, a peer contacts the source anyway if a predefined deadline has passed.

In the message it sends to the source, the peer indicates the number of times it has requested for spare capacity, starting with 1 (the first time). When the source receives the message (with number 1), it only looks for parents for this peer in the first stage of the spare capacity group by randomly picking one eligible parent which has this stripe. Then it calculates what the new contribution for the parent would be. If the new contribution ratio is beyond the quota limit of this stage (20% for the first stage), the parent's record is moved from the current stage to the next higher one (stage 2 in this case).

```
Peer:
  If (current > deadline && has not received all stripes) {
      num = 1;
      while (num_of_try <= 5) {
            send (source,id of all missing stripe, num);
            wait(waiting_time);
            if( still has missing stripes) {
               num++;
            } else {
               return success;
            }
      }}
      return fail;
  }
Source:
  While (1) {
    recv(peer, ids of missing strips, num);
    foreach stripe in missing stripes {
         // find adoption from stage <= num;
         parent = find_adoption_up_to(num);
         if (parent != NULL) {
           send(parent, peer, id of missing strip);
           if (parent.contribution > limit of the current stage)
              move parent to the next higher stage
  }}}
```

Fig. 2. Pseudo code for making the forest complete

If a parent is found, the parent will receive the adoption request of a potential child from the source and then send a request to the potential child that needs to be adopted. Thus the peer with missing stripes can get what it wants.

If the source cannot find a parent in this stage, the peer with missing stripes waits a predefined period of time before it starts the next round of request. When the next round starts, the peer sends another message that has a request number of 2, which tells the source to search for an adoption up to stage 2. However, the source still starts to look for adoption from the first stage in a hope to find some new spare capacity from smaller contributors. Thus each round provides opportunities for the source to find a peer with smaller contribution ratio to adopt. By following this protocol, the source relaxes the quota gradually and finally builds a complete forest in which every peer is in all trees. A pseudo code of this process is illustrated in Figure 2.

We need to mention that the delay between each round of requests for spare capacity and the way the source looks for adoption (always starts from the first stages, and climbs to higher stages gradually) are essential to the effectiveness of FairOM to enforce proportional contributions because they provide an opportunity to utilize resource from newly joined smaller contributors.

3.5 Incorporating Multicast Delay Information into Consideration

The algorithm discussed so far does not consider multicast delay when it performs the forest construction. In this section, we try to minimize the multicast delay of the forest by incorporating the delay information into each of the two phases of the forest construction. Here, the delay perceived by a peer in regard to a particular stripe is defined as the time delay for it to receive the stripe from the source. Performance-wise, the shorter the delay, the better the performance is perceived by this peer.

In the initial forest construction process, each peer sends its delay information along with the message it sends to its neighbors. When a peer receives multiple transmissions of the same stripe, it picks the one with the smallest delay and drops others. Because the dropping process is based on delay, it will not create cycles as proved informally by following example.

Consider three peers A, B and C. Suppose that Peer A chooses B as parent, B chooses C as parent, and C chooses A as parent. In this case, the delay D_a of A is larger than delay D_b of B, that is, $D_a > D_b$. Similarly, we have $D_b > D_c$ and $D_c > D_a$, implying that $D_a > D_a$, which is impossible. Thus the scheme to incorporate delay information is cycle free.

In the second phase of the forest construction, when a peer requests missing stripes from the source, the source chooses several parents for this child (we current use three parents) and the child chooses the parent that gives it the smallest delay.

3.6 Handling Peer Join and Departure

When a peer joins the multicast group after the forest has been built, it first establishes its neighbor list by following the neighborhood establishment procedure. Then it seeks for adoption from its neighbors. Upon receiving this request, a neighbor grants the request if this adoption will still keep itself in the same stage in the spare capacity group. Otherwise, it rejects this request. If no neighbor is willing to adopt the new peer, it contacts the source for spare capacity.

In the case of peer departure, we differentiate two kinds of departures: decent departures and failures. For a decent departure, the departing peer notifies its multicast parents and children so that the parents can reclaim their contribution and its children can start seeking for adoptions by first contacting their neighbors and then contacting the source if none of their neighbors grant their requests. In the case of a failure, this failure will eventually be discovered by the heartbeat checking procedure which is run between each pair of multicast parent and child. After the failure is discovered, the failed peer's parents and children can react accordingly, similar to the case of a decent departure.

3.7 Discussions

Stress Put on the Source: In FairOM, the source is leveraged to manage the spare capacity group. One concern of this is the stress put on the source. We have considered two possible solutions to reduce such stress, but neither of them is completely satisfactory.

The first solution uses a source pool that includes several servers to share and distribute the burden of the source. While this scheme is simple, it assumes that the other peers in the pool are as trustable and stable as the source, which is not usually the case in a dynamic environment such as P2P. The second solution assigns several peers the same responsibility and uses Byzantine protocol to make the final decision and prevent cheating. However, this design complicates the system substantially.

The Security Issue: With the assumption that the peers are trustworthy, FairOM performs well and finally builds a fair-sharing multicast forest. However, when some peers do not work within the rule and cheat on their contributions, the multicast forest would not be fair any more. To prevent this from happening, distributed audit mechanism, as proposed by Ngan et. al [8], can be deployed to detect cheating and remove the peer that cheats from the multicast group.

4 Performance Evaluation

In order to best evaluate the system performance, we choose the Transit-Stub model [10] to simulate a physical network. The Transit-Stub model generates 1452 routers that are arranged hierarchically, like the current Internet structure. Then we generate 1,000 end nodes and attach them to routers randomly with uniform distribution. Further, our simulator models peers' bandwidths by assigning each peer a number that refers to the maximum number of stripes it can forward, which serves as the peer's total outgoing bandwidth. For all the simulations, each peer's total outgoing bandwidth is randomly chosen between 10 and 20.

4.1 Effectiveness of Enforcing Proportional Contributions

We measure the effectiveness of enforcing proportional contribution by *StdR*, the standard deviation of the peers' contributions. In this simulation, we run three configurations with numbers of stripes being 2, 4 and 8, respectively.

In all the simulations, the algorithm satisfies the requirement to build a complete forest and satisfies all peers' bandwidth constraints. Then the mean value and *StdR* are calculated and summarized in Table 1. This result clearly shows that FairOM performs very well when we change the number of stripes from 2 to 8.

Table 1. Mean and Std of contribution ratios

Statistics	FairOM (2)	FairOM (4)	FairOM (8)
Mean	0.131	0.257	0.521
StdR	0.047	0.090	0.106

4.2 Improvement on the Feasibility for Multiple Simultaneous Multicasting Sessions

In this section, we qualitatively argue the effectiveness of FairOM in terms of improving the feasibility for multiple simultaneous multicasting sessions as follows.

Because we assume that each multicast session needs to span the whole network, the feasibility of scheduling multicasting session is determined by the weakest peer in the network. Here, the weakest peer refers to the peer that has the least available outgoing bandwidth when a new multicasting session starts. When its available outgoing bandwidth is not enough to support one stripe, scheduling of that multicasting session becomes infeasible.

We consider two schemes, the SplitStream-like systems, and FairOM. In SplitStream-like systems, when the weakest peer contributes more in one session, it can render the scheduling for additional sessions infeasible. While in FairOM, it enforces that when each new multicast session is scheduled, the contribution ratio of each peer increase proportionally, which implies that the more powerful peers will contribute more to support the multicast, thus leaving enough bandwidth at the small peers' side for them to support more simultaneous sessions.

4.3 Forest Construction Overhead

To evaluate the overhead of the forest construction in FairOM, we use the number of messages received by each peer during the forest construction phase. In the relevant literature, this metric is also denoted as "node stress".

In a typical run, all the peers, except the source, have node stress less than 300. The node stress for the source is 6585. While 6585 appears extremely high compared with other nodes' stress, it is amortized during the whole forest construction and does not induce much bandwidth cost for the source as shown in the following analysis.

In that particular run, the time of the forest construction was 192 seconds. Let us conservatively assume that each packet is of size 1KB, which is much larger than is really needed for the purpose of forest construction according to our experience. These 6585 messages amount to a total size of 6.6MB and receiving these packets in 192 seconds requires a bandwidth of 34.4KB. There is even less data sent out from the source during the forest construction phase (because certain messages, such as spare capacity registration, do not require response but account for a large portion of total messages received by the source). So this should not be a burden for a media server that usually has high-speed Internet connection.

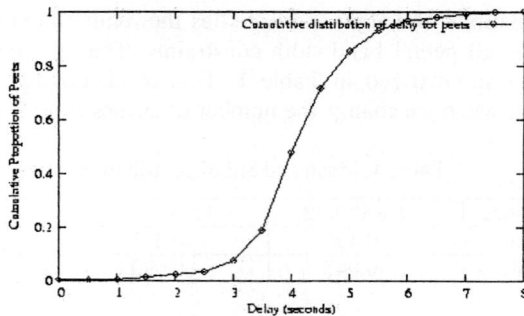

Fig. 3. Cumulative distribution of delay for peers

4.4. Multicast Performance

Figure 3 shows the cumulative distribution of peers' delay in a typical run with 4 stripes. In this figure, a point (x, y) indicates that a fraction y of all the peers have delay less than or equal to x. In this simulation, all peers receive all the stripes within 8 seconds and the average delay is 4.1 seconds. This clearly shows the effectiveness of incorporating multicast delay information into the forest construction process.

4.5. Path Diversity of the Multicast Forest

Path diversity refers to the diversity between the paths from each node to the multicast source. Ideally, the paths should be disjoint with each other so that one peer's failure only causes the loss of one stripe for the receiver. While FairOM mainly uses randomization to achieve diversity, the enforced delay between quota relaxation requests also contributes to the path diversity because it provides opportunities for a receiver to get stripes from different parents.

In the simulation, we randomly fail one peer (not source, of course) in the multicast group. We run the simulation with two configurations. First, we run FairOM with four stripes and then FairOM with eight stripes. The result is shown in Table 2. This result validates the effectiveness of the path diversity of FairOM, which successfully builds such a forest where one peer's failure only costs the loss of a small number of stripes.

Table 2. Max, mean and median # of lost stripes with a single node failure

Statistics	FairOM (4)	FairOM (8)
Max	2	3
Mean	1.02	1.66
Median	1	1

5 Related Work

Seminal work such as Overcast [5] and End System Multicast (ESM) [4] builds a single multicast tree for a multicast source. While these systems proved the feasibility and validity of overlay multicast, the asymmetric nature of tree implies that a single-tree approach can not satisfy P2P's requirement of fairness as the leaves in a tree have no contribution to the multicast transmissions at all.

CoopNet [7, 9] uses a centralized mechanism to build multiple trees. To enforce fairness, CoopNet uses randomization in the tree construction process. There are two main differences between CoopNet and FairOM. First, FairOM utilizes both decentralized initial forest construction and centralized forest improvement while CoopNet is based on a purely centralized algorithm. Second, there is no mechanism in CoopNet to enforce proportional contributions among peers.

SplitStream [3] builds a multicast forest in which each peer only serves as an interior node once, and serves as leaves in all other trees, so is a fair system in the sense that each peer contributes once and only once. The main difference between FairOM and SplitStream lies in the way fairness is defined. Instead of defining fairness by letting each peer that contributes share certain forwarding load, FairOM defines fairness as peers' contributions being proportional to their total available bandwidths. SplitStream also has the concept of spare capacity and uses it as a backup mechanism to build a complete forest; however, the spare capacity group in FairOM is staged and plays a central role to enforce proportional contribution.

Bullet [6] is a representative of mesh based multicast protocol, which builds an overlay mesh to disseminate data. Comparing with a single-tree based multicast, Bullet has the benefit of removing forwarding bottleneck, which helps achieve high bandwidth. The philosophy behind Bullet is to exploit excessive bandwidth while the primary design goal of FairOM is to enforce fair contribution among peers.

Recently, Bharambe et. al [2] present the impact of heterogeneous bandwidth to DHT-based multicast protocols, such as Scribe, the origin of SplitStream. However, their work is based on DHT-based multicast while ours on an unstructured multicast.

6 Conclusion and Future Work

This paper presents the design and evaluation of FairOM, a fair overlay multicasting scheme for Internet-scale distributed systems. Through a two-phase forest construction process, FairOM enforces proportional contribution among peers. Simulation results show that FairOM achieves this design goal and puts low node stress to all the peers. Furthermore, it achieves path diversity which makes it robust to node failure.

In the future, we plan to investigate mechanism to reduce the source's heavy duty and investigate the security issues. Finally, we plan to make this forest adaptive to the dynamic changes of bandwidth after it is initially built.

Acknowledgements

This work is partially supported by the National Basic Research Program of China (973 Program) under Grant No. 2004CB318201.

References

[1] Planet-Lab, http://www.planet-lab.org
[2] R. Bharambe, S. G. Rao, V. N.Padmanabhan, S. Seshan, and H. Zhang. The impact of heterogeneous bandwidth constraints on DHT-based multicast protocols, In IPTPS'05, 2005
[3] M. Castro, P. Druschel, A.-M. Kermarrec, A. Nandi, A. Rowstron, and A. Singh. Splitstream: High-bandwidth multicast in cooperative environment. In *Proc. of the SOSP*, Bolton Landing, New York, USA, October 2003.
[4] Y.-H. Chu, S. G. Rao, S. Seshan, and H. Zhang. A case for end system multicast. IEEE Journal on Selected Areas in Communication (JSAC), Special Issue on Networking Support for Multicast, 20(8), 2002.
[5] J. Jannotti, D. Gifford, K. Johnson, and M. Kaashoek. Overcast: Reliable multicasting with an overlay network. In *Proc. OSDI*, San Diego, CA, 2000.
[6] D. Kostic, A. Rodriguez, J. Albrecht, and A. Vahdat. Bullet: Hight band-width data dissemination using an overlay mesh. In *Proc. of the ACM Symposium on Operating System Principles (SOSP)*, October 2003.
[7] V. N. Padmanabhan, H. J. Wang, and P. A. Chou. Supporting heterogeneity and congestion control in peer-to-peer multicast streaming. In *IPTPS*, 2004.
[8] T.-W. J. Ngan, D. S. Wallach, and P. Druschel. Enforcing fair sharing of peer-to-peer resources. In Proc of IPTPS, 2003
[9] V. N. Padmanabhan, H. J. Wang, P. A. Chou, and K. Sripanidkulchai. Distributing streaming media content using cooperative networking. In *NOSSDAV'02*, Miami, Florida, USA, May 2002.
[10] E. Zegura, K. Calvert, and S. Bhattacharjee. How to model an internetwork. In *INFOCOMM*, San Francisco, California, 1996.
[11] S. Zhuang, B. Zhao, A. Joseph, R. Katz, and J. Kubiatowicz. Bayeux: An architecture for scalable and fault-tolerant wide-area data dissemination. In *NOSSDAV'2001*, June 2001.

An Efficient QoS Framework with Distributed Adaptive Resource Management in IPv6 Networks

Huagang Shao[1,2], Weinong Wang[2], Rui Xie[2], and Xiao Chen[2]

[1] Department of Computer Science and Engineering, Shanghai Jiaotong University
hgshao@cs.sjtu.edu.cn
[2] Regional Network Center of East China of China Education and Research Network,
Floor 4, Haoran Building, 1954 Huashan Road, Shanghai 200030, China
{hgshao, wnwang, sherry, shawn}@sjtu.edu.cn

Abstract. In this paper, we proposed a new QoS framework with Distributed Adaptive Resource Management(DARM). DARM provides end-to-end QoS guarantees to individual flows with minimal overhead, while keeping the scalability characteristic of DiffServ. In DARM, per-flow admission control and resource reservation, in conjunction with a novel IPv6 flow label mechanism, can be processed instantaneously in a fully distributed and independent manner at edge of network without hop-by-hop signaling. In addition, DARM is capable of reconfiguring network resource adaptively according to dynamically changing of traffic load. Through extensive simulations, the results clearly exhibit that DARM has a better overall performance comparing to the IntServ and DiffServ.

1 Introduction

The enlargement of the Internet user community has generated the need for IP-based applications requiring guaranteed Quality of Service (QoS) characters. An Integrated Services (IntServ) model(RFC1633) has been proposed to provision QoS for individual flows through resource reservation and admission control mechanisms. The Resource ReSerVation Protocol(RSVP, RFC2205) is used as the signaling protocol in IntServ. The IntServ/RSVP approach requires every router to maintain per-flow state information. For large networks with millions of simultaneous connections, maintaining the flow state information places a huge storage and processing overhead on the routers. The IntServ/RSVP approach suffers from scalability problems.

Consequently, a Differentiated Services(DiffServ) model has been proposed(RFC2475). In contrast, the DiffServ architecture achieves scalability by limiting QoS functionalities to class-based priority mechanisms. DiffServ makes a distinction between operations performed in the core of the network, and operations at the edges of the network, scheduling and queue management only deal with a few classes of traffic, and can thus remain relatively simple. However, without per-flow admission control and resource reservation mechanism, such an approach only supports weak QoS as compared to IntServ.

To achieve stronger QoS without sacrificing scalability, we have designed a new QoS framework in IPv6 networks with Distributed Adaptive Resource Management(DARM). In conjunction with a novel flow label mechanism, DARM provides end-to-end QoS guarantees to individual flows with much less overhead than IntServ, while keeping the scalability characteristic of DiffServ. DARM makes per-flow admission control and end-to-end bandwidth reservation at the edge of the network, while differentiating the traffic classes as in DiffServ in the core of network.

The remainder of this paper is organized as follows. Section 2 is related work. Section 3 presents the proposed DARM architecture. The details of adaptive resource management mechanism is proposed in section 4. Section 5 shows results based on our simulations. The paper is concluded by section 6.

2 Related Work

The pervasive proposal QoS provisioning architectures were to design a DiffServ enhanced by using a centralized agent, called Bandwidth Broker(BB, RFC2638) to manage the resources within each DiffServ domain and make local admission control decisions. The BB carried the burden of per flow admission control in domain, but there might be some scalability considerations if the BB has to process thousands of requests per second and must maintain per flow information about every flow that is currently active inside its domain. Moreover, BB lacked suitable means to control diversiform network elements and implement traffic engineering efficiently.

In literature[1, 2], a new QoS framework, named DiffServ-aware MPLS Traffic Engineering(DS_TE), was proposed. In this framework, DiffServ was complemented by MPLS Traffic Engineering mechanisms that operate on an aggregate basis across all DiffServ traffic classes. In order to reduce flooding overhead of link state advertisements, Inter Gateway routing Protocol(IGP) extension of per class-type Link State Advertisements(LSA) was used to exchange information on the available bandwidth for each class type. However, the scalability of LSAs was improved by propagating information on a per-class-type basis instead of on a per-class basis, no bandwidth provisioning was enforced for each traffic class within a class type. Flows of different traffic classes within a class type might interfere with each other.

The more related work was done in literature [3], which has proposed a scalability architecture for end-to-end QoS provisioning. In this work, authors adopted similarity flow label function for resources reservation and performed admission control at edge routers in the domain. But the architecture still existed a centralized agent(BB) to control the edge routers, which might more like a two-tier BB architecture. Moreover, the architecture adopted a source routing framework and k-shortest paths algorithm to pre-compute paths between the pair of two edge routers, which has been found inefficiency in consideration of throughput[4].

Most recently, literature [5] has proposed an end-to-end QoS framework with on-demand bandwidth reconfiguration. In this work, path bandwidth allocation can be dynamic reconfigured in a on-demand manner. However, the authors neither gave any details on how to select resource for the admitted flow nor provided any means for how to deploy an admitted flow on corresponding physical resource of underlying network.

3 DARM Architecture

In order to provide per-flow QoS guarantees while keeping the scalability, every network elements need work harmoniously under some reasonable, efficient, and practicable mechanisms. The two of most important issues among them are the plans of admission control and the means of resource reservation. In this section, we will discuss above two key issues in detail.

3.1 Network Model Overview

We consider the communications model of DARM as smart-edge and simple-core, which places much more the functionality to the edge of the network, and maintains a simple core. In DARM, all routers can be categorized into edge routers and core routers. Edge routers are the points where traffic enters and leaves the domain. Core routers connect the edge routers within the same domain. Edge routers fulfill per-flow classifying, shaping and marking, just like what traditional DiffServ edge router does. In DARM, edge routers also carry the burden of per-flow admission control(see section 3.3). Core routers schedule and forward packets according to type of service class and destination address. In DARM, core routers forward QoS guaranteed packets further according to flow label values. The details of forwarding with flow label will be discussed in section 3.2. We assume that routers in the DARM are extended to include a measurement process to track and maintain the local resource reserving state(e.g. local outgoing links residual bandwidth), and support our adaptive resource management mechanism which will be discussed in detail in section 4.

Routing is one of the most important technical issues in networking. In DARM, we decouple QoS-based path selection from QoS-based routing, which always introduces almost impossible dissemination of dynamic state information (e.g. residual bandwidth, delay, and jitter.) in underlying network[6]. In DARM, path selection and adaptive adjusting is performed by our proposed adaptive resource management mechanism. Hence, we assume that all the DARM domains use a standard inter-domain routing protocol, such as the Border Gateway Protocol(BGP, RFC1771), to exchange reachability information with their neighbor domains. All the edge routers in each domain will participate in this information exchanging. Moreover, we assume that a standard link state routing protocol, such as OSPF(RFC2328), operates inside each domain, in order for the routers to advertise and exchange their (relative) static link state information to others.

3.2 Forwarding Packets with Flow Label

An factor of the scalable problem in IntServ is the slowest process in core router to identify the arriving packets to corresponding admitted flows, which involves

IP header multi-field classification. Specifically, when a packet is received at a router, the next hop behavior is decided by looking into several fields on the packet header (e.g. the source and destination addresses, ports, and the transport protocol type), and then finding the appropriate entry at the local database. However, IP addresses longest prefix match-up is a both CPU time and memory storage consuming process. In addition, this operation will be even more complicated for QoS-sensitive flows, since their packets should follow exactly the same path. The worst situation is that these fields may be unavailable due to either fragmentation or encryption. Clearly, these procedures become the bottleneck in a multi-Gbps router of IntServ.

Using IPv6 20-bit flow label, which does not exist in the earlier IPv4, can be a big help in alleviating this problem. In DARM, we introduce concept of Virtual Path(VP), which connects two edge routers in the network. We then assign one flow label value to one of these VPs, and construct new (much smaller) routing tables inside the core routers of the domain, based only on flow labels. Because flow label looking up is an exact match-up, comparing to IP address longest prefix match-up, the data structure of this can be organized in a much simple and efficient manner(e.g. adopt hash technique). Here, we should emphasize that the flow label in our approach is not related to the traditional definition of a flow (i.e., a connection between a certain source-destination pair). Instead, we use the flow label field in the IP header, in order to identify a unique VP within a DARM domain. As a result, any determined VP within a domain will be assigned a specific flow label value, and all the QoS requirement packets that have to follow the path will be marked with exact corresponding flow label value.

3.3 Admission Control

In IntServ, admission control is performed by hop-by-hop signaling through network which is always a tedious process. In BB enhanced DiffServ, BB makes admission control decisions for all the entry flow in the domain. There might be some scalability considerations of a centralized manner. By introducing concept of VP and packet forwarding with flow label mechanism, in DARM, we provide a fully distributed approach where all the edge routers will independently participate in this procedure without hop-by-hop signaling.

In order to make instantaneous and independent admission control decisions for new connection requests, in DARM, edge routers maintain total amount of reserved bandwidth towards the destination. Let p as a Source edge router and Destination edge router pair(SD pair) and R_p as the total amount of reserved bandwidth of p. We assume that there are k_p VPs ($1 \leq k_p \leq K$) connected the SD pair p currently, where K is the maximal number of paths between each SD pair. Then we have $R_p = \sum_{i=1}^{k_p} r_p^i$, where r_p^i represents current reserved bandwidth on i^{th} VP of k_p VPs belonged to the SD pair p.

When a new flow connection request arrives at the source edge router of SD pair p, which includes the destination address and the required amount of bandwidth b, the source edge router will check whether there are enough resource to accommodate this flow. We denote c_p^i as the capacity of ith VP of k_p VPs belonged to the SD pair p. In particular, for each VP belonged to SD pair p, it will check whether have $r_p^i + b \leq c_p^i$, for $i = 1, 2, ..., k_p$. If none of the VP satisfies this inequality, the new flow connecting request will be rejected. Otherwise, the VP with the largest amount of residual bandwidth will be selected. Then, the packets of admitted new flow will be marked with a flow label value, which unique identify the corresponding VP in the domain. Packets marked with corresponding flow label value will be exactly forwarded along this VP through the domain.

4 Adaptive Resource Management

Adaptive resource management is the soul of the DARM framework. The main function of adaptive resource management include how to deploy(redeploy) VPs with a certain resource assigned adaptively between a SD pair, and how to probe available resource for VPs deploying(redeploying). To implement above two issues, we designed an adaptive VP deploying module and an distributed resource probing module.

4.1 Adaptive VP Deploying

In order to deploy VPs adaptively, we extend the source edge router to running a measurement process. Source edge router of each SD pair p will periodically measure (e.g. time slot $\tau = 500ms$) the total amount of reserved bandwidth R_p towards the destination. This means that each of the P routers will keep $(P-1)$ different measurements, where P is the total amount of domain edge routers. Moreover, in order to adaptively increase the capacity of a SD pair, the source edge router of which also monitors the rejected traffic load. Let Q_p as the total amount of reserved bandwidth including the rejected traffic load, which we refer to as potential reserved bandwidth. Q_p is normally updated whenever a new connection is accepted or an existing connection is terminated. However, when a new request is rejected, the edge router will update Q_p as if the request was accepted. It will also assign a virtual finish time, which may be based on some measure average call holding time. When those virtual connections are terminated, Q_p will be updated accordingly.

When we compute R_p and Q_p, exponential averaging formula[7] is adopted. Using an exponential weight gives more reliable estimation of burst traffic, even when the packet inter-arrival time of the aggregate has significant variance. Refer to [7] for detailed discussion.

Every measurement windows T (e.g. $T = 60$ seconds), the source edge router will check the Q_p, C_p, and R_p to determine resource allocation to the SD pair p, where $C_p = \sum_{i=1}^{k_p} c_p^i$ is current total capacity of SD pair p. When the bandwidth utilization $\frac{R_p}{C_p}$ for SD pair p exceeds the predefined upper threshold θ^h, the source edge router of SD pair p will initiate the increasing resource process, adapting to accommodate the increased traffic load. Whereas, if the bandwidth

```
IncreaseResource(p, Q_p, R_p, k_p)
 1:  V_p ← (Q_p − R_p)
 2:  N ← (K − k_p)
 3:  if N = 0 then
 4:      j ← i  for i ∈ { i | Min(c_p^i) ∧ ∀ i ∈ {1...K}}
 5:      PreDeleteVP(j)
 6:      (C_p^{available}, path) ← ResouceProbe(p)
 7:      if C_p^{available} > V_p + c_p^j then
 8:          CreateVP(x, p, path, V_p + c_p^j)
 9:      else
10:          CreateVP(x, p, path, C_p^{available})
11:      end if
12:      DeleteVP(j)
13:      j ← x
14:  else
15:      for i ← (k_p + 1) to (k_p + N)  do
16:          (C_p^{available}, path) ← ResouceProbe(p)
17:          if C_p^{available} < α then
18:              Break
19:          end if
20:          if C_p^{available} > V_p/N then
21:              CreateVP(i, p, path, V_p/N)
22:          else
23:              CreateVP(i, p, path, C_p^{available})
24:          end if
25:      end for
26:      k_p ← i
27:  end if
```

Fig. 1. Pseudo code of increase resource algorithm for a SD pair

utilization is under the lower threshold θ^l, the source edge router will try to shrink the capacity of the SD pair. Due to the space limit, we only give the pseudo code of resource increase algorithm for a SD pair in Fig. 1. In algorithm, source edge router will send control message to routers along the VP when performing the $CreateVP$ and $DeleteVP$ procedure. The corresponding routers will update their local flow label forwarding table upon received control message. In addition, $PreDeleteVP$ procedure is used for virtually releasing resource only for resource probing procedure to compute available resource in more accurate and reasonable way, while the details of resource probing procedure for a SD pair in the network will be discussed in section 4.2.

4.2 Distributed Resource Probing

In general, using shortest path algorithm to find a feasible path between a SD pair is a natural way to look at this problem. However, we argue that path(resource) probing algorithm in our scenario should aim to preserve (to the extent possible) the total flow available between the SD pair instead of simply aiming for the shortest path in order to ensure that the highest number (in volume) of demands are satisfied. Moreover, as reported in literature [8], for about 65% of paths measured in current Internet, there exists better alternative route. Therefore, we adopt a distributed resource probing procedure for our adaptive resource allocation between a SD pair.

Basically, the resource probing mechanism is used to generate Resource Discovery(RD) packets for probing a feasible path in the network. Upon receiving a RD packet, the router consults its local state information and modifies the fields of the RD packets accordingly and then forwards the RD packets to other router along the path to the destination edge router. The destination edge router is responsible for making a decision and sending Resources Acknowledge(RA) packet back to the source edge router.

In order to improve probing efficiency, we adopt a bounded directional probing technique. Specifically, RD packet will only be sent toward non-backward directional links to the destination edge router. Moreover, when there are multiple non-backward directional links available in a transition router, it will control the probing number in parallel. In addition, network topology is relative static state information, comparing to residual bandwidth. Therefore, every router can pre-compute every link directions to each destination edge router based on hop count information.

In practice, we follow the general procedure to represent the network by a graph $G = (V, E)$, where V denotes the set of routers and E denotes the set of communication links connecting the routers. Let s as an arbitrary router of the DARM domain. Then, we denotes $V(s)$ as the set of neighbors of router s, $U(s)$ as the set of edge routers of the domain, $O_{(s,v)}[u]$ as the link (s, v) direction of router s to destination u, and $H_s[u]$ as the shortest distance(hop) computed using the Dijkstra's algorithm from router s to router u. Then, we give pseudo code of direction per-computing algorithm as showing in Fig. 2, which is extended from literature [9]. From pseudo code, we can find that the computational complexity of this procedure is $(1 + |V(s)|)$ times that of Dijkstra's algorithm.

We now consider resource probing between a SD pair by using different combinations of forward and/or neutral links and identify the best path(s). To explore a readily available path and corresponding resource between a SD pair, the source edge router sends a RD packet through its forward links towards the given destination. Each receiving router does the same, i.e., selects one of its forward links and sends the RD packets through that link until the RD packets reach to the destination. Along the followed paths, each router updates the available resource information accumulated in the RD packets and adds its ID to the path vector carried in the RD packets.

Actually, neuter links can also be selected at each router. However, before the next neutral link, we should select at least one forward link so that the possibility of encountering a routing loop will completely disappear.

A key issue is how to select the next links at each router. In this paper, we consider a traffic engineering approach. Let L_t as the set of candidate next links at router t and l is one of its outgoing link, where $t \in V$, $L_t \subseteq E$, and $l \in L_t$.

```
ComputeDirection(G, s)
/*computing every link direction at router s.*/
 1: H_s[ ] ← Dijkstra(G, s)
 2: V(s) ← GetNeighborRouters(G, s)
 3: U(s) ← GetEdgeRouters(G)
 4: for all v ∈ V(s) do
 5:    H_v[ ] ← Dijkstra(G, v)
 6: end for
 7: for all v ∈ V(s) do
 8:    for all u ∈ U(s) do
 9:       if H_s[u] > H_v[u] then
10:          O_(s,v)[u] ← forward
11:       end if
12:       if H_s[u] = H_v[u] then
13:          O_(s,v)[u] ← neutral
14:       end if
15:       if H_s[u] < H_v[u] then
16:          O_(s,v)[u] ← backward
17:       end if
18:    end for
19: end for
```

Fig. 2. Pseudo code of directions computing algorithm

we denote C_l and R_l as bandwidth capacity of link l and residual bandwidth of link l respectively. For each $l \in L_t$, the bandwidth residual ratio u_l is computed as $u_l = \frac{R_l}{C_l}$.

Let F_t is set of selected next links for forwarding, and then F_t must follow condition as Equation (1).

$$\begin{cases} |F_t| \leq \beta \\ u_l \geq \gamma, for\ \forall\ l \in F_t \\ u_j \geq u_k, for\ \forall\ j \in F_t\ and\ \forall\ k \in \{L_t - F_t\} \end{cases} \quad (1)$$

where β and γ is two constant (e.g. $\beta = 3, \gamma = 0.1$), which represent the maximal number of resource probing in parallel and lower threshold of physical link residual bandwidth ratio, respectively.

According to the above conditions, we can find that the resource probing will pursue the maximum residual bandwidth path, which can balance the network load and improve global resource utilization.

For $\forall\ l \in L_t$ and having $u_l < \gamma$, we can conclude $F_t = \emptyset$, which means that no more bandwidth is available at router t. Then the router t will drop the RD packet. We should point out that the transit routers drop the invalid resource probing packets as early as possible, which can help to relieve the parallel probing overheads significantly. When the destination router receives a RD packet, it will still wait δ time expecting to receive all available RD packets. Here, δ is maximal end-to-end packet transmission delay. Then it will select a best result and send a RA packet back to corresponding source edge router. If the source edge router dose not receive RA packet in 3δ after sending RD packet, it will conclude that there are no more available resource between the SD pair.

5 Simulation Results

We simulated the proposed framework in the MCI Internet topology of Fig. 3, which has been widely used in many studies (e.g. [10]). We assume that all the links have a capacity of 2.5 Gbps, and that all the capacity may be allocated to QoS flows. In a real network, though, the service provider will allocate a portion of the available bandwidth to QoS-sensitive traffic, according to some policy.

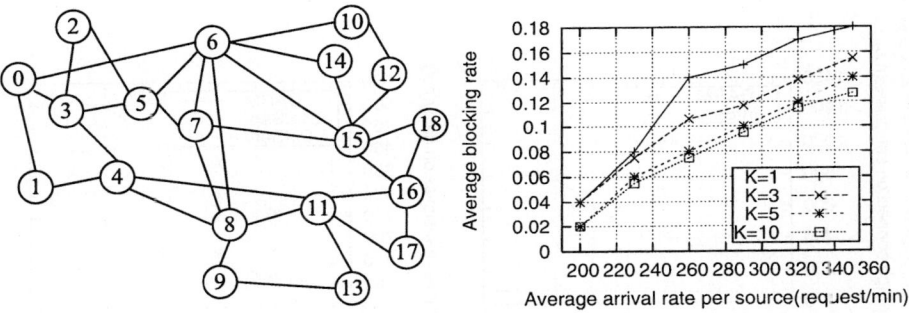

Fig. 3. The simulated network topology(MCI)

Fig. 4. Average blocking rate comparison for different K

The new QoS requests may arrive at any one of the 19 routers. The new QoS requests arriving at each router v follows Poisson distribution with mean λ_v. The arrival rates for the different routers are taken as uniformly distributed in the interval $[1, \lambda_{max}]$. The value of λ_{max} is properly adjusted in order to control the average arrival rate per router. The duration of each admitted connection obeys exponentially distributed with mean 25 minute. The required bandwidth of every QoS request is uniformly distributed in the interval $[64, 1024]$ kbps. The every simulation is last 12 hours. We begin fetch the data after an initial warm-up period.

First, we investigate the impact of the two main parameters of the DARM system, namely the maximal number of paths K between the each SD pair and resource adaptive reconfiguration window T. Fig. 4 illustrates that setting up more than 1 paths per SD pair can improve global performance significantly. However, we also find that the additional performance gain by moving K from 3 to 10 is very small. On the other hand, window T controls the sensitivity of the adaptive reconfiguration and tradeoffs the reconfiguration overheads. From what Fig. 5 showing, $T = 3min$ can gain satisfied performance in the simulation. In the rest of simulation, we adopt $K = 5$ and $T = 3min$ respectively.

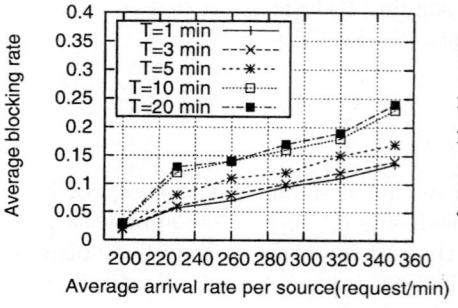

Fig. 5. Average blocking rate comparison for different T

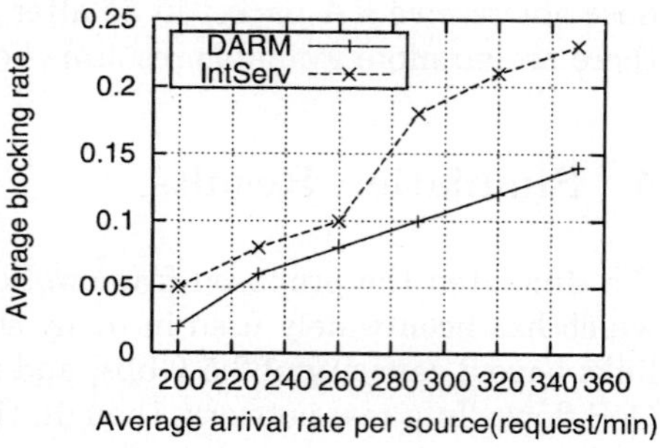

Fig. 6. Average blocking rate comparison between the IntServ and DARM

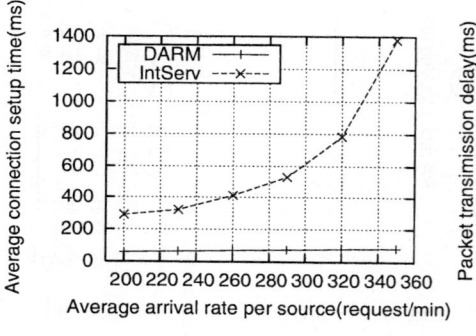
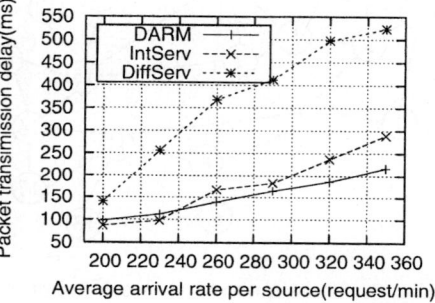

Fig. 7. Average connection setup time comparison between the IntServ and DARM

Fig. 8. Packet transmission delay comparison for IntServ, DiffServ, and DARM

Then, we compare the DARM performance with IntServ and DiffServ scheme. In comparing the performance of DARM and IntServ, the four performance metrics are used, namely average blocking rate, average per connection setup time, and the average and variance of the packet transmission delay. Note that since neither admission control nor signaling messages are employed in DiffServ, only the performance metrics of the average and variance of the packet transmission delay are used in comparing the performance of DARM with what of DiffServ. Fig. 6 and Fig. 7 show the average blocking rate and average per connection setup time of IntServ and DARM. We can find that DARM outperforms the IntServ on both metrics. This is because that due to adaptive resource reconfiguration and distributed resource probing, DARM is capable of providing more bandwidth between the SD pair comparing to IntServ with traditional shortest path first routing mechanism. Moreover, DARM makes admission control decisions in a distributed and local manner without hop-by-hop signaling, which results in a significantly faster process of per connection setup. Fig. 8 and Fig. 9

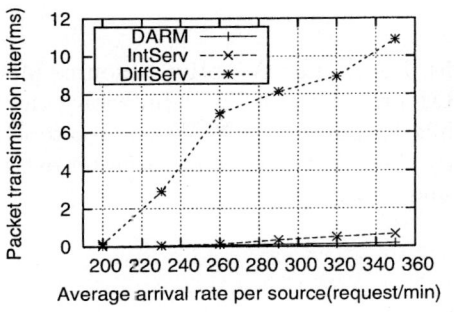 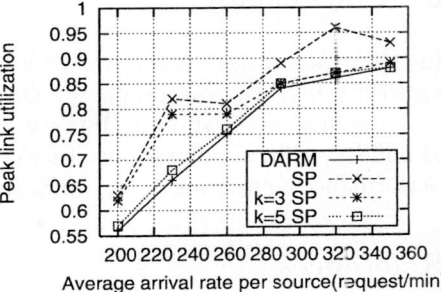

Fig. 9. Packet transmission jitter comparison for IntServ, DiffServ, and DARM

Fig. 10. Peak link utilization comparison between proposed approach and k-shortest path

exhibit average and variance of the packet transmission delay of the simulation traffic for the IntServ, DiffServ, and DARM.

Finally, since the main objective of traffic engineering is to optimize the global utilization of network resource, in the rest of simulation, we compare the performance of proposed distributed resource probing approach in DARM with Shortest Path(SP) scheme and k-shortest path scheme. Shortest path scheme has higher peak link utilization than others(see Fig. 10), which is anticipated, because shortest path scheme tends to overload the links that belong to the shortest paths. For a same level of traffic load, the combination of higher average link utilization and lower average blocking rate generally implies higher throughput. The proposed resource probing approach outperform k-shortest path scheme with higher the average resource utilization and lower blocking rate as showing in Fig. 11 and Fig. 12, respectively.

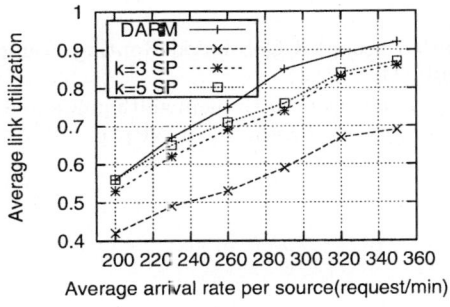 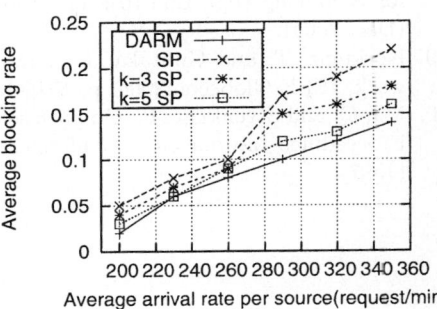

Fig. 11. Average link utilization comparison between proposed approach and k-shortest path

Fig. 12. Average blocking rate comparison between proposed approach and k-shortest path

6 Conclusions

In this paper, a new QoS framework with Distributed Adaptive Resource Management(DARM), was proposed. DARM provides per-flow admission control and resource reservation as IntServ while keeping the salability characteristic as DiffServ. The simulation results clearly show that DARM has a better overall performance comparing to the IntServ and DiffServ.

References

1. Faucheur, F., Wu, L., Davie, B., Davari, S., Vaananen, P., Krishnan, R., Cheval, P., and Heinanen, J.: MPLS support of differentiated services. IETF RFC 3270, (May. 2002).
2. Faucheur, F., Nadeau, T.D., Chiu, A., Townsend, W., Skalecki, D., and Tatham, M.: Requirements for support of Diff-Serv-aware MPLS traffic engineering. Workin progress (Internet draft), (Feb. 2003).
3. Bakiras, S., and Victor, L.:A scalable architecture for end-to-end QoS provisioning, Elsevier computer commnicaitons, vol.27, p.1330-1340, (2004).
4. Acharya, S., Chang, Y. J., Gupta, B., Risbood, P., and Srivastava, A.: Precomputing High Quality Routes for Bandwidth Guaranteed Traffic, IEEE Globecom2004, p. 1202-1207, (Dec. 2004).
5. Yang, M., Huang, Y., Kim, J., Lee, M., Suda, T., and Daisuke, M.: An End-to-End QoS Framework with On-Demand Bandwidth Reconfiguration, IEEE INFOCOMM2004, p. 2072-2083, (Jun. 2004).
6. Korkmaz, T. and Krunz, M.: Hybrid flooding and tree-based broadcasting for reliable and efficient link-state dissemination. IEEE GLOBECOMM2002, volume 3, p. 2400-2404, (Nov. 2002).
7. Stoica, I., Shenker, S., and Zhang, H.: Core-stateless Fair Queueing: Achieving Approximately Fair Bandwidth Allocation in High Speed Networks, in Proceeding of ACM SIGCOMM98, Vancouver, Canada, (1998).
8. Cheng, C., Huang, Y., Kung, H.T., and Wu, C.: Path Probing Relay Routing for Achieving High End-to-End Performance, IEEE Globecom2004, p. 1359-1365, (Dec. 2004).
9. Korkmaz, T. and Guntaka, J.:State-Path Decoupled QoS-based Routing Framework, IEEE Globecom2004, p. 1515-1519, (Dec. 2004).
10. Ma, Q. and Steenkiste, P.: On path selection for traffic with bandwidth guarantees, Proceedings International Conference on Network Protocols (ICNP), p. 191-202, (1997).

Scheduling Latency Insensitive Computer Vision Tasks

Richard Y.D. Xu[1] and Jesse S. Jin[2]

[1] Faculty of Information Technology, University of Technology, Sydney,
Broadway NSW 2007 Australia
richardx@it.uts.edu.au
[2] School of Design, Communication & I.T, The University of Newcastle,
Callaghan, NSW 2308, Australia
jesse@newcastle.edu.au

Abstract. In recent times, there are increasing numbers of computer vision and pattern recognition (CVPR) technologies being applied to real time video processing using single processor PCs. However, these multiple computational expensive tasks are generating bottlenecks in real-time processing. We propose a scheme to achieve both high throughput and accommodation to user-specified scheduling rules. The scheduler is then distributing 'slices' of the latency insensitive tasks such as video object recognition and facial localization among the latency sensitive ones. We show our proposed work in detail, and illustrating its application in a real-time e-learning streaming system. We also provide discussions into the scheduling implementations, where a novel concept using interleaved SIMD execution is discussed. The experiments have indicated successful scheduling results on a high end consumer grade PC.

1 Introduction

In current times, majority of PCs are adopting a single CPU configuration. When application software requires running multiple tasks in parallel on a single CPU, the application level scheduler, are used to determine which thread is being executed on the CPU at a given slice of time by various scheduling methods [1].

Traditionally, most video streaming requires only minimal processing. These processing is limited to video compression, changing resolutions and frame rates. For this reason, the type of video scheduling involved only takes into consideration of information on video bit-stream domain. For example, in [2], author presents two application level scheduling for periodic video processing. These policies are used for hard real-time deadline scheduling. Both of these policies are generated according to video types, frame size and frame rate. The information on video content is completely ignored by the scheduler.

Our motivation lies in our real-time E-learning application [3] where a set of CVPR algorithms are used. These algorithms include object recognition based on SIFT [4] algorithm, frontal face detection using Haar-alike features [5], laser pointer detections using integral features, teaching object and instructor tracking based on mean shift tracking algorithm [6]. In addition, we have used both static and PTZ camera, where in many circumstances, video processing from both streams can occur simultaneously.

Some of these tasks, for example tracking, is executed continuously and dependant on its past processing information (locations of tracked object in previous frame) for current video frame processing. Some task, such as object recognition needs to be executed periodically and independent to its past processing.

Many existing approaches have used specialized processor to achieve real-time processing and high frame rate output, such as using multi-processors and cluster computers [7]. Other literatures are found on parallelizing computer vision algorithms on single processor for real time performance. However most of these contributions are concentrated on parallel processing of a particular CVPR algorithm, rather than a set of continuous tasks [8]. In addition, most existing scheduling methods have focused on maximum throughputs and ignoring end user requirements. In our interactive, peer-to-peer E-learning system, these requirements are important and often vary from application to application.

2 Parallel CVPR Processing Properties in Synchronous E-learning

To address the parallel processing challenges in our current e-learning application, we need to derive am appropriate scheduling method. There are a few properties in a synchronous application, where we can explore them to achieve scheduling more effectively and more meaningful:

The first property is from an application and participant factor, where time response tolerance to a particular vision event needs to be customized from a high level. The second property is the nature of content based video processing:

2.1 Task Latency Sensitivities

In a real time application, each event or algorithm has different levels of sensitivities to time delays, such as video capture, compression and streaming task is highly sensitive to latency, as each frame must be processed and delivered in real time with minimum fluctuation to a pre-specified quality. On the other hand, most video detection tasks can allow longer delays in processing times. For example, if a scheduler policy made teaching object recognition to execute two more seconds, it will not introduce significant quality degradation to the overall student's multimedia viewing. We have listed latency sensitivities for each algorithm used in our work in Table 1:

Table 1. Video task time latency sensitivity

Tasks	Latency sensitivity
Object Recognition	Insensitive
Face identification	Insensitive
Object Tracking	Sensitive, but minor delays is tolerable, if objects or camera has slow motions
Laser Pointer detection	Sensitive
Video capture, compression, streaming	Sensitive

Although some video tasks can be insensitive to latency, however, the spatial information may be inconsistent as current video frame content may vary from when the task first commenced. For example, when the system performs teaching object recognition as shown in Figure 1 (a), when task started, the object is at location indicated by the bounding box. When the task is completed, the object has moved to a different location, shown in Figure 1 (b). This spatial inconstancy has caused unacceptable result in streaming, such as incorrect link building and subsequent tracking would be lost. Therefore, we must also recover the spatial relationships between the detected object with respect to the current video frame. Since this process contributes only overhead to processing, therefore, its computation must be efficient. This is discussed detail in later section 3.3.

Fig. 1. Spatial discrepancy caused by time-delaying processing. (a) The location of object when it is first detected (b) The object moves to a different location in current video frame after detection completes.

2.2 Instructor's High Level Input to Vision Events

As stated in the beginning of this paper, scheduling policy can be made more meaningful if e-learning participant's factor is also being considered. This is because instructor may choose different delay tolerance to an event during a real-time session, or at different times within the same session. Although instructor lacks unawareness to CVPR algorithm used, however, specification can be made from a high-level vision event and propagates to corresponding algorithm(s) by the system. This specification ability allowing greater flexibility to pre-configure the system adapting to different application needs.

For a vision based synchronous e-learning, this awareness in "event processing time" is important to an instructor from an HCI perspective. For example, if an instructor is aware that a four seconds delay in recognition was pre-specified, then during a synchronous session, instructor can be made sure that teaching object must remain in camera view for at least four seconds.

2.2.1 Examples to Instructor's High Level Inputs
An example of such specification is shown in Figure 2. The instructor specifies teaching object recognition event must be executed every 4 seconds interval during particular part of his teaching. At the same time, instructor may consider streaming at 15 FPS is sufficient during a recognition phase.

Another example is that system can be waiting for multiple possible events, such as teaching object recognition, face detection and laser pointer detection to occur during initialization. These events are occurring periodically to avoid CPU congestion. Using the same instructor's high level event scripting, each vision event interval can be specified prior to an e-learning session. Note that instructor's specification are only made as "rules of guidance", where our scheduler is trying to generate policy to best accommodate.

2.2.2 Methods to Instructor's High Level Input

The first problem is that instructor has no knowledge to the nature of the vision algorithms. For this reason, instructor's latency tolerance inputs are made through the scripting interface [3] abstracted to high level vision events. Figure 2 is an event tolerance scripting example:

```
On_Customized_Event (long currentT)
   ...
   If event.Recognition.returnObj = Nothing Then
      Duration.max.Recognition = 3000
      Duration.min.Streaming = 66 // 15FPS
   End if
   ...
```

Fig. 2. Instructor specifies the time tolerance to vision events using high level scripting

Another problem is that instructor lacks default values to vision executions time on his PC, i.e. instructor does not know how long each event really takes. For this reasons, we will perform a benchmark collection to calculate processing time required for each algorithm. This process is only required whenever a PC setting has changed. It will record processing time against various benchmarked video and image, where average processing values are being used as default execution time required for an event.

The same type of off-line benchmarking is also used to construct execution time histogram modeling. For the later case, training is being made in accordance with video frame features generated by EPGF for each entry in a hash table.

In the case of collecting default value for instructor's scripting, the process execution time is simplified to obtaining information according to video frame sizes. As instructor's specification is only an indication to final scheduling policy, accuracy is not critical in the scripting stage.

2.3 Content Dependant Execution

Unlike traditional video scheduling proposed in [2], some CVPR algorithm execution time dose not only depending on its data bit domain, it is also relating to video content features for that algorithm. The processing times may vary dramatically from frames of the same video.

Therefore, in order to 'place' portions of the video processing accurately and fairly into each frame delivery, an execution time prediction method is required prior to or during an initial computation of algorithm's execution.

In our work, our motivation lies into our hypothesis that, for each algorithm, there is some rules can be made, resulted from an "overhead processing". This "overhead processing" can determine how long it will take to execute this algorithm. In addition, if we group the execution times containing similar features together and model them statistically, we can predicate how long a content based vision algorithm will take to execute on the current video frame. Therefore, the remaining challenge is how to derive this processing predication function for each algorithm and how to model them accurately. In addition, we also need to ensure the efficiency of this processing predication function, as this function contributes only overhead. We will also present experimental results proving the validity of our hypothesis.

3 Scheduling System Design

The scheduling system is depicted in the following diagram:

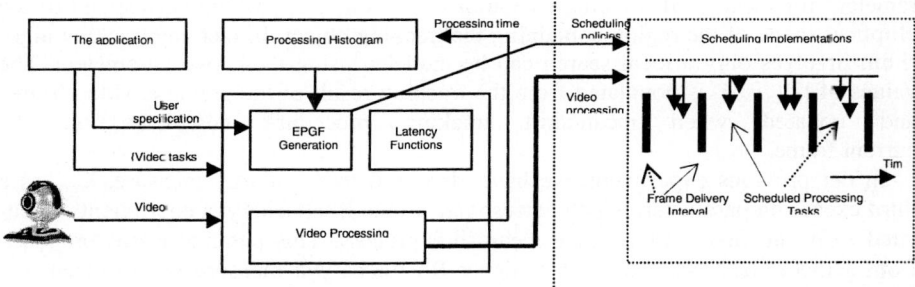

Fig. 3. Scheduler system diagram

The scheduling policy takes account of all the factors influences a video processing including instructor's high level inputs, current video frame and current vision algorithms sets. The scheduler then generates the policy accordingly. There are three modules which we will present in detail as our unique contributions:

1. The Execution Parameter Generation Function (EPGF) subsystem is an "overhead video processing" that generates parameters which predicates the execution time of each algorithm required in our e-learning application. In this paper, we will present EPGF for mean shift tracking and SIFT generation algorithm.
2. The Processing History Modeling subsystem considers the EPGF parameters being generated and produces a predication base on the histogram with similar parameters values.
3. The Latency recovery function subsystem is used to recover spatial discrepancy between a processed and current video frame, as stated in 2.1

3.1 Execution-Time Parameters Generation Function (EPGF)

As we stated previously, our hypothesis is to use an efficient "overhead" processing to predict an entire algorithm execution time. We have also stated we would model such information statistically for later execution predication. Therefore, parameter extraction from these "overhead" processing can achieve both of our purposes. We name such parameter generation, Execution-time Parameter Generation Function (EPGF). EPGF function is unique for every CVPR algorithm. This method was proposed by us in [9].

Currently, in our work, there are various CVPR algorithms needs to be executed in parallel. Note that EPGF is not applicable to some algorithms such as laser pointer detection and face detection based on [5]. Both of these algorithms are using integral images. Integral images have theoretically resulted constant execution times which made predication only dependant on capturing video size.

Therefore, in our work, our current EPGF implementation has been based on the mean-shift Tracking [6] and object recognition using local invariant features, SIFT [4]:

Mean shift tracking. In our work, since tracked object can have variable sizes which determined from an adaptive bandwidth scheme described by [6]. The intuitive parameters for mean-shift tracking execution time is λ_x, λ_y, which correspond to the elliptical shape of the region containing the tracking object. In fact any tracking algorithm involves only a local search can be modeled using these two parameters. The values of [λ_x, λ_y] is populated from the tracking result of the previous video frame, and updated when mean-shift tracking procedure completes on the current frame.

In our previous experiment, we have also used the similarity measure, λ_{barta} as a third execution parameter, which corresponds to the Bhattacharyya coefficients calculated from the first iteration of a mean-shift process. This parameter was proposed from a theoretical assumption that higher Bhattacharyya measure would mean less mean-shift iterations required before this algorithm converges (See [6]for detail). However, the experiment result has found that parameters containing only [λ_x, λ_y] is sufficiently for modeling.

SIFT generation. Since most of computation in object recognition occurs in the SIFT points generations, the post-SIFT computations, include approximate nearest neighbor (ANN) search, Generalized Hough Transform and distance outlier removal are not being used from parameterization.

From analyzing SIFT algorithms, we have used a three parameters EPGF [λ_{width}, λ_{height}, λ_{smooth}] where first two parameters are the size of video frame or region of interest (ROI) for SIFT computation if any pre processing is used. They are both content independent.

λ_{smooth} is a measure to how "smooth" the image is, since SIFT algorithm searches the stable points using Difference of Gaussian (DoG), the more smooth image, the less scale stable points identified, hence less computation is required. In the EPGF modeling, we use binary counts to the first DoG filtered image.

$$DoG = G(x, y, k\sigma_1) * I(x, y) - G(x, y, k\sigma_2) * I(x, y)$$

where G is the Gaussian kernel derivative and I is the current video frame. σ_1 and σ_2 are the first two variable variances used in the Gaussian kernel.

3.1.1 Minimum Overhead EPGF

The above two EPGF are designed which to generate parameters at minimum cost or from an initial part of the algorithm.

For tracking algorithm, the values for [λ_x, λ_y] are obtained from tracking process in the previous video frame. For recognition, parameter λ_{smooth} is generated from a DoG function using the first two variances of Gaussian Kernel derivatives. This computation also forms part of overall SIFT process. The only overhead involved is the binary counting on the DoG image, which can be obtained efficiently. In addition, EPGF itself involves fast computation, which can be computed in < 0.01% of the overall algorithm.

3.2 Execution Time Histogram Modeling

From EPGF, we have obtained two types of information, the feature parameter and the corresponding execution time. We then can model this information statistically.

3.2.1 Necessity of Statistical Modeling

Some reader may argue on the necessity of execution histogram modeling. As we have pointed out that EPGF usually forms an initial part of an algorithm. The software developer can therefore trace through an algorithm code and to determine in exact number of instructions required for the rest of computation based on the outcome of the initial computation.

However, developing computer vision algorithms in current day research are made easier by having many libraries for low level image processing functionaries. In many instances, source code of these libraries is not being made available to developers. In addition, code scan approach takes enormous amount of manual effort. In our work, we have achieved the execution time predication from a high level algorithm approach.

3.2.2 Offline Benchmarking and Online Training

Offline benchmarking is required prior to first real-time streaming or there is a change in instructor's PC setting. This is because initially, the e-learning system has no knowledge to instructor's PC specification and hence there is no scheduler modeling information to begin with. Similar to the method used to collect execution time which allows instructor to script latency tolerance level, the same benchmark is to collect information where execution time can be modeled.

In online execution training, as soon as a video task is completed, its actual execution time and parameters generated are being inserted PC's memory. When a real-time session finishes, the memory is dumped to the database for modeling. This modeling is used for later sessions.

3.2.3 Execution Time Histogram Modeling

Our execution time modeling is inspired by [10], where a running average of pixel color from training/benchmarking is used to classify if a pixel belongs to the background in real-time. Base on the same methodology (different purpose), in our work, we will use histogram to model execution times for predication. Indicated by our hypothesis, that video frame generates similar parameters may contain similar processing times. Therefore, for each algorithm, we use a hash table, and each entry of the hash table contains a Gaussian model fitting. This work is detailed in [11]

3.3 Latency Recovery Functions

Since computational expensive object detection is scheduled to process in a delayed manner. As a result, there may be a spatial discrepancy between the processing and current video frame when object detection completes. An example of this phenomenon was illustrated in Figure 2. In the same section, we also state the necessity to locate the detected object in the current frame by an efficient method. In our current work, the latency recovery procedure is achieved using the following algorithm:

Step 1: When a video recognition task commences, we will buffer the processing image.

Step 2: The detected region is used to calculate target probability distribution function (pdf) used for mean-shift tracking [6].

Step 3: When object recognition execution completes, we will compute the optical flow [12]between the processing and current video frame, using only features from the detected regions.

Step 4: A region is estimated from the result of optical flow, based on which mean-shift tracking starts.

We have performed several experiment on this latency function procedure, and noticed that its computation usually takes less than few milliseconds to complete.

4 Empirical Results on Scheduling

We have tested our scheduling work using PC with specification Pentium M 1.6 GHZ, 512 MB RAM. The objective is to verify if algorithms are being scheduled close to high level specification. Each algorithm is running in its own thread, the start and stop of the thread is according to the scheduling policies determined from instructor's high level input and execution time predication (current video feature and execution modeling).

The results are shown in Table 3 for two sets of latency tolerance levels. In (a), the specification is: recognition at 3 seconds interval maximum; Face detection at 2 second interval maximum; and video frame output rate at 20FPS minimum; In (b), the specification is: recognition at 5 seconds interval maximum; face detection at 0.5 second interval maximum; Video frame output rate at 20FPS minimum; In both cases, the left over CPU burst is allocated to tracking.

The input static camera view is set at 640*480 resolutions and output video is at 320 * 240 resolutions. We have turn off all other applications to ensure maximum CPU availability.

The results have achieved is very close to the specified high level scheduling rules. In both cases, we have achieved desired frame rate around 20 FPS, object recognition task is being scheduled in a delayed but not far from the 0.33 HZ and 0.2 HZ respectively. Face detection is being executed around 0.5HZ and 1.8 HZ. The rest of CPU burst to tracking is performed around 5.2 and 4 HZ respectively. The slight fluctuation to the excepted results may have caused by context switching and other background PC operations.

Table 2. Number of completed tasks

	Video 1	Video 2
Total play time in milliseconds	68330	182820
# processed output frame	1298	3424
FPS	18.99	18.72
Completed SIFT	19	32
Completed Face detection	33	334
Completed Tracking	358	768

5 Discussions

In this paper, we have presented experimental results for a novel approach to schedule multiple content dependent video processing tasks using instructor's PC. We have achieved our aim in showcasing a system that accurately predicate the completion of tasks using unique execution time parameter generation functions (EPGF) and histogram modeling for video tasks incorporated in our e-learning work.

Although in this work, we have used many concepts that may seem only appropriate to e-learning scenarios, such as instructor adjusted latency time and the spatial discrepancy recoverable functions, but we argue that many of the scheduling policy generation can also be applied to other systems requiring multiple CVPR tasks. We also argue that most parts of our framework are also valid, if we are to apply this method to parallel and even distributed processing environment.

6 Attempt to Parallel Execution Using Interleaved SIMD

To further enhancing the scheduling efficiency, one experiment we have performed is to explore the potential use of Interleaved Single Instruction Multiple Data (SIMD) instructions to schedule multiple algorithms.

SIMD is found in most modern day PC. SIMD processing allows multiple data elements to be operated by a single instruction to run sequential instructions in parallel. An abstract illustration of our proposed interleaved SIMD instruction is shown in Figure 4.

In essence, by using interleaved SIMD, we are aiming to achieve fine-grained parallelism based on merging independent processes (vision algorithms) into a single monolithic process in an attempt to artificially induce SIMD parallelism.

During our experiment, several manual modifications to the existing video processing source codes were performed in order to achieve Interleaved SIMD. We forced the program to keep the potentially SIMD merge-able tasks into the same type, using *integer* and *float* data types. We argue its feasibility, as normally, *double float* precision is not required for computer vision applications. We also modified the program in such as way that mutual exclusion was always the case between the merging functions.

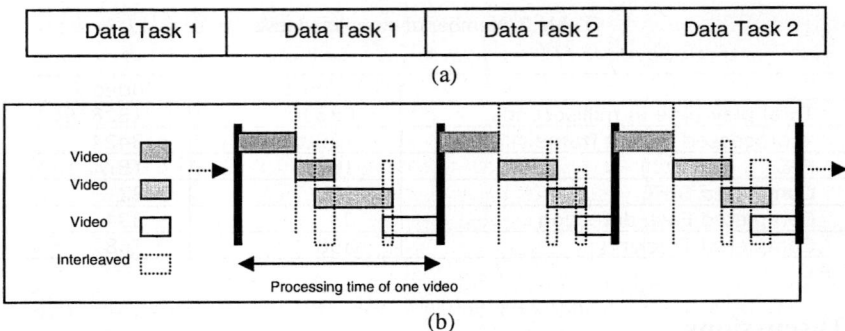

Fig. 4. Parallel scheduling enhancement using interleaved SIMD, (a) shows a 4 SIMD data type registers, (b) is shows the CPU Burst using interleaved SIMD, note some "interleaved" threads are now processed in "true" parallel.

However, contrary to our thoughts, the interleaved SIMD instruction has not achieved much system performance enhancements, where in most cases the degradation was notices. Our preliminary analysis into the root cause was using profile matching and the Superword Level Parallelism (SLP) algorithm [13] shown in Appendix. Therefore, much future studies are required to see how and where we would benefit from including interleaved SIMD execution, a novel and theologically sound method as a candidate for scheduling implementation.

Reference:

1. A. Silberschatz, P. B. Galvin, G. Gagne, *Process Management*, in *Operating System Concepts (7th Edition)*. 2004, John Wiley & Sons. p. 153-189.
2. Tanenbaum, S., *Multimedia Process scheduling on Modern operating systems*, in *Modern Operating Systems*. 2001, Prentice Hall.
3. Richard Y. D. Xu, Jesse S. Jin, John G. Allen. *Framework for Script Based Virtual Directing and Multimedia Authoring in Live Video Streaming.* in *The 11th International Multi-Media Modelling Conference (MMM2005)*. 2005. Melbourne, Australia.
4. Lowe, D., *Distinctive image features from scale invariant key points.* International Journal of Computer Vision, 2004. **60**(2): p. 91-110.
5. P. Viola, M. Jones. *Rapid object detection using a boosted cascade of simple features.* in *CVPR 2001*. 2001.
6. D. Comaniciu, V. Ramesh, P. Meer, *Kernel-Based Object Tracking*. IEEE Trans. Pattern Analysis and Machine Intelligence, 2003. **25**(5): p. 564-575.
7. Gerhard Klimeck, Gary Yagi, Robert Deen, Myche McAuley, Eric DeJong, Fabiano Oyafuso. Near Real-Time Parallel Image Processing using Cluster Computers. in International Conference on Space Mission Challenges for Information Technology (SMC-IT). 2003. Pasadena, CA.
8. A. R. J. François, G. G. Medioni. A Modular Software Architecture for Real-Time Video Processing. in the Second International Workshop on Computer Vision Systems. 2001.

9. Richard Y. D. Xu, John G. Allen, Jesse S. Jin. Constant video frame control under multiple periodic content dependant video processing. in Pan-Sydney Area Workshop on Visual Information Processing (VIP2004). Sydney, Australia.
10. C. Wren, A. Azarbayejani, T. Darrell, A. Pentland, Pfinder:Real-time Tracking of the Human Body. IEEE Trans. on Patt. Anal. and Machine Intell, 1997. 19(7): p. 780-785.
11. Richard Y. D. Xu, Jesse S. Jin. Latency Insensitive Task Scheduling for Real-Time Video Processing and Streaming. in To appear in Advanced Concepts for Intelligent Vision Systems (Acivs2005). 2005. Antwerp, Belgium.
12. Tomasi, J. Shi and C. Good features to track. in IEEE Conf. on Computer Vision and Pattern Recognition (CVPR94). 1994. Seattle.
13. Amarasinghe, S. Larsen and S. Exploiting Superword Level Parallelism with Multimedia Instruction Sets. in SIGPLAN'00 Conference on programming Language Design and Implementation. 2000. Vancouver, B.C.

Appendix: Profile Matching for SIMD execution

We define a *profile* as high or low-level program representation of the independent video tasks that describes the combinations of control statements that make up the program. If two or more task components can be identified as having matching *profiles* (based on a relatively strict set of matching rules) then those components might be merged as shown in Figure 5 in a process similar to the *if-conversion* used in vectorizing compiles. Since this process preserves program semantics and does not prevent the execution of code in vector units, the resulting code might be parallelizable for SIMD hardware even though the original independent tasks were not.

Note that once we have identified components that could potentially merge, it is a necessary phase to determine whether or not it is profitable to do so. Profitable situations might include:

```
proc1() {                                proc() {
    for(init1(); cond1(); incr1())           for(init1(),init2(); cond1()||cond1(); incr1(), incr2())
    body1();                                 {
}                                                if(cond1()) body1();
proc2() {                                        if(cond2()) body2();
    for(init2(); cond2(); incr2())           }
    body1();                             }
}
proc1(float A[]) {                       proc(float A1[], float A2[]) {
    for(i=1; i < N; i++)                     for(i1=0, i2=0; i1 < N1 || i2 < N2; i1++,i2++)
    A[i] = A[i-1] + 1.0;                     {
}                                                A1[i1] = (i1 < N1) ? A1[i1-1] + 1.0 : A1[i1];
proc1(float A[]) {                               A2[i1] = (i2 < N2) ? A2[i2-1] + 4.0 : A2[i2];
    for(i=1; i < N; i++)                     }
    A[i] = A[i-1] + 4.0;                 }
```

Fig. 5. Processes merged using if-conversion and example

- The components contain the same (or similar) sequences of statements
- The components have identical control conditions (which effectively eliminate the requirement of if-conversion) or the program can be transformed to nearly achieve this criteria.

- The components only minimally access memory locations in an indirect manner (indirect memory accesses will make vectorization expensive due total overhead of packing and unpacking data).
- The components have pairings of the same instruction *opcodes* (note: these criteria can be at least partially induced by acyclic condensation of the data dependence graph to determine the singleton nodes for each component.
- The local data for the independent tasks can be packed into adjacent positions on the stack.
- The components are not already completely vectorized for SIMD execution.

Based on these criteria in our initial analyses, it illustrates that only code with very similar execution profiles can gain benefit interleaved SIMD execution.

Throughput Analysis for Fully-Connected Ad Hoc Network with Multiuser Detection[*]

Xiaocong Qian[1,2], Baoyu Zheng[2], and Genjian Yu [2]

[1] Department of Electronic Engineering,
Shanghai JiaoTong University,200030 Shanghai, China
qianxiaocong@sjtu.edu.cn
[2] Institute of Signal and Information Processing,
Nanjing Univ. of Posts and Telecom.,210003 Nanjing, China
{zby, ygj}@njupt.edu.cn

Abstract. The importance of multiuser detection for CDMA-based ad hoc network is addressed in this paper. Conventionally, the terminal in CDMA-based ad hoc network uses matched filter to receive packets, so the performance (e.g., throughput) of the network suffers from multi-access interference (MAI). Different from above scheme, in this paper, each terminal of the ad hoc network is equipped with an adaptive blind linear multiuser detector, so the ability of MAI-resistance is gained. Based on fully-connected network model and Log-distance path loss radio propagation model, the throughput of ad hoc network with multiuser detection is studied. Simulation results show that multiuser detection can remarkably enlarge the throughput of ad hoc network.

1 Introduction

Since Code Division Multi-access(CDMA) system has advantages such as larger capacity, graceful signal degradation, multipath resistance, inherent frequency diversity, etc, it's a wise choice to use CDMA for mobile ad hoc networks. Recently, Bao analyzed the throughput for CDMA-based ad hoc network employing slotted-Aloha random access protocols [1]. In his analysis, each node of ad hoc network was assumed to have the capability of receiving multiple packets simultaneously, and near-far effect was ignored. But for a practical CDMA-based ad hoc system, receiver-based spreading-code protocol [2] is often adopted, thus it is impossible for a node to receive multiple packets destined to it at the same time. Besides, near-far effect should be considered because it usually affects the performance of mobile ad hoc networks greatly. Power control is a method to alleviate near-far effect, at the cost of decreasing the rate of channel utilization or sacrificing system bandwidth [3]. In this paper, we solve near-far effect by signal processing technique. We know that near-far effect is caused by MAI, and multiuser detection is an effective method to suppress MAI. We believe that if multiuser detection is used for a terminal to receive packets, throughput can be raised. A few papers about applying multiuser detection on ad hoc networks have been reported in recent years [4-6]. The throughput of CDMA-based ad hoc network combined with multiuser detection is firstly analyzed by us in [7],

---

[*] Supported by the National Natural Science Foundation of China(No.60372107).

where free space propagation model is adopted during throughput analysis and simulations. But practical radio propagation is much more complicated than free space propagation. Consequently, though the results in [7] have qualitative meaning, they are disaccord with those in practice. In this paper, Log-distance path loss model is adopted to describe the mobile radio propagation, which characterizes indoor radio propagation well. Based on this model, the throughput of ad hoc network with multiuser detection is re-analyzed, and its simulation results are more close to realistic ones.

The organization of this paper is as follows: The system model is given in Section 2. Discussion of multiuser detector is given in Section 3. Based on Log-distance path loss radio propagation model, the throughput of our ad hoc network is deduced and analyzed in Section 4. Simulations and corresponding interpretations are given in Section 5. In Section 6, final conclusion is drawn.

2 System Model

Fully-connected model [1] is considered in our paper, which means that every node can directly communicate with anyone of other nodes in the network, and the total number of nodes in the network is finite. Such model suits indoor circumstance like office or home. Each node is half-duplex, i.e., it can be either a transmitter or a receiver in a slot. Direct sequence CDMA is employed in physical layer. Every node has an unique pseudo-random noise(PN) code, which is taken as spreading-code, and every node knows the knowledge about other nodes' PN code. Receiver-based spreading-code protocol is employed. When node A sends a packet to node B, it will enter "transmitting" mode, use node B's PN code to make spread-spectrum modulation and send the packet to B. Otherwise, it will stay in "receiving" mode. In receiving mode, a node locks on its own PN code, receiving or preparing to receive any possible incoming packet from other nodes. Every data packet must be transmitted within a slot that has specified beginning time and ending time.

Five assumptions are made in the paper to facilitate analysis. A) The network is synchronization on slot. B) The length of DATA packet is fixed, and the duration of one slot is the time that sending or receiving a DATA packet lasts. C) At any slot, for every node, the probability that a node has a packet to transmit is equal to p. And there is no buffer at any node. D) Each node has equal probability to transmit to every other node. E) There is an immediate feedback about the status of the transmission.

3 Multiuser Detector with Bit Error Probability Analysis

Each terminal of our ad hoc network uses multiuser detector instead of conventional detector(i.e., matched filter) to receive packets. Because a terminal only locks on its own PN code, and training sequence is not used in our protocol, so we adopts blind multiuser detector. We suppose that the total number of packets sent in this slot is L, and packet 1 is what we want to detect. At the receiver, the nth bit of mixed signal can be represented by

$$r_n(t) = \sum_{i=1}^{L} A_i b_{i,n} s_i(t) + w(t) \ . \tag{1}$$

Here, A_i is the amplitude when packet i arrives at the receiver; $b_{i,n} \in \{-1,1\}$ with duration T, which is the nth information bit of packet i; $s_i(t)$ is the PN code for packet i; $w(t)$ is the additive white Gaussian noise whose power is σ^2. Sampled by chip-rate, we get vectors $\mathbf{s}_i$ and $\mathbf{r}_n$ from $s_1(t)$ and $r_n(t)$. Let $\mathbf{c}_1$ denote the "weight vector"(i,e., tap coefficients)of the detector. Then, the output of the detector for nth bit of packet 1 is

$$\hat{b}_{1,n} = \text{sgn}\left[\mathbf{c}_1^T \mathbf{r}_n \right] \ . \tag{2}$$

Note the dimension of vector $\mathbf{c}_1$ and $\mathbf{r}_n$ are N (N is spreading gain of CDMA system).

It is shown in [8] that mean output error(MOE) detector is equivalent to minimum mean-sqaure error(MMSE) detector, and has a unique global minimum with respect to $\mathbf{c}_1$. So our blind linear multiuser detector chooses $\mathbf{c}_1$ so as to minimize the mean output error(MOE) cost function

$$E\left\{ \left(\mathbf{c}_1^T \mathbf{r}_n\right)^2 \right\} \ , \tag{3}$$

subject to the constraint

$$\mathbf{c}_1^T \mathbf{s}_1 = 1 \ . \tag{4}$$

To facilitate realization by hardware, adaptive algorithm is recommended to recursively update $\mathbf{c}_1$, minimizing MOE. Let $\mathbf{c}_n$ denote weight vector in nth recursion. Let $r_{n,i}$ and $c_{n,i}$ ($i=1,2,\ldots,N$) denote the elements of $\mathbf{r}_n$ and $\mathbf{c}_n$ respectively. The constrained optimization problem (2) can be transformed into an unconstrained optimization problem, i.e., to compute

$$\min_{\overline{\mathbf{c}}} J_n, \quad J_n \triangleq E\left(\frac{r_{n,1}}{s_{1,1}} + \overline{\mathbf{c}}_n^T \overline{\mathbf{r}}_n \right)^2 \ . \tag{5}$$

where

$$\overline{\mathbf{r}}_i = \left[\left(r_{i,2} - \frac{r_{i,1} s_{1,2}}{s_{1,1}} \right), \cdots, \left(r_{i,N} - \frac{r_{i,1} s_{1,N}}{s_{1,1}} \right) \right]^T, \tag{6}$$

$$c_{n,1} = \frac{1}{s_{1,1}} \left(1 - \sum_{i=2}^{N} s_{1,i} c_{n,i} \right), \tag{7}$$

$$\overline{\mathbf{c}}_n = \left[c_{n,2}, c_{n,3}, \cdots c_{n,N} \right]^T \ . \tag{8}$$

Adaptive Least-Mean-Square(LMS) algorithm [8] can be applied to solve (5), which has a low complexity $O(N)$. Because each terminal in ad hoc network is energy-limited, we hope that the algorithm is as simple as possible. That's the main advantage of multiuser detector using LMS algorithm. Meanwhile, we also hope that the algorithm can converge as fast as possible. For LMS algorithm, though we can raise its convergence velocity by increasing its step size, but its excess mean-square error is also enlarged. Adaptive Recursive-Least -Squares(RLS) algorithm [9] can also be used to solve (5). The rate of convergence for RLS algorithm is very fast, but its complexity is $O(N^2)$, which is too energy-cost to be used in ad hoc terminals. Recently, blind adaptive gradient(BAG) algorithm was apposed in [10]. The performance of BAG algorithm is close to RLS algorithm, while the complexity of BAG algorithm is also $O(N)$. Formulae for BAG algorithm are listed in Eqs.(9-11), where ρ (0<ρ<1, ρ<<1) denotes a forgetting factor applied to the averaging procedure and μ denotes the step size of the tracking algorithm.

$$\hat{\mathbf{c}}_{n+1} = \hat{\mathbf{c}}_n - \mu \bar{\mathbf{r}}_n \left(\frac{r_{n,1}}{s_{1,1}} + \hat{\mathbf{c}}_n^T \bar{\mathbf{r}}_n \right) \tag{9}$$

$$\bar{\mathbf{c}}_{n+1} = (1-\rho)\bar{\mathbf{c}}_n + \rho \hat{\mathbf{c}}_{n+1} \tag{10}$$

$$c_{n+1} = \left[\frac{\frac{1}{s_{1,1}}(1 - \sum_{i=2}^{N} s_{1,i} \hat{c}_{n+1,i})}{\hat{c}_{n+1}} \right] \tag{11}$$

Let p_e be the bit error probability of linear multi-user detection. Given an accurate expression for p_e is very difficult, but Gaussian approximation can be used to get approximate result [11]:

$$p_e \approx Q\left(\frac{1}{\sqrt{\alpha_1^2 + \sum_{i=2}^{L} \beta_i^2}} \right) \tag{12}$$

where $Q(x) = \frac{1}{\sqrt{2\pi}} \int_x^\infty e^{-t^2/2} dt$.

with

$$\alpha_1 \triangleq \frac{\sigma\sqrt{1 + \|\mathbf{c}_1 - \mathbf{s}_1\|^2}}{A_1}, \tag{13}$$

$$\beta_i \triangleq \frac{A_i(\mathbf{s}_i, \mathbf{c}_1)}{A_1}. \tag{14}$$

Here, (x, y) denote the inner-product of vector x and vector y. We see that α_1^2 signifies the effect of noise on p_e, while β_i^2 ($i=2,3,\ldots,L$) signifies the effect of MAI on p_e.

4 Throughput Analysis of Proposed Ad Hoc Network

In this part, we analyze the throughput of our ad hoc network. We suppose that there are M nodes in the ad hoc network, and L nodes have packets to send in current slot. Following Assumptions C in Section 2, we know that the probability of L packets simultaneously being sent in current slot is

$$p_L = \binom{M}{L} p^L (1-p)^{M-L} \quad (L=0,1,2,\ldots,M) . \tag{15}$$

We also define the reception matrix $\mathbf{r}$ as

$$\mathbf{r} = \begin{pmatrix} r_{10} & r_{11} & 0 & \cdots & 0 \\ r_{20} & r_{21} & r_{22} & \cdots & 0 \\ \vdots & & & \ddots & \vdots \\ r_{M0} & r_{M1} & r_{M2} & \cdots & r_{MM} \end{pmatrix} . \tag{16}$$

where r_{ij} is the probability that j packets are received successfully when i packets have been sent in the network for current slot. Considering terminals' half-duplex nature, if M nodes all send packets, there will be no node in receiving mode. So $r_{M0}=1$ and $r_{Mj}=0$ ($j=1,2,\ldots M$).

Now, the task is to solve other non-zero elements of matrix $\mathbf{r}$. Let $\mathbf{N}$ be the random variable for the total number of successfully received packets at the link layer, $\mathbf{L}$ be the random variable for the total number of packets sent in a time slot, and $\mathbf{X}$ be the random variable for the total number of packets intended for nodes which are in receiving mode ($\mathbf{L}$-$\mathbf{X}$ packets are lost due to terminal's half-duplex nature). Then, for $1 \leq L \leq (M-1)$ and $0 \leq n \leq L$, a non-zero element of matrix $\mathbf{r}$ is

$$r_{Ln} = \sum_{x=n}^{L} Prob\{\mathbf{N}=n, \mathbf{X}=x | \mathbf{L}=L\} = \sum_{x=n}^{L} Prob\{\mathbf{N}=n | \mathbf{L}=L, \mathbf{X}=x\} Prob\{\mathbf{X}=x | \mathbf{L}=L\} . \tag{17}$$

Under Assumption D in Section 2, we have

$$Prob\{\mathbf{X}=x | \mathbf{L}=L\} = \binom{L}{x} \left(\frac{M-L}{M-1}\right)^x \left(\frac{L-1}{M-1}\right)^{L-x} . \tag{18}$$

In our protocol, if more than one packet sent to a same terminal in a slot, because they use the same PN code as the receiver's, so the receiver can not distinguish them. Let $\mathbf{Y}$ be the random variable for the total number of packets can be distinguished by the receivers ($\mathbf{X}$-$\mathbf{Y}$ packets fail at their receivers because of collisions). The value of $\mathbf{Y}$ is an integer varying from n to x except for x-1, for the reason that if collision happens at a terminal at least two packets will be involved and be rejected. Now we get

$$Prob\{N=n\mid L=L, X=x\} = \sum_{\substack{y=n \\ y \neq (x-1)}}^{x} Prob\{N=n, Y=y \mid L=L, X=x\} \quad (19)$$

$$= \sum_{\substack{y=n \\ y \neq (x-1)}}^{x} Prob\{N=n \mid L=L, X=x, Y=y\} Prob\{Y=y \mid X=x, L=L\} \cdot$$

To solve (19), we need to determine $Prob\{Y=y \mid X=x, L=L\}$. It was proved in [7] that given L ($0 \leq L \leq M-1$) packets are sent in a time slot (which also means that L nodes are in transmitting mode and remained ($M-L$) nodes are in receiving mode), the probability that y packets are free of collision is:

(1) if $x < (M-L)$, then

$$Prob\{Y=y \mid X=x, L=L\} = \binom{x}{y}\binom{M-L}{y}\left(\frac{M-L-y}{M-L}\right)^{x-y} \frac{y! p_\Delta}{(M-L)^y} ; \quad (20)$$

(2) if $x = (M-L)$, then

$$Prob\{Y=y \mid X=x, L=L\} = \begin{cases} \binom{x}{y}\binom{M-L}{y}\left(\frac{M-L-y}{M-L}\right)^{x-y} \frac{y! p_\Delta}{(M-L)^y} & \text{if } y \leq M-L-2 \\ \frac{(M-L)!}{(M-L)^{M-L}} & \text{if } y = M-L \end{cases} ; \quad (21)$$

(3) if $x > (M-L)$, then

$$Prob\{Y=y \mid X=x, L=L\} = \begin{cases} \binom{x}{y}\binom{M-L}{y}\left(\frac{M-L-y}{M-L}\right)^{x-y} \frac{y! p_\Delta}{(M-L)^y} & \text{if } y \leq M-L-1 \\ 0 & \text{if } y \geq M-L \end{cases} . \quad (22)$$

where

$$p_\Delta = \left(\frac{1}{K}\right)^{x-y} \sum_{m=1}^{\min\left(K, \left\lfloor\frac{x-y}{2}\right\rfloor\right)} \left[\binom{K}{m} \sum_{\substack{j_1+j_2+\cdots+j_m=x-y \\ j_i \geq 2 \ (i=1,2,\ldots,m)}} \prod_{i=1}^{m} \binom{x-y-\sum_{n=1}^{i-1} j_n}{j_i}\right] \quad (23)$$

and $K=M-L-y$.

Next, we need to determine $Prob\{N=n \mid L=L, X=x, Y=y\}$ in (19). This probability relates to the bit error probability p_e in physical layer. When k packets are sent in a slot, from Eqs.(12-14) we have

$$p_e(k) \approx Q\left(1 \bigg/ \sqrt{\frac{\sigma^2(1+\|c_1-s_1\|^2)}{A_1^2} + \sum_{i=2}^{k} \frac{A_i^2}{A_1^2}|(s_i, c_1)|^2}\right). \quad (24)$$

As mentioned in section 2, fully-connected model suits indoor circumstance such as office and home. Let d be the distance between transmitter A and receiver B and d_0

be a known received power reference point. Indoor path loss has been shown by many researchers to follow the distance power law in Eq.(25)

$$PL(d) = PL(d_0) + 10\gamma \log\left(\frac{d}{d_0}\right) + \zeta \text{ (dB)}. \tag{25}$$

Where the value of γ depends on the surroundings and building type and ζ is a normal random variable in decibel having a standard deviation of δ dB. [12]. That is, $\zeta \sim N(0,\delta)$ in decibels. Such model is called as Log-distance path loss model.

Let P_t denote the received power at d_0, then the received power at B($d > d_0$) is

$$P_r = P_t d^{-\gamma} 10^{\frac{\zeta}{10}}. \tag{26}$$

Substitute (25) and (26) into (24), we get

$$p_e(k) \approx Q\left(1 \bigg/ \sqrt{\frac{\sigma^2(1+\|c_1-s_1\|^2)}{P_t d_1^{-\gamma} 10^{\frac{\zeta_1}{10}}} + \sum_{i=2}^{k}\left(\frac{d_i}{d_1}\right)^{-\gamma} 10^{\frac{\zeta_i-\zeta_1}{10}} |(s_i,c_1)|^2}\right). \tag{27}$$

It is seen that $p_e(k)$ is relative to the detection scheme at the receiver. Different detection schemes have different c_1, resulting in different values of $p_e(k)$.

Remark1. If c_1 equals to s_1, then it becomes conventional detector. $p_e(k)$ is proportional to the cross-correlations of PN codes as well as the distance ratios between expected source and interfering sources. That is to say, near-far effect caused by MAI directly deteriorates bit error performance of conventional detector.

Remark2. If c_1 is chosen to force $(s_i, c_1) = 0$ for each s_i, it becomes decorrelating detector. Though MAI is completely suppressed, background noise is magnified as by-product, which will also deteriorate bit error performance of the detector.

Remark3. It has been reported that MMSE detector outperforms decorrelating detector and conventional detector in many papers. When MMSE or equivalent MOE cost function is realized by adaptive iterations, the optimal c_1 is $\mathbf{R}^{-1}\mathbf{s}_1 / \mathbf{s}_1^T \mathbf{R}^{-1}\mathbf{s}_1$, where $R = E\{r_n r_n^T\}$ denotes the autocorrelation matrix of r_n [9]. So algorithm of blind adaptive multiuser detection should converge to the optimal c_1 as fast as possible so as to get a small $p_e(k)$. BAG algorithm recommended in Section 3 is a satisfactory one.

We suppose that nodes in our ad hoc network are uniformly distributed in a square room with $2x_0 \times 2x_0$ m^2. To facility our analysis, we define an assisted random variable $\Psi = d^2/x_0^2$. Then the probability density function (pdf.) of Ψ is

$$f_\psi(\varphi) = \begin{cases} \dfrac{\pi}{4} + \dfrac{\varphi}{16} - \dfrac{\sqrt{\varphi}}{2} & 0 < \varphi \le 4 \\[6pt] \dfrac{\pi - 2\cos^{-1}\left(\dfrac{8}{\varphi}-1\right)}{4} + \dfrac{\sqrt{\varphi-4}}{2} - \dfrac{\varphi}{16} - \dfrac{1}{2} & 4 < \varphi < 8 \\[6pt] 0 & \text{elsewhere} \end{cases} \tag{28}$$

Then we can calculate $p_e(k)$ by a $2k$-dimensional integral:

$$p_e(k) = \int_{\varphi_1} \int_{\varphi_2} \cdots \int_{\varphi_k} \int_{\zeta_1} \int_{\zeta_2} \cdots \int_{\zeta_k} Q\left(1 \middle/ \sqrt{\frac{\sigma^2 x_0\left(1+\|c_1-s_1\|^2\right)}{P_t 10^{\frac{\zeta_1}{10}}}} \varphi_1^{\frac{\gamma}{2}} + \sum_{i=2}^{k}\left(\frac{\varphi_1}{\varphi_i}\right)^{\frac{\gamma}{2}} 10^{\frac{\zeta_i-\zeta_1}{10}} |(s_i,c_1)|^2\right) \quad (29)$$

$$f_\psi(\varphi_1)f_\psi(\varphi_2)\cdots f_\psi(\varphi_k)f_\zeta(\zeta_1)f_\zeta(\zeta_2)\cdots f_\zeta(\zeta_k)d\varphi_1 d\varphi_2 \cdots d\varphi_k d\zeta_1 d\zeta_2 \cdots d\zeta_k$$

Let L_p be the length of a packet (in bits). Provided that at most t bit errors can be corrected by coding, we have the packet success probability on condition that k MAIs exist:

$$p_c(k) = \sum_{i=0}^{t} \binom{L_p}{i} p_e(k)^i \left(1-p_e(k)\right)^{L_p-i}. \quad (30)$$

Now we get

$$Prob\{\mathbf{N}=n \mid \mathbf{L}=L, \mathbf{X}=x, \mathbf{Y}=y\} = \binom{y}{n} p_c(L-1)^n \left(1-p_c(L-1)\right)^{y-n}. \quad (31)$$

Taking Eqs.(20-23) and Eq.(31) into Eq.(19), we solve $Prob\{\mathbf{N}=n \mid \mathbf{L}=L, \mathbf{X}=x\}$. Together with Eq.(18), we can finally determine every non-zero element of **r** by Eq.(17).

Throughput T is defined by the total number of packets received in a slot in the network, which is expressed by

$$T = \sum_{L=1}^{M} p_L \sum_{n=0}^{L} n r_{Ln}, \quad (32)$$

where p_L is given by Eq.(17) and r_{Ln} is the element of matrix **r**.

5 Simulations and Remarks

The scene for simulation is a 20m×20m indoor space, within which M randomly distributed terminals form a fully-connected CDMA-based ad hoc network. The transmission of every data packet is done within a time slot and the length of each data packet is fixed to 800 bits. Distinct 31-bit length gold sequences are pre-assigned to every terminal as spreading codes. The operating frequency is 2.4GHz and the transmission power of every node is fixed to 100mW. The power of ambient noise is -60dBm. Our target is to study the link-level throughput for ad hoc network with BAG-algorithm-based multiuser detector(MUD) scheme, and compare it with the throughput of ad hoc network with conventional detector(CD) scheme. Following five parameters are used in simulations: p - the probability for a terminal to send packet in a time slot; M - the total number of nodes; t - the ability of bit error correction of coding in a packet. And another two parameters are from Log-distance path loss model: γ - the path loss exponent; δ - the standard deviation of Gaussian random variable ζ. In our simulations, p takes values from 0 to 1 with a step of 0.05. We link simulation results for MUD case with solid lines, while link the simulation results for CD case with dashed lines.

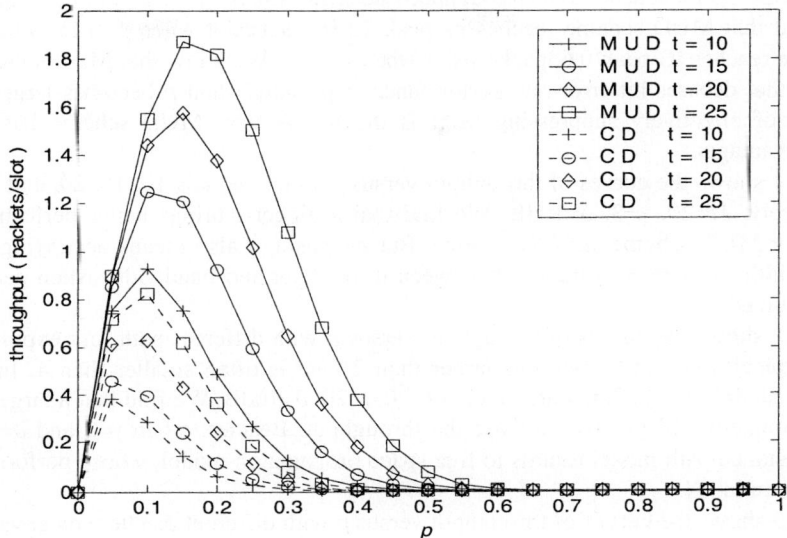

Fig. 1. Throughput vs. p for different t ($M=20$, $\gamma=3$, $\delta=10$dB)

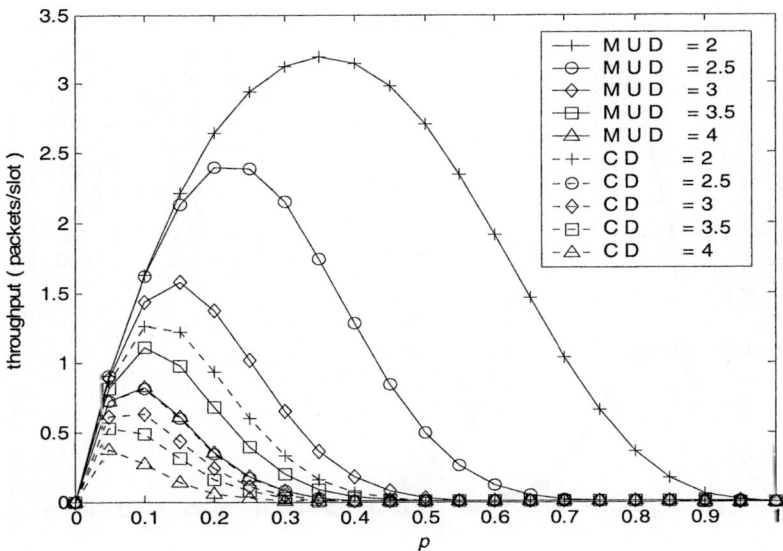

Fig. 2. Throughput vs. p for different γ ($M=20$, $t=20$, $\delta=10$dB)

It is shown in Figs.1-4 that MUD scheme has at least two advantages compared with CD scheme. First, the throughput of MUD scheme is always greatly larger than that of CD scheme. Second, MUD scheme reaches to its throughput's peak at a bigger p while CD scheme reaches to its throughput's peak at a smaller p. (e.g., in Fig.1, for $t=20$, we find that MUD scheme reaches its peak 1.58packets/slot when $p=0.15$, while CD scheme reaches its peak 0.63packets/slot when $p=0.1$.) We know that MAI is the main factor that debases bit-error-rate performance, especially when p becomes larger. The ability of effectively suppressing MAI is the reason why MUD scheme has these two advantages.

Fig.1 shows the curves of throughput versus p when t equals 10, 15, 20, and 25 respectively. $M=20$. $\gamma=3$. $\delta=10$dB. We find that a bigger t brings better performance, both for MUD scheme and CD scheme. But increasing t also means occupying more bandwidth, so there is a trade off between throughput and bandwidth when deciding the value of t.

Fig.2 shows the curves of throughput versus p with different path loss exponent γ. The typical value of indoor γ is larger than 2, and is often smaller than 4. In fig.2 curves of $\gamma=2, 2.5, 3, 3.5, 4$ are given. $M=20$. $t=20$. $\delta=10$dB. We find that a larger path loss exponent will greatly decrease the throughput. Besides, when $\gamma=2$ and $\delta=0$, the Log-distance path model returns to free space propagation model, whose performance was given in [7].

Fig.3 shows the curves of throughput versus p with different δ. The typical value of indoor δ lies between 5dB and 14dB. In fig.3 curves of $\delta=6, 8, 10, 12, 14$ are given. $M=20$, $t=20$, $\gamma=3$. We find when δ grows the throughput will drop slightly.

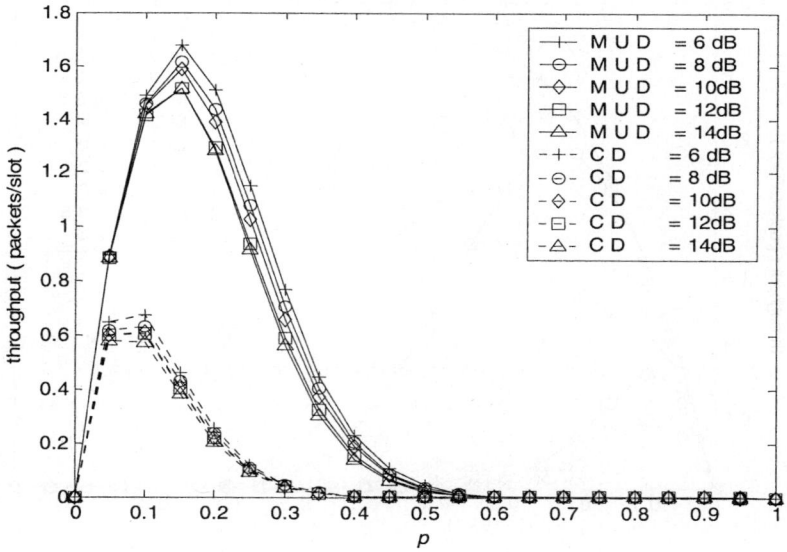

Fig. 3. Throughput vs. p for different δ ($M=20$, $t=20$, $\gamma=3$)

When M grows, because more terminals are involved in communication, it is natural that the throughput of the whole network will rise. To fairly evaluate the effect of nodes' density on the throughput, we divide the throughput by M, and call it "throughput per node". Fig.4 shows the curves of throughput per node versus p when the total number of terminals M varies from 8 to 20 with a step of 4. We find that when M grows, throughput per node will descend, for both MUD and CD scheme. It is because the network becomes denser and the sum of MAIs becomes stronger when M grows. And because MUD scheme is MAI-resistant, the extent of throughput's drop for MUD scheme is slight, while the extent of throughput's drop for CD scheme is remarkable.

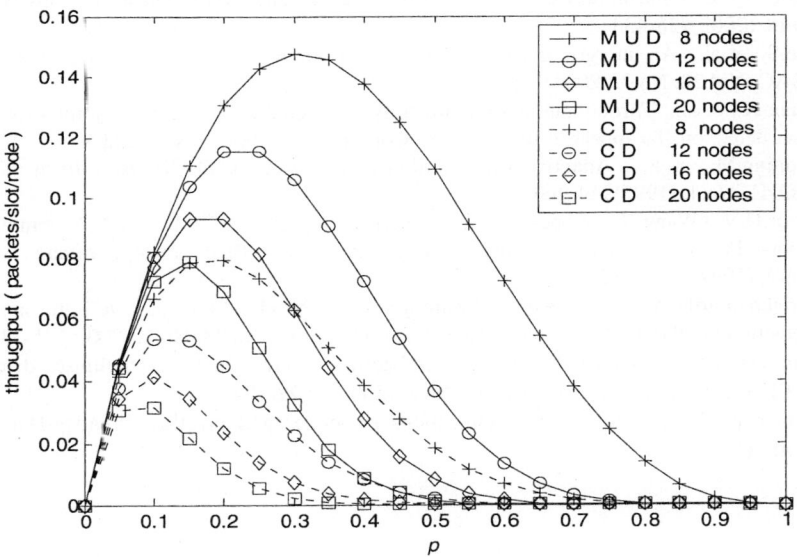

Fig. 4. Throughput per node vs. p for different M ($t=20$, $\gamma=3$, $\delta=10$dB)

6 Conclusion

This paper shows the importance of multiuser detection for fully-connected CDMA-based ad hoc networks. Because of fast convergence and low complexity, BAG is chosen as the algorithm of blind multiuser detector. Based on Log-distance path loss model, the throughput of ad hoc network with multiuser detection is analyzed. Simulations show that compared with conventional scheme using matched filter, proposed scheme can greatly increase the throughput. Besides, the impacts of parameters of Log-distance path loss model (path loss exponent and standard deviation) and network's density on throughput are also studied in the paper.

References

1. Bao,J., Tong,L.: A performance comparison between ad hoc and cellular controlled CDMA wireless LANs. IEEE Trans. on Wireless Communications, Vol.1, No.4, (2000)829-841
2. Sousa,E.S., Silvester,J.A.,: Spreading code protocols for distributed spread-spectrum packet radio networks. IEEE Trans. Commun., Vol.36, No.3, (1988)272-280
3. Muqattash,A., et al,: Solving the near-far problem in CDMA-based Ad hoc networks. Ad Hoc Networks Journal. Vol.1, No.4, (2003)435-453
4. Sankaran,C., Ephremides,A.,: The use of multiuser detectors for multicasting in wireless Ad hoc CDMA networks. IEEE Trans. Inform. Theory. Vol.48, No.11, (2002)2873-2887
5. Cai,Z., et al.,: Minimum average transmission power routing in CDMA Ad hoc networks utilizing the blind multiuser detection. Proc. Parallel and Distributed Processing Symposium. (2002)428-433
6. De,S., et al.,: An intergrated cross-layer study of wireless CDMA sensor networks. IEEE JSAC. Vol.22, No.7, (2004)1271-1284
7. Qian X., et al.,: Throughput analysis for fully-connected ad hoc network joint with multiuser detection. To appear in IEICE Trans. Commun., Vol.E88-B,No.9, 2005
8. Honing,M., et al.,: Adaptive blind multiuser detection. IEEE Trans, Inform. Theory, Vol.41, No.4, (1995)944-960
9. Poor,H.V., Wang,X.,: Code-aided interference suppression for DS/CDMA communications—Part II: parallel blind adaptive implementations. IEEE Trans. Commun., Vol.45, No.9, (1997)1112-1122
10. Krishnamurthy,V.,: Averaged stochastic gradient algorithms for adaptive blind multiuser detection in DS/CDMA systems. IEEE Trans. Commun. Vol.48, No.1, (2000)125-134
11. Burnashev,M.V., Poor,H.V.,: On the probability of error in linear multiuser detection. IEEE Trans. Inform. Theory, Vol.49, No.8, (2003) 1922-1941
12. Rappaport,T.S.,: Wireless communications principles and practice. Prentice-Hall, New York, (1998)

Dynamic Traffic Grooming for Survivable Mobile Networks - Fairness Control

Hyuncheol Kim[1], Sunghae Kim[2], and Seongjin Ahn[3]

[1] Dept. of Electrical and Computer Engineering, Sungkyunkwan University,
300 Chunchun-Dong Jangan-Gu, Suwon, Korea, 440-746
hckim@songgang.skku.ac.kr
[2] Electronics and Telecommunications Research Institutes, Daejon, Korea,
shkim@etri.re.kr
[3] Dept. of Computer Education, Sungkyunkwan University,
53 Myungryun-Dong Jongro-Gu, Seoul, Korea, 110-745
sjahn@comedu.skku.ac.kr

Abstract. The Internet is replacing the traditional telephone network as the ubiquitous network infrastructure. Internet customers are increasing at an exponential rate and will continue to increase in the near future. With the proliferation of mobile communication technologies and wireless personal devices, the demand for mobile communications has grown exponentially over the last decade and is expected to grow even more in the near future. This paper proposes a new bandwidth allocation scheme that guarantees the time independent fairness and fault tolerance in the heterogeneous mobile communication services. It will hold some calls in the second buffer rather than directly discarding it when the residual bandwidth is insufficient. A multimedia call that satisfies all connection requirements has precedence over other calls.

1 Introduction

The Internet is replacing the traditional telephone network as the ubiquitous network infrastructure. Internet customers are increasing at an exponential rate and will continue to increase in the near future. With the proliferation of mobile communication technologies and wireless personal devices, the demand for mobile communications has grown exponentially over the last decade and is expected to grow even more in the near future.

The explosive growth of Internet traffic has led to a dramatic increase in demand for data transmission capacity, which requires high transmission rates beyond the conventional electronic router's capability. This demand has spurred tremendous research activities in new high-speed transmission and switching technologies [1].

In spite of the intrinsic scarcity of wireless bandwidth, mobile networks must have an ability to maintain an acceptable level of service to provide diverse QoS while achieving efficient bandwidth utilization. QoS provisioning is one of the most urgent problem that needs to be solved in the multimedia mobile communications [2][3].

In the view point of the optical network based wireless communication environment, one of the issues is to maintain the multimedia connection regardless of the network failure (position). The management process for multimedia mobile traffic is different from the conventional management process for voice in that a node may have several active connections with different bandwidth requirements and QoS constraints.

The bandwidth management function, then, should ensure that all active connections are rerouted in a seamless manner. In other words, the design goal is to minimize any service disruption and degradation during and after the recovery process. This situation can also be equally applied to broadband multimedia communication services.

The independent multi-class one-step prediction-complete sharing and reservation (IMOSP-CS and IMOSP-RES) incorporates a new resource management, which partitions the available bandwidth to reflect the desired blocking probability profile. Much of the bandwidth is allocated to underprivileged calls if Call Blocking Probability (CBP) ratio between services is greater than the predetermined threshold. The numerical results demonstrate that BPMF actually achieve CBP fairness between wideband and narrowband calls. But, IMOSP controls the reservation partition by simple resource management algorithm so that it often leads to system abnormalities depending on the traffic behavior. Above all, IMOSP cannot guarantee short-term fairness in normal traffic conditions, much less guarantee long-term fairness under heavy traffic conditions [4][5][6].

To make this possible, a new fairness control model is proposed to classify the connection requests to the first buffer using the call identifier. It will hold some calls in the second buffer rather than directly rejecting it when the residual bandwidth is insufficient. A multimedia call that satisfies all connection requirements takes precedence over the others.

The reminders of this paper are organized as follows. We discuss unfairness problem on previous researches in section 1. The proposed scheme is described in section 2 and the reference network is described in section 3. The traffic model and queuing analysis of the scheme is described in section 4. The numerical analysis is explained in section 5. Finally, we end this paper with the conclusion.

2 Survivable Fairness Control Scheme

Fig. 1 shows the strategy used in the proposed scheme to allocate multimedia calls. In the proposed scheme, channels (bandwidths) are split into three subchannels. G_w and G_n channels are dedicated for wideband and narrowband calls, respectively. The shared channels can be used by either type of the traffic.

Narrowband calls are blocked, if all the permitted channels are in use. However, wideband calls have finite queues so as to keep a certain amount when all permitted channels are busy. In most cases, the wideband calls are hardly admitted so that serious CBP unfairness occurs. Thus, we allocate finite buffers for wideband traffic to admit all types of services fairly.

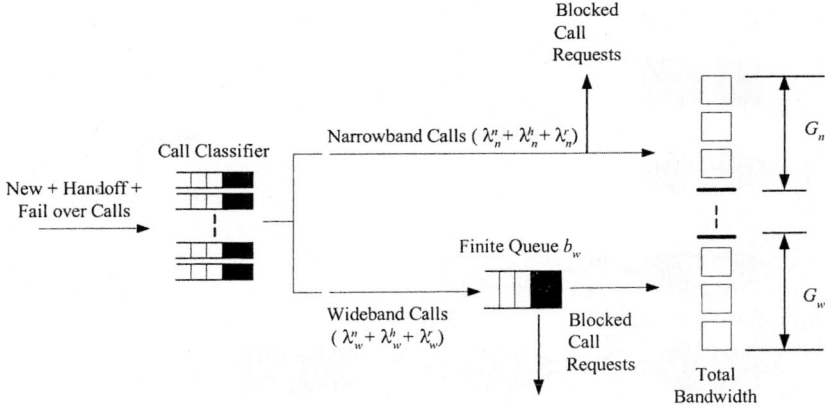

Fig. 1. DPNP Control Scheme

In the proposed scheme, to ensure that all active connections composing a multimedia call are rerouted one at a time, all connection requests are assorted first into the call. In other words, the design goal of the proposed scheme is to minimize any service disruption and degradation during and after the handoff process. This situation can also be applied equally to fail over connections. In the proposed scheme, all active connections composing a multimedia call are executed or blocked all together.

When a new user arrives in a cell, the proposed scheme decides on acceptance or rejection based on each call's current resource occupancy, reservation partition, call state, and dynamic guide channels. A new narrowband call is admitted if the number of existing narrowband calls is less than the number of guard channels G_n. When the number of existing narrowband calls is greater than or equal to the number of guard channels G_n, a new narrowband call is accepted if and only if the total number of used channels are less than the predefined threshold.

Assort the connections requests
if all or almost all connections that belong to the same call
satisfy requirements do
   if narrow new call is requested do
      if narrow new call is less than G_n do
      then Accept
      else if narrow new call is less than T_n do
      then Accept
      else Reject all connections that belong to the same call
   if wide new call is requested do
      if existing used channels is less than C do
      then Accept
      else Reject all connections that belong to the same call

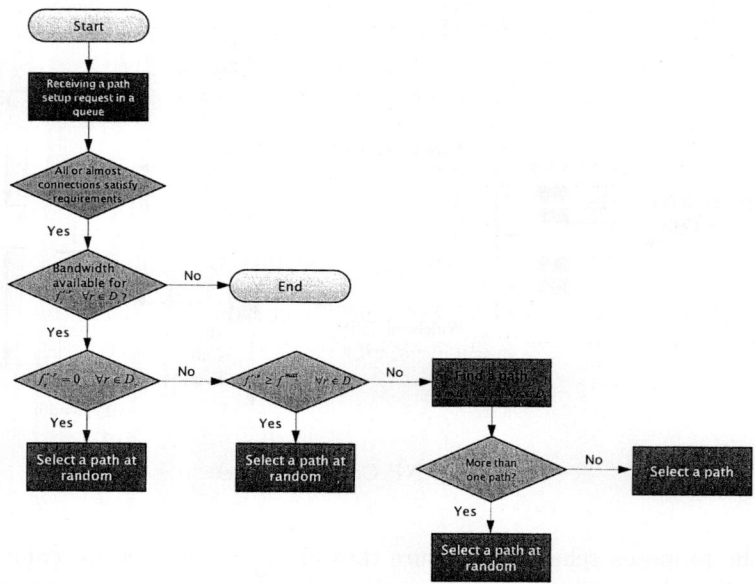

Fig. 2. Procedure of the proposed scheme

2.1 Fairness Control

To describe the proposed fairness control mechanism, the following parameters are defined and Fig. 3 illustrates some examples of the proposed mechanism framework [7].

- D_z: The set of Originator-Destination (O-D) pairs that have lost one or more units of demand upon failure scenario z. Individual O-D pairs of D_z are indexed by r.
- D: The set of all demand quantities exchanged between O-D pairs, with index r, and element value d^r.
- d^r: The number of demand units between end-node pair r.
- p^r: The master set of routes eligible for use in restoration of O-D pair r.
- p_z^r: The set of eligible restoration routes available to O-D pair r for its restoration under failure scenario z.
- F: A set of predefined failure scenarios, specified in terms of failed spans, index z. In ESRLG, path recovery takes place in the context of one specific failure scenario at a time.
- X_z^r: The number of demand units (e.g., individual lightpaths) lost by O-D pair r, for failure scenario z.
- $\delta_{z,j}^{r,p}$: Boolean parameter that is 1, if span j is in the pth eligible route for restoration O-D pair r in the event of failure scenario z.
- $\delta_j^{r,p}$: 1 if span j is in the pth eligible route for O-D pair r.

- $f_z^{r,p}$: The degree of sharing, which refers to the number of lightpaths that can be allocated between one ultimate source-destination node pair on a link.
- f^{max}: The maximum degree of sharing on a link.
- $g^{r,q}$: The amount of working demand flow assigned to the qth working route between node pair r.
- S: The set of spans of the network.
- s_j: The spare capacity on span j.
- w_j: The working capacity on span j.

In equation (1), $\sigma(X)$ denotes a standard deviation of X. An initial statement of the proposed scheme for a given scenario z is:

$$maximize \ \sigma(\sum_{r \in D_z} d^r)$$

$$maximize \left[(1-\alpha) \cdot \sum_{r \in D_z} \sum_{p \in p_z^r} f_z^{r,p} + \alpha \cdot \sum_{r \in D_z} \lambda_r \right] \quad (1)$$

subject to:

$$\sum_{p \in p_z^r} f_z^{r,p} \leq \lambda_r \cdot X_z^r \quad \forall r \in D_z \quad (2)$$

$$\lambda_r \leq 1 \quad \forall r \in D_z \quad (3)$$

$$\lambda_r \geq \lambda_{min} \quad \forall r \in D_z \quad (4)$$

$$\sum_{r \in D_z} \sum_{p \in p_z^r} \delta_j^{r,p} \cdot f_z^{r,p} \leq s_j \quad \forall j \in S \quad (5)$$

$$\sum_{p \in p_z^r} f_z^{r,p} \geq 1 \quad \forall r \in D_z \quad (6)$$

Equation (2) denotes a limited requirement on each commodity, and equation (5) denotes a limited capacity on the network spans. Equation (6) will ensure that all affected O-D pairs enjoy at least one restoration path so they are not disconnected, if this is feasible.

The objective of equation (1) is to maximize the total number of restoration paths provided for the scenario as a whole. This is effected by finding the assignments degree of sharing to the surviving eligible routes for restoration of each pair of affected end-nodes with upper bounds so that no O-D pair can get more restoration than it needs (equation (2)), and by ensuring simultaneous flow assignments do not exceed the spare capacity of any span (equation (5)).

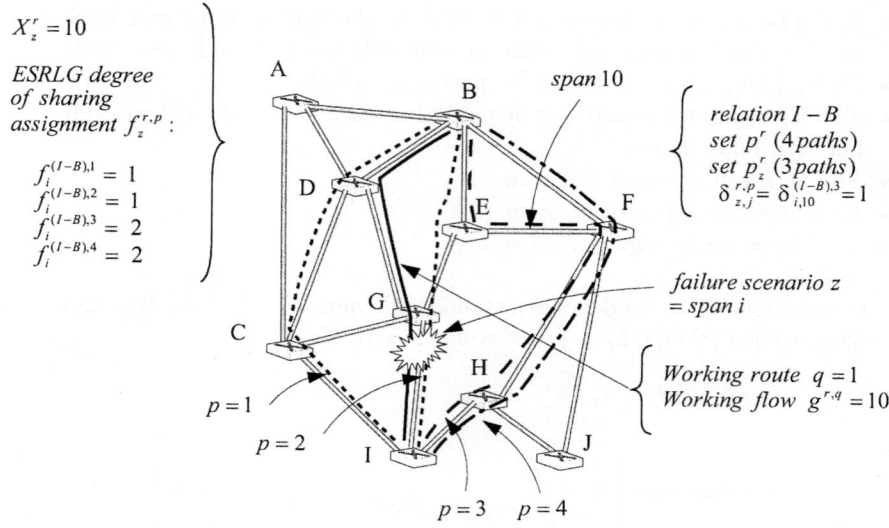

Fig. 3. Context and example terminology for the proposed scheme

3 Examined Network Model

Fig. 4 shows the architectural model for the IP over an optical broadband network to which revised SRLG is applied. Fig. 4 also shows three interfaces according to the overlay model and the peer/integrated model: the User-Network Interface (UNI), the Internal Node-to-Node Interface (I-NNI) within a single sub-network, and the External Node-to-Node Interface (E-NNI) between different sub-networks.

These interfaces require the implementation of a signaling protocol with sufficient capabilities. New messages are being defined by extension of the signaling protocols (i.e., the Label Distribution Protocol (LDP) and Resource reservation Protocol- Traffic Engineering (RSVP-TE)) in the standardization bodies, such as the Internet Engineering Task Force (IETF) and Optical Internet working Forum (OIF) [8].

4 Traffic Model and Analysis

Throughout the paper, we assume that system resources can be shared by two traffic classes, wideband and narrowband calls. The wideband call requires m bandwidths. The narrowband call requires only one basic bandwidth. It is assumed that the new calls, hand-off calls, and fail over calls are arriving in a Poisson process with mean arrival rate of λ_n^n, λ_n^h, λ_n^r and λ_w^n, λ_w^h, λ_w^r, respectively. It also assumed that service time is exponentially distributed with mean service time of $1/\mu_{ns}$ and $1/\mu_{ws}$.

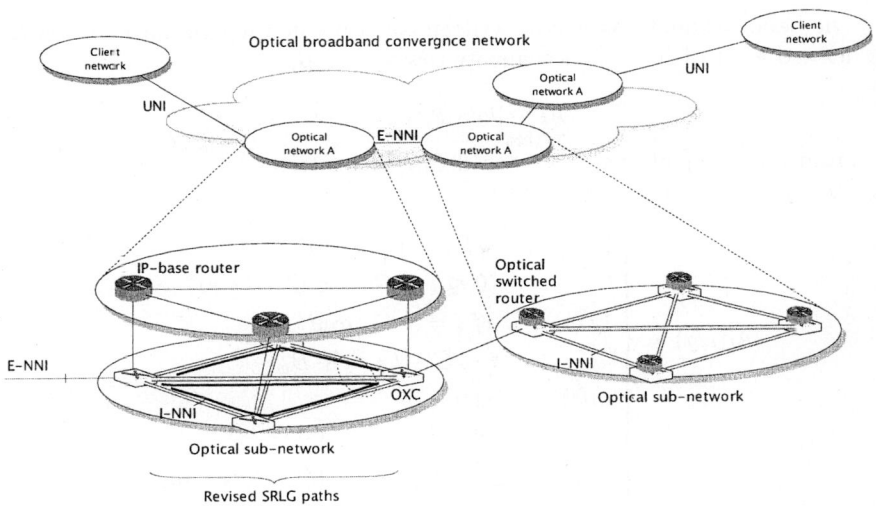

Fig. 4. Network reference model

The time that calls stay in the cell also follows an exponentially distribution with a mean of $1/h_n$, $1/h_w$, and $1/h_r$. We also describe that the narrowband and wideband calls have Poisson distribution with arrival rates of $\lambda_n(\lambda_n^n + \lambda_n^h + \lambda_n^r)$ and $\lambda_w(\lambda_w^n + \lambda_w^h + \lambda_w^r)$, respectively. Channel occupancy times for narrowband and wideband calls are summed with the means of $1/\mu_n(1/(\mu_{ns} + h_n))$ and $1/\mu_w(1/(\mu_{ws} + h_w))$, respectively. We allocate finite buffers B_w for wideband traffic. Let C be the total number of channels and G_n and G_w be the dedicated channels for narrowband and wideband traffic, respectively.

Then, the system can be modeled as a two dimensional Markov process, characterized by $\{i,j\}$, where i and j are the numbers of narrowband and wideband calls in the system, respectively. The state space is represented by the set $\{s(i,j) | 0 \leqslant i < G_n, 0 \leqslant j \leqslant \lfloor(C - G_n + B_w)/m\rfloor$ and $G_n \leqslant i \leqslant C - G_w, 0 \leqslant j \leqslant \lfloor(C - i + B_w)/m\rfloor\}$. $\lfloor x \rfloor$ denotes the greatest integer smaller than or equal to x. Also, let the steady-state probability that the system is in state $s(i,j)$ be $p(i,j)$. The steady-state probability vector $\boldsymbol{p}$ is then partitioned as $\boldsymbol{p} = (\boldsymbol{p}_0, \boldsymbol{p}_1, ...)$.

From the state transition, we can obtain the transition rate matrix $\boldsymbol{Q}$ of the Markov process [9][10]

$$Q = \begin{bmatrix} A_0 & D & & & \\ B_1 & A_1 & D & & \\ & B_2 & A_2 & D & \\ & & \cdots & \cdots & \cdots \\ & & & \cdots & \cdots & \cdots \\ & & & & \cdots \end{bmatrix} \quad (7)$$

Let $\boldsymbol{p}_{i,-1} = 0$ for $0 \leqslant i \leqslant C - G_w$ and $\boldsymbol{p}_{-1,i} = 0$ for $0 \leqslant j \leqslant \lfloor(C - G_n + B_w)/m\rfloor$.

The balance equations maybe written concisely in a matrix form. To do this, we defined a set of $(C - G_w)$ elements row vector $\boldsymbol{p}_i$

$$\boldsymbol{p}_i \equiv [p_{i0},\ p_{i1},\ p_{i2},\ ...] \tag{8}$$

From above equations 8, we can define submatrices for $i, j = 0, 1, ..., C - G_w,\ 0 \leqslant j \leqslant \lfloor (C - G_n + B_w)/m \rfloor$ by

$$A_l(i,j) = \begin{cases} \lambda_n & \text{if } i = j-1 \text{ and} \\ & (0 \leqslant i < G_n | i < C - l*m) \\ (j)\mu_n & \text{if } i = j+1 \text{ and} \\ & i < C - l*m + B_w \\ a_l(i) & \text{if } i = j \\ 0 & \text{otherwise} \end{cases} \tag{9}$$

$$B_l(i,j) = \begin{cases} \min(l,\ \lfloor (C-G_n)/m \rfloor,\ \lfloor (C-i)/m \rfloor)\mu_w \\ \quad \text{if } i = j \text{ and } i < C - l*m + B_w \\ 0 \quad \text{otherwise} \end{cases}$$

$$D(j,k) = \begin{cases} \lambda_w & \text{if } i = j \text{ and } i \leqslant C - l*m + B_w \\ 0 & \text{otherwise} \end{cases}$$

Where $a_i(j)$ is the value that makes the sum of the row elements of $\boldsymbol{Q}$ equal to zero. To solve 8 with this transition rate matrix $\boldsymbol{Q}$, we apply the matrix-geometric solution technique based on Neut's solution process. First we find $\boldsymbol{Q}$ matrix by solving the equation

$$\boldsymbol{R} = \left[\boldsymbol{D} + \boldsymbol{R}^2 \boldsymbol{B}_{n1}\right] \left[\boldsymbol{I} - \boldsymbol{A}_{n1}\right]^{-1} \tag{10}$$

We now start with a trial solution such as $\boldsymbol{R} = 0$ and again iterate until

$$\max_{i.j} \left[\boldsymbol{R}_{ij}(n+1) - \boldsymbol{R}_{ij}(n)\right] < \varepsilon \tag{11}$$

Since all $\boldsymbol{p}_i$ can be expressed in terms of $\boldsymbol{p}_0$ by solving the equation ?? recursively, CBP_n and CBP_w can be easily obtained. Let T_n be the admission threshold of narrow-band traffic. The new call blocking probability of narrow-band traffic $\boldsymbol{p}_n^{nb}$ is given by

$$\boldsymbol{p}_n^{nb} = 1 - \left[\sum_{i=0}^{G_n-1} \sum_{j=0}^{C-G_n+B_w} p_{ij} + \sum_{i=G_n}^{C-G_w-1} \sum_{j=0}^{i+j<T_n} p_{ij}\right] \tag{12}$$

A narrowband hand-off call is accepted if the channels are available. Thus, the hand-off call blocking probability of narrowband traffic $\boldsymbol{p}_n^{hb}$ is given by

$$\boldsymbol{p}_n^{hb} = 1 - \left[\sum_{i=0}^{G_n-1} \sum_{j=0}^{C-G_n+B_w} p_{ij} + \sum_{i=G_n}^{C-G_w-1} \sum_{j=0}^{i+j<C} p_{ij}\right] \tag{13}$$

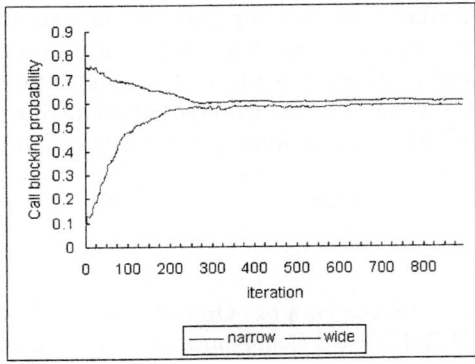

Fig. 5. CBP Fairness

Let T_w be the admission buffer threshold of wideband traffic. The new call blocking probability of wideband traffic $\boldsymbol{p}_w^{nb}$ is given by

$$\boldsymbol{p}_w^{nb} = 1 - \left[\sum_{i=0}^{G_n} \sum_{j=T_w}^{B_w} p_{i,C-G_n+j} + \sum_{i=G_n+1}^{C-G_w} \sum_{j=T_w}^{B_w} p_{i,C-i+j} \right] \quad (14)$$

A wideband hand-off call is accepted if the buffers are available. Thus, the hand-off call blocking probability of wideband traffic $\boldsymbol{p}_w^{hb}$ is given by

$$\boldsymbol{p}_w^{hb} = 1 - \left[\sum_{i=0}^{G_n} p_{i,C-G_n+B_w} + \sum_{i=G_n+1}^{C-G_w} p_{i,C-i+B_w} \right] \quad (15)$$

5 Numerical Analysis

This section presents a numerical analysis of the performance of the proposed scheme in the aspects of CBP fairness and resource utilization. The analysis is done with IMOSP. The cell capacity accommodates 20 units.

As see in Fig. 5, the proposed scheme shows big difference in CBP fairness. In case of proposed scheme, the traffic intensity between wideband and narrowband is wide especially when the wideband call arrives with a larger traffic. IMOSP shows an obvious CBP unfairness between wideband call and narrowband call. On the other hand, proposed scheme shows a fair CBP between two services. We can observe from Fig. 5 that the CBP of wideband decreases as the CBP of narrowband increases. After all, two CBP are converged into their average CBP value.

6 Concluding Remarks

This paper proposed a novel CAC scheme and resource management algorithm that guarantee both short-term and long-term fairness between heterogeneous services with different traffic properties and enhance resource utilization of the system. The proposed method has been analyzed using a two-dimensional Markov chain and Neut's matrix-geometric solutions. By numerical analysis, we demonstrated that our CAC scheme actually achieves fair admitting probability for wideband and narrowband calls and also improves resource utilization regardless of the traffic behavior.

References

1. Dirceu Cavendish, "Evolution of Optical Transport Technologies: From SONET/SDH to WDM," IEEE Communications Magazine, Vol. 38, Issue 6, Jun. 2000, pp. 164-172.
2. Chun Ting Chou and Kang G. Shin, "Analysis of Combined Adaptive Bandwidth Allocation and Admission Control in Wireless Networks," IEEE INFOCOM 2002, pp. 676-684.
3. Mahmoud Naghshineh and Mischa Schwartz, "Distribued call admission control in mobile/wireless networks," IEEE JSAC, Vol. 14, May 1996, pp. 1208-1225.
4. Hyuncheol Kim, Sungkee Noh, Sungjin Ahn, Jinwook Chung, "Analysis of Combined Bandwidth Allocation and Call Admission Control in High-Speed Mobile Networks," Asian Journal of Information Technology, Vol. 4, No. 8, 2005, pp. 751-757
5. Yuan Cheng Lai and Yu Dar Lin, "A Novel Admission Control for Fairly Admitting Wideband and Narrowband Calls," IEEE Communications Letters, Vol. 7, No. 4, Apr 2003, pp. 186-188.
6. M. Naghshineh and A.S. Acampora, "QoS Provisioning in Micro-Cellular Networks Supporting Multiple Classes of Traffic," Wireless Networks, vol. 2, 1996. pp. 195-203.
7. Wayne D. Grover, "Mesh-Based Survivable Networks - Options and Strategies for Optical, MPLS, SONET, and ATM Networking," Prentice Hall, 2004.
8. Tai Won Um, Jun Kyun Choi, Young Ae Kim, Hyeong Ho Lee, Hae Won Jung, and Sang Gug Jong, "Signaling and Control Procedures Using Generalized MPLS Protocol for IP over an Optical Network," ETRI Journal, Vol. 24, No. 2, Apr. 2002, pp. 69-78.
9. M.F. Neuts, "Matrix-Geometric Solutions in Stochastic Models," Johns Hopkins University Press, 1981.
10. YoungHan Kim, ChongKwan Un, "Dynamic Sub-Path Protection for Multi-Granularity Traffic in WDM Mesh Networks," IEEE Transactions On Communications, Vol. 41, 1993. 771-781.

An Efficient Cache Access Protocol in a Mobile Computing Environment*

Jae-Ho Choi and SangKeun Lee

Department of Computer Science and Engineering,
Korea University, Seoul, South Korea
{redcolor25, yalphy}@korea.ac.kr

Abstract. The use of periodic invalidation reports (IRs), has been shown to be a useful technique for conserving wireless bandwidth and battery power. However, IR-based schemes have some drawbacks, such as long query delay and low client caching availability, even if the clients have sufficient local cache capacity. In this paper, we propose an efficient cache access protocol to address these problems. Instead of passively waiting, the clients use the local cache actively. Using our protocol, we can remove the "*false alarm*" that causes unnecessary delay. Based on our threshold-based scheme, the proposed protocol can optimize response time with little loss of data currency. Our simulation results are carried out to evaluate the proposed methodology. Compared to previous IR-based schemes, our scheme can reduce the response time significantly with a very little loss of data currency.

1 Introduction

With the increasing proliferation of mobile devices such as cellular phones, PDAs, and lap-tops, more services will be delivered in a wireless environment [1],[18]. These services may include traffic conditions, weather reports, and financial information. However, theses services are limited by the constraints of mobile environments, such as narrow bandwidth, limitations of battery and frequent disconnections. In a mobile and wireless environment, caching on the client side is an important technique, used to reduce contention on the narrow bandwidth channels and limited battery consumption [4],[5],[14],[16]. However, cached data items may eventually become invalid due to asynchronous updates that simply convey that the replica is not updated, though the source is modified [6]. As a result, when caching is used, cache consistency must be addressed. In most previous work relating to the IR-based cache invalidation scheme, the latest value consistency model is used [1],[4],[5].

Recently, much research has shown that the Invalidation Report (IR)-based cache invalidation scheme is an attractive approach for a mobile environment

---

* This work was done as a part of Information & Communication Fundamental Technology Research Program, supported by Ministry of Information & Communication in Republic of Korea.

[2],[7],[9]. Specifically, in this approach, the server periodically broadcasts IRs. A client uses IRs to keep its cache consistent. However, the IR-based scheme has drawbacks such as long query latency and low client caching availability. If a query is issued from the client side and the client has the data item requested by the query, the client must listen to the next IR whether its cache is valid or not before answering. If an IR interval is long, a client may not submit the answer in a timely manner. We illustrate this using the example below.

Example 1. *Suppose the server broadcasts IRs periodically, and someone who drives his/her own car requests traffic conditions regarding the next junction, and this information resides in the local cache. If the information about the next junction has not already been invalidated, he/she has a valid copy of the information regarding the next junction. With the previous IR-based access protocol, however, he/she must still wait for the next IR to validate the local cache and serve the request. Hence, if he/she passes along the junction before receiving the next IR and no information is updated, the data in the local cache may not be helpful to the driver.*

As shown in Example 1, these traffic information systems may not be able to satisfy client requirements. Though the client receives an IR in a timely manner, it may turn out that the IR leads to a *"false alarm"* [5], while in fact the local cache is valid, causing unnecessary response delay.

There is much work that attacks long query delay [3],[5]. However, most work focuses on a passive client. The client just waits for the IRs passively, though they have a data item in a local cache. In this paper, instead of passively waiting, the client uses its cache actively. There is much research relating to client's cache consistency in mobile environments [6],[10],[12]. For efficient cache access, we adopt a weak consistency model and propose new protocols: the Direct Cache Access Protocol (DCAP) and the Threshold-based Cache Access Protocol (TCAP). In our protocols, if we use an appropriate threshold, the *"false alarm"* problem does not occur. Our simulation results demonstrate that our protocols reduce response time with little loss of data currency.

The rest of this paper is organized as follows: Section 2 introduces some background information on cache invalidation and the system model employed in this paper, and previous work. In Section 3, we describe the proposed protocols. Section 4 evaluates the performance of the proposed protocols. Section 5 provides some concluding remarks.

2 Background

2.1 The System Model

In order to describe the IR/UIR-based algorithms, we describe a system model that is similar to [5]. As shown in Fig. 1, it consists of a single server, one broadcast channel, multiple clients and an on-demand uplink channel. The server broadcasts both the IRs/UIRs and data periodically. The server has three main

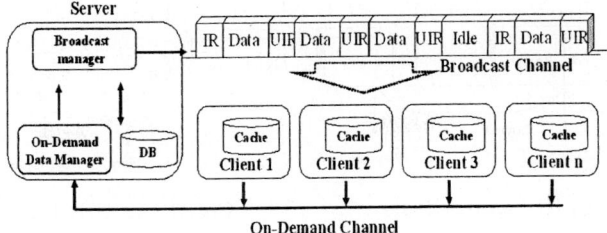

Fig. 1. The system model

components: a broadcast manager component, a database and an on-demand data manager component. The broadcast manager component responsible for sending the IRs/UIRs and data periodically. If the size of the data that will be sent by the server is not sufficient, idle frames will be sent. The database can be accessed and updated only by the server.

2.2 The IR-Based/UIR-Based Cache Invalidation Schemes

The work [2] has proposed the basic IR-based Cache invalidation scheme. In the basic IR-based scheme, the server broadcasts the IRs every L seconds. The IR contains the current timestamp T_i and a list of pairs (d_x, t_x) such that $t_x > (T_i - w*L)$, where t_x is the recent update time stamp of d_x, w is the broadcast window size, d_x is the data item id, and D is the set of data items. Formally, the IR_i defined as follows:

- $IR_i = \{<d_x, t_x> | (d_x \in D) \land (T_i - w*L < t_x \leq T_i)\}$

Since the IRs include the history of w periods, a client can still validate its cache as long as the disconnection time is shorter than $w*L$. However, if the disconnection time is longer than $w*L$, A client must flush its entire caches even if all cached items are valid. Much research has been done to address the long disconnection problem [7],[9]. The fundamentals of the IR technique can be further explained in Fig. 2. When the client receives a new query between T_i and T_{i+1}, and if the client has a local cache data copy, the client must wait for the next IR. Otherwise, the client sends an uplink request to the server. After receiving the next IR broadcast at T_{i+1}, the client determines whether its cache is valid or not. If the data copy is valid, the query can be served locally after the IR broadcast at T_{i+1}. However, if the data copy is not valid, the client will send an uplink request to the server. The query can be served after the IR broadcast at T_{i+2}. The main advantages of the IR-based cache invalidation scheme are its scalability and energy efficiency.

To reduce the long query delay, the concept of the UIR is proposed over the original IR scheme [5],[17]. The UIR schemes use a technique similar to the *(1,m)* indexing [8] to reduce query latency. Proposed *(1,m)* indexing replication reduces the access latency during data broadcasting. Similar to *(1,m)* indexing,

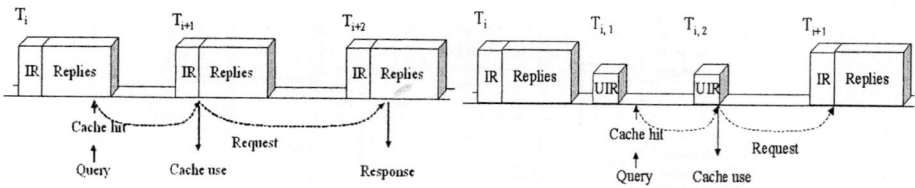

Fig. 2. An IR-based scheme   **Fig. 3.** An UIR-based scheme

the IR is repeated every $\frac{1}{m}$th of the IR interval. Since replicating the complete IR m times may consume a large amount of broadcast bandwidth, the UIR contains the data items id that have been updated after the last IR. Formally, the $UIR_{i,k}$ can be defined as follows:

- $UIR_{i,k} = \{d_x | (d_x \in D) \wedge (T_{i,k-1} < t_x \leq T_{i,k})\}$ where, $(0 < k < m\text{-}1)$, $(m\text{-}1)$ is the number of replicated UIRs within one IR interval.

The idea of the UIR technique can be further explained in Fig. 3. When a client receives a new query between $T_{i,1}$ and $T_{i,2}$, and if a client has a data copy in the local cache, a client must wait for the next UIR. Otherwise, a client sends an uplink request to the server. After receiving the next UIR broadcast at $T_{i,2}$, a client determines whether its cache is valid. If the data copy is valid, the query can be served locally after the UIR broadcast at $T_{i,2}$. If the data copy is not valid, a client will send an uplink request to the server. The query can be served after the IR broadcast at T_{i+1}. Therefore, the UIR-based scheme can reduce the query delay by $\frac{1}{m}$ in case of an average cache hit.

3 The Proposed Protocol

3.1 Motivation

In the IR-based scheme, when a cache hit occurs, the client must wait for the next IR even if the cached items are not updated. Therefore, even if the cache size of clients is large enough to store all data items, the query delay may be longer than when a client has low caching storage due to the "false alarm".

Although the UIR-based solution provides a mobile client with the freshest bounded latency data item, it notably loses the availability benefit of client caching, especially if the data item at the local cache is valid. In addition, it may turn out that the IR leads to a "false alarm" [5], while in fact the local cache is valid, thereby causing unnecessary response delay.

The unnecessary delay is illustrated in the following example (Fig. 4). When a new query is issued between $T_{i,1}$ and $T_{i,2}$, and if a client has a data copy in the local cache, the client waits for the next UIR. If the data is updated at Update A ($T_{i,1}$ < Update A < $T_{cachehit}$) or Update B ($T_{cachehit}$ < Update B < $T_{i,2}$), the UIR broadcast at $T_{i,2}$ contains the requested data id. Therefore, in both cases, the client will send uplink requests. If the client uses a data item

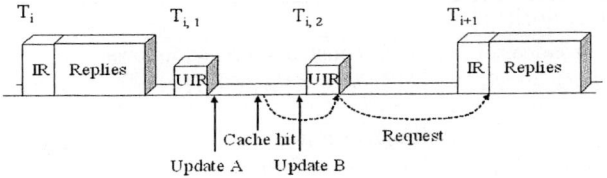

Fig. 4. The example of unnecessary delay

located in the local cache, immediately before Update B, the data item has the highest freshness even if the UIR broadcast at $T_{i,2}$ contains the data id. In this case, the client does not need to wait for the next UIR and the client can use the local cache immediately. The client may acquire fast access time and high availability of client caching without problems. If the client uses a data item located in local cache, immediately after Update A, the response time is shorter than the previous UIR-based schemes but the client may access stale data items.

If a client uses the latest consistency model, the client can acquire high currency. As a previous example, however, if the client wants to acquire fast access time and high availability client caching, the latest-value model is not suitable since it has the *"false alarm"* problem. Since a notion of data consistency is application dependent [1],[5],[6], in this paper, we adopt a weak consistency model to improve the availability of client caching. Specifically, our consistency is based on *the latest-IR consistency model*. In this consistency model, a client must always access the value of a data item, guaranteed by the latest IR/UIR. Therefore, the client can use its local cache more efficiently.

3.2 The Basic Idea

In most previous IR-based algorithms, the latest-value cache consistency model is used for local cache consistency. In these IR-based algorithms, a client just waits for data items requested and uses their cached data items only after listening to the IRs or UIRs. We address the problem by asking the client to actively use cached data items. For example, if a cached data item is updated after a client's request, it is irrelevant whether the client uses its cache directly or waits for the next IRs or UIRs. Therefore, in this case, we can use the client's cache directly. If a cached data item is updated before the client's request, the client may access a stale data item. However, the chance of this case occurring is expected to be very low because all the following requirements should be met: First, the requested data item must be placed in a local cache. Second, the requested data item must be updated during one IR or UIR period. Third, the update must occur before the client's request. Let us denote each probability for the requirements as P_c, P_u and P_{before}. The probability, P_{nf}, that the client cannot obtain an up-to-date data item, is $P_c * P_u * P_{before}$.

Based on these observations, we propose new protocols. In the DCAP, when a client receives a new query, the client uses a data item immediately, if the client has a data copy in the local cache. It may consist of stale data items.

Algorithm 1 Algorithm at server

(A) During the broadcast interval L, construct IR_i as follows:
   $IR_i = \{< d_x, t_x > | \ (d_x \in D) \wedge (T_i\text{-}L*w < t_x \leq T_i)\}$;
   Broadcast IR_i and L_{bcast};
   for each $d_x \in L_{bcast}$ do broadcast data item d_x;
   Execute Step B if the UIR interval reaches. $L_{bcast} = \emptyset$;

(B) At interval time $T_{i,k}$, construct $UIR_{i,k}$ as follows:
   $UIR_{i,k} = \{d_x | (d_x \in D) \wedge (T_{i,k-1} < t_x \leq T_{i,k})\}$, (0<k<m-1)
   Broadcast $UIR_{i,k}$;

(C) Receives a request L_{data} from clients C_j:
   $L_{bcast} = L_{bcast} \cup L_{data}$.

However there is a high probability that the data items are up-to-date and the largest loss of currency, in the worst case, is L, that is one broadcast interval. To obtain fresher data, we propose the TCAP. The simple but effective basic idea of the TCAP is to use the time threshold. Each client may define its own time threshold for the cache access protocol. Based on the time threshold, the client can determine whether to access the cache immediately or not. By using this threshold, the client can reduce P_{before} and loss of currency. For example, when the threshold is $\frac{2}{L}$, P_{before}, P_{before} and the loss of currency is expected to be half the DCAP. When a new query is received before the time threshold, the client uses the local cache immediately. On the other hand, when a new query is received after the time threshold, the client waits for the next IR or UIR, which is similar to the IR-/UIR-based cache invalidation schemes. In the TCAP, the client can adjust the time threshold adaptively, in this manner, if the client wants the highest currency, the client may adjust the time threshold to 0.

3.3 The Server Algorithm

As in [5], the server broadcasts the IRs/UIRs and requests client data periodically. The server guarantees the IR/UIR interval by assigning the highest priority, similar to a beacon broadcast in IEEE 802.11 [15]. The requested data items are served on an FCFS (First Come First Serve) basis. The details of the server side algorithm are described below. The server side algorithm is similar to the previous IR/UIR-based algorithm [5]. L, w, d_x, t_x, D, m and $T_{i,k}$ are defined in the previous section. L_{data} denotes an id list of the data items that a client has requested from the server. L_{bcast} that is initialized to be empty, denotes an id list of the data items that the server received in the last IR interval.

3.4 The Client Algorithm

In our client's algorithm, the client does not wait for the IRs/UIRs to fetch the requested data, if the data is in their local cache. The issued query can be served from the client's local cache immediately. When the client receives a query, the client executes the client algorithm.

Algorithm 2 Algorithm at client

(A) When a client C_j receives IR_i and L_{bcast}:
   if $T_l < (T_i - L*w)$ then drop the entire cache entry;
   for each data item $< d_x, t_x^c >$ in the cache do
      if $((d_x, t_x) \in IR_i) \wedge (t_j^c < t_x)$ then invalidate d_x;
   for each $d_x \in L_{bcast}$ do
      if $(d_x \in L_{data})$ then download d_x into the cache, use d_x to answer the query;
      if d_x is an invalid cache item
         then download d_x, into local cache and $T_l = T_i$;
   if $(L_{data} \neq \emptyset)$ then query (Q_i) and $L_{data} = \emptyset$;
(B) When a client receives a $UIR_{i,k}$:
   if missed IR_i then break and wait for the next IR;
   for each data item $< d_x, t_x^c >$ in the cache do
      if $(d_x \in UIR_{i,k})$ then invalidate d_x;
   if $(L_{data} \neq \emptyset)$ then query $(Q_{i,k})$ and $L_{data} = \emptyset$;
(C) When a client receives a query (d_x):
   if $(T_c - T_t < T_{threshold})$
      if d_x, is a valid entry in the cache then use the cached value immediately;
      else send request(d_x) to the server;
   else $L_{data} = L_{data} \cup d_x$;

(D) Procedure query(Q)
   for each $d_x \in L_{data}$ do send request(L_{data}) to the server;

When $T_{threshold}$ is equal to an IR/UIR period, the TCAP is same as the DCAP. In the DCAP, a client executes this algorithm every time a new query is received. Therefore, the client needs not gather issued queries. This simple but effective algorithm, however, may serve stale data. It means that the client may lose data currency, bound by one IR/UIR period. For higher levels of currency, the TCAP is proposed. In this algorithm, the TCAP selects a threshold based on the UIR scheme. The TCAP is a more general case of the DCAP that is, if the time threshold is set to one UIR period, the TCAP is identical to the DCAP. In the client algorithm, T_t denotes the timestamp of the last received IR, T_c denotes the current time, t_x^c denotes the timestamp of cached data item d_x and $T_{threshold}$ denotes the time threshold($0 \leq T_{threshold} \leq L$). Q_i, $Q_{i,k}$ are the set which contains d_x that has been queried from the threshold to T_i and d_x that has been queried in the interval $[T_{i,k-1}, T_{i,k}]$, respectively.

4 Performance Results

4.1 Simulation Model

For our evaluation purposes, the discrete time simulation package CSIM [13] is used. Using CSIM, we implement the system model of consideration throughout the paper. Our simulation model is similar to that employed in [4],[5].

In this simulation, our protocols are implemented based on the UIR algorithm. Our model consists of a single server, which serves multiple clients, one

Table 1. Simulation parameters

The parameters (Utit)	Contents	The parameters (Utit)	Contents
Database size (data item)	1000	UIR replicate times	4
Number of clients	100	Hot data items	5% of DB
Broadcast interval (sec)	200	Cold data items	95% of DB
Broadcast bandwidth (bits/sec)	10000	Hot data update probability	33%
Cache size (data item)	1 to 500	client's *Zipf.* parameter	0.95
Broadcast window (broadcast interval)	4	Query generate time (data item)	1 to 200

broadcast channel and one uplink request channel. As mentioned in Section 3.1, the server broadcasts both the IR/UIR and requested data items. Data items can be divided into two subsets, hot and cold, hot data consists of frequently updated data items, and cold data consists of others.

In our simulation model, We assume broadcast bandwidth is fully utilized for broadcasting. Basically, we use the LRU cache replacement policy. The client generates a new query one by one. The probability of generating each data item follows the Zipf distribution with 0.95 as a parameter. To measure the access time, we just observe one client, because, in this simulation environment, the activity of a client does not affect the performance of other clients. Each new query is generated by following an exponentially distributed time. The default system parameters are listed in Table 1, which are similar to [4],[5]. To measure the loss of data currency, we examine both time and version difference between the last update and the response of interest. The currency is calculated by the following equation, in this equation, N_{total} denotes the total number of data items that a client received (from the server or the local cache), N_s denotes the number of stale data items that a client received, $Diff_t$ denotes the difference of time between the last update and the response of interest and $Diff_v$ denotes the difference of version between the last update and the response of interest.

The average loss of currency
$$= \frac{N_s * \frac{\sum Diff_t}{N_s}}{N_{total}} = \frac{\sum Diff_t}{N_{total}} \text{ (in terms of time)}$$
$$= \frac{N_s * \frac{\sum Diff_v}{N_s}}{N_{total}} = \frac{\sum Diff_v}{N_{total}} \text{ (in terms of version)}$$

4.2 Evaluation of Average Response Time

First, we evaluate the average response time of varying schemes. Fig. 5 shows the resulting average response time of the IR, UIR, and our protocols. DCAP is a special case of TCAP and has L(in this experiment, L denotes one UIR period) seconds as the time threshold. It can be seen from Fig.5 that DCAP has the lowest average response time and the gap between the UIR and DCAP increases significantly when the cache size increases. This can be explained by the fact that our algorithms use the local cache immediately, through which the client can remove the *"false alarm"*.

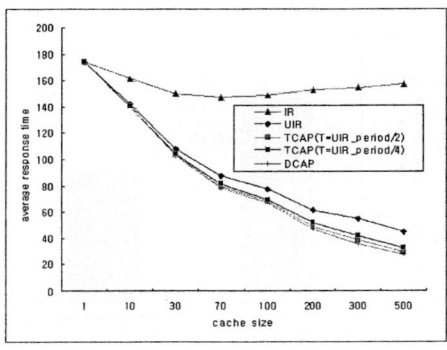 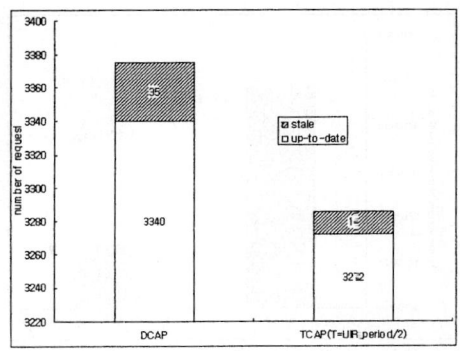

Fig. 5. The average response time ($L=40$)   **Fig. 6.** Total number of client requests

The TCAP (Threshold=$\frac{L}{2}$) outperforms the IR/UIR-based schemes. As can be seen, the performance of the TCAP is similar to DCAP. This can be explained by the following fact. In the TCAP, if a client has a copy of a data item in its local cache, the client does not need to wait for the next UIR before the time threshold. After the time threshold, even if the client must wait for the next UIR, the waiting time is not long. In other words, when the client is in need of an unnecessary long waiting time, the client can use its local cache immediately. For example, when the Threshold=$\frac{L}{2}$, the maximum waiting time does not exceed $\frac{L}{2}$. In the case of the IR, when the cache size is 70, the average response time is smaller than when the client has a larger cache size. This can be explained by the following fact. When the client has many items in its local cache, the probability that data items will be updated will increase. Therefore, although the client has a large local cache, the response time increases.

4.3 Evaluation of Loss of Currency

To evaluate the loss of currency, we observe the details of the client requests. As shown in Fig. 6, the client receives very few stale data items. In the DCAP, about only 1% data items are stale and 99% of date items are up-to-date. Note that the frequency of stale data items is small. In the TCAP, which uses half of the UIR period as the threshold time, about only 0.4% of data items are stale and 99.6% of data items are up-to-date. Furthermore, when we use the threshold, the maximum loss of currency decreases to half of the DCAP.

When stale data items (i.e. that are diagonal lined parts of Fig. 6) are received, the average time loss of currency is shown in Fig. 7(b). When the threshold is used, we can reduce the average time loss. Therefore, total loss of currency decreased in proportion to the threshold. Fig. 7 shows the currency loss in terms of time. In Fig. 7(a), if the client uses the DCAP, the client has a probability of accessing old previously updated data of about $0.005*L$. If the client uses the TCAP, the client has a probability of accessing old data updated before $0.001*L$.

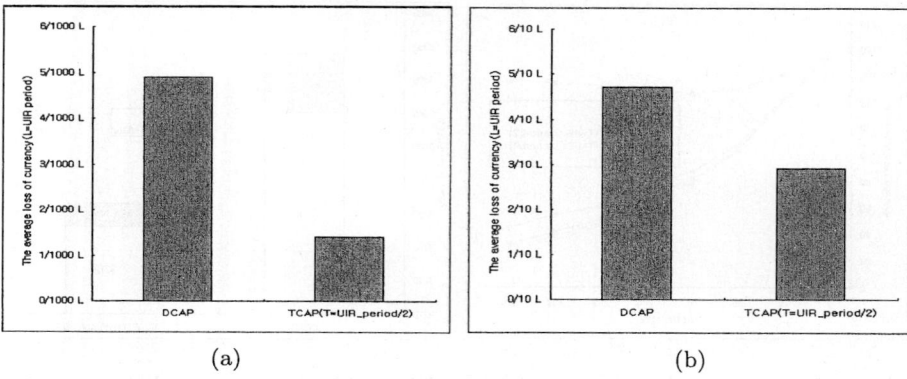

Fig. 7. The average loss of currency(in terms of time)

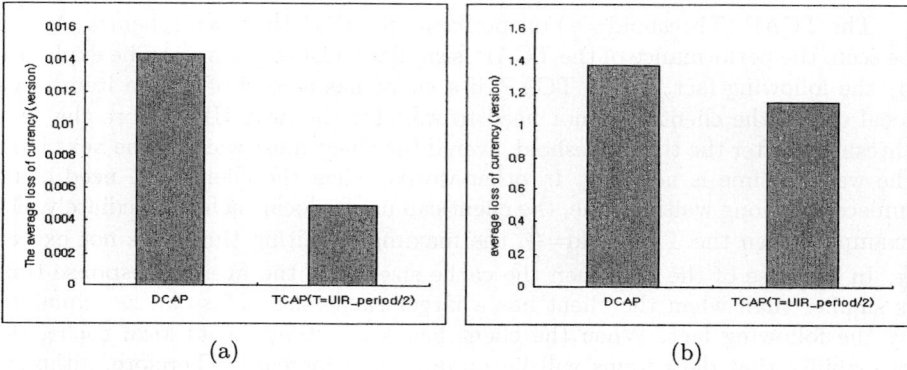

Fig. 8. The average loss of currency(in terms of version)

For example, if the UIR interval is 0.2 sec. and we use the DCAP algorithm, we may access old data, which is updated before an average of 0.001 sec.

Let us look at the loss of currency from a different angle. Fig. 8(a) shows the average loss of currency in terms of version. When the client receives a stale data item, the average loss of currency in terms of version is shown in Fig. 8(b). If the client uses the DCAP, the client may receive average of 0.014 older version, even if the client receives a stale data item, the version of the data is an average of 1.4 older version than up-to-date data. The simulation environment is same as the previous experiment. In these cases, we measure the loss of currency by version. The y axis represents a difference of version between the received data item and up-to-date data items (see Section 4.1). Whenever a data item is updated, its version is increased by one. For example, when the client receives a data item whose version is 8.0 and the current version of the data item is 9.0, the value of the y axis is 1.0. If the client receives up-to-date data items every time, the value of the y axis is 0. In Fig. 8(a), we measure the differences of the version when the client receives a data item. In the case of DCAP, the client accesses an average of 0.014 older version. In the case of the TCAP, the difference is lower than that of the DCAP.

All of these cases occur just when the client has a stale data item in its local cache, and the data item is updated after using the local cache. Furthermore, even if the client uses a stale data item, the differences between the received data item and up-to-date data item, in terms of versions, is not significant.

5 Conclusion

So far, the research into the IR based cache access schemes has focused on the passive role of a client. In this paper, however, we focused on the active role of a client to access a local cache. With this in mind, we have proposed the Direct Cache Access Protocol (DCAP), which is used to access the client's local cache immediately and remove the *"false alarm"* problem. To achieve higher data currency, we have also proposed the Threshold-based Cache Access Protocol (TCAP), a general case of DCAP.

In this paper, we have examined several cache retrieval cache access schemes with the goal of improving access time and cache usability. The experimental results show that the proposed protocols improve response time significantly with minor loss of data currency. In the future, we plan to investigate the effect of varying client access patterns and client disconnections.

References

1. S. Acharya, M. J. Franklin, and S. B. Zdonik. Disseminating updates on broadcast disks. In *Proceedings of International Conference on VLDB*, pages 354–355, 1996.
2. D. Barbar and T. Imielinski. Sleepers and workaholics: Caching strategies in mobile environments. In *Proceedings of ACM SIGMOD Conference on Management of Data*, pages 1–12, 1994.
3. G. Cao. On improving the performance of cache invalidation in mobile environments. *ACM/Baltzer Journal on Special Topics in Mobile Networks and Applications*, 7(4):291–303, 2002.
4. G. Cao. Proactive power-aware cache management for mobile computing systems. *IEEE Transactions on Computers*, 51(6):608–621, 2002.
5. G. Cao. A scalable low-latency cache invalidation strategy for mobile environments. *IEEE Transactions on Knowledge and Data Engineering*, 15(5):1251–1265, 2003.
6. H. Guo, P.-A. Larson, R. Ramakrishnan, and J. Goldstein. Relaxed currency and consistency: How to say "good enough" in sql. In *Proceedings of ACM SIGMOD Conference on Management of Data*, pages 815–826, 2004.
7. Q. Hu and D. L. Lee. Cache algorithms based on adaptive invalidation reports for mobile environments. *Journal of Cluster Computing*, 1(1):39–50, 1998.
8. T. Imielinski, S. Viswanathan, and B. Badrinath. Data on air: Organization and access. *IEEE Transactions on Knowledge and Data Engineering*, 9(3):353–372, 1997.

9. J. Jing, A. K. Elmagarmid, A. Helal, and R. Alonso. Bit-sequences: An adaptive cache invalidation method in mobile client/server environments. *ACM Journal of Mobile Networks and Applications*, 2(2):115–127, 1997.
10. A. Kahol, S. Khurana, S. K. Gupta, and P. K. Srimani. A strategy to manage cache consistency in a disconnected distributed environment. *IEEE Transactions on Parallel Distributed Systems*, 12(7):686–700, 2001.
11. F. J. Ovalle-Martinez, J. S. Gonzalez, and I. Stojmenovic. A parallel hill climbing algorithm for pushing dependent data in clients-providers-servers systems. *ACM/Baltzer Journal on Special Topics in Mobile Networks and Applications*, 9(4):257–264, 2004.
12. D. J. Ram, M. U. Mahesh, N. S. K. C. Sekhar, and C. Babu. Causal consistency in mobile environment. In *Proceedings of ACM SIGOPS Conference*, pages 34–40, 2001.
13. H. Schwetman. *CSIM user's guide(version 18)*. Mesquite Software, Inc., http://www.mesquite.com.
14. K.-L. Tan, J. Cai, and B. C. Ooi. An evaluation of cache invalidation strategies in wireless environments. *IEEE Transactions on Parallel Distributed Systems*, 12(8):789–807, 2001.
15. I. . WG. Draft supplement to part 11: Wireless medium access control (mac) and physical layer (phy) specifications. Technical report, IEEE Std. 802.11e/D4.3, 2003.
16. J. Xu, X. Tang, and D. L. Lee. Performance analysis of location-dependent cache invalidation schemes for mobile environments. *IEEE Transactions on Knowledge and Data Engineering*, 15(2):474–488, 2003.
17. M. K. H. Yeung and Y.-K. Kwok. Wireless cache invalidation schemes with link adaptation and downlink traffic. *IEEE Transactions on Mobile Computing*, 4(1):68–83, 2005.
18. B. Zheng, W.-C. Lee, and D. L. Lee. On semantic caching and query scheduling for mobile nearest-neighbor search. *IEEE Transactions on Wireless Networks*, 10(6):653–664, 2004.

Implementation and Performance Study of Route Caching Mechanisms in DSR and HER Routing Algorithms for MANET

K. Murugan[1], Sivasankar[1], Balaji[1], and S. Shanmugavel[2]

[1] Ramanujan Computing Centre, Anna University, Chennai, India
murugan@annauniv.edu
[2] Telematics Lab, Department of Electronics and Communication Engg,
Anna University, Chennai, India
ssvel@annainiv.edu

Abstract. Route caching strategy is an important on-demand routing protocol for mobile ad hoc networks. On-demand routing protocol for mobile ad hoc networks utilizes route caching in different forms to reduce overheads, peer-to-peer delay. This paper presents a variation in view compared to DSR and HER, to minimize cache staleness, partitions and enhance reliability of service. The variation is with respect to identification of route and cache validation of errors using different techniques namely Update Route Caching (URC), Temporal Cache Validation (TCV), Negative Cache Validation (NCV) and Combined Cache Validation (CCV). The proposed method refreshes cache more often than the DSR and HER thereby initiating route requests earlier, when a route still being used is broken, thus reducing peer to peer delay to transmit packets. The results of GloMoSim simulator validates higher cache hit percentage and reliable delivery of packets in the technique Combined Cache Validation (CCV) when in comparison to DSR and HER

1 Introduction

In a wireless ad hoc network, individual mobile nodes forward packets for other communicating mobile nodes that are out of the transmission range of each other. The network is dynamically self-organizing and self-configuring, with nodes establishing the necessary routes. Dynamic topologies due to mobility and limited bandwidth and battery power make the routing problem in ad hoc networks more challenging than traditional wired networks. A key to designing efficient routing protocols for such networks lies in keeping the routing overhead minimal. In an ad hoc network, many routing protocols, such as DSR [1,2] and HER [3], operate on-demand. These protocols use source routing and each node maintains a cache of all routes that it has previously discovered or overheard in other packets. The source node chooses route for each packet it wishes to dispatch using routes from its route cache. This kind of caching can substantially reduce the overhead of routing protocol and also reduces the delay in delivering data packets when a cached route is already available. Utilizing cached information without robust mechanisms to keep it up-to-date can actually degrade performance and thus making caches counter-productive. However, routing *cache staleness* presents a serious challenge to such protocols. Caches represent learned portions of the network topology, but a cache entry may become invalid due to changes such as two nodes moving out of wireless transmission range of each other.The current specification of DSR lacks a mechanism to determine the relative freshness among routes in the route caches, or even to purge all stale routes from route caches effectively. Performance studies have observed that caches in DSR can report invalid routes frequently, which affects performance negatively. This paper intends to develop and analyze effective caching mechanism along with energy based routing algorithm for the best overall performance. Some trouble spots in DSR are the root cause of the stale cache problem. The work is focused on reducing the invalid cache information by implementing the three techniques namely Update Route Caching (URC), Temporal Cache Validation (TCV) and the use of Negative Cache Validation (NCV) with the existing protocol DSR. Similar techniques for solving cache staleness extend to other ad hoc network routing protocols like HER [3] and compared the performance.

The rest of the paper is organized as follows. Section 2 of this paper gives an overview of the basic operation of the DSR and HER protocol. In Section 3, we describe the route caching in DSR and discusses the problems faced in route caching. In Section 4, we describe the methodology of our simulation study, including our simulator features, the performance metrics we evaluated. In Section 5, we present the Simulation results and analysis. We present the conclusion in section 6.

2 Overview of the Existing Protocols

In this section, two existing version of On-demand routing algorithms for MANET routing protocols, namely DSR and the energy based routing protocol HER are outlined.

2.1 Dynamic Source Routing Protocol

DSR is used in this paper as a base protocol for the development of techniques to ensure cache freshness [1,2]. The operation of DSR is based on *source routing*, where in the source determines the complete sequence of hops to be used as the route for that packet to reach the destination. DSR divides the routing problem in two parts, *Route Discovery* and *Route Maintenance*, both of which operate *entirely* on-demand. In Route Discovery, a node actively searches through the network to find a route to an intended destination node. While using a route to send packets to the destination, Route Maintenance is the process by which the sending node determines if the route has broken. A node that has a packet to send to some destination searches its *route cache* for a route to that destination. If no cached route is found, the sending node initiates Route Discovery by locally broadcasting a ROUTE REQUEST (RREQ) packet containing the destination node address (known as the *target* of the Route Discovery), a list (initially empty) of nodes traversed by this RREQ, and a *request identifier* from the source node. A number of optimizations to the basic DSR protocol have been proposed [1].

2.2 Highest Energy Routing (HER) Algorithm

In this section, a new route selection mechanism for MANET routing protocols, Highest Energy Routing (HER) is described. In this algorithm, the selection of routes is based on the remaining energy levels of the nodes that constitute the route. The modifications in DSR have been proposed in such a way that the destination node knows about the energy levels of the intermediate nodes and hence can choose the most energy efficient route. HER [3] differ from the conventional DSR only in the Route Discovery. The other aspects of DSR remain essentially the same.

In HER, an energy field in the RREQ packet is included, where the intermediate nodes insert their current energy level while forwarding the RREQ packet. The information on the remaining energy levels of intermediate nodes reaches the destination node. Thus this algorithm makes energy information of the various paths traversed available to the destination node. The destination node chooses an energy efficient route from a set of possible routes. In HER, the destination node is designed to wait for a short duration of time (which is directly proportional to the remaining energy level of the node) during which the destination node caches the routes that are being reported to it by different RREQ packets. For this the destination node builds a cache during route discovery that is very similar to the route cache. We call this the *Route-Request cache*. The destination node then send this Route Reply packet to the source by selecting the maximum of the minimum energy in the paths acquired from the RREQ packets. The selection of the route to reply by the destination depends on the energy level of the participating nodes during Route Discovery. Thus, by our algorithm, the destination node selects the route with the highest lifetime from a set of available routes.

3 Route Caching in DSR

All routing information needed by a node participating in ad hoc network using DSR is stored in that node's route cache. A node adds information to its route cache as it learns of new links between nodes in the ad hoc network. Nodes remove information from their route cache as they learn of broken links. By searching for a route in the route cache to a destination, the route cache is indexed by the destination node address.

3.1 Problems Faced in Route Cache

- *In complete error notification*: When a link breaks, route errors are not updated to all caches that have an entry with the broken link. Instead, the route error is unicast only to the source whose data packet is responsible for identifying the link breakage via a link layer feedback. Thus only a limited number of caches are cleaned. Piggybacking the link breakage information onto the subsequent route requests from the source propagates the failure information. But if the route requests are not be updated network-wide, many caches may remain unclean [4].

- *No expiry*: No mechanism to expire stale routes. If not cleaned explicitly by the error corrective mechanism, stale cache entries will stay forever in the cache.

• *Quick pollution:* No method to determine the freshness of any route information. For example, even after a stale cache entry is erased by a route error, a subsequent "in-flight" data packet carrying the same stale route can put that entry right back in. This possibility increases at high data rates, as there will be a large number of "in-flight" upstream data packets carrying the stale route to "un-erase" the route. This problem is compounded by liberal use of snooping. Thus, cache "pollution" can propagate fairly quickly.

3.2 Proposed Solutions to Route Cache Problem

Four mechanisms in DSR and HER protocols are the following:

Update Route Caching (URC): This URC is based on the idea that route errors should be updated very fast in all nodes' cache. In order to increase the speed and the extent of error updating, route errors are now transmitted as broadcast packets. Initially, the node that determines the link breakage, broadcasts the route error packet containing the broken link information. The flow chart and the sequence diagram of URC mechanisms are shown in figures 1 and 2. Upon receipt of route error, nodes update their route cache so that all source paths containing the broken links are truncated. A node receiving a route error propagates (rebroadcasts) it further. By this mechanism, route error information is efficiently disseminated to all the nodes that forwarded packets along the broken route and to the neighbors of such nodes that may have acquired the (broken) route.

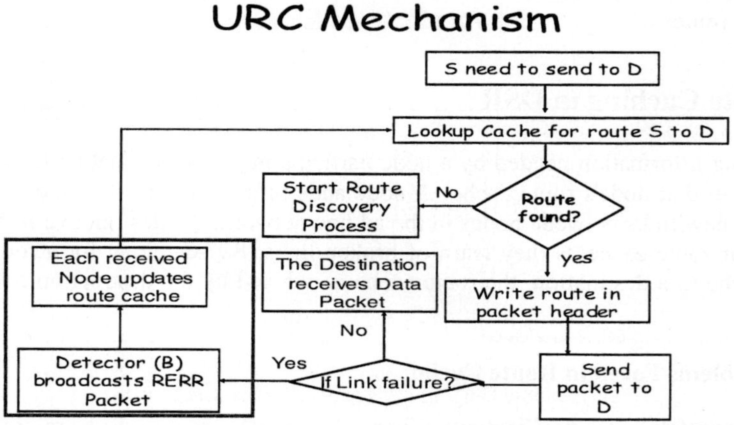

URC Mechanism

Fig. 1. Flow Diagram of URC mechanism

Negative Cache Validation (NCV): This technique is pro-active form to disable the wrong entry of stale routes in the cache. The variation is only in that part where the cache is been updated in the DSR protocol. NCV makes use of another cache structure to store the invalid routes existing in the network. In addition, the negative cache is always checked for broken links before adding a new entry in the route cache.

Figures 3 and 4 illustrate the flow chart and sequence diagram of Negative Cache mechanism. Essentially, route cache and negative cache are mutually exclusive with respect to the links present in them. This prevents the cache pollution problem.

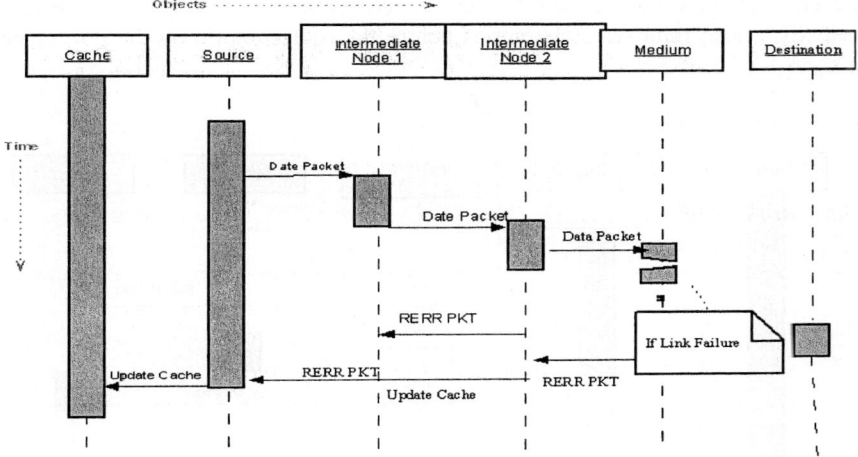

Fig. 2. Sequence Diagram of URC

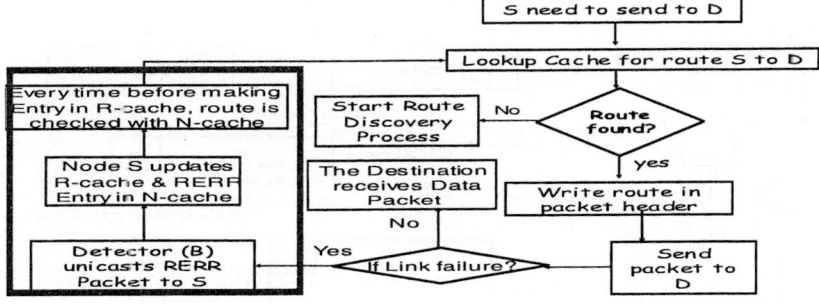

Fig. 3. Flow Diagram of Negative Cache Mechanism

Temporal Cache Validation (TCV): This technique leads to increased search of new routes in the network. TCV makes use of a time-dependent cache, which gets refreshed after some period of time. This refreshment leads to higher good replies by the nodes for the route request packets. The stale routes get expired after some period of time and this leads to a minimized use of cache memory over a period of observation. TCV is a reactive based cache validation. The Sequence diagram of TCV is shown in figure 5. TCV has a timer over which the stale routes are automatically expired.

Combined Cache Validation (CCV): This technique is a conglomeration of the previous techniques to provide consistent routes for routing data packets. CCV is both reactive and pro-active way to update cache in the nodes. Since the validation of the cache is also based on the time, the invalid routes are removed before reception of route error packets and hence the delay in retransmission of request packets is reduced. CCV also removes stale entries before the routes expire by the URC mechanism.

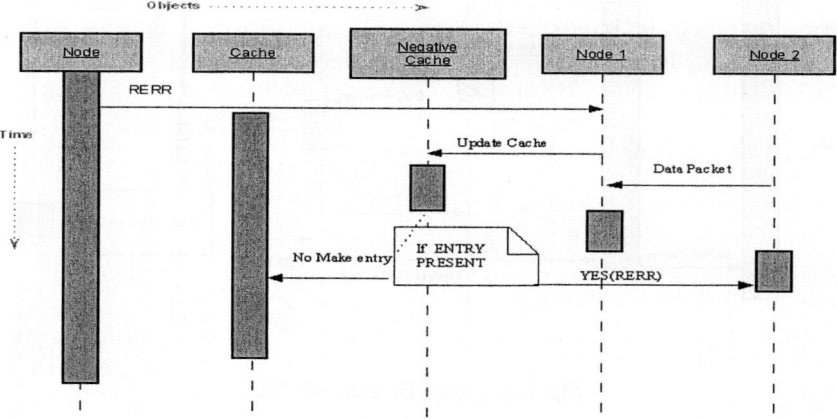

Fig. 4. Sequence Diagram of Negative Cache Mechanism

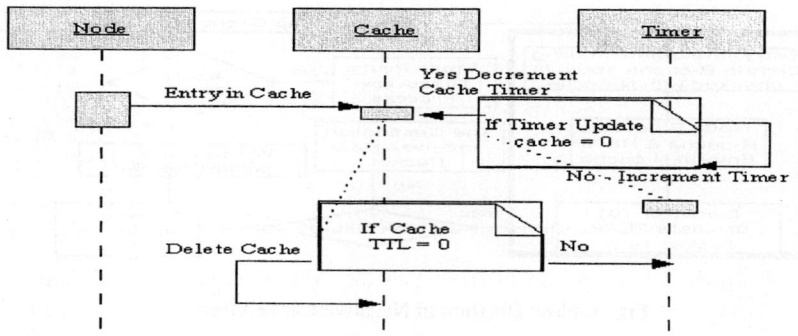

Fig. 5. Sequence Diagram of TCV Mechanism

4 Performance Evaluations

A detailed simulation study is carried out in the next sections to evaluate the effectiveness of the caching mechanism described in the previous section. Their performances are compared with the base DSR protocol and HER protocols.

4.1 Simulation Environment

The routing protocols are simulated within the GloMoSim library [5]. The GloMoSim library is a scalable simulation environment for wireless network systems using the parallel discrete-event simulation capability provided by PARSEC [6]. We simulated a network of mobile nodes placed randomly within a 1000m x 1000m area. Each node has a radio propagation range of 250 meters and channel capacity of 2 Mb/s was chosen for each node. We used the IEEE 802.11 Distributed Coordination function (DCF) as the Medium Access Control (MAC) Protocol. Each simulation was executed for 900 seconds. Multiple runs with different seed values were conducted for each scenario and the collected data was averaged over those runs. A traffic generator was developed to simulate CBR sources. The size of data payload is 512 bytes.

4.2 Performance Metrics

The following metrics are used for comparing the cache performance and evaluate the correctness of route caches in various protocols.
Throughput: Measured as the ratio of the number of data packets delivered to the destination and the number of data packets sent by the sender.
End-to-End delay: It is the time taken between the receipt of the last and the first packet / total number of packets reaching the application layer.
Control Overhead: Measured as the total number of packets transmitted during the simulation period.
Cache Hit ratio: Measured as the total no of hits at a particular node to the total request.
Error Sent: Measured as the number of route errors registered due to link breakages.

5 Simulation Results and Analysis

In this section, the control overhead, throughput, end-to-end delay and energy left with respect to pause time, number of nodes and traffic loads are presented.

5.1 Performance Variation with Respect to Nodal Density

From the figure 5.1, it can be inferred that the combined cache validation is better than the other techniques, though the difference is marginal with respect to hit percentage, but the number of route errors propagating in the network is very less compared to other protocols as shown in figure 5.2. Though link breakages occur due to mobility of the nodes, the updation of the cache in the surrounding of that node causes the data packets to be salvaged by the initiator of the route error by an alternate route to the destination. The throughput from figure 5.3, resemble close to each other for all techniques, but the overhead from figure 5.4 in case of DSR-CCV is comparatively higher than others, as route cache is only refreshed in this technique. But HER-CCV establishes routes considering both cache and energy of a node and hence the number of control packets (Overhead) for this technique is comparatively lesser than the other techniques.

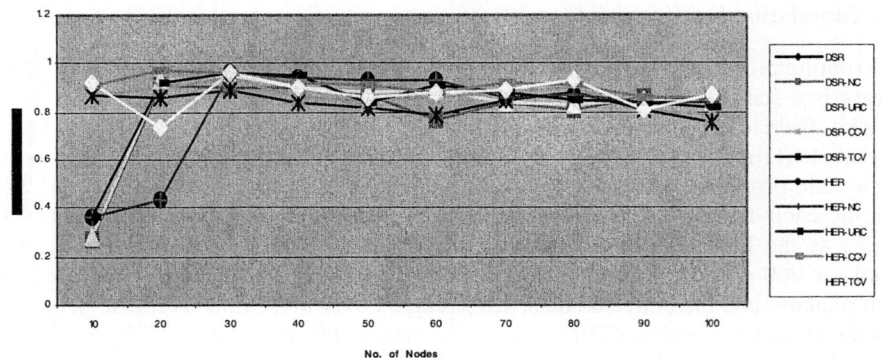

Fig. 5.1. No. of Nodes Vs Hits Percentage

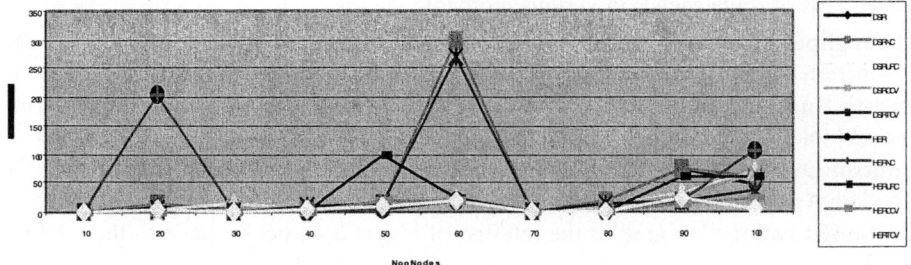

Fig. 5.2. No. of Nodes Vs Error Sent

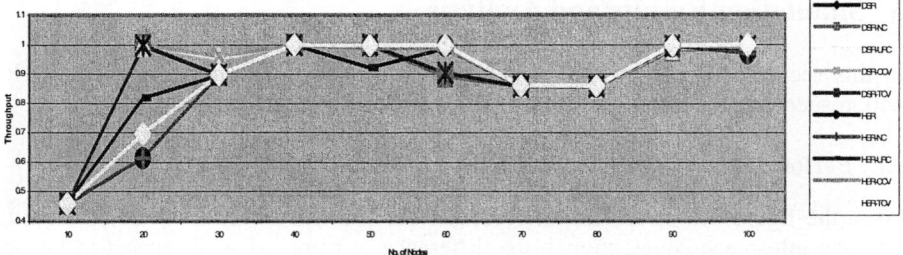

Fig. 5.3. No. of Nodes Vs Throughput

5.2 Performance Variation with Respect to Speed

Mobility of the nodes are an important factor to be considered in Mobile Ad-hoc Networks, as high mobile nodes intersect the ranges of various nodes at a pace proportional to their speed. Hence high validation techniques with energy consideration are needed to propagate data packets in this type of mobile environment.

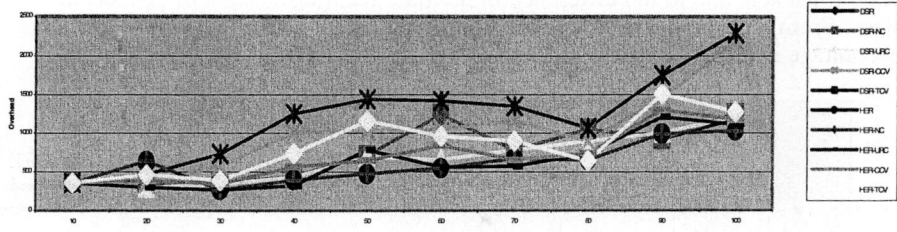

Fig. 5.4. No. of Nodes Vs Overhead

CCV is one of the techniques that are used for cache validation and HER is used for considering the energy of the node for transmission of packets. HER-CCV shows higher hit percentage with lower route errors during data transmission maintaining the same throughput level for a node with marginal differences is shown in figures 5.5, 5.6 and 5.7

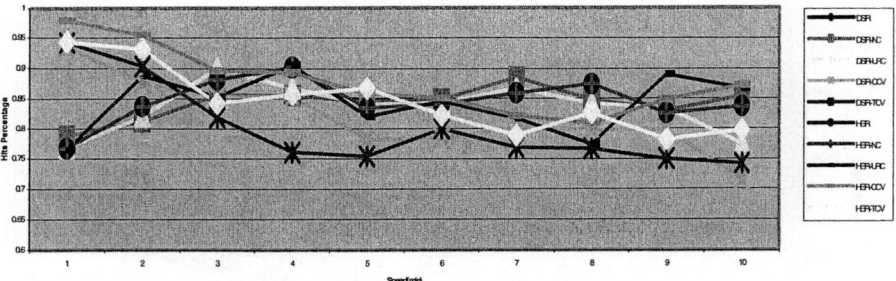

Fig. 5. 5. Speed Vs Hits Percentage

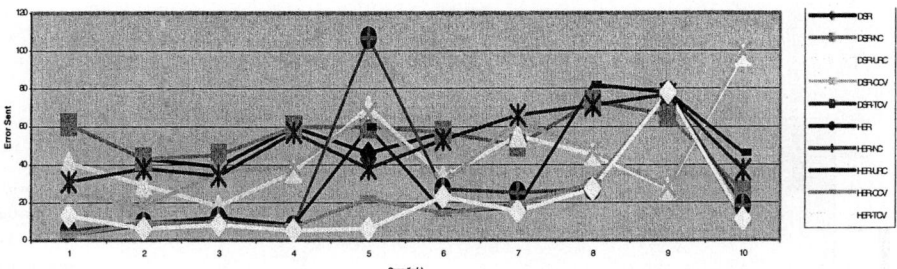

Fig. 5.6. Speed Vs Error Sent

5.3 Performance Variation with Respect to Terrain

Terrain dimensions denote the distribution and scatter in a mobile environment. Though overhead in the case of CCV is higher the average energy left in nodes are comparatively better than the other techniques indicating reliable delivery of bulk data packets as shown in figures 5.8 and 5.9. Bulk data packets consume more energy than control packets due to the difference in the time for transmission of packets of varied sizes. From the figure 5.10 the utilization of the cache is higher in CCV since the hit percentage is compromised with the number of route errors in the environment.

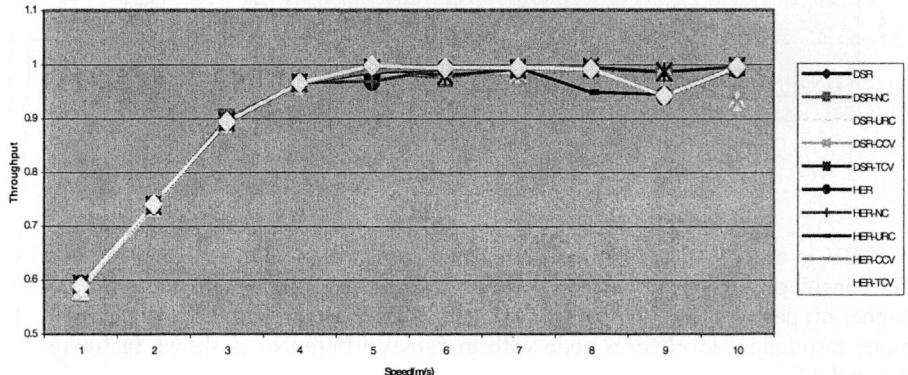

Fig. 5.7. Speed Vs Throughput

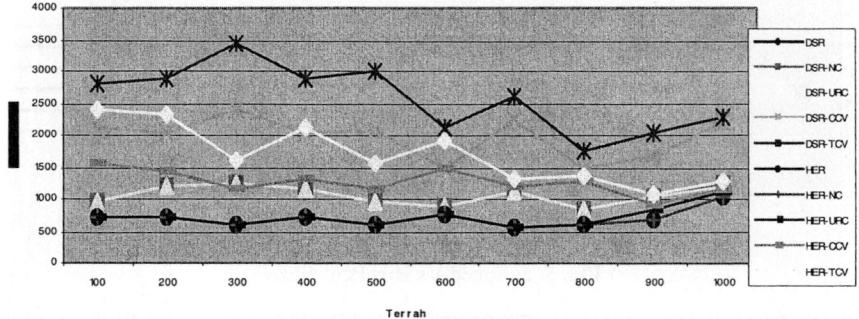

Fig. 5.8. Terrain Vs Overhead

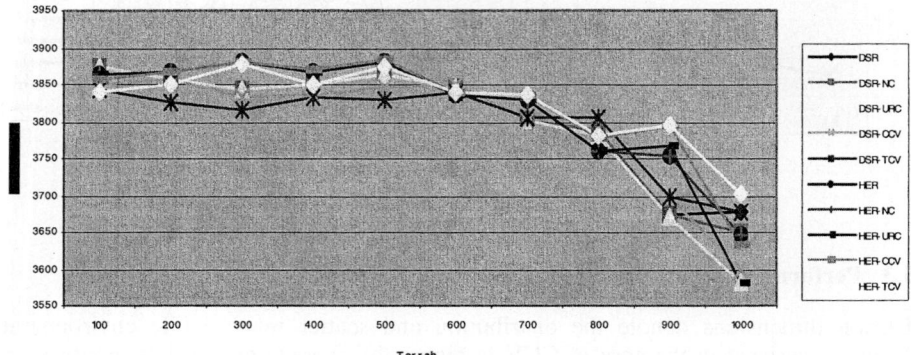

Fig. 5.9. Terrain Vs Average Energy left

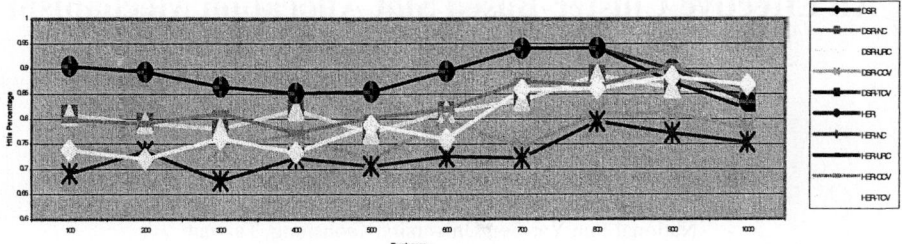

Fig. 5. 10. Terrain Vs Hits Percentage

6 Conclusion

Mobile environments like Dynamic Ad hoc networks should consider both energy and cache metrics to counteract the effects of frequent route changes due to node mobility. Cache in nodes need to be refreshed at a faster rate to inhibit further pollution in the network. Techniques are proposed in this paper to improve caching performance in DSR and HER that primarily focuses on removal of stale entries in the route cache. By frequent flushing of hackneyed entries in the proposed technique, the probability of bad replies made by nodes is reduced, thereby discovering stable routes in shorter periods than the basic routing protocols. The results of the various simulations reveal the credibility of DSR-CCV and HER-CCV techniques in congested, highly mobile environment with lower broadcast range to reduce energy consumption while participating in routing of packets. It is also found that the HER-CCV has good performance with respect to hit ratio, overhead and throughput when compared to other techniques.

References

1. David B. Johnson, David A. Maltz, and Josh Broch. TheDynamic Source Routing Protocol for Multihop Wireless Ad Hoc Networks. In *Ad Hoc Networking*, edited by Charles E. Perkins, chapter 5, pages 139.172. Addison- Wesley, 2001.
2. Josh Broch, David B. Johnson, and David A. Maltz. The Dynamic Source Routing Protocol for Mobile Ad Hoc Networks. Internet-Draft, draft-ietf-manet-dsr-03.txt, October 1999.
3. K.Murugan, C Sapthagiri Saravanan, S.Saravanan, J.Venkatakrishnan, S.Shanmugavel. Delay and Energy Metric Based Routing Algorithms for Improving Efficiency for Mobile Ad Hoc Networks Proceedings of 3rd Asian Mobile Computing Conference (AMOC 2004), May 2004.
4. Mahesh K. Marina and Samir R. Das. Performance of Route Caching Strategies in Dynamic Source Routing. In *Proceedings of the 2nd Wireless Networking and Mobile Computing (WNMC)*, April 2001.
5. Glomosim user Manual http://pcl.cs.ucla.edu/projects/glomosim
6. Richard A.Meyer and Rajive Bagrodia (January 1999), PARSEC User Manual Release 1.1, http://pcl.cs.ucla.edu.

An Effective Cluster-Based Slot Allocation Mechanism in Ad Hoc Networks

Tsung-Chuan Huang and Chin-Yi Yao

Department of Electrical Engineering,
National Sun Yat-Sen University, Kaohsiung, Taiwan
tch@mail.nsysu.edu.tw, takumi.yau@msa.hinet.net

Abstract. This work studies the allocation of bandwidth resources in wireless ad hoc networks. The highest-density clustering algorithm is presented to promote reuse of the spatial channel and a new slot allocation algorithm is proposed to achieve conflict-free scheduling for transmissions. Since the location-dependent contention is an important characteristic of ad hoc networks, in this paper we consider this feature of ad hoc networks to present a new cluster formation algorithm, by increasing the number of simultaneous links to enhance spatial channel reuse. Furthermore, because each cluster has its own scheduler and schedulers operate independently of each other, the transmissions may conflict among the clusters. In this paper, we classify the flows by the locations of their endpoints to prevent this problem. Finally, the proposed mechanism is implemented by simulation and the results reveal that the conflicts can be efficiently avoided without global information and the network throughput is improved without violating fairness.

1 Introduction

An ad hoc wireless network is a collection of wireless mobile nodes that self-configure to form a network without any established infrastructure. The nodes in such a network communicate with each other only if they can reach each other (meaning that they are within each other's radio transmission range).

In traditional wired or cellular networks, either routers or base stations participate in scheduling bandwidth allocation. However, in ad hoc networks, all nodes may be involved in scheduling precious wireless resources. The broadcast characteristic of the wireless medium is such that when a node transmits packets, the nodes within its transmission range can receive the sent packets. All links within vicinity can contend for using the wireless medium due to the nature of wireless propagation. Therefore, the simultaneous transmissions from various nodes without proper coordination may cause serious collisions.

CDMA (Code Division Multiple Access), a multi-channel wireless technology, can address the contention for spatial channel at the physical layer where each channel is defined by a spread spectrum code [5] [10]. Each node schedules its transmission on different channels (codes) in such a way to avoid conflicts with neighboring nodes while making the most efficient use of the available wireless resource. Although this method settles collisions arising from broadcast transmissions, contention still exists because each wireless node is usually equipped with a single transceiver that cannot transmit and receive simultaneously. Namely, a node with just one transceiver can not receive two or more transmissions from variant nodes simultaneously. Besides, a node can not send and receive packets at the same time. Thus, properly coordinating the packets transmission and systematically assigning channel to nodes to get so-called conflict-free scheduling are required.

In addition to conflict-free scheduling, fair scheduling provides nodes sharing bandwidth resource fairly. In recent years, the scheduling of resource allocation in ad hoc networks has focused mainly on achieving fairness and promoting the reuse of spatial channels. Here at least three unique characteristics of ad hoc networks are considered in studying scheduling.

- **Location-dependent contention:** In an ad hoc network, transmissions are locally broadcast, making the channel contention location-dependent. Nodes are prohibited from transmitting if they are in the transmission range to prevent collisions. For instance, Figure 1 depicts a five-node network topology; a dotted line between two nodes indicates that they are within transmission range and the arrow denotes a flow from sender to receiver. The destination of f_1 is node A but node E can also hear f_1, so the flow f_2 cannot transmit packet at this moment, to prevent a collision on node E.

- **Spatial channel reuse:** This is an important means of improving the channel utilization. Location-dependent contention and the nature of multi-hop ad hoc networks enable the reuse of the spatial channel. Any two flows can potentially transmit packets simultaneously if they do not interfere with each other. For example, in Fig. 1, node A, the receiver of flow f_1, is not within the transmission range of the sender of flow f_3 so these two flows can transmit simultaneously.

- **Conflicts between fairness and channel utilization:** Conflicts normally occur in ad hoc wireless networks when the channel utilization is being maximized and an attempt is simultaneously made to ensure fairness among the flows. For instance, in Fig. 1, if flows f_1 and f_3 transmit continuously, the maximum channel utilization is $2C$, where C denotes the capacity of the wireless channel. However, flow f_2 is starved, unfairly to f_2.

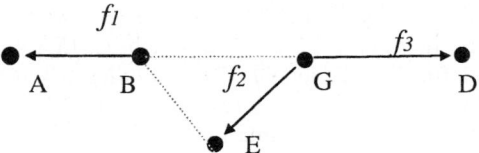

Fig. 1. Spatial channel contention and reuse

The rest of this paper is organized as follows. Section 2 summarizes related works. Section 3 describes the proposed highest-density clustering algorithm and fair slot allocation mechanism. Section 4 presents the simulation results. Section 5 draws conclusions.

2 Related Work

In recent years, research on resource allocation in ad hoc networks has focused on achieving fair scheduling and increasing the network throughput. Numerous works [1] [2] [3] [11] [12] have proposed various solutions, enabling the bandwidth to be shared fairly and the spatial channel to be reused to raise network throughput.

2.1 Fair Scheduling

The mechanisms in [11] [12] are similar in ensuring that all flows fairly share bandwidth. Each new packet is assigned two tags: one is the start tag and the other is the finish tag, as described in [7] [8]. Either tag can be used as the service tag. For instance, in [11], the start tag is the service tag. The packet with the smallest service tag will be sent first. Let S_f^i and F_f^i be the start tag and the finish tag, respectively, for the ith packet of flow f. The tag is assigned by applying the following formula:

$$S_f^i = \max\{v[A(P_f^i)], F_f^{i-1}\} \ ; \ F_f^i = S_f^i + L_f^i / w_f \ , \ i \geq 1$$

where p_f^i, L_f^i and w_f are the ith packet of flow f, the length of p_f^i and the flow weight of flow f, respectively; $A(P_f^i)$ is the arrival time of p_f^i and $v[A(P_f^i)]$ represents the virtual arrival time of p_f^i.

In [1] [2] [3], some slot allocation mechanisms have been presented to make scheduling decisions based on the concept of *credit* rather than timestamp. They compute the excess value as the actual usage minus the accumulated credit value. The flow with smaller excess has higher transmission priority. In this way, all flows can fairly share the slots.

2.2 Increasing Network Throughput

Spatial channel reuse, an important characteristic of ad hoc networks, must be considered in order to increase the network throughput. The nature of multi-hop in ad hoc networks enable channel reuse because any two flows can potentially transmit data packets simultaneously if they do not interfere with each other. To improve channel utilization, in [11] [12] a node graph is firstly converted into a *flow contention graph*(defined in section 3). Then an *independent set* of a flow contention graph, a subset of vertices such that no two vertices in the subset are neighbors in the graph, is found. The flows in the same independent set are *conflict-free* so they can be transmitted simultaneously. However, to maintain the flow contention graph the global node information in the networks must be updated, requiring frequent computations and the storage of related node information.

In [1] [2] [3], the spatial channel reuse is implemented by clustering. The network is logically partitioned into several clusters. Time-Division Multiple Access (TDMA) operates in each cluster. Separate codes are assigned to different clusters to reduce the interference among clusters. Specifically, only one transmission can occur within each cluster, and various orthogonal codes are used in neighboring clusters to reduce the power interference and achieve spatial channel reuse. Consider the following example. Figure 2(a) depicts a network that contains two clusters. These two clusters were formed using the *highest connectivity clustering algorithm* [4]. The square nodes, S1 and S2, are the schedulers. Two separate codes are used in clusters 1 and 2. In this way, the network allows two flows to send packets simultaneously as long as they belong to different clusters, f_2 and f_4 for example. However, since the node distribution in cluster 1 is *sparse* [6], f_1 and f_2 are sufficiently far from each other and can be sent simultaneously. If the node distribution has been taken into account, cluster 1 would be partitioned into two dense clusters, as shown in Fig. 2(b). In the result, the spatial channel is better reused because flows f_1, f_2 and f_4 can send packets simultaneously in various clusters.

In addition, the scheduling in [1] [2] [3] is centralized inside the cluster, but distributed among clusters because different schedulers cannot coordinate with each other. Therefore the flows that are associated with different clusters may be in conflict. Restated, certain time slots may be wasted. Figure 2(a) also explains the conflict between two clusters. In this case, S_1 schedules flow f_2 and S_2 schedules flow f_3. A conflict exists at node D if flows f_2 and f_3 use the same time slot for transmission

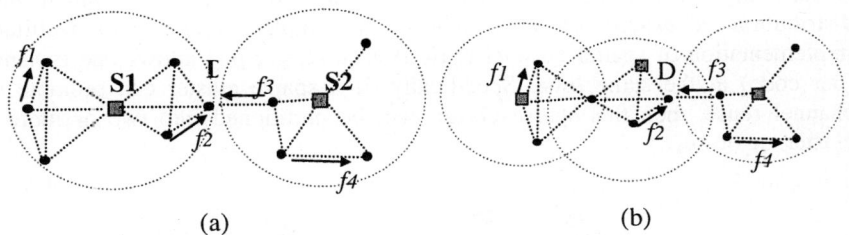

Fig. 2. Example of spatial channel reuse and conflict between clusters

3 Proposed Mechanism

3.1 Assumptions

In this paper, some assumptions are made in the ad hoc networks:

- We assume a time-division multiple access (TDMA) system on a signal channel shared by nodes. To avoid interference among different clusters, we further assume that TDMA is overlaid on the top of a CDMA system. A code assignment algorithm is assumed running in the lower layer of our system as in [1] [2] [3] [4].
- We consider packet-switched multi-hop wireless networks, but do not consider node mobility as in [1] [2] [11] [12].

3.2 Definitions and Basic Concepts

Definition 3.2.1. A set of packets transmitting from one node to another is called a *flow*. Flows f_i and f_j are said to be *conflict* with each other if those packets from these flows cannot be scheduled for transmission simultaneously. Two flows are said to be *conflict-free* if they do not conflict with each other [13] [14].

Definition 3.2.2. A *flow contention graph (or flow graph)* is defined as G= (V, E), where V denotes the set of all flows and an edge (f_i, f_j) belongs to set E if and only if flows f_i and f_j conflict with each other [13] [14].

The flows cannot be scheduled for transmission simultaneously in two situations: (1) the transmitters and receiver of two flows have common node. (2) The receiver of one flow is within the transmission range of the sender of another flow. Figure 3(a) displays a four-node network and its flow contention graph. This network includes three flows. Flow f_1 is in conflict with flows f_2 and f_3 in situation (1). Flow f_2 is in conflict with flow f_3 in situation (2). Figure 3(b) is a complete flow contention graph. Notably, the node topology in Fig. 3(a) is a complete graph. It demonstrates that the corresponding flow contention graph must also be complete, because any two flows in a complete node graph must be in one of the two aforementioned situations. Accordingly, partitioning a network into several dense clusters, in which the node distribution is exactly close to that of a complete graph, will facilitate the implementation of spatial channel reuse if each cluster just allows one transmission (per code) at the same time. Specifically, if a sparse cluster can promote spatial channel reuse, then this sparse cluster will be partitioned into two or more dense clusters to do so.

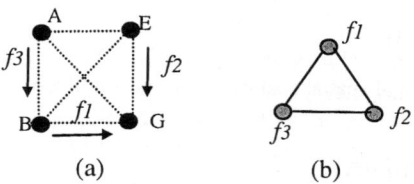

Fig. 3. Node topology and the corresponding flow contention graph

3.3 Highest-Density Clustering Algorithm

A new cluster formation algorithm called the *highest-density clustering algorithm* is proposed. The distributed clustering algorithm is used to partition nodes into various clusters, each with a scheduler (or a cluster-head). The scheduler acts as a local coordinator to schedule time slots to all flows fairly within a cluster. The objective is to find clusters that have two properties: (1) in each cluster, the distribution of nodes is so dense that the node graph is similar to a complete graph. Namely, direct links exist between nearly every pair of nodes within a cluster; (2) two flows in a same cluster will be in conflict if they use the same channel at the same time. Some notations are defined first as follows:

- D_i: The number of neighbors within the transmission range of node i.
- DR_{ij}: Degree Ratio. The ratio of connectivity of node i to that of its neighbor, node j. If a ratio is under one, the nodes within the transmission range of node i will never form a complete graph. But if the ratio exceeds one, a complete graph or almost a complete graph is very likely to be formed.

$$DR_{ij} = D_j / D_i$$

- ZD_i: Zone Density. For node i, the average degree ratio of all neighboring nodes is its zone density. A higher zone density generally implies greater location-dependence.

$$ZD_i = \sum_{j \in N_i} DR_{ij} / D_i = \sum_{j \in N_i} D_{ij} / D_i^2$$

where N_i is the set of neighboring nodes in the transmission range of node i.

The algorithm is described as below.

1. When the network is initialized, each node broadcasts the list of nodes that it can hear (including itself). Then, each node can compute the ZD value and then broadcast it to its neighbors.
2. A node is elected as a scheduler if it has a greater ZD value than all its uncovered neighbors.
    - A node that has not elected its scheduler is called an *uncovered* node. Otherwise, it is a *covered* node.
    - A node that has already elected another node as its scheduler is no longer a scheduler.

Let C represent the capacity of the wireless channel and N be the number of clusters of the network. Then, the network system will have an upper bound NC of the throughput. For instance, Fig. 4(a) depicts a 11-node network topology, where a dotted line between two nodes means that the nodes are within each other's transmission range, and the values near the nodes are their degree and ZD value. The network is partitioned into numerous clusters using two different cluster formation algorithms. In Fig. 4(b), the network is partitioned into two clusters using the *highest-connectivity* clustering algorithm. Separate codes are assigned to each cluster for reducing interference among clusters and only one transmission can be allowed to avoid collisions in the same cluster. Accordingly, its network system throughput has an upper bound of $2C$. No more than two flows are involved in simultaneous transmission in a network. However, in Fig. 4(c) the *highest-density* clustering algorithm is used to organize the network into three clusters, so its throughput has an upper bound of $3C$. if we applying an appropriate scheduling strategy, the three-cluster network throughput may approach to the upper bound of $3C$, which is much better than the upper bound of two-cluster, $2C$.

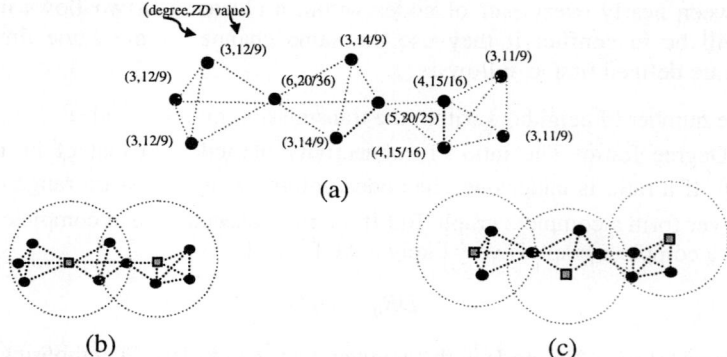

Fig. 4. Examples of cluster formation. (a) Network topology, (b) Highest-connectivity cluster formation and (c) Highest-density cluster formation.

3.4 Scheduling Table

Each scheduler maintains a scheduling table called a *Flow Information Table* (FIT), according to which schedulers can achieve two goals: (1) flows in the cluster can fairly share the time-slots; (2) conflict of flows among clusters can be prevented.

The proposed mechanism involves three parameters for each flow to ensure the fairness of slot allocation; they are *Credit, Total Flow Number and Share Value*.

1. *Credit:* the scheduler assigns time-slots to the flow with the largest credit value.
2. *Total Flow Number:* the number of flows within the cluster.
3. *Share Value:* the sharing ratio of bandwidth for flows in the same cluster.

Since schedulers operate independently, conflicts of transmission may occur among clusters, which will waste slots. To solve this problem, we classify the flows into three types according to the location of their endpoint nodes. The three flow location types are described as follows.

1. *Normal flow: NF.* Both the transmitter and the receiver of the flow are in the same cluster, and neither is a gateway node.
2. *Inside-gateway flow: GF.* Both the transmitter and the receiver of the flow are in the same cluster, and at least one of them is a gateway node.
3. *Across-cluster flow: AF.* The transmitter and the receiver of the flow are in different clusters.

3.5 Slot Allocation Algorithm

In the proposed mechanism, each scheduler maintains a FIT that has two kinds of fields: Basic information and scheduling information. The former has four entries - *flow id, source id, destination id and TN (Total Flow Number)*, and the latter includes three entries - *Credit, SV (Share Value) and FT (Flow Location Type)*.

The scheduler assigns the next slot to a flow using the slot allocation algorithm below, which is repeated as long as a flow is relayed through another node in the ad hoc network. The slot allocation algorithm is described as follows.

1. The scheduler sets the initial value of the scheduling parameters for each flow i in the cluster: *Credit(i)=SV(i) = 1 / (TN)*.
2. For slot k, if k is odd, the scheduler assigns the time slot to the NF-flows or the GF-flows with the greatest credit value; otherwise the scheduler assigns the slot to the NF-flows or the AF-flows with the highest credit value if k is even.
3. If flow i is scheduled to transmit at the next time slot, the scheduler updates the credit value:
   - Decrease the credit value of flow i by one, i.e., *Credit(i)* ← *Credit(i) - 1*.
   - Increase the credit value of each flow j by SV value, i.e., .*Credit(j)* ← *Credit(j) + SV(j)*.

The above three steps are briefly elucidated as below. In step 1, the *SV* value is 1/TN because the next time slot will be shared by TN flows. In step 2, the GF flows are sent at odd time slots and AF flows are sent at even time slots to coordinate flows among clusters, ensuring the flows to be conflict-free. In step 3, when a scheduler assigns a slot to a flow, its transmission priority falls by one and the transmission priority of each flow increases by *SV*.

4 Simulation

In this section, the performance of the proposed mechanism is evaluated by simulation. In the experiment, link throughput and the fairness index are two metrics used to evaluate the performance of the presented highest-density clustering algorithm and the slot allocation scheme, respectively. The evaluation criteria are defined as follows.

1. *Link throughput*: The sum of the throughputs on the links that are simultaneously active in the multi-cluster network. Channel capacity is assumed to be uniform throughout the network, so link throughput is proportional to the number of simultaneous links. Separate codes are assigned to different cluster in order to reduce interference across clusters to facilitate the evaluation of the link throughput. This simulation assumes at least one successful transmission always occurs in each cluster and in each slot. This assumption is acceptable in a comparison among strategies. Accordingly, the cluster has a link throughput of one if at least one link is present in this cluster and the average number of simultaneous active links is approximately equal to the average number of clusters [4].
2. *Fairness index* (FI): This metric represents fairness of the sharing of bandwidth by all flows. If $B(i)$ is the ratio of the bandwidth used by flow i, then $B(i) = Slot(i) / total\ slots$ where $Slot(i)$ is the number of packets received at the destination of flow i (if each packet has fixed packet length and is assumed to occupy one slot). If we further let $X(i) = B(i) / SV(i)$, then FI can be expressed as follows [9].

$$FI = (1/n) \{[\sum_{1}^{n} X(i)]^2 / \sum_{i=1}^{n} X(i)^2\}$$

where n is the number of flows in the network. For any medium access mechanism that achieves fairness, the FI is expected to be close to one.

4.1 Link Throughput

Twenty nodes are randomly distributed over an area of 670m × 670m. The link throughput of two cluster formation algorithms, the proposed *highest-density* cluster algorithm (HD) and the *highest-connectivity* cluster algorithm (HC), are compared. The link throughput and number of clusters are measured and averaged over around 50 random placements of nodes. Figures 5(a) and Figure 5(b) display the average link throughputs in various transmission ranges and the average number of clusters, respectively.

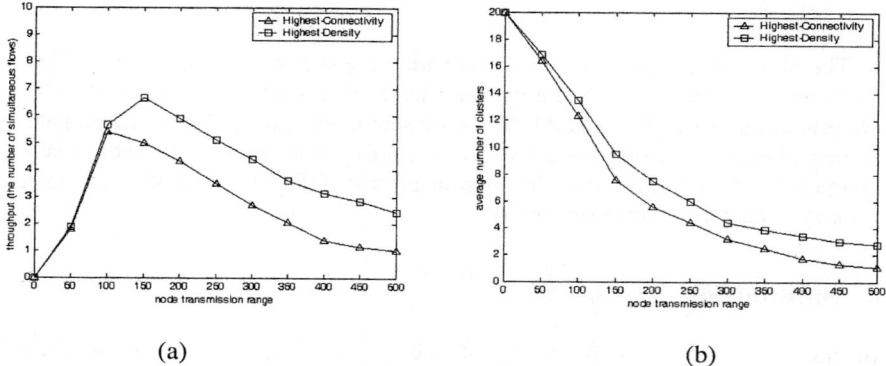

Fig. 5. (a) Throughput comparison. (b) Comparison of number of clusters.

The results demonstrate two facts. First, a tradeoff exists between the transmission range and the throughput. If transmission range is too small, then various single node clusters are formed. Restated, no link that leads to lower throughput is present in the single-node clusters. However, the number of clusters declines as the transmission range increases, so the efficiency of spatial channel reuse decreases, and so does the throughput. Second, the network is partitioned into various dense clusters by the proposed HD algorithm which does not allow the formation of sparse clusters (nodes are sparsely distributed in the cluster). In contrast, sparse clusters cannot be prevented if HC algorithm is applied. Therefore, HD always is associated with more clusters than HC. The average number of simultaneous active links is approximately equal to the average number of clusters, so HD always has better link throughput than HC. A larger link throughput corresponds to better spatial channel reuse.

4.2 Network Throughput and Fairness Index

The simulation scenario is described as follows. Twenty nodes are randomly distributed in a 670m × 670m area. Each node has the same transmission range of 250 meters. The ad hoc network is partitioned into four clusters, each of which has its own scheduler, as shown in Fig. 6(a). Fifteen single-hop flows are randomly generated in the network. Each packet has a fixed packet length and is assumed to occupy one time slot. No node moves during the simulation period. Figure 6(b) is the FIT information of each cluster

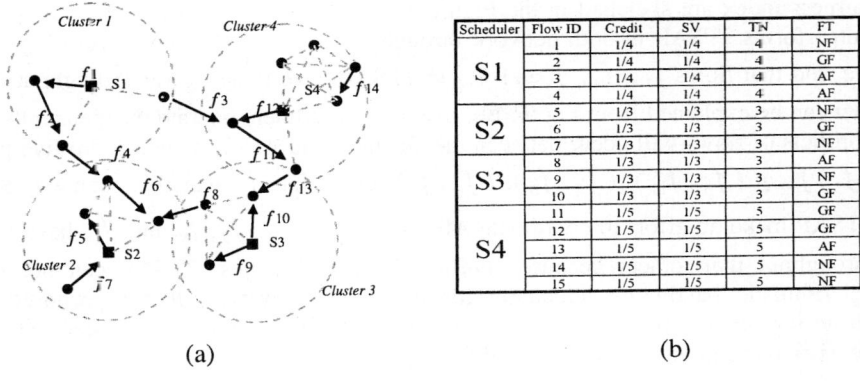

Fig. 6. Simulation example. (a) Network topology. (b) FIT in schedulers.

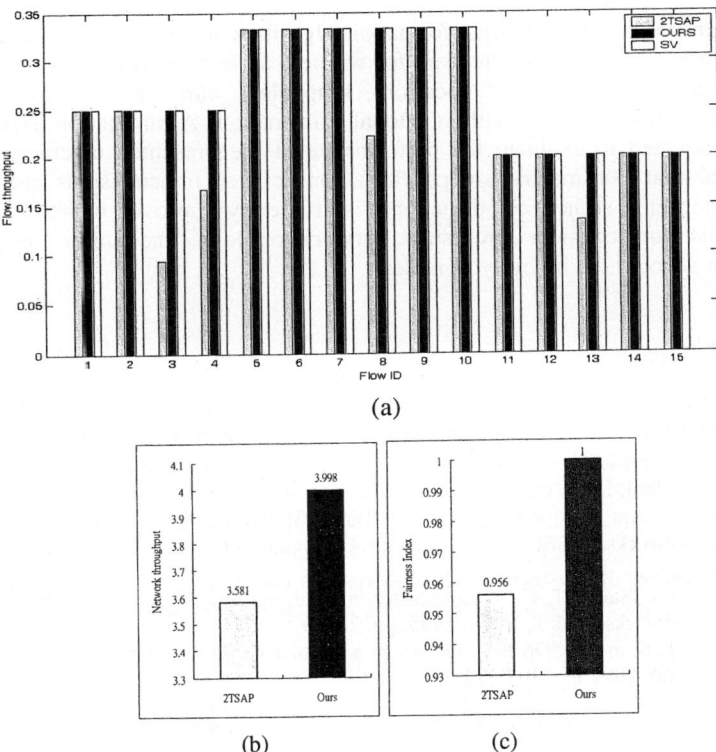

Fig. 7. Comparison between 2TSAP and ours. (a) Flow throughput. (b) Network throughput. (c) Fairness index.

The proposed slot allocation algorithm is compared with the two-tier slot allocation (2TSAP) [1] [2]. The throughput of each flow, the network throughput and the fairness index are sketched in the Figure 7(a), (b) and (c), respectively. Our scheme outperforms 2TSAP in both network throughput and fairness index. From Fig. 7(a), we find that flows f_3, f_4, f_8 and f_{13} in 2TSAP have rather lower throughput. This fact can be explained from Fig. 6. Because four schedulers operate independently, the conflicts of flows will occur between the GF-flow and AF-flow, which are five pairs: (f_3, f_{12}), (f_3, f_{11}), (f_4, f_6), (f_6, f_8) and (f_{10}, f_{13}) in this scenario. Since 2TSAP make no effort to coordinate AF flows, flows f_3, f_4, f_8 and f_{13} have lower throughput than others because conflicts happen. Besides, 2TSAP can not offer deterministic bandwidth allocation for AF-flows. However, if the proposed HD clustering algorithm is applied, cluster 4 will be divided into two clusters, and the network throughput can be enhanced further.

5 Conclusion

This work proposes a new cluster formation algorithm to promote spatial channel reuse and present a fair slot mechanism for wireless ad hoc networks. By classifying the flows according to their location, schedulers can provide conflict-free transmissions among clusters without global information. A simulation experiment was also conducted to evaluate the performance of the presented mechanism. The results reveal that our mechanism provides conflict-free transmissions and higher spatial channel reuse so network throughput is efficiently improved without violating fairness. This work considers only static network topology. The authors' next work will take into account the mobility of nodes.

References

[1] Chao, H. L. and Liao, W.: "Credit-based fair scheduling in wireless ad hoc networks," in Proc. 56th IEEE Vehicular Technology Conf., Vol. 3, Sept. 2002, pp. 1442-1446.
[2] Chao, H. L. and Liao, W.: "Fair scheduling with QoS support in ad hoc networks," in Proc. IEEE Conf. Local Computer Networks, Nov. 2002, pp. 502–507.
[3] Chao, Hsi-Lu and Liao, Wanjiun: "Credit-Based Slot Allocation for Multimedia Mobile Ad Hoc Networks," IEEE J. Select. Areas Commun., Vol. 21, No. 10, Dec. 2003, pp. 1642–1651.
[4] Gerla, M. and Tsai, J. T.-C.: "Multicluster, mobile, multimedia radio network," ACM J. Wireless Networks, Vol. 1, No. 3, 1995, pp. 23–29.
[5] Gilhousen, K.S. et al.: "On the capacity of a cellular CDMA system," IEEE Trans.Veh. Tech., Vol. 40, 1991, pp. 303-312.
[6] Goldsmith, A.J. and Wicker, S.B.: "Design challenges for energy-constrained ad hoc wireless networks," IEEE Wireless Communications, Vol. 9, Issue 4, Aug. 2002, pp. 8 – 27
[7] Goyal, P., Vin, H. M. and Cheng, H.: "Start-time fair queueing: a scheduling algorithm for integrated services packet switching networks," IEEE/ACM Trans. Networking, Vol. 5, Oct. 1997, pp. 690–704.
[8] Hossain, E. and Bhargava, V. K.:"A centralized TDMA-based scheme for fair bandwidth allocation in wireless IP networks," IEEE J. Select. Areas Commun., Vol. 19, Nov. 2001, pp. 2201–2214.

[9] Jain, R. K., Chiu, D. W. and Hawe, W. R.: "A quantitative measure of fairness and discrimination for resource allocation in shared computer system," DEC Tech. Rep., DEC-TR-301, 1984.
[10] Jung, P., Baier, P.W. and Steil, A.: "Advantages of CDMA and spread spectrum techniques over FDMA and TDMA in cellular mobile radio applications," IEEE Trans. Veh. Tech., Vol. 42, 1993. pp. 357-364.
[11] Luo, H. and Lu, S.: "A self-coordinating approach to distributed fair queueing in ad hoc wireless networks," in Proc. IEEE INFOCOM, Apr. 2001, pp. 1370–1379.
[12] Luo, H. and Lu, S.: "A topology-independent fair queueing model in ad hoc wireless networks," in Proc. IEEE Int. Conf. Network Protocols, Nov. 2000, pp. 325–335.
[13] Somani, A.K. and Zhou, Jianwei: "Achieving fairness in distributed scheduling in wireless ad-hoc networks," in Proc. 2003 IEEE Int. Conf. Performance, Computing, and Communications, 9-11 April 2003, pp. 95-102.
[14] Vaidya, N. H. and Bahl, P.: "Fair scheduling in broadcast environments,' Microsoft Research Tech. Rep. MSR-TR-99-61, Aug. 1999.

Author Index

Acosta-Elias, Jesús 90
Ahn, Sanghyun 769
Ahn, Seongjin 1113
Akon, Mohammad Mursalin 431
Ambrosi, Edgardo 972
An, Dong Un 596
An, Zhiping 308

Bai, Hongxing 780
Balaji 1135
Barbosa, J. Javier Gonzalez 678
Bhavsar, Virendra C. 662
Bianchi, Marco 972

Cao, Donglei 945
Cao, Jian 1036
Cao, Jiannong 701, 743, 945, 1024
Cao, Jiuxing 308
Carpenter, Bryan 286
Chang, Chih-Hung 168
Chang, Weng-Long 454
Chen, Ching-Wen 168
Chen, Dao-xu 966
Chen, Daoxu 320
Chen, Guihai 816, 990
Chen, Haiguang 757
Chen, Jian 530
Chen, Jianjun 467
Chen, Kai 668
Chen, Kefei 553
Chen, Li-jun 743
Chen, Lin 1036
Chen, Ling 275
Chen, Mingxue 737
Chen, Shih-Chang 419
Chen, Wei 576
Chen, Xi 780
Chen, Xiao 333, 1077
Chen, Xiaofeng 530
Chen, Yuequan 990
Cheng, Bin 139
Choi, Jae-Ho 1123
Chu, Wanming 150
Chu, William C. 442

Chung, Seung Jong 596
Cong, Lanlan 945
Cui, Gang 407

Dai, Yafei 955
Davis, Adam Brian 491
Deng, Qianni 1001
Diaz, E. Alejandor Macias 678
Dong, Yisheng 645
Du, Ruizhong 371

Feng, Dan 1065
Feng, Guofu 966
Florez, Jose A. Martinez 678
Fox, Geoffrey 286
Fu, Haohuan 1055
Fujita, Satoshi 792

Gaibisso, Carlo 972
Galily, M. 882
Gambosi, Giorgio 972
Gao, Chuanshan 66, 757
Gao, H. 263
Gao, Zhongshan 1024
Ge, JiDong 859
Góes, Luís F.W. 132
Gong, Hai-gang 743
Goswami, Dhrubajyoti 431
Groote, J.F. 263
Gu, Zhimin 845
Guan, Xiaohong 780
Guo, Minyi 320, 454, 804
Gutierrez-Navarro, Omar 90

Habibipour, F. 882
Han, Bo 1055
Han, Gun Heui 853
Han, Saeyoung 49
He, Rui 541
He, Yanxiang 576, 701
Hesselink, W.H. 263
Hirata, Toshiya 662
Ho, Michael (Shan-Hui) 454
Ho, Yu-Chi 780
Honkanen, Risto T. 514

Author Index

Horiguchi, Susumu   3
Hsu, Ching-Hsien   419, 425, 442
Hsu, Wen-Jing   503
Hu, HaiYang   859
Hu, Liang   180, 196
Hu, Mingzeng   298
Huang, Chenrong   737
Huang, Jie   804
Huang, Tsung-Chuan   1146
Hunold, Sascha   58
Huo, Yan-mei   180

Izaiku, Takato   804

Jang, Haeng Jin   596
Jang, Junho   49
Ji, Zhenzhou   298
Jia, Weijia   1055
Jiang, Hong   1065
Jiang, Wenbin   139
Jiang, YuXian   188
Jiang, Zhen   19
Jin, Beihong   945
Jin, Hai   139
Jin, Jesse S.   1089
Jindaluang, Wattana   252
Ju, Jiu-bin   180
Ju, Jiubin   196

Kaneko, K.   479
Kang, Dazhou   1047
Kantabutra, Sanpawat   252
Kautonen, Anssi   524
Khajepour, M.   882
Kim, Beob Kyun   596
Kim, Chang-Soon   725
Kim, Hyuncheol   1113
Kim, Shin-Dug   725
Kim, Sunghae   1113
Knowles, Clinton   491
Ko, Il Seok   853
Kobayashi, Hiroaki   827
Ku, Chang-Jung   168
Kwon, Oh-Young   725

Lai, Chuan-Lin   442
Lan, Chao-Yang   419
Lan, Y.Y.   713
Lawi, Armin   119

Le, Jia-jin   833
Lee, Han-Ku   286
Lee, SangKeun   1123
Leos, E. Chavez   90
Li, Hon Fung   431
Li, Jianhua   383
Li, Kuan-Ching   419, 425, 442
Li, Lei   1012
Li, Minglu   620, 1036
Li, Qian-Mu   890
Li, Shiqun   553
Li, Tingting   596
Li, Weihua   564
Li, Wenwei   870
Li, Wilfred W.   196
Li, Xiangxue   553
Li, Xie   743
Li, Xin   298
Li, Xuhui   701
Li, X.Y.   713
Li, Yamin   150
Li, Yanhui   1047
Liao, Guoqiong   358
Lim, Sang Boem   286
Lim, Yujin   769
Lin, Cheng-Fang   425
Liu, Changshu   608
Liu, D.X.   713
Liu, Feng-Yu   890
Liu, Jian-wei   833
Liu, Jie   491
Liu, Ming   743
Liu, Xiaofeng   358
Liu, Xuejun   645
Liu, Yongqiang   955
Liu, Yunsheng   358
Liu, Zhong   21
Lombardi, Flavio   972
Lu, Jian   859
Lu, Jianjiang   1047
Lu, Ping   859
Lu, Sanglu   320
Lu, Yijun   1065

Mao, Dilin   757
Mao, Ying-chi   966
Martins, Carlos A.P.S.   102, 132
Mo, Ze-Yao   39
Murugan, K.   1135

Na, Yun Ji   853
Ni, Jiarui   126
Niu, Jianwei   541

Ochoa-Cardiel, Alejandro   90
Oda, Kentaro   119

Pan, Wei   564
Pan, Yi   239
Park, Hyoung-Woo   725
Park, Kyung-Lang   725
Park, Sungyong   49
Peng, Shietung   150
Peng, Wenling   576
Perez Ortega, Joaquin   678
Ping, Lingdi   530
Pousa, Christiane V.   132

Qi, Yong   890
Qian, Jiangbo   645
Qian, Qi   620
Qian, Xiaocong   1101
Qin, Yongjin   108
Qiu, Tongqing   816, 990

Ramos, Luiz E.S.   102
Rangel, Rodolfo A. Pazos   678
Rauber, Thomas   58
Recio, Mario   90
Reinemo, Sven-Arne   901
Reyes, B. Pineda   90
Rezazad, Mostafa   984

Sahni, Sartaj   1
Saitoh, Yoshihiro   804
Sarbazi-azad, Hamid   984
Sarker, Biplab Kumer   662
Sawada, N.   479
Schikuta, Erich   33
Shanmugavel, S.   1135
Shao, Huagang   333, 1077
Shao, Zhiyuan   139
Shen, Ji   1055
Shen, Xuemin (Sherman)   431
Shen, Yilin   162
Shen, Zheng   608
Shi, Lei   845
Shi, Yun   845
Shih, Po-Chi   425
Singh, Ajit   431

Sivasankar   1135
Skeie, Tor   901
Song, LiGuo   188
Sumitomo, Kenichi   804
Sun, Caixia   216
Sun, Yuzhong   608
Suzuki, Y.   479

Tagashira, Shigeaki   792
Takemoto, Daisuke   792
Takizawa, Hiroyuki   827
Tan, Zhifang   655
Tang, Jia   630
Tao, XianPing   859
Tatebe, Osamu   196
Techa-angkoon, Prapaporn   252
Tian, Junfeng   371
Tsai, Sien-Tang   454
Tu, Jih-Fu   205

Uehara, Kuniaki   662

Villanueva, J. David Teran   678

Wan, Zheng   530
Wang, Guojun   1024
Wang, Hong   827
Wang, H.Q.   713
Wang, Hui   804
Wang, Jiangdian   503
Wang, Junfeng   1012
Wang, Kai   383
Wang, Peng   1047
Wang, Weinong   333, 1077
Wang, Xugang   1001
Wang, Yijie   108, 933
Wang, Yongli   645
Wang, Yuexuan   588
Wang, Zhi   66
Wei, Lin   845
Wei, Xiaohui   196
Wu, Cheng   588
Wu, Fan   816, 990
Wu, Ming   345
Wu, Ye   78

Xia, Delin   345
Xiang, Yang   395
Xiao, Nong   21
Xiao, Yingyuan   358

Author Index

Xie, Gaogang   870
Xie, Rui   1077
Xu, Baowen   1047
Xu, D.   713
Xu, Fanjiang   1012
Xu, Gaochao   196
Xu, Hongbing   645
Xu, Jian   78
Xu, Man-Wu   890
Xu, Richard Y.D.   1089
Xu, Wuping   345
Xu, Zhiwei   608
Xue, Jingling   224

Yan, Puliu   345
Yan, Wei   955
Yang, Chao-Tung   419, 425, 442
Yang, Guang-Wen   39
Yang, Haijun   608
Yang, Hua   407
Yang, Jihoon   49
Yang, Jinmin   870
Yang, Kan   933
Yang, Min   576, 757
Yang, Xiao-zong   407
Yao, Chin-Yi   1146
Ye, Baoliu   320
Ye, Xinfeng   162
Yew, Pen-Chung   2
Yin, Jian   655
Yoshida, Takaichi   119
Yu, Bo   66, 757
Yu, Genjian   1101

Yu, Jiadi   620
Yu, Shui   927

Zeng, Jianyang   503
Zhang, Bao-Yin   39
Zhang, Chengqi   126
Zhang, Chunfang   275
Zhang, Dafang   870
Zhang, Dalu   78
Zhang, Deyun   308
Zhang, Guangwei   541
Zhang, Lichen   690
Zhang, Lifan   1024
Zhang, Minjie   630
Zhang, Minxuan   216
Zhang, Yuliang   690
Zhang, Zhe   371
Zhao, Dongping   308
Zhao, Q.   713
Zhao, Weidong   371
Zheng, Baoyu   1101
Zheng, Weibin   308
Zheng, Wei-Min   39
Zheng, Yao   467
Zhong, Jiling   239
Zhou, Hongxia   1012
Zhou, Jianying   553
Zhou, Jingyang   701
Zhou, Jipeng   915
Zhou, Wanlei   17, 395, 927
Zhou, Xing-Ming   21
Zuo, Min   383

Lecture Notes in Computer Science

For information about Vols. 1–3672

please contact your bookseller or Springer

Vol. 3781: S.Z. Li, Z. Sun, T. Tan, S. Pankanti, G. Chollet, D. Zhang (Eds.), Advances in Biometric Person Authentication. XI, 250 pages. 2005.

Vol. 3780: K. Yi (Ed.), Programming Languages and Systems. XI, 435 pages. 2005.

Vol. 3777: O.B. Lupanov, O.M. Kasim-Zade, A.V. Chaskin, K. Steinhöfel (Eds.), Stochastic Algorithms: Foundations and Applications. VIII, 239 pages. 2005.

Vol. 3775: J. Schoenwaelder, J. Serrat (Eds.), Ambient Networks. XIII, 281 pages. 2005.

Vol. 3772: M. Consens, G. Navarro (Eds.), String Processing and Information Retrieval. XIV, 406 pages. 2005.

Vol. 3770: J. Akoka, S.W. Liddle, I.-Y. Song, M. Bertolotto, I. Comyn-Wattiau, W.-J.v.d. Heuvel, M. Kolp, J. Trujillo, C. Kop, H.C. Mayr (Eds.), Perspectives in Conceptual Modeling. XXII, 476 pages. 2005.

Vol. 3766: N. Sebe, M.S. Lew, T.S. Huang (Eds.), Computer Vision in Human-Computer Interaction. X, 231 pages. 2005.

Vol. 3765: Y. Liu, T. Jiang, C. Zhang (Eds.), Computer Vision for Biomedical Image Applications. X, 563 pages. 2005.

Vol. 3759: G. Chen, Y. Pan, M. Guo, J. Lu (Eds.), Parallel and Distributed Processing and Applications - ISPA 2005 Workshops. XIII, 669 pages. 2005.

Vol. 3758: Y. Pan, D. Chen, M. Guo, J. Cao, J. Dongarra (Eds.), Parallel and Distributed Processing and Applications. XXIII, 1162 pages. 2005.

Vol. 3756: J. Cao, W. Nejdl, M. Xu (Eds.), Advanced Parallel Processing Technologies. XIV, 526 pages. 2005.

Vol. 3754: J. Dalmau Royo, G. Hasegawa (Eds.), Management of Multimedia Networks and Services. XII, 384 pages. 2005.

Vol. 3752: N. Paragios, O. Faugeras, T. Chan, C. Schnoerr (Eds.), Variational, Geometric, and Level Set Methods in Computer Vision. XI, 369 pages. 2005.

Vol. 3751: T. Magedanz, E.R. M. Madeira, P. Dini (Eds.), Operations and Management in IP-Based Networks. X, 213 pages. 2005.

Vol. 3750: J.S. Duncan, G. Gerig (Eds.), Medical Image Computing and Computer-Assisted Intervention – MICCAI 2005, Part II. XL, 1018 pages. 2005.

Vol. 3749: J.S. Duncan, G. Gerig (Eds.), Medical Image Computing and Computer-Assisted Intervention – MICCAI 2005, Part I. XXXIX, 942 pages. 2005.

Vol. 3747: C.A. Maziero, J.G. Silva, A.M.S. Andrade, F.M.d. Assis Silva (Eds.), Dependable Computing. XV, 267 pages. 2005.

Vol. 3746: P. Bozanis, E.N. Houstis (Eds.), Advances in Informatics. XIX, 879 pages. 2005.

Vol. 3745: J.L. Oliveira, V. Maojo, F. Martin-Sanchez, A.S. Pereira (Eds.), Biological and Medical Data Analysis. XII, 422 pages. 2005. (Subseries LNBI).

Vol. 3744: T. Magedanz, A. Karmouch, S. Pierre, I. Venieris (Eds.), Mobility Aware Technologies and Applications. XIV, 418 pages. 2005.

Vol. 3740: T. Srikanthan, J. Xue, C.-H. Chang (Eds.), Advances in Computer Systems Architecture. XVII, 833 pages. 2005.

Vol. 3739: W. Fan, Z. Wu, J. Yang (Eds.), Advances in Web-Age Information Management. XXIV, 930 pages. 2005.

Vol. 3738: V.R. Syrotiuk, E. Chávez (Eds.), Ad-Hoc, Mobile, and Wireless Networks. XI, 360 pages. 2005.

Vol. 3735: A. Hoffmann, H. Motoda, T. Scheffer (Eds.), Discovery Science. XVI, 400 pages. 2005. (Subseries LNAI).

Vol. 3734: S. Jain, H.U. Simon, E. Tomita (Eds.), Algorithmic Learning Theory. XII, 490 pages. 2005. (Subseries LNAI).

Vol. 3733: P. Yolum, T. Güngör, F. Gürgen, C. Özturan (Eds.), Computer and Information Sciences - ISCIS 2005. XXI, 973 pages. 2005.

Vol. 3731: F. Wang (Ed.), Formal Techniques for Networked and Distributed Systems - FORTE 2005. XII, 558 pages. 2005.

Vol. 3728: V. Paliouras, J. Vounckx, D. Verkest (Eds.), Integrated Circuit and System Design. XV, 753 pages. 2005.

Vol. 3726: L.T. Yang, O.F. Rana, B. Di Martino, J. Dongarra (Eds.), High Performance Computing and Communcations. XXVI, 1116 pages. 2005.

Vol. 3725: D. Borrione, W. Paul (Eds.), Correct Hardware Design and Verification Methods. XII, 412 pages. 2005.

Vol. 3724: P. Fraigniaud (Ed.), Distributed Computing. XIV, 520 pages. 2005.

Vol. 3723: W. Zhao, S. Gong, X. Tang (Eds.), Analysis and Modelling of Faces and Gestures. XI, 4234 pages. 2005.

Vol. 3722: D. Van Hung, M. Wirsing (Eds.), Theoretical Aspects of Computing – ICTAC 2005. XIV, 614 pages. 2005.

Vol. 3721: A. Jorge, L. Torgo, P. Brazdil, R. Camacho, J. Gama (Eds.), Knowledge Discovery in Databases: PKDD 2005. XXIII, 719 pages. 2005. (Subseries LNAI).

Vol. 3720: J. Gama, R. Camacho, P. Brazdil, A. Jorge, L. Torgo (Eds.), Machine Learning: ECML 2005. XXIII, 769 pages. 2005. (Subseries LNAI).

Vol. 3719: M. Hobbs, A.M. Goscinski, W. Zhou (Eds.), Distributed and Parallel Computing. XI, 448 pages. 2005.

Vol. 3718: V.G. Ganzha, E.W. Mayr, E.V. Vorozhtsov (Eds.), Computer Algebra in Scientific Computing. XII, 502 pages. 2005.

Vol. 3717: B. Gramlich (Ed.), Frontiers of Combining Systems. X, 321 pages. 2005. (Subseries LNAI).

Vol. 3716: L. Delcambre, C. Kop, H.C. Mayr, J. Mylopoulos, O. Pastor (Eds.), Conceptual Modeling – ER 2005. XVI, 498 pages. 2005.

Vol. 3715: E. Dawson, S. Vaudenay (Eds.), Progress in Cryptology – Mycrypt 2005. XI, 329 pages. 2005.

Vol. 3714: H. Obbink, K. Pohl (Eds.), Software Product Lines. XIII, 235 pages. 2005.

Vol. 3713: L. Briand, C. Williams (Eds.), Model Driven Engineering Languages and Systems. XV, 722 pages. 2005.

Vol. 3712: R. Reussner, J. Mayer, J.A. Stafford, S. Overhage, S. Becker, P.J. Schroeder (Eds.), Quality of Software Architectures and Software Quality. XIII, 289 pages. 2005.

Vol. 3711: F. Kishino, Y. Kitamura, H. Kato, N. Nagata (Eds.), Entertainment Computing - ICEC 2005. XXIV, 540 pages. 2005.

Vol. 3710: M. Barni, I. Cox, T. Kalker, H.J. Kim (Eds.), Digital Watermarking. XII, 485 pages. 2005.

Vol. 3709: P. van Beek (Ed.), Principles and Practice of Constraint Programming - CP 2005. XX, 887 pages. 2005.

Vol. 3708: J. Blanc-Talon, W. Philips, D. Popescu, P. Scheunders (Eds.), Advanced Concepts for Intelligent Vision Systems. XXII, 725 pages. 2005.

Vol. 3707: D.A. Peled, Y.-K. Tsay (Eds.), Automated Technology for Verification and Analysis. XII, 506 pages. 2005.

Vol. 3706: H. Fuks, S. Lukosch, A.C. Salgado (Eds.), Groupware: Design, Implementation, and Use. XII, 378 pages. 2005.

Vol. 3704: M. De Gregorio, V. Di Maio, M. Frucci, C. Musio (Eds.), Brain, Vision, and Artificial Intelligence. XV, 556 pages. 2005.

Vol. 3703: F. Fages, S. Soliman (Eds.), Principles and Practice of Semantic Web Reasoning. VIII, 163 pages. 2005.

Vol. 3702: B. Beckert (Ed.), Automated Reasoning with Analytic Tableaux and Related Methods. XIII, 343 pages. 2005. (Subseries LNAI).

Vol. 3701: M. Coppo, E. Lodi, G. M. Pinna (Eds.), Theoretical Computer Science. XI, 411 pages. 2005.

Vol. 3699: C.S. Calude, M.J. Dinneen, G. Păun, M. J. Pérez-Jiménez, G. Rozenberg (Eds.), Unconventional Computation. XI, 267 pages. 2005.

Vol. 3698: U. Furbach (Ed.), KI 2005: Advances in Artificial Intelligence. XIII, 409 pages. 2005. (Subseries LNAI).

Vol. 3697: W. Duch, J. Kacprzyk, E. Oja, S. Zadrożny (Eds.), Artificial Neural Networks: Formal Models and Their Applications – ICANN 2005, Part II. XXXII, 1045 pages. 2005.

Vol. 3696: W. Duch, J. Kacprzyk, E. Oja, S. Zadrożny (Eds.), Artificial Neural Networks: Biological Inspirations – ICANN 2005, Part I. XXXI, 703 pages. 2005.

Vol. 3695: M.R. Berthold, R. Glen, K. Diederichs, O. Kohlbacher, I. Fischer (Eds.), Computational Life Sciences. XI, 277 pages. 2005. (Subseries LNBI).

Vol. 3694: M. Malek, E. Nett, N. Suri (Eds.), Service Availability. VIII, 213 pages. 2005.

Vol. 3693: A.G. Cohn, D.M. Mark (Eds.), Spatial Information Theory. XII, 493 pages. 2005.

Vol. 3692: R. Casadio, G. Myers (Eds.), Algorithms in Bioinformatics. X, 436 pages. 2005. (Subseries LNBI).

Vol. 3691: A. Gagalowicz, W. Philips (Eds.), Computer Analysis of Images and Patterns. XIX, 865 pages. 2005.

Vol. 3690: M. Pěchouček, P. Petta, L.Z. Varga (Eds.), Multi-Agent Systems and Applications IV. XVII, 667 pages. 2005. (Subseries LNAI).

Vol. 3689: G.G. Lee, A. Yamada, H. Meng, S.H. Myaeng (Eds.), Information Retrieval Technology. XVII, 735 pages. 2005.

Vol. 3688: R. Winther, B.A. Gran, G. Dahll (Eds.), Computer Safety, Reliability, and Security. XI, 405 pages. 2005.

Vol. 3687: S. Singh, M. Singh, C. Apte, P. Perner (Eds.), Pattern Recognition and Image Analysis, Part II. XXV, 809 pages. 2005.

Vol. 3686: S. Singh, M. Singh, C. Apte, P. Perner (Eds.), Pattern Recognition and Data Mining, Part I. XXVI, 689 pages. 2005.

Vol. 3685: V. Gorodetsky, I. Kotenko, V. Skormin (Eds.), Computer Network Security. XIV, 480 pages. 2005.

Vol. 3684: R. Khosla, R.J. Howlett, L.C. Jain (Eds.), Knowledge-Based Intelligent Information and Engineering Systems, Part IV. LXXIX, 933 pages. 2005. (Subseries LNAI).

Vol. 3683: R. Khosla, R.J. Howlett, L.C. Jain (Eds.), Knowledge-Based Intelligent Information and Engineering Systems, Part III. LXXX, 1397 pages. 2005. (Subseries LNAI).

Vol. 3682: R. Khosla, R.J. Howlett, L.C. Jain (Eds.), Knowledge-Based Intelligent Information and Engineering Systems, Part II. LXXIX, 1371 pages. 2005. (Subseries LNAI).

Vol. 3681: R. Khosla, R.J. Howlett, L.C. Jain (Eds.), Knowledge-Based Intelligent Information and Engineering Systems, Part I. LXXX, 1319 pages. 2005. (Subseries LNAI).

Vol. 3680: C. Priami, A. Zelikovsky (Eds.), Transactions on Computational Systems Biology II. IX, 153 pages. 2005. (Subseries LNBI).

Vol. 3679: S.d.C. di Vimercati, P. Syverson, D. Gollmann (Eds.), Computer Security – ESORICS 2005. XI, 509 pages. 2005.

Vol. 3678: A. McLysaght, D.H. Huson (Eds.), Comparative Genomics. VIII, 167 pages. 2005. (Subseries LNBI).

Vol. 3677: J. Dittmann, S. Katzenbeisser, A. Uhl (Eds.), Communications and Multimedia Security. XIII, 360 pages. 2005.

Vol. 3676: R. Glück, M. Lowry (Eds.), Generative Programming and Component Engineering. XI, 448 pages. 2005.

Vol. 3675: Y. Luo (Ed.), Cooperative Design, Visualization, and Engineering. XI, 264 pages. 2005.

Vol. 3674: W. Jonker, M. Petković (Eds.), Secure Data Management. X, 241 pages. 2005.

Vol. 3673: S. Bandini, S. Manzoni (Eds.), AI*IA 2005: Advances in Artificial Intelligence. XIV, 614 pages. 2005. (Subseries LNAI).